MODERN METHODS
FOR QUALITY CONTROL
AND IMPROVEMENT

SECOND EDITION

MODERN METHODS FOR QUALITY CONTROL AND IMPROVEMENT

HARRISON M. WADSWORTH, JR.
Georgia Institute of Technology, Emeritus

KENNETH S. STEPHENS
Southern Polytechnic State University, Emeritus

A. BLANTON GODFREY
North Carolina State University

WILEY

JOHN WILEY & SONS, INC.

Acquisitions Editor   *Beth Lang Golub*
Editorial Assistant   *Jennifer Battista*
Marketing Manager   *Jessica Garcia*
Senior Production Editor   *Norine M. Pigliucci*
Senior Designer   *Dawn Stanley*
Production Management Services   *TechBooks*
Cover Image   © *Dennis Harms/Stock Illustration Source*

This book was set in Times Roman by TechBooks and printed and bound by Malloy Lithographers. The cover was printed by Lehigh Press.

This book is printed on acid-free paper.

Library of Congress Cataloging in Publication Data:
Wadsworth, Harrison M.
Modern methods for quality control and improvement/Harrison M. Wadsworth, Jr., Kenneth S. Stephens, A. Blanton Godfrey.—2nd ed.
    p. cm.
    Includes bibliographical references.

ISBN 0-471-29973-1 (cloth: alk. paper)
    1. Quality control. 2. Quality control—Statistical methods. I. Stephens, Kenneth S. II. Godfrey, A. Blanton. III. Title.

TS156.W25 2001
658.5'62—dc21   2001026849

Printed in the United States of America

10 9 8 7 6 5 4 3 2 1

To Irene, Gina, and Judy

PREFACE

Much has happened in the field of quality since the first edition of this book was published over fifteen years ago. The purpose of this edition is to introduce these many changes and improvements to the classical developments which were reported earlier.

The most important changes that have occurred have been the emphasis on the management of quality by means of a quality management system and the increased emphasis on total quality. Other changes that have occurred are in the statistical tools that are essential to the control of quality of products or services.

The emphasis on the management of quality has seen two approaches. The first is the introduction of quality prizes. In the United States the principal prize is the Malcolm Baldrige National Quality Award, which is managed by the National Institute of Standards and Technology with the help of the American Society for Quality. In Europe there is the European Quality Award, and many other countries have developed similar awards. In addition, many states in the United States have adopted their own version of the Malcolm Baldrige award. The oldest award is the Deming Prize, which is given by the Japanese, though it is not restricted to Japanese companies. A new chapter has been added to the book to cover these developments as well as other approaches to the concept of total quality management.

The second approach to the management of quality is the standardization and registration to a quality management standard. Many countries had quality management or quality assurance standards before the publication of the first edition of this text, and some of these were discussed in that edition. However, there was then no international agreement on a consistent approach to this standardization. This all changed with the introduction of the ISO 9000 series of standards in 1987. Since then, these standards have become universal and are now the most widely sold standards published by the International Organization for Standardization (ISO). Chapter 3 of this edition discusses these standards and their use in the certification by independent auditors of a company's quality management system. Such certification, or registration as it is called in the United States, has had a profound effect on the quality movement throughout the world. In fact, many companies are now requiring this registration by all of their suppliers. These standards were revised in 1994 and in 2000. The latest revision is discussed in detail in Chapter 3.

Extensions to the ISO 9000 standards have been introduced by the automotive and aerospace industries. The automotive extension of ISO 9001 is called QS 9000. QS 9000 is now in its third edition and is based on the 1994 edition of ISO 9001. It has not been revised to agree with the 2000 edition of ISO 9001 because it was to be replaced by an ISO technical specification, TS 16949, early in 2002. QS 9000 and its successor are being imposed on suppliers to the major automobile and truck manufacturers. The extension introduced by the aerospace industry is called AS 9100. These extensions contain ISO 9001 with additions that are thought to be necessary to their industries. They are also discussed in Chapter 3.

Chapter 4 of this edition discusses, in addition to the quality prizes mentioned earlier, many new concepts that are loosely grouped under the heading of total quality management (TQM). Some of these are quality function deployment, benchmarking, and Six-Sigma^{TM}. Both Chapters 3 and 4 are new to this edition.

This edition is divided into four parts. The first part consists of the four chapters just described, dealing with quality and quality management systems. Chapter 1 presents a history of the quality movement from its earliest beginnings to the present. Chapter 2 is a revision of the material in the first edition. A more comprehensive discussion of quality, quality assurance, quality systems, and quality management is included. A section on quality system developments has been added, along with an extensive list of quality system elements. The discussion of quality policy has been expanded to include vision and mission statements. The material on auditing has been revised, along with corrective and preventive action and product liability. Chapters 3 and 4, discussed above, conclude the first part of the book.

The second part starts with Chapter 5, which serves as an introduction to the statistical tools needed by those who wish to use the remainder of the text. This chapter would not be needed for anyone with some knowledge of statistical concepts. However, the authors believe that it is an essential part of the text that makes it more useful to all readers.

The remainder of this part contains five chapters on statistical process control. The introduction of control charts in Chapter 6 has been shortened from the first edition, where it consisted of two chapters. However, the lucid development of the control chart is retained. Both attributes and variables control charts are introduced with illustrations of both. The general principles of control charts are developed in this chapter.

Control charts for attributes are covered in Chapter 7. The discussion of these charts begun in Chapter 6 is continued to illustrate the detection of changes in the underlying distribution and principles of control charts used for the detection of such changes. The common attributes control charts of np, p, c, and u are covered with many examples of each, along with their operating characteristics.

Control charts for variables are presented in Chapter 8. Again the demonstration of variables control charts begun in Chapter 6 is continued to illustrate the detection of process changes in the underlying distributions. The topic of rational subgrouping is covered in this chapter. The variables control charts for ranges, standard deviations, averages, medians, midranges, and individual values are covered. An introduction to Chapter 9 on special control charts is included, along with the evaluation of variables control charts. In all of the chapters on control charts, statistical software has been used to prepare many of the figures to illustrate and promote its use.

Chapter 9 on special control charts has been revised, especially with respect to CUSUM charts. The original (often acclaimed) coverage of the *V*-Mask design of CUSUM control charts has been retained. To this have been added alternative approaches, including the use of nomographs, for the design of these charts. CUSUM control charts for the various variables and attributes statistics are again covered. This chapter also includes a revision of the material relating to the exponentially weighted moving average (EWMA) control chart, with illustrations using actual data and statistical software. In spite of some controversy, the topic of modifed (or reject) control charts is covered. There are still applications for which this tool is useful, as seasoned practitioners know. Therefore, in the interest of not banishing tools from the toolkit, this topic is included. The discussion of acceptance control charts is retained from the first edition.

Chapter 10 on specification limits, tolerances, and related topics has been moved to this part of the book, where we now believe it belongs. It retains its earlier introduction and discussion of specification limits. The section on process capability indices has been revised extensively including the use of statistical software. A section on Six-Sigma, continuing from the discussion in Chapter 4, has been added. The continuation of the material in Chapter 9 on CUSUM plotting procedures with respect to CUSUM tabulation utilizing specification limits has been retained. The sections on narrow-limit gauging, pre-control, lot-plot, tool wear charts, and statistical addition of tolerances (including mating parts) have been retained from the earlier edition.

Part 3 contains four chapters covering techniques useful for quality improvement. The first chapter, Chapter 11, contains extensive modifications to the former chapters on graphical methods for quality and process control techniques. These two chapters have been combined into Chapter 11 on process control and improvement techniques with extensive additions. The input-output process model is introduced, as are a number of process control and improvement concepts such as the triple role, the 5 Whys, self-control, and special versus common faults or causes. The chapter also includes quality process improvement steps and tools, including checksheets, histograms, Pareto analysis, cause-and-effect diagrams, and scatter plots. The topic of process performance and capability studies is discussed next, with illustrations. The graphical methods that the authors believe are most useful for quality improvement are retained from the earlier edition.

Chapter 12 is an expanded version of the material on industrial experimentation found in the first edition. Simpler analytical techniques are presented. Following this chapter is a new chapter on robust design methods. These are the new design concepts developed by G. N. Taguchi, sometimes called Taguchi methods. Many practitioners have found these design techniques to be useful in recent years.

The relatively brief chapter on reliability analysis has been revised to bring in some new applications of these concepts. This is now Chapter 14, and it concludes Part 3 on quality improvement.

The final section of the book contains material on acceptance sampling. This section, while very important to the field of quality, has been moved to the end of the book to emphasize the primary importance of the control of processes. The section has been reduced from five to four chapters. Many new developments in acceptance sampling have been introduced in this section. Most of these developments have come from international standards work by ISO Technical Committee 69. Chapter 15 on acceptance sampling by attributes has been shortened while still describing completely the theory behind such sampling plans. Chapter 16 discusses the important acceptance sampling standards for attributes. The most important attributes sampling standard is ISO 2859-1. This is an outgrowth of MIL-STD-105E and ANSI/ASQC Z1.4. It has undergone a major change in the 1999 edition. These changes are presented in this chapter. Chapter 17 on acceptance sampling by variables has been updated to bring in the international work of ISO TC 69 in the changes being made to ISO 3951, versions of which have gone by the designation MIL-STD 414 and ANSI/ASQC Z1.9. Although these changes have not yet been approved, their nature is known and reported on in this chapter. The final chapter of this edition presents other acceptance sampling procedures. These include continuous sampling plans, skip-lot plans, and chain sampling plans. An extensive addition has been made that includes ANSI/ASQC S-1, which relates skip-lot sampling to the attributes sampling schemes discussed in Chapter 16.

The book, like the first edition, is designed for either a senior-level or a first-year graduate level course in quality management or quality control for business, engineering, or science students. It could also be used for students majoring in statistics to emphasize some of the very practical applications of statistics. If two semesters or two quarters are available, the entire book can be covered. If only one course is available, the instructor can choose topics that are appropriate for the particular course emphasis. If the course stresses statistical quality control, Chapters 5–10 and 15–18 should be used. If the course is intended to emphasize quality systems, Chapters 2–4, 6–8, 11, 14, and 16 might be used. The book may also be used for nondegree courses for industrial training programs. It will also serve as a reference book for working practitioners, managers, and teams. It contains all the tools needed for Six-Sigma programs.

Throughout the book, many examples are included that are based on real problems with which the authors have been involved. Modern terminology is used, and the text includes references to the most important literature. Although there is no specific portion of the book devoted to the service industry, the methods introduced are used frequently to control and improve the quality of services. Many examples indicating the use of these techniques for that important purpose are included.

Finally, the authors wish to express their appreciation to the reviewers and to our colleagues who suggested many things to improve the book. To our editor, Beth Golub, we wish to express our appreciation for the patience shown to us over a period of several years during which she probably believed no progress was being made. Last, but most important, we wish to express our appreciation to our wives, who put up with our work and actually assisted in developing and reviewing this revision.

Harrison M. Wadsworth
Kenneth S. Stephens
A. Blanton Godfrey

CONTENTS

1

HISTORY AND EVOLUTION OF QUALITY CONTROL AND ASSURANCE

Quality assurance is defined in ISO 9000–2000 as "Part of quality management focused on providing confidence that quality requirements are fullfilled" (American Society for Quality, 2000). Quality control refers to the activities or tools that are used to provide this assurance. The word "quality" here refers to the fitness of a product or service for its intended use. This fitness is usually measured with great difficulty and expense, and by general agreement (in terms of specifications), certain quantities, called *attributes*, are used as fitness surrogates. These attributes should be easy and inexpensive to measure and therefore to control. They should be defined in such a way that when they fall within their specifications, the product or service will be fit for its intended use.

Measurement of these attributes is subject to error, and when measurements vary, the study of variations becomes a statistical matter. The first objective of this book is to present the statistical tools that support decision making concerning these attributes of quality and to demonstrate their use in actual practice. Through these presentations and demonstrations the reader will be able to achieve an understanding of the most modern, powerful, and widely used methods to control a tightly specified product or service.

The second objective of the book is to present modern methods for quality management. These concepts have become much more prevalent since the publication of the first edition of the book. This interest has occurred for several reasons. The primary reason is the increased use of quality as a competitive instrument. This increased use of quality as a means of competing has become worldwide. In fact, many countries have used an increased emphasis on the quality of their goods as a means to improve their balance of payments. The competition between American automobile manufacturers and foreign manufacturers is based on quality. In 1980 the best-selling automobile in the United States was the Chevrolet Citation. In 1990 the best-selling automobile was the Honda Accord. It is well known that we remember a cheap price for a little while but remember a poor-quality device for as long as we own it.

The introduction of quality management standards by the International Organization for Standardization (ISO) is another development that has helped to bring about an increased interest in quality. Many purchasers are requiring their suppliers to conform to these standards as an indication of their intention to produce good-quality products or services. These standards, called the ISO 9000 standards, are discussed in detail in Chapter 3. The automotive industry has introduced a set of quality requirements called QS9000. These requirements are based on the ISO 9000 standards but add a number of additional requirements. Suppliers to the automotive companies are required to meet these requirements. Other industries, such as the aerospace, telecommunications, and medical device industries, have also introduced quality management requirement standards based on the ISO 9000 standards.

Other events relating to the management of quality are the introduction of awards for quality management. The principal ones are the Malcolm Baldrige National Quality Award in the United States, the Deming Prize in Japan, and the European Quality Award in the European Union. Others include awards given by other countries, most of which are quite similar to the Malcolm Baldrige Award, and by many states in the United States and large multilocation companies. These are discussed in Chapter 4. It must be stressed early, however, that the quality management standards and awards cannot be used alone. The tools necessary to obtain and maintain high-quality products and services and to meet these standards are discussed in the remainder of this book.

Although most of the developments in methods for quality assurance and quality control in this book are fairly recent, the need for such procedures and techniques has existed for many years. Perhaps one of the earliest efforts to improve quality was to design and develop a process for speeding the flow of intelligence to the French Republic's central government in the 1790s. To meet this challenge, Claude Chappe developed a system of visually connected (via telescopes) semaphore stations. An unanticipated failure mode was the repeated burning of his apparatus at the Étoile in Paris by "fanatical mobs in the belief that he was communicating with the imprisoned Louis XVI" [Singer et al. (1958)].

Before industrialization individual workers involved with manufacturing were artisans, and they inspected their own work. Gradually, however, as work became more specialized, inspectors were employed to inspect the work of others. This led the production workers to the belief that any defective parts would be found by the inspector. As production levels increased, it was no longer feasible for an inspector to inspect all of the parts being made. This forced them to sample the product. To determine the risks of sampling, the concept of acceptance sampling was developed. Chapters 15–17 in this book cover this topic. In addition, the concept of auditing of quality systems has been developed to the point that certification of quality auditors is being done by the Registration Accreditation Board of the American Society for Quality in the United States and by similar organizations in other countries.

As organizations became larger, the technology of quality control was developed to attempt to control the processes and thus prevent defects, rather than try to detect them. Because it was recognized early in its development that variation in measurements is a statistical phenomenon, much of the technology of quality control is statistically based. To accommodate readers with little or no statistical background, a short survey of fundamental statistics is provided in Chapter 5. In addition, specialized statistical background is included with the introduction of the various techniques included in later chapters.

Specifically, this book covers in detail the tools needed for planning, control, and improvement of quality. These tools include management concepts; the design and use of statistical process control techniques; acceptance sampling procedures, including those plans in wide use today; planning, conducting, and analyzing experiments; reliability methods; and the graphical methods that are so popular today. There is much more to managing quality than statistics-based methods, however. We should consider the costs of inspection, reworking, accepting nonconforming material, and related field failure costs. All these are important facets of quality control that will be discussed along with suggestions for obtaining additional, more detailed information about them.

▶ 1-1 EARLIEST DEVELOPMENTS

One of the earliest references to quality control in the United States was in a report by Alexander Hamilton, then Secretary of the Treasury, to the U.S. House of Representatives in 1791 [Syrett (1966)]. This reference is contained in a report entitled "Report on Manufacturers" and is as follows:

IX. Judicious regulations for the inspection of manufactured commodities

This is not among the least important of the measures, by which the prosperity of manufacturers may be promoted. It is in many cases one of the most essential. Contributing to prevent frauds upon consumers at home and exporters to foreign countries—to improve the quality and preserve the character of the national manufacturers, it cannot fail to aid the expeditious and advantageous sale of them, and to serve as a guard against successful competition from other quarters. The reputation of the flour and lumber of some states, and of the Potash of others has been established by an attention to this point. And the like good name might be procured for those articles, wheresoever produced, by a judicious and uniform system of inspection; throughout the ports of the United States. A like system might also be extended with advantage to other commodities.

Much of the earliest documented work in quality control centered on the Bell Telephone System. Telephone networks are giant series systems. For conversations to be possible over long distances, every piece of the network must function correctly. This means that each telephone, drop wire, and switch and all other transmission facilities must be designed, manufactured, installed, and maintained to exacting standards. The early realization of this fact led to an AT&T document in 1892 emphasizing the importance of managing the quality of all product intended for the rapidly growing network. Fagan (1974) tells us that even before that, in 1882, the contract between the Western Electric Company and the American Bell Telephone Company (an early name of the AT&T Company) states:

At all times during their manufacture and upon their completion the instruments and materials employed shall be subject to the inspection and acceptance . . . by [the American Bell Telephone Company].

Thus, the building of a national communications network created a need for the basic concept of quality assurance—that is, rigorous inspection by an organization for assuring the quality of the product being supplied to another company.

Instead of having each company that receives the products perform redundant inspections, the growing AT&T Company in 1907 reorganized and directed the Western Electric Company to provide inspection and testing for the various Bell Operating Companies under the direction of the Engineering Department of AT&T. The inspection and testing were extended by 1908 to manufactured products, installed products, and purchased materials. Although statistical techniques available in 1908 were very meager, sampling was used extensively, and efforts were made to judge conformity to requirements and to assess durability (reliability). Few statistical techniques were applied. The terms in the special vocabularies of quality control and quality assurance, such as process average, allowable process percent defective, consumer's risk, and sampling error, did not appear until the late 1920s.

By 1922 the function of the Inspection Department of the Western Electric Company was becoming well defined. The inspection of telephones had been extended to factories of the Automatic Electric Company and the Stromberg–Carlson Company. Visiting inspectors made periodic inspections on material repaired at twenty-seven distributing houses and at many non-Western Electric manufacturers' plants. These inspections were called routine check inspections, a term that is still in use. By 1924 inspection had become such a powerful tool of production, the Inspection Department in the famous Western Electric Hawthorne plant had over 5000 members of a total of 40,000 plant employees.

The quality assurance function was now clearly applied to all phases of quality: design, manufacture, and installation. The burden of making the product right was placed on the workers with the command "Do it right the first time." Over seventy years later, this has once again become a rallying cry for American industry in the battle for increasing productivity and lowering costs. However, there is now much greater awareness of the role of top management in achieving quality.

In 1925 a new department was created in the newly formed Bell Telephone Laboratories. This Inspection Department included, among others, Donald A. Quarles, Walter A. Shewhart, Harold F. Dodge, and George D. Edwards. These men were to become the founders of modern quality control and quality assurance methods. Jones (1926) states:

> The duties of the department are closely interrelated with those of the development departments and certain technical groups in the Western Electric Company. With proper interpretations they are described as follows:
>
> 1. To develop the theory of inspection: putting existing mathematical knowledge into available form for use in laboratory and factory and developing new principles where existing knowledge is inadequate.
>
> 2. To develop methods of stating the quality of various types of apparatus and switchboards . . . [and] economic standards of quality. . . .
>
> 3. To maintain oversight of the quality of apparatus, supplies, and systems . . . and to make regular reports on the current quality of these materials.
>
> 4. To studying the quality and performance of telephone plant in service as an aid to further and improved developments.

As their work proceeded in developing the "art and science of inspection engineering," they coined the name "quality assurance." The organization of the department evolved with Edwards as director of quality assurance, Shewhart responsible for theory, and Dodge in charge of methods. By now quality assurance was thought of as supplanting the work of the designer in a most important way. The actual inspection work in the field was delegated to the Western Electric Quality Assurance Department. This growing effort in quality control and quality assurance was in turn supported by another group of brilliant young engineers in the Western Electric plants who worked closely with Dodge and Shewhart. One of the most prominent of these was Joseph M. Juran. Although Juran spent seventeen years with Western Electric, he is best known for his work after World War II as an international consultant. He received the highest Japanese award given to a foreigner. Another early pioneer was Bonnie Small, who edited and wrote most of the Western Electric (now Lucent) *Statistical Quality Control Handbook* [AT&T (1984)].

In the early 1920s it was already becoming clear that inspection and/or rectification was a costly means of trying to improve quality. Even with multiple levels of inspection, some nonconforming product slipped through. Rework and repairs were costly if the defects were detected. When they slipped through to the next stage, they were even more costly.

From 1925 to 1941 the developments of quality control and quality assurance methodology were remarkable. Golomski (1967) writes about this early period:

> On 16 May 1924 . . . Dr. Shewhart prepared a little memorandum only about a page in length. About a third of that page was devoted to a simple diagram which we would all recognize today as a schematic control chart. That diagram, and the short text which preceded and followed it, set forth all of the essential principles and considerations which are involved in what we know today as process quality control.

Shewhart published this concept in the December 1925 issue of the *Journal of the American Statistical Association* [Shewhart (1925)]. In this paper he introduced the control chart, which became a basic manufacturing tool used around the world. Also in 1925 Dodge produced the basic concepts of acceptance sampling by attributes. He defined the notions of consumer's risks and producer's risks. These concepts led to the risks of type I and type II errors in testing of statistical hypotheses [Wilks (1962)]. The application of the principles developed by Shewhart, Dodge, and their associates created a new technology that spread throughout the United States and much of the world. Much of this new technology was published by Shewhart (1931) and Dodge and Romig (1959).

By 1935 many of these methods were already captured in the new British Standard BS 600, *Application of Statistical Methods to Industrial Standardization and Quality Control*, authored by E. S. Pearson. This standard raised considerable interest among technical personnel in industry. In Czechoslovakia, Professor V. List of the Brno Technical University and the Czechoslovak Standards Association developed a standard, CSN 2240 on "Statistical Quality Control," in 1940 [Zaludova (1994)].

▶ 1-2 DEVELOPMENTS IN THE WORLD WAR II ERA

At the beginning of U.S. involvement in World War II, there was an immediate need for large quantities of war material—everything from guns to radar equipment to shoes. United States industry expanded rapidly at the same time that the country's armed forces were expanding. Therefore, many people who had never before worked in a manufacturing organization were employed by these new and expanding factories. The quality of the goods being manufactured naturally suffered from this lack of skilled personnel. As a result, training programs were established by individual companies and by government organizations such as the War Production Board and the Army and Navy. One particular series of courses was set up in a number of training centers throughout the United States. These courses focused on the use of statistical quality control in industry, and topics such as control charts and acceptance sampling plans were taught. The War Department engaged Bell Telephone Laboratories, Edwards, and some of his people to go out to manufacturing plants and teach people simple methods of quality control ["Dr. W. Edwards Deming" (1980)]. Other instructors were selected from local universities.

One of the best-known people working with the War Department was Dr. W. Edwards Deming. In 1938 Deming had persuaded Shewhart to give a series of lectures at the Graduate School of the U.S. Department of Agriculture [Shewhart and Deming (1939)]. Deming, who later became one of the leading quality control consultants, became a close friend of Shewhart. He worked with the War Department two or three days a week on statistical techniques and taught many quality control courses.

Another development during this period was the establishment of two groups of statisticians and engineers to do research in the use of statistics in quality control. One of these was located at the Aberdeen Proving Ground, Maryland. This group was formed by Walter Shewhart and included Harold Dodge as the creative force of the committee, A. G. Ashcroft, General Leslie Simon of the Ordnance Department, Ralph Wareham of General Electric, John Gailland of the American Standards Association, and W. Edwards Deming ["Deming" (1980)]. Their work resulted in three standards for the statistical control of quality.

On July 1, 1942, the Statistical Research Group was formed at Columbia University. "The Statistical Research Group was composed of what surely must be the most extraordinary group of statisticians ever organized, considering both number and quality" [Wallis (1980)]. Results from this group included the development of sequential analysis. Another development was the use of multivariate analysis in quality control with the introduction of the T^2 statistic by Harold Hotelling, who was the principal investigator in the group. Major contributions of this remarkable group included the publication of *Sampling Inspection* (1948), *Techniques of Statistical Analysis* (1947), and *Sequential Analysis of Statistical Data: Applications* (1945). The basic concepts of *Sampling Inspection* survived in revision after revision of the military acceptance sampling standards [Wallis (1980)] that form the core of many national and international standards today.

Both of these groups, and others that were found at various military locations in the United States and other countries, particularly the United Kingdom, were vitally important in the development of the technology of quality. There was never another period in which advances were made so rapidly.

At the end of the war the groups of faculty and many of their graduates in the training centers formed local quality control clubs. Also, at the same time, Dr. Martin Brumbaugh got the idea of publishing a journal dedicated to scientific advances in quality control, which he called *Industrial Quality Control*. This journal was first published in 1944.

In 1946 the various local quality control clubs got together and formed the American Society for Quality Control. George Edwards of Bell Telephone Laboratories was elected the first president of the new society. Brumbaugh's new journal was adopted as the official journal of the society, and he continued as editor. In 1967 the society decided to stop publication of *Industrial Quality Control* and, in its place, to publish two journals. One, *Quality Progress,* was concerned with news of the society as well as nontechnical topics.

The founding editor of the second publication was Dr. Lloyd Nelson, then of General Electric Company. This publication, the *Journal of Quality Technology,* is devoted to the more technical aspects of quality control, much of it of a statistical nature. Another journal that has contained significant technical papers on quality, reliability, and productivity since its beginning is *Technometrics,* a joint publication of. the American Statistical Association and the American Society for Quality Control. The *Journal of the American Statistical Association,* now more than ninety years old, has presented many of the major technical papers in quality and reliability. The publication *Quality* presents papers for managers and engineers in the areas of quality assurance. The ASQ has recently added two new journals to its publication list. These are *Quality Engineering* and *Quality Management Journal. Quality Engineering* has technical articles that are at a somewhat lower statistical level than those in the *Journal of Quality Technology. Quality Management Journal* has articles dealing with research and applications in the field of quality management.

▶ 1-3 MODERN DEVELOPMENTS

Each technique presented in this book starts with its earliest development. Modern developments are then described, along with a discussion of the use of the technique. One of the earliest techniques developed was the control chart. This was first presented by Shewhart, and its use in his original form is still widespread. When used in this way, it is sometimes called a Shewhart chart. Details of the derivation and use of several forms of the Shewhart chart are given in Chapters 6–8.

Other types of control charts have been developed in recent years, and they are presented in Chapters 9 and 10. These include acceptance control charts, which attempt to control both the producer's and consumer's risk and are thus a compromise between the Shewhart chart and an acceptance sampling plan. Another recently developed control chart is the cumulative sum chart, commonly called a CUSUM chart. This chart uses history in its decision-making procedure, whereas the Shewhart chart uses history only in an indirect manner. The CUSUM procedure looks for changes in the slope of the plotted data points, rather than the distance of a point from a central value. As a result, it has the ability to detect small parameter changes quicker than the Shewhart chart. This type of chart is discussed in some detail in Chapter 9.

Several other charts, which are really modifications of the Shewhart chart, are presented in Chapter 9. In addition, procedures for using control charts and the information they can provide for setting tolerance limits and making process capability studies are presented in Chapter 10. These latter concepts are particularly important for modern computer-controlled processes.

Recent developments in acceptance sampling procedures are presented in Chapters 15–17. Included are discussions of sampling standards that have been and are being developed. Many of these standards were originally developed as Military Standards by the U.S. Department of Defense. Some of these have since been canceled by the U.S. Department of Defense and have been replaced by standards published by the American

National Standards Institute (ANSI) as ANSI/ASQ standards in the United States. Others have been published by the International Organization for Standardization as ISO standards. Standards published by ANSI or ISO are called voluntary standards. They are approved by a consensus vote. The ANSI committee concerned with quality control is the Accredited Standards Committee ZI on Quality Assurance. This committee is charged with the responsibility of overseeing the generic quality standards in the United States. All of the authors of this book are or have been members of this committee.

The U.S. Department of Defense is still involved in writing and revising military standards. A 1995 directive has instructed the department to use civilian voluntary standards when an appropriate one is available. Much of the work of the Department of Defense has been conducted with similar groups from other countries. Two outstanding groups with which it participates are the ABCA group (America, Britain, Canada, and Australia) and NATO (North Atlantic Treaty Organization).

In a civilian capacity, ANSI participates as the U.S. member of ISO. ISO has two technical committees (TCs) active in the quality field. These are TC 69 on Statistical Methods and TC 176 on Quality Management and Quality Assurance.

ISO Technical Committee 69 on the Application of Statistical Methods was organized in 1948 in an attempt to standardize statistical terminology and techniques used by industry worldwide. In addition to terminology standards, the early standards produced by this committee included control charts, acceptance sampling, and the statistical control of measurements. This committee has five subcommittees. Subcommittee 1 develops terminology, Subcommittee 3 is concerned with the use of statistics in standardization, Subcommittee 4 with statistical process control, Subcommittee 5 with acceptance sampling, and Subcommittee 6 with interlaboratory tests and the statistics of measurements. (There is no longer a Subcommittee 2.)

In the 1950s through the 1970s these standards were the only ones published by ISO that dealt with quality control. In the meantime, the International Electrotechnical Commission (IEC), a sister organization to ISO, through its Technical Committee 56, was developing standards dealing with reliability, maintainability, and related topics. Thus, in those times, quality practitioners gravitated to those two committees in an effort to standardize the field of quality assurance. However, by the late 1970s it was recognized that standards dealing with the management of quality were needed and that these two committees were unable to meet this need.

To meet this need, Technical Committee 176 on Quality Management and Quality Assurance was established in 1978. This committee deals with the subject of quality assurance by means of the development of international standards for quality systems. This committee has three subcommittees dealing with terminology, quality systems, and quality technology, respectively. The publication of the work of this committee in 1987 of the ISO 9000 standards has done much in recent years to promote the awareness of quality throughout the world. These standards outline the structure of a quality system. They have been used by independent, third-party auditors, called registrars in the United States, to certify that a supplier meets the requirements of one of the standards. As a result of this registration process, many companies require their suppliers to be registered to one of the standards. The ISO 9000 standards are a set of standards. Three of them—ISO 9001, 9002, and 9003—are the contractual standards that are used for auditing purposes. These were revised in 1994, and a third edition was published in 2000. In this latter edition, ISO 9002 and 9003 were dropped so that the only contractual standard is ISO 9001. These standards are discussed in detail in Chapter 3.

Since World War II the subject of reliability has developed rapidly. Much of early work in this field has been in the aerospace and electronics areas. However, applications are now found frequently in most consumer industries, particularly the automobile and medical device industries. From the reliability field, concepts of life testing have evolved. These are applicable to many products, but different types of failures often require different underlying distributions. This subject is discussed in detail in Chapter 14.

▶ 1-4 DEVELOPMENTS IN JAPAN

Perhaps the best-known success stories in quality in recent years have come from Japan. Even before World War II, there were quality control pioneers in Japan in leading companies such as Toshiba and NEC [Nonaka (1993)]. However, there was no organization to promote quality control and few incentives to encourage its use. Imai (1986) discusses quality problems with the post–World War II Nippon Telephone and Telegraph (NTT) public telephone system. Hajirne Karatsu, a technical advisor to Matsushita Electric Industrial Company, recognized these problems from personal experience: "Whenever I tried to call somebody up, I invariably got a wrong number" [Imai (1986)]. General MacArthur's staff requested help from the Western Electric Company. The Western Electric Company personnel quickly identified the need to implement statistical quality control procedures. Imai quotes Karatsu as saying, "In our pride, we told them we were applying quality control at NTT the Japanese way. But when they asked to see our control charts, we didn't even know what a control chart was!" The first one-week course on quality control was conducted near the end of 1945 by W. G. Magil of the Allied Occupation Forces for the managers and engineers of the Japanese telecommunication industries to facilitate military administration [Kondo (1988)] [Kume (1994)].

Kondo (1988) also describes the beginning of the Union of Japanese Scientists and Engineers (JUSE) in 1946 as being established to "contribute to human prosperity through industrial development, achieved by creating, applying, and promoting advanced science and technology." In 1949 JUSE formed the QC Research Group and subsequently developed a "6 month basic QC course," which was attended primarily by engineers "who went on to provide the nucleus of QC activities in their respective companies."

In 1946 and 1948 Dr. W. Edwards Deming had been to Japan "to work on the census of population and of agriculture, on the monthly report on the labor force, and on a number of demographic studies." During his visits there he invited statisticians for a dinner meeting. Dr. Deming "told them how important they were, and what they could do for Japan" [Deming (1994)]. Dr. Deming returned to Japan in 1950 at the invitation of JUSE to "come teach us something about statistical methods in industry."

In July 1950 Dr. Deming conducted an eight-day seminar on the theory of statistical quality control for Japanese engineers. These seminars covered key topics of how to make control charts and how to sample and inspect a product. He conducted these courses first for engineers and then for top managers. He had learned from his experience in the United States that teaching engineers statistical methods was necessary but not sufficient. "I realized that nothing would happen in Japan unless the management learned something about statistical techniques and how to manage them. Why repeat the mistakes of America?"

[Deming (1994)]. Ishikawa (1985) notes that Dr. Deming introduced the Plan Do Check Act (PDCA) cycle in these courses as it relates to design, production, sales, survey, and redesign to enhance and control quality. Dr. Deming's generous decision to donate the proceeds from the sale of his seminars' transcripts led to the establishment of the Deming Prize for Quality Control in Japan in 1951.

Ishikawa (1985) noted that QC "remained a movement among engineers and workers but top and middle-level managers did not show much interest." In 1954, on the basis of the publication of the first edition of Juran's *Quality Control Handbook*, JUSE and the Federation of Economic Organizations (the Keidanren) invited Dr. Juran to Japan. He was asked to conduct the first quality training designed specifically for senior and middle-level Japanese managers. Juran focused on the need to manage quality throughout the organization. He indicated the responsibility of the top executives for [Juran (1954)]:

1. Top policy or doctrine

2. Choice of quality of design, that is, grade

3. The organization of the company with respect to quality

4. Measuring what is actually taking place with respect to quality

5. Reviewing results against goals and taking action on significant variation.

Imai (1986) writes, "This was the first time QC was dealt with from the overall management perspective . . . . From then on, the term QC has been used to mean both quality control and the tools for overall improvement in managerial performance."

Using the solid foundation gained from these seminars, the Japanese gradually established QC departments in their companies. The knowledge of statistical quality control methods spread rapidly throughout the country. Imai (1986) wrote, "The Japanese workers were pleasantly surprised at how well the techniques worked and increasingly tried to use them."

Courses in quality control were taught over the radio starting in 1956. Later, JUSE designed a new magazine for shop workers. The editorial staff, including Kaoru Ishikawa, frequently visited factories and noticed the effectiveness of small study groups in learning and applying the new methods. In the first issue of their new journal, *Genba to QC*, in 1962, they called for "the formation of quality circles by readers of the magazine" [Imai (1986)]. JUSE then organized the QC Circle Headquarters to register the circles.

Iwau Manabe, the head of the machinery section of NTT Corporation, formed the first registered quality circle in Japan in May 1962. Within a year this circle had reduced defects by one third. This success led others on Manabe's staff to join the group [Imai (1986)]. There are now over 400,000 registered quality circles in Japan with over four million members. In 1966, at the annual meeting of the European Organization for Quality Control in Stockholm, Sweden, Dr. Juran first described to the West the growing importance of these activities in Japan. A discussion of quality circles is included in Chapter 2.

▶ 1-5 RECENT DEVELOPMENTS

New concepts of organization of the quality assurance function have evolved in recent years. Many of these developed as a reaction to the outstanding success of such ideas in Japan. These concepts have been proposed to provide attention to the need for quality assurance for all employees in the organization. One of the earlier ideas was called "total quality control." This idea was suggested by A. V. Feigenbaum, then of the General Electric Company, in a book by that name that was first published in 1961 [Feigenbaum (1991)]. Feigenbaum stressed the fact that the responsibility for quality control rested with all departments, not just with the quality control department. His text outlines what each department should be doing to guarantee good quality. Japanese engineers still use the ideas presented by Feigenbaum in that book. However, in recent years the Japanese Union of Science and Engineers (JUSE) has adopted the phrase "total quality management" (TQM) for this concept. In the late 1970s American engineers appeared to rediscover Feigenbaum's ideas, and they are now widely applied in leading U.S. companies.

The entire scope of managing quality has been outlined by Juran (1979). He stresses the necessity for leadership by top management and extensive training programs to make basic quality control techniques available to every worker in the company. He emphasizes a dedication to quality at every step: market research, product design, vendor relations, manufacturing, delivery, and service. His approach stresses the basic business concept of return on investment for selecting and implementing each quality improvement program. Juran discusses this further in his *Quality Handbook* [Juran (1999)].

Another quality leader in the recent past has been Phil Crosby, the founder of the Quality College in Orlando, Florida. Crosby has focused efforts on quality improvement and cutting the cost of quality. He has used twenty-five years of industrial experience (Vice President–Corporate Director of Quality for ITT) to develop ideas such as Zero Defects, the Buck-a-Day cost-saving program, and a fourteen-step quality improvement program ["Phil Crosby: A Change in Career" (1979)]. His books, *Quality Is Free* (1979) and *Quality without Tears* (1984), have been widely read.

One of the most influential individuals in developing and teaching methods for controlling quality has been Professor Kaoru Ishikawa. Much of his work was discussed in Section 1-4. He began his study of quality control concepts in 1950. He first met Dr. Shewhart when he visited AT&T Bell Laboratories as a member of a study team in 1958 [Ishikawa (1967)]. He introduced the control chart method in Japan in 1955 and has made many contributions to quality control methods since that time. Especially elegant and useful is his cause-and-effect diagram, now known by many throughout the world as the Ishikawa diagram. This is discussed in Chapter 11.

Another recent development has been a focus on the quality of the supporting business processes. This concept uses the methodology of quality management and has become known as business reengineering. Companies have introduced the methods of quality control, quality improvement, and quality planning to management, often leading to breakthrough performance improvements of their business processes. They soon discovered that not only were these business processes competitive weapons in the eyes of the customers, but they also had great possibilities for improved efficiencies. There are many examples of these types of improvements. One telephone company reduced the cost of its order-entry process by over 90%. Another company removed 95% of the waste in its direct mail process [Godfrey and Endres (1994)].

With the increasing scope of quality systems came the realization that quality was no longer a tactical issue to be left to quality specialists, but had become a strategic issue requiring senior management leadership. One of the responsibilities of senior management was to ensure that strategic quality goals were integrated into the business planning process.

Senior managers have to participate in the deployment of quality goals across the organization. This is a task that cannot be delegated.

John Jarvis, General Manager of British Telecom's East Anglia District, wrote, "To ensure real added value top management must set time aside and be committed to looking for fundamentally different ways of doing things, . . . addressing the key issues of Vision, Strategy and vital few projects" [Jarvis (1990)]. He reported the key process for ensuring that these activities take place was to integrate "our Annual Operating Plan and Quality Plan to ensure year on year improvements in our overall business performance." He indicated that monthly and annual reviews against operating and quality goals are used as input to performance appraisals with their effect on merit pay and bonuses.

Bowen (1988) described a similar approach at GTE California. GTE also tied its quality performance to incentive compensation. Bowen stated,

> one of the key elements in establishing a clear link between individual accomplishments and the company's strategic quality and cost objectives was to find a statistically sound means of measuring local group contributions to achieving these objectives. . . . GTE California determined how to link GTE's strategic objectives, and an individual's quality objectives by identifying objectives "Key Performance Units," e.g., departments, work groups, whose performance were demonstrably linked (downward) to an individual's objectives and linked (upwards) to GTE's strategic objectives. . . . The performance objectives were at least partially based upon comparisons to the regional Bell telephone companies, other GTE telephone companies and expectations of customers.

This is one of the earliest examples of integrating the results of benchmarking into a strategic planning process.

The combination of statistical quality control, continuous quality improvement, quality planning, modern quality systems, and strategic quality planning came to be called total quality management, or TQM, in the 1980s. This phrase was taken from the Japanese concepts of total quality control or companywide quality control that were developed in the 1970s and 1980s. The modern concept of TQM is discussed in detail in Chapter 4.

A substantial driving force for the adoption of TQM and the goal of a world-class quality system has been the establishment of the national and international quality awards discussed previously. These have been expanded to state awards in the United States and to internal quality awards by multiunit companies such as AT&T and IBM. Many other organizations, such as the American Society for Quality, are also using the award criteria for self-assessments.

An excellent text by Tito Conti (1993) further describes the development of the quality movement. Much of the information in this chapter has been influenced by this work. Conti discusses the development of quality management from early work on product quality to later work on process quality to current work on business process quality management. A review of AT&T's contributions to quality management can be found in an article by Godfrey (1986).

▶ 1-6 TRAINING FOR QUALITY

All the new concepts of making everyone responsible for the quality of the product or service mean that a significant amount of education is necessary. Historically, training in quality control has been an essential component of each phase of progress in beneficial applications of the discipline. As was indicated earlier, the principles and techniques of quality control as developed by Shewhart and others remained for years isolated within Bell Laboratories with only a relatively small number of applications in Western Electric and a few other companies. The massive and widespread training programs that were carried out during World War II finally launched extensive applications of quality control among American manufacturers and businesses. Similar efforts expanded the growth to British firms and others.

The postwar era witnessed still further expansion, diversification, and acceleration of training programs. The importance of training in Japan's rise to international fame in quality of manufactured goods is now history and was discussed in Section 1-4. That country's extensive effort, which outstripped Western efforts, paid off handsomely and has led to a reemphasis among Western firms on training throughout the organization.

An example of Japan's training effort is summarized in the following quotation from Ishikawa (1968), in which he emphasizes the use of public media for quality control training in Japan:

> QC courses through radio began in July 1956. The Nippon Shortwave Broadcasting Co. (NSB) held a 3-month course seven times. Since 1957, NHK (Japan Broadcasting Corporation) held an introductory course called "Management and Quality Control" for 7 weeks (15 minutes per weekday). More than 100,000 copies of this textbook have been distributed. From 1957 to 1962, there were seven NHK radio QC courses. In 1960 and 1961, NHK TV broadcast two courses called Quality Control and Standardization for 4 months.

In one U.S. factory of approximately 4000 employees, some 23,000 work-hours of quality control training were conducted for personnel from top management to inspectors and key shop workers from 1952 to 1963 [Stephens (1965)]. More than 3000 control charts were being used to control the quality of thirty different products. Over the first seven years, savings in production waste and excessive inspection amounted to $27 million. Documentation of the results obtained on a number of specific products is contained in papers by Schin (1959, 1960a, 1960b). This factory was visited by many Japanese (and other) industrial study teams in the mid to late 1950s and is referred to in various papers by Japanese authors.

Extensive efforts have been made in establishing quality control programs in developing countries [Stephens (1978, 1979a, 1979b, 1982)]. Training is still identified as a principal step in the development of quality control programs in these countries and will receive additional emphasis in the future. The ISO 9000 quality system standards discussed in Chapter 3 have a requirement for training. This requirement is that all members of the firm that are in any way associated with quality must be trained and that the training be documented.

Recent surges for quality and quality control among firms in the United States, aided and abetted by Japanese successes, have given rise to increased efforts in training programs and the proliferation of consultants, professional societies, and university courses and seminars. Quality improvement programs on a companywide basis emphasize the importance of training for all managers—not just those in the direct quality function.

▶ 1-7 REFERENCES

American Society for Quality (2000), ANSI/ISO/ASQ Q9000-2000, *Quality Management Systems—Fundamentals and Vocabulary,* ASQ, Milwaukee, WI.

AT&T (1984), *Statistical Quality Control Handbook,* AT&T, Indianapolis, IN.

Bowen, M. D. (1988), "Quality Improvement through Incentive

Compensation," *Juran Institute's IMPRO Proceedings,* pp. 3A-21–24, Juran Institute, Wilton, CT.

British Standards Institution (1935) *BS 600, Application of Statistical Methods to Industrial Standardization and Quality Control,* British Standards Institution, London, U.K.

Conti, Tito (1993), *Building Total Quality,* Chapman & Hall, New York.

Crosby, Philip B. (1979), *Quality Is Free,* McGraw-Hill, New York.

Crosby, Philip B. (1984), *Quality without Tears,* McGraw-Hill, New York.

"Phil Crosby: A Change in Career" (1979), *Quality,* Vol. 18, No. 6, pp. 16–19 (June).

Deming, W. E. (1994), "Transcript of Speech to GAO Roundtable on Product Quality—Japan vs. the United States," *Quality Progress,* Vol. 27, No. 3, pp. 39–44 (March).

"Dr. W. Edwards Deming–the Statistical Control of Quality" (1980), *Quality,* Vol. 19, No. 2, pp. 38–42 (February).

Dodge, H. F., and Romig, H. G. (1959), *Sampling Inspection Tables for Single and Double Sampling,* Second Edition, Wiley, New York.

Fagan, M. D., Ed. (1974), *A History of Engineering and Science in the Bell System, The Early Years* (1875–1925), Bell Telephone Laboratories, Incorporated, New York.

Feigenbaum, A. V., (1991), *Total Quality Control,* Third Edition, McGraw-Hill, New York.

Godfrey, A. B. (1986), "The History and Evolution of Quality in AT&T," *AT&T Technical Journal,* Vol. 65, No. 2, pp. 9–20, (March–April).

Godfrey, A. B, and Endres, A. C. (1994), "The Evolution of Quality Management within Telecommunications," *IEEE Communications Magazine,* Vol. 32, No. 10, pp. 26–34 (October).

Golomski, W. A. (1967), "Walter A. Shewhart—A Man of Quality—His Work, Our Challenge," *Industrial Quality Control,* Vol. 24, No. 2, pp. 83–85 (August).

Imai, M. (1986), *Kaizen,* McGraw-Hill, New York.

Ishikawa, K. (1967), "Tributes to Walter A. Shewhart," *Industrial Quality Control,* pp. 115–16 (August).

Ishikawa, K. (1968), "Education and Training of Quality Control in Japanese Industry," *Tokyo,* pp. 423–26 (October).

Ishikawa, K. (1985), *What Is Total Quality Control?,* Prentice-Hall, Englewood Cliffs, NJ.

Jarvis, J. E. F. (1990), "The Real Leadership Challenge—Making It Stick," *Juran Institute's IMPRO Proceedings,* pp. 6C—24, 64, Juran Institute, Wilton, CT.

Jones, R. L. (1926), "The Viewpoint of Inspection Engineering," *Bell Laboratories Record* (August).

Juran, J. M. (1954), Planning and Practices in Quality Control, July and August, From Juran's Lectures on Quality Control to the Japanese (unpublished materials provided to one of the authors by J. M. Juran) originally translated and distributed by JUSE.

Juran, J. M. (1979), "Japanese and Western Quality—A Contrast," *Quality,* Vol. 18, Nos. 1 and 2, pp. 8–12 and 12–15 (January and February).

Kondo, Y. (1988), "Quality in Japan," in *Juran's Quality Control Handbook,* Fourth Edition, Section 35F, McGraw-Hill, New York.

Kume, H. (1994), Personal communication with one of the authors about the history of quality in Japan (March).

Nonaka, I. (1993), "The History of the Quality Circle," *Quality Progress,* Vol. 26, No. 9, pp. 81–83 (September).

Schin, R. (1959), "Can Quality Control Pay Its Own Way?," *Transactions of the Rutgers All-Day Quality Control Conference,* Rutgers—The State University of New Jersey, New Brunswick, NJ, pp. 107–25 (September 12).

Schin, R. (1960a), "Process Control Is Essential for Reliability of Electronic Devices," *Transactions of the Metropolitan Conference on Quality Control,* New York, pp. 158–67 (February 26–27).

Schin, R. (1960b), "Quality Control Engineering—in Process and Product Control," *Industrial Quality Control,* Vol. 16, No. 10 (April).

Shewhart, W. A. (1925), "The Applications of Statistics as an Aid in Maintaining Quality of a Manufactured Product," *Journal of the American Statistical Association,* pp. 546–48 (December).

Shewhart, W. A. (1931), *Economic Control of Quality of Manufactured Product,* Van Nostrand, New York.

Shewhart, W. A., and Deming, W. E. (1939), *Statistical Methods from the Viewpoint of Quality Control,* Graduate School, Department of Agriculture, Washington, DC.

Singer, C., Holmyard, E. J., Hall, A. R., and Williams, T. I. (1958), *A History of Technology,* Vol. IV, *The Industrial Revolution,* pp. 645–46, Oxford University Press, New York and London.

Statistical Research Group (1945), *Sequential Analysis of Statistical Data: Applications,* Columbia University, New York.

Statistical Research Group (1947), *Techniques of Statistical Analysis,* Columbia University, New York.

Statistical Research Group (1948), *Sampling Inspection,* Columbia University, New York.

Stephens, K. S. (1965), "Quality Control—Small and Large," *Transactions of the 1st Pan American Congress on Quality Control and Statistics in Industry,* Mexico City (May 12) and *Proceedings of the Quality Control Conference,* U.S. Department of Commerce, Bureau of Public Roads, Washington, D.C. (April 6).

Stephens, K. S. (1978), "UNIDO Technical Assistance in Standardization, Certification and Quality Control—With a Thailand Case Study," *Transactions ICQC '78,* Tokyo C3, pp. 31–35.

Stephens, K. S. (1979a), "Nigerian Standards Organization Leads the Way in Nation's QC Development," *Quality Progress,* Vol. 12, No. 8, pp. 11–13 (August).

Stephens, K. S. (1979b), *Preparing for Standardization, Certification and Quality Control,* Asian Productivity Organization, Tokyo, p. 125.

Stephens, K. S. (1982), "Quality Control Training in Turkey," *Quality Progress,* Vol. 15, No. 1, pp. 16–21 (January).

Syrett, H. C., Ed. (1966), *The Papers of Alexander Hamilton, Volume X, December 1791–January 1792,* Columbia University Press, New York.

Wallis, W. A. (1980), "The Statistical Research Group, 1942–1945," *Journal of the American Statistical Association,* Vol. 75, No. 370, pp. 320–30 (June).

Wilks, S. S. (1962), *Mathematical Statistics,* Wiley, New York.

Zaludova, A. (1994), "Brief Report of the Development of Quality Control in the Czech Communications Industry," Private communication to one of the authors (March 7).

2

QUALITY AND
QUALITY SYSTEMS

What is quality? For starters turn to an available dictionary and read the definition of quality. It probably includes some of the following in its definition:

- degree of excellence, or general excellence (. . . has quality)
- attribute or faculty (. . . has many good qualities)
- relative nature, character, or property

These aspects are usually included in the traditional dictionary definitions of quality. Actually, quality has many definitions, as it applies to a very broad range of items. The quality profession takes a much more functional, action-oriented approach to the definition of quality.

Shewhart (1931) argues that quality is often best described as "qualities" (i.e., multiple characteristics), that it is quantifiable, from this perspective, but that there is both an objective and a subjective side to quality.

A widely used definition of quality is:

Quality is conformance to requirements or specifications.

This is the definition used by Crosby (1979), who suggests that such a statement is necessary—that is, to manage quality adequately, we must be able to measure it.

A more general definition of quality is:

Quality is fitness for use.

This definition is attributed to Juran (1988). It places emphasis on the consumer aspect of quality, including design quality. These latter two definitions can and should be the same—they show a need to make the requirements or specifications reflect fitness for use [Stephens (1979)]. Juran does not relegate design responsibility to the inspection department. He emphasizes that requirements and specifications translate fitness for use into measurable quantities. Deming (1986) stresses that "quality should be aimed at the needs of the consumer, present and future." That "Quality begins with the intent, which is fixed by management." "The intent must be translated by engineers and others into plans, specifications, tests, production." Stephens emphasizes that quality doesn't necessarily mean good quality. It means consistency and conformity to a standard or specification, a statement of what the user wants and can afford *and* what the producer can provide. The quality statement should be based on what the existing process can produce economically with reasonable controls and improvements. Hence, the producer and user must cooperate in defining a reasonable and economical specification of quality. This is an important part of quality planning, to match the needs of the customers with the capability of the process and the product design. For example, if a producer of plastic measuring and drawing rulers were to specify a requirement of ±0.5 cm in a length of 30 cm, then even with good conformity to this requirement, the rulers would be unfit for reasonable use. Conversely, if consumers were to request a ±0.01 mm tolerance on the diameter of the body of ballpoint pens, their manufacture would not be practical or economical, while such a tight specification would fail to provide any extra fitness for use.

Feigenbaum (1991) defines product and service quality as follows:

> *The total composite product and service characteristics of marketing, engineering, manufacture, and maintenance through which the product and service in use will meet the expectations of the customer.*

The Japanese term for quality is *shitsu*. It is written by a Chinese character composed of two parts. Lillrank and Kano (1989) explain these parts as follows:

> *The upper part is made of two measures of weight (kin) symbolizing a balance, and the lower part consists of a shell (kai) that was used as money in the old days. Thus* shitsu *implies that quality is a relation, an exchange process where values are measured against each other.*

There have been many additional definitions, however; the most recent one is from ISO 9000-2000 [American Society for Quality (2000)]:

> *Quality: degree to which a set of inherent characteristics fulfils requirements,* with the following notes:
>> NOTE 1: *The term "quality" can be used with adjectives such as poor, good, or excellent.*
>> NOTE 2: *"Inherent" means existing in something, especially as a permanent characteristic.* In further clarification of this definition, "requirement" is defined as,
> *Requirement: need or expectation that is stated, generally implied or obligatory.*

All of these definitions and others have their place in an overall system of quality that considers different viewpoints.

▶ 2-1 QUALITY CONCEPTS AND RELATED ASPECTS

Quality can affect other vital elements of a company such as productivity, cost, and delivery schedules. It may also have an effect on the workplace environment. Quality leaves its imprint on society and on the quality of government.

In recognition of the many aspects of quality, to describe the wide spectrum of applicability, the authors have developed a broad and comprehensive definition of quality.[1]

---

[1]This is an adaptation and expansion from a paper by Dr. Farouk M. Fawzi (1978).

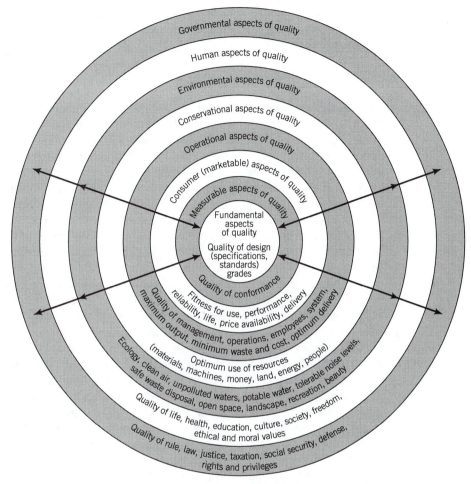

Figure 2-1 Quality's Expanding Influence

It defines quality from several important aspects and illustrates quality's ever-expanding influence. These concepts are portrayed in Figure 2-1. The definitions, including the traditional dictionary definition, cut across the three inner aspects portrayed. The two inner aspects are particularly important for a proper understanding of the "as conceived" and "as made" quality of products and services. Concern for quality is often not exercised adequately, particularly by production and corporate management personnel, because these two inner aspects of quality are not known or understood. Briefly, these aspects of quality are known as "design quality" and "manufactured quality." As emphasized above, the purpose of both should be to provide quality satisfactory to the consumer—the "as delivered" and "as perceived" quality. The double directional arrows on Figure 2-1 imply that inner and outer aspects of quality influence each other.

An excellent discussion of the meaning of quality is also given by Garvin (1984, 1988). He expands the three traditional approaches to defining quality to five and also gives a list of eight dimensions of product quality. Garvin's five approaches to quality are transcendent, product-based, user-based, manufacturing-based, and value-based. His eight dimensions are performance, features, reliability, conformance, durability, serviceability, aesthetics, and perceived quality.

2-1.1 Design versus Manufactured (or Provided) Quality

Manufacturers or other commercial establishments often complain that "Quality costs too much!" When reference is made to the high cost of quality, it is almost always associated with the quality of the design, the product grade. This is, of course, a real cost. Suppliers of a new product or service must decide what will appeal to their potential customers, and consider what it will cost them to produce the product or offer the service and what the customers will pay. Design quality is an important aspect of quality and must be considered in planning the design, manufacture, and marketing of a product or service.

After a product or service has been designed to meet customer expectations, the associated process may not always produce each unit in conformity to the design. Defects in materials, parts, subassemblies, assemblies, and the final product occur. These defects may be related to design of the product, calling for a redesign. Often, these nonconformances are the result of inadequate, poorly planned manufacturing or service processes. Any nonconforming material, assemblies, and finished products that are discarded or reworked during the manufacturing process result in increased cost. These are costs that may not be identified as quality costs by managers who otherwise consider quality too costly. The lost time and effort in producing these nonconforming parts, the loss of business resulting from delays in delivery, and other associated ills of poor quality are the consequence of manufactured quality (i.e., the quality of conformance to the design).

Managers often fail to make the distinction between these two important aspects of quality: design quality and manufactured quality. Making this distinction is important because, with a correct understanding of these aspects of quality, it is realized that good quality and low cost can be achieved simultaneously, with both higher productivity and customer satisfaction. Higher design quality or product grade can mean higher cost, but higher manufactured quality or quality of conformity usually means lower cost. For example, for an automobile, if the design quality is improved by adding such features as air-conditioning, antilock braking systems, automatic transmission, cruise control, or electrically operated windows and door locks, this will result in increased costs. If it is found that camshaft production is resulting in 12% rework and 9% scrap, efforts that are taken to trace the causes, correct the process, and reduce these levels to a negligible amount will contribute to lower costs and greater production of acceptable units.

Insufficient preproduction testing or design qualification—for example, with something as mundane as automobile engine mounts—may result in the recall and repair of as many as 6.7 million units (an actual figure) for extremely costly rework. An inadequate attention to detail, such as tire pressure, in coordination with design, manufacture, and use may result in fatalities and severe liability, especially when earlier warnings are ignored. Understanding these concepts of quality contributes to a correct implementation of its function and to better management of the entire enterprise.

Awareness of the importance of quality and planning for it are essential actions for commercial enterprises, whether small or large. A manufacturer must also be aware of the physical, cultural, operational, and climatic environment in which the product will be used.

When wooden furniture is made in a humid tropical climate for distribution to a frigid or temperate dry climate, it is the producer's responsibility to learn about the effects of this climate, or any artificially produced environment on the long-term performance of the product. It may be necessary to include additional operations or controls in the manufacturing process. If cracks develop in the product after some period of use and the producer is not responsible in this regard, a decline of business after the initial orders should be expected. Costly recalls, warranty claims, or liability judgments may be incurred, depending on the nature of the product or service.

2-1.2 Quality: A Maturing Concept

In addition to management awareness and understanding of quality as an operating discipline, references to quality have become commonplace in the public media. Consumer expectations for quality have risen significantly with respect to performance, reliability, durability, price, and delivery.

In the last several decades, the world has seen tremendous improvements in both design and performance in household appliances, electronic devices, computers, transportation, and services. An increasing quality awareness by society has resulted in mass recalls of automobiles and other manufactured products. Such recalls were unheard of before the late 1960s. The outer rings of Figure 2-1 also reflect a maturing of quality as its principles influence broad-based aspects of society such as the environment and government. These in turn direct changes in the meaning and implementation of the inner ring aspects.

2-1.3 Specifications and Requirements, Quality Characteristics, Standards, and Measurement

As quality of products and services has been defined as conformance to specifications, which ideally reflect fitness for use, such requirements play a significant role in defining and managing quality. Generically, we define a specification as a concise statement of a set of requirements to be satisfied. Individual requirements are often referred to as "quality characteristics." Examples are dimensions, appearance, strength, volume, errors in billing or posting of payments, and product or service life. Individual quality characteristics are the elemental building blocks of quality. They permit measurement, improvement, and control.

A formal definition of a specification is provided by the International Organization for Standardization (1991), *Guide 2,* as follows:

> *Technical Specification: Document that prescribes technical requirements to be fulfilled by a product, process or service.* And additional NOTES, 1 *A technical specification should indicate, whenever appropriate, the procedure(s) by means of which it may be determined whether the requirements given are fulfilled.* And, 2 *A technical specification may be a standard, a part of a standard or independent of a standard.*

The same document also defines a standard:

> *Standard: Document, established by consensus and approved by a recognized body, that provides, for common and repeated use, rules, guidelines or characteristics for activities or their*

results, aimed at the achievement of the optimum degree of order in a given context. And the additional NOTE, *Standards should be based on the consolidated results of science, technology and experience, and aimed at the promotion of optimum community benefits.*

Further elaboration of these terms is necessary for a better understanding of the concepts and their use in measuring, controlling, improving, and managing quality. For example, another definition of a specification is from DOD-STD-480A:

Specification: A document intended primarily for use in procurement, which clearly and accurately describes the essential technical requirements for items, materials, or services including the procedures by which it will be determined that the requirements have been met.

This definition emphasizes further the control aspect by including a reference to "the procedures by which it will be determined that the requirements have been met." This has also been added to the NOTE in the above definition of a technical specification by ISO.

2-1.4 Standards: Foundations for Quality

Standards form an important part of a quality system. Standards cover a broad range of subjects from products to systems themselves. The ISO 9000 series is an excellent example of this at the system level. Verman (1973) has illustrated the concept with his standardization space, which we reproduce as Figure 2-2.[2] Formal systems of standards preparation and implementation have been established in major companies, in trade associations and professional societies, and in governmental and private organizations at the regional and international level.

In today's society of technological advances with extensive efforts to establish order, standards have been developed on an extensive set of items with which we come in contact. The process of standardization continues at an even greater pace. Most of the general public pay little attention to the matter and take for granted the numerous standards affecting such essentials as clothing, food, housing, transportation, and recreation. The principles of standards are often missing in formal educational programs from grade school through university.

2-1.5 Some Examples of Standards

Examining a number of standards will help to obtain a perspective of the quality characteristics that are applicable to certain products, which we may otherwise take for granted.

▶ EXAMPLE 2-1

The ASTM Standard Specification for Knitted Fabrics, D3887-80, specifies requirements on properties of knitted fabrics: yield, weight, width, length, fabric count, bursting strength, extractable matter, and fiber composition. Secondary properties include the moisture regain and thickness. The principal standard references some nine additional standards and provides the necessary test methods for the specified characteristics.

---

[2]Reproduced with permission of Archon Books, Hamden, Connecticut.

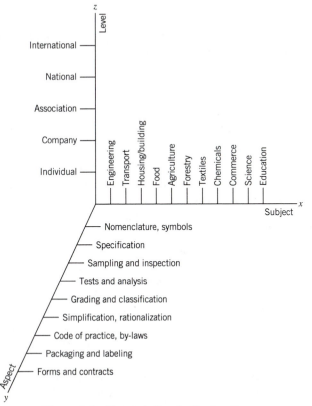

Figure 2-2 Verman's Standardization Space

▶ **EXAMPLE 2-2**

Company standards established for a leading beverage include requirements and test instructions for the following characteristics: syrup-water ratio (syrup content per package size); syrup Brix; syrup age; water (potable; free from off-taste, odor, and suspended matter; maximum alkalinity; maximum chlorine, iron, and aluminum residual); maximum microbiological count limits on water, syrup, final product, and washed bottle; product taste free from off-taste and odors; product appearance free from bottle ring, suspended matter, or any other foreign material, bottle cleaning (minimum temperature and caustic strength); and crown crimp. An extensive set of requirements also applies to new bottle inputs, including finish, roundness, rocker, leaner, dimensions, capacity, pressure strength, and thermal shock strength.

▶ **EXAMPLE 2-3**

As discussed earlier, ISO 9001 is a standard for quality systems. Some of its characteristics are the establishment, documentation, implementation, maintenance, and continual improvement of a quality management system. See Chapter 3 for a more detailed coverage of this standard and its elements.

The Quality of Standards
Because standards are instruments to define and improve the quality of products, services, test methods, and procedures, the standards themselves must be of good quality.

Just as with actual products and services, this is not always the case. In a paper by Stephens (1977), three quality characteristics of standards—clarity of expression, technical acuity, and adequacy and accuracy of compliance sampling procedures—are considered to illustrate some examples of inadequate quality in these characteristics. He offers some solutions for improving the quality of standards. See also the December 1991 issue of ASTM's *Standardization News*.

2-1.6 Severity Classification of Quality Characteristics and Associated Defects

Not all requirements have the same importance regarding the effect of their departure. A departure from a specified requirement is a nonconformity. A sufficient departure from usage requirements is a defect. For example, the definition of a defect as given in the ANSI/ISO/ASQ 9000-2000 is as follows:

> *Defect: nonfulfillment of a requirement related to an intended or specified use. It is accompanied by the following notes:*
>
> NOTE 1: *The distinction between the concepts defect and nonconformity is important as it has legal connotations, particularly those associated with product liability issues. Consequently the term "defect" should be used with extreme caution.*
>
> NOTE 2: *The intended use as intended by the customer can be affected by the nature of the information, such as operating or maintenance instructions, provided by the supplier.*

It is useful to indicate level of severity of defects or nonconformities, and there are various systems to serve this purpose. In many programs of quality control, usually one or more of four categories of severity for correction and prevention are employed. These levels of severity are described as follows in ISO 2859-1 (1999):

Class A	Very Serious	Leads directly to severe injury or catastrophic economic loss
Class B	Serious	Leads directly to significant injury or significant economic loss
Class C	Major	Related to major problems with respect to intended normal, or reasonably foreseeable, use
Class D	Minor	Related to minor problems with respect to intended normal, or reasonably foreseeable, use

Another system in use is the assignment of demerit weights to different severity levels of defects or nonconformities with associated descriptions in specifications containing the requirements or quality characteristics. Common demerit weights are 100, 50, 10, and 1. These are not necessarily aligned with the types of defects or nonconformities described in the fourfold classification above, since very serious defects may be outside these classifications. Demerit classification allows for the computation of a demerit index and the possibility of charting. The system used by AT&T follows this format [see Hoadley (1981)].

A further example is the 3, 5, 15 point system used by Peugeot in auditing completed automobiles. Peugeot's disapproval classification is as follows:

3 Points	Nonconformity that will be accepted by the average customer	To be pointed out but not rectified before delivery

| 5 Points | +0: Important nonconformity that most customers will not accept | To be corrected before delivery |
| 5 Points | +10: Glaring and intolerable blunder that will be noticed by all customers | A 10-point penalty applied, denoting rejection: 5 + 10 = 15 points |

Implementation of the system is aided by a quality audit form with divisions for (1) Vehicle Exterior—Body Shop, Print Shop, Sealer Application, and Carriage Equipment; (2) the same for Vehicle Interior; (3) Mechanical Functioning and Checks; (4) Mechanical Noises and Noises in the Body Work; and (5) Weatherproof.

2-1.7 Measurement of Quality Characteristics

Standards may contain references to other standards that have test methods for measuring quality characteristics. Test methods and equipment for tests are important parts of an overall quality system.

Instruments to measure quality characteristics range from mechanical devices, electrical instruments, and analytical chemistry instruments, to visual inspections and sensory evaluations. For visual inspections it is common to establish visual standards in pictorial, descriptive, or physical example form. The diagram shown in Figure 2-3 illustrates a standardized system of inspection of fabrics and garments used by Sears Roebuck & Company. The small rectangular standard shown to the left of the fabric sample is a replica of levels of severity of various nonconformities, such as slubs and knots. Inspectors are trained to view the fabric or garment sample against the replica to assess the level of severity of any nonconformity that may be present in the sample unit.

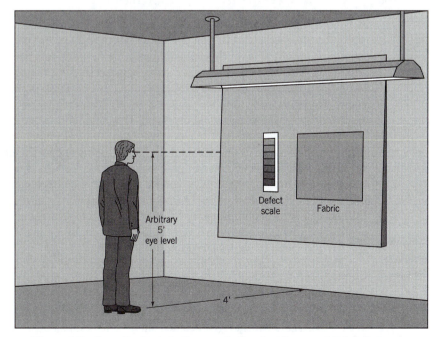

Figure 2-3   Sears Roebuck & Company's Standard System of Fabric Inspection

Sensory evaluations pertain to human judgment regarding appearance, sound, feel, and odor. Because human sensory perception is quite variable, testing is often done via panels made up of a number of selected, trained raters. Error of measurement, important to all forms of measurement, is often incorporated in the rating procedure by asking each rater to rate duplicate samples, with the raters unaware of which sample is the duplicate. Evaluation of a batch is often accomplished as an analysis of the within- and between-rater variation and rating level, based on a semi-variables scale of three to seven levels from very satisfactory to very unsatisfactory. For more details on this procedure, see Dawson (1964, 1967), Herschdoerfer (1967), Pangburn (1967), Stewart (1971), and Furia (1972). See also the paper by Smith and Chambers (1993).

NDT and ATE

Two important areas in the measurement field are nondestructive testing (NDT) and automatic test equipment (ATE). Both are being used in increasing amounts to achieve and ensure quality. NDT is especially useful in detecting flaws, voids, and cracks in solid objects, especially metal parts. Such techniques as radiographic testing, ultrasonic testing, eddy current testing, liquid penetrant testing, and magnetic particle testing are in widespread use. In addition to being supported by manufacturers of equipment, this activity is also supported by the American Society for Nondestructive Testing.

ATE is being used increasingly to replace manual inspection in areas in which it has been determined that 100% inspection is necessary to avoid further processing of nonconforming parts and to prevent such parts from reaching customers. In some cases ATE and NDT are combined by automating certain nondestructive testing.

2-1.8 Metrology: A Broader Perspective of Measurement

A famous quotation by Lord Kelvin is a basic tenet of measurement: "I often say that when you can measure what you are talking about and express it in numbers, you know something about it; but when you cannot measure it, when you cannot express it in numbers, your knowledge is of a meager and unsatisfactory kind." A science of measurement has evolved, known as metrology, the logic or study or science of measurement. The term comes from the Greek words *metron* and *logos*. According to Webster, metrology is the science or system of weights and measures. This latter phrase "weights and measures" is often associated with units of measurement and the legal problem of maintaining accuracy of measurement in the marketplace, "legal metrology." Examples include monitoring of gasoline pumps and market scales.

Industrial metrology is a program for establishing and maintaining an accuracy and precision of measurement necessary to support production of quality goods and services. Exchange of ideas and information on industrial metrology, especially at the factory level, is not supported by international or national organizations, at least not to the degree that weights and measures or legal metrology is supported.

Valuable information for industrial measurement and calibration is available from manufacturers and suppliers of measurement equipment as well as from specialists in laboratory and testing facilities. The national and international measurement system of the United States was the subject of papers by Roberts (1974), McCoubrey (1974), and Podolsky (1974). These papers merit detailed study along with an unsigned article in the same issue of ASTM *Standardization News* on the National Conference on Standards Laboratories (NCSL) [Anon (1974)]. This article contains a Calibration System Specification for use by laboratories or test facilities for control of measuring instruments and physical measurement standards. See also papers by Huntoon (1975), Huntley (1995), and Simpson (1981).

Additional references on calibration are ANSI/NCSL Z540-1, *General Requirements for Calibration Laboratories and Measuring and Test Equipment,* and the International Standard ISO 10012-2002, *Quality Assurance Requirements for Measuring Equipment.*

A Practical Principle of Measurement[3]

A system of measurement that is used by some organizations and countries is known as a hierarchical system, involving formal levels of calibration from a given instrument to a high level measurement authority (such as the national central laboratory or International Bureau of Weights and Measures). From a quality control standpoint, in particular, this system has some drawbacks as explained below.

The metrology and measurement services in the United States are not organized as formally as other countries. Except in a few organizations, such as the U.S. Department of Defense, "calibration chains" or other hierarchical structures do not exist. Each organization is individually responsible for seeing that its measurements are adequate to meet needs.

This approach focuses attention on the quality and adequacy of measurement relative to the need, rather than on the properties of instruments. This has the advantage of forcing one to look at the whole system being tested so that areas needing improvement are discovered even when the instruments are not at fault.

Medical measurements serve as an example of this approach. In this case, success of a metrology organization would be measured by the percentage of correct values obtained on actual patients. The problem that one faces then is how to sample the actual measurements to determine their quality. One could use techniques such as redetermining the value by a more accurate method or perhaps running a reference sample periodically or employing some other appropriate technique.

One has a way of monitoring the quality of the measurements, determining the cause of poor performance, and seeing the effect of changes. By contrast, the usual hierarchical approach confines its attention to the properties of instruments calibrated under successively more restrictive conditions as one approaches the central national laboratory. This would seem to be of doubtful usefulness if one were concerned with the quality of the measurements being made by the instrument.

Internationally, the International Bureau of Weights and Measures (BIPM) located in Sèvres, France, provides for international cooperation in matters relating to primary standards and units of measurement, such as the meter, kilogram, second, ampere, Kelvin, mole, and candela. The BIPM operates under the authority of a diplomatic conference, the General Conference on Weights and Measures, and of a committee of scientific experts, the International Committee for Weights and Measures. The BIPM has the responsibility

---

[3]The measurement principle expounded here is from personal correspondence with one of the authors from Joe Cameron, formerly chief of the NBS (now NIST) Office of Measurement Services. See also the brief article by Kimber (1983).

of establishing new metric standards, conserving the international prototypes, and making comparisons necessary to assure the uniformity of measure throughout the world.

Also at the international level, legal metrology is supported by the International Organization of Legal Metrology (OIML), which was founded in 1955 to "promote intergovernmental cooperation in the field of legal metrology which, broadly relates to the compatibility of standards of measurements and the legislation and Government regulations which may affect such standards of measurement." Aside from its activities as a center of documentation and information exchange in legal metrology, OIML recommends uniform international requirements of scientific and measurement instruments used in industry and commerce and works out model laws and regulations for consideration by member nations.

2-1.9 Laboratory Accreditation

Because many measurements are made in private and public laboratories, programs have been developed for evaluating and accrediting such laboratories. An important goal of accreditation is to provide, in cooperation with the private sector, a national and international voluntary system to examine the technical competence of testing laboratories that serve regulatory and nonregulatory certification needs. A further goal is to establish public confidence in those laboratories that meet the established qualifications under the procedures. Accreditation is important to provide confidence that the output from a laboratory is in fact accurate and in the public interest.

One of the first programs of this type was the Australian Laboratory Accreditation System by the National Association of Testing Authorities (NATA), which began in 1946. NATA accreditation is granted for specific tests, grouped into fields of testing and based on scientific disciplines. They include acoustic and vibration measurement, biological testing, electrical testing, heat and temperature measurement, mechanical testing, metrology, nondestructive testing, and optics and photometry. For more details on the program, see Monaghan (1980).

The U.S. Department of Commerce announced a proposed procedure for a National Voluntary Laboratory Accreditation Program (NVLAP) in the *Federal Register,* Vol. 40, No. 90, on 8 May 1975. After a number of substantive changes in the proposed procedures based on written comments and testimony at public hearings, the rules and regulations for the program were published in the *Federal Register,* Vol. 41, No. 38, on 25 February 1976. The program differs from the NATA program primarily in that it accredits laboratories by specific product and test methods, instead of by discipline.

The purpose of NVLAP is to serve, on a timely basis, the needs of industry, consumers, and government by accrediting testing laboratories. This is pursued by fostering and promoting a uniformly acceptable base of professional and technical competence in testing laboratories and by establishing a background of experience necessary to the orderly evolution of a laboratory accreditation system.

The specific product and test methods for which NVLAP will consider accreditation of one or more laboratories is referred to as a LAP (laboratory accreditation program). A LAP must first be established by the Department of Commerce on request of private sector organizations or federal agencies. LAPs for thermal insulation materials, freshly mixed field concrete, and carpets were the first to be established. For further details on this program, see the referenced sections of the *Federal Register* as well as subsequent notices. The American Council of Independent Laboratories (ACIL) launched a program shortly after the establishment of NVLAP, in October 1976, known as the American Association of Laboratory Accreditation (AALA). It is similar to NATA.

At the international level the International Laboratory Accreditation Conference (ILAC) was established in 1977, primarily to develop a program for reciprocity of test data between laboratories of different countries. ILAC meets annually to review programs of activity and to plan new programs. A new standard on laboratories is ISO 17025 based on the previous ISO/IEC Guide 25, *General Requirements for the Technical Competence of Testing Laboratories.*

► 2-2 QUALITY CONTROL AND QUALITY ASSURANCE

Attention to quality and recognition that quality as a discipline offers sound business strategies are evolutionary and revolutionary forces that have made major contributions to our current way of life. The concepts of quality control and quality assurance have undergone changes in the evolutionary process of refinement and application. Like quality, they have many definitions. One useful definition for quality control [from Juran (1988)] that helps to put the preceding discussion on standards and measurements into an action mode is as follows:

> *Quality control is the regulatory process through which we measure actual quality performance, compare it with standards, and act on the difference.*

Another definition of quality control from the earlier ANSI/ASQC Standard A3 (1987) is as follows:

> **Quality Control:** *The operational techniques and the activities which sustain a quality of product or service that will satisfy given needs; also the use of such techniques and activities.*

Still another definition of quality control from the latest terminology standard, ISO 9000-2000, is:

> **Quality Control:** *part of quality management, focused on fulfilling quality requirements.*

2-2.1 The Evolution of Quality Control

Quality control is the original and most basic term for the application of quality principles. Feigenbaum (1991) ushered in a new development of quality control with his concept of total quality control. He traces the history of the development of total quality control in five steps over a half century.

These steps or stages are named as follows: (1) Operator Quality Control, or craftsmanship; (2) Foreman Quality Control; (3) Inspection Quality Control; (4) Statistical Quality Control; and (5) Total Quality Control. Like many entities undergoing a process of evolution, the various stages of the evolutionary process may coexist. A few companies continue to emphasize only the inspection aspect of quality control, whereas inspection is actually one useful element in an overall quality system [Stephens (2000)]. Some of the early stages are useful in themselves; operator quality control or craftsmanship is still of utmost importance in the creation and production of works of art, including items that are made in considerable quantities such as handwoven and tufted carpets. But even these areas can benefit from a more total or overall approach to quality control (for example, such as yarn and color control and improvement). Quality control circles, quality teams, and other participatory and employee involvement programs for operators are helping to return some quality control to the operator level.

Additional definitions of quality control include the following by Deming (1971), which places emphasis on the statistical aspects applied on an overall or total basis. It also makes explicit the economic objective of quality control:

> *The Statistical Control of Quality is application of statistical principles and techniques in all stages of design, production, maintenance and service, directed toward the economic satisfaction of demand.*

A further, interesting definition of statistical quality control is provided by the AT&T (1984) Statistical Quality Control Handbook, as follows:

Statistical Quality Control

Statistical: With the help of numbers, or data,

Quality: We study the characteristics of our process

Control: In order to make it behave the way we want it to behave

Statistical thinking and techniques still, and always should, play an important role in a total quality program. It is an invaluable discipline for studying processes, achieving and maintaining control, and realizing breakthroughs for continuous improvement.

The definition of total quality control as stated by Feigenbaum (1991) emphasizes the managerial and system aspects (the brackets have been added by the authors):

> *Total quality control is an effective system for integrating the quality—development [planning], quality—maintenance [control], and quality improvement efforts of the various groups in an organization so as to enable production and service at the most economical levels which allow for full customer satisfaction.*

This text, initially published in 1951 and last revised in 1991, is very much applicable to today's management of quality.

2-2.2 Further Evolution

Committees on definitions, nomenclature, and terminology still find considerable difficulty in reaching agreement on common terms. In a discussion among Japanese experts some differences between the American and Japanese concepts of total quality control were pointed out by Ishikawa et al. (1975): "Most American firms have failed to put into practice the total quality control as expounded by Dr. Feigenbaum." The discussion identified what might be called the sixth step or stage in the quality control evolution discussed above: companywide quality control. The following quotation from Ishikawa et al. (1975) explains the distinction:

Ishikawa: Our "TQC" resembles Dr. Feigenbaum's total quality control in that emphasis is put on the necessity of performing quality control in all departments through quality control engineers assigned to proper tasks. Our "company-wide quality control" differs from the American counterpart in that particular stress is placed on the "participation of all in quality control work" from the president downward to foremen and operators.

A paper by Deming (1975) in the same publication helps to reinforce this idea with the following quotation (with the bracketed addition by the present authors):

More important than this list of accomplishments [examples of early results of QC in Japan] was the swiftness with which they were all achieved (all obviously in 1950, 1951, and early 1952). My explanation is that the top people in the companies took hold of the problems of production and quality. All the reports quoted by Mr. Koyanagi (1952) in his paper were written by men with the rank of President of the company, Managing Director, or Chairman of the Board. I know from being out there with them that some of these men were out working in the plant, taking charge of the problems of quality and output and that their reports represented their firsthand participation.

A significant new development in Japan was the decision to make a formal name change from TQC to TQM. The Union of Japanese Scientists and Engineers (JUSE) officially announced this change in April 1996. Shortly thereafter, a TQM Committee was formed to address issues relating to the name change. Further discussion of this topic is contained in Chapter 4.

2-2.3 Quality Assurance

An additional term related to an overall approach to quality control, making the controls more comprehensive, is that of "quality assurance." A generic definition of quality assurance is the following:

Quality assurance is a system of activities whose purpose is to provide an assurance that the overall quality control is in fact being done effectively.

The ANSI/ASQC Standard A3 (1987) definition was:

Quality assurance: *All those planned or systematic actions necessary to provide confidence that a product or service will satisfy given needs.*

The more current definition from ISO 9000-2000 is as follows:

Quality assurance: *part of quality management, focused on providing confidence that quality requirements will be fulfilled.*

It is interesting to note that distinctions between the terms "quality control" and "quality assurance" are not emphasized in Japan, as they are in the United States and other Western cultures. This is primarily because the term "control" in Japan does not bear any negative connotation (as it does to some in the West), such as coercive supervision. The

Japanese word for control is *kanri*. It is said that *kanri* can be translated as management or administration [Lillrank and Kano (1989)]. Hence, the term "quality control" in Japan implies a systematic and fact-based management of quality. This is also the opinion of many practitioners in the West, and strong distinctions are not made between quality control and quality assurance. In fact, Feigenbaum (1991) states, "Total-quality-control programs in their operation include and integrate the actions involved in the work covered by both terms." It isn't the terms that make the programs, but the activities being used.

These activities involve a continual survey of effectiveness of the quality control program to improve it as necessary. For a specific product or service, this may involve verification audits. If used as defined above, quality assurance is ensuring that quality control is doing what it should. Such an effort should be organized within a factory or company and should be motivated by management.

▶ 2-3 QUALITY MANAGEMENT SYSTEMS

An advanced stage of evolution of quality control is expressed by the concept of the quality system, now referred to in the revised ISO 9000-2000 series as the "quality management system." This concept emphasizes the identification of a comprehensive set of elements to be included in the quality control program. Much of the material in the remaining portion of this chapter and the next is devoted to a discussion of the system elements, with some examples that include an example of a quality system itself, that is, the ISO 9000 series. Chapter 4 explores in greater depth the integration of these concepts with emphasis on management.

A definition of the term quality system from ANSI/ASQC Standard A3 (1987) was the following:

> **Quality system:** *The collective plans, activities, and events that are provided to ensure that a product, process, or service will satisfy given needs.*

The more current definition from ISO 9000-2000 is as follows:

> **Quality management system:** *management system to direct and control an organization with regard to quality.*

2-3.1 Quality Management and Total Strategic Quality

Quality management as defined in ISO 9000-2000 is as follows:

> **Quality management:** *coordinated activities to direct and control an organization with regard to quality;* and the accompanying NOTE: *direction and control with regard to quality generally includes establishment of the quality policy and quality objectives, quality planning, quality control, quality assurance and quality improvement.*

Recent years have seen the proliferation of the term "total quality management" and the abbreviation TQM. A word on semantics in the quality disciplines was given above.

In terms of a comprehensive total strategic quality, management is an essential process. Total quality management is defined as follows:

> **Total quality management:** *a process that integrates fundamental management art and techniques with the principles and methodologies of total strategic quality to develop and implement successful business strategies throughout the organization.*

In the evolution to total strategic quality a solid foundation has been laid by defining quality as well as describing stages of quality control development through quality systems to total strategic quality. Much of total strategic quality is covered by these earlier evolutionary stages. However, what sets total strategic quality apart from its earlier evolutionary entities is its emphasis. Building on the strengths of earlier aspects and with recognition of the impact on business strategy, total strategic quality is much more comprehensive. It places emphasis on the following:

- A clear focus on customer needs
- Continuous improvement and innovation of all processes, services, and products
- Effective empowerment and recognition of individuals under a team involvement approach, including essential programs of education and training
- Sound planning for quality with fact-based decision making, variability reduction, defect prevention, and fast response systems that include recognition of the internal customer and the triple role of supplier, processor, and customer
- Integration of and mutual cooperation with suppliers based on long-term partnership relations
- Sensitivity to competitive comparisons via benchmarking, including "best in class" on noncompetitive but significant processes
- Productivity, cost reduction, and profitability enhancements
- Strong leadership by management at all levels

These, together with all of the methodologies of quality systems, constitute total strategic quality. Quality control is an expanding influence on the creation and management of products and services, as well as national and international programs of commerce. Early stages have helped to influence and expand the later stages, which, in turn, have contributed to understanding and expanding the earlier stages as they are continually modified and refined within the overall system. A good example of this is the renewed attention of the operator under a system of employee involvement and empowerment, which can be likened to the recreation of craftsmanship at the mass production level. Similar to that for quality, a diagram presenting the evolution and expansion of quality control has been developed. It summarizes quality control through the multiple stages of evolution and progress and illustrates quality control's ever-expanding influence on business strategy and results. This is shown in Figure 2-4.

During the evolutionary process of development, of particular importance is the move up from detection (inspection QC) to correction and prevention of quality problems (SQC/TQC/QA), to employee involvement and empowerment, to continuous quality improvement, to customer satisfaction. All this is coincident with the expanded scope and

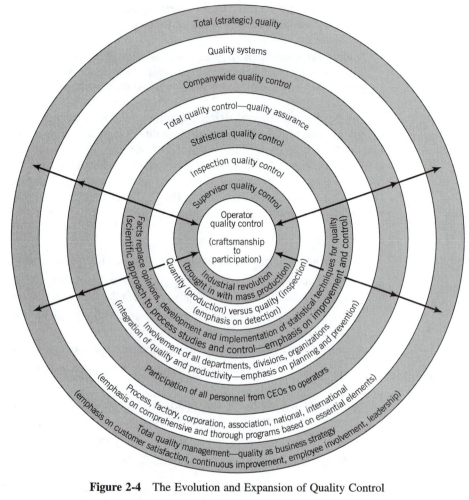

Figure 2-4 The Evolution and Expansion of Quality Control

aspects of quality (see Figure 2-1). This progress of beneficial movement is shown in Figure 2-5. Two levels below defect detection are also shown to emphasize from where we have come.

2-3.2 Benefits of Quality Control and Total Strategic Quality

The benefits realized from QC and TSQ include the following:

- Improving the quality of products and services to meet customer needs
- Increasing the productivity of manufacturing processes and commercial businesses
- Reducing manufacturing and service costs
- Determining and improving the marketability of products and services
- Reducing consumer prices of products and services

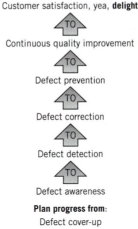

Customer satisfaction, yea, **delight**

TO

Continuous quality improvement

TO

Defect prevention

TO

Defect correction

TO

Defect detection

TO

Defect awareness

Plan progress from:
Defect cover-up
Defect ignorance and indifference

Figure 2-5   Beneficial Progress in the Evolution of Quality Control

- Ensuring on-time deliveries and availability
- Assisting in the management of an enterprise

Quality control as a strategy can bring better quality, price, delivery, and sales, leading to economic prosperity.

The successful users of the quality disciplines are those who have discovered that it doesn't cost money but, on the contrary, saves it [see Crosby (1979)]. Of course, quality control can be applied incorrectly. Its principles and techniques are very flexible. Its implementation can be overdesigned or underdesigned. How effective it is in providing customer satisfaction, creating greater markets, and reducing overall cost resulting from improved quality is a reasonable measure of the correctness of its application. Generally, if it is costing more than it is saving, it is improperly applied. This places great importance on quality cost analysis, a significant element in a quality system that will be explored subsequently.

2-3.3 The Scope of Quality Control and Quality Systems

Quality systems include functions such as marketing surveys and analyses, product design, production planning, vendor policies, receiving inspection, and testing. Further functions are inventory policies, process capability studies, training of employees, failure analysis, reliability, life and environmental testing, instrument calibration, maintainability, product warranty and liability, customer relations, and analyses of field data.

On a national level there are conferences, training programs, certification of practitioners, university degree programs, publications, accreditation of quality system auditors, laboratory accreditation, and regulatory programs on health and safety. These constitute a national quality control system. Stephens (1980) discusses this concept as it applies to developing nations. The multinational companies, bilateral and multilateral aid programs, and international organizations carry the corporate and national programs over to the international level.

2-3.4 Three Important Aspects of Quality Systems

The definition of total quality control given earlier and the expanding evolution of quality control illustrated in Figure 2-4 to total strategic quality include three important aspects of quality systems: planning for quality, control of quality, and improvement of quality. These three basic processes of quality have become known as the Juran trilogy. Because this chapter is concerned with elaboration of the elements of quality systems, especially at the company level, much emphasis is placed on the first of these aspects: planning for quality. Some examples of control of quality and improvement of quality are included in the discussion, again primarily at the corporate or enterprise level. For a more detailed account of control of quality and improvement of quality at the process level, see Chapter 11.

▶ 2-4 ELEMENTS OF QUALITY SYSTEMS

Feigenbaum (1991) mentions ten subsystems that "are typical of the quality system in many companies." He further mentions that "companies which have studied these ten subsystems have learned that at least 300 separate activities are involved within their quality systems." The following is a list of elements to serve as a guide for assessing the thoroughness of a quality system. It was originally based on ANSI/ASQC Z-1.15 (1979) with extensions from the general quality literature and experience. It has been expanded further on the basis of ISO 9004-2000, essentially replacing ANSI/ASQC Z-1.15 (1979), updated literature, and experience with total quality systems. Emphasis is on the functions rather than the organization or individuals that perform the functions. Implementation might well include the sharing of responsibility for these elements with numerous organizational functions throughout a company. Some of the elements may be reserved as the special providence of the organizational quality function.

ANSI/ASQC Z-1.15 was a generic guideline intended to serve as a basis of development of individual industry or corporate standards. It played a major role in the development of ISO 9004. ISO 9004-2000 is a guideline for quality management and quality system elements. The main elements of a quality system are listed as follows, presented in an outline form that can serve as a checklist to check inclusion of system elements. This listing is intended as a reminder of elements that should be considered in developing a quality system. It is more comprehensive than ISO 9004-2000, ISO 9001, or the criteria of the Malcolm Baldrige National Quality Award. The purpose is not to propose that a given quality system must include all of these elements, but to serve as a comprehensive list of elements to consider in designing and implementing a quality system and evaluating the thoroughness of an existing system.

I. Policy, Planning, Organization, and Administration

    A. Quality Policy, Objectives, Commitment, and Characteristics

    B. Quality Planning, Control, and Innovation

        1. Customer Needs Determination and Assessments

    C. Quality Organization

    D. Quality Manual and Documentation System

    E. Quality Assurance—System Auditing, Monitoring

        1. Internal Quality Audit System

    F. Quality Cost Analysis and Management

    G. Administration, Responsibility, and Communications

II. *Product Design Assurance, Specification Development, and Control*

    A. Design Validation

    B. Formal Design Review

    C. Design Verification and Qualification Tests

    D. Acceptance/Rejection Criteria for All Inspections and Tests

    E. Safety, Regulatory Requirement Assurance

    F. Design and Processing Change Control—Configuration Control

III. *Control of Purchased Materials and Component Parts*

    A. Communication of Requirements to Suppliers

    B. Quality Supplier (Source) Selection Methods

    C. Evaluating Supplier's Capability and Performance

    D. Established Proper Vendor-Vendee Relations

    E. Materials and Component Quality Assessment

IV. *Production (In-Process, Operational and Final) Quality Control/Quality Assurance*

    A. Planning, Designing, and Controlling the Process

    B. Employee Selection, Training and Motivation (see VII)

    C. Completed Item and/or Product Inspection and Test

    D. Handling, Packaging, Storage, Preservation, and Shipping

    E. Quality Information

V. *Customer Contact and Field Performance*

    A. Marketing

    B. Sales, Installation, Service, Use, Replacement

    C. Customer Feedback

    D. Other External Feedback

VI. *Corrective and Preventive Action*

    A. Detection and Documentation of Problems, the Five Whys

    B. Quality Reports Leading to Corrective Action

    C. Evaluating the Need for Corrective Action

    D. Responsibility for Corrective Analysis

    E. Initiating Corrective Action, Follow-up, and Control of Corrective Action

    F. Determining the Cause (see Chapter 11)

    G. Application of Corrective/Preventive Action

    H. Nonconforming Product Review and Disposition

    I. Recall of Manufactured Items

VII. Employee Selection, Training, and Motivation

    A. Policy for Employee Quality Performance

    B. Company Work Rules

    C. Recruitment Criteria, Testing, and Evaluation

    D. Employee Job Standards

    E. Workplace Environment

    F. Job Training—Learning Curve

    G. Wage and Salary Administration—Fringe Benefits

    H. Employee Motivation Programs

VIII. Legal Requirements—Product Liability and User Safety

    A. Mandatory Standards and Regulations

    B. Safety and Environmental Criteria and Control

    C. Evaluating and Subscribing Type and Amount of Insurance Coverage

    D. Certification Programs

    E. Company Policy on Product Safety (CPSC)

    F. Design and Design Reviews on Product Safety

    G. Safety Review of User's Manuals and Promotional Material (See V.B)

    H. Product Liability Information

IX. Sampling and Other Statistical Techniques

    A. Acceptance Sampling

    B. Process Control Charts

    C. Special Studies and Experimental Design

    D. Environmental, Life, and Reliability Analysis

2-4.1 Quality Policy, Vision, Mission, Values, and Guiding Principles

As policy, in general, helps to achieve some consistency in other aspects of a business, so a quality policy aids the overall quality system. When decisions must be made such as the disposition of nonconforming batches, the quality policy provides direction.

Examples of Corporate Quality Policy

Quality policies stem from corporate policies and often take the form of statements of vision, mission, values, and guiding principles. Following are four examples of such statements, set forth by corporate management to give direction to the organization.

▶ **EXAMPLE 2-4**

CIBA Vision, a manufacturer and supplier of eye care products and services, has established the following statements:

Our Mission Statement

To be a Worldwide Leader in profitably providing quality eye care products and services which best satisfy our customers' needs and expectations.

Quality Vision
CIBA Vision has many business partners—customers, employees, suppliers, regulatory agencies and society in general. We obtain their confidence and trust by delivering quality products and services which meet or exceed mutually agreed upon requirements.

▶ **EXAMPLE 2-5**

Eastman Chemical Company was one of the winners of the Malcolm Baldrige National Quality Award for 1993. Their brief statements of strategic intent and quality policy help to express the reason for their success:

Strategic Intent
Vision: To be the World's Preferred Chemical Company

Quality Policy
To Be the Leader in Quality and Value of Products and Services

▶ **EXAMPLE 2-6**

The Ford Motor Company has expressed its new direction in terms of missions, values, and guiding principles as follows:

Mission
Ford Motor Company is a worldwide leader in automotive and automotive-related products and services as well as in newer industries such as aerospace, communications, and financial services. Our mission is to improve continually our products and services to meet our customers' needs, allowing us to prosper as a business and to provide a reasonable return for our stockholders, the owners of our business.

In some cases, these principles are carried to the dealership level as expressed by the Customer Satisfaction Standards of a Ford Dealer, depicted in Figure 2-6.

Customer Satisfaction Standards
BANNER FORD

MISSION STATEMENT

All dealership personnel will treat every customer as a potential lifetime purchaser, communicating a professional image that embraces honesty and concern for customer wants and needs.

SALES STANDARDS

1. Customers courteously acknowledged within two minutes of arrival and advised that a Sales Consultant is available upon request.
2. Advisory relationship established by knowledgeable Sales Consultant who listens to customers, identifies needs, and ensures needs are met.
3. Test drive offered to all customers.
4. Pleasant, non-pressured purchase experience and thorough explanation provided by Sales Consultant, Sales Management and F & I personnel.
5. Using checklist, Sales Consultant delivers vehicle in perfect condition when promised.
6. Customers contacted by Sales Consultant within one week after delivery to ensure total satisfaction.

Figure 2-6 Customer Satisfaction Standards of a Ford Dealer

Statements of the kind illustrated serve important roles in the development and implementation of quality systems. An examination of the example statements reveal an association with the tenets and emphases discussed earlier. A vision statement should convey a clear and compelling message of what the organization aspires to become over a given planning horizon (typically, five to eight years). It should be challenging, but it must be achievable. It should be inspiring, involving, and empowering for employees and should rally personnel to a common worthwhile cause. It should reflect the customers' values and needs, be memorable, and engender a positive association with the company.

A further example of a vision statement for an entire country is the now famous quotation from President Kennedy in 1961:

I believe that this nation should commit itself to achieving the goal, before this decade is out, of landing a man on the moon and returning safely to earth.

No specific standard or guideline exists for policy, vision, or mission statements. In fact, examination of numerous examples reveals no particular consistency in title or reference. Policy statements often include statements of vision, mission, values, and guiding principles, as illustrated above, some without specific reference to these divisions. For a discussion of the visioning process, consult Latham (1995).

What is important is that top management takes a leadership role in defining, disseminating, and supporting the quality system. Some direction for this role is provided by Dr. W. Edwards Deming in his fourteen points or obligations of management in assuming proper responsibility for quality and management of the enterprise [see Deming (1982, 1986)]. In brief form, these points are as follows:

1. Create constancy of purpose for improvement of product and service, with the aim to become competitive, to stay in business, and to provide jobs.

2. Adopt the new philosophy. We are in a new economic age, created by Japan. We can no longer live with commonly accepted style of American management or with commonly accepted levels of delays, mistakes, and defective products.

3. Cease dependence on mass inspection to achieve quality. Eliminate the need for inspection on a mass basis by building quality into the product in the first place.

4. End the practice of awarding business on the basis of price tag alone. Instead, minimize total cost.

5. To improve quality and productivity and thus constantly decrease costs, improve constantly and forever the system of production and service.

6. Institute training on the job.

7. Institute leadership. The aim of supervision should be to help people, machines, and gadgets to do a better job. Supervision of management is in need of overhaul, as well as supervision of production workers.

8. Drive out fear so that everyone may work effectively for the company.

9. Break down barriers between departments. People in research, design, sales, and production must work as a team to foresee problems of production and in use that may be encountered with the product or service.

10. Eliminate slogans, exhortations, and targets for the workforce, asking for zero defects and new levels of productivity. Such exhortations only create adversarial relationships, as most causes of low quality and low productivity belong to the system and thus lie beyond the power of the workforce.

11. Eliminate numerical quotas or work standards that prescribe numerical quotas for the day. Substitute aids and helpful supervision.

12a. Remove the barriers that rob hourly workers of their right to pride of workmanship. The responsibility of supervisors must be changed from sheer numbers to quality.

12b. Remove the barriers that rob people in management and in engineering of their right to pride of workmanship. This means, among other things, abolishment of the annual rating or merit rating and management by objective.

13. Institute a vigorous program of education and retraining.

14. Put everybody in the company to work, to accomplish the transformation. The transformation is everybody's job. Take action to accomplish the transformation.

2-4.2 Organization for Quality

Structure is no guarantee of success, but to establish a permanent, stable means of controlling quality, two sets of organizational issues must be faced: (1) the quality organization, the organization of the quality function and its various components, and (2) the organization for quality, including quality-related elements in all organizations within the enterprise. A thorough quality system is equally concerned with the latter as the former. Both aspects are discussed by Feigenbaum (1982) [see also Feigenbaum (1991)].

The quality control department can only help to eliminate "hidden plant" costs if given the following responsibilities:

- *A business responsibility—the opportunity to contribute to business planning and implementation activities. Quality is often asked to react to problems only after they occur.*

- *A system responsibility—the ability to lead a total quality effort that assures quality and controls quality costs from marketing and engineering through production and service.*

- *A technical responsibility—the authority to control operating and assurance activities in quality engineering, process control engineering, quality information equipment engineering, inspection, testing and audit.*

- *Total quality control involves the engineering, production and service functions of the firm; thus quality should not be treated as the specialized activity of a certain group. It should be managed, systems-engineered and promoted with the same thoroughness with which the product is managed, engineered, produced and sold.*

With the emergence of the awareness of quality as a strategic business force, there is more acceptance of responsibility for quality among all personnel. Functional departments recognize the importance of quality and the contribution of the quality disciplines in performing their responsibilities. Thus, there is a greater sharing of the elements of quality among departments. Ultimately, the need for a separate quality department may diminish [see the paper by Cramton and Cofran (1995)]. Meanwhile, quality as a department, in modern quality systems is serving a role of facilitation. It provides specific knowledge of quality technologies to assist other departments in fulfilling their assigned tasks, including quality.

2-4.3 Quality Cost Analysis and Management

A significant aspect of quality systems involves quality costs, their identification, measurement, analysis, and management. Because most enterprises differ considerably in their cost elements, no specific standards have emerged or are likely to emerge with respect to quality costs. Major categories have been identified, and guidelines have been established. Additionally, many examples have been reported in the literature to serve as case studies and motivating forces for other enterprises to seek the benefits of a quality cost system.

The major categories of quality costs as defined by the American Society for Quality Control (ASQC) (1971, 1987, 1989, 1990) are as follows:

Prevention costs: Costs incurred for planning, implementing, and maintaining a quality system that will assure conformance to quality requirements at economic levels

Appraisal costs: Costs incurred to determine the degree of conformance to quality requirements

Internal failure costs: Costs arising when products, components, and materials fail to meet quality requirements before transfer of ownership to customer

External failure costs: Costs incurred when products fail to meet quality requirements after transfer of ownership to the customer

Further discussions of quality costs can be found in *Guide for Reducing Quality Costs* and *Guide for Managing Vendor Quality Costs,* which are both available from ASQ. See also the three part series of articles by Alford (1979). The entire April 1983 issue of *Quality Progress* was devoted to the topic of quality costs.

The principle involved in the technique of quality costs is well illustrated by Figure 2-7. A quality cost system is established. Each of the four major components is evaluated for the first month of measurement. Prevention costs might be zero for some enterprises. Actions to reduce failure and appraisal costs are considered, and appropriate increases in prevention costs are approved and implemented. The situation is reviewed on a periodic basis. Additional prevention costs may be incurred as further opportunities to reduce failure and appraisal costs are uncovered. After operation under a quality improvement program for some time, savings resulting from the program are summarized and reported. The diagram of Figure 2-7 could be part of a monthly management reporting system. The costs might be shown in absolute terms or as a percentage of an appropriate base such as sales, manufacturing costs, or value added.

2-4.4 Product Design Assurance, Specification Development, and Control

Since the advent of total quality control, increasing emphasis has been placed on the design phase of product and service development sequences. Design quality is important for customer appeal, including durability and service features. It is also important

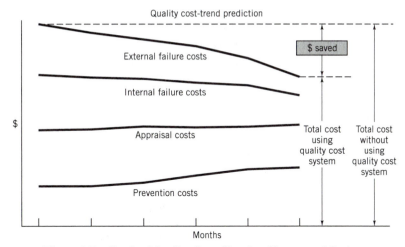

Figure 2-7 Graph of Quality Costs Showing Changes and Savings

in consideration of manufacturability and cost. In the outline of quality systems elements, eleven key activities have been identified with design assurance. Attention at this stage of development has a significant effect on prevention of problems later in the manufacturing and marketing sequence. Costly recalls and liability suits have taught some companies the importance of design assurance. These lessons place further emphasis on this area of the total quality system for any company planning a complete program. Significant new developments include computer-assisted design techniques.

Failure mode, effects and criticality analysis (FMECA), often shortened to FMEA, is a useful methodology for products and processes. By an examination of every component or process step, FMEA provides assistance in the identification of potential failures. It analyzes their effects, their criticality (severity), their expected frequency of occurrence, their potential cause(s), their means of verification, and actions to prevent their actual occurrence or to minimize their effects. Recent attention has been given to the use of this technique at the process planning stage in addition to its earlier use on product design stages. See the discussion of QS 9000 in Chapter 3 and a discussion of the technique in Chapter 14.

Qualification testing includes the formal presentation of a series of specified tests to ensure that the product conforms to each of its requirements. Although the procedures are concerned mainly with design, all failures occurring during testing are important. Some failures will be due to deficiencies of the design and will dictate further design developments. Other failures may occur because the samples or prototypes tested were not made in accordance with the design, revealing valuable information on manufacturability and the necessity for process controls before the complete design of the process. Checks and tests at design qualification also have a very important secondary function. They enable the status of the drawings and standards themselves to be appraised at a defined instant in the development program.

Organized procedures for a new or redesigned product or product system include such phases as (1) concept, (2) definition, (3) preliminary design, (4) detail design, (5) model fabrication and qualification testing, (6) production fabrication, and (7) continued production and operation. In this process certain baselines are often identified, such as (1) program requirements baseline, (2) design requirements baseline, (3) design baseline, (4) development baseline, (5) production baseline, and (6) product configuration baseline. With review, modifications, and approvals at each stage, such a system helps to ensure design assurance and a quality transition into production.

2-4.5 Control of Purchased Materials and Components Parts

To manufacture a high-quality product, procurement of high-quality raw materials, piece parts, or subassemblies from outside suppliers is necessary. This requires careful planning and implementation. In this part of the list of quality system elements are five major activities. These are suggested guidelines for achieving success in procurement quality.

Adequate communication of requirements to suppliers is important. Specifications should be understandable and precise. They should include packaging, handling, and transportation requirements. If inspection is to be performed on incoming deliveries, the specifications should provide information on required quality levels and the verification procedures to be used. In the event of rejections, disposition of rejected batches or consignments should be specified. Process capability requirements on suppliers, together with process controls, can reduce or eliminate inspection of incoming supplies. Certificates of conformance are often used as a basis for acceptance. The following is an example.

▶ **EXAMPLE 2-7**

An example of a certificate of conformance of tallow intended for the manufacture of laundry soap is a cargo superintendent's certification showing the following analysis in comparison with the customer's requirements:

Characteristic	Sample Analysis	Customer Requirement
Titre	41.2°C	42°C maximum
F.F.A.	24.9%	25% maximum
Moisture	1.63%	1.75% maximum
Impurities	0.33%	0.5% maximum
Unsaponifiables	0.65%	0.70% maximum
F.A.C. (Color Value)	23	23 maximum

Samples were drawn in accordance with British Standard 627, *Methods for Sampling Fats and Oils,* from the supplier's shore tanks before loading. Samples drawn were made into a homogeneous mixture; placed in new, clean containers; labeled; sealed; and distributed (1) to the shipper, (2) to a registered laboratory for analysis, and (3) to be retained for reference.

Qualified supplier selection methods evaluate both capability and performance of suppliers. Helpful activities are (1) quality and system audits of the supplier via second-party or third-party assessment programs using, for example, the ISO 9001-2000 standard; (2) assistance to suppliers with training programs on quality control and technical advice; (3) collection, analysis, and use of supplier quality evidence; and (4) certified single sourcing.

Procurement quality assurance includes the establishment of proper vendor relations. Long-term contracts that allow for vendors to invest in process improvements generally produce worthwhile returns. Partnerships help to make suppliers an extension of the business with beneficial results for both parties. The interested reader should consult the publications of the Customer-Supplier Division of ASQ for useful information as well as the discussion on purchasing in ISO 9004-2000.

2-4.6 Production Quality Control

The major planning and implementation efforts for an effective quality system usually lie with the production process. Cross-functional procedures and detailed work instructions are examples of documents that are useful for the establishment and control of processes. See the section on documentation requirements for ISO 9001-2000 in Chapter 3. Computers are being utilized in increasing numbers to assist manufacturing operations and to provide operator instructions via audiovisual devices.

A system of preventive and corrective maintenance is as important to quality as it is to productivity. The analysis and use of maintenance information are vital elements in a quality control system. Machine and instrument downtime may be analyzed by Pareto analysis (see Chapter 11), including the frequency of occurrence caused by specific parts or components. Schedules of preventive maintenance should be developed from considerations of the design of equipment, frequency of use, and statistical analysis of past data.

A system of controlling nonconformities is essential to an overall quality system. A material review board may be organized for this purpose. Specific control of operations and processes includes everything from adequate design of the production processes, selection of materials and machines, training of personnel, collection of process data, and use of control techniques such as control charts and sampling plans.

The establishment and control of in-process inspection and test stations form a part of operation controls. The flowchart technique illustrated in Chapter 11 is a useful procedure for identifying points of inspection and test in a consistent, comprehensive manner.

The techniques of process performance and capability studies are useful for production quality control. Comparison of process capability with specification limits is illustrated in Chapter 11 and provides a basis for decision making and action at the production process level.

In the conduct of process performance and capability studies, it is sometimes necessary to experiment with the process by way of planned changes in materials, process variables, machines, operators, or environments. These techniques provide a further degree of potential improvement. Statistical techniques such as designed experiments, robust designs, multiple regression, and evolutionary operation are often utilized for effectiveness.

Essential to good overall control of processes is control of peripheral devices such as servomechanisms, tools, and measuring equipment. Earlier discussions in this chapter on measurement and calibration pertain to this area.

Minimizing in-process inventories is important to production planning systems, but such systems must provide for an adequate level of inventory to maintain continued flow of operations. Where in-process inventory is essential for production operations, sampling plans may be useful for acceptance inspection between processing stations. A production/inventory/quality control system such as just-in-time should be considered for implementation.

Audits of the process control programs may be done periodically to locate areas of deterioration that require correction, areas needing additional controls, and areas in which controls are no longer necessary. These audits form an essential part of a corporate quality assurance program and are linked to certification systems, such as the ISO 9001-2000 and QS 9000 requirements.

Inspection and test planning are essential to determine the extent of their needs relative to requirements and to provide feedback to the production operations. Inspection may be at a 100% level, a sampling level, or a cursory survey by a quality assurance audit.

The Product Quality Audit

An important element in a quality system is a product quality audit. A definition of such an audit is as follows:

> *A product quality audit is an independent and objective evaluation of the outgoing product quality level, as it would be measured and judged from the viewpoint of the customer, whether that customer is the ultimate user, a dealer, the next department, or another plant.*

ISO 19011-2002 is entitled *Guidelines on Quality and/or Environmental Management Systems Auditing.* It provides a more generic definition that includes quality management systems and service quality audits in addition to product quality audits and audits of environmental management systems.

Product audits provide management with an early view of the product as the customer will eventually see it. This allows immediate correction of potential problems before they are noticed or reported by the customer. This audit is sometimes called a "dock audit." Some key points in planning and conducting quality audits are the following:

- Product auditing should be customer oriented.
- It should measure the outgoing quality level.
- It should not be a substitute for final inspection.
- It should be an ongoing, scheduled activity.
- The audits should be performed on products that have already been released for shipment.
- Audit criteria should be preplanned.
- Consistency should be maintained.
- The confidence level of the results should be estimated.
- Reports should be action oriented and timely and should use a minimum of technical jargon.
- Procedures for completing corrective and preventive action should be indicated.

Reports of the quality audit results are an integral part of the quality reporting system and should reach the highest levels of management.

Acceptance sampling procedures are useful for final product inspection. Sampling plans allow for confirming the results and serve to detect any deterioration in quality. Tests on the final product have a variety of purposes. Some tests emphasize performance characteristics. Others may emphasize effects of environmental conditions that the products may experience during use. Some are to evaluate the life and reliability of the product in use. Special tests may concentrate on safety requirements to ensure quality of service without harm to humans or economic loss. Chapter 14 presents further details on reliability and life testing. The design and use of records, analyses, reports, and the assignment of responsibility are important elements for completing the quality system. For further discussion of product quality audits, see Feigenbaum (1991, pages 291–293, 797–799).

Handling, Storage, Packaging, Preservation, and Delivery

Efforts spent in producing a good-quality product will be wasted if the subsequent operations of handling, packaging, storage, and shipping are not properly executed. Specifications and controls are needed for postproduction operations. In addition to routine procedures and special audits, a system for collecting and analyzing feedback from customers is essential. Postproduction nonconformities do not occur entirely within the plant and cannot be controlled without obtaining outside information. Control of the environment in operations of handling, storage, and shipping is important to prevent deterioration of any of the product quality characteristics that may be sensitive to environmental conditions.

Weights, measures, and quantity control for customer acceptance and to meet applicable local, state, national or international regulations require planning, implementation, and control. The publications by the U.S. National Institute of Standards and Technology (NIST), Handbooks 130 and 133, should be consulted. Related areas include product and carton identification and labeling.

Quality Information

Dissemination of information on quality to key personnel within the company is of importance to an overall quality system. Various reports should be prepared to accomplish this. These include production reports, quality reports, in-process and final product inspection reports, and cost reports. The distribution of voluminous reports (e.g., long computer runs of masses of tabulated figures) should be avoided. Reports should be concise, factual, and action oriented. Graphical methods should be used wherever possible to portray levels and trends. Many of these graphical techniques are presented in Chapter 11. Statistical methods should be used to give validity to reports of significant changes so that long discussions and follow-up activities related to minor changes are avoided. Minor changes are often random occurrences within the production system and attempts to explain them are exercises in futility.

2-4.7 Customer Contact and Field Performance

Planning for customer contact and field performance is another essential activity in an overall quality management system. Listed under the elements of a quality system are four major activities:

- Marketing
- Sales, installation, service, use, replacement
- Customer feedback
- Other external feedback

These serve to provide planning in the area of quality assurance after the product is with the consumer. Many enterprises have incurred considerable financial losses due to external failures. Valuable information for improving product designs may be provided by feedback from consumers. Quality considerations are important to the design, analysis, and eventual feedback to market research programs. Subsequent advertisement and promotion of the product require careful attention to quality.

User literature and product labeling are very important to liability practices. Consideration must be given to the wording and coverage of topics in literature and labels. It should emphasize adequate operating and maintenance instructions and safety warnings and precautions. Product liability prevention is assigned an entire section in the quality system outline (see Section 2-4, VIII).

To offer guarantees to customers, quality considerations are extremely important. Such guarantees must be determined and evaluated against actual performance. As quality, especially quality of conformance, improves warranties can be improved for greater customer appeal. Conversely, as quality deteriorates, excessive warranty claims may seriously erode profit levels.

The quality of installation and service requires the same careful planning and control as does production alone. A system for collecting, analyzing, and responding to consumer returns and complaints is necessary. Systems for studying field-related failures in performance and safety are included in good quality assurance programs.

2-4.8 Corrective and Preventive Action

Comprehensive and integrated activities for achieving corrective and preventive action are essential to a quality system. Listed in the outline under the elements of a quality system are nine major items for consideration in planning and implementing this important area of the quality system. Corrective and preventive action applies to all operations within an enterprise.

Of particular consideration are the phases associated with corrective action. These include the past, present, and future. We should consider how long a problem has existed and how bad the situation is before we determine what remedial action, if any, is required. This may involve recall of products that are already in the hands of consumers. Of immediate interest is to identify the root cause and correct the problem as quickly as possible. However, this might not be possible because of the complexity of the situation or lack of sufficient information. Hence, temporary action is often necessary on an interim basis while further information is being collected and adjustments made. This may lead to a solution that can be instituted, together with controls to prevent a recurrence in the future.

2-4.9 Employee Selection, Training, and Motivation

The evolution of total quality control systems has been accompanied by a recognition of the importance of people in achieving a quality product on a consistent basis. Listed in the quality system outline are eight major items for planning and implementing the quality system regarding employees.

Much publicity has been given to employee motivation programs. There are many other important employee matters related to quality beyond mere motivation schemes. The emergence of total quality control principles has recognized that quality is affected by all employees and departments within an enterprise. Some of the greatest gains in improving the quality and cost position may be in the nonproduction areas.

Employee Motivation Programs

There are four specific programs to enlist the cooperation and participation of employees in efforts to improve products and processes: zero defects, quality control circles, participative quality control, and employee involvement. Some of them are discussed next.

Zero Defects Program. Zero defects had its beginning in 1961–1962, when the Martin Company of Orlando, Florida, delivered a Pershing missile with zero discrepancies to Cape Canaveral. Shortly after this, Brigadier General R. W. Hurst, then deputy commander of the U.S. Army Missile Command, requested the delivery of another Pershing missile one month earlier than scheduled. The Martin Company transmitted the request to its Pershing team, which accepted the challenge to deliver early with zero discrepancies. The result was the inception of the zero defects program.

Indoctrination and motivation toward zero defects are often accomplished by the use of a kickoff campaign, including rallies, posters, pins, and slogans. After the start of the program, each employee is invited to sign the zero defect pledge. The whole program is aimed at motivating the employees to do their best because they want to, not because they have been coerced.

However, motivation of employees to do their best must begin with management. The management team must support the program before they can attempt to motivate their employees into accepting the zero defects program.

For the program to be a success, the employees must believe in it. This may be achieved by convincing the employees of the importance of their jobs. They must be convinced by examples that their jobs are worth doing well. Only then will they see any reason to make the effort that zero defects performance requires.

The maintenance of a zero defects program requires that specific monitoring and correction techniques are given to operators and their supervisors. If they can identify the specific cause of nonconformances, the workers and supervisors are motivated not to repeat the process. Thus, the zero defects program is aimed at keeping the employees doing their best.

A definition of the zero defects program given by Halpin (1966) is as follows:

> *Zero Defects is simply a method of assuring that each individual within an organization realizes his importance to that organization's product or service and conversely, that each member of management realizes and recognizes the important contribution of each person reporting to him.*

One problem with a zero defects program is the attempt to achieve results by motivational techniques alone. Juran (1966) examined the zero defects movement and the concept of motivation. Extensive use of zero defects programs in Japan is reported by Pavsidis (1983).

Quality Control Circles. Perhaps no single quality control concept had more influence on the phenomenal growth of Japan's industrial postwar era than that of the quality control (QC) circle. Ishikawa (1968) explains the early development and objectives of QC circles:

(1) Birth of QC Circle

Needs for more intensive education of the foreman who performs the key functions between management and workers have been felt very strongly by many companies. . . . There was a movement in some companies, under which foremen together with workers got themselves organized to conduct a series of QC discussion meetings at the workshop level. This self-development type training of workers under the leadership of first line supervisors was working very well. At that time the Union of Japanese Scientists and Engineers (JUSE) contemplated the publication of a monthly magazine useful for the QC education of the foreman. . . . As the result the Gemba To QC (Quality Control for the Foreman) . . . magazine . . . came into being in April 1962. . . . New methods, techniques and practices of how to go about making improvement at the production line were introduced. . . .

QC circles have mushroomed in many companies since April 1962 and showed a spectacular growth, totaling some 12,000 circles registered by December 1967. . . . In addition it is estimated that there are today (1968) in operation about 60,000 QC circles organized but not formally registered with JUSE. . . .

(2) What about QC Circle?

A QC circle is but a group of production workers led by a foreman at its nucleus and organized in each workshop or work unit. It is a spontaneously formed group and conducts QC activities on its own, usually independent of other circles also organized at the production level.

Various names have been used for programs similar to QC circles. Some of these are Industrial Democracy, Work Place Democracy, Employee Participation Groups, Participative Quality Control, People Implementing Procedures and Saving (PIPS), and Success Through Everybody's Participation (STEP).

Interest in QC circles in the United States developed in the 1970s and 1980s. This resulted in papers at conferences, exchange visits, journal articles, consulting firms specializing in QC circles, and the International Association of Quality Circles (IAQC) with its own journal entitled *The Quality Circles Journal.* Annual conference proceedings of the American Society for Quality Control from 1976 to 1982 contain many papers on this subject. Articles in *Quality Progress* include those by Alexanderson (1978), Kondo (1978), Swartz and Comstock (1979), Hanley (1980), Cole (1980), Juran (1980), and Konz (1981). The latter is an annotated bibliography of quality circles. An additional early reference is by Niland (1971). The first comprehensive book was by Amsden and Amsden (1976). Beardsley and Devar (1977) published a book, *Quality Circles,* reflecting the manner in which QC circles were introduced into U.S. firms.

QC circles, as a management tool, are based on the following basic principles:

- People want to do a good job.
- People want to be recognized as intelligent, interested employees and to participate in decisions affecting their work.
- People want information to better understand the goals of their organization and to make informed decisions.
- Employees want recognition and responsibility and a feeling of self-esteem.

QC circles became an institution in themselves and were given serious consideration in the development of quality systems. Training was a vital part of their applications. They improved human relations among workers who were trained to cooperate with each other as a team. This resulted in the elevation of workers' morale and promotion of their quality consciousness.

QC circles are still used in Japan. The International Convention on QC Circles is actively promoted and attended. Papers by Nemoto (1993a, 1993b) may be consulted. Although the term "QC circles" is no longer in vogue in the United States and the Western world, its principles have been embedded in numerous programs of employee involvement by means of teams.

Participative Quality Control.   An early pioneer in the involvement of employees in work-related decisions concerning their workplace, environment, processes, and products was Sidney Rubinstein. Recognizing the value of QC circles in working toward this objective, he visited Japan in 1969 and subsequently promoted quality circles in the United States. Rubinstein emphasized participation, as expressed by his firm, Participative Systems Inc., and by papers containing the terms "participative management" [Rubinstein (1972)] and "participative problem solving" [Rubinstein (1977)]. He has done much to establish better relations among workers, management, and labor unions in industry, education, and government.

Employee Involvement.   Modern programs of total strategic quality recognize the importance and contribution of the employee and provide programs of empowerment, teamwork, and recognition. They make use of the concepts, principles, and experiences of earlier programs.

Creating a vision with values, guiding principles, and goals is a beginning. Providing leadership that empowers employees builds on this concept, as does recognizing the differences among people and uniting them using teams with shared responsibilities. Shared accountability for results and shared gains or losses continues the process. Providing training for all employees from top management to first-line workers helps to expand the foundation. Involvement with empowerment requires defined boundaries and delegated authority to allow employees to assume responsibilities and to accept accountability. This, in turn, requires participative management.

Some of the common characteristics of effective work groups are (1) defined mission and standards, (2) common goals, (3) task interdependence, (4) effective communication, (5) documented processes, and (6) tolerance of differences. Networks of such effective work groups throughout an organization contribute to effective systems that enhance quality, productivity, profits, customer and employee satisfaction.

These newer ideas are receiving considerable attention in the quality literature. Of particular significance is the proceedings of the 1995 ASQC Annual Quality Congress. Other papers on this subject are those by Caranicas (1994), Niles and Salz (1994), Sanes (1994), Amsden and Amsden (1992), Bursic (1992), Shannon (1992), and Schenck (1992). The embodiment of many of these principles in a single company is the paper by Cramton and Cofran (1995).

2-4.10 Legal Requirements: Product Liability and User Safety

With the evolution within the U.S. judicial system of strict liability, any enterprise offering a product or service must consider liability prevention. Formal programs of regulatory requirements have been instituted by the government, some of which span many years. Examples include the Federal Meat Inspection Act of 1977; the Poultry Products Inspection Act of 1957; the Radiation Control for Health and Safety Act of 1968; the Federal Food, Drugs and Cosmetic Act of 1938 and its amendments especially related to Current Good Manufacturing Practices in Manufacture, Processing, Packing or Holding of Human Foods of 1969 and the Medical Device Amendments of 1976; and the Consumer Product Safety Act of 1967.

Elements of a quality system should therefore include items pertaining to legal requirements, products liability, and user safety. Eight major items are listed in the elements of a quality system for consideration. These range from mandatory standards and regulations to assessment of potential liability.

Since the creation of the Consumer Product Safety Commission (CPSC) and the signing into law of the Consumer Product Safety Act on 27 October 1967, there has been an acceleration in the preparation, promulgation, and implementation of standards, both in the United States and abroad. In a paper by Shearman (1974), Dr. Lawrence M. Kushner, then a member of CPSC, is quoted as saying, "in the environment created by the Consumer Product Safety Act, one expects an increasing number of engineers to become involved in standardization activities—this time with the encouragement of their management."

As part of an enterprise's quality system, its engineers and scientists should be encouraged to participate in standards preparation. The preparation of sufficient standards by industry to cover safety and performance characteristics of consumer products should be continued. This will contribute further to the reduction in regulation. This possibility was recognized early in CPSC's activities [*Quality Progress* (February 1975)]. A paper by Dennis (1980) discusses a voluntary QC program proposed by the U.S. Department of Agriculture for processed meat and poultry products.

Company policies for safety and environmental considerations should be included in any quality system. A further precaution, beyond actual programs of prevention and control, is an evaluation of the type and amount of insurance coverage needed for product liability claims. Although third-party certification programs are no guarantee of liability prevention, their use is valid evidence in court that systems of control were exercised by the organization. An example of such third-party certification is that of Underwriters Laboratory [Berman (1980)]. A paper by Scott and Kerwin (1995) discusses ISO 9000 compliance and product liability. Goodden (1995) presents the argument that product liability is "a New Frontier for Quality," paraphrasing an earlier paper by one of the authors, Stephens (1977), regarding standards. See also the papers by Lutzel and Lutzel (1995) and that of Benneyan and Kaminsky (1995) concerning liability in the health care area.

The Product Safety and Liability Prevention Technical Committee of the American Society for Quality has promoted improved systems for product liability prevention. Mundel and Jacobs (1994) discuss a recall planning guide for prevention management.

2-4.11 Sampling and Other Statistical Techniques

The last, but still important, element of quality systems outlines some of the more common sampling and other statistical techniques. These techniques are covered in subsequent chapters.

2-4.12 Feedback: A Common Thread in Quality Systems

The outline of the elements of quality systems and the brief discussions following the outline give some detailed areas to include in the design and implementation of a quality system. They do not, however, adequately emphasize the importance of feedback to connect and bind them together. For illustration Figure 2-8 is presented. It includes some of the principal components in the functioning of an enterprise and of a quality system. Additionally, it shows main linkages between these components as well as the feedback links that help to keep the quality system dynamic and flexible. The dual directional arrows on the feedback linkages emphasize the importance of providing feedback in both directions between major functional components.

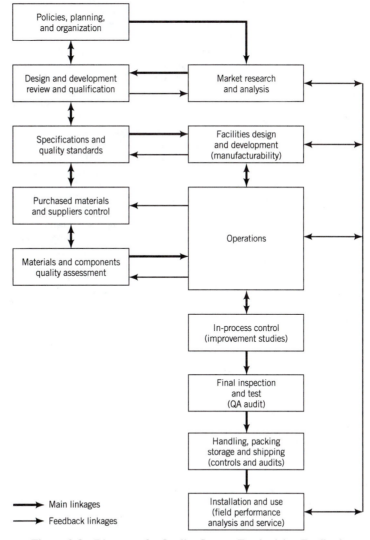

Figure 2-8 Diagram of a Quality System Emphasizing Feedback

► 2-5 REFERENCES

Abbott, R. A. (1995), "Connectivity—Empowering Process Owners under ISO 9000," *ASQC 49th Annual Quality Congress Proceedings,* pp. 23–29.

Alexanderson, B. O. (1978). "QC Circles in Scandinavia," *Quality Progress,* pp. 18–19 (July).

Alford, R. E. (1979), "Quality Costs—Where to Start," *Quality,* Part I, Vol. 18, No. 8 (August); Part II, Vol. 18, No. 9 (September); Part III, Vol. 18, No. 10 (October).

American National Standards Institute (1994), ANSI/NCSL Z540-1, *Calibration Laboratories and Measuring and Test Equipment—General Requirements,* New York.

American Society for Quality Control (1971), *Quality Costs—What and How,* Second Edition, Milwaukee.

American Society for Quality Control (1979) ANSI/ASQC Z1.15, *Generic Guidelines for Quality Systems,* Milwaukee.

American Society for Quality Control (1987), *Quality Costs: Ideas and Applications,* Vol. 1, Second Edition, Milwaukee.

American Society for Quality Control (1987), ANSI/ASQC Standard A3—*Quality Systems Terminology,* American Society for Quality Control, Milwaukee.

American Society for Quality Control (1989), *Quality Costs: Ideas and Applications,* Vol. 2, Milwaukee.

American Society for Quality Control (1990), *Principles of Quality Costs: Principles, Implementation, and Use,* Second Edition, Milwaukee.

American Society for Quality (2000), ANSI/ISO/ASQ Q9000-2000, *Quality Management Systems—Fundamentals and Vocabulary,* ASQ, Milwaukee.

Amsden, D. M., and Amsden, R. T. (1976), *QC Circles: Applications, Tools and Theory,* American Society for Quality Control, Milwaukee.

Amsden, D. M., and Amsden, R. T. (1992), "Institutionalizing Total Quality: A Challenge," *ASQC 46th Annual Quality Congress Proceedings,* pp. 1024–29.

Anon. (1974), "The National Conference on Standards Laboratories," ASTM *Standardization News,* Vol. 2, No. 11, pp. 18–22 (November).

AT&T (1984), *Statistical Quality Control Handbook,* AT&T, Indianapolis, IN.

Beardsley, J. F., and Devar, D. L. (1977), *Quality Circles,* J. F. Beardsley and Associates, International, San Jose, CA.

Benneyan, J. C., and Kaminsky, F. C. (1995), "Successfully Applying SPC to Improve Health Care: Barriers to Improving Quality and Reducing Liability," *ASQC 49th Annual Quality Congress Proceedings,* pp. 570–78.

Berman, H. S. (1980), "Quality Assurance in UL's Follow-Up Programs," *Quality Progress,* Vol. 14, No. 1, pp. 14–17 (January).

Bursic, K. M. (1992), "Strategies and Benefits of the Successful Use of Teams in Manufacturing Organizations," *IEEE Transactions on Engineering Management,* Vol. 39, No. 3, pp. 277–90 (August).

Caranicas, P. C. (1994), "Employee Involvement in the Public Sector: Applies Deming Principles Achieve Cultural Change—A Case Study," *ASQC 48th Annual Quality Congress Proceedings,* pp. 103–108.

Cole, R. E. (1980), "Will QC Circles Work in the U.S.?" *Quality Progress,* Vol. 14, No. 7, pp. 30–33 (July).

Cramton, J., and Cofran, H. H. (1995), "Quality through Commitment: Increasing Involvement and Innovation," *ASQC 49th Annual Quality Congress Proceedings,* pp. 639–40.

Crosby, P. B. (1979), *Quality Is Free,* McGraw-Hill, New York.

Dawson, E. H. (1964), "Sensory Testing Guide for Panel Evaluation of Foods and Beverages," *Food Technology,* Vol. 18, No. 8, pp. 25–31.

Dawson, E. H. (1967), "Sensory Testing of Foods and Beverages," *Food Quality Control,* No. 15, pp. 3–6 (January).

Deming, W. (1971), "Some Statistical Logic in the Management of Quality," *Proceedings of the All India Conference on Quality Control,* New Delhi, 17 March 1971, pp. 98–119.

Deming, W. (1975), "My View of Quality Control in Japan," *Reports of Statistical Applications Research,* Union of Japanese Scientists and Engineers (JUSE), Vol. 22, No. 2, Tokyo, pp. 25–32 (June).

Deming, W. (1982), *Quality, Productivity and Competitive Position,* MIT-CAES, Cambridge, MA.

Deming, W. (1986), *Out of the Crisis,* Massachusetts Institute of Technology, Center for Advanced Engineering Study, Cambridge, MA.

Dennis, F. (1980), "USDA Proposes a Voluntary QC Plan for Processed Meat and Poultry Products," *Quality Progress,* pp. 14–17 (February).

Fawzi, F. (1978), "Conservation of Natural Resources—A New Role for Quality Control," *Transactions ICQC '78,* Tokyo, A2, pp. 15–17.

Feigenbaum, A. V. (1982), "Quality a Productivity Plan—The Motivation," *Quality,* Vol. 21, No. 8, p. Q3 (August).

Feigenbaum, A. V. (1991), *Total Quality Control,* Third Edition, Revised, McGraw-Hill, New York.

Fujita, S. (1994), "Employee Satisfaction—The Source of Customer Satisfaction," *Societās Quālitātis,* Vol. 8, No. 1, pp. 1–3, Union of Japanese Scientists and Engineers (March–April).

Furia, T. E., Ed. (1972), *CRC Handbook of Food Additives,* Vol. I, Second Edition, pp. 535–37, CRC Press, Boca Raton, FL.

Garvin, D. A. (1984), "Product Quality: An Important Strategic Weapon," *Business Horizons,* pp. 40–43 (March–April).

Garvin, D. A. (1988), *Managing Quality, the Strategic and Competitive Edge,* The Free Press, Macmillan, New York.

Goodden, R. (1995), "A New Frontier for Quality: Product Liability," *ASQC 49th Annual Quality Congress Proceedings,* pp. 495–501.

Halpin, J. F. (1966), *Zero Defects—A New Dimension in Quality Assurance,* McGraw-Hill, New York.

Hanley, J. (1980), "Our Experience with Quality Circles," *Quality Progress,* pp. 22–24 (February).

Herschdoerfer, S. M., Ed. (1967), *Quality Control in the Food*

Industry, Vol. I, *Testing Panels: Sensory Assessment in Quality Control* by N. T. Gridgeman, pp. 235–83, Academic Press, London and New York.

Hoadley, B. (1981), "The Quality Measurement Plan (QMP)," *The Bell System Technical Journal,* Vol. 60, No. 2, pp. 215–73 (February).

Huntley, L. (1995), "An Improved Support System for Practical Metrology," *ASQC 49th Annual Quality Congress Proceedings,* pp. 142–49.

Huntoon, R. D. (1975), "Compatibility in Measurement Systems," *NBSIR 75-769,* National Institute of Standards and Technology, Gaithersburg, MD.

International Organization for Standardization (1991), *Guide 2-1991 General Terms and Their Definitions Concerning Standardization and Certification,* Geneva.

International Organization for Standardization (1999), ISO 2859-1 *Sampling Procedures for Inspection by Attributes—Part I: Sampling Schemes Indexed by Acceptance Quality Limit (AQL) for Lot-by-Lot Inspection,* 2nd Ed., Geneva.

International Organization for Standardization (2002), ISO 10012, *Quality Assurance Requirements for Measuring Equipment,* Geneva.

International Organization for Standardization (2002), ISO 19011, *Guidelines on Quality and/or Environmental Management Systems Auditing,* Geneva.

Ishikawa, K. (1968), *QC Circle Activities,* QC in Japan Series No. 1, Union of Japanese Scientists and Engineers (JUSE), 10-11, Sindagaya 5-Chome, Shibayaku, Tokyo (April).

Ishikawa, K., et al. (1975), "Quality Control Activities of Foreign Countries through Japanese Eyes," *Reports of Statistical Applications Research,* Union of Japanese Scientists and Engineers (JUSE), Vol. 22, No. 2, Tokyo, pp. 3–17 (June).

Juran, J. M. (1966), "Quality Problems, Remedies and Nostrums," *Industrial Quality Control,* pp. 647–53 (June).

Juran, J. M. (1980), "International Significance of the QC Circle Movement," *Quality Progress,* pp. 18–22 (November).

Juran, J. M., Ed. (1988), *Quality Control Handbook,* Fourth Edition, McGraw-Hill, New York.

Kimber, R. J. (1983), "The Measurement System Concept," *Quality,* Vol. 22, No. 6, p. 86 (June).

Kondo, Y. (1978), "JUSE—A Center of Quality Control in Japan," *Quality Progress,* Vol. 12, No. 8, pp. 14–15 (August).

Konz, S. (1981), "Quality Circles: An Annotated Bibliography," *Quality Progress,* Vol. 15, No. 4, pp. 30–35 (April).

Koyanagi, K. (1952), *Statistical Control of Quality in Japanese Industry: A Brief Report Submitted to the 1952 American Society for Quality Control Meeting in Rochester,* published by JUSE, Tokyo.

Latham, J. R. (1995), "Visioning: The Concept, Trilogy, and Process" *Quality Progress,* Vol. 28, No. 4, pp. 65–68 (April).

Lillrank, P., and Kano, N. (1989), *Continuous Improvement,* Center for Japanese Studies, The University of Michigan, Michigan Papers in Japanese Studies, No. 19, Ann Arbor, MI.

Lutzel, J. J., and Lutzel, R. J. (1995), "Products Liability &

Total Quality Management," *ASQC 49th Annual Quality Congress Proceedings,* pp. 502–508.

McCoubrey, A. O. (1974), "Expanding the Nation's Measurement System," ASTM *Standardization News,* Vol. 2, No. 11, pp. 14–17 (November).

Monaghan, H. F. (1980), "National Association of Testing Authorities, Australia's Laboratory Accreditation System," ASTM *Standardization News,* Vol. 8, No. 11, pp. 10–13 (November).

Mundel, A. B., and Jacobs, R. J. (1994), "Recall Planning," *ASQC 48th Annual Quality Congress Proceedings,* pp. 827–33.

Murrin, T. J. (1982), "One Major Company's Steps for Improving Quality and Productivity," *Quality Progress,* Vol. 15, No. 10, pp. 14–17 (October).

Nemoto, M. (1993a), "Twelve Articles on the Activation of the QC Circle for Top Management (1)," *Societās Quālitātis,* Vol. 6, No. 6, pp. 2–3, 6, Union of Japanese Scientists and Engineers (January–February).

Nemoto, M. (1993b), "Twelve Articles on the Activation of the QC Circle for Top Management (2)", *Societās Quālitātis,* Vol. 7, No. 1, pp. 5–6, Union of Japanese Scientists and Engineers (March–April).

Niland, P. (1971), *The Quality Control Circle: An Analysis,* McGraw-Hill Far Eastern Publishers, Singapore.

Niles, J. L., and Salz, N. J. (1994), "Why Teams Poop Out," *ASQC 48th Annual Quality Congress Proceedings,* pp. 330–36.

Pangborn, R. M. (1967), "Use and Misuse of Sensory Technology," *Food Quality Control,* No. 15, pp. 7–12 (January).

Pavsidis, C. (1983), "Zero Defect Programs Thriving in Japan," *Quality Progress,* Vol. 16, No. 5, pp. 34–35 (May).

Podolsky, L. (1974), "International Quality Assessment System," ASTM *Standardization News,* Vol. 2, No. 11, pp. 23–28 (November).

Roberts, R.W. (1974), "The National/International Measurement System," ASTM *Standardization News,* Vol. 2, No. 11, pp. 8–13 (November).

Rubinstein, S. (1972), "Participative Management: New Approaches to Human Work Resources," *Professional Engineering,* pp. 17–21 (December).

Rubinstein, S. (1977), "Participative Problem Solving: How to Increase Organizational Effectiveness," *Personnel,* pp. 30–39, AMACOM, American Management Association (January–February).

Sanes, C. (1994), "The Employee Factor in Delivering Differentiated Services," *ASQC 48th Annual Quality Congress Proceedings,* pp. 845–51.

Schenck, D. E. (1992), "Sports—The Empowerment Model Everyone Can Understand," *ASQC 46th Annual Quality Congress Proceedings,* pp. 1013–20.

Scott, G. G., and Kerwin, S. T. (1995), "ISO 9000 and Product Liability," *ASQC 49th Annual Quality Congress Proceedings,* pp. 509–14.

Shannon, W. C. (1992), "Peak Performers in an Empowering Quality Culture," *ASQC 46th Annual Quality Congress Proceedings,* pp. 1021–23.

Shearman, R. W. (1974), "Product Safety and Consumer Protection—

Concerns of Today's Engineer," *Quality Progress,* pp. 8–9 (April).

Shewhart, W. A. (1931), *Economic Control of Quality of Manufactured Product,* D. Van Nostrand Company, Inc., New York, republished by ASQC in 1980.

Simpson, J. A. (1981), "Foundations of Metrology," *Journal of Research of the National Bureau of Standards,* Vol. 86, No. 3, pp. 281–92 (May–June).

Smith, E. C., and Chambers, E. (1993), "Do You Need Sensory Analysis Now or in the Future?," ASTM *Standardization News,* Vol. 21, No. 7, pp. 46–49 (July).

Stephens, K. S. (1977), "Standards: A New Frontier for Quality," *Journal of Quality Technology,* Vol. 9, No. 2, pp. 70–81 (April), and *Quality Assurance* (UK), Vol. 3, No. 4, pp. 125–32 (December).

Stephens, K. S. (1979), *Preparing for Standardization, Certification and Quality Control,* Asian Productivity, Tokyo.

Stephens, K. S. (1980), "A National Quality Control System," *International Trade Forum,* Vol. 16, No. 4, pp. 8–11, 28–30 (October–December), International Trade Center UNCTAD/GATT, Geneva.

Stephens, K. S. (2000), *The Handbook of Applied Acceptance Sampling,* ASQ Quality Press, Milwaukee.

Stewart, R. A. (1971), "Sensory Evaluation of Batch-Type Operations," *Food Technology,* Vol. 25, No. 4, pp. 401–04.

Swartz, G. E., and Comstock, V. C. (1979), "One Firm's Experience with Quality Circles," *Quality Progress,* Vol. 13, No. 9, pp. 14–16 (September).

United States Department of Commerce (1975, 1976), National Voluntary Laboratory Accreditation Program (NVLAP), *Federal Register,* Vol. 40, No. 90, and Vol. 41, No. 38, Washington, D.C.

United States Department of Defense (1978), DOD-STD-480A, *Military Standard Configuration Control—Engineering Changes, Deviations, and Wavers,* Washington, D.C.

Verman, L. C. (1973), *Standardization—A New Discipline,* Archon Books, Hamden, CT.

▶ 2-6 PROBLEMS

1. Prepare a report on a quality system element or technique. It is to represent a summary description of what the element or technique is and how, where, and for what purpose it is used. The report is to reflect extensive reading on the subject from several sources of quality control and related literature, including textbooks, journals, periodicals, company pamphlets, and agency reports. The paper should be six to ten or more typed pages, double-spaced, and include an extensive bibliography of at least six references (more preferred), as exposure to the literature is a major purpose of the assignment. Topics that may be considered for the assignment are the following (others as outlined in Section 2-4 can be used):

Quality costs

Value analysis

Life cycle costing

Vendor-vendee relations

Vendor quality rating plans

QC circles

Zero defects program

Participative QC

Product liability

Government regulatory programs (specific agencies such as FDA, USDA, FTC, CPSC)

Quality warranties and guarantees (general or specific types)

Quality manuals

Self-certification

Third-party certification

Laboratory accreditation

Calibration system

Measurement system— metrology

Automatic test equipment

Computer-assisted design

Computer-assisted manufacture

Nondestructive testing

Product standards (general or specific)

QC in the service industries

Quality auditing systems

Vision, mission statements

Employee involvement

Benchmarking

2. Prepare a report on the quality control system of a specific company, business, enterprise, or agency with information obtained by correspondence, direct visit(s), company report(s), or other contacts. It may include locating the necessary inforrnation in significant publication(s) on the given company (but not limited to a single journal article). It should summarize the system used by the company to achieve a high-quality product or service. It may also include a critique of the system based on the system elements introduced in this chapter. The report can be done for a large or small organization and may include service activities. Brochures or other materials obtained may be included as exhibits or appendixes.

3. Obtain information on a company that has won the U.S. Malcolm Baldrige National Quality Award or a similar award at the state level. Prepare a report on the quality system practiced by the award-winning company. Identify elements of the company's quality system from the list presented in Section 2-4.

CHAPTER

3

THE ISO 9000 QUALITY SYSTEM

In Chapter 2 the ISO 9000 series of standards was discussed briefly as a quality management system consisting of requirements and guidance for its implementation. These standards have been promoted widely, and their adoption has contributed to attracting attention to the quality disciplines. In principle the requirements of the series are sound. They contain the fundamentals of a quality system that will benefit both the customer and the supplier. In Chapter 2 a set of elements for a more complete quality system was presented. This chapter is intended to provide instruction for the use of the ISO 9000 standards. The benefits of going beyond these basic requirements are as follows:

- Improved quality with less variation
- Reduced costs
- Greater productivity
- Greater involvement and satisfaction of employees
- Enhanced customer satisfaction
- Better supplier relations
- Improved leadership from top management

Compliance with the ISO 9001 standard places emphasis on what should be done for an organization's customers: external quality assurance. Going beyond, it places emphasis on what should be done for the organization. Of course, this latter activity will eventually benefit customers, employees, stockholders, and society in general.

▶ 3-1 THE ISO 9000 FAMILY OF STANDARDS

3-1.1 A Historical Perspective

3-1.1.1 American Standards
For the marketplace, standardization is a necessity. Product standards, monetary standards, measurement standards, and others have been with us for thousands of years. This chapter is not addressing these standards. It addresses generic standards that are not product or industry specific. The earliest quality management system standards were developed for contractual purposes. Such standards—for example, MIL Q 9858, issued first in 1959

and later revised as MIL Q 9858A in 1963, and MIL I 45208, first issued in 1961 and revised in 1981—were developed by the U.S. Department of Defense. These were mandatory standards created for the purpose of assuring the defense procurement agencies of the United States that a supplier had the ability to provide high-quality weapons systems. Other countries developed similar standards for quality management systems.

In the United States voluntary national standards, as opposed to the mandatory standards, have been published by several organizations. The most prominent publishers of such standards are the American Society for Testing Materials, the American Society of Mechanical Engineers, the Institute of Electrical and Electronic Engineers, the American Society for Quality, and several others. All of these technical societies publish most of their standards under the auspices of the American National Standards Institute (ANSI). ANSI approves such standards, and most carry a dual designation of both the writing organization and ANSI. There are currently more than 11,000 ANSI standards, most of which are product specific. ANSI itself consists of individual members, approximately 1000 companies, 30 government agencies, and 250 professional, technical, trade, and consumer organizations.

ANSI is the sole U.S. representative to international standards-writing bodies such as the International Organization for Standardization, the International Electrotechnical Commission, and the Pacific Area Standards Congress. To facilitate the development of standards dealing with quality assurance and quality control, the American Society for Quality was accredited by ANSI in 1974 as a standards-writing body. Its Standards Committee was charged with promoting the development and use of such standards. In 1978 the ANSI Accredited Standards Committee Z1 was established, with the ASQ holding its secretariat. One of the early voluntary quality system standards that was developed in the United States was ANSI Standard Z1.8-1971, *Specification of General Requirements for a Quality Program.* This was written by the ASQ and later revised as ANSI/ASQC C1 in 1985. A later, more detailed standard was published by the ASQ as ANSI/ASQC Z1.15-1979, *Generic Guidelines for Quality Systems.* This latter standard was written by a subcommittee of the ANSI Accredited Standards Committee Z1. It later became the basis for the first edition of the international standard ISO 9004, which was published in 1987. In the United States it has been superseded by the American version of ISO 9004, designated as ANSI/ISO/ASQ Q9004. The third edition of this standard has now been issued as ISO 9004-2000 with its corresponding American designation as ANSI/ISO/ASQ Q9004-2000. This standard will be reviewed later in this chapter.

3-1.1.2 European Standards

Other standards similar to MIL-Q 9858A and ANSI/ASQC Z1.15 were being developed at the same time by other countries. A partial list of such early standards follows:

Country	Standard
United Kingdom	BS 4891:1972, *A Guide to Quality Assurance*
France	AFNOR NFX 50-110, *Recommendations for a System of Quality Management for the Use of Companies*
France	AFNOR NFX 50-111, *Quality Assurance Systems for the Use of Companies*
Germany	DIN 55-355, *Basic Elements of Quality Assurance Systems*

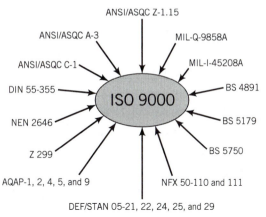

Figure 3-1 Inputs to the Evolution of the ISO 9000 Series

Some standards that were developed during this time were multilevel standards. That is, they had several levels of quality assurance requirements depending on the scope of the organization. They were chiefly developed for use in contractual situations. The following are some of these standards:

Country	*Standard*
United Kingdom	BS 5750-1979, *Specification for Design, Manufacture, and Installation*
Canada	CSA Z299-1978, *Quality Assurance Program Requirements*
Norway	NVS-S-1594, *Requirements of the Contractor's Quality Assurance Program*
South Africa	SABS 0157-1979, *Code of Practice for Quality Management Systems*
Australia	AS 1821-1975, *Suppliers Quality Control System*

These standards and others contributed to the development of the ISO 9000 family of standards as developed by the ISO Technical Committee 176 whose work is discussed next. This process is described in Figure 3-1.

3-1.1.3 International Standards

In 1979 the ISO formed Technical Committee 176, with secretariat given to Canada. The scope of this technical committee, as stated in the 1989 Momento of ISO, is "Standardization in the field of generic quality management, including quality systems, quality assurance, and generic supporting technologies, including standards which provide guidance on the selection and use of these standards." The technical committee published six standards in 1986–1987. Since then, other standards and guides have been published, bringing the total to twenty-seven as of 2001. The six original standards were the principal accomplishments of the committee. The first of the six standards, published in 1986, was ISO 8402, Vocabulary. This standard contained twenty-two terms. It was revised in 1994 with sixty-seven terms. The third edition of the standard, now designated ISO 9000-2000, has eighty terms. In the 2000 edition these terms are divided into ten sections as follows:

- Five terms relating to quality
- Fifteen terms relating to management

- Seven terms relating to organization
- Five terms relating to process and product
- Four terms relating to characteristics
- Thirteen terms relating to conformity
- Six terms relating to documentation
- Seven terms relating to examination
- Twelve terms relating to audit
- Six terms relating to quality assurance for measurement processes

Some of the standards in the ISO 9000 family have been discontinued since publication of the new edition of the basic standards in December 2000. These basic standards are ISO 9000, ISO 9001, and ISO 9004. The original ISO 9002 and 9003 standards, published in 1987 and revised in 1994, have been dropped, leaving ISO 9001 as the only standard containing requirements for quality management systems. ISO 9000-1-1994 contained information about the family of standards and their use. This standard has been combined with ISO 8402 in the new ISO 9000-2000, *Fundamentals and Terminology.* As noted above, TC 176 developed some twenty-seven standards and guides before the publication of the 2000 edition of the basic set of standards. Many of these were deleted or merged with other standards when the 2000 editions of the basic standards were published.

Some standards of note are the three auditing standards. These were designated ISO 10012-1, ISO 10012-2, and ISO 10012-3. Recently a new ISO Technical Committee, TC 207, was formed. This committee is responsible for environmental management systems. That technical committee developed similar auditing standards, designated ISO 14010, ISO 14011, and ISO 14012. The decision was made by both technical committees that these should be merged into one standard. This standard is designated ISO 19011, covering the auditing of both quality and environmental management systems.

The current members of the ISO 9000 family of standards and guides are as follows:

Core Standards

ISO 9000-2000, *Quality Management Systems—Fundamentals and Vocabulary*

ISO 9001-2000, *Quality Management Systems—Requirements*

ISO 9004-2000, *Quality Management Systems—Guidelines for Performance Improvements*

ISO 19011-2002, *Guidelines on Quality and/or Environmental Management Auditing*

Other International Standards

ISO 10012-2001, *Quality Assurance Requirements for Measuring Equipment*

ISO 10015-1999, *Quality Management—Guidelines for Training* (to be revised as a technical report)

Technical Reports

ISO 10006-1997, *Guidelines to Quality in Project Management*

ISO 10007-1995, *Guidelines for Configuration Management*

ISO 10013-1995, *Guidelines for Developing Quality Management System Documentation*

ISO 10014-1998, *Guidelines for Managing the Economics of Quality*

ISO/TR 10017-1999, *Guidance on Statistical Techniques for ISO 9001*

The only standard in this family that may be used for registration, or certification, of a quality management system is ISO 9001. In the two previous editions there were three such requirement standards: ISO 9001, 9002, and 9003. The 9001 standard was the most complete in that it covered all parts of a quality management system. ISO 9002 was identical to 9001 except that the design function was not included. Several other functions were deleted from 9003. The 2000 edition of ISO 9001 allows for the exclusion of some requirements, such as design, if they cannot be applied to an organization owing to its nature. However, conformity to the standard cannot be claimed unless such exclusions are limited to the requirements in Clause 7, Product Realization. The contents of this and other clauses will be discussed next.

3-1.2 Details of the ISO 9001-2000 Standard

3-1.2.1 Process Model

This edition of the standard is based on a process model rather than on the life-cycle model used in the two previous editions. The idea of a process model is that any activity that receives inputs and converts them to outputs is a process. Most processes are linked in that outputs from one process are often inputs to other processes. The systematic identification and management of the processes employed within an organization is the process approach.

This edition of ISO 9001 is one part of a consistent pair of standards, the other being ISO 9004-2000. The two standards have identical clause structures, an important property that was missing in the earlier editions. ISO 9004-2000 gives guidance to the development and operation of the quality management system meant to improve the organization's overall performance beyond that required by ISO 9001-2000. It is not a guideline for implementing ISO 9001-2000 and is not intended for certification or contractual use. The ISO 9001-2000 standard also has a structure similar to that of ISO 14001-1996, *Environmental Management Systems—Specification with Guidelines for Use*, to improve the compatibility between registration of the two management systems.

3-1.2.2 Quality Management Principles

ISO 9000-2000 lists the following steps that should be used to develop a quality management system:

1. Determine the needs and expectations of customers and other interested parties.
2. Establish the quality policy and quality objectives of the organization.
3. Determine the processes and responsibilities necessary to attain the objectives.
4. Determine and provide the resources necessary to attain the quality objectives.
5. Establish methods to measure the effectiveness and efficiency of each process.
6. Apply these measures to determine the effectiveness and efficiency of each process.

7. Determine means to prevent nonconformities and eliminate their causes.

8. Establish and apply a process for continual improvement.

These eight principles form the basis for the ISO 9000 family of standards.

3-1.2.3 Scope of ISO 9001-2000

ISO 9001-2000 specifies requirements for a quality management system when an organization needs to demonstrate its ability to consistently provide products that meet the requirements of customers and regulatory agencies. It also addresses customer satisfaction through the requirements for continual improvement and the prevention of nonconformities.

3-1.2.4 Quality Management System Requirements

ISO 9001-2000 begins with an introduction containing a general clause followed by a clause describing the process approach to quality management including its relationship to the familiar "plan, do, check, act" concept. This is followed by a discussion of the relationship of ISO 9001 and 9004 and other management system standards, specifically the ISO 14001 standard. The introduction is followed by Clause 1, Scope. This includes a clause on application of the standard including some comments regarding requirements that may be deleted in some situations.

The next two clauses are "Normative References" and "Terms and Definitions." Clause 4 of ISO 9001-2000 presents some general requirements of the quality management system. These include requirements for the identification and management of the processes in the system. General documentation requirements are also discussed in this clause. These include requirements for documented procedures, work instructions, manuals, and records and the control of these documents. This clause uses the verb "shall" for the first time, indicating a requirement, on the first line of Subclause 4.1. The use of this verb occurs eleven times in this clause and a total of 140 times in the standard.

The actual, detailed requirements of the standard are stated in the next four clauses entitled:

- Management Responsibility
- Resource Management
- Product Realization
- Measurement, Analysis and Improvement

The requirements found in each of these clauses will be discussed briefly.

3-1.2.4.1 Management Responsibility   Clause 5 of the standard is entitled "Management Responsibility." It designates a requirement for a highly visible management commitment to high quality. This is done by the establishment of a quality policy, the setting of quality objectives, and the establishment of a quality system that emphasizes problem prevention rather than dependence on detection after a problem occurs. Management must develop and state its corporate policy as it relates to quality. This policy must be consistent with all other corporate policies. It is the responsibility of management to ensure that its quality policy is understood, implemented, and maintained. The policy contains management's definition of good quality and its goals for quality improvement.

Quality objectives must be explicitly stated. These include the key elements of quality such as fitness for use, performance, safety, and reliability.

Management's responsibilities also include the organization and operation of the quality system. They are responsible for ensuring that the quality system functions in such a manner that the system is understood and effective. Confidence must be provided that products and services satisfy customer expectations.

This clause also requires the appointment of a management representative charged with the operation and maintenance of the quality system. This person must have direct access to top management. Top management shall review the quality management system at prescribed intervals to ensure its continuing effectiveness. These reviews shall include results of internal and external audits, customer feedback, process performance, status of corrective and preventive actions, and any changes that could affect the quality management system. Output of these reviews shall include actions related to quality improvement and resource needs.

Strong points of this clause include the formulation and dissemination of a quality policy by top management with dissemination to all levels of the organization, the identification of authority for all work affecting quality, and management's review of the system. On the negative side, although on the surface it might seem beneficial to appoint a management representative, it promotes the quality sins of the past by encouraging management to delegate the quality function. This is in contrast to the lessons learned in the evolution to total quality: that top management leadership is essential to achieve long-lasting and significant benefits in quality management.

3-1.2.4.2 Resource Management Clause 6 of the standard requires the provision of resources needed to maintain the quality management system. These include human resources, requiring the identification of competency needs for personnel, the provision of training to satisfy these needs, evaluation of the effectiveness of this training, and the maintenance of appropriate records of education, training, and qualifications of all personnel. There is also a requirement for the maintenance of a proper infrastructure and work environment.

3-1.2.4.3 Product Realization The last two clauses, 7 and 8, are large and contain a number of subclauses. The first subclause of Clause 7 deals with quality planning. This requires a statement of the quality objectives for the product or service and the processes needed. These plans are to be recorded in the form of quality plans, and they include any inspection or tests needed to verify the product quality. The second subclause, 7.2, requires the organization to determine all customer requirements. These include requirements for availability, delivery, and support as well as those not specified by the customer but necessary for the intended use of the product. The organization is also required to review product requirements before a commitment to produce a product to ensure that the organization is able to meet those requirements.

Clause 7.3 deals with the design and development of a product or service. An appropriate planning activity is required that controls the entire design process. Design input states that input must be defined and documented including all functional, regulatory, and legal requirements. The organization must document that knowledge from prior designs is used when it is available. Design output shall be in a form that makes verification against design input feasible. The output must include necessary requirements for production operations, address product acceptance criteria, and explain how the product may be used safely and correctly. The output documents must be approved before release for production.

The design clause requires reviews at appropriate stages using a review team made up of representatives of all functions associated with the product. There must be a verification stage during which the output is matched with the design input. There must also be a design validation stage during which the final product's performance is compared to requirements. Finally, all design changes must be documented and controlled.

Clause 7.4 covers the control of the purchasing function to ensure that the purchased product meets the specified requirements. Criteria for the selection and periodic evaluation of suppliers shall be defined, and results shall be recorded. The organization shall document and implement all activities necessary for the verification of purchased product. A negative aspect of this clause is that single sourcing of material as suggested in Deming's fourth point to management (see section 2-4.1) is ignored.

Clause 7.5 is entitled "Production and Service Operations." The first subclause in the section requires the control of operations relevant to production and services. This is done by making available information including specifications, work instructions, devices needed for measuring and monitoring, and instructions for release and postdelivery activities. The second subclause concerns the validation of special processes. These include any processes in which deficiencies become apparent only after the product is in use or the service has been provided. The third subclause requires the product to be identified and traceable throughout production. Clause 7.5.4 requires the organization to protect and control any customer-owned property. This includes customer-owned tooling, shipping containers, and intellectual property that may be provided in confidence. The last subclause, 7.5.5, requires the preservation of the product during internal processing and delivery to the final destination.

Clause 7.6 deals with the control of measuring and monitoring devices. These devices must be controlled, serviced and calibrated at regular intervals, and protected from damage. The results of calibration must be recorded, and corrective action must be taken if a device is found to be out of calibration, including the reassessment of any previous test results. Calibration is to be against national or international standards if they exist. If they do not exist, the basis for calibration must be documented. Any computer software that is used in monitoring or measuring shall be placed under configuration management. ISO 10012 is referenced in this section for guidance purposes.

3-1.2.4.4 Measurement, Analysis, and Improvement   Clause 8 contains five subclauses, the first of which, 8.1, is a general clause indicating that the organization must define, plan, and implement the measuring and monitoring activities needed to ensure conformity and product improvement. The second clause, 8.2, is entitled "Monitoring and Measurement." It requires the organization to measure customer satisfaction and conduct internal audits at regular intervals to ensure that the quality management system conforms to its own requirements and those of ISO 9001 and is effectively implemented and maintained. The subclause also requires the organization to measure and monitor all processes and products. The requirement for internal audits has been claimed by many users of the standard to be one of its strong points. Internal quality audits should do the following:

- Verify compliance with the organization's quality policy
- Determine the effectiveness of the quality management system
- Be scheduled with reasonable frequency
- Have documented procedures
- Involve follow-up actions
- Document results
- Be brought to the attention of management (of the process audited)
- Generate timely corrective actions on any deficiencies that are found

Reference is made to ISO 19011 for guidance in operating the internal auditing process.

Clause 8.3 covers control of nonconforming product. This is a requirement to identify and control any product that is nonconforming and to take appropriate action to see that it does not reach the customer. It also requires the organization to take appropriate action to see that the problem causing the nonconformities is corrected. The next subclause requires data dealing with the quality system to be collected and analyzed. These data include customer satisfaction, conformance to requirements, characteristics of processes, and suppliers.

Clause 8.5 requires the organization to plan for continual improvement "through the use of the quality policy, quality objectives, audit results, analysis of data, corrective and preventive actions, and management review." The last two subclauses in this clause are entitled corrective action and preventive action. These two requirements were a single clause in the 1994 edition of the standard. This caused some confusion among users of the standard as to the difference between them. Corrective action includes the correction of problems that have occurred, whereas preventive action deals with potential problems that may never have occurred.

3-1.3 ISO 9004-2000: Quality Management Systems—Guidelines for Performance Improvements

ISO 9004-2000 is a guidance document that provides more information regarding the quality management system. As was stated earlier, the clause structure of this standard is the same as that of ISO 9001-2000. It is based on the same quality management principles as ISO 9001-2000. The focus of this standard is the improvement of the processes of the organization to enhance its performance.

When ISO 9001-2000 and ISO 9004-2000 are used together the benefits to an organization are likely to be more than if only one is used. The two standards have identical structures but different scopes. ISO 9004 is not intended to be used as a guidance document for compliance to ISO 9001. The purpose of ISO 9001 is to define the minimum requirements needed to achieve customer satisfaction by meeting specified product requirements. The purpose of ISO 9004 is to provide guidance on the development of a quality management system to improve the overall performance of an organization.

The clauses of ISO 9001-2000 are included in boxes within the clauses of ISO 9004-2000 for immediate reference for users. The verb "shall" is used throughout ISO 9001, whereas the verb used in ISO 9004 is "should."

Clause 8.2.1.5 in ISO 9004-2000 provides a means for self-assessment of an organization's quality management system. The actual methodology, along with appropriate questions to be answered, is included in an annex to the standard.

3-1.4 Other Standards and Guides in the ISO 9000 Family

Most of these were mentioned in Section 3-1.1.3. In addition to those standards and guides there are several that should be mentioned. Three brochures published by ISO relate to the 9000 family:

- *Quality Management Principles and Guidelines on Their Application*
- *Selection and Use of Standards*
- *Small Businesses*

Two other standards were formerly in the 9000 family. The first of these is ISO 9000-3: 1997, *Quality Management and Quality Assurance Standard—Part 3: Guidelines for the Application of ISO 9001-1994 to the Development, Supply, Installation, and Maintenance of Computer Software*. This standard has been transferred to ISO/IEC JTC 1/SC7, which will update it to correspond to the 2000 edition of ISO 9001. The second is ISO 9000-4: 1993, *Quality Management and Quality Assurance Standard—Part 4: Guide to Dependability Program Management*. This standard has been transferred to IEC/TC 56, Dependability, which is updating it for the 2000 edition of ISO 9001. The following standards in the ISO 9000 family have been dropped:

- ISO 8402:1994, *Vocabulary*—now a part of ISO 9000-2000
- ISO 9000-1:1994, *Selection and Use of ISO 9000 Standards*—now part of ISO 9000-2000
- ISO 9002:1994, *Model for Quality Assurance*—now included in ISO 9001-2000
- ISO 9003:1994, *Model for Quality Assurance*—now included in ISO 9001-2000
- ISO 9004-1:1994, *Quality Management and Quality System Elements—Part 1: Guidelines*—now designated ISO 9004-2000
- ISO 9004-2:1991, *Quality Management and Quality System Elements—Part 2: Guidelines for Services*—now included in ISO 9004-2000
- ISO 9004-3:1993, *Quality Management and Quality System Elements—Part 3: Guidelines for Processed Materials*—now included in ISO 9004-2000
- ISO 9004-4:1993, *Quality Management and Quality System Elements—Part 4: Guidelines for Quality Improvement*—now included in ISO 9004-2000
- ISO 10005:1995, *Quality Management—Guidelines for Quality Plans*—now included in ISO 9004-2000

▶ 3-2 QUALITY SYSTEMS DOCUMENTATION AND AUDITING

Two important elements of quality systems that are specifically related to the ISO 9000 series are those of documentation and auditing. These are singled out for some additional discussion here.

3-2.1 Quality Systems Documentation

Importance attached to documenting a quality system is clearly illustrated by the reference to ISO 9001-2000 (see Section 3-1.2.4). Clause 4.2 of the standard discusses this subject. The 2000 edition of this standard, however, places less emphasis on documentation than the earlier editions. Documentation, like standardization, is essential for defining and implementing a quality system.

Key to the documentation of a quality system is a quality manual and its associated procedures, work instructions, forms, records, files, reports, and books. The quality manual is often referred to as the cornerstone of the quality system.

3-2.1.1 Quality Manual

In general, the purpose of a quality manual is to document company policies and procedures affecting quality. It should contain policy and mission statements endorsed and signed by the chief executive officer that define the policy and mission of the organization as it relates to quality. This may include the commitment to quality and perhaps the expectation of what a sound business strategy based on quality principles will do for the organization, for customers, and for society. Examples of several mission statements combined with a quality policy, a quality vision, and related features were presented in Chapter 2.

In addition to policy and mission statements a quality manual should describe the quality system. It should define authority and responsibilities, as well as duties. It should define the quality planning process. With respect to these areas four definitions from ISO 9000-2000 are helpful:

> *3.2.3 **quality management system:** management system to direct and control an organization with regard to quality.*

> *3.2.8 **quality management:** coordinated activities to direct and control an organization with regard to quality. [Note that a more comprehensive definition of total quality management is given in Chapter 2.]*

> *3.2.4 **quality policy:** overall intentions and direction of an organization related to quality as formally expressed by top management.*

> *3.7.5 **quality plan:** document specifying which procedures and associated resources shall be applied by whom and when to a specific project, product, process or contract.*

A quality manual is used to inform the workforce at all levels. It might serve as a marketing tool to inform customers and potential customers of the management policy and objectives for quality. It often serves as the principal document upon which a quality audit is planned or as input to the application for a quality award consideration.

At the systems level, the quality manual may address such details as marketing research strategies; assessment of customer preferences and needs (perhaps via quality function deployment); and strategies for design and development, procurement policies, process planning and development, sales, and distribution.

There is no fixed format or list of topics to be included in a quality manual. There is no general agreement as to how detailed a quality manual should be. Some prefer to exclude all procedures from the quality manual, relegating such procedures to lower-level documents. Even in these preferences there is no general level of agreement as to what constitutes a procedure, as opposed to policies, objectives, responsibilities, or authorities.

Some manuals are entitled "Quality Assurance Manual and Procedures," "Product Assurance Policy and Procedures Manual," or the like. Hence, quality manuals developed by different companies and organizations are bound to be unique. It is their manual, and it should meet their needs. A growing practice in preparing a quality manual is to develop it with sections simply bearing the titles of the requirement clauses and subclauses of ISO 9001. This practice is appreciated, especially by registrars conducting assessment activities, and can assist the enterprise itself in organizing its quality assurance system requirements.

Various factors to consider in the development of a quality manual are the following:

- Recognition of the need and purpose for the manual
- Acceptance by top management and others within the organization
- Recognition as a policy document
- That it be dynamic, requiring review, revision, and document control
- That it be for internal or external use or both
- That it be based on in-house style or a standard pattern
- Authorship—internal or external consultants
- Handling of proprietary and confidential matters
- Levels of documentation and breadth of coverage
- Approval required

An example of a possible structure for a quality manual is as follows:

A. Company policy and mission statements, signed by the chief executive officer

B. A table of contents

C. An introduction to the company, including the products and services it provides, its physical facilities, and its resources

D. Manual control—distribution, review mechanism, revision policy

E. Organizational structure—management structure with authorities and responsibilities

F. Procedure and work instruction reference section(s)

For many company manuals, particularly for large companies, the F section will be a separate manual. The quality manual should refer or otherwise guide the reader to system-level and operational-level procedures and work instructions.

Quality system documentation is often illustrated by triangles or pyramids showing the quality manual at the apex of the figure. An example is shown in Figure 3-2. This model describes the complete documentation of the quality system from manual, to procedures, to work instructions, to forms, records, files, and reports. These are often developed as parts of the complete manual or as multiple sets of manuals such as a quality system policy manual, a system-level procedures manual, an operations-level procedures manual, or work instruction manuals.

Figure 3-2 Quality System Documentation

As referenced earlier, an international standard on *Guidelines for Quality Management System Documentation* (ISO 10013-1995) has been published. It is useful in the preparation of quality manuals as a first step in quality system documentation.

3-2.1.2 Procedures and Work Instructions

Generally, procedures and work instructions inform the workforce in detailed terms how the policies and objectives expressed in the quality manual shall be addressed. They are often confidential, and this provides one mechanism for separating the nonproprietary material that may be placed in a quality manual for external use from those materials and information that should not reach the public.

Procedures and work instructions are the media by which the who, why, what, where, when, and how are conveyed to the workforce. They define how groups of people in the same or in different departments shall work together to meet the organization's objectives. The procedures and work instructions must address each operation and product or service specification to define the organization's total operation from customer order to the delivery of a completed product or service. They may also include after-sales servicing and market research for product redesign or new product innovations. In this sense a standard like ISO 9001 can be helpful as a basis for defining the areas that must be addressed by procedures and work instructions, but it must be understood that quality system standards are generic. They do not address specific product or service specifications, operations, processes, or materials. These must be included in a quality manual or in related procedures and work instructions.

Generally, system-level procedures are horizontal, that is, cross-functional or interdepartmental. This is illustrated in Figure 3-3, which shows several system-level topics that must be written to define all cross-functional inputs and responsibilities. Cross-functional teams for problem solving and quality improvement are another example. Flowcharting is a very useful technique for describing the steps, decisions, and flow in cross-functional procedures. Their use in work instructions is also feasible and instructive.

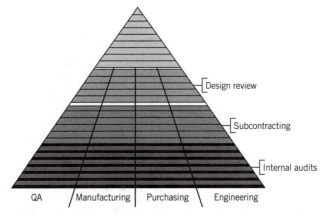

Figure 3-3   System Level Procedures—Interdepartmental

Work instructions are generally intradepartmental and might need to be defined for *each* department separately. They describe in detail how a specific activity is to be conducted. They define the standards of acceptability for a part, assembly, product, or service. Company standards are included in this category. Work instructions may not be in actual manual form. They are often single drawings, pictures, operation sheets, inspection and test schedules, models, or workmanship standards.

3-2.1.3 Forms, Records, and Reports

This category of an organization's quality system documentation confirms that the product or service has been developed and produced in compliance with the specified requirements. This level of strata in the overall documentation is generally loosely structured. It contains the items that are required to support the other levels of the documentation system and to assist in demonstrating the achievements of the objectives. Forms, records, reports, files, and books are generally developed by an organization for its own use and therefore are usually unique.

3-2.2 Auditing and Assessing Quality Systems

ISO 9001-2000 may be used for contractual use. This has its roots in the documents leading up to the publication of the ISO 9000 series, including MIL-Q-9858A. ISO 9004-2000 is intended to assist in developing and implementing quality management systems beyond the basic requirements of ISO 9001 and would be used in a noncontractual situation.

Associated with these two major parts of the ISO 9000 series are various assessment and certification programs. It should be apparent from the above that ISO 9001-2000 is intended to facilitate two-party contractual arrangements for assurance of quality. The purchasing party will want to be assured that the supply party is using a comprehensive quality program as specified in the contract. To gain that assurance, the purchaser may conduct an external audit of the supplier's quality management system. Such an assessment is referred to as a second-party audit.

ISO 9000 Assessment/Certification

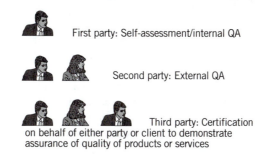

First party: Self-assessment/internal QA

Second party: External QA

Third party: Certification
on behalf of either party or client to demonstrate
assurance of quality of products or services

Figure 3-4 ISO 9000 Series Range of Assessments and Certification

The ISO 9000 series, in particular ISO 9004, may also be used on a first-party basis for self-assessment, design, and implementation of a quality system. The purpose of this exercise is to provide in-house management with assurances of quality. This may be done before, during, or after the system has been approved by a customer. As explained in the review of each of the requirements of ISO 9001-2000, one of the requirements (8.2.2) is for internal quality audits. Hence, after initial approval of a quality system, continual internal audits must be done as a requirement of the standard.

Additionally, the ISO 9001 standard is used on a third-party basis for assessment on behalf of either of two parties and eventual registration. Figure 3-4 illustrates this range of assessments. These programs include the certification of auditors for conducting the registration activities. They also include the accreditation of bodies that are qualified to conduct third-party certification. These topics are discussed in Section 3-3.1 in greater detail.

3-2.2.1 ISO 19011 Guidelines

ISO 19011 has been developed and issued to provide guidelines for auditing management systems. This standard covers material that was previously covered in six ISO standards. ISO 10011-1, 10011-2, and 10011-3 covered quality system auditing, qualification criteria for quality system auditors, and management of audit programs, respectively. ISO TC 207 on environmental management also developed auditing standards, identified as ISO 14010, 14011, and 14012, covering essentially the same material but for environmental auditors. In an effort to make auditing of quality management systems and environmental management systems more compatible, a joint committee of the two technical committees was established. This committee developed ISO 19011, which may be used for both types of audits. This is a big advantage for companies that wish to have both their quality and environmental management systems registered. They may be able to do it with a single audit.

ISO 19011 covers all of the material previously covered in these six standards. The auditing standard covers the responsibilities of auditors, which include the following:

- Determining conformity of the quality or environmental management system
- Determining effectiveness of the system

- Providing a basis for improvement of the system
- Meeting regulatory requirements
- Registering the system
- Verification of conformity and effective implementation of one's own system
- Continuing surveillance of an organization's system

Coverage is given to the auditor's responsibilities and their need for independence from the person or organization being audited. It is recognized that audits may be conducted by one person or a team of auditors and should be under the responsibility of a lead auditor. The lead auditor's responsibilities can be summarized as follows:

- Responsibility for all phases of the audit from planning, to execution, to reporting, to follow-up
- Assisting in selection of the audit team
- Preparing the audit plan
- Liaison with the management of the organization being audited
- Submission of the audit report

The auditor's responsibilities can be summarized as follows:

- Complying with the audit scope and requirements
- Communication and clarification of audit requirements
- Planning and executing assigned areas of responsibilities
- Documenting observations and reporting results to the lead auditor
- Verifying corrective actions
- Safeguarding audit documents
- Maintaining confidentiality

The client's role is as follows:

- Initiating the audit process upon determining needs
- Selecting the auditing organization
- Receiving audit report, determining follow-up actions
- Informing all relevant employees on the scope of the audit
- Appointing staff to accompany auditors
- Providing required resources to the audit team
- Providing access to the facilities and documents
- Cooperating with the auditors
- Initiating corrective actions based on the audit report(s)

The qualifications of auditors are discussed in the standard. These include training, experience, personal attributes, management capabilities, language, and selection of a lead auditor. Minimum education levels are described. Training should include quality or environmental management system standards, auditing techniques, and audit management and administration, including communications. The suggested minimum experience levels are four years practical workplace experience with at least two years in activities related to quality. Audit experience should include participation in at least four audits for a total of at least twenty days.

Personal attributes of auditors should include open-mindedness, maturity, sound judgment, analytical skills and perseverance, the ability to perceive situations realistically, and the ability to understand complex operations and organizations. These attributes should permit an auditor to conduct an audit with thoroughness.

Auditors should maintain their competence with up-to-date knowledge of the appropriate management system standards and auditing techniques, with a performance review by an evaluation panel every three years. Lead auditors are required to have completed at least three audits and to have demonstrated effective communication skills.

3-2.3 Audit Principles and Activities

An audit is defined in ISO 9000-2000 as a "systematic, independent and documented process for obtaining audit evidence and evaluating it objectively to determine the extent to which audit criteria are fulfilled." This definition is further supported by the definition of objective evidence, given by ISO 9000-2000 as "data supporting the existence or verity of something."

Thus, auditing is a process that is documented at the planning, execution, reporting, and follow-up phases. It is based on written procedures, prepared in advance during the planning phase, to ensure that all objectives and requirements of an audit are addressed and verified. It involves direct examination and evaluation of objective evidence. It addresses whether the required elements of a management system have been developed, documented, and effectively implemented. Hence, it involves value judgments on the existence, documentation, and effective implementation of the applicable elements of a management system.

A quality system audit has four phases. Although these may differ somewhat among auditing organizations, the following are identified and discussed here: preliminary planning, execution, reporting, and subsequent follow-up.

3-2.3.1 Preliminary Planning

Initial activities include the decision to conduct an audit, the type, scope, client, objectives, requirements, lead auditor, and the audit team assignment. The early planning activities of the lead auditor include a document review of the organization and the intended audit scope. The organization being audited is required to provide the necessary documents for this review. These may include (1) the vision and mission statements of the organization, (2) the quality policy, (3) the quality manual (or manuals), (4) system and operation procedures, (5) work instructions, (6) an organization chart (if not included in any of the above), (7) specific functional responsibilities of the quality assurance program, (8) the contract(s), existing or contemplated, between the client and or purchaser, (9) any internal or external regulatory requirements.

This documentation database is reviewed by the lead auditor for initial information for the purpose of defining the areas to be audited and developing a detailed checklist and auditing procedures. It should be noted from this that the audit is not a surprise visit to the supplier. The organization should be aware of all audit activities, including preliminary planning ones. Surveillance visits might be part of a registration program once an organization has been approved officially and is aware of the possibility of such visits by the auditing body. This is mentioned as an activity in Section 3-2.3.4.

During the preliminary planning phase the organization that is being audited may be contacted for clarification or additional information. An optional preassessment visit for further familiarization of the auditor(s) might be desirable. Such a visit may contribute to the decisions regarding the number of days and the number of auditors that are required to complete the audit successfully. Such a visit might also include a gap analysis to determine the readiness of the organization for registration.

If all of the above have been conducted by the lead auditor alone, it is then time to select and organize the audit team, including any specialists that are required for the audit. The audit team will then conduct planning meetings to select and assign audit activities, further develop and evaluate the checklists, review documentation, and schedule the actual assessment audit. Upon completion of these activities the lead auditor will contact the organization that is being audited to obtain its agreement to the planned audit schedule. The team members may be introduced, initially by paper, telephone, or electronic media, and a date may be set for the audit.

3-2.3.2 Audit Execution

The initial activity of the on-site audit is the opening meeting. The members of the audit team are introduced, along with the members of the organization's management. The tentative agenda will be reviewed, revised, and approved. The scope, objectives, requirements, areas, and procedures of the audit should be discussed and approved. The schedule for conducting the audit, together with team meetings and debriefing meetings, should be set.

Provisions should be made for administrative and facility needs. Any additional documentation and references should be requested. As part of the audit schedule a tentative time for the closing meeting should be set. Guides from the organization should be assigned to assist the auditors.

As the audit is being executed, the lead auditor should meet daily with the audit team to discuss their observations and findings. The lead auditor should also ensure that the auditors perform their assigned functions. Daily debriefing meetings should be held with management to discuss findings and provide opportunities for clarification, defense, and resolution.

The auditors should document observations and findings, including confirmation by the guides and management or operational staff in the areas in which a finding is to be reported. The concept of objective evidence should be followed. A policy of reporting good conditions as well as nonconforming ones should be followed.

3-2.3.3 Reporting

Besides the debriefing meetings with management, the first complete reporting of audit results should be presented by the lead auditor at the closing meeting. The results, recorded and summarized by the lead auditor in group team meetings, should be presented orally and in written form. Agreement and commitment on the part of management should be obtained on specific actions to correct any nonconformities, and a mutually agreeable time frame should be established.

A complete formal audit report should be compiled by the lead auditor and submitted to the client. This should be within a short period after the closing meeting. All pertinent findings, supported by objective evidence, as gathered from the auditors should be included. Approvals for the release of the report, if required, should be obtained from the client or other interested party.

Expected corrective actions should be spelled out clearly in the report for management follow-up. Completion of corrective actions by the organization should be communicated to the auditor. Follow-up audits may be required to verify correction of nonconformities.

3-2.3.4 Follow-up

Implementation of corrective action and preparation of a response to the auditing organization are initial follow-up activities. Corrective action might have been taken, or at least started, before receipt of the audit report. If possible, complete preventive solutions should be made early. If this is not possible, a temporary solution should be implemented with efforts launched to determine a more complete solution in the near future. A responsibility of management is to locate the root cause of any nonconformity reported to deal adequately and completely with the problem (see the discussion in Section 3-1.3.14).

Follow-up activities of the lead auditor include the review and evaluation of responses to corrective actions taken. A determination of effectiveness must be given serious consideration, always difficult on a remote basis, so that clarification may be required. Eventually, a response to the review and evaluation must be made. If deemed necessary, a follow-up audit should be scheduled to verify whether effective implementation of corrective action has been taken. The follow-up audit may be more precisely directed and briefer than the initial audit. If possible, it should close out the corrective action requests. Otherwise, additional corrective action requests should be issued with a schedule for response.

Upon the satisfactory closing of all corrective action requests and the issuance of a certificate of registration, if applicable, the auditing process is completed. A contract between the two parties may include surveillance visits to the organization to ensure that the quality system has not undergone any major revision or changes that might result in degradation. These surveillance visits should be scheduled periodically during a registration period.

▶ 3-3 ISO 9000: RELATED ASPECTS

Associated with the implementation of the ISO 9000 series are programs to register companies and organizations that are found to be in compliance with the standards. These programs have an infrastructure of registrars, training program providers, auditors, and accreditation bodies establishing criteria to keep some degree of order and uniform practice for these activities.

3-3.1 Registration of Quality Management Systems

Several assessment programs associated with the contractual standard, ISO 9001-2000, have been established. These include third-party programs that are directed toward a more general registration process. These programs have as their purpose the reduction of multiple audits of an organization by multiple purchasers that otherwise might involve considerable outlay of time, effort, labor, and cost. The principle is that if a qualified auditing organization (registrar) conducts a thorough audit leading to the registration of an organization's quality system, this registration can serve all potential customers of the organization. Hence, the initial request for the audit might come from the organization itself as part of its marketing strategy.

These programs require procedures for the certification of auditors of quality systems and accreditation of registrar organizations by nationally or internationally recognized accrediting bodies. Another related program is the accreditation of organizations offering training of auditors and lead auditors.

Third-party certification programs, especially for product certification, have been in existence for many years [see Stephens and Hopper (1973), Stephens (1974), Stephens, Hunter, and Chacko (1974), and Stephens (1975, 1978a, 1978b, 1978c)]. One of the earliest is that of the British Standards Institution (BSI). This product certification mark, known as the "Kitemark" because of its shape, has been in existence since 1903, shortly after the establishment of BSI as a national standards body. Hence, it is not surprising that third-party certification programs for quality management systems were established early and have grown rapidly in the United Kingdom.

To give credibility to certification bodies in the United Kingdom regarding quality system certification, the Secretary of State for Trade and Industry agreed to accredit the certification bodies that could be relied on to be consistent, thorough, and competent. Hence, in 1982 the National Accreditation Council for Certification Bodies (NACCB), funded by the Department of Trade and Industry (DTI), was established with BSI appointed as the secretariat.

Subsequently, in 1985, the Association of Certification Bodies was formed as a forum in which certification bodies could collectively formulate policies. The objective of the association is to encourage improvement in the quality of goods and services manufactured or supplied in the United Kingdom through the promotion of independent certification to specific standards.

Efforts have been under way to standardize and harmonize the accreditation procedure. The European standard, EN 45012, *General Criteria for Certification Bodies Operating Quality System Certification,* was issued in September 1989 in support of these efforts. The accreditation bodies in Europe have come together to form the European Accreditation of Certification.

In the United States the Registrar Accreditation Board (RAB) was incorporated in November 1989 as an independent, wholly owned subsidiary of the American Society for Quality (ASQ) [see Lofgren (1990)]. The American National Standards Institute (ANSI, the U.S. member of ISO) and RAB/ASQ jointly operate the American National Accreditation Program for Registrars of Quality Systems. ANSI and RAB have also concluded a memorandum of understanding with counterparts in the Netherlands (RVA), Australia and New Zealand (JAS-ANZ), and the United Kingdom (NACCB) to "achieve mutual recognition of each other's accreditation of quality system registrars." In January 1993 ANSI and RAB joined with these three counterparts, as well as organizations from Japan, Canada, and Mexico, to form the International Accreditation Forum, with ANSI as secretariat.

ISO itself has now joined this effort. Its council approved establishing a special group to propose the membership rules, organizational structure, and financing mechanisms for a worldwide system to ensure the international recognition of ISO 9000 certificates. See *ISO 9000 News,* Vol. 2, No. 4, July-August 1993, pp. 1–3, and Vol. 2, No. 5, September-October 1993, pp. 1, 3, and 4.

Another significant development in the United Kingdom was the formulation of the National Registration Scheme for Assessors of Quality Systems (RBA). This was an element of the National Quality Campaign following the issue of the government's white paper "*Standards, Quality and International Competitiveness*" in 1982. At the same time that NACCB was established, the RBA was also sponsored by DTI to be managed by an independent board of management with the Institute of Quality Assurance appointed to provide the secretariat. The function of the RBA is to support the National Quality Initiative by setting qualifications and experience requirements for the accreditation of Assessors of Quality Systems.

To qualify for certification by the RBA, individuals must be able to score a specified number of credits for a combination of academic qualifications, work experience, and experience in auditing quality systems to the ISO 9000 series. In addition, it is a mandatory requirement that candidates must have successfully completed one of the training courses accredited by the RBA. RBA/IQA operates another program for accreditation of an assessor training course.

In the United States, RAB operates a certification program for auditors of quality systems and an accreditation of lead assessor courses.

3-3.1.1 Some Observations and Concerns

These programs of registration also have both positive and negative aspects (see Section 3-3.2). On the positive side, third-party programs contribute to the minimization of multiple audits, saving time, effort, labor, and costs. On the negative side, registration programs must be carefully monitored by the international and national community to ensure that they do not become barriers to trade. Small businesses have unique problems and have expressed concerns about these programs. The registration and accreditation process must be carefully implemented to avoid business opportunists with no long-term interests in quality. Sayles (1992) mentions a deplorable practice of issuance of conditional certificates simply to promote continued business.

In the discussion of the Japanese adoption of the ISO 9000 series in the next section (Section 3-3.2), reference is made to a JISC report indicating that business interests were influential in the decision to adopt the standards, including the establishment of local registrars and accreditation bodies. Hutchins (1992), a U.K. quality professional, is critical of the practice of third-party certification because it may dilute the effectiveness of quality systems. He expresses the opinion that "third party accreditation has probably cost the United Kingdom ten years of leadership in quality."

A particularly bad scenario is the situation in which companies feel forced to comply, often in response to assessment failures. This, in turn, may result in a fragmented quality system that no one is using, relegating quality control to a police role rather than as a significant aid to business strategy—the very type of system from which we have evolved.

3-3.2 The ISO 9000 Series and Quality Systems in Perspective

With the 2000 revisions of the ISO 9000 series, including their widespread adoption and implementation, these international standards on quality management systems continue to generate attention. This is deserving but needs understanding as to what the ISO 9000 series is and what it is not. Such an understanding will contribute significantly to the correct implementation and use of these standards and guidelines.

It is important to realize that quality systems or even standards for quality systems were not invented by ISO 9000. Inputs to the evolution of the ISO 9000 series are discussed in Section 3-1.1 and reflected in Figure 3-1, which portrays the historical and widespread influences in the development of ISO 9000.

Many terms of the modern disciplines of quality have been borrowed from Japanese innovative and successful applications. Some of these terms are as follows:

- *Kaizen* (improvement)
- *Hoshin-kanri* (management by policy)
- *Kanban* (visible record or order ticket, as an integral part of the kanban system of management by policy and just-in-time production management)
- *Jishu kanri* (self-management)
- *Poka-yoke* (foolproofing/prevention)
- *Seiri* (organization)
- *Seiton* (neatness)
- *Seiso* (cleaning)
- *Seiketsu* (standardization)
- *Shitsuke* (discipline)

The latter five are referred to as the 5 S's [see Osada (1991)]. Other terms that took on English references directly include the following:

- *QCC* (quality control circles)
- *CWQC* (companywide quality control)
- *QFD* (quality function deployment)
- *CE* (cause-and-effect) *Diagrams*
- *JIT* (just-in-time production/inventory management system)
- *TPM* (total productive maintenance)

To these must be added Deming's fourteen points for management, emanating from Japanese applications and innovations.

Most of these concepts are not an integral part of the ISO 9000 series, and none of these terms, concepts, and techniques represent quality system assessment or registration. The system that is so successful in achieving quality in Japanese products was not based on quality system registration. However, this is the system that has attracted the attention of corporate management and the quality profession worldwide, often with provocative exhortations by Western consultants, such as Deming and Juran. It is also the system that has been implemented with beneficial results by many of the world's leading corporations and enterprises. It has had many names, some of which were mentioned in Chapter 2. These inputs to the evolution and development of quality systems are reflected in Figure 3-5.

3-3.2.1 The ISO 9000 Series: A Minimum Foundation

The ISO 9000 series is a family of standards. Thus, it has both the advantages and disadvantages of standards. As a standard, it is subject to periodic review and revision. Two

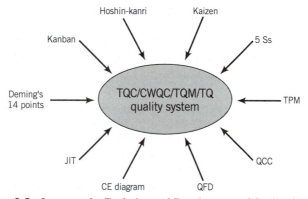

Figure 3-5 Inputs to the Evolution and Development of Quality Systems

cycles of that process have been realized with the 1994 and 2000 revisions, referred to as phase I and phase II revisions [see Tsiakals (1994)]. The standards should be understood to ensure correct and beneficial implementation, combined with other elements of a total quality system that are not a part of the series. It is extremely important for managers to understand that ISO 9001-2000 is not intended as a standard on total quality! A total quality system must go beyond ISO 9001-2000. ISO 9004-2000 is intended to provide a platform for organizations to accomplish this.

On the positive side, the strengths of ISO 9001-2000 lie in the structure that sets forth a uniform, consistent set of requirements that can be applied universally, within limitations of interpretation and individual implementation. It provides a basis for designing, implementing, evaluating, specifying, and certifying (registering) a quality management system. With widespread adoption, it provides a common language for international trade. It requires a sound, well-documented contractual relationship between customer and supplier. Hence, it establishes a common understanding between these parties, based on agreed requirements.

For further understanding, ISO 9001-2000 is generic in two significant aspects. It is not product or process specific. The quality management system will, of necessity, contain specific subsystems related directly to the processes and to the products to which it is being applied. It does not specify a fixed system with regard to how the requirements are to be met for every organization. This is, of course, not a criticism. It provides considerable flexibility to the organization to design and document its own system within the framework of the requirements. It then directs attention to evaluating conformance to its management system.

On the negative side, as for many standards passing through negotiation, debate, review, and consensus, ISO 9001-2000 represents a least common denominator in its coverage of the quality management system. Everyone should understand that it is not a standard on total quality and realize that the quality system that is optimum for a given organization might go well beyond the requirement of ISO 9001-2000. It is encouraging that many companies implementing quality management systems do go beyond the requirements of ISO 9001-2000 and incorporate other elements of total quality.

There are many aspects of total quality systems that are not incorporated in ISO 9001-2000. The name one gives to these systems is not as important as the content. We see references to TQC, TQM, IQM (integrated quality management) [see Asian Productivity Organization (1990)], SQM (strategic quality management), TQ [see Hutchins (1992)], re-engineering, whole system architecture, six sigma, and others. At this juncture a historical note may be entered. The quality sciences have always been plagued by problems of semantics and the NIH (not invented here) syndrome. Some proponents of total quality management (TQM), for example, are ignorant of, or ignore, the fact that programs and systems with previous names as simple as quality control or total quality control, which existed twenty-five to thirty-five years ago, included many of the concepts and methodologies of TQM. This is not to say that important strides in refining and exposing these concepts to a wider audience have not been made in recent years. But overzealous proponents of certain concepts have shown tendencies to ignore the situations calling for a full range of tools (including statistical and others) for the total job of achieving quality.

The following topics, generally considered to be a part of total quality management, are either missing or less than adequately covered in ISO 9000-2000:

- Quality cost analysis and applications (other than as an element in ISO 9004-2000 and in ISO 10014)
- Project-by-project improvement, pursued with revolutionary rates of improvement
- Joy and pride in work and employee participation, involvement, and empowerment via project teams and quality circles
- Variation reduction, statistical process control, process capability, and process management
- Production and inventory management systems such as JIT with TQC
- Benchmarking of competitors as well as best-in-class products, processes, and systems
- Marketing research together with quality function deployment to determine customer needs and translation of these needs into new products
- Deming's fourteen points for management and the recognition of the benefits and the necessity for transformation

Juran (1994) lists the following exclusions from ISO 9001 as essentials to attain world-class quality:

- Personal leadership by the upper managers
- Training the hierarchy in managing for quality
- Quality goals in the business plan
- A revolutionary rate of quality improvement
- Participation and empowerment of the workforce

Additional resources for total quality management systems assessments and criteria for designing and implementing such systems are the various quality awards. Among these are the Deming Prize, the Malcolm Baldrige Award, and the European Quality Award. The latter, in particular, encourages self-appraisal. See Chapter 4 for a further discussion of these and other awards.

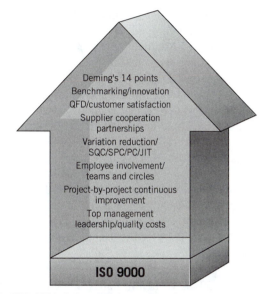

Figure 3-6   ISO 9001 Only a Minimum Foundation for Total Quality Systems

With consideration of these additional resources, the resultant system should be better, more dynamic, more comprehensive, more effective, and more economical than that of ISO 9001-2000 alone. This is illustrated by Figure 3-6, with ISO 9001 shown as a basic foundation for a total quality system that for completeness includes other techniques and procedures.

3-3.2.2 ISO 9000 Series, Quality System, Summary

No single standard (or set of standards) has had more universal results in increasing the awareness of quality than has the ISO 9000 series with its direct linkage to the unified market of the European Union. Every country, trade association, and corporation that wishes to compete in international trade must give serious consideration to the use of ISO 9001-2000 or ISO 9004-2000 for establishing and demonstrating assurance of quality of their products or services. The publication of the ISO 9000 Series in 1987 and its revisions in 1994 and 2000, together with the accompanying terminology standard (ISO 8402, now ISO 9000-2000), has brought harmonization on an international scale and has supported the growing impact of quality as a factor in international trade. The ISO 9000 series has quickly been adopted by many nations and regional bodies and is rapidly supplanting prior national and industry-based standards. It is a basis for promoting and disseminating quality management systems globally. The ISO 9000 series is fundamental to total strategic quality.

▶ 3-4 OTHER QUALITY SYSTEMS

3-4.1 QS-9000 Requirements for Automotive Suppliers

The Automotive Industry Action Group (AIAG) published a set of requirements entitled *Quality System Requirements, QS-9000* in August 1994. The document was revised in

February 1995 because of comments that had been received, particularly from European divisions of Chrysler, Ford, and General Motors. It was further revised in March 1998 [AIAG (1998a)]. This document is an agreement between the three major American auto manufacturers and five truck manufacturers. QS-9000, together with six supplementary manuals [AIAG (1992, 1994, 1995a, 1995b, 1995c, 1998b)], replaces the individual requirements previously used by each company. These requirements, which are now withdrawn, were Chrysler's Supplier Quality Assurance Manual, Ford's Q101 Quality System Standard, General Motor's NAO Targets for Excellence, General Motor's Europe General Quality Standard for Purchased Materials, and the Truck Manufacturers' quality system manuals. QS-9000 does not qualify theoretically as a standard because a consensus process was not used in its development. Quality system requirements for tooling and equipment suppliers have also been developed as TE-9000.

The European auto manufacturers together with the American ones have now published a technical specification that is to take the place of QS 9000. It has been designated TS 16949 [ISO (1999)]. The first edition of the specification was based on the 1994 edition of ISO 9001. The revised edition, based on ISO 9001-2000, will be published early in 2002. QS-9000 and TS 16949 contain all of ISO 9001-1994, which is its foundation. ISO 9001-1994 is written in italics in the document, and all interpretations and supplementary requirements are in roman type. The goal for QS-9000 is stated in the introduction as "the development of fundamental quality systems that provide for continuous improvement, emphasizing defect prevention and the reduction of variation and waste in the supply chain." As in ISO 9001, the verb "shall" indicates a mandatory requirement, whereas "should" indicates a preferred approach. However, in this case an organization must show its customer that the approach used will meet the requirements and intent of QS-9000.

3-4.1.1 Section I of QS-9000

This section contains all twenty subclauses of ISO 9001-1994, Clause 4. Not all clauses have supplementary requirements, but most have something added.

Clause 4.1, "Management Responsibility," has additional requirements. To the section on organization, 4.1.2, pertaining to personnel, has been added the representation of the needs of the customer in internal functions concerning the requirements of QS 9000. Additionally, systems must be in place for the management of concept development through to production using a multidisciplinary approach to all decision-making activities. This includes communication in a customer-prescribed format. The section on management review (4.1.3) contains a requirement that all management reviews must include all elements of the system. An additional clause contains a requirement for a business plan (not subject to third-party audit). Other clauses refer to the analysis and use of company-level data and requirements for the consideration of customer satisfaction.

Clause 4.2, "Quality System," has a number of additional requirements for quality planning. These consist of advanced product quality planning, identification of special characteristics, feasibility reviews, product safety, the inclusion of process failure mode and effects analysis (process FMEAs), mistake proofing, and the development of a control plan.

Clause 4.3, "Contract Review," contains, in addition to the ISO requirements, a statement referring to some customer-specific requirements found in Section II of QS-9000.

Clause 4.4, "Design Control," applies only to design-responsible suppliers. It contains extensive requirements additional to those of ISO 9001. Specifically, it requires use of previous design projects; it lists required skills of design personnel; it includes the use of CAD/CAE techniques; it requires the use of statistical techniques such as design of experiments and QFD; it includes the use of geometric dimensioning and tolerancing; it requires analysis of cost data; it requires the use of feedback from testing, production, and the field; and it requires the use of design FMEAs.

Clause 4.5, "Document and Data Control," contains a requirement for the control of all reference documents with a list of what they are. There is also a requirement for a timely review of all engineering specifications (in business days, not weeks or months).

Clause 4.6, "Purchasing," contains additional requirements for the approval of materials, subcontractor development, and subcontractor delivery performance.

Clause 4.7 contains an additional requirement on the marking of customer-owned tools.

Clause 4.8 contains a note striking out the phrase "where appropriate" from the ISO 9001 requirement.

Clause 4.9, "Process Control," contains extensive additional requirements. Cleanliness of premises is required, as is the preparation of contingency plans for continual operation of the facilities. Particular care is required for special characteristics. These are defined as characteristics that can affect safe vehicle operation, compliance with government regulations, fit/function, and so on. Specific requirements are spelled out for the preventive maintenance of production equipment. Clauses have been added for process monitoring and operator instructions, maintaining process control, modified process control requirements, verification of job setups, process changes, and appearance items.

Clause 4.10, "Inspection and Testing," contains some extensive additional requirements. There is a paragraph covering acceptance criteria. Various methods for determination of incoming product quality are enumerated. Layout inspection and functional testing shall be performed at a frequency established by the customer and shall be available for customer review. A final process audit is specified. An extensive subclause on laboratories is included. This clause requires a scope statement for each laboratory and accreditation requirements for outside laboratories.

Clause 4.11, "Control of Inspection, Measuring and Test Equipment," contains a further requirement on the use of calibration services. Two additional clauses have been added that require the maintenance of calibration records and measurement system analysis, namely, a gage R & R study.

Clause 4.12, "Inspection and Test Status," contains two explanatory paragraphs dealing with product location and supplemental verification.

Clause 4.13, "Control of Nonconforming Product," contains a statement that this element applies to suspect as well as nonconforming product. It also contains two new requirements for control of reworked product and engineering approved product authorizations.

Clause 4.14, "Corrective and Preventive Action," contains requirements for the use of disciplined problem solving methods as well as mistake proofing. Returned product analysis is required as is the application of corrective action applications to other areas.

Clause 4.15, "Handling, Storage, Packaging, Preservation, and Delivery," contains several additional requirements. The first, under storage, requires the use of an inventory management system. The second concerns packaging and labeling according to customer requirements. Another requirement is for the maintenance of 100% on-time delivery and the use of order-driven production scheduling, including electronic communication and a shipment notification system.

Clause 4.16, "Control of Quality Records," specifies a record retention time for quality records. Production part approvals, tooling records, purchase orders, and amendments shall be kept as long as the part is active plus one year. Quality performance records, including control charts and inspection results, shall be kept for one year after the year in which they were created. Records of internal quality audits shall be kept for three years.

Clauses 4.17, 4.18, and 4.19, "Internal Quality Audits," "Training," and "Servicing," respectively, contain some explanatory notes.

Clause 4.20, "Statistical Techniques," contains the statement requirement that the selection of statistical tools shall be made during advance quality planning. It also requires that basic statistical concepts be understood throughout the supplier's organization.

3-4.1.2 Section II of QS 9000

This section is entitled "Customer-Specific Requirements." It lists some specific requirements of Chrysler, Ford, and General Motors.

3-4.1.3 The Appendices of QS 9000

Ten appendices are included in QS 9000. These cover the following topics:

A. Implementation of the QS-9000 system.

B. Code of practice for quality system certification bodies/registrars. Registrars must be accredited by an accrediting agency. They must conform to the standard ISO/IEC Guide 62:1996.

C. Standard characteristics/special characteristics and symbols. Special symbols used by GM, Ford, and Chrysler are included in this appendix.

D. Local equivalents for ISO 9001 and 9002. The designations of sixteen countries for these two standards as well as the ISO member with telephone and fax numbers are included in this appendix.

E. Acronyms and their meanings. This appendix contains a list of eighteen acronyms.

F. Change summary. This appendix contains a list of the changes in the 1998 (third) edition of QS-9000.

G. QS-9000 accreditation body implementation requirements. This appendix contains specific requirements of accredited registrars including automotive experience of auditors.

H. QS-9000 registration audit-day requirements. This appendix contains a table showing the minimum number of audit-days required to audit organizations of varying sizes for compliance to QS-9000. The table contains figures for both the initial audit and required six-month/twelve-month surveillance audits.

I. Additional QS-9000 registration requirements. Some forty-one additional items are covered in this appendix.

J. Control plans. This appendix provides a form for a control plan.

It should be noted that a supplier is required to meet all the requirements of QS-9000 with no major or minor nonconformities. Registration to ISO 9001 generally is allowed with a few minor nonconformities. Many of the additional requirements of QS 9000 have been included in ISO 9001-2000.

3-4.2 Other Industry Specific Requirements

The International Aerospace Quality Group has published a set of requirements similar to QS 9000. These requirements are included in a document entitled AS 9100:1999, *Quality Systems—Aerospace—Model for Quality Assurance in Design, Development, Production, Installation and Servicing.* These requirements will be updated to correspond to the 2000 edition of ISO 9001.

The medical device industry, through the work of ISO Technical Committee 210, Quality Management and Corresponding General Aspects for Medical Devices, has two standards based on ISO 9001-1994 and ISO 9002-1994, entitled *ISO 13485-1996, Quality Systems—Medical Devices—Particular Requirements for the Application of ISO 9001* and *ISO 13488-1996* (ISO 9002). These two standards will be updated on the basis of ISO 9001-2000 in 2001 or 2002. In this case TC 210 plans to retain ISO 13488 for those medical device manufacturers that are not involved in the design process.

The telecommunication industry has developed a similar set of requirements, entitled *TL 9000:1999, Quality System Requirements,* Book One, Release 2.5. The authors of this requirement, the Quality Excellence for Suppliers of Telecommunications (QuEST) Forum, have indicated they plan to update the document to correspond to the ISO 9001-2000 standard. This should be accomplished in 2002.

3-4.3 Good Manufacturing Practices (GMPs)

Good manufacturing practices (or GMPs), whether for the manufacture of food, drugs, or medical devices, are other forms of quality assurance models representing parts of a total quality system. The term "minimum" is used within the regulations themselves, in a manner similar to how we used it in our discussion of the ISO 9000 series.

In contrast to ISO 9001, GMPs are mandatory for the defined categories. This might not be seen as much different from a manufacturer whose principal customer(s) demands compliance with ISO 9001 as a condition for doing business. It is hardly voluntary!

The food, drug, and medical device manufacturers are looking at the ISO 9000 series requirements to replace the GMPs in order to show compliance with their quality assurance provisions. Although this might be useful and beneficial, we recommend going beyond the quality system defined by the ISO 9000 series to that of a total quality system. The major differences, as illustrated in Chapter 4, are methodologies and techniques that have quality improvement objectives rather than mere assurance or control.

GMPs are less generic than the ISO 9000 series counterpart. They contain more specific requirements suited to the target product, food, drugs, and medical devices. Examples include direct references to buildings and facilities, including lighting, ventilators, air filtration, heating and cooling, and sanitation. There are also direct references to equipment, including design, size, location, construction, cleaning, and filtration. Additionally, there are references to containers and closures and to product and process specifics such as laboratory animals and drug contamination.

More common ground between the GMPs and the ISO 9000 series includes the existence and responsibilities of a quality control unit. There is further emphasis on records and documentation similar to the ISO 9000 series. Handling, storage, packaging, and delivery requirements share common ground. Process control and inspection and test requirements are similar. The ISO 9000 series places more emphasis on the structure and content of a quality management program as part of an overall quality system.

Hence, the joint use of GMPs, where required and otherwise recommended for borderline cases, and ISO 9001 is appropriate. There are definite complementary features, GMPs providing requirements that are more product and process specific, while ISO 9001 provides more comprehensive structure for the quality system.

Our purpose here is not to render a treatise on GMPs. That has been done, rather adequately, by other publications. Our purpose has been to recognize the relevance of GMPs as partial QA models and to compare some differences and similarities with the ISO 9000 series.

▶ 3-5 REFERENCES

American Society for Quality (1996), ANSI/ASQC C1-1996, *Specifications of General Requirements for a Quality Program,* also designated as Z1-8, Milwaukee.

American Society for Quality (1979), ANSI/ASQC Z1.15-1979, *Generic Guidelines for Quality Systems,* Milwaukee.

Asian Productivity Organization (1990), *New Waves in Quality Management—An Integrated Approach for Product, Process and Human Quality,* Workshop on Quality Management: An Integrated Approach, September 4–8 (Taipei), Tokyo.

Automotive Industry Action Group (1992), *Statistical Process Control Reference Manual,* Detroit.

Automotive Industry Action Group (1994), *Advanced Product Quality Planning and Control Plan Reference Manual,* Detroit.

Automotive Industry Action Group (1995a), *Potential Failure Mode and Effects Analysis Reference Manual,* 2nd Edition, Detroit.

Automotive Industry Action Group (1995b), *Measurement Systems Analysis Reference Manual,* 2nd Edition, Detroit.

Automotive Industry Action Group (1995c), *Production Part Approval Process,* 2nd Edition, Detroit.

Automotive Industry Action Group (1998a), *Quality System Requirements, QS-9000,* 3rd Edition, Detroit.

Automotive Industry Action Group (1998b), *Quality System Assessment,* 2nd Edition, Detroit.

Hutchins, D. (1992), *Achieve Total Quality,* Director Books, Cambridge, UK.

International Aerospace Quality Group (1999), *AS9100:1999, Quality Systems—Aerospace—Model for Quality Assurance in Design, Development, Production, Installation, and Servicing,* Washington, D.C.

International Organization for Standardization (1989), *ISO Momento,* Geneva.

International Organization for Standardization (1993), *ISO 9000-4-1993, Quality Management and Quality Assurance Standard—Part 4: Guide to Dependability Program Management,* Geneva.

International Organization for Standardization (1995), *ISO 10013-1995, Guidelines for Quality Manuals,* Geneva.

International Organization for Standardization (1996), *ISO 14001-1996, Environmental Management System—Specification with Guidance for Use,* Geneva.

International Organization for Standardization (1997), *ISO 9000-3-1997, Quality Management and Quality Assurance Standard—Part 3: Guidelines for the Application of ISO 9001-1994 to the Development, Supply, Installation, and Maintenance of Computer Software,* Geneva.

International Organization for Standardization (1999), *ISO/TS 16949, Quality Systems—Automotive Suppliers—Particular Requirements for the Application of ISO 9001:1994,* Geneva.

International Organization for Standardization (2000a), *ISO 9000-2000, Quality Management Systems—Fundamentals and Vocabulary,* Geneva.

International Organization for Standardization (2000b), *ISO 9001-2000, Quality Management Systems—Requirements,* Geneva.

International Organization for Standardization (2000c), *ISO 9004-2000, Quality Management Systems—Guidelines for Performance Improvements,* Geneva.

International Organization for Standardization (2001), *ISO 10012, Quality Assurance Requirements for Measuring Equipment,* Geneva.

International Organization for Standardization (2002), *ISO 19011,*

Guidelines on Quality and/or Environmental Management Auditing, Geneva.

Juran, J. M. (1994), "The Upcoming Century of Quality," *Keynote Address to the ASQC Quality Congress,* American Society for Quality, Milwaukee, p. 15.

Lofgren, George Q. (1990), "Accreditation of Quality System Registrars," *ASQC Quality Congress Transactions—San Francisco,* American Society for Quality, Milwaukee, pp. 979–82.

Osada, T. (1991), *The Five Keys to a Total Quality Environment,* Asian Productivity Organization, Tokyo.

Quality Excellence for Suppliers of Telecommunications Forum (1999), *TL 9000:1999, Quality Systems Requirements,* Book One, Release 2.5, New York.

Sayle, A. J. (1992), "Audits—The Key to the Future," *1st Annual Quality Audit Conference, ASQC, St. Louis,* American Society for Quality, Milwaukee, Feb. 27–28, 1992.

Stephens, K. S., (1974), "The Modern Concepts of Quality Methodology and Techniques of Quality Control and Inspection," *Study Tour Workshop on Quality Control and Certification Marking for Industrial Products,* Singapore, May 20–25, 1974, UNIDO, ID/WG 180/2, 29 April 1974.

Stephens, K. S. (1975), "Thailand's Certification and Quality Marks Programme," *Transactions of the ASQC Annual Technical Conference,* American Society for Quality Control, Milwaukee, pp. 345–56.

Stephens, K. S. (1978a), "UNIDO Standards Aid—The Nigeria Experience," *Transactions of the ASQC Annual Technical Conference,* American Society for Quality Control, Milwaukee, pp. 97–104.

Stephens, K. S. (1978b), "UNIDO Technical Assistance in Standardization, Certification and Quality Control—With a Thailand Case Study," *Transactions ICQC '78,* Tokyo, pp. 31–35.

Stephens, K. S. (1978c), "Training-Consulting Workshops on Quality Control Principles and Techniques," *UNIDO Technical Report No. 2, NIR/75/070,* UNIDO, Vienna, Austria.

Stephens, K. S., and Hopper, R. (1973), "Standards and Certification in a Developing Country," *BSI News,* London, UK, April 1973.

Stephens, K. S., Hunter, W. G., and Chacko, E. (1974), "Creating Effective National Programs in Developing Countries for Standardization, Certification, and Quality Control," *International Technical Cooperation Center Review,* Vol. 3, No. 4, October 1974, Tel Aviv, pp. 1–38.

Tsiakals, J. J. (1994), "Revision of the ISO 9000 Standards," *ASQC Quality Congress Transactions,* American Society for Quality, Milwaukee, pp. 873–81.

▶ 3-6 PROBLEMS

1. Prepare a literature report on quality system documentation involving at least two items on the subject. Each student should look for and conduct literature searches on all matters pertaining to documentation of quality systems and subsystems, beyond the textbook, preferably in journal articles or company-related literature. A potential source of such literature is the Internet, and each student is encouraged to become familiar with literature searching on the Internet. Articles for the literature project may be found by using this source. This exercise has the purpose of expanding your horizon to the literature of the field beyond the textbook. For documentation this may include actual examples of quality manuals, procedures, or work instructions, that are not proprietary (or can be neutralized). Practical (real-life) reports/manuals/articles that show applications of documentation, methods thereof, requirements thereof, or other documents are encouraged. For journal articles, a complete bibliographical reference should accompany each report, including the title, name(s) of the author(s), name of the publication in which it appeared, volume number, issue number, number of the first and last page, and date of publication. A brief abstract should accompany each of the two items selected. The report should contain observations and a discussion of the material submitted as to its content, relevance to quality systems, structure, agreements or disagreements (whether the student agrees or disagrees with any aspect of the item and why), perceived controversies, and ideas for further developments related to the subject, as applicable. Certain items of documentation, such as quality manuals, procedures, or work instructions, of a proprietary nature (that cannot be totally neutralized) may be requested for the instructor's review only, as deemed necessary.

2. Repeat Exercise 1 on the subject of auditing.

3. Visit or correspond with a registrar of quality systems to obtain their approach to the assessment of quality management systems. Obtain the registrar's available materials and prepare a report on the methodology, suggested activity schedule, and timetable for the evaluation, feedback, and subsequent surveillance of results of third-party audits. If available, obtain a copy of the checklist used by the registrar; obtain examples of other forms such as noncompliance reports used by the registrar and include these in your report with appropriate explanations.

4. Your instructor will conduct one or more case studies on quality management system assessments on an individual or team basis.

5. Visit a local company that has become registered to ISO 9001 and/or QS 9000. Prepare a report on the company's program that summarizes the approach to its preparation, documentation, implementation, costs (if available), and results.

4

TOTAL QUALITY MANAGEMENT

As described in Chapter 1, "The History and Evolution of Quality Control," many advances have been made to the art and science of managing quality over the years. In Chapter 2, "Quality and Quality Systems," quality was defined and the development of quality management systems was discussed. In Chapter 3, the "ISO 9000 Quality System" was discussed in detail along with its development and use. The ISO 9000-2000 family and its American version, ANSI/ISO/ASQ/Q9000-2000, is the most widely used quality system in the world. The rapid development of this view of quality and of these company, national, and international quality system standards has been the result of three forces: the rapid globalization of trade, the increasing power of the consumer, and continuing advances in methods and technologies.

The globalization of trade has made high-quality low-cost products available throughout the world. Most leading companies now compete in multinational markets, and even residents of small villages may have the opportunity to select from a wide variety of products and services. Products such as automobiles and consumer electronics are highly visible examples of this trade. Less visible but becoming just as pervasive are services such as financial services and telecommunications. Consumers can now buy retail products at multinational retail chains by visiting local branches, or shopping by electronic commerce on line from anywhere in the world. A credit card can be selected from a local bank or from a national or international credit card provider. A person can buy telecommunications services from local, national, and international providers offering a vast array of products, services, and prices.

This rapidly increasing global competition has given new power to the consumer to demand and receive high-quality goods and services at reasonable prices. The power came first from the increased competition and reduced trade and distribution barriers, but now the power is also coming from increased information. Numerous organizations provide accurate information about product and service quality. Consumer groups and magazines continually rank products in many different dimensions of quality. The Internet has become a widely used method to obtain product and service information. Consumers are using this information to make more intelligent purchase decisions. Products that are ranked at the top of the lists are often sold out quickly. Products at the bottom of the lists sometimes are almost impossible to sell. Books that are recommended on one talk show in the United States become overnight bestsellers. One state is even publishing death rates for each heart surgeon practicing in that state.

Technologies such as computer-based testing, automated inspection, laser measurements, scanning electron microscopes, and advanced simulation devices have made much testing and inspection feasible and practical that in the past was impossible or too costly. New methodologies in quality improvement, cross-functional management, process engineering and reengineering, and teamwork have also contributed breakthroughs in product and service quality.

A small number of companies have radically transformed their business performance in recent years. Many of the concepts and methods they have used are now collectively called "total quality" or "total quality management." Some other terms include "business transformation," "performance excellence," "business excellence," and "Six Sigma." The successes of these companies have dramatically changed how they and others see both quality and business management.

▶ 4-1 INTRODUCTION TO TOTAL QUALITY MANAGEMENT

In the 1980s and 1990s many organizations throughout the world were under tremendous pressure from competition in quality and cost. Some were battered by international competition, others were confronted by new entrepreneurial companies that redefined businesses, and others were seriously challenged by new technologies that created formidable alternatives to their products and services. Some leading companies rapidly changed under these pressures. Some of the new companies have now become major competitors. Other companies are still engaged in daily battles for survival. Many other companies disappeared.

During these years there has been an increasing global emphasis on quality management. In global competitive markets quality has become the most important single factor for success. Quality management has become the competitive issue for many organizations. Juran has even stated that "Just as the 20th Century was the century for productivity, the 21st Century will be the quality century" [Juran (1998)].

Curt Reimann, then director for quality programs at the National Institute of Standards and Technology of the U.S. Department of Commerce, stated this clearly in testimony to the U.S. Congress: "There is now far clearer perception that quality is central to company competitiveness and to national competitiveness" [Reimann (1992a)].

In October 1991, *Business Week* published a bonus issue devoted entirely to the subject of quality. The editor-in-chief, Stephen Shepard called this bonus issue "the most ambitious single project" in *Business Week*'s sixty-two-year history. Mr. Shepard further commented that quality "may be the biggest competitive issue of the late 20th and early 21st centuries." This issue sold out in a matter of days. The demand was so high that *Business Week* had to make two additional printings of the magazines. At the end of the year, the magazine editors of America named this issue the "Magazine of the Year," the top honor for magazines in the United States.

During 1991, the U.S. General Accounting Office completed a study of Malcolm Baldrige National Quality Award winners and site visited companies. They studied carefully the relationship between quality management activity and success and profitability. This report, GAO Report 91-190, became GAO's all time best-selling report. In early 1995 the National Institute of Standards and Technology of the U.S. Department of Commerce issued a new report contrasting the stock market success of companies that had won the Malcolm Baldrige National Quality Award and site visited companies with average companies. The results were convincing. The National Quality Award Program in the United States does not maintain information on individual organization's financial results, but for the fourth year in a row a special stock comparison study has shown significant differences [Port (1998), p. 113]. The Malcolm Baldrige National Quality Award recipients as a group have outperformed the Standard & Poor's 500 by nearly a 2.5 to 1 margin. The fifty-two publicly traded site visited companies (the top-scoring organizations on the written applications) outperformed the Standard & Poor's 500 by 80%. They achieved a 216% rate of growth versus a 119% rate of growth for average companies [Port 1998), p. 113].

In Europe the creation of the European Foundation for Quality Management in 1988 has already had a significant impact on the understanding of quality management as a leadership issue. The introduction in 1992 of the European Quality Award has had a major effect in raising senior executive awareness and understanding of quality management concepts. The oldest award is the Deming Application Prize, which was started in 1951 by the Union of Japanese Scientists and Engineers (JUSE). This prize stimulated the adoption of quality control in virtually every sector of Japanese industry and over time evolved into the concept of Company Wide Quality Control (CWQC) and Total Quality Control (TQC) [Kondo, Kume, and Schimizu (1995), p. 4].

It should be mentioned here that the generic term "total quality management" will be used to mean the vast collection of philosophies, concepts, methods, and techniques that are being used throughout the world to manage quality. Other terms are frequently used. "Total quality management" (TQM) is probably the most frequently used term in the United States. Kondo uses the equivalent term "Companywide Quality Management" [Kondo (1995)]. In 1997 the JUSE announced a formal change from the term "total quality control" to "total quality management" [The TQM Committee (1997a), p. 1]. This name change was made both to adopt a more internationally accepted term and to give them an opportunity to revisit the origin of quality control and rebuild the concept to meet new environmental challenges in business management. The TQM Committee of JUSE explained this change in three publications [The TQM Committee (1997a, 1997b, and 1997c)]. A summary of their thinking is provided by the diagram in Figure 4-1.

In JUSE's view, TQM is a management approach that strives for the following in any business environment. (The numbers in the following correspond to the numbers in Figure 4-1):

- Under strong top management leadership (1), establish clear mid- and long-term vision and strategies (1).
- Properly utilize the concepts, values (2), and scientific methods (3) of TQM.
- Regard human resources (4) and information (5) as vital organizational infrastructures.
- Under an appropriate management system (6), effectively operate a quality assurance system (7) and other cross-functional management systems such as cost, delivery, environment, and safety (8).
- Supported by fundamental organizational powers such as core technology, speed, and vitality (9a), ensure sound relations with customers, employees, society, suppliers, and stockholders (9b).

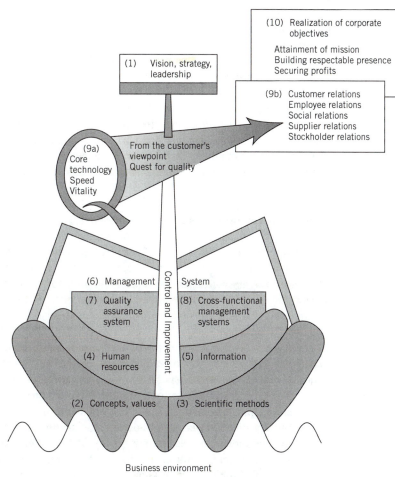

Figure 4-1   JUSE View of Total Quality Management

- Continuously realize corporate objectives in the form of achieving an organization's mission, building an organization with a respectable presence, and continuously securing profits (10).

4-1.1 The Results of Total Quality

The almost universally accepted goals of total quality are lower costs, higher revenues, delighted customers, and empowered employees. There has been a movement away from believing that managing quality just means conformance to specifications and requirements. Good quality also means meeting and even exceeding the needs and expectations of customers. It means having the right features, correct documentation, error-free invoices, on-time delivery, and no failures. Good quality means reducing all the costs of poor quality.

Lower Costs

Higher quality can mean lower costs by reducing errors, rework, and non-value-added work. Organizations around the world have repeatedly proven that higher quality frequently means lower costs. The costs associated with preventing errors during design are often far less than the costs of correcting the errors during production. The costs of preventing errors during production are far less than the costs of correcting the errors after final inspection, and the costs of finding and correcting errors during final inspection are far less than correcting the errors after the customer has received the goods or services. An understanding of these costs has grown rapidly [Godfrey (1998), p. 18]. Sörqvist (1998, pp. 36–39) categorizes these costs in five basic levels: traditional poor-quality costs, hidden poor-quality costs, lost income, customers' costs, and socioeconomic costs.

Higher Revenues

Higher quality can mean more satisfied customers, increased market share, and premium prices. Customers are increasingly beginning to demand high-quality goods and services. By exceeding the levels of quality offered by competitors in the marketplace, organizations can add new customers, retain old customers, and move into new markets. Often informed customers are willing to pay a premium price for higher levels of quality that provide new and useful features or reduce total life cycle costs.

Empowered Employees

For many years organizations believed that empowered employees were a means for achieving lower costs, higher revenues, and satisfied customers. Now most leading organizations realize that empowered employees are also a major goal of total quality management. These organizations not only want to solve the problems of today, but also want to create an organization that can solve, or even avoid, the problems of tomorrow.

The concept of empowered employees embraces many new ideas. Empowered employees have the means to measure the quality of their own work processes, and to act when the process is not in control. But the concept of empowered employees goes far beyond self-control. Employees also know how to change the process and how to improve performance, increasing both the effectiveness and the efficiency of the process.

They also understand how to plan for quality. They understand who their customers are, what the customers expect, how to design new goods and services to meet these expectations, how to develop and use the necessary quality measurements, and how to continuously improve the processes.

4-1.2 The Three Fundamental Concepts

Many leading companies have revisited the fundamental concepts of quality management: customer focus, continuous improvement, and the value of every individual.

4-1.2.1 Customer Focus

Calling customer focus a fundamental concept of quality management seems obvious. Organizations exist to provide products to customers. Aren't all organizations customer focused?

For some organizations the answer to this question is a resounding no. During the evolutionary progress of almost every industry, the first phase is a focus on quality of the new product in the most basic terms. The goal is to make the product work. The early automobiles, airplanes, and telephones are dramatic examples. There were no customers in the beginning, only obsessed inventors trying to make something no one had seen before. Later in this chapter we trace the basic evolution of quality in typical organizations and industries.

A major challenge facing organizations is their understanding of customers' needs and their measurements of how well they meet these needs. More and more companies are finding that keeping customers is far more profitable than acquiring new ones. Xerox found in a study that sales to current customers were over 20% more profitable than sales to new customers. The other critical factor is what percentage of the customer's business the company has. Becoming the dominant supplier can have outstanding business results.

In *The Loyalty Effect,* Reichheld (1996) documents many examples of how companies have gone beyond customer satisfaction and customer retention to customer loyalty. Building customer loyalty is a bedrock of corporate strategic planning and process management.

4-1.2.2 Continuous Improvement

In early 1995 the thirtieth anniversary edition of Juran's book *Managerial Breakthrough* [Juran (1995)] was published. In 1964 this book had documented, for the first time, the structured approach that many companies would use to achieve breakthrough improvements by the thousands. In more recent years rapid change has become a way of life in many organizations.

But this was not always the case. For thousands of years societies and governments have been organized to prevent change. In some societies doing something in a different way was punishable by death. In *The Egyptian,* Waltari describes how a physician in ancient Egypt was trained to perform 128 different procedures. Only these could be performed, and there was only one way to perform each. Artists were trained carefully in the only way to draw a bird, a crocodile, or a person [Waltari (1949)].

In medieval Europe the various trade guilds established rigid guidelines for the making of each object. Daring to experiment in the ways in which things were made or materials were used was grounds for expulsion from the guild. In the Byzantine Greek language the word for *change* was the same as the word for *danger.* Change in societies, in production practices, in armies, and in governments came slowly. Many societies endured mentally incompetent rulers rather than risk changing the form of government.

Organizations often mirrored society, and this lasted well beyond the medieval era. They were governed by thick policy manuals and corporate executive instructions in multivolume sets. Promotions were given to those who did not encourage change. Strong hierarchies were created to control all operations and individual work. The Taylor system was used to carefully define each step in the work process and each person's role. Job descriptions defined clearly what one did and what one did not do.

Things began to change rapidly in the years following World War II. The Japanese were so far behind in many areas of commercial production that they had to improve rapidly to survive. The continuous improvement methods that they perfected worked very well. Faced with severe competition, many U.S. firms started copying these ideas, some with great success.

The literature contains many examples of astonishing improvements. These improvements are being made in all types of manufacturing and service organizations. The means that are used to achieve these results have become quite familiar: cross-functional teams, quality control circles, reengineering, quality action teams, creative idea suggestion systems, process improvement teams, and many others.

4-1.2.3 The Value of Every Associate

The value of each associate in an organization is another idea that sounds simple on the surface. For years companies have had clear statements about the strength of their organizations being the people who work for them. But many companies are still blindly following the Taylor system of "scientific management." A few planners, managers, or engineers are planning all the steps of every process, defining carefully worded job descriptions, and enforcing the unthinking following of instructions.

Even the most cursory review of history illuminates how radical an idea it is to have each person thinking, creating ideas, and making changes to the system. Entire armies marched side by side with spears pointed forward at exactly the same angle. Musketeers marched in ranks, fired precisely timed volleys, reloaded and fired again. They acted only on the orders of the commander. Individuals were trained in apprentice programs by demanding masters. The early factories contained rows and rows of workers, each doing each task exactly the same way.

The average number of implemented ideas per employee per year in the United States in one study was only 0.16. That is one idea implemented for every six employees per year. In organizations that truly value the ideas and personal contributions of each employee, the number is dramatically higher. Toyota is achieving eight implemented ideas per employee at their Georgetown, Kentucky manufacturing facilities. Overall, Toyota receives 4,000,000 ideas from its 80,000 employees. Since over 95% are implemented, this is over forty-six implemented ideas per employee per year [Yasuda (1991)].

Some companies in the United States have achieved similar results. Globe Metallurgical and Milliken and Company have averaged over one implemented idea per employee per week. Milliken is now one of the country's leaders at sixty-eight ideas implemented per associate per year. One employee in a Marriott hotel contributed sixty-three improvement suggestions in one month [Fromm and Schlesinger (1993)]!

But ideas contributed are just one measure of individual contributions. Other contributions may be even more important. These include participation on quality improvement teams, membership on business process reengineering teams, work on statistical quality control, and working as members of self-directing work teams.

4-1.3 The Three Strong Forces: Alignment, Linkage, and Replication

There are three primary drivers of performance excellence: alignment, linkage, and replication. To achieve breakthrough results, the organization must focus its efforts on the most important issues. It must have its strategy correct and the organization's goals, resources, and activities aligned with the strategy. The organization must also understand the cross-functional nature of work, that is, the linkages across the organization. Sometimes called "systems thinking" or "process thinking," this understanding of the way work is done is crucial. The organization must also be able to replicate successes quickly. A simple improvement may be worth only a few thousand dollars. But replicated one hundred times, it might become a major contribution to the organization's success.

4-1.3.1 Alignment

A 1996 study by the Association of Management Consulting Firms in the United States found that executives, consultants, and university professors agree that business strategy is now the single most important management issue and will remain so for at least the next five years [Byrne (1996), p. 46]. In recent years there has been a new understanding of the importance of strategy. This strategy must include the following:

1. A clear vision of where the company is going

2. Clear definitions of the small number of key objectives that must be achieved if the company is to realize its vision

3. Translation of these key objectives throughout the entire organization so that each person would then know how performing his or her job helps the company to achieve these objectives

One of the biggest changes in the strategic planning process has been the inclusion of many layers of the workforce, customers, suppliers, and even competitors in the planning process. These changes are creating a whole new set of buzzwords: business ecosystems, business designs, and core competencies. The key differences include the creation of networks of new relationships with customers, suppliers, and rivals to gain competitive advantages and new markets.

The second big change has been the inclusion of employees of all ages, levels, and job functions in the planning process. Several years ago, Electronic Data Systems Corp. (EDS) launched a major strategy initiative involving 2500 of its 55,000 employees. A core group of 150 worked full time for a year coordinating the input from the larger group. Finland's Nokia Group involved 250 employees in a strategic review in 1995. Nokia's head of strategy development, Chris Jackson, reports that the involvement of a large number of people makes their ability to implement the strategy more viable and wins a high degree of commitment to the process [Byrne (1996), p. 52].

The third change has been the intense focus on customers. The new strategic planning starts with them. Hewlett-Packard brings both customers and suppliers together with general managers from many different business units to work on strategies. For example, the company brought together managers from divisions making service bay diagnostic systems for Ford with those making workstations for auto plants and those developing electronic components for cars. Many of the ideas for new opportunities came directly from the customers.

Far too many companies have stopped with creating their strategic plan. Their plans are beautifully developed and packaged, but nothing happens. Somehow they assume that packaging and distributing the plans to a select number of managers is actually going to make things happen. To see results, these plans must be carefully deployed throughout the entire organization. The organization must then clearly define the specific work projects that support the plans.

4-1.3.2 Linkage (Process Management or Systems Thinking)

During the 1980s and 1990s many companies embraced the concept of reengineering with a fervor that defied description. Pioneered in the early 1980s by companies such as IBM, Ford, AT&T, and NCR, reengineering became a common tool for corporations throughout the world. The definition of reengineering by Hammer as "the radical redesign of business processes for dramatic improvement" captured and excited the imagination of managers around the world. Hammer later realized that "the key word in the definition of reengineering is 'process': a complete end-to-end set of activities that together create value for a customer" [Hammer (1996), p. xii].

As companies have discovered the importance of linking their activities across all functions and departments, they have also realized how critical it is to understand how many activities are actually in series. Unless efforts are linked across all parts of the company, they fail to achieve the needed results.

With this critical emphasis on linkage, or process management, the worlds of total quality management and reengineering converge. A fundamental tenet of quality management since Shewhart in the 1920s, if not before, has been the importance of controlling the process. Deming further developed Shewhart's ideas of statistical process control with the PDCA cycle, and Juran pioneered the concepts of process improvement with his text *Managerial Breakthrough* [Juran (1995)]. As leading companies moved into rapid improvement activities in the 1980s, the need for process management became clear. In manufacturing plants the series nature of work was apparent. If any part of an assembly line failed or created a bottleneck, the whole line suffered. What wasn't so clear was how many administrative processes were also series systems. If a mistake is made in the order entry step, it may not be possible to complete the delivery of the product or service correctly and on time.

The critical steps to managing the linkages and making dramatic and continuous improvements to the key processes are well defined. The first step is to identify the organization's key processes. The next step is to create the necessary measurements. Most of these measurements will be focused on departmental activities or the budget.

The final step in managing the critical linkages is to make major changes in the structure of the organization. Although quality management has been about process control, improvement, and planning for many years, it still has not developed all of the understanding needed. This is a major challenge for the future.

The single most important word in the definition of process is "customer." As has been discovered in recent years, the customer sees the company only as the output of processes. The customer does not care how the company is organized, who reports to whom, what the various titles are, or where the different departments are located. The customer requests products, wants them delivered exactly when promised, wants the required service to be available when needed, and wants the bills to be exactly as agreed upon.

The second key to managing processes is to determine exactly what value is added by each step in the process. When there is a purchase order for a $30.00 book with six signatures that has taken six weeks to process, obviously there is a better way. What value has this process added? Organizations have been surprised to learn how many steps they have in key processes, the number of useless handoffs that occur, and how much effort is wasted.

Just focusing on cycle time reductions can illuminate how unmanaged many of the key processes are. The Royal Leicester Infirmary in the United Kingdom reduced a neurological testing procedure from forty days to one day and removed 40% of the administrative costs by redesigning the process of how fourteen departments worked together. Motorola reduced the six-week process of taking a pager order and producing and shipping the pager to less than 100 minutes.

The third critical area of managing the critical linkages is the realization that almost all key processes cut across many different areas of the organization. To manage these processes successfully requires a team-based approach involving employees with new skills and an understanding of the company's strategy, goals, and competitors.

4-1.3.3 Replication

Probably the most powerful and least understood way to dramatically accelerate the results of quality and productivity improvement efforts is the third strong force: replication. An example from a leading international service company makes this clear. The CEO was justifiably proud of some of the company's accomplishments. In one location a true chronic problem had been solved, and the savings were over $350,000 per year. In another location a different chronic problem had been reduced by 75%. The increased revenues were also in the hundreds of thousands of dollars.

It was not hard for the CEO to do the math. If each of his more than 250 locations could duplicate these results, the company would exceed its aggressive financial goals for the next year. But he knew how hard it would be to get each of the locations to understand what had been done in these two locations, to modify the approach to fit their situations, and to apply a similar problem-solving methodology to achieve similar results.

When replication is addressed, resistance to change becomes apparent, along with the entrenched beliefs that every location is different. Problems then remain unsolved, opportunities are missed, and companies have slow rates of change with disappointing results. The successful companies act to make things happen. They use passive means to encourage replication, they use active means to force replication, and they make replication a requirement, not an option.

Active sharing systems force the issue. At Honda's annual facilitator network meetings (attended by over 3000 people worldwide), each participant is expected to share one completed and well-documented project and to study thoroughly four others that could be used in his or her location. Upon returning to this location, the person is expected to implement these four projects. The support structure is in place to assist them, and results are expected.

4-1.4 The Three Critical Processes for Quality Management

The three critical quality management processes—quality planning, quality control, and quality improvement—are not new. They are the same ones that have been used for years to manage finance. This commonality is helpful to managers. Their long experience in managing for finance becomes useful when they enter the world of managing for quality. These three processes are closely interconnected.

4-1.4.1 Quality Planning

The logical place to start is quality planning. This consists of a universal sequence of events—a quality planning procedure. First identify the customers and their needs, and then design products and services that meet those needs. Next design processes that can produce these goods and services. Finally, the plan is given to the operating forces, which then have the responsibility of conducting operations. The quality planning process is summarized in Figure 4-2.

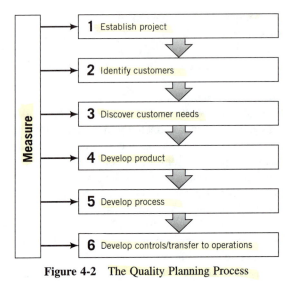

Figure 4-2 The Quality Planning Process

In later chapters there is in-depth coverage of some of the more technical tools that are used in quality planning. These techniques include experimental design (Chapters 12 and 13) and reliability prediction and reliability estimation (Chapter 14).

No matter how well the methods and techniques of quality planning are applied, most processes are not perfect. They have associated with them some chronic waste: time delays, errors, rework, non-value-added work, and scrap. This waste is built into the plan. First, the control systems that are necessary to maintain quality at the planned levels must be provided. Next, opportunities to make dramatic improvements in the levels of quality achieved are needed. Figure 4-3 makes these relationships clear.

In this figure the cost of poor quality is plotted on the vertical scale, so what goes up is bad. These are the costs associated with imperfection. Despite best efforts at planning the costs in this example, they are about 20%. These costs could be from defects, or they could be even harder to see. Examples of hard-to-detect costs are work-in-process inventory, non-value-added work, underutilized capacity, and unnecessary delays.

The first job is to build a quality control system that ensures that quality performance is at least as good as planned. In Figure 4-3 a spike is seen, a major deviation from the planned level of performance. In this example the quality control system is working well. Because this point is a spike, it indicates that the problem was detected and the cause of the problem was discovered and quickly removed. Little time elapsed before the quality performance was back at the planned levels.

In many cases quality control systems do not function this well. Several days or even weeks may go by before a problem is discovered. Then more days or weeks are spent investigating the possible causes, and more days or weeks developing remedies.

4-1.4.2 *Quality Control*

What the operating forces can do is to minimize this waste. They do this through quality control. Quality control relies on five basics: a clear definition of quality; a target; a way

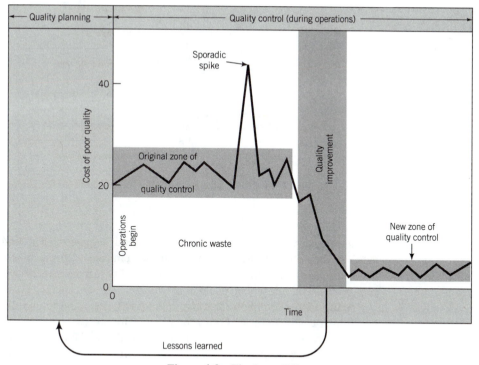

Figure 4-3 The Juran Trilogy

to measure actual performance; a way to interpret the measurement and compare with the target; and a way to adjust the process if necessary. Quality control is discussed in Chapters 6–9. Other methods for quality control, such as establishing specification and tolerances, are covered in Chapter 10.

4-1.4.3 Quality Improvement

All of this activity only keeps quality at the planned level. Deliberate, specific actions must be taken if we wish to change this level. As Deming states in *Out of the Crisis,* "Putting out fires is not improvement of the process. Neither is discovery and removal of a special cause detected by a point out of control [the sporadic spike in Figure 4-3]. This only puts the process back to where it should have been in the first place (an insight of Juran, years ago)." [Deming (1982), p. 51].

In *Managerial Breakthrough,* Juran (1995) describes the quality improvement process individuals and organizations use to make breakthrough changes in levels of performance. The quality improvement process is directed at long standing performance levels.

4-1.5 The Total Quality Management Infrastructure

Figure 4-4 shows the main elements of the total quality infrastructure. These elements include the quality system, customer-supplier partnerships, total organization involvement, measurement and information, and education and training.

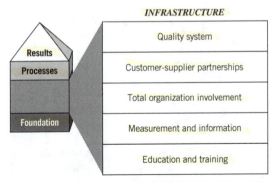

Figure 4-4   The Total Quality Management Infrastructure

4-1.5.1 The Quality System

The total quality infrastructure consists of several key pieces. The first, and one of the most important, is the quality management system. Best defined by ISO Standard 9004-2000, this is a critical building block for total quality management. The ISO Quality Management System is described in detail in Chapter 3 [American Society for Quality (2000)].

A key element of the infrastructure is measurement and information. Donald Peterson, former chairman of the Ford Motor Company, stresses the importance of having the right information. When Ford benchmarked Mazda, the Ford management was quite impressed with how well Mazda managed this part of the business. Peterson states, "Perhaps, most important, Mazda had been able to identify the types of information and records that were truly useful. It didn't bother with any other data. [At Ford] we were burdened with mountains of useless data and stifled by far too many levels of control over them" [Peterson (1992)].

The last and perhaps the most important part of the infrastructure is education and training. Organizations must train the team members to work as teams and to diagnose problems and provide remedies. This type of training should be directed at changing behavior. The training should be provided as the team is ready to address the real problems. Training in how to improve quality should be done during actual improvement projects. The training should be designed to help the teams complete these projects quickly and successfully.

▶ 4-2 THE EVOLUTION OF TOTAL QUALITY

4-2.1 Product Quality

All organizations began their quality management efforts with a focus on product quality as illustrated in Figure 4-5. At the first introduction of a product, this is necessarily a definition of product quality from the producer's point of view. Because the product is unknown to the customers, they have little input in defining the product or in defining quality. Some organizations might try to survey the customers to ascertain their wants, but in the case of a truly new product their inputs are ambiguous and somewhat vague.

In a recent study of the evolution of quality in telecommunications, this was clearly the case [Godfrey and Endres (1994)]. The telephone was truly a new product. Potential

Figure 4-5 First Phase of the Evolution of Quality Management: Product Quality

customers were amazed that it worked at all and had no idea how it worked. The driving forces for defining quality were the engineers who were trying to make it work well enough to be a salable product. As early as 1892, the Bell System was developing inspection procedures to ensure that the specifications developed by the engineers were being met by the production personnel.

This focus on product quality has continued up to the present. Telecommunications companies extended their efforts beyond initial quality to reliability in the field, then to availability, usability, maintainability, and other definitions of product quality. Some of the methods used to manage these broadened definitions of product quality have become quite sophisticated. In health care, much recent work on clinical outcomes would be in this category. Researchers have extended the traditional definitions of outcome to include patient performance, lack of pain, and ability to work.

4-2.2 Process Quality

The next phase of the evolution for telecommunications quality began in 1924 with the creation of the control chart as indicated in Figure 4-6. For some time it had been evident that controlling product quality by final inspection was quite expensive. In the installation forces of the rapidly growing American Telephone & Telegraph company, the emphasis had become "Do it right the first time." Finding the wiring errors in complex switching machines after the machine had been assembled was a time-consuming, costly process. It was far more economical to ensure functioning parts and carefully control the assembly than to go back and try to find the problems. There is evidence that during World War I the British developed rather sophisticated control procedures for ensuring proper tensioning of the wires between the wings of the biplane fighters.

But it was the creation of the control chart that made it clear how easily process control could be transferred to the operating forces. This would reduce the reliance on final inspection and free people for productive work.

This stage of product process quality—focus on the processes producing the products—has also continued to the present. Many sophisticated methods have been added, engineering process control, experimental design, robust design, and, more recently, process simplification and reengineering.

Figure 4-6 Second Phase of the Evolution of Quality Management: Product Process Quality

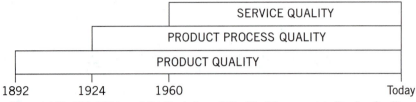

Figure 4-7   Third Phase of the Evolution of Quality Management: Service Quality

In health care there are numerous examples: patient-focused care, care maps, clinical guidelines, protocols. Any methods that try to improve the outcomes of work by improving the processes by which those outcomes are created are in the product process phase. In other industries, these have focused on the cost side of producing the product.

4-2.3 Service Quality

The next phase, indicated in Figure 4-7, for some industries began in the early 1960s. For other industries it probably began much earlier, and for still others not until the 1980s or even 1990s. This was the expansion of the traditional definition of product quality to include the services surrounding the product. For telecommunications this expansion includes repair and maintenance services, order entry, billing, and modular phones that customers could easily install and maintain themselves. In health care many new ideas emerged. These are sometimes called the features or the salability part of quality.

Many manufacturing companies were introduced to this aspect of quality in the 1960s and 1970s. The customer was no longer interested just in the quality of the car. Service provided by the dealers, roadside assistance, financing, and many other aspects of the supplier-customer relationship became part of the competitive quality battleground. In the late 1980s this was accelerated with the introduction of the Japanese luxury cars with their special dealerships and new service relationships. GM has taken this down to the basic car with the Saturn division.

4-2.4 Service Quality Process

In the 1980s, as indicated in Figure 4-8, a new focus on quality occurred. Led by IBM, companies started focusing on the costs of providing the quality of services. Many of the

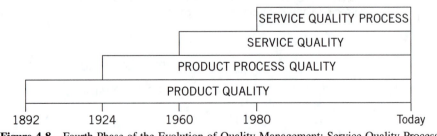

Figure 4-8   Fourth Phase of the Evolution of Quality Management: Service Quality Process

same techniques used in product process quality were applied for the first time to processes that cut across organizations and were often totally unmanaged.

Some new ideas also emerged. The concept of a process owner and a process team expanded the power of a quality council by continuously identifying opportunities for team interventions in critical business processes. In many ways these process teams acted as focused councils deploying improvement, control, and planning teams to the processes.

Again the focus was primarily on costs. These reengineering or business process quality efforts were directed at reducing cycle times, reducing numbers of steps or handoffs, and improving overall efficiency. Many of these business process interventions also improved the quality of the output.

We began to see a cycle emerging. The evolutionary process of total quality management seems to alternate between a focus on quality and a focus on the costs of attaining that quality.

4-2.5 Business Planning

Many companies have started to integrate quality management into their business planning cycles as indicated in Figure 4-9. This integration of the quality goals with the financial goals has been a major thrust of these companies. This integration was listed as the major effort underway by the respondents to a Business Roundtable survey on TQM.

The setting of quality goals—subdivided into subgoals, annual goals, and projects— and their deployment throughout the organization have become major breakthroughs for many organizations. This goal setting has been called hoshin kanri, hoshin planning, policy deployment, and strategic quality planning. Some companies are actually going beyond the annual business planning cycle and incorporating these methods in their five-year or longer-term plans.

This leads to the question as to what are the next steps in the evolution of total quality. The immediate next step in the pyramid is strategic quality planning. Some companies are beginning to go even further: They have implemented integrated strategic planning, in which they are involving customers and suppliers.

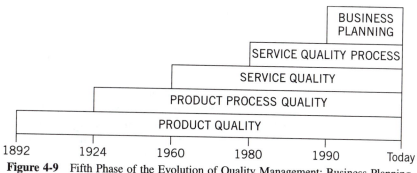

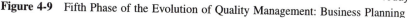

Figure 4-9 Fifth Phase of the Evolution of Quality Management: Business Planning

▶ 4-3 THE IMPACT OF NATIONAL AND INTERNATIONAL QUALITY AWARDS ON TOTAL QUALITY MANAGEMENT

One of the most useful trends in the past decade has been the self-assessment activities of many organizations. They are using the criteria of the Malcolm Baldrige National Quality Award, the European Quality Award, the Deming Application Prize, and others to assess their current performance against a set of guidelines for total quality.

One of the benefits of these national and international quality awards has been the increase in senior management contact with the leaders in total quality. For the first time in the history of the United States, senior managers are hearing what other companies have achieved in quality, how they obtained these results, and what the executive leadership's role was in these achievements.

This benchmarking, on both a personal and an organizational level, is one of the most important trends in modern quality management. When asked by *Boardroom Reports* whether there was a single most important thing a company could do to change the company culture and achieve remarkable results, the chairman of Ford Motor Company, Donald Peterson answered, "There sure is. Each company must find out which other companies in the world are best in that industry. Then, each company must benchmark operations against the most efficient—and most profitable—foreign and domestic businesses. . . . those that do—such as Xerox—have had incredible results" [Peterson (1992)].

4-3.1 The Creation of the Malcolm Baldrige National Quality Award

During the 1980s there was growing interest in the United States in promoting what is now called total quality. Many leaders in the United States thought that a national quality award, similar to the JUSE's Deming Application Prize, would help to stimulate the quality efforts of U.S. companies.

A number of individuals and organizations proposed such an award, leading to a series of hearings before the U.S. House of Representatives Subcommittee on Science, Research and Technology. Finally, on 6 January 1987, the Malcolm Baldrige National Quality Improvement Act of 1987 was passed. The act was signed by President Ronald Reagan on 20 August 1987 and became Public Law 100-107. This act provided for the establishment of the Malcolm Baldrige National Quality Award Program. The purpose of this award program was to help improve quality and productivity by:

> *"(A) helping stimulate American companies to improve quality and productivity for the pride of recognition while obtaining a competitive edge through increased profits,*
>
> *(B) recognizing the achievements of those companies which improve the quality of their goods and services and providing an example to others,*
>
> *(C) establishing guidelines and criteria that can be used by business, industrial, governmental and other organizations in evaluating their own quality improvement efforts, and*
>
> *(D) providing specific guidance for other American organizations that wish to learn how to manage for high quality by making available detailed information on how winning organizations were able to change their cultures and achieve eminence" [House Resolution 812, U.S. Government (1987)].*

The act provided that up to two awards could be presented to companies in each of three categories:

- Small businesses
- Companies or their subsidiaries
- Companies that primarily provide services

The act also stated that to be eligible for the award, a company must submit an application in writing. And the company must permit a "rigorous evaluation of the way in which the business and other operations have contributed to improvements in the quality of goods and services."

In 1995 pilot examinations of health care and educational organizations were conducted, and in 1999 the Malcolm Baldrige National Quality Award was expanded to include such organizations.

The act also called on the Director of the National Bureau of Standards (now the National Institute of Standards and Technology) to

rely upon an intensive evaluation by a competent board of examiners which shall review the evidence submitted by the organization and, through a site visit, verify the accuracy of the quality improvements claimed. The examination should encompass all aspects of the organization's current quality management in its future goals. The award shall be given only to organizations which have made outstanding improvements in the quality of their goods or services (or both) and which demonstrate effective quality management through the training and involvement of all levels of personnel in quality improvement.

In addition to the establishment of the board of examiners, the act also called for the establishment of a board of overseers consisting of at least five individuals who have demonstrated preeminence in the field of quality management.

4-3.2 The Malcolm Baldrige National Quality Award Core Values

In creating the Malcolm Baldrige National Quality Award, the first step was to develop the criteria that would be used to evaluate the organizations applying. The director of the National Bureau of Standards selected Dr. Curt Reimann as director of the Malcolm Baldrige National Quality Award. Dr. Reimann immediately began calling on individuals and organizations throughout the United States and the world for their suggestions and contributions to creating the criteria and the process by which these criteria would be evaluated. Dr. Reimann and his staff collected much information on other awards, such as the JUSE Deming Prize and the NASA quality award, as background information. They then selected a small team of volunteers to help create the first draft of the criteria. Selected experts from organizations throughout the United States reviewed these draft criteria in intensive focus group sessions.

One of the most important actions taken by the director, his team, and the volunteers at this stage was to create a clear design strategy for the award program. The elements of the strategy were as follows:

- To create a national value system for quality
- To provide a basis for diagnosis and information transfer

- To create a vehicle for cooperation across organizations
- To provide for a dynamic award system that would evolve through consensus and be continuously improved

The design strategy has been followed carefully. The award criteria have been improved each year. In this chapter we do not try to discuss the evolution of the criteria, but rather describe the most recent, 2001 criteria. These criteria are described in detail in a booklet that is available free from the National Institute of Standards and Technology (National Institute of Standards and Technology (2001)].

The Malcolm Baldrige National Quality Award Criteria are the basis for the awards and providing feedback to the applicants. The criteria also have three other important purposes.

- To help raise quality performance standards and expectations
- To facilitate communication and sharing among and within organizations of all types based upon a common understanding of key quality and operational performance requirements
- To serve as a working tool for planning, training, assessment, and other uses

Ten core values and concepts are embodied in the award criteria. These core values and concepts are discussed in the following sections.

4-3.2.1 Customer-Driven Quality

Emphasis here is placed on product and service attributes that contribute value to the customer and lead to customer satisfaction. The concept goes beyond just meeting basic customer requirements and also includes those that enhance the product and service attributes and differentiate them from competing offerings. Customer-driven quality is thus described as a strategic concept directed towards customer retention and market share gain.

This focus on the customer was even emphasized by President George H. W. Bush: "In business, there is only one definition of quality—the customer's definition. With the fierce competition of the international market, quality means survival" (quoted in the *1993 Award Criteria*, Malcolm Baldrige National Quality Award).

The emphasis on quality management and the customer has crossed administrations and political parties in the United States as shown by this statement by former President Clinton:

> *Quality is one of the keys to the continued competitive success of U.S. businesses. The Malcolm Baldrige National Quality Award, which highlights customer satisfaction, workforce empowerment and increased productivity, has come to symbolize America's commitment to excellence (quoted in the* 1988 Criteria for Performance Excellence, *Malcolm Baldrige National Quality Award)*

4-3.2.2 Leadership

A key part in the award's focus is on senior executive leadership. The leaders must create a customer orientation, clear and visible quality values, and high expectations. This concept stresses the personal involvement required of leaders. Involvement extends to areas of public responsibility and corporate citizenship as well as to areas of development of the entire workforce. This concept also emphasizes such activities as planning, communications, review of company quality performance, recognition, and serving as a role model.

4-3.2.3 Continuous Improvement and Learning

This includes both incremental and breakthrough improvement activities in every operation, function, and work process in the organization. It stresses that improvements may be made through enhancing value to customers; reducing defects and waste; improving cycle time performance; improving productivity and effectiveness; and improving the company's performance and leadership position in fulfilling its public responsibilities and corporate citizenship.

4-3.2.4 Valuing Employees

This concept stresses the fact that a company's success depends increasingly on the knowledge, skills, and motivation of its workforce. Employee success depends increasingly on having opportunities to learn and to practice new skills. Companies should invest in the development of the workforce through education, training, and opportunities for continued growth. There is an increasing awareness in the United States that overall organization performance depends increasingly on workforce quality and involvement. Factors that bear on the safety, health, and morale of employees need to be part of the company's continuous improvement objectives.

4-3.2.5 Fast Response

The value of shortening time cycles is also emphasized. Faster and more flexible response to customers is becoming each year a more critical requirement of business management. Improvements in these areas often require redesigning work processes, eliminating unnecessary work steps, and making better use of technology. Measures of time performance should be among the quality indicators.

4-3.2.6 Design Quality and Prevention

Throughout the criteria the importance of prevention-based quality systems are highlighted. Design quality is a primary driver of downstream quality. This concept includes fault-tolerant (robust) products and processes. It also includes the entire time for the design, development, production, and delivery to customers of new goods and services.

The concept of continuous improvement and corrective action is also included here. This concept stresses that changes should be made as far upstream as possible for the greatest savings. It also recognizes that major success factors in competition include the design to introduction cycle times. To meet the demands of rapidly changing national and international markets, companies should promote concurrent engineering of activities from basic research to commercialization.

4-3.2.7 Long-Range View of the Future

This concept stresses the need to take a long-range view of the organization's future and consider all stakeholders: customers, employees, stockholders, and the community. Planning must consider new technologies, the changing needs of customers, the changing customer mix, new regulatory requirements, and competitors' strategies. Emphasis is also placed on long-term development of employees and suppliers and on fulfilling public responsibilities.

4-3.2.8 Management by Fact

This concept stresses the need to make decisions based on reliable data, information, and analyses. These data need to accurately reflect the needs, expectations, and perceptions of the customers. They must give accurate descriptions of the performance of products sold. They should reflect clearly the market situation and portray accurately the offerings, performance levels, and satisfaction levels of competitors' products. They also should provide clear findings of employee-rated issues and accurately portray cost and financial matters. The role of analysis is stressed. Emphasis is placed on the role of benchmarking in comparing organizational quality performance with competitors' or best-in-class organizations' performance.

The need for organization-wide performance indicators is also stressed. These indicators are measurable characteristics of products, processes, and company operations. They should be clearly linked to show the relationships between strategic goals and all activities of the company.

4-3.2.9 Partnership Development

The need to develop both internal and external partnerships to accomplish overall goals is also emphasized. These partnerships may include labor-management relationships; working relationships with key suppliers; agreements with technical colleges, community colleges, and universities.

4-3.2.10 Results Focus

The Malcolm Baldrige National Quality Award stresses results throughout the criteria. It emphasizes that performance measurements need to focus on key results. But these results should not be just financial. Results should be guided and balanced by the interests of all stakeholders. Company strategy should explicitly include their requirements. The use of a balanced composite of performance measurements offers an effective means to communicate short- and long-term priorities, to monitor actual performance, and to marshal support for improving results.

4-3.3 The Malcolm Baldrige National Quality Award Criteria

The core values and concepts described above are embodied in seven categories:

1.0 Leadership

2.0 Strategic Planning

3.0 Customer and Market Focus

4.0 Information and Analysis

5.0 Human Resource Focus

6.0 Process Management

7.0 Business Results

The dynamic relationships among these seven categories are best described by Figure 4-10, which was originally presented in the 2001 Award Criteria booklet published by the National Institute of Standards and Technology (2001).

Leadership, Strategic Planning, and Customer and Market Focus represent the leadership triad. These categories are placed together to emphasize the importance of a leadership focus on strategy and customers. Human Resource Focus, Process Management,

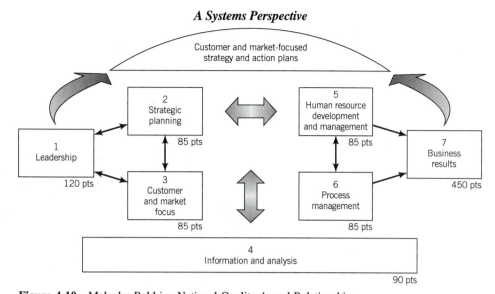

Figure 4-10 Malcolm Baldrige National Quality Award Relationships

Source: National Institute of Standards and Technology, *2001 Criteria for Performance Excellence, Malcolm Baldrige National Quality Award,* Gaithersburg, MD, 2001.

and Business Results represent the results triad. A company's employees and its supplier partners, through its key processes, accomplish the work of the organization that yields the business results. The Information and Analysis category is critical to effective management and to a fact-based system for improving company performance and competitiveness. It also serves as the foundation for the performance management system.

The seven categories are further subdivided into eighteen examination items, each focusing on a major requirement. Each item contains one or more areas to address. There are twenty-nine areas to address. The seven categories and the points for each category are shown in Figure 4-10.

The areas to address give specific instructions regarding what information should be contained in the application form. Notes supporting each section give further explanation and clarification. The notes also help the applicant to understand where certain data should be reported when there are several possibilities.

4-3.4 The Emphasis on Results in the Malcolm Baldrige National Quality Award

During the first years of the Malcolm Baldrige National Quality Award, some people thought that too much emphasis was placed on quality systems and too little emphasis was placed on quality results. Tito Conti compared the strengths and weaknesses of the Deming Application Prize, the European Quality Award, and the Malcolm Baldrige National Quality Award in an incisive paper [Conti (1992)]. Conti's criticisms of systems-based assessments are right on the mark. The proof of the effectiveness of any quality system must be in the results produced by the system.

Conti points out the Malcolm Baldrige National Quality Award's apparent overfocus on systems and underfocus on actual results. In fact, the applicants for the award have always emphasized results, sometimes even entering charts and data in inappropriate places in the application form. The examiners also looked for results in almost every area addressed.

However, the language in the application form was not clear in the early years, and it was possible to interpret the application process as only giving 10% weight to customer satisfaction results and 10% weight to internal results. Some companies and reviewers read the guidelines this way. The 2001 revision makes it absolutely clear that the focus is on results. Criterion 7.0, Business Results, is now worth 450 points out of 1000.

The actual applications are full of charts, graphs, tables, and other forms of results. The winning companies are well on the way to "management by fact," and it is not surprising that they report their activities in fact-rich documents. The examiners expect this and often refuse to score any examination item highly that doesn't have convincing data to support a statement. One of the most common statements on a scored application is "Lack of evidence to support claim of . . ."

Another misconception about the scoring is a belief that the examiners and judges rely wholly on a total score in making their final decisions on applicants. This is not the case. The seven category scores are always highly visible to all examiners and judges, and individual category scores are discussed at length. It is highly unlikely that a company that scored poorly in any single category would be selected for an award.

The scores—individual categories and total—are used mainly in the early stages of the awards process. High-scoring applications are selected for the consensus review stage. High-scoring applications after consensus scoring are selected for site visits. After site visits, scores are *not* recalculated. The actual findings of the site visit teams are submitted to the judges, and the judges get further information from the site visit members. At this stage of judging, scores have become much less important and are rarely used. The site visit teams concentrate very much of their activity on finding the evidence to support claims in the applications, verifying results, and examining supporting documents. These visits focus very much on results, not just approach or deployment. Examiners verify data, interview employees, and review actual operations and facilities.

During the site visit, examiners look for measurements of both internal and external quality. They look for measures of suppliers' quality levels. They interview employees and ascertain the results of the training, teamwork, and quality improvement processes. They look at customer satisfaction data, competitive evaluations, and benchmarks. They look for evidence of actual, sustained improvement and world-class performance.

4-3.5 Administration of the Malcolm Baldrige National Quality Award

The Malcolm Baldrige National Quality Award is administered through a complex set of processes under the management of the U.S. Department of Commerce, Technology Administration, National Institute of Standards and Technology, and administration for the Award is provided by the American Society for Quality. Most of the actual work of reviewing and scoring applications, site visits, judging, and developing the management processes is done by several hundred volunteers from U.S. companies, universities, government, consultants, and other organizations. These volunteers perform several key roles.

The board of overseers is a small group of people who have established preeminence in quality management. For example, a recent chair of the board of overseers was Robert

Galvin, the chairman of the Executive Committee of Motorola. Motorola was one of the first winning companies of the award. Armand V. Feigenbaum, University of Chicago Professor William Golomski, Harvard University Professor David Garvin, and Joseph M. Juran have all served as members of the board of overseers.

The overseers are concerned mostly with questions of process. They ensure that proper processes for managing the award are in place, are working, and are continuously improved. They review recommendations by the judges as to process improvements, but the overseers are not involved in the actual evaluation and judging of the applicants. Issues of concern for the overseers include the number of awards, award categories, changes to the Malcolm Baldrige National Quality Improvement Act, and technology sharing and transfer based on lessons learned.

The board of examiners consists of approximately 400 people who are selected according to expertise, experience, and peer recognition. They do not represent companies or organizations, but serve as volunteers for the common good. All members of the board of examiners receive three days of rigorous training using case studies, scoring exercises, and team-building sessions. They become a powerful network for quality improvement throughout the United States.

The board of examiners consists of three distinct groups: judges, senior examiners, and examiners. There are nine judges. The judges oversee the entire process of administering the award, help to select examiners, review the scored applications, select the organizations to receive site visits, and review the results of the site visits. They then decide which, if any, organizations to recommend for the Malcolm Baldrige National Quality Award. The U.S. Secretary of Commerce makes the final decision for the awards after further background evaluations of the recommended organizations. The secretary may not add any organization to the list and has no other influence on the awards process.

The judges are involved in oversight at every stage of the process but get involved in the review of actual applications only after many hours of work by the examiners. These evaluations, screenings, and site visits provide the foundation on which the award process is built.

There are approximately seventy senior examiners, and they play a crucial role. They are selected for their experience and expertise, and many have been examiners for several years or directly involved in winning organizations' quality management. They score applications and manage the consensus review process.

The rest of the board of examiners make up the examiners. They score all the applications, perform site visits with the senior examiners, and provide input each year on how to improve the application guidelines, the scoring process, and the entire awards process.

The award process follows several carefully defined steps. The first is the annual improvement of the criteria, the guidelines, and the entire awards process. The next step is the completion of the eligibility determination form by the company. Applicants must have their eligibility approved before applying for the award. The applicants then complete and file the application. The award applications then go through four stages of review:

Stage 1: Independent review by at least five members of the board of examiners

Stage 2: Consensus review and evaluation for applications that score well in Stage 1

Stage 3: Site visits to applicants that score well in Stage 2

Stage 4: Judge's review and recommendations

The scoring system used by the board of examiners is described in the application guidelines. It is based on three evaluation dimensions: approach, deployment, and results. All examinations items require applicants to furnish information relating to one or more of these dimensions.

Each year, after the recommendations for the winning companies are forwarded to the Secretary of Commerce, the judges review the entire process. Feedback is solicited from all members of the board of examiners, the applying companies, the administrator of the award process (ASQ), the staff of the National Quality Award Office, and other interested parties. The suggestions for improvement are carefully considered, and each year a number of changes are made to the award criteria, the application guidelines, and the award process. This constant improvement is one of the greatest strengths of the Malcolm Baldrige National Quality Award.

▶ 4-4 THE EUROPEAN QUALITY AWARD

In *Building Total Quality,* Tito Conti (1993) presents a comprehensive view of a total quality system. In this text Conti uses the European Quality Award as the fundamental model for total quality and gives many expansions of this model tied to business performance. Conti was a key architect of the European Quality Award as a member of the European Foundation for Quality Management executive committee. In 1990 Conti proposed separating the enablers from results and attributing to each 50% of the total score. These ideas, published in 1991 [Conti (1991)], became a fundamental part of the structure of the European Foundation for Quality Management Model for Business Excellence. This structure also contributed greatly to the value of the EFQM model's usefulness for self-assessment.

Conti's view of a total quality system is well worth understanding. He breaks the system down into five first-level subdivisions: the role of management, corporate values/culture, infrastructure, involvement/use/role of human resources, and the adequacy/use of technical resources. These are shown in Figure 4-11.

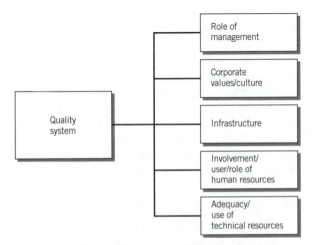

Figure 4-11 Conti's First-Level View of the Quality System

Source: Conti, Tito (1993), *Building Total Quality,* Chapman and Hall, London, p. 112.

Conti also suggests a further deployment of this model from the first-level criteria to the second-level criteria. He admits that the choice of criteria is more subjective at this level and based on experience. He suggests that when the criteria are used by different companies or different market sectors, it is essential to assign appropriate weights to the different criteria. In fact, some of the assigned weights might be zero for certain companies. Conti's second-level criteria are shown in Figure 4-12.

Role of management
- Leadership
- Definition/dissemination of quality policies
- Creation/management of the quality system
- Definition of goals/strategies and strategic planning
- System audits
- Creation of values
- Management team unity
- Responsibility versus public bodies/society/environment

Corporate values/ culture
- Customer orientation
- Excellence and continuous improvement
- Team spirit/matrix mentality
- Mangement by facts
- Respect for the individual
- Participatory management

Infrastructures
- Management by goals and means. Vertical alignment
- Process management/horizontal integration
- Information/data collection/analysis/transmission/uses
- Customer satisfaction measurement/improvement organization
- Strategic/operational improvement planning operation
- Improvement organization/teams
- Assessments/audits
- Involvement of external partners
- Standardization
- Benchmarking organization
- Product/service quality assurance

Involvement/use/ role of human resources
- Motivation/involvement
- Communication
- Teamwork
- Internal supplier-customer relations
- Attitude to improvement
- Interpersonal relationships
- Empowerment/participatory management/decision-making processes
- Policies/standards/procedures
- Job rotation
- Education and training
- Reward system

Adequacy/use of technical resources
- Diffusion/application of statistical knowhow
- Process management methodologies/tools
- Problem-solving methodologies/tools
- Policy deployment diffusion/use
- Quality function deployment diffusion/use
- Information technology diffusion/use
- Standardization methodologies/tools (SDCA)

Figure 4-12 Conti's View of the Second Level of the Quality System

Source: Conti, Tito (1993), *Building Total Quality,* Chapman and Hall, London, p. 113, used with permission.

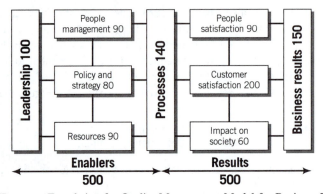

Figure 4-13 European Foundation for Quality Management Model for Business Excellence and Scores for Each Criterion

Source: *The European Quality Award 1997 Information Brochure,* European Foundation for Quality Management, used with permission.

The European Quality Award (EQA) shares many concepts and criteria elements with the Malcolm Baldrige National Quality Award (MBNQA), but the two awards differ in some important ways. Conti illustrates the differences clearly and openly discusses strengths and weaknesses of both approaches, as well as comparing them both with the Deming Application Prize.

The logical model of the EQA is quite clear (see Figure 4-13). The first element is leadership that leads people management, policy and strategy, and resources. These in turn promote processes that control people satisfaction, customer satisfaction, and impact on society. These three promote business results.

One of the major differences between the Malcolm Baldrige National Quality Award and the EQA is the emphasis the EQA puts on self-assessment. The EQA makes the principle of self-assessment an entry requirement for companies applying for the award. Conti (1997) stresses this in a new text, *Organizational Self-Assessment.*

A second difference between the EQA and the Baldrige Award, which Conti believes is a weakness, is the apparent absence in the EQA of the fundamental internal results category. Some people argue that internal results are implicit in other categories, but Conti thinks that "it is inadmissible that such an important category should be absent or implicit in some other category" [Conti (1993)].

Another difference between the Baldrige Award and EQA is the way in which the awards are administered. The Baldrige Award is competitive; it is given to a maximum of two companies in each of three categories: manufacturing, service, and small business. So far this has not been a problem, since the maximum number of companies has never been reached. The EQA is essentially noncompetitive; every company that reaches the pass mark receives a "prize." The award is given to the best prize winner. In some ways this makes the EQA even more competitive, since companies have a great desire to win the award, not just a "prize."

▶ 4-5 THE DEMING APPLICATION PRIZE

Another major contribution to the development of total quality has been the JUSE's Deming Application Prize. In his book *Companywide Quality Control,* Yoshio Kondo describes the creation and evolution of the Deming Prize [Kondo (1995)]:

> *In recognition of Deming's friendship and contributions to Japan, the Deming Prize was established in 1951 at JUSE's suggestion to encourage the development of QC in Japan. The prizes were originally funded with Deming's generous gift of the royalties from transcripts of his eight-day QC course lectures and the Japanese translation of his book* Some Theory of Sampling, *along with other donations.*

There are two types of Deming Prizes: the Deming Prize for individuals and the Deming Application Prize for companies and divisions.

> *Deming Application Prizes are awarded to companies or operating divisions that have achieved outstanding results through the skillful application of CWQC [Companywide Quality Control] based on statistical methods, and are considered likely to continue to do so in the future, where CWQC is defined as "the activity of economically designing, producing, and supplying products and services of the quality demanded by customers, based on customer-focused principles and with full consideration of the public welfare" [Kondo (1995)].*

In the over fifty-year existence of the Deming Application Prize, there have been many modifications and improvements to the prize criteria and the administration of the prize. The Deming Application Prize is not competitive; every company whose application is accepted may win. The examiners are selected by the JUSE from a small group of scholars and other experts associated with not-for-profit organizations who share a uniform approach to quality management [Conti (1993)]. Conti (1993) gives a simple chart illustrating the first-level deployment and example of second-level deployment for the assessment model of the Deming Application Prize. This model is shown in Figure 4-14.

There are several differences between the Malcolm Baldrige National Quality Award and the Deming Application Prize. There is no limit to the number of companies that may receive a Deming Application Prize in any one year, and there is a stronger emphasis on the use of statistical methods than in the Baldrige Award. The company decides itself when it is to receive an objective assessment of whether its activities have reached the level capable of passing the Deming Application Prize examination. Usually, the company engages a team of consultants from JUSE to provide ongoing consulting support during the four or five years preceding the official examination.

Kondo indicates that one of the main differences between the Deming Application Prize and the Malcolm Baldrige National Quality Award is that the checklist of items that applicants must satisfy to win a Baldrige Award is far more detailed, extending to twenty-three pages. Due to interest from around the world, the Deming Prize Committee created new regulations in 1984 making it possible for countries outside Japan to apply. In 1989 a U.S. electric utility, Florida Power & Light, became the first overseas company to win. In 1991 Phillips Taiwan became the second winner of the Deming Application Prize for Overseas Companies, and in 1994 the AT&T Power Systems division became the third.

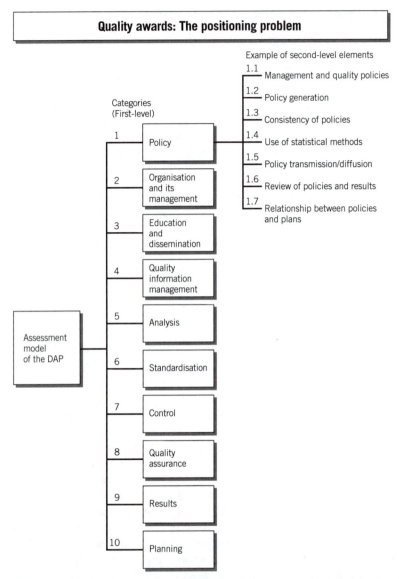

Quality awards: The positioning problem

Example of second-level elements

Categories
(First-level)

1.1 Management and quality policies
1.2 Policy generation
1.3 Consistency of policies
1.4 Use of statistical methods
1.5 Policy transmission/diffusion
1.6 Review of policies and results
1.7 Relationship between policies and plans

Assessment model of the DAP

1 Policy
2 Organisation and its management
3 Education and dissemination
4 Quality information management
5 Analysis
6 Standardisation
7 Control
8 Quality assurance
9 Results
10 Planning

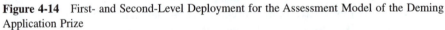

Figure 4-14 First- and Second-Level Deployment for the Assessment Model of the Deming Application Prize

Source: Conti, Tito (1993), *Building Total Quality,* Chapman and Hall, London, p. 281, used with permission.

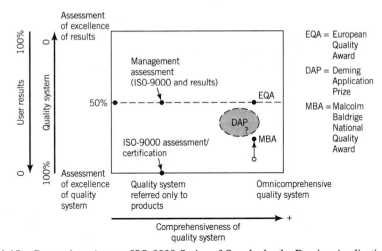

Figure 4-15 Comparison Among ISO 9000 Series of Standards, the Deming Application Prize, the Malcolm Baldrige National Quality Award, and the European Quality Award

Source: Conti, Tito (1993), *Building Total Quality,* Chapman and Hall, London, p. 283, and as modified by Conti (1999), used with permission.

▶ 4-6 COMPARISON OF NATIONAL/INTERNATIONAL QUALITY AWARDS AND INTERNATIONAL STANDARDS

Over the past few years there have been attempts to compare the ISO 9000 series of standards with the Deming Application Prize, the Malcolm Baldrige National Quality Award, and the European Quality Award. Conti (1993) provides one comparison, shown in Figure 4-15. The ISO 9000 series of standards are covered in depth in Chapter 3.

In Conti's chart shown in Figure 4-15, the ISO 9000 series of standards provide a way of assessment and certification for the excellence of a quality system that is at the far left of the *x*-axis. That is, the ISO system focuses on products and is the least comprehensive of the systems. It is also at the bottom of the *y*-axis, indicating no assessment of excellence of results but just of the system.

Conti sees the Baldrige Award, the Deming Application Prize, and the EQA as roughly equal in their focus on comprehensiveness of the quality system but the EQA as somewhat more focused on results. The Baldrige Award has changed since Conti's comparisons, and it is now more focused on results, perhaps equal to the EQA.

▶ 4-7 SIX SIGMA AND OTHER EXTENSIONS OF TOTAL QUALITY MANAGEMENT

In the past few years there have been many new definitions of total quality management. TQM has become an umbrella term for many different collections of concepts, methods, and tools. As new concepts are created, they are often added as extensions to the basic collection. Sometimes the creators of these ideas attempt to differentiate them from TQM and energetically stake out a separate place for their efforts. But most organizations integrate the new methods with the older successful methods and discard what is not working along the way.

A few years ago a great effort was made to stake a claim that reengineering was somehow different from other methods that are considered part of TQM. Some companies actually created new departments of reengineering separate from the quality departments or continuous improvement departments. Soon these efforts were merged.

4-7.1 Introduction to Six Sigma Quality

In the late 1970s many U.S. companies were in serious trouble. Some were losing market share. Some were selling off unprofitable businesses. Others were losing money. One of the most troubled was Motorola. During an executive retreat, a senior vice president challenged the company to improve quality. He stated, "Our products stink! I am ashamed to tell people I work for Motorola." The chairman and CEO at the time, Robert Galvin, would later relate that that moment was the turning point. Everyone had to agree with the statement, and everyone agreed that it was time to do something about it. Thus started one of the most remarkable stories in American quality management. Within nine years Motorola not only had solved most of its quality problems, but had also become the first large company to win the Malcolm Baldrige National Quality Award.

The story of what Motorola did is the beginning of the Six Sigma journey. In the first years Motorola embarked on a focused continuous quality improvement effort. One of the leaders of the Japanese quality revolution, Joseph M. Juran, was brought in with Frank M. Gryna to provide training to over 700 of the company's top executives. These leaders quickly brought the training down to the entire company. At the first training for the improvement teams focused on just the basic quality improvement tools such as flowcharts, histograms, Pareto diagrams, cause-and-effect diagrams, scatter plots, and control charts (see Chapter 11). These methods were quite useful in getting the teams started, and much progress was made in problem solving.

Several key concepts were stressed by both Juran and Gryna during these early training sessions. Perhaps the most important was the key role of upper management. The senior leaders were to select the projects to be undertaken and were to personally write the mission statements. The quality improvement teams were to collect data and analyze the symptoms, theorize as to causes, test the theories, establish what the root causes were, implement and test remedies, and establish controls to hold the gains [Juran and Godfrey (1999)]. This emphasis on senior management involvement in selecting the projects and personally selecting the team leaders and often even the team members was key. Although this was a basic tenet of earlier continuous quality improvement initiatives and TQM efforts, it was more in speech than in practice. Robert Galvin of Motorola made it very much the practice.

By 1983 the teams at Motorola found that many of their problems resisted solving by the basic tools. They started exploring other methods to see which were easy enough for the teams to use and also powerful enough to solve more difficult problems. Multivari analysis, created and championed by Dorian Shainin, was one of these statistical tools. Later Motorola looked for more advanced techniques and brought in formal programs in experimental design and reliability. For some of these methods, such as multivari analysis and design of experiments, they went right to the sources using the originators (e.g.,

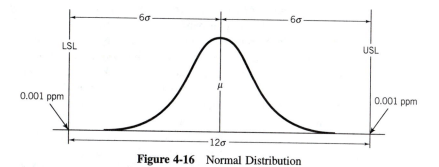

Figure 4-16 Normal Distribution

Shainin) or leading experts as instructors. Other times they shamelessly borrowed methods that had been developed in other leading companies, such as reliability estimation and prediction.

By 1985 the statistical methods toolboxes at Motorola were so full of new methods that company managers decided that they needed a new name for their quality initiative. They had performed a number of studies in various plants and noticed that many of their processes shifted over time. The maximum shift of the process mean seemed to be about 1.5 standard deviations. They decided to build this shift into their calculations. They wanted to strive for absolute perfection in product quality and decided to calculate the nonconformities in parts per million if their processes were so well in control that there were six standard deviations from the process mean to the specification limits when the process was centered. When the process mean shifted toward either the upper specification limit or the lower specification limit by 1.5 standard deviations, there would be only 4.5 standard deviations from the shifted process mean and one of the specification limits. From the normal distribution tables (see Table A in the Appendix), this gives only 3.4 parts per million nonconforming.

In Figure 4-16 we can easily see how few defects would be beyond the specification limits if we had six standard deviations from the process mean to the specification limits. The tail area of the distribution in this case (the amount outside the specification limits) is only about one part per billion on each side. The process is truly producing almost perfect products. But if the process shifts one and a half standard deviations toward either the upper or the lower specification limit (see Figure 4-17), now the process average is only 4.5 standard deviations from the specification limit, and the tail area is 3.4 parts per million.

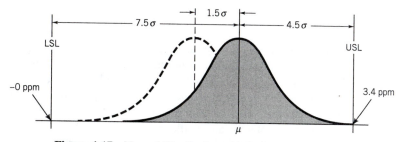

Figure 4-17 Normal Distribution with Process Mean Shifted

Note that on the other side, the process mean is 7.5 standard deviations from the limit, which means quality even far better than the original one part per billion.

When Motorola won the Malcolm Baldrige National Quality Award in 1988, the concept of six sigma quality became widely known. Motorola generously presented details of its efforts at conferences throughout the United States and internationally and published papers and books describing the program. It also offered courses through Motorola University. Many other companies became interested in Motorola's methods and started similar initiatives. Two of the most publicized have been AlliedSignal (now Honeywell) and General Electric. Both of these well-known companies are watched carefully by other executives because of their size and outstanding leadership. The six sigma explosion in the United States and quickly worldwide was fueled by General Electric's annual reports in 1997, 1998, and 1999, in which outstanding results were reported. These companies, as did Motorola, also put pressure on their suppliers to implement similar programs.

As companies such as AlliedSignal and General Electric implemented their own versions of six sigma quality, many variations were introduced. New methods were added, new case studies and examples were incorporated into the training, and new software was utilized to make complex statistical methods easy to use. In addition to the original breakthrough improvement model of six sigma for problem solving, a new set of methods was developed for "design for six sigma" quality. But despite the many variations, a basic methodology has emerged and in one form or another is followed by most organizations.

4-7.2 The Six Sigma Process

The first step is a decision by senior management to engage in such an effort. Because it will require significant resources of the organization this decision must be made by the chief executive and his or her direct reports. There is then an executive seminar, usually one or two days, for the executive team to learn the basic approach and discuss their personal roles. One of the key roles is selecting the "Champions," senior managers who will oversee the actual work of the six sigma teams. The company then provides a special course for the Champions, usually three to five days long. During this course the fundamental methods of six sigma are introduced, and the Champions begin to understand the hard work in which the team leaders (often called Black Belts) will be engaged. Some companies called these "process improvement teams" and "process improvement specialists," but the acronyms proved to be undesirable, and the karate term "Black Belt" emerged as quite popular.

4-7.3 Black Belt Training

During the training courses for the Champions project, opportunities are reviewed and usually both the first projects and the Black Belts to lead the project teams are selected. The Champions become familiar with the problem-solving steps the teams will use, the training the teams and Black Belts will receive, and the active roles they will personally play. Most companies select ambitious problems for these Black Belts. In the United States most of the problems are worth over $100,000. The Black Belt candidates are usually leaders within the organization and are asked to work on the project full time.

The Black Belt training is the heart of the six sigma quality effort. This training is usually four or five weeks long, and each week of training is separated by three or four weeks of hard work as the Black Belts and their teams apply the methods to the problem. During each week of training, new methods are introduced, and the Black Belts present their work to the instructors and other Black Belt candidates. This open review provides both good feedback during the project and a great deal of peer pressure. Often the Champions and even members of the senior executive team sit in on the project presentations.

The exact form of the Black Belt training has evolved over the years in the different organizations using six sigma methodology. Not surprisingly, because the purpose of the training is to enable the Black Belts to achieve significant results, this training has become quite effective and efficient. The training incorporates many of the modern ideas of cognitive theory in the instructional methods [see Lovett and Greenhouse (2000)].

In the Black Belt courses new methods are usually introduced by the instructor's giving an example of a problem and how the problem is solved using a combination of new and previously introduced methods. The instructor walks through an example, showing how the methods fit together to solve this type of problem. Then the students follow the instructor in solving a similar type of problem. This is usually done first with a simple problem, and the methods are applied by hand for maximum understanding. Then the instructor introduces a more realistic problem, often with real data, and the students follow the instructor in solving this problem using software. The students apply the software in each step from opening the data set, to testing assumptions, to manipulating the data if necessary and then in applying the correct methods to solve the problem.

Next the students work in small groups of two or three to solve several similar problems. Most often the data are already on disks to minimize time that might be required just to type in long lists of numbers for realistic problems. Students are selected to present solutions to the rest of the class. The presenter receives questions and feedback both from other students and from the instructor.

At each stage the students are integrating new methods with earlier methods learned and solving more complex problems. Several times during the week the students will be divided into small groups to conduct actual experiments. During the weeks between classes the Black Belt candidates are leading their own teams on their project using the methods they have learned in the training up to that point. During the following class each Black Belt will give a project review to the entire class, again receiving comments, feedback, and suggestions from the other participants and from the instructor.

From the above we can see that the evolution of six sigma training has also incorporated many of the educational reforms being introduced in the past few years [Lovett and Greenhouse (2000)]:

- Collaborative learning: Students work together in class on small teams solving problems, conducting small experiments, and with actual project teams applying the lessons learned to real problems.

- Active learning: Students apply methods learned to realistic problems and solve these problems in an open environment.

- Target misconceptions: At many stages students are encouraged to solve problems incorrectly, often using methods that they have been using on the job. The students see how easily one can get misleading results or spend far more time and money to get inferior results.

• Use of technology: In Black Belt training, the students have either personal laptops or desktop computers with the same software as other students. This software will also be used on their actual projects and work assignments.

Many companies have organized their Black Belt training using a five-step approach often called by its acronym, DMAIC. The five steps are define, measure, analyze, improve, and control. For each of these steps, special methods and tools are taught to the Black Belts and used by them on their projects. Hahn, Hill, Hoerl, and Zinkgraf (1999) give an example of a typical Black Belt training curriculum based on their experience with Motorola, General Electric, AlliedSignal, and Polaroid. Presented here is a similar typical curriculum based on work with two of these companies and with other organizations.

4-7.3.1 Define
The first week of training covers the basic methods. The introduction to six sigma is given, along with a review of how the new methods and ideas relate to what the students have already been using in their company. In the introduction the instructor will discuss how these methods may be incorporated into six sigma and give examples of new ideas and methods that will be used. The instructor will also present an overview of the five major steps: define, measure, analyze, improve, and control.

The focus during this first step is on writing the problem statement and the mission statement for the project. The concept of critical to quality (CTQ) is introduced. The CTQ parameters, the Ys, are the customer needs or the company needs that must be met. (See Chapter 10 for a discussion on specification limits and tolerances.) The concepts of quality function deployment (QFD) are reviewed and used to capture the primary customers for the product or process and the critical needs. Techniques such as Functional Deployment Matrices and Failure Mode and Effects Analysis are used to formally determine priorities for these CTQs. An excellent guide for Potential Failure Mode and Effects Analysis has been prepared by the Automotive Industry Action Group (1995).

During the define phase students also review simple statistical techniques such as Pareto diagrams, cause-and-effect diagrams, simple descriptive graphical methods, and flowcharts (see Chapter 11). For most students the only new part here is using special software to apply these methods quickly. During this phase teamwork principles are also introduced, and the Black Belts start selecting the team that will work with them on solving the problem.

4-7.3.2 Measure
In a five-week training program the second week of training focuses on measurement. In four-week programs the define and measure phases may be combined in the first week. When the Black Belts do a formal measurement system analysis, often called gage repeatability and reproducibility, they are frequently shocked at how poor their measurement system is. In most classes the students will design a measurement system analysis for both a variables problem and an attributes problem. For example, students may be given micrometers and a selection of parts to measure. Different students measure the same parts with the same micrometer, and then they perform a measurement system analysis to

determine repeatability and reproducibility. For details on this process see Automotive Action Group (1995). For attributes analysis, color samples of fabrics might be compared to a color standard.

A second subject that is covered during the measurement phase is the cost of poor quality. This is another subject that has been discussed in quality literature but not often used in practice. These costs can be between 15% and 30% of a company's total revenues. By performing formal studies of costs of poor quality, the Black Belts are able to focus their projects on areas of high potential impact to the company's profit margin. Using modern concepts of cost of poor quality analyses [see Sörqvist (1998)], many overlooked areas such as work-in-process inventory, non-value-added work, order-processing costs, and selling costs are included.

The third area covered during the measurement phase is process capability analysis (see Chapter 10). The students conduct an in-class experiment, perform a process capability analysis, and then prepare an action plan for conducting a formal process capability analysis for their projects. During the three weeks between classes, the student will then conduct the cost of poor quality study, the measurement system analysis, and the process capability study. See Fowlkes and Creveling (1995) for good examples of in-class analyses.

4-7.3.3 Analysis

The analysis week introduces the students to the concept of the Xs, the input factors that will drive the Ys. Although the basic concept of $Y = f(X)$ has been introduced in the first week of training, the emphasis there was on the CTQ parameters, or the Ys. During the analysis week the students start to list and examine the possible root causes of the variation in the Ys or the causes for the Ys to be at the wrong levels.

The analysis week is where the students first meet many of the new methods. This week starts with a review of all methods discussed in the define and measure phase followed by a review of probability and statistics (see Chapter 5). The review of probability and statistics is supported by both physical experiments such as the bead box and the Quincunx (see Chapter 6). Simulations are presented, using the software to generate numerous distributions and statistics from samples. These include averages from samples of varying sizes from several different and highly nonnormal distributions. The concepts of confidence intervals, confidence limits, and alpha and beta risk are covered here.

Also during this week concepts of correlation and tests of hypothesis are introduced. The students explore the association between numerous variables and discuss the meaning of the correlation. Many misconceptions surface during these discussions. After correlation the next step is to introduce simple regression and the fitted line. Here many of the methods that were introduced earlier come back into the analysis as the students create both probability intervals and confidence intervals. At this stage many Black Belts are also ready to explore multiple regression and use the software to perform simple stepwise and best subset regressions.

The main purpose of the analysis methods used and introduced during this week is to assist in reducing the number of suspected factors, the Xs. As different Xs are shown to have no effect or only minor effects on the CTQ parameters (the Ys), they can be removed, simplifying the problem. During the week each Black Belt presents his or her project and discusses which methods were used.

4-7.3.4 Improve

Again the week starts with a thorough review of the first three steps and introduces the basic concepts that will be introduced. During the week each Black Belt will present a review of his or her project and show how the earlier tools and concepts were used on the project. The purpose of this week is to find the optimum levels for the Xs that were identified during the earlier weeks.

For most Black Belts the most interesting week is the improve step. Many engineers, physicists, and chemists have been carefully taught in college to perform one-factor-at-a-time experiments and are quite amazed to find that not only are these experiments inefficient, they often give wrong answers. The week starts with an introduction to analysis of variance and moves toward more complex experiments (see Chapter 12). The Black Belts will start with full factorial designs and progress to 2^K experiments and then to fractional factorial experiments.

As with other topics, each of the experimental design methods is introduced with an example, and the Black Belts work through an example with the instructor while learning to use the software. The Black Belts then work in small groups to prepare examples and then by themselves on several problems.

Many companies use the catapult experiment as part of the experimental design week. [See Fowlkes and Creveling (1995) for a good discussion of this tool.] Small teams of students design an experiment, usually a fractional factorial, conduct the experiment by varying five or six parameters of the catapult and operator, enter and analyze the data, and then present their results. The instructor then conducts a final contest in which the teams must use their derived equations to predict the proper settings to hit a target at a new distance and then demonstrate their accuracy in front of the other teams.

4-7.3.5 Control

The final week of instruction again starts with a review of the preceding weeks and again the Black Belts present their projects during the week. The Black Belts have now found the optimum levels for the Xs, the input factors, that optimize the Ys, the CTQ values. The issue at this stage is to establish the controls that will keep the gains.

The main techniques introduced in this week are control charts and mistake proofing. Companies may use the little book *Mistake-Proofing for Operators* by Productivity Press (1996) to introduce the concepts of poka-yoke. Student exercises and examples fill the gaps and create an understanding of the fundamental ideas of creating processes in which mistakes can not happen.

The Black Belts learn how to design and deploy basic control plans using the basic control charts as tools (see Chapters 6–9). The final steps of closing the projects include preparing manufacturing operating procedures, control plans, an updated failure mode and effects analysis, a new process flowchart, a new process capability analysis, and a new measurement system analysis.

4-7.4 Summary of the Six Sigma Approach

A number of leading companies are using the six sigma quality approach to obtain outstanding results. In many ways the approach is an evolution of total quality management ideas with some important additions. The bottom line is stressed, with clear financial goals and measurements established before projects begin. Senior management plays an important and well-defined role. Black Belt team leaders, working half to full time, lead projects. The Black Belts received in-depth "grad school" training supported by modern hardware and software technologies. Projects are reviewed frequently, and Black Belt project leaders receive feedback, comments, and suggestions from peers, instructors, and senior management. Modern instructional concepts are thoroughly integrated in the entire training program. Training is active and interactive. Students apply what they learn in class and again on their projects following each session.

A majority of the statistical methods used in six sigma are contained in this text. The text can serve as a valuable reference for these methods. When supplemented by the appropriate special texts such as the Automotive Industry Action Groups FMEA, SPC, and MSA booklets [Automotive Industry Action Group (1991, 1995a, and 1995b)]; Productivity Press's *Mistake-Proofing;* and supplemental reading on topics such as multi-vari analysis and hypothesis testing, this text can be the fundamental reference for six sigma training.

▶ 4-8 REFERENCES

American Society for Quality (2000), ANSI/ISO/ASQ Q9004-2000 *Quality Management Systems—Guidelines for Performance Improvements,* Milwaukee.

Automotive Industry Action Group (1991), *Statistical Process Control (SPC),* Troy, MI.

Automotive Industry Action Group (1995a), *Potential Failure Mode and Effects Analysis (FMEA),* Second Edition, Troy, MI.

Automotive Industry Action Group (1995b), *Measurement Systems Analysis (MSA),* Second Edition, Troy, MI.

Business Week (1991), "The Quality Imperative—What It Takes to Win in the Global Economy," October 25.

Byrne, J. A. (1996), "Strategic Planning," *Business Week,* August 26.

Conti, T. (1991), "Company Quality Assessments," *Total Quality Management.* June and August.

Conti, T. (1992), "A Critical Review of the Current Approach to Quality Awards," *Proceedings of the EOQ Conference,* Brussels, June, pp. 130–39.

Conti, T. (1993), *Building Total Quality,* Chapman and Hall, London.

Conti, T. (1997), *Organizational Self Assessment,* Chapman and Hall, London.

Conti, T. (1999), "Modification of Il posizionamento delle valutazioni e dei premi," Personal communication from the author, January 20.

Deming, W. E. (1982), *Out of the Crisis,* Massachusetts Institute of Technology, Center for Advanced Engineering Study, Cambridge, MA.

Fowlkes, W. Y., and Creveling, C. M. (1995), *Engineering Methods for Robust Product Design,* Addison-Wesley, Reading, MA.

Fromm, B., and Schlesinger, L. (1993), *The Real Heroes of Business and Not a CEO among Them,* Currency Doubleday, New York.

Godfrey, A. B. (1998), "Hidden Costs to Society," *Quality Digest,* Vol. 18, No. 6, p. 18.

Godfrey, A. B., and Endres, A. C. (1994), "The Evolution of Quality Management within Telecommunications," *IEEE Communications Magazine Journal,* Vol. 32, No. 10, pp. 26–34, October.

Hahn, G. J., Hill, W. J., Hoerl, R. W., and Zinkgraf, S. A. (1999), *American Statistician,* Vol. 53, No. 3, pp. 208–15.

Hammer, M. (1996), *Beyond Reengineering,* Harper Business Division of Harper Collins Publishers, New York.

Juran, J. M. (1995), *Managerial Breakthrough,* 30th Anniversary Edition, McGraw-Hill, New York.

Juran, J. M. (1998), *The Upcoming Century of Quality,* Presentation at IMPRO 98, Juran Institute's 15th Annual Conference on Managing for Quality, Las Vegas, September 25.

Juran, J. M., and Godfrey, A. B., Eds. (1999), *Juran's Quality Handbook,* Fifth Edition, McGraw-Hill, New York.

Kondo, Y. (1995), *Companywide Quality Control: Its Background and Development,* 3A Corporation, Tokyo.

Kondo, Y., Kume, H., and Schimizu, S. (1995), "The Deming Prize," in *The Best on Quality: Targets, Improvement, Systems,* Vol. 5, Quality Press, Milwaukee, pp. 3–19.

Lovett, M. C., and Greenhouse, J. B. (2000). "Applying Cognitive Theory to Statistics Instruction," *American Statistician,* Vol. 54, No. 3, August, pp. 196–206.

National Institute of Standards and Technology (2001), *2001 Criteria for Performance Excellence, Malcolm Baldrige National Quality Award,* Gaithersburg, MD.

Peterson, D. (1992), "How Donald Peterson Turned Ford Around," Interview in *Boardroom Reports,* June 15, p. 1, New York.

Port, O. (1998), "Quality Claims Its Own Bull Market," *Business Week,* March 16, pp. 113.

Productivity Press Development Team (1996), *Mistake-Proofing for Operators: The ZQC System,* Productivity Press, Portland, OR.

Reichheld, F. F. (1996), *The Loyalty Effect,* Harvard Business School Press, Boston.

Reimann, C. W. (1992), "Testimony on the Malcolm Baldrige National Quality Award before the Sub-Committee on Technology and Competitiveness of the Committee on Science, Space and Technology, U.S. House of Representatives, February 5, U.S. Government Printing Office.

Sörqvist, L. (1998), *Poor Quality Costing,* Doctoral Thesis No. 23, Royal Institute of Technology, Stockholm.

The TQM Committee (1997a), "A Manifesto of TQM (1)—Quest for a Respectable Organization Presence," *Societas Qualitas,* Vol. 10, No. 6, pp. 1–4.

The TQM Committee (1997b), "A Manifesto of TQM (2)—Quest for a Respectable Organization Presence," *Societas Qualitas,* Vol. 11, No. 1, pp. 1–4.

The TQM Committee (1997c), "A Manifesto of TQM (3)—Quest for a Respectable Organization Presence," *Societas Qualitas,* Vol. 11, No. 2, pp. 1–4.

U.S. Government (1987), House Resolution 812, Washington, D.C.

Waltari, M. (1949), *The Egyptian,* Werner Söderström Osakeyhtiöm, Helsinki.

Yasuda, Y. (1991), *40 Years, 20 Million Ideas: The Toyota Suggestion System,* translated by Fredrich Czupryna, Productivity Press, Cambridge, MA.

▶ 4-9 PROBLEMS

1. Identify three companies that are engaged in six sigma quality efforts and summarize briefly the main points of their program. The summaries should be less than one page each and just capture the main ideas. You might find this information on the Internet, in business magazines or journals, or from personal contacts, including telephone interviews.

2. Identify three companies that have won the Malcolm Baldrige National Quality Award in the past two years. Summarize what major concepts or methods each one has used. What were the most significant results these companies attribute to their quality efforts?

3. What are the main differences in the ISO 9000-2000 standards and the earlier versions of these standards with respect to measurement and calibration systems?

4. A few years ago the Malcolm Baldrige National Quality Award program was expanded to include education and health care categories.

(a) What are the main differences between the criteria for health care and the criteria for small business, manufacturing companies, and service businesses?

(b) What are the main differences between the criteria for education and the criteria for small business, manufacturing companies, and service businesses?

5. How many states in the United States now have quality awards similar to the Malcolm Baldrige National Quality Award? How many awards have these states given in total since the awards were created?

6. What are the main differences between the European Quality Award and the Malcolm Baldrige National Quality Award?

7. Describe the main differences between quality control and quality improvement.

8. What is the single most important word in the definition of process?

9. What does Michael Hammer believe is the key word in the definition of reengineering?

10. Why is replication such an important concept in total quality management? Describe an example of replication in a company or organization with which you are familiar.

11. Describe what is meant in the core values of the Malcolm Baldrige National Quality Award that "changes should be made as far upstream as possible for the greatest potential savings."

12. What does the term "stakeholder" mean in total quality management?

5

REVIEW OF FUNDAMENTAL STATISTICAL CONCEPTS

This chapter reviews the fundamental concepts underlying statistical quality control that are discussed in this book. It is necessarily brief, with a minimum of mathematical proofs. More detailed explanation of any topic in this chapter may be found in any of the recognized texts on statistics such as those in the end-of-chapter references.

If the reader has some previous statistical background, this chapter will serve as a review. If not, with the help of a good instructor, the reader can learn enough of the fundamentals to proceed through the remaining chapters of the book.

Another purpose of this chapter is to provide a handy reference for readers who might, during the reading of later chapters, run across a statistical concept or idea that has been forgotten or is not clear.

▶ 5-1 PROBABILITY

Statistics can be defined as the science of collecting, analyzing, and interpreting data through the application of probability concepts. Therefore, this review of statistics is started with a brief summary of some of the concepts of probability. Probability is a measure that describes the chance that an event will occur. It is a dimensionless number that ranges from zero to one, with 0 meaning an impossible event and 1 referring to an event that is certain to occur. A probability of 0.5 means that the event is just as likely to occur as not.

The probability of an event occurring is measured in several ways. The most obvious is the concept of *a priori* probability. This is the ratio of the number of ways an event may occur to the total number of possible outcomes of the experiment under consideration. It corresponds to reality when all the outcomes are equally likely.

The set of all possible outcomes of an experiment is called the sample space. The denominator in the above ratio is thus the total number of points in the sample space. An event A can be written

$$P(A) = \frac{n_A}{N} \qquad (5\text{-}1)$$

where

$P(A)$ = the probability of event A

n_A = the number of ways A can occur

N = the number of points in the sample space

The above equation could be used, for example, to determine the likelihood of a part selected at random being found to be nonconforming to specifications. For a lot of 100 parts, of which five are nonconforming in some way, select one part in such a way that any part, nonconforming or not, is equally likely to be selected. The probability that a nonconforming one is selected will be, from (5-1),

$$P(d) = \frac{5}{100} = 0.05$$

Conversely, if the number of nonconforming pieces in the lot is not known, a few of them may be observed, a sample, and the sample results used to estimate the number (i.e., the quality) in the lot. Suppose, for example, it is decided to inspect ten of the lot of 100 and two of them are found to be nonconforming. Our sample result may be used to infer that 20% of the lot is nonconforming—that is, there are twenty nonconforming pieces in the lot. Before making such statements, however, the statistical properties of such estimates should be investigated. This will be done in the following pages. Another question that naturally arises is: How many parts constitute an adequate sample? The answer to this question is not simple, but depends on many factors that will be considered in this text.

The above discussion is centered on some fairly simple concepts, predicting the outcome of a future sample from *a priori* knowledge of the lot quality or taking a single sample from a lot and estimating the lot quality based on the sample. Now, however, some more involved ideas must be considered concerning probability. Start by defining four rules dealing with the computation of the probability of occurrence of multiple events:

Rule 1. Addition rule for mutually exclusive events:

$$P(A \text{ or } B) = P(A) + P(B) \qquad (5\text{-}2)$$

Rule 2. Multiplication rule for independent events:

$$P(A \text{ and } B) = P(A)P(B) \qquad (5\text{-}3)$$

Rule 3. General addition rule:

$$P(A \text{ or } B) = P(A) + P(B) - P(A \text{ and } B) \qquad (5\text{-}4)$$

Rule 4. General multiplication rule:

$$P(A \text{ and } B) = P(A)P(B|A) \qquad (5\text{-}5)$$

where $P(B|A)$ is the probability of B, given that A has occurred

The first rule applies to the case in which two events cannot both occur. For example, a steel rod cannot be both too short and too long. Thus, if a manufacturing process is making 1% of steel rods too short and 2% too long, Rule 1 says that 3% of the rods made by the process are either too short or too long. If this is the only nonconformity to be considered, the process is operating at a 3% nonconforming level.

Rule 2 gives a means to compute the probability that two events can both happen when they are independent, that is, the occurrence of one event does not affect the chance that the other may occur. Suppose for example, that a process is producing parts with two possible nonconformities: out of round and too short. Furthermore, assume that the presence of one does not affect the probability of the occurrence of the other. Then if 2% of the parts made on the process are out of round and 3% are too short, the probability that a given part selected at random fails to conform to both requirements is

$$P(AB) = (0.02)(0.03) = 0.0006$$

That is, only six parts in ten thousand will have both nonconformities.

Rule 3 is the addition rule obtained when the mutually exclusive requirement is removed. That is, it provides a means to compute the probability of either or both of two events happening. If they are really mutually exclusive, get Rule 1 by setting $P(A \text{ and } B)$, the probability they both occur, equal to zero.

Thus, for the example used to illustrate Rule 2, the probability that a part will be either out of round or too short is

$$P(A \text{ or } B) = 0.02 + 0.03 - 0.0006 = 0.0494$$

The necessity of subtracting the joint probability from the sum may be illustrated by Figure 5-1, which is called a Venn diagram.

The entire rectangle would represent the process, P. The ratio of the area of circle A to the area of rectangle P represents the probability of A occurring. Similarly, the ratio of the area of circle B to P represents the probability that B occurs. The ratio of the area of

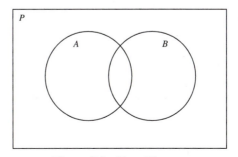

Figure 5-1   Venn Diagram

the intersection of both circles to P represents the probability both A and B will occur, the joint probability. Thus, the probability of A or B occurring can be computed by adding the areas of both circles A and B and dividing by P. However, then area AB (the intersection) will be added twice, so it must be subtracted.

Rule 4 considers the possibility that two events are not independent. Under this rule, consider the fact that the probability B occurs is different depending on the prior occurrence of A. For example, if A refers to the supplier that supplies parts A, and B refers to the occurrence of a certain class of nonconformance, the probability of B occurring will depend on the supplier chosen. Thus, for example, 2% of parts from supplier A_1 may be nonconforming while only 1% of those from A_2 are nonconforming. Furthermore, 40% of the parts may come from A_1 while 60% are from A_2. The probability of a part being nonconforming and from A_1 is $(0.40)(0.02) = 0.008$, while the similar probability regarding A_2 is $(0.60)(0.01) = 0.006$. The percent nonconforming in this mixed batch is then given by

$$P(d) = P(A_1) \, P(B|A_1) + P(A_2) \, P(B|A_2) \tag{5-6}$$
$$= 0.40(0.02) + (0.60)(0.01) = 0.014 \text{ or } 1.4\%$$

5-1.1 Counting Rules

There are often a great many different ways in which an event, such as a certain type of nonconformance to specifications, can occur. Thus, some rules are needed to assist in counting. For example, consider the number of different samples of ten, containing one nonconforming part, that may be selected from a large lot. This means that there are, in each sample, one nonconforming and nine conforming parts. Because the nonconforming part can occur at any one of the ten places, intuition tells us that the answer is ten. Formally, this can be calculated by considering first that there are 10! (ten factorial) ways to arrange the ten parts in the sample. That is, any of the ten parts could have been selected first, leaving nine for the second selection, eight for the third, etc. The number of ways, is then, $10 \cdot 9 \cdot 8 \cdots 2 \cdot 1$. This is called 10 factorial and is written ten 10!

Now the ten parts are divided into two classes (good and bad). There are 9! ways to arrange the good parts for every arrangement in the sample of the nonconforming one. Thus, the number of ways of obtaining (or permutations of) one bad and nine good units is given by

$$\frac{10!}{1!9!} = 10$$

This is usually called the number of combinations of ten things taken one at a time. Symbolically, write this as the binomial coefficient:

$$\binom{n}{x} = \frac{n!}{x!(n-x)!} \tag{5-7}$$

The above example was obvious enough to have been computed without the aid of Equation (5-7). However, many times these computations get much more cumbersome.

For example, to compute the number of ways of selecting from a manufacturing process a sample of 100 pieces that contains five nonconforming pieces use (5-7), to obtain

$$\binom{n}{x} = \binom{100}{5} = \frac{100!}{5!95!} = 75,287,520$$

The above discussion assumed that there are only two classes of parts. If there are k classes, the resulting expression is called a multinomial coefficient and would be written as

$$\binom{n}{x_1 x_2 \cdots x_k} = \frac{n!}{x_1! x_2! \cdots x_k!}, \; x_i \geq 0, \, n, \, x, \, \text{integers} \tag{5-8}$$

where

$$\sum_{i=1}^{k} x_i = n$$

For example, suppose there are four ways in which a part may fail to conform to specifications, and there are 100 pieces in our sample. Of these, five have the first type of nonconformity, twenty-five have the second, fifteen have the third, five the fourth, and fifty have no nonconformity. The number of possible permutations or arrangements of these is

$$\frac{100!}{5!25!15!5!50!} = 1.0506 \times 10^{52}$$

▶ 5-2 FREQUENCY DISTRIBUTIONS

Most of the above discussion related to computing probabilities when the structure of the distribution is known. Typically, this is not the case. Thus, consider what should be done to compute probabilities when the structure of the population is unknown. For example, a large sample might be taken, or the entire population or lot of material might be observed to determine the nature of the variable under consideration.

It will usually be informative, however, to tabulate the data in the form of a frequency distribution to consider the frequency (number) of values falling in each of several intervals. Suppose for example, there are 100 measurements on parts selected from a process. The first task in constructing a frequency distribution is to decide on the number of class intervals (and, therefore, the width of each interval) and the location of the intervals. Some considerations that can be used to select the number of intervals are as follows:

1. There should be enough intervals to show the variability in the data. Typically, this would require six to eighteen or so intervals, depending on the amount of data present. A rule of thumb is to use approximately as many intervals as the square root of the number of observations.

2. There should not be so many intervals that many of them are empty or that adjacent intervals have widely different contents.

3. If possible, the intervals should all be of the same width.

A graph of a frequency distribution is called a histogram. The above rules are most easily followed if the histogram of the data collected is drawn.

TABLE 5-1   100 Measurements of Metal Sleeve Diameters

22	25	15	13	27	30	18	10	16	12
19	27	24	22	27	27	30	18	19	23
15	20	20	27	25	29	17	15	26	24
32	14	20	20	27	21	15	22	16	19
25	27	18	13	23	25	25	27	24	32
27	30	22	24	16	19	23	25	30	30
27	22	21	22	24	29	17	19	22	26
23	21	24	26	30	32	15	19	20	20
17	22	20	27	29	19	26	30	16	20
17	23	16	22	24	23	24	23	22	22

The second consideration, the location of the intervals, should be made so that data cluster roughly around the center of as many as possible of the intervals. Thus for example, if the data come from an inspector, it may be discovered that he or she seems to favor measurements in millimeters ending in 5 or 0. Then construct the frequency distribution so that these numbers fall in the middle of the classes. This is justified because it actually represents the subconscious rounding the inspector was making.

As an example, consider the data in Table 5-1, which represent 100 measurements of the diameter of a metal sleeve in millimeters.

Table 5-1 may be examined, but not much can be observed from it except that data range from 10 to 32 mm with most of the measurements from 20 to 27. Table 5-2 shows the same data grouped in the form of a frequency distribution. The distribution has eight intervals of 3 mm width. In the table, f refers to the frequency, or number of measurements, in each interval.

Figure 5-2 illustrates the histogram of the distribution tabulated in Tables 5-1 and 5-2. In the figure the abscissa represents the sleeve diameter in mm (x), and the ordinate represents the frequency of each interval (f). Note that if too few intervals were used, some of the variability would be missed; the number of measurements near 23 is substantially larger than the number near 20 or 26. This information would be lost with too few intervals. Conversely, with too many intervals variability that is not really substantial

TABLE 5-2   Frequency Distribution of 100 Measurements

Class Interval	Midpoint	f
9.6–12.5	11	2
12.6–15.5	14	8
15.6–18.5	17	12
18.6–21.5	20	18
21.6–24.5	23	26
24.6–27.5	26	21
27.6–30.5	29	10
30.6–33.5	32	3
Total		100

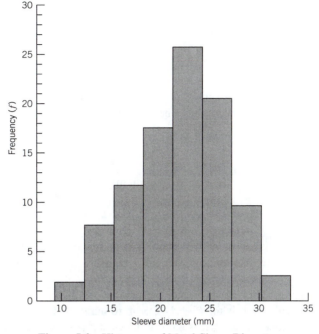

Figure 5-2 Histogram of Metal Sleeve Diameters

would be seen; the number of 23's is less than the number of 22's or 24's, but probably this is just a chance occurrence.

The histogram indicates the distribution to be centered on 22 or 23 with a skewed pattern of variation. The skewness results because there are a few more small measurements than large ones. Such skewness might indicate the occurrence of extreme values that should be investigated for the presence of measurement errors. It might also indicate a flinching effect caused by an inspector's being reluctant to say that a piece is too large unless it is considerably larger than a specified upper limit.

▶ 5-3 MEASUREMENTS OF CENTRAL TENDENCY

In the above example, it was observed that the measurements seemed to be centered on 22 or 23. To make a more definitive statement, compute the value on which the data are centered. Such a value is called a measure of central tendency or average.

There are several types of averages, all of which have their uses. The most common one and the one that is used most in quality control work is the arithmetic mean. In fact, this one is so common that unless some other type is specified, when the average is used, it will be the arithmetic mean.

The symbol for the arithmetic mean of a sample is $\bar{x}$. The mean of a population or lot from which the sample is taken is μ. The sample average, $\bar{x}$, is an estimate of the mean of the population, μ, which is usually unknown.

The arithmetic mean of a sample of size n may be computed by

$$\bar{x} = \frac{1}{n} \sum_{i=1}^{n} x_i \tag{5-9}$$

That is, it is the sum of all the measurements in the sample divided by the sample size (Σ denotes the sum of the x_i). In the case of a finite, known population of size N, the population mean, μ, would be calculated as

$$\mu = \frac{1}{N} \sum_{i=1}^{N} x_i \tag{5-10}$$

For the 100 sample measurements in Table 5-1, the arithmetic mean is

$$\bar{x} = \frac{2234}{100} = 22.34$$

Recall that the earlier guess, obtained by observing the histogram, was 22–23.

Another measure of central tendency that is sometimes useful is the median. This is the middle number in an ordered set of numbers. More specifically, it is the $(n + 1)/2$ number, counting from either end, in an ordered list of numbers. Thus, if there are five numbers, it is the $(5 + 1)/2$ or third number. If there are six numbers, it is the 7/2 or 3.5 number. That is, it is halfway between the third and fourth numbers.

For the 100 measurements in Table 5-1, it is the $101/2 = 50.5$ number. Because both the 50th and 51st measurements are 22, it can be said that the median is 22.

Another measure of central tendency sometimes used is the mode. This is the most frequently occurring number. For the data in Table 5-1 there are eleven 22's and eleven 27's. Therefore, there are two modes.

In the case of grouped data, such as those in Table 5-2, the arithmetic mean can be computed by considering all the measurements in an interval to be equal to the midpoint of that interval. This leads to Equation (5-11):

$$\bar{x} = \frac{1}{n} \sum_{i=1}^{k} f_i x_i \tag{5-11}$$

where

x_i = the midpoint of the ith interval

k = the number of intervals

f_i = number of observations in interval i

n = sample size

$$n = \sum_{i=1}^{k} f_i$$

For the example in Table 5-2, the arithmetic mean is calculated with the assistance of Table 5-3:

$$\bar{x} = \frac{2228}{100} = 22.28 \text{ mm}$$

TABLE 5-3   Calculation of Arithmetic Mean

Class Interval	x_i	f_i	$f_i x_i$
9.6–12.5	11	2	22
12.6–15.5	14	8	112
15.6–18.5	17	12	204
18.6–21.5	20	18	360
21.6–24.5	23	26	598
24.6–27.5	26	21	546
27.6–30.5	29	10	290
30.6–33.5	32	3	96
Total		100	2228

When a random sample of n observations is taken from a finite population whose entire size is N, the sample mean approximates the population mean, defined by Equation (5-10). The population mean, μ, is rarely known, since the entire population is often something inaccessible such as "all the conceivable observations of shaft diameter that could be made under the same conditions as those under which the actual n observations are made." Equation (5-9) simply averages the observations that *were* taken and gives an estimate $\bar{x}$ of what the population mean *would* have turned out to be if all the conceivable observations had been taken. The estimate $\bar{x}$ as given in Equation (5-9) is the only estimate of the population mean, μ, that makes much sense; compared to any other mathematical operations that could have been performed on the observations x_i, adding them up and dividing by their number is the only procedure giving an estimate that is a maximum-likelihood estimate and an unbiased one. That is, from statistical theory, $\bar{x}$ is both the value of the (unknown) population mean that would have given greatest likelihood of having a sample from it turn out exactly as observed and the value such that if repeated samples of size n were observed, it is the quantity that the average of the $\bar{x}$'s would be expected to approach.

Another result from statistical theory is that the accuracy of any estimate including the estimate $\bar{x}$ of μ tends to increase as the square root of n; this means that doubling the sample size decreases the error by a factor of about $\sqrt{2} = 1.414$, or by 41%.

If n is large enough and if the sample is close enough to being truly random, we can be confident the true mean μ is close to the sample mean $\bar{x}$. Much of the art of statistical quality control, treated in many places in the following pages, concerns the issue of making sure samples are random and the related issue of checking that the samples are from the population intended to be studied. These are largely qualitative issues. Sample size issues are more quantitative and await a discussion of dispersion.

▶ 5-4 MEASURES OF DISPERSION

Dispersion, or how much an individual observation varies from the mean, is at the heart of statistical quality control. Quality control, viewed narrowly, aims at controlling dispersions to stay within acceptable limits. This dispersion may be measured in several ways. The two that are used most often by quality control practitioners, however, are the sample standard deviation and the range. The former is sometimes expressed in its squared form as the sample variance. Both are used to estimate the population standard deviation (or variance).

5-4.1 Sample Standard Deviation

The dispersion of a single observation is measured by its deviation from the sample mean; the deviation of the ith observation is $x_i - \bar{x}$, which can be positive, zero, or negative. The sum of all the deviations [as can easily be seen by subtracting $\bar{x}$ for both sides of Equation (5-9)] is always zero, but the sum of the squares of deviations is positive unless all the deviations are zero.

The whole population has a *population variance,* which is denoted by σ^2 and defined as the average of the squares of all the deviations. Its square root, which is in the same units as the observations, is called the population standard deviation and is denoted by σ. It is defined as follows:

$$\sigma = \sqrt{\frac{\sum_{i=1}^{N}(x_i - \mu)^2}{N}} = \sqrt{\frac{\sum x_i^2}{N} - \mu^2}$$

where

σ = population standard deviation

μ = population mean

N = size of the population

Note that μ was used instead of $\bar{x}$, since for the full $n = N$ sample, $\bar{x}$ is exactly μ by definition.

Now if there is a sample of size n, less than the full population size N, estimate σ by the same strategy used for the mean, namely by taking the squares of the deviations that have been observed and hoping their average approximates the average for the whole population. However, since after a sample is taken μ is unknown but only its estimate, $\bar{x}$ is known, the situation is slightly different when the average $(x_i - \bar{x})^2$ is substituted for the average $(x_i - \mu)^2$. It turns out from statistical theory that this would give a maximum-likelihood estimate (the estimated variance would be the one that makes the observed deviations most likely to have occurred), but not an unbiased estimate. If many samples of size n were taken, their average squared deviation would tend to be too small by a factor $(n - 1)/n$. Therefore, so that sample variances will not be biased, the sample standard deviation is defined with $n - 1$ instead of n, as follows:

$$s = \sqrt{\frac{\sum(x - \bar{x})^2}{n - 1}} = \sqrt{\frac{n\sum x^2 - (\sum x)^2}{n(n - 1)}} \tag{5-13}$$

The expression on the right in Equation (5-13) is easier computationally. Most preprogrammed pocket calculators use this expression to calculate s, the sample standard deviation.

5-4.2 Range

The range is the simplest measure of dispersion. It is merely the difference between the largest and smallest observations in a sample. Because it would obviously be greatly affected by the occurrence of an extreme value, it should be used only for small sets of data, say less than ten. The symbol R is used for the range, and a formula for it would be

$$R = x_L - x_S \qquad (5\text{-}14)$$

where

x_L = largest observation

x_S = smallest observation

There are many applications for the range. However, when it is used, it must be remembered that only two of the observations are used, and if one of them is a bad reading, there is not the advantage of using all the other data points to help recognize that fact.

The distribution of the range will of course depend on the magnitude of the numbers but it may be standardized as the statistic w, where

$$w = \frac{R}{\sigma} \qquad (5\text{-}15)$$

and σ = the standard deviation of the population from which the samples were drawn. The mean of the distribution of w is a function of the sample size. When the samples from which the ranges are computed are drawn from a normal distribution (to be discussed later), this mean is the factor d_2 found in Table H in the Appendix. The population standard deviation may then be estimated by means of collecting a series (usually 20 to 25) of samples, computing the range of each, and averaging them. The estimate of the standard deviation would then be

$$\hat{\sigma} = \frac{\overline{R}}{d_2} \qquad (5\text{-}16)$$

where the symbol ^ is used to represent an estimate.

5-4.3 Properties of These Estimators

The sample standard deviation, s, is a biased estimator of the population standard deviation, σ. However, the square of s (i.e., the sample variance) is an unbiased estimator of σ^2, the population variance. Equations (5-17) and (5-18) express these facts:

$$E(s^2) = \sigma^2 \qquad (5\text{-}17)$$
$$E(s) = c_4\sigma \qquad (5\text{-}18)$$

where c_4 is a measure of the bias in s and is a function of sample size (again when the samples from which the standard deviations are computed are drawn from a normal distribution). The E is the expected value or mean. This is discussed in Section 5-5.1.

The expression for c_4 is given in Equation (5-19).

$$c_4 = \sqrt{\frac{2}{n-1}} \; \frac{\left(\dfrac{n-2}{2}\right)!}{\left(\dfrac{n-3}{2}\right)!} \qquad (5\text{-}19)$$

Thus an estimate of σ is the value s/c_4. To improve on this estimate, take a series of k samples of the same size, average the sample standard deviations to get the statistic $\bar{s} = 1/k\sum_{i=1}^{k} s_i$, and then use as an estimate of σ:

$$\hat{\sigma} = \bar{s}/c_4 \tag{5-20}$$

As Equation 5-19 indicates, c_4 can be tabulated by n, the sample size, and is so tabulated in Table H in the Appendix. This procedure is similar to the one expressed previously by Equation 5-16 using the average range.

This estimate ($\bar{s}/c_4$) will be used in control chart applications in Chapter 8, where the s chart will be presented for control of process variability. While $\bar{s}/c_4$ is used in control charts, an estimate of σ more frequently used in other statistical work takes advantage of the unbiased property of s^2 as an estimate of the population variance, σ^2. Thus, if for k (usually twenty to twenty-five) samples from a population with unknown standard deviation, σ, another useful estimate of σ is

$$\hat{\sigma} = \sqrt{\frac{1}{k}\sum_{i=1}^{k} s_i^2} \tag{5-21}$$

if they are all based on the same size sample. If the sample size varies, however, weight the sample variances according to their sample sizes as shown in Equation (5-22):

$$\hat{\sigma} = \sqrt{\frac{(n_1 - 1)s_1^2 + (n_2 - 1)s_2^2 + \cdots + (n_k - 1)s_k^2}{n_1 + n_2 + \cdots + n_k - k}} \tag{5-22}$$

These last two estimates do not require use of the constant, c_4.

If our sample data are in the form of a frequency distribution, the sample standard deviation may be computed by the use of (5-23),

$$s = \sqrt{\frac{\sum f_i(x_i - \bar{x})^2}{n - 1}} = \sqrt{\frac{n\sum f_i x_i^2 - (\sum f_i x_i)^2}{n(n - 1)}} \tag{5-23}$$

▶ 5-5 PROBABILITY DISTRIBUTIONS

The distribution of data can be described in terms of a theoretical distribution instead of a frequency distribution, as in the previous section. This is particularly helpful when it is not practical to obtain large samples as in Table 5-1. Thus, it is necessary to write mathematical equations to describe the data. Such equations are called probability distribution functions or density functions.

There are several properties that probability distribution functions must have in order to qualify. For a discrete distribution (e.g., the number of nonconforming pieces in a sample), let p_i be the probability of outcome x_i. For continuous distributions let $f(x)$ represent the density of probabilities of outcomes of a continuous variable, x, such that the integral of $f(x)$ over an interval is the probability that x lies in the interval. The properties then are

1. For x discrete:

$$p_i = \text{probability that } x = x_i$$
$$p_i \geq 0, \text{ all } i$$
$$\sum_{\text{all } i} p_i = 1$$

2. For x continuous:

$$\int_a^b f(x)\, dx = \text{probability of } a < x < b$$

$$f(x) \geq 0, \quad -\infty < x < \infty$$

$$\int_{-\infty}^{\infty} f(x)\, dx = 1$$

For example, consider the probability distribution associated with the number of heads obtained in tossing three coins. For the variable $x = $ number of heads, the distribution is discrete and may be described as follows:

x_i	p_i
0	1/8
1	3/8
2	3/8
3	1/8
Total	1

An equation representing this is given later [Equation (5-40)].

An example of a continuous distribution might be given by the equation

$$f(x) = 6x(1 - x), \quad 0 \leq x \leq 1$$

The probability that x lies between 0 and 1/4, for example, is

$$\int_0^{1/4} 6x(1 - x)\, dx = 5/32$$

For this density function

$$\int_0^1 6x(1 - x)\, dx = 1$$

and for all x ($0 \leq x \leq 1$), $f(x)$ is positive. Figure 5-3 is a graph of this function. The reader will recall from calculus that the area under the curve in Figure 5-3 is 1.

Continuous distributions are useful for measurement data. Even though the measuring device might make the data seem like discrete data, they are theoretically continuous and treated as such. Conversely, count type data (e.g., number of nonconforming items) are clearly discrete.

5-5.1 Expected Values and Variances

The mean of a distribution is often called the expected value. The symbol $E(x)$ is used for the expected value, where $E(x) = \mu$. This may be defined as

$$E(x) = \begin{cases} \displaystyle\sum_{\text{all } i} x_i p_i & x \text{ discrete} \\[2em] \displaystyle\int_{-\infty}^{\infty} x f(x)\, dx & x \text{ continuous} \end{cases} \tag{5-24}$$

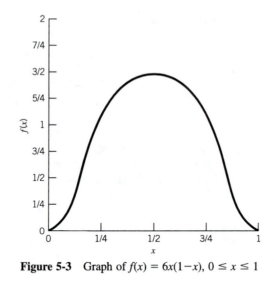

Figure 5-3   Graph of $f(x) = 6x(1-x),\ 0 \le x \le 1$

The expected number of heads for three tosses of a coin may be computed by the following table:

x_i	p_i	$x_i p_i$	$x^2 p_i$
0	1/8	0	0
1	3/8	3/8	3/8
2	3/8	6/8	12/8
3	1/8	3/8	9/8
		12/8	24/8

Thus, the expected number of heads is

$$E(x) = \frac{12}{8} = 1.5$$

Similarly, the variance (σ^2) can be defined as $E(x - \mu)^2$ or, equivalently, $E(x^2) - \mu^2$, where $E(x^2)$ is defined as

$$E(x)^2 = \begin{cases} \displaystyle\sum_{\text{all } i} x_i^2 p_i & x \text{ discrete} \\[2ex] \displaystyle\int_{-\infty}^{\infty} x^2 f(x)\, dx & x \text{ continuous} \end{cases} \tag{5-25}$$

and μ^2 is $E(x)^2$. The standard deviation is the positive square root of the variance.

For the above example the variance is

$$\sigma^2 = \Sigma x_i^2 p_i - (\Sigma x_i p_i)^2 = \frac{24}{8} - (1.5)^2 = 0.75$$

and

$$\sigma = \sqrt{0.75} = 0.87$$

Similarly, the mean, variance, and standard deviation may be calculated for the continuous example:

$$Ex = \mu = \int_0^1 6x^2(1 - x)\,dx = 0.5$$

$$Ex^2 = \int_0^1 6x^3(1 - x)\,dx = \frac{6}{20}$$

$$\sigma^2 = \frac{6}{20} - \left(\frac{1}{2}\right)^2 = \frac{1}{20} = 0.05$$

and

$$\sigma = \sqrt{0.05} = 0.22$$

Some specific probability distributions that occur in quality control applications will now be discussed. The normal, chi square, t, and F are continuous while the hypergeometric, binomial, and Poisson are discrete. Other theoretical distributions that have a more specialized application will be discussed later in the text when that application is encountered.

5-5.2 The Normal Distribution

The most important continuous probability distribution to quality control practitioners, as well as many other users of applied statistics, is the normal or Gaussian distribution. This distribution is often a good model for observations of natural phenomena and has been characterized as the appropriate distribution for most measurement type data. An obvious exception to this statement is in measurement of the life of a device such as is found in reliability analysis. Distributions useful in reliability analysis are discussed in Chapter 14.

The normal distribution is a continuous, symmetrical distribution theoretically having a range including all real numbers. The density function can be written as

$$f(x) = \frac{1}{\sqrt{2\pi}\sigma} e^{-\frac{(x-\mu)^2}{2\sigma^2}}, \qquad -\infty < x < \infty \tag{5-26}$$

where the two parameters, μ and σ, are the mean and standard deviation, respectively $(-\infty < \mu < \infty, 0 \le \sigma < \infty)$.

As can be seen from Equation (5-26), the normal distribution is really a family of distributions, each member with unique values of μ and σ. To facilitate tabulation of this distribution any of these normal distributions may be transformed into a normal distribution with zero mean and unit standard deviation. Thus, setting $\mu = 0$ and $\sigma = 1$ in Equation (5-26) will yield

$$f(x) = \frac{1}{\sqrt{2\pi}} e^{-\frac{x^2}{2}} \tag{5-27}$$

This distribution is called the standard normal and is plotted in Figure 5-4. As indicated in Figure 5-4, virtually all the distribution is within three standard deviations of the mean.

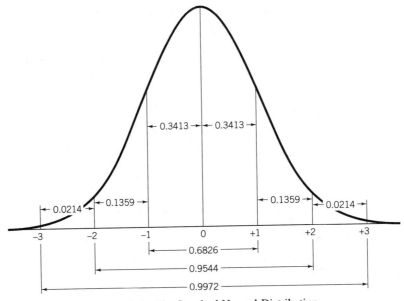

Figure 5-4 The Standard Normal Distribution

Any normal distribution may be transformed into the standard normal by means of the transformation indicated in Equation (5-28):

$$z = \frac{x - \mu}{\sigma} \tag{5-28}$$

where

$z =$ the transformed value of x

$\mu =$ the mean of the x values

$\sigma =$ the standard deviation of the x values

Thus for example, for a normal distribution with a mean of 60 and a standard deviation of 2, an x value of 63 would give a z of 1.5, computed as follows:

$$z = \frac{63 - 60}{2} = 1.5$$

Similarly, an x of 57 would correspond to a z of -1.5.

The standard normal distribution is tabulated in Table A in the Appendix. The values in the body of the table are the areas from $-\infty$ to z, called $\Phi(z)$. Since the total area under the curve is 1, these areas represent the probability that a random observation from the standard normal distribution will be less than the corresponding value of z. For the above example the probability of randomly selecting a value of x corresponding to a z of less than -1.50 is 0.0668 and the probability of an observation corresponding to a z greater than 1.50 is $1 - 0.9332 = 0.0668$. That is, $P(z < -1.5) = \Phi(-1.5) = 0.0668$, $P(z > 1.5) = 1 - \Phi(1.5) = 0.0668$, that is, $\Phi(z = 1 - \Phi(-z)$.

The Distribution of the Sample Mean

If a variable X has a normal distribution with mean μ and standard deviation σ, the distribution of the means of random samples of size n taken from this population is also a normal distribution with mean μ but with standard deviation equal to $\sigma/\sqrt{n}$. Furthermore, a well-known theorem known as the central limit theorem tells us that the distribution of sample means converges to this normal distribution as n increases, even if the underlying distribution is not normal. The convergence is faster for distributions that have properties like the normal, such as being symmetric or, if not symmetric, having one mode.

Most distributions found in practice are of the type that reasonable convergence is attained for very small sizes, such as four or five. About the only time such convergence may not occur this quickly is for distributions that contain mixtures of two different lots. In this case the resulting collection may be bimodal, as in Figure 5-5. In such a case, analysis of the data should be made using the two separate distributions. Even here, though, the distribution of sample means will tend to converge to a normal distribution with a mean value at a point in between two distributions.

As a result of this convergence of the distribution of the sample mean to the normal distribution, the following equation may be used to compute probabilities regarding the sample mean:

$$z = \frac{\bar{x} - \mu}{\sigma/\sqrt{n}} \tag{5-29}$$

As an illustration of Equation (5-29), suppose a measurement has a mean value of 0.500 in. with a standard deviation of 0.002 in. If samples of size 5 are drawn from this population, what is the probability that the sample mean will be greater than 0.501 in.? It might also be asked within what interval 95% of the sample means may be expected to fall.

To answer the first question, use Equation (5-29):

$$z = \frac{0.501 - 0.500}{0.002/\sqrt{5}} = 1.12$$

From Table A

$$P(\bar{x} > 0.501) = 1 - \Phi(1.12) = 1 - 0.8686 = 0.1314$$

Approximately 13% of sample means drawn from this population may be expected to be larger than 0.501. $100(1 - \alpha)\%$ of the sample means are expected to fall in the interval $\mu \pm z_{\alpha/2}(\sigma/\sqrt{n})$. This interval, for this example, for $\alpha = 0.05$ will be $0.500 \pm 1.96(0.002/\sqrt{5}) = 0.500 \pm 0.0018$. That is, 95% of the means of samples of size 5 are

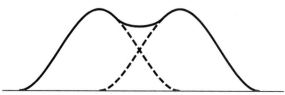

Figure 5-5   A Lot Containing Two Separate Populations

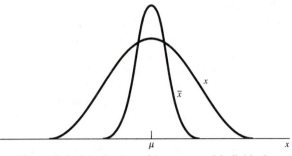

Figure 5-6   Distribution of Averages and Individuals

expected to be in the interval 0.4982 to 0.5018 in. Recall that 95% of the individual measurements will be expected to be in the interval

$$\mu \pm z_{\alpha/2}\sigma = 0.500 \pm 1.96(0.002) = 0.500 \pm 0.0039 \text{ or } 0.4961 \text{ to } 0.5039$$

This is illustrated in Figure 5-6 in which the larger distribution is the distribution of individuals and the smaller, more compact one is the distribution of sample averages. The use of the normal distribution to describe the distribution of sample averages is the basis of the control chart for averages. Further detailed discussion of the normal distribution is given in the succeeding chapters on control charts.

5-5.3 The Chi Square Distribution

The sample means have been observed to follow a normal distribution. The sample standard deviation however, does not, except for very large samples. In considering the distribution of the sample standard deviation, it is usually easier to work with the square of the standard deviation—that is, the variance. The distribution of the statistic $(n - 1)s^2/\sigma^2$ follows a chi square distribution with degrees of freedom $n - 1$, where σ^2 is the variance of the normal population from which the sample size n was drawn and s^2 is the sample variance.

The expected value of the sample variance is σ^2 and the variance of the distribution of sample variances is $2\sigma^4/(n - 1)$. Thus, the sample variance is an unbiased estimator of the population variance. As observed in Section 5.4.2, the same cannot be said about the sample standard deviation, s. The distribution of the sample standard deviation has a mean, or expected value, as shown in (5-18), of $E(s) = c_4\sigma$, where c_4 was given in Equation (5-19). The constant c_4 can be seen from Equation (5-19) to be a function of the sample size, n. It is tabulated by n in Table H in the Appendix. This constant approaches 1 as n increases and for $n > 25$ can be taken as 1. Thus, the bias becomes less important as the sample size increases but for small n it may be important. The standard deviation of the distribution of sample standard deviations, s, from a normal population is

$$\sigma_s = \sigma\sqrt{1 - c_4^2} \tag{5-30}$$

From Equation (5-30), after substitution and simplification, σ_s is approximately $\sigma/\sqrt{2n}$ whereas the standard deviation of the distribution of sample variances is $\sigma/\sqrt{2/(n - 1)}$.

The chi square distribution may be used to make probability statements about the sample variance or the sample standard deviation. In other words, using s, probabilities associated with the statistic

$$\sqrt{\frac{(n-1)s^2}{\sigma^2}} = \frac{s\sqrt{n-1}}{\sigma} \tag{5-31}$$

may be computed from the chi square distribution.

To illustrate this last result, suppose samples of size 5 are taken from a normal population of measurements with a standard deviation known to be 0.005 in. The probability that a sample standard deviation, s, is greater than 0.008 in. would be computed from

$$\chi^2 = \frac{(n-1)s^2}{\sigma^2} = \frac{4(0.008)^2}{} = 10.24$$

From Table B in the Appendix, for a chi square distribution with degrees of freedom $(n-1) = 4$, the probability that χ^2 is greater than 10.24 is approximately 0.04. This then is the probability that s^2 exceeds $(0.008)^2 = 0.000064$ or that s exceeds 0.008.

The chi square distribution may be generated by considering the sum of squares of independent standard normal variables. That is, if the squares of n independent standard normal variables are added, a chi square distribution with n degrees of freedom is obtained:

$$\sum_{i=1}^{n} z_i^2 = \chi^2_{(n)} \tag{5-32}$$

Proof of this relationship may be found in most standard texts on statistics such as Bowker and Lieberman (1972), Dudewicz (1978), or Duncan (1986). Because only $n-1$ of the observations in a sample from a population of unknown mean can be said to be independent (once $n-1$ of the observations have been selected, the last remaining one is fixed by estimation of the average), the relationship given previously as $(n-1)s^2/\sigma^2$ clearly has a chi square distribution with $(n-1)$ degrees of freedom.

If X has a chi square distribution, the density function of x is given by

$$f(x) = \frac{1}{2^{\nu/2}\Gamma(\nu/2)} x^{(\nu/2)} e^{-x/2}, \qquad x \geq 0, \quad \nu > 0 \tag{5-33}$$

where $\Gamma(a)$ is a gamma function, defined by

$$\Gamma(a) = \int_0^\infty x^{a-1} e^{-x} \, dx \tag{5-34}$$

The only parameter in the chi square distribution is ν, called the degrees of freedom. For the statistic described in this section, ν is equal to $n-1$. The mean of the chi square distribution is ν, the degrees of freedom, and the variance is 2ν.

The chi square distribution is tabulated in Table B in the Appendix. The values in the body are the chi square value exceeded by the fraction α given in the heading for each value of degrees of freedom, ν.

5.5.4 Student's *t* Distribution

It has been indicated previously that the expression $(x - \mu)/\sigma$ has a standard normal distribution when x is normal with mean μ and variance σ^2. Additionally, for the same random variable x, statistical theory indicates that the relationship $(x - \mu)/s$ has a slightly different distribution, called the t distribution, or Student's t. This is of importance, since typically the value of the universe standard deviation would not be known, and instead the estimate, s would be used.

The t distribution, like the standard normal, is symmetric about zero, its mean value. It is more spread out than the standard normal, but this difference becomes less as the sample size increases. There is a single parameter, again called the degrees of freedom, associated with this distribution. The distribution itself is tabulated by degrees of freedom in Table C in the Appendix. For most cases considered in this text, degrees of freedom is one less than the sample size, that is, $(n - 1)$.

If t has a Student's t distribution, the density function of t is

$$f(t) = \frac{\Gamma[(\nu + 1)/2]}{\sqrt{\pi\nu}\,\Gamma(\nu/2)} \cdot \frac{1}{[1 + t^2/\nu]^{(\nu+1)/2}}, \qquad -\infty < t < \infty \qquad (5\text{-}35)$$

where $\Gamma(\nu/2)$ is a gamma function defined in Equation (5-34) and ν is the degrees of freedom. The only parameter of this distribution is ν. Its mean value is zero, and its variance is $n/(n - 2)$.

As an illustration of the application of this distribution, consider a normal population with mean $\mu = 60$. Now suppose samples of size 5 are taken from this distribution. The values of $t = (\bar{x} - 60)/(s/\sqrt{5})$ would form a t distribution with $(n - 1) = 4$ degrees of freedom. The probability that t is less than -2.13 or greater than 2.13 is 0.05, illustrated by the shaded areas in Figure 5-7. If such a sample is taken and the standard deviation is found to be 2, a confidence interval may be constructed of width:

$$2t_{(0.95;4)}\left(\frac{s}{\sqrt{n}}\right) = 2\left[2.132\left(\frac{2}{\sqrt{5}}\right)\right] = 3.81$$

Ninety percent of intervals computed in such a manner would contain the true mean. If the mean of the sample were 61, it could then be concluded, with a confidence of 90% of being correct, that the true mean lies in the interval

$$\bar{x} \pm t_{(0.95;4)}\left(\frac{s}{\sqrt{n}}\right) = 61 \pm (2.132)\left(\frac{2}{\sqrt{5}}\right)$$

$$= 61 \pm 1.91 \text{ or } (59.09 \text{ to } 62.91)$$

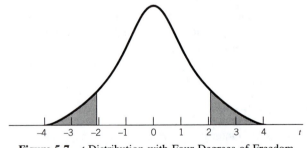

Figure 5-7 t Distribution with Four Degrees of Freedom

If it is believed or hypothesized that the true mean was 60 and the sample mean was found to be 57.5 with the same standard deviation as above (and a confidence interval width of ±1.91), there would be cause to doubt that the true mean was really 60. Other applications of this distribution will be found later in the text. Now consider a final continuous distribution.

5-5.5 The *F* Distribution

The ratio of two chi square statistics divided by their respective degrees of freedom, ν_1, ν_2, generates a distribution commonly called the *F* distribution. Thus, for example, consider the ratio

$$F = \frac{\chi_1^2/\nu_1}{\chi_2^2/\nu_2} = \frac{\dfrac{(n_1 - 1)s_1^2}{\sigma_1^2(n_1 - 1)}}{\dfrac{(n_2 - 1)s_2^2}{\sigma_2^2(n_2 - 1)}} = \frac{s_1^2/\sigma_1^2}{s_2^2/\sigma_2^2} \tag{5-36}$$

where the subscripts (1, 2) refer to the respective sample and universe variances and sample sizes associated with two random samples, Now if both samples were chosen from the same population, the two variances σ_1^2 and σ_2^2 are the same and may be canceled in the above expression. Therefore, for two samples drawn from the same population,

$$F = \frac{s_1^2}{s_2^2} \tag{5-37}$$

generates an *F* distribution with degrees of freedom ($n_1 - 1$, $n_2 - 1$). Note that each of the two chi square expressions in (5-36) has an associated degree of freedom, and therefore their ratio, *F*, has a set of two degrees of freedom.

The probability density function of the *F* distribution is

$$f(F) = \frac{[(\nu_1 + \nu_2 - 2)/2]!}{[(\nu_1 - 2)/2]![(\nu_2 - 2)/2]!} (\nu_1/\nu_2)^{\nu/2} \frac{F^{(\nu_1 - 2)/2}}{[1 + (\nu_1 F)/2]^{(\nu_1 + \nu_2)/2}} \tag{5-38}$$

Its mean is $\nu_2/(\nu_2 - 2)$, $\nu_2 > 2$ (approximately 1), and its variance is

$$[2\nu_2^2(\nu_1 + \nu_2 - 2)]/[\nu_1(\nu_2 - 2)^2(\nu_2 - 4)], \qquad \nu_2 > 4$$

The *F* distribution is tabulated in Table D of the Appendix. As an example of the use of this distribution, it may be concluded that if two samples of sizes 5 and 10, respectively, are drawn from the same population, the ratio of their sample variances will be no larger than $F_{(0.95;4,9)} = 3.63$ with probability 0.95. Other applications will be presented later in this text.

5-5.6 The Hypergeometric Distribution

In drawing samples from a lot of finite size containing a certain number of nonconforming parts, the probability of, say, the fourth piece selected being nonconforming depends on the number of nonconforming pieces among the first three pieces selected. This statement, of course, is based on the usual assumption that selected parts are not replaced after they are inspected—that is, sampling is without replacement. The question of sampling with or without replacement becomes less important as the ratio of sample size to lot size becomes smaller. It makes no important difference when this ratio is less than 10% (i.e., $N \geq 10\,n$).

However, if the lot or population size is less than ten times the sample size, the hypergeometric distribution is used to evaluate probabilities of certain outcomes. For example, suppose cartons with twenty-four light bulbs each and five bulbs from each carton are to be tested. Then each carton is to be accepted if no nonworking bulbs are found among the five bulbs tested. The probably of acceptance is then given by $P(x = 0)$, where x is the number of nonworking bulbs in the sample.

Let D be the number of nonworking bulbs in the carton, and let N and n be the carton and sample sizes, respectively, then compute the probability of x bad bulbs in the sample as

$$P(x) = \frac{\binom{D}{x}\binom{N - D}{n - x}}{\binom{N}{n}} \tag{5-39}$$

where

$x = 0, 1, 2, \cdots, \min(n, D)$

$n = 0, 1, \cdots, N$

$N = 0, 1, \cdots$

$D = 0, 1, \cdots, N$

The numerator of Equation (5-39) is the number of ways in which one can get x bad bulbs from the D nonworking ones in the carton times the number of ways to get $(n - x)$ good bulbs from the $(N - D)$ good bulbs in the carton. The denominator of (5-39) is the total number of possible samples of size n one can get from the N items in the carton.

For this example, for a carton with two bad bulbs among the twenty-four, the probability of not finding any of them in a random sample of five would therefore be

$$P(x = 0) = \frac{\binom{2}{0}\binom{22}{5}}{\binom{24}{5}} = 0.62$$

5-5.7 The Binomial Distribution

Now, for the situation in which the result of each trial, or piece inspected, is independent of the results of previous trials, the binomial distribution applies. This independence would occur for sampling with replacement, which is rarely, if ever done, or if the population were of an infinite size. The latter case would occur if the sample is selected randomly from a continuous process that is assumed to continue at the same level for the foreseeable future. This independence of trials also may be approximately correct if the lot or population size is large relative to the sample size. Stated another way, the limit of the hypergeometric distribution as $N \to \infty$ and D/N remains fixed is the binomial distribution.

Now, suppose that one of the above conditions is met and interest is in the probability of getting x nonconforming parts in a sample of size n for which the probability of each part being nonconforming is θ. This parameter θ might be the number of noncon-forming parts randomly distributed in the lot divided by the lot size or it might be the constant probability of a nonconforming part from a continuous process. The multiplica-tion rule of probability discussed in Section 5-1 is used to say that the probability of ob-taining x nonconforming items and $n - x$ conforming items is

$$P(x) = \binom{n}{x} \theta^x (1 - \theta)^{n-x} \tag{5-40}$$

where

$x = 0, 1, \ldots n$

$n = 0, 1, \ldots$

$0 \le \theta \le 1$

The mean value of x in this expression is $n\theta$, and the variance is $n\theta(1 - \theta)$.

Now return to the previous example in which there is a batch of light bulbs with two out of twenty-four bulbs nonoperating. If this ratio is a long-run average for all such cartons of bulbs, there is a process with $\theta = 2/24 = 0.0833$. Now reason that the previous sample of five bulbs was taken from an infinite process operating at a quality level of 8.33% nonoperating. It is not known for sure how many bad bulbs are in the carton from which the sample came, but on the average, there are two such bulbs in each carton.

Then compute the probability of getting all good bulbs in the sample of five as

$$P(x = 0) = \binom{5}{0}(0.0833)^0(0.9167)^5 = 0.6473$$

Thus, it is known that approximately 65% of such samples would have no nonoperating bulbs, whereas, if there were two bad bulbs in the carton, the previous section indicated that only 62% of such samples would be all operating. The cumulative binomial distri-bution is tabulated in Table E of the Appendix. The table shows for various n and θ the probability that $x \le c$.

5-5.8 The Poisson Distribution

Another distribution that will prove quite useful in this text is the Poisson distribution. A useful way to think of this distribution is in the "rare event" situation. That is, with a large sample for which the probability of each piece not conforming to specifications is very small for each trial and the overall number of nonconforming pieces per sample, that is, $n\theta$, is of moderate size. In fact, it can be shown mathematically that the limit of the bi-nomial distribution as $n \to \infty$ and $\theta \to 0$ while $n\theta$ remains constant is the Poisson dis-tribution. This distribution is given by Equation (5-41) for the probability of x noncon-forming pieces in a sample when there are an average of $\lambda = n\theta$ nonconforming items in the population from which the sample was drawn:

$$P(x) = \frac{\lambda^x}{x!} e^{-\lambda}, \, x = 0, 1, 2, \ldots, \qquad 0 \le \lambda \tag{5-41}$$

The mean and variance of this distribution are λ.

Now, returning to the light bulb example, consider the probability of a carton containing exactly two nonoperating bulbs. Recall that the process average percent nonconforming was 8.33%. The sample size would now be $n = 24$ (assuming the cartons are randomly filled). The product λ will thus be, as before,

$$\lambda = 24(0.0833) = 2.00$$

The probability of two bad bulbs in a particular carton is

$$P(x = 2) = \frac{2^2}{2!} e^{-2} = 0.27$$

The cumulative Poisson distribution is tabulated in Table F in the Appendix. The table shows for various λ the probability that $x \leq c$. In other words, the values in the body of the table are

$$\sum_{x=0}^{c} \frac{\lambda^x}{x!} e^{-\lambda} \qquad (5\text{-}42)$$

5-5.9 The Normal Approximation to the Binomial

When the use of the Poisson as an approximation to the binomial is not valid, the normal distribution may sometimes be used. In particular, if the percent nonconforming exceeds 10% or if the product $n\theta > 5$, the normal is generally better than the Poisson. This will be illustrated in Table 5-4.

The binomial may be approximated by a normal distribution with $\mu = n\theta$ and $\sigma^2 = n\theta(1 - \theta)$. This is the distribution of x, the number of nonconforming pieces in a sample. If instead, interest is in the variable $p = (x/n)$, the sample fraction nonconforming, use a normal distribution with mean θ and variance $\theta(1 - \theta)/n$. To illustrate this, suppose there is a continuous process operating at a 15% nonconforming rate. Determine the probability that a sample of 50 pieces will contain more than 10 nonconforming pieces. This may

TABLE 5-4   Probability of c or Fewer Nonconforming Items in Samples Drawn from Finite Lots

p	N	n	c	Hyper-geometric	Binomial	Poisson	Normal
0.02	50	10	1	1.000	0.984	0.982	0.998
	100	10	1	0.991	0.984	0.982	0.998
	1000	10	1	0.985	0.984	0.982	0.998
0.05	100	10	1	0.923	0.914	0.910	0.927
	1000	10	1	0.915	0.914	0.910	0.927
	1000	100	2	0.106	0.118	0.125	0.125
0.10	100	10	1	0.739	0.736	0.736	0.701
	1000	10	1	0.737	0.736	0.736	0.701
	1000	100	2	0.000	0.002	0.003	0.006
0.15	100	10	1	0.538	0.544	0.558	0.500
	1000	10	1	0.544	0.544	0.558	0.500
	1000	100	10	0.088	0.099	0.118	0.104

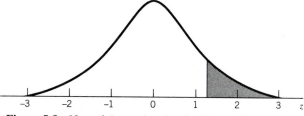

Figure 5-8   Normal Approximation for Binomial Probability

be computed by first using Equation (5-43) or (5-44) to calculate z and then using Table A in the Appendix.

$$z = \frac{(x \pm 0.5) - n\theta}{\sqrt{n\theta(1 - \theta)}} \tag{5-43}$$

$$z = \frac{\left(p \pm \dfrac{1}{2n}\right) - \theta}{\sqrt{\dfrac{\theta(1 - \theta)}{n}}} \tag{5-44}$$

The 0.5 added or subtracted in Equations (5-43) and (5-44) is to correct for the fact that a continuous distribution is being used to evaluate a discrete situation. If $x < n\theta$, use plus and if $x > n\theta$, use minus. If $x = n\theta$, use 0. Another way of thinking of this is, for example, that ten nonconforming pieces would be represented in the normal distribution as the area between 9.5 and 10.5.

Using (5-43) for this example, get

$$z = \frac{10.5 - (50)(0.15)}{\sqrt{(50)(0.15)(0.85)}} = 1.19$$

This is illustrated in Figure 5-8, where the shaded area is the desired probability. From Table A in the Appendix, find the probability that there will be more than ten nonconforming pieces in a sample of 50 to be 0.1170.

Equation (5-44) may be used by considering $p = x/n = 10/50 = 0.20$. Using (5-44) we get

$$z = \frac{\left(0.20 + \dfrac{1}{100}\right) - 0.15}{\sqrt{\dfrac{(0.15)(0.85)}{50}}} = 1.19$$

This of course, yields the same answer obtained using (5-43). That is, the probability that a sample of fifty will be more than 20% nonconforming is 0.1170.

5-5.10 The Geometric Distribution

One further discrete distribution will be discussed because of its application to continuous sampling plans. This distribution describes the number of parts tested in a series of independent trials before a nonconforming part is found. Thus, for example, suppose a procedure calls for a switch to sampling from 100% inspection if a certain number of successive conforming parts is found.

If x is the trial for which a nonconforming part is found and θ is the probability of a part nonconforming, the probability the first nonconformance is found on trial x is $(1 - \theta)^{x-1}\theta$. That is, there are $(x - 1)$ conforming parts followed by one bad one. Thus,

$$P(x) = (1 - \theta)^{x-1}\theta, \qquad x = 1, 2, \ldots \tag{5-45}$$

The cumulative distribution function is

$$\sum_{x=0}^{n} (1 - \theta)^{x-1}\theta = 1 - (1 - \theta)^n$$

This is the probability that the first nonconforming part will be found somewhere among the first n parts inspected.

The geometric distribution has an interesting property that is not found in other discrete distributions. That is, it is memoryless. In other words, if an event has not occurred in the first s trials, the probability that it will not occur during the next t trials is the same as the probability that it will not occur during the first t trials. Proof of this statement may be found in Feller (1957). A continuous distribution that has this same property is the exponential distribution that will be discussed later, in the chapter on reliability (Chapter 14).

The mean of the geometric distribution is $1/\theta$, and the variance is $(1 - \theta)/\theta^2$. Now return to the previous example in which light bulbs from a population known to have 8.33% that will not work are inspected. If the bulbs are inspected one at a time, the first bad one will be expected in the μth trial, where

$$\mu = \frac{1}{\theta} = \frac{1}{0.833} = 12$$

That is, on the average, eleven bulbs will be tested before finding a bad one. The memoryless property indicates that even if several bulbs have been tested before counting starts, the first bad one would still be expected to be the twelfth bulb tested.

5-5.11 Comparison of Hypergeometric Approximations

To summarize this discussion, a few points will be reviewed. For discrete data, x is an integer in all cases. If sampling is done without replacement from a finite-sized population, the correct distribution is the hypergeometric. However, if the ratio $n/N \leq 0.10$, the binomial would become a good approximation. If the sample size is large and the probability of each observation is small but the product $\lambda = n\theta$ is of moderate size, the Poisson distribution may be used to approximate the binomial. If $\theta > 0.10$ or $n\theta > 5$, the normal may be used to approximate the binomial. Table 5-4 illustrates these concepts for several values of θ, N, c, and n. The probability of c or fewer nonconforming items in samples of size n selected from lots of size N is computed by using, respectively, the hypergeometric, binomial, Poisson, and normal distributions. Finally, since computational aids, in the form of small computers and sophisticated calculators, are currently available at a relatively reasonable cost, the need for these approximations is certainly much less than in past years.

▶ 5-6 STATISTICAL INFERENCE

Statistical inference deals with making an inference about a population based on the results of a sample. In most cases this inference is about the value of a parameter. Statistical inference can be based on an assumption of an underlying distribution from which the sample was taken, or it can be based on no such assumption. The latter case is called nonparametric statistical inference.

In most cases dealing with data such as those obtained from measurements of manufactured parts, an underlying normal distribution is assumed as discussed in Section 5-5.2. This brief review of statistical inference will be restricted to that situation.

There are two forms of statistical inference: estimation and hypothesis testing. The first deals with the inferring of a parameter value on the basis of sample results. The second deals with the testing of the reasonableness of a hypothesis, or statement, about the value of a parameter. These two forms will be taken up in turn.

5-6.1 Estimation

The purpose of estimation is to make an inference about a parameter value, such as the mean thickness of a flange, μ, or the true fraction of a lot of material which is nonconforming, θ. If from a sample $\bar{x}$ is computed, in the first case, or p, in the second, these statistics would be used as estimates of the respective parameters. This makes some sense because they are known to be unbiased and reasonably efficient estimators of the parameters. However, it is not known whether they are correct. Therefore a statement cannot be made expressing confidence in them. How close they are likely to be to the true value of the parameters depends on the dispersion of the statistics—measured by the variance or standard deviation. This standard deviation of a statistic is often called the *standard error.* This term will be used to distinguish it from the population standard deviation.

With these considerations the value may be stated in the form of an interval within which it is believed, with a stated confidence, the unknown parameter lies. In Section 5-5.2 an interval was presented, $\mu \pm z_{\alpha/2}\sigma/\sqrt{n}$, which contains $100(1 - \alpha)\%$ of the sample averages, where α is some small fraction and $z_{\alpha/2}$ is the value of the standard normal distribution exceeded by an area of $\alpha/2$. In the present situation, μ is not known, but $\bar{x}$ could be used as its estimate. Thus an interval about $\bar{x}$ could be constructed and infer that the interval contains the parameter μ with a confidence of $(1 - \alpha)100\%$ of being correct. If the process standard deviation is known, such an interval would be

$$\bar{x} \pm z_{\alpha/2}\sigma/\sqrt{n} \tag{5-46}$$

If the true standard deviation were unknown, the t distribution described in Section 5-5.4 would need to be used, rather than the normal. For this situation Equation (5-46) would become

$$\bar{x} \pm t_{(\alpha/2;n-1)}s/\sqrt{n} \tag{5-47}$$

where $t_{(\alpha/2;n-1)}$ is the value of the t distribution with $n - 1$ degrees of freedom exceeded by $\alpha/2$. Examples illustrating these concepts will follow.

If the true standard deviation, σ, of measurements is to be estimated from a process, the fact that the statistic $(n - 1)s^2/\sigma^2$ has a chi square distribution (see Section 5-5.3) could be used. Thus, write

$$P\left[\frac{(n - 1)s^2}{\chi^2_{(\alpha/2;n-1)}} < \sigma^2 < \frac{(n - 1)s^2}{\chi^2_{(1-\alpha/2;n-1)}}\right] = 1 - \alpha \qquad (5\text{-}48)$$

for confidence intervals for the variance. Note that this interval is not symmetric about the sample variance, s^2, as the confidence interval is for the mean. Using Equation (5-48), the upper and lower confidence bounds for the population standard deviation, σ, can be written as

$$L = \frac{s\sqrt{n - 1}}{\sqrt{\chi^2_{(1-\alpha/2;n-1)}}} \qquad (5\text{-}49)$$

$$U = \frac{s\sqrt{n - 1}}{\sqrt{\chi^2_{(1-\alpha/2;n-1)}}}$$

For confidence interval estimates of θ, the process or lot fraction nonconforming, use $p = x/n$ as the initial estimate, where x is the number of nonconforming pieces observed in a sample of n pieces. If binomial tables are available, appropriate confidence intervals may be computed as follows:

$$\sum_{i=0}^{x}\binom{n}{i}\theta_L^i(1 - \theta_L)^{n-i} = \alpha/2 \qquad (5\text{-}50)$$

$$\sum_{i=x}^{n}\binom{n}{i}\theta_U^i(1 - \theta_U)^{n-i} = \alpha/2$$

where θ_L and θ_U are the lower and upper confidence interval estimates of θ. Since x, the number of nonconforming pieces in the sample, must be an integer, the desired values of $\alpha/2$ might not be available. However, select probabilities as close to them as possible. Curves to facilitate the use of Equation (5-50) have been developed [Clopper and Pearson (1934)].

In quality control, especially for the control charts discussed in Chapter 7, the normal approximation is often used to develop confidence interval estimates of θ. Thus, a $(1 - \alpha)100\%$ confidence interval estimate for θ would be

$$p \pm z_{\alpha/2}\sqrt{\frac{p(1 - p)}{n}} \qquad (5\text{-}51)$$

Care must be exercised in the use of Equation (5-51), since the binomial is not symmetric unless θ is 0.5. Also, Equation (5-51) might result in a negative value for the lower confidence limit. In that case, use zero for the lower limit. In general, Equation (5-51) may be used when $p \geq 0.10$ and $n \geq 50$.

5-6.2 Hypothesis Testing

To test a hypothesis is to ascertain the reasonableness of a statement or hypothesis about the value of a parameter. For example, say that a process is manufacturing parts that have a mean diameter of 1.25 in. Then take a sample and if the sample average is not reasonably close to 1.25 in., reject the hypothesis that it is 1.25 in. In making this decision the possibility of making two kinds of errors is incurred:

1. Say the hypothesis is false when it is really correct.
2. Say it is correct when it is really false.

The first kind of error is commonly called a Type I error. The probability of making this type of error is given the symbol α. Quality control practitioners often call α the "producer's risk." That is, it is the risk of rejecting a process when the process mean is really correct [Grant and Leavenworth (1988)].

The second type of error is called a Type II error. The probability of making this type of error is given the symbol β. In quality control β is called the "consumer's risk" when it represents the risk of saying a process mean is correct when it is not. The value of β, the consumer's risk, depends on the true parameter value. It is therefore a conditional probability, depending on the true value of the parameter such as μ or θ. The function is called an operating characteristic or OC function. The OC function is usually shown as a curve plotting the probability of accepting a hypothesis versus the value of the parameter about which the hypothesis is made.

The appropriate test is based on the underlying distribution of the statistic used to estimate this parameter. Thus, if the parameter to be estimated is the process mean, the sample average may be used with the test statistic shown in Equations (5-52) or (5-53), depending on whether the process standard deviation, σ, is known:

$$z = \frac{\bar{x} - \mu_0}{\sigma/\sqrt{n}} \tag{5-52}$$

$$t = \frac{\bar{x} - \mu_0}{s/\sqrt{n}} \tag{5-53}$$

The test statistic in Equation (5-52) is compared to a standard normal distribution while that in Equation (5-53) to a t distribution with $n - 1$ degrees of freedom. In both equations μ_0 is the hypothesized mean.

To test a hypothesis about the variance of a process, make use of the chi square distribution and the test statistic would be

$$\chi^2 = \frac{(n - 1)s^2}{\sigma_0^2} \tag{5-54}$$

where σ_0^2 is the assumed process variance. The test statistic in Equation (5-54) is compared to the chi square distribution with $n - 1$ degrees of freedom.

To compare two processes, one might, for example, wish to test the hypothesis that the two have equal mean values. For this test, the test statistics in Equations (5-55) or (5-56) are used, depending on whether the process standard deviations are known:

$$z = \frac{\bar{x}_1 - \bar{x}_2}{\sqrt{\dfrac{\sigma_1^2}{n_1} + \dfrac{\sigma_2^2}{n_2}}} \tag{5-55}$$

$$t = \frac{\bar{x}_1 - \bar{x}_2}{s_p\sqrt{\dfrac{1}{n_1} + \dfrac{1}{n_2}}} \tag{5-56}$$

where

$\bar{x}_i$ = sample mean of process i ($i = 1, 2$)

σ_i^2 = process variance of process ($i = 1, 2$)

n_i = sample size ($i = 1, 2$)

s_i = sample standard deviation ($i = 1, 2$)

$$s_p = \sqrt{\frac{(n_1 - 1)s_1^2 + n_2 - 1)s_2^2}{n_1 + n_2 - 2}}$$

The statistic s_p is the pooled estimate of the process standard deviation using Equation (5-22). This pooling or averaging should only be done if the two sample standard deviations can be assumed to be estimates of the same population standard deviation. To determine this, test the hypothesis that the two processes have equal variances, that is, $\sigma_1^2 = \sigma_2^2$.

Section 5-5.5 indicated that if this is true, the statistic

$$F = s_1^2/s_2^2 \tag{5-57}$$

will be an F statistic with $n_1 - 1$ and $n_2 - 1$ degrees of freedom. Thus compute this ratio of sample variances and compare it to critical values from the F table.

To test whether a process fraction nonconforming is equal to some hypothesized value, use the statistic

$$z = \frac{(x \pm 0.5) - n\theta_0}{\sqrt{n\theta_0(1 - \theta_0)}} \tag{5-58}$$

or

$$z = \frac{\left(p \pm \dfrac{1}{2n}\right) - \theta_0}{\sqrt{\dfrac{\theta_0(1 - \theta_0)}{n}}} \tag{5-59}$$

where θ_0 is the hypothesized value of θ, x is the number of nonconforming pieces in a sample of size n pieces, and $p = x/n$. The test statistic, z, is compared to a standard normal distribution. Similar tests are available using the binomial, hypergeometric, and Poisson distributions. These will be used in appropriate places in the following chapters on control charts and acceptance sampling.

The charts in Tables 5-5 and 5-6 summarize the decision process discussed in this section [Gutman et al. (1982), Hines and Montgomery (1990)].

TABLE 5-5   Decisions Regarding Hypothesis Testing

	H_0 True	H_0 Not True
Accept H_0	Correct decision	Type II error
Reject H_0	Type I error	Correct decision

TABLE 5-6   Probabilities Associated with Table 5-5

	H_0 True	H_0 Not True
Accept H_0	$1 - \alpha$	Consumer's risk = β
Reject H_0	Producer's risk = α	$1 - \beta$

5-6.3 Examples

▶ **EXAMPLE 5-1**

A process manufacturing metal washers is supposed to be operating with a mean diameter, μ, of 1.250 in. and a standard deviation, σ, of 0.002 in. A random sample of 25 pieces was taken from washers made by the process with the following results:

$$\bar{x} = 1.256 \text{ in.}$$

$$s = 0.003 \text{ in.}$$

The first hypothesis to be tested was that $\sigma = 0.002$ in. as specified. If this hypothesis is not rejected, the value of $\sigma = 0.002$ will be used to test the mean value. Thus, test the hypothesis that $\sigma = 0.002$ versus the alternative that it is greater than 0.002. That is,

$$H_0: \sigma = 0.002$$

$$H_1: \sigma > 0.002$$

It was decided that a producer's risk of 5% would be used. Thus, if $\chi^2 > \chi^2_{(0.05,24)} = 36.4$ (see Table B), we would reject H_0. For this example,

$$\chi^2 = \frac{(24)(0.003)^2}{(0.002)^2} = 54$$

Therefore, conclude that the process standard deviation is greater than 0.002.

One would then test the process mean. Because it cannot be assumed that σ is 0.002 (or 0.003 based on only twenty-five observations), use the t statistic in Equation (5-54) to test the hypothesis that $\mu = 1.250$ in. In this case, the interest is in whether the mean is either smaller or larger than 1.25, so use a two-sided alternative. That is, reject the hypothesis that $\mu = 1.25$ if the test statistic indicates it to be either larger or smaller. If again α is chosen to be 0.05, the test would be

$$H_0: \mu = 1.25 \text{ in.}$$

$$H_1: \mu \neq 1.25 \text{ in.}$$

and reject H_0 in favor of H_1 if $t < -t_{(0.025;24)}$ or $t > t_{(0.025;24)}$. Table C indicates that $t_{(0.025;24)} = 2.064$. For this example

$$t = \frac{1.256 - 1.250}{0.003/\sqrt{25}} = 10.0$$

Because 10 is greater than 2.064, conclude that the process mean is not 1.250 in.

Now estimate the values of μ and σ, since the hypothesized values were rejected. A 95% confidence interval for σ is, using Equation (5-49),

$$L = \frac{s\sqrt{n-1}}{\sqrt{\chi^2_{(.025;24)}}} = \frac{0.003\sqrt{24}}{\sqrt{39.4}} = 0.0023 \text{ in.}$$

$$U = \frac{s\sqrt{n-1}}{\sqrt{\chi^2_{(0.975;24)}}} = \frac{0.003\sqrt{24}}{\sqrt{12.4}} = 0.0042 \text{ in.}$$

Similarly, use Equation (5-47) to get a 95% confidence interval for μ as

$$\bar{x} \pm t_{(0.025;24)}s/\sqrt{n} = 1.256 \pm 2.064(0.003/\sqrt{25})$$

$$= 1.256 \pm 0.0012 = 1.2548 \text{ to } 1.2572 \text{ in.}$$

Note that neither confidence interval contains the original hypothesized values of $\mu_0 = 1.25$ and $\sigma_0 = 0.002$.

▶ **EXAMPLE 5-2**

Another machine was also making these washers. A sample of twenty washers was selected from the second machine with the following results:

$$\bar{x} = 1.23 \text{ in.}$$
$$s = 0.0025 \text{ in.}$$

It is necessary to test the hypotheses that these two machines have the same mean and standard deviation. As indicated above, first test the hypothesis they are alike as to standard deviation. That is, test

$$H_0: \sigma_1^2 = \sigma_2^2$$
$$H_1: \sigma_1^2 > \sigma_2^2$$

Here assume, if H_0 is rejected, that the first machine has more variability. The test statistic is

$$F = s_1^2/s_2^2 = (0.003)^2/(0.0025)^2 = 1.44$$

This ratio (1.44) is compared to the value of $F_{(0.05;24,19)}$ found in Table D to be 2.11. Since the test statistic is less than 2.11, conclude the two machines may have the same variability. Next pool the two sample variances to get an estimate of the process standard deviation:

$$s_p^2 = \frac{(n_1 - 1)s_1^2 + (n_2 - 1)s_2^2}{n_1 + n_2 - 2} = \frac{(24)(0.003)^2 + (19)(0.0025)^2}{25 + 20 - 2}$$
$$= 0.00000778$$

The pooled estimate of the standard deviation is 0.0028. The test statistic, t, is then computed as

$$t = \frac{\bar{x}_1 - \bar{x}_2}{s_p\sqrt{\dfrac{1}{n_1} + \dfrac{1}{n_2}}} = \frac{1.256 - 1.253}{0.0028\sqrt{\dfrac{1}{25} + \dfrac{1}{20}}} = 3.57$$

If again a two-sided test with a producer's risk, α, of 0.05 is used, the hypothesis to be tested and the alternative are

$$H_0: \mu_1 = \mu_2$$
$$H_1: \mu_1 \neq \mu_2$$

The critical value from Table C is $t_{(0.025;43)} = 2.02$. Since the test statistic (3.57) exceeds this, reject the hypothesis that the machines are producing washers with the same mean diameter.

A confidence interval estimate of the difference between the two mean diameters is

$$(\bar{x}_1 - \bar{x}_2) \pm t_{(\alpha/2;n_1+n_2-2)}s_p\sqrt{\frac{1}{n_1} + \frac{1}{n_2}}$$

For this example, a 95% confidence interval for the difference in the two mean values is

$$(1.256 - 1.253) \pm 2.02(0.0028)\sqrt{\frac{1}{25} + \frac{1}{20}} = 0.003 \pm 0.0017 = 0.0013 \text{ to } 0.0047$$

Note that zero is not contained in this confidence interval. This is consistent with the hypothesis test.

▶ **EXAMPLE 5-3**

If the requirements for the washers in the previous examples are 1.250 ± 0.010 in., the results of the samples may be used to obtain estimates of the fraction nonconforming for the two machines.

For the first machine, using a normal approximation, with the pooled estimate for σ of (0.0028), obtain

$$z_U = \frac{1.260 - 1.256}{0.0028} = 1.43$$

$$z_L = \frac{1.240 - 1.256}{0.0028} = -5.71$$

This indicates, from Table A, that 7.64% of the washers from machine 1 are outside the tolerance limits. Similarly, for the second machine,

$$z_U = \frac{1.260 - 1.253}{0.0028} = 2.50$$

$$z_L = \frac{1.240 - 1.253}{0.0028} = -4.64$$

Appendix Table A indicates that 0.62% of the washers from the second machine are out of tolerance.

▶ **EXAMPLE 5-4**

The process in the above examples was assumed to be operating at a 5% nonconforming level. The first machine may be tested with $\alpha = 0.05$ for this level as follows:

$$H_0: \theta = 0.05$$
$$H_1: \theta > 0.05$$

If the test statistic exceeds $z_{(0.05)} = 1.645$ (from Table A), reject the hypothesis that the fraction nonconforming is 5%. The test statistic is

$$z = \frac{p - \theta_0}{\sqrt{\dfrac{\theta_0(1 - \theta_0)}{n}}} = \frac{0.0764 - 0.0500}{\sqrt{\dfrac{0.0500(0.9500)}{25}}}$$

$$= 0.606$$

Because this value is less than 1.645, it cannot be assumed that the process percent nonconforming is greater than 5% on the basis of this relatively small sample.

It should be noted here that the normal approximation to the binomial was used even though $n\theta$ was less than 5. This was done to illustrate the use of this approach. A more theoretically correct procedure would have been the use of the binomial distribution. In this case, $n\theta = 25\,(0.0764) = 1.91 \approx 2$. Table E in the Appendix indicates that for a sample size of 25 and $\theta = 0.05$, the probability of getting two or fewer nonconforming parts is 0.873. The probability of more than two nonconforming parts is 0.127. On the basis of this result, it would again be assumed that this result is reasonably likely and the hypothesis that $\theta = 0.05$ would not be rejected.

▶ **5-7 QUALITY CONTROL AS AN AREA OF STATISTICS**

This chapter has dealt with a review of some fundamental statistical concepts. In closing a brief discussion of the problems of statistics as suggested by Enoch Ferrell (1953) is presented.

Ferrell suggested four general problems of statistics by way of the illustration shown in Figure 5-9. In Figure 5-9 (Ferrell's Figure 1), the check mark (✓) indicates the information known, while the question mark (?) indicates the conclusions to be reached or, in

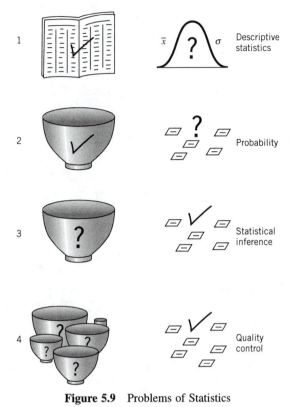

Figure 5.9 Problems of Statistics

other words, the problem to be solved. The four problems are *descriptive statistics,* in which the aim is to reduce data to a small number of statistics that summarize the relevant information in the data; *probability,* in which the aim is to predict characteristics of samples before the samples are drawn or in lieu of drawing them, given the characteristics of a population; *statistical inference,* in which the aim, conversely, is the inference of characteristics of a population from samples drawn from it; and *quality control,* in which the aim is to recognize from a sample whether it deviates too far from a desired or previous condition.

The remaining chapters of this text provide details, techniques, and applications pertaining to this last area. A sample is drawn of the values of one or several variables and, on the basis of how greatly they individually or collectively deviate from the expected, a conclusion is drawn: Either the process is "in control," as indicated by relatively small deviations reasonably attributable to factors other than breakdown of our assumptions regarding it, or it is "out of control," as indicated by relatively large deviations. Taking action to isolate, reduce, or eliminate out-of-control states is the principal task of quality control, and its statistical methods seek, early detection when something is wrong, and, on the other hand, avoidance of unnecessary action when something is not.

▶ 5-8 REFERENCES

Bowker, A. H., and Lieberman, G. J., (1972). *Engineering Statistics*, Second Edition, Prentice-Hall, Englewood Cliffs, NJ.

Clopper, C. J., and Pearson, E. S. (1934), "The Use of Confidence or Fiducial Limits," *Biometrika*, Vol. 26, p. 410.

Dudewicz, Edward J. (1976), *Introduction to Statistics and Probability*, Holt, Rinehart and Winston, New York.

Duncan, Acheson J. (1986), *Quality Control and Industrial Statistics*, Fifth Edition, Richard D. Irwin, Homewood, IL.

Feller, William (1957), *An Introduction to Probability Theory and Its Applications*, Vol. 1, Second Edition, Wiley, New York.

Ferrell, Enoch B. (1953), "Control Charts Using Midrange and Medians," *Industrial Quality Control*, Vol. 9. No. 5, pp. 30–54 (March).

Grant, L., and Leavenworth, R. S. (1988), *Statistical Quality Control*, Sixth Edition, McGraw-Hill, New York.

Guttman, I., Wilks, S. S., and Hunter, J. S. (1982), *Introductory Engineering Statistics*, Third Edition, Wiley, New York.

Hines, W. W., and Montgomery, D. C. (1990), *Probability and Statistics in Engineering and Management Science*, Third Edition, Wiley, New York.

▶ 5-9 PROBLEMS

1. Yarn used in the manufacture of woolen knitwear has specifications on nominal count expressed at (2/9), representing 2 ply with 9 meters per gram in each ply. Sample specimens of yarn are taken from various spinning spindles and measured for count prior to the doubling operation to see if the 9 meters per gram is being well maintained. Data for 100 measurements are given below. Prepare a frequency distribution and histogram for these data. Do these data seem to support the existence of a single underlying population? Tolerances on the count characteristic are plus and minus 5% about nominal. Does the present process meet these tolerance limits? (Determine the number and percent of measurements outside the tolerances.)

9.4	9.0	9.4	8.0	9.0	9.0	8.2	8.2	8.6	9.3
9.6	9.2	9.2	9.2	9.6	9.0	8.6	8.8	9.2	10.0
8.2	9.4	9.4	9.8	10.6	9.2	9.0	9.4	9.0	9.0
9.2	9.2	9.8	9.4	9.2	9.4	8.2	9.0	9.0	9.0
9.0	9.0	9.2	9.6	10.6	8.2	8.4	9.2	8.6	8.6

9.0	8.4	9.0	8.6	8.6	8.6	8.6	8.6	9.7	8.6
8.6	9.6	8.8	8.6	9.6	8.6	8.6	9.4	9.2	9.4
9.4	9.6	9.6	8.2	9.4	9.2	8.6	8.9	9.0	9.0
8.2	9.4	9.0	8.8	10.0	8.8	9.4	9.2	9.1	9.0
8.6	8.6	8.6	9.0	8.4	9.6	8.4	8.6	8.7	8.4

2. Data on count are obtained from a second factory producing the same yarn as in the previous problem. Measurements from 112 specimens are shown here. Repeat the previous problem for these data. How do the factories compare?

Another measure of variation often used in textile work is the coefficient of variation (*cv*), the ratio of the standard deviation and the mean ($s/\bar{x}$); it serves to compare the performance of production units such as between spinning frames, between factories, etc. Compute the *cv* (expressed in percent) for the data of the previous problem and for this problem. Which factory has the smaller *cv*?

9.1	9.1	9.1	9.1	9.2	8.9	9.3
9.1	9.1	9.1	9.1	8.9	8.8	9.3
8.9	9.2	9.2	9.1	9.2	8.8	9.2
9.2	8.6	8.6	9.1	8.8	8.5	9.5
9.1	8.8	8.8	8.8	9.2	8.6	9.0
8.9	9.2	9.2	8.9	8.8	8.9	9.1
8.6	8.9	8.9	9.1	8.8	8.8	9.1
9.3	9.0	9.0	8.8	8.8	8.6	9.2

9.0	8.8	8.8	8.9	9.1	9.1	9.2
8.5	8.9	8.8	8.8	9.0	9.2	9.5
8.8	8.8	8.6	8.9	9.2	8.9	9.4
8.6	8.5	8.7	8.8	9.1	9.3	9.5
8.9	8.6	8.7	8.7	8.9	9.3	9.7
8.8	8.5	8.9	8.7	8.9	8.9	9.4
8.7	8.6	8.6	9.0	8.9	9.0	9.6
8.8	8.8	8.8	9.0	8.8	8.8	8.8

3. A study is conducted on the filled volume of bottles of a popular beverage. During one day's production 120 bottles are sampled, and measurements are made of the volume in each bottle in milliliters (ml). The data are given here. Prepare a frequency distribution and histogram for these data. Compute the mean, variance, and standard deviation. If the labeled volume is 290 ml net, how well does the filling process fare? What is the estimated probability a bottle will contain less than the labeled volume?

288	277	302	295	276	295	281	300	296	288
294	296	287	278	296	300	298	300	297	292
278	277	300	286	304	282	292	299	295	291
294	277	288	280	296	295	294	302	296	300

283	295	279	300	274	283	299	304	298	296
300	303	282	284	294	295	296	299	307	298
296	299	288	300	274	299	293	288	284	297
278	299	282	300	295	303	296	314	298	285

296	304	299	292	298	297	295	302	285	298
285	298	297	291	280	300	277	293	284	307
300	288	280	277	299	300	282	298	298	283
303	302	282	280	293	300	292	278	300	297

4. It is desired to control the mass to a nominal of 33.5 grams for a PVC bottle used for 1 liter sale of cooking oil. Samples collected from the blow molding machine throughout one day of production reveal the following results:

32.20	32.51	33.02	32.58	32.45	33.18	32.81
32.21	32.38	33.02	32.41	32.39	32.48	32.75
32.57	32.58	32.88	32.59	32.70	32.40	32.84
32.80	32.51	33.06	33.11	32.78	32.54	32.38
32.99	32.47	32.43	33.06	32.70	32.88	32.37

32.88	32.75	32.37	33.05	32.75	32.85	32.42
32.77	32.70	32.43	32.31	32.82	32.94	32.57
32.68	32.72	32.10	32.21	32.81	33.02	32.55
32.67	33.30	32.20	32.27	33.05	32.96	32.62
32.44	33.14	32.18	32.46	33.13	32.91	

(a) Prepare a frequency distribution and a histogram for these results.
(b) Compute the mean, variance, and standard deviation.
(c) How well is the process meeting the desired nominal?

5. Cord produced for the production of fish nets has a requirement of 195 ± 15 for the number of twists per meter. Data are collected from a certain factory producing this cord by measuring the twist number on 100 cord specimens. The data are as follows:

189	204	196	193	192	201	196	201	203	193
197	205	197	205	187	195	201	204	191	201
193	197	192	209	195	192	192	193	195	200
196	204	197	196	197	204	200	196	197	192
200	193	196	200	201	189	191	192	196	196

201	205	197	202	202	196	189	200	192	193
192	192	201	201	199	193	201	197	200	195
189	205	204	195	196	195	200	205	196	200
201	205	196	192	201	197	205	201	193	196
188	193	200	196	191	192	202	206	201	197

(a) Prepare a frequency distribution and a histogram for these data.
(b) Compute the mean, variance, and standard deviation.
(c) Comment on the performance of the process with respect to the specification limits.

6. The following data are the measurements of the net mass for 120 units of margarine, filled by an automatic filling machine into plastic cups labeled at 250 grams:

251.65	250.92	251.38	250.25	251.02	251.33
252.26	251.20	251.82	250.56	251.46	251.16
251.45	251.45	249.60	249.81	250.05	250.29
251.60	249.63	251.74	250.70	249.10	250.09
249.87	251.10	250.29	250.05	251.01	249.56

250.94	250.75	251.16	251.06	249.96	251.54
250.66	251.18	250.73	250.66	249.43	251.94
252.13	251.56	250.55	251.32	249.84	252.03
250.30	249.18	251.01	249.92	249.74	251.00
251.79	251.73	249.93	250.70	249.74	251.10

252.72	249.00	250.75	249.70	251.15	251.53
251.85	251.55	251.30	249.48	248.87	250.37
251.15	251.30	250.05	250.81	251.60	251.44
250.54	251.82	250.96	250.70	250.60	249.77
249.65	250.34	249.13	251.74	250.75	250.32

250.54	251.91	249.43	251.35	250.90	250.87
250.08	249.25	249.54	251.26	248.86	250.30
249.70	251.28	250.98	251.52	251.02	249.53
251.46	249.80	249.75	250.37	249.48	250.94
250.26	251.88	250.70	249.58	251.48	251.02

(a) Prepare a frequency distribution and a histogram for these data.
(b) Compute the mean, variance, and standard deviation.
(c) Comment on the apparent nature of the distribution.
(d) Does it appear that the filling process is capable of meeting tolerances of ±1% of labeled mass? Is there an advantage to the company in producing less variation than the allowed tolerance?

7. The following are the counts of the number of match sticks in 100 boxes randomly selected from the filling machine during a day's production:

56	55	52	58	50	53	51	54	51	51
52	51	48	56	47	50	53	54	56	53
52	54	47	50	45	51	50	54	54	51
53	54	47	54	45	55	52	52	50	53
49	51	58	51	49	49	50	50	51	49
50	50	58	50	47	53	53	54	53	54
54	51	60	55	46	52	53	53	54	52
52	53	53	52	41	56	51	51	50	53
50	50	55	49	49	47	48	52	52	53
55	51	52	46	40	57	47	55	50	53

(a) Prepare a frequency distribution and a histogram for these data.

(b) Compute the mean, variance, and standard deviation for these data.

(c) Assuming that the normal distribution is a good approximation to the underlying distribution of match count, use Table A to estimate the percentage of match boxes having a count below 50 and a count below 45. Remember to use the half correction for the discrete values of count.

(d) A requirement is proposed that in a package of ten boxes there must be 500 matches—or that the average of ten boxes must be equal or greater than 50. Is the above factory able to meet this requirement with the present setting of the filling machine? If not, what adjustment in meant fill is needed? Assuming that the adjustment in mean value can be made but that the standard deviation remains the same, repeat part (c).

8. Data for a second match factory are as follows:

56	60	56	56	54	56	51	48	56	57
55	57	51	55	55	57	56	54	54	53
52	57	51	54	54	51	62	59	54	54
48	58	54	55	58	54	60	53	52	48
49	57	51	60	53	54	50	58	57	50
51	57	59	56	55	53	51	51	58	52
56	56	53	58	57	59	59	54	55	54
53	56	46	56	55	62	53	49	49	52
53	61	44	55	53	58	54	58	54	49
53	57	42	52	55	51	61	51	57	47

Repeat the previous problem for this factory.

9. A case containing twenty-four cans of vegetables has three defective cans. If five cans are selected randomly from the case, what is the probability that the sample contains:
(a) No defective cans?
(b) One defective can?
(c) Two or more defective cans?

10. A person holds two aces in a bridge hand of thirteen cards. What is the probability that his or her partner holds exactly one ace?

11. Enough well-mixed dough to make 500 raisin cookies contains 4000 raisins. What is the probability that a given cookie contains eight raisins?

12. A case of fifty manufactured parts is 8% nonconforming. If a sample of ten pieces is taken from the case, find the probability of getting one or less nonconforming part in the sample using each of the following distributions:
(a) Hypergeometric
(b) Binomial
(c) Poisson

(d) Under what assumptions would each of these procedures be correct?

13. Find the mean and variance of the following probability distributions:

(a)

x_i	p_i
0	1/16
1	3/16
2	5/16
3	5/16
4	1/8

(b) $f(x) = \begin{cases} 12x^2(1-x), & 0 < x < 1 \\ 0, & \text{otherwise} \end{cases}$

14. A random sample of fifteen parts is taken from a process, and a particular measurement is to be made on each of these pieces. If the process average is 50 and the process variance is 12, what is the probability that the mean of the sample will exceed 51.5? Assume the distribution of the measurements is normal.

15. It is proposed that a manufacturing process be inspected once each hour. It is suggested that a sample of five pieces each hour be taken, then compute the sample mean, $\bar{x}$. The process standard deviation is assumed to be constant at 0.255 in. Within what limits would one expect 95% of the sample means to be if the process average is stable at $\mu = 4.500$ in.? Assume that the measurements are from a normal population.

16. What is the probability that a sample mean would lie outside the limits determined in Problem 15 if the mean changes to 4.200?

17. A gauge manufacturer is attempting to sell a new type of gauge. The current one you are using has a standard deviation of 0.010 mm. The new gauge is much cheaper and, according to the sales agent, is just as good as far as the standard deviation goes. You make a series of 6 measurements on a carefully machined block with the new gauge and find the sample standard deviation of your measurements to be 0.015 mm. What is the probability that you would get such a result if the true standard deviation, σ, is 0.010 mm?

18. A random sample of twenty-five shafts was selected from a large lot by a receiving inspector. The requirements for diameter of this part is that the mean should not exceed 3.250 in. The following are the results of the sample. What should the inspector's decision be? Use $\alpha = 0.01$.

$$\bar{x} = 3.350 \text{ in.}$$
$$s = 0.150 \text{ in.}$$

19. For the situation in Problem 18, what is your estimate of the percentage of the lot falling above an upper limit of 3.800 in.? Use the sample data as your estimate of the parameter values.

20. A random sample of nine parts was selected from a normal population with unknown mean and variance. The following statistics were computed from the sample:

$$\bar{x} = 152.6$$
$$s = 16.3$$

(a) Determine a 90% confidence interval estimate of the mean, μ.

(b) Determine a 90% confidence interval estimate of the standard deviation, σ.

(c) Test the hypothesis that $\mu = 164$ versus the alternative that $\mu < 164$ with $\alpha = 0.05$.

(d) Test the hypothesis that $\sigma = 25$ versus the alternative that $\sigma < 25$ with $\alpha = 0.05$.

21. A large lot of manufactured goods is 10% nonconforming. A sample of twenty-five pieces is selected randomly from the lot. Compute the probability that there will be five or more nonconforming pieces in the lot using the normal approximation to the binomial.

22. Determine a 90% confidence interval estimate for the mean μ, if a sample of 10 observations yields the following results.

$$\bar{x} = 84.6$$
$$s = 10.5$$

23. For the sample results in Problem 22, determine a 90% confidence interval estimate for σ.

24. If a second sample of 10 is taken, find a 95% confidence interval estimate for the ratio of the two variances, σ_1^2/σ_2^2, where Sample 1 is the sample taken in Problem 22 and the results of Sample 2 are

$$\bar{x}_2 = 92.4$$
$$s_2 = 4.1$$

25. Find a 95% confidence interval estimate of the difference in the means of the populations from which these two samples were drawn, that is, $(\mu_2 - \mu_1)$ using the data in Problems 22 and 24.

CHAPTER

6

INTRODUCTION TO CONTROL CHARTS

Concern over variation in the measured qualities of parts and products produced for the Bell System plus related studies of sampling results from statistical models of distributions led Dr. Walter Shewhart to the development of the control chart as early as 1924.[1] Early applications were on fuses, heat coils, and station apparatus at the Hawthorne (Chicago) Works of the Western Electric Company. By 1927–1928, applications throughout the Western Electric Company were initiated by another Bell Laboratories quality control pioneer, Harold F. Dodge, in two shop-related areas: as an adjunct to all sampling inspection plans and as a basic device for demerits-per-unit charts for quality assurance ratings. Quality reports of the Bell Laboratories and of Western Electric used a number of control charts. By 1935 Dodge had prepared the *ASTM Manual on Presentation of Data* with many types of control charts.

In 1941 and 1942 Dodge served as chairman of the American Standards Association (ASA) Committee Z1, which published the ASA Standards, Z1.1, Z1.2, and Z1.3 on control charts [American Society for Quality (1985a, 1985b, 1985c)]. Widespread use of control charts followed the publication of these standards. Training courses on quality control principles and techniques sponsored by the Office of Production Research and Development of the War Production Board were instrumental in extending applications. Control charts are now widely used in every industry. They represent one of the principal sets of tools for statistical process control and related process improvement programs such as six sigma. Extensions and modifications are expanding their applications and effectiveness.

▶ 6-1 VARIATION AND THE CONTROL CHART

Shewhart observed that variation occurs everywhere in our world. There is the variation in each of a multiple of characteristics of human beings. No two snowflakes or tree leaves are exactly alike, even in their individual attributes such as shape, length, and color. The same is true of industrial and commercial processes and services—variation abounds.

The study of the behavior of this variation on important quality characteristics and help in reducing the variation for process improvements are objectives of the control chart

---

[1]An unpublished memorandum of 16 May 1924 by Walter A. Shewhart contains the first known control chart. Subsequent memoranda and papers developed the concept more completely. See, for example, Shewhart (1926a, 1926b, 1927). Further to these is his classic book [Shewhart (1931)].

as a tool of quality control. The next several chapters deal with the characterization of variation and some of the ways in which control charts are useful for its study.

6-1.1 Phenomena of Variation

Observations from any process exhibit variation and lead to the establishment of the following fundamental phenomena:

1. Everything varies—no two items or occurrences are exactly alike.
2. Individual observations are unpredictable.
3. Groups of observations either tend to form predictable patterns or produce evidence that no predictable pattern exists without some process change.

These phenomena support the acceptance of two important principles as necessary "firsts" in our scientific approach to the solution of industrial and commercial problems: (1) variation is inevitable and (2) single observations form little basis for objective decision making. It is the rational selection of samples and the application of some basic statistics and analytical tools that permit us to find recognizable and predictable patterns in the characteristics of a product, process, or service.

6-1.2 Patterns of Variation

Several significant types of patterns of variation are obtained by examining observations in various ways. Observations obtained by testing a product, process, or service for its quality characteristics may be examined by viewing a graph of the measurements in the order in which the units were measured. Another way is to plot statistics obtained from the observed values, such as single observations, averages, ranges, standard deviations, proportions, counts of nonconformities, or other functions. This is illustrated in Figure 6-1 and is often referred to as a run chart.

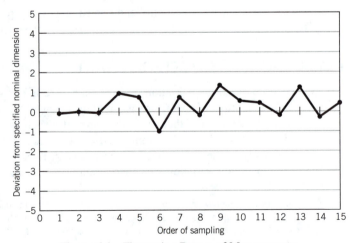

Figure 6-1 Fluctuating Pattern of Measurements

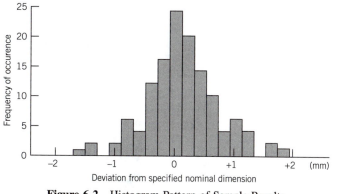

Figure 6-2 Histogram Pattern of Sample Results

Another pattern is the composite picture of a group of such measurements and the occurrence of items (frequency) having these observed values. This pattern of variation is commonly referred to as a distribution and is illustrated by the histogram of sample results shown in Figure 6-2 and discussed previously in Chapter 5. Extensions and modifications of these two basic patterns form the basis for most analyses of variation.

Devices to Demonstrate Variation

Some useful tools for demonstrating variation empirically in a classroom setting are a bead box of colored beads with sampling paddles as pictured in Figure 6-3, a quincunx as illustrated in Figure 6-4, and a bowl and numbered chips as shown in Figure 6-5.[2] These

[2]These photos are courtesy of STATCO Products, Inc., P.O. Box 65, Clawson, Michigan 48017.

Figure 6-3 Bead Box and Paddles for Sampling Demonstrations

Figure 6-4   Quincunx for Demonstrating Variation

Figure 6-5   Bowl and Numbered Chips for Demonstrations

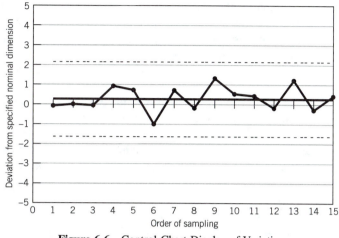

Figure 6-6 Control Chart Display of Variation

devices are used to simulate variation in the qualities or characteristics of a product or process and are very useful for teaching and learning the principles of statistical process control. The bead box and paddle are used for sampling, and the quincunx is used to describe the normal distribution. Use of the bead box is demonstrated in Section 6-2.1 and use of the quincunx in Section 6-3.1. Figures 6-1 and 6-2 represent typical data produced by these devices as representative of industrial, scientific, or natural processes. They are useful to demonstrate the kind of variation one may expect when sampling results from a fixed population representing a stable process. Additionally, they are useful to demonstrate the ability of control charts to detect changes in the population, affording some degree of confidence and understanding in the use of control charts.

The Control Chart

The control chart is a useful tool for studying variation. It employs some of the statistical theory discussed in Chapter 5 to place limits of expected variation for a fluctuating pattern. Typical is the control chart shown in Figure 6-6, which shows limits placed about the fluctuating pattern of Figure 6-1.

These limits give the control chart analytical power to enable its user to determine whether a process can be considered stable and thus predictable or unstable and unpredictable. Such information about an important quality characteristic can enable one to continue to control, in the case of a stable process operating at an acceptable level, or gain control, in the case of an unstable process. This is accomplished by repeated rational sampling of the process and analysis of the data plotted on the control chart. Unstable patterns are often associated with special or sporadic causes in the process. Stable patterns operating at unacceptable levels are often associated with common or chronic causes in the process.[3]

---

[3]The terms "special" and "common" are attributed to Ed Deming; the associated terms "sporadic" and "chronic," respectively, are attributed to Joe Juran.

A control chart is a graphic representation of the variation in the computed statistics being produced by the process. It has a decided advantage over the frequency distribution method of presenting data (e.g., Figure 6-2). It shows how the variation of a particular set of data, representing process characteristics, was produced. The frequency plot of observations shows the overall amount and form of variation during the period of time sampled, but it fails to indicate how or when that variation was produced. The control chart's advantage over the histogram is in the use of limits. The fluctuating plot of observations shows the amount and nature of variation by time, but it is scale dependent and doesn't indicate the presence or lack of statistical control. The control chart shows the amount and nature of variation by time, indicates statistical control or lack of it, and enables pattern interpretation and detection of changes in the process under study.

6-1.3 Attributes and Variables Data

There are generally two types of data that are helpful in the study of quality characteristics: attributes data and variables data. Attributes data are the mere counting, or conversion of counts to proportions or percentages, of the presence or absence of some characteristic or attribute in the units examined. They can be a measure of the number of satisfactory or unsatisfactory items in a sample for one or for many quality characteristics. They can be the number of people who favor a certain product or political candidate or have a certain disease. They can be the number of invoices with errors or the number of errors per invoice. Variables data refer to an actual measurement along a scale of a quality characteristic or process property capable of being measured. Examples are length, diameter, voltage, temperature, volume, and score.

Control charts for both types of data are available and are analytical visualizations of the corresponding distribution of the computed statistics on quality characteristics. The following demonstrations will provide some understanding of the principles of control charts as applied to the analysis of attributes and variables data. Attribute control charts are explored in greater detail in Chapter 7. Variables control charts are covered in Chapter 8.

▶ 6-2 AN ATTRIBUTE CONTROL CHART

A useful attribute control chart is the percentage control chart, or *p* chart. It is used here to demonstrate the basic behavior of attributes variation in samples drawn from a process having a stable percentage level of certain characteristics. It is used further in Chapter 7 to demonstrate how the control chart detects changes in the process resulting in a different level of the characteristics.

6-2.1 Behavior of Attributes Variation

Attribute sampling may be demonstrated by the device shown in Figure 6-3. The box of beads can represent a batch or a lot of product. The individual beads can represent discrete units of product, with beads of different colors representing units having different characteristics or attributes. The percentage level for one or more characteristics can be fixed to study the effect of variation when sampling from a stable process. For example, the bead box of Figure 6-3 has the composition of beads shown in Table 6-1.

TABLE 6-1 Composition of Bead Box

Color of Beads	Number of Beads	Percentage
White	1456	91
Red	80	5
Yellow	48	3
Black	16	1
Total	1600	100

Sampling is facilitated by a paddle with a fixed number of holes, such as the ones shown in Figure 6-3, with 25, 50, and 100 holes. For example, samples of 100 can be taken by dipping the appropriate paddle in the box of well-mixed beads. The sample is thus drawn without replacement of the individual units, a typical procedure for process inspection. However, to demonstrate results of repeated sampling from the same process, the entire sample of 100 beads is replaced and well mixed between subsequent samples.

To relate these results to an everyday process, suppose the box of beads represents a lot of glass bottles produced in a certain time period. White beads denote conforming bottles, that is, bottles having no departures from specified requirements. Red beads might denote nonconforming bottles that have too small or too large openings, as measured by the inside diameter of the mouth. For simplicity we will limit our discussion to this single quality characteristic. The first sample of 100 beads is drawn, and seven red beads are observed, a sample result of 7% nonconforming. This is an individual observation of the statistic under study. If nothing is known about this process, it would represent the best estimate of the percentage of nonconforming bottle openings with deviation from the true level by plus 2% as seen in Table 6-1. If past information were available to indicate a process capability of 5%, this sample result of 7% could represent a signal of process trouble with unnecessary investigation and adjustment.

The second sample result is six red beads. Variation in sample results is immediately apparent. Again, this might be interpreted as a 1% improvement in the process over the period represented by the first sample.

Now ask for a prediction of the next sample result and perhaps do so without placing too high a stake on being correct. The third outcome is two red beads. The production supervisor might be bragging about having reduced the process nonconforming to 2% by careful supervision and prowess with the process.

Of course these sample results are known to have come from the same bead box, representing the process. These results serve to illustrate the first two phenomena of variation introduced earlier in this chapter: Results vary, and individual observations are unpredictable. Were it not known that we were sampling from a fixed process, we might question whether this was the case. To answer such a question requires invoking the third phenomenon of variation and is directly aided by the control chart. Next obtain a larger group of sample observations. The results of twenty samples are recorded in Table 6-2. For an estimate of the true percentage of red beads, the average of the twenty samples can serve, provided that the results are from the same process. This assumption, when sampling in an unknown situation, can be verified by the use of a control chart. The control chart will be developed momentarily. From Table 6-2 we obtain the average percentage of

TABLE 6-2 Results of Twenty Samples

Sample Number	Sample Size, n	Number of Red Beads, x	Percentage of Red Beads, $p = 100(x/n)$
1	100	7	7
2	100	6	6
3	100	2	2
4	100	7	7
5	100	8	8
6	100	4	4
7	100	5	5
8	100	4	4
9	100	5	5
10	100	5	5
11	100	4	4
12	100	2	2
13	100	2	2
14	100	6	6
15	100	4	4
16	100	6	6
17	100	7	7
18	100	8	8
19	100	6	6
20	100	5	5
Totals	2000	103	

red beads (nonconforming bottle openings) as $\bar{p} = \Sigma x_i / \Sigma n_i = 103/2000 = 0.0515$, or 5.15%, a reasonable estimate of the known percentage, from Table 6-1, of 5%.

This illustrates the third phenomenon of variation: the degree of predictability evolving from groups of observations. Now, how much variation is to be expected when sampling from this process? Observe variation in the twenty samples ranging from two in 100 to eight in 100. This variation is centered at about five. To explore this further, conduct additional sampling to obtain 200 samples of size 100 from this process. Because the interest is in the overall amount and form of the variation, use a frequency distribution to summarize the results. The tally mark form of a frequency distribution is used as shown in Table 6-3.

Now observe variation ranging from zero in 100 to twelve in 100, though these extremes have occurred infrequently and values of 3, 4, 5, 6, and 7 are predominant. The significant fact is that this variation has been obtained in sampling from a fixed process. As observed, it is not unlikely to obtain samples where the largest values are three or four times the smallest values.

Equal care must be exercised in comparing today's result with yesterday's, or the 10:00 A.M. result with the 9:00 A.M. result. Some serious errors in judgment can be committed. How to cope with this variation so that unnecessary process adjustments are not made? The answer is the control chart.

TABLE 6-3 Frequency Distribution of 200 Samples

Number of Red Beads	Tally Marks of Occurrences	Observed Frequency
0	//	2
1	////	4
2	𝓣𝓗𝓛 𝓣𝓗𝓛 𝓣𝓗𝓛	15
3	𝓣𝓗𝓛 𝓣𝓗𝓛 𝓣𝓗𝓛 𝓣𝓗𝓛 𝓣𝓗𝓛	25
4	𝓣𝓗𝓛 𝓣𝓗𝓛 𝓣𝓗𝓛 𝓣𝓗𝓛 𝓣𝓗𝓛 𝓣𝓗𝓛 𝓣𝓗𝓛 /	36
5	𝓣𝓗𝓛 𝓣𝓗𝓛 𝓣𝓗𝓛 𝓣𝓗𝓛 𝓣𝓗𝓛 𝓣𝓗𝓛 𝓣𝓗𝓛	35
6	𝓣𝓗𝓛 𝓣𝓗𝓛 𝓣𝓗𝓛 𝓣𝓗𝓛 𝓣𝓗𝓛 𝓣𝓗𝓛 /	31
7	𝓣𝓗𝓛 𝓣𝓗𝓛 𝓣𝓗𝓛 𝓣𝓗𝓛	20
8	𝓣𝓗𝓛 𝓣𝓗𝓛 ///	18
9	𝓣𝓗𝓛 𝓣𝓗𝓛	10
10	//	2
11	/	1
12	/	1
	Total	200

6-2.2 Constancy in Variation

The control chart was developed to recognize constant patterns of variation. When observed variation fails to satisfy criteria for controlled patterns, the chart indicates this. A control chart indicates when to attempt to locate assignable causes.[4]

The placement of expected limits of variation about a fluctuating pattern of observations distinguishes the control chart and gives it analytical capability. In view of the variation observed in the demonstration, as shown in Table 6-3, where are the control limits to be set and on what basis?

Underlying Distribution

Sampling for attribute data is known to follow the binomial distribution introduced in Chapter 5. This is characterized by the following probability function:

$$b(x) = \binom{n}{x}(\theta)^x(1 - \theta)^{n-x} \tag{6-1}$$

where

n = the sample size

θ = the true proportion of units in the universe having the characteristics of interest

---

[4]"Assignable causes" is the term used by Shewhart to denote those causes operating in the process that result in changes in the parameters of the underlying distribution and hence lack of statistical control on control charts. He reasoned that proper use of control charts would allow these causes to be located or "assigned" and thus removed by action on the process. As was mentioned earlier, these are also referred to as "special" or "sporadic" causes.

x = the random variable denoting the number of units in the sample having the characteristics of interest with integer values ranging from 0 to n

$b(x)$ = the probability that x units will be observed in a sample of size n

Since $\theta = 0.05$, sampling results should obey the following probability law:

$$b(x) = \binom{100}{x}(0.05)^x(0.95)^{100-x} \tag{6-2}$$

Under the condition of an unknown situation, as is usual for industrial processes, substitute the computed average, $\bar{p}$, of 0.0515 as an estimate for θ, based on knowledge of the initial twenty samples. These two cases, (1) knowledge of the population and use of known or standard parameter values and (2) no prior knowledge of the population and use of statistics computed from sample results, are known in control chart work as the cases of *standard given* and *no standard given*, respectively. They are presented in greater detail in subsequent chapters.

Just how well do these results obey the above probability law? By using the data of Table 6-3, observed frequencies can be compared to the expected frequencies obtained from the probability law. This comparison is shown in Table 6-4.

Visual agreement is seen to be close and is a further illustration of the third phenomenon of variation. This comparison may be subjected to a more analytical scrutiny via various statistical tests. The assumption of an underlying binomial distribution is justified. One can then develop expected limits of variation or control limits for the control chart on the percentage or proportion of red beads (nonconforming bottles) in the demonstration.

Control Limits, Risks, and Decision Errors

Control charts allow us to distinguish between controlled and uncontrolled processes. They must do this in light of sampling variation in the computed statistic and based on

TABLE 6-4 Observed versus Expected (Binomial) Variation

Number of Red Beads, x	Observed Frequency Count, f	Observed Frequency Proportion, $f(x)$	Expected Frequency Proportion, $b(x)$
0	2	0.0100	0.00592
1	4	0.0200	0.03116
2	15	0.0750	0.08118
3	25	0.1250	0.13958
4	36	0.1800	0.17814
5	35	0.1750	0.18002
6	31	0.1550	0.15002
7	20	0.1000	0.10603
8	18	0.0900	0.06487
9	10	0.0500	0.03490
10	2	0.0100	0.01672
11	1	0.0050	0.00720
12	1	0.0050	0.00281
Totals	200	1.0000	0.99855

the underlying distribution. Prescribed control limits, denoting the expected limits of variation, must therefore consider the amount of variation and the distribution of the statistic under study. Where are the limits to be drawn in the above example? Are limits of 0 to 12 to be used or 1 to 10, with some risk of exceeding the limits with the occasional occurrence of a 0, an 11, a 12, or even a 13, when sampling from the same process?

It is unreasonable to draw limits that will distinguish with *absolute perfection* between the above process and another at a different underlying percentage nonconforming level. There will be some risks of wrong conclusions or decisions in the use of the control chart. Control limits are designed to balance somewhat two important risks of errors associated with their use: (1) the risk of declaring an out-of-control condition when there has been no change in the underlying process and (2) the risk of not detecting an actual change in the process. These errors were referred to in Chapter 5 as error of the first kind (Type I error) and error of the second kind (Type II error). Symbols to express values of the risks of making these errors are α and β. The development of the basic concepts of these errors was a major contribution of Shewhart to statistical theory.

For a fixed population it is possible to select the level of the risk of making the first type of error. Common practice is to select a very small value for this risk, of the magnitude of 3 in 1000. Because the second type of error is associated with a departure of a parameter from a fixed value, with varying degrees of departure possible, this risk is allowed to go unspecified. It is a consideration in the selection of such factors as sample size or location of control limits. Control charts for averages that allow for specification of both risks are referred to as *acceptance control charts* and are discussed in Chapter 9.

Two general practices in the setting of control limits have evolved. One is based on the principle of obtaining control limits by an estimate of the average of the statistic under study plus and minus ($\pm$) a multiple (commonly 3) of an estimate of the standard deviation of the statistic being plotted. The other is based on the establishment of limits for specified probability values, commonly 0.001, 0.002, or 0.005. The first is of U.S. origin; the second is of British origin. Subsequent chapters consider this matter in greater detail. For convenience in most of the common control charts, the first method is preferred. For most applications three standard deviations suffice, as this satisfies the objective of setting a very small value on the risk of a Type I error.

For the attribute chart in our demonstration, derivation of control limits by the first practice mentioned above is therefore based on the following formula:

$$\text{Control limits} = \theta \pm 3\sigma_p, \quad \text{when } \theta \text{ is known or assumed}$$

If a standard value of θ is to be used (the standard given case), p_0, which is the standard, will be substituted for θ, and control limits will be obtained as $p_0 \pm 3\sigma_p$. In the no standard given case, an estimate of θ must be used. This estimate is usually $\bar{p} = \bar{x}/n$ (for constant n).

Choose as before, $p_0 = 0.05$ as a standard, based on knowledge of the population, in contrast to using $\bar{p} = 0.0515$ as an estimate of θ. Therefore develop control limits under the case of standard given since the parameter is known. For the standard deviation, σ_{p_0}, obtain the following formula from the binomial probability function $b(x)$, Equation (6-1) with parameter p_0 substituted for θ:

$$\sigma_{p_0} = \sqrt{\frac{p_0(1 - p_0)}{n}} \tag{6-3}$$

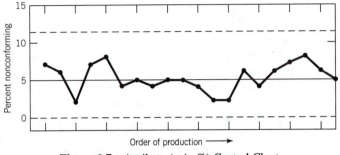

Figure 6-7   Attribute (p in %) Control Chart

Hence, control limits for the p chart of this demonstration are

$$\text{Control limits} = p_0 \pm 3 \sqrt{\frac{p_0(1 - p_0)}{n}} \tag{6-4}$$

$$= 0.05 \pm 3 \sqrt{\frac{(0.05)(0.95)}{n}}$$

$$= 0.115 \text{ and } 0.0$$

where the lower control limit is fixed by convention in not using a negative lower control limit (in this case, -0.0154), since by the nature of the statistic, p cannot be negative. Thus truncate the lower control limit at zero when a negative value is computed.

The control chart for the data of Table 6-2 with the above control limits is shown in Figure 6-7. The pattern is seen to fall within the control limits and to fluctuate about the centerline of 5% in a random manner. This control within limits is indicative of constancy in variation, denoting that the variation is what would be expected in samples from a stable process.

This control chart could now be used to monitor the process—for example, the glass bottle process—to determine whether and when the percentage of nonconforming bottle openings undergoes a change in level. Points falling above the upper control limit or a sufficient pattern of points falling above the centerline serve to indicate a shift to a greater level of nonconformance. Such a condition would warrant process investigation to trace causes of the shift. Then take action to return the process to the previous level or, if possible, to a more desirable lower level of nonconformance. Management of the glass bottle factory should not be satisfied with a percentage level of 5% nonconforming bottle openings, even though the control chart indicates a controlled pattern at that level.

One might, in fact, prefer an out-of-control pattern, indicating the presence of assignable causes, that, when located and eliminated, would result in a reduced level of nonconformance. If there is a pattern indicating a stable process at a level of nonconformance that is considered too high for economic production, one is often forced to make major process changes to reduce the level of nonconformance.[5] The above control chart could be used to continue to monitor results to confirm progress in reducing the level of nonconformance

---

[5]A significant evolution of the work of Shewhart (1931) is the recognition of two major types of quality problems, defined by Juran as sporadic and chronic and by Deming as special and common. Whereas Shewhart's developments concentrated on the sporadic or special causes, Juran and Deming have successfully placed emphasis on breakthroughs accomplished by addressing the chronic or common causes of quality problems.

as indicated by a sufficient pattern of points falling below the centerline. To detect such shifts in the process to a lower level requires pattern interpretation as part of the criteria for judging out-of-control conditions. Both of these situations, shifts to the high side and shifts to the low side, are demonstrated in Chapter 7.

▶ 6-3 VARIABLES CONTROL CHARTS

Variables control charts are employed when it is necessary to examine a scaler, or measurement, characteristic as opposed to the presence of an attribute. Control charts for averages ($\bar{x}$) and ranges (R) are often used for such scaler variables. Other variables' control charts exist, and they will be presented in Chapter 8.

6-3.1 Behavior of Variables Data

First examine the basic behavior of variation in variables data from a fixed or stable process. The initial device to be used for the study of variables type data is the quincunx, or "statistical pinball machine," pictured in Figure 6-4. Balls or beads representing the basic raw materials are dropped through rows of pins representing steps in the process by which the raw materials are formed, with variation imparted, into the final product. Collection channels at the bottom represent measurements made on an important quality characteristic on a scale of 1 through 25. The device includes a feeding mechanism and an adjustable funnel for direction of the beads or raw materials to the pins or process operations. Think of these adjustments as representing management actions. Suppose 250 balls are allowed to fall through the pins and collect in the measurement channels. The result is the sample distribution shown by the histogram of Figure 6-8.

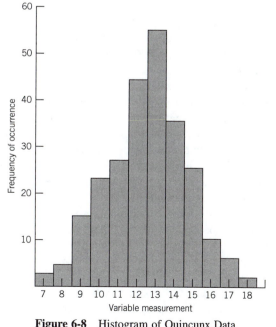

Figure 6-8 Histogram of Quincunx Data

TABLE 6-5   Extended Quincunx Data

Observed Value	Cumulative Sums of Frequency of Occurrence					
	1	4	8	12	16	20
4	—	—	—	—	1	1
5	—	—	1	1	1	2
6	—	—	—	1	2	3
7	3	7	11	17	26	33
8	5	24	47	72	95	118
9	15	47	99	140	191	236
10	23	117	229	324	448	567
11	27	125	272	439	600	751
12	44	197	349	587	768	957
13	55	201	381	562	728	895
14	35	125	279	426	558	688
15	25	93	175	261	350	436
16	10	41	76	115	150	208
17	6	18	31	47	66	87
18	2	5	5	6	13	14
19	—	—	—	—	1	1
20	—	—	—	2	2	3
Totals	250	1000	2000	3000	4000	5000

The variation is seen to range from 7 to 18 on the 1 to 25 scale. The frequency of occurrence increases for the measured values of 7 to 13 and then decreases again up to values of 18. Values of 12 and 13 are predominant, with values on either side decreasing in frequency.

This sample result is indicative of an underlying theoretical population or process. The phenomena of variation (Section 6-1.1)—especially the third, that groups of observations can form patterns—provide direction regarding this process. Now collect twenty additional samples of 250 balls. To see how the patterns become clearer with increasing numbers of samples, compute cumulative sums of the frequency of occurrences for each observed value in increments of four samples. The results are displayed in Table 6-5. Using a frequency polygon approach, these results are displayed in a more pictorial form of distributions in Figure 6-9.

With increasing cumulation a smoothing of the lines connecting the points of frequency of occurrence for the integer values of our variable is observed. There is a settling-in to a particular distributional form. But of what form? The answer is somewhat obscured in the patterns of Figure 6-9 owing to the lack of continuity in the values of the variable. Proceed to remove the discreteness and simultaneously explore the fit of the data to the normal distribution, a functional form that is known to occur with striking universality to variables' characteristics in industrial processes.

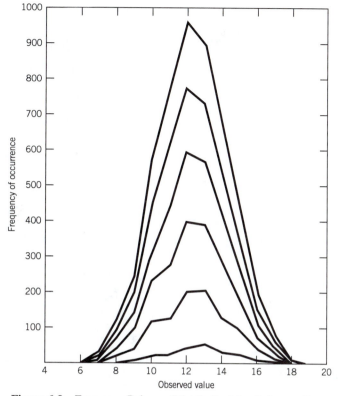

Figure 6-9 Frequency Polygon (Distribution) for Quincunx Data

6-3.2 Normal Distribution

The normal distribution was introduced in Chapter 5 as Equation (5-26). It was characterized by the following probability density function:

$$f(x; \mu, \sigma) = \frac{1}{\sqrt{2\pi}\sigma} e^{-1/2[(x-\mu)/\sigma]^2}, \qquad -\infty < x < \infty \tag{6-5}$$

where the parameters μ and σ denote the mean and standard deviation, respectively; the random variable x denotes the value of the measurable quality characteristic with continuous domain ranging from $-\infty$ to $+\infty$; $f(x)$ denotes the ordinate of the function; and $\int_a^b f(x) \, dx$ denotes the probability that the random variable x will lie between a and b.

Because there is no prior knowledge of the parameters of this function as a possible explanation for the variation in the demonstration process, estimates for these parameters from the available data must be obtained. Use the sample mean, $\bar{x}$, and sample standard deviation, s, computed from the sample distribution in the far right column of Table 6-5. The results to three decimal places are as follows:

$$\bar{x} = \hat{\mu} = 12.338, \qquad s = \hat{\sigma} = 2.068$$

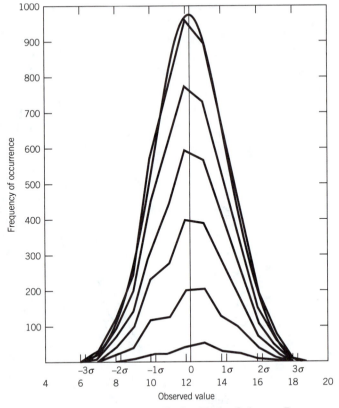

Figure 6-10 Normal Distribution Fit for Quincunx Data

Substitute these values for μ and σ in Equation (6-5). First, obtain the resultant ordinates, $f(x)$, for each of a series of values of x such as from 4.5 in increments of 0.5 to 19.5, including some special intermediate values of x such as 8.202 (representing $-2\hat{\sigma}$), 10.270 ($-1\hat{\sigma}$), 12.338 ($\bar{x}$), 14.406 ($+1\hat{\sigma}$), and 16.474 ($+2\hat{\sigma}$). Each of these ordinates is then multiplied by 5000 to obtain scaled values for comparison with the uppermost frequency polygon of Figure 6-9, representing the frequency distribution in the far right column of Table 6-5. These scaled values are then plotted on Figure 6-9. The result is shown in Figure 6-10. The central tendency and the dispersion of the normal distribution have been shown by drawing in the centerline at $\bar{x}$ and showing the scale in terms of standard deviations, $\hat{\sigma}$, from the centerline. This serves to illustrate the properties of the parameters μ and σ of the normal distribution, in that almost all (99.73%) of the values fall in the interval $\mu \pm 3\sigma$.

Next obtain for the observed data and the normal distribution the comparison equivalent to Table 6-4 for the binomial distribution. The observed frequencies are obtained as relative proportions by division by 5000 for each of the frequencies of occurrence in the far right column of Table 6-5. Corresponding expected frequencies from the normal distribution (with $\mu = 12.338$ and $\sigma = 2.068$) are obtained by successive integration of $f(x)$

TABLE 6-6   Observed versus Expected (Normal) Variation

Observed Value, x	Observed Frequency Count, f	Observed Frequency Proportion, $f(x)$	Expected Frequency Proportion, $F(x + 0.5) - F(x - 0.5)$
4	1	0.0002	0.000075
5	2	0.0004	0.000397
6	3	0.0006	0.001907
7	33	0.0066	0.007277
8	118	0.0236	0.022078
9	236	0.0472	0.053245
10	567	0.1134	0.102081
11	751	0.1502	0.155597
12	957	0.1914	0.188563
13	895	0.1790	0.181686
14	688	0.1376	0.139187
15	436	0.0872	0.084777
16	208	0.0416	0.041050
17	87	0.0174	0.015802
18	14	0.0028	0.004835
19	1	0.0002	0.001176
20	3	0.0006	0.000227
Totals	5000	1.0000	0.999960

over intervals of one unit width, with the corresponding integer values of our variable as the center points of the intervals. For example,

$$\int_{9.5}^{10.5} f(x)dx = F(10.5) - F(9.5) = 0.102081$$

where $F(x)$ represents the cumulative normal distribution function, which is readily evaluated by the cumulative standard normal distribution, $\Phi((x - \mu)/\sigma)$ tabulated in Table A in the Appendix. Details on using Table A are found in Section 5-5.2. The comparison is shown in Table 6-6.

Visual agreement is observed to be very close. It seems reasonable to assume the normal distribution to be the underlying universe for this demonstration device. If a more definitive statement is required, a goodness-of-fit test such as the chi square test could be used. The data might also be plotted on normal probability paper. For references to these procedures, see Shapiro (1990) and Chapter 8.

The normal distribution is a very remarkable phenomenon. It is beyond the scope of this book to explore it in complete detail. However, because it is so important in quality control work and is referenced frequently in the text, one of its properties which helps to explain the reason for its predominance will be explored.

When a fair die is tossed, expect its six sides to occur face up with equal probability. Assume the six integer values, 1 through 6, occur with probability 1/6 each, and this describes the theoretical distribution for the die-tossing experiments. If a pair of dice is

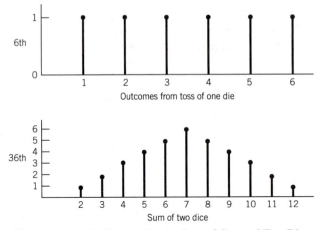

Figure 6-11   Distributions for the Sum of One and Two Dice

tossed, each die follows its own individual distribution as above. But when one considers combining the results in the toss of a pair of dice (or one die twice) in terms of the sum of the faces showing, a different distribution results. Simple probability principles permit the calculation of the probabilities for the sums ranging in integers from 2 through 12. The distributions for one die and the sum of two dice are shown in Figure 6-11.

The distributions for the sums of three dice and of six dice are shown in Figure 6-12. The form of the normal distribution is already apparent for the sum of three dice and is quite striking for the sum of six dice, in spite of the fact that the variables (sums) are discrete. This phenomenon is not without theory. As early as the 1730s, Abraham DeMoivre developed the function as an approximation to the binomial. His work and the later work of Laplace and Gauss combine to give us the first form of what is now known as the Central Limit Theorem.[6] Simply stated, this theorem tells us that the form of the distribution of sample sums approaches the form of a normal distribution as the size of the sample increases, regardless of the form of the distribution from which the samples were drawn.

This is often regarded as one of the most remarkable theorems of mathematics. But the practical behavior of sums is even more remarkable. The theorem applies to the limiting case, yet observe in the case of dice tossing, the rapid manner with which sums take on the form of the normal distribution. This is considering sums of variables, each having a distribution that is quite nonnormal and discrete (as seen in Figure 6-11). This phenomenon applies to sums in general; and as averages are but a scale change (sum divided by its sample size), the distribution of averages of even small samples (3, 4, or 5) will be approximately a normal distribution.

This behavior of sums has significant implications for its association with many variable quality characteristics in industrial and scientific processes. Many measured quality characteristics of products and services are the result of a summing components, particles, or

---

[6]DeMoivre's *The Doctrine of Chances* appeared in 1718. But his development of the function now known as the *normal* appeared later as an appendix. Laplace's *Theorie Analytique des Probabilités* appeared in 1812. Gauss gave us the normal distribution in its usual bell-shaped form in his *Disquisitions Arithmeticae* in 1801. In fact, the distribution is often given his name.

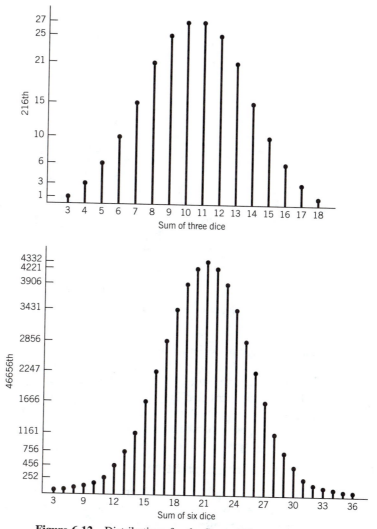

Figure 6-12   Distributions for the Sum of Three and Six Dice

processes. For example, consider a length of yarn. It has been formed from fibers, natural or synthetic, by carding and spinning of multiple fibers. The strength of a length of yarn is the composite strength of its component fibers. It is therefore not surprising for this characteristic to be normally distributed. This same example may be extended to the making of woven or knitted fabrics. Many quality characteristics—for example, length, width, thickness, weight, and strength of the finished fabric—are the result of additions of yarn characteristics. Filling an order may consist of multiple steps, each with a different variable time, so that the time it takes to fill an order will be a sum. So it is with many quality characteristics.

With some reflection on the universality of this principle to variables characteristics, one may be tempted to wonder where the normal distribution does not apply. There are

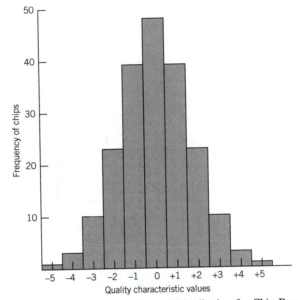

Figure 6-13 Approximate Normal Distribution for Chip Bowl

many relationships besides arithmetic summing, such as geometrical and exponential effects. For example, although the length and width of a manufactured article might be normally distributed, its surface area (the product of its length and width) will not necessarily be normally distributed. Hence, other distributions will also be considered for variables characteristics. However, certain departures from normality do not seriously affect the use of control charts with control limits based on the assumption of normality.

6-3.3 Control Charts for Averages and Ranges

Having examined the behavior of variables data and established a rationale for the applicability of the normal distribution, a demonstration of the average $(\bar{x})$ and range (R) control charts will be used for introduction. Previously quincunx and dice were used for demonstrations; now return to the box of beads (Section 6-2.1). Using the bead box, assume a process about which everything is known by preassigning frequencies to values of a hypothetical quality characteristic. Make it a bowl with chips, as shown in Figure 6-5. Figure 6-13 shows the initial distribution to be used, in histogram form, representing an approximate normal distribution with parameters of 0.0 for the mean, μ, and 1.72 for the standard deviation, σ.

For the variables chart, explore initially the constancy in variation of averages and ranges of small samples from a fixed or stable process.[7] In Chapter 8 the ability of the variables control charts for averages and ranges are demonstrated to detect changes in the

---

[7]The normal distribution, as for others such as the binomial distribution for the attribute control chart demonstrated earlier, can be simulated on a computer with samples drawn by a random number generator with appropriate functional transformations. The statistical software package MINITAB has this capability, for example.

process. In this case, companion use of the average and range control charts permits the detection of different kinds of changes in the underlying distribution. This will serve to emphasize basic characteristics of distributions as well as the use of control charts to trace causes of process difficulties.

Averages and Ranges

Organizations are generally interested in individual items, such as units of product, and the values of one or more quality characteristics on these individual items. Averages and ranges computed from small samples or subgroups of individual items provide sensitive measures of the underlying process. They permit one to control, predict, and otherwise make decisions about the process. Control charts for individual measurements are also available for use and are discussed in Chapter 8. Their use is generally reserved for characteristics for which it is impractical to replicate observations and to form subgroups of observations to aid in the study of process variation. If averages of many observations before and after a change are compared, the change can more rapidly and accurately be detected. Additionally, the range from these subgroups, as a measure of the variability in the process, provides further information and control of the process performance. These two statistics are used to study a process.

Initially, assume that the process is producing the distribution of Figure 6-13 consistently each time a sample is drawn. Suppose the measurements represent deviations from a specified net weight in grams of a medicated cream packaged in glass jars.

Select for this demonstration a commonly used sample size, n, of five units. Mix the chips in the bowl and randomly draw five chips without replacement, since the bias from not replacing each chip is small. However replace each sample of five chips and mix again before drawing the next sample. Each sample of five might represent five consecutive jars from a single filling head or station.

The first sample result is as follows, arranged in descending order within the subgroup:

$$2, 1, 0, -1, \text{ and } -2$$

Sampling variation in the individual measurements is apparent. The average, $\bar{x}$, for the subgroup is the arithmetic mean of n values, as follows:

$$\bar{x} = \sum_{i=1}^{n} x_i/n = 0/5 = 0 \tag{6-6}$$

The range, R, for the subgroup is the difference between the largest, x_{max}, and the smallest, x_{min}, observations in the subgroup, as follows:

$$R = x_{max} - x_{min} \tag{6-7}$$
$$= (+2) - (-2) = 4$$

The second sample result is

$$1, 0, -2, -3, -3$$

resulting in an average ($\bar{x}$) of -1.4 and a range (R) of 4. Thus, variation in the computed statistics, $\bar{x}$ and R, is also apparent. The results of twenty samples of five are shown in Table 6-7. Calculations of the totals, averages, and ranges are shown for each sample.

TABLE 6-7   Data for Twenty Samples of Size 5

	2	1	3	0	3	3	1	1	2	2
	1	0	0	0	2	0	1	0	0	1
	0	−2	−1	−2	1	0	0	0	0	0
	−1	−3	−2	−2	0	0	0	0	−1	−1
	−2	−3	−3	−3	−1	−1	−1	−1	−1	−3
Total	0	−7	−3	−7	5	2	1	0	0	−1
Average $(\bar{x})$	0.0	−1.4	−0.6	−1.4	1.0	0.4	0.2	0.0	0.0	−0.2
Range (R)	4	4	6	3	4	4	2	2	3	5
	1	3	2	2	2	1	2	5	1	4
	0	1	2	1	−1	1	1	2	1	1
	0	1	1	0	−2	0	−1	2	−1	0
	−1	1	1	−1	−2	−1	−1	1	−1	0
	−1	−1	1	−2	−3	−2	−3	−1	−2	0
Total	−1	5	7	0	−6	−1	−2	9	−2	5
Average $(\bar{x})$	−0.2	1.0	1.4	0.0	−1.2	−0.2	−0.4	1.8	−0.4	1.0
Range (R)	2	4	1	4	5	3	5	6	3	4

To set up control charts for each of these statistics, expected limits of variation (control limits) must be determined for each statistic. Just how much do these statistics vary among samples drawn from a stable process? What are the distributions for these statistics?

Averages

It has already been observed that averages are approximately normally distributed regardless of the distribution of the individual measurements from which the averages are computed. In sampling from a normally distributed universe, the underlying distribution for averages is normal even for the smallest sample size. From this theory, how do the parameters of the distribution of averages compare with those of the population of individual values from which the averages are computed? Explore this initially using an empirical approach and confirm the conjectured relationships by mathematical derivation. The distribution of sample averages of 250 samples of five is presented in Table 6-8. The expected normal shape is apparent. Computation of the overall average $(\bar{\bar{x}})$, the average of averages, and the standard deviation of the averages, $s_{\bar{x}}$, reveals values of 0.065 and 0.794. The overall average, $\bar{\bar{x}}$, is located near the mean of the universe of individual values as might be expected. The standard deviation, $s_{\bar{x}}$, is less than the standard deviation, σ, of the universe of individual values. This result is also expected, as it is unlikely for all values in a sample (in this case of size 5) to come from one tail of the universe. Averages will tend to have smaller spreads than individual observations. For our empirical data a ratio of $\sigma/s_{\bar{x}} = 1.72/0.794 = 2.17$ is obtained. The spread or dispersion of the averages is less than one half the spread of the individuals. For the expected relationship between the spread of averages and individuals, this single result is insufficient for making a general conclusion. To approach this empirically would require a large number of experimental results, including the use of different sample sizes.

TABLE 6-8   Frequency Distribution of Averages for 250 Samples

Average, $\bar{x}$	Tally Marks of Occurrences	Observed Frequency
2.0	///	3
1.8	////	4
1.6	𝓣𝓗𝓛	5
1.4	𝓣𝓗𝓛	5
1.2	𝓣𝓗𝓛 ///	8
1.0	𝓣𝓗𝓛 𝓣𝓗𝓛 /	11
0.8	𝓣𝓗𝓛 𝓣𝓗𝓛 𝓣𝓗𝓛 //	17
0.6	𝓣𝓗𝓛 𝓣𝓗𝓛 ////	14
0.4	𝓣𝓗𝓛 𝓣𝓗𝓛 𝓣𝓗𝓛 𝓣𝓗𝓛 𝓣𝓗𝓛 /	26
0.2	𝓣𝓗𝓛 𝓣𝓗𝓛 𝓣𝓗𝓛 𝓣𝓗𝓛 ////	24
0.0	𝓣𝓗𝓛 𝓣𝓗𝓛 𝓣𝓗𝓛 𝓣𝓗𝓛 𝓣𝓗𝓛 ////	29
−0.2	𝓣𝓗𝓛 𝓣𝓗𝓛 𝓣𝓗𝓛 𝓣𝓗𝓛 ////	24
−0.4	𝓣𝓗𝓛 𝓣𝓗𝓛 𝓣𝓗𝓛 𝓣𝓗𝓛 ////	24
−0.6	𝓣𝓗𝓛 𝓣𝓗𝓛 𝓣𝓗𝓛 /	16
−0.8	𝓣𝓗𝓛 𝓣𝓗𝓛 /	11
−1.0	𝓣𝓗𝓛 𝓣𝓗𝓛	10
−1.2	𝓣𝓗𝓛 ////	9
−1.4	////	4
−1.6	///	3
−1.8	//	2
−2.0		0
−2.2	/	1
	Total	250

Instead refer to a mathematical derivation to discover this relationship. These relationships were derived in Chapter 5. The results are as follows:

$$\text{Mean of averages, } E(\bar{x}) = \mu \qquad (6\text{-}8)$$

Standard deviation of averages $(\sigma_{\bar{x}})$	equals	Standard deviation of individuals (σ)	divided by	Square root of the sample size $(\sqrt{n})$

$$\sigma_{\bar{x}} = \sigma/\sqrt{n} \qquad (6\text{-}9)$$

These relationships are important in quality control work and are used in the derivation of control limits for the average ($\bar{x}$) control chart.

Following the earlier discussion on the development of an attribute control chart, and using the three standard deviation principle for obtaining control limits, those for the average ($\bar{x}$) control chart are based on the following formulas:

$$\text{Control limits} = \mu \pm 3\sigma_{\bar{x}} = \mu \pm 3\sigma/\sqrt{n}$$

when μ and σ are known, and this result is expressed more simply as

$$\text{Control limits} = \bar{x}_0 \pm A\sigma_0 \qquad (6\text{-}10)$$

where $\bar{x}_0$ and σ_0 are standards or known values of μ and σ and $A = 3/\sqrt{n}$. A, as a function of the sample size (n), is tabulated in Table G in the Appendix, and

$$\text{Control limits} = \bar{\bar{x}} \pm 3\sigma_{\bar{x}}$$

when μ and σ are unknown, and $\bar{\bar{x}}$ is used as an estimate for μ. Although it is possible to compute $s_{\bar{x}}$ from a series of averages to be used as an estimate of $\sigma_{\bar{x}}$, an alternative estimate that makes use of Equation (6-9) and the average range ($\bar{R}$) is preferred. It is developed next under discussion of ranges.

Ranges

The range is an order statistic in that its measure depends on the ordering of the individual values in a sample. It is the difference between the largest and smallest values. The theory and techniques of order statistics may be studied in depth; however, that is outside the scope of this text. This statistic will be presented using an empirical approach for initial understanding. Ranges for the 250 samples of five have the distribution shown in Table 6-9. The ranges are seen to vary from 0 through 8. The pattern is reasonably symmetrical, though perhaps skewed somewhat to the high side, a characteristic of the distribution of the range statistic. It is fairly well centered at 4, which is the distribution mode. The computed average range ($\bar{R}$) and the standard deviation of the ranges (s_R) are 3.996 and 1.457, respectively.

Early interest in the range and its properties including quality control applications was shown in a series of papers by Tippett (1925), Pearson (1926), McKay and Pearson (1935), Pearson and Hartley (1942), and Hartley (1942). This work has generated tables giving the mean value and standard deviation of the range from random samples drawn from the normal distribution as well as tables of the probability integral of the range. Since the range is a measure of dispersion, two significant relationships have evolved from the referenced work as follows:

The standard deviation of individuals (σ)	equals	True average range (μ_R)	divided by	Constant of proportionality factor (d_2)

$$\sigma = \mu_R/d_2 \tag{6-11}$$

The standard deviation of individuals (σ)	equals	Standard deviation of range (σ_R)	divided by	Constant of proportionality factor (d_3)

$$\sigma = \sigma_R/d_3 \tag{6-12}$$

where d_2 and d_3 are functions of the sample size (n) from which the ranges (R) are obtained. They are tabulated in Table H in the Appendix.

These relationships are important in quality control work and are used along with those of Equations (6-8) and (6-9) in the derivation of control limits for the average ($\bar{x}$) and range (R) control charts. First examine how well these relationships estimate σ for the empirical data. The factors d_2 and d_3 for sample size 5 are 2.326 and 0.864. The computed values of $\bar{R}$ of 3.996 and $s_R = 1.457$ give the estimate

TABLE 6-9   Frequency Distribution of Ranges for 250 Samples

Range, R	Tally Marks of Occurrences	Observed Frequency
8	////	4
7	𝟙𝟙𝟙𝟙 𝟙𝟙𝟙𝟙	10
6	𝟙𝟙𝟙𝟙 𝟙𝟙𝟙𝟙 𝟙𝟙𝟙𝟙 𝟙𝟙𝟙𝟙 ////	24
5	𝟙𝟙𝟙𝟙 𝟙𝟙𝟙𝟙 𝟙𝟙𝟙𝟙 𝟙𝟙𝟙𝟙 𝟙𝟙𝟙𝟙 𝟙𝟙𝟙𝟙 𝟙𝟙𝟙𝟙 𝟙𝟙𝟙𝟙 //	42
4	𝟙𝟙𝟙𝟙 𝟙𝟙𝟙𝟙 𝟙𝟙𝟙𝟙 𝟙𝟙𝟙𝟙 𝟙𝟙𝟙𝟙 𝟙𝟙𝟙𝟙 𝟙𝟙𝟙𝟙 𝟙𝟙𝟙𝟙 𝟙𝟙𝟙𝟙 𝟙𝟙𝟙𝟙 𝟙𝟙𝟙𝟙 𝟙𝟙𝟙𝟙 𝟙𝟙𝟙𝟙 𝟙𝟙𝟙𝟙 𝟙𝟙𝟙𝟙 //	77
3	𝟙𝟙𝟙𝟙 𝟙𝟙𝟙𝟙 𝟙𝟙𝟙𝟙 𝟙𝟙𝟙𝟙 𝟙𝟙𝟙𝟙 𝟙𝟙𝟙𝟙 𝟙𝟙𝟙𝟙 𝟙𝟙𝟙𝟙 𝟙𝟙𝟙𝟙 𝟙𝟙𝟙𝟙 𝟙𝟙𝟙𝟙	55
2	𝟙𝟙𝟙𝟙 𝟙𝟙𝟙𝟙 𝟙𝟙𝟙𝟙 𝟙𝟙𝟙𝟙 𝟙𝟙𝟙𝟙 𝟙𝟙𝟙𝟙 ///	33
1	////	4
0	/	1
		Total 250

$$\hat{\sigma} = \overline{R}/d_2 = 3.996/2.326 = 1.718$$

$$\hat{\sigma} = s_R/d_3 = 1.457/0.864 = 1.686$$

where $\sigma = 1.72$ in the universe sampled.

Using the three standard deviation principle for obtaining control limits for the range control chart yields the following formulas:

$$\text{Control limits} = \mu_R \pm 3\sigma_R = d_2\sigma \pm 3d_3\sigma, \qquad \text{from (6-11) and (6-12)}$$

$$= (d_2 \pm 3d_3)\sigma$$

when σ is known. For the standard given case this result is expressed as

$$UCL_R = D_2\sigma_0 \tag{6-13}$$

where

$$D_2 = d_2 + 3d_3$$

σ_0 = known or standard value of σ

$$LCL_R = D_1\sigma_0 \tag{6-14}$$

where $D_1 = d_2 - 3d_3$, and D_1 and D_2, along with d_2 and d_3, are functions of the sample size (n) and are tabulated in Table H in the Appendix.

$$\text{Control limits} = \overline{R} \pm 3\hat{\sigma}_R$$

when σ is unknown, where $\overline{R}$ is used as an estimate for μ_R. Although it is possible to compute s_R from a series of ranges to be used as an estimate of σ_R, combining Equations (6-11) and (6-12) allows the expression of $\hat{\sigma}_R$ in terms of $\overline{R}$ as follows:

$$\sigma_R = d_3\sigma, \qquad \text{from Equation (6-12)}$$

$$\hat{\sigma}_R = d_3(\overline{R}/d_2), \qquad \text{from Equation (6-11)} \tag{6-15}$$

Hence,

$$\text{Control limits} = \overline{R} \pm 3\hat{\sigma}_R = \overline{R} \pm 3d_3(\overline{R}/d_2)$$

$$= (1 \pm 3d_3/d_2)\overline{R}$$

which, again for convenience, is expressed more simply as

$$UCL_R = D_4\overline{R} \tag{6-16}$$

where

$$D_4 = (1 + 3d_3/d_2)$$

$$LCL_R = D_3\overline{R} \tag{6-17}$$

where

$$D_3 = (1 - 3d_3/d_2)$$

and D_3 and D_4 are functions of the sample size (n) and are tabulated in Table H in the Appendix.

Armed with Equations (6-9) and (6-11), now return to the derivation of the control limits for the average ($\overline{x}$) control chart, when μ and σ are unknown. The result follows:

$$
\begin{aligned}
\text{Control limits} &= \overline{\overline{x}} \pm 3\hat{\sigma}_{\overline{x}} \\
&= \overline{\overline{x}} \pm 3(\hat{\sigma}/\sqrt{n}), && \text{from Equation (6-9)} \\
&= \overline{\overline{x}} \pm (3/\sqrt{n})(\overline{R}/d_2), && \text{from Equation (6-11)} \\
&= \overline{\overline{x}} \pm (3/d_2\sqrt{n})\overline{R}
\end{aligned}
$$

and for convenience this result is expressed as

$$\text{Control limits} = \overline{\overline{x}} \pm A_2\overline{R} \tag{6-18}$$

where

$$A_2 = 3/d_2\sqrt{n}$$

and A_2 is a function of the sample size (n) and is tabulated in Table G in the Appendix.

6-3.4 Constancy of Variation: Average and Range

Now return to the initial variables data of Table 6-7 to set up the control charts for averages and ranges. For contrast with the attribute chart demonstration, the case of no standard given will be used to compute the control limits. For this situation it is recommended that at least fifteen to twenty-five samples be obtained to serve as a performance study.

For the twenty subgroups of Table 6-7 the grand average ($\overline{\overline{x}}$) and the average range ($\overline{R}$) are as follows. These statistics estimate the expected values reasonably well:

$$\overline{\overline{x}} = \sum_{i=1}^{20} \overline{x}_i/20 = 0.820 = 0.04$$

$$\overline{R} = \sum_{i=1}^{20} R_i/20 = 74/20 = 3.70$$

Control limits for the R chart use Equations (6-16) and (6-17), where D_3 and D_4 for a sample size of 5 are 0 and 2.114, are as follows:

$$UCL_R = D_4\overline{R} = 2.114(3.70) = 7.82$$
$$LCL_R = D_3\overline{R} = 0.0(3.70) = 0.0$$

Control limits for the $\bar{x}$ chart use Equation (6-18), where A_2 for a sample size of 5 is 0.577, as follows:

$$\text{Control limits} = \bar{\bar{x}} \pm A_2\bar{R} = 0.04 \pm (0.577)(3.70) = 0.04 \pm 2.13$$
$$UCL_{\bar{x}} = 2.17$$
$$LCL_{\bar{x}} = -2.09$$

The control charts for the data of Table 6-7 with the above control limits are shown in Figure 6-14. It is common practice to place the $\bar{x}$ chart above the R chart with points corresponding to the same subgroups in vertical alignment.

The points tend to fluctuate about the centerlines and remain within the control limits on both the $\bar{x}$ and R control charts. This is indicative of controlled patterns and is a further illustration of constancy in variation. Patterns of this general nature would continue with repeated sampling from the same population and represent the amount of variation that can occur in statistics when the process is stable. These control charts may now be used to monitor and control the medicated cream filling process so that unnecessary adjustments will not be made when the patterns remain in control. When out-of-control points or patterns occur, action should be initiated to determine the cause of the change in the process and adjustments should be made to correct the problem.

The fact that the control charts are in control, indicating a stable process for the quality characteristic under study, does not necessarily mean that the process is satisfactory. There are many factors besides statistical control that determine satisfaction with a process.

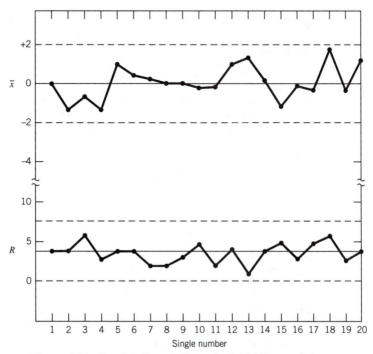

Figure 6-14 $\bar{x}$ and R Control Charts for Initial Twenty Subgroups

Three examples are (1) ability to meet specifications on individual units and overall customer requirements, (2) compatibility with other parts or processes, and (3) cost. Because the patterns are in control, the relationships (6-9) through (6-11) can be used to predict the nature of the process. Estimate σ as $\overline{R}/d_2 = 3.7/2.326 = 1.59$; and estimate μ as $\overline{\overline{x}} = 0.04$. Assuming an approximately normal distribution (preparing a histogram of the 100 individual values from the twenty subgroups of size 5 is a rough check on this assumption), one can predict individual values in the range of $0.04 \pm 3(1.6)$, or 4.84 to -4.76.

It is conceivable that for a labeled fill of 100 grams, this amount of variation would not be economically desirable. This would require a setting of an amount larger than 100 grams to provide assurance that no jar contains less than the labeled weight. Because the process is stable, it might require a redesigned process to reduce the variability so that the nominal setting may be lowered to be closer to the label weight. The resultant savings, with amortization for an acceptable rate of return, would justify the expense for the redesigned process.

▶ 6-4 GENERAL PRINCIPLES OF CONTROL CHARTS

Principles of control charts have been introduced for understanding in the demonstrations of the attribute control chart (p chart) and the variables control charts ($\overline{x}$ and R charts). Certain principles have been reserved for more detailed discussion in this section, including natural and unnatural patterns and tests for lack of statistical control.

6-4.1 Natural Patterns

Chapters 7 and 8 will illustrate the importance of the interpretation of patterns in drawing sensible conclusions from control charts about the nature of the underlying process. A stable process, under statistical control or constancy of variation, will generally produce a natural pattern. It will produce random data points that possess several basic characteristics, caused by the underlying distribution and the sampling regime that it depicts. It has shown that control limits reflect the tails of the underlying distribution of the statistic being plotted and studied. It is understandable that these random data arrays from a stable process should have the following characteristics on control charts:

1. Most of the points occur near the centerline.
2. A few of the points occur near the control limits.
3. Only an occasional point occurs beyond the control limits.
4. The points occur in a random manner with no clustering, trending, or other departure from a random distribution of the points.

6-4.2 Unnatural Patterns

Unnatural data patterns can be defined as those lacking one or more of the characteristics of random arrays. It is instructive to take this approach, as this directs us to consider certain unnatural patterns that might not be commonly understood. In the consideration of certain unnatural patterns, the importance of knowing the method of sampling and the process from which the observations came are emphasized.

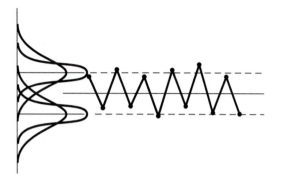

Figure 6-15   Mixture Pattern, $\bar{x}$ Chart

Consider the absence of the first of the characteristics of random arrays above: a failure of most of the points to be near the centerline. This can occur on the $\bar{x}$ chart for many reasons. If the mean changes because of a machine with two or more cutting heads, two machines, or two people, most of the points can be near lines above and below the control chart centerline rather than near the centerline. Figure 6-15 illustrates this situation. If the dispersion greatly increases, there will be no recognizable tendency for the points to lie close to the centerline. From a review of the sampling and subgrouping and some knowledge of the process, the source of the problem producing the unnatural pattern can be identified. Thus, correction could readily follow.

Now consider the absence of the second of the characteristics of random data arrays above: a failure of a few of the points to be near the control limits. This can occur on the $\bar{x}$ chart from a situation quite similar to the above but with a different manner of sampling and forming of the subgroups. Figure 6-15 illustrates a process for which the subgroups are drawn intermittently from distributions having different process means. Figure 6-16 shows the same changes but with each subgroup drawn from a mixture of two processes with different means. The sample averages tend to fluctuate about the center of the mixture, and the subgroup ranges, from which the control limits for $\bar{x}$ are obtained, will tend to be inflated. This unnatural pattern, called stratification, can be misinterpreted

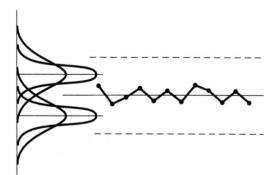

Figure 6-16   Stratification Pattern, $\bar{x}$ Chart

as representing the desirable feature of less variation, since the $\bar{x}$ chart is steady. The range chart, however, will indicate the greater variability that results from such stratification.

Data patterns lacking the third characteristic of random arrays, that is, having points occurring beyond the control limits, usually indicate either frequent changes in the underlying distribution, or an increased dispersion.

For the fourth and last of the characteristics of random arrays, examples of unnatural patterns are sudden shifts in level, trends, bunching, or clustering. A more detailed treatment of this subject is contained in the AT&T Technologies *Statistical Quality Control Handbook* (1984), where a dictionary of control chart patterns is developed.

6-4.3 Rules for Detecting Out-of-Control Conditions

If the process is truly in control, there is about a risk of 0.0013, or 0.13%, of investigating a change in the parameter needlessly (α risk) because of a point occurring above the upper control limit. There is an equal risk on the low side, for a total α risk of 0.0026. If the process is out of control, a point outside the control limits is more likely. The control limits are set arbitrarily (see Section 6-2.2) for a low α risk. Limits much wider than three sigmas would save only a few needless investigations and would cause some delay in detecting out-of-control situations. Much narrower limits would increase the number of needless investigations while not appreciably reducing delay in detection. The rule of investigating each point beyond the limits is then a compromise.

Once the limits are set, the control chart contains additional information that is not exploited by this rule. For example, it is about equally likely to have *two out of three successive points outside two sigmas,* or *four out of five successive points outside one sigma,* or *eight successive points on one side of the centerline* as to have one point outside three sigmas. Why not use these, or rules based on runs in addition to the three-sigma rule?

The three additional rules italicized above have proved practical and were advocated in 1956 by the Western Electric Company's quality control program. Their use is optional and applies only to control limits that are reasonably symmetrical. Collectively, their use increases the α risk in a controlled situation but decreases the β risk in an uncontrolled situation (see Section 6-2.2), since looking for all of several indicators increases the chance of finding something wrong, whether validly (β) or not (α).

The control limits on an $\bar{x}$ chart are usually symmetrical, barring some truncation of the quality characteristic. However, the control limits for other control charts, for specific sample sizes and values of the parameters, are sometimes asymmetrical. In these cases the rules can be applied roughly by dividing the lower, asymmetric, region into three equal zones and requiring slightly stronger reactions. Desired use of the rules may be considered in designing the control charts to have reasonably symmetrical control limits.

▶ 6-5 SUMMARY

This chapter has introduced in some detail the concepts of control charts as used for statistical process control, using the statistical principles first introduced in Chapter 5. The next several chapters will continue this discussion in much greater detail.

Chapter 7 presents many different types of attributes control charts, and Chapter 8 does the same for variables control charts. Chapters 9 and 10 present some newly developed control charts with a somewhat specialized use that have become popular in recent years. All of these chapters make extensive use of the principles presented in this chapter.

This chapter closes with the statement of two common principles generally associated with Shewhart type control charts:

1. Control charts are named according to the statistic being plotted. This helps to identify the statistic being used to assist in interpreting as well as in formulating the correct control limits.

2. Control limits are most often based on the principles of an estimate of the expected value of the statistic being plotted, or the parameter if known, plus and minus three times an estimate of the standard deviation of the statistic being plotted.

▶ 6-6 REFERENCES

American Society for Quality (1985a), ANSI Z1.1-1985, *Guide for Quality Control,* Milwaukee.

American Society for Quality (1985b), ANSI Z1.2-1985, *Control Chart Method of Analyzing Data,* Milwaukee.

American Society for Quality (1985c), ANSI Z1.3-1985, *Control Chart Method of Controlling Quality during Production,* Milwaukee.

AT&T Technologies (1956), *Statistical Quality Control Handbook,* Indianapolis.

Hartley, H. O. (1942), "The Range in Random Samples," *Biometrika,* Vol. 32.

McKay, A. T., and Pearson, E. S. (1935), "A Note on the Distribution of Range in Sample Sizes of n," *Biometrika,* Vol. 27.

Pearson, E. S. (1926), "A Further Note on the Distribution of Range in Samples Taken from a Normal Distribution," *Biometrika,* Vol. 18, p. 173.

Pearson, E. S., and Hartley, H. O. (1942), "The Probability Integral of the Range in Samples of n Observations from a Normal Population," *Biometrika,* Vol. 32, p. 301.

Shapiro, Samuel S. (1990), *How to Test Normality and Other Distributional Assumptions,* Vol. 3 of *The ASQC Basic References in Quality Control: Statistical Techniques,* ASQ, Milwaukee.

Shewhart, W. A. (1926a), "Quality Control Charts," *Bell System Technical Journal,* October, pp. 593–603.

Shewhart, W. A. (1926b), "Finding Causes of Quality Variations," *Manufacturing Industries,* February, pp. 125–28.

Shewhart, W. A. (1927), "Quality Control," *Bell System Technical Journal,* October, pp. 722–35.

Shewhart, W. A. (1931), *Economic Control of Quality of Manufactured Product,* Van Nostrand-Reinhold, New York. (A reprint of this classic work has been published and is available from the American Society for Quality, Milwaukee.)

Tippett, L. H. C. (1925), "On the Extreme Individuals and the Range of Samples Taken from a Normal Population," *Biometrika,* Vol. 17, p. 364.

▶ 6-7 PROBLEMS

1. Develop a box of beads similar to that of Table 6-1. Draw twenty samples of size 50 from the box as shown in the chapter demonstration. Record the number of red beads in each sample. Compute the percentage, p_i, for each sample. Compute $\bar{p}$ and the control limits for the p control chart (in percentages). Do not assume knowledge of the true parameter. Plot and interpret the control chart in view of the known universe from which the sample results were obtained.

2. For Problem 1, compute control limits (warning limits) based on a multiple of two standard deviations of p ($2\sigma_p$) instead of three. Plot these limits on the control chart and interpret the result.

3. Do Problems 1 and 2 for samples of size 25.

4. What minimum sample size would you consider practical for the p control chart? Explain.

5. Electronic components are assembled by individual operators. A process checker collects a sample of fifty units each half day and inspects all units to determine the number of nonconforming units. Records for ten days for a certain operator are as follows:

Sample Size	Number of Nonconforming Units	Sample Size	Number of Nonconforming Units
50	3	50	1
50	4	50	5

(continued)

Sample Size	Number of Nonconforming Units	Sample Size	Number of Nonconforming Units
50	3	50	1
50	2	50	3
50	6	50	3
50	2	50	1
50	3	50	3
50	2	50	2
50	1	50	1
50	5	50	2

Set up a p control chart for these data. Does the control chart appear to be in control? Interpret the control chart and speculate on the associated process. What is the level of nonconformances? Discuss.

6. Records for a second operator for the situation of Problem 5 are as follows:

Number of Nonconforming Units
(same sample size as for Problem 5)

0, 2, 3, 2, 0, 1, 1, 0, 1, 0, 1, 0, 0, 2, 1, 1, 0, 0, 1, 0

Set up a p control chart for these data. Does the control chart appear to be in control? Interpret the control chart and speculate on the associated process. What is the level of nonconformances? How does this compare with the operator of Problem 5? Discuss.

7. When applied to $\bar{x}$ charts, the rules for out-of-control conditions are seen to represent single points or combinations of points falling beyond certain values of a normal distribution. The probability that a given point falls in or beyond the respective sigma zones can be determined from Table A in the Appendix, giving areas under the normal distribution. These probabilities can then be used in the binomial probability function to determine the probabilities associated with each of the rules, Rule 1 being the trivial case of one trial. Determine these probabilities and compare them with each other.

8. Devise a distribution similar to Figure 6-13 in spread and frequency of occurrence of the values of the quality characteristic but with a mean of 7. Set up this distribution on tags or chips as well as the distribution of Figure 6-13, keeping them in separate bowls. Draw a series of twenty samples of size 5 as carried out in the chapter demonstrations, systematically drawing one sample from the distribution of Figure 6-13 followed by a sample from the distribution with mean of 7. Repeat this procedure ten times, maintaining the order of sampling. Compute $\bar{x}$ and R values for the twenty samples. Compute $\bar{\bar{x}}$, $\bar{R}$, and con-

trol limits for each control chart. Set up and plot the $\bar{x}$ and R control charts, and interpret the patterns on each of the control charts.

9. Combine the distributions of Problem 8 into one bowl. Draw twenty samples of size 5 from this bowl. Compute $\bar{x}$ and R values for the twenty samples; compute $\bar{\bar{x}}$, $\bar{R}$, and control limits for each control chart. Set up and plot the $\bar{x}$ and R control charts, and interpret the patterns on each of the control charts. Compare with the control charts of Problem 8.

10. Measurements of gain in decibels are made on an electronic circuit with the following results. Small samples of size five were taken from the process each hour to form the subgroups for $\bar{x}$ and R control charts used to monitor the process for this quality characteristic; $\bar{x}$ and R values are computed for the first ten of the twenty subgroups given. Complete the $\bar{x}$ and R computations for the remaining subgroups. Set up and plot the $\bar{x}$ and R control charts for these data. Do the control charts appear to be in control? Prepare a histogram for the 100 individual data points. Interpret the control charts and histogram. Discuss.

Subgroup	1	2	3	4	5
	11.1	9.6	9.7	10.1	12.4
	9.4	10.8	10.0	8.4	10.0
	11.2	10.1	10.0	10.2	10.7
	10.4	10.8	9.8	9.4	10.1
	10.1	11.0	10.4	11.0	11.3
Total	52.2	52.3	49.9	49.1	54.5
Average ($\bar{x}$)	10.44	10.46	9.98	9.82	10.90
Range (R)	1.8	1.4	0.7	2.6	2.4

Subgroup	6	7	8	9	10
	10.1	11.0	11.2	10.6	8.3
	10.2	11.5	10.0	10.4	10.0
	10.2	11.8	10.9	10.5	8.8
	11.2	10.0	11.2	10.5	9.5
	10.1	11.3	11.0	10.9	9.8
Total	51.8	55.6	54.3	52.9	46.4
Average ($\bar{x}$)	10.36	11.12	10.86	10.58	9.28
Range (R)	1.1	1.8	1.2	0.5	1.7

Subgroup	11	12	13	14	15
	10.6	10.8	10.7	11.3	11.4
	9.9	10.2	10.7	11.4	11.2
	10.7	10.5	10.8	10.4	11.4
	10.2	8.4	8.6	10.6	10.1
	11.4	9.9	11.4	11.1	11.6
Total					
Average ($\bar{x}$)					
Range (R)					

(continued)

Subgroup	16	17	18	19	20
	10.1	10.7	11.9	10.8	12.4
	10.1	12.8	11.9	12.1	11.1
	9.7	11.2	11.6	11.8	10.8
	9.8	11.2	12.4	9.4	11.0
	10.5	11.3	11.4	11.6	11.9
Total					
Average $(\bar{x})$					
Range (R)					

11. Coded measurements of oxide thickness in angstroms are obtained on samples of size 4 drawn every four hours from the oxidation process for three days. For the following data, obtain the $\bar{x}$ and R values, set up and plot the $\bar{x}$ and R control charts for these data, and interpret the control charts.

Subgroup	1	2	3	4	5
	94	105	44	−34	210
	149	127	185	−78	183
	91	103	−16	−75	223
	38	186	38	−121	205

Subgroup	6	7	8	9	10
	73	−30	41	−72	−26
	108	23	94	−32	−21
	75	127	176	−20	−96
	93	64	248	22	−120

Subgroup	11	12	13	14	15
	143	99	−79	127	8
	−10	−127	−172	−78	−76
	24	−23	−179	−26	−35
	−115	−23	−171	22	−33

Subgroup	16	17	18
	−187	15	−194
	−110	−90	−96
	−220	−37	−184
	−105	−38	−286

12. Using a computer subroutine (or software package) for random number generation together with the binomial distribution function and a routine for p control chart calculations and plotting, repeat Problems 1 to 3 by computer analysis, using whatever computer language (or software) is most familiar.

13. For Problem 12, repeat Problems 8 and 9, using computer subroutines (or software packages) for generating normally distributed random variables having the prescribed means and variances, together with $\bar{x}$ and R chart calculations and plotting routines.

7

CONTROL CHARTS
FOR ATTRIBUTES

The basic concepts of control charts were developed in Chapter 6. To illustrate these concepts, charts were introduced for attributes (p) and variables ($\bar{x}$ and R). Control charts for situations in which a standard is given and used to compute the control limits were discussed as well when no standard is stated and the limits are computed from estimates obtained from data. Both situations have important applications. The first (standard given) is useful when a process is to be maintained in a state of statistical control at a predetermined level. The second (no standard given) is useful to maintain a process at its current level.

This chapter extends these same concepts in some detail for attributes data. The following chapter will do the same for variables data. In this chapter the measurable quantity is of the count type. It considers the number of pieces in a sample that possess a quality characteristic (np charts) or the related percent or fraction of the sample that contains the characteristic (p charts). Charts for the number of nonconformities in the sample (c charts) and a fourth type of chart, the u chart, which is a standardized form of a c chart are also included.

The first of these quality measures is the number of items in a sample that contain one or more nonconformities. This has been called the number or percent defective by many quality professionals. However, the use of the words "defect" and "defective" really means only that there is a quality variant. For example, a gasoline might have needlessly high octane and therefore be called defective. Nonconforming is a more accurate term for most situations. Further discussion of this point may be found in ANSI/ISO/ASQ A3534-2-2001, which may be obtained from the American Society for Quality (2001).

This chapter develops attribute control charts for each quality measure for situations both with standard given and with no standard given. First, continue the demonstration started in the preceding chapter to show the manner by which attribute control charts detect changes in the process. This is fundamental to an understanding and proper use of control charts.

▶ 7-1 DETECTION OF CHANGES WITH ATTRIBUTE CHARTS

An increase in the percentage level of nonconforming bottle openings is readily simulated with the bead box having the composition shown in Table 6-1, by considering red, yellow,

TABLE 7-1   Additional Sample Results

Sample Number	Sample Size, n	Number of Red Beads, x_1	Number of Yellow Beads, x_2	Number of Black Beads, x_3	Sum, x	Percent, p
21	100	5	5	2	12	12
22	100	6	5	4	15	15
23	100	6	2	1	9	9
24	100	7	3	0	10	10
25	100	5	4	0	9	9
26	100	3	2	0	5	5
27	100	5	5	1	11	11
28	100	4	0	1	5	5
29	100	6	3	0	9	9
30	100	7	2	1	10	10

and black beads as nonconforming bottle openings. This yields a change in the process parameter, θ, from 5% to 9%. The results of ten additional samples are shown in Table 7-1.

The control chart, with these additional points plotted, is shown in Figure 7-1. It reveals an out-of-control condition with the first and second points exceeding the upper control limit. These are the only two of the ten to exceed the limit, and they are marked with an $\times$ to denote "out-of-control." If the process continued to run, by inability to locate and correct the problem immediately or by an increase in the sampling frequency, the resultant pattern would illustrate the change in level of the process. Other points are marked to indicate "out-of-control" in accordance with the rules given in Chapter 6. The control chart has detected the change. There is a risk of delay, as some of the points falling within the control limits might have been the first few points observed. This emphasizes the caution with which this statistical tool must be used for specifying the frequency of sampling or the sampling interval. Had the increased level of nonconformance been smaller, one would have been totally dependent on pattern interpretation to detect the increase, resulting in a delay.

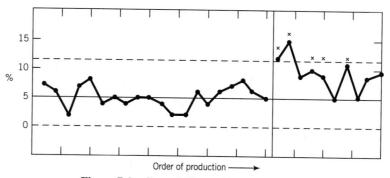

Figure 7-1   Control Chart with Extended Data

TABLE 7-2 Additional Sample Results

Sample Number	Sample Size, n	Number of Yellow Beads, x	Percent, p
31	100	2	2
32	100	6	6
33	100	1	1
34	100	1	1
35	100	2	2
36	100	2	2
37	100	5	5
38	100	1	1
39	100	4	4
40	100	6	6

Until the detection and correction process is complete, a greater percentage of nonconforming pieces will be present.

Detection of a decrease in the process nonconforming level is demonstrated by considering only the yellow or black beads as nonconforming bottle openings. By selecting the yellow beads for consideration, a change in the parameter, θ, from 5% to 3%, is demonstrated. Because this is a smaller change than that demonstrated on the increase and is associated with the lower portion of the control chart, pattern interpretation is necessary. The results of ten additional samples are shown in Table 7-2, recording only the yellow bead count. The continuing control chart, with these additional ten points plotted, is shown in Figure 7-2.

On a point-by-point basis we observe that the first three points present no particular reason for concluding that the process has changed. During these three sampling intervals efforts made to reduce the level of nonconformance appear not to have been successful. It is on the fourth point that a signal is received, based on the rules for out-of-control conditions given in Chapter 6. This and additional points satisfying the rules are marked to

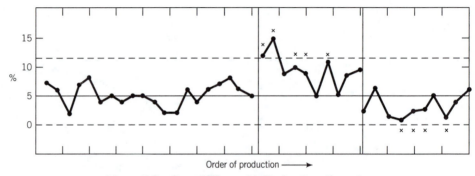

Figure 7-2 Control Chart with Further Data Extension

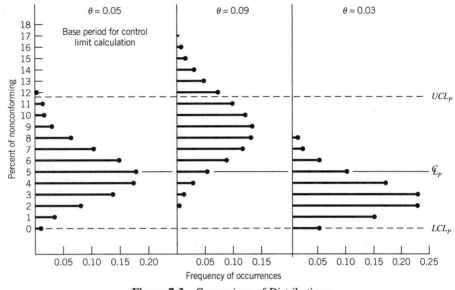

Figure 7-3 Comparison of Distributions

indicate a change from the level on which the control limits are based. A strong signal of quality improvement has been received. The control chart may continue to be used to monitor the level of nonconforming bottle openings after an adjustment in the centerline and control limits to reflect this improved performance has been made.

The necessity to use pattern interpretation on control charts for detection of process changes is vividly seen by a summary of the underlying distributions, the initial one of Chapter 6 and each of the two cases demonstrated above. There is a fair amount of variation in the computed statistics at each of the several process percent nonconforming levels. This results in overlap in the underlying distributions, especially when the parameter changes are not large. The control chart must contend with the inherent variation in the underlying distributions, in addition to the overlap, to detect changes.

This comparison of the distributions for each of the three cases—the initial distribution of Chapter 6 and the two demonstrated above—is shown in Figure 7-3. The first is that of Table 6-3 from Equation (6-2). The second and third are obtained by substituting $\theta = 0.09$ and 0.03, respectively, for θ in the binomial probability function, Equation (6-1). While the basic distributions from Equation (6-1) are in terms of number of nonconforming pieces, x, they are converted to fraction nonconforming, p, with division by the sample size, n, that is, $p = x/n$, and in our case, $n = 100$. The percent scale ($100p = 100x/n$) is shown in Figure 7-3 for direct association with the control chart. The control chart centerline and control limits are superimposed on the figure.

The second distribution (with $\theta = 0.09$) will be used to present an illustration of the type II error discussed in Chapter 6. The proportion of the distribution inside the control limits represents the probability that a point will fall inside the control limits and is therefore the risk that the change will not be detected, using the criterion of a single point outside the control limits. This is seen to have a β value of 0.814. The third distribution with

$\theta = 0.03$ is seen to lie entirely within the control limits. Detection of this change from the original distribution is entirely dependent on pattern interpretation.

Additional details on attribute control charts are presented next. This demonstration has been designed to present the principles of control charts in general and the attribute control chart in particular.

▶ 7-2 CHARTS FOR NUMBER OF PIECES NONCONFORMING

7-2.1 Standard Given

If each inspected part is classified good or bad according to whether it contains one or more quality variants, a chart will now be presented to observe the sample variation in the number of parts found nonconforming. In order to make valid comparisons with such a chart all samples must be of the same size. If n is the sample size and x the number of nonconforming pieces ($x = 0, 1, \ldots, n$) and a stable, continuing process exists, use the binomial distribution presented in Equations (5-40), (6-1), and again in (7-1):

$$b(x) = \binom{n}{x}(\theta)^x(1 - \theta)^{n-x}, \qquad x = 0, 1, \ldots, n \tag{7-1}$$

In Equation (7-1), θ is the true fraction nonconforming of the process. Recall from Chapter 5 that the mean or expected number of nonconforming items is $n\theta$ and the standard deviation is $\sqrt{n\theta(1 - \theta)}$. Chapter 5 also indicated that a normal distribution with mean and standard deviation equal to these two values may be used to approximately describe the binomial distribution of Equation (7-1).

Let p_0 be a specified standard in terms of fraction nonconforming and n the sample size. Then substitute p_0 for θ in Equation (7-1) and in the expressions for the mean and standard deviation. Note that p_0 is a standard that might or might not be equal to θ, the true fraction nonconforming. The product, np_0, is the expected number of items nonconforming if the standard is met. Thus, np_0 will be the centerline, and the control limits will be, using Shewhart's suggested three standard deviation limits and the normal approximation to the binomial distribution,

$$np_0 \pm 3\sqrt{np_0(1 - p_0)} \tag{7-2}$$

To illustrate this, a manufacturer of dry cell batteries desired to maintain a 1.5% nonconforming level for one of the processes. The process is suspected currently to be running at different quality levels. It sometimes runs higher and sometimes lower than this 1.5% level. The company wished to have a means of determining when the process is higher so that efforts can be made to stabilize it at the 1.5% level or below. It was decided that samples of fifty cells would be taken each hour and tested for conformance to specifications. The process ran two shifts per day; there would thus be sixteen samples taken each day.

Control limits were established by using Equation (7-2) as follows:

$$UCL = 50(0.015) + 3\sqrt{50(0.015)(0.985)}$$
$$= 0.75 + 2.58 = 3.33$$
$$LCL = 50(0.015) - 3\sqrt{50(0.015)(0.985)}$$
$$= -1.83 = 0$$

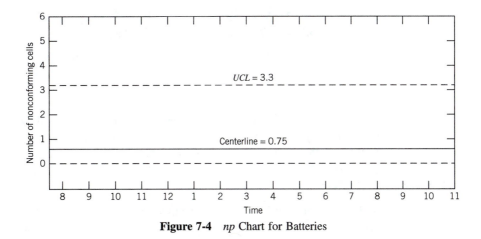

Figure 7-4 *np* Chart for Batteries

Equation (7-2) results in a negative lower control limit; we therefore set the lower limit at zero. An upper limit of 3.3 means that three or fewer nonconforming cells are acceptable but four or more are not.

The chart is then set up as illustrated in Figure 7-4. The company placed the control chart on the process, and after one day, the chart appeared as shown in Figure 7-5. The process did not indicate the desired random pattern around a level of 0.75 nonconforming cell per sample (1.5%). An effort was made to determine the cause of the out-of-control condition during the middle of the day shift and during the first five hours of the second shift. After some discussion it was determined that the second shift inspector had gone home at 8:30 P.M. because he was ill, and the supervisor made the last three inspections. Considering this fact, it was then decided that, on the basis of this one day's data, the second shift appeared to be operating at a higher percent nonconforming level than the first shift. No good reason was found for the two out-of-control points during the first shift except that there was an apparent slump that often occurs during midmorning. The chart was kept on the process for the rest of the week and at the end of this time it was determined that the first shift could be expected to maintain the desired 1.5% nonconforming level, but the second shift appeared to

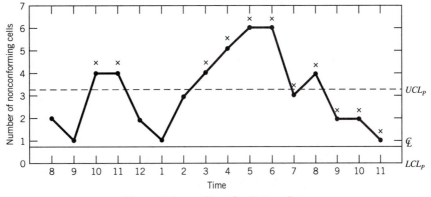

Figure 7-5 *np* Chart for Battery Data

be operating at a 3% level. Separate charts were then set up for each shift with the first shift as indicated in Figure 7-5, while the second shift had control limits at

$$UCL = 50(0.03) + 3\sqrt{50(0.03)(0.97)}$$
$$= 1.5 + 3.62 = 5.1$$
$$LCL = 1.5 - 3.62 = 0$$

By working with the second shift whenever points appeared above the new upper control limit (i.e., when more than five nonconforming cells were observed in a sample), the quality level of the shift was gradually brought to that of the first shift.

7-2.2 No Standard Given

Many times no standard is established by management. This situation occurs when the process to be controlled is operating at an unknown level or, if known, it is determined that the level is satisfactory and should be maintained. In the previous example a no-standard-given approach might well have been used for the second shift.

In this case, rather than start with a predetermined standard value of p_0, some preliminary data must be obtained from which to compute an estimate of the number of nonconforming pieces expected per sample of size n in order to determine the centerline of the chart. This estimate is the arithmetic mean of the number of nonconforming units per sample. Use this estimate to determine the control limits using Equations (7-3). If x_i is the number of nonconforming pieces in the ith sample, then $p_i = x_i/n$ is the fraction nonconforming for sample i. The average of the p_i's is $\bar{p}$.

$$\bar{p} = \frac{1}{k}\sum_{i=1}^{k} p_i = \frac{1}{kn}\sum_{i=1}^{k} x_i = \bar{x}/n$$

where

$$\bar{x} = \frac{1}{k}\sum_{i=1}^{k} x_i$$

Thus, the centerline will be

$$n\bar{p} = n\bar{x}/n = \bar{x}$$

The standard deviation can also be stated in terms of $\bar{x}$ as

$$\hat{\sigma}_{np} = \sqrt{n\bar{p}(1 - \bar{p})}$$
$$= \sqrt{n(\bar{x}/n)(1 - \bar{x}/n)}$$
$$= \sqrt{(\bar{x})(1 - \bar{x}/n)}$$

Thus, the centerline and control limits will be

$$\text{Centerline} = \bar{x} \text{ as defined above}$$
$$UCL = \bar{x} + 3\sqrt{(\bar{x})(1 - \bar{x}/n)} \qquad (7\text{-}3)$$
$$LCL = \bar{x} - 3\sqrt{(\bar{x})(1 - \bar{x}/n)}$$

where

$\bar{x}$ = average number of nonconforming units

k = number of samples taken

n = sample size

TABLE 7-3 Number of Nonconforming Batteries

Day	Time	Number Nonconforming	Day	Time	Number Nonconforming	Day	Time	Number Nonconforming
Mon.	4	5	Tues.	4	4	Wed.	4	6
	5	6		5	4		5	4
	6	6		6	5		6	4
	7	3		7	3		7	2
	8	4		8	5		8	2
	9	2		9	3		9	3
	10	2		10	3		10	5
	11	1		11	6		11	2

Suppose, for example, for the second shift on the battery manufacturing process discussed in the previous example over a period of three days (twenty-four samples) the number of nonconforming batteries per sample of fifty were as shown in Table 7-3. The average number nonconforming is first determined. Then the control limits are calculated:

$$\bar{x} = 90/24 = 3.75$$
$$UCL = 3.75 + 3\sqrt{3.75[1 - (3.75/50)]}$$
$$= 3.75 + 5.59 = 9.34$$
$$LCL = 3.75 - 5.59 = 0$$

The upper control limit was computed to be 9.3, which means that ten or more nonconforming units in a sample indicate an out-of-control condition. Because none of the above data points are above the upper limit, it was concluded that this is the proper chart for the second shift. The data are plotted on the chart in Figure 7-6. The solid horizontal line in Figure 7-6 indicates the centerline (3.75), and the upper control limit (9.3) is indicated by a dashed line. The lower control limit is at zero. The chart was then installed

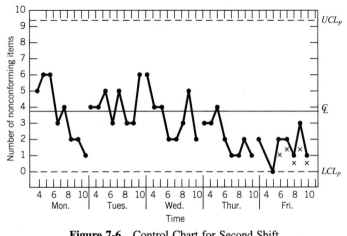

Figure 7-6 Control Chart for Second Shift

on the process, and the data for Thursday and Friday are also indicated in Figure 7-6. The data for Thursday and Friday were reviewed by the quality control engineer, who, together with the supervisor, agreed that a new lower level for the chart seemed to be indicated. Actually, what had occurred was that the charting of the data served as an extra motivation for the operators to improve the quality of their work. This led to the almost immediate improvement indicated in Figure 7-6.

The data for Thursday and Friday were then used to determine a new centerline and control limits. The new centerline was found to be 1.8 and the new control limits to be 5.8 and zero. These were computed as follows by using Equations (7-3):

$$\bar{x} = 29/16 = 1.8$$
$$UCL = 1.8 + 3\sqrt{1.8[1 - (1.8/50)]}$$
$$= 1.8 + 4.0 = 5.8$$
$$LCL = 1.8 - 4.0 = 0$$

The new limits were then used on the second shift chart for the next week. Further improvements in quality were made in subsequent weeks, but the rate of improvement was considerably less dramatic than this first change.

▶ 7-3 CHARTS FOR PERCENT NONCONFORMING

7-3.1 Standard Given

The chart for number of pieces nonconforming discussed in the previous section has one serious drawback. To use it, all sample sizes must be the same. This problem can be overcome by working with the percent of each sample that is nonconforming instead of with the number of nonconforming pieces. If all pieces produced in an inspection period are to be inspected or if the sample size is some function of the production quantity, this situation clearly exists. The control chart for percent of a sample that is classified as nonconforming to some quality standard was used in Chapter 6 to illustrate the overall concepts and philosophy of control charts, and is used again here. First review the case in which a quality standard is given and then, in the next section, consider the situation in which a standard is not given.

Again p_0 will be the specified standard fraction nonconforming, and n is the sample size, which may vary. For this chart, the centerline will be merely the stipulated p_0. The control limits will be at $p_0 \pm 3\sigma_p$, where we recall that

$$\sigma_p = \sqrt{p_0(1 - p_0)/n}$$

If n does not vary, this will result in one common set of control limits; but if n varies, the control limits also vary, coming closer together as n increases. An example of this chart using a constant sample size was found in Chapter 6. An example using a variable n follows.

The situation is one in which dry cell batteries are being tested for proper voltage mechanically. The cells travel down a pathway, first passing a mechanical counter, then passing a voltmeter. This voltmeter is constructed so that each cell meeting a specified minimum voltage is allowed to pass. Cells that fail this voltage test are ejected into a scrap bin, tripping another counter as they go. Thus, the first counter gives n and the second gives x, the number of nonconforming cells. The quotient of these two (x/n) is the variable to be plotted on the control chart. The test results are plotted each thirty minutes, and the standard required is an average of 1% below the cutoff voltage.

The cells are purchased, and therefore the order of production is lost. The assumption is then made that nonconforming cells are randomly mixed in each lot of cells.

Equations (7-4) specify the control chart limits with the additional understanding that a negative value for the lower control limit will be taken as zero:

$$\text{Centerline} = p_0$$
$$UCL = p_0 + 3\sqrt{p_0(1 - p_0)/n} \tag{7-4}$$
$$LCL = p_0 - 3\sqrt{p_0(1 - p_0)/n}$$

For this example, using Equation (7-4), obtain

$$\text{Centerline} = 0.01$$
$$UCL = 0.01 + 3\sqrt{0.01(0.99)/n} = 0.01 + 0.2985/\sqrt{n}$$
$$LCL = 0.01 - 0.2985/\sqrt{n}$$

Now consider the sample size, n. There are several alternative possibilities for this:

1. Use variable limits and change the limits each half hour. Although this is a theoretically correct procedure, it may be confusing to the inspector.

2. Calculate an average n and use it in Equations (7-4). As a result samples may be accepted or rejected erroneously. The only time this is likely to happen, however, is when the sample results are close to the control limits.

3. Use an average n as in procedure 2, but whenever the sample result is close to the control limit, recompute the limit using the actual n.

Procedure 3 is the procedure recommended here. Now continue with this example using procedure 3. For alternative approaches, see Nelson (1989) and Rocke (1990). From past data it was determined that the average number of cells that run past the tester in half an hour is 350. Now compute the control limits as follows:

$$UCL = 0.01 + 0.2985/\sqrt{350} = 0.01 + 0.0160 = 0.0260$$
$$LCL = 0.01 - 0.2985/\sqrt{350} = 0.01 - 0.0160 = 0$$

The control chart has an upper limit at 2.60%, a centerline at 1.00%, and a lower control limit at zero.

Following the establishment of these limits, the data in Table 7-4 for fourteen run periods of the voltage tester were collected. The fourteen data points were then plotted on the control chart in Figure 7-7. As the chart illustrates, periods 4, 5, 7, and 8 are close enough to the upper control limit to warrant calculation of the exact limits. Point number 9 is clearly out of control, and the remainder are clearly in control. The exact control limits for the four questionable points are as follows:

Period Number	n	x	p (%)	UCL (%)
4	260	7	2.7	2.85
5	465	12	2.6	2.38
7	508	11	2.2	2.32
8	241	5	2.1	2.92

TABLE 7-4 Voltage Test Results

Period No.	n	x	p (%)
1	312	4	1.3
2	356	6	1.7
3	412	6	1.5
4	260	7	2.7
5	465	12	2.6
6	362	4	1.1
7	508	11	2.2
8	241	5	2.1
9	216	9	4.2
10	292	4	1.4
11	396	6	1.5
12	452	8	1.8
13	480	7	1.5
14	405	5	1.2
Totals	5157	94	

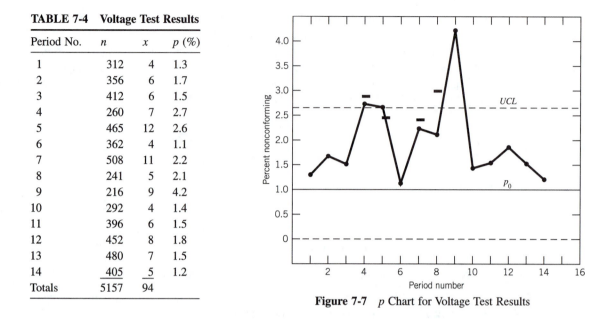

Figure 7-7 p Chart for Voltage Test Results

The exact control limits are marked on Figure 7-7, and it is seen that only periods 5 and 9 are out of control, while the remainder are within the control limits. Another consideration indicating an out-of-control condition is that all fourteen points are on the same side of the centerline. This exceeds the number stipulated in Section 6-4.3: eight successive points.

7-3.2 No Standard Given

The above example illustrated a process that was not meeting the required standard of 1% nonconforming. After learning this, the management stated that it would then like a chart centered around the current level of quality so it would know whether the quality deteriorated from that level. Thus, the company had temporarily abandoned the 1% standard in favor of a more realistic standard. Using the data of Table 7-4, the average percent nonconforming was determined. If these fourteen points are representative of the usual batteries, compute the chart using this average p as indicated in Equations (7-5):

$$\text{Centerline} = \bar{p}$$
$$UCL = \bar{p} + 3\sqrt{\bar{p}(1 - \bar{p})/n} \tag{7-5}$$
$$LCL = \bar{p} - 3\sqrt{\bar{p}(1 - \bar{p})/n}$$

where

$$\bar{p} = \frac{\displaystyle\sum_{i=1}^{k} x_i}{\displaystyle\sum_{i=1}^{k} n_i}$$

k = number of samples

x_i = number of nonconforming units in sample i

n_i = number of sample units in sample i

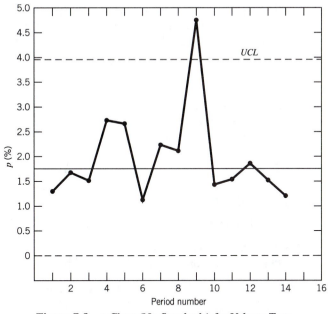

Figure 7-8 *p* Chart (No Standards) for Voltage Tests

For this example, $\bar{p} = 94/5157 = 0.0182$, or 1.82%. The control limits are

$$UCL = 0.0182 + 3\sqrt{0.0182(1 - 0.0182)/n} = 0.0182 + 0.4010/\sqrt{n}$$
$$LCL = 0.0182 - 0.4010/\sqrt{n}$$

The new control chart is shown in Figure 7-8 with the data of Table 7-4 plotted on it. An average *n* of 350 was again used to compute the control limits for Figure 7-8 as follows.

$$UCL = 0.0182 + 0.4010/\sqrt{350} = 0.0182 + 0.0214 = 0.0396$$
$$LCL = 0.0182 - 0.0214 = 0$$

The chart now indicates all points except number 9 to be in control (at a higher level than before). Because period number 9 is now near the control limit, the exact limit for that point was calculated. This calculation is $0.0182 + 0.4010\sqrt{216} = 0.0455$. This limit (4.55%) is indicated on the chart, and it is now concluded that all points are in control and the process is operating at a stable level of 1.8% nonconforming.

7-3.3 Sample Size

When either a *p* or *np* chart is to be used with a constant sample size, the question of preferred sample size sometimes arises. There are several ways to answer this question. One is that the sample size should be large enough to reject a sample a certain fraction of the time when the true value of *p* is at a certain level. To illustrate, assume that for inspection of a certain part a sample size is needed so that the probability of rejecting a sample is 0.90 when the true level of *p* is 8% nonconforming. Find *n* such that $P(\text{acceptance}|\theta = 0.08) = 0.10$.

The solution to this problem may be obtained by trial-and-error methods using a binomial table; however, a simpler method is to use the Poisson approximation to the binomial discussed in Chapter 5. Recall that the Poisson distribution is

$$P(x) = \frac{\lambda^x}{x!}e^{-\lambda}, \qquad x = 0, 1, \ldots$$

Now if x is the number of nonconforming items in the sample, use m as an estimate of the parameter λ, where m is the product of n and a standard, p_0. The probability of accepting a sample will then be

$$\sum_{x=0}^{c_2} \frac{(np_0)^x}{x!}e^{-np_0} \qquad (7\text{-}6)$$

where

c_2 = the largest integer resulting in a point just inside the upper control limit

A similar expression may be obtained for the lower control limit if it is nonzero. This would lead to an expression for the probability of acceptance as

$$P_a = \sum_{x=c_1}^{c_2} \frac{(np_0)^x}{x!}e^{-np_0} \qquad (7\text{-}7)$$

where

c_1 = the integer resulting in a point just above the lower control limit if it is nonzero. Otherwise, c_1 is zero.

There are a number of possible solutions to this situation, each dealing with a different value of c_2. To resolve this, choose a value of c_2. For example, say that the sample size is to be determined so that there is a 90% chance that a sample value of x will lie above the upper control limit when the process is 8% nonconforming and as many as five nonconforming parts are in a sample. Table 7-5 may be used for this purpose. In Table 7-5, p_a represents the value of θ for which that fraction is not exceeded. For example, when $\lambda = n\theta$ is 2.996, c is zero 5% of the time. In the table, $n\theta$ is written as np.

For this example, for a c of 5, the value of $n\theta$ that has a 10% chance of acceptance (i.e., $p_{0.10}$) is 9.27. The sample size will then be

$$n = np_{0.10}/p_{0.10} = 9.27/0.08 = 116$$

Table 7-5 may be used for any of five probabilities and for c from 0 to 15, inclusive. Because it is based on the Poisson distribution, values of np_α may be obtained without the use of this table from a Poisson table such as Table F in the Appendix. For each c, the value of np_α may be obtained by going down the column under that c until the appropriate value of α is found. Then np_α may be read from the left margin.

For the above example the sample size of 116 may then be used for an np or a p chart, and a point will be above the upper limit 90% of the time when the process average is 8% nonconforming or higher. In this example the lower control limit would be zero.

Another approach favored by some authors [see Rice (1947)] is to use a p or np chart for which there is a 90% chance of getting at least one nonconforming item per sample. If the true fraction nonconforming is 2%, again use Table 7-5 and find np such

TABLE 7-5 Values of np_α

c	$np_{0.05}$	$np_{0.10}$	$np_{0.50}$	$np_{0.90}$	$np_{0.95}$
0	2.996	2.303	0.693	0.105	0.0513
1	4.744	3.890	1.678	0.532	0.355
2	6.296	5.322	2.674	1.102	0.818
3	7.754	6.681	3.672	1.745	1.366
4	9.154	7.994	4.671	2.433	1.970
5	10.513	9.274	5.670	3.152	2.613
6	11.842	10.532	6.670	3.895	3.286
7	13.148	11.771	7.669	4.656	3.981
8	14.434	12.995	8.669	5.432	4.695
9	15.705	14.206	9.669	6.221	5.426
10	16.962	15.407	10.668	7.021	6.169
11	18.208	16.598	11.668	7.829	6.924
12	19.442	17.782	12.668	8.646	7.690
13	20.668	18,958	13.668	9.470	8.464
14	21.886	20.128	14.668	10.300	9.246
15	23.098	21.292	15.668	11.135	10.035

that $P(x \geq 1) = 0.90$ or $P(c < 1) = 0.10$. This is the value of $np_{0.10}$ corresponding to $c = 0$ or 2.303. The required minimum value of n then would be

$$n = 2.303/0.02 = 115$$

A third approach to the solution of the sample size problem would be to specify that the sample size should be large enough to have a 50% chance of rejecting a sample when the true value of θ increases by a certain amount from the value used for the centerline. The chart should be constructed so that, if the normal approximation to the binomial distribution is used, the upper control limit will be at the mean of the normal distribution as shown in Figure 7-9. In Figure 7-9 recall that the mean of this normal distribution is np_0

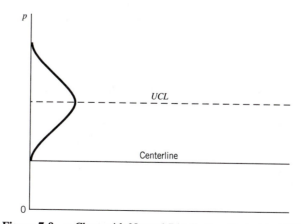

Figure 7-9 p Chart with Normal Distribution Centered at *UCL*

and the distance between the UCL and the centerline is $3\sqrt{p_0(1 - p_0)/n}$. Thus, with a p chart centered at, say, 0.05 and for a 50% chance of catching a shift in θ of 0.04, the sample size would be determined as follows:

$$3\sqrt{p_0(1 - p_0)/n} = d$$
$$n = 9p_0(1 - p_0)/d^2 \tag{7-8}$$

or

$$n = 9(0.05)(0.95)/(0.04)^2 = 267$$

A sample size at least equal to 267 is needed to meet this situation.

▶ 7-4 CHARTS FOR NUMBER OF NONCONFORMITIES

7-4.1 Standard Given

Now consider a situation in which each sample unit may have a number of different types of quality variants or nonconformities. The variable of interest becomes the number of nonconformities rather than the number of units that have one or more nonconformities. An example of a situation in which this type of chart is applicable is the case of inspecting tables in a furniture factory. The interest is in the number of minor surface blemishes on the table tops. Theoretically, the situation is that there are an infinite number of places for a blemish to occur, and the probability of such a blemish occurring in any given place is very small (virtually zero). However, there may still occur an average of c blemishes per table top. This is clearly a situation in which n is large, θ is small, $n\theta = \lambda$ is a finite number, and the Poisson distribution would apply.

The variable charted will be the number of nonconformities in each sample unit, and the sample unit must remain constant from sample to sample. The opportunity for a nonconformity must remain constant. For example, this means that if some tables have twice the surface area of others, two of the small or one of the larger tables must be considered as a sample unit.

This chart is usually called a c chart, where c is the number of nonconformities per sample unit. The standard value of c will be c_0, and the average c is denoted $\bar{c}$. Because the standard deviation of the Poisson distribution is the positive square root of the mean, the 3σ control limits will be, for the standard given case,

$$UCL = c_0 + 3\sqrt{c_0} \tag{7-9}$$
$$LCL = c_0 - 3\sqrt{c_0}$$

As an example, suppose a control chart is needed to record the results of inspections of tables and the standard will be an average of four surface blemishes per table. The control limits would then be at

$$4 \pm 3\sqrt{4} = 4 \pm 6 = 0 \text{ to } 10$$

If there are ten or more blemishes on a table, the table will be returned for refinishing.

7-4.2 No Standard Given

This chart will be the same as the standard given chart, except that the average value of c will be estimated empirically. The control limits would then be

$$UCL = \bar{c} + 3\sqrt{\bar{c}} \qquad (7\text{-}10)$$
$$LCL = \bar{c} - 3\sqrt{\bar{c}}$$

This type of chart is useful wherever the quality characteristic is such that the number of quality variants is important rather than the presence or absence of one or more variants. Further examples might be the number of defective welds in an aircraft fuselage, the number of blemishes in a bolt of cloth, the number of accidents on a shift, or the number of typing errors in a letter.

7-4.3 Variable Unit Size

If the area of opportunity varies from sample to sample, the unit size may be standardized and the standardized c chart or u chart be used, where $u = c/k$ and k is the number of inspection units in each sample. As an example, suppose that the table-manufacturing facility makes tables of various sizes, and interest is in controlling the number of blemishes per tabletop. Table 7-6 contains the results of the inspection of twenty such tables. For a standard given situation the control chart would be constructed as follows:

$$UCL = u_0 + 3\sqrt{u_0/k} \qquad (7\text{-}11)$$
$$LCL = u_0 - 3\sqrt{u_0/k}$$

TABLE 7-6 Inspection Results of Tables

Table No.	Surface Area in Square Meters	No. of Blemishes	No. of Blemishes per Square Meter
1	2.0	4	2.0
2	2.0	5	2.5
3	2.0	1	0.5
4	4.0	9	2.3
5	5.0	14	2.8
6	2.5	3	1.2
7	3.0	6	2.0
8	3.0	6	2.0
9	3.0	3	1.0
10	4.2	10	2.4
11	2.8	4	1.4
12	2.8	8	2.9
13	3.2	8	2.5
14	3.2	16	5.0
15	3.2	8	2.5
16	3.2	8	2.5
17	4.2	8	1.9
18	4.2	12	2.9
19	2.8	6	2.1
20	2.8	8	2.9
Totals	63.1	147	

where u_0 is the standard value. Note that this means that the control limits will vary with k. If there is no standard given, u_0 must be estimated by $\bar{u}$, the average of past results.

For the data in Table 7-6, compute $\bar{u}$ as the total number of blemishes divided by the total surface area in all twenty samples:

$$\bar{u} = 147/63.1 = 2.33$$

Note that $\bar{u}$ is not the simple arithmetic mean of the u values in the right-hand column of Table 7-6. To use them, each value must be weighted by its surface area. If that is done, the same result would be obtained.

Now construct the control chart using the value of $\bar{u}$ calculated above:

$$UCL = 2.33 + 3\sqrt{2.33/k} = 2.33 + 4.58/\sqrt{k}$$
$$LCL = 2.33 - 3\sqrt{2.33/k} = 2.33 - 4.58/\sqrt{k}$$

Again consider the three procedures for handling this situation that were used to handle the variable sample size application of the p chart. These procedures are as follows:

1. Use variable control limits.

2. Use an average k value to compute the control limits.

3. Use an average value of k to compute control limits, and use the actual k for points near these limits.

The first of the methods for this example is illustrated by Table 7-7. Figure 7-10 illustrates the control chart with the data plotted on it. Observation of Figure 7-10 tells us

TABLE 7-7 Control Limits for u Chart

Sample No.	k	UCL	LCL
1	2.0	5.57	0
2	2.0	5.57	0
3	2.0	5.57	0
4	4.0	4.62	0.04
5	5.0	4.38	0.28
6	2.5	5.23	0
7	3.0	4.97	0
8	3.0	4.97	0
9	3.0	4.97	0
10	4.2	4.56	0.10
11	2.8	5.07	0
12	2.8	5.07	0
13	3.2	4.89	0
14	3.2	4.89	0
15	3.2	4.89	0
16	3.2	4.89	0
17	4.2	4.56	0.10
18	4.2	4.56	0.10
19	2.8	5.07	0
20	2.8	5.07	0

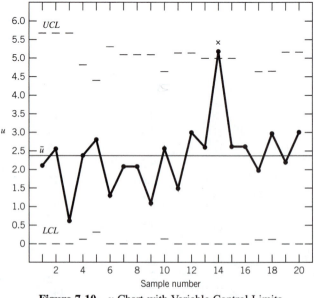

Figure 7-10 u Chart with Variable Control Limits

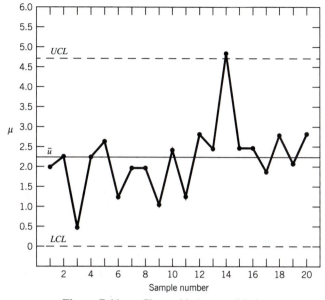

Figure 7-11 u Chart with Average Limits

that table number 14 has an excessive number of scratches, while the remainder seem to present a reasonably random pattern about $\bar{u}$.

The second method would use an average surface area of

$$\bar{k} = 63.1/20 = 3.16 \text{ square meters}$$

The control limits would then be

$$UCL = 2.33 + 4.58/\sqrt{3.16} = 2.33 + 2.58 = 4.91$$
$$LCL = 2.33 - 2.58 - 0$$

A quick review of Table 7-6 indicates that table number 14 is again above this limit, so the same conclusion would be reached using this procedure as with the variable limits.

Using the third procedure, draw the chart as indicated in Figure 7-11 using 3.16 as the average value of k. The upper control limit is 4.91, and the lower limit is zero. Observation of the control chart in Figure 7-11 indicates that exact limits should be computed for points 3 and 14. All the rest are significantly away from the control limits. Point 3 needs the exact lower limit, and the exact upper limit is needed for point 14. These limits were calculated in Table 7-7 and were zero for the LCL for table 3 and 4.89 for the UCL for table 14. The first is no change from that using an average k. The second, 4.89, is also no appreciable difference from the 4.91 value used in Figure 7-11. Thus, the conclusion is again that only table number 14 has an excessive number of blemishes.

▶ 7-5 OC CURVES FOR ATTRIBUTES CONTROL CHARTS

7-5.1 *p* Charts

The operating characteristic (OC) curve for any statistical technique is a plot of the probability of accepting a hypothesis about a parameter versus the true value of that parameter.

TABLE 7-8 OC Curve for p Chart

θ	$n\theta$	$\sigma_p = \sqrt{\dfrac{\theta(1-\theta)}{100}}$	$\dfrac{0.115 - \theta}{\sigma_p}$	P_a
0	0			1.000
0.05	5			0.995
0.08	8			0.89
0.10	10			0.70
0.13	13	.0336	−0.45	0.33
0.20	20	.0400	−2.13	0.02

In this case consider the probability that a sample estimate, $\hat{p}$, will fall within the control limits versus the true value of θ. Similar considerations will be made about other parameters in later chapters. The purpose of the OC curve is to describe the ability of the control chart to detect parameter shifts.

To illustrate this concept, assume there is a p chart with $p_0 = 0.05$ and $n = 100$. This means that the upper control limit will be at $0.050 + 0.065$ or 0.115. This means that for the number of nonconforming pieces in a sample, eleven or fewer would be within the control limits, while twelve or more would be outside. The lower control limit would be zero.

The probability of a sample p being inside the control limits (i.e., the probability of eleven or fewer nonconforming pieces) may be computed from the binomial distribution as

$$P_a = \sum_{x=[nLCL+1]}^{[nUCL]} \binom{n}{x}(\theta)^x(1-\theta)^{n-x} \tag{7-12}$$

where $[*]$ = the largest integer that is less than $*$. This computation may be approximated by either the normal distribution or the Poisson. A good rule is to use the Poisson for values of θ less than or equal to 0.10 and the normal for larger values. Table 7-8 illustrates the calculations needed. Figure 7-12 shows the resulting plot of the OC curve.[1]

7-5.2 c Charts

To compute the operating characteristic curve for a c chart, the appropriate distribution is the Poisson. Therefore, no approximations would be necessary, and Table F in the Appendix would be used to compute probabilities for all values of c. As an illustration of this procedure, use a control chart with $c_0 = 4.0$ nonconformities per sample unit. The upper control limit for the c chart would be at $c_0 + 3\sqrt{c_0} = 10$. Because $c_0 - 3\sqrt{c_0}$ would be a negative number, the lower limit would be zero. Table 7-9 illustrates the procedure to be used to construct the OC curve. In the table λ represents the true value of c, that is, the true number of nonconformities per sample unit.

Figure 7-13 is a graph of the OC curve for this control chart. From Figure 7-13 one can observe that if a process is operating at a quality level of $\lambda = 9$ nonconformities per

---

[1]An exact computation may be made with the incomplete beta function used to compute a cumulative binomial, but because values of θ are assumed here, the approximations presented are appropriate.

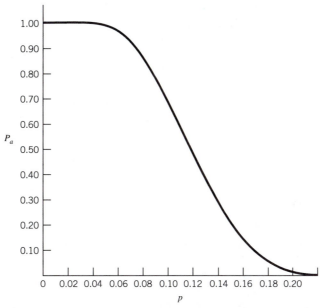

Figure 7-12 OC Curve for p Chart with $p_0 = 0.05$ and $n = 100$

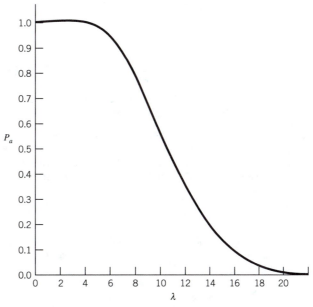

Figure 7-13 OC Curve for c Chart with $c_0 = 4.0$

TABLE 7-9 Computations for OC Curve for c Chart

λ	$P(c \leq 10)$	λ	$P(c \leq 10)$
0	1.000	10	0.583
4	0.997	12	0.347
6	0.957	15	0.118
8	0.815	20	0.010

unit, the probability of not detecting this change from 4.0 on the next sample is 0.7. That is, the probability of detecting it is 0.3. Similarly, the probability that at least one of the next two samples will be out of control is $1 - (0.7)^2 = 1 - 0.49 = 0.51$.

Similar OC curves may be produced for all the other attribute control charts discussed in this chapter. Details of the development of such charts are left to the reader. For a discussion of the design of attribute control charts see papers by Chiu (1975, 1976), Gibra (1978, 1981), Montgomery (1980), Montgomery, Heikes, and Mance (1975), Montgomery and Heikes (1976), Vaughn and Peters (1991), and Williams, Looney, and Peters (1985, 1990).

▶ 7-6 SUMMARY

This chapter has extended the discussion of control charts for attributes that was begun in Chapter 6. The demonstration that was started there has been continued to illustrate how the attribute (p) chart is able to detect changes in the parameters of the process under study. This extension has consisted of detailed discussions of four types of attributes control charts: the np chart, p chart, c chart, and u chart. Illustrations of the use of each control chart have been given. Evaluations of the performance characteristics of the p and c charts have been presented.

The next chapter continues this extension of the introduction begun in Chapter 6 by developing control charts for variables. Still other types of charts are presented in later chapters.

▶ 7-7 REFERENCES

American Society for Quality, ANSI/ISO/ASQ A3534-2-2001, *Statistics—Vocabulary and Symbols—Applied Statistics,* ASQ, Milwaukee.

Chiu, W. K. (1975), "Economic Design of Attribute Control Charts," *Technometrics,* Vol. 17, No. 1, pp. 81–87.

Chiu, W. K. (1976), "Economic Design of np Charts for Processes Subject to a Multiplicity of Assignable Causes," *Management Science,* Vol. 23, pp. 404–11.

Gibra, I. N. (1978), "Economically Optimal Determination of the Parameters of np Control Charts," *Journal of Quality Technology,* Vol. 10, No. 1, pp. 12–19.

Gibra, I. N. (1981), "Economic Design of Attribute Control Charts for Multiple Assignable Causes," *Journal of Quality Technology,* Vol. 13, No. 2, pp. 93–99.

Montgomery, D. C. (1980), "The Economic Design of Control Charts: A Review and Literature Survey," *Journal of Quality Technology,* Vol. 12, No. 2, pp. 75–87.

Montgomery, D. C., Heikes, R. G., and Mance, J. F. (1975), "Economic Design of Fraction Defective Control Charts," *Management Science,* Vol. 21, No. 11, pp. 1272–84.

Montgomery, D. C., and Heikes, R. G. (1976), "Process Failure Mechanisms and Optimal Design of Fraction Defective Control Charts," *AIIE Transactions,* December, pp. 467–72.

Nelson, L. S. (1989), "Standardization of Shewhart Control Charts," *Journal of Quality Technology,* Vol. 21, No. 4, pp. 287–89.

Rice, W. B. (1947), *Control Charts in Factory Management,* Wiley, New York, p. 82.

Rocke, D. M. (1990), "The Adjusted p Chart and u Chart for Varying Sample Sizes," *Journal of Quality Technology,* Vol. 22, No. 3, pp. 206–209.

Vaughn, T. S., and Peters, M. H. (1991), "Economic Design of Fraction Nonconforming Control Charts with Multiple State Changes," *Journal of Quality Technology,* Vol. 23, No. 1, pp. 32–43.

Williams, W. W., Looney, S. W., and Peters, M. H. (1985), "Use of Curtailed Sampling Plans in the Economic Design of np Control Charts," *Technometrics,* Vol. 27, No. 1, pp. 57–63.

Williams, W. W., Looney, S. W., and Peters, M. H. (1990), "Improved Curtailed Sampling Plans for np Control Charts," *Journal of Quality Technology,* Vol. 22, No. 2, pp. 118–27.

▶ 7-8 PROBLEMS

1. Continue Problems 1 and 2 and/or 3 of Chapter 6 extending the control limits as computed (both regular and warning limits). Take ten additional samples, recording the *total* number of colored beads (red, yellow, and black) as denoting an increased level of nonconformities of the red type. Calculate p_i (%) and plot these results on the extended control chart. Interpret the results.

2. Plot the data of Table 7-2 on Figure 7-2. Determine approximate (more than ten points are usually preferred) control limits for the *p* chart to be used to monitor subsequent production and to maintain control of the process at the improved level. Do not assume knowledge of the true percentage.

3. Repeat Problem 1 by computer analysis.

4. An *np* chart is to be used following an operation on an assembly line. A roving inspector takes a sample of 100 pieces every hour and checks for nonconforming pieces. The inspector posts the results to the chart and has authority to shut down the line if a sample is out of control. The chart is based on a standard value of $p_0 = 0.04$.
(a) What are the centerline and control limits for the *np* chart?
(b) If the true process average fraction nonconforming is 0.12, what is the probability the inspector will shut down the line following his next inspection?

5. An *np* chart is to be based on samples of fifty units taken four times a shift. What are the control limits if the results of twenty samples indicate an average of 3% nonconforming?

6. Construct an OC curve for the control chart in Problem 5. Determine the OC function at $\theta = 0.04, 0.10$, and 0.15.

7. For the inspection results tabulated below, present a *c* chart analysis with graphic representation.

Sample Number	No. of Nonconformities	Sample Number	No. of Nonconformities
1	11	11	21
2	23	12	36
3	35	13	20
4	19	14	48
5	22	15	29
6	25	16	13
7	28	17	22
8	14	18	26
9	50	19	18
10	23	20	30

8. Determine variable control limits for the following five lots of finished parts. *N* is the lot size, and *x* is the number of nonconforming parts in each lot. On the basis of your results, do the lots appear to come from the same controlled process?

Lot	N	x
1	500	32
2	50	10
3	800	10
4	100	18
5	150	20

9. A *p* chart is being used in connection with the inspection of a certain process. The results of the last ten samples are as follows:

Sample Number	No. Inspected	No. Nonconforming	p
1	100	5	0.050
2	90	1	0.011
3	500	20	0.040
4	400	10	0.025
5	100	2	0.020
6	100	8	0.080
7	60	5	0.083
8	50	5	0.100
9	400	10	0.025
10	200	4	0.020

Compute the final control limits for the process.

10. The following are the results of the inspection of fifteen sample units.

No.	No. of Nonconformities	No.	No. of Nonconformities
1	4	9	9
2	2	10	4
3	8	11	7
4	10	12	3
5	9	13	15
6	16	14	4
7	2	15	5
8	6		

Present a *c* chart analysis of the data. Does the analysis indicate the process to be in control?

11. The following are the results of the inspection of fifteen samples of 100 units each:

No.	No. Nonconforming	No.	No. Nonconforming
1	7	9	4
2	2	10	2
3	3	11	3
4	7	12	0
5	1	13	2
6	0	14	0
7	0	15	6
8	5		

(a) Present a p chart analysis with graphic presentation.
(b) If the quality level changed to 8% nonconforming, what is the probability that the next sample would be out of control on your control chart?

12. The following are the results of the inspection of eight samples:

Sample Size	No. of Nonconforming Pieces
100	7
49	2
64	3
100	4
100	5
25	1
81	5
81	3

Present a p chart with graphic presentation using variable control limits.

13. Compute OC curves for the following:
(a) A c chart with $\bar{c} = 10$ nonconformities per sample
(b) A p chart with $\bar{p} = 0.06$ and sample size 100

14. The following data refer to the results of the inspection of shirts in a factory. The number of imperfections in each bundle inspected is indicated. The number of shirts in each bundle varies. Determine a u chart to use for monitoring this process. Show the OC curve for this chart. Is the process in control?

Bundle No.	No. of Shirts	No. of Imperfections
1	12	5
2	4	3
3	18	10

(continued)

Bundle No.	No. of Shirts	No. of Imperfections
4	18	8
5	20	18
6	6	8
7	8	2
8	10	5
9	6	12
10	14	10
11	16	12
12	16	20
13	12	3
14	20	18
15	5	4
16	6	5
17	12	15
18	12	8
19	16	18
20	10	9

15. Completely assembled combines are subjected to a visual inspection (including operation of functional mechanisms) before being released for sale. Necessary repairs are made when required. Additionally, feedback of results to the assembly and parts sections was initiated to reduce the number of repairs and attempt to prevent nonconformities. The following data were collected over the month during which the special studies were undertaken. Prepare a c chart for the month's data. Is the process in control? Does it appear that the efforts made at reducing nonconformities have been successful?

Day	No. of Nonconformities	Day	No. of Nonconformities
1	12	16	12
2	9	17	11
3	8	18	13
4	12	19	12
5	12	20	9
6	14	21	7
7	8	22	9
8	8	23	10
9	13	24	7
10	12	25	10
11	14	26	9
12	8	27	8
13	12	28	5
14	12	29	7
15	14	30	5

16. The following is a record of the number of glass beer bottles containing stones and seeds in daily samples for a period of one month of continuous operation. The daily samples consist of 2400 bottles compiled from samples of 100 taken each hour of production. Do the data indicate that the production process was in control for these quality characteristics during the month? Prepare a p chart and interpret.

Day	No. of Nonconforming Bottles	Day	No. of Nonconforming Bottles
1	209	17	223
2	146	18	252
3	166	19	223
4	142	20	254
5	168	21	307
6	154	22	274
7	146	23	168
8	144	24	156
9	175	25	168
10	178	26	137
11	137	27	154
12	180	28	170
13	190	29	180
14	180	30	149
15	206	31	139
16	324		

17. A bottling company of a popular beverage maintains daily records of the occurrences of unacceptable units flowing from the filling and capping machine. Nonconformities such as (1) improper filling height, (2) bottles with no caps, (3) dirty bottles, (4) broken or cracked bottles, and (5) bottles with foreign matter are noted. Data for two months' production are given below. Prepare p charts for these data. Do the charts indicate the process is in control? Does it appear that improvement in the level of nonconformities may be possible?

November Data:

Units Produced	No. of Nonconformities	Fraction
3870	111	0.0287
4694	143	0.0305
1265	52	0.0411
3783	120	0.0317
4340	143	0.0329
6414	244	0.0380
2079	61	0.0293

(continued)

Units Produced	No. of Nonconformities	Fraction
2530	59	0.0233
2380	59	0.0248
2441	87	0.0356
1718	40	0.0233
2260	46	0.0204
2190	66	0.0301
3553	251	0.0706
2533	78	0.0308
3300	60	0.0182
4100	81	0.0198
2118	70	0.0331
1969	59	0.0300
2964	74	0.0250
3545	62	0.0175
2110	54	0.0256
2067	173	0.0837
2017	124	0.0615

December Data:

Units Produced	No. of Nonconformities	Fraction
2273	119	0.0524
2427	72	0.0297
2790	75	0.0269
2700	56	0.0207
2275	66	0.0290
2430	24	0.0099
2709	75	0.0277
2384	60	0.0252
3017	110	0.0365
2257	70	0.0310
2815	86	0.0306
2502	30	0.0120
2577	52	0.0202
2550	107	0.0420
1576	75	0.0476
3085	125	0.0405
3662	120	0.0328
4500	106	0.0236
1790	77	0.0430
3190	70	0.0219
2500	43	0.0172
2550	64	0.0251
2904	107	0.0368
3840	137	0.0357
3560	155	0.0435
2356	94	0.0399

18. Automotive headlamps produced in a small parts factory involve a process of vacuum deposition of reflector material on the reflector surface. The following data represent two months of production during which some difficulties were experienced with the deposition unit. Analyze these data by a control chart, and propose controls for future production.

Date	Units Produced	No. of Nonconforming Units
Nov. 12	181	2
13	381	3
14	173	2
15	105	16
16	258	2
20	404	3
22	480	0
26	251	10
27	415	15
28	365	15
29	625	123
Dec. 4	66	1
5	30	2
11	133	11
18	372	72
20	527	100
26	117	2
28	487	11
29	154	3
Jan. 2	435	3
9	295	1
10	401	3
11	358	3
14	209	2
15	179	1

19. (a) A factory that produces video cassettes inspects a random sample of forty units each day at a final inspection station. The following data represent results for fourteen days:

Day	No. of Nonconformities	Day	No. of Nonconformities
1	28	8	30
2	21	9	21
3	23	10	19
4	32	11	34
5	29	12	37
6	33	13	24
7	19	14	18

Discuss the type(s) of control chart(s) to be used to study this process; compute the necessary statistics and control limits; plot and interpret the control chart.
(b) Data on the same product from other factories is to be combined on the same chart for comparison of factory-to-factory quality. However, the sample size used for inspection varies between factories, from twenty to forty. How would you modify your control chart of part (a) to accommodate this new objective?

20. The following data are the results of inspecting samples of cloth for nonconformities introduced during processing. Discuss the type of control chart to be used to study this process; compute the necessary statistics and control limits; plot and interpret the control chart.

Square meters of cloth inspected:

200	80	100	300	120	90	250	50	100	70

Nonconformities found:

5	7	3	15	4	6	10	1	6	2

21. During spot welding of thin hot sheets to the frame of insulating heat shields in the production of aircraft, pinholes are seen to develop in the hot sheets. These nonconformities must be found, marked, repaired, and verified. A number of preventive measures are to be instituted to reduce these nonconformances and their associated extra costs. It is decided to use a control chart to inform operating personnel and supervision on the shield-to-shield variation, the level of nonconformance, and whether the preventive measures are effective, as well as to take further corrective action on out-of-control conditions occurring on specific shields. The following data are records for the first twelve heat shields since instituting the process study. Analyze these data by an appropriate control chart. Propose any adjustments in the control chart for future control.

Shield Series	Number of Pinholes	Shield Series	Number of Pinholes
0032	6	0038	4
0033	4	0039	5
0034	4	0040	2
0035	6	0041	0
0036	7	0042	1
0037	14	0043	2

8

CONTROL CHARTS FOR VARIABLES

Chapter 6 presented the principles of control charts, including an introduction to the variables control charts of averages ($\bar{x}$) and ranges (R). This chapter develops a more methodical and comprehensive coverage of these and other variables control charts. The demonstration begun in Chapter 6 is continued to understand how changes in the process are detected. Additional control charts for variables are introduced. These include charts for individual measurements and for variability including the range and the standard deviation. Charts for central tendency including averages, medians, and midranges are also presented. Control charts for central tendency and for variability are usually used together as discussed in Chapter 6. Applications of these charts include situations with standard given and no standard given.

▶ 8-1 DETECTION OF CHANGES WITH VARIABLES CHARTS

Chapter 6 discussed the benefit in detecting different kinds of changes in the underlying distribution by the companion use of control charts for averages and ranges. These ideas are presented next.

8-1.1 Change in Process Mean

To illustrate the behavior of the $\bar{x}$ and R control charts when the process changes, replace the chip bowl distribution described in Figure 6-14 with another having a larger mean (μ) but with the same dispersion (σ). This represents a shift in the mean of the distribution. Such a shift may occur in the hypothetical filling process (recall from Section 6-3.3 that the measurements represent deviations from nominal net weights in manual filling of jars) by a number of factors. These changes may be changes in glass jar capacity from a new shipment with visual filling to the same level, changes in fill operator, or a change in temperature, viscosity, or other properties of the formulation. The new chip bowl from which samples are to be drawn is shown, again in histogram form, in Figure 8-1. The mean (μ) has been increased two units to 2.0. The standard deviation (σ) remains at 1.72. The results of ten additional subgroups of five from this distribution are shown in Table 8-1.

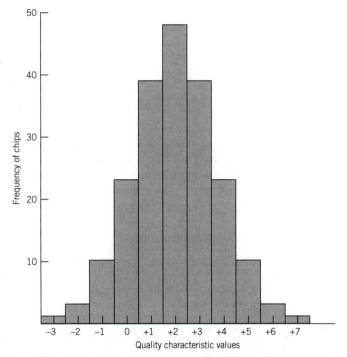

Figure 8-1   Second Normal Distribution for Chip Bowl: Shift in Mean

The control charts with the original limits extended and with these additional points plotted are shown in Figure 8-2. Were the control charts being used for process monitoring and control, these points, in $\bar{x}$ and R pairs, would be generated sequentially in time according to the prescribed frequency. Observe that the very first subgroup produces an average ($\bar{x}$) exceeding the upper control limit on the $\bar{x}$ chart, indicating an out-of-control condition. The corresponding range (R) for this subgroup is inside the control limits on the R chart. The $\bar{x}$ chart has detected the change in universe mean on the first sample of five observations! Investigation and correction of the problem should result in adjustment immediately back to the original level.

TABLE 8-1   Additional Sample Results

	2	6	0	3	3	3	3	2	3	4
	0	1	1	2	2	4	−1	1	2	2
	2	3	1	1	4	5	1	1	3	1
	7	3	1	0	2	1	2	2	3	4
	5	3	3	2	5	−1	2	2	4	0
Total	16	16	6	8	16	12	7	8	15	11
Average ($\bar{x}$)	3.2	3.2	1.2	1.6	3.2	2.4	1.4	1.6	3.0	2.2
Range (R)	7	5	3	3	3	6	4	1	2	4

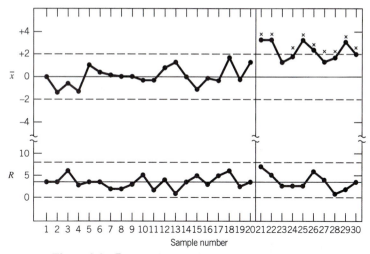

Figure 8-2 $\bar{x}$ and R Control Charts with Extended Data

Ten samples have been selected and plotted on the $\bar{x}$ and R charts to indicate the nature of the patterns resulting from this changed process, revealing important properties of the control charts. It is significant to note two particular characteristics of these new data: (1) Some of the $\bar{x}$ points fall inside the upper control limit, and (2) the pattern on the R chart is similar to that of the original twenty points; it lies inside the control limits in a controlled pattern.

Principles involving the first of these characteristics were discussed in the attribute control chart demonstrated in Chapter 7. A delay in detecting such a change is possible, because some portion of the new distribution of averages lies between the control limits for averages obtained from the original distribution of averages. The first few points could come from that portion of the distribution inside the limits, causing a delay in detection of the change. The new pattern on the $\bar{x}$ chart, as developed over ten points, is quite different from the original and reveals the nature and approximate amount of the process change. An increase in the mean is now estimated to be $\bar{\bar{x}} = 2.3$ (whereas $\mu = 2.0$).

The important principle here is that varying amounts of shift or change in the underlying distribution may require more than one point for detection. A slight increase in the mean (μ) may result in points above the centerline but within the upper control limit. This leads to the use of pattern interpretation utilizing several rules, not just a single point outside the control limits, for detecting changes. These rules were developed in Chapter 6.

While the mean of the distribution has changed, its dispersion remains the same. As the R chart measures this dispersion, it indicates no change in this property. The $\bar{x}$ and R control charts are separate monitors of these two important properties of the quality characteristic.

8-1.2 Change in Process Dispersion

Now increase the dispersion while maintaining the original process mean at 0.0, to illustrate the effects of such a change on the R chart and on the $\bar{x}$ chart. The new distribution is shown in Figure 8-3. The mean (μ) remains at 0.0. The standard deviation (σ) is increased to a

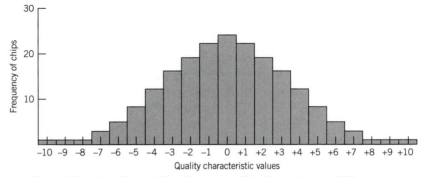

Figure 8-3   Third Normal Distribution for Chip Bowl: Increased Dispersion

value of 3.47, slightly more than double the original. For the medicated cream filling process, this distribution could result from a new operator exercising less consistency in the filling operation. Increased variability in the capacity of the jars is another possible cause.

The results of ten additional subgroups of five from this new distribution are shown in Table 8-2. The control charts, with the original limits extended further and with the additional points plotted, are shown in Figure 8-4.

Again, the $\bar{x}$ and R pairs would normally come one pair at a time, allowing a decision after each. Both the $\bar{x}$ and R values for the first subgroup are within their respective limits, illustrating the risk of a delay in detecting such changes. The R value for the second sample exceeds the upper control limit signifying an out-of-control condition for the process dispersion. The R chart has detected the change. The $\bar{x}$ value for the second subgroup is within control limits, indicating no change in the mean. Action based on the out-of-control signal from the R chart should lead to correction of the problem and a return to the original distribution.

Ten samples have again been selected and plotted on the $\bar{x}$ and R charts to reveal the nature of the patterns on the control charts resulting from this changed process. There is the higher pattern on the R chart, including some points within control limits. The higher pattern on the R chart developed over the ten points is different from the earlier patterns and reveals the nature and approximate amount of the change. This is an increase in dispersion with a standard deviation estimated as $\hat{\sigma} = \bar{R}/d_2 = 7.4/2.326 = 3.18$ (whereas $\sigma = 3.47$).

TABLE 8-2   Additional Sample Results

	−3	0	1	1	0	10	2	0	−6	−5
	3	3	−3	−1	−6	−1	0	3	5	0
	2	2	2	2	−5	−1	−1	4	2	0
	−2	−6	5	−2	−7	−2	−1	1	1	3
	3	−7	4	1	−3	0	2	5	1	3
Total	3	−8	9	1	−21	6	2	13	3	1
Average ($\bar{x}$)	0.6	−1.6	1.8	0.2	−4.2	1.2	0.4	2.6	0.6	0.2
Range (R)	6	10	8	4	7	12	3	5	11	8

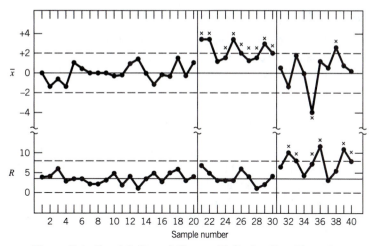

Figure 8-4 $\bar{x}$ and R Control Charts with Further Data Extension

For an increased dispersion there is a corresponding increase in the dispersion of averages as given by Equation (6-9). The mean of the new distribution of averages will be unchanged relative to the original distribution as indicated in Equation (6-8). This results in a certain proportion of the distribution of averages exceeding the control limits on both the low and high sides. This phenomenon must be considered when interpreting the patterns on $\bar{x}$ and R charts.

A comparison of the distributions for each of the three cases demonstrated above is shown in Figure 8-5. The corresponding distributions of averages are superimposed on each, as are the control limits for the $\bar{x}$ chart. Relating this visual illustration of the distributions to the control chart patterns should provide a better understanding of the principles. Additional details on the performance of variables control charts are presented next.

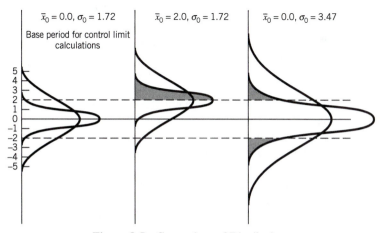

Figure 8-5 Comparison of Distributions

▶ 8-2 RATIONAL SUBGROUPS: DESIGN OF DATA COLLECTION

Control charts for variables, except for charts for individuals, involve the collection of small samples, from which the statistics for charting are computed. How the data collection is designed is important to the effective use of control charts in analyzing and controlling processes.

There are different types of variation in most processes, depending on the design of the process itself. Processes may consist of multiple machines, some newer and of different design than others. Different machines may be at different settings, affecting the centering of the underlying distribution of the quality characteristic of interest. Some may have more variability. Others may be using different batches of raw materials. Some may be automatic, semiautomatic, or mostly manual. Operators of machines and assembly processes will vary in skill, training, or attentiveness. Machines or processes may involve multiple heads or cavities, with units of product passing through only one position or many positions.

Processes will vary in the ease with which adjustments may be made and how they respond to adjustments. In some processes, the simple turning of a valve can regulate the process temperature, flow rate, amount of chemical additions, and so on. Others may involve complicated interactions, requiring careful balancing of adjustments.

These and other characteristics of processes must be considered in designing and collecting the data. Different types of process variation should be studied. There is long-term variability of a process, covering weeks or months. There is short-term variability of a process (of hours or days). There is piece-to-piece variability, variation between different pieces of product. This may be used to measure the short- and long-term variability. It denotes the inherent capability of the process as reflected by consecutive pieces.

More detailed studies may probe deeper into the nature of the variability produced by a process. There is within-piece variability at different locations on the same piece. Still more fundamental is study of the measurement process. This is essential for the analysis of any process, since statistical control of measurements is necessary to study other sources of variability [see Stephens (2000), Chapter 10].

Variables control charts are ideally suited to the study of all these forms of variability by a careful design and collection of the data used in constructing the charts, and in their interpretation. Rational samples should be selected in a manner that makes each sample as homogeneous as possible and to allow for maximum changes between the samples. Often the individual units in a sample are selected sequentially as they are produced. In such a design for data collection it should be recognized that piece-to-piece, within-piece, and measurement variability are contained within the sample and are reflected on the chart for dispersion. With a frequency between samples of fractions of hours, the short-term variability can be studied and controlled.

Since differences between samples are an indication of process changes, while differences within samples are an indication of inherent variability, the sample size selected is important. If the process is suspected of cycling with a period of N pieces, the sample size should not exceed $N/2$ pieces, as larger samples will mask the variations.

The sequence in the use of variables control charts generally consists of the following:

1. An unnatural pattern is observed.

2. After reviewing how the sample was obtained, the form of the underlying distribution that produced the unnatural pattern is determined.

3. The condition of the process producing the expected distributional form and unnatural pattern is considered.

4. Action to correct and prevent further occurrences of the undesirable condition of the process is taken.

5. The control chart is continued to confirm the desired effects of the corrective action.

Some brief examples of this sequence, emphasizing the subgrouping and control chart patterns, are presented in the latter part of Chapter 6.

Each practitioner must gain experience in the use of control charts and the above principles. Knowledge of the process by at least one member of the quality team conducting the study is essential. See also the papers by Nelson (1988), Amin and Miller (1993), and Daudin (1992) for interesting principles and alternative approaches.

▶ 8-3 RANGE (R) CHART

The most common control chart for measuring dispersion in the underlying distribution of an important quality characteristic is the range or R chart. Its popularity is mainly due to the ease with which ranges are computed. Its efficiency in estimating process dispersion, primarily for samples of small size, is almost as high as the sample standard deviation.

This chart was used to introduce variables control charts in Chapter 6. It is used as a companion chart with all three of the control charts for central tendency. Common uses for the R chart, usually in conjunction with one of the charts for central tendency, are the following:

1. To conduct process performance and process capability studies. During the process capability study, the charts serve to indicate the nature of effects of process adjustments and help to improve the process.

2. The ability of the process to meet specifications can be determined based on the capability information provided by the charts. The information serves to establish specifications for a new or modified process.

3. To serve as a basis for process control. To locate and determine the nature of production difficulties.

4. With specially prepared control limits to serve as a basis for acceptance or rejection of process runs or batches.

The basic procedure for using the R chart, usually in conjunction with one of the charts for central tendency, is as follows:

1. Select a measurable characteristic of the product or process.

2. Choose a basis for obtaining rational subgroups.
   a. Decide on the sample size (generally less than 10 and of equal size: 4 or 5 for general use, 2 for expensive experimentation).
   b. Decide on design and frequency of sampling from the process.

3. Obtain enough samples for a trial study (fifteen or more).

4. For each sample, calculate the range (difference between the largest and smallest value in the sample, i.e., $R = x_{max} - x_{min}$).

5. Decide on using standard given or no standard given for control limits. For the latter case, calculate $\bar{R}$ from the series of samples in the initial study. Calculate control limits using one of the formula sets given below.

6. Set up the control chart on the lower portion of a sheet of graph paper, reserving the upper portion for the companion chart for central tendency, with plotted points, control limits, and centerline.

7. Interpret the pattern from the trial study.
   a. If satisfactory, extend control limits as a guide for future samples, or
   b. Revise control limits as needed by removing out-of-control data points and adjusting the centerline to assist in maintaining or improving the process.
   c. For a controlled pattern, estimate the process standard deviation as $\hat{\sigma} = \bar{R}/d_2$ for the case of no standard given.

8. Periodically assess the effectiveness of the control chart, revising or discontinuing it as needed.

8-3.1 Computing Control Limits

Control limits for the R chart use the common principle $\bar{R}_0 \pm 3\sigma_R$ for the standard-given case and $\bar{R} \pm 3\sigma_R$ for the no-standard-given case. These limits and others are developed below.

No-Standard-Given Case
The most common practice under this case is the use of the average range, $\bar{R}$, to estimate σ_R. Equations (6-16) and (6-17) contain the following control limit formulas:

$$UCL_R = D_4\bar{R} \tag{8-1}$$

$$LCL_R = D_3\bar{R} \tag{8-2}$$

where D_3 and D_4, as functions of the sample size (n), are tabulated in Table H in the Appendix. See Example 8-1, later in this chapter, for an application of the range chart with no standard given.

Median Range.
When the range chart is used in conjunction with the median ($\tilde{x}$) chart, it is a common practice to base the centerline of the range chart on the median range ($\tilde{R}$). Control limits are obtained by estimating σ_R by means of the relationship.[1]

---

[1] Early papers on the use of medians and midranges for control charts are by Ferrell (1953, 1961, 1964) and Clifford (1959). However, factors for control limits used here are based on two later papers by Stephens (1964, 1974). The derived values of D_5 and D_6 are not the same as those of Ferrell and Clifford. Their derivation of D_5 and D_6 for the range chart with median range centerline is based on the principle of making the width of the limits the same as the range chart with average range centerline—a not unreasonable approach! However, this is not the same as the common procedure of placing limits of ±3 standard deviations of the statistic being plotted about the centerline. The factors and corresponding values, which are derived here, do not differ significantly from theirs and have the desirable feature of consistency.

The standard deviation of individuals	equals	True median range	divided by	Constant of proportionality factor
(σ)		$(\tilde{\mu}_R)$		(d_4)

$$\sigma = \tilde{\mu}_R/d_4 \tag{8-3}$$

where d_4, as a function of the subgroup size (n), is tabulated in Table H in the Appendix. Control limits for this case are as follows:

$$\text{Control limits} = \hat{\tilde{\mu}} \pm 3\hat{\sigma}_R = \tilde{R} \pm 3d_3\hat{\sigma} \qquad \text{from Equation (6-12)}$$
$$= \tilde{R} \pm 3d_3\tilde{R}/d_4, \qquad \text{from Equation (8-3)}$$
$$= (1 \pm 3d_3/d_4)\tilde{R}$$
$$UCL_R = D_6\tilde{R} \tag{8-4}$$
$$LCL_R = D_5\tilde{R} \tag{8-5}$$

where $D_6 = 1 + 3d_3/d_4$ and $D_5 = 1 - 3d_3/d_4$ and values, as functions of the sample size (n), are tabulated in Table H in the Appendix. Example 8-4, following discussion of the median $(\tilde{x})$ chart, later in the chapter, is an application of the range chart using the median range.

Conversions to the Range Chart. To complete the computation of control limits for the range chart for the no-standard-given case, consider a situation that may occur in some applications. Although not common, this situation arises when, after computing standard deviations, s, for each sample during a trial study, it is decided to use the R chart for subsequent samples for control. Only the formulas are given here for direct use. Derivation is left to the reader, using the relationships introduced under the standard deviation control charts and those used previously.

For this situation the average of subgroup standard deviations is available from a controlled pattern. Hence, the centerline for the R chart is

$$\text{Centerline} = (d_2/c_4)\bar{s} \tag{8-6}$$

Control limits are

$$UCL_R = (D_2/c_4)\bar{s} \tag{8-7}$$
$$LCL_R = (D_1/c_4)\bar{s}$$

where the ratios (d_2/c_4), (D_2/c_4), and (D_1/c_4), as functions of the subgroup size (n), are tabulated in Table H in the Appendix. They are expressed in the form of ratios of common control chart constants, so as not to proliferate an undue number of additional symbols.

Standard-Given Case

When σ is assumed known, control limits for the range chart were developed in Equations (6-13) and (6-14). These control limit formulas are as follows:

$$\text{Centerline} = R_0 = d_2\sigma_0 \tag{8-8}$$

where

$$\sigma = \sigma_0$$

$$UCL_R = D_2\sigma_0 \qquad (8\text{-}9)$$

$$LCL_R = D_1\sigma_0 \qquad (8\text{-}10)$$

where D_1 and D_2, as functions of the sample size (n), are tabulated in Table H in the Appendix.

▶ 8-4 STANDARD DEVIATION CHART

With the relative ease with which it is possible to compute standard deviations by calculators with built-in functions or by spreadsheets or statistical software, the standard deviation control chart is growing in use as the control chart for measuring dispersion in the underlying distribution. It offers greater efficiency in estimating dispersion than the range chart and is more flexible for applications involving larger and unequal subgroup sizes.

Common uses for the standard deviation chart, usually with the average ($\bar{x}$) chart for central tendency, are primarily those listed under the range chart above. The usual expression for computing the sample standard deviation was given in Chapter 5 and is shown here as Equation (8-11):

$$s = \sqrt{\frac{\sum\limits_{i=1}^{n}(x_i - \bar{x})^2}{(n-1)}} = \sqrt{\frac{\sum\limits_{i=1}^{n}x_i^2 - (\Sigma x_i^2)/n}{(n-1)}} \qquad (8\text{-}11)$$

Early users of control charts employed a slightly different method of computing the standard deviation of a sample. This was discussed in Chapter 5 and is mentioned here again for emphasis. The alternative is the square root of the sum of the squared deviations of observations from their mean divided by the number of observations rather than ($n - 1$). This statistic will be called the root mean square deviation and is computed by

$$s_{(\text{rms})} = \sqrt{\frac{\Sigma(x - \bar{x})^2}{n}} = \sqrt{\frac{\Sigma x^2 - (\Sigma x)^2/n}{n}} \qquad (8\text{-}12)$$

The choice of the two statistics revolves around the common controversy: Shall n or ($n - 1$) be used in the denominator? The answer is, for most quality control work, it does not matter much! The primary purpose of the control chart is to determine whether a state of statistical control exists. Either statistic serves that purpose well for dispersion in the underlying process. Estimation of the process parameter, σ, is a purpose also, but a secondary one. Both s and $s_{(\text{rms})}$ are biased estimators of σ, but s^2 is an unbiased estimator of σ^2, while $s_{(\text{rms})}^2$ is biased. The term $s_{(\text{rms})}$ has some physical and mathematical appeal, it is the maximum likelihood estimator of σ, and with the use of the appropriate correction factor, either gives the same estimate of σ. It is customary in most industrial applications and by most statisticians to use s as defined in Equations (5-13) and (8-11) rather than $s_{(\text{rms})}$.

The important factor in the choice is consistency and use of the correct relationships and associated constants. These are developed subsequently. Because of the above-mentioned common practice, s will be used throughout the remainder of this chapter, but references to $s_{(\text{rms})}$ will be made for completeness. For those wishing to use $s_{(\text{rms})}$, consult Table H in the Appendix for the necessary tabulations of associated constants.

The basic procedure for using the standard deviation chart, usually in conjunction with the average ($\bar{x}$) chart for central tendency, is as follows:

1. Select a measurable characteristic of the product or process you wish to study. Applications for existing data, even where sample sizes are not equal, are possible.
2. Choose a basis for obtaining rational subgroups.
   a. Decide on sample size, generally less than 10 and of equal size, but if specific conditions warrant, much larger sample sizes can be used, and they do not have to be equal for application of the control chart.
   b. Decide on the design and frequency of samples from the process.
3. Obtain enough samples for a trial study, fifteen or more.
4. For each sample, calculate the standard deviation.
5. Decide on using standard given or no standard given for control limits. For the latter case, calculate the weighted average standard deviation, $\bar{s}$, accounting for unequal sample sizes if present, in the series of samples in the initial study.
6. Calculate control limits using the appropriate formula given below. This may be done for each of the sample sizes represented in the study. If only a few points are of different size, control limits for the principal sample size may be calculated. After observing the position of these standard deviations on the chart, calculate control limits for other sample sizes. The calculations may be performed if these data points fall near the control limits of the common subgroup size.
7. Set up the control chart on the lower portion of the graph paper, reserving the upper portion for the companion chart for averages, with plotted points, control limits, and centerline.
8. Interpret the pattern from the trial study.
   a. If satisfactory, extend control limits as a guide for future samples, or
   b. Revise the control limits as needed by removing out-of-control data points, adjusting the centerline, etc., to assist in maintaining or improving the process.
   c. For a controlled pattern, it may be desirable to estimate the process standard deviation as $\hat{\sigma} = \bar{s}/c_4$ (as introduced in Chapter 5) for the case of no standard given.
   d. Periodically assess the effectiveness of the control chart, revising or discontinuing it as appropriate.

8-4.1 Computing Control Limits

The common principle, $\sigma_0 \pm 3\sigma_s$, for the standard-given case and $\bar{s} \pm 3\sigma_s$, for the no-standard-given case, is used for developing control limits for the standard deviation control chart. Basic relationships are used to derive from this principle control limits using common parameters or statistics with applications.

No-Standard-Given Case
When σ is unknown, estimates must be obtained from the data. The value of $\bar{s}$ is computed as follows, using the s_i values obtained for the samples in the trial study:

$$\bar{s} = \sqrt{\frac{\sum\limits_{i=1}^{k} (n_i - 1)s_i^2}{\sum n_i - k}} \tag{8-13}$$

for unequal sample sizes, or

$$= \sum_{i=1}^{k} s_i/k, \qquad \text{for k equal size subgroups}$$

Derivation of control limits proceeds from the following relationships, linking μ_s and σ_s with σ:

The standard deviation of individuals	equals	Average standard deviation	divided by	Constant of proportionality factor
(σ)		(μ_s)		(c_4)

$$\sigma = \mu_s/c_4 \tag{8-14}$$

The standard deviation of individuals	equals	Standard deviation of standard deviations	divided by	Constant of proportionality factor
(σ)		(σ_s)		(c_5)

$$\sigma = \sigma_s/c_5 \tag{8-15}$$

where c_4 and c_5 as functions[2] of the subgroup size (n) are tabulated in Table H in the Appendix.

Hence, control limits for the s chart are

$$\text{Control limits} = \hat{\mu}_s \pm 3\hat{\sigma}_s$$
$$= \bar{s} \pm 3c_5\hat{\sigma}, \qquad \text{from Equation (8-15)}$$
$$= \bar{s} \pm 3c_5(\bar{s}/c_4), \qquad \text{from Equation (8-14)}$$
$$= (1 \pm 3c_5/c_4)\bar{s}$$
$$UCL_s = B_4\bar{s} \tag{8-16}$$
$$LCL_s = B_3\bar{s} \tag{8-17}$$

where $B_4 = (1 + 3c_5/c_4)$ and $B_3 = (1 - 3c_5/c_4)$ are tabulated in Table H in the Appendix.

---

[2]These constants c_4 and c_5, as well as corresponding constants c_2 and c_3 for $s_{(rms)}$, are also functions of each other. Since, for example, each $s_{(rms)}$ value is $\sqrt{(n-1)/n}$ times the corresponding s_i (i.e., for the same sample), it follows that $\bar{s}_{(rms)} = \sqrt{(n-1)/n}\,\bar{s}$ and, hence, $c_2 = \sqrt{(n-1)/n}\,c_4$. The value of c_4 is derived directly in terms of n as follows:

$$c_4 = (2/(n-1))^{1/2}[((n-2)/2)!/((n-3)/2)!]$$

Furthermore,

$$c_2 = (2/n)^{1/2}[((n-2)/2)!/((n-3)/2)!] = c_4((n-1)/n)^{1/2}$$
$$c_3 = ((n-1)/n - c_2^2)^{1/2}$$
$$c_4 = c_2((n/(n-1))^{1/2}$$
$$c_5 = c_3(n/(n-1))^{1/2} = (1 - c_4^2)^{1/2}$$

See, for example, Mosteller (1946) and Duncan (1986).

Corresponding control limits for use with $\bar{s}_{(rms)}$ may be developed by using the constants c_2 and c_3 in place of c_4 and c_5 (see footnote 2). The resulting limits would be at $B_4\bar{s}_{(rms)}$ and $B_3\bar{s}_{(rms)}$ for the upper and lower control limits, respectively.

Example 8-2, later in this chapter, is an application of the standard deviation (s) chart with no standard given.

Conversions to Standard Deviation Charts. Situations sometimes occur when it may be desired to develop a standard deviation control chart after computing ranges for each sample in a trial study. Only the formulas are given here for direct use. Derivation is left to the reader using the relationships developed for the standard deviation and the range control charts. For an s chart with $\bar{R}$ available from a controlled pattern

$$\text{Centerline} = (c_4/d_2)\bar{R} \tag{8-18}$$
$$UCL_s = (B_6/d_2)\bar{R} \tag{8-19}$$
$$LCL_s = (B_5/d_2)\bar{R} \tag{8-20}$$

where the ratios (c_4/d_2), (B_6/d_2), and (B_5/d_2) are tabulated in Table H in the Appendix. As with the R chart conversion they are expressed in the form of ratios of common control chart constants so that an undue number of additional symbols are not proliferated.

Standard-Given Case

When σ is assumed known or a standard value, σ_0, is to be used, control limits for the standard deviation chart are obtained directly from the common control limit principles (8-14) and (8-15) as follows:

$$
\begin{aligned}
\text{Control limits} &= \mu_s \pm 3\sigma_s \\
&= c_4\sigma_0 \pm 3c_5\sigma_0, \qquad \text{from Equations (8-14) and (8-15)} \\
&= (c_4 \pm 3c_5)\sigma_0,
\end{aligned}
$$

$$\text{Centerline} = c_4\sigma_0 \tag{8-21}$$
$$UCL_s = B_6\sigma_0 \tag{8-22}$$
$$LCL_s = B_5\sigma_0 \tag{8-23}$$

where $B_6 = (c_4 + 3c_5)$ and $B_5 = (c_4 - 3c_5)$ are tabulated in Table H in the Appendix. The lower control limit for the standard deviation chart is fixed by convention at zero for sample sizes of five and under to avoid a negative lower control limit for this positive-valued statistic. Example 8-3, later in this chapter, is an application of the standard deviation chart with standard given.

► 8-5 AVERAGE ($\bar{x}$) CHART

The most common control chart for central tendency in the underlying distribution of an important quality characteristic is that of the average or $\bar{x}$ chart. Its relative ease of computation and application and its sensitivity in detecting changes in the mean of the underlying distribution (as demonstrated in Section 8-1) account for its popularity. Common uses of the $\bar{x}$ chart, usually in conjunction with one of the charts for dispersion (R or s), are outlined under the range chart earlier in this chapter.

The basic procedures for using the $\bar{x}$ chart are similar to those for the range and standard deviation charts. The average ($\bar{x}_i$) is computed for each sample. For the case of no standard given, the weighted grand average ($\bar{\bar{x}}$) for the samples in the trial study is computed for use as the centerline of the chart. It is also the estimate of the mean for a controlled process.

8-5.1 Computing Control Limits

Control limits for the $\bar{x}$ chart use the common principle $\mu \pm 3\sigma_{\bar{x}}$ or $\bar{x}_0 \pm 3\sigma_{\bar{x}}$ for the standard-given case and $\hat{\mu} \pm 3\hat{\sigma}_{\bar{x}}$, for the no-standard-given case. Important relationships were indicated in Chapter 6, and control limit formulas for use with the range chart were developed. These are summarized here together with the development of control limit formulas for use with the standard deviation control charts.

No-Standard-Given Case

With Range Chart. Using Equations (6-9) and (6-11), control limit formulas were developed as Equation (6-18) as follows:

$$UCL_{\bar{x}} = \bar{\bar{x}} + A_2\bar{R} \tag{8-24}$$

$$LCL_{\bar{x}} = \bar{\bar{x}} - A_2\bar{R} \tag{8-25}$$

where A_2 values are tabulated in Table G in the Appendix.

With Standard Deviation (s) *Chart.* Equations (6-9) and (8-14) are used to develop control chart formulas for an $\bar{x}$ chart to be used in conjunction with the s chart as follows:

$$\text{Control limits} = \bar{\bar{x}} \pm 3\hat{\sigma}_{\bar{x}}$$

$$= \bar{\bar{x}} \pm 3(\hat{\sigma}/\sqrt{n}), \qquad \text{from Equation (6-9)}$$

$$= \bar{\bar{x}} \pm (3/\sqrt{n})(\bar{s}/c_4), \qquad \text{from Equation (8-14) with } \bar{s} \text{ used for } \mu_s$$

$$UCL_{\bar{x}} = \bar{\bar{x}} + A_3\bar{s} \tag{8-26}$$

$$LCL_{\bar{x}} = \bar{\bar{x}} - A_3\bar{s} \tag{8-27}$$

where $A_3 = 3/c_4\sqrt{n}$ is tabulated in Table G in the Appendix.

Standard-Given Case

When μ and σ are known or standard values, $\bar{x}_0$ and σ_0, are given; control limits for the $\bar{x}$ chart are obtained directly from the basic relationship of Equation (6-9), as developed in Equation (6-10). This results in the following control limit formulas:

$$UCL_{\bar{x}} = \bar{x}_0 + A\sigma_0 \tag{8-28}$$

$$LCL_{\bar{x}} = \bar{x}_0 - A\sigma_0 \tag{8-29}$$

where A, as a function of the subgroup size (n), is tabulated in Table G in the Appendix.

Three examples follow to illustrate the computations and some uses for $\bar{x}$ and R, and $\bar{x}$ and s control charts.

► **EXAMPLE 8-1**

The melt index of an extrusion-grade polyethylene compound is to be studied to determine variation in this property and to relate it to raw material, shift, and other changes in the process. Ability of the process to produce within maximum and minimum specification limits is also to be studied. A sample of four is selected to correspond to the melt index values produced and tested by one shift. Data for seven days, yielding twenty samples, are used as an initial study. The data with computation of the averages and ranges are shown in Table 8-3.

Control limit computation for the average ($\bar{x}$) and range (R) control charts is as follows:

$$\bar{\bar{x}} = \Sigma \bar{x}_i/20 = 4700.75/20 = 235.0375$$
$$\bar{R} = \Sigma R_i/20 = 375/20 = 18.75$$

$$UCL_{\bar{x}} = \bar{\bar{x}} + A_2\bar{R} = 235.04 + 0.729(18.75) = 248.71, \qquad \text{from Equation (8-24)}$$
$$LCL_{\bar{x}} = \bar{\bar{x}} - A_2\bar{R} = 235.04 - 13.67 = 221.37, \qquad \text{from Equation (8-25)}$$
$$UCL_R = D_4\bar{R} = 2.282(18.75) = 42.8, \qquad \text{from Equation (8-1)}$$
$$LCL_R = D_3\bar{R} = 0.0(18.75) = 0.0, \qquad \text{from Equation (8-2)}$$

The control charts are shown in Figure 8-6, with marking of out-of-control points by the rules of Chapter 6.

Both charts show out-of-control conditions. The R chart shows instability followed by a decreasing trend, indicating better within-shift control. The $\bar{x}$ chart shows gradual changes in level together with abrupt changes in level. Shift changes appear to have no particular significance to the variation observed. Further investigation of raw material changes showed adjustments in two resins resulting in most of the changes in level. Estimation of the possible capabilities of the process to meet specification limits of 200 to 270 is made by revising the average range ($\bar{R}$) with removal

TABLE 8-3 Samples of Melt Index Measurements

Date:	Aug. 1			Aug. 2			Aug. 3			Aug. 7
Shift:	3	1	4	3	1	4	2	1	4	2
	218	228	280	210	243	225	240	244	238	228
	224	236	228	249	240	250	238	248	233	238
	220	247	228	241	230	258	240	265	252	220
	231	234	221	246	230	244	243	234	243	230
Total:	893	945	957	946	943	977	961	991	966	916
Average:	223*	236	239	236	236	244	240	248	242	916
Range:	13	19	59	39	13	33	5	31	19	18

Date :		Aug. 8			Aug. 9				Aug. 10	
Shift:	4	3	1	4	3	1	4	3	1	4
	218	226	224	230	224	232	243	247	224	236
	232	231	221	220	228	240	250	238	228	230
	230	236	230	227	226	241	248	244	228	230
	226	242	222	226	240	232	250	230	246	232
Total:	906	935	897	903	918	945	991	959	926	928
Average:	226	234	224	226	230	236	248	240	232	232
Range:	14	16	9	10	16	9	7	17	22	6

*Averages are rounded to three places only.

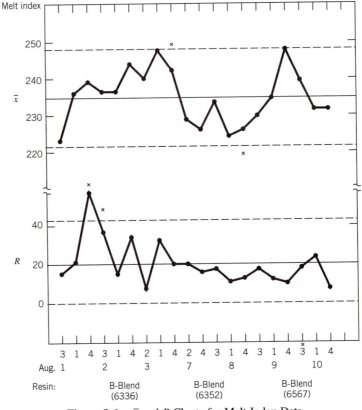

Figure 8-6 $\bar{x}$ and R Charts for Melt Index Data

of the two out-of-control points (3 and 4). This yields a revised $\bar{R}$ of 15.4, which may be conservative considering the reduced level in the R chart over the last four days. Estimating the universe standard deviation, σ, as $\bar{R}/d_2$ results in a value of approximately 7.5 (here $d_2 = 2.059$ for subgroups of size 4). Assume that the mean level can be maintained at 235 and that most of the dispersion will be $\pm 3\hat{\sigma}$ about the mean value. A natural process spread of $235 \pm 22.5 = 212.5$ to 257.5, within specifications, is then estimated. This may require more careful control of raw material adjustments to prevent overadjustment as well as controls to prevent material over or under specifications. Use of the control charts will serve to monitor and control and aid further improvement of the process. Additional study may be warranted to determine the effect on the final product of variation in levels within the specification limits. If such level changes are satisfactory, special control limits for the $\bar{x}$ chart may be devised to control the product to specifications rather than to a single distribution. For a discussion of this procedure, consult Chapter 9.

▶ **EXAMPLE 8-2**

A variables sampling plan is used for the acceptance or rejection of batches of flares' ability to meet the minimum candlepower required. Batch rejections are too frequent, and it is desired to study the sampling data by $\bar{x}$ and s control charts, since sample sizes vary from 4 to 20. Data from twelve samples over three days are obtained for the initial study. This is shown in Table 8-4 with sample size, and $\bar{x}$ and s computations. The data are coded results, adjusted to set the minimum specification for candlepower at the value of zero (0.0).

TABLE 8-4 $\bar{x}$ and s Values for Candlepower Measurements

Date	n	$\bar{x}$	s	Date	n	$\bar{x}$	s
Sept. 9	4	9.425	4.180	Sept. 10	10	5.370	5.484
	5	16.660	3.559		20	17.700	3.893
	5	10.580	4.258	Sept. 13	5	10.380	4.303
	5	10.780	2.476		7	9.343	3.814
Sept. 10	5	5.480	4.917		7	8.486	5.990
	10	9.890	5.800		20	12.905	5.914

Control limit computations for the average ($\bar{x}$) and standard deviation (s) control charts are as follows:

$$\bar{\bar{x}} = \Sigma n_i \bar{x}_i / \Sigma n_i = 1196 - 6/103 = 11.62$$

$$\bar{s} = \sqrt{\Sigma (n_i - 1)(s_i)^2 / (\Sigma n_i - k)} \qquad \text{per Equation (8-13)}$$

$$= \sqrt{2199.37/91} = \sqrt{24.169} = 4.92$$

For $n = 5$,

$$UCL_{\bar{x}} = \bar{\bar{x}} + A_3 \bar{s} = 11.62 + 1.427(4.92), \qquad \text{from Equation (8-26)}$$

$$= 11.62 + 7.02 = 18.64$$

$$LCL_{\bar{x}} = \bar{\bar{x}} - A_3 \bar{s} = 4.60, \qquad \text{from Equation (8-27)}$$

$$UCL_s = B_4 \bar{s} = 2.089(4.92) = 10.28, \qquad \text{from Equation (8-16)}$$

$$LCL_s = B_3 \bar{s} = 0.0(4.92) = 0.0, \qquad \text{from Equation (8-17)}$$

Control limits for the other sample sizes—namely, 4, 7, 10, and 20—are obtained similarly. The control charts, giving the control limits for the various subgroup sizes, are shown in Figure 8-7.

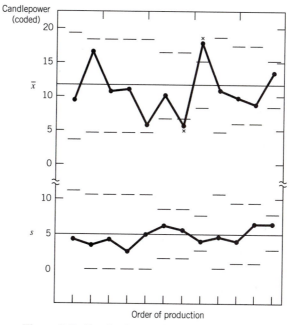

Figure 8-7 $\bar{x}$ and s Charts for Candlepower Data

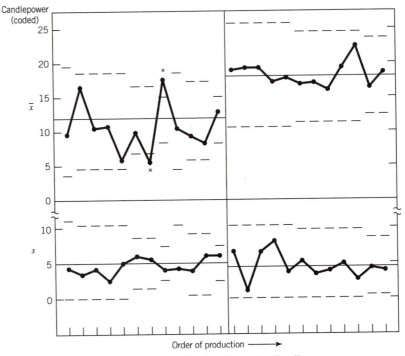

Figure 8-8 Extended $\bar{x}$ and s Charts for Candlepower

The s chart shows a controlled pattern, while the $\bar{x}$ chart shows two points out of control, as marked by ×'s. Estimating the standard deviation of the underlying distribution, $\hat{\sigma}$, using s with $n = 5$ (the most prevalent subgroup size), yields

$$\hat{\sigma} = \bar{s}/c_4 = 4.92/0.94 = 5.2$$

Assuming an approximately normal distribution for the quality characteristic indicates that a mean in excess of 16 ($3\hat{\sigma}$) is required for the product units to meet the minimum specification of 0.0. Experimentation with the product formulation and process operations resulted in the additional data points shown in the $\bar{x}$ and s charts of Figure 8-8. Although there is some suspicion of stratification in the early portion of these extended charts, the improvement is further confirmed by acceptance of the batches under a variables sampling plan.

▶ **EXAMPLE 8-3**

Considerable experience with an automatic fill operation reveals an estimate of the standard deviation of the underlying distribution of fill weight to be 0.85 gram. This dispersion is also known to apply at different average fill levels. Periodic adjustments are required to keep the mean fill level at 251 grams. Average ($\bar{x}$) and standard deviation (s) control charts with a sample size of 5 are used at the fill operation to monitor the need for adjustments. The control limits are obtained as follows.

$$\text{Assuming } \bar{x}_0 = 251, \qquad \sigma_0 = 0.85$$
$$UCL_{\bar{x}} = \bar{x}_0 + A\sigma_0 = 251 + 1.342(0.85), \qquad \text{from Equation (8-28)}$$
$$= 251 + 1.14 = 252.14$$

$$LCL_{\tilde{x}} = \tilde{x}_0 - A\sigma_0 = 249.86, \qquad \text{from Equation (8-29)}$$

$$\text{Centerline} = c_4\sigma_0 = 0.940(0.85) = 0.799, \qquad \text{from Equation (8-21)}$$

$$UCL_s = B_6\sigma_0 = 1.964(0.85) = 1.699, \qquad \text{from Equation (8-22)}$$

$$LCL_s = B_5\sigma_0 = 0.0(0.85) = 0.0, \qquad \text{from Equation (8-23)}$$

▶ 8-6 MEDIAN ($\tilde{x}$) CHART

Another measure of the central tendency in the underlying distribution of a quality characteristic that may be studied is the median ($\tilde{x}$). It is commonly used in conjunction with the range chart to monitor dispersion in the underlying process. It is often associated with small rational subgroups, as are the $\bar{x}$ and R control charts. This is appropriate, since the efficiency of the median in estimating the true mean decreases with increasing sample size.[3] In quality control work using control charts, the interest is in detecting changes in a process. Ferrell (1953) presents a comparison of both the efficiency of estimation and detection of disturbances by averages, ranges, average of averages, and average range with medians, midranges, median of midranges, and median range. He indicates an advantage of these less conventional measures in detecting outliers, as well as changes in dispersion, while not losing much in detecting a change in central value.

Median and range control charts are useful for the same purpose as the more common variables control charts, $\bar{x}$ and R. For some situations it is better to further simplify the calculations for each sample by using the median. This is useful for maintaining control of operations on the shop floor and utilizing operators or similar persons to draw the samples, compute the statistics, plot the control charts, and take direct action on the process when necessary. Odd-sized samples, such as 3, 5, and 7, are often used to locate the sample median by a visual scan of the values with no computation. The range is also a simple computation. Computation of control limits for trial studies and shop control may use the average or median of the statistics observed.

The basic procedure for using the $\tilde{x}$ chart is similar to that listed under the range chart for selection of the quality characteristic and size and number of samples. The median ($\tilde{x}_i$) is obtained for each sample. Generally, these charts are used only for the no-standard-given case, for which the average or the median of the medians is used as the centerline of the chart.

8-6.1 Computing Control Limits

The common principle, $\hat{\mu} \pm 3\hat{\sigma}_{\tilde{x}}$ is used as the basis for deriving control limits for the median chart, for the no-standard-given case. Estimates of the mean and the standard

---

[3]Because the median of an odd number of values arranged in arithmetic order is the middle number and for an even number is halfway between the two middle numbers, the efficiency is higher for even sample sizes than for odd sizes. For larger sample sizes, the efficiency approaches 0.637 in comparison with the arithmetic mean. That is, the sample mean of a sample of sixty-four would have the same precision for estimating the population mean as the median of a sample of 100. The efficiency of one statistical procedure relative to a second is the ratio of the sample size of the second to the first, in which both procedures have equal power. Dixon and Massey (1969) show the efficiency of the median with respect to the arithmetic mean to be as follows:

Sample size	2	3	4	5	6	7	8	9	10	∞
Efficiency	1.00	0.74	0.84	0.69	0.78	0.67	0.74	0.65	0.71	0.64

deviation of medians must be obtained from the data. The latter is estimated by the following relationship:

The standard deviation of individuals	equals	The standard deviation of medians	divided by	Constant of proportionality factor
(σ)		$(\sigma_{\tilde{x}})$		(e_4)

$$\sigma = \sigma_{\tilde{x}}/e_4 \qquad (8\text{-}30)$$

where e_4, as a function of the sample size (n), is tabulated in Table H in the Appendix.

With Median Range

Most common applications of the median chart make use of the median range $(\tilde{R})$ and the relationship of Equation (8-3) listed earlier in this chapter.

Control limits for this case are as follows:

$$\begin{aligned}
\text{Control limits} = \hat{\mu} \pm 3\hat{\sigma}_{\tilde{x}} &= \tilde{\tilde{x}} \text{ or } \bar{\tilde{x}} \pm 3e_4\hat{\sigma}, && \text{from Equation (8-30)} \\
&= \tilde{\tilde{x}} \text{ or } \bar{\tilde{x}} \pm 3e_4(\tilde{R}/d_4), && \text{from Equation (8-3), with } \tilde{R} \text{ used for } \tilde{\mu}_R \\
&= \tilde{\tilde{x}} \text{ or } \bar{\tilde{x}} \pm A_5\tilde{R} \\
UCL_{\tilde{x}} &= \tilde{\tilde{x}} \text{ or } \bar{\tilde{x}} + A_5\tilde{R} && (8\text{-}31) \\
LCL_{\tilde{x}} &= \tilde{\tilde{x}} \text{ or } \bar{\tilde{x}} - A_5\tilde{R} && (8\text{-}32)
\end{aligned}$$

where $A_5 = 3e_4/d_4$ and values, as functions of the sample size (n), are tabulated in Table G in the Appendix.

With Average Range

Computation of control limits may make use of the average range $(\overline{R})$ and Equation (6-11). Control limits for this case are as follows:

$$\begin{aligned}
\text{Control limits} = \hat{\mu} \pm 3\hat{\sigma}_{\tilde{x}} &= \tilde{\tilde{x}} \text{ or } \bar{\tilde{x}} \pm 3e_4\hat{\sigma}, && \text{from Equation (8-30)} \\
&= \tilde{\tilde{x}} \text{ or } \bar{\tilde{x}} \pm 3e_4(\overline{R}/d_2), && \text{from Equation (6-11), with } \overline{R} \text{ used for } \mu_R \\
&= \tilde{\tilde{x}} \text{ or } \bar{\tilde{x}} \pm A_7\overline{R} \\
UCL_{\tilde{x}} &= \tilde{\tilde{x}} \text{ or } \bar{\tilde{x}} + A_7\overline{R} && (8\text{-}33) \\
LCL_{\tilde{x}} &= \tilde{\tilde{x}} \text{ or } \bar{\tilde{x}} - A_7\overline{R} && (8\text{-}34)
\end{aligned}$$

where $A_7 = 3e_4/d_2$ and values, as functions of the sample size (n), are tabulated in Table G in the Appendix. The following example will illustrate the computations and construction of the charts involved in using median $(\tilde{x})$ and range (R) control charts.

► **EXAMPLE 8-4**

The CO_2 content of a popular beverage should be monitored hourly to control the level at a nominal value of 7 grams per liter. Samples of five consecutive bottles are drawn from the line each hour, and the CO_2 value is obtained for each bottle. The data for a trial study of fifteen samples are shown in Table 8-5, with computation of the median and ranges.

TABLE 8-5 Samples of CO$_2$ Measurements

	7.6	6.3	6.6	6.8	6.2	5.8	7.0	7.3	6.9	7.1	6.3	6.7	6.1	6.3	6.9
	6.9	6.7	6.6	7.0	6.5	6.9	7.0	6.9	7.1	6.5	6.7	6.9	6.9	7.1	6.7
	7.1	6.7	6.3	7.3	7.1	6.7	6.8	6.7	7.1	7.2	6.7	7.3	7.1	7.3	7.1
	7.6	6.5	6.7	8.0	6.5	6.9	7.0	6.5	6.7	6.9	7.1	6.5	6.5	7.0	6.5
	6.9	6.1	6.9	7.1	7.1	6.9	6.7	6.7	6.7	6.7	7.1	6.9	6.7	6.9	6.9
$\tilde{x}$	7.1	6.5	6.6	7.1	6.5	6.9	7.0	6.7	6.9	6.9	6.7	6.9	6.7	7.0	6.9
R	0.7	0.6	0.6	1.2	0.9	1.1	0.3	0.8	0.4	0.7	0.8	0.8	1.0	1.0	0.6

Control limit computations for the median ($\tilde{x}$) and range (R) control charts are as follows:

$$\tilde{\tilde{x}} = 6.9 \text{ and } \tilde{R} = 0.8, \qquad\qquad \text{by observation in Table 8-5}$$

$$UCL_{\tilde{x}} = \tilde{\tilde{x}} + A_5\tilde{R} = 6.9 + 0.681(0.8) = 7.44, \qquad \text{from Equation (8-31)}$$

$$LCL_{\tilde{x}} = \tilde{\tilde{x}} - A_5\tilde{R} = 6.9 - 0.544 = 6.36, \qquad \text{from Equation (8-32)}$$

$$UCL_R = D_6\tilde{R} = 2.148(0.8) = 1.72, \qquad \text{from Equation (8-4)}$$

$$UCL_R = D_5\tilde{R} = 0.0(0.8) = 0.0, \qquad \text{from Equation (8-5)}$$

The control charts are shown in Figure 8-9. Both charts exhibit patterns of control, though the overall median is on the low side. The limits have been adjusted to achieve control about a median of 7, requiring adjustment of the CO$_2$ mixer. These limits are shown on the $\tilde{x}$ chart, extended for future control. The process variation, estimated by $\tilde{R}/d_4 = \hat{\sigma}$, yields a value of 0.8/2.257 = 0.354 for $\hat{\sigma}$, considered to be too large for good product quality. But as the controlled patterns on the control charts indicate a single, stable process, reduction of the variation may require a major change in the process to achieve improvement (an example of a common or chronic quality problem).

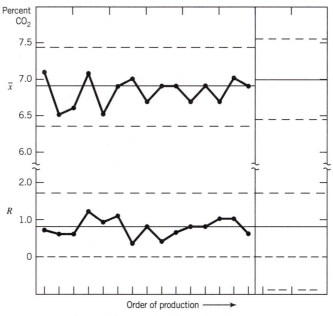

Figure 8-9 $\tilde{x}$ and R Charts for CO$_2$ Data

▶ 8-7 MIDRANGE (M) CHART

A further measure of central tendency in the underlying distribution of a variable quality characteristic is the midrange (M). Like the median, it is used with the range chart and offers an alternative to the average ($\bar{x}$) control chart when ease of computation is desired. Many of the references for the median chart also address the midrange chart (see footnote 1). The procedure differs from the median chart only in the computation of the midrange, $M = (x_{max} + x_{min})/2$, as the average of the two extreme values in the sample, the same values that are used to obtain the range. Again, either the average or the median of the midranges may be used as the centerline of the chart.

8-7.1 Computing Control Limits

The common principle, $\hat{\mu} \pm 3\hat{\sigma}_M$, is used as the basis for deriving control limits for the midrange chart for the no standard given case. Estimates of μ and σ_M are obtained from the data. The latter involves the following relationship:

The standard deviation of individuals	equals	The standard deviation of midranges	divided by	Constant of proportionality factor
(σ)		(σ_M)		(e_3)

$$\sigma = \sigma_M/e_3 \tag{8-35}$$

where e_3, as a function of the subgroup size (n), is tabulated in Table H in the Appendix.

With Median Range
The midrange chart is used typically with the range chart and the median range. Control limits for this case are as follows:

$$
\begin{aligned}
\text{Control limits} = \hat{\mu} \pm 3\hat{\sigma}_M &= \tilde{M} \text{ or } \overline{M} \pm 3e_3\hat{\sigma}, && \text{from Equation (8-35)} \\
&= \tilde{M} \text{ or } \overline{M} \pm 3e_3(\tilde{R}/d_4), && \text{from Equation (8-3), with } \tilde{R} \text{ used} \\
&= \tilde{M} \text{ or } \overline{M} \pm A_4R && \text{for } \tilde{\mu}_R
\end{aligned}
$$

$$UCL_M = \tilde{M} \text{ or } \overline{M} + A_4\tilde{R} \tag{8-36}$$
$$LCL_M = \tilde{M} \text{ or } \overline{M} - A_4\tilde{R} \tag{8-37}$$

where $A_4 = 3e_3/d_4$; and values, as functions of the sample size (n), are tabulated in Table G in the Appendix; and $\tilde{M}$, $\overline{M}$, and $\tilde{R}$ are the median midrange, average midrange, and median range, respectively.

With Average Range
Computation of control limits may use the average range ($\overline{R}$) and Equation (6-11). Control limits for this case are as follows:

$$
\begin{aligned}
\text{Control limits} = \hat{\mu} \pm 3\hat{\sigma}_M &= \tilde{M} \text{ or } \overline{M} \pm 3e_3\hat{\sigma}, && \text{from Equation (8-35)} \\
&= \tilde{M} \text{ or } \overline{M} \pm 3e_3(\overline{R}/d_2), && \text{from Equation (6-11)} \\
&= \tilde{M} \text{ or } \overline{M} \pm A_6\overline{R}
\end{aligned}
$$

$$UCL_M = \tilde{M} \text{ or } \overline{M} + A_6\overline{R} \tag{8-38}$$

$$LCL_M = \tilde{M} \text{ or } \overline{M} - A_6\overline{R} \tag{8-39}$$

where $A_6 = 3e_3/d_2$ is tabulated in Table G in the Appendix.

▶ ## 8-8 INDIVIDUALS (x) CHART

A basic variables control chart is that for individual measurements of a variables characteristic. Following the common principles of Chapter 6, this is called an x chart or individuals chart. The individuals (x) chart is also called the chart with moving range control limits or the moving range chart, since the moving range of the individual observations is typically used in the determination of the control limits. Following the principle of naming charts according to the statistic of the chart, the second of these alternative names is particularly undesirable, as the moving range is a valid statistic itself, for which a control chart can be developed and used.

The x chart is commonly used for the following:

1. The study of process or product variables (e.g., temperature, pressure, etc.) for which it is difficult, costly, or impractical to obtain several measurements during a short period and it is therefore not feasible to use $\bar{x}$ control charts.

2. Accounting, clerical, or service characteristics or other commercial data such as ratios, efficiency, and quality costs.

3. Attributes data for which the sample size is so large that the control limits, as determined by the binomial distribution, will be more sensitive than is desirable for assessing significant changes.

4. Any other purpose for which a sample of one must suffice.

The basic procedure for using x charts is as follows:

1. Select the measurable characteristic to be studied.

2. Determine the frequency of obtaining the measurements and collect enough for a trial study (twenty or more observations). The frequency, or interval between observations, should be large enough to detect and take action on changes in the characteristic as they may occur.

3. Calculate control limits and centerline for the trial study using one of the methods given below.

4. Set up the control chart, plotted points with control limits and centerline, interpreting the pattern from the trial study and extending the limits as a guide for future observations, or

5. Revise control limits as needed by removing out-of-control data points to assist in maintaining or improving the process. The centerline might be adjusted to set a goal.

6. Periodically assess the effectiveness of the control chart, revising or discontinuing it as appropriate.

8-8.1 Computing Control Limits

Control limits for the x chart are based on the common principle outlined in Chapter 6. This principle dictates the following formulas for the more common no-standard-given case, where m denotes any desired multiple of standard deviations:

$$UCL_x = \hat{\mu} + 3\hat{\sigma} \text{ or } \hat{\mu} + m\hat{\sigma} \tag{8-40}$$
$$LCL_x = \hat{\mu} - 3\hat{\sigma} \text{ or } \hat{\mu} - m\hat{\sigma}$$

The arithmetic mean, $\bar{x}$, is used to estimate the mean of the process characteristic. For the standard-given case, the known or standard mean, $\bar{x}_0$, and the standard deviation, σ_0, are used directly.

8-8.2 Estimating the Standard Deviation

There are two methods of estimating the standard deviation, σ, for the process characteristic from the observations: by the moving range between consecutive observations and by the overall sample standard deviation, s. Although these are optional, they are not necessarily equivalent. The first method, using the moving range, is preferred for relative ease of computation and for the type of variation it estimates.

Moving Range

The moving range is defined as the difference between the largest and smallest observations in consecutive sets of n observations, with the samples formed by moving through the observations in unit steps, adding the next ith observation to each new set while discarding the $(i - n)$th.

In a set of k observations there will be $k - n + 1$ moving ranges. The first is associated with the nth observation. It is common to use consecutive pairs $(n = 2)$ of observations to compute the moving ranges. The following formula applies for this case:

$$MR_i = |x_i - x_{i-1}|, \quad i = 2, \ldots, k \tag{8-41}$$

This procedure yields $(k - 1)$ moving ranges from which the average moving range, $\overline{MR}$, is computed as

$$\overline{MR} = \sum_{i=2}^{k} MR_i/(k - 1) \tag{8-42}$$

Derivation of control limits for the x chart, when the moving range is used to estimate the standard deviation, makes use of the relationship between the universe standard deviation and ranges. This was developed in Chapter 6, where the constant of d_2 was introduced. Control limits are derived as follows:

$$
\begin{aligned}
\text{Control limits}_x &= \hat{\mu} \pm 3\hat{\sigma}, &&\text{from Equation (8-40)} \\
&= \bar{x} \pm 3\overline{MR}/d_2, &&\text{from Equation (6-11) with } \overline{MR} \text{ used for } \mu_R \\
&= \bar{x} \pm E_2\overline{MR} &&\text{(8-43)}
\end{aligned}
$$

where $E_2 = 3/d_2$ and values of E_2, as a function of n, are tabulated in Table G in the Appendix. For the common practice of using moving pairs of observations (with $n = 2$), $E_2 = 2.66$, that is, $3/1.128$, and the control limit formula becomes

$$\text{Control limits}_x = \bar{x} \pm 2.66\overline{MR}, \quad \text{with } n = 2 \tag{8-44}$$

TABLE 8-6   Tensile Strength Measurements

x (N/mm²)	MR	x (N/mm²)	MR	x (N/mm²)	MR
186.0	—	183.9	6.9	181.2	11.2
185.5	0.5	185.8	1.9	184.8	3.6
194.9	9.4	183.8	2.0	187.6	2.8
183.3	11.6	189.3	5.5	185.4	2.2
183.2	0.1	195.1	5.8	186.6	1.2
190.8	7.6	192.4	2.7	188.5	1.9
				$\Sigma x_i = 3368.1$	$\Sigma MR_i = 76.9$

To determine control limits based on multiples of standard deviations, m, other than 3, it is necessary only to multiply $E_2\overline{MR}$, for the general n case, or $2.66\overline{MR}$ for the case of $n = 2$, by the ratio $m/3$.

▶ **EXAMPLE 8-5**

Tensile strength measurements are made on eighteen specimens aluminum sheets. The observations, in Newtons per square millimeter, and the calculations of the moving ranges are shown in Table 8-6.
The centerline and control limits for an x chart for these data are as follows:

$$\bar{x} = \Sigma x_i/18 = 3368.1/18 = 187.12$$

$$\overline{MR} = \Sigma MR_i/17 = 76.9/17 = 4.52$$

$$UCL_x = 187.12 + 2.66(4.52)$$

$$= 187.12 + 12.02 = 199.14$$

$$LCL_x = 175.10$$

The x chart is shown in Figure 8-10.
After this initial study, the limits were adjusted to a desired mean of 190 N/mm² with multiples of $2\hat{\sigma}$ for later control, having a larger α risk. These limits are shown in Figure 8-10, to the right, extended for monitoring the process.

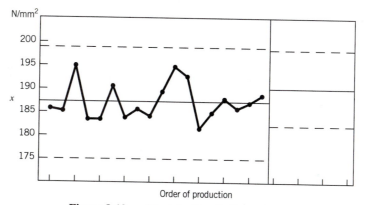

Order of production

Figure 8-10 x Chart for Tensile Strength Data

Sample Standard Deviation

In some instances we may want to estimate the standard deviation of the process characteristic by the sample standard deviation, s, as follows, repeating Equations (5-13) and (8-11):

$$s = \sqrt{\frac{\sum_{i=1}^{k}(x_i - \bar{x})^2}{(k-1)}} = \sqrt{\frac{\sum_{i=1}^{k}x_i^2 - (\Sigma x_i^2)/k}{(k-1)}} \qquad (8\text{-}45)$$

Equations (8-40) are then used for computing control limits directly, with $\hat{\sigma} = s$. For Example 8-5, $s = 4.008$, compared with $4.007(\overline{MR}/d_2)$ by the moving range method, in this case giving the same result for the control limits.

Estimating σ on the basis of moving range will emphasize the variation between consecutive observations, while estimating σ by Equation (8-45) will emphasize the overall variation among the observations. When there is a trend or other moving instability in the data, significantly different values of $\hat{\sigma}$ may be obtained by $\overline{MR}$ and s. Consider the data of Table 8-7, in which a trend is apparent. From Table 8-7,

$$\hat{\sigma} \text{ (by } MR) = \overline{MR}/d_2 = 1.67/1.128 = 1.48, \qquad \text{while } \hat{\sigma} \text{ (by } s) = 5.22$$

The moving range method is preferred to highlight the out-of-control condition, represented by the trend when computing control limits.

The same observations occurring randomly and not associated with a changing process in the form of a trend, might appear as in Table 8-8.

From Table 8-8, $\hat{\sigma}$ (by MR) = 4.33, while $\hat{\sigma}$ (by s) = 5.22, as before. They are no longer significantly different. Either might be used for establishing control limits. The moving range method is most common for quality control work. If $n > 2$, a moving s might be made to obtain a more accurate measure of variability. When $n = 2$, the MR and moving s would result in equal accuracy. Papers by Roes, Does, and Schurine (1993) and by Cryer and Ryan (1990) may be consulted for further information.

The x chart yields best results in monitoring a process characteristic if the underlying distribution is normal, or at least symmetrical. It is not very sensitive to changes in the parameters of the process, as it is based on a sample size of 1. Smaller multiples of $\hat{\sigma}$ or the additional criteria for judging out-of-control conditions developed in Chapter 6 may be used to increase sensitivity.

TABLE 8-7 Data Example with Trend Effect

x	MR	x	MR
50	—	43	1
49	1	40	3
48	1	39	1
46	2	37	2
44	2	35	2
		$\Sigma x_i = 431$	$\Sigma MR = 15$

TABLE 8-8 Data of Table 8-7 Arranged Randomly

x	MR	x	MR
35	—	48	2
39	4	37	11
46	7	40	3
44	2	43	3
50	6	49	6
		$\Sigma x_i = 431$	$\Sigma MR_i = 44$

▶ 8-9 OTHER VARIABLES CONTROL CHARTS

In addition to the control charts presented, there are many other control charts for variables data. It is possible to develop control charts for many statistics by means of the principles developed and illustrated in this chapter. Where an application may justify this approach, the practitioner should proceed accordingly. Examples of other statistics for variables data are discussed below.

For the type of data that are collected for the x chart, control charts for moving ranges or moving averages may be developed. The midrun and runrange statistics have been defined and illustrated by Ferrell (1964).

For the type of data collected for $\bar{x}$ and R or s charts, control charts for sample totals, variances, or $\bar{\bar{R}}$ have been developed, where $\bar{\bar{R}}$ is defined as the average of ranges from subsamples of large samples. Control charts on the extreme values, x_{max} or x_{min} or both, have been used. An individuals control chart may be used with sample data by plotting each individual value in the sample on the same vertical line associated with the given time period. The average, median, or midrange may also be identified on this plot and emphasized by connecting lines. Control charts for quasi-ranges (difference between largest and second smallest or second largest and second smallest, etc.) have been developed.

Control charts for standardized statistics are in use, converting a measurement or statistic, x, by the transformation $(x - x_0)/\sigma_0$. Reasons for doing this include simplifying the statistic and creating a common scale upon which different characteristics, streams, processes, products, or even plants may be compared.

Control charts for the graphical analysis of data from designed experiments, known as analysis of means (ANOM), have been developed by Ott (1967) and extended by Schilling (1973) and Sheesley (1980). The January 1983 issue of the *Journal of Quality Technology* is devoted to this topic and it is discussed in Chapter 12.

Control charts using cumulative results of past and present data have also been developed. These include the exponentially weighted moving average (EWMA) chart and cumulative sum (CUSUM) charts. The latter charts have been applied to variables statistics such as averages, ranges, standard deviations, variances, and averages and standard deviations combined. Coverage of these control charts is included in Chapter 9, including references for further study.

Multivariate control charts incorporating more than a single quality characteristic have been developed. A statistic called T^2 has been used for these control charts. For a discussion of such procedures, see Alt (1985), Holmes and Mergen (1993), Jackson (1985), Montgomery and Klatt (1972), Montgomery and Wadsworth (1972), Tracy, Young, and Mason (1992), and Wade and Woodall (1993).

Still other variables control charts represent modifications of the common ones to serve specific purposes and applications. Examples include fitting a trend line to an $\bar{x}$ chart to account for allowed variation due to tool wear or other trend producing patterns and modifying the control limits on $\bar{x}$ charts to maintain control of the underlying individuals distribution to specification limits including acceptance decisions. Others are cause-selecting charts for interdependent process stages; job shop charts, including Q charts for fast startup; zone control charts; group control charts; multi-vari charts; control charts adjusted for autocorrelated data; and trimmed mean control charts to deal with nonnormality. See Chapter 9 for coverage of some of these control charts, including extensive references.

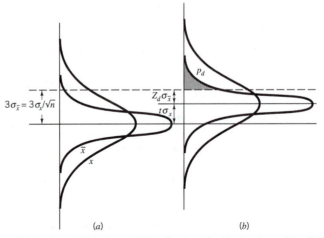

Figure 8-11 Control Limits and Distributions for Evaluation of the $\bar{x}$ Chart

▶ 8-10 EVALUATION OF AVERAGE CONTROL CHARTS

Sensitivity of the $\bar{x}$ chart to detect a change in mean of the underlying distribution is demonstrated earlier in this chapter. It is possible to subject this behavior to a more comprehensive analysis. This is accomplished by developing an operating characteristic curve[4] for the $\bar{x}$ chart, plotting the amount of shift in multiples of process standard deviations versus the probability of not detecting the shift using one or more out-of-control criteria. This is developed readily for the criterion of a single point out of the control limits and the assumption of a stable normal distribution.

8-10.1 Operating Characteristic Curves

The concept is illustrated in Figure 8-11 where in part (a) the universe and sampling distribution of averages are shown in the zero (0.0) shift position. The control limits for averages are shown at the $3\sigma_{\bar{x}}$ tail with only the upper control limit considered for this case. In part (b) the distributions are shown after an upward shift in the mean of $t\sigma$ with no change in σ. The shaded area of the distribution of averages outside the control limit is the probability of detecting the shift, P_d. The distance of the new mean from the control limit, z_d, in $\sigma_{\bar{x}}$ units, is as follows:

$$z_d\sigma_{\bar{x}} = 3\sigma_{\bar{x}} - t\sigma, \qquad \text{from Figure 8-11}$$
$$= 3\sigma_{\bar{x}} - t\sqrt{n}\sigma_{\bar{x}}, \qquad \text{from Equation (6-9)}$$
$$= (3 - t\sqrt{n})\sigma_{\bar{x}} \tag{8-46}$$

Hence, $P_d = 1 - \Phi(3 - t\sqrt{n}) = \Phi(t\sqrt{n} - 3)$. This is evaluated by using the table of areas under the normal curve given in Table A in the Appendix. A brief table for samples of size 4 is shown in Table 8-9.

---

[4]Used here in its generic sense to denote a measure of performance of the procedure. A specific form of an operating characteristic curve (OC curve), commonly used, is defined for the attribute control charts in Chapter 7, Section 7-7. A different form of operating (performance) characteristic is used here for the $\bar{x}$ chart.

TABLE 8-9   Probabilities for Various Shifts

t	$t\sqrt{n}-3$	P_d
0.0	−3	0.00135
0.5	−2	0.0228
1.0	−1	0.1587
1.5	0	0.5000
2.0	1	0.8413
2.5	2	0.9773
3.0	3	0.99865

The operating characteristic curves, derived as above, for sample sizes of 1, 2, 3, 4, 5, 7, 9, and 16, are shown in Figure 8-12. The sample size, 1, curve is that for the individuals chart with control limits at the 3σ tail of the distribution. It illustrates the sensitivity of the average chart over that for individuals in detecting changes in the universe mean. Figure 8-12 can serve as a nomograph for selecting a sample size for the $\bar{x}$ control chart, when shifts of a certain amount must be detected with a desired probability. For example, if it is needed to detect shifts of as much as 2σ with a probability of approximately 0.95, with a single sample, then samples of size 5 or 6 should be used.

8-10.2 Average Run Length

Another measure of the performance characteristics of decision mechanisms, such as the control chart, is the average run length (*ARL*) to the detection of a shift. This is also developed for the average control chart under the assumptions used above. In this case the *ARL* is the expected number of samples required to get an average outside of the control limit for a given shift in the mean. The probability of detection is P_d as developed above.

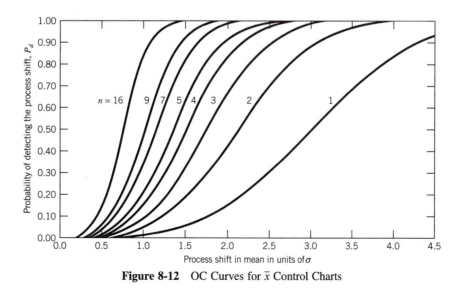

Figure 8-12   OC Curves for $\bar{x}$ Control Charts

Hence, the run length, L, is 1 with probability P_d, is 2 with probability $(1 - P_d)P_d$, is 3 with probability $(1 - P_d)^2 P_d$, ad infinitum, or

$$ARL = \sum_{L=1}^{\infty} L(1 - P_d)^{L-1}P_d$$

$$= P_d \Sigma L(1 - P_d)^{L-1} \qquad (8\text{-}47)$$

The infinite series $1 + 2Q + 3Q^2 + 4Q^3 + 5Q^4 + \ldots$ is easily produced by algebraic division of 1 by $(1 - Q)^2$. Hence, if we let $Q = 1 - P_2$, then ARL is as follows:

$$ARL = P_d(1/P_d^2) = 1/P_d \qquad (8\text{-}48)$$

The expected number of individual units required for detection of a shift, I, equals $n \times ARL = n/P_d$. Table 8-10 extends Table 8-9 to add ARL and I computations for $n = 4$. The ARLs are for either upper or lower control limits. If both upper and lower control limits are considered simultaneously, then P_d for $t = 0.0$ is twice 0.00135, or 0.0027; ARL is half 740.74, or 370.37; and I is half 2962.96, or 1481.48. For values of $t > 0.0$, the effects on P_d, ARL, and I diminish rapidly.

The ARL and I curves, derived as shown above, for sample sizes of 1, 2, 3, 4, 5, 7, 9, and 16, are shown in Figures 8-13 and 8-14, respectively. These curves may also be

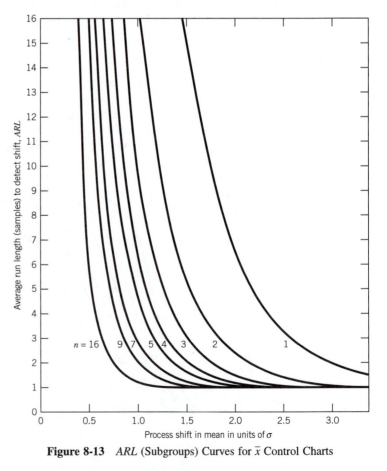

TABLE 8-10 Average Run Lengths for Various Shifts

t	P_d	ARL	I
0.0	0.00135	740.74	2962.96
0.5	0.0228	43.86	175.44
1.0	0.1587	6.30	25.20
1.5	0.5000	2.00	8.00
2.0	0.8413	1.19	4.75
2.5	0.9773	1.02	4.09
3.0	0.99865	1.00+	4.01

Figure 8-13 ARL (Subgroups) Curves for $\bar{x}$ Control Charts

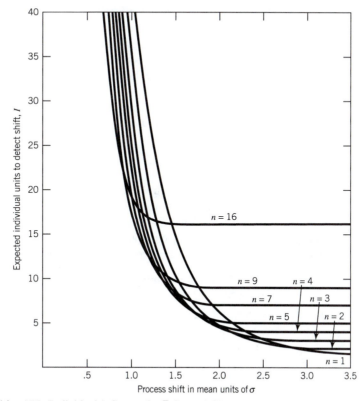

Figure 8-14 *ARL* (Individuals) Curves for $\bar{x}$ Control Charts

used as nomographs in selecting sample sizes for $\bar{x}$ chart applications. Figure 8-14 shows the optimum sample size (for minimum I) for various shifts in the mean.

▶ 8-11 OTHER EVALUATIONS

Similar evaluations may be made for the other control charts. More complicated evaluations may be made under different assumptions (multiple criteria for out-of-control, unstable universe, etc.). For further study of these types of evaluations, consult papers by King (1925), Scheffé (1949), and Duncan (1951, 1986).

▶ 8-12 ECONOMIC DESIGN AND EVALUATION OF CONTROL CHARTS

There are two broad philosophies for setting control chart limits: statistical and economic. The statistical approach, which is emphasized in this book and is most frequently used in professional work, is flexible enough to preclude the need for explicit economic criteria. If the economic consequences are different for high values of a variable than for low values, or if there are limiting values that are not symmetric around the central value, it might not always be obvious where to place the centerline and limits. In such cases it may be appropriate to derive economic or cost models to optimize the design of control charts. Cost models often utilize operations research methods to find that combination of design parameters which minimizes expected net cost or maximizes expected net profit.

Many studies and papers have been devoted to this topic. See, for example, Chiu and Wetherill (1974), Duncan (1956), Jaraiedi and Zhuang (1991), McWilliams (1989), Montgomery (1980), Rahim (1993), Saniga (1991), and von Collani (1986). These may be studied for applications for which the necessary costs are readily available or may be obtained at less cost than the additional cost of using a somewhat suboptimum control chart.

▶ 8-13 CONCLUSIONS

Experience with the use of control charts and various methods and models for their design and evaluation has shown that for many applications, sample sizes of 4 or 5, with 3 sigma control limits and with a frequency of checking based on knowledge of likely changes in the process, will yield optimum or near optimum results. Evaluations seem to support intuition in the use of control charts. For example:

1. If small changes in the universe are important to detect, then a larger sample size is required.

2. If the cost, effort, or time to check a process to conclude that no change has occurred is low, then a larger risk may be warranted, by using a lower multiple of sigma (say, 2.5 or 2.0) for control limits.

3. If the cost, effort, or time is very high, then higher multiples of sigma (say, 3.5) may be warranted.

4. If the cost of taking the sample or the cost of obtaining the measurement is high, then smaller samples (say, 2 or 3) may be warranted at a lower frequency, depending on the nature of changes the process may undergo.

Many applications may not require great sensitivity in the detection of small shifts as they may occur from day to day. Using larger samples just to be sure may actually be counterproductive when too much time is spent checking the process for unimportant changes signaled by an oversensitive control chart.

▶ 8-14 REFERENCES

Alt, F. B. (1985), "Multivariate Quality Control," *Encyclopedia of the Statistical Sciences,* Vol. 6, eds. N. L. Johnson, S. Kotz, and C. R. Read, John Wiley & Sons, New York, pp. 111–22.

Amin, R. W., and Miller, R. W. (1993), "A Robustness Study of x̄ Charts with Variable Sampling Intervals," *Journal of Quality Technology,* Vol. 25, No. 1, Jan.; pp. 36–44.

Chiu, W. K., and Wetherill, G. B. (1974), "A Simplified Scheme for the Economic Design of x̄-Charts," *Journal of Quality Technology,* Vol. 6, No. 2, April; pp. 63–69.

Clifford, Paul C. (1959), "Control Charts without Calculations," *Industrial Quality Control,* Vol. 15, No. 11, May; pp. 40–44.

Cryer, J. D., and Ryan, T. P. (1990), "The Estimation of Sigma for an x Chart: MR/d_2 or S/c_4?," *Journal of Quality Technology,* Vol. 22, No. 3, July; pp. 187–92.

Daudin, J. J. (1992), "Double Sampling x̄ Charts," *Journal of Quality Technology,* Vol. 24, No. 2, April; pp. 78–87.

Dixon, W. J., and Massey, F. J. (1969), *Introduction to Statistical Analysis,* Third Edition, pp. 238–39, McGraw-Hill, New York.

Duncan, A. J. (1951), "Operating Characteristics of R Charts," *Industrial Quality Control,* Vol. 7, No. 5, March; pp. 40–41.

Duncan, A. J. (1956), "The Economic Design of x̄ Charts Used to Maintain Current Control of a Process," *Journal of the American Statistical Association,* Vol. 51, No. 274, March; pp. 228–42.

Duncan, A J. (1986), *Quality Control and Industrial Statistics,* Fifth Edition, p. 139, Richard D. Irwin, Homewood, IL.

Ferrell, Enoch B. (1953), "Control Charts Using Midranges and Medians," *Industrial Quality Control,* Vol. 9, No. 5, pp. 30–34.

Ferrell, Enoch B. (1961), *Notes on Data Analysis,* Unpublished Paper, Bell Telephone Laboratories, Inc., Murray Hill, NJ.

Ferrell, Enoch B. (1964), "A Median, Midrange Chart Using Run-Size Subgroups," *Industrial Quality Control,* Vol. 20, No. 11, April; pp. 22–25.

Holmes, D., and Mergen, E. A. (1993), "Improving the Performance of the T^2 Control Chart," *Quality Engineering,* Vol. 5, No. 4, pp. 619–25.

Jackson, J. E. (1985), "Multivariate Quality Control," *Communications in Statistics—Theory and Methods,* Vol. 14, pp. 2657–88.

Jaraiedi, M., and Zhuang, Z. (1991), "Determination of Optimal Design Parameters of $\bar{x}$ Charts When There Is a Multiplicity of Assignable Causes," *Journal of Quality Technology,* Vol. 23, No. 3, July; pp. 253–58.

King, E. P. (1925), "The Operating Characteristic of the Control Chart for Sample Means," *Annals of Mathematical Statistics,* Vol. 23, pp. 384–95.

McWilliams, T. P. (1989), "Economic Control Chart Designs and the In-Control Time Distribution: A Sensitivity Study," *Journal of Quality Technology,* Vol. 21, No. 2, April; pp. 103–10.

Montgomery, D. C. (1980), "The Economic Design of Control Charts: A Review and Literature Survey," *Journal of Quality Technology,* Vol. 12, No. 2, April; pp. 75–87.

Montgomery, D. C., and Klatt, P. J. (1972), "Economic Design of T^2 Control Charts to Maintain Current Control of a Process," *Management Science,* Vol. 19, No. 1, pp. 76–89.

Montgomery, D. C., and Wadsworth, H. M. (1972), "Some Techniques for Multivariate Control Chart Applications," *Annual Technical Conference Transactions,* American Society for Quality Control, Milwaukee, pp. 427–35.

Mosteller, F. (1946), "On Some Useful Inefficient Statistics," *The Annals of Mathematical Statistics,* Vol. 17, Dec.; pp. 377–408.

Nelson, L. S. (1988), "Control Charts: Rational Subgroups and Effective Applications," *Journal of Quality Technology,* Vol. 20, No. 1, Jan.; pp. 73–75.

Ott, E. R. (1967), "Analysis of Means—A Graphical Procedure," *Industrial Quality Control,* Vol. 24, No. 2, Aug.; pp. 101–09.

Rahim, M. A. (1993), "Economic Design of $\bar{x}$ Control Charts Assuming Weibull In-Control Times," *Journal of Quality Technology,* Vol. 25, No. 4, Oct.; pp. 296–305.

Roes, K. C. B., Does, R. J. M. M., and Schurink, Y. (1993), "Shewhart-Type Control Charts for Individual Observations," *Journal of Quality Technology,* Vol. 25, No. 3, July; pp. 188–98.

Saniga, E. M. (1991), "Joint Statistical Design of $\bar{x}$ and R Control Charts," *Journal of Quality Technology,* Vol. 23, No. 2, April; pp. 156–62.

Scheesley, J. H. (1980), "Comparison of k Samples Involving Variables or Attributes Data Using the Analysis of Means," *Journal of Quality Technology,* Vol. 12, No. 1, Jan.; pp. 47–52.

Scheffé, H. (1949), "Operating Characteristics of Average and Range Charts," *Industrial Quality Control,* Vol. 5, No. 6, May; pp. 13–18.

Schilling, E. G. (1973), "A Systematic Approach to the Analysis of Means," *Journal of Quality Technology,* Vol. 5, No. 3, July; pp. 93–108; No. 4, Oct.; pp. 147–59.

Stephens, K. S. (1964), *Derivation of Control Limits for Range and Midrange Control Charts Using the Median as a Centerline,* Western Electric Company Technical Report CC879, Princeton, NJ.

Stephens, K. S. (1974), "A Unified Approach to Range Control Limit Derivation," *The Q R Journal,* Vol. 1, No. 2, May; pp. 89–92.

Stephens, K. S. (2000), *The Handbook of Applied Acceptance Sampling,* Quality Press, American Society for Quality, Milwaukee.

Tracy, N. D., Young, J. C., and Mason, R. L. (1992), "Multivariate Control Charts for Individual Observations," *Journal of Quality Technology,* Vol. 24, No. 2, April; pp. 88–95.

von Collani, E. (1986), "A Simple Procedure to Determine the Economic Design of $\bar{x}$ Control Charts," *Journal of Quality Technology,* Vol. 18, No. 3, July; pp. 145–51.

Wade, M. R., and Woodall, W. H. (1993), "A Review and Analysis of Cause-Selecting Control Charts," *Journal of Quality Technology,* Vol. 25, No. 3, July; pp. 161–69.

► 8-15 PROBLEMS

1. A manufacturer produces weights for use in a space mechanism that is essential in the re-entry process of a spacecraft. To study this component and the automatic machine process, samples of size 4 are selected twice each day: once in the morning and once in the afternoon. Data for twelve days are as follows:

1	2	3	4	5	6	7	8
1.028	1.026	1.027	1.028	1.015	1.013	1.027	1.020
1.030	1.026	1.028	1.030	1.028	1.023	1.039	1.029
1.025	1.019	1.025	1.028	1.043	1.029	1.028	1.012
1.025	1.030	1.026	1.030	1.020	1.037	1.029	1.025

9	10	11	12	13	14	15	16
1.025	1.025	1.016	0.998	1.013	1.039	1.036	1.026
1.033	1.031	1.020	1.022	1.025	1.025	1.024	1.029
1.020	1.020	1.034	1.018	1.031	1.031	1.031	1.032
1.024	1.021	0.997	1.036	1.025	1.027	1.026	1.020

17	18	19	20	21	22	23	24
1.036	1.039	1.039	1.031	1.021	0.988	1.024	1.013
1.038	1.041	1.037	1.028	1.014	1.013	1.012	1.018
1.038	1.043	1.021	1.038	1.021	0.997	1.013	1.022
1.034	1.039	1.024	1.023	1.024	0.988	1.010	1.019

Prepare $\bar{x}$ and R control charts as a trial study for the process. Plot and interpret the charts. Investigations of the process based on these control charts revealed (1) a mixture of alloys occurred on the sixth day (samples 11 and 12), (2) an overweight lot of stock was used on the ninth day (samples 17 and 18), and (3) defective stock, containing voids, was used on the afternoon of the 11th day (sample 22). It is expected that these difficulties with the raw material supply can be eliminated by additional controls on the vendor and incoming inspection. Eliminate these data, estimate the process standard deviation, σ, and revise the control limits. Will the process be able to meet specifications of 1.040 and 1.010?

2. In the production of cotton yarn, samples are taken from the spinning frames at eight positions daily. Four measurements of yarn count are obtained for each position to form a sample. Three days' results are given below. Prepare variables control charts, $\bar{x}$ and (R or s) for these data to serve as a basis for future control. Interpret the trial study and estimate the coefficient of variation, $100\,\sigma/\mu$ (in %), which is required to be no larger than 3.0. The data are for 30-count yarn.

Position	8	10	12	14	16	18	20	24
Jan. 15	31.5	31.2	31.0	31.5	31.0	30.5	31.7	30.5
	31.4	31.5	30.7	31.0	31.0	32.5	30.0	31.8
	30.8	31.0	31.3	31.0	30.0	31.5	34.0	31.0
	33.0	32.5	31.5	31.0	32.0	32.0	31.5	32.5

Position	7	9	11	13	17	19	21	23
Jan. 16	32.0	30.5	30.0	31.0	30.5	33.5	32.0	33.5
	31.5	32.0	31.0	29.0	30.0	32.0	30.0	30.8
	32.0	31.0	31.0	31.5	32.0	30.0	30.0	30.0
	31.8	31.0	31.5	31.0	32.5	34.5	30.5	30.5

Position	8	10	12	14	16	20	22	24
Jan. 17	32.5	32.5	34.0	31.5	30.8	31.5	31.0	32.5
	32.8	31.0	31.0	30.7	30.5	30.4	30.5	30.4
	32.0	30.5	31.5	29.0	30.5	31.5	31.0	30.8
	32.5	34.0	30.5	31.0	29.8	30.0	31.0	31.5

3. A margarine company is packing 250-gram containers for retail sales using an automatic filling engine. They wish to study the capability of the filling operation. Samples are formed by selecting five consecutive containers each half hour during a trial study of the process. Data for twenty samples are given below. Prepare variables control charts for these data, and interpret and estimate the process ca-

pability for a desired nominal of 250 grams. Propose control charts for future process monitoring.

1	2	3	4	5
251.65	250.94	252.72	250.54	250.92
252.26	250.66	251.85	250.08	251.20
251.45	252.13	251.15	249.70	251.45
251.60	250.30	250.54	251.46	249.43
249.87	251.79	249.65	250.26	251.10

6	7	8	9	10
250.75	249.00	251.91	251.38	251.16
251.18	251.55	249.25	251.82	250.73
251.56	251.30	251.28	249.60	250.55
249.18	251.82	249.80	251.74	251.01
251.73	250.34	251.88	250.29	249.93

11	12	13	14	15
250.75	249.43	250.25	251.06	249.70
251.30	249.54	250.56	250.66	249.48
250.05	250.98	249.81	251.32	250.81
250.96	249.75	250.70	249.92	250.70
249.13	250.70	250.05	250.70	251.74

16	17	18	19	20
251.35	251.02	249.96	251.15	250.90
251.26	251.46	249.43	248.87	248.86
251.52	250.05	249.84	251.60	251.02
250.37	249.10	249.74	250.60	249.48
249.58	251.01	249.74	250.75	251.48

4. Equation (8-7) for control limits for the range chart is used when the range chart is desired for future control after having conducted a trial study based on computation of s_i for each sample and $\bar{s}$ for the series. Beginning with the basic principle for range control chart limits, $\hat{\mu}_R \pm 3\hat{\sigma}_R$, derive Equations (8-6) and (8-7). Repeat for Equations (8-18), (8-19), and (8-20).

5. A sample is obtained from every batch of flares produced. The samples vary in size from 4 to 20, depending on the batch size. The length of burn time is measured, and an acceptance decision is made concerning the batch using a variables sampling plan. It is also desired to study the amount and nature of the variation in this quality characteristic. With the variable samples, use $\bar{x}$ and s control charts. Prepare the control charts for the trial data of fifteen samples given below. Interpret the control chart patterns and the ability of the process to meet the specified requirements of 8 ± 2 seconds.

1: 8.0, 8.1, 8.5, 8.5; **2:** 8.3, 8.1, 8.3, 8.3; **3:** 8.1, 7.9, 8.6, 8.2; **4:** 8.7, 9.1, 8.5, 8.7; **5:** 8.9, 9.0, 8.5, 8.6; **6:** 8.4, 8.1, 8.3, 8.4, 8.3; **7:** 8.5, 8.7, 8.9, 8.5, 7.1; **8:** 8.5, 8.3, 8.9, 8.5, 8.6; **9:** 8.9, 8.4, 8.1, 8.6, 8.4; **10:** 8.0, 7.8, 8.3, 7.9, 8.0, 7.5, 7.8, 8.3; **11:** 8.2, 7.9, 7.9, 8.3, 8.1, 8.4, 7.7, 8.3, 8.3, 8.6; **12:** 8.4, 8.5, 8.6, 8.7, 8.1, 8.6, 8.2, 8.4, 8.7, 8.3, 8.3, 8.4, 8.5, 8.3, 8.9, 9.1, 8.8, 9.0, 8.7, 8.4; **13:** 8.7, 8.9, 9.1, 8.7, 8.8, 8.6; **14:** 8.6, 9.0, 8.7, 8.2, 8.3, 8.6, 8.8; **15:** 8.7, 8.5, 8.7, 8.8, 8.7, 8.6, 9.0.

6. In the manufacture of tractor parts it is important to control the journal diameter of the rear wheel axle to dimensions of 44.975 to 44.990 mm. An automatic grinding machine is used for this part. A trial study is conducted with the selection of four consecutive pieces each hour, for twenty samples. The data are as follows, recording the last three places for the measurement:

1	2	3	4	5	6	7
0.985	0.985	0.980	0.975	0.975	0.975	0.980
0.985	0.980	0.985	0.975	0.975	0.980	0.983
0.990	0.980	0.980	0.975	0.983	0.980	0.985
0.990	0.980	0.978	0.975	0.980	0.983	0.983

8	9	10	11	12	13	14
0.980	0.980	0.980	0.980	0.980	0.983	0.975
0.980	0.978	0.980	0.980	0.980	0.983	0.978
0.985	0.975	0.978	0.983	0.983	0.980	0.980
0.983	0.975	0.980	0.983	0.983	0.978	0.978

15	16	17	18	19	20	
0.973	0.975	0.980	0.980	0.980	0.980	
0.978	0.975	0.978	0.983	0.978	0.980	
0.975	0.970	0.975	0.978	0.978	0.978	
0.973	0.970	0.978	0.975	0.978	0.980	

Prepare control charts for median (or midrange) and range for this trial study. Plot and interpret the patterns. It was noted that a grinding wheel profile correction was made following sample 16. Propose control limits for future process control.

7. A popular beverage bottling company has two filling machines in operation for different brands of product. The company wishes to study the level and variation of the duration of daily machine stoppages and to prepare an x chart for management reporting, goal setting, and control of this process characteristic for future production. The machine stoppages (in minutes) for a one-month study are shown below for both machines. Prepare the x control charts for each machine, interpret, and propose control limits for future control.

Machine 1: 10, 20, 25, 10, 20, 5, 15, 10, 10, 20, 25, 15, 10, 15, 10, 10, 5, 20, 35, 30, 10, 5, 20, 20

Machine 2: 15, 10, 10, 10, 10, 30, 10, 25, 10, 10, 10, 10, 20, 15, 10, 30, 20, 10, 10, 15, 20, 10, 90, 10

8. The company of Problem 7 also wishes to study the fill variation of one of its most popular beverages. In an initial trial study (before more detailed investigations), samples of four bottles are removed from the line for each case produced. Filling volume measurements in ml are obtained for each bottle in the samples. The data for twenty-four cases are shown below. Prepare variables control charts for these data, and interpret and estimate the filling machine capability for a desired nominal of 300 ml. Is further investigation warranted?

Case No.	1	2	3	4	5	6
	288	277	302	295	276	295
	294	296	287	278	296	300
	278	277	300	286	304	282
	294	277	288	280	296	295

Case No.	7	8	9	10	11	12
	281	300	296	288	283	295
	298	300	297	292	300	303
	292	299	295	291	296	299
	294	302	296	300	278	299

Case No.	13	14	15	16	17	18
	279	300	274	283	299	304
	282	284	294	295	296	299
	288	300	274	299	293	288
	282	300	295	303	296	314

Case No.	19	20	21	22	23	24
	298	296	296	304	299	292
	307	298	285	298	297	291
	284	297	300	288	280	277
	298	285	303	302	282	280

9. Tablets compressed from a granulation generated by a continuous extrusion process are tested for hardness. Tablets are sampled at the beginning, middle, and end of the compressing operation. Each batch of tablets, depending on batch size, contains from three to seven samples of size 14. Average and standard deviation computations are made for each sample and plotted on control charts for monitoring the compression operation. Data for five batches are given below. Prepare the $\bar{x}$ and s control charts and interpret the results.

Batch No.	Date	$\bar{x}$	s
0001	July 8	11.82	0.59
		8.07	0.87
		10.25	1.18
		10.39	0.93
		10.35	1.47
0002	July 9	10.75	0.83
		10.36	1.33
		9.79	0.72
0003	July 10	11.29	1.90
		9.18	1.41
		10.61	0.96
		9.07	1.62
		10.18	1.02
0004	July 11	10.21	1.05
		10.14	1.57
		9.57	0.53
		10.64	1.76
		8.64	0.77
0005	July 13	9.25	0.99
		9.29	1.04
		9.04	1.38
		10.11	0.89
		10.11	1.10

10. A company is engaged in extracting oil from cotton seed. They are able to sell the extracted cake to animal feed producers, but they must control the protein content. Variations are due mainly to the amount of shell added to the meat for pressing the oil. More shell increases the oil yield but reduces the protein in the extracted cake. A ten-day study of percent protein gives the following results: 35.4, 36.7, 37.6, 36.6, 33.3, 34.7, 35.2, 35.6, 38.1, and 35.5. Variations of from 33.3 to 38.1 are considered too excessive, and additional controls are exercised on shell content. An additional twelve days' worth of data are collected with the following results: 35.8, 35.5, 35.7, 34.6, 36.2, 35.2, 35.3, 36.3, 36.1, 36.8, 36.0, and 35.5. Prepare an individual (x) chart from this latter data for use in controlling this characteristic for future production.

11. Temperature measurements, in degrees Celsius, are taken on a gas flame at an important burner position in a glass stem sealing machine. Two measurements per day are made, in the morning and afternoon. The data for ten days are as follows:

Day	Temp	Day	Temp	Day	Temp
1	554	2	566	3	554
	571		543		543

Day	Temp	Day	Temp	Day	Temp
4	527	7	543	9	538
	510		566		538
5	527	8	538	10	543
	538		532		560
6	539				
	560				

Prepare an x chart for these data and interpret the chart.

12. Daily electrical meter readings on a private residence are begun when it is suspected that an electrical drainage is occurring, with some minor shocks resulting from contact with a number of appliances. The initial readings confirm that daily power consumption, in kilowatt hours, is too high for the usage level of the residence. A thorough investigation is made on September 20, and a short in the fuse box is located and corrected. The data for four weeks are as follows:

Sept.	12	60.0	Sept.	26	24.4
	13	54.5		27	19.6
	14	60.1		28	23.4
	15	53.7		29	20.9
	16	58.3		30	17.5
	17	59.3	Oct.	1	20.9
	18	59.3		2	20.1
	19	55.9		3	18.7
	20	42.3		4	19.6
	21	26.4		5	23.5
	22	25.7		6	22.9
	23	32.3		7	24.0
	24	19.6		8	18.0
	25	24.7		9	19.3

Prepare an x chart for these data, and interpret the chart. Determine revised control limits to be used to monitor daily power usage so as to detect significant changes in this characteristic in the future.

13. It is desired to monitor by control chart the results of daily 100% inspection of a critical component in an electronic assembly operation. Studies are underway to reduce the number and percent of nonconformities in the supply of these components to the assembly line. An initial control chart for percent nonconformities based on the binomial distribution proves to be too sensitive for these data for which the average sample size is over 1400. It is decided to develop an x chart for these data. The data are listed below. Prepare an individuals chart for these data using two sigma control limits based on moving ranges between successive values of percent nonconformities, treating them as individual (x) values. Interpret the control chart and establish control limits for continued monitoring.

Date	Number Inspected	NCs	Percent NCs
Aug. 11	1723	118	6.85
12	2035	169	8.30
15	1214	88	7.25
16	215	24	11.16
17	1384	77	5.56
18	1195	115	9.62
19	467	36	7.71
20	1524	70	4.59
22	1275	53	4.16
23	1821	132	7.25
24	1496	91	6.08
25	1213	32	2.64
26	1371	55	4.01
29	1248	69	5.53
30	1123	67	5.97
Sept. 2	1517	159	10.48
6	1488	94	6.32
7	2052	105	5.12
8	1696	37	2.18
9	1427	58	4.06
10	1277	75	5.87
12	1613	73	4.53
13	1987	145	7.30
14	1360	41	3.01
15	1439	50	3.47

As an alternative exercise, develop the corresponding p chart and compare with the x chart.

14. A form of instability in data is that of large fluctuations between consecutive observations (perhaps denoting a systematic mixture). For such data the moving range is inflated over the standard deviation computation. An example set of data is as follows:

Obs.	x	Obs.	x	Obs.	x	Obs.	x
1	45	4	41	7	45	10	41
2	39	5	46	8	42	11	44
3	44	6	40	9	47	12	39

For these data, compute the standard deviation estimates by (a) moving range, and (b) by Equation (8-45); compare

and consider which estimate might be used for control limits for subsequent investigation and control of the process characteristic.

15. Loss of compression time of a pharmaceutical tablet awaiting laboratory results of the disintegration test during machine setup, following batch formulation, is causing a company considerable difficulty. The company decides to prepare an x chart to display the current results in a graphical form for management information and action. Data for the last six weeks are as follows:

Week	Day	Time (mins)	Week	Day	Time (mins)
1	M	170	4	M	105
	T	360		T	400
	W	210		W	65
	Th	420		Th	120
	F	150		F	145
2	M	180	5	M	390
	T	380		T	85
	W	180		W	370
	Th	410		Th	85
	F	170		F	360
3	M	320	6	M	45
	T	70		T	90
	W	90		W	390
	Th	150		Th	120
	F	130		F	400

Prepare the x control chart for these data, and interpret the results.

16. For the $\bar{x}$ and R control charts demonstrated in the chapter using the underlying distributions of Figures 6-14, 8-1, and 8-3, devise a fourth distribution representing a reduced dispersion, perhaps with zero mean. Use these distributions to demonstrate use of the R chart to detect a reduction in variability of a measured quality characteristic. Set up your distribution on tags or chips, and draw ten samples of five as in the chapter demonstration. Extend the control limits of Figure 8-4, and plot the $\bar{x}$ and R points from these samples. Interpret the patterns on the R and $\bar{x}$ control charts, including use of the rules for out-of-control conditions.

17. Repeat Problem 16 using a computer analysis.

9

SPECIAL CONTROL CHARTS

Chapters 6 through 8 presented the basic control charts commonly attributed to Walter Shewhart. In fact, they are often referred to as Shewhart control charts. Several other types of charts are also available and may be preferred for certain applications (some were mentioned in Section 8-9). This chapter will examine the cumulative sum (CUSUM) chart, the exponentially weighted moving average (EWMA) chart, the modified average ($\bar{x}$) control chart, and the acceptance control chart.

▶ 9-1 CUMULATIVE SUM CONTROL CHARTS

CUSUM charts differ from the common Shewhart control charts in several ways. Instead of plotting the individual value of the statistic of interest, such as x, $\bar{x}$, R, s, p, np, or c, a statistic based on the cumulation of these statistics is created. Often the cumulative statistic is the sum of the deviations of the individual statistic from a target value, for example, $\Sigma(x_i - x_0)$, or $\Sigma(R_i - R_0)$. For these charts, the target value becomes more important than in the Shewhart charts. Sometimes the statistic for CUSUM charting is the direct sum of the individual values of the statistic of interest, for example, ΣR_i, or Σd_i (d_i being the number of nonconformities), as if a target value of zero were used. For some applications, zero may be the required target value for a process statistic. In these cases, even under a state of statistical control, a horizontal pattern is not maintained on the control chart. A sloping pattern results.

CUSUM charts differ further from the Shewhart charts with reference to the control limits or decision criteria. A common practice is to use a "V" mask consisting of a vertex, a location point at a lead distance from the vertex, and two sloping lines serving as the decision lines. These and other characteristics of the V mask will be introduced later. Another practice is to tabulate a cumulative statistic in relation to a reference value(s), with designated restarts, and with action based on violation of a decision interval. This can also be plotted. It can be incorporated into computerized automatic instrumentation for signaling out-of-control conditions. This tabulation procedure will be discussed later.

The principal interest in CUSUM charts or CUSUM monitoring via tabulations is the ability of the procedures to detect small changes in the underlying process more quickly than Shewhart charts. Although Shewhart charts are effective for detecting changes in the mean level of a process of more than 2σ (of the reference statistic), they are not very

TABLE 9-1 CUSUM of Sample Averages from Table 6-6

$\bar{x}_i$	$\Sigma(\bar{x}_i - \bar{x}_0)$	$\bar{x}_i$	$\Sigma(\bar{x}_i - \bar{x}_0)$	$\bar{x}_i$	$\Sigma(\bar{x}_i - \bar{x}_0)$	$\bar{x}_i$	$\Sigma(\bar{x}_i - \bar{x}_0)$
0.0	0.0	0.4	−2.0	−0.2	−2.2	−0.2	−1.2
−1.4	−1.4	0.2	−1.8	1.0	−1.2	−0.4	−1.6
−0.6	−2.0	0.0	−1.8	1.4	0.2	1.8	0.2
−1.4	−3.4	0.0	−1.8	0.0	0.2	−0.4	−0.2
1.0	−2.4	−0.2	−2.0	−1.2	−1.0	1.0	0.8

$$\text{CUSUM} = \sum_{i=1}^{m}(\bar{x}_i - \bar{x}_0) = \sum_{i=1}^{m}\bar{x}_i$$

effective in detecting changes of the magnitude of 0.5 to 1.5σ. CUSUM charts may be created that significantly improve the chances of such detection.

In the following sections, CUSUM charts for several of the more common variables and attributes statistics are presented. Some examples are given to assist with applications of the charts. For a more thorough understanding of CUSUM techniques, the interested reader is referred to the related literature in Chapter 8 References and at the end of this chapter.

9-1.1 The CUSUM Chart for Sample Averages

One of the most popular statistics used with CUSUM procedures is that of sample averages. For this technique individual values (x) are only a special case of averages with $n = 1$ and $\sigma_{\bar{x}} = \sigma_x$.

To start the development, consider the data of Table 6-6. Instead of plotting the averages as in Figure 6-17, form a cumulative sum of deviations from a target value, $\bar{x}_0$, of zero as shown in Table 9-1.

A plot of the CUSUM values is shown in Figure 9-1. The pattern is generally horizontal, as expected from a knowledge of the underlying distribution of Figure 6-14, representing a single system with a true mean of 0.0. If to the data of Table 9-1 we add the data of Table 8-1, we obtain the results shown in Table 9-2.

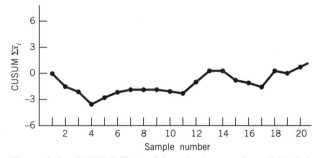

Figure 9-1 CUSUM Chart of Sample Average from Table 9-1

TABLE 9-2 Additional CUSUM of Sample Averages from Table 8-1

$\bar{x}$	$\Sigma(\bar{x}_i - \bar{x}_0)$	$\bar{x}$	$\Sigma(\bar{x}_i - \bar{x}_0)$
3.2	4.0	2.4	15.6
3.2	7.2	1.4	17.0
1.2	8.4	1.6	18.6
1.6	10.0	3.0	21.6
3.2	13.2	2.2	23.8

These data, added to the graph of Figure 9-1, are shown in Figure 9-2. Starting with the twenty-first value, the CUSUM pattern takes an abrupt turn upward at a relatively steep slope. The pattern alone indicates a change, as may be expected from the universe of Figure 7-1 with a true mean of 2.0. Like the fluctuating pattern of variation in Figure 6-1, it is scale dependent and lacks decision lines or control limits that compensate for any scale compression.

What test is to be used to determine if this noticeable increase in CUSUM represents a direct signal that the population mean has changed? If such a signal is obtained, how can the new mean level be estimated? Answers to these questions will now be developed.

The V Mask for CUSUM Decision Limits

A signal of change for the CUSUM pattern is provided by using a *V* mask as shown in Figure 9-3. We first develop and apply the *V* mask as a basis for detecting changes in the underlying process. This was the early procedure for designing CUSUM charts. Following this development alternate procedures for tabulating and charting are introduced and discussed. Some alternative approaches to the design of CUSUM charts are also presented.

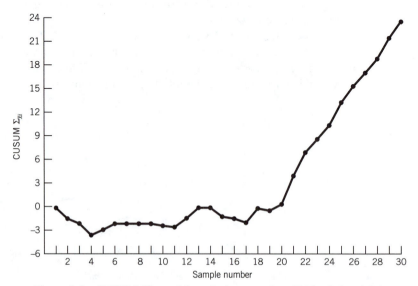

Figure 9-2 CUSUM Chart of Sample Averages from Tables 9-1 and 9-2

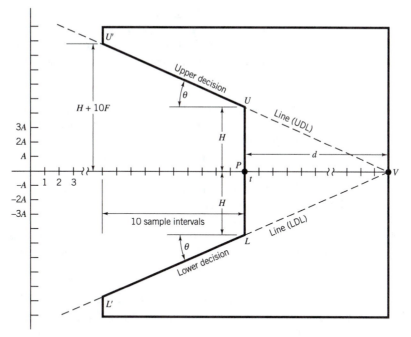

Figure 9-3 *V* Mask Design for CUSUM Decision Limits

Measures identified on the *V* mask are as follows:

t   The present time, representing the cumulation over *t* samples since the plotting began or was restarted. It is the number of sample intervals in a CUSUM sequence for which a test of change of level is conducted.

P   The location point, where the mask is located over the *t*th point of the CUSUM statistic with the horizontal axis of the mask placed parallel to the sequence axis of the chart for testing for a change in level.

d   The lead distance (segment *PV*), the distance between the location point and the vertex of the mask measured along the sequence axis; a parameter of mask design.

V   The vertex of the *V* mask.

H   The decision interval, the half height of the mask at the location point (segments *UP* and *PL*) measured along the CUSUM axis. It is also the cumulative sum of deviations from a reference value required to yield a signal related to CUSUM tabulations. It is a parameter of mask design.

h   The decision interval in multiples of standard error, that is, $H = h\sigma_v$.

θ   The half angle of the *V* mask; the angle the decision lines make to the horizontal axis of the mask. It is a parameter of mask design.

F   The slope of the decision lines per sample interval. It is also the difference between the target and reference values for a CUSUM tabulation. It is a parameter of mask design used for practical construction of masks.

f   The slope of the decision lines per sample interval in multiples of standard error, that is, $F = f\sigma_v$.

$U'U$ The upper decision line for detecting a decrease in mean level or change to the lower side of the target value. A signal is generated when any point of the previous CUSUM sequence is covered by the V mask with the mask located over a later point.

$L'L$ The lower decision line for detecting an increase in mean level or change to the upper side of the target value.

A The scale factor; the number of units of the plotted CUSUM statistic, measured on the CUSUM axis, corresponding to one sample interval on the sequence axis of the CUSUM chart. It is a parameter of the CUSUM chart design. It is recommended to use A values of approximately $2\sigma_v$.

a The scale factor in multiples of standard error, that is, $A = a\sigma_v$. ($a = 2$ is recommended.)

There are several other terms, not reflected in the diagram in Figure 9-3, but used in CUSUM techniques. CUSUM charts also employ terms from Shewhart control charts and statistics in general. Those are not repeated here. For example, α and β are the risks of incorrectly deciding that a shift in process level has occurred when the process is still on the target level and the risk of failing to detect that a shift in process level of D units has occurred.

T The target value; the target or standard value from which detection of a departure is desired.

K The reference value; the value from which differences are calculated for a CUSUM tabulation. $K_1 = T + F$ for monitoring against an upward shift, and $K_2 = T - F$ for monitoring against a downward shift.

σ_v The standard error of a sample statistic; the measure of variation of a sample statistic used in CUSUM. For example, $\sigma_{\bar{x}}$ for averages or σ_R for ranges.

D The smallest shift in process level to be detected, in the original units of the CUSUM axis.

δ The smallest shift in process level to be detected, in multiples of standard error of the sample statistic, that is, $D = \delta\sigma_v$.

From CUSUM theory (based on sequential analysis) the following relationships concerning the above parameters are obtained:

$$d = 2 \ln [(1 - \beta)/\alpha]/\delta^2 \tag{9-1}$$

For small β this is approximately

$$d = -2 \ln \alpha/\delta^2 \tag{9-2}$$

$$\theta = \arctan (D/2A) \tag{9-3}$$

Other results following from these relationships are

$$\tan \theta = D/2A \text{ (from 9-3)} = \delta\sigma_v/2a\sigma_v = \delta/2a \tag{9-4}$$

and since d, in terms of CUSUM scale units, equals dA,

$$\tan \theta = H/dA = h\sigma_v/da\sigma_v = h/da \tag{9-5}$$

and since $F = f\sigma_v$ is the slope of the decision line per sample interval and one sample interval is $A = a\sigma_v$ units on the CUSUM scale,

$$\tan \theta = F/A = f\sigma_v/a\sigma_v = f/a \tag{9-6}$$

From Equations (9-4), (9-5), and (9-6) the following is obtained

$$F = D/2, f = \delta/2, d = h/f, F = H/d$$

the latter term when stated in proportional terms helps to understand the V mask of Figure 9-3 in that F is to one sample interval as H is to d sample intervals.

Returning to the CUSUM chart for averages as shown in Figure 9-2, now armed with the above development of the V mask, a V mask to answer the first of the two questions posed just before the development can be constructed. Is there an out-of-control signal? Choose $\alpha = 0.005$ and $\delta = 1.0$, which results in the following calculations for d, f, and h:

$$d = 10.5966$$
$$f = 0.5$$
$$h = 5.2983$$

For ease of constructing the mask, round these figures to

$$d = 10$$
$$f = 0.5$$
$$h = 5.0$$

which has the effect of modifying our original choice of α and δ to $\alpha = 0.005$, $\delta = 1.06$; $\alpha = 0.0067$, $\delta = 1.0$; or other combinations that produce the same parameters.

To apply these parameters to the construction of a decision mask, an estimate of σ_v or, in this case, of $\sigma_{\bar{x}}$ will be needed. For the example data, the underlying population is known. Hence, it is possible to adopt a standard given approach using

$$\sigma_{\bar{x}} = \sigma_x/\sqrt{n} = 1.72/\sqrt{5} = 0.7692$$

For practical applications, σ is seldom known. However, a chart may be set up for process control purposes on a characteristic that has been studied in some depth during process capability studies. In such cases a sufficient estimate of σ would be available to allow the standard given approach.

In other cases an estimate of σ or $\sigma_{\bar{x}}$ may be obtained from the data of the current study. In Chapter 6 (Section 6-3.4) for the twenty samples of Table 6-6, $\bar{R} = 3.70$. Hence,

$$\hat{\sigma} = \bar{R}/d_2 = 3.70/2.326 = 1.59$$

and

$$\hat{\sigma}_{\bar{x}} = \hat{\sigma}\sqrt{n} = 1.59/2.236 = 0.71$$

Although this underestimates the true value of $\sigma_{\bar{x}}$, it may still be used to construct the decision mask, and in some cases may be the only available estimate. There are other ways to estimate $\sigma_{\bar{x}}$. It is possible that the measure of within-sample variation provided by R and $\bar{R}$ may not be available. In such cases as estimate of the standard error of the sample statistic, in this instance the sample average, may be obtained as the standard deviation of a set of statistics from the present study. For the twenty averages ($\bar{x}_i$) of Table 9-1 the following result is obtained:

$$\hat{\sigma}_{\bar{x}} = s_{\bar{x}} = \sqrt{[\Sigma\bar{x}_i^2 - (\Sigma\bar{x})^2/n]/(n-1)} = 0.874$$

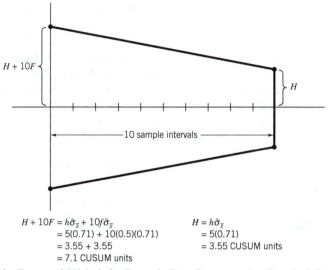

$H + 10F = h\hat{\sigma}_{\bar{x}} + 10f\hat{\sigma}_{\bar{x}}$ $H = h\hat{\sigma}_{\bar{x}}$
$= 5(0.71) + 10(0.5)(0.71)$ $= 5(0.71)$
$= 3.55 + 3.55$ $= 3.55$ CUSUM units
$= 7.1$ CUSUM units

Figure 9-4   Truncated V Mask for Example Data Demonstrating Practical Construction

There is a possible danger in using this estimate. In the event of a large between-sample component of variation, such an estimate may be inflated.

An alternative estimate from a series of values of a sample statistic is obtained via successive differences or moving ranges as discussed in Chapter 8 (see Section 8-8.2). Applying this approach to the series of averages in Table 9-1 produces the following result:

$$\hat{\sigma}_{\bar{x}} = \overline{MR}/d_2 = 0.9368/1.128 = 0.831$$

For the example data, estimates obtained by all three methods do not differ much. This is a reflection of the underlying stable universe from which the samples were drawn. For some sets of data it is recommended that different estimates be obtained to estimate the validity of the estimate.

Using $\hat{\sigma}_{\bar{x}} = 0.71$, as estimated from the within-sample variation, a truncated V mask for the CUSUM chart of Figure 9-2 is constructed as shown in Figure 9-4. The recommended convention of using $A = 2\hat{\sigma}_{\bar{x}}$ has been adopted with rounding to $A = 1.5$ (from $2\hat{\sigma}_{\bar{x}} = 1.42$). This was used to plot Figures 9-1 and 9-2.

This mask is illustrated in Figure 9-5 positioned at the twenty-first point, for which there is an immediate signal. The seventeenth point falls below the lower decision line at that position. Signals are produced for every point thereafter. The CUSUM chart has detected the change in level on the very first point after the change, as did the Shewhart chart of Figure 8-2. As for the $\bar{x}$ chart, there is also a risk that the CUSUM chart would require more than one point to detect the change. Actually, the shift to $\mu = 2.0$ is a shift of $2.0/0.7692 = 2.6\sigma_{\bar{x}}$ for which the average run length, ARL, is approximately 3 for the decision criteria used.

Now consider the second question posed just before the development of the V mask in connection with estimating the new mean level. On a CUSUM chart the mean level is determined from the slope. For a slope of zero, the level is the target value T. A change in mean level appears as a change in slope of the pattern. For a sustained pattern at a

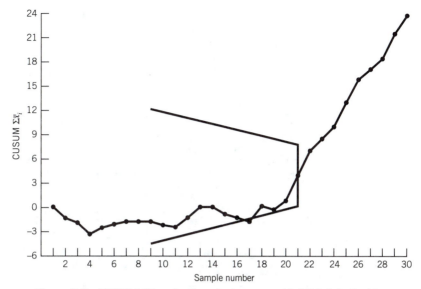

Figure 9-5 CUSUM Chart for Sample Averages with V Mask in Position

consistent slope over a segment of the sample sequence, the mean level of the segment can be obtained from the CUSUM data. Let C_i be the CUSUM value at sequence i. Then the estimated average level $\bar{x}_{i+1,j}$ for the segment from i to j is as follows:

$$\hat{\mu} = \bar{x}_{i+1,j} = T + \frac{C_j - C_i}{j - i} \qquad (9\text{-}7)$$

Apply this result to the CUSUM chart of Figure 9-5, over the segment $i = 20$ to $j = 30$, where i is selected as the point just before the change was signaled.

$$\bar{x}_{21,30} = 0.0 + \frac{23.8 - 0.8}{10} = 2.3$$

This is an estimate of the true mean, μ, which somewhat overestimates the true mean of $\mu = 2.0$, during this period.

To demonstrate the ability of the CUSUM chart to detect smaller shifts in mean level, return to the population of Figure 6-14, shift the mean to $\mu = 1.0$, and draw ten samples of size 5. The resultant data are shown in Table 9-3.

TABLE 9-3   Ten Samples with $\mu = 1.0$

	1	2	4	5	1	1	2	1	0	3
	1	-2	2	1	1	1	2	2	3	2
	-1	-1	0	0	1	1	1	2	3	0
	-1	1	1	-3	0	0	0	4	3	0
	-1	1	2	1	-1	0	0	0	-2	1
Total	-1	1	9	4	2	3	5	9	7	6
$\bar{x}$	-0.2	-0.2	1.8	-0.8	-0.4	0.6	1.0	1.8	1.4	1.2
R	2	4	4	8	2	1	2	4	5	3

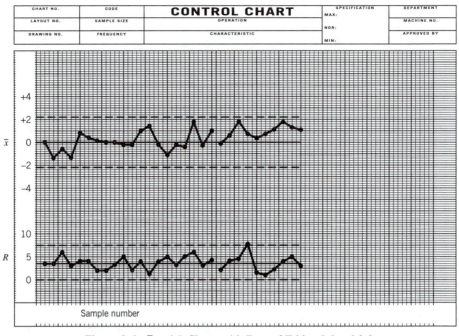

CHART NO.	CODE	CONTROL CHART	SPECIFICATION MAX:	DEPARTMENT
LAYOUT NO.	SAMPLE SIZE	OPERATION	NOR:	MACHINE NO.
DRAWING NO.	FREQUENCY	CHARACTERISTIC	MIN:	APPROVED BY

Figure 9-6 $\bar{x}$ and R Charts with Data of Tables 6-6 and 9-3

These results are shown in Figure 9-6, appended to the $\bar{x}$ and R charts of Figure 6-17, similar to that of Figure 8-2, where a shift to $\mu = 2.0$ was used. As seen, no direct signal of out-of-control occurs, considering a single point outside control limits. A signal does occur on the ninth point, using the rules of Section 6-4.3, in that eight consecutive points, from two to nine, fall above the centerline. The R chart remains in control.

Now consider these averages on a CUSUM basis. Some additional features of CUSUM charts are illustrated, including the ability to detect smaller shifts in the mean. The first question that arises is: Where are these points to be plotted? Should they be appended to the CUSUM chart of Figure 9-2 or Figure 9-5? To do so is rather unwieldy, since the last point plotted is far from the target level. However, if there is no evidence that corrective action has been taken and the process returned nearly to the target level, there may be no alternative. In this sense, CUSUM charts are more awkward to use than Shewhart charts.

If corrective action has been taken, whether known to be totally effective or not, the convention is to restart the pattern. The CUSUMS are as shown in Table 9-4.

The CUSUM chart with these points appended to the chart of Figure 9-1, with a gap for restart, is illustrated in Figure 9-7. The V mask, as developed in Figure 9-4, is shown in position at the eighth point in the new sequence where the second point in the new sequence falls below the decision line. The CUSUM chart has detected the change in level. The new mean can be estimated by using Equation (9-7) as

$$\hat{\mu} = \bar{x}_{2,10} = 0.0 + \frac{9.0 - (-0.2)}{9} = 1.02$$

TABLE 9-4   CUSUMS with $\mu = 1.0$ from Table 9-3

$\bar{x}$	$\Sigma(\bar{x}_i - 0.0)$	$\bar{x}_i$	$\Sigma(\bar{x}_i - 0.0)$
−0.2	−0.2	0.6	3.6
0.2	0.0	1.0	4.6
1.8	1.8	1.8	6.4
0.8	2.6	1.4	7.8
0.4	3.0	1.2	9.0

One may argue that the CUSUM chart provides no great advantage over the $\bar{x}$ chart in this case because the detection is on the eighth point with the CUSUM chart and on the ninth point with the $\bar{x}$ chart. In this connection the following remarks are pertinent. For most comparisons of CUSUM charts with Shewhart charts the performance of the CUSUM chart is contrasted with the performance of the Shewhart chart using the decision criteria of (1) a single point outside of three sigma control limits or (2) the single point criterion and two consecutive points outside warning limits of two sigma. Neither of these signals has occurred on the $\bar{x}$ charts of Figure 9-6. So, on that basis, the contrast between Figures 9-6 and 9-7 is no signal versus a definite signal on the eighth point. The CUSUM signal is considered by some to be more definite (stronger) than the signal provided by a run of points. Each practitioner must develop experience and confidence in the various approaches to use them to their fullest.

CUSUM Tabulation and Alternate Charting with Decision Limits

Use the earlier development to illustrate CUSUM tabulation and alternate charting, which may be preferred over the V mask approach. The procedure is as follows:

1. Form the CUSUM as $C_1 = \Sigma(\bar{x}_i - K_1)$, where $K_1 = T + F$, to detect an upper trend.
2. Form the CUSUM as $C_2 = \Sigma(\bar{x}_i - K_2)$, where $K_2 = T - F$, to detect a lower trend.
3. Tabulate these quantities sequentially with $\bar{x}_i$, ignoring negative values of C_1 and positive values of C_2; that is, reset to zero the upper CUSUM when it is negative and the lower CUSUM when it is positive.

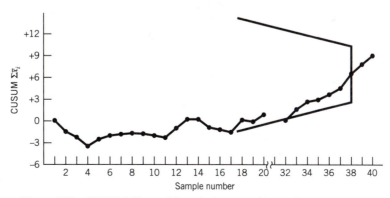

Figure 9-7   CUSUM Chart of Sample Averages from Tables 9-1 and 9-3

4. Watch the progress of the C_1 and C_2 values. When such values equal or exceed $H = h\hat{\sigma}_{\bar{x}}$, in absolute value, a signal is produced.

Use the data of Table 9-4 as an example, with ten sample averages added, drawn from a universe similar to Figure 6-14 but with $\mu = -1.0$ to illustrate detection of a downward slope. Recall for this example that $T = 0.0$, $F = 0.5\hat{\sigma}_{\bar{x}}$, $H = 5\hat{\sigma}_{\bar{x}}$, and $\hat{\sigma}_{\bar{x}} = 0.71$.

Hence,

$$C_1 = \Sigma(\bar{x}_i - K_1) = \Sigma[\bar{x}_i - (T + F)] = \Sigma(\bar{x}_i - 0.355)$$

and

$$C_2 = \Sigma(\bar{x}_i - K_2) = \Sigma[\bar{x}_i - (T - F)] = \Sigma(\bar{x}_i + 0.355)$$

The decision interval is $H = 5(0.71) = 3.55$.

The CUSUM tabulation is given in Table 9-5. An upper signal occurs on the eighth point as for the CUSUM chart of Figure 9-7. A lower signal occurs on the 14th point, just 4 points after the change in mean to $\mu = -1.0$. Signals are indicated by an asterisk in the table.

A CUSUM tabulation as shown in Table 9-5 can be charted as a control chart taking on more of the form of the common Shewhart chart with horizontal control limits placed at H and $-H$ to monitor upward shifts with C_1 and downward shifts with C_2. Both CUSUM statistics may be active simultaneously as shown for samples 11 to 13 in Table 9-5. The chart is shown in Figure 9-8.

TABLE 9-5 CUSUM Tabulation for Data of Table 8-4 with Additions

	Sample Mean	Upper $\bar{x}_i - K_1$	CUSUM, C_1 $\Sigma(\bar{x}_i - K_1)$	Lower $\bar{x}_i - K_2$	CUSUM, C_2 $\Sigma(\bar{x}_i - K_2)$	Remarks
i Sequence	$\bar{x}_i$	$\bar{x}_i - 0.355$		$\bar{x}_i + 0.355$		
1	−0.2	−0.555	<0	0.155	>0	
2	0.2	−0.155	<0	+	>0	
3	1.8	1.445	1.445	+	>0	
4	0.8	0.445	1.890	+	>0	
5	0.4	0.045	1.935	+	>0	
6	0.6	0.245	2.180	+	>0	
7	1.0	0.645	2.825	+	>0	
8	1.8	1.445	4.270*	+	>0	Upper signal
9	1.4	1.045	5.315	+	>0	
10	1.2	0.845	6.160	+	>0	
11	−0.8	−1.155	5.005	−0.445	−0.445	
12	−1.4	−1.755	3.250	−1.045	−1.490	
13	−1.6	−1.955	1.295	−1.245	−2.735	
14	−1.2	−1.555	<0	−0.845	−3.580*	Lower signal
15	−2.2	—	<0	−1.845	−5.425	
16	−1.4	—	<0	−1.045	−6.470	
17	−0.6	—	<0	−0.245	−6.715	
18	−0.6	—	<0	−0.245	−6.960	
19	−1.4	—	<0	−1.045	−8.005	
20	−1.6	—	<0	−1.245	−9.250	

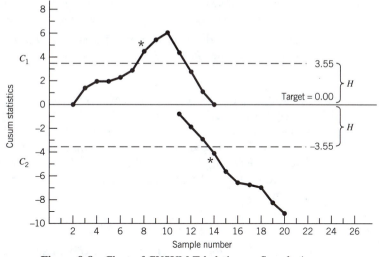

Figure 9-8 Chart of CUSUM Tabulation on Sample Averages

It is possible to prepare CUSUM tabulations and charts for monitoring only one side of the target value. It is also possible to prepare two-way tabulations in which the target values differ on the side, T_1, and lower side, T_2, $T_1 \neq T_2$. See Chapter 10 for an example.

Alternative Approaches to the Design of CUSUM Charts

Woodall and Adams (1993) recommend that CUSUM charts should be designed on the basis of ARL performance, rather than on the use of α probabilities, as used for the earlier designs. This recommendation is based on an earlier work by Adams, Lowry, and Woodall (1992) in which they argue that 2α, as a false alarm probability, is ambiguous and that the corresponding β probability (error of the second kind in failing to detect a change) has no clear interpretation for the CUSUM chart.

Now what should be made clear here is that ARL is also a measure of performance of the CUSUM charts designed with parameters, α and δ, as above. After designing a CUSUM procedure, obtaining d, f, and h, it is possible to determine the ARLs associated with various shifts in the process mean. These ARLs then serve as a measure of performance of the CUSUM procedure and can be used to compare it with other procedures. In fact, later in the chapter a number of standard CUSUM procedures that may serve for numerous practical applications are introduced. The ARLs associated with these standardized procedures are also given to assist in their selection for specific applications.

The approach recommended by Woodall and Adams (1993) is as follows:

1. Select a δ as before, with δ as defined earlier in the chapter.

2. Determine f (note that our f corresponds to their k) as $\delta/2$. This is based on the observed property that such a value for f in the design of a CUSUM procedure comes close to minimizing the ARL for a process shift of size δ.

3. Select a desired value for the "in-control" ARL that would be desirable for the procedure to exhibit, when there is no change in the process (0 shift).

4. Determine h, as defined earlier in the chapter, that provides the desired in-control ARL, as specified in Step 3.

The problem with this approach is in Step 4. It is not a simple procedure to determine h. Given f and h, there are a number of procedures (and computer programs) for determining ARLs. See, for example, Woodall (1983, 1986), Fellner (1990), Vance (1986), Goel and Wu (1971), Hawkins (1992a, 1992b), Park (1987), and Siegmund (1985). Any of these procedures could be used on a trial-and-error basis, with iterations of h values, to determine the value of h that produces the desired in-control ARL. For example, Woodall and Adams (1993) recommend the approximation by Siegmund (1985), as follows,

$$ARL = \{\exp\left[-2\Delta(h + 1.166)\right] + 2\Delta(h + 1.166) - 1\}/2\Delta^2 \qquad (9\text{-}8)$$

where $\Delta = E(z_i) - f$, for the upper one-sided CUSUM and $\Delta = -E(z_i) - f$ for the lower one-sided CUSUM, and $E(z_i)$ is the actual shift in the mean, in σ units, for which the ARL is to be determined. For $E(z_i) = f$ on the upper side and $E(z_i) = -f$ on the lower side, Equation (9-8) will not yield the ARL, since Δ cannot be zero (0).

For two-sided procedures, the ARL can be obtained from the ARLs of the respective one-sided CUSUM procedures by the following, shown by Kemp (1961), where ARL_U and ARL_L are the upper and lower ARLs:

$$ARL_2 = 1/[1/ARL_U + 1/ARL_L] \qquad (9\text{-}9)$$

This approximation will be demonstrated using a set of standardized CUSUM procedures for comparison.

Understandably, this trial-and-error approach to obtaining h by iterations of the ARL formulas is tedious and time consuming. Woodall and Adams (1993) provide an expression based on numerical analysis.

For some practical simplicity in deriving a host of potential CUSUM procedures, four nomographs from Gan (1991a) with different ranges of the feasible values of f and h are reproduced in enlarged form as Figures 9-9 through 9-12. They apply to two-sided produres. Gan (1991b) also gives similar nomographs for CUSUM procedures with "head starts" of $h/2$. He also provides nomographs for exponential CUSUM procedures in Gan (1994).

With these nomographs available, return to the four steps mentioned earlier to derive a CUSUM procedure. Suppose a two-sided procedure with $\delta = 0.75$ and a desired ARL = 350 is desired, close to that of the Shewhart control chart. Take $f = \delta/2 = 0.375$ (from Step 2). This value of f is on the scale of Figure 9-10. Entering the abscissa with $f = 0.375$ and tracing up to ARL = 350 (by visual interpolation), a value of h of approximately 5.95 is obtained. For this procedure, Equation (9-8) yields an ARL of approximately 717, and Equation (9-9) yields an ARL_2 of $717/2 \approx 358$.

If a one-sided procedure is desired with $\delta = 1.0$ and a desired ARL = 750, begin with Equation (9-9) to obtain the two-sided ARL of 375 (assuming symmetry on upper and lower sides). Then with $f = \delta/2 = 0.5$ enter Figure 9-11 to obtain $h \approx 4.75$. Equation (9-8) yields an estimate of 728 for this ARL.

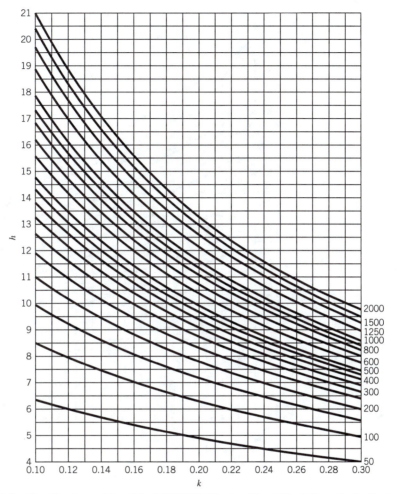

Figure 9-9 Combinations of *k* and *h* of CUSUM Charts without Head Starts for In-Control ARLs 50(50) 500(100) 1000(250) 2000.

A Set of Standard CUSUM Charts for Sample Averages

Using the *V* mask design criteria illustrated above, with real valued quantities such as α and δ, or the alternate design criteria of δ and an in-control ARL one can derive an infinite set of CUSUM charts. In practice, however, a very limited set of parameters may be useful for many applications. This is the approach taken by the British Standards Institution (BSI) in the preparation and publication of a series of guides to CUSUM techniques. These guides are numbered BS 5703 and are available in four parts. For more information on this set consult the references at the end of this chapter.

Six basic CUSUM schemes for averages are in Table 9-6, which is reproduced from Table 6 of BS 5703, Part 3: 1981 with permission of the British Standards Institution. The same set of CUSUM schemes is shown in Appendix H of ISO/TR7871:1997 (E).

As shown, two subsets of three schemes each are labeled C1 and C2. These designations relate to the magnitude of the average run length, at acceptable process levels.

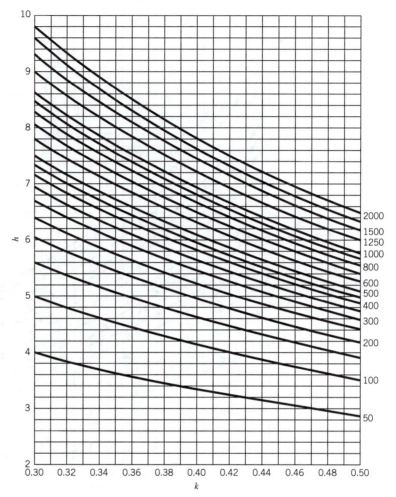

Figure 9-10   Combinations of k and h of CUSUM Charts without Head Starts for In-Control ARLs 50(50) 500(100) 1000(250) 2000.

TABLE 9-6 Parameters for Six Standard CUSUM Schemes

Critical Shift from Target, in Units of Standard Error	C1 Schemes (*La* 700 to 1000)		C2 Schemes (*La* 140 to 200)	
δ	h	f	h	f
(a) <0.75	8	0.25	5	0.25
(b) 0.75 to 1.5	5	0.50	3.5	0.50
(c) >1.5	2.5	1.00	1.8	1.00

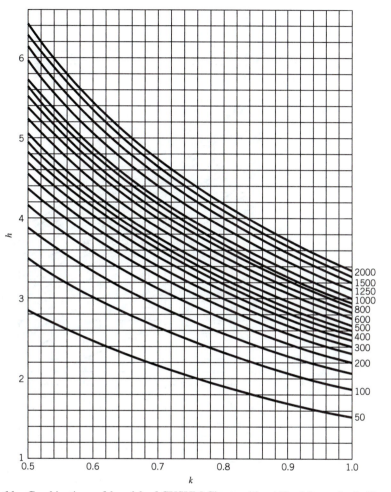

Figure 9-11 Combinations of k and h of CUSUM Charts without Head Starts for In-Control ARLs 50(50) 500(100) 1000(250) 2000.

The shorter notation, La, is used to express the idea. The C1 schemes have been devised to yield La values in the range of 700 to 1000. The C2 schemes have been devised to allow for a larger risk of checking on the process when no departure from an acceptable process level has occurred. This is reflected in values of La in the range of 140 to 200. ARL was used in the evaluation of $\bar{x}$ charts in Chapter 8. It is the most popular measure for evaluating the performance of CUSUM schemes. The ARLs for the referenced schemes are for one-sided application.

The three CUSUM schemes under each of the two subsets, C1 and C2, are classified according to ranges of δ—the critical shift from target in units of standard error (in this case $\sigma_{\bar{x}}$). Schemes are devised to detect small changes (a) with $\delta < 0.75$; medium changes, (b) with $0.75 \le \delta \le 1.5$; and larger changes, (c) with $\delta > 1.5$. The six schemes may be referenced with designations such as C1(a), C1(b), . . . , C2(b), C2(c).

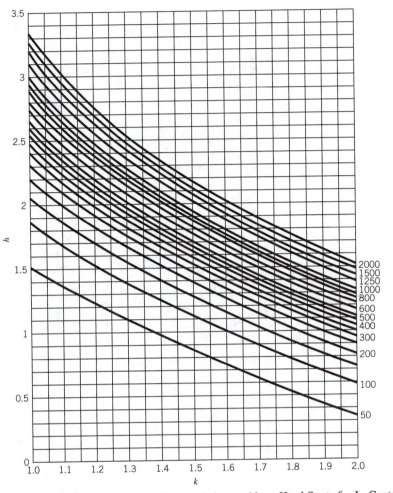

Figure 9-12 Combinations of k and h of CUSUM charts without Head Starts for In-Control ARLs 50(50) 500(100) 1000(250) 2000.

The parameters provided in Table 9-6 (namely, h and f) are sufficient to construct a V mask as detailed in Figures 9-3 and 9-4 or to develop the criteria for CUSUM tabulation and charting. Only a target level, T, and an estimate of the standard error of sample averages, $\hat{\sigma}_{\bar{x}}$, are needed to complete the setup of the CUSUM technique.

To assist in the selection of the appropriate scheme among the set of six standard schemes provided in Table 9-6, information on the average run lengths is provided in the referenced British and ISO standards. This is shown in Table 9-7, taken from Table 7, BS 5703, Part 3: 1981 and from ISO/TR 7871: 1997 (E).

An additional column of *ARLs* is provided in the standard for the C1(b) scheme fitted with a parabolic shaped mask, designed to improve detection of larger shifts. Consult the BSI Guide for further information. In addition to the *ARLs* for the six basic schemes, *ARLs* are provided for comparison for two Shewhart $\bar{x}$ charts with specific action and warning limits. These are designated S1 and S2. Procedure S1 relates to an $\bar{x}$ chart with the following control limits:

TABLE 9-7 *ARL* **Information for CUSUM and Shewhart Schemes (One-Sided)**

Shift from Targets in Units of $\sigma_{\bar{x}}$	C1 Schemes (a)	(b)	(c)	S1	C2 Schemes (a)	(b)	(c)	S2
0	730	930	715	640	140	200	170	167
0.25	85	140	205	256	38	55	68	76
0.5	29	38	68	126	17	22	30	38
0.75	16.4	17	27	52	10.5	11.5	15	20
1.0	11.4	10.5	13.4	26	7.4	7.4	8.8	11.7
1.5	7.1	5.8	5.4	8.9	4.7	4.3	4.0	5.0
2.0	5.2	4.1	3.25	4.15	3.5	3.0	2.5	2.8
2.5	4.2	3.2	2.3	2.46	2.8	2.4	1.9	1.86
3.0	3.5	2.6	1.85	1.75	2.4	2.0	1.5	1.44
4.0	2.6	1.9	1.32	1.19	1.9	1.5	1.12	1.09

Note: Boxes and arrows indicate range of shifts for which each scheme has been designed for greater effectiveness.

$$\text{Action lines at } T \pm 3.09 \; \hat{\sigma}_{\bar{x}}$$
$$\text{Warning lines at } T \pm 1.96 \; \hat{\sigma}_{\bar{x}}$$

with the rules for a signal of change, one point falling on or beyond the action lines or two consecutive points falling on or beyond the warning lines on the same side of T.

Procedure S2 relates to an $\bar{x}$ chart with the following control limits and the same rules in using the limits:

$$\text{Action lines at } T \pm 2.65 \; \hat{\sigma}_{\bar{x}}$$
$$\text{Warning lines at } T \pm 1.65 \; \hat{\sigma}_{\bar{x}}$$

A comparison of the ARLs shown in Table 9-7 with those estimated by Equation (9-8) is presented in Table 9-8. The ARLs for the six CUSUM schemes are calculated by Equation (9-8).The greatest deviations appear to be with the (c) schemes. Otherwise the approximations are reasonable.

TABLE 9-8 *ARL* **Comparisons Between Table 9-7 and Equation 9-8**

Shift from Targets in Units of $\sigma_{\bar{x}}$	C1 Schemes (a)	(b)	(c)	C2 Schemes (a)	(b)	(c)
0.0	738	938	760	142	201	185
0.25	—	142	212	—	56	71
0.50	29	—	69	17	—	31
0.75	16.3	17	27	10.3	11.4	15.4
1.0	11.3	10.3	—	7.3	7.4	—
1.5	7.0	5.7	5.4	4.6	4.2	4.0
2.0	5.1	3.9	3.2	3.4	2.9	2.5
2.5	4.0	3.0	2.2	2.6	2.2	1.8
3.0	3.3	2.4	1.7	2.2	1.8	1.4
4.0	2.4	1.7	1.2	1.6	1.3	0.9

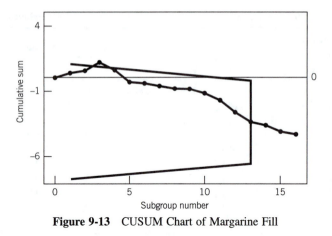

Figure 9-13 CUSUM Chart of Margarine Fill

▶ **EXAMPLE 9-1**

Control of an automatic filling engine for packaging plastic tubs of margarine is desired. An earlier capability study showed the process to maintain a stable distribution with a standard deviation estimated at 0.9 gram. Maintaining the proper average level to balance the cost of overfilling against the risk of producing too many tubs below 250 grams becomes the principal problem. It is decided to aim the average level at 251 grams. A CUSUM chart for averages of samples of size 5 is to be used to monitor the average level using the target of 251 grams. A large *ARL* is desired if the process average is on target so that unnecessary checks are not required. It is necessary to detect small departures from target in the magnitude of $0.75\hat{\sigma}_{\bar{x}}$ or less as quickly as possible. Hence, the C1(a) scheme of Table 9-6 is chosen for design of the decision criteria.

The truncated *V* mask shown in Figure 9-4 is constructed with $h = 8$, $f = 0.25$, $\hat{\sigma}_{\bar{x}} = 0.40$, yielding $H = 3.20$ and $H + 10F = 4.20$. A scaling factor of $A = 2\hat{\sigma}_{\bar{x}} = 0.8$ is chosen for plotting the CUSUM statistics. The process is adjusted, and a sample is drawn each hour during two shifts to obtain sixteen sample averages. The CUSUM chart (via MINITAB) is shown in Figure 9-13 with the *V* mask positioned over the thirteenth point, where a signal of a shift below target level occurs, requiring an upward adjustment in the filling mechanism. The average level for the segment from $i = 3$ to 16 is estimated as follows:

$$\hat{\mu} = \bar{x}_{4,16} = 251 - \frac{(-4.33) - (1.16)}{16 - 3} = 250.58$$

▶ **EXAMPLE 9-2**

To illustrate the availability of computer software for analyzing data, including CUSUM charting, a CUSUM chart has been prepared for the example using measurements of the width of fiberboards, as given in ISO/TR 7871: 1997 (E). The data are shown in Table 9-9, where each value represents the average width of ten measurements from five fiberboard panels. A CUSUM scheme with parameters $h = 5.0$ mm and $f = 0.215$ mm is used (this is scheme C2(a) of Table 9-6). The upper and lower CUSUMs, C_1 and C_2, are also shown in Table 9-9 in spreadsheet form. A CUSUM chart, as prepared by MINITAB, is shown in Figure 9-14. It shows signals on the low side at point number 6 and on the high side at points 9, 12, 18, 19, and 20. Note that MINITAB begins with a zero value as sample number 0.

Based on the earlier developments, using the sample average statistic as a foundation for discussion and following the standardized approach, it is now possible to present

TABLE 9-9 Mean Width of Fiberboards and CUSUM Statistics

X-Bar	$\bar{x}$-1200.125	C_1	$\bar{x}$-1199.875	C_2
1199.5	−0.625	0	−0.375	−0.375
1201.9	1.775	1.775	2.025	0
1199.8	−0.325	1.45	−0.075	−0.075
1199.5	−0.625	0.825	−0.375	−0.45
1199	−1.125	0	−0.875	−1.325
1198.5	−1.625	0	−1.375	−2.7
1202.1	1.975	1.975	2.225	0.475
1199.8	−0.325	1.65	−0.075	−0.55
1201.2	1.075	2.725	1.325	0
1199.7	−0.425	2.3	−0.175	−0.175
1200.2	0.075	2.375	0.325	0
1200.7	0.575	2.95	0.825	0
1199.2	−0.925	2.025	−0.675	−0.675
1199.1	−1.025	1	−0.775	−1.45
1200	−0.125	0.875	0.125	−1.325
1199.5	−0.625	0.25	−0.375	−1.7
1201.3	1.175	1.425	1.425	−0.275
1201.3	1.175	2.6	1.425	0
1202.2	2.075	4.675	2.325	0
1199.7	−0.425	4.25	−0.175	−0.175

CUSUM schemes for other statistics, including range, standard deviation, number of non-conformities, and number of nonconforming items.

9-1.2 CUSUM Charts for Sample Range and Standard Deviation

Because the estimate of standard error for sample averages plays an important role in the construction and use of the CUSUM for averages, it is wise to continue to monitor the variability within the samples from which the averages are obtained. Additionally, for

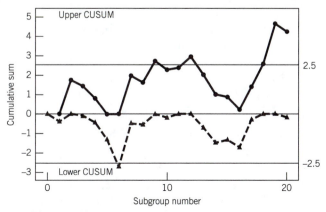

Figure 9-14 Average Width of Five Fiberboard Panels

TABLE 9-10   CUSUM Schemes for Ranges in Samples from a Normal Universe

		Sample Size, n						
		2	3	4	5	6	8	10
	a_n	1.5	1.0	0.85	0.75	0.65	0.55	0.50
C1	h	2.5	1.75	1.25	1.00	0.85	0.55	0.50
	f	0.85	0.55	0.50	0.45	0.45	0.40	0.35
C2	h	2.5	1.75	1.25	1.00	0.85	0.55	0.50
	f	0.55	0.35	0.30	0.30	0.30	0.25	0.25

some processes the emphasis for control may be on the sample variability as measured by the range or standard deviation. The range or standard deviation charts are useful for this purpose and often accompany the CUSUM chart for averages.

These statistics are also suitable for CUSUMS. The parameters for a set of standard CUSUM schemes for sample ranges are shown in Table 9-10 for samples ranging from $n = 2$ to 10. This table is adapted from Table 10 of BS 5703, Part 3: 1981, with permission of the British Standards Institution. Values for the scaling factor are again based on multiples of two (i.e., $2\hat{\sigma}_R$). The values shown are multiples of the average range at the target level, denoted $\bar{R}_T$ (i.e., $a_n \bar{R}_T$). They are derived as follows:

From Chapter 6, Equation 6-15, we have

$$\hat{\sigma}_R = d_3(\bar{R}/d_2)$$

Hence,

$$2\hat{\sigma}_R = (2d_3/d_2)\bar{R}$$

so

$$a_n \approx 2d_3/d_2$$

The values shown in Table 9-10 have been rounded for convenience.

Parameters for two subsets are provided with notation C1 and C2. As before, the C1 schemes supply relatively long ARLs at target while the C2 schemes are more liberal with the α risk and have shorter ARLs at target in order to shorten the ARLs associated with actual shifts in the mean. More rapid response to a given change in level is provided by larger sample sizes. A design parameter used in the development of these schemes is to give the smallest possible ratio of $\bar{R}_5/\bar{R}_T$, where $\bar{R}_5$ is the level of average range that yields an ARL of 5. ARL tables for these schemes are provided in the BSI Guide.

The parameters provided in Table 9-10 for CUSUM schemes for sample ranges are used in the following way to set up the CUSUM chart:

1. Obtain an estimate of μ_R (e.g., $\bar{R}$) or to choose a target value for the average range, $\bar{R}_T$.

2. Choose the desired sample size; 2 to 6, 8, and 10 are provided in Table 9-10. Choose the type of control desired and the appropriate scheme, C1 or C2. Obtain from Table 9-10 the parameters h, f, and a_n.

3. Develop the V mask as in Figure 9-4, with the decision interval, $H = h\overline{R}_T$; the slope of the decision line, $F = f\overline{R}_T$, and the CUSUM scale factor, $A = a_n\overline{R}_T$. Note that the parameters, h and f, given in Table 9-10 are designed to detect upward shifts in the mean value of R. Hence, only the lower decision line of the mask is intended for use. Because the distribution of the range is not symmetric, if a symmetrical V mask is used the upper decision line provides a conservative decision criterion. If violated, there is very convincing evidence that a real reduction in process dispersion has occurred.

4. Compute the sequence of CUSUM statistics, C_j, from the sequence of sample ranges, R_i, as

$$C_j = \sum_{i=1}^{j} (R_i - \overline{R}_T)$$

5. Plot this sequence using a CUSUM scale with approximately $a_n\overline{R}_T$ (rounded to a reasonable scale value) as the value of one vertical scale division, where the same scale division corresponds to each sample on the horizontal axis.

6. Position the mask lower decision interval on each point in the sequence to detect a signal of change in mean range from the target value.

For CUSUM tabulation procedures involving ranges, the reference value, $K = k\overline{R}_T$, is obtained with $k = 1 + f$. The CUSUM tabulation statistic is then

$$C_j = \sum_{i=1}^{j} (R_i - K)$$

reverting to zero whenever negative and providing a signal if C_j equals or exceeds the decision interval, H.

The parameters for a set of standard CUSUM schemes for sample standard deviations, s, are shown in Table 9-11 for samples ranging from $n = 2$ to 20. This table is adapted from Table 12 of BS 5703, Part 3: 1981, with permission of the British Standards Institution. The scaling factor is $2\hat{\sigma}_s$ and is rounded from $2\hat{\sigma}_s = (2c_5/c_4)\overline{s}$; that is, the values shown are multiples of the average standard deviation at the target level, denoted $\overline{s}_T$ (i.e., $a_n\overline{s}_T$). Recall Equations (8-14) and (8-15).

The above discussion for ranges, including the step-by-step procedure, applies to the case of standard deviations with the appropriate changes in statistics and parameters from Table 9-11. For parameters for sample sizes larger than 20, consult the BSI Guide.

TABLE 9-11 CUSUM Schemes for Standard Deviations in Samples from a Normal Universe

		Sample Size, n									
		2	3	4	5	6	8	10	12	15	20
	a_n	1.5	1.0	0.85	0.75	0.65	0.55	0.5	0.45	0.4	0.35
C1	h	2.0	1.6	1.15	0.9	0.8	0.6	0.5	0.4	0.35	0.3
	f	0.5	0.35	0.35	0.35	0.32	0.3	0.3	0.3	0.27	0.23
C2	h	2.0	1.6	1.15	0.9	0.8	0.6	0.5	0.4	0.35	0.3
	f	0.25	0.15	0.2	0.2	0.2	0.2	0.2	0.2	0.18	0.16

9-1.3 The CUSUM Chart for Count of Nonconformities

CUSUM procedures for the attribute control charts in Chapter 7 may also be developed. The basic principles are the same as those presented for sample averages, ranges, and standard deviations. Only certain details, peculiar to the statistics involved, differ.

For the statistic representing the number of nonconformities, a set of standard CUSUM schemes is presented in Table 9-12. This table is adapted from Table 5 of BS 5703, Part 4: 1982, with permission of the British Standards Institution. It lists parameters H and F associated with a series of mean target rates, c_T, from 0.1 to 25, for two subsets, C1 and C2, as before.

The procedures for using the parameters of Table 9-12 to set up a CUSUM chart for number of nonconformities, c_i, are as follows:

1. Obtain an estimate of c (e.g., $\bar{c}$) or choose a target value for the mean rate of occurrences of nonconformities, c_T. Obtain $\hat{\sigma}_c$ as $\sqrt{c_T}$ based on the Poisson distribution.

2. Choose the type of control desired and the appropriate scheme, C1 or C2. For c_T, or the nearest value to c_T, obtain from Table 9-12 the parameters H and F. For

TABLE 9-12   CUSUM Schemes for Number of Nonconformities

Target Mean Rate c_T	C1 Schemes		C2 Schemes	
	H	F	H	F
0.10	1.5	0.650	2.0	0.150
0.125	2.5	0.375	2.5	0.125
0.16	3.0	0.340	2.0	0.340
0.20	3.5	0.300	2.5	0.300
0.25	4.0	0.250	3.0	0.250
0.32	3.0	0.680	4.0	0.180
0.40	2.5	1.100	3.0	0.600
0.50	3.0	1.000	2.0	1.000
0.64	3.5	0.860	2.0	1.360
0.80	5.0	0.700	3.5	0.700
1.00	5.0	1.000	5.0	0.500
1.25	4.0	1.750	5.0	0.750
1.60	5.0	1.400	4.0	1.400
2.00	7.0	1000	5.0	1.000
2.50	7.0	1.500	5.0	1.500
3.20	7.0	1.800	5.0	1.800
4.00	8.0	2.000	6.0	2.000
5.00	9.0	2.000	7.0	2.000
6.40	9.0	2.600	9.0	1.600
8.00	9.0	3.000	9.0	2.000
10.00	11.0	3.000	11.0	2.000
15.00	16.0	3.000	11.0	3.000
20.00	20.0	3.000	14.0	3.000
25.00	24.0	3.000	17.0	3.000

values of c_T between 10 and 25 not given in the table, intermediate schemes may be obtained by linear interpolation in both H and F.

3. Develop a chart scaling based on $2\hat{\sigma}_c$ (rounded to a reasonable value) as the value of one vertical scale division on the CUSUM axis corresponding to the same scale division on the horizontal axis. For $c_T < 1.0$ and hence $\hat{\sigma}_c < 1.0$, determine the average number of samples required to yield one "success" or nonconformity—that is, $1/c_T$. Round this value up to a convenient integer, and use this integer for the horizontal sequence scale division. Mark off the vertical scale devision of the same width as consecutive even integers above and below zero (e.g., 0, +2, −2, +4, −4, etc.).

4. Develop the V mask as in Figure 9-4 with the values of H and F and the scale developed in Step 3. As for the range and standard deviation, the parameters are designed to detect upward shifts in the mean rate of c. Hence, only the lower decision line of the mask is intended for use.

5. Compute the sequence of CUSUM statistics, C_j, from the sequence of sample number of nonconformities, c_i, as

$$C_j = \sum_{i=1}^{j}(c_i - c_T)$$

6. Plot the CUSUM sequence with the scale developed in Step 3.

7. Position the mask lower decision interval on each point in the sequence as it appears necessary to detect a signal of change in mean rate from target value.

For CUSUM tabulation procedures involving number of nonconformities, the reference value, $K = F + c_T$, is used. The CUSUM tabulation and alternate charting statistic is then

$$C_j = \sum_{i=1}^{j}(c_i - K)$$

reverting to zero whenever negative and providing a signal if C_j equals or exceeds the decision interval, H.

9-1.4 The CUSUM Chart for Number of Nonconforming Units

For the statistic representing the number of nonconforming units in a sample of size n based on the binomial distribution, several options are available for applying CUSUM techniques. For certain values of the parameters n and p the Poisson function is an adequate model, and the CUSUM procedures and tables of the preceding section are applicable. For other values of the parameters a normal approximation may be used, and the CUSUM techniques and tables developed for sample averages apply. For still other values, CUSUM parameters may be developed, based directly on the binomal distribution.

For the latter case a set of standard CUSUM schemes is presented in Table 9-13. This table is adapted from Table 9 of BS 5703, Part 4: 1982, with permission of the British Standards Institution. It lists parameters H and F associated with a series of sample sizes, n, ranging from 10 to 100 and target fraction nonconforming, p_T, ranging from 0.1 to 0.5 for two subsets, C1 and C2 as before. For each combination of n and p_T the mean occurrence of nonconforming units, np_T, is also shown.

TABLE 9-13   CUSUM Schemes for Number of Nonconforming Units

Sample Size n	Target Mean Proportion p_T	Mean Occurrence np_T	C1 Schemes H	C1 Schemes F	C2 Schemes H	C2 Schemes F
10	0.1	1	4	1	3	1
	0.2	2	6	1	4	1
	0.3	3	7	1	5	1
	0.4	4	7	1	5	1
	0.5	5	7	1	5	1
15	0.1	1.5	4	1.5	3	1.5
	0.2	3	8	1	6	1
	0.3	4.5	7	1.5	5	1.5
	0.4	6	10	1	7	1
	0.5	7.5	7	1.5	5	1.5
20	0.1	2	4	2	3	2
	0.2	4	10	1	7	1
	0.3	6	6	2	5	2
	0.4	8	7	2	5	2
	0.5	10	13	1	9	1
25	0.1	2.5	6	1.5	4	1.5
	0.2	5	7	2	5	2
	0.3	7.5	11	1.5	8	1.5
	0.4	10	9	2	7	2
	0.5	12.5	12	1.5	8	1.5
35	0.1	3.5	8	1.5	6	1.5
	0.2	7	9	2	7	2
	0.3	10.5	14	1.5	10	1.5
	0.4	14	12	2	9	2
	0.5	17.5	10	2.5	7	2.5
50	0.1	5	8	2	6	2
	0.2	10	12	2	10	2
	0.3	15	15	2	11	2
	0.4	20	12	3	9	3
80	0.1	8	12	2	8	2
	0.2	16	18	2	13	2
	0.3	24	16	3	12	3
100	0.1	10	14	2	10	2
	0.2	20	22	2	16	2

For values of the parameters not given in the table, the following steps are recommended:

For $p_T < 0.10$, follow the preceding section with $c_T = np_T$ and proceed accordingly.

For $np_T > 20$, use the section on sample averages with $T = np_T$ and $\sigma_v = \sqrt{np_T(1 - p_T)}$. Obtain H as the nearest integer to $h\sigma_v$ and F as $f\sigma_v$ (rounded as desired, perhaps to one decimal place).

For combinations of n and p_T for which parameters are given in Table 9-13, proceed as for the chart for number of nonconformities with np_T, $\sigma_v = \sqrt{np_T(1 - p_T)}$, $C_j = \Sigma_{i=1}^{j} (x_i - np_T)$, where x_i are the number of nonconforming units in each sample.

Many additional topics relating to the use of CUSUM procedures are discussed in the referenced BSI Guides. Tables of ARLs are presented for the various schemes introduced above. Normalizing transformations are covered along with related statistical tests, computer routines, nomographs, and examples. Some of the earlier papers on CUSUM are referenced in Chapter 8. Other early papers are Bissell (1979, 1981), Elder, Provost, and Ecker (1980), Lucas (1976, 1982, 1985), Lucas and Crosier (1982a, 1982b), and Westgard, Groth, Aronsson, and de Verdier (1977). Other references that may be consulted are Brook and Evans (1972), Ewan (1963), Fellner (1990), Hawkins (1987), Johnson (1961), Johnson and Leone (1962), Van Bobben De Bruyn (1968), Vardeman and Ray (1985), Woodall (1984), Woodall and Ncube (1985), and Yaschin (1993).

► 9-2 THE EXPONENTIALLY WEIGHTED MOVING AVERAGE CONTROL CHART

Another of the special control charts is the exponentially weighted moving average (EWMA) chart. It was introduced by Roberts (1959). Since then, an extensive literature has developed exploiting this technique in the quality disciplines. Applications have been made in many areas, including the process and chemical industries, as well as to financial and management control systems, for which single observations, x_i, per time period may be available (i.e., where subgrouping may be impractical). The single observation may be an average, an individual, a ratio, a proportion, or a similar measurement. Only a brief introduction is presented here. For a detailed study of this technique the interested reader should consult the related bibliography given in the reference section of this chapter.

The plotted statistic is as follows:

$$\bar{x}_{t+1} = (1 - \alpha)\bar{x}_t + \alpha x_t \tag{9-10}$$

where

$\bar{x}_{t+1}$ = the exponentially weighted moving average at the next time period

$\bar{x}_t$ = the weighted moving average at the present time period

x_t = the present observation

α = the weighting factor for the present observation, where $0 < \alpha < 1$

For the above statistic, if the sequence, $x_1, x_2, x_3, \ldots, x_t, \ldots$ are independently distributed random variables, each with variance, σ_x^2, then the variance of the EWMA statistic for time period $t + 1$ is as follows:

$$\text{Var}(\bar{x}_{t+1}) = \sigma_x^2[\alpha/(2 - \alpha)][1 - (1 - \alpha)^{2t}] \tag{9-11}$$

It should be noted that for this result to hold, the variance of $\bar{x}_1$ must be zero, that is, $\text{Var}(\bar{x}_1) = 0.0$. This is a feasible result if $\bar{x}_t$ for $t = 1$ in Equation (9-10)—that is, the EWMA statistic—is considered to be the constant mean, μ_x, the mean of the x_i sequence, with variance zero. This implies that the starting value of the EWMA statistic, $\bar{x}_1$, in Equation (9-10) should be the mean of the process. Because the mean may not be known, an approximation

TABLE 9-14   Alpha Values Corresponding to Integer Values of n

n:	2	3	4	5	6	7	8	9
α:	0.667	0.5	0.4	0.333	0.286	0.25	0.222	0.2

consisting of an earlier sample average may be used. If earlier information is not available, the starting value may be the mean of the first several observations in the x_i sequence.

Now with α between 0 and 1, the term $(1 - \alpha)^{2t}$ in the variance Equation (9-11) will diminish as t increases and the variance for the EWMA statistic becomes

$$\text{Var}(\bar{x}_{t+1}) = \sigma_x^2[\alpha/(2 - \alpha)] \tag{9-12}$$

Wortham and Ringer (1971) demonstrated that the statistic $\bar{x}_t$ for normally distributed x_i with mean μ_x and variance σ_x^2 and for large t is normally distributed with

$$E(\bar{x}_t) = \mu_x$$
$$\text{Var}(\bar{x}_t) \approx \sigma_x^2[\alpha/(2 - \alpha)]$$

They also observed that if you choose $\alpha = 2/(n + 1)$, the variance approximation reduces to

$$\text{Var}(\bar{x}_t) \approx \sigma_x^2/n, \qquad \text{the variance of averages of sample size } n$$

For integer n (2 to 9), the corresponding α values are shown in Table 9-14. On this basis, control limits for the EWMA statistic can take various forms as follows:

$$\text{Control limits} = \hat{\mu}_x \pm 3\hat{\sigma}_x\sqrt{[\alpha/(2 - \alpha)][1 - (1 - \alpha)^{2t}]} \tag{9-13}$$

and for large t these become

$$UCL = \hat{\mu}_x + 3\hat{\sigma}_x\sqrt{[\alpha/(2 - \alpha)]} \tag{9-14}$$
$$LCL = \hat{\mu}_x - 3\hat{\sigma}_x\sqrt{[\alpha/(2 - \alpha)]} \tag{9-15}$$

Under the conditions reflected in Table 9-14 the control limits for large t become

$$UCL = \hat{\mu}_x + 3\hat{\sigma}_x/\sqrt{n} \tag{9-16}$$
$$LCL = \hat{\mu}_x - 3\hat{\sigma}_x/\sqrt{n} \tag{9-17}$$

which demonstrate that the choice of α narrows the limits to $\bar{x}$ chart type control limits.

Consider as an example the data of Table 6-6 (also used in Table 9-1). Applying the EWMA calculations with $\alpha = 0.20$ results in the control chart of Figure 9-15. Note the variable control limits for the first eight or nine subgroups ($t = 1$ to 9). This is another example of plotting with MINITAB.

Appending to this chart the data of Table 8-1 (also used in Table 9-2) with a mean of 2.0, with the same control limits based on the first twenty samples as in Figure 9-15, results in the chart shown in Figure 9-16. As with the $\bar{x}$ chart of Figure 8-2, the first sample after the change (sample 21) exceeds the upper control limit. This corresponds to a shift in the mean of about 1.2 sigmas (2.0/1.72).

A further example is to append to the data of Table 9-1 (Table 6-6) the data given in Table 9-3, corresponding to a change in the mean from 0.0 to 1.0, instead of 2.0. This is a shift in the mean of about 0.58 sigma (1.0/1.72). An EWMA chart of these data with the control limits based on the first twenty samples as in Figures 9-15 and 9-16 is shown in Figure 9-17. A very positive indication of a change in the mean occurs on the eighth point, as it does for the CUSUM chart of Figure 9-7.

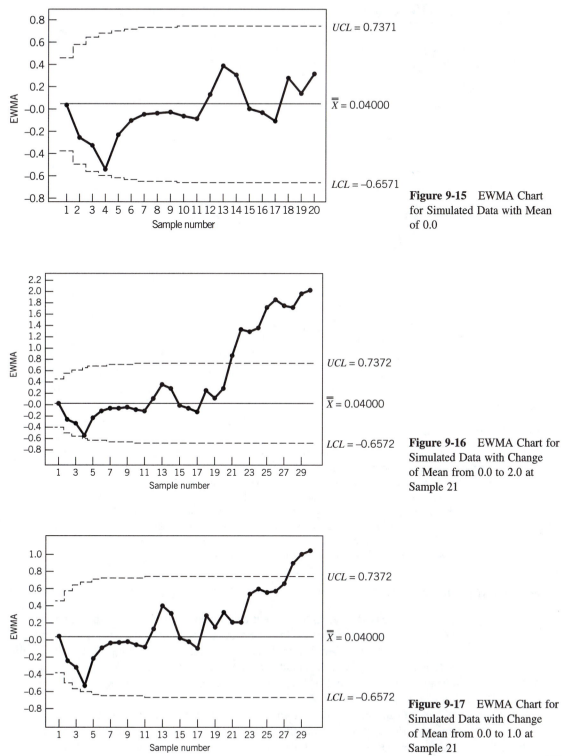

Figure 9-15 EWMA Chart for Simulated Data with Mean of 0.0

Figure 9-16 EWMA Chart for Simulated Data with Change of Mean from 0.0 to 2.0 at Sample 21

Figure 9-17 EWMA Chart for Simulated Data with Change of Mean from 0.0 to 1.0 at Sample 21

TABLE 9-15   Ratio of Value of Product Losses to Value of Product Shipped

January	0.30	June	0.27	December	0.24	May	0.24
February	0.38	August	0.27	January	0.26	June	0.21
March	0.34	September	0.29	February	0.30	August	0.18
April	0.37	October	0.28	March	0.32	September	0.14
May	0.28	November	0.25	April	0.29	October	0.17

Figure 9-18   Ratio of Product Losses to Product Shipped

▶ **EXAMPLE 9-3**

A management reporting system includes a charting of losses occurring in production as a ratio of the value of such losses to the value of good product produced and shipped. Data for an eleven-month year (based on a July shutdown) are given in Table 9-15.

An EWMA chart of these data is shown in Figure 9-18, with control limits based on the first eleven data points (January through December of the previous year), to monitor the next year's results with a management goal set to reduce the losses (ratio) significantly during the year. An earlier goal of 0.30 had been set. The results of the improvement efforts are seen to break through the lower control limit in June of the following year.

▶ **9-3 MODIFIED OR REJECT CONTROL LIMITS FOR $\bar{x}$ CHARTS**

In the preceding charts, both in the present chapter and in earlier ones, the emphasis was on statistical control of the process. In some cases adjustment of the mean value may have been required, and since specification limits are so much an integral part of most quality characteristics, many examples included reference to such limits. A detailed discussion of specification limits is found in Chapter 10. Modified limits are a means of integrating such limits with control charts.

When $\bar{x}$ charts are used for *controlling the fraction nonconforming of products exceeding specification limits* rather than detecting lack of statistical control in the process, two useful approaches have been developed. One involves the use of modified or reject control limits developed in this section. The second approach is that of acceptance control charts presented in the next section.

The following is a formal definition of the modified control chart

Modified Control Chart (Control Chart with Modified Limits): A control chart for evaluating the process level in terms of the subgroup average, $\bar{x}$, modifying the usual Shewhart control limits to relate to product or service specifications.

The term "reject limits" is interchangeable with "modified limits" and reflects the rejection of the process, subjecting it to investigation and adjustment when averages of samples from the process exceed the modified or reject limits. The single term, modified limits, will be used.

One of the most popular derivations of modified control limits is in terms of the process standard deviation, σ, from which factors labeled V are derived for various samples. [See, for example, Grant and Leavenworth (1996)]. In terms of previous control chart discussion this is generally applicable to the case of standard given.

For various applications of the $\bar{x}$ chart, with no standard given, either the ranges, R, or the sample standard deviations, s, may be used with the averages of samples. In these cases, employing the V factor requires a separate estimate of σ by $\bar{R}$ or $\bar{s}$. A more direct approach, for the case of no standard given, is possible. This section presents a standardized and comprehensive derivation of the modified control limit formulas and associated factors for the following three common cases:

1. No standard given, $\bar{x}$ and R values, $\bar{\bar{x}}$ and $\bar{R}$ calculated from a set of samples.
2. No standard given, $\bar{x}$ and s values, $\bar{\bar{x}}$ and $\bar{s}$ calculated from a set of samples.
3. Standard given, $\bar{x}$ and R or $\bar{x}$ and s values calculated from a set of samples.

9-3.1 Derivation Principles

Two basic principles are used for the derivation of modified control limits. These are as follows:

1. The upper and lower modified centerlines are based on the principle of placing these centerlines three times an estimate of the process standard deviation inside the specification limits, U and L. This multiple of three may be varied for certain applications, including cases in which the limits are based on probability values. In these cases, appropriate adjustments must be made in the derivations and resultant factors. See the next section on acceptance control charts for variation of these multiples.
2. The modified control limits, UML and LML, are based on the principle of placing these limits three times an estimate of the standard deviation of averages above the upper modified centerline and below the lower modified centerline.

Derivation of Modified Control Limits

On the basis of the above principles and the relationships developed earlier for Shewhart control charts, the derivation of modified control limits for the three common cases follows. Some necessary conditions and assumptions are given first:

1. A natural, controlled pattern is evidenced by the $\bar{R}$ or s control chart; that is, the variability is in statistical control. Derivation of the formulas assumes a normal

distribution, though some departure from normality is not serious. One of these charts (i.e., R or s with regular control limits) should be maintained along with the $\bar{x}$ chart with modified control limits to monitor continuously the process variability. Action should be taken on any changes in the spread of the underlying distribution.

2. The specification limit(s) is (are) correct for the item under consideration.

3. Strict statistical control of the individual distribution mean within the specification limit(s) is not necessary—only that the individual distribution does not shift too far beyond the specification limit(s). It is assumed that the center of the underlying distribution can be adjusted as desired and that it may change on occasion as it is affected by various process factors.

4. The universe variability, σ, as estimated by $\hat{\sigma} = \bar{R}/d_2$ or $\bar{s}/c_4$ is sufficiently small that the inequality $U - L \geq 6\hat{\sigma}$ holds for the case of two-sided specification limits.

No Standard Given Using $\bar{x}$ and R with $\bar{\bar{x}}$ and $\bar{R}$ Calculated

For each of the three common cases, the diagram in Figure 9-19 graphically describes the modified control limit problem. Based on the diagram and relationships developed in earlier chapters, the following results hold:

$$\text{Upper centerline} = U - 3\hat{\sigma} = U - 3\bar{R}/d_2 \qquad (9\text{-}18)$$
$$= U - E_2\bar{R}$$

where $E_2 = 3/d_2$ and values, as functions of the sample size (n), are tabulated in Table G of the Appendix.

$$UML = U - 3\hat{\sigma} + 3\hat{\sigma}_{\bar{x}} = U - 3\bar{R}/d_2 + 3\hat{\sigma}/\sqrt{n}$$
$$= U - (3/d_2)\bar{R} + (3/d_2\sqrt{n})\bar{R} = U - (E_2 - A_2)\bar{R} \qquad (9\text{-}19)$$
$$= U - C_2\bar{R}$$

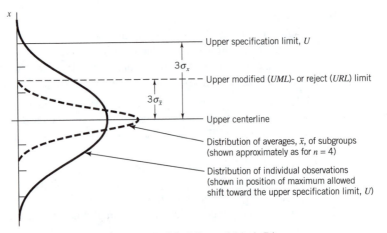

Figure 9-19 Modified Control Limit Diagram

where $C_2 = E_2 - A_2$ and values, as functions of the sample size (n), are tabulated in Table H of the Appendix.

Similarly,

$$\text{Lower centerline} = L + E_2\bar{R} \tag{9-20}$$

$$LML = L + C_2\bar{R} \tag{9-21}$$

No Standard Given Using $\bar{x}$ and s, with $\bar{\bar{x}}$ and $\bar{s}$ Calculated

On the basis of the diagram of Figure 9-19 and relationships developed in earlier chapters, the following results hold:

$$\text{Upper centerline} = U - 3\hat{\sigma} = U - 3\bar{s}/c_4$$
$$= U - E_3\bar{s} \tag{9-22}$$

where $E_3 = 3/c_4$ and values, as functions of the sample size (n), are tabulated in Table G of the Appendix.

$$UML = U - 3\hat{\sigma} + 3\hat{\sigma}_{\bar{x}} = U - 3\bar{s}/c_4 + 3\hat{\sigma}/\sqrt{n}$$
$$= U - (3/c_4)\bar{s} + (3/c_4\sqrt{n})\bar{s} = U - (E_3 - A_3)\bar{s} \tag{9-23}$$
$$= U - C_3\bar{s}$$

where $C_3 = E_3 - A_3$ and values, as functions of the sample size (n), are tabulated in Table H of the Appendix.

Similarly,

$$\text{Lower centerline} = L + E_3\bar{s} \tag{9-24}$$

$$LML = L + C_3\bar{s} \tag{9-25}$$

Standard Given Using $\bar{x}$ and R or $\bar{x}$ and s

On the basis of the diagram of Figure 9-19 and relationships developed in earlier chapters, the following results hold:

$$\text{Upper centerline} = U - 3\sigma_0 \tag{9-26}$$
$$UML = U - 3\sigma_0 + 3\sigma_{\bar{x}} = U - 3\sigma_0 + 3\sigma_0/\sqrt{n}$$
$$= U - (3 - A)\sigma_0$$
$$= U - C\sigma_0 \tag{9-27}$$

where $C = 3 - A$ and values, as functions of the sample size (n), are tabulated in Table H of the Appendix.

Similarly,

$$\text{Lower centerline} = L + 3\sigma_0 \tag{9-28}$$

$$LML = L + C\sigma_0 \tag{9-29}$$

9-3.2 Modified Control Chart Examples

Several examples will serve to illustrate the use of the above formulas in computing and applying modified control limits on $\bar{x}$ charts.

▶ **EXAMPLE 9-4**

Example 8-1 relates to a study of the melt index of an extrusion-grade polyethylene compound for which $\bar{x}$ and R control charts are used with samples of size 4. Some stability of the R chart is seen in the last twelve samples for which a revised computation of $\bar{R}$ produces the following result:

$$\bar{R} = 163/12 = 13.58$$

This provides an estimate for the process standard deviation of

$$\hat{\sigma} = \bar{R}/d_2 = 13.58/2.059 = 6.6$$

Assume that the specification limits of $U = 270$ and $L = 200$ have been found to be realistic and necessary and that the conditions given above are reasonably valid. Then modified control limits may be computed and used for further control of the process. It can be seen that $U - L = 70 > 6\hat{\sigma} = 39.6$.

The computations are as follows:

$$\text{Upper centerline} = U - E_2\bar{R}$$
$$= 270 - 1.457(13.58) = 270 - 19.79 = 250.2$$
$$UML = U - C_2\bar{R}$$
$$= 270 - 0.728(13.58) = 270 - 9.89 = 260.1$$
$$\text{Lower centerline} = L + E_2\bar{R}$$
$$= 200 + 19.79 = 219.8$$
$$LML = L + C_2\bar{R}$$
$$= 200 + 9.89 = 209.9$$

The $\bar{x}$ and R control charts, using the last twelve data points of Table 8-3 and 8-6 with regular control limits and with the above modified control limits extended for future control on the $\bar{x}$ chart, are shown in Figure 9-20. Several features of these charts may be noted. The modified limits on the $\bar{x}$ chart for future control may be thought of as stretching the single centerline of the regular limits into a central band within which the mean of the distribution may fluctuate. The modified control limits represent the signal based on averages that the distribution has moved too far toward either specification limit. The specification limits may be shown as arrows on the scale for reference purposes. The $\bar{x}$ chart of the trial study is not in statistical control, nor is this necessary for establishing and using modified control limits.

The R chart is in control and regular control limits are extended to monitor the spread of the distribution in the future. Should out-of-control points occur, especially on the high side, action should be taken to locate and correct the cause. Otherwise, with an increased spread of the underlying distribution, the modified control limits for the $\bar{x}$ chart are no longer valid.

▶ **EXAMPLE 9-5**

Example 8-2 presents a variables sampling plan for batch acceptance of flares with overall monitoring by means of $\bar{x}$ and s control charts. An alternative approach is to employ modified (reject) control limits on the $\bar{x}$ chart and base acceptance of batches on meeting these control limits. From the computations given in Example 8-2 the following results for $\bar{s}$ are obtained:

$$\bar{s} = \sqrt{24.169} = 4.92$$

From Equation (9-24) for $n = 5$ the lower centerline is calculated:

$$\text{Lower centerline} = L + E_3\bar{s}$$
$$= 0.0 + 3.191(4.92)$$
$$= 15.7$$

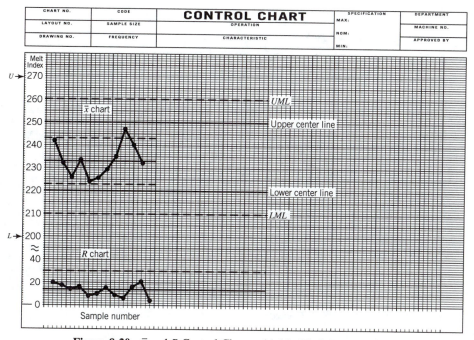

Figure 9-20 $\bar{x}$ and R Control Charts with Modified Control Limits

The lower modified limit is obtained by using Equation (9-25):

$$LML = L + C_3\bar{s}$$
$$= 0.0 + 1.764(4.92)$$
$$= 8.68$$

Similar computations of the lower centerline and lower modified limit for the other sample sizes may be made with the same equations and appropriate constants, E_3 and C_3. Because only a lower specification limit applies, the upper centerline and upper modified limit are not obtained.

The $\bar{x}$ and s control charts from Figure 8-7 are shown in Figure 9-21, but with the lower centerlines and lower modified control limits shown for the second set of 12 data points for the respective sample sizes. The pattern of higher average candlepower values shows that no points come close to the lower modified control limits. There is no signal or alarm concerning the ability of individual units to meet the lower specification limit of 0.0. The s chart is maintained to monitor the spread of the distribution. The regular Shewhart control limits and centerline ($\bar{s}$) are extended from the trial study for the s chart.

► **EXAMPLE 9-6**

Modified control limits are employed in the application to be discussed in Example 11-25 pertaining to the weld strength of support legs for the cathode sleeve of an electron tube. The modified control limits for the $\bar{x}$ chart are shown in Figure 11-53. The computations are as follows:

$$\bar{R} = 1.2, \qquad L = 2.0, \qquad n = 5$$
$$\text{Lower centerline} = L + E_2\bar{R} = 2.0 + 1.29(1.2)$$
$$= 2.0 + 1.548 = 3.55$$

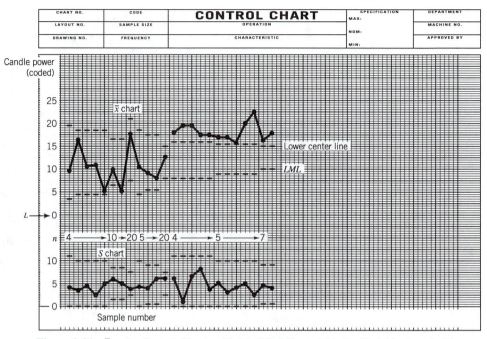

Figure 9-21 $\bar{x}$ and s Control Charts with Modified Control Limits: Variable Sample Size

$$LML = L + C_2\bar{R} = 2.0 + 0.713(1.2)$$
$$= 2.0 + 0.8556 = 2.86$$

9-3.3 Other Forms of Modified Control Limits

The formal procedure for modified limits has been for the $\bar{x}$ control chart in relation to specification limits. The principles associated with modified control limits also apply to other control charts. Control limits for any control chart may be modified to suit the specific needs of the user. The use of different multiples of the estimated standard deviation (other than 3) represents a modification of control limits. A type of modified control limits is the use of warning limits at 2σ and control limits at 3σ. Limits are sometimes modified to achieve a certain goal. Limits for attribute control charts may also be modified. See, for example, Figure 7-6 and the computation of new control limits based on recognition of an improved level for future control.

The following example illustrates the modification of control limits for the R chart as well as the $\bar{x}$ chart in an attempt to achieve a desired level of control with respect to specification limits.

▶ **EXAMPLE 9-7**

The journal diameter of a machine-ground shaft is to be controlled to achieve conformance to a set of tight specification limits with $U = 11.996$ mm and $L = 11.986$ mm. A brief study is conducted by drawing twelve samples of size 4 and obtaining the diameter measurements from which $\bar{x}$ and

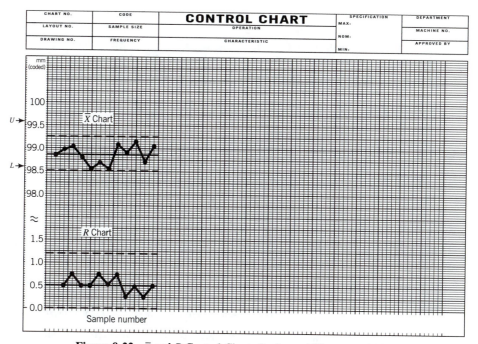

Figure 9-22 $\bar{x}$ and R Control Charts for Journal Diameter of Shaft

R control charts, as shown in Figure 9-22, are prepared. The upper specification limits U and L are shown by arrows on the $\bar{x}$ coded scale with 11 subtracted from the original values and with multiplication by 100. Because these apply to individual units and the width of the control limits for averages are almost as wide, a specification conflict is indicated. The lower specification limit is higher than the lower control limit for averages. The situation is illustrated in Figure 9-23. The approximate distribution of individual units is obtained from the control chart information as follows:

$$\hat{\sigma} = \bar{R}/d_2 = 0.00529/2.059 = 0.00257$$
$$6\hat{\sigma} = 0.0154 > U - L = 11.996 - 11.986 = 0.010$$

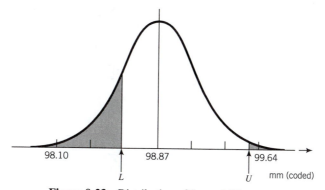

Figure 9-23 Distribution of Journal Diameters

Approximately 15% of the units are below the lower specification limit, L. Even if the distribution were centered at the specification nominal (i.e., 11.991 or 99.10 on the coded scale), approximately 2.6% of individual units would fall outside each specification limit.

From a consideration of the process, it is believed that the distribution can be centered and that a smaller process variation may be possible. The improvement program is implemented along with the continued use of the $\bar{x}$ and R control charts. The control limits on both charts are to be modified to indicate statistically by means of averages and ranges when the individual units are meeting the specification limits. The modified limits are then obtained.

For the R chart, an $\bar{R}_0$ is determined that corresponds to 6σ, equaling the width of the total tolerance, that is, $U - L$:

$$U - L = 0.010 = 6\hat{\sigma} \quad \text{so that } \hat{\sigma} = 0.00167$$
$$\bar{R}_0 = d_2\hat{\sigma} = 2.059(0.00167) = 0.00343$$
$$UCL_R = D_4\bar{R} = 2.28(0.00343) = 0.00782$$
$$LCL_R = D_3\bar{R} = 0.0(0.00343) = 0.0$$

For the $\bar{x}$ chart, $\bar{x}_0$ is taken as the specification nominal with $\bar{R}_0$ as the measure of the distribution spread:

$$UCL_{\bar{x}} = \bar{x}_0 + A_2\bar{R}_0 = 11.991 + 0.73(0.00343)$$
$$= 11.991 + 0.0025 = 11.9935$$
$$LCL_{\bar{x}} = \bar{x}_0 - A_2\bar{R}_0 = 11.991 - 0.0025 = 11.9885$$

These control limits are extended to the control charts of Figure 9-22 for monitoring the process. Samples of size 4 were continued to be drawn approximately every fifteen minutes, and the $\bar{x}$ and R values were plotted on these modified control charts. The results of fourteen additional samples are shown in Figure 9-24. Initially, there was still some difficulty producing the shafts

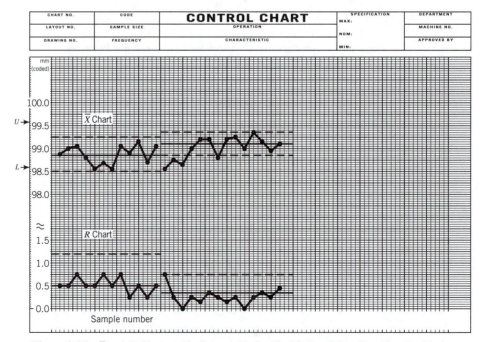

Figure 9-24 $\bar{x}$ and R Charts with Control Limits Modified to Meet Specification Limits

within control limits on the $\bar{x}$ chart. The operator had a tendency to grind the shafts too much, resulting in low values. Aided by the control charts, the grinding technique was improved and the data points indicate control of the average at a level that meets the specification limits. The expected improvement of a reduced spread is also indicated by the pattern on the modified R chart.

▶ 9-4 ACCEPTANCE CONTROL CHARTS

The second approach to using $\bar{x}$ charts for controlling the fraction nonconforming of product exceeding specification limits is that of acceptance control charts. As given in ANSI/ISO/ASQ A3534-2 (2002), the following is a formal definition of acceptance control charts:

> **Acceptance Control Chart:** *control chart intended primarily to evaluate whether or not the plotted measure can be expected to satisfy specified tolerances.*

This requires the use of a companion chart for sample variability such as an R or s chart together with the acceptance control chart for averages.

9-4.1 Background and Scope

The initial development was by Freund (1957, 1960), who presented a generalized solution of the problem of using the $\bar{x}$ chart to accept a process with reference to specification limits on a variable quality characteristic. His solution considers both the risk of rejecting a process operating at a satisfactory level (the α risk) and the risk of accepting a process operating at an unsatisfactory level (the β risk). This is in contrast to the technique of the last section: that of using modified or reject control limits on the $\bar{x}$ chart, which accounts for controlling only the first of these risks (the α risk), allowing the second risk (β) to float according to the factors present in each application.

The techniques are related. The relationship between acceptance control limits and ordinary modified control limits will be examined later. The examination leads to the development of an intermediate approach to the derivation of acceptance control limits. By fixing the relationship between the specification limits and the modified centerlines at $3\hat{\sigma}$ and for fixed relationships between the α and β risks—three such relationships are considered, namely, $\alpha = \beta$, $\alpha = \beta/2$, and $\alpha = \beta/4$—"modified acceptance control charts" are developed. The quality practitioner is thus offered a choice among alternative procedures and some rationale for making the choice.

9-4.2 Definitions, Derivation Principles, and Assumptions

As an extension of Figure 9-19, the diagram in Figure 9-25 summarizes the acceptance control chart-modified control limit problem and assists in the derivation of useful results. It considers the upper portion of the control chart in relation to the upper specification limit. The lower portion is similar with respect to the lower specification limit. On the basis of the diagram, the following definitions apply:

> **Acceptable Process Level, APL:** *centerline or mean level of the underlying distribution of the applicable quality characteristic that results in a satisfactory quality in terms of an allowed*

proportion (p₁) *of units exceeding the specification limit. Specific symbols,* UAPL *and* LAPL, *designate the* APL *associated with the upper and lower specefication limits, respectively. Acceptability is in terms of the α risk, that is to accept the process almost all (1 − α) of the time that this situation or a better one exists.*

Rejectable Process Level, RPL: *centerline or mean level of the underlying distribution of the applicable quality characteristic that constitutes an unsatisfactory quality in terms of an unacceptable proportion* (p₂) *of units exceeding the specification limit. Specific symbols,* URPL *and* LRPL, *designate the* RPL *associated with the upper and lower specification limits, respectively. Rejectability is in terms of the β risk, that is to reject the process almost all (1 − β) of the time that this situation or a worse one exists.*

Acceptance Control Limit, ACL: *action criterion for sample averages. Specific symbols,* UACL *and* LACL, *designate the* ACL *associated with the upper and lower acceptance control limits, respectively.*

Further terms (via symbols) are shown in Figure 9-25 to assist derivation of equations and related discussion. These are described as follows:

z_1 multiples of σ (or $\hat{\sigma}$) between U and $UAPL$ or L and $LAPL$.

p_1 proportion of individual units from the underlying distribution exceeding the specification limit when the mean of the distribution is at the position of the APL, that is, a multiple of $z_1\sigma$ from the specification limit. $p_1 = 1 - \Phi(z_1)$, where $\Phi(x) = P(X \leq x)$ for the standard normal distribution can be determined from Table A in the Appendix.

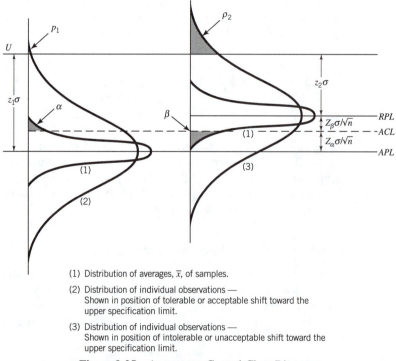

(1) Distribution of averages, $\bar{x}$, of samples.

(2) Distribution of individual observations —
    Shown in position of tolerable or acceptable shift toward the
    upper specification limit.

(3) Distribution of individual observations —
    Shown in position of intolerable or unacceptable shift toward the
    upper specification limit.

Figure 9-25   Acceptance Control Chart Diagram

z_2 multiples of σ (or $\hat{\sigma}$) between U and $URPL$ or L and $LRPL$.

p_2 proportion of individual units from the process exceeding the specification limit when the center of the distribution is at the position of the RPL, that is, a multiple of $z_2\sigma$ from the specification limit. $p_2 = 1 - \Phi(z_2)$ can be determined from Table A in the Appendix when the normal distribution is applicable.

α risk (proportion) that sample averages will fall outside the ACL causing a reject decision when the mean of the distribution is at the APL.

β risk that a sample average will fall inside the ACL causing an accept decision when the mean of the distribution is at the RPL.

z_α multiples of the standard deviation of averages, $\sigma/\sqrt{n}$ (or $\hat{\sigma}/\sqrt{n}$), between APL and ACL.

z_β multiples of the standard deviation of averages, $\sigma/\sqrt{n}$ (or $\hat{\sigma}/\sqrt{n}$), between RPL and ACL.

     The acceptance control limit(s) is (are) derived on the basis of *jointly* associating (1) an α risk of averages falling outside the limit(s) when the mean of the underlying distribution has shifted to the position of $z_1\hat{\sigma}$ inside the specification limit(s) and (2) a β risk of averages falling inside the limit(s) when the mean of the underlying distribution has shifted to the position of $z_2\hat{\sigma}$ inside the specification limit(s).

Necessary Conditions and Assumptions

Similarly, to the derivation of modified control limits for $\bar{x}$ charts given in the preceding section, some necessary assumptions apply to the derivation of acceptance control charts. The first three of those for modified control limits also apply. For the fourth condition, $U - L \geq 2z_1\hat{\sigma}$, that is, the universe variability, σ, as estimated by $\hat{\sigma} = \overline{R}/d_2$ or $\overline{s}/c_4$ must be sufficiently small that the difference between the upper and lower specification limits equals or exceeds $2z_1\hat{\sigma}$. In relating this to condition 4 of the last section, it should be noted that for modified control limits z_1 is generally fixed at a value of 3, yielding an inequality of $U - L \geq 6\sigma$.

9-4.3 Derivations of Acceptance Control Chart Limits

Consider three common cases for the derivation of acceptance control charts: (1) the general case of acceptance control charts, (2) the special case of modified control limits, to be examined considering acceptance control chart principles, and (3) modified acceptance control charts, to provide a practical alternative for many applications.

The General Case

For all conceivable values of p_1, p_2, α, and β, the following results apply. In Figure 9-25 we may observe the following relationship:

$$z_1\sigma = z_2\sigma + z_\beta\sigma/\sqrt{n} + z_\alpha\sigma/\sqrt{n}$$

which yields the following equation for n:

$$n = [(z_\beta + z_\alpha)/(z_1 - z_2)]^2 \tag{9-30}$$

     Hence, the sample size is determined after selection of a set of parameters, p_1, p_2, α, and β. Because n must be an integer, the sample size is usually taken as the next largest integer above the value obtained from Equation 9-30.

The z_p values are obtained from a table of areas of the standard normal distribution as given in Table A in the Appendix, such that $P(Z \geq z_p) = p$, where p is p_1 for z_1, p_2 for z_2, α for z_α, and β for z_β. For example, for $p_1 = 0.005$, $z_1 = 2.576$.

Because acceptance control charts relate to control in regard to specification limits, it is reasonable to derive control limits using the specification limits directly instead of in terms of the *APL*. In Figure 9-25 we have the following relationships:

$$UAPL = U - z_1\hat{\sigma} \qquad (9\text{-}31)$$

and

$$UACL = U - [(z_2 + z_\beta/\sqrt{n})]\hat{\sigma} \qquad (9\text{-}32)$$

Similarly,

$$LAPL = L + z_1\hat{\sigma} \qquad (9\text{-}33)$$

and

$$LACL = L + [(z_2 + z_\beta/\sqrt{n})]\hat{\sigma} \qquad (9\text{-}34)$$

For the three common cases of (1) no standard given, $\bar{x}$ and R, calculated; (2) no standard given, $\bar{x}$ and s calculated; and (3) standard given (i.e., a standard σ_o selected) substitute for $\hat{\sigma}$ in Equations (9-31) through (9-34), (1) $\bar{R}/d_2$, (2) $\bar{s}/c_4$, and (3) σ_0, respectively.

If the *APL* and/or *RPL* values are set or specified on grounds other than associated values of p_1 and p_2, equations for *ACL* in terms of *APL* and/or *RPL* may be obtained directly from Figure 9-25. Similarly, an equation for n may be obtained by substituting the following relationship in Equation (9-30): $z_1 - z_2 = (RPL - APL)/\hat{\sigma}$.

The Special Case of Modified Control Limits

Using the diagram of Figure 9-25, ordinary modified control limits, as presented in Section 9-3, apply under the following conditions:

1. $z_1 = 3$, that is, $UAPL =$ Upper centerline $= U - 3\hat{\sigma}$.

2. Hence, $p_1 = 0.00135$ (for the normal distribution).

3. $z_\alpha = 3$, i.e., $UACL = UAPL + 3\hat{\sigma}/\sqrt{n}$
   $$= U - 3\hat{\sigma} + 3\hat{\sigma}/\sqrt{n}$$
   $$= U - (3 - 3/\sqrt{n})\sigma$$

4. Hence, $\alpha = 0.00135$ (for the normal distribution).

The other factors, z_β, β, z_2, and p_2, are generally unassigned and are allowed to vary according to the application. Normally, the sample size, n, is selected for a given application, either arbitrarily for convenience or by computation to achieve a given objective. Explore the latter of these selection criteria for some additional insight into the relationship of modified control limits to acceptance control charts.

Upon selection of n, choose a value of β (thus fixing z_β) and determine the corresponding values of z_2 and p_2, or choose a value of p_2 (thus fixing z_2) and determine the corresponding values of z_β and β. Values of p_2 and β can be chosen, thus fixing z_2 and z_β, to determine n. This selection of sample size, n, to achieve desired values of β and p_2

for modified control limit applications (with $z_1 = z_\alpha = 3$) can be made more convenient by the preparation of a table of values of n, β, and p_2. From the derivations of Section 9-3 or from Figure 9-25 the following relationships are noted:

$$UACL = U - (3 - 3/\sqrt{n})\sigma = U - C\sigma$$

Hence,

$$z_2 + z_\beta/\sqrt{n} = C \qquad \text{(for the standard given case)}$$

and

$$z_2 = C - z_\beta/\sqrt{n}$$

Now

$$p_2 = 1 - \Phi(z_2) \qquad \text{(for the normal distribution)}$$

Thus, for

$$\beta = 0.50, \qquad z_\beta = 0.0$$

and

$$z_2 = C, \qquad \text{for all } n$$

For

$$\beta = 0.25, \qquad z_\beta = 0.6745$$

and

$$z_2 = C - 0.6745/\sqrt{n}$$

Using the above relationships, Table 9-16 presents values of p_2 for values of β of 0.01, 0.05, 0.10, 0.15, 0.25, to 0.50 and with n ranging from 2 to 20. From Table 9-16 note that for a given sample size, p_2 decreases with increasing β risk; and for a given β risk, p_2 can be decreased by an appropriate increase in sample size n. The practitioner can use this to achieve a sufficiently low β risk of failing to detect undesirable shifts in the distribution, resulting in $100p_2\%$ of units exceeding the specification limit for some unacceptable value of p_2. For example, if we desire p_2 to be equal to or less than 8%, a β of 5% is possible with a sample size of 9. If a β risk of 1% is desired, then a sample size of 12 will be necessary.

Several relatively large β risks (0.50, 0.25, 0.15, and 0.10) have been included in Table 9-16 to permit a wide range of comparisons. Beyond this purpose, there are applications of modified control limits in which it may be reasonable to permit β risks of these magnitudes. For many applications of modified control limits, decisions for action are based on a series of points in addition to a single point with the frequency between samples not too great—minutes in some cases. In these situations detection of a change in distribution level after several sampling intervals is not a major catastrophe; for example, with $\beta = 0.50$, the average run length (*ARL*) to detection is *two* sampling intervals. From Table 9-16 we note that with a sample of size 5 and a β risk of 0.50, p_2 is less than 5%.

The technique of modified control limits is further aided by this discussion relating it to acceptance control charts. This gives some consideration to levels of unacceptable quality and the associated β risk.

TABLE 9-16 Values of p_2 to Facilitate Selection of Desired β and n Values for Modified Control Limits

			β			
n	0.01	0.05	0.10	0.15	0.25	0.50
2	0.7782	0.6120	0.5111	0.4420	0.3439	0.1898
3	0.5299	0.3752	0.2988	0.2516	0.1898	0.1024
4	0.3681	0.2490	0.1952	0.1631	0.1225	0.0668
5	0.2682	0.1781	0.1390	0.1161	0.0874	0.0486
6	0.2045	0.1349	0.1053	0.0882	0.0668	0.0379
7	0.1618	0.1067	0.0836	0.0702	0.0536	0.0310
8	0.1320	0.0873	0.0686	0.0579	0.0445	0.0262
9	0.1104	0.0733	0.0579	0.0490	0.0379	0.0228
10	0.0941	0.0629	0.0499	0.0424	0.0330	0.0201
11	0.0816	0.0549	0.0437	0.0373	0.0292	0.0181
12	0.0718	0.0485	0.0389	0.0333	0.0262	0.0164
13	0.0639	0.0435	0.0350	0.0300	0.0238	0.0151
14	0.0574	0.0393	0.0318	0.0274	0.0218	0.0140
15	0.0521	0.0359	0.0291	0.0251	0.0201	0.0130
16	0.0476	0.0330	0.0268	0.0232	0.0187	0.0122
17	0.0438	0.0303	0.0249	0.0216	0.0175	0.0115
18	0.0405	0.0284	0.0233	0.0202	0.0164	0.0109
19	0.0377	0.0265	0.0218	0.0190	0.0155	0.0104
20	0.0352	0.0249	0.0206	0.0180	0.0147	0.0099

9-4.4 Modified Acceptance Control Charts

An alternative approach to the derivation of acceptance control limits is possible, one that is a compromise between modified control limits and acceptance control charts. This approach retains conditions 1 and 2 as outlined under the case of modified control limits above (i.e., $z_1 = 3$ with $p_1 = 0.00135$). However, conditions 3 and 4 are relaxed to permit the α risk to vary.

Under these conditions it is possible to derive control limits and associated factors that permit computation of the control limits directly from the specification limits. This retains the simplicity of the determination of control limits provided by the modified control limit approach. Then, by fixing the relationship between the α and β risks, (1) the control limits can be evaluated for their effectiveness in detecting changes in terms of β and p_2, or (2) for desired values of β and p_2 the necessary sample size can be determined for computation of the limits.

The necessary conditions set forth earlier for modified control limits and acceptance control charts apply here. Because $z_1 = 3$, condition 4 becomes the inequality, $U - L \geq 6\hat{\sigma}$.

The derivation of control limits for modified acceptance control charts is developed here for the three cases of (1) no standard given, $\bar{x}$ and R calculated, (2) no standard given, $\bar{x}$ and s calculated, and (3) standard given, that is, σ assumed known.

No Standard Given, x̄ and R Calculated

On the basis of the diagram of Figure 9-25, the following results hold:

$$UAPL = \text{Upper centerline} = U - E_2\bar{R}, \quad \text{as in Equation (9-18)}$$

$$UACL = U - 3\hat{\sigma} + z_\alpha\hat{\sigma}/\sqrt{n}$$
$$= U - 3\bar{R}/d_2 + z_\alpha\bar{R}/(d_2\sqrt{n})$$
$$= U - [3/d_2 - z_\alpha/(d_2\sqrt{n})]\bar{R}$$
$$= U - C_{2,\alpha}\bar{R} \tag{9-35}$$

where

$$C_{2\alpha} = 3/d_2 - A_{2,\alpha} = E_2 - A_{2,\alpha}$$

Values for sample sizes ranging from 2 (1) 25 are given in Table L in the Appendix. The $A_{i,\alpha}$ factors were developed by Freund (1957). The $C_{i,\alpha}$ factors were developed by Stephens (1975b). The factors for $i = 1$ are reserved for the less common case of no standard given, $\bar{x}$ and s using n instead of $(n - 1)$ as the divisor calculated for each sample. Similarly,

$$LAPL = \text{Lower centerline} = L + E_2\bar{R}$$
$$LACL = L + C_{2,\alpha}\bar{R} \tag{9-36}$$

No Standard Given, x̄ and s Calculated

On the basis of the diagram of Figure 9-25, the following results hold:

$$UAPL = \text{Upper centerline} = U - E_3\bar{s}, \quad \text{as in Equation (9-22)}$$

$$UACL = U - 3\bar{s}/c_4 + z_\alpha\bar{s}/(c_4\sqrt{n})$$
$$= U - [3/c_4 - z_\alpha/(c_4\sqrt{n})]\bar{s}$$
$$= U - C_{3,\alpha}\bar{s} \tag{9-37}$$

where

$$C_{3,\alpha} = 3/c_4 - A_{3,\alpha} = E_3 - A_{3,\alpha}$$

Values for sample sizes ranging from 2 to 25 are given in Table L in the Appendix. Similarly,

$$LAPL = \text{Lower centerline} = L + E_3\bar{s}$$
$$LACL = L + C_{3,\alpha}\bar{s} \tag{9-38}$$

Standard Given, x̄ and R or x̄ and s Calculated

On the basis of the diagram of Figure 9-25, the following results hold:

$$UAPL = \text{Upper centerline} = U - 3\sigma_0, \quad \text{as in Equation (9-26)}$$

$$UACL = U - 3\sigma + z_\alpha\sigma_0/\sqrt{n}$$
$$= U - (3 - z_\alpha/\sqrt{n})\sigma_0$$
$$= U - C_{0,\alpha}\sigma_0 \tag{9-39}$$

where

$$C_{0,\alpha} = 3 - A_{0,\alpha}$$

Values of $C_{0,\alpha}$ for sample sizes ranging from 2 (1) 25 are given in Table L in the Appendix.

Similarly,

$$LAPL = \text{Lower centerline} = L + 3\sigma$$
$$LACL = L + C_{0,\alpha}\sigma \tag{9-40}$$

It should be noted that in the derivations of the $C_{i,\alpha}$ factors, the β risk was not used. These control limit factors may apply to the computation of control limits for different relationships between α and β. Three such relationships are considered here to serve as practical applications of the techniques: (1) $\alpha = \beta$, (2) $\alpha = \beta/2$, and (3) $\alpha = \beta/4$.

For the first of these relationships, from Figure 9-25 with $z_1 = 3$ and $\alpha = \beta$, the following relationships are determined:

$$z_2\sigma = 3\sigma - (2z_\alpha/\sqrt{n})\sigma$$

or

$$z_2 = 3 - 2z_\alpha/\sqrt{n} = 3 - 2A_{0,\alpha}$$

and

$$p_2 = 1 - \Phi(z_2) \quad \text{(for the normal distribution)}$$

With these results Table 9-17 has been prepared presenting values of p_2 for values of $\alpha = \beta$ of 0.001, 0.0025, 0.005, 0.010, 0.025, 0.050, and 0.100 and with n ranging from 2 to 20.

TABLE 9-17 Values for p_2 to Facilitate Selection of Desired β and n Values for Modified Acceptance Control Charts, with $\alpha = \beta$

	$\alpha = \beta$						
n	0.001	0.0025	0.005	0.010	0.025	0.050	0.100
2	0.9146	0.8339	0.7399	0.6139	0.4098	0.2503	0.1176
3	0.7150	0.5953	0.4898	0.3767	0.2306	0.1356	0.0643
4	0.5359	0.4235	0.3358	0.2502	0.1492	0.0877	0.0429
5	0.4066	0.3123	0.2432	0.1789	0.1062	0.0632	0.0319
6	0.3167	0.2394	0.1849	0.1355	0.0808	0.0488	0.0254
7	0.2533	0.1899	0.1462	0.1072	0.0645	0.0395	0.0211
8	0.2075	0.1550	0.1193	0.0877	0.0533	0.0331	0.0182
9	0.1736	0.1295	0.0998	0.0736	0.0452	0.0285	0.0160
10	0.1478	0.1103	0.0852	0.0631	0.0392	0.0250	0.0143
11	0.1278	0.0956	0.0740	0.0551	0.0345	0.0223	0.0130
12	0.1120	0.0839	0.0652	0.0488	0.0309	0.0202	0.0119
13	0.0992	0.0745	0.0581	0.0437	0.0279	0.0184	0.0110
14	0.0888	0.0669	0.0523	0.0395	0.0254	0.0170	0.0103
15	0.0801	0.0605	0.0475	0.0360	0.0234	0.0158	0.0097
16	0.0728	0.0552	0.0434	0.0331	0.0217	0.0147	0.0092
17	0.0667	0.0507	0.0400	0.0306	0.0202	0.0138	0.0087
18	0.0614	0.0468	0.0371	0.0285	0.0189	0.0131	0.0083
19	0.0568	0.0434	0.0345	0.0266	0.0178	0.0124	0.0079
20	0.0528	0.0405	0.0323	0.0250	0.0169	0.0118	0.0076

It is apparent from an examination of Table 9-17 that for these small α and β risks, larger sample sizes are required to reduce p_2 to a relatively low value. Table 9-17, like Table 9-16, provides a basis for selecting sample size, n, for modified acceptance control charts to achieve desired values of β and p_2, with $\alpha = \beta$. For example, if p_2 is to be equal to or less than 6%, a β ($= \alpha$) risk of 0.01 is possible with a sample size of 11. If a β ($= \alpha$) risk of 0.001 is desired, then a sample size of 19 is required.

For the second relationship between α and β, namely, $\alpha = \beta/2$, from Figure 9-25 with $z_1 = 3$ and $\beta = 2\alpha$, the following relationships are obtained:

$$z_2\sigma = 3\sigma - (z_\alpha\sigma/\sqrt{n} + z_{2\alpha}\sigma/\sqrt{n})$$

or

$$z_2 = 3 - (z_\alpha + z_{2\alpha})/\sqrt{n}$$

and

$$p_2 = 1 - \Phi(z_2) \qquad \text{(for the normal distribution)}$$

With these results, Table 9-18 has been prepared, presenting values of p_2 for values of $\alpha = \beta/2$ of 0.001, 0.0025, 0.005, 0.010, 0.025, and 0.050 with n ranging from 2 to 20.

In comparing Table 9-18 with Table 9-17, there is a relaxation of sample size required to achieve a specified p_2 value for a particular α risk. This is because of the larger associated β risk. For example, if p_2 is to be equal to or less than 6%, an α risk of 0.01 ($\beta = 0.02$) is possible with a sample size of 10 instead of 11.

TABLE 9-18 Values of p_2 to Facilitate Selection of Desired β and n Values for Modified Acceptance Control Charts with $\beta = 2\alpha$

	0.002	0.005	0.010	0.020	0.050	0.100	β
n	0.001	0.0025	0.005	0.010	0.025	0.050	α
2	0.8888	0.7900	0.6795	0.5387	0.3260	0.1761	
3	0.6721	0.5430	0.4326	0.3187	0.1791	0.0951	
4	0.4936	0.3789	0.2915	0.2090	0.1156	0.0622	
5	0.3703	0.2767	0.2096	0.1489	0.0826	0.0454	
6	0.2865	0.2112	0.1590	0.1128	0.0632	0.0355	
7	0.2283	0.1672	0.1256	0.0894	0.0508	0.0291	
8	0.1867	0.1364	0.1026	0.0733	0.0422	0.0247	
9	0.1561	0.1140	0.0860	0.0618	0.0361	0.0215	
10	0.1329	0.0972	0.0736	0.0532	0.0314	0.0190	
11	0.1150	0.0843	0.0640	0.0465	0.0279	0.0171	
12	0.1008	0.0741	0.0565	0.0413	0.0250	0.0156	
13	0.0893	0.0659	0.0505	0.0371	0.0227	0.0143	
14	0.0800	0.0592	0.0455	0.0337	0.0208	0.0133	
15	0.0723	0.0537	0.0414	0.0308	0.0193	0.0124	
16	0.0658	0.0490	0.0380	0.0284	0.0179	0.0117	
17	0.0603	0.0451	0.0351	0.0263	0.0168	0.0110	
18	0.0555	0.0417	0.0325	0.0246	0.0158	0.0104	
19	0.0515	0.0388	0.0304	0.0230	0.0149	0.0099	
20	0.0479	0.0362	0.0285	0.0217	0.0141	0.0095	

TABLE 9-19 **Values of p_2 to Facilitate Selection of Desired β and n Values for Modified Acceptance Control Charts with $\beta = 4\alpha$**

	0.004	0.010	0.020	0.040	0.100	0.200	β
n	0.001	0.0025	0.005	0.010	0.025	0.050	α
2	0.8555	0.7355	0.6079	0.4534	0.2396	0.1072	
3	0.6237	0.4855	0.3719	0.2590	0.1296	0.0589	
4	0.4487	0.3323	0.2467	0.1682	0.0839	0.0395	
5	0.3328	0.2406	0.1763	0.1197	0.0606	0.0295	
6	0.2560	0.1829	0.1335	0.0908	0.0468	0.0236	
7	0.2033	0.1446	0.1056	0.0723	0.0380	0.0197	
8	0.1660	0.1180	0.0864	0.0595	0.0319	0.0170	
9	0.1387	0.0987	0.0726	0.0504	0.0275	0.0150	
10	0.1182	0.0843	0.0623	0.0436	0.0241	0.0134	
11	0.1023	0.0732	0.0544	0.0383	0.0216	0.0122	
12	0.0897	0.0645	0.0481	0.0341	0.0195	0.0112	
13	0.0796	0.0575	0.0431	0.0308	0.0178	0.0104	
14	0.0714	0.0517	0.0390	0.0280	0.0164	0.0098	
15	0.0646	0.0470	0.0356	0.0257	0.0153	0.0092	
16	0.0589	0.0430	0.0327	0.0238	0.0143	0.0087	
17	0.0540	0.0396	0.0303	0.0222	0.0134	0.0083	
18	0.0498	0.0367	0.0282	0.0207	0.0127	0.0079	
19	0.0462	0.0342	0.0263	0.0195	0.0120	0.0076	
20	0.0431	0.0320	0.0247	0.0184	0.0115	0.0073	

Similarly, Table 9-19 has been prepared for the relationship $\beta = 4\alpha$. A further relaxation of sample size is required to achieve a given p_2 value for a given α risk. For example, if p_2 is to be equal to or less than 6%, an α risk of 0.01 ($\beta = 0.04$) is possible with a sample size of 8 instead of 10 (Table 9-18) or 11 (Table 9-17).

Tables such as Tables 9-17, 9-18, and 9-19 may be developed for any relationship between α and β, and for emphasis, for a given sample size n, and α value, the control limit factors, $C_{i,\alpha}$, are the same. For example, for $n = 10$, $\alpha = 0.005$, the same control limit, ACL, applies to (1) $\beta = 0.005$, $p_2 = 0.0852$ from Table 9-17; (2) $\beta = 0.010$, $p_2 = 0.0736$ from Table 9-18; and (3) $\beta = 0.020$, $p_2 = 0.0623$ from Table 9-19.

9-4.5 Acceptance Control Chart Examples

▶ **EXAMPLE 9-8**

Still another approach to the problem presented in Example 8-2 and again in Example 9-5 is the use of the acceptance control chart. For purposes of operating at defined risks, it is agreed that the sample size can be kept constant. It is further decided that the following set of parameters is desirable for the application: $p_1 = 0.005$, $p_2 = 0.06$, $\alpha = 0.01$, and $\beta = 0.05$. Corresponding to these values, $z_1 = 2.576$, $z_2 = 1.555$, $z_\alpha = 2.33$, and $z_\beta = 1.645$, respectively. Using these results in Equation (9-30) yields a sample size of 15.16, or 16.

As in Example 8-2, take an estimate of σ of 5.2. Then, with $L = 0.0$ and $n = 16$, the following limits are obtained:

$$LAPL = L + 2.576\hat{\sigma}, \qquad \text{using Equation (9-33)}$$
$$= 0.0 + 2.576(5.2)$$
$$= 13.4$$
$$LACL = L + [(1.555 + 1.645/\sqrt{16})]\hat{\sigma}, \qquad \text{using Equation (9-34)}$$
$$= 0.0 + 1.966(5.2)$$
$$= 10.2$$

The control chart of Figure 9-21 should then be used with these limits for the $\bar{x}$ chart. Corresponding limits for the s chart, with $n = 16$, would be computed by using Equations (8-16) and (8-17).

▶ **EXAMPLE 9-9**

Adjusting a relay requires specification limits of 16.65 to 17.55 milliamperes. An initial study of this operation with $\bar{x}$ and R control charts reveals a reasonably controlled pattern on the R chart, with an average range, $\bar{R}$, of 0.34 ma based on samples of 5. This, in turn, yields an estimate, $\hat{\sigma} = \bar{R}/d_2 = 0.34/2.326 = 0.146$, so that $6\hat{\sigma} = 0.876$ compared to a difference of 0.9 between U and L.

The conditions for modified acceptance control charts are accepted for this application—that is, $p_1 = 0.00135$. Shifts of the distribution in either direction resulting in 2% or more of the units outside the specification limit should be detected with a β risk not exceeding 0.10. However, an α risk of this same magnitude is considered too large. Table 9-18 is used with an $\alpha = 0.05$, resulting in a sample size of 10 to achieve the desired results.

Some alternatives are needed to set up the acceptance control chart, since no $\bar{R}$ figure is available for sample size 10, in order to compute limits directly from Equations (9-35) and (9-36). Some possibilities are (1) to use the previous control chart information, including the estimate of σ (i.e., $\hat{\sigma} = 0.146$) to develop the acceptance control chart for the case of standard given with Equations (9-39) and (9-40), together with an R chart for $n = 10$; (2) to conduct a further capability study using $\bar{x}$ and R control charts with $n = 10$ and set up the acceptance control charts based on the new information using Equations (9-35) and (9-36); or (3) for alternative (1), to switch to computation of $\bar{x}$ and s with an appropriate s chart for $n = 10$.

For the first alternative, the control limits are computed as follows:

$$UACL = U - C_{0, 0.05}\hat{\sigma}, \qquad \text{from Equation (9-39)}$$
$$= 17.55 - 2.48(0.146)$$
$$= 17.19$$
$$UAPL = 17.55 - 3(0.146), \qquad \text{from Equation (9-26)}$$
$$= 17.11$$
$$LACL = U + C_{0, 0.05}\hat{\sigma}, \qquad \text{from Equation (9-40)}$$
$$= 16.65 + 0.362$$
$$= 17.01$$
$$LAPL = 16.65 + 0.438, \qquad \text{from Equation 9-28}$$
$$= 17.09$$

9-4.6 Choice between Modified and Acceptance Control Limits

In Section 9-3 a standardized derivation of modified control limits was presented. This enables direct computation of modified centerlines and control limits in relation to the specification limits.

Section 9-4 examines the general case of acceptance control charts and relates the ordinary modified control limits to them with some rationale for their use (Table 9-16). It further develops a modified acceptance control chart that enables computation of the control limits for these charts directly from the specification limits and computed (or standard) statistics. Some rationale is also presented for selection of parameters for their use (Table 9-17, 9-18, and 9-19).

With this material the practitioner has a choice between (1) ordinary modified control limits, (2) modified acceptance control charts, or (3) acceptance control charts. The following summarizes the nature of these choices and presents an additional technique for using the modified acceptance control chart.

If satisfied with $p_1 = 0.00135$ ($3\hat{\sigma}$ between extreme position of centerlines and specification limits, i.e., with $z_1 = 3$) and $\alpha = 0.00135$ ($3\hat{\sigma}_{\bar{x}}$ between centerlines and control limits, i.e., with $z_\alpha = 3$), use the ordinary modified control limits of Section 9-3, Equations (9-18) through (9-29), and with control limit factors C, C_2, and C_3 of Table H in the Appendix. Use of Table 9-16 allows a rational selection of values of n, β, and p_2 for various applications.

If satisfied with $p_1 = 0.00135$ (as above)[1] and fixed relationships between α and β (such as $\alpha = \beta$, $\alpha = \beta/2$, $\alpha = \beta/4$), use modified acceptance control charts with the formulas of Section 9-4.4. Use of Tables 9-17, 9-18, and 9-19 allows for a rational selection of values of n, α, and β, and p_2 for various applications.

If complete flexibility to choose p_1, p_2, α, β, and the $U - L$ spacing is desired, use acceptance control charts with the formulas given in Section 9-4.3, Equations (9-30) through (9-34). For an example of acceptance control charts applied to attribute data, see the paper by Mhatre, Scheaffer, and Leavenworth (1981).

▶ 9-5 REFERENCES

Adams, B. M., Lowry, C., and Woodall, W. H. (1992), "The Use (and Misuse) of False Alarm Probabilities in Control Chart Design," *Frontiers in Statistical Quality Control 4*, edited by H. J. Lenz, G. B. Wetherill, and P. Th. Wilrich, Physica-Verlag, Heidelberg, pp. 155–68.

American Society for Quality Control (2002), ANSI/ISO/ASQ A3534-2-2002, *Statistics—Vocabulary and Symbols*, ASQ, Milwaukee.

Bissell, A. F. (1979), "A Semi-Parabolic Mask for CUSUM Charts," *The Statistician*, Vol. 28, pp. 1–7.

Bissell, A. F. (1981), "Correction to a Semi-Parabolic Mask for CUSUM Charts," *The Statistician*, Vol. 30, p. 77.

British Standards Institution (1980a), *BS 5703: Part 1: 1980, Guide to Data Analysis and Quality Control Using CUSUM Techniques, Part 1. Introduction to CUSUM Charting*, BSI, London.

---

[1]A technique that can be employed to effectively vary z_1, and hence p_1, while still using the control limit formulas and constants, $C_{i,\alpha}$, is to derive "modified specification limits," U' and/or L' as follows: $U' = U - (3 - z_{p1}) = U - 3 + z_{p1}$ and $L' = L + (3 - z_{p1}) = L + 3 - z_{p1}$, where z_{p1} is the standard normal deviate cutting off an area of p_1 on the positive (upper) side. For example, if $p_1 = 0.005$, rather than 0.00135, is desired, then $U' = U - 3 + z_{0.005} = U - 3 + 2.576 = U - 0.424$ and $L' = L + 3 - z_{0.005} = L + 3 - 2.576 = L + 0.424$. U' and/or L' is then used in place of U and/or L in the associated equations for computing the modified acceptance control limits.

British Standards Institution (1980b), *BS 5703: Part 2: 1980,* Guide to Data Analysis and Quality Control Using CUSUM Techniques, Part 2. Decision Rules and Statistical Tests for CUSUM Charts and Tabulations, BSI, London.

British Standards Institution (1981), *BS 5703: Part 3: 1981,* Guide to Data Analysis and Quality Control Using CUSUM Techniques, Part 3, CUSUM Methods for Process/Quality Control by Measurement, BSI, London.

British Standards Institution (1982), *BS 5703: Part 4: 1982,* Guide to Data Analysis and Quality Control Using CUSUM Techniques, Part 4, CUSUMS for Counted Attributes Data, BSI, London.

Brook, D., and Evans, D. A. (1972), "An Approach to the Probability Distribution of CUSUM Run Lengths," *Biometrika,* Vol. 59, pp. 539–49.

Elder, R. S., Provost, L. P., and Ecker, D. M. (1980), "United States Department of Agriculture CUSUM Acceptance Sampling Procedures," *Journal of Quality Technology,* Vol. 13, No. 1, Jan.; pp. 59–64.

Ewan, W. D. (1963), "When and How to Use CUSUM Charts," *Technometrics,* 5, No. 1, Feb.; pp. 1–22.

Fellner, W. H. (1990), "Average Run Lengths for Cumulative Sum Schemes," *Applied Statistics, Journal of the Royal Statistical Society (Series C),* Vol. 39, No. 3, pp. 402–12.

Freund, R. A. (1957), "Acceptance Control Charts," *Industrial Quality Control,* Vol. 14, No. 4, Oct.; pp. 13–23.

Freund, R. A. (1960), "A Reconsideration of the Variables Control Charts," *Industrial Quality Control,* Vol. 16, No. 2, May; pp. 35–41.

Gan, F. F. (1991a), "An Optimal Design of CUSUM Quality Control Charts," *Journal of Quality Technology,* Vol. 23, No. 1, Jan.; pp. 279–86.

Gan, F. F. (1991b), "Computing the Percentage Points of the Run Length Distribution of an Exponentially Weighted Moving Average Control Chart," *Journal of Quality Technology,* Vol. 23, No. 4, Oct.; pp. 359–65.

Goel, A. L., and Wu, S. M. (1971), "Determination of ARL and a Contour Nomogram for Cusum Charts to Control Normal Mean," *Technometrics,* Vol. 13, No. 3, Aug.; pp. 221–30.

Grant, E. L., and Leavenworth, R. S. (1996), *Statistical Quality Control,* Seventh Edition, McGraw-Hill, New York.

Hawkins, D. M. (1987), "Self Starting CUSUMS for Location and Scale," *The Statistician,* Vol. 36, pp. 299–315.

Hawkins, D. M. (1992a), "Evaluation of Average Run Lengths of Cumulative Sum Control Charts for an Arbitrary Data Distribution," *Communications in Statistics—Simulation and Computation,* Vol. B21, pp. 1000–20.

Hawkins, D. M. (1992b), "A Fast Accurate Approximation of Average Run Lengths of CUSUM Control Charts," *Journal of Quality Technology,* Vol. 24, No. 1, Jan.; pp. 37–43.

Johnson, N. L. (1961), "A Simple Theoretical Approach to Cumulative Sum Control Charts," *Journal of the American Statistical Association,* Vol. 56, pp. 835–40.

Johnson, N. L. and Leone, F. C. (1962), "Cumulative Sum Control Charts, Parts I, II, & III," *Industrial Quality Control,* Vol. 18, pp. 15–21; Vol. 19, pp. 29–36.

Kemp, K. W. (1961), "The Average Run Length of the Cumulative Sum Control Chart When a V-Mask Is Used," *Journal of the Royal Statistical Society,* Vol. B 23, pp. 149–53.

Lucas, J. M. (1976), "The Design and Use of V-Mask Control Schemes," *Journal of Quality Technology,* Vol. 8, No. 1, Jan.; pp. 1–12.

Lucas, J. M. (1982), "Combined Shewhart-CUSUM Quality Control Schemes," *Journal of Quality Technology,* Vol. 14, No. 2, April; pp. 51–59.

Lucas, J. M. (1985), "Counted Data CUSUM's," *Technometrics,* Vol. 27, No. 3, May; pp. 129–44.

Lucas, J. M., and Crosier, R. B. (1982a), "Fast Initial Response for CUSUM Quality-Control Schemes: Give Your CUSUM a Head Start," *Technometrics,* Vol. 24, No. 3, Aug; pp. 199–205.

Lucas, J. M., and Crosier, R. B. (1982b), "RobustCUSUM: A Robustness Study for CUSUM Quality Control Schemes," *Communications in Statistics—Theory and Methods,* Vol. 11, pp. 2669–87.

Mhatre, S., Scheaffer, R., and Leavenworth, R. (1981), "Acceptance Control Charts Based on Normal Approximations to the Poisson Distribution," *Journal of Quality Technology,* Vol. 13, No. 4, Oct.; pp. 221–27.

Park, C. A. (1987), "A Corrected Wiener Process Approximation for CUSUM ARLs," *Sequential Analysis,* Vol. 6, pp. 257–65.

Roberts, S. W. (1959), "Control Chart Tests Based on Geometric Moving Averages," *Technometrics,* Vol. 1, No. 3, Aug.; pp. 239–50.

Siegmund, D. (1985), *Sequential Analysis: Tests and Confidence Intervals,* Springer-Verlag, New York.

Stephens, K. S. (1975b), "Some Standardized Derivation of Control Limits, Part II, Modified Acceptance Control Charts," *The QR Journal,* Vol. 11, No. 1, Jan.; pp. 33–37.

Vance, L. C. (1986), "Average Run Lengths of Cumulative Sum Control Charts for Controlling Normal Means," *Journal of Quality Technology,* Vol. 18, No. 3, July; pp. 189–93.

Van Bobben De Bruyn, C. S., (1968), *Cumulative Sum Tests: Theory and Practice,* Griffin, London.

Vardeman, S., and Ray, D. (1985), "Average Run Lengths for CUSUM Schemes When Observations Are Exponentially Distributed," *Technometrics,* Vol. 18, No. 3, pp. 189–93 (July).

Westgard, J. O., Groth, T., Aronsson, T., and de Verdier, C. (1977), "Combined Shewhart-CUSUM Control Chart for Improved Quality Control in Clinical Chemistry," *Clinical Chemistry,* Vol. 23, No. 10, pp. 1881–87.

Woodall, W. H. (1983), "The Distribution of the Run Length of One-Sided CUSUM Procedures for Continuous Random Variables," *Technometrics,* Vol. 25, No. 4, Oct.; pp. 295–301.

Woodall, W. H. (1984), "On the Markov Chain Approach to the Two-Sided CUSUM Procedure," *Technometrics,* Vol. 26, No.1, Feb.; pp. 41–46.

Woodall, W. H. (1986), "The Design of CUSUM Quality Control Charts," *Journal of Quality Technology,* Vol. 18, No. 2, April; pp. 99–102.

Woodall, W. H., and Adams, B. M. (1993), "The Statistical Design of CUSUM Charts," *Quality Engineering,* Vol. 5, No. 4, pp. 559–70.

Woodall, W. H. and Ncube, M. M. (1985), "Multivariate CUSUM Quality Control Procedures," *Technometrics,* Vol. 27, No. 4, Oct.; pp. 285–92.

Wortham, A. W., and Ringer, L. J. (1971), "Control Via Exponential Smoothing," *The Logistics Review,* Vol. 7, No. 3, pp. 33–40.

Yashchin, E. (1993), "Performance of CUSUM Control Schemes for Serially Correlated Observations," *Technometrics,* Vol. 35, No. 1, Feb.; pp. 37–52.

▶ 9-6 PROBLEMS

1. A manufacturer of toothpaste wishes to maintain the pH of the product at a nominal level of 7.7. Detailed studies over the last fifty batches show a variation, discounting several out-of-control batches, that is generally stable at an estimated standard deviation of 0.08. A process control chart is desired to monitor this characteristic on a batch-by-batch basis.
(a) Design a CUSUM chart, including V mask, for this purpose. It is desired to detect shifts of one sigma in the nominal level.
(b) Design a CUSUM chart with the same delta as in part (a) and a desired two-sided in-control ARL of 800.

2. The manager of the margarine factory of Example 9-1 would like to know whether the filling engine, as currently set, could maintain an average fill of 250.5 grams. Data for an additional shift are collected without an adjustment being made, following the signal during the second shift by the CUSUM chart of Figure 9-13. The sample averages for the three shifts are as follows:

Shift 1	Shift 2	Shift 3
251.35	250.97	250.53
251.16	250.68	249.74
251.65	250.44	250.59
250.41	250.08	250.35
250.10	250.27	250.49
250.88	250.73	251.52
250.80	250.51	250.69
250.82	250.82	250.53

(a) Complete the calculations for Figure 9-13 using the first sixteen sample averages and the parameters of Example 9-1.
(b) Set up a CUSUM chart for the twenty-four sample averages using a target average level of 250.5 grams and the same parameters as in Example 9-1. Plot the CUSUM chart and apply the V mask. Is there a signal denoting a change from the new target value? Perform any other relevant analysis.

3. Develop a CUSUM chart for the range data of Table 6-6 in Chapter 6, selecting a scheme from Table 9-10. Append to this chart the ranges of Table 8-2, and test each point for a signal of change in level. Use $\bar{R}$, computed from the data of Table 6-6, as the target value, $\bar{R}_T$.

4. Do Problem 3 using a CUSUM tabulation procedure.

5. Devise a distribution similar to Figure 8-3, but with a smaller spread, say, from -7 to $+7$. Draw ten samples of size 5 from this distribution, calculate the ranges, and append to the range data of Table 6-6. Develop a CUSUM chart for sample ranges from Table 9-10 and test the data for a change in level. Use $\bar{R}_T$ as developed in Problem 3.

6. Develop a CUSUM chart for the data of Example 8-5, selecting a scheme from Table 9-6. Use 190 N/mm^2 as the target value.

7. (a) Develop a CUSUM chart for the sample averages of Problem 2 of Chapter 8 using a target value of 30.
(b) Develop the companion CUSUM chart for sample standard deviations using the computed $\bar{s}$ as a target value. Select the scheme from Table 9-11.

8. Repeat the instructions of Problems 7(a) and 7(b) for Problem 8 of Chapter 8 using a target value of 300 ml.

9. For the data of Table 6-2, develop a CUSUM chart under the Poisson approximation, selecting a scheme from Table 9-12. Append to this chart the data of Table 7-1, and test each point for a signal of change in level. Use a target value of $p = 0.05$ or $np = 5$.

10. Develop a CUSUM chart for the data of Table 7-2, including a V mask for testing a change in level, using the Poisson approximation and Table 9-12. Append to this chart the data of Table 6-2, and test each point for a signal of change in level. Use a target of $p = 0.03$ or $np = 3$.

11. Repeat Problem 9 using a CUSUM tabulation and/or charting procedure.

12. Repeat Problem 10 using a CUSUM tabulation and/or charting procedure.

13. Develop a CUSUM chart for the data of Problem 11 in Chapter 7. Use a target value based on the computed $\bar{p}$.

14. Develop a CUSUM chart for the data of Problem 10 in Chapter 7. Use a target value based on the computed $\bar{c}$.

15. For the suture manufacture of Example 10-2, the following set of twenty samples of size 5 were drawn from the process every two hours, and tensile strength measurements (in kg force) were taken. Prepare an initial performance study using $\bar{x}$ and s control charts for these data. From the initial study prepare the modified control limit and centerline for a lower specification limit (L) of 2.0 kg and display these lines on the $\bar{x}$ control chart for future control.

	2.068	2.409	2.182	2.386	2.432
	2.205	2.409	2.273	2.432	2.477
	2.250	2.636	2.341	2.477	2.523
	2.409	2.795	2.523	2.477	2.659
	2.659	2.932	2.659	2.773	2.932
$\bar{x}$	2.318	2.636	2.395	2.509	2.605
s	0.226	0.232	0.193	0.152	0.202
	2.341	2.091	2.227	2.227	2.273
	2.364	2.318	2.364	2.250	2.455
	2.523	2.545	2.455	2.614	2.568
	2.614	2.591	2.500	2.682	2.659
	2.841	2.727	2.795	2.773	2.727
$\bar{x}$	2.536	2.455	2.468	2.509	2.536
s	0.204	0.251	0.211	0.253	0.179
	2.227	2.318	2.364	2.341	2.318
	2.341	2.386	2.455	2.432	2.409
	2.614	2.523	2.455	2.545	2.500
	2.636	2.614	2.591	2.682	2.568
	2.795	2.932	2.659	2.864	2.795
$\bar{x}$	2.523	2.555	2.505	2.573	2.518
s	0.232	0.240	0.119	0.207	0.181
	2.341	2.341	2.227	2.227	2.273
	2.341	2.523	2.273	2.341	2.341
	2.500	2.568	2.432	2.545	2.364
	2.568	2.659	2.455	2.591	2.455
	2.750	2.773	2.591	2.659	2.705
$\bar{x}$	2.500	2.573	2.395	2.473	2.427
s	0.172	0.161	0.147	0.181	0.168

16. The data given for the number of twists per meter in cord for fish nets in Problem 5 of Chapter 5 are arranged in twenty subgroups of size 5. Prepare $\bar{x}$ and R control charts for these data, and use the results to determine modified control limits and centerlines for the specification limits of 195 ± 15. Display these lines on the $\bar{x}$ chart for future control to the specification limits.

17. For the data in Problem 6 in Chapter 8 on the journal diameter of a tractor rear wheel axle, prepare $\bar{x}$ and R control charts. Use the results to determine modified control limits and centerlines for the specification limits of $U =$

0.990 and $L = 0.975$. Display these lines on the $\bar{x}$ chart for future control to the specification limits.

18. Data for Figure 11-45 of Example 11-20 on case hardness depth (in mm) are given below. On the basis of these data and the calculations shown in Example 11-20, determine modified control limits and centerlines for the specification limits of $U = 10.5$ and $L = 3.5$ mm. Extend the control limits of Figure 11-45 with these modified limits for future control to the specification limits.

Sample Number									
1	2	3	4	5	6	7	8	9	10
4.9	5.8	5.9	5.9	6.2	6.0	5.2	5.1	5.8	5.2
5.5	5.5	6.2	5.9	5.9	5.7	4.6	5.8	6.1	5.4
5.3	5.6	5.9	6.4	5.7	5.7	5.4	6.2	5.7	5.2
5.6	6.3	5.8	5.3	4.9	6.3	6.1	5.9	6.5	5.8
5.1	5.7	5.4	5.2	5.9	6.0	5.2	5.6	5.2	4.6

11	12	13	14	15	16	17	18	19	20
5.2	6.2	4.9	6.1	5.3	6.3	5.4	5.6	4.7	6.0
4.6	5.8	4.9	6.2	5.4	5.6	5.3	5.0	4.7	5.3
5.4	5.1	4.9	5.9	5.4	5.9	5.4	5.2	5.6	5.6
6.1	5.2	4.9	4.5	5.4	4.7	5.2	4.9	5.0	5.0
5.2	5.4	4.6	5.6	5.2	6.2	5.2	4.7	5.2	5.2

21	22	23	24	25	26	27	28	29	30
5.1	5.6	5.5	4.9	4.7	6.0	5.5	5.2	5.0	5.5
6.2	6.1	6.0	4.8	4.9	5.1	5.0	4.9	5.2	5.1
5.0	5.8	5.7	6.1	5.2	5.3	6.0	5.2	6.0	5.3
5.2	5.9	5.0	5.3	6.0	4.9	5.7	5.0	4.9	4.1
5.7	5.8	4.9	5.2	5.7	6.1	5.0	5.3	6.1	5.0

19. For the x data of Problem 17 in Chapter 11 representing water content in margarine by the rapid method, prepare ten subgroups of size 4. For these subgroups, determine $\bar{x}$ and R (or s) values, and set up the corresponding control charts. From the control chart data prepare the modified control limit and centerline for a maximum limit of $U = 20$.

20. Prepare modified control limits to specification limits of 20.3 ± 1 gram for the data of Problem 21 in Chapter 11 on the mass of black bobbins in the manufacture of dry cell batteries.

21. For the data of Problem 1 in Chapter 7, after eliminating the indicated samples, prepare an acceptance control chart for the specification limits of $U = 1.04$ and $L = 1.01$ with the following parameters: $p_1 = 0.02$, $p_2 = 0.06$, $\alpha = 0.005$, $\beta = 0.010$.

22. Repeat Problem 15, developing the acceptance control chart lower limits with $\alpha = 0.0025$, $\beta = 0.010$ (using Table 9-19) such that $p_2 \leq 0.10$.

23. Repeat Problem 16, developing the modified acceptance control chart limits for averages of size 5 with $\alpha = 0.025$ and $\beta = 0.050$. What p_2 value is associated with these control limits? What sample is required to reduce p_2 to a value equal to or less than 2.5%? What are the corresponding acceptance control chart limits?

24. Repeat Problem 17, developing the modified acceptance control chart limits for averages of size 4 with $\alpha = \beta = 0.05$. What p_2 value is associated with these control limits? What sample size is required to reduce p_2 to a value equal to or less than 2.5%? What are the corresponding acceptance control chart limits? If we can relax β to a value of 0.10, what p_2 value is associated with the control limits for size 4? For the relaxed β, what sample size is re-

quired for $p_2 \leq 2.5\%$? What are the corresponding acceptance control chart limits?

25. Repeat Problem 18, developing the modified acceptance control chart limits for averages of size 5 with $\alpha = 0.01$ and $\beta = 0.04$. What p_2 value is associated with these control limits? What sample size is required to reduce p_2 to a value equal to or less than 5.0%? What are the corresponding acceptance control chart limits?

26. Repeat Problem 20 for $\bar{x}$ and s control charts, developing the modified acceptance control chart limits for averages of size 6 with $\alpha = 0.01$ and $\beta = 0.02$. What p_2 value is associated with these control limits? For the same control limits, if β is relaxed to $\beta = 0.04$, what p_2 value applies? What sample size is required (with $\beta = 0.02$) to reduce p_2 to a value equal to or less than 3.0%? What are the corresponding acceptance control chart limits?

CHAPTER

▼

10

SPECIFICATION LIMITS, TOLERANCES, AND RELATED TECHNIQUES

Quality requirements are usually given in the form of specification limits on quality characteristics of individual units of product. Examples of specification limits or tolerances include those for knitted fabrics of ASTM D3887-80 referred to in Example 2-1. The referenced standard shows a tolerance of ±5% on yield, weight, and fabric count; a ±2% tolerance on length, and a ±10% tolerance on bursting strength.

Similarly, the problems in Chapter 5 include specification limits of 9 m/g ± 5% on count of woolen yarn, 195 ± 15% on the twist number per meter on cord for fish nets, and 250 grams ± 1% on the net filled mass of margarine cups. Examples in Chapter 8 include specification limits of 200–270 on the melt index of an extrusion-grade polyethylene compound (Example 8-1) and a coded minimum specification limit of zero on the candlepower value of a flare (Example 8-2). The problems in that chapter include specification limits of 1.01–1.04 on the mass of weights for a space mechanism, 8 ± 2 seconds on the burn time of a flare, 44.975–44.990 on the journal diameter of a rear wheel axle, and a maximum of 3.0 on the coefficient of variation of cotton yarn. Many other examples are included in other chapters throughout this book.

▶ 10-1 SPECIFICATION LIMITS AND TOLERANCES

The ISO Standard 3534-2 (2002) defines specification limits as follows:

specification limit: *conformance boundary specified for a characteristic*

These limits may be of the two-sided type with both upper and lower limits or the one-sided type with either an upper or lower limit.

These specifications on quality characteristics are sometimes defined in terms of the distribution of the quality characteristics. They may, for example, apply to some statistic of a sample of individual units. In this chapter the concentration is on specification limits as defined above. The presentation in other chapters as well as in this chapter will help the reader to understand other types of requirements.

A related area that will have some usefulness in helping to establish specification limits is that of statistical tolerance limits. These may be defined as follows:

> *Statistical Tolerance Limits:* limits of the interval for which it can be stated with a given level of confidence that it contains at least a specified proportion of the population.

Such limits are the results of statistical computations on observations of a given quality characteristic from one or more samples. They may therefore differ from specification limits that represent requirements on individual units. When design considerations alone do not dictate what specifications should be established on individual units, it is possible to consider some measure of process capability to establish the requirements. Control charts are very useful for this purpose. Statistical tolerance limits provide an alternative or a complementary procedure.

▶ 10-2 RELATIONSHIP TO PROCESSES AND CONTROL CHARTS

The capability of the process to meet specification limits, to produce individual units that conform as required, is of major interest to manufacturers. Consequently, assessments, studies, evaluations, and controls associated with the ability of processes to meet specification limits are concerns of quality control practitioners. An important body of techniques and principles has been developed to cope with these matters.

10-2.1 Some Process Specification Conflicts

Variables control charts are particularly effective in identifying, clarifying, and helping to solve conflicts between process performance and specification limits. One such conflict occurs when the specification limits are two-sided and narrower than 6σ, so that either the inherent variability of the process is too great or the specification limits are too narrow. This is called a type I conflict. Another conflict occurs when the specification limit is one-sided and closer than 3σ from the process mean. This type of conflict is a type II conflict. A third conflict occurs when the specification limits are too wide for acceptable quality. This conflict, which is a conflict between the specifications and the actual requirements, is a type III conflict. These three types will now be discussed in more detail.

Type I: Distribution Too Wide for Double Specification Limits
This conflict occurs when a process has been brought to a state of statistical control at the desired nominal for a given quality characteristic. Parameter estimates have been obtained from a large number of samples, or a frequency distribution has been prepared. The standard deviation estimate or the frequency distribution indicates the spread of the distribution to be wider than the specification limits. Some nontrivial proportion of the distribution of individual units for the given quality characteristic is outside the specification limits. If the process quality characteristic is assumed to be normally distributed, the percent nonconforming may be estimated by using Table A in the Appendix.

Possible actions to be taken in the event of a type I specification conflict are (1) changing the process; (2) changing the specification; (3) setting up an inspection/sorting operation to find, remove, or repair the units of product falling outside either specification limit; and (4) adjusting the centering of the distribution to strike a balance among relative costs such as the cost of scrap versus the cost of rework. One or more of these actions may be taken depending on the circumstances. Further explanation for each action follows.

Action 1, changing the process, should be preceded by a thorough investigation of the actual validity of the specification limits. If the specification limits are found to be valid, the necessity for a change in the process is based on the existing process having been brought to a state of statistical control. Therefore, some fundamental change in the process will be necessary to reduce the spread of the underlying distribution.

The nature of the change in process required to reduce the spread of the distribution will vary considerably with different processes, products, and quality characteristics. Beyond the use of control charts to continue to monitor the characteristic as changes are made, designed experiments (see Chapters 12 and 13) may be useful to study the effects of changes such as new materials, new methods, different settings on principal process variables, new machines, or new or retrained operators. These techniques provide a basis for learning quickly whether the proposed changes show promise for improving the process by reducing the spread of the distribution to within the specification limits. They may reduce the spread to an economic level but still not meet the specification limits, in which case action 2, changing the specification limits, may be warranted in combination with the process improvement.

Action 2 is often a sensible and economical activity. The basis for it is the manner in which some specification limits are established, often without consideration of process controls used during the manufacture of the product. When an organization is not following an integrated total quality control system, there may be a lack of coordination between those who set the specification limits (often R&D personnel) and production personnel. Some specification limits may be set tighter than necessary to keep the distribution of the quality characteristic from moving too far from the design intent (see Example 10-1). Many R&D personnel in the past have had little confidence in the production personnel's ability to maintain control to the requirements. Hence, needlessly tight specifications were often established. With the advent of a total quality control system, the specification limits may be reviewed in the light of better controls and adjusted accordingly.

For new products a lack of complete knowledge about the behavior of certain characteristics may dictate setting the specification limits on the *safe side*. As new knowledge becomes available, often aided by quality control techniques, these specifications may be changed or even eliminated. They may also have to be tightened instead of loosened. Some specification limits are taken from previous designs or directly from handbooks or other accepted general engineering practices. Objective information from process capability studies may indicate that some quality characteristics deserve or require more (type III) or less (type I) tightening than is specified by general practice.

For these and other reasons, specification limits should not be untouchable or "cast in concrete." There is often a valid basis for questioning the necessity for a given requirement and acting to change it. Quality control techniques, especially variables control charts, are invaluable aids for this purpose. Example 10-1 is an illustration of setting specification limits tighter than necessary with the solution of the conflict based on maintaining statistical control of the characteristic at the desired nominal value.

► **EXAMPLE 10-1**

The designer of a product insists on very tight specification limits, which result in an excessive, continuing proportion of the product being discarded because it does not meet the specified requirements. If a more expensive process is installed, enabling the product to meet the limits that have been established, the cost of every unit will be increased substantially. Millions of the items are made. Is there any solution to this situation?

An investigation revealed that what the designer actually wanted was a nominal value with reasonable variation about the desired nominal, as in Figure 10-1, for example, which shows the standardized distribution with the design nominal coded at zero. The investigation revealed the process was capable of meeting this level of variation. The designer did not trust the production department, since there was a general awareness that controls were not being maintained. Emphasis was simply on the inspection function. If specification limits of ±3 were to be established, the designer was afraid that the distribution would be allowed to shift away from the desired nominal, as shown by the distribution in Figure 10-2.

The designer established specification limits of ±1 to prevent this from happening. The level of nonconforming pieces associated with such a shift was so severe that even inadequate inspection routines would cause corrective action to be instituted. By so doing, even the distribution with the desired nominal contains a large proportion of nonconforming pieces on each side of these tight specification limits, as shown in Figure 10-3.

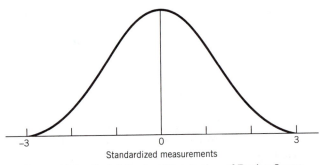

Standardized measurements

Figure 10-1   Coded Product Distribution of Design Intent

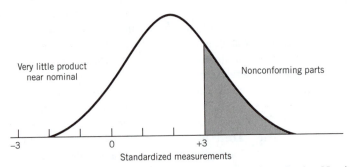

Very little product
near nominal

Nonconforming parts

Standardized measurements

Figure 10-2   Coded Product Distribution Shifted away from Design Nominal

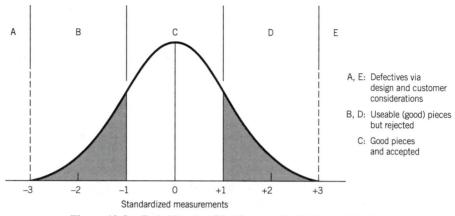

Figure 10-3 Coded Product Distribution with Tight Specification

This was the type I specification conflict that led to an investigation, revealing the above information and potential solution. By placing variables control charts on this quality characteristic at the process level to maintain the nominal value, the designer was satisfied and was willing to establish specification limits of ± 3 instead of ± 1.

Before leaving the discussion of action 2, it is necessary to say that most items have multiple quality characteristics, and two or more may be related or correlated. Changing specifications on one quality characteristic, perhaps allowing the distribution to be altered, may result in problems with other quality characteristics. In a thorough quality control effort, all quality characteristics must be considered.

Now return to a brief discussion of action 3—setting up an inspection/sorting operation—and action 4—adjusting the center associated with a type I specification conflict. Sometimes there is a type I specification conflict in which it is not feasible to change the specification limits or possible to make a change in the process in a short time. Setting up an inspection/sorting operation to find and remove the units of product that fall outside of either specification limit may then be necessary. But it should be considered an interim procedure while efforts are made to seek a more permanent solution. This incurs additional appraisal costs. It requires controls to maintain the correct criteria and calibrate and maintain the inspection instruments. If feasible, the use of automatic test equipment (ATE) should be considered. This may reduce costs and improve control compared to manual inspection.

Action 4 (adjusting the center) is based on the principle that the severity and costs of parts beyond the upper and lower specification limits may differ. An example is the machining of a certain journal diameter of a shaft. Shafts with diameters exceeding the upper specification limit may be returned to the machining operation for rework, at a cost of the labor, energy, and materials involved in the remachining. However, shafts with diameters falling below the lower specification limit may need to be scrapped or used for a smaller diameter part at a higher cost. It would be better to adjust the centering of the distribution to a position that minimizes combined costs of the nonconforming parts above the upper specification limit and below the lower specification limit. For cases in which the variable is normally distributed, the following cost equation pertains, where $\Phi(x)$ is the cumulative normal probability $P\ (X \leq x)$; C_u and C_L are the costs associated with the upper and lower specification limits U and L, respectively; μ and σ are the mean and standard deviation; and C is the combined relative cost that is to be minimized by choosing the optimum mean value:

$$C = C_U \Phi\left(\frac{\mu - U}{\sigma}\right) + C_L \Phi\left(\frac{L - \mu}{\sigma}\right) \tag{10-1}$$

With an estimate of σ, Table A of the Appendix may be used to find the optimum value of μ by trial and error.

For some processes, it may not be easy to adjust the mean value of the underlying distribution to a desired value. Additionally, design considerations should be considered, as Example 10-1 illustrates. This situation represents a variation on a type I specification conflict in which the mean is difficult to adjust to meet the requirements of two-sided specification limits or to minimize the cost of not meeting the specifications. Statistical techniques may be used to reduce the variation of the distribution and to adjust the mean value.

Type II: Distribution Not Centered Correctly for Single Specification Limit

With estimates of the standard deviation and mean value from a controlled process or with a frequency distribution of a large number of individual values, the approximate underlying distribution for the given quality characteristic may be sketched. From the sketch or the parameter estimates, it may be determined whether some proportion of the distribution is outside the specification limit. If so, under the assumption of a normal distribution, the proportion of items outside the specification limit may be estimated using Table A in the Appendix.

Possible actions to be taken in the event of a type II specification conflict are (1) attempting to center the process at a value far enough from the specification limit to avoid individual items outside of the limit; (2) changing the specification limit; and (3) setting up an inspection/sorting operation to find and remove or repair the units of product that fall outside the specification limit.

Action 1 should be preceded by an investigation of the necessity for the given specification limit. If found valid, work on the process should proceed to adjust the mean value of the distribution. For some processes this may be relatively easy; for others it may require experimentation or a fundamental change in the process itself. The necessary value for the mean can be estimated as $U - 3\hat{\sigma}_x$ or $L + 3\hat{\sigma}_x$, where U and L refer to the upper and lower specification limits and $\hat{\sigma}_x$ is an estimate of the standard deviation of the underlying distribution. This is valid for a normal distribution and will hold approximately for most distributions. A multiple of $\hat{\sigma}_x$ of between 3 and 4 will provide a safer level for the mean value. As attempts are made to adjust the centering of the distribution to the estimated desired mean value, an $\bar{x}$ chart can be used to monitor the progress. Such a chart may be fitted with modified control limits as explained in Chapter 9.

A reduced spread may allow for meeting the specification for the original centering of the distribution, or a combination of adjusted mean and reduced spread may eliminate this conflict. Reduction in the spread of the distribution may also have positive economic benefits. As an example, consider a minimum specification on filled volume of a bottled product. If the mean value alone must be increased to meet the minimum specification, an added cost is incurred. However, if the spread of the distribution of filled volume can be reduced, even at a certain investment, savings in overall costs may result while still meeting the specification.

For action 2, changing the limit of a type II specification conflict, the above discussion for a type I conflict is sufficient. The caution concerning correlated quality characteristics is particularly relevant.

Also, for action 3, sorting the product, the discussion for type I pertains. Again, it should be considered an interim measure only and the process should be improved as rapidly as possible.

Type III: Specification Limits Too Wide for Acceptable Product

An estimate of the standard deviation from a controlled process shows that the spread of the distribution is considerably less than the width of the specification limits. For example, if $6\hat{\sigma}_x < U - L$ for double specification limits, or $\bar{\bar{x}} < U - 3\hat{\sigma}_x$ or $\bar{\bar{x}} > L + 3\hat{\sigma}_x$ for single specification limit cases, then a type III conflict may exist.

This occurs if during the initial capability study or during subsequent control, it is seen that some items, though meeting the specified limits, do not produce satisfactory results. These units do not perform their intended function and are considered nonconforming, though they have met the specification limit(s). The specification limits are then suspected of being incorrect, either at the wrong value or, particularly for double specifications, too wide, allowing for too much movement of the distribution.

Possible actions to be taken in the event of a type III specifications conflict are (1) conducting more formal programs of process experimentation to determine what range of values cause nonconformities, (2) tightening the specification limit(s), and (3) establishing shop or manufacturing limits on a temporary basis until final values are determined.

In some organizations where a well-integrated quality system has not been implemented and the design function is quite separate from production, the designers may object to production or quality control people being involved in their activities. Thus, action 1, changing the process, or action 2, changing the specifications, must involve a team of people including design personnel as early as possible.

A type III conflict often arises for those quality characteristics that the designers consider to be of no particular importance and to which they may have applied some blanket, general practice, or handbook tolerance. It occurs especially on products for which some theory or knowledge is still missing. For these cases valuable feedback may be obtained from production process experimentation, as indicated in Chapter 12.

Action 3, establishing shop limits, has its counterpart with the inspection/sorting operation of type I and II conflicts, and it should be considered a temporary procedure. This can be done by control charts requiring strict statistical control at a nominal value that is believed to produce good results. If some latitude is believed permissible in the movement of the distribution, modified control limits or acceptance control charts may be used based on the shop limit(s).

10-2.2 Specification Limits and Process Capability

The Process Capability Index

One of the most common measures of process capability in relation to specification limits is the process capability index, Cp. The following equation describes Cp, where U and L

are the upper and lower specification limits and $\hat{\sigma}$ is an estimate of the standard deviation of the underlying distribution for the given quality characteristic:

$$Cp = (U - L)/6\hat{\sigma} \tag{10-2}$$

This type of a measure allows for evaluation of processes in relationship to the required specification limits. It also permits establishment of specification limits and assists in setting requirements on processes. An example of the second purpose is to require a certain value of Cp from suppliers of parts or products. The required values may be specified in purchase documents. A common value for such a requirement is that $Cp \geq 1.33$. An examination of Equation (10-2) reveals that such a requirement would mean that, in terms of the process standard deviation, the specification limits would have to be at $\pm 4\hat{\sigma}$ or that $U - L = 8\hat{\sigma}$. The producer would see this from a different perspective. That is, for the required specification limits, the process would have to be designed and controlled at a standard deviation that is only 1/8th of the width of the specified total tolerance, $U - L$.

Equation (10-2) indicates that larger values of Cp mean a better situation with respect to the capability of the process to meet established specification limits. A value of 1.0 for Cp indicates that the natural spread of the process just equals the width of the specification limits, assuming a normal distribution. Any shift in the mean will result in some (more than the expected 0.00135 outside $3\hat{\sigma}$ from the mean) product outside the specification limit in the direction of the shift. Values of $Cp < 1.0$ indicate a type I specification conflict. In any particular situation the validity of the specification limits is important, and without verification of this validity, the process capability index is meaningless. For example, a type III specification conflict might exist when a Cp value of 3.0 is obtained for the process. Additionally, when the Cp value is large—say, 2.0 or more—and the specifications are valid, it may be possible to develop a less expensive process. The use of modified control limits or acceptance control charts may also be warranted.

Other Process Capability Measures

Other measures of process capability relative to specification limits are used by some quality control practitioners, especially in Japan, as an adjunct to control charts. The following is a scaled measure of how far the process average varies from the specification nominal value:

$$K = |T - \bar{x}|/[(U - L)/2] \tag{10-3}$$

where T is the specification nominal (or target) and $\bar{x}$ is an estimate of the current process average. When $\bar{x} = T$, $K = 0$; when $\bar{x} = U$, $K = +1$; and when $\bar{x} = L$, $K = +1$; assuming that the target value lies equally between U and L.

Another measure of process capability is

$$Cpk = Cp(1 - K) \tag{10-4}$$

Cpk also measures shifts in the process mean level but on a scale relative to the Cp value. For example, when $\bar{x} = T$, $Cpk = Cp$; when $\bar{x} = U$, $Cpk = 0$; and when $\bar{x} = L$, $Cpk = 0$.

A relative measure of how far the upper limit exceeds the mean is

$$CPU = (U - \bar{x})/3\hat{\sigma} \tag{10-5}$$

CPU measures shifts in the process mean level with emphasis on the upper specification limit by associating values less than *Cp* with shifts towards the upper limit. For example, when $\bar{x} = T$, $CPU = Cp$; when $\bar{x} = U$, $CPU = 0$; and when $\bar{x} = L$, $CPU = 2Cp$.

The corresponding measure for the lower limit is

$$CPL = (\bar{x} - L)/3\hat{\sigma} \qquad (10\text{-}6)$$

When $\bar{x} = T$, $CPL = Cp$; when $\bar{x} = U$, $CPL = 2Cp$; and when $\bar{x} = L$, $CPL = 0$. These latter two measures allow for a second expression to that given above for *Cpk*, comparable to *Cp*, that accounts for off-center processes, as follows:

$$Cpk = \min (CPU, CPL) \qquad (10\text{-}7)$$

Thus, for a capable process in which $U - L > 6\hat{\sigma}$, with a corresponding $Cp > 1$, if the mean is not centered between the specification limits, *Cpk* will reflect a lower value, for example, even less than 1 when either $U - \bar{x}$ or $\bar{x} - L$ is less than $3\hat{\sigma}$. Otherwise, *Cpk* reflects the lower (minimum) of the two values relating the process capability index to the position of the process mean. In this sense it can be argued that *Cpk* is a more complete measure of process capability than *Cp*, in that when the process is centered, it yields the same result that *Cp* yields.

There are examples in which all of these measures are used simultaneously. This is totally unnecessary and, in fact, redundant. For example, note that for the values of $\bar{x} = T, U,$ and L above, $Cpk = CPL$. This is not accidental, since for the assumption that $T = (U + L)/2$ or, equivalently, $U - L = 2(T - L)$, $Cpk = CPL$. Additionally, *CPU* and *CPL* are functionally related by $(U - L)/3\hat{\sigma}$ or $2Cp$, that is, $CPU = 2Cp - CPL$. One of the above measures is sufficient when it is desired to maintain a running account of the current process performance relative to the specification limits.

Chan, Cheng, and Spiring (1988a) have introduced still another measure of process capability, which they refer to as *Cpm* in a further effort to establish a single value that accounts for variability and centering simultaneously. Their expression for *Cpm* is as follows:

$$Cpm = (U - L)/6\sqrt{\hat{\sigma}^2 + (\bar{x} - T)^2} \qquad (10\text{-}8)$$

It can be seen that when $\bar{x} = T$, $Cpm = Cp = Cpk$. Otherwise, it has different properties than *Cpk*. It is also referred to as the "Taguchi capability index." See, for example, Boyles (1991), who illustrates, among other things, that *Cpm* is a better measure of centering than is *Cpk*, because of its similarity to the Taguchi loss function, discussed in Chapter 13.

The Taguchi loss function involves a term similar to that in the denominator of Equation (10-8):

$$E(L) = kE(\bar{x} - T)^2 \qquad (10\text{-}9)$$

Expected loss is viewed as a quadratic function of departure of the process mean from the target value. See Taguchi (1986) for a more complete development of this concept.

The technique of process capability indices is available in numerous software packages relating to statistical analysis. See, for example, the references to software in Flaig (1996). The following examples illustrate the analysis available by MINITAB.

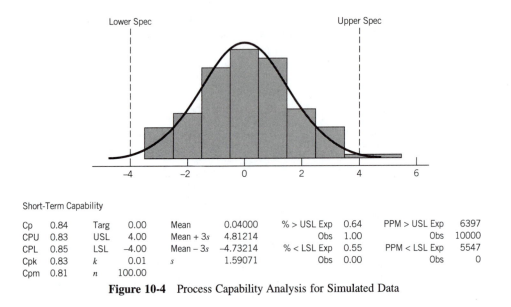

Figure 10-4 Process Capability Analysis for Simulated Data

Short-Term Capability

Cp	0.84	Targ	0.00	Mean	0.04000	% > USL Exp	0.64	PPM > USL Exp	6397
CPU	0.83	USL	4.00	Mean + 3s	4.81214	Obs	1.00	Obs	10000
CPL	0.85	LSL	−4.00	Mean − 3s	−4.73214	% < LSL Exp	0.55	PPM < LSL Exp	5547
Cpk	0.83	k	0.01	s	1.59071	Obs	0.00	Obs	0
Cpm	0.81	n	100.00						

▶ EXAMPLE 10-2

For the simulated data of Table 6-6 the capability analysis prepared by MINITAB is shown in Figure 10-4. With a target value of 0.0 (coded data) and with specification limits set at ±4.0, the capability analysis shows that the process is not capable of meeting the indicated specification limits. In this case the three measures *Cp*, *Cpk*, and *Cpm* are approximately equal and well under 1.0.

▶ EXAMPLE 10-3

For the tensile strength data of Example 8-5, with a target value of 190N/mm² and a lower specification of 175, the capability analysis of MINITAB is shown in Figure 10-5. This is a one-sided

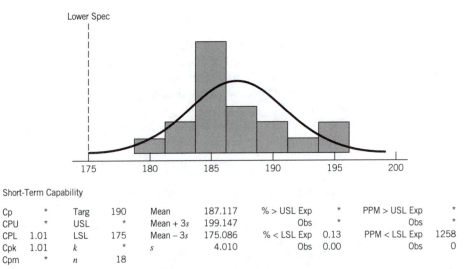

Short-Term Capability

Cp	*	Targ	190	Mean	187.117	% > USL Exp	*	PPM > USL Exp	*
CPU	*	USL	*	Mean + 3s	199.147	Obs	*	Obs	*
CPL	1.01	LSL	175	Mean − 3s	175.086	% < LSL Exp	0.13	PPM < LSL Exp	1258
Cpk	1.01	k	*	s	4.010	Obs	0.00	Obs	0
Cpm	*	n	18						

Figure 10-5 Tensile Strength

(unilateral) specification example. Note that the control chart of Figure 8-10 indicates reasonable statistical control and some evidence of process capability, allowing for a valid estimate of process variability. More will be said about this later. With the present process mean of just over 187 N/mm^2, the process is just capable of meeting the lower specification value with *CPL* and *Cpk* values of just over 1.0. As illustrated in Figure 8-10, a desired improvement in the process mean to a level of 190 would further improve the capability of the process to meet the lower specification. A reduction in process variability, usually a more difficult undertaking, would also enhance process capability.

As observed by the authors. the process capability index technique is one of the most misused procedures in the quality disciplines. What is often observed is that a single, rather small sample is taken from a process, measurements made on an important variable quality characteristic, and the mean and standard deviation are computed for the sample observations. These values are then substituted into the formulas for one or more process capability indices, and the process capability is declared according to the results of the computation. No attempt is made to verify or achieve a state of statistical control, or check normality, for the process and quality characteristic in question. In fact, the indices are used in situations where the actual process capability has not been established. For additional arguments and essential criteria before use of capability indices, see Pignatiello and Ramberg (1993). The following example is an illustration of this erroneous practice.

► **EXAMPLE 10-4**

For the Melt Index data of Example 8-1 the MINITAB capability analysis is shown in Figure 10-6, for the twenty samples of size 4 (total sample of 80) given in Table 8-3. With the estimated process mean of 235.037 and process standard deviation of 9.1, the process appears to be meeting the specification limits with *Cp* and *Cpk* values of 1.28 as well as a *Cpm* value of 1.02. Is this truly indicative of the process capability? Actually, this example is more conservative than most, for reasonably well-planned rational samples have been obtained that permit further analysis. A much larger total sample has been obtained than is often used. The $\bar{x}$ and *R* charts for these data are shown

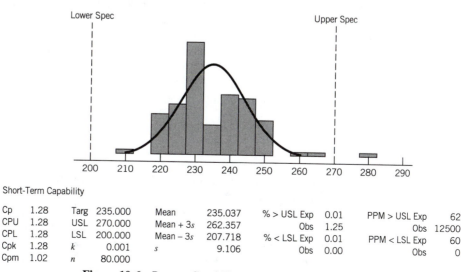

Short-Term Capability

Cp	1.28	Targ	235.000	Mean	235.037	% > USL Exp	0.01	PPM > USL Exp	62
CPU	1.28	USL	270.000	Mean + 3s	262.357	Obs	1.25	Obs	12500
CPL	1.28	LSL	200.000	Mean − 3s	207.718	% < LSL Exp	0.01	PPM < LSL Exp	60
Cpk	1.28	k	0.001	s	9.106	Obs	0.00	Obs	0
Cpm	1.02	n	80.000						

Figure 10-6 Process Capability Analysis for Melt Index Data

in Figure 8-6. The process is clearly out of control for the period of study discussed in Example 8-1. The histogram of Figure 10-6 helps to reinforce the interpretation of the $\bar{x}$ chart for mixtures of distribution at different levels, and instability of the R chart for the early portion. With the reduced R chart over the last four days, if the process mean can be controlled at the desired target of 235, the process capability may be considerably better than indicated by this erroneous initial analysis.

In Chapter 11 a distinction is made between *performance* and *capability* in the study of process control and improvement techniques. One approach to capability indices as discussed above is to make this type of distinction with respect to the type and extent of data and process knowledge obtained to date in the study of processes. If the study is relatively incomplete or relates to new processes for which there is a lack of knowledge of the overall variability, it is a good practice to recognize this situation by using different symbols for process capability indices. One approach is to substitute Pp for Cp, essentially with the same formula but with recognition that the estimate of the standard deviation in the denominator reflects an incomplete measure of total, overall variability of the process for the quality characteristic of interest. Likewise, one could substitute Ppk for Cpk (and other capability measures). This substitution, however, does not relieve the practitioner from the task of checking whether the process appears to be exhibiting a state of control before using the available data to obtain an estimate of the standard deviation representing potential capability.

Six Sigma

A topic related to specifications and process capability is Six Sigma[TM]. This subject is also discussed in a different light in Chapter 4. Developed and promoted by Motorola and Texas Instruments and with a growing number of adoptions, Six Sigma is a program for establishing and improving process capability. It represents for many a stretch goal for process design and improvement via variation reduction to achieve a process capability that represents a Cp of 2.0 and a Cpk of 1.5. To achieve a Cp of 2.0, the process variability must a be a reduced proportion of the specification range to the extent of a $\pm 6\sigma$, hence the name Six Sigma. With the recognition that over time the process mean may shift away from the target between specification limits, an allowance of a $\pm 1.5\sigma$ shift in the mean is included in the concept. This means that the process mean could move to within $6.0\sigma - 1.5\sigma = 4.5\sigma$ of either the upper or lower specification limit. Hence a Cpk of $4.5/3.0 = 1.5$ is a stated objective.

For the normal distribution, an area of 99.73% is contained within $\pm 3\sigma$, leaving some 0.27% outside of $\pm 3\sigma$ limits. In terms of parts per million (ppm) this equates to 2700 ppm. A better than 99% process yield may seem excellent, but there are many industries and many product characteristics in which this is not adequate. This is especially true in considering complex systems of multiple parts in series in which success of the system is dependent on success of all components. For a simple example, a 99% yield on each of ten independent components in series results in a system yield of only $0.99^{10} \approx 0.90$, or 90%. Twenty components lowers this to approximately 82%.

The Six Sigma concept with a minimum of 4.5σ between the process mean and either specification limit results in a defect rate of only 3.45 ppm per tail area, or a total of 6.9 ppm. See the extended normal curve tail areas in Table 10-1, from 3.00 to 4.99σ. For

TABLE 10-1 Extended Normal Curve Tail Areas

z	0.00	0.01	0.02	0.03	0.04	0.05	0.06	0.07	0.08	0.09
3.00	0.00134997	0.00130631	0.00126394	0.00122284	0.00118296	0.00114428	0.00110675	0.00107036	0.00103507	0.00100085
3.10	0.00096767	0.00093550	0.00090432	0.00087410	0.00084481	0.00081642	0.00078891	0.00076226	0.00073644	0.00071143
3.20	0.00068720	0.00066374	0.00064102	0.00061901	0.00059771	0.00057709	0.00055712	0.00053780	0.00051910	0.00050100
3.30	0.00048348	0.00046654	0.00045014	0.00043429	0.00041895	0.00040411	0.00038977	0.00037589	0.00036248	0.00034952
3.40	0.00033698	0.00032487	0.00031316	0.00030184	0.00029091	0.00028034	0.00027013	0.00026028	0.00025075	0.00024156
3.50	0.00023267	0.00022410	0.00021582	0.00020782	0.00020010	0.00019266	0.00018547	0.00017853	0.00017184	0.00016538
3.60	0.00015915	0.00015313	0.00014734	0.00014175	0.00013635	0.00013115	0.00012614	0.00012131	0.00011665	0.00011216
3.70	0.00010783	0.00010366	0.00009964	0.00009577	0.00009204	0.00008844	0.00008498	0.00008165	0.00007844	0.00007535
3.80	0.00007237	0.00006951	0.00006675	0.00006409	0.00006154	0.00005908	0.00005671	0.00005444	0.00005225	0.00005014
3.90	0.00004812	0.00004617	0.00004429	0.00004249	0.00004076	0.00003909	0.00003749	0.00003595	0.00003447	0.00003305
4.00	0.00003169	0.00003037	0.00002911	0.00002790	0.00002674	0.00002562	0.00002455	0.00002352	0.00002253	0.00002158
4.10	0.00002067	0.00001979	0.00001895	0.00001815	0.00001738	0.00001663	0.00001592	0.00001524	0.00001458	0.00001396
4.20	0.00001335	0.00001278	0.00001222	0.00001169	0.00001118	0.00001070	0.00001023	0.00000978	0.00000935	0.00000894
4.30	0.00000855	0.00000817	0.00000781	0.00000746	0.00000713	0.00000681	0.00000651	0.00000622	0.00000594	0.00000567
4.40	0.00000542	0.00000517	0.00000494	0.00000472	0.00000450	0.00000430	0.00000410	0.00000391	0.00000374	0.00000356
4.50	0.00000340	0.00000324	0.00000309	0.00000295	0.00000282	0.00000268	0.00000256	0.00000244	0.00000233	0.00000222
4.60	0.00000211	0.00000202	0.00000192	0.00000183	0.00000174	0.00000166	0.00000158	0.00000151	0.00000144	0.00000137
4.70	0.00000130	0.00000124	0.00000118	0.00000112	0.00000107	0.00000102	0.00000097	0.00000092	0.00000088	0.00000083
4.80	0.00000079	0.00000076	0.00000072	0.00000068	0.00000065	0.00000062	0.00000059	0.00000056	0.00000053	0.00000050
4.90	0.00000048	0.00000046	0.00000043	0.00000041	0.00000039	0.00000037	0.00000035	0.00000034	0.00000032	0.00000030

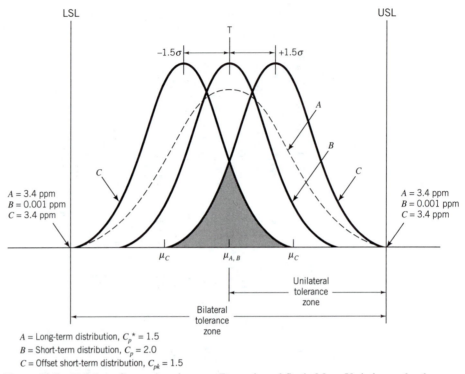

A = Long-term distribution, $C_p^* = 1.5$
B = Short-term distribution, $C_p = 2.0$
C = Offset short-term distribution, $C_{pk} = 1.5$

Figure 10-7 Tail Area Comparison between Dynamic and Static Mean Variation under the Constraint of a Symmetrical Bilateral Tolerance

a more extensive table, see Harry and Lawson (1992). Figure 10-7 is a graphical illustration of the Six Sigma concept.

The Six Sigma movement is further evidence of the validity and usefulness of specification limits set on the basis of design, engineering, production, economic, and customer considerations. Otherwise, anyone could achieve Six Sigma quality quickly by determining the process variation and setting specifications at $\pm 6\sigma$ about the desired target value, without regard to technical, economic, and customer requirements.

Setting Specification Limits

When a state of statistical control is reached for a quality characteristic, as evidenced by controlled patterns on control charts, the control chart statistics provide an estimate of the standard deviation of the underlying distribution. This estimate, $\hat{\sigma}$, is necessary to establish specification limits. Then, if customer, technical, and economic considerations allow, the specification limits can be set, for example, at $\pm 4\hat{\sigma}$ to give a $Cp = 1.33$.

When control chart information is not available, the technique of statistical tolerance limits, introduced in Section 10-1, may be useful. These limits are useful for estimating the natural spread of the process. This in turn permits setting specification limits that may be somewhat wider than the estimated natural spread if customer, technical, and economic considerations permit. Such limits may serve as interim specification limits until a more complete process capability study can be conducted. The following example illustrates the technique.

► **EXAMPLE 10-5**

A leading suture manufacturing company produces a new type of suture by first extruding a tape from a protein-based raw material. This tape, which is collected on spools in continuous lengths, is tanned by passing through various chemical solutions and drying cycles. The tape is then split into string, and the processed string is cut into standard lengths. A random sample is then taken for measurement of tensile strength. The following is a random sample of thirty such measurements from a certain production lot, expressed in kilogram-force:

2.80	2.34	2.57	2.68	2.61	2.23
2.34	2.66	2.52	2.70	2.57	2.82
2.50	2.34	2.73	2.45	2.70	2.23
2.14	2.52	2.30	2.34	2.77	2.36
2.52	2.52	2.39	2.57	2.75	2.55

From these data obtain estimates of the mean and variance as $\bar{x} = 2.517$ and $s^2 = 0.0342$. A probability plot indicates normality of the underlying distribution. Similarly, computation of the Shapiro-Wilk W Test for normality yields a W value that does not allow rejection of the hypothesis of normality [see Shapiro (1980) or Hahn and Shapiro (1967)].

Obtain a lower one-sided statistical tolerance limit as follows:

1. From Table I of the Appendix, with $1 - \alpha = 0.99$, $P = 0.99$, and $n = 30$, the coefficient, $k_2 = 3.45$ is obtained.

2. The tolerance limit is

$$\bar{x} - k_2 s = 2.517 - 3.45\sqrt{0.0342}$$
$$= 2.517 - 3.45(0.1849)$$
$$= 2.517 - 0.638$$
$$= 1.879$$

On the basis of this calculation a lower specification limit of 1.8 or 1.85 might be proposed. However, for technical reasons a larger value is desired so that all accepted sutures will be strong enough to perform properly. Additionally, it is expected that some process improvement, a larger mean value or a reduced spread, will result from further studies and process adjustments. Because of this, a value of 2.0 is set for the lower specification limit. Further process capability studies are initiated to evaluate this limit and to achieve the desired process improvements.

Statistical Tolerance Intervals

Determining statistical tolerance limits or intervals is a reasonably simple procedure that is summarized as follows:

1. Obtain a sample of n observations, or multiple samples representing the overall process performance.

2. Subject the sample(s) to some basic statistical tests such as tests for outliers, control charts, or normality tests and adjust as necessary.

3. For the accepted data, obtain parameter estimates as $\bar{x}$ and s^2.

4. Select the desired confidence level, $1 - \alpha$, and the desired population proportion to be covered by the limit(s), P.

For one-sided limits:

5. Enter Table I of the Appendix[1] to obtain the appropriate k_2 $(n, P, 1 - \alpha)$ value.

6. Obtain the required limit as $\bar{x} + k_2 s$ (upper limit) or $\bar{x} - k_2 s$ (lower limit).

For two-sided limits:

7. Enter Table J of the Appendix to obtain the appropriate k_2' $(n, P, 1 - \alpha)$ value.

8. Obtain the required limits as $\bar{x} \pm k_2' s$.

▶ 10-3 CUSUM CHARTS AND SPECIFICATION LIMITS

CUSUM charts or tabulations, as developed in Chapter 9, may be extended to the application of control of specification limits. An example using CUSUM tabulations in which the target values differ on the upper side and lower side follows and is used to illustrate the application of CUSUM to specification limit control.

In general, any target value, T, used in a CUSUM charting or tabulation procedure may be developed by consideration of a specification limit. Such a target value may correspond to an upper or lower modified centerline as used in modified control charts or to an upper or lower acceptable process level (APL) to be used with acceptance control charts. For dual specification limits (upper and lower), two target values, T_1 and T_2, may be specified and used, with $T_1 \neq T_2$. Example 10-6 will be used to illustrate this procedure.

▶ **EXAMPLE 10-6**

For the problem presented in Example 9-9, it is decided to employ a CUSUM tabulation procedure, selecting from Table 9-6 the C_1 (b) scheme with parameter $h = 5, f = 0.50$. Target values related to the specification limits are computed as $T_1 = U - 3\hat{\sigma}$. This results in target values of $T_1 = 17.11$ and $T_2 = 17.09$, the $UAPL$ and $LAPL$ values obtained in Example 9-9.

Following the CUSUM tabulation procedure (a) through (d) in Chapter 9, illustrated by Table 9-5, obtain the following results:

a.
$$C_1 = \Sigma(\bar{x}_1 - K_1), \quad \text{with } K_1 = T_1 + F$$
$$= 17.11 + 0.5\hat{\sigma}_{\bar{x}}$$
$$= 17.11 + 0.5(0.065)$$
$$= 17.14$$

b.
$$C_2 = \Sigma(\bar{x}_1 - K_2), \quad \text{with } K_2 = T_2 - F$$
$$= 17.09 - 0.0325$$
$$= 17.06$$

c. The tabulations of C_1 and C_2, ignoring negative values of C_1 and positive values of C_2, are shown in Table 10-2.

d. The decision limit, $H = h\hat{\sigma}_{\bar{x}} = 5(0.065) = 0.325$, is applied as $+H$ to C_1 and $-H$ to C_2 in Table 10-2 to indicate when signals occur.

A sequence of twenty-five means of samples of 5, representing measurements of the relay adjustment, are tabulated in Table 10-2 with the corresponding CUSUM tabulations and signal

---

[1]Tables I and J are reproduced from Tables 7 and 8, respectively, of ISO 3207 Statistical Interpretation of Data—Determination of a Statistical Tolerance Interval by permission of the International Organization for Standardization, Geneva. The entire standard should be consulted for further information on statistical tolerance intervals.

TABLE 10-2 CUSUM Tabulation for Relay Adjustment Means

i Sequence	Sample Mean $\bar{x}_i$	Upper $\bar{x}_i - K_1$ $\bar{x}_i - 17.14$	CUSUM, C_1 $\Sigma(\bar{x} - K_1)$	Lower $\bar{x}_i - K_2$ $\bar{x}_i - 17.06$	CUSUM, C_2 $\Sigma(\bar{x}_i - K_2)$	Remarks
1	17.18	0.04	0.04	0.12	>0	
2	17.26	0.12	0.16	0.20	>0	
3	17.24	0.10	0.26	0.18	>0	
4	17.20	0.06	0.32	0.14	>0	
5	17.39	0.25	0.57*	0.33	>0	Upper signal
6	17.30	0.16	0.37	0.24	>0	
7	17.41	0.27	1.00	0.35	>0	
8	17.35	0.21	1.21	0.29	>0	
9	17.37	0.23	1.44	0.31	>0	
10	17.39	0.25	1.69	0.33	>0	
11	17.18	0.04	1.73	0.12	>0	
12	16.93	−0.21	1.52	−0.13	−0.13	
13	17.12	−0.02	1.50	0.06	−0.07	
14	17.05	−0.09	1.41	−0.01	−0.08	
15	16.98	−0.16	1.25	−0.08	−0.16	
16	16.80	−0.34	0.91	−0.26	−0.42*	Lower signal
17	16.99	−0.15	0.76	−0.07	−0.49	
18	16.85	−0.29	0.47	−0.21	−0.70	
19	16.95	−0.19	0.28	−0.11	−0.81	
20	16.81	−0.33	<0	−0.25	−1.06	
21	17.15	0.01	0.01	0.09	−0.97	
22	16.97	−0.17	<0	−0.09	−1.06	
23	17.08	−0.06	<0	0.02	−1.04	
24	16.98	−0.16	<0	−0.08	−1.12	
25	16.92	−0.22	<0	−0.14	−1.26	

*Denotes the first occurrence of a signal.

remarks. Plotting of these results as in Figure 9-8 is also possible. An upper signal is detected on sample 5. An adjustment of the mean value of the underlying distribution to a lower value is apparent around the eleventh sample. There appears to be an overadjustment, as a lower signal occurs on the sixteenth sample and continues throughout the remainder of the sequence.

▶ 10-4 SOME MISCELLANEOUS PROCEDURES

Other techniques relating to control of processes to specification limits have been developed. These may be considered in the general category of miscellaneous procedures. Only a brief description is provided here for familiarity with the techniques. References are provided for a more detailed study of each procedure for possible applications.

10-4.1 Narrow-Limit Gauging

This idea was developed as early as 1944 by Dudding and Jennett (1944), extended by Stevens (1948) and Mace (1952), and given a particularly practical boost by the paper of Ott and Mundel (1954). The technique is essentially a single sampling plan with parameters of sample size n and acceptance number c together with a third parameter, t, denoting the location of the narrowed limit(s) of $t\sigma$ inside the required specification limit(s). By gauging to the narrowed limit(s) nearer the mean of the underlying distribution, more units will tend to exceed the narrowed limit(s), even for relatively small samples. Then, by increasing the acceptance number, c, of allowed units in the sample exceeding the narrowed limit(s), an adequate compensation can be made to achieve a desired control of the number of items in the underlying distribution exceeding the actual required specification limit(s).

A large selection of available narrow-limit gauging plans for practical application is provided in the paper by Schilling and Sommers (1981). They relate the plans to attribute sampling plans (see Chapter 15) and to associated variables sampling plans (see Chapter 17). Stephens (2001) provides a spreadsheet application for the evaluation of the operating characteristics of narrow-limit sampling plans, and provides a procedure to design narrow-limit plans.

10-4.2 Pre-Control

This technique is useful for the control of processes without charting or computations using a small number of sample units on a periodic frequency basis. A popular variation of the technique calls for setting pre-control (PC) lines one fourth of the way in from specification limits. The following simple procedure is then used to control the related process:

1. Select and measure the first unit produced. If it is outside either specification limit, adjust the process and proceed with Step 6.

2. If it is inside specification limits but outside either PC limit, select and measure the second unit produced.

3. If the second unit is outside the same PC limit, adjust the process and proceed with Step 6.

4. If the second unit is inside the PC limit, continue producing units, following Step 6.

5. If the second unit is outside the opposite PC limit, action should be taken to check and reduce process variation.

6. Continue to select and measure consecutive units produced. When five successive units fall between the PC limits, select subsequent units on a frequency basis, adjusting the process only as indications 1, 3, or 5 occur on selected units. If before reaching five successive units between the PC limits, a unit exceeds a PC limit or specification limit, proceed as in Steps 1 through 5. The frequency of checking should be so that the average number of checks between process adjustments during which frequency checking is made is 25. If more than twenty-nine checks are made without a process adjustment, reduce the frequency of checking; if a process adjustment is made before twenty-one checks are made, increase the frequency of checking.

For more details on this procedure, see papers by Shainin (1965), Brown (1966), and Wadsworth (1999).

10-4.3 Lot Plot

This technique was developed by Shainin (1950, 1952) primarily for application in receiving inspection to variable quality characteristics of incoming items. It is also applicable to in-process control, with emphasis on the relationship between the probable underlying distribution and the required specification limits. It uses a histogram (see Chapter 5) of fifty observations (the lot plot) together with estimates of the mean and standard deviation of the lot to further estimate proportions of the lot exceeding the specification limits. For further instructions and possible applications consult the papers by Shainin referenced above as well as those by Ashley (1952) and Wilson (1952). Moses (1956) contains a statistical caution on the technique.

10-4.4 Tool Wear Control Chart

The technique of tool wear charts was developed by Manuele (1945) for application to situations in which dimensions of units may change as a tool wears during production. The process at any time may have the capability to produce a distribution of individual parts well within the prescribed specification limits. As a result of tool wear, the mean of the distribution may undergo a fairly constant trend until the distribution begins to exceed one of the specification limits. An example of this is the operation of drawing wire through a die. Ordinary modified control limits or acceptance control charts may be used for this situation without concern for the degree of trend or slope of the change in the distribution. This establishes control limits on averages to indicate when the distribution has shifted too far toward the specification limit. A further refinement is to determine the approximate trend that would result from adjusting the process to a safe level near one specification and then allowing the distribution to change until it reaches an undesirable position near the other specification limit. Hence, the centerline of the control chart and the control limits can be determined by using regression techniques and plotted as trend lines. Such limits would allow for monitoring the degree of trend in addition to the overall movement of the distribution. If a factor is introduced into the process that has the effect of changing the trend, it may be detected and necessary corrective action taken.

The technique assumes that the trend line is a part of the process, can be estimated from past results, and would not change unless an assignable cause enters the process. The chart is used for a given cycle—for example, movement of the distribution from just within the lower specification limit to just within the upper specification limit. The process is then adjusted to the lower side and the chart is redrawn to monitor the next cycle.

For further instructions in use of this technique, consult the paper by Manuele (1945).

▶ 10-5 STATISTICAL ADDITION OF TOLERANCES

The discussion has so far only considered quality characteristics individually. The various techniques presented may be applied separately to any number of characteristics. Another important aspect of specification limits and tolerances is to evaluate their joint effect, for example, an assembly of parts. Some quality characteristics considered for application of the previous techniques may be the result of the combined effect of two or more dimensions.

The study of the combined effect of quality characteristics, such as assemblies of various kinds, is often useful to develop control of the dimensions or characteristics for each characteristic under study. It is also useful to establish tolerances on an assembly based on the tolerances of the parts from which it is made. A third use is to evaluate the existing tolerances specified on assembly characteristics to determine whether they are compatible with the tolerances specified on individual parts of the assembly.

As an introduction to this subject, consider only those characteristics that are simple linear combinations of others, such as the following relationship:

$$y = a_1 x_1 \pm a_2 x_2 \pm a_3 x_3 \pm \cdots \pm a_n x_n \tag{10-10}$$

where the x_i are characteristic of parts, the a_i represent integer multiples of such parts, and y is a resultant assembly characteristic.

The distribution of y, including its mean and standard deviation, is determined by statistical theory. For example,

$$\mu_y = \sum_{i=1}^{n} a_i \mu_{x_i} \tag{10-11}$$

and if the x_i are independent,

$$\sigma_y^2 = \sum_{i=1}^{n} a_i^2 \sigma_{x_i}^2 \tag{10-12}$$

$$\sigma_y = \sqrt{\sigma_y^2} \tag{10-13}$$

To explore the practical effects of these results, consider the assembly shown in Figure 10-8 consisting of five parts, A through E. The concern is with the overall length of the assembly, y, which is determined by the simple sum of the widths of five parts, x_A through x_E. For simplicity, assume that the distributions for the five parts are independent and normally distributed with the same spread, σ, that is, $\sigma_A = \sigma_B = \cdots = \sigma_E = \sigma = 0.1$, and the following means, $\mu_A = 2$, $\mu_B = 5$, $\mu_C = 6$, $\mu_D = 7$, and $\mu_E = 3$.

Equation (10.11) gives the following mean value for y:

$$\mu_y = \mu_A + \mu_B + \mu_C + \mu_D + \mu_E$$
$$= 2 + 5 + 6 + 7 + 3 = 23$$

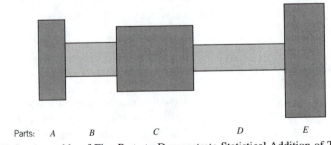

Parts: A   B   C   D   E

Figure 10-8   Assembly of Five Parts to Demonstrate Statistical Addition of Tolerances

Considering the distributions for all five parts and the property of the normal distribution, that virtually all units will fall $\pm 3\sigma_x$ about the mean value, then

Part A will vary as 2 ± 0.3, or from 1.7 to 2.3

Part B will vary as 5 ± 0.3, or from 4.7 to 5.3

Part C will vary as 6 ± 0.3, or from 5.7 to 6.3

Part D will vary as 7 ± 0.3, or from 6.7 to 7.3

Part E will vary as 3 ± 0.3, or from 2.7 to 3.3

Sum: 21.5 to 24.5

From the sum of the minimum and maximum values, it is possible for the assembly to vary from 21.5 to 24.5, that is, 23 ± 1.5. However, from Equation (10-13) it is determined that

$$\sigma_y = \sqrt{\sigma_A^2 + \sigma_B^2 + \cdots + \sigma_E^2}$$
$$= \sqrt{5(0.01)^2} = 0.2236$$

With the expectation that y will also vary in the interval $\pm 3\sigma_y$ about its mean value, the assemblies will vary as 23 ± 0.67, or from 22.33 to 23.67.

This variation is considerably smaller than would result from the direct sum of the spread of the individual parts (i.e., ± 0.67 as opposed to ± 1.5, in this case a multiple of $1/\sqrt{5}$). The above results, in particular Equation (10-13), indicate that *random assemblies of independently selected parts can be held to narrower spreads than would be indicated by totaling the spreads of the parts.* Now this property can also be applied to tolerances. Suppose that the tolerances established on the five parts just equal the natural spread of the process (i.e., ± 0.3). The assemblies are then able to meet tolerances of ± 0.67 instead of ± 1.5. This phenomenon is referred to as the statistical addition of tolerances. The result is not unreasonable since it is unlikely that in random assemblies (random selection of parts from their individual distribution) all five parts would be at their minimum or maximum values; or even several of the five at these extremes on the same assembly. Of course, the extremes of 23 ± 1.5 for the assemblies are physical possibilities as they may occur from the spreads indicated for the parts. However, the probability of such a result is very small, as this is associated with normal random variables beyond $\pm 3\sigma$ from the mean.

10-5.1 Control Aspect

There is an important control aspect to this phenomenon. Suppose the process producing the parts allows a shift in the mean of 1 standard deviation in only one of the parts—for example, part C is now varying at 6.1 ± 0.3. The mean value of the assembly, μ_y, is now 23.1 with the same standard deviation as before (i.e., $\sigma_y = 0.2236$), so the assemblies vary from 22.43 to 23.77. If it is necessary to hold tolerances on the assemblies of 23 ± 0.67, the upper tolerance is exceeded by approximately 0.5%. If such a shift in the means of two of the five parts should occur, the upper tolerance of the assemblies is exceeded by 1.8%.

The assembly length is in itself an individual quality characteristic. It can be monitored by control charts for variables. Should there be difficulties in maintaining control and meeting tolerances, it may be necessary to monitor and control the dimensions of the individual parts as they affect the assembly dimensions.

10-5.2 Establishing and Evaluating Tolerances

Now return to Figure 10-8 and place somewhat more realistic tolerances on the five parts. For example, suppose the following tolerances are specified:

Part	Specification Limits (Tolerances)
A	2 ± 0.005 cm
B	5 ± 0.010 cm
C	6 ± 0.010 cm
D	7 ± 0.015 cm
E	3 ± 0.008 cm
	23 ± 0.048 cm

If these tolerances are held, if the parts dimensions are independent, and if assembly is at random, then a tolerance of less than ± 0.048 can be met by the assemblies. In fact, under the assumptions indicated the assemblies can meet the following tolerance:

$$\text{Assembly nominal} = \Sigma \text{ Parts nominals}$$
$$= 2 + 5 + 6 + 7 + 3 = 23 \quad \text{as before}$$
$$\text{Assembly tolerances} = \pm \sqrt{\text{sum (Parts tolerance)}^2}$$
$$= \pm \sqrt{(0.005)^2 + 2(0.010)^2 + (0.015)^2 + (0.008)^2}$$
$$= \pm \sqrt{(0.000514)} = \pm 0.02267$$

A tolerance of 23 ± 0.023 cm is not unreasonable for the length of the assembly. Tolerances set in this manner are often referred to as overlapping tolerances.

10-5.6 Selective Assembly

Suppose now for design considerations, this tolerance on the assemblies is too large? If a tolerance of ± 0.016, or even ± 0.010, is required, for example, how is this requirement to be met? An obvious consideration is to return to the individual parts and examine the tolerances and process capabilities associated with each to determine if the part tolerances can be reduced. If it is found that the individual parts tolerances cannot be reduced, is there anything that can be done to meet these tighter limits? The technique for managing this problem is that of selective assembly, as opposed to random assembly. This is done by measuring individual parts and placing them into cell groupings. This will permit selection of parts making up assemblies so that resulting assemblies will be within a small tolerance about the nominal value. By this means, assemblies with very tight tolerances can be produced.

An alternative to selective assembly is partial selective assembly or random/selective assembly. For some situations it may be possible to achieve the necessary assembly tolerances by doing a random selection of one or more of the parts, thus building a subassembly, and selective assembly for the remaining parts. For example, suppose it is necessary to meet assembly tolerances of ±0.016 for the above case. Assume that parts *A, B,* and *C* are just meeting their tolerances, are independent, and are assembled into a subassembly by random selection. The tolerance range of the subassemblies, using Equations (11-8) and (11-10), will be 13 ± 0.015. By careful selective assembly of parts *D* and *E,* the prescribed tolerance on the overall assembly can be met. Random assembly may also be used for any adjacent set of two parts, and selective assembly for the remaining three parts.

10-5.7 Mating Part Tolerances

A special form of assembly is that of mating parts such as a pin and a sleeve or a shaft and a bushing. The above principles apply equally well to these types of assemblies. However, some differences in the analysis apply to this special case.

Explore this case initially by way of a hypothetical example. Consider the shaft and mating bearing shown in Figure 10-9 with their corresponding specifications. The parts are manufactured according to their tolerances, and pairs of parts are assembled. The parts can be made so that the natural spread of each process just equals its specified tolerance range and the parts are independent with normal distributions.

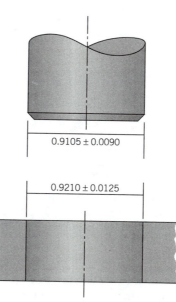

0.9105 ± 0.0090

0.9210 ± 0.0125

Figure 10-9 Specifications for Shaft and Bearing to Demonstrate Mating Parts Tolerances

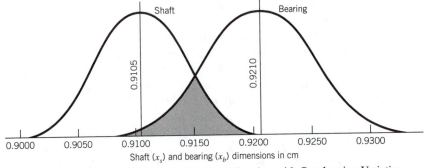

Figure 10-10 Distributions for Shaft and Bearing with Overlapping Variation

The shafts will vary in the range 0.9105 ± 0.0090 cm, or from 0.9015 to 0.9195. The range of bearing measurements will be 0.9210 ± 0.0125 cm, or from 0.9085 to 0.9335. Overlapping tolerances are apparent, since the range of variation of the shafts includes values larger than the minimum value of the bearings. This can be seen more vividly in Figure 10-10, which shows the distributions for each characteristic drawn on a common scale. There is a region of overlap in the distributions. The question then is "How will random selections of such shafts and bearings fit together? Is the overlap too much for satisfactory assembly?"

An Analysis
The situation pictured in Figure 10-10 can be analyzed as follows: Let

$$x_s = \text{a value for the shaft O.D.}$$
$$x_b = \text{a value for the bearing I.D.}$$
$$\mu_s = 0.9105, \qquad \mu_b = 0.9210$$
$$d = x_b - x_s$$

Hence,

$$\mu_d = \mu_b - \mu_s = 0.0105$$

The standard deviation for the shaft O.D., σ_s, may be approximated as

$$\sigma_s = (0.9195 - 0.9015)/6 = 0.003$$

Similarly, the standard deviation for the bearing I.D., σ_b, may be approximated as

$$\sigma_b = (0.9335 - 0.9085)/6 = 0.00417$$

The standard deviation for the difference, σ_d, may be approximated by using Equation (10-13) with $a_1 = 1$ and $a_2 = -1$ as follows:

$$\sigma_d = \sqrt{\sigma_s^2 + (-\sigma_b)^2} = \sqrt{(0.003)^2 + (0.00417)^2}$$
$$= 0.005134$$

This distribution of the difference, d, will be normal, since x_s and x_b are normal, with the approximate mean value and standard deviation obtained above. This situation is pictured in Figure 10-11.

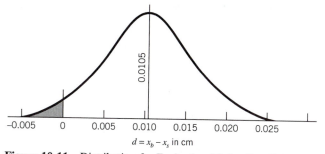

Figure 10-11   Distribution for Evaluating Mating Part Tolerances

The area to the left of zero represents the proportion of bearings having smaller I.D.s than the O.D.s of the corresponding shafts. It is estimated as follows:

$$z = (0 - 0.0105)/0.005134 = -2.045$$

with

$$\Phi(-2.045) = 0.0204, \quad \text{or } 2.04\%$$

The actual proportion of difficult fits between shafts and bearings may be higher because of ovality, taper, or surface roughness. But this percentage is strikingly small in comparison to the amount of overlap of the distributions in Figure 10-10. This example demonstrates the manner of dealing with mating part tolerances and illustrates that Equations (10-11) to (10-13) may be used for this situation.

Clearance Fits and Interference Fits

The overlap of tolerances illustrated by the example of Figure 10-10 may be specified for various applications. It has been standardized to facilitate specifications, application, and reduction in variety. British Standard series BS 4500, Parts 1, 2, and 3, provide useful working information on the "Specification for ISO Limits and Fits." Several definitions are presented here for initial interest and understanding:

Fit   The relationship resulting from the difference, before assembly, between the sizes of the two parts that are to be assembled.

Clearance   The difference between the sizes of the hole and the shaft, before assembly, when this difference is positive.

Interference   The magnitude of the difference between the size of the hole and shaft, before assembly, when this difference is negative.

Clearance Fit   A fit that always provides a clearance. (The tolerance zone of the hole is entirely above that of the shaft.)

Interference Fit   A fit that always provides an interference. (The tolerance zone of the hole is entirely below that of the shaft.)

Transition Fit   A fit that may provide either a clearance or an interference. (The tolerance zones of the hole and the shaft overlap.)

Some examples from the referenced standards to illustrate these definitions are as follows:

Clearance fit (Shaft Basis: G7, h6)

Nominals of from 120 to 180 mm

tolerances of $\{+0, -0.025\}$ mm on shaft

tolerances of $\{+0.054, +0.014\}$ mm on hole

(For example: shaft 150 $\{+0, -0.025\}$, hole 150.034 ± 0.020)

Transition Fit (Shaft Basis: K7, h6)

Nominals of from 120 to 180 mm

tolerances of $\{+0, -0.025\}$ mm on shaft

tolerances of $\{+0.012, -0.028\}$ mm on hole

(For example: shaft 150 $\{+0, -0.025\}$, hole 149.992 ± 0.020)

Interference Fit (Shaft Basis: P7, h6)

Nominals of from 120 to 180 mm

tolerances of $\{+0, -0.025\}$ mm on shaft

tolerances of $\{-0.028, -0.068\}$ mm on hole

(For example: shaft 150 $\{+0, -0.025\}$, hole 149.952 ± 0.020)

▶ 10-6 REFERENCES

Ashley, R. L. (1952), "Modification of the Lot Plot Method of Acceptance Sampling," *Industrial Quality Control,* Vol. 8, No. 5, March; pp. 30–31.

Boyles, R. A. (1991), "How Reliable is Your Capability Index?", *Journal of Quality Technology,* Vol. 23, Jan.; pp. 17–26.

British Standards Institution, BS 4500, *British Standards Specification for ISO Limits and Fit; Part 1. General, Tolerances and Deviations; Part 2, Inspection of Plain-Work Pieces; Part 3. Working Limits on Untoleranced Dimensions,* BSI, London.

Brown, N. R. (1966), "Zero Defects the Easy Way with Target Area Control," *Modern Machine Shop,* July, pp. 96–100.

Chan, L. K. Cheng, S. W., and Spiring, F. A. (1988a), "A New Measure of Process Capability: Cpm," *Journal of Quality Technology,* Vol. 30, April; pp. 162–75.

Dudding, B. P., and Jennett, W. J. (1944), *Quality Control Chart Technique When Manufacturing to a Specification,* Gryphon Press, Arlington, VA.

Flaig, J. J. (1996), "A New Approach to Process Capability Analysis," *Quality Engineering,* Vol. 9, No. 2, pp. 205–11.

Hahn, G. J., and Shapiro, S. S. (1967), *Statistical Models in Engineering,* Wiley, New York.

Harry, M. J., and Lawson, J. R. (1992), *Six Sigma Producibility Analysis and Process Characterization,* Addison-Wesley, Reading, MA.

International Standard Organization (1975), Standard 3207-1975, *Statistical Interpretation of Data—Determination of a Statistical Tolerance Interval,* ISO, Geneva.

International Organization for Standardization (2002). *ISO 3534-2, Statistics—Vocabulary and Symbols—Part 2: Applied Statistics,* ISO, Geneva.

Mace, A. E. (1952), "The Use of Limit Gauges in Process Control," *Industrial Quality Control,* Vol. 8, No. 4, Jan.; pp. 28–31.

Manuele, J. (1945), "Control Charts for Determining Tool Wear," *Industrial Quality Control,* Vol. 1, No. 6, May; pp. 7–10.

Moses, L. E. (1956), "Some Theoretical Aspects of the Lot Plot Sampling Inspection Plan," *Journal of the American Statistical Association,* Vol. 51, pp. 84–107.

Ott, E. R., and Mundel, A. B. (1954), "Narrow-Limit Gauging," *Industrial Quality Control,* Vol. 10, No. 5, March; pp. 21–28.

Pignatiello, J., and Ramberg, J. (1993), "Process Capability Indices: Just Say No!", *Transactions of ASQC Quality Congress,* Boston, May 24–26, pp. 92–104.

Schilling, E. G., and Sommers, D. J. (1981), "Two-Point Optimal Narrow Limit Plans with Applications to MIL-STD-105D," *Journal of Quality Technology,* Vol. 13, No. 2, April; pp. 83–92.

Shainin, D. (1950), "The Hamilton Standard Lot Plan Method of Acceptance Sampling by Variables," *Industrial Quality Control,* Vol. 7, No. 1, July; pp. 15–34.

Shainin, D. (1952), "Recent Lot Plot Experiences around the Country," *Industrial Quality Control,* Vol. 8, No. 5, Sept.; pp. 20–29.

Shainin, D. (1965), *Techniques for Maintaining a Zero Defects Program,* Bulletin 71, American Management Association, New York.

Shapiro, Samuel S. (1980), The ASQC Basic References in Quality Control: Statistical Techniques, Vol. 3: How to Test Normality and Other Distributional Assumptions, ASQC, Milwaukee, WI.

Stephens, K. S. (2001), *The Handbook of Applied Acceptance Sampling*, ASQ Quality Press, Milwaukee.

Stevens, W. L. (1948), "Control by Gauging," *Royal Statistical Society Journal*, Series B, Vol. 10, pp. 54–108.

Taguchi, G. (1986), *Introduction to Quality Engineering*, Asian Productivity Organization, Tokyo, Japan.

Wadsworth, H. M. (1999), "Statistical Process Control," in *Juran's Quality Handbook*, Fifth Edition, McGraw-Hill, New York, Section 45.

Wilson, R. (1952), "A Convenient Shortcut in the Use of Lot Plot," *Industrial Quality Control*, Vol. 8, No. 5, pp. 32–33 (March).

▶ 10-7 PROBLEMS

1. Collect and list examples of specification limits for ten quality characteristics from engineering drawings, company standards, and so on, and, where possible, obtain explanations concerning the process by which these specification limits were set.

2. Review some national and/or international standards, and list at least ten quality characteristics with associated specification limits.

3. Obtain and list examples of process capability indices specified for some quality characteristics for in-process operations and/or purchasing requirements.

4. For Problem 10 in Chapter 6, assume that difficulties in maintaining control of the average gain can be overcome with process improvements and control and that a mean of 10.5 decibels can be sustained. Further assume that the within-sample variability (as given by $\bar{R}$ over the twenty samples) represents the process capability. Estimate the process capability standard deviation using $\bar{R}$, and complete a capability analysis to determine whether specification limits of 8.5 to 12.5 decibels can be met.

5. The target value for the data of Problem 11 in Chapter 6 is zero, and the data as given represent deviation from target. As for Problem 4 above, assume that difficulties in maintaining control of the average oxide thickness can be solved and that a mean at the target value can be achieved and sustained. Also assume that the within-sample variability (as given by $\bar{R}$ over the eighteen samples) represents the process capability. Estimate the standard deviation using $\bar{R}$, and compute relevant capability indices to

determine how well the specification limits of ± 200 angstroms can be met.

6. For Problem 1 in Chapter 8, further revise the data by eliminating samples 23 and 24 (in addition to samples 11, 12, 17, 18, and 22 as suggested in that problem). Complete a capability analysis for the revised data, estimating the revised σ, computing Cp, CPU, CPL, Cpk, and Cpm, using $U = 1.040$, $L = 1.010$, and $T = 1.025$. Is the process (as revised, and assumed to be maintained at the new mean and standard deviation) capable of meeting the specifications? If not, what further improvements are necessary?

7. For the data on fish net cord, number of twists per meter, given in Problem 5 in Chapter 5:
(a) Perform a capability analysis (including determination if capability has been achieved).
(b) Prepare a CUSUM tabulation procedure using the scheme with parameters $h = 8$, $f = 0.25$ [C1 (a) from Table 9-6], and with $T_1 = 196$ for the upper target, and $T_2 = 194$ for the lower target.

8. Given the assembly sketch in Figure 10-12 of three parts whose manufacture is believed to be independent and for which random selection is made for the assembly, determine the minimum tolerances that might safely be set on the assembly, assuming further that the parts might just meet their respective tolerances.

9. Given the assembly sketch in Figure 10-13 of two parts whose manufacture is believed to be independent and for which random selection is made for the assembly, determine the minimum tolerances that might safely be set on

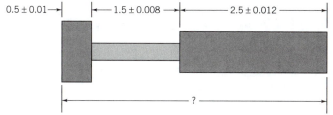

Figure 10-12 Assembly Sketch of Three Parts

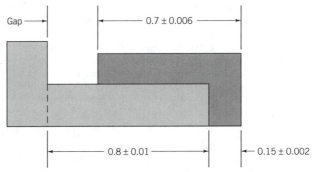

Figure 10-13 Assembly Sketch of Two Parts

the indicated gap dimension, assuming further that the parts might just meet their respective tolerances.

10. For the specification of a transition fit (K7, h6 on shaft basis) on parts with a nominal dimension of 160 mm, it has been found that the shaft diameter is normally distributed with a mean of 159.99 and a standard deviation of 0.003 and that the hole diameter is also normally dis-

tributed with a mean of 159.996 and a standard deviation of 0.005.

(a) Do the parts meet their respective tolerance requirements?

(b) Assuming independent parts and random assembly, approximately what percent of holes will be smaller than the chosen shaft?

11

PROCESS CONTROL AND IMPROVEMENT TECHNIQUES

Among the most powerful techniques for producing good quality are those of statistical process control or SPC, and process improvement. A well-designed process will produce good products, of the desired amount, on time, and at the lowest cost. This assumes that the product is well designed, reflecting the needs of the customer. Good process control can also contribute to identifying any areas of product design that need improvement. It will also help to identify aspects of the process design that need controls and improvements.

▶ 11-1 PRINCIPLES, METHODOLOGIES, AND TECHNIQUES

Understanding what is meant by a process will enhance understanding of process control and process improvement. A process is defined in ISO 9000-2000 as follows:

> *Process: set of interrelated or interacting activities which transforms inputs into outputs.*
>
> *NOTE 1: Inputs to a process are generally outputs of other processes*
>
> *NOTE 2: Processes in an organization are generally planned and carried out under controlled conditions to add value.*
>
> *NOTE 3: A process where the conformity of the resulting product cannot be readily or economically verified is frequently referred to as a "special process."*

An input-transformation-output model for a process is a very useful one for understanding process operation, control, and improvement. Visualize a process in its simplest form as follows:

$$\text{Inputs} \rightarrow \text{Transformations} \rightarrow \text{Outputs}$$

A process may also be defined as a sequence of activities that are characterized as having (1) measurable inputs, (2) value-added transformations, (3) measurable outputs, with the activities repeatable, definable, and predictable. The sequence of activities may be referred to as processes themselves. To simplify the discussion, subprocesses are often referred to as processes, similar to the concept of systems and subsystems.

This sequence of activities is of importance to process control and improvement. Often quality control has been limited to the final operation or process and thus limited to inspection following that final process step. The control of quality is then oriented toward the final product, rather than the processes producing the product. Even if defective product units are found and prevented from reaching the customer, the control is too late to prevent losses such as scrap, rework, or regrading. This final inspection is not perfect, and it may still allow nonconforming product to reach customers. This results in even further losses due to warranties, recalls, or product liability judgments.

Process control and improvement have traditionally concentrated on the production processes from raw materials to the final product. This includes postproduction processes such as packaging, storage, handling, shipping, and installation. As discussed in Chapter 2, emphasis is on moving from detection and correction to prevention. Process control and improvement are enhanced by a number of concepts. Among these are the triple role, the 5 Whys, self-control, and special versus common faults—simple tools for identifying problems and their solutions. Four of these are introduced next.

11-1.1 The Triple Role

To better understand processes, process control, and improvement, a useful concept is that of the *triple role.* All processes are simultaneously fulfilling three roles. They are supplier, processor, and customer, and every processor has suppliers and customers. Figure 11-1 illustrates this concept.

Every process receives inputs from suppliers, possibly the previous process step, and is therefore a customer. Each process sends outputs to customers, possibly the next process step, and is therefore a supplier. The inputs are coming from suppliers, the outputs are going to customers, and the process is making a transformation and adding value. As a processor, one should understand the supplier, know the customers' requirements, and plan the processes to meet their needs. There should be procedures for receiving feedback from customers and for providing them with product quality information. Monitoring, control, and improvement techniques should be applied that use all of the principles for process control and improvement.

What is significant about the triple role concept is that it is universal. The processor can be a business, a department, or an individual. The process can be the first step, any intermediate step, or the final step in a sequence of operations.

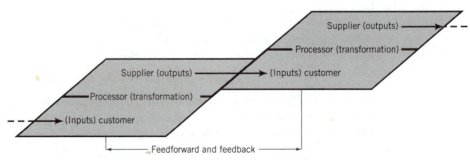

Figure 11-1   The Input/Output Triple-Role Model of Processes

The customer may be a business or an individual. It may be the next step in a sequence of operations. That is, it may be an external customer or an internal customer. The internal customer is the next step or process within an organization. This has significance in planning for customer satisfaction. If this is implemented correctly, faults that go beyond one process step should be prevented or at least minimized.

The supplier may also be a business or an individual. It also may be an external or an internal supplier. An internal supplier is the previous step or process within an organization.

The triple role is an important concept for planning and implementing process control and improvement. It helps to promote the concept of cross-trained operators who know previous and subsequent operations. It can be enhanced further by inviting external customers to address operators on the importance of quality features.

11-1.2 The 5 Whys

A useful technique to investigate quality and other problems in the pursuit of process control and improvement is that of the 5 Whys. The premise upon which this is based is that the real cause of a problem is seldom seen on first observation. The real root cause(s) of a quality problem is (are) often hidden beneath the initial occurrence of the problem. The problem may occur at a work location occupied by a particular operator. There is a tendency of management to blame that particular operator for the problem. The root cause(s) of the problem may be many operations before the location at which the problem first appears, and in a totally different functional area. The technique of the 5 Whys is to continue any investigation at least to the level of asking a minimum of five Whys. An example will help to illustrate this principle.

▶ EXAMPLE 11-1

In a garment factory, fabricating men's dress shirts, it was noticed that an excessive amount of rejects were being produced because of sewing errors. A question was asked: "Why are these rejects occurring?" The initial answer was that the seams were uneven, erratic, and with some bunching up of the thread stitches. A second question was asked: "Why are the seams uneven, erratic, and with some bunching up of stitches?" A quick answer by some supervisors was that the operators were careless, some being new and inexperienced. After further study, it was seen that the thread was breaking frequently during the sewing operations, causing multiple start-ups. A third question was then asked: "Why is the thread breaking?" This required further study of the process, including sampling and testing of the thread supplies for tensile strength. The study included a review of the sewing machine manuals for minimum recommended tension and tensile strength of the thread. A review of the thread specification was also conducted. These studies concluded that the thread in stock did not meet the recommended tensile strength of the sewing machine manufacturer. A fourth question was asked: "Why doesn't the thread meet the required tensile strength?" On investigation of the purchasing function, it was learned that the purchasing manager had found a supplier of less expensive thread. Hence, he placed an order with that supplier, bypassing the normal receiving inspection, because of a requirement for cost reduction.

The example could stop here at the fourth level of Whys, and corrective action could be taken. Following a comparison of this cost reduction with the extra costs of rejects, seconds, and lower productivity, an even further study could ask a fifth question: "Why would the purchasing manager be able to purchase off-specification thread?" A more thorough investigation revealed that top management was placing pressure on departments to cut costs because of a desire to achieve short-term profits.

This example reveals a phenomenon that is often present in such process studies. The deeper the investigation proceeds, the more Whys are asked, the more the finger points upward to management and away from individual operators. This is directly related to the matter of special (sporadic) causes versus common (chronic) causes of quality problems. Many quality problems are the fault of the system even though they may appear on the surface, in response to the first Why, to be related to particular operators.

11-1.3 Self-Control: Principles, Concepts, and Techniques

Juran and Gryna (1993) have developed a very useful set of criteria for assessing self-control. Creating a state of self-control on the part of every employee, from operators to management, is an important part of achieving control and improvement of quality. The criteria that every employee should have are as follows:

1. Knowledge of what they are supposed to do
2. Knowledge of what they are, in fact, doing
3. The means for regulating or adjusting the process back to standard when (2) above reveals that (1) is not being met
4. A state of mind so that they will actually use their facilities and skills to meet the standards established for the process

The significance of these criteria is that they can be used to establish control and to assess whether control has been established. Only management can provide the means for meeting these criteria. Hence, any failure to meet these criteria is a failure of management, and any faults when these criteria have not been met are beyond the control of the operators. The concept is related closely to the principles of special versus common causes discussed later in this section, as well as to the 5 Whys. In view of these criteria and an awareness of them by management, tendencies to pin blame on operators should be tempered by the state of self-control.

Management should ask the following questions related to self-control: Has a state of self-control been established at all operations? Is knowledge of what is supposed to be done communicated to all employees via training and documentation? Is knowledge of what is being done adequately measured, and is this being communicated to all employees? Has a means for regulating the process been established? Has a positive attitude been established by means of motivation, empowerment, and leadership?

11-1.4 Special versus Common Faults or Causes

Deming consistently included management among those requiring understanding, education, and fact-based decision making regarding the quality processes. This was based on a conviction that most quality problems that are encountered are faults of the system rather than faults of individual or groups of operators. He was convinced that if a problem is investigated deeply enough, it will reveal areas where the system is deficient. These are areas in which individual operators or groups of operators are helpless or powerless to take corrective actions.

Deming developed this concept by dividing causes of quality problems into two broad categories: *special causes* and *common causes*. Special causes relate to the failure of individuals to perform as required on a given job. They may be due to out-of-control variations in the process caused by inconsistencies in processes, machines, materials, methods, or procedures. His common causes relate to faults of the system, the design of the products or processes, the installation and instructions, or the specifications.

A second quality pioneer, Juran, addresses these same matters using the terms *sporadic* and *chronic*. That is, Deming's special causes are Juran's sporadic causes, and Deming's common causes are Juran's chronic causes. A quotation from Deming (1967) helps to explain this concept:

> *Confusion between common causes and special causes is one of the most serious mistakes of administration in industry, and in public administration as well. Unaided by statistical techniques, man's natural reaction to trouble of any kind, such as an accident, high rejection rate, stoppage of production (of shoes, for example, because of breakage of thread), is to blame a specific operator or machine. Anything bad that happens, it might seem, is somebody's fault, and it wouldn't have happened if he had done his job right.*

As process knowledge is developed by the analysis of process variation, statistical techniques help to identify whether action is required to (1) remove special cause variation and bring processes into control or (2) reduce unsatisfactory common cause variation, often by a process change. In either case reduced variation is a strategy that leads to improved quality and satisfied customers.

Included in these considerations is that statistical control of processes, however useful that is to eliminate assignable causes, may not result in a satisfactory situation. Control may be at the wrong average level, not on the desired target, or the controlled variation may be too large for good product performance and customer satisfaction. These conditions are indicative of common (chronic) causes that may call for a change of process, since a state of statistical control has already been reached with the present process.

Deming (1975) attached relative percentages to the occurrence of common and special causes. In the paper cited he uses the figures of 85% for common causes and 15% for special causes. Later Deming (1986) said,

> *I should estimate that in my experience most troubles and most possibilities for improvement add up to proportions something like this: 94% belong to the system (responsibility of management) 6% special.*

Management may ask the following questions related to special and common causes: Is the distinction between common and special causes understood? Is it understood that management is responsible for most of the problems that occur? Is it understood that statistical methods are useful to identify faults of the system as well as those of individual operators?

An example may help to illustrate the extent to which special and common causes merge into common causes.

▶ **EXAMPLE 11-2**

A group of thirty women are employed in the assembly area for mounting the filament to the base of a small special lamp. Data on the number and type of defects produced by each operator are analyzed. A few operators continue to produce significantly higher levels of defects. This indicates a special cause related to these specific operators. On further study of the problem it is learned that these operators lack visual acuity and require prescription eyeglasses. The question now arises whether this is their personal responsibility or that of management. The conclusion is that if these women were not employed outside the home, sight correction would be their personal responsibility. But because this represents a characteristic of the job, prescription eyeglasses are just another tool for job performance and a clear responsibility of management. This is not exactly a common cause in that it doesn't affect everyone alike, but it is a job-related requirement. Sight examinations and prescription eyeglasses were provided by management for these specific operators.

▶ 11-2 QUALITY (PROCESS) IMPROVEMENT

As presented in Chapter 2, the processes of quality may be divided into three major categories: planning for quality, control of quality, and improvement of quality. Much of Chapters 2, 3, and 4 are devoted to the first of these categories (planning) as it applies to achieving improvement and control. Chapters 5 through 9 present in some detail development of commonly used statistical techniques with only a minor coverage of applications. This chapter will present a discussion, with examples, of control and improvement.

To relate this to the earlier developments, consider the following situation: A process capability study on a plastic molding process revealed that the process can produce 99.7% good parts (a process capability index of 1.0 or greater), but it was producing 100% nonconforming parts because the wrong plastic was being used. Here the concept of a process capability study is introduced; however, the above example indicates that the benefits must be integrated with overall systems of planning and control.

Quality control should be considered to be more than a set of techniques. It is concerned with using these techniques to achieve improved quality, reduced costs, less waste, greater productivity, and customer acceptance. When a proper attitude has been communicated throughout the organization and quality planning is being accomplished, consideration of the latter two categories (quality improvement and quality control) at the process level will achieve positive results.

These two aspects of quality control are closely related and complementary. There is no rule concerning which should be applied first. This will vary with the process, product, or service. Applying these procedures to achieve control of quality may reveal places where improvement is needed and possible. Similarly, application of techniques to improve quality will often indicate where procedures are necessary.

11-2.1 Some Proven Steps in Quality Investigations

Six simple steps have proven useful in studies of manufacturing and service processes [Stephens (1965a, 1965b)]. A prerequisite for success in applying these steps is to develop a quality consciousness concerning product variation and defect prevention. Another requirement is management awareness of their responsibility for quality improvement. For each step there are related techniques, some as simple as recording and summarizing data, others involving control charts, and a few beyond the scope of this text.

1. Determine the magnitude of nonconformities, customer complaints, warranty claims, or other measures of undesirable process conditions. These may include off-target centering or variability too excessive for customer satisfaction.

Useful measures of these characteristics may be attribute data. Variables data on important quality characteristics showing central tendency and variability are also important. Another effective measure is cost. Experience has shown that many applications of SPC have begun with a critical study of troublesome characteristics of a finished product or service. An in-depth study of the process (upstream) is then performed to trace possible causes of a specific problem. This step has the purpose of identifying and quantifying problems. Techniques that are useful for this step are data sheets, checksheets, graphs, and data summary procedures. Both past data and new data may be used, but past data should be examined or verified for validity. New data collections should be planned carefully to detect correct information.

2. Stratify the data on the selected characteristics and processes by comparisons involving production paths such as the following:

    a. Different products or procedures
    b. Different shifts or teams of employees
    c. Different departments, machines, or individual operators
    d. Different time periods
    e. Different measurement instruments or analysis methods
    f. Different environmental conditions
    g. Different suppliers

This step emphasizes that for investigative purposes it is necessary to obtain as much detail as possible to locate causes of trouble to achieve improvement. The purpose of this step is to narrow the problem area and to locate possible causes. Steps 1 and 2 require good records. In the absence of these records, initial collection of the data often constitutes the beginning of an SPC study. Plotting of the data on control charts or other types of graphs is useful in making comparisons. Pareto analysis and geographical analysis with graphing are useful. If significant differences are observed between shifts, machines, or operators, easily rendered corrective and preventive action to eliminate these differences may be all that is necessary to improve the process. For some studies, the cause of the problem may be evident and a solution implemented after proceeding through only two or three steps.

3. Analyze the nonconforming units. In this physical examination consider the following:

    a. Are they actually nonconforming or defective?
    b. Can they be categorized according to severity?
    c. Is the same nonconformity present on most units?
    d. Are there many different nonconformities or defects? What is the frequency of occurrence of each?
    e. Can causes of nonconformities be determined?
    f. Can centering be adjusted?
    g. Can causes of excessive variability be identified and reduced?

This step involves an objective evaluation, more than just inspection. Production, engineering, design, and marketing personnel should analyze nonconformities jointly with inspection personnel. They should review inspection criteria, determine the most prevalent nonconformities, and assess their severity. Such an evaluation usually indicates causes that can then be investigated by additional data collection and analysis. This step also narrows the problem area and locates possible causes. Tools that are useful for this step involve test instruments and various aids for visual examination. Data summary procedures, such as Pareto analysis and other graphical displays are also useful. Lists of factors and possible causes or cause-and-effect (CE) diagrams may be developed for guiding further investigations.

4. Form ideas about the causes of the undesirable conditions under study. This step includes a knowledge of the process under study, both technically through engineering or scientific training and practically through shop experience. It has the express purpose of identifying possible causes of trouble and directing further study. Since it involves planning for further investigations, useful tools include checklists and CE diagrams. Brainstorming exercises among key personnel, quality circles, and quality teams have been used successfully.

5. Collect data for process capability studies under the following conditions:
   a. No process change: New or additional data on suspected variables are collected without making any process changes is an important initial step.
   b. Process change: A change is made to confirm or refute suspected areas of difficulty.

This step requires a careful analysis of critical variables identified in Steps 3 and 4. Where process capabilities, as seen by control charts, are not immediately attainable, experience has shown that continued use of control charts (even though the initial data may be out of control) can aid in attaining process improvement. Such studies have been called "performance studies," as distinguished from process capability studies. They often lead to the attainment of the process capability and the establishment of process controls. The purpose of this step is to investigate the possible causes of problems, to achieve process capability, and to establish process controls.

Useful tools include control charts, performance studies, process capability studies, special process control techniques, and sampling plans. When the interplay of several variables is suspected as the cause of difficulty, designed experiments are often needed to study their effect. See Chapters 12 and 13 for more details on these procedures.

6. On learning the causes of difficulties, take the necessary corrective action and institute controls to prevent future problems. The success of any quality improvement effort is dependent on the effective implementation of the corrective action and process controls. For example, if it is realized that $\bar{x}$ and R charts should be maintained on a machine to guide the operator in the grinding of a critical diameter, it may be difficult to convince the operator and the production supervisor of this necessity. Yet without their cooperation the control would be ineffective. If the problem is cheaper raw materials, action must be taken to improve or change suppliers. The purpose of this step is to achieve the improvement and prevent recurrences. The capability of the process may appear to be achieved by a state of statistical control on all control charts maintained on critical quality characteristics. However, there may still be a problem with excessive nonconformances, off-centered variable characteristics, or excessive variability. Further studies must then be conducted on the causes of these problems, essentially repeating Steps 2 to 5, with corrective and preventative actions of this sixth step. Useful tools for this step include good personnel relations, good organization, and effective management. Process control procedures are also useful to establish control for prevention of recurrences of difficulties.

11-2.2 Some Techniques, with Examples

There are a number of techniques that are useful in conducting investigations to achieve improvements. The following presentation of some of these techniques is integrated with examples and broadly follows the six steps outlined above. These examples help to illustrate the close relationships among the steps in that certain techniques are used for two or more steps simultaneously. Some departments within the organization may have already started a program of data collection and may have needed information.

Data Sheets and Checksheets: Initial Data Collection
Most organizations starting on a program of improvement and control of quality will design special data sheets for use in collecting information. These data sheets may vary from simple checksheets to sophisticated forms.

► **EXAMPLE 11-3**

A company manufacturing polyester continuous filament uses machines with four extrusion heads and take-up bobbins. During a shift's production ten filament specimens were selected from each position for a particular machine and tested for tensile strength. The results were recorded as tally marks on simple checksheets as shown in Table 11-1.

Shown on the checksheet is a line below 600 indicating the minimum desired tensile strength. The results of this simple check reveal troubles meeting this minimum specification on the three positions: A_2, B_1, and B_2. The study indicates the need to examine this characteristic more thoroughly to determine the factors contributing to low tensile strength and to devise process controls on a continuing basis.

A properly designed checksheet is an easy way to collect data, analyze it, and present the results. This is often enough to start the action required to solve a problem. A checksheet

TABLE 11-1   Checksheet of Tensile Strength Measurements

Tensile Strength (grams)	Positions A_1	A_2	B_1	B_2
640–649				
630–639	//			
620–629	ᵗᴴᴸ	/	//	
610–619	///	///	ᵗᴴᴸ/	///
600–609		///	/	ᵗᴴᴸ
590–599		//	/	//
580–589		/		

Circuit Board		Date	
Final Test		Location	
Test & Workmanship		Inspector	
Sample Size D		Lot No.	

Type	# of Nonconformities	
Functional Test	ЖЖ ЖЖ //	12
Soldering	ЖЖ ЖЖ ЖЖ ЖЖ ЖЖ ЖЖ ЖЖ ЖЖ /	41
Plating	///	3
Others	ЖЖ ///	8
TOTAL		64

Figure 11-2　A Tallysheet

can be a simple tally, as in Table 11-1 or Figure 11-2, in which the occurrences of different nonconformities are checked. This type of checksheet is often part of a control chart that gives a quick picture of the process control and the kinds of problems occurring.

Location Plots: Geographical Analysis

▶ **EXAMPLE 11-4**

Another simple checksheet is the location plot. In Figure 11-3 the checksheet was used to plot solder defects on a circuit pack. On this circuit pack, over 100 components were inserted and mass-soldered by a wave soldering process. The location of each solder defect was plotted by an ×, ○, or △ on the picture where the defect occurred. An unusual pattern was soon observed: The defects seemed to be clustered on the left and right sides. They appeared to be where one would hold the board. An investigation indicated that the defects occurred exactly where the operator cleaning the boards was holding them. The operator's hands were keeping the boards from being thoroughly cleaned after soldering, which caused test set failures later in the process.

▶ **EXAMPLE 11-5**

Another location plot on a circuit pack revealed quite a different problem. Figure 11-4 shows that over 70% of the soldering defects occur in one region of the circuit pack. By overlaying this plot on a schematic of the circuit pack (Figure 11-5), it was observed immediately that one of the hybrid integrated circuits was oriented 90° out of phase with the others. This is an actual example from AT&T Bell Laboratories that showed a simple design error causing almost three fourths of the soldering problems.

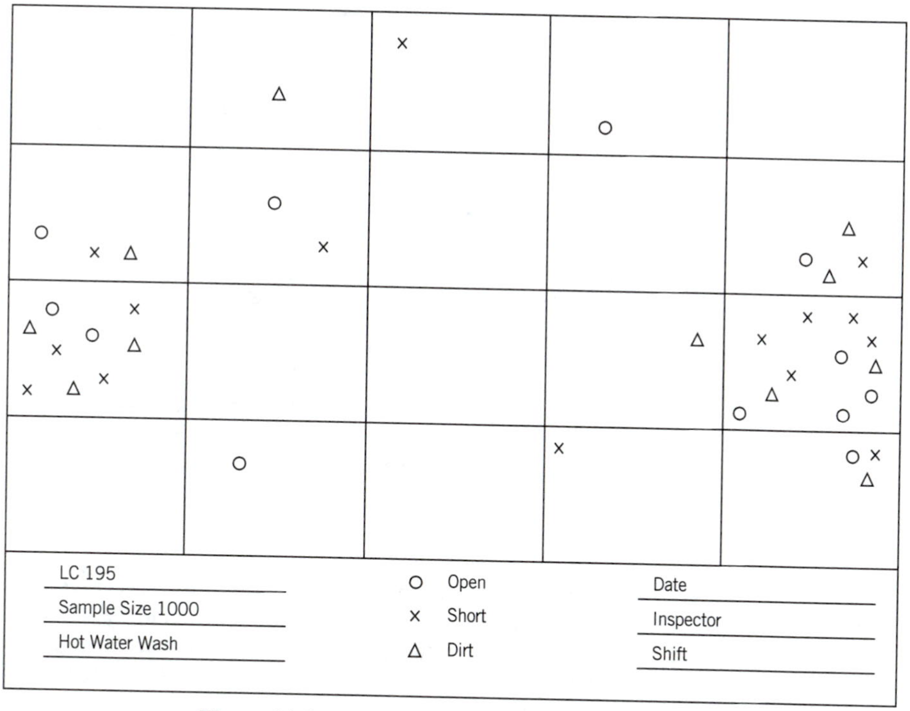

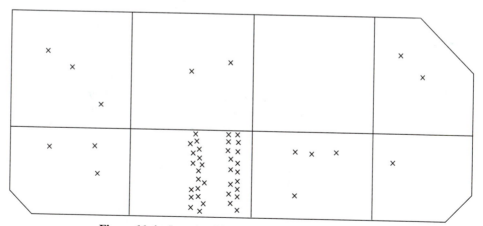

Figure 11-3 Location Plot Showing Solder Defects

LC 195

Sample Size 1000

Hot Water Wash

○ Open

× Short

△ Dirt

Date

Inspector

Shift

Figure 11-4 Location Plot of Clustering of Solder Defects

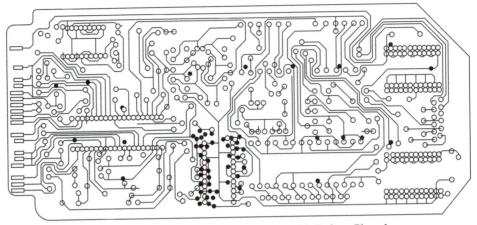

Figure 11-5   Schematic of Circuit Pack With Defects Plotted

▶ EXAMPLE 11-6

A very interesting example of the power of location plots occurred during the Second World War. Analysts were trying to discover the weaknesses in airplanes. Why did some crash when hit and others still return even though full of holes? The breakthrough occurred when someone suggested plotting all the holes on a location plot (Figure 11-6). The crucial information was in the locations where there were no holes in planes that returned safely. Because it was reasonable to expect that the holes would be uniformly distributed, the places on the plots without holes would be the critical places. Planes that were hit there were the ones that did not return. These places were examined, critical controls were duplicated or rerouted, and extra armor plating was strategically placed. The vulnerability of the planes was reduced substantially.

▶ EXAMPLE 11-7

In a factory manufacturing protective gloves for use with aggressive chemicals, a problem encountered was perforation of the gloves. This was a major defect for these gloves, and an investigation was planned. To obtain information about the source of the trouble, samples were inspected for perforation. A special form was designed for recording results consisting of a drawing of the glove on which the location of any perforation could be marked. This is shown in Figure 11-7.

   An analysis of these forms for several days, by mold number and operators, found that more than 80% of the perforations were concentrated at one single location of one mold. Inspection of the mold showed that it contained a sharp edge, caused by the stamping of the brand-mark on the mold. Removal of the sharp edge virtually eliminated this defect. The uneven distribution of the defects by location and mold constitutes the Pareto principle together with geographical analysis. The study, carried through to Step 3, led to a very obvious cause (Step 4) and correction (Step 6) for solution of the problem. More in-depth studies may then be necessary to reduce the remaining percentage of perforations and other nonconformities.

▶ EXAMPLE 11-8

A manufacturer of plate glass by the method of vertical drawing from a molten interface maintains daily records on the overall yield of plate glass panels produced relative to total glass drawn (Step 1). Day-by-day fluctuations and monthly levels of yield are unsatisfactory. A control chart (x) for one

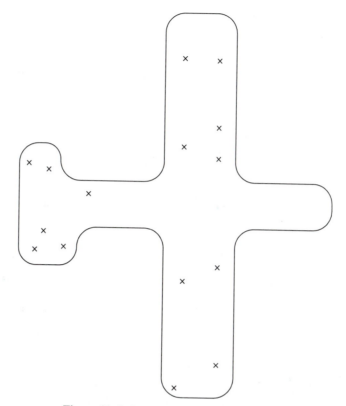

Figure 11-6 Location Plot of Airplane Holes

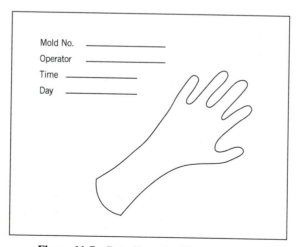

Mold No. _____
Operator _____
Time _____
Day _____

Figure 11-7 Data Sheet for Glove Inspection

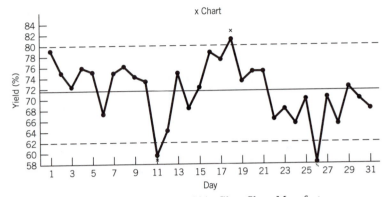

Figure 11-8 *x* Chart on Yield in Glass Sheet Manufacture

month's production is shown in Figure 11-8. An average yield of 71.3% is seen with excessive out-of-control variations. This is related to a maximum possible yield of 84%, since 16% of glass drawn serves as vertical edges for drawing purpose and is reprocessed as cullet. Improvement in this average is desired. Following Step 2, the company decided to prepare charts separately for each of eight machines, three shifts, and five thicknesses, ranging from 3 to 7 mm. They also established quality teams, consisting of the furnace-level and upper-level supervisors and production and engineering managers, to follow the study and take necessary corrective action.

Yield data, as shown in the previous example, is often recorded on a data sheet similar to that shown in Figure 11-9. This form is also useful for recording the results of sampling plans as developed in Chapters 15 through 17.

▶ **EXAMPLE 11-9**

Quality improvement studies conducted with a small manufacturer of gumboots identified the occurrence of nonconformities at the grading section of finished boots as an important area of data summary and analysis. A simple data sheet was devised to allow identification of nonconformities by type, shift, size of boot, and press number. An overall summary of data for 11 days revealed the results shown in Table 11-2.

Following Step 2 of the preceding section, these data were broken down by day, size, and press to assist in the identification of causes of nonconformities. The data by day for press number 5 with size changes are shown in Table 11-3.

Similar data breakdown for other presses and sizes by press revealed the principal nonconformities for each press size. Some time-related factors were evident—for example, the LF and HOC variation on press 5 for size 8L in Table 11-3. Isolated occurrences of certain nonconformities for specific sizes resulted in direct improvements. Because of the frequent occurrence of the foxing nonconformance (LF and UF), a change in molding was introduced. The two-part design—vamp and upper pieces—was changed to a three-part design—vamp, upper back, and upper front pieces—to reduce trapping of air in the mold, which leads to foxing.

▶ **EXAMPLE 11-10**

An effective type of checksheet for scanning multiple types of problems is shown in Figure 11-10. In this checksheet the workers have been divided by position and by machine. The data have been

| | Part no.
Product
Sampling plan
L. D. no. | | | | | | List of Characters | | | | | | | | | | | | | | | |
|---|---|---|---|---|---|---|---|---|---|---|---|---|---|---|---|---|---|---|---|---|---|---|
| | Code or lot no. | Date and/or time inspected | Lot size | Sample size | | | | | | | | | | | | | Total nonconformities or nonconformance | % Nonconformance | Initials | Remark no. | Disposition of lot |
| 1 | | | | | | | | | | | | | | | | | | | | | |
| 2 | | | | | | | | | | | | | | | | | | | | | |
| 3 | | | | | | | | | | | | | | | | | | | | | |
| 4 | | | | | | | | | | | | | | | | | | | | | |
| 5 | | | | | | | | | | | | | | | | | | | | | |
| 6 | | | | | | | | | | | | | | | | | | | | | |
| 7 | | | | | | | | | | | | | | | | | | | | | |
| 8 | | | | | | | | | | | | | | | | | | | | | |
| 9 | | | | | | | | | | | | | | | | | | | | | |
| 10 | | | | | | | | | | | | | | | | | | | | | |
| 11 | | | | | | | | | | | | | | | | | | | | | |
| 12 | | | | | | | | | | | | | | | | | | | | | |
| 13 | | | | | | | | | | | | | | | | | | | | | |
| 14 | | | | | | | | | | | | | | | | | | | | | |
| 15 | | | | | | | | | | | | | | | | | | | | | |
| 16 | | | | | | | | | | | | | | | | | | | | | |
| 17 | | | | | | | | | | | | | | | | | | | | | |
| 18 | | | | | | | | | | | | | | | | | | | | | |
| 19 | | | | | | | | | | | | | | | | | | | | | |
| 20 | | | | | | | | | | | | | | | | | | | | | |
| 21 | | | | | | | | | | | | | | | | | | | | | |
| 22 | | | | | | | | | | | | | | | | | | | | | |
| 23 | | | | | | | | | | | | | | | | | | | | | |
| 24 | | | | | | | | | | | | | | | | | | | | | |
| 25 | | | | | | | | | | | | | | | | | | | | | |
| 26 | | | | | | | | | | | | | | | | | | | | | |
| 27 | | | | | | | | | | | | | | | | | | | | | |
| 28 | | | | | | | | | | | | | | | | | | | | | |
| 29 | | | | | | | | | | | | | | | | | | | | | |
| 30 | | | | | | | | | | | | | | | | | | | | | |
| 31 | | | | | | | | | | | | | | | | | | | | | |
| 32 | | | | | | | | | | | | | | | | | | | | | |
| 33 | | | | | | | | | | | | | | | | | | | | | |
| 34 | | | | | | | | | | | | | | | | | | | | | |
| 35 | | | | | | | | | | | | | | | | | | | | | |
| 36 | | | | | | | | | | | | | | | | | | | | | |
| 37 | | | | | | | | | | | | | | | | | | | | | |
| 38 | | | | | | | | | | | | | | | | | | | | | |
| 39 | | | | | | | | | | | | | | | | | | | | | |
| 40 | | | | | | | | | | | | | | | | | | | | | |
| 41 | | | | | | | | | | | | | | | | | | | | | |
| 42 | | | | | | | | | | | | | | | | | | | | | |
| 43 | | | | | | | | | | | | | | | | | | | | | |
| 44 | | | | | | | | | | | | | | | | | | | | | |
| 45 | | | | | | | | | | | | | | | | | | | | | |
| 46 | | | | | | | | | | | | | | | | | | | | | |
| 47 | | | | | | | | | | | | | | | | | | | | | |
| 48 | | | | | | | | | | | | | | | | | | | | | |
| 49 | | | | | | | | | | | | | | | | | | | | | |
| 50 | | | | | | | | | | | | | | | | | | | | | |
| 51 | | | | | | | | | | | | | | | | | | | | | |
| 52 | | | | | | | | | | | | | | | | | | | | | |
| 53 | | | | | | | | | | | | | | | | | | | | | |

Figure 11-9 Data Sheet for Inspection Results

TABLE 11-2 Overall Summary of Gumboot Production and Nonconformities

Boots Produced	Boot Classification				Nonconformities											
	I	II	M	R	LF	UF	UP	HOC	SNC	LLO	LP	SOC	HNC	LS	LB	Total
4420	4156	169	58	37	82	62	46	39	23	19	16	14	9	3	2	315
	94.03%	3.82%	1.31%	0.84%	0.26	0.20	0.15	0.12	0.07	0.06	0.05	0.04	0.03	0.01	0.006	

Abbreviations: I—First Grade, II—Second Grade, M—Miniboot (with cut-off top), R—Rejected boot, LF—Lower Foxing, UF—Upper Foxing, UP—Upper Pinching, HOC—Heel Overcured, SNC—Sole Not Cured, LLO—Lining Latex Out, LP—Lower Pinching, SOC—Sole Overcured, HNC—Heel Not Cured, LS—Lining Short, LB—Lining Black.

TABLE 11-3 Gumboot Data by Day (Time) for Press No. 5

Date	Press No.	Size	Boots Produced	Classification				Nonconformities											
				I[a]	II	M	R	LF	UF	UP	HOC	SNC	LLO	LP	SOC	HNC	LS	LB	Total
08-24	5	8L	62	58	2	1	1	3	1	1	—	—	—	—	—	—	1	—	6
08-25	5	8L	56	55	0	1	0	—	—	1	—	—	—	—	—	—	—	—	1
08-26	5	8L	46	44	0	1	1	1	—	1	—	—	1	—	—	—	—	—	3
08-27	5	8L	67	65	1	0	0	1	—	1	—	—	—	—	1	—	1	—	4
08-28	5	8L	44	42	2	0	0	2	—	—	—	—	—	—	—	—	—	—	2
08-31	5	8L	72	68	4	0	0	1	—	1	—	2	—	—	—	2	1	—	7
09-01	5	9L	59	56	0	1	2	—	—	1	—	—	2	1	—	—	—	—	4
09-02	5	9L	66	64	2	0	0	2	—	—	—	—	—	—	—	—	—	—	2
09-04	5	9L	72	72	0	0	0	—	—	—	—	—	—	—	—	—	—	—	0
09-09	5	8L	70	59	11	0	0	6	1	—	3	—	—	—	—	1	—	—	11
09-10A	5	8L	72	61	10	0	1	3	1	—	5	—	—	—	2	—	—	—	11
09-10B	5	8L	44	41	3	0	0	1	—	—	2	—	—	—	—	—	—	—	3
			730	685	35	5	5	20	3	6	10	2	3	1	3	3	3	0	54
				93.8%	4.8%	0.7%	0.7%	0.37	0.06	0.11	0.19	0.04	0.06	0.02	0.06	0.06	0.06	—	—

[a]See Table 11-2 for list of abbreviations.

Equipment	Worker	Mon AM	Mon PM	Tues AM	Tues PM	Wed AM	Wed PM	Thur AM	Thur PM	Fri AM	Fri PM	Sat AM	Sat PM	Sun AM	Sun PM
Machine 1	A	△ △	~ △	△			△				△~ △ △	△		~ △	○
	B	△ ~ ~	~	△		△					△ ~	~ ○○	○○ ~× △△	× ×	△ × ○
Machine 2	C	△ ~ ○										△			
	D	△ ~					△								
Machine 3	E					×					~				
	F	~ ×	△ ○	△ ○ ○	○ × ×	○	○	○	× ○ ~	× ×	×○ O~ △△	×		○	
Machine 4	G	~			~				△		×				
	H	○ ~							~				△		
Totals		15	6	5	2	4	2	1	5	2	14	7	7	5	4

~ Scratch △ Dig
○ Hole × Shape

Figure 11-10 Multiple Case Checksheet

split by day of week and time of day and plotted using symbols to indicate the type of nonconformance. One can quickly see that some problems appear to be clustered on Monday morning, others on Friday afternoons. One worker appears not to be well trained. The number of nonconformities associated with this worker's position are quite high. Machine 1 appears to need adjusting, recalibrating, or maybe even rebuilding. It is producing far more nonconformities than the others. It is obvious that proper training has not been provided to the workers on the weekend shifts.

Looking at the data by type of nonconformity, it is readily discovered that there are too many digs and scratches. This may indicate poor handling procedures or rough surfaces in the machine or feeding conveyors. It may also be seen that the first place to look would be at Machine 1.

Histograms

A histogram is a very direct way of showing frequencies of occurrences or counts. The basic principles for constructing a histogram were discussed in Chapter 5. A number of intervals or bins are selected, the width of each bin is specified, the data are sorted, and the number lying within each bin is determined and then plotted either by raw count or by percentage.

In Figure 11-11, a simple histogram illustrates resistances of fifty wires in a telephone cable. Histograms are very useful for determining the distribution of the data. In Figure 11-11

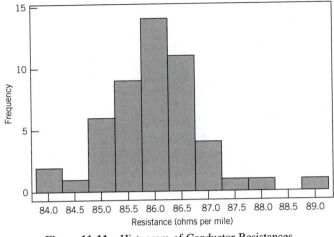

Figure 11-11 Histogram of Conductor Resistances

it may be seen immediately that the data have one mode, the mean and median are 86 ohms per mile, and the data appear to be symmetrically distributed. The variation of the data is also apparent.

Some simple rules can help to construct useful histograms. The intervals should have reasonable breakpoints, either whole numbers or common fractions. The intervals should be of equal width. There should be enough intervals to show the distribution's shape but not to create excessive "jumpiness." Ishikawa (1976) suggested a simple table, shown in Table 11-4, that appears to work well in practice. Another method for determining the number of intervals to use for 500 or fewer observations is to take the square root of the number of observations and round upwards or downwards. For example, for fifty observations, use seven intervals; for 100 observations, use ten intervals.

Diaconis and Freedman (1981) give a more complete treatment of selecting the number of bins and constructing the histogram in their discussion on using histograms to estimate probability density functions. Whenever available, a statistical software package should be used to obtain the results and information as quickly as possible. For example, the histogram of Figure 11-11 was prepared directly from the raw data by means of the MINITAB[1] software package.

[1]Information on MINITAB is available from MINITAB, Inc., 3081 Enterprise Drive, State College, PA 16801-3008; phone: 814-238-3280; fax 814-238-4383; email: sales@minitab.com; Internet: www.minitab.com.

TABLE 11-4   Estimation of Number of Histogram Bins

Number of Observations	Number of Bins
Under 50	5–7
50–100	6–10
100–250	7–12
Over 250	10–20

Source: Based on Ishikawa, K. (1976), *Guide to Quality Control,* Asia Productivity Organization, Tokyo, p. 9.

By designing a checksheet carefully, the data can be collected and a histogram constructed in one step. An example from Ishikawa (1976) illustrates this point (shown in Figure 11-12). In this figure, the bins are determined before the study starts, the specification lines are drawn on the chart, and the data are recorded as collected by making tally marks in the correct bins. The shape of the distribution is apparent, the observations falling below the lower specification limit or above the upper limit are obvious, and the center of the distribution can be noted. It is then easy to decide whether the mean should be shifted, the variability reduced, or both, to eliminate the observations outside the specification limits.

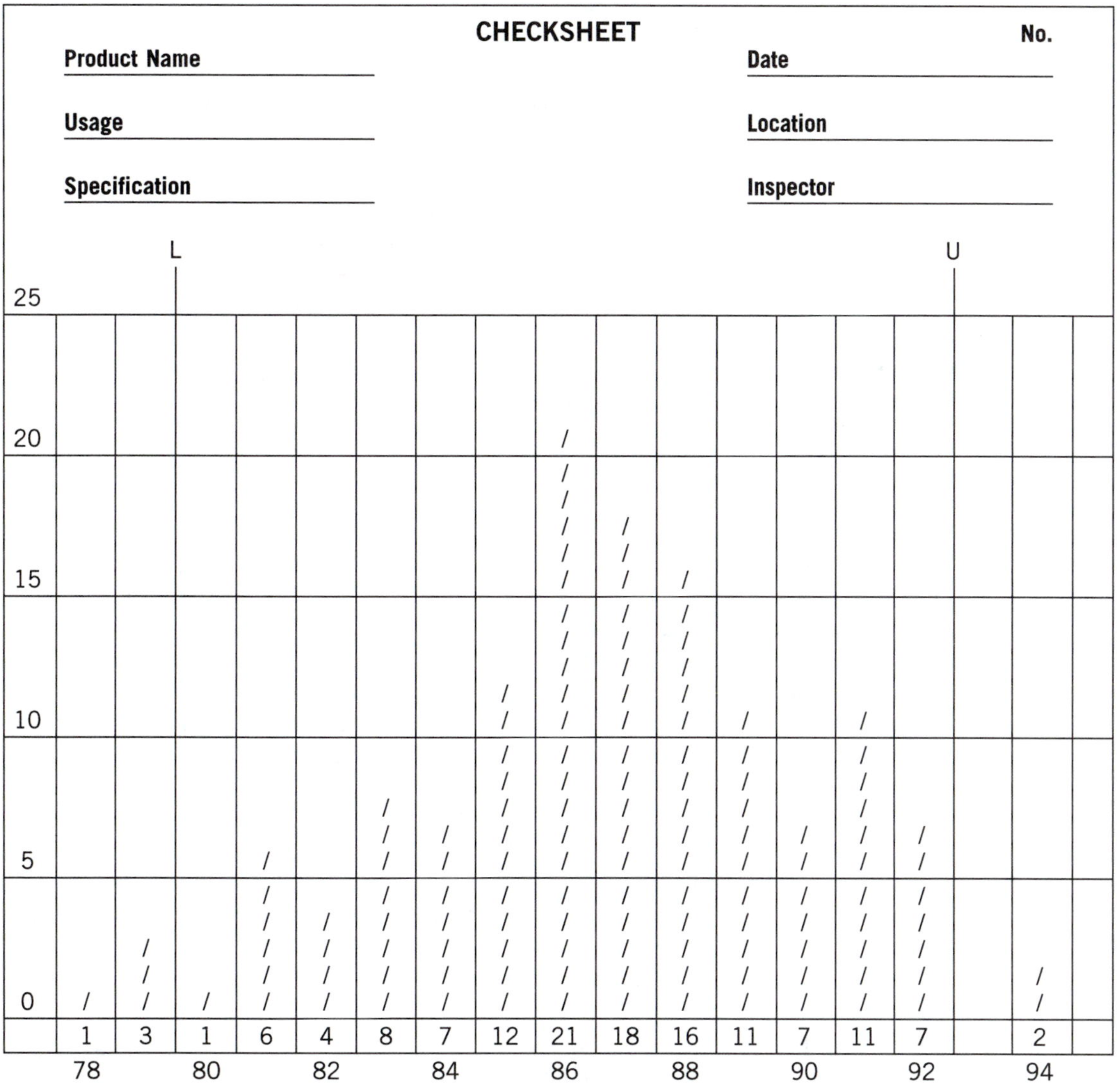

CHECKSHEET   No.

Product Name   Date

Usage   Location

Specification   Inspector

Count	1	3	1	6	4	8	7	12	21	18	16	11	7	11	7		2	
Value	78		80		82		84		86		88		90		92		94	

Figure 11-12   Tally Marks as a Histogram

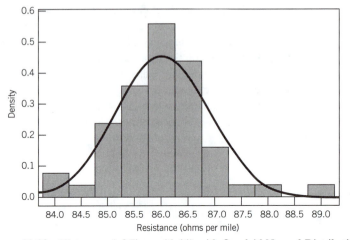

Figure 11-13   Histogram (of Figure 11-11) with Overlaid Normal Distribution

In his book *Quality, Productivity and Competitive Position,* Deming (1982) gives an excellent example of the use of the histogram. A histogram of the distribution of measurements on the diameters of 500 steel rods shows a gap to the left of the lower specification. Measurements have piled up just inside the specification. The data are obviously distorted.

In another example Deming (1982) shows how histograms can be misused. A computer was being utilized to measure copper ingots, and all the data were plotted as a histogram. The histogram's function was "to show the operator how he is doing." Actually, the operator was adjusting the machine up or down after every ingot and widening the variance. A control chart would enable the operator to avoid adjusting the machine except when there was a statistical signal of a special cause.

When using the histogram to check for the shape of the distribution, it may be difficult to see whether the data appear to come from a particular assumed distribution. It helps if the assumed distribution is drawn over the histogram. In Figure 11-13 a normal distribution is superimposed over the histogram of Figure 11-11. Visually, the fit is reasonable.

Other analyses can be conducted to determine whether it is reasonable to assume a given distribution function as the underlying process distribution that generated a sample of the data. This may involve hypothesis testing for distributional form. A graphical test that can be done fairly readily with the use of a statistical software package such as MINITAB, mentioned earlier, is that of probability plotting. A normal probability plot of the data of Figure 11-11 is shown in Figure 11-14. It shows that the majority of the data fall very closely around a straight line that is expected if the data follow the normal distribution. The greatest deviation from the straight line is the largest value of the sample data.

Before leaving the discussion of histograms, another useful type of histogram suggested by John Tukey (1972) is introduced: the stem-and-leaf plot. As Tukey states (1972, p. 296), "If we are going to make a mark, it may as well be a meaningful one. The simplest and most useful meaningful mark is a digit." To construct a stem-and-leaf

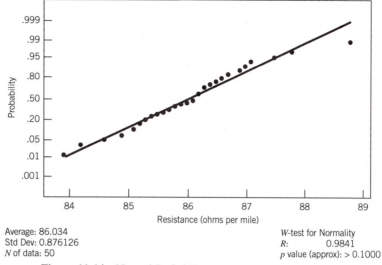

Average: 86.034
Std Dev: 0.876126
N of data: 50

W-test for Normality
R: 0.9841
p value (approx): > 0.1000

Figure 11-14   Normal Probability Plot of Data of Figure 11-11

plot simply use the numbers themselves and designate the bin (the stem) by the first part of the number (one or more digits) and the plotted point is the remaining digit (the leaf).

By replotting Figure 11-11 as a stem-and-leaf plot (shown in Table 11-5), it can be seen that the information about the shape of the distribution can be preserved, but the individual values of the original observations are kept.

As can be seen from Table 11-5, the smallest value in the data set from which the histogram of Figure 11-11 was prepared, is 83.9. Next larger values are 84.2, 84.6, and 84.9. The largest value in the data set is 88.8. These values can be seen readily in the stem-and-leaf plot of Table 11-5.

Pareto Principle, Diagram, and Analysis

The Pareto principle was espoused by Juran many years ago to urge managers to focus on "the critical few rather than the trivial many." In his book *Managerial Breakthrough* (1964), Juran gives many examples in which relatively few defect types account for most of the total defects, a few sales accounts result in 80% of the orders, and a small number of problems account for most of the money lost.

TABLE 11-5   Stem-and-Leaf Plot of Data of Figure 11-11

Cell Count	Stem	Leaf
1	83	9
3	84	269
17	85	11122334456777889
23	86	01112222222333455567779
5	87	00158
1	88	8

Pareto analysis is a tool for data summary and evaluation for assisting the identification of the principal causes of problems. The Pareto principle occurs with striking regularity in industrial and commercial processes. Briefly, this principle states that when many items in a system are subject to variation, a few of the items will vary more than the others. Applied to the quality arena, this principle is often expressed by the uneven distribution of the occurrences of nonconformities for a given product or service.

Data collected that isolate the nonconforming characteristics that occur more frequently enable one to identify those that require the most attention to achieve the greatest benefit. For example, the principle implies that a relatively large percentage (such as 80% or 90%) of process difficulties are caused by a relatively small percentage (such as 10% or 20%) of the related factors. Application of this principle helps to identify the important few from the trivial many in process investigations.

This principle should not be construed to apply only to bad factors. For example, a producer of an elite line of products or a provider of an elite service may want to identify and locate the few members of the society who are wealthy enough to be interested. In inventory analysis a distribution of the items by value, mass, or size may isolate the relatively few items deserving special attention.

▶ **EXAMPLE 11-11**

From Table 11-2 observe that the Pareto principle applies to the occurrence of nonconformities on gumboots. The nonconformities are listed in decreasing order of occurrence in the table. A graphical summary of these occurrences is possible in a Pareto diagram. The gumboot data are shown in Figure 11-15. The graph has several notable features. The frequency of the nonconformities is shown on the left-hand ordinate scale as a proportion. The frequency for each nonconformity is depicted

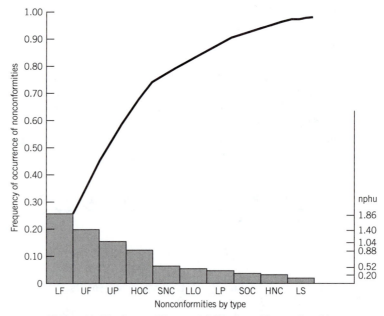

Figure 11-15 Pareto Diagram of Gumboot Nonconformities

as a rectangular bar whose height reflects the numerical proportion. It is computed as the ratio of the number of nonconformities of the specific type and the total nonconformities (e.g., for LF it is 82/315). The type of the nonconformity is labeled below the bar. A cumulative frequency of occurrence is shown by points and a connecting line. This enables the observation of the cumulative effect of as many of the nonconformities as desired. For example, approximately 60% of the total nonconformities result from the three (30%) highest-occurring characteristics. Because the first two of these, LF and UF, represent the same type of nonconformity (foxing) at different locations (lower and upper), it is apparent that action to eliminate this nonconformity will be beneficial. (See the discussion in Example 11-9).

A further feature of Figure 11-15 is the ordinate scale on the right side. This is often considered optional but may be useful to observe the magnitude of the nonconformities relative to overall production. The scale of nonconformities per hundred units (nphu) is computed as 100 times the ratio of the number of nonconformities of the specific type and the total number of units produced (e.g., for LF it is 82/4420 times 100).

It would be possible to apply the same type of analysis to the data of Table 11-3 for Press No. 5 and to the other presses and sizes. As observed in Table 11-3, the frequency of occurrence of the nonconformities does not follow the same order as for the overall results.

▶ **EXAMPLE 11-12**

A breakdown by cause of rejections of truck cylinder blocks at the foundry showed the following ordered list of characteristics with percent of occurrence: (1) Blow hole, 37.8%, (2) Sandwash, 30.2%, (3) Misrun, 9.4%, (4) Lap, 5.7%, (5) Scab, 3.7%, (6) Slag, 1.9%, (7) Core Broken, 1.9%, (8) Crack, 1.9%, (9) Miscellaneous, 7.5%. These data in Pareto diagram form are shown in Figure 11-16.

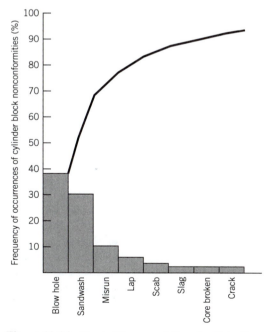

Figure 11-16 Pareto Diagram of Foundry Rejections

The analysis directs attention to the search for causes of blow holes and sandwash nonconformities to achieve process and product improvement.

▶ **EXAMPLE 11-13**

The Pareto diagram in Figure 11-17 shows the causes of circuit pack failures. The component failures are almost half of the total failures. Only three failure modes account for over 80% of the problems.

More information can be added to the plot by breaking down the data by week in this example. The data were collected during a one-month quality improvement study to determine whether the same types of problems were occurring each week. In Figure 11-18 the bars were segmented to show the number of nonconformities of each type by week produced. In this study, the numbers of nonconformities in each week by type of nonconformity were consistent across the four weeks of the study.

Before-and-After Studies. A common use of Pareto diagrams is to organize data to help focus action on the primary causes of the problems. After the quality improvement action has been taken, the same type of data should be collected again and the results compared to previous data. Pareto diagrams are usually plotted as in Figure 11-18 with the scale in percent of total nonconformities. If the before-and-after diagrams are plotted side by side on the same scale (Figure 11-19), it will only evoke the response "So what is the big deal? All that has been done was to change the types of nonconformities. Nothing has been improved." The truth may be that the total number of nonconformities has been cut in half. A better way of showing this comparison is to plot total numbers of nonconformities rather than percentages or to take percentages of the original numbers of nonconformities. The same results shown in Figure 11-19 are replotted in Figure 11-20. Now the dramatic improvement is evident.

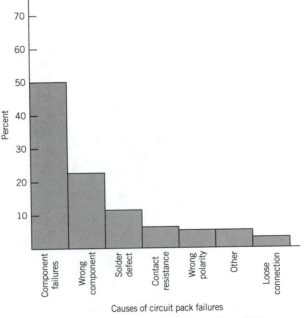

Figure 11-17 Pareto Diagram of Circuit Pack Failures

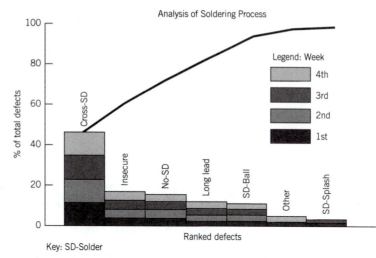

Figure 11-18 Pareto Diagram with Segmented Bars

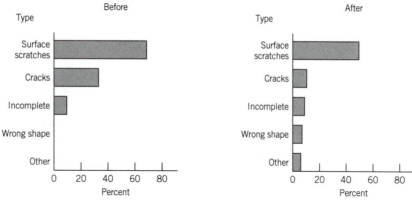

Figure 11-19 Pareto Diagrams Side by Side for Comparisons

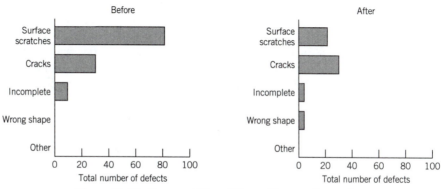

Figure 11-20 Improved Plot of Pareto Diagram Comparison

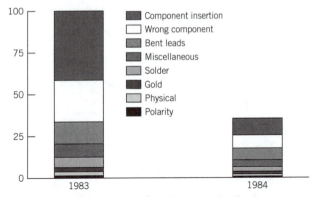

Figure 11-21   Segmented Bars to Compare Quality Improvement

Another way that is even more effective in many cases is to use segmented bar plots in place of the entire Pareto diagram. In Figure 11-21 the two Pareto diagrams have been replaced with single bars to compare 1983 and 1984 results on circuit pack failures. Within a bar, differently coded blocks indicate the types of nonconformities. This plot is based on actual data and the result of a quality improvement program in a manufacturing plant. The plot shows an interesting phenomenon. Although the quality improvement program manager used a Pareto diagram to identify the primary type of nonconformity and all directed efforts were focused on the causes of that type, a remarkable improvement was seen in many of the types. The explanation for this phenomenon appears to be the Hawthorne Effect. This phenomenon was first recorded in the 1920s during industrial engineering experiments at the Western Electric Hawthorne works that showed that workers performed better when they received attention. In the circuit pack quality improvement program, the mere existence of the study and the importance management placed on determining and eliminating causes of nonconformities, created a team spirit in which each worker in the process helped to identify and eliminate other problems.

The Pareto Pyramid.   Even with the segmented bars placed side by side, it is often difficult to compare numbers of nonconformities by type. A combination of the demographic population pyramid and the Pareto diagram has been found to be very effective for comparisons. By laying the Pareto diagrams on their sides and keeping the labeling of types of nonconformities consistent, a direct comparison that is easy to understand may be achieved. In Figure 11-22 data from before and after studies are compared by using a Pareto pyramid. It is seen that the major types of nonconformities have been reduced significantly, but now there are two new types that were not seen before.

Cause-and-Effect (CE) or Ishikawa Diagrams
Another of the useful techniques for process investigation is the orderly listing and consideration of factors that may have a direct bearing on the problem. A way of presenting this list of factors and subfactors is by way of cause-and-effect (CE) diagrams. Such diagrams formalize the simple listing of expected causes used earlier than the development

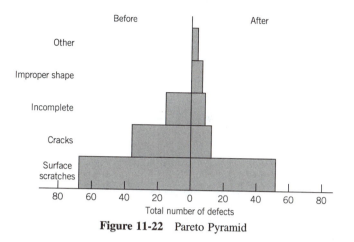

Figure 11-22   Pareto Pyramid

of CE diagrams by Ishikawa. They also focus attention, in a more methodical way, on the factors and subfactors that may warrant further study as the investigation proceeds.

The CE diagram is sometimes called the Ishikawa diagram. It is also called the fishbone diagram because of its appearance. It is called the cause-and-effect diagram because of its use. By any name, it is an effective graphical method. Ishikawa (1976) described three basic uses of the CE diagram:

- Dispersion analysis
- Production process classification
- Cause enumeration

In fact, people working in the areas of quality control and quality assurance are applying it to a far wider set of problems. One of the best applications is a structured brainstorming session. The CE diagram is effective to collect and order the ideas generated in a session where people are trying to list the possible causes of dropouts, rework, scrap, or excessive variation. Quality circles and quality improvement teams have found them very useful.

Construction of the Cause-and-Effect Diagram

Construction is simple. First, the variable to be studied is selected. In Figure 11-23 circuit pack yield is selected as the target for a troublesome manufacturing process. In this process, yield is defined as the percentage of circuit packs that go through the production process with no adjustments, rework, or component replacements. From the middle baseline pointing to the yield figure, main spines are constructed for each major cause of yield problems. In this example soldering, machine insertion, hand insertion, and electrical test are the main groups. Within major groupings, the subgroups of problem areas are identified and plotted as small horizontal spines.

In Figure 11-23, the percent yield at each of the primary processes and subprocesses has been indicated on the spines. Although this is a simple example, it is easy to see where the problems are and where efforts should be focused.

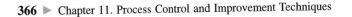

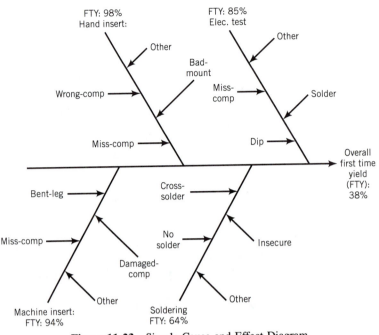

Figure 11-23   Simple Cause-and-Effect Diagram

How to Use the Cause-and-Effect Diagrams

The application of cause-and-effect diagrams is very wide. In Figure 11-24 a cause-and-effect diagram is used to outline a household budget. This use led to a better understanding of expenses, especially of energy-use–related expenses, and where improvements would be most cost effective.

The *QC Handbook* prepared by Komatsu Ltd. has an excellent discussion on how to prepare a cause-and-effect diagram. They list the following four basic steps (pp. 20–21):

1. Clarify the object effect.
   - A numerical measure should be used for the effect to determine the degree of improvement after actions are taken.

2. Pick causes.
   - Gather related people for a brainstorming session to choose causes that influence the effect.
   - Observe the actual effect with its environment.
   - Use a large blackboard or write on a big sheet of white paper with a marking pen to prevent missing possible causes.
   - Direct causes of the effect should be drawn as branches, and direct causes of branches as subbranches. Use arrows to show the cause-and-result relationships.
   - Because cause-and-result relationships are complicated, always ask whether each cause position is proper while writing the CE diagram. The end cause must be

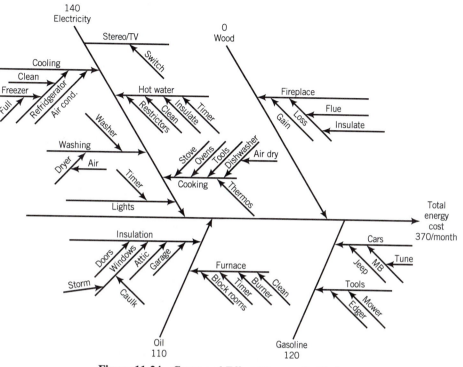

Figure 11-24 Cause-and-Effect Diagram for Budget

represented definitely to facilitate later actions. Use numerical values as much as possible.

- If the diagram becomes too complicated, review the effect (problem) that was initially selected. If necessary, the diagram may be divided by causes into several diagrams.

3. Determine the priority causes.

- To determine priority causes out of many, ranking based on a Pareto diagram and actual past data is desirable. If this method is impractical, select several causes that the team regards as important, determine the ranking of their influence on the effect by voting, and enter the ranking in the diagram.

4. Work out the counteractions for priority causes.

- Take advice from many people and exercise your ingenuity.

The example from Komatsu Ltd. is also excellent. It has been reproduced as Figure 11-25. The example shows a CE diagram used to study the problem of trying to obtain good copies from a copy machine.

The following is an example of an early recorded study using the steps outlined in the first part of this chapter, including the simple list of factors like a "shopping list" for seeking a solution. It is from Schin (1960).

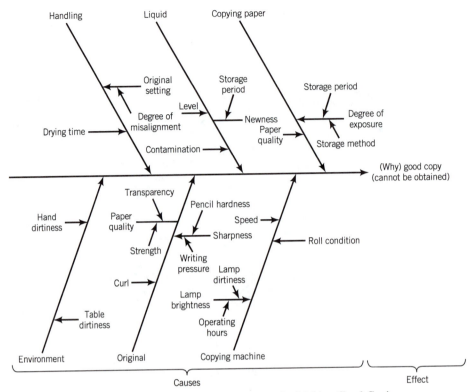

Figure 11-25   Cause-and-Effect Diagram for Making Good Copies

▶ **EXAMPLE 11-14**

In the manufacture of a silicon alloy varistor, concern over a low yield instituted a concentrated quality control effort to study the causes of the low yield and to achieve improvement. The study was begun by summarizing the level of rejects at various process stages in the manufacturing operation. The measure used was the cost of the rejects (see Figure 11-26a). It was noted that the largest losses were occurring at the tested varistor or final stage of production. This led to an examination and breakdown of the frequency of occurrence of test failures by final product quality characteristics. The Pareto principle was apparent (see Figure 11-26b). Factors affecting the most frequent cause of failures, high reverse current, were then listed by process operations to help direct the improvement study. This list of factors is shown in Figure 11-26c. Process performance and capability studies were then conducted on these factors. See Example 11-17.

▶ **EXAMPLE 11-15**

An electronics firm manufacturing filled reflectors using LEDs (light-emitting diodes) identifies a problem of excessive open circuits occurring at seven positions of the figure eight configuration. In addition to an overall program of quality control (see Example 11-20), a special study is devoted to this problem. An early step in the investigation was to prepare the CE diagram shown in Figure 11-27.

Initial investigation of the handling of the lead frame revealed that a reversal of the orientation of the frame as it is inserted into the reflector filled with epoxy resulted in a significant

Silicon Alloy Varistor Junk		Breakdown of Test Defects		Factors Affecting High Reverse Rejects	
Operation	Net $ Value Junk (One Month)	Type Defect	% of Defects	Prior Operation	Factor
Cut wire	14.84	Forward voltage	5.3%	Silicon dicing	Wafer width
Wire stud	22.57	Slope	0.3%	Alloying	Temperature
Copper pin	10.20				Belt speed
Wire stud assembly	128.41	Reverse current	59.7%	Wafer assembly	Chips & cracks
Silicon wafer	271.39				Off-center buttons
Alloyed wafer	926.13	Open	4.9%		Cleanliness
Etched pin—wafer assembly	2959.31	Shorts	10.6%	Pin assembly	Alignment
		Zener voltage	19.2%		Shape of "S" bend
Assembled varistor	338.36			(Control charts placed at each operation to study level and variation of factors)	
Tested varistor	8213.45				
Total	12884.66				
(a)		(b)		(c)	

Figure 11-26 Data Summary and Breakdown and Factor List for Silicon Alloy Varistor Study

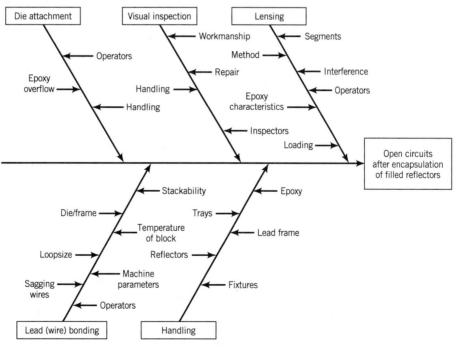

Figure 11-27 CE Diagram for Quality Improvement Study on Filled Reflectors

369

improvement in open circuits, a reduction of around half of the difficulty from 8% to 4%. This change was also motivated by a Pareto/geographical analysis revealing that more opens were occurring at the end position of the frame, the last to be inserted, and that this end was less rigid than the opposite end. Further studies on the other factors resulted in redesigned fixtures, reduction and better training of lensing operators, less handling during visual inspection, and some form of control on most of the factors listed. This reduced the occurrences of open circuits to less than 0.5%.

Scatter Plots (Line Graphs, Run Charts, Time Series Plots)

Scatter plots were first used around 1750–1800 [Tufte (1983)]. Sometimes called *x-y* plots or crossplots, scatter plots are easy and effective. The idea is just to plot bivariate data (x_i, y_i) by constructing a scale on the *x*-axis that covers the range of *x* values and a scale on the *y*-axis that covers the range of the *y* values. Scatter plots are a first step in many quality investigations or data analyses. They are often the last step in an analysis, since they are useful in checking the residuals. Various forms of scatter plots are referred to as line graphs or run charts. When the *x* variable is time, they are also referred to as time series plots. Later in this chapter there is a discussion of the scatter diagram, which is more closely aligned with correlation studies.

A glance through an excellent text on data analysis such as Daniel and Wood (1980) shows a wide use of scatter plots. They can be simple dot plots in which each bivariate pair is represented by a point or the points may be connected as in a time series or replaced by numbers or symbols. Transformations can be made to one or both scales. Additional information such as moving medians or quartiles or other smoothers may be overlaid. The fitted model or theoretical model can be plotted through the data points. In this section only the basic plots are discussed.

▶ EXAMPLE 11-16

The following example shows how useful a basic scatter plot can be in quality investigations. Here the incoming percent nonconforming of a critical part (a programmable read-only memory) has been plotted against time. The results are from a 100% incoming test, since the test is simply programming the memories; if they fail to program correctly, they are called nonconforming. At the time of this study, this part was the state of the art and very difficult to manufacture. The suppliers gave assurance that they were constantly doing everything possible to improve the quality. The shop using the parts thought that quality was not improving and might be, in fact, getting worse.

The first scatter plot constructed (Figure 11-28) reveals two outliers together with an underlying pattern that appears to be a favorable trend. On recognition that these data involve two different suppliers, the data points for each supplier were separated. Figure 11-29 is a multiple scatter plot, using spreadsheet software, showing plots for the total (as in Figure 11-28) and separate plots for suppliers 1 and 2. Supplier 1 appears to have a favorable trend. The results can be seen even more clearly by making two scatter plots, one for each supplier. These are shown in Figures 11-30 and 11-31.

What is found is that supplier 1 appears to be improving the quality of the memories constantly. Supplier 2 is not having as much success but at least is not getting worse. There are two points in the data that are very suspicious. An investigation determined that these points were caused by a malfunctioning of the device used to program the memories.

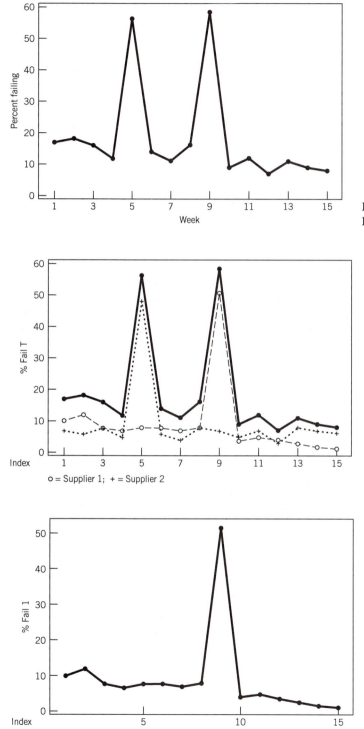

Figure 11-28 Scatter Plot of Percent Failing over Time

o = Supplier 1; + = Supplier 2

Figure 11-29 Multiple Scatter Plots of Total and Suppliers 1 and 2

Figure 11-30 Scatter Plot of Supplier 1

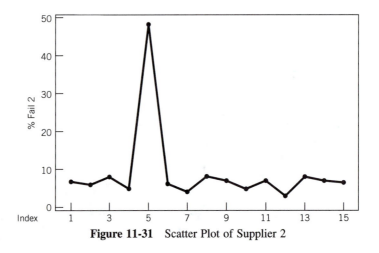

Figure 11-31   Scatter Plot of Supplier 2

Smoothing.   Often there is a need to reduce the amount of information in a scatter plot by a statistical summary to see clearly what is really happening. Earlier, one method was used—stratification—to compare two suppliers. When there are hundreds or even thousands of data points, the confusion level may be reduced by summarizing using moving averages or moving medians or other techniques. These methods also frequently contribute to the understanding of even small data sets and can help to visualize general patterns or trends.

In general, when fitting a model to data, we have [Hoaglin, Mosteller, and Tukey (1983)]

$$\text{Data} = \text{Fit} + \text{Residual}$$

A smooth sequence of fitted values is just another kind of fit, so we have

$$\text{Data value} = \text{Smooth} + \text{Residual}$$

The terminology that is used in data analysis calls the smooth sequence of fitted values the *smooth* and calls the rule for determining a smooth the *smoother.* The residual sequence is calculated by subtraction. The weighted means have traditionally been used as smoothers, but they are so sensitive to even one outlying value in a sequence that better smoothers are needed.

One of the simplest and most frequently used smoothers is a median of size 3. In the plot of supplier 1's results (Figure 11-30), the y values, percent nonconforming, are replaced with the medians of size 3, that is,

$$z_t = \text{median } (y_{t-1}, y_t, y_{t+1})$$

The result is shown in Figure 11-32. The sets of three data points that are used to calculate the medians are called a window of size 3. These plots are insensitive to single outliers or multiple outliers when separated by at least two data points.

There is a small problem about what to do with the end values of the smooth, z_1, and z_n. Let

$$z_1 = y_1, \qquad z_n = y_n$$

or

$$z_1 = \text{median } (y_1, y_2), \ z_n = \text{median } (y_{n-1}, y_n)$$

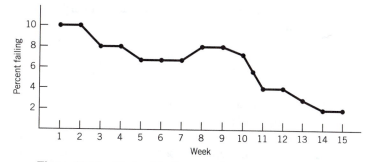

Figure 11-32 Moving Medians as a Smooth of Supplier Data

Tukey (1977) suggests that the following rule be used to determine the end values:

$$z_1 = \text{median } (z_2, y_1, 3z_2 - 2z_3)$$
$$z_n = \text{median } (z_{n-1}, y_n, 3z_{n-1} - 2z_{n-2})$$

A fortunate property of this type of smoothing is that it can be repeated with excellent results. The smoothing can be resmoothed with medians of size 3. This can be repeated until the result no longer changes. A second smoothing of Figure 11-30 is shown in Figure 11-33.

Other window sizes can be used to calculate moving medians. Moving medians of even length, for example, size 2 or 4, have the advantage of being somewhat smoother than comparable odd length moving medians because each smooth value is the average of two data values.

Another smoother that has wide applicability is one called "hanning" by Tukey (1977) after Julius van Hann, who used it to smooth weather data. This smoother is a weighted mean technique with weights of 1/4, 1/2, and 1/4. The transformation is

$$z_t = 1/4(y_{t-1}) + 1/2(y_t) + 1/4(y_{t+1})$$

This smoother is especially useful for increasing or decreasing data. Other smoothers that can be very useful in data analysis include *splitting* to modify peaks and valleys and

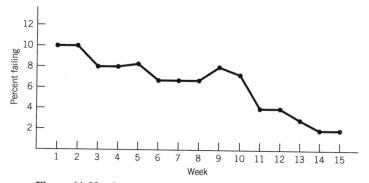

Figure 11-33 Second Smooth of Data with Moving Medians

twicing, which operates on the residuals to improve the fit. A discussion of these smoothers can be found in Tukey (1977).

Process Performance and Capability Studies

In addition to the use of scatter plots for the study of trends, they may, in the form of control charts, be used for process studies. Control charts were introduced and discussed in Chapters 6 through 9, and some examples of their use will be given in this chapter. If an investigation reaches the stage of a CE diagram, the techniques of process performance and capability studies will be useful for the various factors, variables, or operations identified by the diagram. The terms "process performance study" and "process capability study," as used here, refer to the study of processes by means of various statistical techniques, principally control charts. Performance relates to the current behavior of the process, generally over a relatively short period, under the prevailing operating conditions. It may represent the capability of the process in that further improvement of the process variation may not be possible without changing the process itself. The current performance of the process may involve excessive variation, lack of statistical control, the wrong average level, or too high a level of nonconformities; one or all may be improved by action on the process.

Capability relates to the limits of inherent variability in which the process can operate upon removal of these causes of excessive variation, lack of statistical control, wrong average level, or excessive nonconformities. It is generally related to a state of statistical control as demonstrated by control charts prepared and maintained over a reasonable period of operation of the process under the prevailing conditions to control the variation within statistical limits. Still another aspect of capability is the ability of the process to meet prescribed specification limits. Discussion of that aspect was given in Chapter 10.

Capability does not necessarily imply acceptability. For a process, a series of performance studies may be completed, each contributing to reduced variation, eventually reaching a state of stability and process control. For the given need, this may still not be satisfactory. This allows us to make an important distinction. If performance studies are conducted utilizing control charts and a state of statistical control has not been realized, there are still some assignable causes remaining that may be located and removed to improve the process. However, when a state of statistical control has been achieved and the process is still not satisfactory, a different type of action must be taken. It may require a redesigned process involving new designs, equipment, materials, personnel, or training.

Because process performance and capability studies make use of control charts, all the discussion in Chapters 6 through 9 apply. The examples in Chapter 7 are performance studies involving attributes control charts. Some carry the study to process capability. Similarly, the examples in Chapter 8 are performance studies involving variables control charts. In Example 8-1 the inherent capability is apparent, but the average level is desired to be at a different value, leading to a control chart developed for subsequent process control. A minimum specification limit (see Chapter 10 for a more detailed discussion) is the principal concern in Example 8-3. The initial performance study reveals an inability of the current production to meet the limit, resulting in a change in formulation to achieve a capability at a satisfactory average level.

Example 8-5 is a case in which the process capability is apparent during the initial performance study but the variability is larger than desired. The hypothetical case created in Chapter 6 for the attribute (p) chart is another example in which the current capability is apparent on the initial study. However, the level of nonconformities of the controlled state is far from satisfactory for economical production.

► EXAMPLE 11-17

In Example 11-14, control charts were placed at each operation to study the level and variation associated with each of the factors identified in the list. Two such control charts are shown in Figures 11-34 and 11-35 to illustrate the nature of the initial performance study and the improvement achieved by action taken on the process based on the interpretation of the control charts. The control charts have been marked with notes reflecting some of the action required and are reasonably self-explanatory.

The results achieved were part of an overall savings of 26.2 million dollars in reduced merchandise losses and inspection. These savings were accomplished over a period of seven years by similar studies on a variety of products.

► EXAMPLE 11-18

A study was undertaken on the mass of a PVC bottle produced on a blow molding machine. Records showed insufficient production of bottle units for PVC consumption. This initial concern was examined in greater detail by a study of one month's data on PVC consumption, actual production,

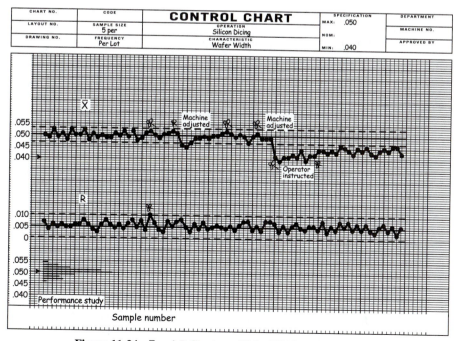

Figure 11-34 $\bar{x}$ and R Charts on Wafer Width at Silicon Dicing

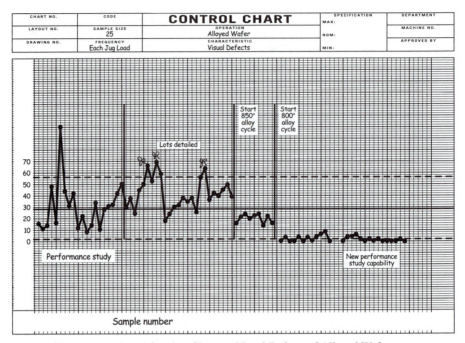

Figure 11-35 Percent Nonconforming Chart on Visual Defects of Alloyed Wafer

and expected production based on a desired nominal mass. The data are shown in Table 11-6 with explanation of the columns and computations. As seen from the last figure in column 8, a cumulative loss of expected production of 3531 bottles has occurred during the month by not maintaining control of the average mass to the desired nominal of 33.5 grams. Column 9 reflects the average mass in grams of the daily production and reveals the excess over 33.5 grams.

It was decided to develop a daily control chart for these data plotting the difference statistic, column 7, on an individuals (x) chart, initially as a fluctuating pattern without control limits. Data for July were added to those of Table 11-6. On July 9 a decision was made to replace the extrusion mandrel, which was believed to be worn excessively, after which plotting of the data continued. The control chart with data through September 30 is shown in Figure 11-36. Two sigma control limits are shown from July 10 based on the data up to September 30 using moving ranges to estimate the standard deviation (see Section 8-8.2). The two high values on August 8 and September 14 were excluded, as they were believed to be the combined result of erroneous counts and underweight bottles. These limits were developed as a basis to monitor future performance.

The study also focused on the blow molding machine itself. Motivated by the potential savings from the process change the next step was to study the variation in the bottle mass to better control this characteristic. In addition to achieving maximum production for PVC consumption at the average mass of 33.5 grams per bottle, it was believed that control of the uniformity of the bottle might allow a reduced nominal. This would require careful monitoring of the strength with uniform wall thickness, resulting in even further savings.

An initial process performance study of the blow molding machine was conducted with samples of five consecutive bottles drawn from each of the two molds every fifteen minutes. The bottles were allowed to cool and were weighed in the factory laboratory, a procedure resulting in a time lag between production and the reporting of results. To present the results of the initial study, the data and control charts ($\bar{x}$ and R) are shown in Figure 11-37.

TABLE 11-6 Summary of One Month's Production Data on PVC Bottles

Date	(1) PVC (kg)	(2) Regrind (kg)	(3) Scrap (kg)	(4) Consumption (kg)	(5) Expected Production	(6) Actual Production	(7) Difference (From Std.)	(8) Cum. Diff.	(9) Average Mass (g)
06-01	225	50	51.7	223.3	6666	6107	−559	−559	36.6
06-02	150	25	35.8	139.2	4152	4065	−87	−646	34.2
06-03	150	25	35.7	139.3	4158	3990	−168	−814	34.9
06-04	150	50	39.9	160.1	4779	4622	−157	−971	34.6
06-05	250	50	57.6	242.4	7236	7000	−236	−1207	34.6
06-08	250	50	56.9	243.1	7257	6760	−497	−1704	36.0
06-09	225	50	53.7	221.3	6606	6330	−276	−1980	35.0
06-10	225	75	57.4	242.6	7242	7100	−142	−2122	34.2
06-12	100.6	—	33.0	67.6	2018	1619	−399	−2521	41.8
06-15	199.4	100	56.8	242.6	7242	6956	−286	−2807	34.9
06-17	225	75	56.1	243.9	7281	7235	−46	−2853	33.7
06-22	225	60	57.4	227.6	6794	6567	−227	−3080	34.7
06-24	150	60	40.5	169.5	5060	4785	−275	−3355	35.4
06-29	175	58.4	53.3	180.1	5376	5200	−176	−3531	34.6

Columns (1), (2), (3), and (6) from actual records, Column (4) = (1) + (2) − (3), Column (5) = (4) ÷ 0.0335 based on desired nominal of 33.5 grams per bottle, Column (7) = (6) − (5), Column (8) = Σ(7), Column (9) = (4) + 1000(6).

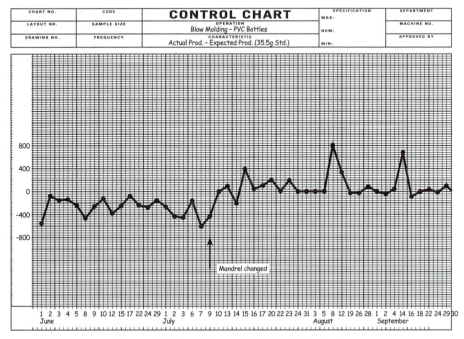

Figure 11-36 x Chart on PVC Bottle Production

VARIABLES CONTROL CHART (X̄ & R)

	PART NAME (PRODUCT)							PART NO.		CHART NO.
	PVC Plastic Bottles									

OPERATION (PROCESS)				SPECIFICATION LIMITS	
Blow Molding – Mass of Bottles					

OPERATOR	MACHINE	GAGE	UNIT OF MEASURE grams	ZERO EQUALS

DATE	July 31, 1981													
TIME	10:25		10:40		10:55		11:10		11:25		11:40		11:55	
SAMPLE MEASUREMENTS 1	33.6	33.4	33.5	33.6	33.5	33.6	33.4	33.5	33.5	33.4	33.4	33.2	33.7	33.9
2	33.6	33.7	33.3	33.3	33.4	33.5	33.4	33.5	33.5	33.4	33.3	33.4	33.9	33.9
3	33.6	33.3	33.4	33.4	33.4	33.5	33.4	33.4	33.4	33.3	33.3	33.2	33.9	33.8
4	33.8	33.6	33.5	33.5	33.4	33.5	33.3	33.4	33.4	33.5	33.3	33.4	33.9	33.8
5	33.7	33.7	33.3	33.3	33.5	33.3	33.3	33.3	33.4	33.4	33.5	33.4	33.8	33.8
SUM														
AVERAGE, X̄	33.66	33.64	33.40	33.40	33.46	33.52	33.36	33.36	33.44	33.48	33.38	33.32	33.84	33.84
RANGE, R	0.2	0.1	0.3	0.2	0.1	0.1	0.1	0.1	0.1	0.1	0.2	0.2	0.2	0.1
NOTES (Mold)	4	5	3	5	5	6	5	5	4	5	4	5	5	5

AVERAGES
33.8
33.7
33.6
33.5
33.4

RANGES
.4
.2
0

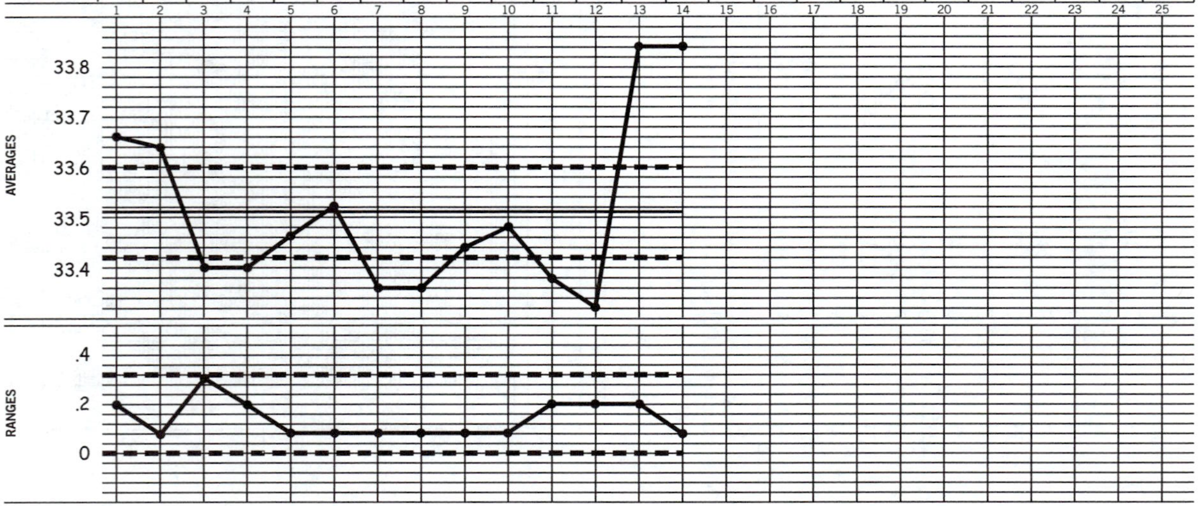

Figure 11-37 Initial Performance Study on PVC Bottle Mass

Information gained from this initial study included the following:

1. The great sensitivity of the mass of the bottle to changes in adjustment of the machine, parameters drifting with time as well as operator adjustments. The erratic out-of-control pattern on the $\bar{x}$ chart of Figure 11-37 reflects this sensitivity.

2. A tendency on the part of operators to overadjust the machine, especially the screw speed with the controls conveniently located at the work position.

3. A range chart reflecting a consistent short-term variability within samples.

4. A sufficient similarity of the molds to conduct future studies using samples from one mold only.

5. A need to study the correlation between the mass and width of the bottom piece versus the bottle mass. This bottom piece is formed by the mold pressing out the excess PVC extruded to the mold. In view of a correlation between the width of the bottom piece and the bottle mass, measurement of the width could be made at the machine. This allows a real-time control without the time lag required to cool and weigh the bottles. A negative correlation was suspected.

A second process performance study was conducted in which ten samples of three consecutively produced bottles were drawn directly from the machine at 5-minute intervals for mold 4. The machine operator was instructed not to make any adjustments in the screw speed as the samples were drawn. However, when an increase was noted in the width of the bottom piece directly at the machine over some thirty minutes (six samples), a change in the screw speed from 40 rpm to 39.5 rpm was executed and recorded. The initial machine parameters were also set to achieve a nominal mass of approximately 33 grams as an attempt to produce a uniform bottle of sufficient strength at the lower mass.

The bottle and bottom pieces were weighed in the factory lab and the masses recorded. Measurements were also made on the widths of the bottom pieces. The $\bar{x}$ and R charts for the mass of the bottle, together with the width of the bottom piece, are shown in Figure 11-38. The negative correlation is apparent. This affords an opportunity to illustrate an additional technique, introduced earlier, often useful in process studies, the scatter diagram and its related correlation or regression analysis.

The Scatter Diagram

A scatter diagram is drawn using the width of the bottom piece as the independent variable, x, and the mass of the bottle as the dependent variable, y. The related statistical analysis is referred to as a regression study. Scatter diagrams can be prepared for cases in which both variables are considered dependent, and the related statistical analysis is then referred to as a correlation study. If it can be established that a relationship exists between the width of the bottom piece and the mass of the bottle, the width measurement taken directly at the machine can be used to control the bottle mass.

A further example of usefulness of scatter diagrams is to establish a possible relationship between the hardness measurement of a metallic piece and its tensile strength. If such a relationship can be established, the hardness measurement can be used to control the tensile strength, replacing a destructive test with a nondestructive test at considerable savings.

Returning to the above example, the scatter diagram of the width of the bottom piece (x) versus the mass of the bottle (y) is shown in Figure 11-39. The diagram consists of the thirty coordinate pairs from the ten samples of size 3. A negative relationship of a linear form is apparent. By applying further statistical analysis, the line of best fit via least squares has been obtained and drawn on the scatter diagram. The y-intercept, slope, and correlation coefficient have been labeled on the diagram for reference purposes. It is seen that to

VARIABLE CONTROL CHART ($\bar{X}$ & R)

PART NAME (PRODUCT)	OPERATION (PROCESS)	PART NO.	CHART NO.
PVC Plastic Bottle	Blow Molding	SPECIFICATION LIMITS	

OPERATOR	MACHINE	GAGE	UNIT OF MEASURE	ZERO EQUALS

Mass of Bottle

DATE / TIME	1420	1425	1430	1435	1440	1445	1447	1450	1450	1500
Sample Measurements 1										
2	33.01	32.93	33.01	32.80	32.73	32.43	33.09	33.18	33.14	33.12
3	33.08	33.17	32.82	32.86	32.57	32.54	33.11	33.18	33.38	33.98
4	33.24	33.07	32.91	32.89	32.65	32.61	33.09	33.22	33.18	33.04
5										
SUM										
AVERAGE, $\bar{X}$	33.11	33.06	32.91	32.78	32.65	32.53	33.10	33.19	33.23	33.05
RANGE, R	0.23	0.24	0.19	0.23	0.16	0.18	0.02	0.04	0.24	0.14
NOTES										

Width of Bottom Piece

DATE / TIME	1420	1425	1430	1435	1440	1445	1447	1450	1455	1500
Sample Measurements 1										
2	25.0	26.0	25.5	26.5	27.0	30.0	24.0	23.0	23.5	23.5
3	24.0	23.0	27.0	28.5	28.0	28.0	23.5	23.0	22.0	25.0
4	23.5	23.0	26.0	25.5	26.5	26.0	23.5	23.5	23.5	24.5
5										
SUM										
AVERAGE, $\bar{X}$	24.2	24.7	26.2	26.8	27.2	28.0	23.8	23.2	23.0	24.3
RANGE, R	1.5	3.0	1.5	3.0	1.5	4.0	0.5	0.5	1.5	1.5
NOTES										

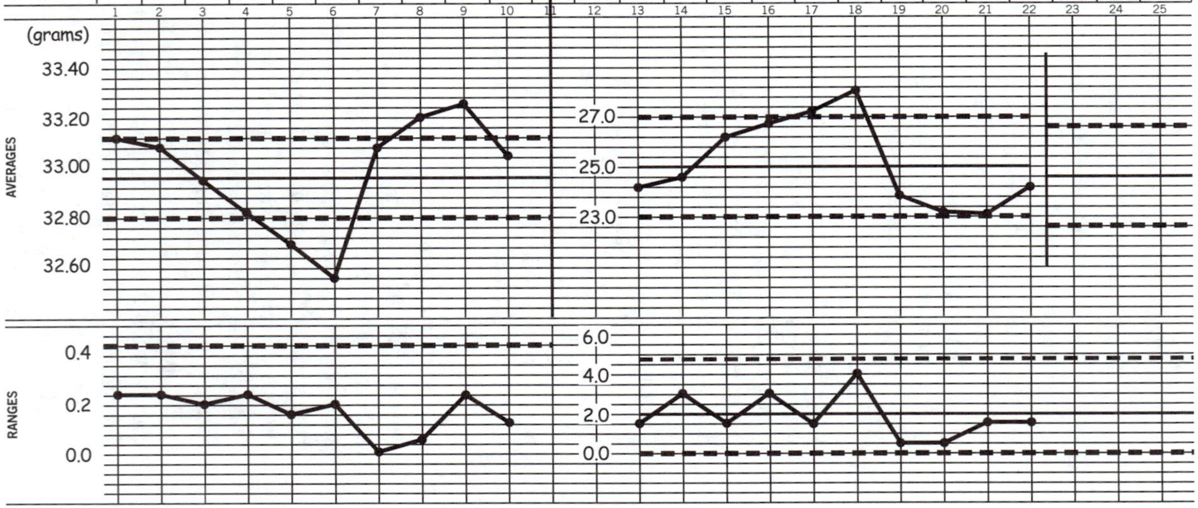

(grams)
33.40
33.20
33.00
32.80
32.60
AVERAGES
0.4
0.2
0.0
RANGES
27.0
25.0
23.0
6.0
4.0
2.0
0.0

Figure 11-38 Second Performance Study—Bottle Mass and Width of Bottom Piece

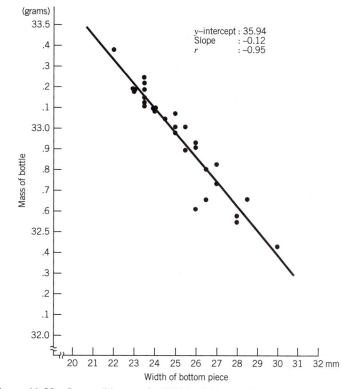

Figure 11-39 Scatter Diagram for Width of Bottom Piece versus Bottle Mass

control the bottle mass at an average of 33 grams requires control of the width of the bottom piece at an average of approximately 24.7 mm. The control limits on the x chart of Figure 11-38 have been adjusted to that level and extended for subsequent control.

As future control is exercised on the width of the bottom piece, using $\bar{x}$ and R charts directly at the blow molding machine, it will be necessary to verify that the relationship continues to hold. Adjustments in other machine parameters such as air pressure, PVC mix, zone temperatures, pressure, and nozzle configuration may affect the basic relationship. A sample is drawn periodically to obtain the mass of the bottle, together with the width of the bottom piece. If the relationship changes for specific setup variables, appropriate adjustments are made in the target value of the width of the bottom piece. It also was necessary to improve, by means of stabilization, the air pressure supplied to the machine and to improve the feed rate controls to make finer adjustments possible.

For further examples of process improvement studies using a variety of principles, the interested reader is referred to the many "Practical Aids" articles written or edited by Ellis R. Ott for *Industrial Quality Control*. Many of these form the basis for his book, *Process Quality Control* [Ott (1975)]; Ott and Schilling (1990)]. A related article appears in *Quality* [Ott (1980)]. Further illustrations are contained in the AT&T *Statistical Quality Control Handbook* [AT&T Technologies (1984)]. A systematic approach to measurement and separation of sources of variability in process capability analysis is given by Seder and Cowan (1956).

▶ 11-3 CONTROL OF QUALITY

As a follow-up to programs of quality improvement, process control is an essential element in any quality system within a manufacturing or commercial organization. Most of the examples discussed earlier in this chapter and in previous chapters have an element of control or lead to a control procedure. A natural result of a process performance or capability study is the development of an effective process control chart or other technique to prevent the recurrence of the trouble(s) corrected. Control charts serve the dual role of assisting in process improvement investigations and serving as a basis for monitoring and controlling process variables.

Because an important aspect is the control to specification limits of individual items the techniques of Chapter 10 form an important aspect of this control. There is no general rule about whether improvement of quality or control of quality should be emphasized first. Either can lead to the other. Just as there are certain principles for improvement of quality, so are there for its control. The elements of quality systems discussed in Chapters 2, 3, and 4 are directed to the control of quality.

11-3.1 Some Essential Areas for Process Control

The necessary areas that must be controlled are as follows:

- Manufacturing or operations information, including precise instructions for all employees
- Purchasing and storage of raw materials and piece parts
- Operators, including their selection, training, and motivation
- Process steps including the establishment of control procedures
- Finished product
- Measuring and test equipment, including calibration and maintenance
- Corrective and preventive action

Some Useful Tools for Process Control
With a subject as broad as process control, there are many techniques. Only a few are included here. Some pertain to process steps in general; others relate to individual process characteristics. Others are discussed in other chapters.

Flowchart of Operations
Planning for process control requires consideration of the steps involved in the overall process. It is often aided by a flowchart of operations. On completion, with control points indicated, the flowchart serves as instruction for processing and control. Development of the flowchart, with points of control, is often assigned to a multidisciplinary quality team.

As stated by Carlsen and Lewis (1979), "[The flowchart] is the graphic method for displaying a system's operation and sequence." A very familiar type of flowchart is the program flowchart. The program flowchart, sometimes called the logic diagram, is widely used in displaying data collection, processing analysis, and results steps in a software program. It is a useful technique that is routinely employed both in the planning stage of programming and in summarizing a completed program.

In this section the systems flowchart that focuses on the flow of information throughout all parts of a system is described. Carlsen and Lewis (1979) describe two kinds of systems flowcharts. One type is task oriented and is used to describe the flow of data in terms of the work being performed. The second type is forms oriented and is used to describe the flow of forms through the functional structure of the system. In this section the basic elements of flowcharting are discussed along with the basic symbols used in constructing flowcharts. Much of the following material is based on Carlsen and Lewis's description of flowcharting in *The System Analysis Workbook* (1979). Another description of how to use flowcharts in defining procedures is by Turnbull and Higby (1985).

Basic Flowcharting Symbols

Figure 11-40 illustrates the basic flowcharting symbols that are used in systems analysis. Their use is fairly obvious. Process refers to any manual, machine, or automatic operation or function. It also refers to work done. Machine insertion of components, visual inspection, and teaching are all processes.

A key element of a flowchart is the decision step. This is often a simple yes-or-no decision, but it can be a complex switching type operation in which many different paths

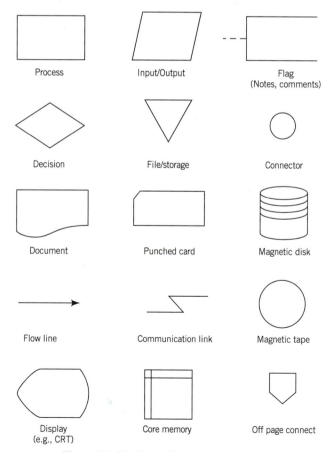

Figure 11-40 Basic Flowcharting Symbols

are possible. A simple example is from acceptance sampling inspection, in which the decision is to accept or reject a lot. A slightly more complex example would be double sampling, in which the decision is accept, reject, or take a second sample.

The symbols for files and storage show how the data are stored for both input and output. In a complex manufacturing process access to a variety of databases or information sources may be needed. For output files may be sent to disks or magnetic storage, but ideally, some form of quick graphical display of key results will be available.

The small circle representing a connector is very useful. It indicates that the flow continues somewhere else on the chart or on a following chart. A symbol resembling home plate is sometimes used for indicating an off-page connection. The flags are used for notes and comments to provide additional information about the flowchart steps.

Flow lines and communication links are used to show direction and means of transmission of data and information. The document symbol indicates any kind of report, form, instruction, drawing, specification, or other material used in the system.

Using the Flowchart

Although a flowchart is usually prepared by the process engineer when the process is first defined, preparing a flowchart describing the actual process that is being used is often a good first step for any quality improvement program. Over time, the process usually evolves and is redefined and improved so many times that any resemblance to the flowchart in the files is accidental.

Sometimes, flowcharting the process leads to a major improvement without much detailed analysis or recommendations. When the process is clearly defined so that everyone understands what each step is, improvements become obvious. An example of this comes from a study of a service order process some years ago. The process was quite complex and had twenty-four steps. At one point in the process, the steps were as follows:

- Print out results from computer
- Give computer printout to waiting taxi
- Deliver to office across town
- Have operator key input results to computer

Needless to say, when the manager reviewed this flowchart, a way was found to have the first computer "talk" directly to the second one. Not only did this elimination of unnecessary steps save time and money, but two sources of error were avoided.

In Figure 11-41 a simple flowchart shows how the service process for ticketing passengers was done for many years by the major airlines. In examining the flowchart, it is easy to see some obvious places where the process could be improved. Most airlines now routinely give seat assignments to customers when they make reservations. These customers, if they have only carry-on baggage, may proceed directly to the gate and avoid waiting in two lines. The airlines also save time in processing these customers.

When flowcharts are used to describe a complex manufacturing process, it is often found that it is informative to use many flags with quantified results. Key information at manufacturing steps includes inventory at each step, waiting times, dropouts or rework, number of inspectors, machine down time, and processing times. These details may lead the investigation to probable areas that are seriously affecting quality and productivity.

Additional examples of flowcharts applied to different processes follow.

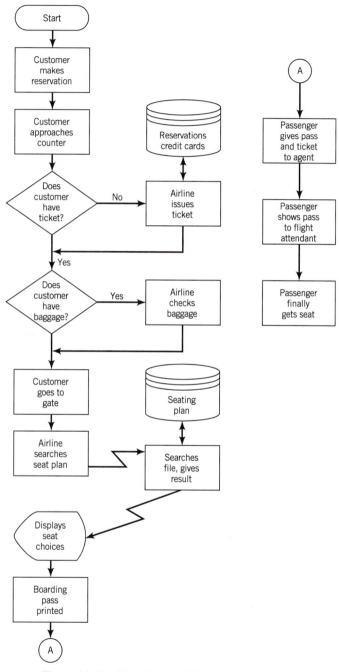

Figure 11-41 Flowchart of Airline Ticketing Process

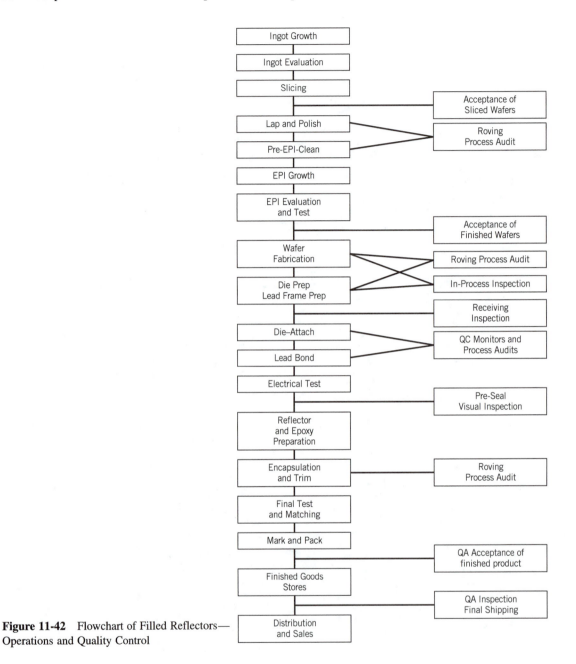

Figure 11-42 Flowchart of Filled Reflectors—
Operations and Quality Control

▶ **EXAMPLE 11-19**

As was mentioned in Example 11-15, an overall process control program was in operation for the electronics firm manufacturing filled reflectors. The flowchart of operations and control points is shown in Figure 11-42. The study described in Example 11-15 helps to emphasize the merger of quality improvement with quality control.

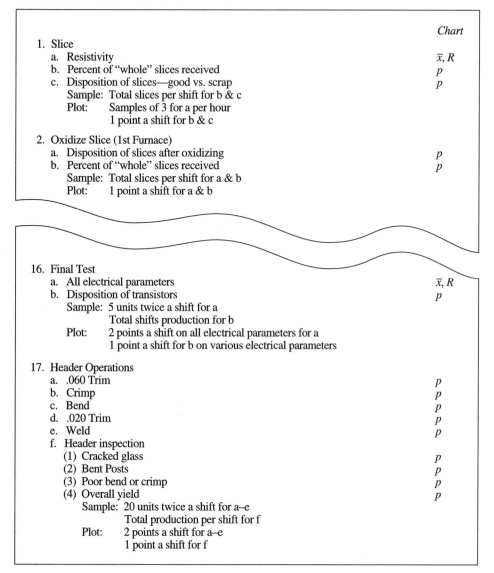

Figure 11-43 Transistor Process Control Program—List

▶ **EXAMPLE 11-20**

A manufacturer of transistors decides to develop a program of process control with emphasis on the application of control charts at significant process steps. The task is undertaken by the quality team assigned to the production line. The program developed is shown in Figure 11-43. It illustrates a variation in the flowchart method that can be shown in list form by operation to enumerate more details such as the nature and frequency of samples drawn and data plotted.

PROD. ENG. __RBT-4270__ MANUF. __FCE-8126__ **PROCESS CONTROL LAYOUT** DATE __12-29-62__ NO. __IL-3163__

SERVICE ENG. _____ Q. C. ENG. __FDR-230__ FOR USE WITH SI 213 SHEET __1__ OF __2__ ISSUE ____5____

MANUFACTURING DEPARTMENT DIFFUSED SILICON TRANSISTOR

Operation	Characteristic	Code	Drawing No.	Chart No.	Type of Chart	Sample Size	Frequency	Origin of Data	Record of Data	Facilities	Note
1. Received Slice	Thickness (1/4″ from edge)	16A, 21A, 23A, 16C	P-49B295	1	$\bar{x}$, R	4 slices/lot	4 lots/shift	P.C.	AP-510F	VN-305840-D	
2. Lapping (after detailing)	Thickness (1/4″ from edge)	All	P-49B293	2	$\bar{x}$, R	4 slices	4 checks/shift	P.C.	AP-510F	VN305840-D	
3. Gallium Diffusion	Sheet Resistance	All (Except Epitax)	P-49B293	3	$\bar{x}$, R	4 slices	1 check a shift/furnace	Operator	AP-510F	ESE 1-1629	
4. Phosphorous Pre-deposit	Sheet Resistance	All (Except Epitax)	P-49B302	4	$\bar{x}$, R	4 slices	1 check a shift/furnace	Operator	AP-510F	ESE 1-1629	
5. Final Diffusion	Sheet Resistance	All (Except Epitax)	P-49B302	5	$\bar{x}$, R	4 slices	1 check a shift/furnace	Operator	AP-510F	ESE 1-1629	
6. Photo Resist (after etching)	Check for: a. Scratched slice b. Peeling c. Uneven sides d. Insufficient etching (determine by color of emitter area) e. Foreign deposits (dust or dirt) f. Pitted slice g. Small emitter h. Spiked emitter	All	P-49B293	6	p	30	2 slices twice/shift	P.C.	Special Form	Toolmaker's Microscope	#1

Operation	Check for		Part No.								
7. Mesa Etch (after etching)	Check for: a. Poor photo resist b. Cut emitter c. Emitter short d. Undercut mesa e. Scratched mesa f. Poor mesa g. Insufficient etching h. Dirty wafers i. Heat probe	All	P-49B300	7	*p*	30	2 slices twice/ shift	P.C.	Special Form	Toolmaker's Microscope	#1
8. Evaporation	Check for: a. Poor emitter stripe b. Missing emitter stripe c. Emitter short d. Poor alignment e. Dirty wafer f. Missing base stripe g. Poor photo resist h. Insufficient aluminum (area and pile-up)	All	P-49B301	8	*p*	30	2 slices twice/ shift	P.C.	Special Form	ESE 1-1328 Toolmaker's Microscope	#2 #1

#1—Check 6 emitters (or wafers) at approximately five equidistant areas on the slice.
#2—Take 4 probes (approx. 90° apart) on each sample slice. Notify the supervisor if a defect is found.

Figure 11-44 Process Control Layout for Transistors

These examples illustrate the use of flowcharts or lists of operations with designated control points and characteristics checked. As with process capability studies, no two will be exactly alike.

The Process Control Layout: The Inspection Layout

Another device for process control is a layout of instructions. This may be a formal document of manufacturing or operations information and specifications. They are often called process control layouts for in process operations and inspection layout for end point operations involving an inspection function such as acceptance sampling. The program illustrated in Figure 11-43 may be placed on such a document for direct implementation in the shop. Brief examples follow, which serve to illustrate the idea.

▷ **EXAMPLE 11-21**

A portion of a process control layout for diffused silicon transistors is shown in Figure 11-44. The specification covers such items as operation, quality characteristic, product code, drawing number (reference to other applicable specifications), chart number, type of chart, sample size, frequency, origin of data, record of data, facilities, and note(s). It is a direct instruction to the manufacturing department to conduct the specified checks on the process. The layout is prepared by the quality control engineer assigned to the product line, after consultation with the quality team. It is the responsibility of the quality control and reliability engineering department.

▷ **EXAMPLE 11-22**

A portion of an inspection layout is shown in Figure 11-45. It pertains to the final inspection of header assemblies for transistors for which multiple sampling plans (see Chapter 15) are specified for major and minor defect classification. Another sampling plan, not shown, of the single-variables type is specified for the lead bend test, including $\bar{x}$ and R control charts to monitor any significant changes in the lead strength properties. The layout is also the responsibility of the quality control and reliability engineering department and is prepared by the quality control engineer in cooperation with the quality team.

Process Control Charts: Shop Charts

Besides being used for process performance and process capability studies control charts play a significant role in process control. Often, process improvement studies are translated into process control techniques utilizing control charts. Most of the examples presented previously contain an aspect of control.

Process control charts should be implemented on manufacturing or service operations with a specific purpose in mind. Choosing the purpose is an important part of process control planning. All parties involved in the operation should be aware of the control charts and their purposes. Again the quality team approach is recommended. Two examples follow, and other examples were presented in Chapter 10, with particular emphasis on specification limits.

▷ **EXAMPLE 11-23**

An important process in the manufacture of an electron tube for microwave amplification is the attachment of the support legs to the cathode sleeve. This is performed by an individual operator

| INSPECTION LAYOUT | Issue 8 | No. IL-3000 |
| | Date 1-25-85 | Sheet 1 of 6 |

	Issue 8	No. IL-3000
INSPECTION LAYOUT	Date 1-25-85	Sheet 1 of 6
	Mfg. Dept. Header assembly	
	Insp. Dept. Final inspection	
HEADER	Asso. Dwgs. P-49B892 A-499787 P-49B286 P-49B895	
	29, 17, 21 & 16 Types Used on "J" Type Encapsulation Transistors	

Operations and Methods	Facilities

SAMPLING PLAN
2.5% AQL FOR MAJORS—PARA. 1.0
4.0% AQL FOR MINORS—PARA. 2.0

Lot Size 801 to 1300

		AQL 2.5%		AQL 4.0%	
n	Cum. n	Ac	Re	Ac	Re
30	30	0	4	0	4
30	60	2	5	3	7
30	90	3	8	5	9
30	120	4	9	7	11
30	150	6	10	9	13
30	180	8	12	12	15
30	210	11	12	14	15

Select a random sample from each lot in accordance with the applicable table above and inspect for the following characteristics:

1.0 Major Defect Classification per P-49B892, A-499787, etc.

1.1 Loose burrs on leads	10× Microscope
1.2 Trimmed lead length (.002″ over max. allowable)	VN-305763
1.3 Glass Cracks (Para. 2.1.8)	10× Microscope
1.4 Surface connecting bubbles (Para. 2.1.5)	"
1.5 Bubbles at seal interface (Para. 2.1.1, 2.1.9, & 2.1.10)	"
1.6 Crackle at seal interface (Para. 2.1.7)	"
1.7 Poor seals (Para. 2.1.6)	"

2.0 Minor Defect Classification per A-499787, P-49B892, etc.

2.1 Lead length (air side) less than .438″	
2.2 Lead Alignment	VN-306104B
2.3 Lead Concentricity	"
2.4 Trimmed lead length (if > .002″ under min. allowable)	VN-305763
2.5 Random bubbles in glass (not in seal area)	

Product Eng.	Service Eng.	Manufacturing	Inspection	Proc. Control
WKA-4240	CSF-4180	EJB-2265	CCF-223	AHT-230

Figure 11-45   Inspection Layout for Header Assemblies

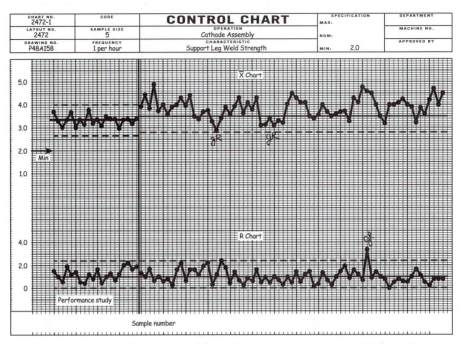

Figure 11-46 $\bar{x}$ and R Control Charts on Cathode Support Leg Weld Strength

using a small bench-type welder and a positioning fixture. Rigidity of the cathode is crucial to proper functioning of the amplifier. The support leg welding process is early in the sequence of operations to fabricate the electron tube. It is also covered by other parts early during subsequent assembly, so that it cannot be inspected or repaired at a later stage. Hence, control directly at the welding operation is essential. The quality team decides to install a process control check together with $\bar{x}$ and R control charts on the strength of the welds.

An initial performance study reveals patterns of control on both the $\bar{x}$ and R charts. The study reveals that the average level of weld strength ($\bar{\bar{x}}$) is slightly low, relative to the inherent variation of the distribution, as measured by $\bar{R}$, and the minimum specification on weld strength. The quality team decides to install the control charts with control limits on the $\bar{x}$ chart modified (shifted upward) to indicate conformance of the distribution of individual welds with the minimum specification (see Chapter 9). Only a lower control limit is used. Concurrently, adjustments on the welder are made in expectation of stronger welds. The control charts are shown in Figure 11-46. This illustrates another control chart form suitable for process control charts, that allows the plotting of a greater number of points than the form introduced earlier in this chapter for use on process performance studies (see Figure 11-37).

The pattern on the $\bar{x}$ chart reveals that the adjustments have been effective in increasing the weld strength. Continued monitoring of the process with this process control indicates periods during which the weld strengths become lower. Such trends are detected early enough to keep the welder, including dressing of the electrodes, adjusted at an adequate level.

▷ **EXAMPLE 11-24**

For the product of Example 11-23, a percent defective (p) control chart is maintained at the final test operation of the completed electron tube to monitor the rejects from the gas test related to the vacuum achieved in the sealed tube. A level of just over 3% rejects has been achieved and is a

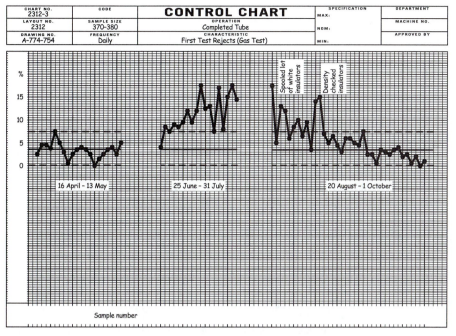

CHART NO. 2312-3	CODE	**CONTROL CHART**	SPECIFICATION MAX:	DEPARTMENT
LAYOUT NO. 2312	SAMPLE SIZE 370-380	OPERATION Completed Tube	NOM:	MACHINE NO.
DRAWING NO. A-774-754	FREQUENCY Daily	CHARACTERISTIC First Test Rejects (Gas Test)	MIN:	APPROVED BY

Figure 11-47 *p* Chart on Gas Test Rejects

measure of the capability of the process. A typical pattern is shown on the left portion of the control chart of Figure 11-47. Because this is a final test characteristic, a large number of factors at various stages of fabrication and assembly affect its performance. The control chart has been set up to detect changes in such factors.

The center portion of the control chart in Figure 11-47 shows that for a certain period the level of rejects are increasing, revealing an out-of-control situation caused by a deterioration at one or more process steps. This signaled the need for investigation by the quality team assigned to the production line. Initial attempts at checking and adjustments to factors that are known to affect this characteristic in the past were unsuccessful. A more thorough investigation was required.

During the investigation some attention was drawn to the ceramic insulator used in the assembly, which is a purchased part. It was obvious that the problems originated with receipt of a new shipment of insulators. This triggered some process experimentation with different lots of insulators. During the detailed investigation the density of the insulators was checked and the new shipment found to contain insulators that were very porous, contributing to difficulties in outgassing the electron tube. There were discussions with the supplier of the insulators, with emphasis on meeting the density requirements. A new shipment of insulators was obtained, and a density check was initiated on receipt of subsequent shipments. The right portion of the control chart in Figure 11-47 shows the period of the investigation including the return to control. Some evidence of a new capability at a lower level of percent rejects became evident as a result of the actions taken during the investigation.

Some lessons learned from this example are as follows:

1. No matter how thorough the controls may be on a given process there may still exist some factor(s) in the process that may cause significant changes in important quality characteristics. These may need to be controlled in the future.

2. The control charts that are maintained on important quality characteristics indicate the necessity for process investigation.

▶ 11-4 FURTHER GRAPHICAL METHODS FOR QUALITY IMPROVEMENT AND CONTROL

Techniques for achieving process control and improvement have been introduced in this chapter with applications to show their usefulness. Many of these techniques are of a graphical nature. One of the earliest and still most effective techniques in the quality disciplines is that of the control chart. It is simple to construct and relatively easy to use and understand. Other good graphical methods share these properties, including many that were not introduced previously in this chapter.

The ease with which graphical methods can be used has been enhanced by the computer and its software. Spreadsheet software packages are being used routinely and contain many of these methods. Graphical routines are being incorporated in word processing software packages. There has been a proliferation of specialized statistical software packages containing large numbers of these methods. See, for example, each April issue of ASQ's *Quality Progress Magazine* for a directory of such software.

Some additional graphical methods are introduced next for possible use by practitioners and others in analyzing processes and operations to achieve improvement and control. They are not exhaustive of methods available. An historical perspective is also included to help challenge the imagination in making applications and to illustrate that applications outside of the manufacturing arena are not only feasible, but beneficial.

11-4.1 A Brief History of Graphical Methods

The use of graphical methods goes back far before the modern practice of quality control. In fact, this use was widespread when statistical summaries were made for the rulers of countries and only one copy of the report was published [Fienberg (1979)]. Some of these early reports had beautifully drawn charts in many colors and very innovative plots. William Playfair's *Commercial and Political Atlas, 1786* contained not only a wealth of economic data but the first recorded bar charts. The printing press had a chilling effect on graphical methods. Typesetting enabled multiple printing of articles and books, but the reproduction of charts and pictures became prohibitively expensive. The use of graphical methods in published reports appears to have declined until recent years.

The resurgence in graphical methods is due to several factors. One driving force is the tremendous quantity of data collected. It is not uncommon to collect millions of observations on the quality of a product line every month. These data are collected for many reasons:

- Automated test facilities
- Multiple tests per item
- Tests at multiple stages in production
- 100% inspections of some components
- Large production numbers
- Computer-controlled processes

Many of our usual statistical procedures break down under this data load. Outliers (or data errors) cause havoc with averages and standard deviations. Computations become prohibitively expensive. The data handling procedures become so complex that all efforts are diverted to the collection and storage of the data with no time for analysis. The analyst becomes overwhelmed by the quantity of data.

Turning Data into Information

One of the best examples of handling staggering quantities of data is from the early days of navigation in the U.S. Navy [Whipple (1984)]. While recovering from a broken leg, a young Navy lieutenant named Mathew Maury was brash enough to draft proposals for several needed reforms in the Navy. Because one of his reforms included retiring half of the admirals on half pay, Maury was not exactly everyone's favorite young officer. Upon his recovery in 1842, the Navy assigned Maury to one of the worst jobs in the Navy: chief of metrology.

Maury soon discovered that he was also the keeper of the logbooks, rooms and rooms full of completed logs of every naval voyage by American Navy ships. In these logs were the direction and speed of the currents, water depths and temperatures, and prevailing wind strengths and directions. One of Maury's loves was navigation, and he was appalled at the poor aids the American sea captains had. In a letter to the War Office Maury explained that when an American ship sailed even into the Chesapeake Bay, the captain had to rely on charts provided by the English admiralty.

Maury soon began to compile the hundreds of thousands of records he had in his possession. His goal was to "generalize the experience of navigators in such a manner that each should have before him, at a glance, the experience of all" [Whipple (1984)]. He finally developed a set of simple graphics. He plotted prevailing wind as an arrow pointing downwind with the length of the arrow proportional to the strength of the wind. The current speed he plotted numerically under a finger pointing in the direction the current was flowing. Water temperatures were plotted and underlined.

A Captain Jackson in the bark *WHDC Wright* was one of the first to use Maury's new charts on a voyage from Baltimore to Rio de Janeiro. Maury's charts showed that sailing far to the east to avoid going under Brazil's jutting Cape Sao Roque was unnecessary. The currents and winds under the cape were not treacherous but favorable. The *Wright* reached Rio in thirty-eight days—seventeen days faster than the previous record.

The *Flying Cloud* set sail on her maiden voyage armed with Maury's charts from New York to San Francisco on June 2, 1851, around Cape Horn. She reached San Francisco in eighty-nine days—twenty-one hours less than a full month under the record. She broke this new record on her return trip. Using Maury's charts, the *Flying Cloud* had repaid her investors her full purchase price of $90,000 in six months.

Navy captains were cutting one third from around-the-world cruises soon afterward. Maury's charts provided each captain with the full knowledge of all who had sailed before, and each captain was building on this knowledge to improve his ship's performance.

In 1853, at Maury's urging, the first International Maritime Meteorological Conference was held in Brussels. Unanimously, the ten nations attending agreed to share information using Maury's revised abstract log. Maury promised a new edition of his charts to each sea captain who returned a log. In the next fifty years, ten nations submitted millions of completed abstract logs. "Maury had almost single-handedly brought navigation into the modern age, changing nearly every captain's traditional hunch and guesswork to scientific observation" [Whipple (1984)].

Turning Data into Action

The basic problem in quality assurance and quality control can be thought of as that of turning data into information that causes action. Mathew Maury had very few problems with getting action after he published his charts. After the first voyage using his charts had set new records, sea captains immediately saw the great advantage and were clamoring for the charts. In this case a clear presentation of the results was enough to secure the desired action.

In quality analyses there is often a more hostile reaction. Analyses often point to major problems and hint at causes. Managers and workers can be very defensive. Instead of treating the nonconforming product or process and the cause as the enemy, individuals often react by attacking the data, the analysis, or the results. The results must be made clear enough that everyone focuses on the problem and how to eliminate the cause.

A great example of facing a hostile audience and winning through perseverance with the help of innovative graphical methods is Florence Nightingale's fight with the British Army Medical Corps in the Crimean War. When asked by Sidney Herbert, the Secretary at War, to organize, train, and lead a team of thirty-eight nurses to the Crimea to work in the military hospitals, she accepted. But when she reached the Crimea, she found the conditions appalling. "The hospital barracks were infested with fleas and rats." Under the buildings, as a commission of inquiry later reported, "were sewers . . . loaded with filth . . . through which the wind blew sewer air up the pipes . . . where the sick were lying on straw mats" [Cohen (1984)].

Her criticisms of the military medical establishment carried little weight. She was only a nurse, and she was a woman. She immediately began collecting data on the casualties in the hospitals, but she faced not only the task of turning these data into information, but also the more difficult challenge of inventing ways to make the summaries and presentations of the results so clear that action would have to be taken. She was an ardent admirer of the Belgian astronomer statistician Lambert-Adolphe-Jacques Quetelet. "Ms. Nightingale . . . early displayed a predilection for collecting and analyzing data" [Cohen (1984)]. When she returned to England, she met William Farr, a pioneer in the use of graphical statistics. She used his bar plots to great advantage and invented what are now called radial or polar plots to make her points dramatically. From Figure 11-48 it can be seen how bad the situation was in 1854 and 1855. By January 1855 the annualized death rate from contagious diseases was so great that the army would have to be replaced every year just from that one cause. The death rate from contagious diseases was roughly twice the death rate from wounds and all other causes.

The results of Florence Nightingale's efforts appear dramatically in Figure 11-49. By June 1855 the death rate from contagious diseases was one ninth of what it had been in February. In fact, by the end of the Crimean War the death rate for the soldiers in the Crimea was lower than the death rate of those stationed in England.

On returning to England, Florence Nightingale immediately attacked the problems of the home soldier. Figure 11-50 shows how she compared the death rates of English soldiers and civilian males in the same age groups. The comparisons are shocking. Soldiers had a death rate that was twenty times higher for contagious diseases. Her charts were presented to the newly established Medical Practices Commission through a third party

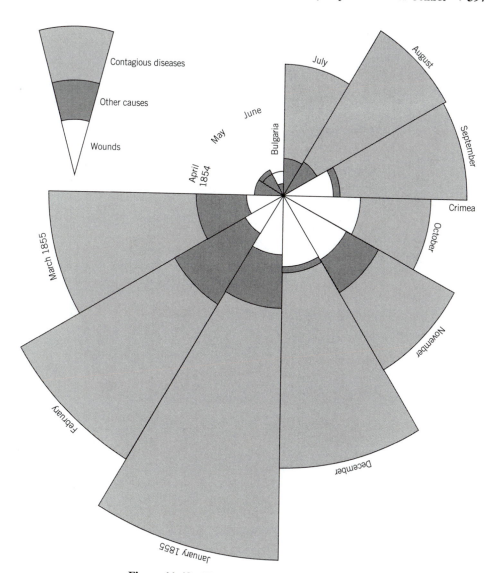

Figure 11-48 Florence Nightingale's Polar Chart

(a woman could not appear before the commission). By now Prince Albert and Queen Victoria had become interested, and the Army Medical Service was forced to yield to the clearly presented facts. Major reforms were instituted.

11-4.2 Some Additional Graphical Methods

The preceding sections concentrated on several simple graphical methods that may have widespread applicability throughout a company. At least a basic understanding of each method should be part of each employee's training. In this section three more graphical methods are described that are widely used in quality and productivity studies. Some of

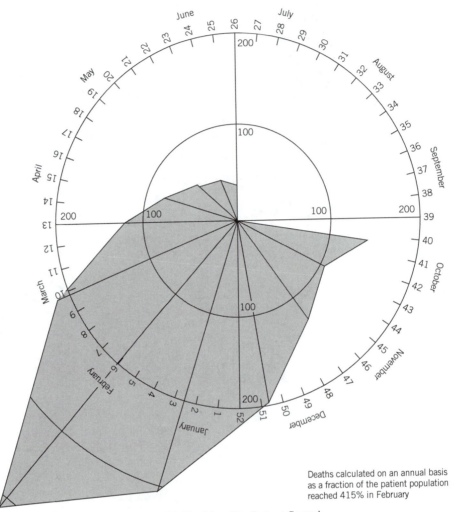

Figure 11-49   Mortality Rate at Scutari

these are as easy to use as the earlier ones, some require more effort, but the results are easily understood. Many of these methods are widely used in certain companies by every level of management and worker. These graphical methods are:

- Bar plots
- Box plots
- Quantile-quantile plots

Barplots
One of the most widely used graphics is the bar plot. Earlier, the simple bar plots used by Florence Nightingale with great effect were presented. It was also noted that the earliest recorded use appears to be by William Playfair in 1786 [Playfair (1801)]. The Pareto

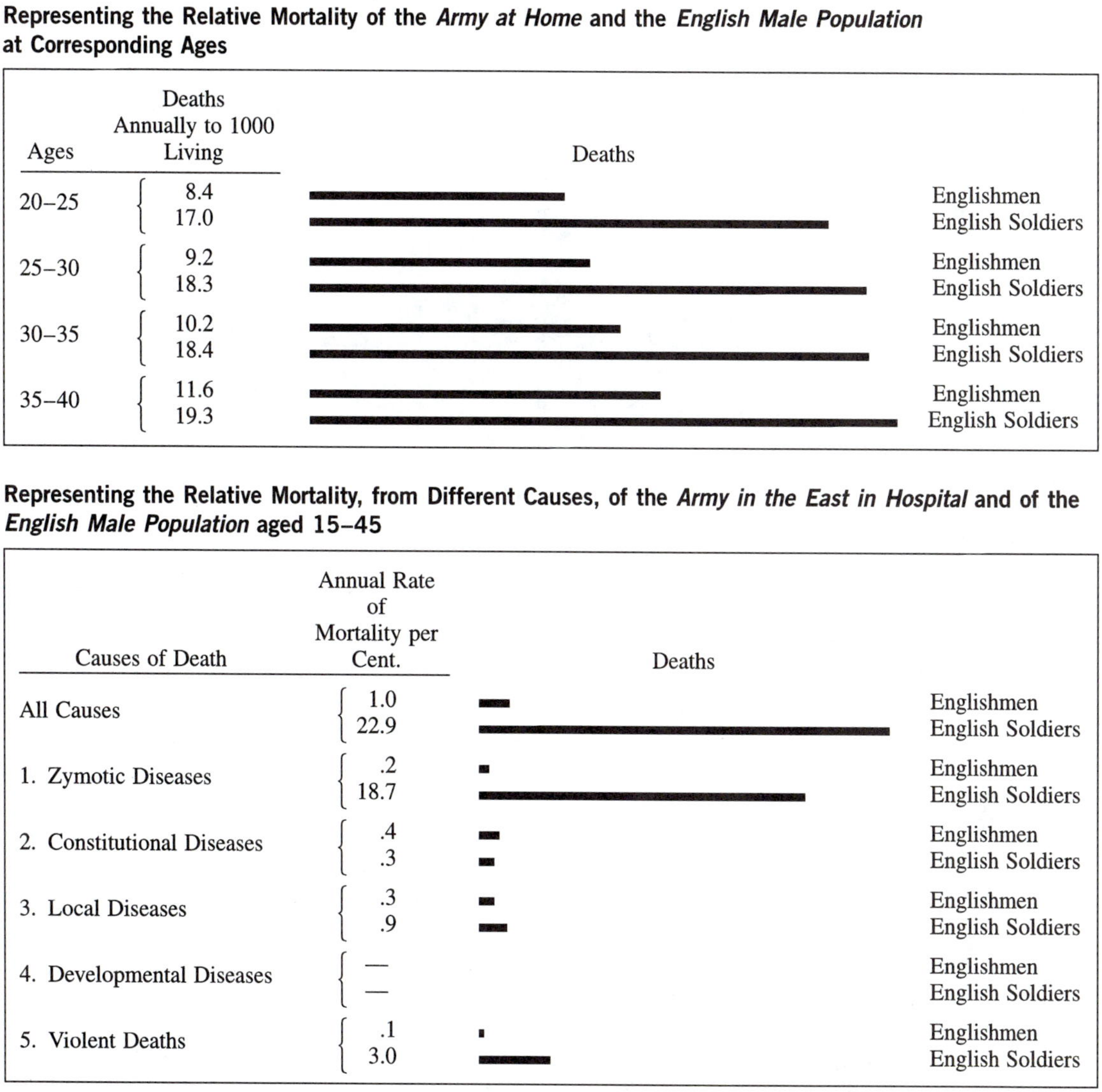

Representing the Relative Mortality of the *Army at Home* and the *English Male Population* at Corresponding Ages

Ages	Deaths Annually to 1000 Living	Deaths	
20–25	{ 8.4	▬▬▬▬▬▬▬	Englishmen
	17.0	▬▬▬▬▬▬▬▬▬▬▬▬▬▬▬	English Soldiers
25–30	{ 9.2	▬▬▬▬▬▬▬▬	Englishmen
	18.3	▬▬▬▬▬▬▬▬▬▬▬▬▬▬▬▬	English Soldiers
30–35	{ 10.2	▬▬▬▬▬▬▬▬	Englishmen
	18.4	▬▬▬▬▬▬▬▬▬▬▬▬▬▬▬▬	English Soldiers
35–40	{ 11.6	▬▬▬▬▬▬▬▬▬	Englishmen
	19.3	▬▬▬▬▬▬▬▬▬▬▬▬▬▬▬▬	English Soldiers

Representing the Relative Mortality, from Different Causes, of the *Army in the East in Hospital* and of the *English Male Population* aged 15–45

Causes of Death	Annual Rate of Mortality per Cent.	Deaths	
All Causes	{ 1.0	▬	Englishmen
	22.9	▬▬▬▬▬▬▬▬▬▬▬▬▬▬▬▬▬▬	English Soldiers
1. Zymotic Diseases	{ .2	▪	Englishmen
	18.7	▬▬▬▬▬▬▬▬▬▬▬▬▬▬▬	English Soldiers
2. Constitutional Diseases	{ .4	▬	Englishmen
	.3	▬	English Soldiers
3. Local Diseases	{ .3	▬	Englishmen
	.9	▬▬	English Soldiers
4. Developmental Diseases	{ —		Englishmen
	—		English Soldiers
5. Violent Deaths	{ .1	▪	Englishmen
	3.0	▬▬▬▬	English Soldiers

Figure 11-50 Florence Nightingale's Bar Plots

diagram that was discussed earlier is a version of a bar plot. The histogram can also be thought of as a special bar plot. Ishikawa (1976) calls bar graphs (bar plots) one of the three most fundamental graphs. (Pie charts and line graphs are the other two.)

Bar plots can have the bars running horizontally or vertically. Bars can extend above the line, below the line, or both. They can be split vertically or horizontally to show subgroups. Bar plots are usually two-dimensional representations, but a third dimension can be added. Bar plots are a favorite of computer software purveyors because they are easy to compute and understand and they lend themselves to vivid colors. Schmid (1983) devotes an entire chapter to bar plots.

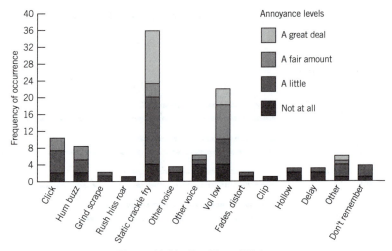

Figure 11-51   Bar Plot of Noises

Simple Bar Plots.   The simplest bar plots are just representations of numbers or percentages by a column. They are often used to compare things across time or across production facilities or locations. Figure 11-51 shows, for the small number of customers having transmission difficulties, what kind of noise it was they heard. It is easy to see from this bar plot which types of noises were the biggest problems.

Another simple bar plot is the paired bar plot. Ishikawa (1976) uses a paired bar plot to show advertising expenditures for two years by type of media (Figure 11-52).

Segmented Bar Plots.   Bar plots can easily be segmented to show subgroup effects. Earlier, a segmented bar plot was used to show weekly results of a soldering process quality improvement program using Pareto diagrams (Figure 11-18). Figure 11-53 shows the amount of effort of a quality organization by type of function. Notice the very different impression one gets of their activities with the segmented bar plot than one would have with just a standard bar plot.

Three-Dimensional Bar Plots.   The bar plot can sometimes be extended easily to a third dimension to bring new insight to a problem. In Figure 11-54, circuit pack failures are plotted by issue date and by type of component. Several things are clear at once. The first issue had many problems. Component 8 was most failure prone; but components 6, 7, 5, and 1 were also problems. By issue C most component problems had been eliminated, but component 8 was still in trouble. Finally by the fourth issue (D), the component failures had been substantially reduced.

Box Plots

One of the simplest and most useful ways of summarizing data is the box plot [Tukey (1977)]. The box plot is simply a five-number summary of the data. The upper and lower quartiles form the ends of a box, the median is a line dividing the box, and the minimum and maximum of the data are drawn as points at the end of lines ("whiskers") extending

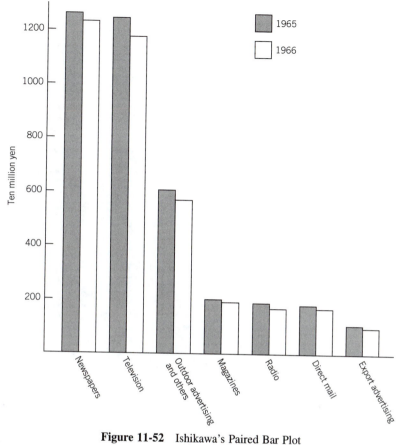

Figure 11-52 Ishikawa's Paired Bar Plot

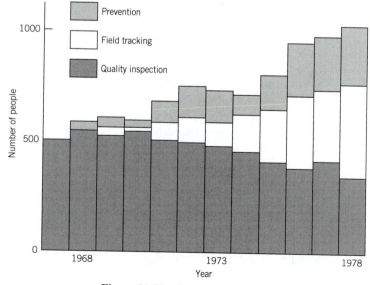

Figure 11-53 Segmented Bar Plot

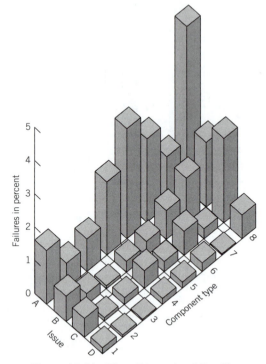

Figure 11-54 Three-Dimensional Bar Plot

from the box. A simple box plot of the observations of fifty resistances of wires from a cable is shown in Figure 11-55.

In this plot, some evidence of symmetry can be seen. It is quickly seen that 50% of the resistances are well between 85 and 87 ohms per mile and that all the resistances in the sample lie between 83 and 89 ohms per mile. The median is just over 86 ohms per mile.

Notched Box Plots.   In Figure 11-56 samples from each of eight cables are compared. The box plots are notched to indicate variability of the median [McGill, Tukey, and Larsen (1978)]. The notch widths are calculated so that if the notches around two medians do not overlap, the medians are roughly different at a 5% significance level. In this plot there were fifty observations from each cable. In studying the plot, it is seen that there is some evidence of drift toward higher resistances in the middle and then a correction back toward the standard of 86.5 ohms per mile.

Variable-Width Box Plots.   When there are different numbers of observations in the boxes, it is useful to indicate the sample size. In Figure 11-57 box plots with widths proportional to the log of the sample size are plotted. Here the results are from chemical analyses and are taken month by month. Differences are easily spotted by month in both median and variability. Outliers are identified as points that are more than 1.5 times the interquartile distance from either quartile. These are plotted as asterisks. Some computer programs automatically identify these points and label them.

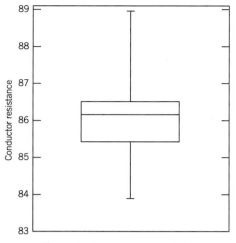

Figure 11-55   Simple Box Plot

Box plots are easy to construct and effective in displaying large quantities of data in a digestible form. Imagine the 500 observations in Figure 11-56 plotted as a simple scatter plot and how difficult it would be to estimate the average, changes over time, or differences between cables. Next another kind of box plot will be observed in which confidence intervals are used to define the box rather than empirical data.

Box Plots with Sampling Variability.   Schmid (1983) has a chapter devoted to presentation of errors in data, which he calls "a neglected problem in statistical graphics." He shows how bar plots can be modified to show confidence limits by overlaying bars or by shading. He also gives examples of confidence levels overlaid on line plots. One of the

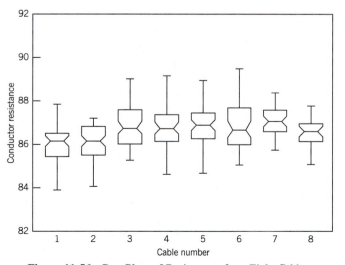

Figure 11-56   Box Plots of Resistances from Eight Cables

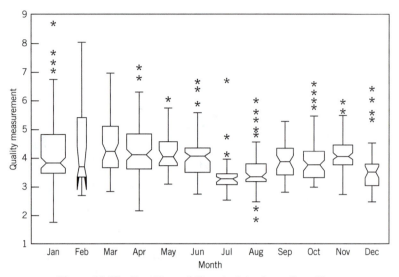

Figure 11-57   Box Plots of Chemical Analyses Over Time

best methods for displaying the sampling variability is the box plot. He uses a plot of educational attainment of adult males from Golladay (1977) as an excellent example of this (Figure 11-58). In her plot, Golladay displays the average as the center of the box, the 68% confidence interval as the ends of the box, and the 95% confidence interval as the whiskers.

The Quality Measurement Plan

A very interesting and important use of the box plot was developed by Bruce Hoadley (1981). He devised a very sophisticated way of using modern statistical methods to better report results from AT&T's quality audits. The Quality Measurement Plan (QMP) provided a good estimate of process quality and a good indication of whether the process was producing product that met quality objectives. The QMP uses data from a current sample and the five previous samples weighted appropriately.

Figure 11-59 shows the definition of the QMP box plot. Several estimates of quality are calculated for each period (a six-week sampling period). The current sample index, the long-run average of thirty-six weeks, and the best measure of quality are all plotted inside the box and whiskers. In Figure 11-60, the boxes and whiskers are defined. The boxes form a 90% confidence interval around the best estimate, and the ends of the whiskers form a 98% confidence interval. That is, the bottom of the whisker is the first percentile, the bottom of the box the fifth percentile, and the best estimate (the center line) is the fiftieth percentile.

By transforming the quality standards to indices in which standard quality is represented as one, products with different quality objectives could still be compared. Quality can be checked by a quick glance at the results. In Figure 11-60 it may be seen that when the box covers the standard quality line (or is above it), quality is considered good. When the box does not cover the standard quality line but the whiskers do, there is an "alert" condition, indicating that quality is suspect. When neither the box nor the whiskers cover

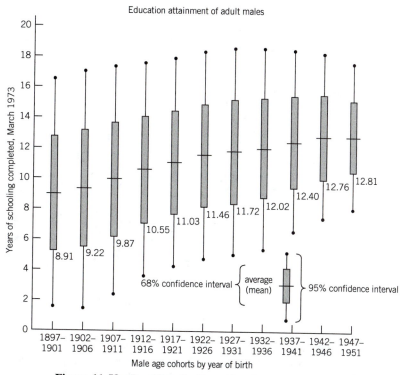

Figure 11-58 Box Plots for Portraying Sampling Variability

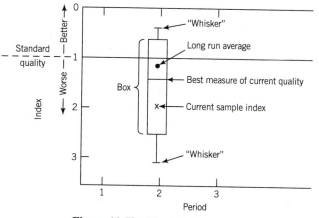

Figure 11-59 The QMP Box Plot

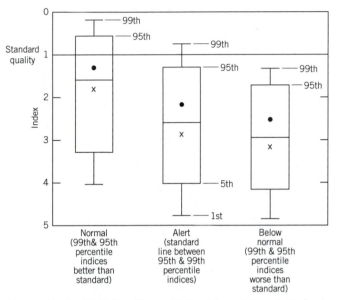

Figure 11-60 QMP Box Plots with Confidence Intervals Defined

the standard quality line, the quality is called below normal, and corrective action must be taken immediately. Thus, when the ninety-ninth percentile index, represented as the top of the whisker, falls below the standard quality line, there is more than 99% confidence that the product or service tested is not meeting its quality standard.

Hoadley based his calculations of the best estimate and confidence intervals on empirical Bayes statistics and the calculations are nontrivial. For a thorough discussion, see Hoadley (1981). In simple terms, the best estimate is a weighted function of the six sets of data. The best estimate is

$$BE = w(\text{average of first five}) + (1 - w)(\text{Current sample})$$

where w is a calculated weight. The w is a function of process stability and sample variability. Thus, if the process has little variability and only a small current sample is taken, w will be close to 1. When the process variability is high and a large current sample is taken, w will be small, and most of the weight will be on the current sample results.

Quantile-Quantile Plots
One of the most useful graphical techniques is the quantile-quantile plot of Wilk and Gnanadesikan (1968). Empirical quantile-quantile plots can be used to make detailed comparisons of the distributions of two data sets. Quantile-quantile plots can also be used to compare a sample from an unknown distribution with an assumed theoretical distribution.

Empirical Quantile-Quantile Plots. The empirical quantile-quantile plot is easy to construct. If there are two samples from unknown distributions, say, x_i, $i = 1, \ldots, n$ and y_i, $i = 1, \ldots, n$, just order the values in each sample and plot x_i against y_i, and so on. If the samples are from the same distribution, the points will lie on or close to a straight line.

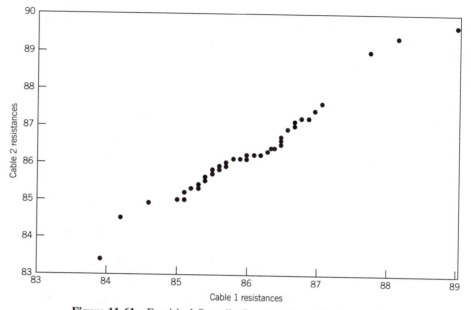

Figure 11-61 Empirical Quantile-Quantile Plot of Resistance Data

The way in which the points differ from a straight line gives clues to how the distributions differ. If the samples are of different sizes it is a little more difficult. The empirical quantiles for any range of values, say, p_i, $i = 1, \ldots, m$ can be calculated. For example, the median ($p = 0.5$) from x is plotted against the median from y, the upper quantiles are plotted against each other, and so on.

Chambers, Cleveland, Kleiner, and Tukey (1983) suggest the following when making empirical quantile-quantile plots from unequal data sets. Use the entire set of ordered values from the smaller data set, and interpolate a corresponding set of quantiles from the larger set. They give an excellent explanation of quantile-quantile plots along with several good examples.

Figure 11-61 illustrates an empirical quantile-quantile plot of resistance from two cables. The straightness of the line indicates that the underlying distributions are the same, the slope of 45° indicates that the samples have the same standard deviations, and the nearness of the medians indicates similar location parameters also.

Theoretical Quantile-Quantile Plots. Another important use of quantile-quantile plots is in testing the assumption that a particular set of data is from a particular distribution. The ability to assume that observations are from a known distribution is the first step in building many models. One is then able to model phenomena in a very concise way by estimating the parameters. Understanding the distribution also frequently leads to insight into physical or engineering effects.

The idea of a theoretical quantile-quantile plot is quite simple. Just as before, with the empirical quantile-quantile plot, two sets of ordered data are plotted against each other. This time, however, one of the sets of ordered data is generated from the assumed

Table 11-7 Cumulative Distribution Functions for Nine Distributions

Distribution	$F(y)$	Abscissa	Ordinate
Uniform	$\dfrac{y-\mu}{\sigma}$	p_i	y_i
Normal	$\Phi\left(\dfrac{y-\mu}{\sigma}\right)$	$\Phi^{-1}(p_i)$	y_i
Lognormal	$\Phi\left[\dfrac{\ln(y)-\alpha}{\beta}\right]$	$\Phi^{-1}(p_i)$	$\ln(y_i)$
Exponential	$1-\exp\left[-\left(\dfrac{y-\mu}{\sigma}\right)\right]$	$\ln[1/(1-p_i)]$	y_i
Extreme-Value	$1-\exp\left[-\exp\left(\dfrac{y-\mu}{\sigma}\right)\right]$	$\ln\{\ln[1/(1-p_i)]\}$	y_i
Weibull	$1-\exp\left[-\left(\dfrac{y}{\alpha}\right)^{\beta}\right]$	$\ln\{\ln[1/(1-p_i)]\}$	$\ln(y_i)$
Laplace	$\begin{cases}\dfrac{1}{2}\cdot\exp\left(\dfrac{y-\mu}{\sigma}\right), & y\le\mu \\[2mm] 1-\dfrac{1}{2}\exp\left(-\dfrac{y-\mu}{\sigma}\right), & y>\mu\end{cases}$	$\begin{cases}\ln(2-p_i), & p_i\le\dfrac{1}{2} \\[2mm] \ln[1/(2-2p_i)], & p_i>\dfrac{1}{2}\end{cases}$	y_i
Logistic	$1/\left[1+\exp\left(-\dfrac{y-\mu}{\sigma}\right)\right]$	$\ln[p_i/(1-p_i)]$	y_i
Cauchy	$\dfrac{1}{2}+\dfrac{1}{\pi}\cdot\arctan\left(\dfrac{y-\mu}{\sigma}\right)$	$\tan\left[\pi\cdot\left(p_i-\dfrac{1}{2}\right)\right]$	y_i

theoretical distribution. If there are y_i, $i = 1, \ldots, n$, values from an unknown distribution to be compared with one that came from a normal (Gaussian) distribution with mean 0 and variance 1, n quantiles for x_i, $i = 1, \ldots, n$. In this case the x_i when ordered correspond to the order statistics with quantiles $p_i = (i - 0.5)/n$.

If the $F(y)$ is the cumulative distribution function of the assumed distribution then the quantiles to be plotted are the inverses of the assumed distribution:

$$F^{-1}(p_i), \qquad i = 1, \ldots, n$$

These quantiles are easy to compute as long as F is easy to invert. Table 11-7 contains the cumulative distribution functions for nine frequently used distributions and the corresponding quantile-quantile plotting points.

Figure 11-62 shows the results of an investigation of a distributional assumption for the cable resistances. The fifty observations are plotted against fifty quantiles from the standard normal distribution. The intercept of 86.0 ohms per mile gives an estimate of the average and the slope, which is less than the 45° angle indicates a standard deviation less than 1.

Quantile-Quantile Plots in Reliability. Quantile-quantile plots and probability plots are widely used in reliability analysis (see Chapter 14). Special probability paper is available

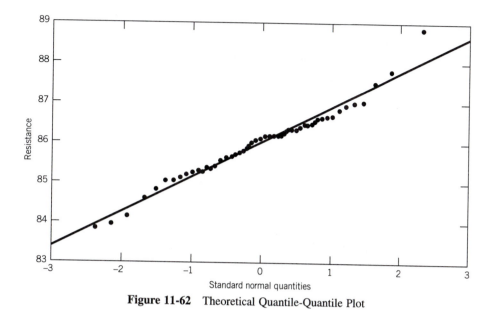

Figure 11-62   Theoretical Quantile-Quantile Plot

for many families of distributions. No special paper is necessary as long as the distribution F can be inverted or tables of standard quantiles exist. Quantile-quantile plots are so frequently used that many computer software packages include quantile-quantile plotting functions.

The main problem to be faced in reliability when using quantile-quantile plots is that reliability data are often censored (see Chapter 14). Michael (1979) addresses the problem of quantile-quantile plots with censored data. An excellent discussion of the problem appears also in Chambers, Cleveland, Kleiner, and Tukey (1983).

Limitations of Quantile-Quantile Plots.   As Michael (1983) points out, the main drawback of quantile-quantile plotting is its subjectivity. Only with experience are users able to judge whether an apparent deviation from linearity is significant or not. The variability of the plotted points depends on the sample size, the order of the points, and the distribution. There is high correlation between neighboring points. An alternative to these subjective judgments is the use of goodness-of-fit statistics. As Michael indicates, the use of such a test statistic is a drastic reduction of the data and has virtually no exploratory value. When the test statistic falls in the critical region, there is little indication how the data differed from the assumed distribution.

Michael (1983) shows how the quantile-quantile plot and goodness-of-fit statistics can be regarded as complementary methods. He creates the stabilized probability plot with accompanying graphical goodness-of-fit tests. These graphical methods give nice bounds on the quantile-quantile plots and not only show when the test statistic falls in the critical region, but also indicate why.

Chambers, Cleveland, Kleiner, and Tukey (1983) devote an entire chapter to assessing distributional assumptions about data. Their discussions about the use of quantile-quantile plots are excellent and very thorough. The interested reader should also consult

Wilk and Gnanadesikan (1968). Other interesting examples of probability plotting used to detect errors are given in Deming (1982). An example of this type of graphical technique is the normal probability plot of Figure 11-14 in the earlier discussion of histograms.

▶ 11-5 CONCLUSIONS

This chapter has presented applications of the principles and techniques of earlier chapters as well as graphical methods, with applications, found useful in analyzing situations for improvement and control. It has attempted to tie together some of the material presented earlier. A clear message is that whenever work is started to solve a problem, it is never known in advance exactly what techniques should be used.

The chapter has concentrated on two very important functions in the quality disciplines, the improvement and control of quality. By means of example a relatively simple set of six steps for quality improvement has been delineated. Following this, procedures for the control of many phases of production and service were presented. The next chapters discuss further techniques of process and product improvement.

▶ 11-6 REFERENCES

AT&T Technologies (1984), *Statistical Quality Control Handbook*, AT&T Technologies, Indianapolis, IN.

Carlsen, R. D., and Lewis, J. A. (1979), *The Systems Analysis Workbook*, Second Edition, Prentice-Hall, Englewood Cliffs, NJ.

Chambers, J. M., Cleveland, W. S., Kleiner, B., and Tukey, P. A. (1983), *Graphical Methods for Data Analysis*, Wadsworth International Group, Belmont, CA.

Cohen, I. B. (1984), "Florence Nightingale," *Scientific American*, Vol. 250, No. 3, March; pp. 128–37.

Daniel, C., and Wood, F. S. (1980), *Fitting Equations to Data*, Second Edition, Wiley, New York.

Deming, W. E. (1967), "What Happened in Japan?" *Industrial Quality Control*, Vol. 24, No. 2, March; pp. 89–93.

Deming, W. E. (1975), "On Some Statistical Aids toward Economic Production," *Interfaces, The Institute of Management Science*, Vol. 5, No. 4, Aug.; pp. 1–15.

Deming, W. E. (1982), *Quality, Productivity, and Competitive Position*, Massachusetts Institute of Technology, Center for Advanced Engineering Study, Cambridge, MA.

Deming, W. E. (1986), *Out of the Crisis*, p. 315, Massachusetts Institute of Technology, Cambridge, MA.

Diaconis, P., and Freedman, D. (1981), "On the Maximum Deviation between the Histogram and the Underlying Density," *Zeitscript fur Wahrscheinlichkeitstheori*, Vol. 57, pp. 453–76.

Fienberg, S. E. (1979), "Graphical Methods in Statistics," *American Statistician*, Vol. 33, No. 4, Nov.; pp. 165–78.

Golladay, Mary A. (1977), "The Condition of Education," *Part 1, HEW National Center for Education Statistics*, U.S. Government Printing Office, Washington, D.C., p. 104.

Hoadley, B. (1981), "The Quality Measurement Plan (QMP)," *The Bell System Technical Journal*, Vol. 60, No. 2, Feb.; pp. 215–73.

Hoaglin, D. C., Mosteller, F., and Tukey, J. W. (1983), *Understanding Robust and Exploratory Data Analysis*, Wiley, New York.

Ishikawa, K. (1976), *Guide to Quality Control*, Asian Productivity Organization, Nordica International Ltd., Hong Kong. (Available in the United States from UNIPUB, New York.)

Juran, J. M. (1964), *Managerial Breakthrough*, McGraw-Hill, New York.

Juran, J. M. and Gryna, F. M., Jr. (1993), *Quality Planning and Analysis*, Third Edition, McGraw-Hill, New York.

McGill, R., Tukey, J. W., and Larsen, W. A. (1978), "Variations of Box Plots," *The American Statistician*, Vol. 32, No. 1, Feb.; pp. 12–16.

Michael, J. R. (1979), "Fundamentals of Probability Plotting with Applications to Censored Data," Private Communication.

Michael, J. R. (1983), "The Stabilized Probability Plot," *Biometrika*, Vol. 70, No. 1, March; pp. 11–17.

Ott, E. R. (1975), *Process Quality Control*, McGraw-Hill, New York.

Ott, E. R. (1980), "Process Improvement with Quality Control," *Quality*, April; pp. 31–33.

Ott, E. R., and Schilling, E. G. (1990), *Process Quality Control*, McGraw-Hill, New York.

Playfair, W. (1801), *Commercial and Political Atlas*, Third Edition, London: Stockdale.

Schmid, C. F. (1983), *Statistical Graphics*, Wiley, New York.

Schin, R. (1960), "Quality Control Engineering—In Process and Product Control," *Industrial Quality Control*, Vol. 16, No. 10, April; pp. 2–8.

Seder, L. A., and Cowan, D. (1956), "The Span Plan Method Process Capability Analysis," *ASQC General Publications No. 3.*

Stephens, K. S. (1965a), "Quality Control—Small and Large," *Proceedings of the Quality Control Conference*, U.S. Department of Commerce, Bureau of Public Roads, Washington, D.C., April 6, 1965.

Stephens, K. S. (1965b), "Process Capabilities—Small and Large," *Transactions of the 1st Pan American Congress on Quality Control and Statistics in Industry,* Mexico City, May 12, 1965.

Tufte, E. R. (1983), *The Visual Display of Quantitative Information,* Graphics Press, Cheshire, CT.

Tukey, J. W. (1972), "Some Graphic and Semigraphic Displays," in *Statistical Papers in Honor of George W. Snedecor,* edited by T. A. Bancroft, Iowa State Press, Ames, IA.

Tukey, J. W. (1977), *Exploratory Data Analysis,* Addison-Wesley, Reading, MA.

Turnbull, D. M., and Higby, C. W. (1985), "Writing Quality Procedures," *Quality Progress,* Feb.; pp. 18–23.

Whipple, A. B. C. (1984), "Stranded Navy Man Who Charted the World's Seas," *Smithsonian,* March; pp. 171–86.

Wilk, M. B., and Gnanadesikan, R. (1968), "Probability Plotting Methods for Analysis of Data," *Biometrika,* Vol. 55, March; pp. 1–17.

▶ 11-7 PROBLEMS

1. A bottletop crowning problem was being experienced by a bottling company. In an attempt to quantify and possibly isolate the nature of the problem, a simple data sheet was prepared on which to record the results of a critical inspection on the crowns of ten bottles from each of the crowning heads every fifteen minutes. Data on twenty samples (intervals) are shown below. Only an indication of satisfactory (S) or unsatisfactory (U) was recorded.

				Crowning Head					
Interval	1	2	3	4	5	6	7	8	9	10
1	S	S	S	U	S	S	U	U	U	S
2	U	U	S	S	S	S	U	U	S	S
3	S	S	U	U	U	S	U	S	S	U
4	S	S	S	U	S	S	U	U	U	S
5	S	S	S	S	S	U	U	S	S	U
6	S	S	U	S	S	S	U	U	S	S
7	S	S	U	S	S	S	U	U	U	S
8	S	U	U	S	S	S	U	U	U	U
9	S	S	U	S	S	S	U	S	S	S
10	U	S	U	S	U	S	U	U	S	S
11	S	S	S	S	U	U	U	S	S	U
12	S	U	S	S	S	U	S	U	S	S
13	S	S	S	S	S	S	S	S	U	S
14	S	S	S	S	U	S	U	U	S	S
15	S	S	S	S	U	S	S	U	S	S
16	S	S	S	U	S	S	U	S	S	U
17	S	S	U	S	S	U	U	S	S	S
18	S	S	S	S	S	S	U	U	S	S
19	S	S	S	U	S	S	U	S	S	S
20	S	S	S	S	S	S	U	U	S	S

Analyze the data by time and by crowning head. What conclusions would you make from this initial study?

2. An analysis of the types of nonconformities occurring in the manufacture of bottles for a popular soft drink reveals the following:

Stones	58.5%
Seeds	19.5
Pressure check	6.3
Lip check	3.8
Check under bead	3.3
Marks	3.2
High strain	1.3
Out of roundness	1.2
Others	2.9

Prepare a Pareto diagram from these data.

3. The following data are obtained from a breakdown by cause of rejected castings in an iron foundry over a six-month period:

Total rejections	16.9%	Shrink	0.9%
Blow holes	3.3	Lap	0.5
Sandwash	3.7	Swell	0.2
Misrun	1.5	Scab	0.1
Shift	0.4	Slag	0.3
Core shift	2.2	Miscellaneous	3.8

Prepare a Pareto diagram from these data, including the secondary scale of the actual percent of rejections by cause. Comment on the nature of the data collection.

4. A bottling company prepares a breakdown of causes of lost time of production to study this characteristic for improvement. The following data are obtained:

Breakdown and repair	38.7%
Cleaning and maintenance	20.8
Electricity	2.0
Water	3.0
Lack of manpower	1.5
Lack of bottles	1.0
Defective caps	0.4
Worker transportation service	0.4
Lack of forklift	0.2
Lack of CO_2	0.1
Other	31.9

Additionally, data on the actual lost time in hours (nearest quarter) is recorded for 26 days as follows:

Day	Lost Time	Day	Lost Time
1	4.0	14	3.5
2	3.5	15	4.5
3	2.0	16	6.5
4	2.75	17	4.25
5	3.5	18	2.75
6	2.75	19	3.0
7	2.0	20	3.25
8	3.5	21	3.75
9	2.0	22	3.5
10	3.0	23	2.0
11	3.0	24	2.5
12	3.25	25	4.0
13	3.25	26	3.0

Prepare a Pareto diagram from these data. Comment on the nature of the data collection. Prepare an x chart for analysis of lost time. Is this characteristic in control for the period studied?

5. Data for the port detentions (rejections) of exports from Latin American countries by principal causes for the year 1990 is as follows. Prepare and interpret a Pareto diagram for these data.

Cause	*No. of Detentions*
Insect and rodent filth/damage	273
Pesticides	171
Mold	133
Contaminated packaging	101
New or not authorized drugs	84
Aflatoxin	76

Decomposition	72
Labeling	71
Unknown process	34
Dirty	26
Prohibited colorants	17
E. coli	16
Histamines	16
Defective packaging	14
Hipoglicina	13
Process not hygienic	10
Other additives	7
Consumer protection law violation	9
Salmonella	4
Extraneous moisture	3
Poisonous substance	1
Prohibited substance	1

6. For ten important world commodities, the following is the average value (in millions of U.S. $) of exports for the period 1990–1995. Prepare a Pareto diagram for these data.

Commodity	Value of World Exports	Commodity	Value of World Exports
Sugar	4040	Cocoa	1247
Coffee	3052	Tin	838
Copper	2881	Jute	646
Cotton	2534	Tea	626
Rubber	1428	Sisal	229

7. The following data represent a production process on circuit packs, and are the nonconformities found in 1000 assemblies per week.

Numbers of Nonconformities by Type

Week	Missing Compo- nent	Wrong Compo- nent	Too Much Solder	Insuffi- cient Solder	Failed Compo- nent
1	93	120	18	24	57
2	81	132	29	42	31
3	62	91	31	39	61
4	57	88	42	27	34
Totals	293	431	120	132	183

Make a Pareto diagram of the nonconformities. Split the data into two parts, weeks 1 and 2 versus weeks 3 and 4, and plot two Pareto diagrams and compare. Has there been improvement?

8. For purposes of developing instructional material and courses in the art of communication, a study revealed the following data with respect to the percentage of use of four principal modes of communication: (1) Listening—45%, (2) Speaking—30%, (3) Reading—15%, and (4) Writing—10%. Does the Pareto principle appear to apply to this topic?

9. A polypropylene tape is obtained by extruding the polymer, slitting the extruded sheet, and winding the tapes on take-up reels. The problem of excessive waste on the extruder was a concern to company management and the extruder department personnel. A meeting of knowledgeable persons was held and the following list of factors and subfactors was compiled.

A. *Machines*

Maintenance	Stock Control
Inspection	Identification of
Replacement Parts	Vital Parts

B. *Settings*

Temperature	Air Blower
Extruder Speed	Tower Height
Take-up Speed	Stretch Ratio
Winders	

C. *Materials*

Quantity	Mixing
Quality	Preparation
Moisture	Instructions
Foreign Matter	Cleanliness
Purity	Homogeneity
Granular Size	

D. *Operators*

Training	Temperature Control
Experience	Extruder
Absenteeism	Stretching
Attentiveness and Speed	Winder
Film Thickness	Feeding
Width Control	

E. *Operation*

Start-up	Screen Change
Shut-down	Bobbin Change

F. *Measuring Equipment*

Precision	Thickness Gauge
Thermo-Controls	Speedometer

G. *Power Failure*

Frequency	Maintenance
Generator	Controls

Prepare a CE diagram from this information.

10. Use a CE diagram to explore the relationship between a student's activities during the term and the student's final grade. Identify at least four or five major branches and several subbranches.

11. The following prices of used four-door Honda Accords were taken from newspaper ads in 1984:

Year	Miles	Price	Year	Miles	Price
1979	80,000	3,500	1981	42,000	7,000
1979	65,000	4,200	1981	58,000	6,300
1979	71,000	3,900	1981	50,000	7,700
1980	41,000	6,000	1982	30,000	8,000
1980	54,000	5,800	1982	28,000	7,500
1980	64,000	4,900	1983	20,000	8,600
1981	36,000	7,900	1983	19,000	8,700
1981	40,000	6,700			

Plot year against price and miles against price. By using coding for price or miles, plot all three variables. Identify the cars that appear to be the best buys.

12. Pick one operation with which you are familiar, and construct a flowchart. Mark on the flowchart the points at which quality control or quality assurance checks are made (or should be made). Are there obvious places where the operation could be improved?

13. Arrange a visit to a local factory, bank, insurance office, shipping agent, public transportation company, restaurant, or other business. Develop a flowchart of operations pertaining to a product, a subassembly, and/or a service performed. Discuss with a responsible person the nature of controls needed at various points in the operation, and add these to your flowchart.

14. Find an example of the use of graphical statistics in recent newspapers or popular magazines. Discuss why the graph helps or hinders your understanding of the data.

Replot the data in a way that improves understanding, using any of the methods discussed in this chapter.

15. Replot the scatter plots in Problem 11 using median smoothing.

16. You have the following thirty-five observations of weights of piece parts from a metal-stamping process. Make a histogram of the data, and then make a stem-and-leaf plot. If it is critical that no piece be under 20 grams, what would you recommend?

Weights in Grams of Piece Parts

20.7	21.7	20.3	26.8	24.9	24.1	25.5
25.9	21.2	22.4	22.5	23.7	23.0	24.5
23.7	23.2	23.5	22.1	22.8	24.4	25.4
24.9	23.3	23.3	21.4	21.8	20.5	24.3
24.4	23.2	23.9	23.9	22.1	22.7	21.0

17. A requirement on the production of margarine is that the fat content should not be lower than 80%. This is controlled indirectly in the factory by controlling the water content. The mean water content is desired at 19% with a maximum limit of 20%. Two methods of determination of water content are available. One method is performed in the laboratory as the official analytical method. However, this procedure is time consuming with respect to the test itself as well as the necessity to carry the test sample to the laboratory and the results back to the factory floor, where batching is performed. The second method is a rapid test water content analyzer housed in an area close to the production operation, allowing for quick results that permit adjustments to be made before extrusion. The second method is known to give measurements that are not as accurate as the official analytical method. However, if a sufficient relationship exists between the rapid method and the analytical method, the rapid method will serve the purpose. This is especially true if the overall variation is such that the maximum limit is not exceeded. A study is performed in which forty test samples are selected from production over several weeks. Each sample is subjected to both methods of measurement. The results are presented below, with x representing the rapid method and y representing the analytical method. Analyze these data with a scatter diagram and any other statistical methods available to you. What conclusions do you reach?

x	y	x	y	x	y	x	y
19.10	19.11	19.25	19.31	19.20	19.23	19.20	19.18
19.10	19.19	18.85	18.92	19.10	19.12	19.05	19.16
19.15	19.24	19.10	19.10	19.05	19.11	18.90	18.93

x	y	x	y	x	y	x	y
19.10	19.27	19.10	19.28	19.25	19.26	18.95	19.03
18.95	19.10	19.00	19.05	18.95	19.04	19.10	19.13
19.10	19.16	19.20	19.30	19.05	19.03	19.25	19.23
19.05	19.05	19.10	19.19	19.15	19.14	19.05	19.07
19.10	19.21	18.90	19.01	19.00	19.09	18.90	18.93
18.90	18.98	19.05	19.12	19.15	19.19	19.00	19.11
19.20	19.33	19.15	19.18	19.00	19.02	19.00	19.05

18. A spinning mill preparing woolen yarn for knitting woolen garments performs a doubling operation at assembly winding. Two cones are sampled each hour, and two specimens are taken from each cone. Count measurements are obtained for each of the four specimens. A standard 9 Nm (metric count representing 9 meters per gram) is desired. Twenty-four samples of size 4 are given below. Develop a performance study on the process from these data. What conclusions do you reach?

8.9	9.3	9.1	9.3	9.0	8.8	9.2	8.8	9.4	9.2	9.0	9.0
8.8	8.9	9.2	9.0	9.0	9.3	9.6	9.4	9.3	8.8	9.4	9.4
9.0	9.2	9.1	8.7	8.8	8.7	9.3	9.4	9.4	9.4	9.5	9.4
9.0	9.1	8.9	9.0	9.1	9.2	9.2	9.0	9.5	8.8	9.0	9.2
9.1	9.1	9.3	9.1	9.3	8.9	8.9	9.2	9.1	8.9	9.1	8.9
9.1	9.2	9.2	8.9	9.3	9.0	9.1	8.4	9.1	8.6	9.5	9.4
9.0	9.1	9.0	9.0	9.1	8.9	8.3	8.9	9.3	8.9	9.1	9.0
9.0	9.2	9.1	9.1	9.1	8.9	8.6	8.5	9.0	8.8	9.2	8.6

19. A second spinning mill for woolen yarn of the same standard used in Problem 18 selects five cones, five times during each day, obtaining a count measurement for each cone. Data for four days are listed. Develop a performance study on this process. How does their performance compare with that of the mill in Problem 18?

9.4	9.0	9.0	8.4	9.4	9.0	8.0	8.6	9.0	8.6
9.6	8.6	9.2	9.6	9.2	8.8	9.2	8.6	9.6	9.6
8.2	9.4	9.4	9.6	9.4	9.6	9.8	8.2	10.6	9.4
9.2	8.2	9.2	9.4	9.8	9.0	9.4	8.8	9.2	10.0
9.0	8.6	9.0	8.6	9.2	8.6	9.6	9.0	10.6	8.4
9.0	8.6	8.2	8.8	8.2	8.6	8.6	9.7	9.3	8.6
9.0	8.6	8.6	8.6	8.8	9.4	9.2	9.2	10.0	9.4
9.2	9.2	9.0	8.6	9.4	8.4	9.0	9.9	9.0	9.0
9.4	8.8	8.2	9.4	9.0	9.2	9.0	9.1	9.0	9.0
8.2	9.6	8.4	8.4	9.2	8.6	8.6	8.7	8.6	8.4

20. For the manufacture of a specialty toilet soap, it is desired to maintain a nominal of 100 grams in one of the sizes of bars marketed. An initial study is performed, sampling 5 bars each half hour from the molding operation.

The data, shown as deviations from 100, for thirty samples are given below. Develop the initial performance study. Is the process in control? By eliminating certain out-of-control data values, obtain an estimate of the standard deviation that may be maintained by the process under a state of control. (a) Develop the control limits for $\bar{x}$ and R charts to serve as process control charts for this quality characteristic. (b) Develop a CUSUM chart for sample averages to serve the same purpose.

0.70	0.50	0.35	0.50	0.05
0.60	0.20	0.44	0.02	0.05
0.80	−0.02	−1.30	−0.07	−1.25
0.40	0.45	0.08	−0.83	0.05
0.70	0.00	0.55	−0.43	−0.80
0.60	0.40	−0.02	−2.70	0.02
0.60	0.35	0.02	0.28	0.18
0.80	−0.15	0.09	0.13	−0.24
0.45	0.15	−0.25	−0.22	−0.32
0.25	0.00	−0.13	−0.23	0.34
0.37	0.15	−1.30	0.80	0.50
0.18	0.35	0.40	0.20	−0.11
0.40	0.30	0.77	0.33	0.10
0.45	−0.23	0.10	−0.15	0.35
−0.05	0.20	−0.13	-0.30	−0.45
0.30	0.57	−0.75	0.15	0.15
0.40	0.90	0.45	0.56	0.55
0.30	−0.65	0.35	0.37	0.35
0.50	0.55	0.50	−0.53	0.10
0.12	0.05	0.40	0.45	0.75
0.65	−0.03	−0.35	−0.30	0.15
0.40	−0.15	0.00	−0.80	0.15
−0.15	0.30	−0.10	−0.30	0.30
0.30	−2.85	−0.40	−0.10	0.20
0.25	−0.05	−0.10	0.25	0.50
−0.25	0.25	0.05	−0.95	0.25
−0.40	0.14	0.55	0.20	0.05
−0.40	−0.15	0.20	0.50	0.15
−2.10	0.23	0.75	0.25	0.70
−0.50	0.17	−0.20	−0.35	0.15

21. The mass of the black bobbin (dolly) in the manufacture of dry cell batteries is critical to the service output of the cells. During the pressing operation, six consecutive dollies are sampled twice per shift of production. These are weighed to the nearest tenth of a gram. The data for nine consecutive shifts of production are given below. Prepare a performance study for these data. Prepare process control charts to be used to maintain a nominal of 20.3 grams for future production.

20.5	20.9	20.3	20.1	20.5	20.0	20.2	20.3	20.0
20.3	20.2	20.2	20.3	20.5	19.8	20.1	20.1	20.0
20.0	20.2	20.5	20.0	20.3	20.2	20.1	20.1	19.5
20.0	20.1	20.2	20.2	20.5	19.7	20.0	20.0	20.0
20.0	20.0	20.2	20.2	20.3	19.8	20.0	20.0	20.3
20.0	19.6	20.1	20.0	20.3	20.3	20.0	20.1	20.0
20.2	20.1	20.3	19.8	19.8	20.2	19.8	19.6	20.5
20.0	20.1	20.4	20.2	19.6	20.5	20.0	20.0	20.4
20.2	20.0	20.2	20.1	20.1	20.2	19.8	20.5	20.4
20.1	20.2	20.3	19.7	19.6	20.4	20.2	20.3	20.4
20.0	20.0	20.5	20.0	19.6	20.5	19.6	20.5	20.3
20.0	20.0	20.2	20.0	20.0	20.3	20.3	20.5	20.3

22. The following are fictitious faculty salaries. Use box plots to compare the salaries by department. Which department has the highest median salary? Which department has the widest range?

				Salaries/Year in $1000				
Department	1	2	3	4	5	6	7	8	9
English	40	51	43	49	68	42	39	43	48
Mathematics	61	47	42	53	49	58	42	47	49
Statistics	39	52	71	63	47	61	44	52	46
Computer Science	37	54	61	65	70	39	58	71	55
Biology	43	55	41	39	52	47	53	52	41

23. Compare the fictitious salaries of faculty members (Problem 22) in computer science with faculty members in biology using the empirical quantile-quantile plot. What do you conclude?

12

INDUSTRIAL
EXPERIMENTATION

Continuous processes, such as chemical, textile, or rubber processes or large-scale integrated circuit manufacture, have some special problems that will be considered in this chapter. Many times it is believed that the process variables could be changed to provide an improved yield. Improved yield here means that a quality characteristic may be improved or the yield of a desired product may be increased. Yield may refer to the fraction of product that is deemed acceptable. For example, in the initial stages of integrated circuit manufacture, such yields are often 5–10%, that is, 5–10% of chips manufactured perform all functions they are designed to do. This may be improved with procedures such as those to be discussed in this chapter to as much as 70–90% or better. There may be 400 or more chips to a wafer with all chips tested functionally. The acceptable chips are then sent to succeeding manufacturing stages; thus the concept of increased yield. Increased yield in a chemical process might mean an increase of a desired output from a chemical reaction with correspondingly less tar or an otherwise useless product.

Well-known principles of experimental design may be used in the laboratory to determine the levels of each process variable that will result in improved yields. However, many times what occurs in a laboratory or pilot plant operation cannot be reproduced in a production setting. Principles of experimental design used in the laboratory setting are not considered here. There are many excellent texts covering virtually all aspects of that topic.

G. E. P. Box (1966) stated, "To find out what happens to a system when you interfere with it you have to interfere with it (not just passively observe it)." This chapter considers methods of interfering with a process in a controlled manner rather than random interference as may happen in uncontrolled procedures.

The first procedure discussed concerns designing an experiment to determine the best levels at which to operate a process. A technique to do this, called PLEX, was presented by Hill and Wiles (1975). This is a designed experiment using production equipment. Because of the cost, such an experiment is usually done only once and therefore requires substantial planning and supervision. Since the full experiment is a one-time experimental process, the levels of the process variables must be altered enough that an observable effect on the process is expected. Such an effect may mean that decisions concerning needed data points must be changed during the experimental runs to avoid serious quality problems. Early runs may indicate that the yield is deteriorating or that, while the quantity is increasing as expected, the resulting output is of an inferior quality. It may be discolored, have a lowered tensile strength, or other problems. There is a necessity for skilled people to be in attendance during the experimentation process. The presence of such individuals, in addition to introducing a possibly large cost factor, may alter the outcome of the process from what it would be if only the usual production personnel were in attendance.

A second procedure to be discussed in this chapter is evolutionary operations, usually called EVOP. This procedure was developed by G. E. P. Box (1957) and has been discussed in several papers as well as a text by Box and Draper [see, for example, Box and Hunter (1959); Hunter and Kittrel (1966); Box and Draper (1969)]. The advantage of this procedure is that it requires only the usual production personnel and does not necessitate close surveillance by skilled persons. A possible disadvantage is that is may take substantially longer to obtain an answer to the questions raised regarding the effect of production variables. Because normal plant conditions are maintained, the answer may be more valid.

Another technique dealing with process experimentation that will be discussed in this chapter is the analysis of means (ANOM) proposed by Ellis Ott (1967). This technique provides a control-chart-like approach to the analysis of experimental data.

▶ 12-1 ONE-TIME EXPERIMENTS

Excessive variability may be present in a process with its cause a mystery. One way to understand and explain this variability is to run a series of controlled experiments to see which process variables might affect the process and thus produce this variability. Since usually many different possible variables are to be considered, and since the answer should be obtained with a minimum amount of experimentation, proper design techniques must be followed. This procedure may involve a one-shot look at the process or a series of looks using various experimental conditions. Because information must be obtained immediately, the process must be changed more drastically than with EVOP techniques. Because of this, skilled people must be in attendance in addition to the regular operating personnel. Close cooperation must be present between the two.

▶ EXAMPLE 12-1

As an example of such a situation, consider a particular chemical process. Percent yield is the response variable to be increased. A plot of yield for production days in October produced the results shown in Figure 12-1. Note that the yield varied from a low of 27% to a high of 70%. Because of this excessive variability, it was impossible to isolate probable causes. Therefore, an experimental design approach was needed. After reviewing the possible cause of this variability, it was decided that four variables were the most likely culprits: temperature, pressure, catalyst concentration, and reaction time. Practical high and low limits must then be established for each of these variables, as well as the normal operating condition for them. An experiment was proposed that would make use of ten different treatment configurations of the four variables. This is half of a full factorial design with two center points at the normal operating conditions for each of the variables.

A factorial design is a design in which experimental runs are made at all combinations of each of the independent or control factors. A fractional factorial design is one for which only some fraction of the possible runs are made. Thus, a full factorial design with four factors each at two levels

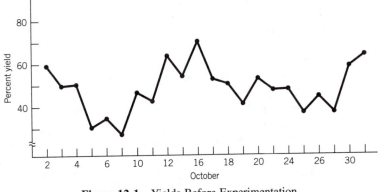

Figure 12-1   Yields Before Experimentation

(e.g., high and low) would require 2^4, or 16, runs. Half of this design would be 2^{4-1}, or 8, runs. The eight runs are chosen in such a way that analysis of the effect of each of the factors is still possible. With only eight runs, isolation of interaction effects is not possible. However, effects of the four factors may be analyzed independently. The purpose of the two center points is to obtain an error estimate with which to determine significant effects. Details of the construction of such designs may be found in many texts on experimental designs, such as Hicks (1973), Montgomery (1991), Box, Hunter, and Hunter (1978), or Nelson (1998).

The levels of the variables and the results of the ten experimental runs are shown in Table 12-1. The levels are coded so that $+1$ means the high and -1 the low levels for each variable. The 0 refers to the normal or central level.

Analysis of the data indicates that the temperature is the most important factor. In this case the effect of going from the low to the high level of each factor is indicated in Table 12-2. The effect of increasing the temperature caused an average loss of 6.13%. The next most important factor was catalyst concentration, with an average increase of 2.23% when going from the low to the high level of this factor.

TABLE 12-1   Initial Experimental Design

Run No.	Temperature	Pressure	Catalyst Concentration	Reaction Time	% Yield
1	-1	-1	-1	-1	69.9
2	$+1$	-1	-1	$+1$	60.7
3	-1	$+1$	-1	$+1$	71.5
4	$+1$	$+1$	-1	-1	58.8
5	-1	-1	$+1$	$+1$	67.7
6	$+1$	-1	$+1$	-1	64.4
7	-1	$+1$	$+1$	-1	68.5
8	$+1$	$+1$	$+1$	$+1$	69.2
9	0	0	0	0	67.0
10	0	0	0	0	68.3

TABLE 12-2   Results of Experimentation

Factor	Average Effect
Temperature	−6.13
Pressure	1.33
Catalyst Concentration	2.23
Reaction Time	1.88

Similarly, the corresponding effect of changing reaction time is 1.88%, and that of changing pressure is 1.33%. These effects are easily calculated by observing the plus one and minus one designations in Table 12-1. Thus the four main effects are as follows:

Temperature: $\frac{1}{4}(-69.9 + 60.7 - 71.5 + 58.8 - 67.7 + 64.4 - 68.5 + 69.2) =$
$24.5/4 = -6.13$

Pressure: $\frac{1}{4}(-69.9 - 60.7 - 71.5 + 58.8 - 67.7 - 64.4 + 68.5 + 69.2) =$
$5.3/4 = 1.33$

Catalyst Concentration: $\frac{1}{4}(-69.9 - 60.7 - 71.5 - 58.8 + 67.7 + 64.4 + 68.5 + 69.2) =$
$8.9/4 = 2.23$

Reaction Time: $\frac{1}{4}(-69.9 + 60.7 + 71.5 - 58.8 + 67.7 - 64.4 - 68.5 + 69.2) =$
$7.5/4 = 1.88$

The two center points may be used for an error term as

$$s_y^2 = \frac{\Sigma y^2 - \dfrac{(\Sigma y)^2}{n}}{n - 1} = \left[9{,}153.89 - \frac{(135.3)^2}{2}\right]/(2 - 1) = 0.845$$

The estimate of the standard deviation is $\sqrt{0.845} = 0.92$. Using this figure, the effect of each factor may be tested for significance. The t statistic, discussed in Chapter 5, may be employed. Thus, for example, for the temperature effect, using Equation (5-56):

$$t = \frac{-6.13}{0.92\sqrt{\frac{1}{4} + \frac{1}{4}}} = -9.42$$

Similarly, the other factors may be tested. The t statistics for pressure, catalyst concentration, and reaction time are 2.04, 3.43, and 2.89, respectively.

The temperature effect is the only one that appears to have any significant effect on the yield. Because this effect is negative, further experimentation was made at lower temperatures, resulting in considerably higher yields.

▶ EXAMPLE 12-2

The following example was provided by Raghu Kackar of the National Institute of Standards and Technology from a tutorial on experimental design he prepared while at Bell Laboratories. A company manufacturing 125 mm silicon wafers to be used in integrated circuits was concerned about proper manufacturing procedures. Specifically, the problem related to the mean thickness of the photoresist layer on the wafers. It was specified as 15.000 (×1000 Angstroms) with a range less than 0.500 (×1000 Angstroms). The factors to be controlled were (a) final spin speed, (b) acceleration to

TABLE 12-3 Factors for Example 12-2

	Test Levels	
Factors	1	2
A. Final spin speed	2000 RPM	3000 RPM
B. Acceleration to speed	Low	High
C. Method of photoresist applications	Dynamic	Radial
D. Method of initial acceleration	Pulse	Ramp

final spin, (c) method of photoresist (PR) application, and (d) method of initial acceleration. A study was conducted with the following goals:

1. To study any cause-and-effect relationships.

2. To reduce the process variability.

3. To get the mean thickness as close to the nominal as possible.

The first goal was stated by the research and development group while the last two were goals of the quality engineers.

It was decided to use two levels for each of the four factors. These levels were indicated for each factor in Table 12-3.

An initial study was made, altering one factor at a time. For this study, spin speed and method of acceleration were used, with the following results. The two spin speeds were first compared using the pulse method of acceleration. The results are shown in Table 12-4. They indicate the average effect of increasing spin speed from 2000 to 3000 RPM is $13.266 - 13.433$ or -0.167 units.

Is this a real difference, or could it have occurred due to chance? To answer that question, consider the variability in the measurements. This can be measured by means of the pooled standard deviation. For two samples, this was shown in Equation (5-22) to be

$$s_p = \sqrt{\frac{(n_1 - 1)s_1^2 + n_2 - 1)s_2^2}{n_1 + n_2 - 2}}$$

In this case

$$s_p = \sqrt{\frac{3(0.5956)^2 + 3(0.2686)^2}{4 + 4 - 2}} = 0.4620$$

The standard error for each test speed is

$$s_e = s_p/\sqrt{n} = 0.4620/\sqrt{4} = 0.2310$$

The standard error of the difference in the two test speeds is

$$s_{(\bar{y}_1 - \bar{y}_2)} = \sqrt{2s_e^2} = 0.3267$$

TABLE 12-4 Results of Varying Spin Speed

	Replications					Standard
Speeds	1	2	3	4	Averages	Deviations
2000	13.965	13.817	13.301	12.648	13.433	0.5956
3000	13.349	12.867	13.409	13.439	13.266	0.2686

TABLE 12-5   Results of Varying Method of Acceleration

Method of Acceleration	Replications				Averages	Standard Deviations
	1	2	3	4		
Pulse	13.965	13.817	13.301	12.648	13.433	0.5956
Ramp	18.810	18.218	18.023	18.768	18.455	0.3945

Thus a 95% confidence interval estimate of the difference in the two test speeds is given by the following, from Equation (5-47)

$$100(1 - \alpha)\% \ CI = (\bar{y}_1 - \bar{y}_2) \pm t_{(1-\alpha/2;\nu)}s_{(\bar{y}_1-\bar{y}_2)} \tag{12-1}$$

where $t_{(1-\alpha/2;\nu)}$ = Student's t value with ν degrees of freedom:

$$\nu = n_1 + n_2 - 2$$

Here, this is

$$95\% \ CI = (-0.167) \pm 2.447(0.3267)$$
$$= (-0.167) \pm 0.799$$
$$= (-0.966, 0.632)$$

Because this interval contains zero, there appears to be no significant effect of spin speeds on photoresist. The method of acceleration keeping spin speed constant at 2000 RPM may also be considered. When this is done the results obtained are shown in Table 12-5. The average effect here is $(18.455 - 13.433)$, or 5.022, with ramp being the higher level. The pooled standard deviation is 0.5052, and the standard error of the difference in test point averages is

$$s_{(\bar{y}_1-\bar{y}_2)} = s_p\sqrt{\tfrac{2}{4}} = 0.5052\sqrt{.5}$$
$$= 0.3572$$

A 95% confidence interval estimate of the difference in two means is

$$5.022 \pm 2.447(0.3572) = 5.022 \pm 0.874 = (4.148, 5.896)$$

Since this interval does not contain zero, the conclusion is that the method of acceleration does affect the result.

There is no significant effect observed of spin speed. Either spin speed using the pulse method of acceleration results in layers that are too thin (13.350). Using 2000 RPM, the pulse method gave too thin layers (13.433), whereas the ramp method gave layers that were too thick (18.455). Sixteen trials were required to study two factors, one at a time.

What would the same experiment run as a two-factor factorial experiment produce? Table 12-6 describes the four test points needed for a two-factor experiment. The data from the experimental

TABLE 12-6   Test Points for Two-Factor Factorial Design

(A) Spin Speed	(D) Method of Acceleration	Factor Levels	
		A	D
2000	Pulse	−	−
3000	Pulse	+	−
2000	Ramp	−	+
3000	Ramp	+	+

TABLE 12-7 Data for Two-Factor Experiment

Test Points		Replications					Standard
A	D	1	2	3	4	Averages	Deviations
−	−	13.965	13.817	13.301	12.648	13.433	0.5956
+	−	13.349	12.867	13.409	13.439	13.266	0.2686
−	+	18.810	18.218	18.023	18.768	18.455	0.3945
+	+	15.396	16.063	16.266	15.384	15.777	0.4548

runs are shown in Table 12-7. Note that the first three sets of runs were reported earlier while the fourth set (i.e., 3000 RPM and ramp method) is new.

For each factor there are now eight readings at each level. The average effect for method of acceleration (factor D) is

$$(18.455 + 15.777 - 13.433 - 13.266)/2 = 3.767$$

The average effect for spin speed (factor A) is

$$(13.266 + 15.777 - 13.433 - 18.455)/2 = -1.423$$

Now also consider the effect of interaction between the two factors—that is, whether the effect of A is the same at both levels of D and vice versa. This is measured by first getting the effect of factor A (speed) at each level of factor D (method), then subtracting the A effect at the low level of D from that at the high level and dividing by 2. The two A effects are

$$15.777 - 18.455 = -2.678$$
$$13.266 - 13.433 = -0.167$$

The interaction effect is $[(-2.678) - (-0.167)]/2 = -1.256$.

The measure of variability may be obtained by first pooling the four standard deviations shown in Table 12-7:

$$s_p^2 = \frac{3(.5956)^2 + 3(.2686)^2 + 3(.3945)^2 + 3(.4548)^2}{4(4) - 4}$$

$$= [(.5956)^2 + (.2686)^2 + (.3945)^2 + (.4548)^2]/4$$

$$= 0.1973$$

$$s_p = \sqrt{0.1973} = 0.444$$

The standard error for each test point is

$$s_e = s_p/\sqrt{4} = 0.222$$

Now construct 95% confidence interval estimates for each test point average using this estimate of the standard error and a Student's t statistic with $4(4) - 4 = 12$ degrees of freedom.

Effect A: $-1.432 \pm 2.179(0.222) = (-1.907, -0.939)$

Effect D: $3.767 \pm 2.179(0.222) = (3.283, 4.251)$

Interaction AD: $-1.256 \pm 2.179(0.222) = (-1.740, -0.772)$

Since none of the intervals contains zero, it may be concluded that all effects, including the interaction, are significant. The significance of the interaction indicates that for at least one level of each

TABLE 12-8 Data for Four-Factor Experiment

	Factors				Response	
Run	A	B	C	D	Mean	Range
1	−	−	−	−	13.965	0.426
2	+	−	−	−	13.349	0.316
3	−	+	−	−	13.817	0.359
4	+	+	−	−	12.867	0.478
5	−	−	+	−	13.301	0.693
6	+	−	+	−	13.409	0.351
7	−	+	+	−	12.648	0.332
8	+	+	+	−	13.459	0.276
9	−	−	−	+	18.810	0.536
10	+	−	−	+	15.396	0.149
11	−	+	−	+	18.218	0.315
12	+	+	−	+	16.063	0.575
13	−	−	+	+	18.023	0.223
14	+	−	+	+	16.266	0.361
15	−	+	+	+	18.768	0.332
16	+	+	+	+	15.384	0.633

factor, the other factor is significant. In this case, it was observed in the one-factor-at-a-time experiment that, when using the pulse method of acceleration, the spin speed did not matter. The interaction now indicates that when using the ramp method it must matter. Therefore, referring to Table 12-7, it is seen that the best results (closest to 15) occur with the ramp method and with 3000 RPM spin speed. This result was completely missed by the one-factor-at-a-time procedure, which ended in total frustration regarding the best way to improve the process.

Recall at the start of this example that four factors were to be considered. If a factorial experiment is designed containing all combinations of all levels of each factor, it will require sixteen test points. Table 12-3 contains the levels of each factor. In addition, there was originally interest in the mean photoresist thickness and the variability in thickness. The variability may be measured by the range in thickness. It was to be as small as possible and no greater than 0.500.

Table 12-8 shows the results of sixteen runs that correspond to a full factorial design. The factor levels are shown for each run with a minus (−) representing level 1 and a plus (+) representing level 2 as indicated in Table 12-3. Table 12-8 may be interpreted as, for example, for run 7, spin speed (A) was 2000 RPM, acceleration to final speed (B) was high, method of photoresist application (C) was radial, and the pulse method of acceleration (D) was used. There was no replication in this case, so each reading is shown as the mean and range for one wafer.

The three- and four-factor interactions probably have no real meaning and were therefore pooled together as an error term. These error terms for the mean and range are shown in Tables 12-9 and 12-10, respectively. The effects of the main factors and their interactions are computed as they were for the two-factor experiment. For example, the effect of factor A is formed by subtracting the eight responses for level one of factor A from the eight readings for level two and dividing the difference by 8. That is, the effect of factor A for the mean is

$$[(13.349 + 12.867 + \cdots + 15.384) - (13.965) + 13.817 + \cdots + 18.768)] \div 8 = -1.42$$

The effects of the other factors for both the mean and range are computed similarly. For the two-factor interaction the effect of one factor at the low level of the second is subtracted

TABLE 12-9   Effects on Mean

Factors	Effects	95% Confidence Interval
A	−1.42	−1.42 ± 0.70 = −2.12, −0.73*
B	−0.16	−0.16 ± 0.70 = −0.86, 0.54
C	−0.16	−0.16 ± 0.70 = −0.86, 0.54
D	3.77	3.77 ± 0.70 = 3.08, 4.47*
AB	−0.002	−0.002 ± 0.70 = −0.70, 0.69
AC	0.36	0.36 ± 0.70 = −0.34, 1.06
AD	−1.26	−1.26 ± 0.70 = −1.96, −0.57*
BC	−0.03	−0.03 ± 0.70 = −0.73, 0.67
BD	0.15	0.15 ± 0.70 = −0.55, 0.85
CD	0.14	0.14 ± 0.70 = −0.56, 0.84
ABC	−0.234	
ABD	−0.082	
ACD	−0.255	
BCD	−0.027	
ABCD	−0.488	

*Significant.

TABLE 12-10   Effects on Range

Factors	Effects	95% Confidence Interval
A	−0.077	−0.077 ± 0.204 = −0.28, 0.13
B	0.034	0.034 ± 0.204 = −0.17, 0.24
C	0.006	0.006 ± 0.204 = −0.20, 0.21
D	0.014	0.014 ± 0.204 = −0.19, 0.22
AB	0.166	0.166 ± 0.204 = −0.04, 0.37
AC	0.002	0.002 ± 0.204 = −0.20, 0.21
AD	0.088	0.088 ± 0.204 = −0.12, 0.29
BC	−0.045	−0.045 ± 0.204 = −0.25, 0.16
BD	0.116	0.116 ± 0.204 = −0.09, 0.32
CD	−0.013	−0.013 ± 0.204 = −0.19, 0.22
ABC	−0.054	
ABD	0.037	
ACD	0.122	
BCD	0.088	
ABCD	−0.068	

from that at the high level, and the difference is divided by 8. For interaction AB, for the mean, this is

$$\tfrac{1}{8}\{[(12.867 + 13.439 + 16.063 + 15.384) - (13.817 + 12.648 + 18.218 + 18.768)]$$
$$- [(13.349 + 13.409 + 15.396 + 16.266) - (13.965 + 13.301 + 18.810 + 18.023)]\}$$

$$= \tfrac{1}{8}[(57.753 - 63.451) - (58.420 - 64.099)] = \tfrac{1}{8}[-5.698 - (-5.679)]$$

$$= -0.019/8 = -0.0024$$

The effects for the other two factor interactions are computed in a similar manner.

The 95% confidence interval estimates are computed as before using a Student's t factor with five degrees of freedom corresponding to the four three-factor and one four-factor interaction effects that make up the error term. The error term is computed by squaring the effects due to the high order interactions, adding, dividing by 5, and taking the square root. For the mean thickness the standard error is

$$s_e = \sqrt{[(-0.234^2 + \cdots + (-0.488)^2]/5} = 0.27$$

The 95% confidence interval, for factor A, for the mean is

$$-1.42 \pm 2.571(0.27) = -1.42 \pm 0.70 = (-2.12, -0.73)$$

For the range in thickness the standard error is

$$s_e = \sqrt{[(-0.054)^2 + (0.037)^2 + \cdots + (-0.068)^2]/5} = 0.079$$

The 95% confidence interval for factor A for the range is

$$-0.010 \pm 2.571(0.079) = -0.010 \pm 0.204 = (-0.21, 0.19)$$

From Table 12-9 it is seen that for the mean thickness, factors A, D, and interaction AD are the only significant effects. None of the effects in Table 12-10 are significant. Interaction AB has the largest effect and factor C and all interactions containing C are negligible. Therefore factor C could be eliminated from further consideration. The method of photoresist application apparently does not affect either the mean thickness or the range.

TABLE 12-11 Factors A and D (Mean)

No.	A	D	Mean	No.	A	D	Mean
1	−	−	13.965	9	−	+	18.810
2	+	−	13.349	10	+	+	15.396
3	−	−	13.817	11	−	+	18.218
4	+	−	12.867	12	+	+	16.063
5	−	−	13.301	13	−	+	18.023
6	+	−	13.409	14	+	+	16.266
7	−	−	12.648	15	−	+	18.768
8	+	−	13.349	16	+	+	15.384

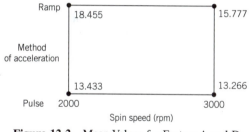

Figure 12-2 Mean Values for Factors A and D

For the mean thickness, Table 12-11 shows the data points for each combination of factors A and D only. The average of the four readings for each treatment combination is obtained. These are plotted in Figure 12-2. The AD interaction can be interpreted by the figure as demonstrating that spin speed has little effect using the pulse method, but has a significant effect when using the ramp method. The ramp method using a spin speed of 3000 RPM is closest to the desired 15.000 value.

Table 12-12 describes the factor combinations for factors A, B, and D. The averages for the two tests at each factor combination are shown in Figure 12-3. From the figure it may be observed that for the high level of factor B, increasing A increases the range, while for the low level it decreases it. This is particularly noticeable for the high level of factor D. In considering the mean photoresist thickness, it was determined that the high levels of factors A and D were superior. From Figure 12-3 it is observed that, using these conditions, the low level of factor B results in the smallest range. Therefore, the final selection will be a spin speed (A) of 3000 RPM, the ramp method of acceleration (D), and the low acceleration to final speed (B).

For this example one can optimize both response variables with the same factor combinations. At times this cannot be done, and other considerations, such as economic ones, must be introduced

TABLE 12-12 Factors A, B, and D (Range)

No.	A	B	D	Range
1	−	−	−	0.426
2	+	−	−	0.316
3	−	+	−	0.359
4	+	+	−	0.478
5	−	−	−	0.693
6	+	−	−	0.351
7	−	+	−	0.332
8	+	+	−	0.276
9	−	−	+	0.536
10	+	−	+	0.149
11	−	+	+	0.315
12	+	+	+	0.575
13	−	−	+	0.223
14	+	−	+	0.361
15	−	+	+	0.332
16	+	+	+	0.632

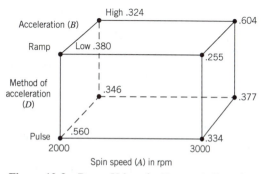

Figure 12-3 Range Values for Factors A, B, and D

to select the best factor combinations, which may be a compromise between two or more response variables.

In concluding this example, it might be pointed out that a fractional factorial design might have been used instead of the full factorial that was employed. If that had been done, eight runs would have been used instead of the sixteen that were run. The information would still have been obtained regarding main effects but it would have been impossible to investigate the two-factor interactions. Other designs are also available that might have reduced the number of runs needed. The reader is referred to texts such as those in the references in this chapter on the design of experiments for further details.

12-1.1 The Analysis of Variance

This experiment may also be analyzed by means of an algorithm called *analysis of variance (ANOVA)*. This is often a quicker and easier method of analysis although the results are the same. To illustrate this technique use the full four factor experiment described in Table 12-8. The complete data are shown in Table 12-13. The run numbers correspond to those in Table 12-8. In Table 12-13 subscript 1 refers to the low level, and subscript 2 refers to the high level of each factor. Run numbers are indicated on the upper line of each cell of the table.

The analysis is conventionally shown in the form of a table. The columns of the table consist of the source of variation, such as main effects and interactions, the sum of squares, the degrees of freedom, the mean squares, and the variance ratio. For this example the analysis of variance table is shown as Table 12-14.

The sum of squares for main effects are calculated by adding the responses for each level of the factor, squaring these totals, and adding the squares. This sum is then divided by the number of responses in each total, and a correction factor is subtracted. The correction factor (CF) is found by squaring the grand total and dividing by the total number of responses. For the main effects these calculations are

$$SS(A) = \frac{(13.965 + \cdots + 18.787)^2 + (13.349 + \cdots + 15.386)^2}{8} - \frac{(243.723)^2}{16}$$

$$= 8.090$$

TABLE 12-13   Complete Data for the Four-Factor Experiment

		A_1		A_2	
		B_1	B_2	B_1	B_2
C_1	D_1	1	3	2	4
		13.965	13.817	13.349	12.867
	D_2	9	11	10	12
		18.810	18.218	15.396	16.063
C_2	D_1	5	7	6	8
		13.301	12.648	13.409	13.439
	D_2	13	15	14	16
		18.023	18.768	16.266	15.384

TABLE 12-14   Analysis of Variance

Source	Sum of Squares	Degrees of Freedom	Mean Squares	Variance Ratio
A	8.090	1	8.090	27.61*
B	0.108	1	0.108	—
C	0.097	1	0.097	—
D	56.750	1	56.750	194*
AB	0.001	1	0.001	—
AC	0.523	1	0.523	1.78
AD	6.304	1	6.304	21.57*
BC	0.003	1	0.003	—
BD	0.089	1	0.089	—
CD	0.083	1	0.083	—
Error	1.465	5	0.293	
Total	73.511	15		

*Indicates a significant effect.

TABLE 12-15 AD Interaction (Totals)

	A_1	A_2
D_1	53.731	53.064
D_2	73.819	63.109

$$SS(B) = \frac{(13.965 + \cdots + 16.266)^2 + (13.817 + \cdots + 15.384)^2}{8} - \frac{(243.723)^2}{16}$$

$$= 0.108$$

$$SS(C) = \frac{(13.965 + \cdots + 16.063)^2}{8} - C.F. = 0.097$$

$$SS(D) = \frac{(13.965 + \cdots + 15.384)^2}{8} - C.F. = 56.750$$

Similarly, the sum of squares for two-factor interactions is calculated by adding the responses for each combination of the factors being considered, squaring these totals, adding, and dividing the sum by the number of responses in each total. For example, for the AD interaction, Table 12-15 contains the totals for each factor combination.

The sum of squares for this interaction is then

$$SS(AD) = \frac{53.731^2 + \cdots + 63.109^2}{4} - 8.090 - 56.570 - C.F.$$

$$= 6.304$$

Other interactions are calculated in a similar manner, but as indicated in Table 12-14, none are significant.

The total sum of squares is the sum of squares of each response minus the correction factor:

$$SS(Total) = 13.965^2 + \cdots + 15.384^2 - C.F. = 73.511$$

The three-factor and four-factor interactions are pooled and used as an error term. The degrees of freedom for main effects are one less than the number of levels of each factor. In this example all factors have two levels, so the degrees of freedom for each main effect is 1.

Interaction degrees of freedom are the product of the degrees of freedom of the factors in the interaction. Again, these are all one. Since four three-factor interactions and one four-factor interaction were pooled for the error term, the error degrees of freedom is $4 + 1$ or 5.

The mean squares are found by dividing each sum of squares by its degrees of freedom. The mean square for the error term is then used as the divisor in each variance ratio.

If a factor is significant, its mean square divided by the error mean square will be significantly greater than one. This is determined by reference to the F table found in Table D in the Appendix. For this example, the 0.05 value of F with 1 and 5 degrees of freedom is 6.61.

Table 12-14 indicates the only significant factors are main effects A and D and interaction AD. Table 12-15 is useful in understanding the meaning of interaction AD. If

TABLE 12-16   AD Interaction (Averages)

	A_1	A_2
D_1	13.433	13.266
D_2	18.456	15.777

the values in Table 12-15 are divided by 4, the results are in Table 12-16. The values in Table 12-16 are the same as those plotted in Figure 12-2. The resulting conclusions are thus the same as those discussed earlier.

▶ 12-2 EVOLUTIONARY OPERATIONS

Evolutionary operations, often called EVOP, were first discussed by G. E. P. Box (1957) in an article in *Applied Statistics*. This paper was based on an earlier one given at the International Conference on Statistical Quality Control in Paris in July 1955. The introduction to Box's 1957 paper states, "The rate at which industrial processes are improved is limited by the present shortage of technical personnel. Dr. Box describes a method of process improvement that supplements the more orthodox studies and is run in the normal course of production by plant personnel themselves. The basic philosophy is introduced that industrial processes should be run so as to generate not only product, but also information on how the product can be improved."

The point of the procedure is that each plant run may contribute information about the effect of one, two, or three processing variables on a response variable such as yield by slightly displacing each of the processing variables from its normal value. The amount of this displacement is determined in consultation with production personnel. It should be as much as possible but not enough to cause a problem in the eyes of the production personnel. This means that the amount of displacement will typically be slight, and one cycle through our design will probably not produce any significant effects. However, by using the arithmetic mean of the responses at each design point, the knowledge that the standard deviation of the arithmetic mean (discussed in Chapter 5) is $\sigma/\sqrt{n}$ may be used. Thus, the ability to detect significant effects increases as the number of cycles increases.

Box (1957) suggested that an EVOP committee be formed with appropriate members from research, development, production, quality control, and others. This committee would meet periodically to review results. The results would be posted daily in an appropriate place on an information board such as that illustrated in Figure 12-4. The example found in Figure 12-4 is set up for two processing variables and a maximum of three response variables.

An EVOP study would start with a planning stage during which the EVOP Committee would go through the following steps:

1. Select two or three key processing variables. This might be difficult because ten or more may be immediately suggested. The committee will then need to set some of them aside for later studies and decide which to consider in their initial study.

2. Select levels for each processing variable that will not produce substandard material.

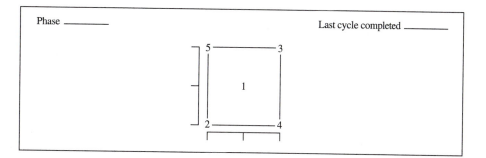

Response			
Requirement			
Running averages			
95% Error limits for averages	±	±	±
Effects with 95% error limits — × — Change in mean	± ± ± ±	± ± ± ±	± ± ± ±
Standard deviation			
Prior estimate σ	( )	( )	( )

Figure 12-4 Evolutionary Operation Information Board

3. Choose appropriate test criteria.

4. Estimate the number of cycles needed to detect significant improvements in the process. This information is used to determine the frequency of future meetings.

Box and Hunter (1959) suggested the use of a worksheet such as that shown in Figure 12-5 to carry out the computations. This sheet is set up for two processing variables and one response variable. If another response variable is used, a separate worksheet would be needed. In the case of three processing variables, the three-factor designs may be divided into two half replicates and a worksheet such as Figure 12-5 may be used for each. Details of this procedure may be found in the Box and Hunter (1959) article.

An EVOP cycle is a single performance of a complete set of operating conditions. A set of operating conditions for two processing variables consists of the four corner points in a 2^2 design plus a center point. The five points are indicated in Figure 12-6. In Figure 12-6 the corner points correspond to the high and low levels of each factor.

Figure 12-5 EVOP Worksheet

CALCULATION OF STANDARD DEVIATION

PREVIOUS SUM S _____

NEW S = RANGE = K _____ × _____ = _____

NEW SUM S _____ = _____

NEW AVERAGE S_A _____ =

NEW SUM S/(N−1)

= _____ / _____ =

PREVIOUS AVERAGE S_A = _____

CALCULATIONS OF 95% ERROR LIMITS

FOR NEW AVERAGES

L _____ = S_A _____ = ± _____
FOR NEW EFFECTS A, B, AB

L _____ = S_A _____ = ± _____
FOR TOTAL CHANGE-IN-MEAN EFFECT

M _____ = S_A _____ = ± _____

FACTORS

N	K	L	M
2	0.30	1.96	1.76
3	0.35	1.33	1.19
4	0.37	1.09	0.98
5	0.38	0.95	0.85
6	0.39	0.85	0.76
7	0.40	0.78	0.70
8	0.40	0.72	0.65

EVOLUTIONARY OPERATION
TWO VARIABLE WORK SHEET

PRODUCT _____

RESPONSE _____

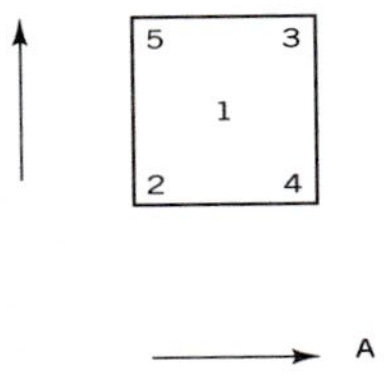

PHASE _____ CYCLE (N) _____

BY _____ DATE _____

CALCULATIONS OF AVERAGES

	1	2	3	4	5
OPERATING CONDITIONS					
SUM FROM PREVIOUS CYCLE					
AVERAGE FROM PREVIOUS CYCLE					
NEW OBSERVATIONS					
DIFFERENCES (WATCH SIGNS)					
NEW SUMS (N. S.)					
NEW AVERAGES (N. S./N)	A)	B)	C)	D)	E)

CALCULATIONS OF EFFECTS

A EFFECT

C   B
D   E
F   G

2 _____   2 _____
+ _____   − _____

B EFFECT

C   B
E   D

2 _____   2 _____
+ _____   − _____

AB EFFECT

B   D
C   E

2 _____   2 _____
+ _____   − _____

CHANGE-IN-MEAN EFFECT

F   A
G

5 _____ = _____
+ _____   4

5 _____
− _____

DESIGN

```
5   3
  1
2   4
```

B ←   → A

REMARKS:

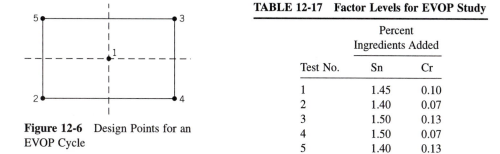

Figure 12-6 Design Points for an EVOP Cycle

TABLE 12-17   Factor Levels for EVOP Study

	Percent Ingredients Added	
Test No.	Sn	Cr
1	1.45	0.10
2	1.40	0.07
3	1.50	0.13
4	1.50	0.07
5	1.40	0.13

The five runs may be made on the five days of the week, and must be made in the order indicated on the figure. For example [Bingham (1963)], if the process under consideration is the manufacture of Zircalloy-2 metal, the processing variables might be the amount of tin and chromium added. The levels of tin might be 1.45 ± 0.05 percent, while those for chromium are 0.10 ± 0.03 percent. Table 12-17 shows the factor levels for each cycle.

An EVOP phase refers to the repeated running through of cycles at one set of operating conditions. A new phase begins when a new set of operating conditions is introduced. For example, after several cycles of the operating conditions in Table 12-17 a decision may be made to move to the set of conditions with tin at 1.55 ± 0.05 and chromium at 0.16 ± 0.03.

At the end of each cycle, the EVOP committee decides whether a new phase should be introduced or whether more cycles should be run with the present phase. If it appears that further moving of the present variables will not help, the committee may decide to delete one or more and introduce new variables into the study for subsequent phases. When the effect of a variable (including interaction) exceeds its indicated error, it is considered significant. If the effect of a variable does not exceed its indicated error, the real effects are small or more cycles are needed. To further explain this technique, an example found in Box and Hunter (1959) will be used.

The reader who desires further examples should refer to the literature cited, particularly DeBusk (1962), Koehler (1958), Hunter and Kittrell (1966), Box and Draper (1969), and Hahn and Dershowitz (1974). Russell and Stephens (1970) and Stephens (1997) present an EVOP game that has been used successfully for training plant personnel in this technique.

▶ **EXAMPLE 12-3**

This example is taken from Box and Hunter (1959). Table 12-18 contains yield data corresponding to four cycles of a manufacturing process. The processing variables are time (60 ± 10 minutes) and temperature ($120 \pm 10°C$). That is, the high and low levels of time are 70 and 50 minutes, respectively, while those for temperature are 130° and 110°C, respectively.

Figure 12-7 shows the worksheet after the first cycle has been run. The new data (cycle 1) are added on the line labeled "new observations." Because this is the first cycle, these responses

CALCULATIONS OF STANDARD DEVIATION

PREVIOUS SUM S _____

NEW S = RANGE = K

NEW SUM S = _____ × _____ = _____

NEW AVERAGE S_A = _____

NEW SUM S/(N-1)

= _____ / _____ = _____

PREVIOUS AVERAGE S_A _____

CALCULATIONS OF 95% ERROR LIMITS

FOR NEW AVERAGES

L $\frac{1.96}{}$ = S_A _____ 1.8* = ± 3.5

FOR NEW EFFECTS A, B, AB

L $\frac{1.96}{}$ = S_A _____ 1.8* = ± 3.5

FOR TOTAL CHANGE-IN-MEAN EFFECT

M $\frac{1.78}{}$ = S_A _____ 1.8* = ± 3.2

CALCULATIONS OF AVERAGES

	1	2	3	4	5
OPERATING CONDITIONS					
SUM FROM PREVIOUS CYCLE					
AVERAGE FROM PREVIOUS CYCLE					
NEW OBSERVATIONS	63.7	62.8	63.2	67.2	60.5
DIFFERENCES (WATCH SIGNS)					
NEW SUMS (N. S.)	63.7	62.8	63.2	67.2	60.5
NEW AVERAGES (N. S./N)	A) 63.7	B) 62.8	C) 63.2	D) 67.2	E) 60.5

CALCULATIONS OF EFFECTS

A EFFECT

C 63.2   B 62.8
D 67.2   E 60.5
F 130.4 G 123.3
         123.3
2 ⌐ 7.1
+   3.6

B EFFECT

C 63.2   B 62.8
E 60.5   D 67.2
123.7   130.0
         123.7
2 ⌐ 6.3
+   3.2

AB EFFECT

B 62.8   D 67.2
C 63.2   E 60.5
126.0   127.7
         126.0
2 ⌐ 1.7
+   0.9

CHANGE-IN-MEAN EFFECT

F 130.4   A 63.7 = 4
G 123.3
253.7   254.8
          253.7
5 ⌐ 1.1
-   0.2

DESIGN

```
5     3
   1
2     4
```

→ A

B (arrow)

FACTORS

N	K	L	M
2	0.30	1.96	1.76
3	0.35	1.33	1.19
4	0.37	1.09	0.98
5	0.38	0.95	0.85
6	0.39	0.85	0.76
7	0.40	0.78	0.70
8	0.40	0.72	0.65

EVOLUTIONARY OPERATION
TWO VARIABLE WORK SHEET

PRODUCT _____
RESPONSE _____Yield_____
PHASE __1__ CYCLE (N) __1__
BY _____ DATE _____

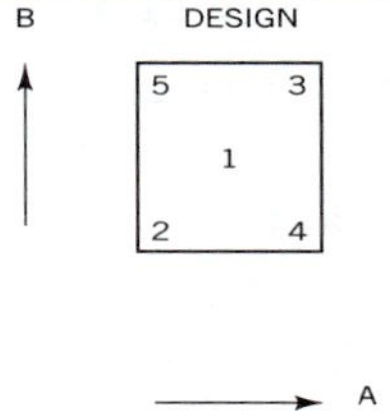

REMARKS:

*Prior estimate $\hat{\sigma}$ = 1.8

Figure 12-7 Worksheet for EVOP Cycle 1

432

TABLE 12-18   Batch Yields for EVOP Study

Cycles	Conditions				
	1	2	3	4	5
1	63.7	62.8	63.2	67.2	60.5
2	62.1	65.8	65.5	67.6	61.3
3	59.6	62.1	62.0	65.3	64.1
4	63.5	62.8	67.9	62.6	61.7

are carried down as new sums and new averages ($n = 1$). The new averages are used as indicated in the "calculation of effects" portion of the worksheet. For example, for the A effect (time) the smaller of the sums F and G is placed under the larger. The difference is then obtained. This difference is positive or negative depending on whether F or G is larger. Thus, the A effect is the average of runs 3 and 4 minus the average of runs 2 and 5. The other effects are calculated similarly. The change in mean effect is the difference between the center point and the average of the four corners. If this is significant, it would mean that the center corresponds to a maximum or minimum response.

Since there is only one set of data for cycle 1, a previous estimate of the standard deviations was used to determine error limits. Even though the A effect exceeds the 95% error limit a second cycle was run. Figure 12-8 is the worksheet following cycle 2. The data on the first two lines come from the worksheet for cycle 1. The difference is the previous cycle average minus the new observations. The largest and smallest differences are circled, and the range is calculated from these circled values and noted where indicated in the upper right-hand portion of the worksheet.

The new observations are added to the previous sums to get the new sums. The new sums are divided by the cycle number (2 in this case) to get the new averages. These new averages are then used to calculate the effects.

The range of the differences is multiplied by factor K to obtain an estimate of the standard deviation. For derivations of factors K, L, and M the reader is referred to Box and Hunter (1959), Bingham (1963), or Box and Draper (1969). The factor K is computed from Equation (12-2).

$$K = c_t[(n - 1)/n]^{1/2}$$
(12-2)

where c_t is the constant [obtained from Pearson and Hartley (1954)] by which the range from a normal population must be multiplied to obtain an unbiased estimate of the standard deviation, σ, from t observations. Factors L and M are just the appropriate values of the Student's t statistic divided by the square root of n, the number of cycles, modified by a factor that considers the fact that the range is being used to estimate the standard deviation.

Figure 12-8, the results of cycle 2, does not indicate any significant effects. Therefore cycle 3 is run. The worksheet following cycle 3 is shown as Figure 12-9. After cycle 3, the prior estimate of the standard deviation is no longer being used but the estimate calculated in Figure 12-9 is used. Once again, no significant effects are observed, so the fourth cycle is run.

Figure 12-10 is based on the results following cycle 4. This worksheet indicates a significant increase in yield for factor A. That is, the A effect is 2.6 ± 2.46, an interval that does not contain zero. This indicates the time of the process might be increased; however, the temperature has no significant effect on the yield. A new phase may now be proposed keeping the temperature the same while increasing the time. Alternatively, temperature might be dropped from the new phase and another processing variable added.

Figure 12-8 Worksheet for EVOP Cycle 2

CALCULATIONS OF AVERAGES

OPERATING CONDITIONS	1	2	3	4	5
SUM FROM PREVIOUS CYCLE	63.7	62.8	63.2	67.2	60.5
AVERAGE FROM PREVIOUS CYCLE	63.7	62.8	63.2	67.2	60.5
NEW OBSERVATIONS	62.1	65.8	65.5	67.6	61.3
DIFFERENCES (WATCH SIGNS)	1.6	-3.0	-2.3	-0.4	-0.8
NEW SUMS (N. S.)	125.8	128.6	128.7	134.8	121.8
NEW AVERAGES (N. S./N)	A) 62.9	B) 64.3	C) 64.4	D) 67.4	E) 60.9

CALCULATIONS OF EFFECTS

A EFFECT

```
C  64.4    B  64.3
D  67.4    E  60.9
F 131.8    G 125.2
          125.2
        2 | 6.6
        + | 3.3
```

B EFFECT

```
C  64.4    B  64.4
E  60.9    D  67.4
  125.3      131.7
             125.3
           2 | 6.4
           + | 3.2
```

AB EFFECT

```
B  64.3    D  67.4
C  64.4    E  60.9
  128.7      128.3
             128.3
           2 | 0.4
           + | 0.2
```

CHANGE-IN-MEAN EFFECT

```
F 131.8    A  62.9 = 4
G 125.2        251.6
  257.0        251.6
               251.6
             5 | 5.4
             + | 1.1
```

DESIGN

```
 5     3
    1
 2     4
```

B ←   A →

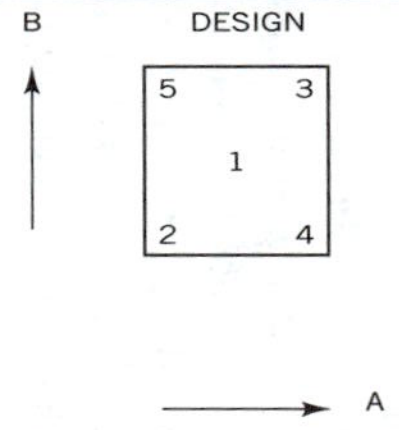

REMARKS:

*Prior estimate $\hat{\sigma}$ = 1.8

CALCULATION OF STANDARD DEVIATION

PREVIOUS SUM S

NEW S = RANGE = K

= 4.6 × 0.30 = 1.38

NEW SUM S = 1.38

NEW AVERAGE S_A =

NEW SUM S/(N-1)

= 1.38 / 1 = 1.38

PREVIOUS AVERAGE S_A

CALCULATIONS OF 95% ERROR LIMITS

FOR NEW AVERAGES

L 1.96 = S_A 1.8* = ± 3.5

FOR NEW EFFECTS A, B, AB

L 1.96 = S_A 1.8* = ± 3.5

FOR TOTAL CHANGE -IN-MEAN EFFECT

M 1.78 = S_A 1.8* = ± 3.2

FACTORS

N	K	L	M
2	0.30	1.96	1.76
3	0.35	1.33	1.19
4	0.37	1.09	0.98
5	0.38	0.95	0.85
6	0.39	0.85	0.76
7	0.40	0.78	0.70
8	0.40	0.72	0.65

EVOLUTIONARY OPERATION
TWO VARIABLE WORK SHEET

PRODUCT _____

RESPONSE ___Yield___

PHASE ___1___ CYCLE (N) ___2___

BY _____ DATE _____

434

CALCULATIONS OF AVERAGES

OPERATING CONDITIONS	1	2	3	4	5
SUM FROM PREVIOUS CYCLE	125.8	128.6	128.7	134.8	121.8
AVERAGE FROM PREVIOUS CYCLE	62.9	64.3	64.4	67.4	60.9
NEW OBSERVATIONS	59.6	62.1	62.0	65.3	64.1
DIFFERENCES (WATCH SIGNS)	(3.3)	2.2	2.4	2.1	(−3.2)
NEW SUMS (N. S.)	185.4	190.7	190.7	200.1	185.9
NEW AVERAGES (N. S./N)	A) 61.8	B) 63.6	C) 63.6	D) 66.7	E) 61.9

CALCULATION OF STANDARD DEVIATION

PREVIOUS SUM S _____ 1.38

NEW S = RANGE = K

NEW S = $\underline{6.5}$ × $\underline{0.35}$ = 2.28

NEW SUM S _____ 3.66

NEW AVERAGE S_A =

NEW SUM S/(N−1)

= $\underline{3.66}$ / $\underline{2}$ = 1.83

PREVIOUS AVERAGE S_A = 1.38

CALCULATIONS OF 95% ERROR LIMITS

FOR NEW AVERAGES

L $\underline{1.33}$ = S_A $\underline{1.83}$ = ± 2.43

FOR NEW EFFECTS A, B, AB

L $\underline{1.33}$ = S_A $\underline{1.83}$ = ± 2.43

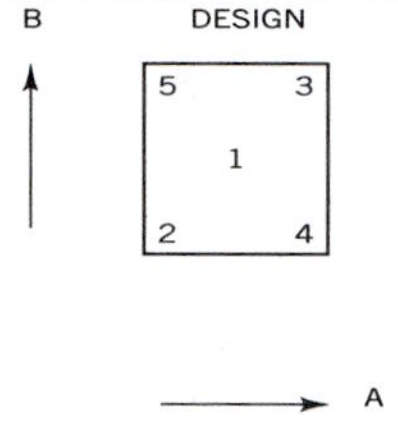

FOR TOTAL CHANGE-IN-MEAN EFFECT

M $\underline{1.19}$ = S_A $\underline{1.83}$ = ± 2.18

FACTORS

N	K	L	M
2	0.30	1.96	1.76
3	0.35	1.33	1.19
4	0.37	1.09	0.98
5	0.38	0.95	0.85
6	0.39	0.85	0.76
7	0.40	0.78	0.70
8	0.40	0.72	0.65

EVOLUTIONARY OPERATION
TWO VARIABLE WORK SHEET

PRODUCT _____

RESPONSE __Yield__

PHASE __1__ CYCLE (N) __3__

BY _____ DATE _____

CALCULATIONS OF EFFECTS

A EFFECT

C 63.6 B 63.6
D 66.7 E 61.9
F 130.3 G 125.5
125.5
2 ⌊ 4.8   2 ⌊
+ ⌊ 2.4

B EFFECT

C 63.6 B 63.6
E 61.9 D 66.7
125.5   130.3
125.5
2 ⌊   2 ⌊ 4.8
+   − 2.4

AB EFFECT

B 63.6 D 66.7
C 63.6 E 61.9
127.2   128.6
127.2
2 ⌊   2 ⌊ 1.4
+   − 0.7

CHANGE-IN-MEAN EFFECT

F 130.3   A   61.8 = 4
G 125.5
255.8   247.2
247.2
5 ⌊ 8.6
+ ⌊ 1.7

DESIGN

5	3
	1
2	4

B →   A →

REMARKS:

Figure 12-9 Worksheet for EVOP Cycle 3

CALCULATIONS OF STANDARD DEVIATION

PREVIOUS SUM S   3.66

NEW S = RANGE = K

$\underline{8.4} \times \underline{0.37} = \underline{3.11}$

NEW SUM S = 6.77

NEW AVERAGE S $_A$ =

NEW SUM S/(N–1)

= $\dfrac{6.77}{3} = \underline{2.26}$

PREVIOUS AVERAGE S $_A$ 1.83

CALCULATIONS OF 95% ERROR LIMITS

FOR NEW AVERAGES

L $\underline{1.09}$ = S $_A$ $\underline{2.26}$ = ± $\underline{2.46}$

FOR NEW EFFECTS A, B, AB

L $\underline{1.09}$ = S $_A$ $\underline{2.26}$ = ± $\underline{2.46}$

FOR TOTAL CHANGE-IN-MEAN EFFECT

M $\underline{0.98}$ = S $_A$ $\underline{2.26}$ = ± $\underline{2.21}$

FACTORS

N	K	L	M
2	0.30	1.96	1.76
3	0.35	1.33	1.19
4	0.37	1.09	0.98
5	0.38	0.95	0.85
6	0.39	0.85	0.76
7	0.40	0.78	0.70
8	0.40	0.72	0.65

EVOLUTIONARY OPERATION
TWO VARIABLE WORK SHEET

PRODUCT _____ **Yield**

RESPONSE _____

PHASE ___1___ CYCLE (N) ___4___

BY _____ DATE _____

CALCULATIONS OF AVERAGES

OPERATING CONDITIONS	1	2	3	4	5
SUM FROM PREVIOUS CYCLE	185.4	190.7	190.7	200.1	185.9
AVERAGE FROM PREVIOUS CYCLE	61.8	63.6	63.6	66.7	61.9
NEW OBSERVATIONS	63.5	62.8	67.9	62.6	61.7
DIFFERENCES (WATCH SIGNS)	–1.7	0.8	(–4.3)	(4.1)	0.3
NEW SUMS (N. S.)	248.9	253.5	258.6	262.7	247.4
NEW AVERAGES (N. S./N)	A) 62.2	B) 63.4	C) 64.7	D) 65.7	E) 61.9

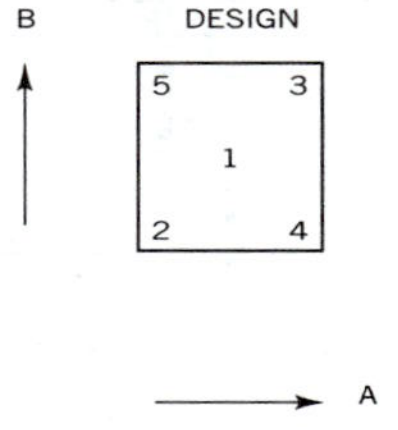

CALCULATIONS OF EFFECTS

A EFFECT

```
C  64.7     B  63.4
D  65.7     E  61.9
F 130.4     G 125.3
           125.3
        2 | 5.1
        +   2.6
```

B EFFECT

```
C  64.7     B  63.4
E  61.9     D  65.7
  126.6       129.1
            126.6
          2 | 2.5
          –   1.3
```

AB EFFECT

```
B  63.4     D  65.7
C  64.7     E  61.9
  128.1       127.6
            127.6
          2 | 0.5
          +   0.3
```

CHANGE-IN-MEAN EFFECT

```
F 130.4    A  62.2 = 4
G 125.3       248.8
  255.7
  248.8
5 | 6.9
+   1.4
```

DESIGN

```
      5   3
        1
      2   4
```

B ←   → A

REMARKS:

Figure 12-10 Worksheet for EVOP Cycle 4

436

12-2.1 Comments on EVOP

Box (1957) recommended that the EVOP procedure be continued with an information board posted daily in the plant manager's office. The manager could change the process whenever results indicate a change to be appropriate. This would lead to a continuing quality improvement effort.

Spendley et al. (1962) suggested using a simplex design instead of the full factorial design used by Box. This design would result in fewer observations per cycle (three instead of five). A simplex design in two factors is an equilateral triangle rather than a square. There would be three corner points; in general, a simplex design in k factors requires $k + 1$ points. The simplex EVOP procedure operates differently from the factorial procedure. After each cycle the point in the simplex that yielded the poorest response is dropped and a new simplex is formed using the reflection of the deleted point with the other k points. A move is made after each cycle, rather than waiting to obtain a statistically significant change. It is thus more dynamic and less conservative than the factorial approach.

Hahn and Dershowitz (1974) reported on an informal survey that they conducted in 1972 to evaluate the extent and nature of EVOP in industry. The results of the survey indicated that EVOP is being used much less extensively than the respondents thought it should be. The main reason for not using it was the "reluctance to perturb manufacturing processes." However, there is no evidence that such a program ever led to deleterious effects. One of the comments reported by Hahn and Dershowitz was "The major problem in encouraging the use of EVOP has been an absence of responsibility for process improvement at the operating level. Operating personnel are not sure they will be praised for process improvement—they know they will be criticized for disturbing throughput." The success of an EVOP program, as with other quality control programs discussed in this text, is dependent on active commitment, participation, and leadership of those responsible for the manufacturing process.

▶ 12-3 ANALYSIS OF MEANS

The analysis of means (ANOM) procedure was first developed by Ott (1967) and later extended by Schilling (1973) to address interactions and main effects for a variety of experimental designs. Schilling called his extensions the analysis of means for treatment effects (ANOME), in which k means being compared are not necessarily independent. Ott's original concepts of ANOM is a method of comparing k independent means. The procedure is based on the multiple significance test proposed by Halperin et al. (1955). They computed upper and lower bounds on the 5% and 1% critical values and conjectured the true values were close to the lower bound. Ott (1967) used the upper bounds and called them H_α. Schilling's critical values simplified interactions and were called h_α, where

$$h_\alpha = H_\alpha \sqrt{k/(k-1)} \tag{12-3}$$

Tables for h_α are given by L. S. Nelson (1974) for $\alpha = 0.10, 0.05, 0.01,$ and 0.001.

Tables of exact critical values for k means with equal sample size are given by L. S. Nelson (1983a) for the same values of α, numbers of means from 3 to 20, and degrees of freedom from k to ∞. These tables for $\alpha = 0.05$ and $\alpha = 0.01$ are reproduced as Table K in the Appendix. Nelson (1983a) also gives approximation functions for these tables and discusses the case for unequal sample sizes.

The procedure can be considered an alternative to the more well-known analysis of variance (ANOVA) procedure described in Section 12-1.1 and in most basic texts on statistics. The ANOM, however, is easier to interpret than the analysis of variance and lends itself more readily to a graphic presentation. It therefore takes on similarities to the Shewhart control charts discussed earlier in this text. An ANOM chart contains decision lines, similar to control limits so that statistical differences may be assessed easily.

Computer programs for this procedure have been developed by Sheesley (1980), Schilling et al. (1980), and P. R. Nelson (1983). The last program, along with the previously mentioned tables of L. S. Nelson (1983a), a reprint of Ott (1967), and other articles relative to ANOM are included in the January 1983 issue of *Journal of Quality Technology,* which is devoted entirely to this topic in honor of Professor Ott. P. R. Nelson (1998) discusses the ANOM procedure and compares it with the ANOVA procedure. He includes many examples using both techniques.

12-3.1 The ANOM for Variables Data—One-Factor Analysis

Ramig (1983) describes the ANOM procedure very clearly. Her step-by-step procedure to use the techniques will be described here. As a first example, assume that all samples are of the same size n. All samples are assumed to come from normal populations with the same variance, σ^2. As with the $\bar{x}$ chart in Chapter 8, the average of the averages is denoted $\bar{\bar{x}}$. The pooled estimate of the common standard deviation (σ) is obtained using Equation (5-22) and is denoted here as s_p. Since equal sample sizes are assumed, s_p is just the square root of the average of the k sample variances. Ott (1967) used the range statistic to obtain an estimate of the common standard deviation, while Schilling (1973) used both the standard deviation and the range, and showed how s_p could be estimated for ANOME even with only one observation per cell. The sample standard deviations, s_i, are used here because they are easy to compute with modern calculators.

Ramig (1983) lists six steps to carry out the ANOM:

1. Compute the average and standard deviation of each sample. Denote them $\bar{x}_i$ and s_i.

2. Compute the grand average, $\bar{\bar{x}}$.

3. Compute s_p, the pooled standard deviation.

4. Obtain h_α from Table K in the Appendix or from L. S. Nelson (1983a) for the appropriate significance level (α) number of averages (k) and degrees of freedom $[k(n - 1)]$.

5. Compute the upper and lower decision lines from Equation (12-4):

$$UDL = \bar{\bar{x}} + h_\alpha s_p \sqrt{(k - 1)/kn}$$
$$LDL = \bar{\bar{x}} + h_\alpha s_p \sqrt{(k - 1)/kn} \tag{12-4}$$

6. Plot the sample averages. Any of the averages lying outside the decision lines is an indication that there is a statistically significant difference among the samples. It is unlikely the samples came from populations with the same underlying means.

TABLE 12-19   Data for Example 12-4

	1	2	3	4	5
	\multicolumn{5}{c}{Supplier}				
	3.46	3.59	3.51	3.38	3.29
	3.48	3.46	3.64	3.40	3.46
	3.56	3.42	3.46	3.37	3.37
	3.39	3.49	3.52	3.46	3.32
	3.40	3.50	3.49	3.39	3.38
$\bar{x}$	3.458	3.492	3.524	3.400	3.364
s	0.0687	0.0630	0.0688	0.0354	0.0650

▶ **EXAMPLE 12-4**

A manufacturer of metal products suspects variations in iron content of raw material supplied by five suppliers. Five ingots were randomly selected from each of the five suppliers. Table 12-19 contains the data for the iron determinations on each ingot in percent by weight.

Following the six-step procedure, the following is obtained:

1. The averages and standard deviations are indicated in Table 12-19.

2. $\bar{\bar{x}} = \frac{1}{5}\Sigma\bar{x}_i = 3.448$.

3. $s_p^2 = \frac{1}{5}\Sigma s_i^2 = \frac{1}{5}[(0.0687)^2 + \cdots + (0.00650)^2]$

   $= 0.00378$

   $s_p = 0.0615$

4. For $\alpha = 0.05$, $k = 5$ and degrees of freedom $= 20$, we find in Table K that $h_\alpha = 2.79$.

5. $UDL = 3.448 + 2.79(0.0615)\sqrt{4/25} = 3.517$

   $LDL = 3.448 - 2.79(0.0615)\sqrt{4/25} = 3.379$

6. Figure 12-11 shows the decision lines for $\alpha = 0.05$ along with the five plotted averages. The figure indicates that the suppliers are statistically different in iron content. The ingots from supplier 3 have more iron, while those from supplier 5 have less than the others.

Two-Factor Analysis

For a two-factor factorial design, consider the means for each level of each factor as well as the effect of any interactions between the two factors. For each main effect the decision lines are given by Equation (12-5).

$$UDL = \bar{\bar{x}} + h_\alpha s_p\sqrt{q/N}$$
$$LDL = \bar{\bar{x}} - h_\alpha s_p\sqrt{q/N}$$

(12-5)

where q is the number of degrees of freedom associated with that factor (the number of levels of the factor less one) and N is the total number of observations.

For the interaction effect the decision lines are given by Equation (12-6):

$$UDL = h_\alpha^* s_p\sqrt{q/N}$$
$$LDL = -h_\alpha^* s_p\sqrt{q/N}$$

(12-6)

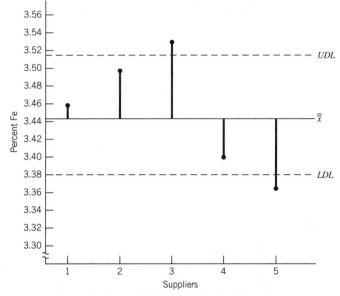

Figure 12-11 ANOM Chart for Metal Suppliers

where q is the number of degrees of freedom for interaction, h_α^* is computed as the upper $\alpha*/2$ percentage point of the Student's t distribution, and

$$\alpha* = 1 - (1 - \alpha)^{1/k} \tag{12-7}$$

In Equation (12-7) α is the desired significance level, and k is the number of averages (based on the two-factor combination). To avoid interpolating in the t table, Figure 12-12 may be used to get the percentage point. This nomograph is from L. S. Nelson (1975). To use it, draw a straight line from the right scale through the tail area desired to the left scale, which is the value of t desired.

▶ **EXAMPLE 12-5**

Duncan (1986, p. 702) gives an example in which three analysts, A_1, A_2, and A_3, each make two determinations of the melting point of hydroquinine in degrees centigrade with each of four different thermometers, T_1, T_2, T_3, and T_4. Each reading is recorded in Table 12-20. Table 12-21 shows the average and standard deviation for each of the cells in Table 12-20.

Again, following the six steps for each factor, for Steps 1 and 2, the averages for each level of each main factor are calculated and shown in Table 12-20 along with the overall average, $\bar{\bar{x}}$. The averages and standard deviations for each factor combination are shown in Table 12-21.

3. The estimate of the standard deviation, s_p, is obtained by averaging the squares of the twelve standard deviations in Table 12-21 and taking the square root of the result:

$$s_p = \sqrt{\frac{(0.35)^2 + \cdots + (0.35)^2}{12}} = 0.47$$

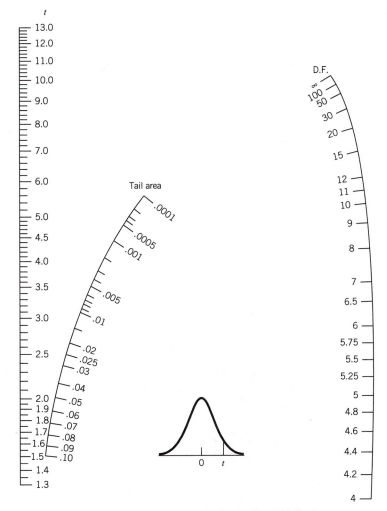

Figure 12-12 Nomograph for Student's *t* Distribution

TABLE 12-20 Thermometer Readings

Analyst	Thermometer T_1	T_2	T_3	T_4	Averages
A₁	174.0	173.0	171.5	173.5	
	173.5	173.5	172.5	173.5	173.13
A₂	173.0	172.0	171.0	171.0	
	173.0	173.0	172.0	172.0	172.13
A₃	173.5	173.0	173.0	172.5	
	173.0	173.5	173.0	173.0	173.06
Averages	173.33	173.00	172.17	172.58	172.77

TABLE 12-21 Averages and Standard Deviations for Cells of Table 12-20

Analyst		Thermometer T_1	T_2	T_3	T_4
A₁	$\bar{x}$	173.75	173.25	172.0	173.5
	s	0.35	0.35	0.71	0.00
A₂	$\bar{x}$	173.0	172.50	171.50	171.50
	s	0.00	0.71	0.71	0.71
A₃	$\bar{x}$	173.25	173.25	173.00	172.75
	s	0.35	0.35	0.00	0.35

4. For $\alpha = 0.05$, h_α is found in Table K in the Appendix for twelve degrees of freedom. For thermometers, $k = 4$ and h_α is 2.85 while for analysts, $k = 3$ and h_α is 2.67. For the interaction effect h_α^* is computed as follows:

$$\alpha^* = 1 - (1 - 0.05)^{1/12} = 0.0043$$

In Figure 12-12 there are 12 degrees of freedom for s_p, and the tail area is $\alpha^*/2 = 0.0021$, giving a value of h_α^* of 3.52.

5. For thermometers,

$$UDL = 172.77 + 2.85(0.47)\sqrt{3/24}$$
$$= 172.77 + 0.47 = 173.24$$
$$LDL = 172.77 - 0.47 = 172.30$$

For analysts,

$$UDL = 172.77 + 2.67(0.47)\sqrt{2/24}$$
$$= 172.77 + 0.36 = 173.13$$
$$LDL = 172.77 - 0.36 = 172.41$$

For the interaction effects,

$$UDL = 3.52(0.47)\sqrt{6/24} = 0.83$$
$$LDL = -0.83$$

6. The ANOM charts for thermometers and analysts are shown in Figures 12-13 and 12-14, respectively. The interaction effects for each of the twelve factor combinations are computed as follows:

$$T_{ij} = \bar{x}_{ij} - \bar{x}_i - \bar{x}_j + \bar{\bar{x}} \tag{12-8}$$

In Equation (12-8), T_{ij} is the interaction effect for row i and column j. The cell averages are $\bar{x}_{ij}$, $\bar{x}_i$ are the row averages, $\bar{x}_j$ are the column averages, and $\bar{\bar{x}}$ is the overall average. Table 12-22

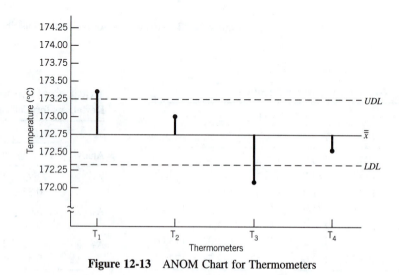

Figure 12-13 ANOM Chart for Thermometers

TABLE 12-22   Interaction Effects

Analyst	Thermometer			
	T_1	T_2	T_3	T_4
A_1	0.06	−0.11	−0.53	0.56
A_2	0.31	0.14	−0.03	−0.44
A_3	−0.37	−0.04	0.54	−0.12

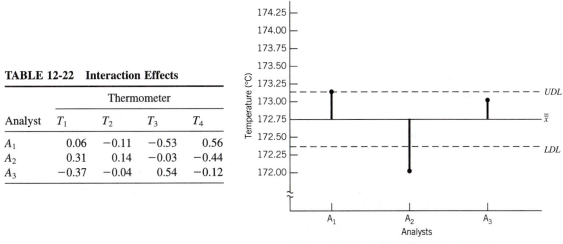

Figure 12-14   ANOM Charts for Analysts

contains the interaction effects for this sample. The twelve effects are plotted, along with the decision lines on Figure 12-15. The ANOM charts indicate significant differences among the thermometers and analysts, but no significant interaction effects. Figure 12-13 shows thermometer one to be consistently high while thermometer three is low. Figure 12-14 indicates that analyst two is consistently reading lower than the other two analysts.

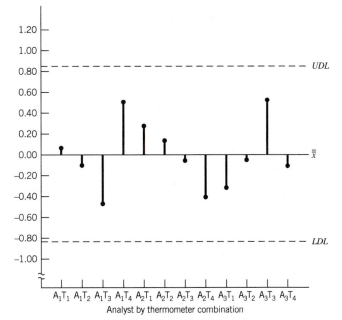
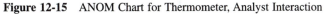

Figure 12-15   ANOM Chart for Thermometer, Analyst Interaction

12-3.2 The ANOM for Attributes Data

Ott (1975) extended the ANOM to attributes-type data. This procedure makes use of the fact that both the binomial and Poisson distributions may be approximated by the normal distribution. Recall that the same approximation was used in Chapters 6 and 7 with attributes control charts. Ramig (1983) again suggests that the following six steps be followed for ANOM for attributes data:

1. Obtain k samples of equal size n. Determine the number of items $x_i (i = 1, \ldots, k)$ in each sample that contain the attribute of concern (e.g., nonconforming).

2. Compute the k sample proportions, $p_i = x_i/n$ $(i = 1, 2, \ldots, k)$ for proportion data. For count data (e.g., number of nonconformities per sample), the x_i obtained in step one is the variable of interest.

3. Obtain the overall mean, $\bar{p} = \Sigma p_i/k$ (or $\bar{c} = \Sigma x_i/k$, for count data).

4. Compute the standard deviation

$$s = \sqrt{\frac{\bar{p}(1 - \bar{p})}{n}} \qquad \text{for proportions data}$$

   or

$$s = \sqrt{\bar{c}} \qquad \text{for count data}$$

5. Determine the decision lines. For proportions data these are

$$UDL = \bar{p} + h_\alpha s \sqrt{(k - 1)/k} \tag{12-9}$$
$$LDL = \bar{p} - h_\alpha s \sqrt{(k - 1)/k}$$

   For count data the decision lines are

$$UDL = \bar{c} + h_\alpha s \sqrt{(k - 1)/k} \tag{12-10}$$
$$LDL = \bar{c} - h_\alpha s \sqrt{(k - 1)/k}$$

6. Plot the sample results (fraction nonconforming or number of nonconformities) and the decision lines on an ANOM chart. Interpret the results as with variables data.

▶ **EXAMPLE 12-6**

Table 12-23 shows inspection results on twenty-four samples of batteries, all of size 50. Table 12-23 also indicates the fraction nonconforming for each example. The six-step procedure will be again followed for ANOM:

1, 2. The results of the first two steps are indicated in Table 12-23.

3. $\bar{p} = (0.10 + 0.12 + \cdots + 0.04)/24 = 0.075$

4. $s = \dfrac{\sqrt{0.075(1 - 0.075)}}{50} = 0.0372$

5. For $k = 24$ and degrees of freedom $\leq$ infinity (the normal case), go to Table K in the Appendix. However, k is listed only for 20 or less. An approximation that may be used is given by L. S. Nelson (1983b) as

$$h_\alpha, k, \nu = B_1 + B_2\,k_1^{B_3} + (B_4 + B_5k_1)\,V_1 + (B_6 + B_7k_2 + B_8k_2^2)\,V_1^2 \tag{12-11}$$

TABLE 12-23 Nonconforming Batteries

Sample Number	Number Nonconforming	Fraction Nonconforming	Sample Number	Number Nonconforming	Fraction Nonconforming
1	5	0.10	13	5	0.10
2	6	0.12	14	3	0.06
3	6	0.12	15	3	0.06
4	3	0.06	16	6	0.12
5	4	0.08	17	6	0.12
6	2	0.04	18	4	0.08
7	2	0.04	19	4	0.08
8	1	0.02	20	2	0.04
9	4	0.08	21	2	0.04
10	4	0.08	22	3	0.06
11	5	0.10	23	5	0.10
12	3	0.06	24	2	0.04

where

k = number of samples

$k_1 = \ln(k)$

$k_2 = \ln(k - 2)$

ν = degrees of freedom for error

$V_1 = 1/(\nu - 1)$

B_1 = constants depending on α

Table 12-24 contains values of B_1 through B_8 for $\alpha = 0.05$ and 0.01. Using these constants, for $k = 24$, $\nu = \infty$, and $\alpha = 0.05$, we get

$$k_1 = \ln(24) = 3.1781$$

$$k_2 = \ln(22) = 3.0910$$

$$\nu = \infty$$

$$V_1 = 1/\infty = 0$$

TABLE 12-24 Constants for Approximating h_α

Constants	$\alpha = 0.05$	$\alpha = 0.01$
B_1	1.7011	2.3539
B_2	0.6047	0.5176
B_3	0.7102	0.7107
B_4	1.4605	4.3161
B_5	1.9102	2.3629
B_6	0.2250	4.6400
B_7	0.6300	1.8640
B_8	−0.2202	0.3204

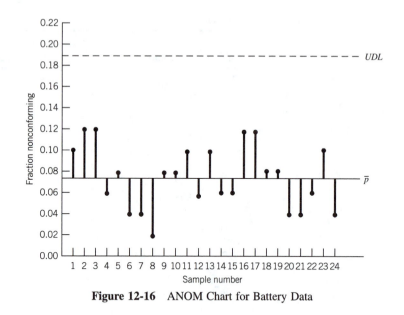

Figure 12-16   ANOM Chart for Battery Data

Since V_1 is 0, the last two terms of Equations (12-11) drop out, and

$$h_\alpha = 1.7011 + (0.6047)\,(3.1781)^{.7102}$$
$$= 3.08$$

The reader is referred to L. S. Nelson (1983b) for the development of Equation (12-11). The decision lines may now be computed as

$$UDL = 0.075 + 3.08(0.0372)\ \sqrt{23/24}$$
$$= 0.075 + 0.112 = 0.187$$
$$LDL = 0.075 - 0.112 = 0$$

6. The ANOM chart is shown in Figure 12-16. This chart may be compared with the *np* chart shown in Figure 7-6. Both indicate the process to be in a state of statistical control. The data in Table 12-23 are for the first three days in Figure 7-6.

▶ EXAMPLE 12-7

Problem 7 in Chapter 7 contains inspection data for the situation in which the number of nonconformities (*c*) was given for twenty samples of equal size. The data for the first ten samples are reproduced here as Table 12-25. Again, follow the six-step procedure:

1, 2. The individual values are shown in Table 12-25.

3. $\bar{c} = 250/10 = 25.0$

4. $s = \sqrt{25} = 5.0$

5. h_α, for $\alpha = 0.05$, $k = 10$, and degrees of freedom ∞ is, from Table K in the Appendix, 2.80.

$$UDL = 25.0 + 2.80(5.0)\sqrt{9/10}$$
$$= 25.0 + 13.3 + 38.3$$
$$LDL = 25.0 - 13.3 = 11.7$$

TABLE 12-25 Number of Nonconformities

Sample Number	Number of Nonconformities
1	11
2	23
3	35
4	19
5	22
6	25
7	28
8	14
9	50
10	23
Total	250

6. The ANOM chart is shown in Figure 12-17. The chart shows that there are significant differences among the samples. Specifically, sample one is slightly less than the others while sample nine is much too high. Figure 12-17 may be compared to the c-chart in Chapter 7, recalling that an α of 0.05 was used here while the c-chart is set up using $\pm$ 3 standard deviation limits (an α of approximately 0.0027).

12-3.3 Summary of ANOM

The ANOM for variables data assumed an underlying normal distribution. As discussed in Chapter 6, this is often a reasonable assumption with most measurement data. For attributes data the normal distribution was also used as an approximation to the appropriate

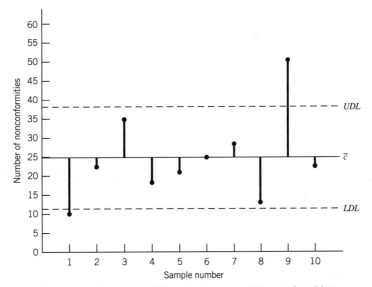

Figure 12-17 ANOM Chart for Number of Nonconformities

distribution. Chapter 7 discussed its use for such data for control charts. The ANOM procedure is somewhat more sensitive to a lack of normality, particularly for small sample sizes. Nevertheless, for such situations the data may be transformed. A suitable transformation is the arcsin transformation

$$W = \arcsin \sqrt{\frac{x}{N+1}} + \arcsin \sqrt{\frac{x+1}{N+1}} \tag{12-12}$$

given in L. S. Nelson (1983b). Other possible transformations are also mentioned in the Nelson paper.

The ANOM is sometimes referred to as an alternative to the analysis of variance. Its advantage over the ANOVA procedure is that the data are plotted and thus the results may be quickly interpreted. It may also be compared to conventional Shewhart control charts. However, such comparisons may not be justified in many cases. For process control, the control chart is ideal. ANOM is useful only to determine whether significant differences exist in past data.

▶ 12-4 SUMMARY

This chapter has concentrated on techniques that are useful for the improvement of quality rather than the control of quality. It has only touched on many of these topics, however, and the reader is urged to pursue the concepts presented here and in other texts that discuss them. The concept of experimental design is critical to the improvement of quality and is the foundation of most quality improvement studies including six sigma programs. These procedures are the difference between maintaining quality at its current level and improving it. To remain competitive, such quality improvement efforts must be made.

Professor Taguchi [see Taguchi (1981) or Taguchi and Wu (1979)] proposes a somewhat different approach to quality improvement studies using experimental design procedures. He considers two classes of factors: control factors and all others, which he refers to as noise. He then works with the concept of the signal-to-noise ratio to analyze the data. He also considers the cost of making improvements along with their savings. The experimental designs used may be of two- or three-level factors or a combination of them, thus quadratic effects may be observed. However, interactions are assumed not to be significant with his procedures. These methods are being widely used in Japan and by some leading U.S. companies. Details, with examples, of Taguchi's approach to the design and analysis of experiments is the subject of Chapter 13.

▶ 12-5 REFERENCES

Bingham, R. S. (1963), "EVOP for Systematic Process Improvement," *Industrial Quality Control*, Sept.; pp. 17–23.

Box, G. E. P. (1957), "Evolutionary Operation: A Method for Increasing Industrial Productivity," *Applied Statistics*, Vol. 6, pp. 81–101.

Box, G. E. P. (1966), "Use and Abuse of Regression," *Technometrics*, Vol. 8, No. 4, Nov.; pp. 625–29.

Box, G. E. P., and Draper, N. R. (1969), *Evolutionary Operations*, Wiley, New York.

Box, G. E. P., and Hunter, J. S. (1959), "Condensed Calculations for Evolutionary Operations Programs," *Technometrics*, Vol. 1, No. 1, Feb.; pp. 79–95.

Box, G. E. P., Hunter, J. S., and Hunter, W. G. (1978), *Statistics for Experimenters*, Wiley, New York.

DeBusk, R. E. (1962), "Experience in Evolutionary Operations at Tennessee Eastman Company," *Industrial Quality Control*, Oct.; pp. 15–21 (October).

Duncan, A. J. (1986), *Quality Control and Industrial Statistics*, Fifth Edition, Richard D. Irwin, Homewood, IL.

Hahn, G. J., and Dershowitz, A. F. (1974), "Evolutionary Operations Today—Some Survey Results and Observations," *The Journal of the Royal Statistical Society, Series C (Applied Statistics)*, Vol. 23, No. 2, pp. 214–18.

Halperin, M., Greenhouse, S. W., Cornfield, J., and Zalokar, J. (1955), "Tables of Percentage Points for the Studentized Maximum Absolute Deviate in Normal Samples," *Journal of the American Statistical Association*, Vol. 50, pp. 185–95.

Hicks, C. R. (1973), *Fundamental Concepts in the Design of Experiments*, Holt, Rinehart and Winston, New York.

Hill, W. J., and Wiles, R. A. (1975), "Plant Experimentation (PLEX)," *Journal of Quality Technology*, Vol. 7, No. 3, July; pp. 115–22.

Hunter, W. G., and Kittrell, S. R. (1966), "Evolutionary Operations: A Review," *Technometrics*, Vol. 8, No. 3, pp. 389–97.

Koehler, T. L. (1958), "Evolutionary Operations: Some Actual Examples," *Transactions of the Second Stevens Symposium on Statistical Methods in the Chemical Industry*, pp. 5–8, Stevens, NJ.

Montgomery, D. C. (1991), *Design and Analysis of Experiments*, Third Edition, Wiley, New York.

Nelson, L. S. (1974), "Factors for the Analysis of Means," *Journal of Quality Technology*, Vol. 6, No. 4, Oct.; pp. 175–81.

Nelson, L. S. (1975), "A Nomograph of Student's *t*," *Journal of Quality Technology*, Vol. 7, No. 4, Oct.; pp. 200–201.

Nelson, L. S. (1983a), "Exact Critical Values for Use with the Analysis of Means," *Journal of Quality Technology*, Vol. 15, No. 1, Jan.; pp. 40–44.

Nelson, L. S. (1983b), "Transformation for Attribute Data," *Journal of Quality Technology*, Vol. 15, No. 1, Jan.; pp. 55–56.

Nelson, P. R. (1983), "The Analysis of Means for Balanced Experimental Designs," *Journal of Quality Technology*, Vol. 15, No. 1, Jan.; pp. 45–54.

Nelson, P. R. (1998), "Design and Analysis of Experiments," in Wadsworth, H. M., Ed., *Handbook of Statistical Methods for Engineers and Scientists*, Second Edition, McGraw-Hill, New York.

Ott, E. R. (1967), "Analysis of Means—A Graphical Procedure," *Industrial Quality Control*, Vol. 24, No. 2, pp. 101–09.

Ott, E. R. (1975), *Process Quality Control*, McGraw-Hill, New York.

Pearson, E. S., and Hartley, H. O. (1954), *Biometrika Tables for Statisticians*, Vol. 1, p. 46. The University Press, Cambridge, England.

Ramig, P. F. (1983), "Applications of the Analysis of Means," *Journal of Quality Technology*, Vol. 15, No. 1, Jan.; pp. 19–25.

Russell, E. R., and Stephens, K. S. (1970), "An EVOP Teaching Game Using a Simulated Process," *Journal of Quality Technology*, Vol. 2., No. 2, pp. 61–66.

Schilling, E. G. (1973), "A Systematic Approach to the Analysis of Means," *Journal of Quality Technology*, Vol. 5, No. 3, July; pp. 93–108, No. 4, Oct.; pp. 147–59.

Schilling, E. G., Schlotzer, G., Schultz, H. E., and Sheesley, J. H. (1980), "A FORTRAN Computer Program for Analysis of Variance and Analysis of Means," *Journal of Quality Technology*, Vol. 12, No. 2, April; pp. 106–13.

Sheesley, J. H. (1980), "Comparison of Samples Involving Variables or Attributes Data Using the Analysis of Means," *Journal of Quality Technology*, Vol. 12, No. 1, Jan.; pp. 47–52.

Spendley, W., Hext, G. R., and Himsworth, F. R. (1962), "Sequential Applications of Simplex Designs in Optimization and EVOP," *Technometrics*, Vol. 4, No. 4, Nov.; pp. 441–61.

Stephens, K. S. (1997), *EVOP Revisited*, 17th Southeastern Quality Conference, ASQ, Atlanta, GA.

Taguchi, G. (1981), *On Line Quality Control*, Japanese Standards Association, Tokyo, Japan.

Taguchi, G., and Wu, Y. (1979), *Introduction to Off-Line Quality Control*, Central Japanese Quality Control Association, Nagoya, Japan.

▶ 12-6 PROBLEMS

1. Analyze the following three-factor factorial design using the methods of Section 12-1. Factor A represents two grades of raw material. Factor B represents two production processes, while factor C represents high and low temperatures. The response variable is product yield in pounds minus 150 pounds.

	A_1		A_2	
	B_1	B_2	B_1	B_2
C_1	18	32	−2	−16
	28	24	3	−20
C_2	30	46	13	−6
	38	36	13	−12

2. Use the analysis of means procedure to analyze the following data, which represent the results of five random samples taken from different machines. The data depict diameters of metal sleeves in mm.

M_1	M_2	M_3	M_4	M_5
1.02	1.06	0.99	0.99	1.05
0.99	1.02	1.00	0.94	1.02
0.99	1.05	0.94	0.96	1.01
1.00	1.07	0.96	0.98	1.01

3. Analyze the data for July 11, batch 0004 in Problem 9 of Chapter 8 using the ANOM procedure.

4. Analyze the data in Problem 3 of Chapter 8 using ANOM procedures.

5. Analyze the data in Problem 10 of Chapter 7 using the analysis of means.

6. Analyze the data in Problem 11 of Chapter 7 using the analysis of means.

7. The following are weekly sales results of an electronic product in nine different cities of approximately the same size. Analyze the data using the analysis of means procedure to determine any differences among the cities in regard to sales of the product. Each mean and standard deviation is based on thirty weeks.

Cities	Average Sales	Standard Deviations
1	37.10	14.50
2	20.00	8.49
3	40.37	21.23
4	51.60	21.63
5	24.07	18.77
6	32.22	25.30
7	44.56	27.18
8	62.10	19.51
9	37.33	15.46

8. A two-variable EVOP program has been proposed to increase the yield of a chemical reaction. The two variables considered are moisture concentration (A) and temperature (B). High and low levels were selected for each variable and the table below gives the response for six cycles. Follow the EVOP procedure to formulate a recommendation for a new phase.

	Operating Conditions				
Cycle	1	2	3	4	5
1	60.3	64.8	58.3	56.4	55.9
2	62.0	60.2	57.2	51.7	57.8
3	58.4	61.0	59.6	50.2	62.2
4	58.6	59.3	52.0	58.9	66.6
5	55.8	61.0	57.1	59.6	57.4
6	61.3	53.3	59.5	54.3	62.5

CHAPTER

13

ROBUST DESIGN

In the 1960s a small ceramic tile company in Japan was facing a serious problem. Too many of the ceramic floor tiles it produced were failing final inspection and had to be scrapped. The main reason for the failures appeared to be misshaped tiles, primarily tiles that were not within the specified dimensions.

An investigation pointed to a culprit; the root cause of the defective tiles appeared to be the kiln in which the tiles were fired. Tiles fired in the center of the kiln were fine. Those fired on the edges of the kiln had high variability in their dimensions. The heating elements and temperature-controlling devices were old and unable to provide a uniform firing temperature. The unevenness of the temperature caused the problems.

The solution seemed to be easy but expensive: Replace the kiln with a new one. This solution would cost approximately half a million dollars. This caused an energetic debate. Could the company justify the return on this quality improvement investment? Would the savings in reduced defects and scrapped tiles be greater than the cost of the new oven? How long would it take to recover the investment?

While this debate was raging, someone suggested an alternative approach. Was there any way, he wondered, to get proper tiles out of the existing process? Was there some way other than replacing the oven to produce proper tiles? The company started experimenting with different mixtures of the clay formulas used in its ceramic tiles. It was soon discovered that by changing the mixture of lime and clay, a tile formulation that was robust to temperature variations in the oven could be produced. Even with the existing oven, high-quality tiles with the correct dimensions were produced.

▶ 13-1 THE CONCEPT OF ROBUST DESIGN

This concept of changing some variables in a process to make the process impervious to variation in other variables has become known as robust design in the United States [Godfrey, Phadke, and Shoemaker (1986)]. The idea is not a difficult concept to understand. But the application of the idea can be time consuming, and it often requires advanced mathematical skills and a thorough understanding of the process one is trying to manage.

In the United States the first demonstration of the power of robust design was in the design and manufacture of new microprocessors at AT&T Bell Laboratories and Western Electric [Phadke, Kacker, Speeney, and Grieco (1983)]. Taguchi and Phadke designed experiments that pointed to a way to reduce variation in microprocessor window openings by a factor of 4. These changes in the process design reduced defects by two thirds and cut the processing time in half.

One of the tough problems in making integrated circuits is getting an absolutely uniform layer of photographic emulsion on the silicon. Other experiments reduced the sensitivity of the pattern-etching process to the variation of emulsion thickness. This increase in "robustness" reduced visual defects to less than 20% of the original level. Another experiment led to a 40% increase in machine utilization. The savings were over $1.2 million.

These robust design methods can be applied to a wide variety of problems in many different industries. First develop a thorough understanding of five key concepts. These concepts are not new, but many of them are not fully understood in many companies or even entire industries. In some cases work must be done before robust design methods can be used.

The five key concepts in robust design are measurement, the loss function, control variables, noise variables, and planned experimentation. Each of these key concepts are discussed in this chapter, as they relate to robust design.

Figure 13-1 is a simple picture of these concepts. All work is a process. It receives some kind of input; effort is added to that input in the form of tasks, procedures, and interventions; and an output is produced. There is a target for this output—what must be achieved. Some variables can be controlled. These are called the *control variables*. These variables are set at what are expected to be the optimal values and the output is observed. Over time it is possible to become quite skilled at how to manipulate the control variables to obtain the desired output.

Unfortunately, in every situation there are a number of other variables that cannot be controlled or that are too expensive to control. These are the noise variables, confounders in epidemiological terms. Some of the noise variables may be unknown along with their effect on the outcome.

What is not evident in Figure 13-1 is the role of planned industrial experimentation (see Chapter 12). Robust design is an attempt to efficiently experiment with the control variables in the presence of the noise variables to learn the optimum settings for those variables that can be controlled. In the first example given at the start of this chapter, the main noise variable was the variation of temperature in the ovens. In the work on improving the yields of the microprocessor production line, one of the key noise variables was the variation in thickness of the photographic emulsions. For a medical example the control variables may be the type of medication, the dose, and the timing of the treatment. For each type of patient, one wishes to know the optimum treatment [Godfrey (1992)].

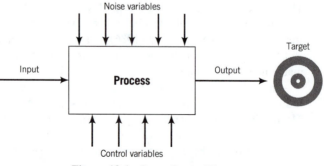

Figure 13-1 Input-Output Diagram

▶ 13-2 MEASUREMENT

There is no more fundamental concept in robust design than measurement. To make significant improvements, one must be able to measure the changes. For many companies, especially in the service industries, quality measurements are not well developed. The companies are using weak sets of product quality (goods and services) that have been developed for delivered quality. They have only rudimentary measurements of process quality, measurements that will allow the organization to predict the final quality. Instead, they rely too much on quality by inspection and sort the good from the bad at the end of the line. Other companies, especially service companies, rely on quality by recovery. These companies try to retain customers by providing excellent warranties or by generous allowances and gifts after mistakes are made. The construction industry, airlines, and hotels are notorious for the high percentage of mistakes and pervasive use of recovery strategies to attempt to mitigate the effect of numerous errors.

Other industries such as pharmaceutical and health care depend on a limited set of measurements, often defined by an outside regulating agency. Many of these companies are missing even those critical measurements that would enable them to study, compare, and manage the critical outcomes of their key processes. For many of these organizations, measurements from the customer point of view are often lacking. Other organizations have created extensive sets of measurements for production or operational processes but have few measurements on administrative processes, even though they may significantly affect costs and customer satisfaction.

There has been much work done in recent years to develop better measurements in health care quality. Some hospitals and managed care organizations have created first-class health care quality measurement groups. These groups have contributed greatly to the understanding of how to measure clinical outcomes, treatment effectiveness, and care efficiencies.

13-2.1 Attributes Measurements

The simplest, but often least useful, measurement of quality is an attribute measurement, a one-dimensional, binary outcome measurement. The nonconformance to quality requirements is an example. Counting nonconformities is a good way to start measuring quality. It is better to define nonconformities and count their number than to not measure quality at all. But it must be remembered that attributes measurements have some inherent limitations. First, everything must be categorized as either good or bad, conforming or not conforming. This involves drawing a line, often rather arbitrarily, that divides conforming from nonconforming. On one side of the line items are considered good; on the other side they are considered bad.

For some quality characteristics this is perfectly adequate and even the right thing to do. For example, after an electrical test it is found that the item either worked or didn't work. The car either started or didn't start. The patient either survived the operation or did not survive the operation. But for other applications the use of nonconformities is quite constraining. When an arbitrary line is set for miles per gallon in measuring fuel efficiency for an automobile and the car is considered nonconforming below the line and conforming above the line, several unnecessary and counterproductive simplifications are made.

A better measure of fuel efficiency would be the variables measurement that gives a good estimate of the fuel efficiency of the automobile. The fuel efficiency could be reported as 32.3 miles per gallon, or the average fuel efficiency of the twenty automobiles tested could be reported as 31.1 miles per gallon.

13-2.2 Variables Measurements

Variables-type measurements are continuous measurements. The actual variables measurement, like miles per gallon or patient waiting times, may be used with little more effort than comparing the measurement to a specification, requirement, or standard. The actual measurement may be more difficult, the recording of the measurement may be more time consuming, and the analysis may take more effort. When measurements are made and recorded by hand, these may be real concerns. But most of these concerns have been eliminated by the widespread use of automated measurement devices and electronic data processing and analysis.

Many current service organizations use attributes data such as rooms not ready, percent of planes late, unsatisfactory loss on telephone calls, deaths, complications, or fever. Perhaps some of these are candidates for variables measurements instead. The actual temperature could be recorded rather than just noting that it was over 100.4. The exact number of minutes that planes are late or the actual loss during telephone calls can be measured. Many such service measurements have been recorded and used routinely as variables for many years.

13-2.3 Weighted Measurements

The next problem encountered with the simplest quality measurements is the implicit assumption that all measurements are equal. In using these simplest measurements, it is implied the car that does not start in the morning is as bad as the car whose brakes fail on an interstate highway. Are either of these failures equal to the car with an unnecessary rattle in the glove box? Failure to accurately weight measurements could imply that medicine that is delivered to the patient ten minutes late is the same as the wrong medicine delivered to the patient.

Nonconformities are not all the same. Some may cause minor inconveniences; others may cause severe damage, extreme risks, significant loss or even death. A simple solution to this problem is to assign weights to measurements of different quality characteristics. These weights may be developed through basic research, customer focus groups, simulations of customer behavior, expert analysis, or sophisticated modeling of failure probabilities.

Many other methods are used to weight simple measurements to relate to severity of outcomes or customer dissatisfaction. Some organizations use continuous scales and sophisticated loss functions to indicate the seriousness of the problem.

13-2.4 Compound Measurements

Quality measurements have been discussed as if everything had only one quality dimension. However, this is far from the truth. Most things are quite complex and have several dimensions of quality. One of the harder problems of quality measurement is combining the measurements of different quality requirements into meaningful summary statistics.

Most organizations have learned that they cannot possibly work with the numerous, often hundreds of measurements of product (both goods and services) quality outcomes, customer satisfaction, on time deliveries, and others. They have learned that a one-number summary of all these measurements is also inadequate. The problem is how to combine many measurements into a small, useful set that accurately portrays what is actually happening and gives clear indications about methods for improvement.

Adding nonconformities is easy. Adding weighted nonconformities is somewhat harder. Adding variables or weighted variables is still harder. Unfortunately, many organizations have chosen to minimize their mathematical problems rather than maximize the usefulness of their information.

13-2.5 Complex Measurements

This discussion has considered only the simplest kinds of measurements. The assumption has been that for every quality dimension or outcome, there is one measurement that can be made. This, of course, is not the case. There are many choices of what to measure, how to measure it, when to measure it, and how to interpret the results.

An entire class of measurements has been overlooked in the above discussion: measurements of variation. In many industrial quality problems and in many service organizations' quality problems, the measurement of variation may be even more important than the measurement of current value (or location in statistical terms).

Many important measurement questions, such as measurement accuracy, repeatability, reproducibility and uncertainty, are currently ignored. But the reduction of variation is crucial for robust design. The interest is not only in the outcome, but also in the variation of the outcome. For many applications reducing the variation of the result may be more important than moving the result closer to the target.

▶ 13-3 LOSS FUNCTIONS

One of the most important concepts of robust design is the idea of the loss function. In robust design it is assumed that any deviation from the desired target has a loss associated with it.

A well-known example from the automobile industry shows how this works. Several years ago, when the automobile companies manufactured transmissions, they used simple quality measures for the various gears and shafts used to assemble the transmissions. For each part they had a specified diameter with tolerance limits—allowable plus and minus variation. The parts either were within the tolerance limits or were not.

The problem was that it was possible that two gears, both on the high end of the tolerance limits, could be selected for the same assembly. This transmission would be stiff and hard to shift. Or two gears on the low end of the tolerance limits could be selected, and the transmission would in the customer's opinion now be loose or sloppy. The automobile manufacturers could have just tightened the tolerance limits. This would have been an improvement, but they still would not have the information needed for continuous improvement. They would have only attributes data—the percent outside the new limits.

They chose instead to develop a new measure based on a quadratic loss function (just the squares of the distances from the desired target) to indicate lack of quality. This is an easy measurement to use. Squaring the distances from the desired target results in positive numbers that can easily be added. Multiplying by a constant adjusts the measurement any way one desires. This measure did what was hoped. The attention was focused on continuously reducing this number, that is, continuously reducing the variation around the target diameter.

The use of a loss function to indicate to the customer and producer the loss as a function of the amount of deviation from a desired target is not a new idea. Mathematical statisticians have used loss functions, especially quadratic loss functions, for many years. AT&T Bell Laboratories rediscovered the usefulness of loss functions in the early 1970s while developing a new measurement system for the transmission quality dimensions of telephone cables manufactured in AT&T's cable plants.

Under the previous quality measurement system, for example, resistances of the copper wires were measured in ohms per mile, and the measurement was compared to a specification with upper limits. For 22-gauge copper wire the target resistance was 86.5 ohms per mile, and the upper tolerance limit was 91 ohms per mile. Wires with resistance under the limit were called good, and those exceeding the limit were labeled bad. That meant that wires with a resistance of 90.9 ohms per mile were considered good and wires with a resistance of 91.1 ohms per mile were considered bad.

Of course, there is little practical difference between 90.9 ohms per mile and 91.1 ohms per mile. There is, however, considerable difference between 86.5 ohms per mile (the target value) and 90.9 ohms per mile. This naive measurement system had serious consequences even though the standard, less than one nonconformity per million, was being met. As manufacturing processes became more sophisticated, plant managers moved the production process closer and closer to the tolerance limit. The higher resistance caused high electrical loss in the field, customer complaints, expensive maintenance operations and even more expensive overengineering on the telephone network. By changing the quality measurement system to a loss function around the target resistance, the managers obtained a tool for attaining the quality needed in the field.

Phadke's (1989) figure, shown here with permission as Figure 13-2, shows how a quadratic loss function can be used to indicate that loss increases as the distance from the

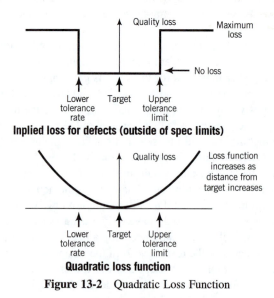

Figure 13-2   Quadratic Loss Function

target increases. When nonconformities based on specified tolerances are used, it is implied that there is no loss within the tolerance limits, and maximum loss is incurred just outside the tolerance limits.

▶ 13-4 CONTROL VARIABLES

The outcome of the process is influenced by the input and by a large number of variables: the noise variables and the control variables. The variables under control are called the control variables. Examples of control variables in a manufacturing process include temperature, flow rate settings, spin rates, electrical charge, and line speed. Control variables in health care include type of medication, dose, timing of medication, therapy, and many other medical interventions. In other service organizations control variables may include room temperatures, water temperatures, waiting times, noise on telephone lines, bit and block error rates for data, appearance, taste, and temperature of food and drinks.

The objective of the planned experiments in robust design is to determine the optimum settings for the control variables. A number of criteria may be used in defining the best levels. One may wish to minimize costs or maximize effectiveness. The idea of robustness is insensitivity to noise variables [Phadke (1986)].

▶ 13-5 NOISE VARIABLES

The noise variables are the uncontrollable variables or variables that cannot be controlled. These variables are not controlled because of costs of control or difficulty of control or for other reasons. The noise variables may be unknown.

The influence of the noise variables on the output may not be well understood. The influence may change from time to time, from one process to another, or from one environment to another. Only the statistical characteristics of the noise variables may be known, not the actual values [Phadke (1986)]. The noise variables can and do cause the output to deviate from the target value. This leads to quality loss.

Examples of noise variables include diet, smoking, other medications, other medical conditions, and stress. George Box describes a simple problem of designing a competitive cake mix. In the past the research and development labs of the food-processing companies would optimize the mix using the high-tech ovens in the design labs. The problem was that the ovens that are used in the average homes are quite variable. The temperatures in the ovens vary from the settings, the average timer is not perfect, and the cook is not always there to remove the cake at exactly the set time. The challenge was to develop the best possible cake mix for the ovens in the homes of the customers, not for the ovens in the design labs.

▶ 13-6 PLANNED EXPERIMENTATION

Now the stage is set for a difficult problem. There are an input, a set of noise variables, a set of control variables, and a desired output: the target. A decision must be made about which settings of the control variables will give the best output in the presence of the noise variables. There are hundreds, even thousands, of experiments that might be run to gain this information.

Kacker and Shoemaker (1986) present a straightforward approach for planning and conducting robust design experiments. There are several basic differences between these experiments and the randomized controlled trials described in Chapter 12. Noise variables are explicitly identified and considered in the experiments. The output to be optimized is a function of both the variation of the response (the outcome) and the average value of the response.

13-6.1 Formulating the Problem

This is a crucial first step. The analysis team should clearly state the objectives and specify the output measurements that reflect these objectives. The team members next list all control and noise variables.

The first step is often begun by brainstorming. The analysis team should include a wide variety of professional specialties and staff specialists with solid experience. Then there is a good chance of identifying the most important objectives and key noise and control variables.

This group should include people who understand all process steps and how the work actually flows and what measurements and data are available. Kacker and Shoemaker (1986) emphasize the importance of choosing continuous, fundamental output measurements rather than discrete measurements.

After the team clearly identifies the output measurements, the team members list all known variables that they believe affect the outcome. They then classify each variable as controllable (control variables) or difficult to control (noise variables). During this step the team must also list the pairs of control variables that may interact in their effect on the outcome.

13-6.2 Deciding on Settings for Control Variables

At this stage the team must decide on trial settings for each of the control variables. The first decision they must make is how many settings to use for each variable. If they feel the relationship between the control variable and the outcome is fairly simple—for example, linear—they may choose to use only two settings: one on each side of the nominal value. When the team is worried that the relationship may be more complex, they may choose three or four different settings for the control variable.

The team must also decide how far apart to make these settings of the control variables. If they make the settings too close together, they may not be able to see the effect on the outcome. If they spread the settings too far apart, they may get unexpected or confusing results. For example, in a manufacturing process, setting the temperature too high for a chemical reaction process could cause a fire or explosion.

13-6.3 Constructing the Control Array

The experimental plan in robust design has two parts: a control array and a noise plan. The control array is a plan for varying the settings of the control variables in the experiment. The noise plan is the scheme for measuring the noise variables.

In a completely controlled experiment, the noise variables may be able to be set at different levels to study their effect on the response. The more usual case is that the levels of the noise variables cannot be controlled even in an experiment. Instead, a plan is constructed for taking multiple measurements of the noise variables during the experiment. In this way the effect of the noise variables on the outcome responses may be studied.

13-6.4 Constructing the Noise Plan

The team is now ready to construct the noise plan. Here, the purpose is to systematically introduce real-world variation into the experiment [Kacker and Shoemaker (1986)]. The example given above by George Box illustrated these noise variables. The control factors for the food producer designing a new cake mix include the dry mix, the amount of liquid to be added, the baking time, and the temperature.

There are several things not under the producer's control, the noise variables. The ovens in general use are not perfect; there is variation in the actual temperatures obtained. The timers used in homes are also not perfect; there will be some variation in baking times. People also live at different altitudes. So the task is not to develop the best cake that can be produced in a test kitchen, but to develop the best cake that will be produced in a home.

It is not always possible to directly introduce important noise variables into the experiment. This is likely to be the case, especially in administrative functions, service companies, and health care. It is also the case in many manufacturing process design problems. The sources of noise here are often variation in raw materials; personnel changes; equipment wear; and environmental variations such as humidity, dust, light, electrical surges, and other electromagnetic interferences.

In these cases noise variables are introduced indirectly by taking replications of the experiment in a way designed to capture the effects of these noise variables. The normal variations are allowed to occur and the noise levels for each experimental run are measured.

The introduction of a noise plan in an experiment adds to the overall cost of the experiment as there must be many more replications to study interactions between control variables and noise variables. This added complexity further strengthens the case for using well planned experimental designs to reduce the number of replications necessary for good estimates. If all possible combinations of variables are to be studied, impossible situations may soon occur. For example, even a simple experiment with seven variables at three levels, each with only one replicate at each possible combination, would take over 2000 runs.

The noise plan matrix or array is constructed in a similar fashion to the control array described briefly above. Kacker and Ghosh (1998) give an excellent discussion of how the control variables array is crossed with every row of the noise variables array. Wedderburn (1987) gives a short but useful discussion with an example of a furnace productivity study.

13-6.5 Conducting the Experiment

This is the simplest part of robust design conceptually and the hardest in practice. Each experimental run involves setting the control variables to the values indicated in the experimental design plan and setting or observing the levels of the noise variables for each run. The results are carefully measured for each run.

13-6.6 Analyzing the Results

There are many ways to analyze the results of a well-designed experiment. Taguchi (1985), Box (1986a, 1986b), Phadke (1989), and Kacker and Ghosh (1998) give excellent discussions on the pros and cons of different methods. Taguchi has recommended the use of performance criteria he calls signal-to-noise ratios for the analysis. These signal-to-noise ratios are constructed using prior knowledge about the process and the outcomes. For each type of problem a signal-to-noise ratio is constructed so that the optimization of the performance measure minimizes the expected loss. In Section 13-7 two graphical methods are suggested for use in complex dynamic robust designs.

13-6.7 Confirming the Results

The final and one of the most important steps in robust design is running a confirmation experiment. The experimental design may have predicted that the optimal results will be obtained at settings of control variables that were not in the original experiment. One final run should then be made at the indicated control variables settings to confirm the results. How to achieve the best possible outcome for a very complex process with a number of noise variables now becomes obvious.

▶ 13-7 ROBUST DESIGNS WITH DYNAMIC CHARACTERISTICS

The concept of robust design has proven to be a cost-effective approach to reduce variation and improve the quality of products and processes. Since being introduced in Japan by Taguchi and then later in the United States and Europe, robust design has been used extensively in a wide range of applications including the automobile, the electronics, food processing, and medical equipment industries. Recently, there have been interesting extensions of the basic methodology to new applications involving so-called dynamic systems. These new methods cover the general condition in which the systems output, Y, depends on a signal factor, M, that also varies. Lunani, Nair, and Wasserman (1997) give a detailed discussion of robust designs with dynamic characteristics and suggest new graphical methods for analyzing the results of these designs.

The original ideas for these dynamic robust designs were presented in Taguchi (1991a, 1991b). Lunani, Nair, and Wasserman extend Taguchi's methods and suggest new methods of analysis that cover more general conditions and are easier to use. In Figure 13-3 an illustration is provided of this general situation. The main difference in these designs and those of static parameter designs is that the target values, Y, vary with the signal factors, M, which can have a range of values.

Lunani, Nair, and Wasserman (1997) give many different examples of systems with dynamic characteristics. For example, consider the design of a water pump. The response variable, Y, to be optimized is the flow rate. The signal, M, is the input speed of the water, which can vary. The control factors, d, are the pump material, impeller design, and scroll design. The noise factors, n, are contamination, temperature, and the aging of the pump.

Lunani, Nair, and Wasserman (1997) also give an example of a robust system design for an injection molding process. The response variables, Y, in this example are the

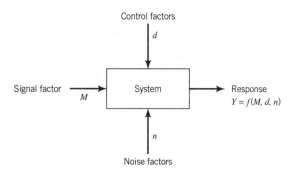

Figure 13-3 System with Dynamic Characteristics

product dimensions coming out of the mold. The signals, M, are the mold dimensions. Many different molds may be used in the injection molding process to make different products. The control factors, d, include mold temperature, mold materials, and resin temperature. The noise factors, n, include moisture, mold wear, and materials variability.

One third example that Lunani, Nair, and Wasserman (1997) give is for a measurement system design for an engine coolant temperature sensor. The response variable, Y, is the output voltage. The signal variable, M, is the coolant temperature. The control factors, d, include sensor configurations and materials. The noise factors, n, are sensor position, degradation, and product variability.

One of the best approaches to the analysis of these designs is a two-step approach such as that suggested by Leon, Shoemaker, and Kacker (1987). This type of approach facilitates achieving the dual goals of reducing variability and minimizing the distance from the intended target values. Lunani, Nair, and Wasserman (1997) suggest the following procedure for the analysis. Let $Y(i, j, k)$ denote the observation (response) corresponding to the ith setting of the control factors, jth setting of the signal factor, and kth setting of the noise factors for $i = 1, 2, \ldots, I, j = 1, 2, \ldots, J$, and $k = 1, 2, \ldots, K$. Under the assumption of a linear function with no intercept, the correct model is

$$Y(i, j, k) = \beta(i)M(j) + \epsilon(i, j, k) \qquad (13\text{-}1)$$

In this model, $\beta(i)$ is the sensitivity measure and $\sigma^2(i) = \text{Var}[\epsilon(i, j, k)]$. Both depend on the control factor settings $d(i)$, that is, $\beta(i) = \beta[d(i)]$ and $\sigma^2(i) = \sigma^2[d(i)]$, for $i = 1, 2, \ldots, I$.

Lunani, Nair, and Wasserman (1997) suggest that the general relationship is appropriate for many realistic situations. This is an extension of generalized signal-to-noise ratios suggested by Nair and Pregibon (1988) for the static parameter designs. In practice, y is unknown and has to be estimated from the data. Lunani, Nair, and Wasserman (1997) develop a λ plot similar to the λ plots introduced by Box (1988).

How to perform a dynamic robust design experiment can be better understood by following the example of engine idling performance given by Lunani, Nair, and Wasserman (1997). This example is from a real application conducted at the Powertrain Engineering Division of the Ford Motor Company [Alashe, Barnes, Bath, Jacobsen, and O'Keefe (1994)]. In this example the signal factor, M, is fuel flow and the response variable, Y, is the indicated mean effective pressure.

**TABLE 13-1 Control Array, Estimated Sensitivity, and
Standard Deviation for Engine Idling Performance Data**

A	B	C	D	E	F	H	G	b	s	S/N

| \multicolumn{8}{Control Array} | | | |

Control Array

A	B	C	D	E	F	H	G	b	s	S/N
1	1	1	1	1	1	1	1	9.67	3.67	8.39
1	1	2	2	2	2	2	2	10.18	3.57	8.91
1	1	3	3	3	1	3	3	10.44	3.61	9.20
1	2	1	1	2	2	3	3	8.05	4.10	5.67
1	2	2	2	3	1	1	1	10.87	3.99	8.65
1	2	3	3	1	1	2	2	10.94	2.74	11.67
1	3	1	2	1	1	2	3	9.52	3.68	8.24
1	3	2	3	2	1	3	1	10.19	3.37	9.53
1	3	3	1	3	2	1	2	9.71	4.17	7.18
2	1	1	3	3	2	2	1	11.66	2.66	11.96
2	1	2	1	1	1	3	2	7.94	3.79	6.47
2	1	3	2	2	1	1	3	11.19	3.46	10.1
2	2	1	2	3	1	3	2	8.99	3.87	6.77
2	2	2	3	1	2	1	3	12.54	2.46	13.33
2	2	3	1	2	1	2	1	8.82	3.88	6.99
2	3	1	3	2	1	1	2	12.07	3.47	11.27
2	3	2	1	3	1	2	3	8.64	4.18	5.81
2	3	3	2	1	2	3	1	8.96	3.36	8.68

There were eight control factors in the actual study: A, cylinder head; B, fuel injectors; C, spark plug gap; D, ignition timing; E, air-fuel ratio; F, spark plug penetration; G, engine speed; and H, injection timing. An orthogonal array design L18 [see Phadke (1989)] was used, with two factors (A and F) set at two levels and the other six factors set at three levels. There were two noise levels, n, representing a low engine mileage and a high engine mileage. For the signal variable the fuel flows were observed at different load points. Four different load settings were used. The control array and estimates of sensitivity and standard deviation are for the engine idling performance data are given in Table 13-1.

The estimates $b(i)$ are usually made by fitting a linear model to the $b(i)$ values as a function of the control factors and identifying the important effects using ANOVA (see Chapter 12) or half-normal plots. The estimates of the dispersion effects, $s(i)$, are made by fitting a linear model to the estimated signal-to-noise ratios as a function of the control factors using an ANOVA table or half-normal plots.

Lunani, Nair, and Wasserman (1997) suggest using graphical methods for the following analysis. In Figure 13-4 the multiple SS plots are reproduced for engine idling performance. These SS plots are extensions of the mean-variance plot described in Nair and Pregibon (1986).

In Figure 13-4 the plot in the top left-hand frame shows that the standard deviation decreases as sensitivity increases which indicates a negative value of γ. The value of γ can be estimated by fitting a line through the SS plot. Lunani, Nair, and Wasserman (1997) use a least-squares fit to give an estimated value of -1.6. They also use a λ plot shown

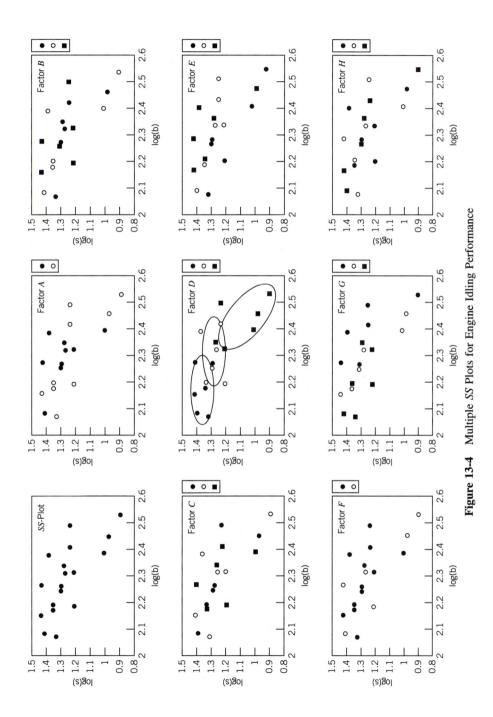

Figure 13-4 Multiple SS Plots for Engine Idling Performance

463

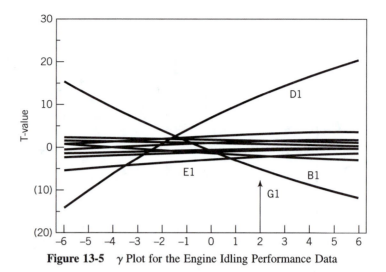

Figure 13-5 γ Plot for the Engine Idling Performance Data

in Figure 13-5 to estimate γ as −1.5 in terms of parsimony and separation. See Box (1988) for a discussion of how to calculate the λ plots which are generated in a similar fashion to the γ plots.

Examination of the frames in Figure 13-4 allows one to make several observations. In the frame for Factor E the points corresponding to the three different levels of the factor appear to fall on three separate lines, which suggests that factor E has a dispersion effect. For factors D and G the separation is primarily along the x-axis which suggests a sensitivity effect.

▶ 13-8 A SPECIAL CASE STUDY

This case study was initially presented as a paper by the executives of Electroporcelains Division, BHEL, Bangalore, at a national forum in India. The paper "A Quality Improvement of 33 D Cap" was presented at the Fifth National Convention on Quality and Reliability Organized by the Indian Association for Quality and Reliability (IAQR) held at New Delhi between 4 and 7 December 1985. This paper was shared with the authors to use as a case study by B. K. Pal, one of the leading statistical consultants in India.

Juran suggests that upper management make three breaks with tradition with regard to quality management. They are an annual improvement plan, a massive training for all individuals in the organization, and hands-on leadership. Regarding the choice of improvement projects, the emphasis has to be on chronic problems rather than sporadic problems.

Deming designates these chronic problems as problems of the system and emphasizes that they are management problems, while sporadic ones are control problems. For example, if the rejection rate of a component is 20% but it is found to be under statistical control, there is a problem of the system. The method of manufacturing requires modification. How does one do this systematically?

Dr. G. Taguchi suggested various methods of determining the levels of different manipulable parameters of production so that a better system (Deming) is evolved or a breakthrough (Juran) is achieved. This is done through a planned experimental approach.

Statistical design of experiments is needed to achieve reproducible and precise results at a minimum cost of experimentation. The whole procedure of planning of statistically designed experiments was so complex that its application has not become an integral part of an engineer's life.

This study demonstrates a new method of experimentation and analysis, as suggested by Taguchi. Standard orthogonal arrays are chosen to accommodate the manipulable factors in the experiment. The special feature of this method of analysis is its ability to optimize both the average response and the variation through one concurrent measure: the signal-to-noise ratio.

The Malleable Iron Foundry of Electroporcelains Division, Bharat Heavy Electricals Ltd., Bangalore, is the prime producer of various sizes and shapes of metal parts needed for high-tension insulators. About thirty different items are being produced in this foundry, amounting to about 100 tons per month.

The porcelain insulators and metal parts are assembled with cement bond. This assembled insulator has to sustain both electrical and mechanical stresses. Quality of metal parts is as important as that of the porcelainware and cement bond to ensure reliable functioning of the insulators.

Both the product quality of the insulators and the rejection percentage are evaluated and monitored from time to time. This study is concerned with efforts to reduce the rejection of castings at various stages. The recovery percentage (ratio of accepted castings to those produced, expressed as a percentage) was improved from about 54% to about 80%. The effort is continuous and a further target of 85% was set. This was done through a technostatistical approach.

Step 1: Problem Identification

Problem identification was done by using Pareto analysis. One single product, 33 D Cap, contributed 40% of the total rejections. Further Pareto analysis on the nature of nonconformities revealed that about two thirds of the nonconformities were contributed by gas trap, sand inclusion, and shift. Gas porosity and shrinkage were found to be major sporadic problems.

Step 2: Shop Floor Actions

Several countermeasures were tried based on experience and knowledge. The ratio of fresh sand was increased to improve permeability and to reduce gas trap. The height of the riser was increased from 100 mm to 120 mm but was again brought back to the original setting. The riser volume was increased by 10%. Vents were provided in the boss region where the gas trap was found to be localized. Later gas trap was diagnosed as shrinkage, and position of the chills were changed from the core to the mold. Small chills were also tried. Experiments were conducted by increasing the temperature of the molten metal and ingate area for feeding the molten metal. Several such actions were tried but did not succeed in reducing the rejections.

Step 3: Planning for Experimentation

It could be observed that ad hoc actions based on experience alone do not produce results in all cases. A new approach was needed to plan the experimentation, after considering

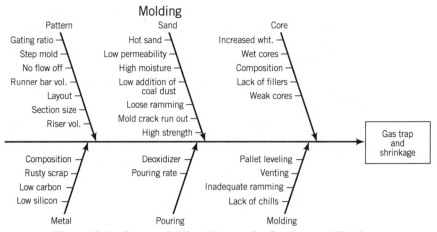

Figure 13-6 Cause-and-Effect Diagram for Gas Trap and Shrinkage

the totality of the situation. To start, a group of concerned technical people assembled and a cause-and-effect diagram was drawn by means of organized brainstorming. Available literature was also surveyed to supplement the cause-and-effect diagram (see Figure 13-6).

Parameters that were thought to be responsible for nonconformities such as gas trap, shrinkage, sand inclusions, and gas porosity were first identified from cause-and-effect analysis. Each of the causes was further scrutinized for its controllability and need for further investigation. Cause parameters (factors) that are controllable and whose effects were to be investigated were chosen as experimental factors. The domain of experimentation for each of the chosen factors was also chosen as levels. Table 13-2 indicates the factors and levels for experimentation.

Nine factors each with three levels and two factors each with two levels, that is, $3^9 \times 2^2$ factor level combinations were chosen for experimentation. No interaction was considered,

TABLE 13-2   Factors and Levels for Experimentation

Factors			Experimental Level		
			1	2	3
Pattern	A	Gating ratio	X	Y	Z
	B	Ingate position	Top	Bot	Top
Molding	C	Coal dust (%)	0.5	0.8	1.0
	D	Bentonite (%)	0.9	1.0	1.1
	E	Fresh sand (%)	10.0	15.0	20.0
	F	Water (%)	2.8	3.0	3.2
Core Shop	G	Core age	Immediate	One day	Two days
	K	Chills	Core	Mold	Core
Melting	H	Silicon (%)	0.9	1.1	1.3
	I	Carbon (%)	2.5	2.6	2.7
	J	Pig iron (%)	0.0	5.0	10.0

$X = 1:1.5:0.5,\ Y = 0.75:1.2:0.5,\ Z = 0.75:1.2:0.6.$

TABLE 13-3 Physical Layout of Experimentation

Column	1	2	3	4	5	6	7	8	9	10	13
Code	A	B	C	D	E	F	G	H	I	J	K

Expt. No.	Factor	GR	IP	CD	B	FS	W	CA	SI	C	PI	CH
1		X	Top	0.5	0.9	10	2.8	IM	0.9	2.5	0	Core
2		X	Top	0.5	0.9	15	3.0	1D	1.1	2.6	5	Mold
3		X	Top	0.5	0.9	20	3.2	2D	1.3	2.7	10	Core
4		X	Bot	0.8	1.0	10	2.8	IM	1.1	2.6	5	Core
5		X	Bot	0.8	1.0	15	3.0	1D	1.3	2.7	10	Core
6		X	Bot	0.8	1.0	20	3.2	2D	0.9	2.5	0	Mold
7		X	Top	1.0	1.1	10	2.8	IM	1.3	2.7	10	Mold
8		X	Top	1.0	1.1	15	3.0	1D	0.9	2.5	0	Core
9		X	Top	1.0	1.1	20	3.2	2D	1.1	2.6	5	Core
10		Y	Top	0.8	1.1	10	3.0	2D	0.9	2.6	10	Core
11		Y	Top	0.8	1.1	15	3.2	IM	1.1	2.7	0	Core
12		Y	Top	0.8	1.1	20	2.8	1D	1.3	2.5	5	Mold
13		Y	Bot	1.0	0.9	10	3.0	2D	1.1	2.7	0	Mold
14		Y	Bot	1.0	0.9	15	3.2	IM	1.3	2.5	5	Core
15		Y	Bot	1.0	0.9	20	2.8	1D	0.9	2.6	10	Core
16		Y	Top	0.5	1.0	10	3.0	2D	1.3	2.5	5	Core
17		Y	Top	0.5	1.0	15	3.2	IM	0.9	2.6	10	Mold
18		Y	Top	0.5	1.0	20	2.8	1D	1.1	2.7	0	Core
19		Z	Top	1.0	1.0	10	3.2	1D	0.9	2.7	5	Mold
20		Z	Top	1.0	1.0	15	2.8	2D	1.1	2.5	10	Core
21		Z	Top	1.0	1.0	20	3.0	IM	1.3	2.6	0	Core
22		Z	Bot	0.5	1.1	10	3.2	1D	1.1	2.5	10	Core
23		Z	Bot	0.5	1.1	15	2.8	2D	1.3	2.6	0	Mold
24		Z	Bot	0.5	1.1	20	3.0	IM	0.9	2.7	5	Core
25		Z	Top	0.8	0.9	10	3.2	1D	1.3	2.6	0	Core
26		Z	Top	0.8	0.9	15	2.8	2D	0.9	2.7	5	Core
27		Z	Top	0.8	0.9	20	3.0	IM	1.1	2.5	10	Mold

GR = Gating ratio, IP = Ingate position, CD = Coal dust (%), B = Bentonite (%), FS = Fresh sand (%), W = Water (%), SI = Silicon (%), C = Carbon (%), PI = Pig iron (%), CA = Core age, CH = Chills.

$X = 1:1.5:0.5$, $Y = 0.75:1.2:0.5$, $Z = 0.75:1.2:0.6$.

since the interest was to locate robust levels of factors with strong main effects. This experimentation was planned using L_{27} (3^{13}) and the layout is given in Table 13-3. The ingate position, B, has only two levels: top and bottom. Top was repeated in place of the third level. Similarly, chill position has only two levels. Here, chill in the core was repeated in place of level 3.

It was decided to take a sample of size 30 for each experimental combination. A large sample size for each combination was needed, since the data were attributes type, that is, number of nonconformities of various types, such as gas trap.

The number of castings found nonconforming because of (a) gas trap, (b) sand inclusion, (c) gas porosity, and (d) shrinkage for each experimental combination was the experimental result (response). Other characteristics of the castings—carbon percent, silicon percent, permeability, green compressive strength, and moisture—were recorded for any future investigation.

Step 4: Conduct the Experiments

The experimentation was conducted according to the physical layout given in Table 13-4. The levels of factors not used in the experiment were also included. Identification marks were placed on each casting to indicate its particular experimental combination. These were followed through each stage. Nonconformities of all types were recorded. The results are given in Table 13-5.

TABLE 13-4 Experimental Results: Nonconforming Castings

Expt. No.						Factors								No. of Nonconformities in Different Castings			
	1	2	3	4	5	6	7	8	9	10	13	11	12	GT	SI	GP	SK
	A	B	C	D	E	F	G	H	I	J	K						
1	1	1	1	1	1	1	1	1	1	1	1	1	1	0	6	17	1
2	1	1	1	1	2	2	2	2	2	2	2	2	2	0	9	7	1
3	1	1	1	1	3	3	3	3	3	3	1	3	3	0	3	0	0
4	1	2	2	2	1	1	1	2	2	2	1	3	3	2	0	14	3
5	1	2	2	2	2	2	2	3	3	3	1	1	1	0	0	0	5
6	1	2	2	2	3	3	3	1	1	1	2	2	2	0	2	0	20
7	1	1	3	3	1	1	1	3	3	3	2	2	2	0	4	0	0
8	1	1	3	3	2	2	2	1	1	1	1	3	3	0	10	15	1
9	1	1	3	3	3	3	3	2	2	2	1	1	1	0	6	0	2
10	2	1	2	3	1	2	3	1	2	3	1	1	2	0	18	0	6
11	2	1	2	3	2	3	1	2	3	1	1	2	2	0	4	0	2
12	2	1	2	3	3	1	2	3	1	2	2	3	1	0	7	0	0
13	2	2	3	1	1	2	3	2	3	1	2	3	1	0	0	9	6
14	2	2	3	1	2	3	1	3	1	2	1	1	2	0	0	0	3
15	2	2	3	1	3	1	2	1	2	3	1	2	3	0	1	0	3
16	2	1	1	2	1	2	3	3	1	2	1	2	3	0	6	3	0
17	2	1	1	2	2	3	1	1	2	3	2	3	1	0	5	15	0
18	2	1	1	2	3	1	2	2	3	1	1	1	2	0	4	8	2
19	3	1	3	2	1	3	2	1	3	2	2	1	3	1	4	3	0
20	3	1	3	2	2	1	3	2	1	3	1	2	1	0	1	5	1
21	3	1	3	2	3	2	1	3	2	1	1	3	2	0	2	0	0
22	3	2	1	3	1	3	2	2	1	3	1	3	2	0	0	17	3
23	3	2	1	3	2	1	3	3	2	1	2	1	3	3	0	0	4
24	3	2	1	3	3	2	1	1	3	2	1	2	1	0	2	0	15
25	3	1	2	1	1	3	2	3	2	1	1	2	1	2	1	3	0
26	3	1	2	1	2	1	3	1	3	2	1	3	2	0	1	21	0
27	3	1	2	1	3	2	1	2	1	3	2	1	3	0	1	27	0

Note: Sample size = 30.

GT = gas trap, SI = Sand inclusion, GP = Gas porosity, SK = Shrinkage.

TABLE 13-5   Gas Trap: Experimental Data

| Level | | | | | | Observations | | | | | | | S/N |
Factor		1	2	3	4	5	6	7	8	9	Total	$\bar{x}$	Ratio
A	1	0	0	0	2	0	0	0	0	0	2	0.22	21.27
	2	0	0	0	0	0	0	0	0	0	0	0.00	27.32
	3	1	0	0	0	3	0	2	0	0	6	0.66	16.43
B	1	0	0	0	0	0	0	1	0	0	1	0.11	24.30
	1	0	0	0	0	0	0	2	0	0	2	0.22	22.53
	2	2	0	0	0	0	0	0	3	0	5	0.55	17.24
C	1	0	0	0	0	0	0	0	3	0	3	0.33	19.49
	2	2	0	0	0	0	0	2	0	0	4	0.44	18.23
	3	0	0	0	0	0	0	1	0	0	1	0.11	24.30
D	1	0	0	0	0	0	0	2	0	0	2	0.22	21.27
	2	2	0	0	0	0	0	1	0	0	3	0.33	19.49
	3	0	0	0	0	0	0	0	3	0	3	0.33	19.49
E	1	0	2	0	0	0	0	1	0	2	5	0.55	17.24
	2	0	0	0	0	0	0	0	3	0	3	0.33	19.49
	3	0	0	0	0	0	0	0	0	0	0	0.00	27.32
F	1	0	2	0	0	0	0	0	3	0	5	0.55	17.24
	2	0	0	0	0	0	0	0	0	0	0	0.00	27.32
	3	0	0	0	0	0	0	1	0	2	3	0.33	19.49
G	1	0	2	0	0	0	0	0	0	0	2	0.22	21.27
	2	0	0	0	0	0	0	1	0	2	3	0.33	19.49
	3	0	0	0	0	0	0	0	3	0	3	0.33	19.49
H	1	0	0	0	0	0	0	1	0	0	1	0.11	24.30
	2	0	2	0	0	0	0	0	0	0	2	0.22	21.27
	3	0	0	0	0	0	0	0	3	2	5	0.55	17.24
I	1	0	0	0	0	0	0	0	0	0	0	0.00	27.32
	2	0	2	0	0	0	0	3	2	0	7	0.77	15.75
	3	0	0	0	0	0	0	1	0	0	1	0.11	24.30
J	1	0	0	0	0	0	0	0	3	2	5	0.55	17.24
	2	0	2	0	0	0	0	1	0	0	3	0.33	19.49
	3	0	0	0	0	0	0	0	0	0	0	0.00	27.32
K	1	0	0	0	0	0	0	0	0	0	0	0.00	27.32
	1	0	2	0	0	0	0	0	0	2	4	0.22	21.27
	2	0	0	0	0	0	0	1	3	0	4	0.44	8.23

Step 5: Perform the Analysis and Determine Results

The objective of the data analysis was to determine the best levels for each of the process parameters so that the number of nonconformities due to gas trap, shrinkage, gas porosity, and sand inclusion is reduced to a minimum, along with their variability. The interest is not only in achieving these targets, but also in reducing the variation.

Instead of working with the mean and the standard deviation separately, Taguchi suggests optimizing these concurrently through a new transformed variable signal-to-noise

(S/N) ratio. Different formulas of S/N ratio have been developed to suit different situations. Here the response is the number of nonconforming items in a sample of thirty. The S/N ratio is calculated by the following formula:

$$S/N \text{ ratio} = 10 \text{ Log}_{10} (1/p - 1) \qquad \text{when } 0 < p < 1$$
$$= 10 \text{ Log}_{10} (2n) \qquad \text{when } p = 0$$
$$= 10 \text{ Log}_{10} (n/2) \qquad \text{when } p = 1$$

where

p = fraction nonconforming

= Number of nonconforming items/Number inspected

Among the factors chosen for experimentation, factors such as gating ratio (A), ingate position (B), and position of chills (K) can be controlled easily. Factors such as coal dust percent (C) and silicon percent (H) cannot be controlled at a given level precisely but can be controlled around any given level within certain limits. The intent should be to choose the levels of manipulable factors of the former group first and then to choose the levels of the factors of the second group if necessary.

Robust process design is the factor-level combination that will be immune to the normal fluctuations of other factors. In this case, nine factors, each with three levels, and two factors, each with two levels, were used in a L_{27} orthogonal array. The usual type of analysis is to make an analysis of variance with each response parameter, such as gas trap, sand inclusion, gas porosity, and shrinkage, and then decide the best factor level combination. The method adopted here is different.

Analysis has been made using the concept of determining the robust level. For a three-level factor, each level has been tried nine times under different combinations of the levels of the other factors. Using the nine observations, the S/N ratio was calculated for each level. The case for two-level factors is similar. The higher the S/N ratio, the better the level. For example, in the case of gas trap, it can be seen from Table 13-5 that the A_2 resulted in no nonconforming items for all combinations of the other factor levels. The S/N ratio of A_2 is also the highest. A_2 is called the robust level with respect to gas trap. It is expected that even if the other parameters are assumed to vary in the experimental range, it will not affect gas trap as long as the gating ratio is maintained at level two.

The robust levels of different process parameters were obtained by maximizing the S/N ratios. For multiple responses the choice of the robust level is more difficult. The method applied in optimizing the levels is discussed in the remarks column of Table 13-6. As is seen from Table 13-6, the combination $A_2B_1C_3D_2E_3F_1G_2H_3I_1J_1K_1$ was found to be robust.

The change of the level of any process parameter involves either (1) no cost, (2) only initial cost, (3) only recurring cost, or (4) a combination of the latter two. Factors such as water percent and position of chills come under category (1); factors such as ingate position and gating ratio come under category (2); factors such as pig iron, silicon, carbon, fresh sand, Bentonite, and coal dust come under category (3). Change of levels of the third category should be done only as a last resort. For example, coal dust has been recommended at 1%, Bentonite at 1%, fresh sand at 20%, silicon at 1.3%, carbon at 2.5%, and pig iron at 10%. Although there is no possibility of reduction of silicon percent, coal dust percent, and Bentonite percent, the feasibility of reduction of pig iron and fresh sand had to be examined. Pig iron percent is supposed to improve the incidences of gas trap and

TABLE 13-6 S/N Ratios for Gas Trap, Sand Inclusion, Gas Porosity, and Shrinkage

Factor and Level			Gas Trap	Sand Inclusion	Gas Porosity	Shrinkage	Optimum	Remarks
A. Gating ratio	1	X	21.3	7.6	6.1	8.6	A_2	Sand inclusion and gating ratio not related
	2	Y	27.3	6.7	8.3	10.5		
	3	Z	16.4	13.3	4.1	10.3		
B. Ingate position	1	Top	22.6	6.9	5.2	15.2	B_1	Top ingate gave rise to higher sand inclusion. QC group modified the design of core to eliminate the defect of sand inclusion.
	2	Bot	17.2	17.2	7.6	5.2		
C. Coal dust (%)	1	0.5	19.5	8.3	4.8	9.7	C_3	Best level for all defects
	2	0.8	18.2	8.4	5.0	8.1		
	3	1.0	24.3	9.4	8.7	12.0		
D. Bentonite (%)	1	0.9	21.3	10.5	3.4	12.6	D_2	Higher S/N ratio for shrinkage and best level for combined effect
	2	1.0	19.5	10.1	6.6	18.6		
	3	1.1	19.5	6.3	8.7	8.6		
E. Fresh sand (%)	1	10	17.2	7.7	4.9	11.2	E_3	Best level for gas trap, sand inclusion, gas porosity; shrinkage has no relation with this factor
	2	15	19.5	9.0	5.2	11.7		
	3	20	27.3	9.9	8.3	7.3		
F. Water (%)	1	2.8	17.3	10.1	5.0	12.6	F_1	Best for sand inclusion and shrinkage
	2	3.0	27.3	6.6	5.3	8.4		
	3	3.2	19.5	9.9	7.8	9.0		
G. Core age	1	IMMED	21.3	10.1	4.3	10.1	G_2	No level was found good for all. One day aging was found convenient for operation.
	2	1 day	19.5	8.1	6.1	12.3		
	3	2 day	19.5	8.0	7.8	9.0		
H. Silicon (%)	1	0.9	24.3	6.5	4.5	6.9	H_3	Most important factor for gas porosity and equally important for shrinkage
	2	1.1	21.3	9.9	3.2	11.0		
	3	1.3	17.2	10.3	16.4	13.3		
I. Carbon (%)	1	2.5	27.3	8.6	3.4	9.2	I_1	Most important factor for gas trap
	2	2.6	15.7	7.3	7.7	11.2		
	3	2.7	24.3	10.5	7.5	9.0		
J. Pig iron (%)	1	0	17.2	9.2	6.2	8.1	J_1	10% was best for gas trap and shrinkage.
	2	5	19.5	8.3	6.6	10.1		
	3	10	27.3	8.6	5.1	11.5		
K. Chills	1	Core	21.3	8.6	6.3	10.2	K_1	Chills in the cores was best for gas trap and shrinkage.
	2	Mold	18.2	8.7	5.2	8.9		

shrinkage. Gas trap could be effectively improved by gating ratio, ingate position, and chills. Similarly, shrinkage could be reduced by ingate position and silicon percent. It is therefore recommended that a higher percent of pig iron and a lower level of fresh sand be used: 10% to start. If the results with regard to shrinkage are not satisfactory, a higher level of pig iron can be used. Similarly, addition of more fresh sand can be considered if gas porosity problems are observed.

Step 6: Confirmation Experiment

On the basis of the analysis the combination, $A_2B_1C_3D_2E_2F_1G_2H_3I_1J_1K_1$ (i.e., gating ratio) Y (0.75:1.2:0.5), ingate position Top, 1.0% coal dust, 1.0% Bentonite, 15% fresh sand, 2.8% water, 1 day core age, 1.3% silicon, 2.5% carbon, 0% pig iron, and chills in core was tried for trial production. During the trial production 2400 molds of 33 D Cap were produced, out of which 34 (1.4%) were found nonconforming due to gas trap, 108 (4.5%) due to sand inclusion, and none (0%) due to gas porosity. The incidence of gas trap has definitely decreased, but that of sand inclusion has not decreased as expected. Ingate position at top was found to have many advantages but the one disadvantage of giving rise to higher sand inclusion. Sand inclusion was observed because of rubbing of the pad core. This problem was discussed by a quality circle, which suggested a change in the design of the core while ensuring the ingate position at the top.

This was tried and the results were as follows:

No. inspected	1638
Gas trap	1.15%
Sand inclusion	0.91%
Gas porosity	0.0%
Shrinkage	30.9%

Although sand inclusion was reduced, shrinkage increased drastically.

The problem was further discussed, and a single gating system was suggested instead of a double one while keeping the gating ratio and feeding at the optimum levels of experimentation, that is, Y (0.75:1.2:0.5), and feeding from the top, respectively. This was tried, and the results were found to be satisfactory. Large-scale implementation was done and the results were as follows:

No. inspected	1067
Gas trap	1.2%
Sand inclusion	1.3%
Gas porosity	0.0%
Shrinkage	5.4%

Step 7: Implementation and Follow-Up

The final recommendation was made based on the experimental results and the outcome of the various production trials. The final results are summarized in Table 13-7.

This recommendation has been issued to the shop floor as the modified production method for 33 D Cap. It will ensure the control of the following factors:

- Gating ratio
- Ingate position

TABLE 13-7 Robust Combination Recommended

Parameters	Recommended Level
1 Gating ratio	Y (0.75 : 1.2 : 0.5)
2 Ingate position	Top
3 Coal dust	1.0%
4 Bentonite	1.0%
5 Fresh sand	15%
6 Water	2.8%
7 Core age	1 day
8 Silicon	1.3%
9 Carbon	2.5%
10 Pig iron	Nil
11 Position of chills	Core
12 Core design	Embedded
13 Feeding	Single-sided

- Position of chills
- Design of core
- Feeding

A core age of one day has been assured through communication, supervision, and audit. Factors such as fresh sand percent, coal dust percent, Bentonite percent, and water percent can be more easily assured because the sand plant of the factory is mechanized. An audit check will be useful to ensure that these values are maintained. The major problem will be the control of metal composition, carbon percent, and silicon percent at recommended levels. This will be done with the use of control charts.

Step 8: Review Final Results
Rejections caused by sand inclusion, shrinkage, gas trap, and gas porosity were reduced as a result of the experimentation. Rejection of 33 D Cap has been reduced from 30% to 15%. This in turn has helped the overall recovery to be increased by 5%.

As a consequence of using a single gating system, yield has improved by about 19%, thus saving molten metal of about 250 MT per year at the current rate of production. Pad core consumption and grinding operations of 33 D Cap castings have been reduced by 50%. Savings due to fewer rejections and reduced consumption of molten metal, pad cores, grinding time, and wheels accounted for about Rs.16.25 lakhs per annum at the current rate of production.

▶ 13-9 SUMMARY

Robust design has been widely used in many different manufacturing industries in product and process design. More recently, leading organizations are beginning to use dynamic robust design methods to extend these methodologies to new applications. A few service organizations have now begun to apply robust design to designing new services and the processes which create these services. An article by Godfrey (1992) speculates on how robust design might work in health care. A simple example in a medical setting might be the control of blood-clotting times through the use of the drug warfarin (coumadin). Once the patient leaves the hospital, there are a number of noise variables that can be only partially controlled. These include what the patient eats, when the patient takes the medicine, how often the patient forgets to take the medicine, what other medications the patient takes, the patient's basic metabolism, the daily activities of the patient, and variations in the medication. There are limited control variables with which to work. The right dose must be prescribed, the patient is taught how to take the medication, the patient's prothrombin time may be monitored, and the dose must be adjusted for other drug and dietary factors. The job is to control both the outcome, the blood-clotting rate, and the variation of that outcome around the desired target. The problem in this simple example is to understand which of the control variables are important and what are the right control levels in the presence of the noise variables.

In applying these methods, it should be remembered that robust design demands an advanced level of mathematical and statistical sophistication. These methods are familiar to mathematical research centers, operations research and industrial engineering support departments, special analysts in many service organizations, and medical researchers. In many companies there may not be the necessary support, and the methods are difficult to teach to large numbers of managers or other personnel.

Robust design is an exciting tool for modern quality control and management. It is very appropriate for analyzing complex processes. It is particularly useful for online research. In complex manufacturing, service, or design processes, there are many possible control variables and even more noise variables, or variables that cannot be controlled. It is necessary to achieve the best possible outcome in spite of the uncontrolled variation. Robust design provides a means for studying these difficult cases and finding the best parameter levels for attaining desirable outcomes.

▶ 13-10 REFERENCES

Alashe, W. D., Barnes, E. B., Bath, K. L., Jacobsen, K. E., and O'Keefe, M. K. (1994), "Engine Idle Quality Robustness Using Taguchi Methods," *Proceedings of the Symposium on Taguchi Methods,* American Supplier Institute Press, Dearborn, MI, pp. 111–21.

Box, G. E. P. (1986a), *Studies in Quality Improvement: Signal to Noise Ratios, Performance Criteria and Statistical Analysis: Part I, Report 4,* Center for Quality and Productivity Improvement, University of Wisconsin, Madison, WI.

Box, G. E. P. (1986b), *Studies in Quality Improvement: Signal to Noise Ratios, Performance Criteria and Statistical Analysis: Part II, Report No. 4,* Center for Quality and Productivity Improvement, University of Wisconsin, Madison, WI.

Box, G. E. P. (1988), "Signal-to-Noise Ratios, Performance Criteria and Transformations," (with discussion), *Technometrics,* Vol. 30, Feb.; pp. 1–40.

Godfrey, A. B. (1992), "Robust Design—A New Tool for Health Care Quality," *Quality Management in Health Care,* Volume 1, No. 1, pp. 55–63.

Godfrey, A. B., Phadke, M. S., and Shoemaker, A. C. (1986), "The Development & Application of Robust Design Methods—

Taguchi's Impact in the United States," (In Japanese). *The Journal of the Japanese Society for Quality,* Vol. 16, No. 2, pp. 33–41.

Kacker, R. N., and Ghosh, S. (1998), "Robust Design Methods," Chapter 20 in *Handbook of Statistical Methods for Engineers and Scientists,* Second Edition, edited by Harrison M. Wadsworth, McGraw-Hill, New York.

Kacker, R. N. and Shoemaker, A. C. (1986), "Robust Design: A Cost-Effective Method for Improving Manufacturing Processes," *AT&T Technical Journal,* Vol. 65, pp. 39–50.

Leon, R. V., Shoemaker, A. C., and Kacker, R. N. (1987), "Performance Measures Independent of Adjustment: An Explanation and Extension of Taguchi's Signal-to-Noise Ratios," *Technometrics,* Vol. 29, Aug.; pp. 253–65.

Lunani, M., Nair, V. N., and Wasserman, G. S. (1997), "Graphical Methods for Robust Design with Dynamic Characteristics," *Journal of Quality Technology,* Vol. 29, No. 3, July, pp. 327–38.

Nair, V. N. and Pregibon, D. (1986), "A Data Analysis Strategy for Quality Engineering Experiments," *AT&T Technical Journal,* Vol. 65, pp. 73–84.

Nair, V. N. and Pregibon, D. (1988), "Discussion of Signal-to-Noise Ratios, Performance Criteria, and Transformations," *Technometrics,* Vol. 30, Feb.; pp. 24–30.

Phadke, M. S. (1986), "Design Optimization Case Studies," *AT&T Technical Journal,* Vol. 65, No. 2, pp. 51–68.

Phadke, M. S. (1989), *Quality Engineering Using Robust Design,* Prentice Hall, Englewood Cliffs, NJ.

Phadke, M. S., Kacker, R. N., Speeney, D. V., and Grieco, M. J. (1983), "Off-Line Quality Control in Integrated Circuit Fabrication Using Experimental Design," *The Bell System Technical Journal,* Vol. 62, No. 5, pp. 1273–1309.

Taguchi, G. (1985), "Quality Engineering in Japan," *Communications in Statistics: Theory and Methods,* Vol. 14, No. 11, pp. 2785–01.

Taguchi, G. (1991a), *Taguchi Methods, Research and Development, Vol. 1,* American Supplier Institute Press, Dearborn, MI.

Taguchi, G. (1991b), *Taguchi Methods, Signal-to-Noise Ratio for Quality Evaluation, Vol. 3,* American Supplier Institute Press, Dearborn, MI.

Wedderburn, H. (1987), "Product and Process Improvement Using the Taguchi Method of Experimental Design," *Proceedings of the International Conference on Quality Control,* Tokyo.

► 13-11 PROBLEMS

1. In planning a new experiment, an engineer has identified seven critical factors. The objective is to improve the tear strength of a new material. Working closely with the design and process engineers and the plant operations people, the engineer is quite certain that these factors are: the line speed, the processing temperature, the pressure generated by the rollers, the type of fibers, the bonding resins, the moisture content of the fibers, and the humidity in the plant. The plant is quite large and is not air conditioned. It would be quite expensive to dry the fibers or to control their moisture content as they come in large bales and are stored on trucks or in a warehouse. What would you select as the control variables in this experiment? What would be your noise variables?

2. The engineer working on the previous problem has found that the process engineers want to run the experiment at three different line speeds using four different types of fibers. The design engineers suggest testing three different resins. The plant operations people want to use all four settings of roller pressure and three settings of temperature. As the designer of the experiment it is believed that four different humidity levels and three different levels of moisture content of the fibers should be tested. If a full-factorial experiment is to be run on all seven of these factors at the recommended levels with two replications at each possible combination, how many total runs should be made?

3. An engineer is trying to improve the quality of injection molded plastic parts for an important customer. The customer has been complaining that the parts are often too large or too small for his manufacturing process to use. In deciding how to measure the critical dimensions of these parts, what types of measurements should the engineer use? Why?

4. In problem 3 above, what is the engineer trying to optimize: the smaller the better, the larger the better, or the closer to target the better? Why?

5. In problem 3 above, should the engineer just be trying to get the average (mean) on target or should he/she be worried about the variance also? Why? Suggest an appropriate signal-to-noise ratio to use in this experiment.

6. This chapter discusses the use of orthogonal arrays as a way of assisting in planning the experiment. Because of the extremely high number of possible combinations of experiments, usually only a small fraction of the possible experiments are run. What is one of the main dangers in running such a small number of experiments?

7. Why should there always be a confirmation experiment run?

8. The basic problem being addressed by robust design is how to optimize output in the face of factors that cannot be controlled or are not controlled because of the expense, the "noise variables." In many real-world situations the levels of these noise variables cannot be set during the experiment. What should be done then?

RELIABILITY

Performance tests are often done on products at the end of the manufacturing cycle to ensure that the product meets or exceeds all specified performance parameters. But initial performance is only one aspect of quality. Customers are interested in how long the product will last, how many products will fail per year, and how many will last more than some number of years. In the simplest cases, one can use the quality control and acceptance testing procedures described in other chapters to measure performance to some standard, such as percent passing all tests for one month or percent failing before one year. Often, since longitudinal testing (testing over time) usually causes unacceptable delays in results, the engineer will measure quality attributes or variables that are believed to be highly correlated with long useful life or will devise accelerated aging tests to simulate long usage in a short time. The quality engineer who uses standard procedures makes implicit assumptions about the failure rate, the uniformity of products on test, and the ability of the tests to simulate normal operating conditions.

Reliability refers generally to a product's ability to maintain good performance for a long time. In this chapter the basic concepts of reliability will be discussed and some distributions that are useful in reliability modeling will be presented along with how to estimate the parameters of these distributions, and check the accuracy of the model. Examples will be given that show why these models work in many cases and why some of these concepts are so useful. Life testing will then be discussed. This discussion will include designing a life test, conducting the test, analyzing the data, and interpreting the results. Problems of censoring will be described, and how the analysis is handled when not all of the items can be tested until they fail. The final subject to be discussed in this chapter is accelerated life testing. It is often not practical to conduct a life test long enough to get accurate results for the time one would like to be able to portray the product's performance. Many models exist for accelerating the aging of the product by heat, humidity, higher voltages, mechanical shocks, and thermal shocks. These models permit the quality engineer to predict the performance of a product for a period much longer than the test.

▶ 14-1 BASIC CONCEPTS OF RELIABILITY

The definition of reliability that is used in this chapter is simply the probability that a product is functioning as its designer intended for a given time. That is,

$$R(t) \equiv \text{Prob}\{X > t\} \equiv 1 - F(t) \equiv \overline{F}(t) \tag{14-1}$$

where X is a random variable representing the lifetime of the product[1] and t is time measured in some appropriate units. $F(t)$ is the cumulative distribution function introduced in Chapter 5, and $R(t) \equiv 1 - F(t) \equiv \overline{F}(t)$ is the reliability or survival function or the cumulative hazard function.

A useful measure of reliability is the conditional failure rate or hazard rate:

$$\lambda(t) = \lim_{t \to 0} \frac{P(t \le X < t + \Delta t \,|\, X > t)}{\Delta t} = \frac{f(t)}{\overline{F}(t)} \tag{14-2}$$

where $f(t)$ is the probability density function introduced in Chapter 5. Recall that the density function does not always exist, but when it does, it is the derivative of the cumulative distribution function. Equation (14-2) can be rewritten as

$$\lambda(t) = \frac{-d \log \overline{F}(t)}{dt} \tag{14-3}$$

Then

$$\overline{F}(t) = \exp \left\{ -\int_0^t \lambda(u) \, du \right\} \tag{14-4}$$

and

$$f(t) = \lambda(t) \exp \left\{ -\int_0^t \lambda(u) \, du \right\} \tag{14-5}$$

See Barlow and Proschan (1975) or Kalbfleisch and Prentice (1980) for more details. Another concept that is useful in reliability analyses is that the failure rate changes monotonically with time. Thus, $\lambda(t)$ is an increasing failure rate (IFR) if $\lambda(t)$ is not decreasing in t and $\lambda(t)$ is a decreasing failure rate (DFR) if $\lambda(t)$ is not increasing in t [Barlow and Proschan (1975)]. Equivalently, it can be seen that if

$$\lambda(t + \Delta t) \ge \lambda(t) \qquad \text{for all } t$$

the distribution defined by $\lambda(t)$, $f(t)$, or $F(t)$ is an IFR distribution. A somewhat broader class of distribution is defined by the idea of increasing (decreasing) failure rate average, IFRA (DFRA). That is, if

$$1/t \int_0^t \lambda(t) \, dt$$

is increasing (decreasing) for all t, then the distribution defined by $\lambda(t)$, $f(t)$, or $F(t)$ is an IFRA (DFRA) distribution.

To illustrate the concepts of failure rate and hazard rate, consider some common examples. The first example is the failure (death) rate for human beings in Figure 14-1. The failure rate is extremely high for the first few months of life, drops sharply, remains fairly constant for many years, and then slowly climbs as the person ages. Failure rates for human beings differ by sex, race, nationality, and other factors, but all failure rates for humans appear to exhibit this distinctive "bathtub curve." A common assumption made by electrical

---

[1]For simplicity of presentation in this chapter it is assumed throughout that X is continuous. When X is a discrete random variable taking values $x_1 < x_2 < \cdots$ with probability function $f(x_i) = P(X = x_i)$, see Kalbfleisch and Prentice (1980) or Barlow and Proschan (1975).

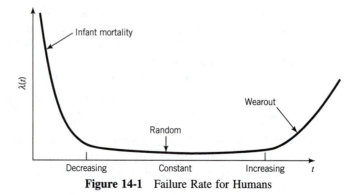

Figure 14-1 Failure Rate for Humans

engineers is that the distribution of the lifetime of a product is exponential. Although the basis for this assumption is probably for mathematical tractability (the hazard rate is constant), models based on the exponential distribution seem to work quite well for a wide variety of products. In the next section some distributions that are useful in reliability will be presented, and it will be seen that the failure rate for an exponential distribution is constant for all t.

Solid-state electronic devices often exhibit a very high failure rate when first used, and the failure rate then decreases very rapidly. Their early failure rates look very much like those for human populations. In fact, they are said to have high "infant mortality." These failure rates often decrease to something that appears to be a constant failure rate. This is shown in Figure 14-2. There are several explanations for this behavior. One of the most common phenomena is when the devices actually have a mixture of distributions. Some devices are made correctly, and some have imperfections leading to high failure

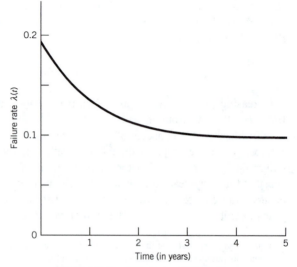

Figure 14-2 Decreasing Failure Rate

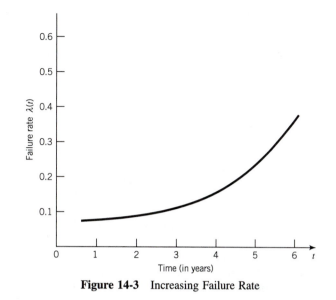

Figure 14-3   Increasing Failure Rate

rates. When a sample from the mixture of devices is placed on test, the imperfect ones fail early, and the correctly made devices fail with a much lower failure rate. As the imperfect devices fail, the percentage of imperfect devices in the test sample declines until finally only the correctly made devices are left on test. The example in Figure 14-2 used a very simple model in which ninety items with constant failure rates, $\lambda(t) = \lambda$, were put on test with ten items with constant failure rates $\lambda(t) = 10\lambda$. The failure rate of this population of 100 devices is plotted. Many products wear out with use. These products often exhibit the increasing failure rate shown in Figure 14-3.

▶ 14-2 DISTRIBUTIONS USEFUL IN RELIABILITY

14-2.1 Exponential Distribution

As was mentioned earlier the exponential distribution is most frequently used by engineers. The cumulative distribution function can be written as

$$F(t) = 1 - e^{-\lambda t} \tag{14-6}$$

The density function is

$$f(t) = \lambda e^{-\lambda t} \tag{14-7}$$

which is derived from Equation (14-5) by letting $\lambda(t) = \lambda$, a constant. The reliability or survival function is then simply

$$\overline{F}(t) = e^{-\lambda t} \tag{14-8}$$

and the failure or hazard rate is constant:

$$\lambda(t) = \frac{f(t)}{\overline{F}(t)} = \frac{\lambda e^{-\lambda t}}{e^{-\lambda t}} = \lambda \tag{14-9}$$

14-2.2 Weibull Distribution

The distribution that engineers use most frequently, other than the exponential, is the two-parameter Weibull. The Weibull has a cumulative distribution function that can be written as

$$F(t) = 1 - e^{-(\lambda t)^\beta} \tag{14-10}$$

The density function is

$$f(t) = \lambda\beta(\lambda t)^{\beta-1}e^{-(\lambda t)^\beta} \tag{14-11}$$

and the failure rate is

$$\lambda(t) = \frac{\lambda\beta(\lambda t)^{\beta-1}e^{-(\lambda t)^\beta}}{e^{-(\lambda t)^\beta}} = \lambda\beta(\lambda t)^{\beta-1} \tag{14-12}$$

By taking natural logarithms of both sides of Equation (14-12), a quick check of the usefulness of the Weibull distribution for a particular set of data and rough estimates of the parameters λ and β can be made. Make empirical estimates of the failure rate at different time intervals, and plot (using natural logarithms) log [$\lambda(t)$] versus log (t) on log-log paper. Since log $\lambda(t)$ = log ($\lambda\beta$) + (β − 1) log (λ) + (β − 1) log (t), a linear regression can be seen in the form

$$\log (\text{observation}) = \alpha_0 + \alpha_1 \log (t) \tag{14-13}$$

yields approximate estimates of λ and β by solving the equations

$$\alpha_0 = \log (\lambda\beta) + (\beta - 1) \log (\lambda) \tag{14-14}$$

and

$$\alpha_1 = (\beta - 1) \tag{14-15}$$

Later in this chapter better estimates of failure rates and parameters of the distribution will be discussed.

The failure rates for several Weibull distributions are plotted in Figure 14-4 [from Barlow and Proschan (1975), p. 78]. The exponential distribution is just a special case

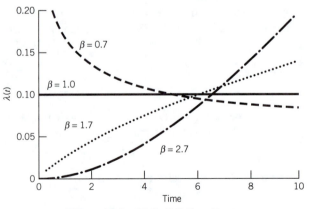

Figure 14-4 Weibull Failure Rates

in which $\beta = 1$. For $\beta > 1$ the Weibull is an IFR distribution, and for $\beta < 1$ the Weibull is a DFR distribution. For $\beta \approx 3.5$ the Weibull resembles the normal distribution, which is often used for modeling wearout situations (with increasing failure rate).

14-2.3 Normal Distribution

The normal distribution is often used for devices or systems in the wearout phase (increasing failure rate) of their life. The normal distribution was discussed in Chapter 5. The failure rate for the normal distribution is

$$\lambda(t) = \frac{\dfrac{1}{\sigma\sqrt{2\pi}} \exp\left[-\dfrac{1}{2\sigma^2}(t - \mu)^2\right]}{1 - \Phi\left(\dfrac{t - \mu}{\sigma}\right)} \tag{14-16}$$

where

$\Phi(t)$ = the normal area up to time t

μ = mean life

σ = standard deviation

In Figure 14-5 failure rates from normal distributions with three different values of μ are shown.

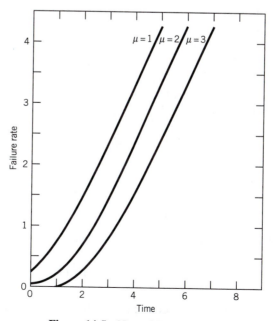

Figure 14-5 Normal Failure Rates

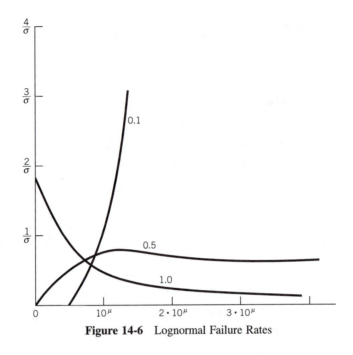

Figure 14-6 Lognormal Failure Rates

14-2.4 Lognormal Distribution

A distribution that is also sometimes used in reliability is the lognormal, although it is a subject of some controversy. Many engineers think that there are few realistic models that lead naturally to the characteristic failure rate exhibited by the lognormal shown in Figure 14-6. A very good discussion of the lognormal distribution can be found in Johnson and Kotz (1970).

The lognormal distribution is formed by taking the logarithms of normally distributed random variables. Its probability density function is

$$f(t) = \frac{0.4343}{\sqrt{2\pi}\, t\sigma} \exp\left[-\frac{1}{2\sigma^2} (\log t - \mu)^2 \right], \qquad t > 0 \qquad (14\text{-}17)$$

where

$\mu = $ log mean

$\sigma = $ log standard deviation

The cumulative distribution function is

$$F(t) = \Phi\left(\frac{\log (t) - \mu}{\sigma} \right) \qquad (14\text{-}18)$$

For σ approximately equal to 0.5, the failure rate is constant; for σ less than 0.2, the failure rate is increasing; for σ greater than 0.8, the failure rate is decreasing.

▶ 14-3 RELIABILITY PREDICTIONS

Purchasers use reliability predictions to compute life cycle costs for comparing competing products. Designers use reliability predictions in the design process to ensure that performance objectives will be met. Service and maintenance operations personnel use reliability predictions to stock spares, allocate maintenance, and plan service activities. As is explained in MIL-STD-756B (1981), "Prediction provides a rational basis for design decisions such as the choice between alternative concepts, choice of part quality levels, derating to be applied, use of proven versus state-of-the-art techniques, and other factors."

The performance of a product in field use is affected by many variables. Operator errors, acts of nature, software failures, and failures of other products or services (e.g., public power systems) can all cause the product to fail. These exogenous failures are usually not included in the reliability prediction model. In using reliability models, it must be remembered that they account for only a fraction of the total system failures. However, these predictions (when the model is correct) can be valid estimates of the failures that may be expected because of the product's failure or failures resulting from its included components.

When the results of reliability predictions are combined with appropriate maintenance parameters such as repair times, many service-affecting parameters can be calculated [Bell Communications Research (1984)]. Examples of these calculations are:

- Frequency of outages per year
- Frequency of outages in first months of service
- Expected downtime per year or per outage
- Availability

The reliability of a system or product may be determined by operating a large number of systems or products for the necessary length of time and observing the failures. These procedures are called life tests and will be discussed later in this chapter. Life test procedures are effective but expensive. They are often used for components and small parts when the cost of the items and the test facilities is not prohibitively expensive and it is practical to simulate the actual operating environment.

For complex products or systems it is usually more practical to develop procedures for mathematically determining the reliability by studying the system architecture and component reliability.

14-3.1 System Reliability

For a system that contains items connected in series, assuming independence of their individual failures, the reliability of the system is the product of the reliabilities of the individual items:

$$R_s(t) = R_1(t)R_2(t) \cdots R_M(t) \tag{14-19}$$

where

$R_s(t)$ = system reliability at time t

$R_i(t)$ = probability item i will operate at least until time t

M = number of items in series

It can be seen that if there are M identical parts, with each part independently having reliability $R(t)$, then the system reliability is

$$R_s(t) = [R(t)]^M \qquad (14\text{-}20)$$

From either Equation (14-19) or (14-20) it can be seen that in a series system all units must operate, or the system fails. If there are three items in series, each with reliability 0.95 at time t, the system reliability at time t will be

$$(0.95)^3 = 0.86$$

In systems with large numbers of components in series, each component must have excellent reliability for the system to give satisfactory performance. An example of how difficult it is to build high-reliability series systems is the transatlantic ocean telephone cable system. With 300 regenerators in series, even a reliability of 0.999 at time t for each regenerator would result in a far from satisfactory system reliability of 0.741. In fact, the first transatlantic cable installed by AT&T was retired after over twenty years of service with no electronic failures.

How are such high reliabilities achieved? One way is by introducing redundant parts. For example, suppose two parts are in parallel and that the system operates if at least one part operates. In this system the probability that the system fails is equal to the probability that both components fail. If the failures are assumed to be independent, the reliability of the system is thus

$$R_s(t) = 1 - [1 - R_1(t)][1 - R_2(t)] \qquad (14\text{-}21)$$

If the reliability of each component is 0.95 at time t, then the reliability of the system is

$$R_s(t) = 1 - (1 - 0.95)(1 - 0.95)$$
$$= 1 - (.05)(.05) = 0.9975$$

By adding a redundant part, the reliability of the system has been increased at time t from 0.95 to 0.9975. In the example of the transatlantic cable system, if each regenerator is a parallel pair, the reliability of each pair could be improved at time t from 0.999 to 0.999999. The system reliability at time t would then be improved to 0.99970.

The assumption has been that both parts are operating whenever the system is on and that failure of one part does not affect the operation of the other part. This is sometimes called hot stand-by and is not always practical. There may be a need to provide a cold stand-by in which the second part is switched into service when the first one fails. Then one must also consider the reliability of the switch. If there are, as before, two components with reliability 0.95 at time t and a switching device with reliability 0.98 at time t, the system reliability at time t is

$$R_s(t) = 0.95 + (0.05)(0.95)(0.98) = 0.9966$$

The above equation is just the probability that the first part is operating plus the probability that the first part fails times the probability that the second part operates times the probability that the switch operates.

If the failure rate is constant with time, the above example can be put in terms of the exponential distribution discussed in Section 14-2.1. The system reliability would then be

$$R_s = e^{-\lambda t} + P_s(t)\, \lambda t e^{-\lambda t} \qquad (14\text{-}22)$$

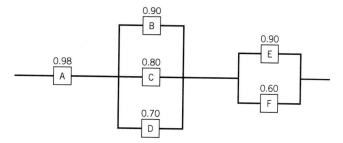

Figure 14-7 A Simple System with Series and Parallel Parts

where

$$e^{-\lambda t} = \text{probability of no failures of a part at time } t$$
$$\lambda t e^{-\lambda t} = \text{probability that part one fails and the stand-by unit operates}$$
$$P_s(t) = \text{probability that the switch operates at time } t$$

In the example, $\lambda = 0.0001$ failures per hour, and the required operating time was 500 hours. Thus, the reliability of each part was $e^{-\lambda t} = 0.95$. The probability of the switch operating at time $t = 500$ hours was assumed to be 0.98.

The following example shows how reliability prediction with simple systems can actually be done. First, it is necessary to study the system architecture to determine which parts are in series and which are in parallel. The example in Figure 14-7 [Wadsworth (1984)] has six parts. One group of three is in parallel, another group of two is in parallel, and the first part and the two groups are in series. The reliabilities of each part R_A through R_F at the system operating time t are given in the figure. The system reliability can thus be calculated as

$$R_s = R_A[1 - (1 - R_B)(1 - R_C)(1 - R_D)][1 - (1 - R_E)(1 - R_F)]$$
$$= 0.98[1 - (0.10)(0.20)(0.30)][1 - (0.10)(0.40)]$$
$$= (0.98)(0.994)(0.960) = 0.935$$

Reliability has been discussed in terms of the survival function or reliability function and the failure rate (hazard rate). Other measures of reliability are also useful. Some of the more useful measures are mean life and mean time between failures. The mean life is a measure used with parts or systems that are not repaired and is the mean time to failure for these parts or systems. Mean time between failures (often written MTBF) is used for parts or systems that may be repaired. The mean life or MTBF is usually denoted by the symbol θ.

The conditional failure rate defined in Equation (14-2) is often used to describe the reliability of a part or system. The failure rate may be expressed as the reciprocal of the mean life or MTBF. Thus, $\lambda = 1/\theta$. If a device has a mean life of 10,000 hours, its failure rate is 0.0001 per hour. For devices with an exponential distribution of failure times, this is an accurate estimate of failure rate. For devices with increasing failure rates or decreasing failure rates, it is more informative to use the instantaneous failure rate at the time of interest.

Failure rates are often expressed as numbers of failures per hour, per 100 hours, or per 10^6 hours. For electronic parts the most common failure rate expression is FITS, or failures in 10^9 hours.

14-3.2 MIL-HDBK-217 and MIL-STD-756

As with control charts and acceptance sampling plans, reliability prediction is such a common tool of ensuring product quality that many national and international standards have been published to explain standard procedures. The most widely used procedure for reliability prediction is given in MIL-HDBK-217. Not only does it contain the basic procedures for parts count reliability prediction and parts stress analysis prediction, but it also contains many pages of failure rates for a wide variety of commonly used parts.

The base failure rates for many electronic and some mechanical parts are tabulated along with factors that modify the base failure rate to consider specific usage. The parts are assumed to have independent exponential failure distributions and are connected in a system in series.

The MIL-HDBK-217 models of the stress-analysis type for resistors are as follows:

$$\lambda_p = \lambda_b(\pi_Q \cdot \pi_R \cdot \pi_E) \tag{14-23}$$

where

λ_p = failure rate for the part in failures per 10^6 hours

λ_b = base failure rate

π_Q = quality factor

π_E = environmental factor

π_R = resistance factor

For a microelectronic part the model is

$$\lambda_p = \lambda_b \pi_Q \cdot \pi_L[C_1 \pi_T + (C_2 + C_3)\pi_E] \tag{14-24}$$

where

π_L = learning factor

π_T = temperature factor

$\quad = 0.1 e^{A[T_R^{-1} - T_j^{-1}]}$

A = temperature acceleration factor

T_R, T_j = reference junction temperatures

C_1, C_2, C_3 = complexity factors, and the other terms are as defined before

The parts count method requires less information than the parts stress analysis method. The parts count method is applicable during bid proposals and early design phases. The information needed to apply the method is as follows:

1. Generic part types (including complexity for microelectronics) and quantities of each part type

2. Part quality levels

3. Equipment environment

Since MIL-HDBK-217 treats only the case in which the reliability distribution is exponential, the failure rate can be expressed as λ, independent of time. The general expression for equipment or system failure rate with the parts count method is for a given equipment or system environment:

$$\lambda_s = \sum_{i=1}^{n} N_i (\lambda_G \pi_Q)_i \qquad (14\text{-}25)$$

where

λ_s = total system failure rate (failures/10^6 hours)

λ_G = generic failure rate for the ith generic part (failures/10^6 hours)

π_Q = quality factor for the ith generic part

N_i = quality of the ith generic part

n = number of different generic parts

The above expression applies only if the entire system is being used in the same environment. If the system consists of several units that will operate in different environments, Equation (14-25) is applied to each portion of the system for its environment, and then the failure rates are added for the total system failure rate.

The generic failure rates (λ_G) to be used are given in tables in great detail. For example, the generic failure rates for random logic microelectronic semiconductor devices in hermetic packages are given by number of gates (twelve groups from 1–20 to 15,001–20,000), by technology (bipolar and MOS) and for ten application environments. The quality factors to be used are located in specified additional tables. Multiquality levels are presented for microelectronics, discrete semiconductors, and established reliability (*ER*) resistors and capacitors. Microelectronic devices have an additional multiplying factor, π_L, called the learning factor.

Generic failure rates are not given for all devices. For example, no generic failure rates are provided for hybrid devices.

The parts stress analysis method requires more information than the parts count method and is applicable when most of the design is completed and a detailed parts list including part stresses is available. The parts stress analysis method is often used during later design phases for reliability trade-offs versus part selection and stresses. In the MIL-HDBK-217 section describing this method, parts are grouped by major categories and, when appropriate, subgrouped within categories. There are fourteen major parts categories.

The information needed for the parts stress analysis method includes the following:

1. Specific part types, including complexity for microelectronics

2. Part quantities

3. Part quality levels

4. System environment

5. Part operating stresses

The general expression for system failure rate for the parts stress analysis method is

$$\lambda_s = \sum_{i=1}^{n} N_i (\lambda_p \pi_Q)_i \qquad (14\text{-}26)$$

where

λ_s = system failure rate

λ_p = specific failure rate for the ith part

π_Q = quality factor for the ith part

N_i = quantity of the ith part

n = number of different specific part categories

As with the parts count method, the time to failure of the parts is assumed to be exponentially distributed. The system failure rate is determined directly by the summation given above if all parts in the system reliability model are in series or can be assumed to be in series for the purpose of an approximation. If the reliability model has nonseries elements, the system reliability can be approximated by considering only the series elements or by calculating an equivalent series failure rate for the nonseries elements of the model.

MIL-STD-756 gives detailed procedures for reliability modeling. The standard shows how to construct reliability block diagrams to show interdependencies among all elements or functional groups. The reliability block diagrams demonstrate by concise visual shorthand the various series-parallel block combinations that result in system success. A complete understanding of the system's mission definition is required to produce the reliability block diagram.

The basic rules for probability computations covered in Chapter 5 are provided in MIL-STD-756 for analyzing the reliability block diagrams. The standard covers series, parallel, and k-out-of-n systems. The term "k-out-of-n systems" refers to systems that operate when any k parts out of the n total parts are functioning.

In addition to the limitation of the exponential distribution assumption and the assumption of independence, there are some other limitations of MIL-HDBK-217. O'Connor, Head, and Joy (1983) point out the following:

1. It does not consider the fact that modern electronic devices are really subsystems, the reliability of which may be affected by system application and software.

2. It does not adequately distinguish between part-level and system-level failures.

3. The model used in some ways does not adequately represent the underlying failure physics so as to facilitate derivation of parameter estimates.

14-3.3 Other Reliability Predictions

Many electronic parts exhibit decreasing failure rates characterized by high infant mortality and then excellent performance for many years. The reliability prediction models that assume an exponential time to failure also assume a constant failure rate. This assumption will often cause unrealistic predictions. Models allowing the parts to have decreasing failure rates have been developed, but the calculations become very difficult. Most of these calculations must be done with the aid of a computer.

Some approximate methods have been developed. The Bellcore Technical Advisory [Bell Communications Research (1984)] describes a method in which a failure rate multiplier is used during the first year of system life (8760 hours) and then the constant failure rate is used for the steady state performance. The Bellcore Technical Advisory also gives two methods other than parts count. In one, laboratory data can be combined with parts count predictions. In the other method, statistical predictions from field tracking are allowed.

Some companies (e.g., AT&T) have developed internal procedures for calculating reliability predictions. One method uses Weibull models for the first 10,000 hours of life (slightly longer than one year) and then the exponential model for steady state reliability.

▶ 14-4 RELIABILITY ESTIMATION

A key part of any quality program is the assurance that the products produced meet performance objectives. It is not enough to just predict the reliability; solid evidence is needed of what the reliability really is. Many different methods are used to estimate product reliability, including formal life tests, field tracking studies, analyses of repair data, and accelerated life testing.

The problems faced in designing a life test are very similar to those faced in deciding on an acceptance sampling plan. The life test designer must decide what performance parameters are to be tested, how long the tests should last, and how many items should be placed on test. The number of items on test and the length of the life test are closely related questions.

If the failure distribution is known, a more efficient life test can be designed than if an assumption about the failure distribution is not made. However, it is necessary to ensure that the life test design permits a check that the assumed model fits the data fairly well.

As for reliability prediction, in reliability estimation the exponential distribution is the model most frequently used. This distribution assumes a constant failure rate and may not be an appropriate model for some products. When it is an appropriate model, it has a great advantage that the time on test and the number of items on test can be traded off. One hundred items on test for ten days will give the same information as ten items on test for 100 days. The critical parameter is total time on test. However, if the life distribution of the product being tested is not exponential (the product does not have a constant failure rate), then one cannot rely only on total time on test.

14-4.1 Censored Data

Other complications must be considered in designing life tests. Rarely is complete life test data available. That is, there are incomplete measurements of the times to failure. Suppose 100 items are placed on test for six months. During the six months, twenty-three of the items fail, and the failure times are recorded. For the other seventy-seven items, all that is known is that they survived for six months; their failure times were greater than six months. These data are called censored.

There are actually three types of censoring. The most common, described above, is called right censoring. Failure times for items that are removed from the test before the items fail are right censored. Many times a test is designed that does not permit exact failure times to be obtained. For example, testing may be in a simulated operating environment in a sealed chamber. At the end of the test time, the items are removed and tested. The items that have failed are said to be left censored. It is known only that they failed some time between the start of the test and the end of it. Another type of censoring that is similar to left censoring is interval censoring. Sometimes observations may be made only at specified times. When a failed item is found, it is known only that it failed some

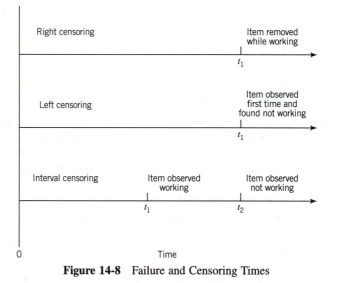

Figure 14-8   Failure and Censoring Times

time between the last check and this check. These three types of censoring are illustrated in Figure 14-8.

14-4.2 Reliability Data Analysis

When the reliability data are complete, that is, every item has been run until it fails, ordinary probability plotting techniques can be used to begin the analysis. However, most reliability data are censored as described above. Nelson (1983) points out that even for some censored reliability data, probability plotting methods may be used. When all the sample units start on test together and the failure times of all failed items are below the running time of the units that did not fail, he calls the data singly censored. The method for probability plotting of singly censored data is the same as the method for complete data. The ith ordered observation is plotted against a plotting position

$$F_i = 100(i - 0.5)/n$$

Nelson (1983) gives the plotting positions for $i = 1, \ldots, 35$ and $n = 6, \ldots, 35$ in the appendix of his guide.

Example of Plotting Singly Censored Data

Nelson (1983) gives the results of life tests on electric cords for a small appliance. These cords are flexed by a test machine until they fail. Each week twelve cords were put on the machine, and at the end of the week the cords were replaced by a new sample of cords.

In Table 14-1 the data are reproduced from Nelson's test. Note that for the old cords, seventeen failed during the test and seven were removed without failing. For the new cords, nine failed during the test and three were removed without failing.

Figure 14-9 shows Nelson's plot of the results of the life tests on new cords and old cords. He plotted the samples on normal probability paper, which provided a reasonably

TABLE 14-1   Nelson's Appliance Cord Data

	Old			New	
Rank i	Hours	$100i/(n+1)$	Rank i	Hours	$100i/(n+1)$
1	57.5	4	1	72.4	7.7
2	77.8	8	2	78.6	15.4
3	88.0	12	3	81.2	23.4
4	96.9	16	4	94.0	30.8
5	98.4	20	5	120.1	38.4
6	100.3	24	6	126.3	46.1
7	100.8	28	7	127.2	53.8
8	102.1	32	8	128.7	61.5
9	103.3	36	9	141.9	69.2
10	103.4	40	10	164.1+	X
11	105.3	44	11	164.1+	X
12	105.4	48	12	164.1+	X
13	122.6	52			
14	139.3	56			
15	143.9	60			
16	148.0	64			
17	151.3	68			
18	161.1+	X			
19	161.2+	X			
20	161.2+	X			
21	162.4+	X			
22	162.7+	X			
23	163.1+	X			
24	176.8+	X			

X removed from test before failure.

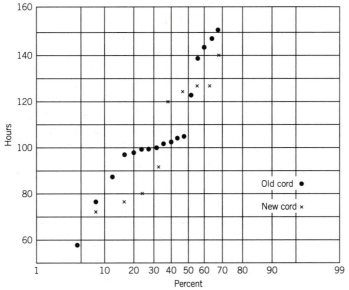

Figure 14-9 Normal Probability Plot of Appliance Cord Data

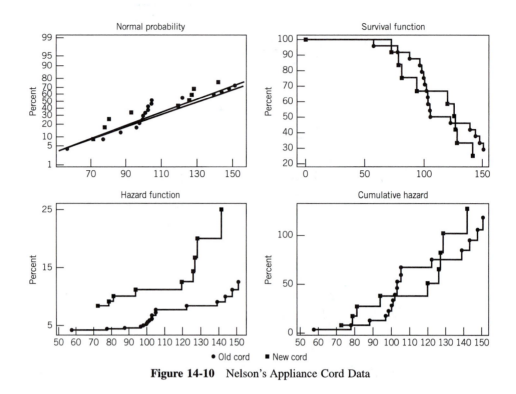

Figure 14-10 Nelson's Appliance Cord Data

straight plot. Nelson concludes that the lines of the electric appliance cords with respect to failures from flexing are comparable.

As for quality routines, software also plays an important role in reliability analysis. To demonstrate some available software and to examine alternative analyses, Figure 14-10 shows the fourfold overview plots of the normal probability plot, comparable to Figure 14-9; the survival function or reliability plot; the hazard function or failure rate plot; and the cumulative hazard plot for the data of Table 14-1, as produced by MINITAB. The alternative to the normal probability plot, the Weibull probability plot for the same data as produced by MINITAB, is presented in Figure 14-11. The associated parameter estimates for the old cord and the new cord for the two-parameter Weibull are as shown in Table 14-2.

The shape parameter, β, for both sets of data is just over 3 and helps to reinforce the use of the normal distribution in the earlier analysis (note mention in Section 14-2.2 of an approximate normal distribution for $\beta \approx 3.5$). The second parameter estimated by MINITAB is referred to as the *characteristic life*, often designated by θ,

TABLE 14-2 **Weibull Parameter Estimates for Appliance Cord Data**

	Old Cord	New Cord
β (shape)	3.17	3.28
$\theta = 1/\lambda$ (characteristic life)	148.63	142.82

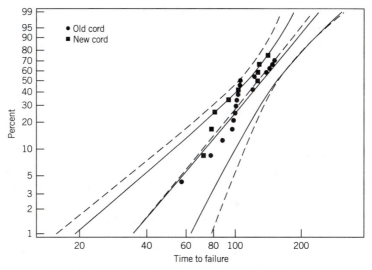

Figure 14-11 Probability Plot for the Old Cord and New Cord

and is equal to $1/\lambda$ as given in Equation (14-11). The Weibull density function is sometimes written as

$$f(t) = [\beta/t][t/\theta]^{\beta} \exp[-[t/\theta]^{\beta}] \tag{14-27}$$

with parameters, β, and $\theta = 1/\lambda$. θ is estimated as the time value corresponding to the 100% cumulative hazard value. See the discussion that follows. It is also the 63.2nd percentile on the probability scale, which could be estimated from Figure 14-11.

Hazard Plotting
A type of probability plotting that is used frequently in reliability analyses is called hazard plotting. The theory of hazard plotting is explained very clearly in Nelson (1972c), and applications of hazard plotting are covered in Nelson (1972c, 1982, 1983). Holcomb and Saperstein (1979) give a very clear explanation with examples of hazard plotting. Recall from Section 14-1 the definition of the conditional failure rate or hazard rate [Equation (14-2)]

$$\lambda(t) = \frac{f(t)}{\overline{F(t)}}$$

The cumulative hazard rate is defined by

$$H(t) = \int_0^t h(x)\,dx \tag{14-28}$$

The cumulative hazard rate, $H(t)$, is related to the cumulative distribution function by

$$F(t) = 1 - e^{-H(t)} \tag{14-29}$$

For multiply censored data it is convenient to plot simple estimates of $H(t)$ against theoretical values of $H(t)$ based on proposed reliability models.

Hazard Plotting with Weibull Data

The Weibull distribution, as discussed in Section 14-2.2, is frequently used in reliability models and analyses. Recall from Equation (14-12) that the Weibull failure rate or hazard rate can be written as

$$\lambda(t) = \lambda\beta(\lambda t)^{\beta-1}$$

The cumulative hazard rate is then

$$H(t) = (\lambda t)^{\beta} \tag{14-30}$$

This particularly simple form of $H(t)$ makes it very convenient to do graphical analyses of Weibull data. Suppose, for example, that there are n devices to test. At the end of the study at time t there are observed k failures with the corresponding k ordered failures times, $t_1, t_2, \ldots t_k$. Some devices ($n - k$ to be exact) have survived until the end of the study. If it is assumed that no devices are replaced during the study, there are $n_i = n - i + 1$ items on test at t_i, the instant of failure for the ith failure. The observed conditional failure rate or hazard rate at time t_i is i/n_i. The observed cumulative hazard rate at time t_i is

$$\hat{H}(t) = \sum_{j=1}^{i}(1/n_j) \tag{14-31}$$

The theoretical cumulative hazard rate from Equation (14-30) is $(\lambda t)^{\beta}$. If $H(t)$ is estimated with $\hat{H}(t)$ and the $\hat{H}(t_i)$ are plotted versus the times t_i on log-log paper, there will be a straight line with intercept $\log(\lambda^{\beta})$ and slope β if the underlying distribution is, in fact, a Weibull. Plotting $\hat{H}(t)$ versus the times of failure gives a simple way of checking the distributional assumption and estimating λ and β.

Multiply Censored Life Data

Unfortunately, not all reliability data are so well behaved. It is not uncommon, especially in field studies, to have units placed on test at different times, and to have running times without failure shorter than times to failure. Nelson (1983) calls these data multiply censored. He explains in detail how to handle these data with hazard plotting. The procedure is actually quite simple.

The sample times are ordered without regard to whether the times are running times or failure times. The instantaneous failure rate or hazard rate is then estimated as

$$\hat{\lambda}(t_i) = \frac{1}{n_i} \tag{14-32}$$

for each failure time t_i. The n_i refer to the number of items on test at time t_i. Cumulative hazard rates are calculated by summing the hazard rate and the cumulative hazard area of the preceding failure. Cumulative hazard rates may be greater than 1 (or 100%) and have no physical interpretation.

The probability paper corresponding to the assumed distribution is then chosen. For Weibull, log-log paper is used. The time scale is marked to include the range of test times. Each cumulative hazard rate is then plotted against its corresponding failure time. If the plot of the points is reasonably straight, the model fits the data fairly well. A straight line through the data points can then be fitted. The hazard plot is then interpreted like a probability plot.

Example of Weibull Hazard Plot for Multiply Censored Data

Nelson (1983) gives an example of seventy diesel generators tested for fan failures. The data he presents are the hours to failure of the fan for twelve diesel generators and the running times without a fan failure for fifty-eight diesel generators. The engineers wished to estimate the percentage of fan failures during the 8000-hour warranty period. The engineers also wanted to estimate whether the fan failures exhibited an increasing or decreasing failure rate. Nelson (1983) states that the results of these tests and analyses helped the engineers and management to decide whether to replace the unfailed fans with a better fan.

The data from Nelson's example are presented in Table 14-3. There are five columns: items on test, indication of failures, times to failure or removal from test, the estimate of the instantaneous failure rate or hazard rate in percent, and the estimate of the cumulative hazard rate in percent. Fans that failed are indicated by an X in the failures column. The

TABLE 14-3   Nelson's Diesel Generator Fan Data

Items on Test	Failures	Hours on Test	Estimated Hazard Rate (Percent)	Estimated Cumulative Hazard Rate (Percent)
70	X	450	1.4	1.4
69		460		
68	X	1150	1.5	2.9
67	X	1150	1.5	4.4
66		1560		
65	X	1600	1.5	5.9
64		1660		
63		1850		
62		1850		
61		1850		
60		1850		
59		1850		
58		2030		
57		2030		
56		2030		
55	X	2070	1.8	7.7
54	X	2070	1.9	9.6
53	X	2080	1.9	11.5
52		2200		
51		3000		
50		3000		
49		3000		
48		3000		
47	X	3100	2.1	13.6
46		3200		
45	X	3450	2.2	15.8

(continued)

TABLE 14-3 *(continued)*

Items on Test	Failures	Hours on Test	Estimated Hazard Rate (Percent)	Estimated Cumulative Hazard Rate (Percent)
44		3750		
43		3750		
42		4150		
41		4150		
40		4150		
39		4150		
38		4300		
37		4300		
36		4300		
35		4300		
34	X	4600	2.9	18.7
33		4850		
32		4850		
31		4850		
30		4850		
29		5000		
28		5000		
27		5000		
26		6100		
25	X	6100	4.0	22.7
24		6100		
23		6100		
22		6300		
21		6450		
20		6450		
19		6700		
18		7450		
17		7800		
16		7800		
15		8100		
14		8100		
13		8200		
12		8500		
11		8500		
10		8500		
9		8750		
8	X	8750	12.5	35.2
7		8750		
6		9400		
5		9900		
4		10100		
3		10100		
2		10100		
1		11500		

calculations are simple. Recall from Equation (14-32) that the estimates of the hazard rates are just 1 divided by the number of items on test given in column 1. Thus for the first failure,

$$\hat{\lambda}(t_i) = \frac{1}{n_i} = \frac{1}{70} = 0.014 = 1.4\%$$

For the second and third failures, which occur at 1150 hours,

$$\hat{\lambda}(t_i) = \frac{1}{n_i} = \frac{1}{68} = 0.015 = 1.5\%$$

$$\hat{\lambda}(t_i) = \frac{1}{n_i} = \frac{1}{67} = 0.015 = 1.5\%$$

The estimate of the cumulative failure rate at 1150 hours is then [from Equation (14-31)]

$$\hat{H}(t_i) = \frac{1}{70} + \frac{1}{68} + \frac{1}{67} = 0.044 = 4.4\%$$

Nelson's Weibull hazard plot is reproduced in Figure 14-12. He marked the time scale on Weibull paper from 100 to 100,000 hours. He plotted the calculated cumulative

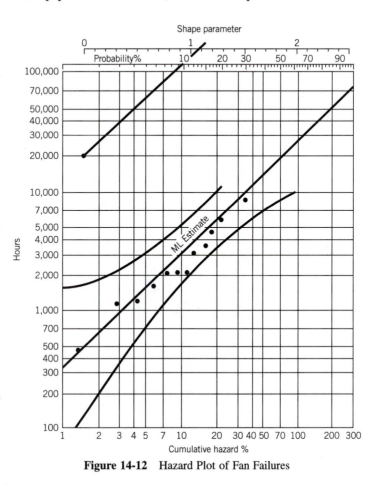

Figure 14-12 Hazard Plot of Fan Failures

hazard rates on the horizontal scale. Note that Weibull paper also gives you an easy way to estimate the shape parameter, β. By drawing a line parallel to the fitted line intercepting the circle in the upper left of the hazard paper, the shape parameter can be estimated by reading the value where the line intercepts the shape parameter scale. Note in this example that the estimate of the shape parameter is 1.1 Recall that a Weibull distribution with a shape parameter equal to 1 is the same as an exponential distribution. This means that the data in this example indicate that the fan failures have a failure rate that is almost constant. Replacing the unfailed fans with new ones of the same type will not change the reliability of the diesel generators.

Once the hazard plot has been created, it can be used to make several estimates quickly. To estimate the percentage of the population that will fail by a certain operating time, enter the plot at that time, go across to the fitted line, and then vertically up to the probability scale. For example, at 6000 hours about 20% of the fans will have failed. The time at which a certain percentage of the fans will have failed can be estimated. For example, 5% of the fans will have failed at about 1500 hours.

Additional software is available in the reliability field. Figure 14-13 presents the Weibull two-parameter probability plot for the generator fan data using ReliaSoft®. And as is noted above with β estimated as 1.058, the exponential distribution is a reasonable

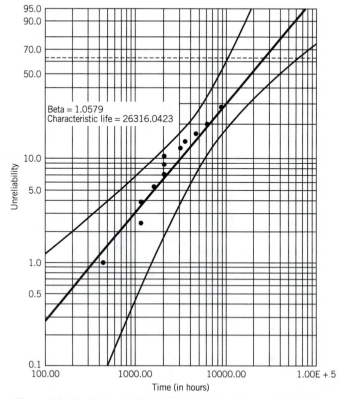

Figure 14-13   Nelson's Diesel Generator Fan Data—Weibull Plot

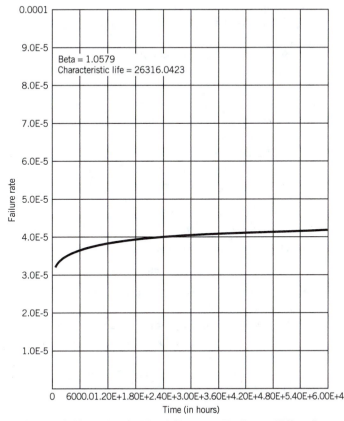

Figure 14-14   Nelson's Diesel Generator Fan Data—Failure Rate

alternative model for these data, with constant failure rate. To illustrate this the failure rate curve as produced by ReliaSoft® is shown in Figure 14-14, which shows the failure rate to be almost constant. In support of the following discussion it is interesting to point out that the parameter estimates shown on Figures 14-13 and 14-14 are obtained by maximum likelihood estimation within the software.

Maximum Likelihood Estimation

Holcomb and Saperstein (1979) explain that although hazard plotting is a very valuable tool, it does have some drawbacks. Hazard plotting uses only the number of items on test to make each estimate of the hazard rate. If there is extensive censoring between observed failure times as in the diesel generator fan example, hazard plotting is far from optimal. The example in Holcomb and Saperstein (1979) makes this very clear. Start with 100,000 items on test and at some time between the first and second failure remove 50,000 of the items. The cumulative hazard rate calculated at the second failure is

$$\hat{H}(t_2) = \frac{1}{100,000} + \frac{1}{50,000} = 0.00003$$

whether the 50,000 devices were removed the second after the first failure or a minute before the second failure. If the first failure occurred at the end of the third day and the second failure at the end of the first year, the time when the 50,000 other items are removed from test should make a difference.

There are several analytical methods that overcome this problem. The most widely used is the method of maximum likelihood. This method is described in basic statistics texts. With maximum likelihood techniques, censored data can be treated in a wide variety of ways. The accuracy of the maximum likelihood estimates may also be calculated in a straightforward manner.

To illustrate the method of maximum likelihood, an example from Holcomb and Saperstein (1979) is used. This example has one exact failure time and one device with each of the three types of censoring discussed earlier. There are four devices in total:

1. Device 1 failed at time t_1.

2. Device 2 failed some time between time t_2 and t_3.

3. Device 3 had failed before time t_4, but the exact time is not known.

4. Device 4 survived the entire test and was finally removed at time t_5.

Other than the obvious constraint that time $t_3 > t_2$, the other times are arbitrary and could be in any order.

To illustrate the method of maximum likelihood, the Weibull model discussed in Section 14-2.2 is used, and the likelihood or probability associated with each observation is calculated.

For the first device the likelihood is just the probability of failing at time t_1. Equation (14-11) shows

$$f(t_1) = \lambda\beta(\lambda t_1)^{\beta-1}e^{-(\lambda t_1)^\beta} \tag{14-33}$$

For the second device the likelihood is the probability of failing in the interval $[t_2, t_3]$, which from (14-10) is

$$[F(t_3) - F(t_2)] = e^{-(\lambda t_2)^\beta} - e^{-(\lambda t_3)^\beta} \tag{14-34}$$

For the third device the likelihood is just the probability of failing by t_4:

$$F(t_4) = 1 - e^{-(\lambda t_4)^\beta} \tag{14-35}$$

The fourth device has survived until at least time t_5. This event has probability

$$1 - F(t_5) = e^{-(\lambda t_5)^\beta} \tag{14-36}$$

The likelihood of these four events taken together is the product of the four expressions given in Equations (14-33) through (14-36). It can now be seen that by using these four building blocks, the likelihood function for any set of data can be constructed no matter how it may have been censored.

That is the good news. Unfortunately, now the values of λ and β must be found that maximize this function. The typical likelihood function for reliability data is so complicated that it is usually not at all tractable, or even possible, to solve for the parameters in a closed form. Numerical methods on a reasonably good computer are usually necessary. Hazard plotting is a required adjunct to this method. Not only can computation time be saved by using the parameter estimates as starting points for the iterative procedure, but the hazard plot can help to avoid the potential pitfalls of any numerical method.

Holcomb and Saperstein (1979) have one other piece of advice. They recommend plotting the estimates of the conditional failure rates or hazard rates directly. These plots are more likely to show the typical or irregular bits of data that can cause major problems with the analysis.

Confidence intervals for the hazard rate estimate can be constructed by estimating the variance of the parameter estimates $\hat{\lambda}$ and $\hat{\beta}$ and then estimating the variance of the function of these estimates (the hazard rate). Maximum likelihood theory states that when the sample is large enough the estimates of the hazard rate, $\hat{\lambda}(t)$, behave reasonably like normal random variables with mean $\lambda(t)$ and with a variance that can be calculated as indicated above. Confidence intervals around the estimated hazard rate can be calculated by using standard methods.

Figure 14-15 shows a plot from Holcomb and Saperstein (1979) of the estimated failure rates (in FITS) over a time period of 10,000 hours. There are three parts to the life test: an oven period in which the devices are operated at elevated temperatures, a power cycling burn-in, and a field tracking study. Since the oven test appeared to have an uncharacteristically high failure rate in the first ten hours due to heat sensitive failures and items that were dead when placed on test, these data were excluded from the estimates. The estimated hazard rates are plotted as bars, and the maximum likelihood estimate of

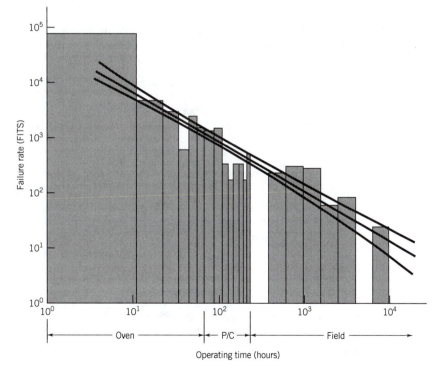

Figure 14-15 Maximum Likelihood Fit and 90% Confidence Intervals for Manufactured Product

the hazard rate and 90% confidence bounds are also plotted. The fit of the Weibull model appears to be reasonably good.

▶ 14-5 ACCELERATED LIFE TESTING

It is often not practical to run a life test long enough to obtain sufficient data to estimate accurately a product's reliability. Many products that are manufactured today have very high reliability. A life test that would produce enough failures to make good reliability estimates would require many units on test and very long test times. Designers, manufacturers, and sometimes buyers frequently use accelerated life tests to estimate the reliability of products. When failure mechanisms are well understood, these accelerated life tests provide valuable information about life distribution characteristics. In accelerated life testing, the basic idea is to test units at stress levels higher than the normal operating levels. Statistical models are then employed to relate the observed failure rates at the accelerated stress levels to a predicted failure rate at normal operating conditions.

14-5.1 Basic Models

The main difficulty in using accelerated life tests is that there must be a reasonable model of the relationship between stress and the failure rate. Inaccuracies in the model can lead to serious errors in an understanding of the true failure rate at normal operating conditions. In this chapter the purpose is only to give a general overview of the concept of accelerated life testing. Many excellent articles and books give comprehensive treatment to the subject, and some of these are referenced in this chapter.

A model that is often used in accelerated life testing is based on the Weibull distribution introduced in Section 14-2.2. Assume that the time T to failure of a unit at any stress level follows the Weibull distribution with cumulative distribution function

$$F(t) = 1 - e^{-(\lambda t)\beta} \tag{14-37}$$

Following the discussion in Meeker and Michael (1980), assume that the Weibull scale parameter, λ, is a power function of applied voltage V; that is,

$$\lambda(V) = e^{\gamma_0}(V)^{-\gamma_1} \tag{14-38}$$

where the model parameters γ_0 and γ_1 are to be estimated from the data. This is usually referred to as the inverse power rule. Also assume that the Weibull shape parameter, β, does not depend on the stress level. This model has been used successfully for modeling time to failure in many applications [see, for example, Nelson (1970a) and Nelson (1972a)].

Again following the development of Meeker and Michael (1980), the natural logarithm of the time to failure, T, follows a smallest extreme value distribution with cumulative distribution function

$$G(y) = 1 - e^{-\exp[(y-\mu)/\sigma]} \tag{14-39}$$

where $\mu = -\log(\lambda)$ and $\sigma = 1/\beta$ are the location and scale parameters, respectively. The natural logarithms of Weibull data can now be analyzed with this model in a straightforward manner. The inverse power rule, Equation (14-38), can now be expressed as

$$\mu = \gamma_0 + \gamma_1 \log(V) \tag{14-40}$$

If a product is to be tested at several different voltages (stress levels), with different scale parameters

$$\mu_i = \gamma_0 + \gamma_1 \log (V_i) \qquad (14\text{-}41)$$

Then, again from Meeker and Michael (1980), the maximum likelihood estimates of the pth quantile of the life distribution at stress level i is

$$\hat{y}_p(i) = \hat{\mu}_i + u_p \hat{\sigma} \qquad (14\text{-}42)$$

where $u_p = \log [-\log (1 - p)]$ is the pth quantile of the standard ($\mu = 0$, $\sigma = 1$) smallest extreme value distribution. The maximum likelihood estimate for the corresponding Weibull quantile is

$$\hat{t}_p(i) = e^{\hat{y}_p(t)} \qquad (14\text{-}43)$$

Now competing accelerated life test plans can be compared by observing the asymptotic variance of $\hat{y}_p(i)$ at a specified stress level. As Meeker and Michael (1980) point out, minimizing this asymptotic variance is equivalent to minimizing the coefficient of variation, or relative error, of the estimator of the corresponding Weibull quantile.

Mann, Schafer, and Singpurwalla (1974) give an excellent discussion of accelerated life tests and the physics of failure. Since the exponential distribution is widely used in practice, they discuss four different relationships between the failure rate, λ, and the stress level, V, for the exponential distribution.

One of the most commonly used accelerated life testing models is the Arrhenius model, which expresses the time degradation of some device parameter as a function of the operating temperature. The model can be expressed as

$$\lambda_i = \exp [A - B(V_i^{-1} - \overline{V})] \qquad (14\text{-}44)$$

for all values V_i within the specified range, where $\overline{V}$ is the weighted mean of the V_i^{-1}'s. Mann, Schafer, and Singpurwalla (1974) develop the maximum likelihood estimates for this model. They also describe and discuss the Eyring model for a single stress and the generalized Eyring model. The generalized Eyring model is applicable if the device being tested is subjected to the constant application of two types of stress (a thermal stress and a nonthermal stress).

Even with accelerated stress levels, one may not obtain enough failures within practical test duration to make good estimates of failure rates. Step stress testing is sometimes used to reduce test times and to ensure that failures occur during the planned test duration. Nelson (1980) gives an excellent review of models and data analyses for step stress accelerated life testing. The basic concept is that products are run through a series of tests at different stress levels in a predetermined pattern, each for a specified time. Different products may be tested with different step stress patterns. He also supplies an example in which the objective was to estimate cable insulation life at a design stress of 400 volts/mil. Each specimen in the sample was held for 10 minutes each at 5000 volts, 10,000 volts, 15,000 volts, and 20,000 volts before it went to Step 1 at 26,000 volts. There were ten different stress steps ranging from 26,000 to 48,500 volts with holding times from 15 minutes to 16 hours. The analysis with step stress models is more difficult than that with constant stress. Nelson (1980) uses the inverse power rule that was discussed earlier for his analysis. A simpler procedure using a graphical analysis of incomplete accelerated life test data is described by Hahn and Nelson (1971). Step stress models have been used successfully for many years in testing transistors [see Dodson and Howard (1960) and Siuta (1961)].

14-5.2 Planning an Accelerated Life Test

Several important decisions must be made in planning an accelerated life test. Meeker and Michael (1980) present a careful discussion of the entire process. The general and specific objectives of the accelerated life test should be clear. Examples of common objectives are to compare reliability performance with reliability requirements and to judge two products or designs on the basis of the time it takes 10% of the items on test to fail.

The amount of time, money, test facilities, and other resources available is a major factor in planning the test. It must be decided which method of stressing to accelerate life will be used. The failure mechanisms must be understood to be reasonably certain that failures produced under the accelerated conditions are related in a known way to failures under operating conditions. The accelerated conditions should not cause other failure modes that are not normally encountered. Many common failure modes may not be accelerated in the test, and this must be understood. For example, in testing an automobile on a test rack for various wearout mechanisms, metal aging due to thermal change or corrosion (rust) cannot be accelerated.

There may be physical constraints on the type of tests that can be run. These constraints can arise from the type of test facilities, the units available for tests, or other constrained resources. A plan must be designed for sampling the units from the population of interest, assigning the units to test positions and stress levels, and deciding how many units will be assigned to each stress level. A decision must be made regarding how many stress levels to use, what the levels will be, and whether to keep the stress levels constant or use step stressing.

Many of the above problems are covered in traditional experimental designs [see Chapter 12 and Box, Hunter, and Hunter (1978)]. Some problems are unique to accelerated life testing (e.g., number of stress levels, level of stress). Previous experience or results from similar tests on similar products can give valuable information that can be used in planning the test.

Because inaccurate estimates can be made when the model is incorrect, one should always have a provision for testing the model. Frequently, it is impractical to verify the appropriateness of a model over the entire range of stresses of interest. Meeker and Michael (1980) state that often an accelerated life test is planned so that a moderate number of failures will be observed over that range of stress. If the relationship appears to be linear, one then makes the critical assumption that the relationship is linear down to normal operating conditions.

Meeker and Michael (1980) discuss the specific design of an accelerated life test plan. A major problem to be considered is that at high levels of stress, failure modes may occur that are not present at normal operating conditions. The highest stress level to be well within a safe bound will usually be selected. Engineering judgment, previous experience with similar products, or results of preliminary tests are used to select the highest stress level. Usually, three or more levels of stress are used to provide useful information. There are several papers discussing optimum plans in which least squares estimation is used to fit a linear regression model to complete data. Nelson and Meeker (1978) review these papers. Other papers discuss planning accelerated life tests in which maximum likelihood estimates will be used to fit an accelerated life test model to censored data. Chernoff (1962) gives results for the exponential distribution with right censoring. Nelson and Kielpinski (1976) and Kielpinski and Nelson (1975) also give optimum plans for other distributions. Meeker and Nelson (1975) and Nelson and Meeker (1978) give optimum plans for the extreme value and Weibull distributions. Meeker and Hahn (1977) give asymptotically optimum plans for tests with a logistic model. These optimum plans consist of two stress levels with the lowest stress level chosen to minimize the asymptotic variance of the quantile of interest. Consequently, several authors have suggested compromise plans in which small proportions of units are placed at intermediate stress levels. See, for example, Nelson and Kielpinski (1976) and Meeker and Hahn (1977).

▶ 14-6 RELIABILITY MONITORING AND DESIGN CONSIDERATIONS

Similar to quality, reliability requires continuous monitoring, control, and improvement. Information on present and past reliability and, in particular, unreliability or failures of components and systems provides important data that contributes to improved designs for future applications. Information on reliability, including failures, serves at least three purposes: (1) to establish a history and databank of failures, their causes, and their effects so that improvements can be made to avoid repeats of those failures; (2) to discover deficiencies or limitations in systems and equipment for effective and efficient maintenance; and (3) to confirm that systems and components are meeting their reliability objectives. Formal procedures have been developed to facilitate data collection and analysis and design efforts. A number of these are discussed below.

14-6.1 Failure Reporting, Analysis, and Corrective Action System

Failure Reporting, Analysis, and Corrective Action System (FRACAS) is a requirement (task 104) of MIL-STD-785. Consequently, it is referenced in numerous related handbooks and standards such as MIL-HDBK-338, MIL-STD-781, MIL-STD-1543, and MIL-STD-1635. Contractors providing supplies and services to the military are required to comply. Many procedures that were developed for military application have been adopted by civilian companies on the basis of their logic and usefulness. Recall that MIL-Q-9858 is the grandfather of the ISO 9000 series (see Chapter 3).

FRACAS is a closed-loop system with defined significant feedback for collecting and reporting on failures (what failed, how it failed), analyzing failures (why it failed), and determining and implementing corrective actions based on the failures (how future failures can be prevented). This includes feedback of information to design, manufacturing, and test processes. The analysis phase requires in-depth investigation of the root causes of failures. As stated in MIL-STD-785,

The closed loop system shall include provisions to assure that effective corrective actions are taken on a timely basis by a follow-up audit that reviews all open failure reports, failure analyses, and corrective action suspense dates, and the reporting of delinquencies to management. The failure cause for each failure shall be clearly stated.

FRACAS includes reliability estimation as discussed in Section 14-4, utilizing failure information collected. As for general quality systems and the organization of a material review board for product disposition decisions, FRACAS often includes a failure review board.

For more details on this procedure, see the earlier referenced documents as well as NAVAIR 01-1A-32 [Naval Air Systems Command (1977)] and Arsenhault and Roberts (1980).

14-6.2 Failure Mode, Effects, and Criticality Analysis

Even more popular (especially among non-defense companies) than FRACAS is Failure Mode, Effects, and Criticality Analysis (FMECA) as a significant procedure in the concept and design phases and in the manufacturing process phase to prevent failures from occurring. It is also a requirement of MIL-STD-785 (task 204) with the following stated purpose (paraphrased):

To identify potential design weaknesses through systematic, documented consideration of (1) all likely ways in which a component or equipment can fail, (2) causes for each mode of failure, (3) the effects of each failure, and (4) the criticality to other components, assemblies, equipment, and systems including the likelihood of failure and the method and degree of detectability.

As such, FMECA is a procedure that emphasizes failures before the fact, that is, before components or systems are deployed and failures actually occur. It attempts to identify all potential failures that may occur, and it does this early enough in the concept or design phase to effect prevention in the actual final concept and design. This eliminates or at least reduces the multiplicities of failure redesign, costly and time-consuming sequences. Besides its reference in MIL-STD-785, it is also referenced and discussed in MIL-HDBK-338, MIL-STD-1543, MIL-STD-1635, and others. Additionally, an entire standard is devoted to the subject: MIL-STD-1629.

FMECA is often considered as the combination of two activities or procedures, that is, FMEA and CA—or Failure Mode and Effects Analysis and Criticality Analysis. These are defined as follows:

FMEA—A procedure by which each potential failure mode in a system (component, assembly, equipment) is analyzed to determine the results or effects thereof on the system and to classify each potential failure mode according to its severity.

CA—A procedure by which each potential failure mode is ranked according to the combined influence of severity and probability of occurrence (and ease or difficulty of detection).

FMEA has gained some additional popularity by its inclusion in the requirements of QS 9000 (see Chapter 3). The Ford Motor Company, in particular, has placed considerable emphasis on the procedure for design and process. Ford's design FMEA procedure is summarized in Figure 14-16. A form that is utilized in conducting design FMEA is shown in Figure 14-17.

Make a list of product/design requirements.

| Develop a list of what the product is expected to do, and what it is expected not to do. Incorporate all known product requirements. |

Translate requirement into potential failure mode.

| The failure mode is the manner in which a part or assembly could potentially fail to meet the design intent, performance requirements, and/or customer expectations. |

Identify potential effects and causes of associated failure.

| Effects should always be stated in terms of vehicle or system performance.

If the effect involves potential non-compliance with government regulations or could potentially affect safe vehicle operations, it must be so indicated.

A potential cause of failure is defined as an indication of a design weakness. (Be specific.) |

Yes — Another Potential Failure Mode?

No

Determine Design Verification (DV)

| Design Verification is meant to prevent the failure cause(s) from occurring, or to detect the cause or resultant failure mode should either occur. |

Assign severity, occurrence, and detection rankings

| To ensure consistency, use the tables in the FMEA Manual to help determine the rankings.

Severity is an assessment of the seriousness of the effect of the failure mode to the next assembly, the vehicle, or the customer.

Occurrence is how frequently the failure mode is projected to occur as a result of the specific cause.

Detection is an assessment of the ability of the design verification program to identify a potential design weakness before the part or assembly is released for production. |

Calculate Risk Priority Number (RPN)

Another Failure
Yes Mode/Effect/ Cause Combination?

| Multiply the severity, occurrence, and detection rankings together. |

No

Rank the RPNs in pareto fashion and determine Recommended Actions

| The concerns with the highest RPNs should be considered for recommended actions first. The intent is to reduce the severity, occurrence and/or detection rankings. A Design FMEA will be of limited value without positive and effective corrective actions. |

Record the actions taken and determine the resulting RPN

| Record a description of what action was taken and its effective/completion date. Estimate and record the resulting severity, occurrence and detection rankings; calculate the new RPN. If necessary, take action to further reduce the RPN. |

Follow-Up

| The design engineer is responsible for assuring that all recommended actions have been implemented or adequately addressed. |

Mode Examples
Deformed
Worn
Leaking
Fractured

Effect Examples
Unstable
Operation impaired
Rough
Vehicle out of control

Cause Examples
Over-stressing
Imbalance
Incorrect torque specification
Incorrect material specification

Figure 14-16 Design FMEA Procedure

507

Page _____ of _____

POTENTIAL
FAILURE MODE AND EFFECTS ANALYSIS
(DESIGN FMEA)

Subsystem/Name ______________ Suppliers and Plants Affected ______________ Prepared By ______________

Design Responsibility ______________ Model Year/Vehicle(s) ______________ FMEA Date (Orig) _____ (Rev) _____

Other Areas Involved ______________ Engineering Release Date ______________

Part Name & Number / Part Function	Potential Failure Mode	Potential Effect(s) of Failure	Severity	▽	Potential Cause(s) of Failure	Occurrence	Design Verification	Detection	RPN	Recommended Action(s)	Area/Individual Responsible & Completion Date	Action Results: Actions Taken	Action Results: Severity	Action Results: Occurrence	Action Results: Detection	Action Results: RPN

Figure 14-17 FMEA Form

NOTE: Reference Failure Mode and Effects Analysis Instruction Manual with permission from Ford Motor Company.

An example of such a form (a variation of Figure 14-17) applied to FMEA of a heat exchanger is shown in Figure 14-18.

Severity classification categories (MIL-STD-1629) are as follows:

a. Category I—Catastrophic.—A failure which may cause death or weapon system loss (i.e., aircraft, tank, missile, ship, etc.).

b. Category II—Critical.—A failure which may cause severe injury, major property damage, or major system damage which will result in mission loss.

c. Category III—Marginal.—A failure which may cause minor injury, minor property damage, or minor system damage which will result in delay or loss of availability or mission degradation.

d. Category IV—Minor.—A failure not serious enough to cause injury, property damage, or system damage, but which may result in unscheduled maintenance or repair.

Each failure mode is classified according to the following definitions of levels of probability of occurrence:

a. Level A—Frequent. A high probability of occurrence during the item operating time interval. High probability may be defined as a single failure mode probability greater than 0.20.

b. Level B—Reasonably probable. A moderate probability of occurrence during the item operating time interval. Probable may be defined as a single failure mode probability of occurrence which is more than 0.10 but less than 0.20.

c. Level C—Occasional. An occasional probability of occurrence during item operating time interval. Occasional probability may be defined as a single failure mode probability of occurrence which is more than 0.01 but less than 0.10.

d. Level D—Remote. An unlikely probability of occurrence during item operating time interval. Remote probability may be defined as single failure mode probability of occurrence which is more than 0.001 but less than 0.01.

e. Level E—Extremely unlikely. A failure whose probability of occurrence is essentially zero during item operating time interval. Extremely unlikely may be defined as a single failure mode probability of occurrence which is less than 0.001.

For further details on the FMEA (CA) procedures, see the referenced documents. Among some related procedures that should be consulted for application are FTA (Fault Tree Analysis) and THERP (Technique for Human Error Rate Prediction). See the discussion of these procedures in MIL-HDBK-338 and MIL-STD-1472 and their related references.

▶ 14-7 THE BODY OF KNOWLEDGE FOR RELIABILITY ENGINEERING

The American Society for Quality administers and maintains programs of certification, including one for reliability engineers. Associated with this program a body of knowledge for reliability engineering has been established to define subject areas from which

FAILURE MODE AND EFFECT ANALYSIS

ITEM	FUNCTION	FAILURE MODE AND POSSIBLE CAUSE(S)	FAILURE EFFECT ON SUBSYSTEM PERFORMANCE
Heat Exchanger	The heat exchanger converts liquid oxygen supplied by the turbopump to gaseous oxygen (using hot turbine exhaust gas) for vehicle LOX tank pressurization.	1. INTERNAL LIQUID OXYGEN LEAK FROM COIL PACK. CAUSES: Weld joint or parent material failures.	1A. None 1B. Heat exchanger burn-out may occur from combustion of hot exhaust gas & oxygen & lead to damage and loss of pressurization capability to the vehicle LOX tank.
		2. EXTERNAL HOT GAS LEAK. CAUSES: a) Hot gas seal failure. b) Weld joint or parent material failure in heat exchanger shell.	2A. None 2B. Hot gas leak may affect Heat Exchanger performance.
		3. TUBE BLOCKAGE. CAUSES: Contamination or denting during assembly or operation.	3A. None 3B. Possible tube burn through or reduced HEX performance. May result in fire & loss of pressurization capability.
		4. EXTERNAL LOX LEAK FROM BYPASS LINE AT ORIFICE INTERFACE. CAUSES: Seal/seal groove discrepancy.	4A. None. 4B. Reduced LOX/GOX Flowrate & pressure.
		5. EXTERNAL LEAK, FLEX LINE, DOME TO HEAT EXCHANGER INLET CAUSES: a) Seal—Joint alignment or defect. b) Hose failure.	5A. None 5B. Reduced LOX/GOX Flowrate & pressure.
		6. EXTERNAL HOT GAS LEAK, EXHAUST DUCT, DOWNSTREAM OF HEAT EXCHANGER. CAUSES: a) Joint alignment or defect. b) Duct failure.	6A. None 6B. None

Figure 14-18 FMEA of a Heat Exchanger

FAILURE MODE AND EFFECT ANALYSIS

FAILURE EFFECT ON SYSTEM PERFORMANCE	FAILURE EFFECT ON MISSION	SINGLE POINT FAILURE MODE	SEVERITY CATEGORY	OCCURENCE PROBABILITY LEVEL	METHOD OF FAILURE DETECTION
1A. None	1A. None	1A. No	1A. N/A	Level D	1,3,4,5,6
1B. Engine performance degradation due to decreased LOX Tank Pressure, or fire, explosion in boattail. Loss of pressurization to the vehicle LOX Tank and possible fire, explosion.	1B. Possible mission loss, loss of pressurization to the vehicle LOX Tank and possible fire, explosion.	1B. Yes	1B. II	Level D	
2A. None	2A. None	2A. No	2A. N/A	Level D	1,3,4,5,6
2B. Engine performance degradation due to decreased LOX Tank Pressure, or fire, explosion in boattail.	2B. Possible mission loss from fire damage or engine performance degradation.	2B. No	2B. III	Level D	
3A. None	3A. None	3A. No	3A. N/A	Level D	1,3
3B. Reduced or no pressurization capability to the vehicle LOX Tank, possible fire damage.	3B. Mission degradation or loss due to LOX Tank pressure reduction or fire damage.	3B. Yes	3B. II	Level D	
4A. None	4A. None	4A. No	4A. N/A	Level D	1,3,4,5,6
4B. Reduced LOX Tank pressure or excessive temp to LOX Tank. Possible boattail fire damage.	4B. Mission degradation or loss due to LOX Tank pressure reduction or fire damage.	4B. Yes	4B. II	Level D	
5A. None	5A. None	5A. No	5A. N/A	Level D	1,5,6
5B. Reduced LOX Tank pressure or excessive temp to LOX Tank. Possible boattail fire damage.	5B. Reduced performance and possible mission loss.	5B. Yes	5B. II	Level D	
6A. None	6A. None	6A. No	6A. N/A	Level D	1,5,6
6B. Possible component damage due to hot gases leaking into boattail.	6B. Possible mission loss due to fire damage.	6B. No	6B. III	Level D	

examination questions are drawn. This serves as an outline of subject areas identified with the reliability field. This body of knowledge is reproduced below to serve as a summary and outline of topics that should be studied for a degree of competence in this field. This chapter has dealt with some of these topics in a fairly cursory manner. The interested reader should consult the references in this chapter as well as other sources of information for more details on the general subject of reliability.

I. Basic Principles, Concepts, and Definitions

A. Design Reliability, Specifying Reliability, Test for Reliability

B. Reliability Engineering and Quality Engineering Relationships

C. Definitions of Reliability, Maintainability, MTFF, MTBF, Failure Rates, Stress-Strain Analysis, Product Safety, etc.

D. Basis of Prediction, Allocation, Modes of Failure, and Estimates of Failure Rates

E. System Reliability and Effectiveness

F. Software Reliability Methodology

II. Management Control

A. Systems Effectiveness

B. Mission Evaluation

C. Cost Effectiveness

D. Quantitative Methods for Assessment

E. Reliability Program Management Principles

F. Computer Use for Reliability Applications

III. Prediction, Estimation, and Apportionment Methods

A. Mathematical Prediction Methods

B. Prediction of Wearout, Catastrophic Failures, Parts Failure Systems, Reliability (from Parts Failure Rates, from Degradation, from Accelerated and Reliability Testing, from Design Redundancy)

C. Estimation of Distribution Parameters

D. Estimation of Reliability

E. Confidence Intervals; Chi-square, F, Normal Distributions, etc.

F. Reliability Allocation—Parallel versus Series Circuit

G. Allocation for Availability, Reliability, Maintainability

H. Hypothesis Testing

I. Software Methods

IV. Failure Mode, Effect, and Criticality Analysis (Hardware and Software)

A. Criticality Analysis

B. Environmental Requirements and Influence

C. Fault-Tree Analysis

D. Differences Between Part Function, Part Failure Mechanism, Failure Effect, Failure Detection, Failure Mode

V. Part Selection and Derating

A. Evaluation of Parts for Reliability

B. Parts Application and Specification

C. Reliability Testing for Parts

D. Vendor Evaluation of Part Reliability

E. Derating Methods, Principles, Techniques

VI. Reliability Design Review

A. Checklists, Follow-up, Preventive and Corrective Action

B. Design Review Evaluation

C. Management Relation to Design Review

VII. Maintainability and Availability

A. Maintainability—Preventive and Corrective

B. Maintainability and Availability Parameters—Measurement, Definition, and Interpretation

C. Availability

VIII. Product Safety

A. Contingency Analysis

B. Fault-Tree Analysis

C. Malfunction and Multiple Failure Analysis

IX. Human Factors in Reliability

A. Human Factors in Design and Design Principles

B. Man-Machine Function Allocation

C. Human Factors in Production

D. Human Factors in Field Testing

X. Reliability Testing and Planning

A. Objectives—Detect Modes of Failures, Verify Failure Rate, Verify Specification Requirements, Monitor Reliability Trends, Demonstration, Qualification

B. Type of Test—Functional Tests, Environmental Tests, Reliability Life Tests, Computer Software

C. Mathematical Distributions Applied to Testing

D. Truncated Tests—Sequential Order

E. Economic Factors in Reliability Testing

XI. Data Collection, Analysis, and Reporting

A. Recording and Processing

B. Analysis

C. Corrective Action

D. Follow-up

E. Factors for Planning

XII. Mathematical Models

A. Normal and Log Normal Distribution

B. Exponential, Binomial, Poisson, Hypergeometric, and Geometric Distribution

C. Weibull Distribution

D. Gamma and Beta Distribution

E. Chi-Square, *F*, and Student's *t* Distributions

F. Propagation of Errors

G. Monte Carlo Simulation

H. Distribution Characteristics—pdf, cdf, moments, mean, variance

I. Bayes Probability Analysis

▶ 14-8 REFERENCES

Arsenhault, J. E., and Roberts, J. A. (1980), *Reliability and Maintainability of Electronic Systems,* Computer Science Press, Potomac, MD.

Barlow, R. E., and Proschan, J. (1975), *Statistical Theory of Reliability and Life Testing,* Holt, Rinehart, and Winston, New York.

Bell Communications Research (1984), "Reliability Prediction Procedures for Electronic Equipment," Bellcore Technical Advisory TA-000-2360-84-01 1P-10425.

Box, G. E. P., Hunter. J. S., and Hunter, W. G. (1978), *Statistics for Experimenters,* Wiley, New York.

Chernoff, H. (1962), "Optimal Accelerated Life Designs for Estimation," *Technometrics,* Vol. 4, No. 3, Aug.; pp. 381–408.

Dodson, G. A., and Howard, B. T. (1960), "High Stress Aging to Failure of Semiconductor Devices," Paper presented at the Seventh National Symposium on Reliability and Quality Control, Philadelphia.

Hahn, G. J., and Nelson, W. (1971), "Graphical Analysis of Incomplete Accelerated Life Test Data," *Insulation/Circuits,* September, pp. 79–84.

Holcomb, D. P., and Saperstein, B. (1979), "Analysis of Infant Mortality Data," Private communication.

Johnson, N. L., and Kotz, S. (1970), *Continuous Univariate Distributions,* Vols. 1 and 2, Houghton Mifflin, Boston.

Kalbfleisch, J. D., and Prentice, R. L. (1980), *The Statistical Analysis of Failure Time Data,* Wiley, New York.

Kielpinski, T. J., and Nelson, W. (1975), "Optimum Censored Ac-

celerated Life Tests for Normal and Lognormal Distributions," *IEEE Transactions on Reliability,* Vol. R-24, pp. 310–20.

Mann, N. R., Schafer, R. E., and Singpurwalla, N. D. (1974), *Methods for Statistical Analysis of Reliability and Life Data,* Wiley, New York.

Meeker, W. Q., and Hahn, G. J. (1977), "Asymptotically Optimum Over-stress Tests to Estimate the Survival Probability at a Condition with a Low Expected Failure Probability," *Technometrics,* Vol. 19, No. 4, Nov.; pp. 381–99.

Meeker, W. Q., and Michael, J. R. (1980), "Planning Accelerated Life Tests," Private communication.

Meeker, W. Q., and Nelson, W. (1975), "Optimum Accelerated Life Tests for the Weibull and Extreme Value Distributions," *IEEE Transactions on Reliability,* Vol. R-24, pp. 321–32.

MIL-HDBK 217 (1982), *Reliability Prediction of Electronic Equipment,* U.S. Department of Defense, Washington, D.C.

MIL-HDBK 338, *Electronic Reliability Design Handbook,* U.S. Department of Defense, Washington D.C.

MIL-STD 756B (1981), *Reliability Modeling and Prediction,* U.S. Department of Defense, Washington, D.C.

MIL-STD 781, *Reliability Testing for Engineering Development, Qualification, and Production,* U.S. Department of Defense, Washington, D.C.

MIL-STD 785, *Reliability Program for Systems and Equipment Development and Production,* U.S. Department of Defense, Washington, D.C.

MIL-STD 1543, *Reliability Program Requirements for Space and*

Launch Vehicles, U.S. Department of Defense, Washington, D.C.

MIL-STD 1629, *Procedures for Performing a Failure Mode, Effects and Criticality Analysis,* U.S. Department of Defense, Washington, D.C.

MIL-STD 1635, *Reliability Growth Testing,* U.S. Department of Defense, Washington, D.C.

MINITAB (1996), *Reference Manual, Release 11,* State College, PA.

Naval Air Systems Command (1977), NAVAIR 01-1A-32, *Reliability Engineering Handbook,* Washington, D.C.

Nelson, W. (1970), "Statistical Methods for Accelerated Life Test Data—the Inverse Power Law Model," General Electric Company R&D TIS Report TIS 71-C-011, Schenectady, NY.

Nelson, W. (1972a), "Graphical Analysis of Accelerated Life Test Data with the Inverse Power Law Model," *IEEE Transactions of Reliability,* Vol. R-21, pp. 2–11.

Nelson, W. (1972b), "Theory and Applications of Hazard Plotting for Censored Failure Data," *Technometrics,* Vol. 14, No. 4, Nov.; pp. 945–66.

Nelson, W. (1980), "Accelerated Life Testing-Step-Stress Models and Data Analysis," *IEEE Transitions of Reliability,* Vol. R-29, June; pp. 103–108.

Nelson, W. (1982), *Applied Life Data Analysis,* Wiley, New York.

Nelson, W. (1983), *ASQC Basic References in Quality Control: Statistical Techniques,* Volume 6: *How to Analyze Reliability Data,* American Society for Quality, Milwaukee, WI.

Nelson, W., and Kielpinski, T. (1976), "Theory for Optimum Accelerated Life Tests for Normal and Lognormal Life Distributions," *Technometrics,* Vol. 18, No. 1, Feb.; pp. 105–14.

Nelson, W., and Meeker, W. Q. (1978), "Theory for Optimum Accelerated Censored Life Tests for Weibull and Extreme Value Distributions," *Technometrics,* Vol. 20, No. 2, May; pp. 171–77.

O'Connor, P. D. T., Head, M. G., and Joy, M. (1983), "Reliability Predictions for Microelectronic Systems," *1983 Proceedings of the Annual Reliability and Maintainability Symposium,* IEEE, Orlando, FL.

Siuta, A. J. (1961), "A Correction Factor for Temperature Step-Stress Aging to Failure," Engineering Series on Transistors, Fourth Interim Technical Report, AT&T Bell Laboratories, Chapter 3, pp. 19–24.

Wadsworth, H. M. (1984), "Reliability Prediction Techniques," Paper Presented at Rochester ASQC Annual Technical Meeting (March).

► 14-9 PROBLEMS

1. Assume that the distribution of the lifetime of a component is exponential. If the failure rate is 0.1, what is the probability of the component surviving 5 years? If the failure rate (hazard rate) is 1.0, what is the probability of the component surviving 5 years?

2. Assume that the distribution of the lifetime of a second component is Weibull with $\beta = 0.7$. If $\lambda = 0.1$, what is the probability of this component surviving 5 years?

3. If the two components described in Problems 1 and 2 are put in series, what is the probability of this simple system surviving 2 years if $\lambda = 0.1$ for both components? What is the probability of the system surviving 2 years if $\lambda = 0.5$ for both components?

4. You are designing a simple circuit with three parts in series. The probabilities that each part fails within 5 years are as follows:

Part	Prob. of Failure
1	0.1
2	0.1
3	0.2

What is the probability of your circuit lasting 5 years?

You decide to increase the reliability of your circuit by putting Part 3 in parallel with a duplicate of Part 3. What is the probability of your new circuit lasting 5 years? Draw the reliability block diagrams (see Figure 14-7 for both systems).

5. You have two parts in parallel with one on cold standby. If each part has a probability of operating at mission time t of 0.90 and the switch has a probability of 0.99 of operating when needed, what is the probability of this system operating at mission time t?

6. If the components in Figure 14-7 all have probability of operating of 0.95 at time t, what is the system reliability at time t?

7. In a series system with ten parts, each with failure rate 0.01, what is the failure rate of the system if the parts are independent?

8. Given the following observed hazard rates and times, use the simple method described in Section 14-2.2 to estimate the parameters of a Weibull distribution:

Time t	Observed Hazard Rate
0.25	0.17
0.50	0.16

Time t	Observed Hazard Rate
0.75	0.13
1.00	0.14
1.25	0.12
1.50	0.13
1.75	0.11
2.00	0.12
2.25	0.10
2.50	0.11
2.75	0.11
3.00	0.11
3.25	0.10
3.50	0.10
3.75	0.10
4.00	0.10

Plot the observed hazard rates and the estimated Weibull hazard rate. Calculate the residuals and plot. Comment on the results.

9. Use the simple method described in Section 14-2.2 to estimate the parameters of the Weibull distribution for Nelson's generator fan data in Table 14-2. Compare your results with those Nelson obtained using hazard plotting.

10. While conducting a life test on five items the following results were obtained for $t_1 < t_2, < \cdots < t_5$:

Item 1 failed at time t_1
Item 2 failed at time t_2
Item 3 failed between time t_3 and time t_4
Items 4 and 5 did not fail and were removed from the test at time t_5.

Assume the Weibull model discussed in Section 14-2.2 and construct the likelihood function.

CHAPTER

15

ACCEPTANCE SAMPLING FOR ATTRIBUTES

Sampling refers to the observation or inspection of a portion of a population or lot for the purpose of obtaining some information. Quality control is usually concerned with what is called *acceptance sampling*. This is defined in ISO 3534-2 and its American version, ANSI/ISO/ASQ A3534-2: 2002 as "Sampling in which decisions are made to accept or not to accept a lot or other grouping of product, materials, or service, based on sample results." Acceptance sampling itself does little for the quality of the product, as this has already been fixed by the manufacturer. Instead, it is a decision-making tool by which a conclusion is reached regarding the acceptability of the lot or process. Indirectly, by eliminating or rectifying poor lots, acceptance sampling may improve the overall quality of the product. A rejected lot is frequently a signal to a manufacturer that the process should be improved. This is not to imply that acceptance sampling should ever take the place of process control. However, because it is in wide use and often necessary, it should be included in this text.

Some of the reasons for taking a sample are economic. Sampling allows an economical use of the inspection labor force. Dealing with samples rather than a complete lot often enables the inspector to evaluate more carefully the items selected in the sample. If inspection is in any way harmful to the product, it must be done on a sampling basis. Even if it is not harmful, sampling may be the only economically feasible way to inspect a large lot of material

The next four chapters will introduce a number of procedures that may be used for acceptance sampling. Before any specific procedures are presented, the consequences of sampling should be discussed. There will then be a brief review of the types of procedures available.

▶ 15-1 SAMPLING RISKS

Sampling will always incur certain risks. Because an entire lot or batch of material is not being inspected, not everything about it is known. Only the sample is known. This incurs the risk of making two types of errors in the accept–not accept decision. A lot may be rejected that should be accepted. The risk of doing this is often called the *producer's risk*.

The second error is that a lot may be accepted that should have been rejected. The risk of doing this is called the *consumer's risk*. Although sampling always incurs these two risks, they can be measured if proper statistical procedures are used.

The producer's risk is stated in terms of a probability or risk level denoted by the Greek letter alpha (α). This is the probability that a lot whose quality is at a certain specified level or better is not accepted by the sampling procedure. The consumer's risk, denoted by the Greek letter beta (β), is the probability that a lot whose quality is at or worse than a specified unacceptable level is accepted. The first, acceptable, level is called the *producer's risk quality (PRQ)* in the terminology standard ISO 3534-2: 2002. Another related term is *acceptance quality limit (AQL)*. This second term (AQL) has historically been interpreted as "acceptable quality level." However, this terminology has led to misinterpretations of the term, since the only really acceptable quality level must be zero nonconforming items. Therefore, AQL will be interpreted to mean the acceptance quality limit. This is really what is meant by the term. This term should be reserved for use in acceptance sampling systems for a continuing series of lots such as those discussed in Chapter 16. In many of these systems the producer's risk varies with the lot size. When not considering a continuing series of lots, the term PRQ will be used.

The second (unacceptable) level is called the *consumer's risk quality (CRQ)* in the terminology standard. Related terms that are sometimes found in the literature are *limiting quality level (LQL)*, *limiting quality (LQ)*, and *lot tolerance percent defective (LTPD)*. Again, these latter terms should be reserved for use in sampling systems for a continuing series of lots. The terms are not synonyms, and their meanings will be described later.

Both the PRQ and the CRQ are usually expressed as percent nonconforming or number of nonconformities per hundred items. In designing sampling plans, one goal would be to design a procedure resulting in lots whose quality is equal to or better than the PRQ being accepted $100(1 - \alpha)\%$ or more of the time. In this text, for ease of notation, the symbol p_1 will be used for the lot quality (θ) that has a probability of acceptance of $(1 - \alpha)$. Similarly, p_2 will be used to designate the value of the lot quality that has a probability of acceptance of β. Lots whose quality are equal to the CRQ or worse should be accepted no more than $100\beta\%$ of the time.

A word of caution should be stated here regarding the interpretation of the PRQ. To allow for anything other than complete (i.e., 100%) inspection of a lot, the PRQ must be greater than zero. This does not mean that there is approval of a certain fraction of the lot to be nonconforming to specifications. It means recognizing that without complete inspection of a lot, it is possible for a small number of nonconforming items to be present. If a series of lots are submitted with quality level equal to or better than the PRQ, the sampling procedure will reject only a small fraction (α) or less of them. The PRQ may be made as small as necessary, but then a larger fraction of the lot must be inspected.

If the product is of a critical nature such that a nonconforming item may cause death or serious malfunction and inspection is not destructive, complete inspection may be necessary. Even complete inspection may not be enough to completely ensure that no variant parts are present. This is because of errors of inspection. If there are a large number of pieces to be inspected, the chance for such inspection errors increases rapidly. For this reason complete inspection may actually result in more nonconforming pieces passing the inspector than sampling in which more care may be made in inspection and the risks are known.

▶ 15-2 TYPES OF SAMPLING PLANS

Like control charts, sampling plans can be classed as variables or attributes plans. This chapter, along with Chapter 16 and Chapter 18, discusses attributes plans. Chapter 17 examines variables sampling procedures. Attributes sampling is the most commonly used procedure and has the advantages discussed in connection with attributes control charts. More than one type of quality characteristic may be considered for each sample, and measurements are usually simpler to make. They may be of the go–no go variety, or they may be visual nonconformities. Attributes sampling plans require a larger sample size than variables sampling plans. Variables plans need measurement-type data, and each decision regarding lot or batch acceptance must be based on only one such measurement characteristic.

The simplest type of sampling plans are those involving a single sample. In the attributes case a sample of size n is selected from the lot, and the lot is accepted if no more than c nonconforming parts are found in the sample. Double sampling involves taking a second sample when the results of the first sample indicate marginal quality. For very good lots and very bad lots a smaller first sample will give the same protection against errors as a single sample. Lots of intermediate quality may require a second sample and thus more inspection, but there will usually be a saving in average sample size over single sampling plans. This saving may be counteracted by the increased complexity of a double sampling procedure.

The concept of double sampling may be extended to multiple sampling and item-by-item sequential sampling. In multiple sampling, decisions may be made on any number of smaller samples. Usually, multiple plans require an accept–reject decision after no more than five to seven samples. Sequential sampling requires one of three decisions to be made after each piece is inspected: Accept the lot, do not accept the lot, or inspect another piece. This process is continued until one of the first two decisions is made.

Multiple sampling results in a smaller average sample size than double sampling, and sequential sampling results in an average sample size savings over multiple plans. However, each sampling procedure is progressively harder to administer, so administrative costs must be balanced against cost savings due to decreased sample sizes.

In some cases it may not be convenient or even possible to divide the product to be inspected into lots. It may be better to inspect the product on the assembly line as it is being produced and not wait for a convenient amount to be assembled at the end of the line. Such inspection procedures are called *continuous sampling plans* and usually involve alternate periods of 100% inspection and sampling. Such sampling schemes will be discussed in Chapter 18.

Finally, variables sampling will be presented in Chapter 17. Variables sampling may require significantly smaller sample sizes than attributes sampling schemes. For this reason most variables plans are single sampling plans. An exception to this involves life tests. Since life tests are destructive in nature, the use of very small samples becomes essential. For these applications sequential procedures have been developed. Sampling in life test situations is discussed in Chapter 14.

▶ 15-3 SINGLE SAMPLING

A single sample attributes plan might call for the inspection of eighty pieces from a large lot. If two or fewer of the pieces do not conform to specifications, the lot is to be accepted;

otherwise, it is not. Thus, some decision must be made concerning the acceptability of the lot based on the results of a single sample.

This general attribute single sampling situation may be expressed as a probability problem. Suppose a simple random sample of size n is taken from a lot of size N, $n \leq N < \infty$. What is the probability of obtaining exactly x, $x \leq n$, nonconforming pieces in the sample if there are d, x, $\leq d \leq N$, nonconforming items in the lot? To answer this question, turn to the hypergeometric distribution presented in Chapter 5. The following situation is presented:

		Lot		*Sample*
	d	nonconforming items	x	nonconforming items
	$N - d$	conforming items	$n - x$	conforming items
Total	N	lot size	n	sample size

Next recall from Chapter 5 that the number of ways in which the above results may be obtained in the sample (x out of d nonconforming items and $n - x$ out of $N - d$ conforming items) is

$$\binom{d}{x}\binom{N-d}{n-x}$$

Similarly, the number of possible samples of size n obtained from a lot of N (without regard for whether they satisfy the requirement of having x conforming items) is

$$\binom{N}{n}$$

Then the probability of obtaining a sample with exactly x nonconforming items is

$$P(x) = \frac{\binom{d}{x}\binom{N-d}{n-x}}{\binom{N}{n}} \tag{15-1}$$

Equation (15-1) is the hypergeometric distribution. This would be the proper way to compute the probability of a stated number of nonconforming parts drawn randomly without replacement, as would be the case in an inspection situation, from a finite lot with a known number of nonconforming items.

To illustrate the use of this distribution, assume that material is submitted to an inspector in lots of twenty items each. The inspector is instructed to select five items from each lot in a random manner. The inspector is then to reject the lot if two or more of the items in the sample do not conform to specifications. If there is zero or one nonconforming item, the inspector is to pass the lot. Now, assume a lot is submitted that has exactly four nonconforming items. To compute the probability such a lot will be accepted, use Equation (15-1) to obtain

$$P(1) = \frac{\binom{4}{1}\binom{16}{4}}{\binom{20}{5}} = 0.470$$

$$P(0) = \frac{\binom{4}{0}\binom{16}{5}}{\binom{20}{5}} = 0.282$$

The probability that the inspector will not find sufficient nonconforming items in the sample to reject the lot is $0.470 + 0.282 = 0.752$. The probability of acceptance of such a lot is therefore 0.752.

15-3.1 The Use of the Binomial Distribution

If the lot size is large relative to the sample size, the binomial distribution may be used. In particular, this approximation is quite satisfactory for situations in which the lot size is more than ten times the sample size. The binomial distribution would be theoretically correct if each item withdrawn from the lot were inspected and returned to the lot before the next item was withdrawn. There would then be sampling with replacement. This, of course, would not be done in a practical situation. If the lot size is large relative to the sample size, regardless of which items were selected for the sample, the fraction nonconforming of the remaining lot would not be appreciably affected.

Another way of justifying the use of the binomial distribution is to consider the present lot as a subset of a larger superlot, which may be called a manufacturing process. Theoretically this superlot may be of infinite size and contain a series of lots from which the current lot was randomly selected. That is, the current lot was selected from a process for which θ is the fraction of items nonconforming to specifications.

Consider p to be the fraction nonconforming of a lot taken from a superlot or process with θ fraction nonconforming; then the probability of obtaining x nonconforming items in a sample of size n is

$$P(x) = \binom{n}{x} p^x q^{n-x} \tag{15-2}$$

which is the binomial distribution. Note that the notation is such that θ is a process fraction nonconforming, while p is the lot fraction nonconforming.

15-3.2 The Poisson Distribution

Chapter 5 discussed the Poisson distribution as a satisfactory approximation for the binomial distribution when the sample size is fairly large and the nonconforming fraction of the lot is small. In particular, if $np < 5$ and $p < 0.10$, it is a good approximation. If $p \geq 0.10$, the normal distribution is generally a better approximation to the binomial distribution than is the Poisson. The normal approximation was used for the control chart applications of Chapters 6 and 7.

Table 5-4 tabulates the probability of acceptance of lots of various sizes that have several quality levels and to which several acceptance sampling schemes have been applied. These probabilities are calculated using each of the applicable distributions, the binomial, Poisson, and hypergeometric. They illustrate the closeness of the approximations under the various sampling situations. Since the Poisson is the simplest distribution to use for probability calculations and is a satisfactory approximation in most practical situations, it is often used for attribute sampling calculations. For most of the purposes in this text the Poisson distribution will be used to compute appropriate probabilities of events while using attribute sampling plans.

15-3.3 The Operating Characteristic Curve

One of the most useful considerations of a sampling plan is its operating characteristic function. Whenever a statistical sampling plan is derived, its description is not complete until its operating characteristic function has been described. This is usually by means of a curve called the operating characteristic (OC) curve. This curve shows the probability of acceptance of lots with varying quality that might be submitted for inspection under the specified procedure.

Figure 15-1 is the OC curve for the single attribute sampling plan $n = 150$, $c = 4$. The probabilities on this curve have been calculated by using the Poisson distribution. If the lot size is large enough to be ignored, this curve describes the ability of the sampling procedure to discriminate between good and bad lots without regard to lot size. In spite of this consideration, it will be seen in later chapters that most sampling procedures do increase the sample size as the lot size increases. This is often done because it becomes increasingly difficult to get small samples from large lots that are representative enough to adequately describe the quality of the lot. This is not a statistical problem but an operational one. A very large lot will not have a truly random distribution of nonconforming pieces.

Three points are indicated on the OC curve of Figure 15-1 as p_1, p_2, and p_3. The first, p_1, is a quality level that should be accepted with a relatively high probability, referred to as producer's risk quality (PRQ) in Section 15-1. The probability that a lot

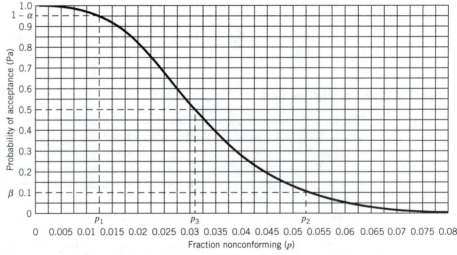

Figure 15-1 OC Curve for the Sampling Plan, $n = 150$, $c = 4$

whose fraction nonconforming is equal to p_1 will be rejected is the producer's risk (α). Recall that this value, α, is the probability of making a type I error discussed earlier in Chapter 5. The value of the OC function when $p = p_1$ is therefore $1 - \alpha$. Some authors refer to p_1 as the AQL and α as the producer's risk. However, in using AQL as an index for a sampling plan as is done in Chapter 16, there is not a fixed producer's risk associated with it. Therefore, these stipulated values will be referred to as merely p_1 and α.

The second point, p_2, is a fraction nonconforming that should be accepted with a relatively low probability. The probability that a lot whose fraction nonconforming is equal to p_2 will be accepted is β. This corresponds to the probability of making a type II error. All of these concepts were discussed earlier in this chapter and in Chapter 5. Some authors refer to p_2 as the limited quality level (LQL) or as the lot tolerance percent defective (LTPD). Again as seen in Chapter 16, the LQL is used as an index for sampling plans. When used in this manner, it does not have a fixed probability of acceptance or consumer's risk associated with it. As with p_1 and α, this point will be referred to as p_2 with probability of acceptance β.

Generally, p_1 is selected as a lot quality to be accepted most or $100(1 - \alpha)\%$ of the time, while p_2 refers to a lot quality to be rejected most or $100(1 - \beta)\%$ of the time. These two points on the OC curve, $(p_1, 1 - \alpha)$ and (p_2, β), may be used to identify or to specify the requirements for a sampling plan.

The third point, p_3, is commonly called the *indifference quality level (IQL)*. This is the lot quality for which there is a 0.50 probability of acceptance. There is an equal chance of accepting or rejecting a lot whose fraction nonconforming is equal to p_3. This point is occasionally used to specify requirements for a sampling plan, and plans making use of the IQL will be discussed later.

Many authors [e.g., Duncan (1986)] refer to two different OC curves. A type A curve is one that applies to a single finite sized lot and describes the probability of accepting a lot as a function of the lot quality. This curve would be drawn using the hypergeometric distribution. The second or type B curve applies to the series-of-lots situations and describes the frequency of lot acceptance as a function of the process average. For a single lot, as the lot size increases, the type A OC curve converges to the type B curve. Thus, the type B curve, which uses the binomial (or Poisson) distribution may be thought of as the limiting case of the type A curve. Unless otherwise indicated, type B OC curves will be used in this text.

Effect on the OC Curve of Changes in n *and* c

If the sample size is reduced, the OC curve tends to flatten out as illustrated in Figure 15-2. As can be seen by the figure, if n is reduced while the ratio between n and c is kept constant, both the producer's and consumer's risks are increased.

If the acceptance number, c, is changed without changing the sample size, the OC curve will move to the left or right without much change in curvature. This is illustrated in Figure 15-3. This figure shows that a reduction in c has the effect of increasing α while it decreases β. Of particular interest is that the curve for $c = 0$ indicates a high value of α. In other words, there is little protection for the producer when no nonconforming items are allowed in the sample. For this reason, sampling plans should allow acceptance of a lot when at least one nonconforming item appears in the sample if it is at all practical.

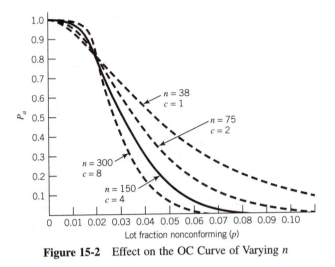

Figure 15-2 Effect on the OC Curve of Varying n

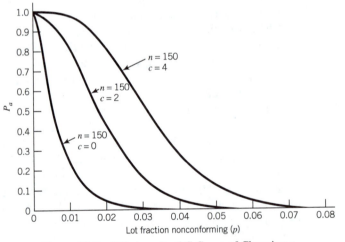

Figure 15-3 Effect on the OC Curve of Changing c

15-3.4 Rectifying Inspection Procedures

If rectifying inspection is used by an inspection department, additional characteristics of a sampling procedure may be used to describe it. Rectifying inspection is a procedure whereby a lot rejected by sampling inspection is 100% inspected. It is also assumed that this screening as well as the inspection of the sample is 100% effective and that all non-conforming items discovered at either stage are replaced by conforming items. This rectification may be done by the consumer or by the supplier, and either may be responsible for the cost.

Average Outgoing Quality

The average quality, in terms of fraction nonconforming, leaving the inspection operation, including both lots that are screened and those that are only sampled, is called the average outgoing quality (AOQ). An expression may be derived for this quite simply by recalling that a screened lot has no nonconforming items and there are none among those items making up the sample after its inspection. The remainder of the lot, for accepted lots, has fraction nonconforming, p. Therefore, the average outgoing quality is

$$AOQ = \frac{P_a p (N - n)}{N} \qquad (15\text{-}3)$$

If the lot size is large relative to the sample size, this may be approximated by

$$AOQ = P_a p \qquad (15\text{-}4)$$

Equation (15-4) indicates that the average outgoing quality for any p may be approximated by the product of the abscissa and ordinate of the operating characteristic curve.

The AOQ curve for the sampling plan $n = 150$, $c = 4$ is shown in Figure 15-4. As this illustration indicates, for extremely good lots and extremely bad lots the value of the AOQ is quite low. The AOQ rises to a maximum for some intermediate value of p, say, p_m, and falls off as the quality deteriorates further.

The maximum value of the AOQ is called the average outgoing quality limit (AOQL). This is the worst average quality that will be obtained, regardless of what lot quality is submitted for inspection. One should remember that it is an average, and any particular lot will have a quality of $p[N - n]/N$ or 0% nonconforming after the inspection process.

The AOQL may be used as a measure of a sampling inspection scheme. In fact, it will be seen later that for some situations, such as continuous sampling, it is more appropriate than the PRQ, the CRQ, or any designated points on the OC curve. The AOQL

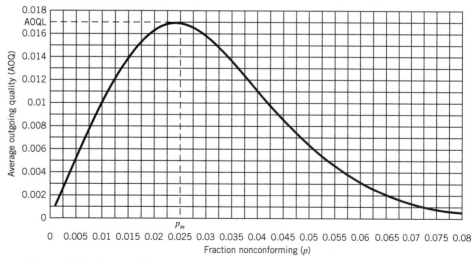

Figure 15-4   Average Outgoing Quality Curve for Single Sampling Plan, $n = 150$, $c = 4$

TABLE 15-1   Maximum Values of $(P_a)(pn)$

c	Max $P_a pn$	c	Max $P_a pn$	c	Max $P_a pn$
0	0.3679	14	9.404	28	20.11
1	0.8408	15	10.12	29	20.91
2	1.372	16	10.87	30	21.75
3	1.946	17	11.63	31	22.54
4	2.544	18	12.38	32	23.40
5	3.172	19	13.14	33	24.22
6	3.810	20	13.88	34	25.08
7	4.465	21	14.66	35	25.94
8	5.150	22	15.42	36	26.83
9	5.836	23	16.18	37	27.68
10	6.535	24	16.97	38	28.62
11	7.234	25	17.73	39	29.50
12	7.948	26	18.54	40	30.44
13	8.677	27	19.30		

Source: Reprinted with permission from Dodge and Romig, *Sampling Inspection Tables—Single and Double Sampling,* 2nd Edition, New York, Wiley, 1959.

may be calculated for any single sampling plan from Table 15-1, which shows the maximum value of $P_a pn$ for any value of the acceptance number, c, from 0 through 40. For example, Table 15-1 gives, for the plan $n = 150$, $c = 4$,

$$AOQL = \frac{\text{Max } P_a pn}{n} = \frac{2.544}{150} = 0.017$$

If the Poisson distribution is applicable, the maximum value of $P_a pn$ may be obtained from Table F of the Appendix by obtaining the maximum product of the number in the left column (np) and the value in the body of the table, the probability of c or less. This is what has been done for each value of c in Table 15-1. If an exact value of the AOQL is desired, it may be obtained from Equation (15-5):

$$AOQL = \frac{\text{Max } P_a pn}{n} \left(\frac{N - n}{N} \right) \tag{15-5}$$

For the previous example, assume that the samples are from lots of size 5000 with sampling plan $n = 150$, $c = 4$, Equation (15-5) gives

$$AOQL = \frac{2.544}{150} \left(\frac{5000 - 150}{5000} \right) = 0.0163$$

The difference between these two results depends on the relative sizes of the lot and sample.

Average Total Inspection

If rectifying inspection is used, there is one more characteristic of a sampling inspection scheme that is often considered. This is the average total inspection. This is the average

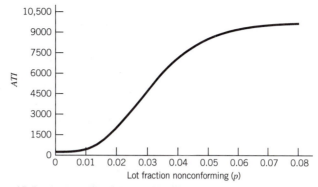

Figure 15-5 Average Total Inspection Curve for the Single Sampling Plan,
$n = 150$, $c = 4$, $N = 10,000$

number of pieces inspected, considering those lots accepted on the basis of the sample and those rejected and 100% screened. The average number of items inspected will depend on the quality of the submitted lot, since the probability of having to screen the lot depends on this quality. If $p = 0.0$, the average total inspection will be just n, the sample size. If $p = 1.00$, the average total inspection will be N, the lot size, since there is then no chance of accepting the lot without complete screening. The average total inspection for any value of p will be

$$ATI = n + (1 - P_a)(N - n) \tag{15-6}$$

where P_a is the probability the sampling inspection scheme will accept a lot whose quality is equal to p. For example, when $N = 10,000$, $n = 150$, $c = 4$, and $p = 0.04$,

$$ATI = 150 + 0.715(9850) = 7193$$

This calculation indicates that, on the average, 7193 pieces are inspected from a lot of 10,000 pieces that is 4% nonconforming. Either 150 or 10,000 pieces are inspected, depending on whether the lot is accepted or rejected. This 7193 figure is an average.

Figure 15-5 is the average total inspection curve for the sampling plan, $n = 150$, $c = 4$, for lots of 10,000 items.

It will be seen later that sampling schemes are sometimes devised that minimize the average total inspection for some specified incoming quality and satisfy constraints or other criteria such as p_2 or AOQL.

15-3.5 Derivation of a Single Sampling Plan

There are several procedures that may be used to derive a single sampling plan for attributes. Four ways to derive such a plan are

$$p_1, \alpha$$
$$p_2, \beta$$
$$\text{AOQL}$$
$$\text{ATI}$$

If any two of these are stipulated, a unique plan will be obtained. Methods for obtaining a plan that fits the first two will be presented first. This procedure would work for determining a plan whose OC curve goes through any two designated points. For example, the $p_1(1 - \alpha)$ point and the indifference quality level (IQL, 0.5), could be used.

Second, a procedure for deriving a plan that uses the second and fourth measures will be presented. The third procedure discussed will be derivation of a plan that fits designated values for the last two criteria. These last two procedures are used in the sampling plans by Dodge and Romig (1959) to be discussed in Chapter 16.

Derivation Using Two Points on the OC Curve

If two points on the OC curve are designated, a single sampling plan can be derived. Usually these two points will be $(p_1, 1 - \alpha)$ and (p_2, β). That is, designate a lot quality level to be accepted $100(1 - \alpha)\%$ of the time and a second quality level to be accepted only $100\beta\%$ of the time. One procedure makes use of Table 7-3, which includes, for acceptance numbers 0 through 15, the product of np_α, for $\alpha = 0.05, 0.10, 0.50, 0.90,$ and 0.95. Thus to find a plan with an acceptance number of 3 and an IQL of 0.05, n is found from Table 7-3.

$$n = \frac{np_{0.50}}{p_{0.50}} = \frac{3.672}{0.05} = 74$$

The plan would thus be $n = 74$, $c = 3$.

Now if it is not set in advance, it is necessary to make use of two points on the OC curve. For example, suppose a plan is needed to have $p_1 = 0.01$, $\alpha = 0.05$, $p_2 = 0.08$, and $\beta = 0.10$. To derive such a plan, divide the $np_{0.10}$ values in Table 7-3 by the corresponding $np_{0.95}$ value to get the values in the right column of Table 15-2. Since n cancels in

TABLE 15-2   Values for Single Sampling Plans

c	$np_{0.10}$	$np_{0.95}$	$np_{0.10}/np_{0.95}$
0	2.303	0.0513	44.84
1	3.890	0.355	10.96
2	5.322	0.818	6.51
3	6.681	1.366	4.89
4	7.994	1.970	4.06
5	9.274	2.613	3.55
6	10.532	3.286	3.21
7	11.771	3.981	2.96
8	12.995	4.695	2.77
9	14.206	5.426	2.62
10	15.407	6.169	2.50
11	16.598	6.924	2.40
12	17.782	7.690	2.31
13	18.958	8.464	2.24
14	20.128	9.246	2.18
15	21.292	10.035	2.12

Source: Taken, with permission, from F. E. Grubbs, "On Designing Single Sampling Inspection Plans," *Annals of Mathematical Statistics,* Vol. XX (1949), p. 256. The probabilities are based on the Poisson distribution.

the ratio $np_{0.10}/np_{0.95}$, this ratio is just p_2 divided by p_1. For this example, $p_2/p_1 = 0.08/0.01 = 8.0$. Observe in Table 15-2 that 8.0 is about halfway between the values of this ratio for $c = 1$ and $c = 2$. Therefore, consider the corresponding plans to see which is better. For $c = 1$, $np_{0.10} = 3.890$ and $np_{0.95} = 0.355$. Divide $np_{0.10}$ by $p_{0.10}$ (i.e., p_2), to get

$$n = \frac{np_{0.10}}{p_2} = \frac{3.890}{0.08} = 49$$

and divide $np_{0.95}$ by $p_{0.95}$ (i.e., p_1) to get

$$n = \frac{np_{0.95}}{p_1} = \frac{0.355}{0.01} = 36$$

Similarly, using $c = 2$,

$$n = \frac{np_{0.10}}{p_2} = \frac{5.322}{0.08} = 67$$

and

$$n = \frac{np_{0.95}}{p_1} = \frac{0.818}{0.01} = 82$$

Thus there are four possible plans:

A. $n = 49$, $c = 1$
B. $n = 36$, $c = 1$
C. $n = 67$, $c = 2$
D. $n = 82$, $c = 2$

Plans A and C have β fixed at 0.10, and plans B and D have α fixed at 0.05. To help the decision as to the choice of a sampling plan, compute α for plans A and C and β for B and D. This can be done using the Poisson approximation. For plan A, $np_1 = 49(0.01) = 0.49$, from which $P_a = P(x \leq 1) = 0.910$; therefore, $\alpha = 0.09$. For plan B, $np_2 = 36.(0.08) = 2.88$, from which $P_a = P(x \leq 1) = 0.21 = \beta$. For plan C, $np_1 = 67(0.01) = 0.67$, from which $\alpha = 1 - P(x \leq 2) = 1 - 0.970 = 0.03$. Finally, for plan D, $np_2 = 82(0.08) = 6.56$, and $\beta = P(x \leq 2) = 0.042$.

In summary, the four plans and their associated risks are as follows:

Plan	n	c	α	β
A	49	1	0.09	0.10
B	36	1	0.05	0.21
C	67	2	0.03	0.10
D	82	2	0.05	0.042

Plans C and D meet or exceed both required risks; therefore, plan C would probably be chosen, as this has the smaller sample size.

Instead of using the Poisson table to determine the sampling plan, Figure 15-6 may be used. This figure plots the probability of c or fewer nonconforming items for various acceptance numbers and values of np. To illustrate the use of this figure, refer to the previous example. For $P_a = 0.10$ and $c = 1$, $np = 3.89$ and $n = 3.89/0.08 = 49$. To get α for

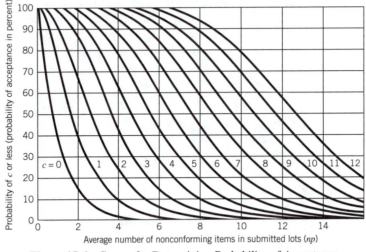

Figure 15-6 Curves for Determining Probability of Acceptance

this plan, multiply 49 by 0.01 to get 0.49. Then go up from 0.49 on the abscissa to the curve for $c = 1$ and get $\alpha = 1 - P(c \leq 1) = 1 - 0.91 = 0.09$. These are, of course, the same results derived by using the table, but the use of the curve may be somewhat quicker. However, a curve such as this may also be more difficult to read with any precision.

Sampling plans have been computed by stipulating the $(p_{0.95}, 0.95)$ and the $(p_{0.10}, 0.10)$ points on the OC curve. As was stated earlier, any other point could have been used with Figure 15-6—that is, the $(p_{0.50}, 0.50)$ point, the $(p_{0.99}, 0.99)$ point and so on. This is an additional advantage of this procedure.

Derivation of a Plan Using p_2 and ATI

To use the ATI consider a finite lot size and assume that rejected lots are screened. Furthermore, the ATI is to be minimized for a certain expected quality level, p_0. A sampling plan that uses one quality in its derivation may not give minimum ATI for some other quality level. The following example will illustrate the derivation of such a sampling plan.

Assume that lots of size 900 are being submitted for inspection. Also assume a value of p_2 of 7% and a consumer's risk (β) of 10%. A sampling plan is needed that minimizes the average total inspection when the lot quality is at a 2% nonconforming level. The computations will be illustrated using a trial-and-error procedure. Furthermore, to facilitate the computations, the Poisson approximation will be used even though for a finite lot the hypergeometric should be used. The approximation will be very close for lots of this size.

As a first approximation, use an acceptance number of zero. Table 15-2 gives a value of $np_{0.10}$ of 2.303. When this is divided by $p_{0.10} = 0.07$ a sampling plan of $n = 33$, $c = 0$ is obtained. For this plan and $p = 0.02$, $np = 33(0.02) = 0.66$. The Poisson table gives, for $np = 0.66$, the probability of acceptance, that is, $P(x = 0)$, of 0.52. Then substitute these values into Equation (15-6):

$$ATI = n + (1 - P_a)(N - n)$$
$$ATI = 33 + (0.48)(900 - 33) = 449$$

Because this result seems quite large, try a larger acceptance number. For example, try $c = 2$. The resulting computations give a sampling plan $n = 76$, $c = 2$, and $ATI = 238$. This is a considerable improvement. Now try $c = 4$ to get a plan of $n = 114$, $c = 4$, and $ATI = 184$. With $c = 6$, the plan is $n = 150$, $c = 6$, and the ATI is 176. Since this is slightly smaller than that for $n = 114$, $c = 4$, try $c = 7$. This results in the plan $n = 168$, $c = 7$, and $ATI = 184$. Since this is larger than the $c = 6$, plan, go next to $c = 5$. This gives a plan of $n = 132$, $c = 5$ with an ATI of 171, which is the smallest. These results indicate that the best plan is $n = 132$, $c = 5$. The following list contains the plans and the average total inspections for these situations and acceptance numbers 0 through 7:

c	n	ATI
0	33	449
1	56	316
2	76	238
3	95	196
4	114	184
5	132	171
6	150	176
7	168	184

As the list indicates, the ATI is fairly flat near the minimum value. However, the following indicates the ATI for the optimum plan, $n = 132$, $c = 5$, for other values of p. The plan $n = 132$, $c = 5$ is the optimum only when $p = 0.02$. When p is 4% nonconforming, the optimum plan would be $n = 254$, $c = 12$, giving an ATI of 390. The plan being used gives an ATI for $p = 4\%$ of 470. On the average, inspection of 21% more items would be needed in using the proposed plan than if the correct plan had been selected.

p	ATI
0.005	132
0.01	134
0.02	171
0.03	296
0.04	470
0.05	627
0.06	746

Derivation of a Plan Using AOQL and ATI

Again assume that screening of rejected lots is required and that product arrives in lots of 900 items each. Now the interest is in maintaining the AOQL at, for example, 4% nonconforming. In addition, determine a sampling plan for which the ATI is a minimum when the process average is 2%. Equation (15-3) gave the expression for AOQ as

$$AOQ = \frac{P_a p(N - n)}{N} \qquad (15\text{-}7)$$

and

$$AOQL = \frac{P_a p_m(N - n)}{N} \qquad (15\text{-}8)$$

where p_m is the process average for which the AOQ is a maximum. If now the value for the AOQL is given, the values of n and c may be obtained, since P_a and p_m depend on these values. Using a trial-and-error procedure, c can be designated and Equation (15-8) can be solved for n. Then the ATI for that plan at the designated process average is determined. Try a different c until the minimum ATI is found.

The simplest procedure to solve Equation (15-8) for n is to use Table 15-1. Thus, if the values in Table 15-1 are designated as y, Equation (15-8) can be written as

$$AOQL = \frac{y}{n}\left(\frac{N - n}{N}\right) \tag{15-9}$$

Rearranging Equation (15-9),

$$n = \frac{yN}{(AOQL)N + y} \tag{15-10}$$

Now, to illustrate the procedure, continue with the example. For $c = 0$, Equation (15-10) gives

$$n = \frac{(0.3679)900}{(0.04)(000) + 0.3679} = 9$$

and for the plan $n = 9$, $c = 0$, the ATI at $p = 0.02$ is

$$ATI = 9 + (1 - 0.835)(900 - 9) = 156$$

Now jump to $c = 2$, to get the sampling plan $n = 33$, $c = 2$, and the ATI is 59. For $c = 4$ the plan is $n = 59$, $c = 4$ and the ATI is 65. Since this is an increase, try $c = 3$ to get $n = 46$ and ATI = 58. The results of these calculations are as follows:

c	n	ATI
0	9	156
2	33	59
3	46	58
4	59	65
5	73	76

As indicated, the desired plan will be $n = 46$, $c = 3$. The Poisson approximation has been used to obtain all these results. If the hypergeometric had been used, the results would have been a little different. The sampling plans of Dodge and Romig (1959) contain single and double plans that minimize the ATI for a designated process average and stated p_2 (designated LTPD) or AOQL. Readers are referred to these plans if they desire to use plans that correspond to these situations. A discussion of these plans is in Chapter 16.

▶ **15-4 DOUBLE SAMPLING PLANS**

Double sampling plans are characterized by two sample sizes along with two sets of acceptance and rejection numbers. The two sample sizes may or may not be equal, but in most applications the second sample size is either equal to the first or twice the first. The procedure calls for a sample of size n_1 to be taken. If the number of nonconforming items is equal to or less than the first acceptance number, c_1, the lot is accepted. If the number of nonconforming items is equal to or greater than the first rejection number, r_1, the lot is rejected. If the number of nonconforming items is between c_1 and r_1, a second sample of size n_2 is taken. Then, if the number of nonconforming items from the total $n_1 + n_2$ items is less than or equal to c_2, the acceptance number for the combined samples, the lot is accepted. If there are more than c_2 items nonconforming, the lot is rejected. That is, $r_2 = c_2 + 1$.

Usually, if the second rejection number, r_2, is reached during inspection of the second sample, inspection is curtailed. Inspection of the complete first sample is often required to provide a lot-by-lot quality history. If curtailing on the rejection number for the second sample is done, double sampling will give a lower average sample size, ASN, for any incoming quality than single plans with equivalent OC curves. If curtailing is not done, there may be some lot qualities for which the ASN for doubling sampling is larger than that for the equivalent single plan, but for most quality levels, it will still be lower.

15-4.1 OC Curves for Double Attribute Plans

The OC curve for double plans is more difficult to compute than that for single plans. The probability of acceptance is the probability of acceptance on the first sample plus the conditional probability of acceptance on the second, given that a second sample was taken. To explain this, use as an example the following double plan:

$$n_1 = 80 \qquad c_1 = 2 \qquad r_1 = 5$$
$$n_2 = 80 \qquad c_2 = 6 \qquad r_2 = 7$$

Recall that the second accept–reject numbers refer to the entire 160 pieces, not just the second 80.

To simplify the calculations, again use the Poisson approximation to compute the probabilities needed for the OC curve. Start by computing the value of the OC curve for the point $p = 0.03$. When $p = 0.03$, the probability of acceptance by the first sample will be the probability of two or fewer nonconforming pieces in a sample of eighty. For $p = 0.03$, $n_1 p = 2.40$, and, from the Poisson table, the probability of two or fewer nonconforming pieces is 0.570. Curve A in Figure 15-7 is the curve consisting of the acceptance probabilities for the first sample. Curve B describes the probability of not rejecting the lot on the first sample. The difference between the two curves is the probability of taking a second sample. For $p = 0.03$, the probability of not rejecting on the first sample is the probability of four or fewer nonconforming items. For $n_1 p = 80(0.03) = 2.40$, the Poisson table indicates the probability to be 0.904. Thus, for a process average of $p = 0.03$, the probability of taking a second sample, P_2, is $0.904 - 0.570 = 0.334$.

Now, to obtain the OC curve for the double plan, the probability of acceptance on the second sample must be obtained. The lot may be accepted on the second sample if there are three on the first and three or fewer on the second or if there are four on the first and two or fewer on the second. These are the only possible ways to do it. The probabilities of these two events when $p = 0.03$ are again computed by using the Poisson approximation. Since $n_2 p = n_1 p = 2.40$ as before, these values may be easily obtained from the Poisson table. If P_a is the probability of acceptance on the ith sample and x_i is the number of nonconforming pieces in the ith sample,

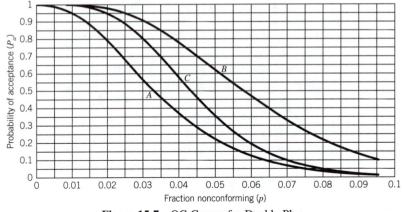

Figure 15-7   OC Curves for Double Plan

$$P_{a_2} = P(x_1 = 3)P(x_2 \le 3) + P(x_1 = 4)P(x_2 \le 2)$$
$$= (0.779 - 0.570)(0.779) + (0.904 - 0.779)(0.570)$$
$$= (0.209)(0.779) + (0.125)(0.570)$$
$$= 0.234$$

and the probability of acceptance for the double plan is

$$P_a = P_{a_1} + P_{a_2} = 0.570 + 0.234 = 0.804$$

This is plotted as curve C in Figure 15-7, which is the final OC curve. The probability of acceptance for the double sampling plan (curve C on Figure 15-7) may be written as

$$P_a = P(x_1 \le c_1) + P(x_1 = c_1 + 1)P(x_2 \le c_2 - x_1) + P(x_1 = c_1 + 2)P(x_2 \le c_2 - x_1)$$
$$+ \cdots + P(x_1 = r_1 - 1)P(x_2 \le c_2 - x_1)$$

$$= P(x_1 \le c_1) + \sum_{i=c_1+1}^{r_1-1} P(x_1 = i)P(x_2 \le c_2 - i) \tag{15-11}$$

15-4.2 ASN Curve for Double Attribute Plans

The first sample is always inspected, and the second sample is inspected when a decision is not made on the first. That is, inspect n_1 with probability P_1 or otherwise inspect $n_1 + n_2$ items. A decision can be made on the basis of the first sample whenever x_1, the number of nonconforming pieces in the first sample, is less than or equal to c_1 or is greater than or equal to r_1. That is, P_1, the probability of making a decision on the basis of the first sample, is

$$P_1 = P_{a_1} + P_{r_1} = P(x_1 \le c_1) + P(x_1 \ge r_1) \tag{15-12}$$

The average sample number will therefore be

$$ASN = n_1 + n_2(1 - P_1) = n_1 + n_2 P_2 \tag{15-13}$$

where

$$P_2 = 1 - P_1$$

For our example, $n_1 = n_2 = 80$, $c_1 = 2$, $c_2 = 6$, $r_1 = 5$, $r_2 = 7$, and $p = 0.03$, gives $n_1p = 2.40$. Using the Poisson distribution, obtain

$$P_1 = P(x_1 \leq 2) + P(x_1 \geq r_1) = P(x_1 \leq 2) + [1 - P(x_1 \leq r_1 - 1)]$$
$$P_1 = 0.570 + (1 - 0.904) = 0.666$$
$$P_2 = 1 - P_1 = 0.334$$
$$ASN = 80 + 80(0.334) = 107$$

As was mentioned earlier, inspection is usually curtailed and the lot is rejected as soon as the rejection number for the second sample, r_2, is reached. If this is done, the ASN will be smaller than that computed by Equation (15-13). Burr (1957) developed the following expression for the ASN for curtailment on r_2:

$$ASN = n_1 + \sum_{i=c_1+1}^{r_1-1} P(x_1 = i)[n_2P(x_2 \leq c_2 - i) + \frac{r_2 - i}{p}P(x_3 \geq r_2 - i + 1)] \qquad (15\text{-}14)$$

where

$n_1 = $ size of first sample

$n_2 = $ size of second sample

$r_1 = $ rejection number for first sample

$c_1 = $ acceptance number for first sample

$c_2 = $ acceptance number for combined samples

$r_2 = $ rejection number for combined samples

$x_1 = $ number of nonconforming items in a sample of size n_1

$x_2 = $ number of nonconforming items in a sample of size n_2

$x_3 = $ number of nonconforming items in a sample of size $n_2 + 1$

Table 15-3 illustrates the computations needed for evaluation of the ASN using Equation (15-14). For this illustration again consider the sampling plan, $n_1 = 80$, $n_2 = 80$, $c_1 = 2$, $c_2 = 6$, $r_1 = 5$, $r_2 = 7$, and let $p = 0.01, 0.03, 0.05$. From Table 15-3, for $p = 0.01$,

$$ASN(0.01) = 80 + 0.0383[80(0.991) + 400(0.00150)]$$
$$+ 0.00767[80(0.953) + 300(0.00942)]$$
$$= 80 + 3.06 + 0.61 = 83.7$$

TABLE 15-3 Computations of ASN for Double Sampling with Curtailed Inspection

p	i	$c_2 - i$	$P(x_1 = i)$	$P(x_2 \leq c_2 - i)$	$P(x_3 \geq r_2 - i + 1)$	$\dfrac{r_2 - i}{p}$
0.01	3	3	0.0383	0.991	0.00150	400.00
0.01	4	2	0.00767	0.953	0.00942	300.00
0.03	3	3	0.209	0.779	0.0998	133.33
0.03	4	2	0.125	0.570	0.228	100.00
0.05	3	3	0.195	0.433	0.381	80.00
0.05	4	2	0.195	0.238	0.576	60.00

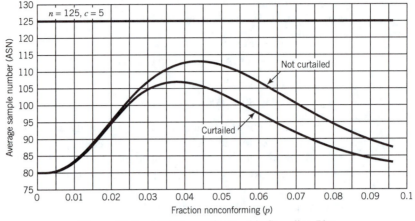

Figure 15-8 ASN Curves for Double Sampling Plan

Similarly, for $p = 0.03$ and $p = 0.05$

$$ASN(0.03) = 80 + 0.209[80(0.779) + 133.33(0.0998)]$$
$$+ 0.125[80(0.570) + 100(0.228)]$$
$$= 80 + 15.81 + 8.55 = 104.4$$
$$ASN(0.05) = 80 + 0.195[80(0.433) + 80(0.381)]$$
$$+ 0.195[80(0.238) + 60(0.576)]$$
$$= 80 + 12.70 + 10.45 = 103.2$$

The two ASN curves for this plan, along with that for a single sampling plan with approximately the same operating characteristic curve, are plotted in Figure 15-8. It will be observed that the ASN for the curtailed procedure is consistently less than that of the noncurtailed plan except where decision on the first sample is virtually certain. Both procedures result in an ASN everywhere less than that for the single sampling procedure.

15-4.3 Derivation of a Double Sampling Plan

A procedure will be discussed next that is useful for the derivation of a double sampling attributes plan. In addition to the choice of p_1, p_2, α, and β needed for derivation of a single sampling attributes plan, the relationship between the two sample sizes and acceptance numbers must be decided in advance. Table 15-4 is adapted from a similar table by Schilling and Johnson (1980). This table contains matched single, double, and multiple plans based on the ratio of $p_{0.10}$ to $p_{0.95}$. The double plans are restricted to the equal sample size requirement.

An example may be used to illustrate the use of Table 15-4. Suppose there is a desire to determine a double plan for which $n_1 = n_2$ and for which the probability of acceptance at $p_1 = 0.02$ is 0.95 and the probability of acceptance at $p_2 = 0.0725$ is 0.10. The ratio R in Table 15-4 is $n_1 p_{0.10}/n_1 p_{0.95}$ or $p_{0.10}/p_{0.95}$. For this example,

$$R = \frac{p_{0.10}}{p_{0.95}} = \frac{0.0725}{0.02} = 3.625$$

TABLE 15-4 Values for Construction of Single, Double, and Multiple Sampling Plans ($n_1 = n_2 = \cdots = n_K$)

Plan	$R = \dfrac{p_2}{p_1}$	Accept–Reject		$P_a = 0.95$	$P_a = 0.50$	$P_a = 0.10$
0S	44.89	Ac = 0	np	0.0513	0.693	2.303
		Re = 1				
0D	32.66	Ac = # 1	np	0.0501	0.573	1.636
		Re = 1 2	ASN/n_1	1.951	1.564	1.195
0M	33.25	Ac = # # 0 0 1 2 3	np	0.0252	0.294	0.838
		Re = 1 1 2 2 3 4 4	ASN/n_1	2.973	2.538	1.732
1S	10.958	Ac = 1	np	0.355	1.678	3.890
		Re = 2				
1D	12.029	Ac = 0 1	np	0.207	1.006	2.490
		Re = 2 2	ASN/n_1	1.168	1.368	1.206
1M	8.903	Ac = # # 0 0 1 1 2	np	0.103	0.416	0.917
		Re = 2 2 2 3 3 3 3	ASN/n_1	3.501	3.640	2.601
2S	6.506	Ac = 2	np	0.818	2.674	5.322
		Re = 3				
2D	5.357	Ac = 0 3	np	0.635	1.816	3.402
		Re = 3 4	ASN/n_1	1.443	1.564	1.306
2M	6.244	Ac = # 0 0 1 2 3 4	np	0.217	0.683	1.355
		Re = 2 3 3 4 4 5 5	ASN/n_1	2.789	3.165	2.261
3S	4.891	Ac = 3	np	1.366	3.672	6.681
		Re = 4				
3D	4.398	Ac = 1 4	np	1.000	2.465	4.398
		Re = 4 5	ASN/n_1	1.245	1.470	1.293
3M	4.672	Ac = # 0 1 2 3 4 6	np	0.348	0.910	1.626
		Re = 3 3 4 5 6 6 7	ASN/n_1	2.820	3.288	2.450
4S	4.058	Ac = 4	np	1.970	4.671	7.994
		Re = 5				
4D	4.102	Ac = 3 5	np	1.633	3.789	6.699
		Re = 6 6	ASN/n_1	1.077	1.341	1.242
4M	4.814	Ac = # 1 2 3 4 5 6	np	0.440	1.141	2.118
		Re = 3 4 4 6 6 7 7	ASN/n_1	2.300	2.618	2.021
5S	3.550	Ac = 5	np	2.613	5.670	9.275
		Re = 6				
5D	3.547	Ac = 2 6	np	1.630	3.490	5.781
		Re = 5 7	ASN/n_1	1.199	1.405	1.243
5M	3.243	Ac = # 1 2 3 5 7 9	np	0.700	1.410	2.270
		Re = 4 5 6 7 8 9 10	ASN/n_1	2.906	3.516	2.677
7S	2.957	Ac = 7	np	3.981	7.669	11.771
		Re = 8				
7D	2.951	Ac = 3 8	np	2.427	4.599	7.162
		Re = 7 9	ASN/n_1	1.215	1.492	1.352
7M	2.892	Ac = 0 1 3 5 7 10 13	np	1.023	1.921	2.959
		Re = 4 6 8 10 11 12 14	ASN/n_1	2.586	3.325	2.397

Table 15-4 indicates that plan 5D has an R of 3.547. This is the closest value to the prescribed R of 3.625; therefore, plan 5D will be used.

Table 15-4 gives the acceptance and rejection numbers. The sample sizes may be obtained by dividing the values of np in Table 15-4 by the stipulated value of p. Thus, to maintain the $p_{0.95}$ point, divide the $np_{0.95}$ by $p_{0.95}$. For this example this would be

$$n_1 = n_2 = \frac{1.630}{0.02} = 82$$

The sampling plan, holding the $p_{0.95}$ point, would be

$$n_1 = 82, \quad c_1 = 2, \quad r_1 = 5$$
$$n_2 = 82, \quad c_2 = 6, \quad r_2 = 7$$

Similarly, for $p_{0.10}$,

$$n_1 = n_2 \frac{np_{0.10}}{p_{0.10}} = \frac{5.781}{0.0725} = 80$$

The double sampling plan would then be, for the $p_{0.10}$ point,

$$n_1 = 80, \quad c_1 = 2, \quad r_1 = 5$$
$$n_2 = 80, \quad c_2 = 6, \quad r_2 = 7$$

The ASN curve and the OC curve may also be obtained from Table 15-4. Points on the OC curve may be obtained by dividing the values of np by n_1. Therefore, for the $p_{0.10}$ plan,

P_a	np	p
0.95	1.630	0.020
0.50	3.490	0.044
0.10	5.781	0.072

The plot of these probabilities is shown as curve C in Figure 15-7, which was the OC curve for this plan.

The ASN curve may also be obtained from Table 15-4. In this table, immediately below the np values are the values of the ASN/n_1. Thus, the ASN figures corresponding to the points on the OC curve above may be obtained by multiplying these values by n_1 (80 in the example).

p	ASN/n_1	ASN
0.020	1.199	95.9
0.044	1.405	112.4
0.072	1.243	99.4

These values of ASN are computed by assuming that the second sample is completely inspected.

As was discussed previously, if inspection of the second sample is curtailed, when the rejection number is reached, the ASN will be lower than that indicated in the above table. This ASN curve is shown as the curve labeled "Not curtailed" in Figure 15-8. It may be noted that a single sampling plan with approximately the same OC curve requires a sample size of 125 items.

A table similar to Table 15-4 but with $n_2 = 2n_1$ may be found on page 193 of Duncan (1986). ANSI/ASQC Z1.4 (1993) and its predecessor, MIL-STD 105E (1989), along with its international version, ISO 2859-1 (1999), which will be discussed in the next chapter, contain tables of single, double, and multiple sampling plans indexed by AQL and lot size. The Dodge and Romig (1959) tables contain single and double plans indexed by LQL, designated as LTPD, and AOQL. OC curves are presented for all of these plans.

▶ 15-5 SEQUENTIAL SAMPLING PLANS

It was demonstrated in Section 15-4 that by using a double sampling plan with the same protection as a single sampling plan, as evidenced by the OC curve, the total number of items that must be inspected on the average will be reduced (i.e., the ASN). The reason for this saving is that very good quality lots and very poor quality lots are disposed of with a smaller sample. Lots with marginal quality may require both samples and therefore more inspection. Even for marginal lots, there will be savings on inspection if sampling is curtailed when the rejection number is reached on the second sample. Extending this concept to more than two samples will now be considered.

First examine the ultimate concept of making one of three decisions based on the cumulative results following the inspection of each individual sample item. This procedure is called item-by-item sequential sampling or simply sequential sampling.

a. The lot is to be rejected.

b. The lot is to be accepted.

c. Inspect one more item.

The inspection will be continued until either decision a or b is made. Wald and Wolfowitz (1948) have shown that no other attributes sampling plan whose OC curve passes through two points that are the same as those for the sequential plan will have a smaller ASN at those two points. Thus, as far as ASN goes, this procedure would be the best that can be obtained. Of course, other considerations must also be weighed. Even though fewer pieces may be inspected, additional administrative costs may be incurred with such a procedure that might far outweigh the sample size advantage.

For this reason a decision may be made on the basis of a small group of sample items rather than on a single item. This would be a compromise between double and sequential sampling. The result is an increase in the ASN over sequential sampling but a reduction in the administrative complexity and thus the total cost of the procedure. Such a procedure might be called a *group sequential plan* or, more typically, a *multiple sampling plan*.

15-5.1 Theory of Sequential Sampling

There have been two principal approaches to sequential sampling. The first was developed by Wald when he was a member of the Statistical Research Group at Columbia University during World War II. The procedure and tables developed by Wald and his coworkers were considered so important to the U.S. war effort that they were classified until 1945 when the war ended. Then they were published as a series of pamphlets [Statistical Research Group (1945a, 1945b)] and later in a book by Wald (1947). The second approach was developed by Barnard in England at about the same time [Barnard (1946)]. In the United States, Wald's approach is the one that is almost always used and will be the one used in this text. The two procedures are essentially equivalent. In the Barnard approach, merits and demerits are given when the items are found to be good or bad. The score of these merits is kept, and when certain critical scores are reached, the lot is rejected or accepted. In this chapter only the attributes sampling (binomial) situation will be covered. Sequential sampling by variables was introduced in Chapter 14.

The basic concept in Wald's approach to sequential sampling is the use of the *sequential probability ratio* (*SPR*), which is the ratio of the probability of a particular outcome in terms of number of items sampled and number of nonconforming items observed under hypothesis H_1 to that under H_0, where H_1 and H_0 are as follows:

$$H_0: p = p_1$$
$$H_1: p = p_2 > p_1$$

p_1 is the quality for which the probability of acceptance is $1 - \alpha$, and p_2 is the quality for which the probability of acceptance is β. Both α and β are small, and thus p_1, α, p_2, and β describe two points on the OC curve. If p_1 and p_2 are the PRQ and CRQ, as described in Section 15-1, α and β would be the producer's risk and consumer's risk, respectively.

In terms of the fraction of a lot that is nonconforming, this ratio would be, using the binomial distribution,

$$SPR = \frac{Kp_2^d(1 - p_2)^{n-d}}{Kp_1^d(1 - p_1)^{n-d}} = \frac{p_2^d(1 - p_2)^{n-d}}{p_1^d(1 - p_1)^{n-d}} \tag{15-15}$$

where

n = number of sample items observed

d = number of nonconforming items observed

K = number of ways of getting to the result (n, d)

$$K \le \binom{n}{d}$$

The SPR is computed after inspection of each item until the result is such that it is greater than or equal to $A = (1 - \beta)/\alpha$ or less than or equal to $B = \beta/(1 - \alpha)$. In the first case the lot is rejected; in the second it is accepted.

Graphically, this result may be shown as in Figure 15-9, which depicts two parallel straight lines each with slope s and intercepts $-h_1$ and h_2. The region below the lower decision line is the accept region, while that above the upper decision line is the reject region. No decision is made as long as the results remain between the two lines. Sampling would start at $n = 0$ and $d = 0$. As long as no nonconforming items are observed, continue along the n axis. Each time a nonconforming item is observed, move to the next higher value of d. In Figure 15-9, there is a need to have the first thirty-nine items conforming to specifications in order to accept the lot at the earliest time. If the first two pieces inspected were nonconforming, the lot would be rejected.

To introduce this procedure further, develop an item-by-item sequential sampling procedure that would have a 95% chance of accepting a lot for which $p = 0.02$ and a

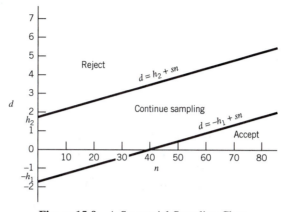

Figure 15-9 A Sequential Sampling Chart

10% chance of accepting a lot for which $p = 0.08$. For any pair of values (n, d) the SPR will be

$$SPR = \frac{(0.08)^d (0.92)^{n-d}}{(0.02)^d (0.98)^{n-d}}$$

Now, setting the SPR equal, first to A, the rejection value, and second to B, the acceptance value, gives Equations (15-16) and (15-17), respectively:

$$SPR = A = \frac{1 - \beta}{\alpha} \qquad (15\text{-}16)$$

$$SPR = B = \frac{\beta}{1 - \alpha} \qquad (15\text{-}17)$$

These equations may be solved by taking logarithms of both sides to give, after some simplification,

$$\text{for rejection:} \quad d = h_2 + sn \qquad (15\text{-}18)$$

and

$$\text{for acceptance:} \quad d = -h_1 + sn \qquad (15\text{-}19)$$

where

$$h_1 = \frac{b}{v_1 + v_2}$$

$$h_2 = \frac{a}{v_1 + v_2}$$

$$s = \frac{v_2}{v_1 + v_2}$$

$$a = \log\left(\frac{1 - \beta}{\alpha}\right)$$

$$b = \log\left(\frac{1-\alpha}{\beta}\right)$$

$$\nu_1 = \log\left(\frac{p_2}{p_1}\right)$$

$$\nu_2 = \log\left(\frac{1-p_1}{1-p_2}\right)$$

Equations (15-18) and (15-19) are the equations for the reject and accept lines, respectively, as shown in Figure 15-9. It does not matter what base is used for the logarithms, since the base would cancel out.

For the example, using natural logarithms (base e),

$$\nu_1 = \log\left(\frac{p_2}{p_1}\right) = \log\left(\frac{0.08}{0.02}\right) = 1.3863$$

$$\nu_2 = \log\left(\frac{1-p_1}{1-p_2}\right) = \log\left(\frac{0.98}{0.92}\right) = 0.0632$$

$$a = \log\left(\frac{1-\beta}{\alpha}\right) = \log\left(\frac{0.90}{0.05}\right) = 2.8904$$

$$b = \log\left(\frac{1-\alpha}{\beta}\right) = \log\left(\frac{0.95}{0.10}\right) = 2.2513$$

$$s = \frac{\nu_2}{\nu_1 + \nu_2} = \frac{0.0632}{1.3863 + 0.0632} = 0.0436$$

$$h_1 = \frac{b}{\nu_1 + \nu_2} = \frac{2.2513}{1.4495} = 1.5532$$

$$h_2 = \frac{a}{\nu_1 + \nu_2} = \frac{2.8904}{1.4495} = 1.9941$$

The procedure is therefore as follows:

1. Reject the lot when the results pass above the line

$$d = 1.9941 + 0.0436n$$

2. Accept the lot when the results pass below the line

$$d = -1.5532 + 0.0436n$$

3. Continue inspecting as long as the results are between these two lines.

Graphically, this procedure is shown in Figure 15-10.

Now suppose inspecting is started, and the twenty-third and forty-second pieces inspected were found to be nonconforming. If no more nonconforming items were observed the lot would be accepted after the eighty-sixth piece as shown by the solid line in Figure 15-10. If the sixtieth, sixty-fifth, seventy-second, and eightieth pieces were also found to be nonconforming as shown by the broken line on the figure, the lot would be rejected after the eightieth item is inspected.

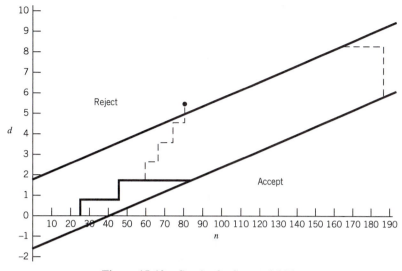

Figure 15-10 Graph of a Sequential Plan

It may be more convenient to construct a table for the use of the inspector rather than use the graphical procedure discussed here. To do this, acceptance and rejection numbers for each n must be determined. For example, the previously developed plan would not allow acceptance until thirty-six items have been inspected with none found to be nonconforming. This value is determined by solving the following two equations simultaneously:

$$d = -1.5532 + 0.0436n$$
$$d = 0$$

Similarly, the first point at which the acceptance decision may be made with one nonconforming part is found by solving the following two equations simultaneously:

$$d = -1.5532 + 0.0436n$$
$$d = 1$$

This gives $n = 59$. The acceptance number for all n from 36 to 58 will thus be 0. From 59 to 82 it will be 1. Of course, if no nonconforming items were found after inspection of thirty-six items, inspection would stop and therefore never get to the n values of 37 to 58.

Similar concepts may be used to determine the rejection numbers. The rejection line equation may be considered with the line $d = n$. That is, each unit inspected is nonconforming. The lines $d = 1.9941 + 0.0436n$ and $d = n$ intersect at $n = 2.09$. Therefore, the earliest that rejection may be made is with $n = 3$ and $d = 3$. Now solve the lines $d = 3$ and $d = 1.9941 + 0.0436n$ simultaneously to get $n = 23.1$. If the third nonconforming item is observed anywhere between the third and the twenty-third item inspected inclusive, reject the lot, but if the twenty-fourth item was the third nonconforming item the lot would not be rejected, but sampling would continue. The rejection number for n from 3 to 23, inclusive, is 3, while that for $n = 24$ to 46 would be 4. By continuing in this manner, a table similar to Table 15-5 may be developed.

TABLE 15-5   Sequential Sampling Table

n	Ac	Re	n	Ac	Re
1	*	*	⋮	⋮	⋮
2	*	*	104	2	7
3	*	3	105	3	7
⋮	⋮	⋮	⋮	⋮	⋮
23	*	3	114	3	7
24	*	4	115	3	8
⋮	⋮	⋮	⋮	⋮	⋮
35	*	4	127	3	8
36	0	4	128	4	8
⋮	⋮	⋮	⋮	⋮	⋮
45	0	4	137	4	8
46	0	5	138	4	9
⋮	⋮	⋮	⋮	⋮	⋮
58	0	5	150	4	9
59	1	5	151	5	9
⋮	⋮	⋮	⋮	⋮	⋮
68	1	5	160	5	9
69	1	6	161	5	10
⋮	⋮	⋮	⋮	⋮	⋮
81	1	6	173	5	10
82	2	6	174	6	10
⋮	⋮	⋮	⋮	⋮	⋮
91	2	6	183	6	10
92	2	7	184	6	11
			⋮	⋮	⋮

15-5.2 Truncation

Theoretically, a sequential plan could require inspection of a very large number of sample items. To guard against such an unlikely event, the procedure may be truncated at some large value of n. Wald (1947, pp. 104–105), suggested that this be done for a value of n equal to two and one-half times the ASN for a fraction nonconforming value equal to the slope, s. As will be shown presently, the ASN for $p = s$ is $h_1/h_2/s(1 - s)$. For this example this gives

$$ASN(s) = \frac{(1.5532)(1.9941)}{(0.0436)(0.9564)} = 74.3$$

Thus, the truncation number would be 2.5(74.3) or 186.

At $n = 186$ the acceptance number is 6, as indicated in Table 15-5, and the rejection number is 11. The average of these two numbers is 8.5. This means that if there are nine or more nonconforming pieces after 186 have been inspected, the lot would be rejected. If there are eight or fewer, it would be accepted. This would change Figure 15-10 and Table 15-5. To Figure 15-10 a horizontal line would be added connecting the rejection line and the point $n = 186$, $d = 8.5$. A vertical line would also be

TABLE 15-6 Sequential Sampling Table with Truncation at $n = 186$

n	Ac	Re
150	4	9
151	5	9
⋮	⋮	⋮
173	5	9
174	6	9
⋮	⋮	⋮
185	6	9
186	8	9

TABLE 15-7 Sequential Sampling Table with Truncation at $n = 100$

n	Ac	Re
68	1	5
69	1	5
⋮	⋮	⋮
81	1	5
82	2	5
⋮	⋮	⋮
99	2	5
100	4	5

added connecting the point $n = 186$, $d = 8.5$ with the acceptance line. Both lines are shown in Figure 15-10 as dashed lines. The effect of the truncation on Table 15-5 is that for $n \geq 161$ the rejection number remains at 9, and at $n = 186$ the acceptance number becomes 8. That is, Table 15-5 from $n = 150$ to $n = 186$ becomes Table 15-6.

Under this procedure the largest sample size is $n = 186$. It is of interest to note that a single sampling plan whose OC curve passes through the same two points is $n = 100$, $c = 4$. Some authors recommend truncating at the corresponding single sample size rather than the more conservative value recommended by Wald. If truncation had been at $n = 100$, the value $d = 4.5$ would be obtained as the average of 2 and 7. Thus Table 15-5 from $n = 68$ on would become Table 15-7.

15-5.3 Average Sample Number

The average sample number depends on the value of p, the fraction nonconforming in the lot. When p is very low or very high, it will have a small ASN. The maximum will occur at about $p = s$. In particular, when p is equal to 0, the ASN will be equal to the value of n at which the accept line crosses the n axis; that is, it is the intersection of lines $d = 0$ and the accept line. This is h_1/s. Similarly, if $p = 1.0$, the ASN will be the value of n at the intersection of the reject line and the line $d = n$. This is $h_2/(1 - s)$. For these and other values of p, the ASN is given by Equation (15-20):

$$ASN = \begin{cases} \dfrac{h_1}{s}, & p = 0.0 \\[2mm] \dfrac{(1 - \alpha)h_1 - \alpha h_2}{s - p_1}, & p = p_1 \\[2mm] \dfrac{h_1 h_2}{s(1 - s)}, & p = s \\[2mm] \dfrac{(1 - \beta)h_2 - \beta h_1}{p_2 - s}, & p = p_2 \\[2mm] \dfrac{h_2}{1 - s}, & p = 1.0 \end{cases} \qquad (15\text{-}20)$$

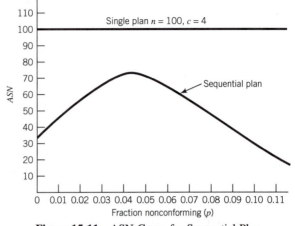

Figure 15-11 ASN Curve for Sequential Plan

The ASN values given by Equation (15-20) should be enough to draw an ASN curve. If more points are necessary, Wald (1947, p. 53) gives a general expression for the ASN as

$$ASN = \frac{P_a \log\left(\dfrac{\beta}{1-\alpha}\right) + (1 - P_a) \log\left(\dfrac{1-\beta}{\alpha}\right)}{p \log\left(\dfrac{p_2}{p_1}\right) + (1 - p) \log\left(\dfrac{1-p_2}{1-p_1}\right)} \tag{15-21}$$

where p and P_a refer to the two coordinates of the OC curve for any specific point.

The ASN curve for this example is computed as follows:

p	ASN
0.0	36.6
0.02	58.3
0.0436	74.3
0.08	45.0
1.0	2.1

This curve is shown in Figure 15-11. For comparison purposes the corresponding single sampling plan, $n = 100$, $c = 4$, is also shown in Figure 15-11. ASN for a single plan is, of course, constant at $ASN = n$.

15-5.4 Operating Characteristic Curve

The OC curve for a sequential plan may be drawn from the two points $(p_1, 1 - \alpha)$ and (p_2, β), along with an intermediate point such as $p = s$. For this latter point, Wald found that $P_a = h_2/(h_1 + h_2)$ [see Statistical Research Group (1945a), pp. 2, 48]. If other points are needed, they may be obtained from the following parametric equations also developed by Wald (1947, p. 51):

$$p = \frac{1 - \left(\dfrac{1 - p_2}{1 - p_1}\right)^t}{\left(\dfrac{p_2}{p_1}\right)^t - \left(\dfrac{1 - p_2}{1 - p_1}\right)^t}$$

$$P_a = \frac{\left(\dfrac{1 - \beta}{\alpha}\right)^t - 1}{\left(\dfrac{1 - \beta}{\alpha}\right)^t - \left(\dfrac{\beta}{1 - \alpha}\right)^t}$$

(15-22)

Equations (15-22) give, for any arbitrary values of t, the p and P_a coordinates of the OC curve. For $t = 1$, $p = p_1$ and $P_a = 1 - \alpha$, and for $t = -1$, $p = p_2$ and $P_a = \beta$. For $t = 0$, direct substitution would give an indeterminant number, but Wald shows this to be equivalent to $p = s$ and $P_a = h_2/(h_1 + h_2)$. If a value of p between p_1 and s is needed, choose $t = 0.5$. Similarly, a value of $t = -0.5$ would give a p between s and p_2. A value of t less than -1, such as -1.5, would give a p greater than p_2 if it were desired.

For this example the following results are obtained:

p	Pa
0	1.0
0.02	0.95
0.03	0.83
0.0436	0.56
0.06	0.27
0.08	0.10
0.102	0.034

The results for $p = 0.03$ and $p = 0.06$ were obtained by using $t = \pm 0.5$ in Equation (15-22), and those for $p = 0.102$ were obtained by using $t = -1.5$. The OC curve for this plan is illustrated in Figure 15-12.

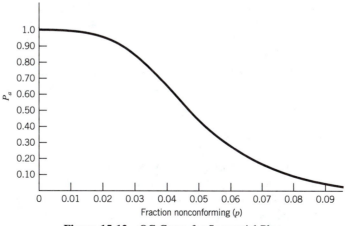

Figure 15-12 OC Curve for Sequential Plan

TABLE 15-8   Group Sequential Plan

Stage	n_i	Σn_i	AC	Re
1	23	23	*	3
2	23	46	0	5
3	23	69	1	6
4	23	92	2	7
5	23	115	3	8
6	23	138	4	9
7	23	161	5	9
8	23	184	8	9

▶ 15-6 GROUP SEQUENTIAL PLANS

A study of Figure 15-10 reveals that for many values of n acceptance is not possible. For example, if there is one nonconforming item after thirty-six items sampling is continued. If there are no more nonconforming items, accept on number 59. If there were no nonconforming items, acceptance would have been at $n = 36$. There is therefore no way the lot can be accepted for any n between 36 and 59. This suggests that one might simplify the administration of a sequential procedure by selecting small groups of items and making a decision after inspection of the group. This procedure will affect the ASN and OC curve a little because rejection could occur for any n (beyond 3 in this example). Such a procedure might be called group sequential sampling. If, in addition, the procedure is truncated, it is commonly called a multiple sampling plan.

Duncan (1986, p. 201) indicates that if h_1 and h_2 are integers and the group size is the integer just larger than $1/s$, group sequential sampling will give the same results as item-by-item sequential sampling. The error is not appreciable when h_1 and h_2 are not integers.

A group sequential (or multiple) plan for the example that has been used may now be developed. The group sample size would thus be $n_i = 1/s = 1/0.0436 = 23$. Earlier, it was determined that the item-by-item procedure would be truncated at $n = 186$ with rejection on 9 and acceptance on 8 or less. With this information the procedure indicated in Table 15-8 can be developed. The acceptance and rejection numbers may be obtained by using the appropriate cumulative sample size in the two acceptance and rejection equations. In doing this, always round up for the rejection number and round down for the acceptance number. The asterisk means that no acceptance is allowed following the first stage. (Recall that thirty-six items must be inspected with none nonconforming before acceptance is allowed.)

▶ 15-7 DERIVATION OF MATCHED PLANS

Schilling and Johnson (1980) have published a set of tables that may be used to develop single, double, or multiple plans that are very closely matched at two points on their OC curves. These tables were introduced in Section 15-4.3 for double plans. The two points are those points that have a 0.95 chance of acceptance and a 0.10 chance of acceptance, respectively. The procedure is to choose these two points and compute $R = p_{0.10}/p_{0.95}$.

This ratio R, called the operating ratio, is then used to enter the table. Choose the single, double, or multiple plan closest to your computed R value.

Table 15-4 contains a portion of the material in the Schilling and Johnson table. It lists, in addition to the acceptance and rejection numbers, values from which the OC curves, ASN curves, and sample sizes may be computed. To illustrate its use, assume that it is desired to obtain a set of matched plans for which there is a 95% chance of accepting material that is 1% nonconforming and a 10% chance of accepting lots with 6% nonconforming items. The operating ratio is

$$R = \frac{p_{0.10}}{p_{0.95}} = \frac{0.06}{0.01} = 6.00$$

Table 15-4 indicates the set of plans with operating ratio nearest to 6 would be 2S, 2D, and 2M. Plan 2S has acceptance number 2, rejection number 3, and sample size

$$n = \frac{np_{0.95}}{p_{0.95}} = \frac{0.818}{0.01} = 82 \quad \text{or} \quad \frac{np_{0.10}}{p_{0.10}} = \frac{5.322}{0.06} = 89$$

The first, $n = 82$ holds $\alpha = 0.05$, while the second has $\beta = 0.10$. As a compromise, choose $n = 85$. For $n = 85$, compute $p_{0.95}$ and $p_{0.10}$ as

$$p_{0.95} = \frac{np_{0.95}}{n} = \frac{0.818}{85} = 0.0096$$

$$p_{0.10} = \frac{np_{0.10}}{n} = \frac{5.322}{85} = 0.0626$$

which are reasonably close to the values specified, that is, $p_{0.95} = 0.01$ and $p_{0.10} = 0.06$.

The sample sizes for our double plan may be determined from Table 15-4 as follows:

$$n_1 = n_2 = \frac{0.635}{0.01} = 64$$

or

$$n_1 = n_2 = \frac{3.402}{0.06} = 57$$

Again, as a compromise choose $n_1 = n_2 = 60$.

For this size sample,

$$p_{0.95} = \frac{0.635}{60} = 0.0106$$

or

$$p_{0.10} = \frac{3.402}{60} = 0.0567$$

Again, both are reasonably close to 1% and 6% nonconforming.

The sample sizes for the corresponding multiple plan are

$$n_1 = n_2 = \cdots = n_7 = \frac{0.217}{0.01} = 22$$

or

$$n_1 = n_2 = \cdots = n_7 = \frac{1.355}{0.06} = 23$$

Since these values are adjacent, $n_i = 22$ might be chosen. For $n_i = 22$

$$p_{0.95} = \frac{0.217}{22} = 0.0099$$

and

$$p_{0.10} = \frac{1.355}{22} = 0.0616$$

Table 15-4 may be used to determine the difference between the plans at the $P_a = 0.50$ point. This would give another idea as to how closely they are matched. For the single plan, the $p_{0.50}$ point is $p_{0.50} = 2.674/85 = 0.0315$. For the double plan, $P_{0.50} = 1.816/60 = 0.0303$. The multiple plan gives $0.683/22 = 0.0310$. Again, all three appear to be matched reasonably closely. To summarize, the three plans are as follows:

Single:		$n = 85,$	$c = 2$	
Double:			Ac	Re
	$n_1 = 60$		0	3
	$n_2 = 60$		3	4

Multiple:	*Stage*	$\mathbf{n_i}$	$\mathbf{\Sigma n_i}$	*AC*	*Re*
	1	22	22	#	2
	2	22	44	0	3
	3	22	66	0	3
	4	22	88	1	4
	5	22	110	2	4
	6	22	132	3	5
	7	22	154	4	5

The ASN curves may be plotted using the three points given in Table 15-4. For the single plans the ASN is just equal to the sample size. For the double and multiple plans, the ASN may be determined at the $p_{0.95}$, $p_{0.50}$, and $p_{0.10}$ points by multiplying the appropriate values in the table by n_1.

For the example, for the double plan

$$ASN\ (p = 0.0106) = 60(1.443) = 86.6$$
$$ASN\ (p = 0.0303) = 60(1.564) = 93.8$$
$$ASN\ (p = 0.0567) = 60(1.306) = 78.4$$

and for the multiple plan

$$ASN\ (p = 0.0099) = 22(2.789) = 61.4$$
$$ASN\ (p = 0.0310) = 22(3.165) = 69.6$$
$$ASN\ (p = 0.0616) = 22(2.261) = 49.7$$

Figure 15-13 is a plot of the ASN functions for the three matched plans. Recall that for each plan, the 0.95 point is approximately 1%, the 0.50 point is approximately 3%,

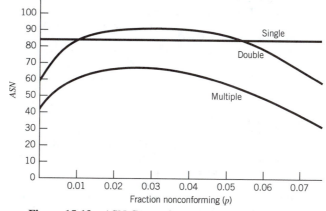

Figure 15-13 ASN Curves for Matched Sampling Plans

and the 0.10 point is approximately 6% nonconforming. This figure may be used to compare the three plans. The ASN values determined by using Table 15-4 do not assume curtailment for the double and multiple sampling plans. If curtailment is used, the high points on the curves will be somewhat lower. The double plan would be more affected by curtailment.

Other methods have been suggested in the literature to derive multiple plans [see, for example, Statistical Research Group (1948), U.S. Department of the Army (1953), Enters and Hamaker (1951)]. However, for the purpose of this text, these procedures seem to be sufficient. Some of these other approaches are reviewed briefly by Duncan (1986).

▶ 15-8 SUMMARY

This chapter has presented the most used attribute sampling procedures. These procedures have been standardized in the form of national and international standards, many of which are discussed in Chapter 16.

In addition to the procedures of acceptance sampling for attributes, covered in this chapter, many other types of procedures exist. These other procedures are often called "special" attribute sampling procedures. These include continuous sampling plans—CSP, skip-lot sampling plans—SkSP, and chain sampling plans—ChSP. The reader interested in any of these sampling plans may refer to Stephens (1995a, 1995b, or 2001) for detailed coverage of the techniques. The material is also covered in Chapter 18.

Some of these special attributes sampling procedures have also been standardized. Continuous sampling plans are included in MIL-STD 1235C (1988) and MIL-STD 1916 (1999). Skip-lot plans related to the ISO 2859-1 (1999) are contained in ISO 2859-3 (1991). Chain sampling plans are used in ISO 2859-1 (1999).

▶ 15-9 REFERENCES

American Society for Quality (1993), ANSI/ASQ Z1.4, *Sampling Procedures and Tables for Inspection by Attributes,* ASQ, Milwaukee.

American Society for Quality (2002), ANSI/ISO/ASQ A3534-2, *Statistics—Vocabulary and Symbols—Part 2: Applied Statistics,* Milwaukee.

Barnard, G. A. (1946), "Sequential Tests in Industrial Statistics," *Journal of the Royal Statistical Society, Series B,* Vol. 8, pp. 1–21.

Burr, I. W. (1957), "Average Sample Number under Curtailed or Terminated Sampling," *Industrial Quality Control,* February, pp. 5–7.

Dodge, H. F., and Romig, H. G. (1959), *Sampling Inspection Tables, Single and Double Sampling,* Second Edition, Wiley, New York.

Duncan, A. J. (1986), *Quality Control and Industrial Statistics,* Fifth Edition, Richard D. Irwin, Homewood, IL.

Enters, J. H., and Hamaker, H. C. (1951), "Multiple Sampling in Theory and Practice," in *Statistical Methods in Industrial Production,* Royal Statistical Society, Sheffield, England.

International Organization for Standardization (1999), *Sampling Procedures for Inspection by Attributes—Part 1: Sampling Plans Indexed by Acceptance Quality Limit (AQL) for Lot-by-Lot Inspection,* ISO, Geneva, Switzerland.

International Organization for Standardization (2002), ISO 3534-2, *Statistics—Vocabulary and Symbols—Part 2: Applied Statistics,* Geneva, Switzerland.

Schilling, E. G. and Johnson, L. J. (1980), "Tables for the Construction of Matched Single, Double, and Multiple Sampling Plans with Applications to MIL-STD 105D," *Journal of Quality Technology,* Vol. 12, No. 4, Oct.; pp. 220–29.

Statistical Research Group, Columbia University (1945a), *Sequential Analysis of Statistical Data: Applications,* Columbia University Press, New York.

Statistical Research Group, Columbia University (1945b), *Sequential Analysis of Statistical Data: Theory,* Columbia University Press, New York.

Statistical Research Group, Columbia University (1948), *Sampling Inspection,* McGraw-Hill, New York.

Stephens, K. S. (1995a), "How to Perform Continuous Sampling" *The ASQ Basic References in Quality Control: Statistical Techniques,* Vol. 2, American Society for Quality, Milwaukee.

Stephens, K. S. (1995b), "How to Perform Skip-Lot and Chain Sampling," *The ASQ Basic References in Quality Control: Statistical Techniques,* Vol. 4, American Society for Quality, Milwaukee.

Stephens, K. S. (2001), *The Handbook of Applied Acceptance Sampling,* Quality Press, American Society for Quality, Milwaukee.

U.S. Department of the Army, Chemical Corps Engineering Agency (1953), *Master Sampling Plans for Single, Double, and Multiple Sampling,* Manual No. 2, Army Chemical Center, MD.

U.S. Department of Defense (1988), *Single and Multi-Level Continuous Sampling Procedures and Tables for Inspection by Attributes,* MIL-STD 1235C, Washington, D.C.

U.S. Department of Defense (1989), *Sampling Procedures and Tables for Inspection by Attributes (MIL-STD 105E),* U.S. Government Printing Office, Washington, D.C.

U.S. Department of Defense (1999). *DoD Preferred Methods for Acceptance of Product,* MIL-STD 1916, Washington, D.C.

Wald, A. (1947), *Sequential Analysis,* Wiley, New York.

Wald, A., and Wolfowitz, J. (1948), "Optimum Character of the Sequential Probability Ratio Test," *Annals of Mathematical Statistics,* Vol. 19, pp. 326–39.

▶ 15-9 PROBLEMS

1. Construct the OC curves for the following single sampling plans:
(a) $n = 100, c = 2$
(b) $n = 200, c = 4$
(c) $n = 50, c = 1$
(d) $n = 400, c = 8$

2. Construct the OC curves for the following single sampling plans:
(a) $n = 100, c = 1$
(b) $n = 200, c = 2$
(c) $n = 50, c = 0$
(d) $n = 400, c = 4$

3. Compute the AOQLs and plot the ATI curves for the sampling plans in Problem 1, assuming lot sizes of 2000 items.

4. Compute the AOQLs for the plans in Problem 2, assuming the following lot sizes:
(a) 1000
(b) 2000
(c) 500
(d) 4000

5. Derive single sampling plans that come closest to meeting the following criteria:
(a) $p_{0.95} = 0.025, p_{0.10} = 0.08$
(b) $p_{0.95} = 0.005, p_{0.10} = 0.06$
(c) $p_{0.95} = 0.040, p_{0.10} = 0.10$
(d) $p_{0.95} = 0.060, p_{0.10} = 0.12$

6. Derive single sampling plans that minimize the ATI when $p_0 = 0.02$ for the following lot sizes and values of $p_{0.10}$:
(a) $p_{0.10} = 0.04, N = 5000$
(b) $p_{0.10} = 0.06, N = 2000$
(c) $p_{0.10} = 0.08, N = 4000$
(d) $p_{0.10} = 0.10, N = 10,000$

7. Derive single sampling plans that minimize the ATI when $p_0 = 0.01$ for the following lot sizes and AOQLs:
(a) $N = 5000, AOQL = 0.02$
(b) $N = 2000, AOQL = 0.04$

(c) $N = 4000$, $AOQL = 0.01$

(d) $N = 10,000$, $AOQL = 0.03$

8. For the following double sampling plans, derive the values of the operating characteristic at the indicated fraction nonconforming:

(a) $n_1 = 80$, $n_2 = 80$; $c_1 = 1$, $r_1 = 4$; $c_2 = 6$, $r_2 = 7$; $p = 0.04$

(b) $n_1 = 50$, $n_2 = 50$; $c_1 = 1$, $r_1 = 4$; $c_2 = 4$, $r_2 = 5$; $p = 0.04$

(c) $n_1 = 50$, $n_2 = 100$; $c_1 = 0$, $r_1 = 3$; $c_2 = 5$, $r_2 = 6$; $p = 0.02$

(d) $n_1 = 200$, $n_2 = 200$; $c_1 = 5$, $r_1 = 9$; $c_2 = 12$, $r_2 = 13$; $p = 0.02$

9. Compute the ASN curves for the plans in Problem 8 assuming that:

(a) curtailment is not practiced on r_2.

(b) curtailment on r_2 is practiced.

10. Derive double sampling plans that meet the criteria listed in Problem 5.

11. Determine the OC curves and the ASN curves for the double sampling plans developed in Problem 10.

12. Derive item-by-item sequential attributes sampling plans for the following criteria:

(a) $p_1 = 0.025$, $\alpha = 0.05$

  $p_2 = 0.08$, $\beta = 0.10$

(b) $p_1 = 0.01$, $\alpha = 0.05$

  $p_2 = 0.05$, $\beta = 0.10$

(c) $p_1 = 0.02$, $\alpha = 0.10$

  $p_2 = 0.10$, $\beta = 0.10$

(d) $p_1 = 0.03$, $\alpha = 0.05$

  $p_2 = 0.10$, $\beta = 0.10$

13. Construct the OC curves and ASN curves for the plans derived in Problem 12.

14. Determine the truncation point for each of the plans derived in Problem 12. Show the graph of the plans with truncation.

15. Derive a group sequential plan for each of the situations in Problem 12.

16. Derive multiple sampling plans for each of the criteria in Problem 12 using Table 15-4.

17. Determine OC and ASN curves for the multiple plans derived in Problem 16 and compare them with the curves derived in Problem 13.

18. Inspection is carried on using the sequential procedure, and the following pieces are found to be nonconforming: numbers 10, 12, 22, 50, 83, 102, 120, 140. At what point would a decision be made under each of the plans derived in Problem 12?

19. Inspection is continued using the sequential procedure with pieces number 25, 82, 134, and 182 found to be nonconforming. At what point would a decision be made using the plans in Problem 12?

CHAPTER

16

ATTRIBUTE SAMPLING TABLES

In the preceding chapter, acceptance sampling by attributes was discussed. The main concepts were described, and procedures for designing acceptance sampling plans were introduced. Over the years, particularly during and after World War II, many systems of acceptance sampling plans have been developed, and several are in common use today. In this chapter three of the most common attributes sampling systems will be explained: MIL-STD-105E:1989 (now replaced by ANSI/ASQC Z1.4:1993 and ISO 2859-1:1999), the Dodge-Romig system, and the limiting quality level system (ISO 2859-2:1994). In the next chapter the most common variables sampling plan—ANSI/ASQC Z1.9:1993 and its equivalent systems, ISO 3951 and MIL-STD-414—will be explored. First, before proceeding, three terms must be defined. The definitions are from ISO 2859-1:1999.

1. A sampling plan is a "combination of sample size(s) to be used and associated lot acceptability criteria."

2. A sampling scheme is a "combination of sampling plans with rules for changing from one plan to another." A scheme is indexed by lot size and AQL, LQ, or AOQL.

3. A sampling system is a "collection of sampling plans, or of sampling schemes, each with its own rules for changing plans, together with sampling procedures including criteria by which appropriate plans or schemes may be chosen."

The first widespread use of a published acceptance sampling system was during the U.S. involvement in World War II. Shortly after America's entry into the war the government invited a group of distinguished engineers from the Bell Telephone Laboratories to Washington to develop a sampling inspection program for the Army Ordinance [Dodge (1969)]. Bell Laboratories' engineers had formulated many sampling plans for use by the Bell System's manufacturing arm, the Western Electric Company, and this system of plans had been used successfully for many years. From this work Army Ordinance tables and procedures were prepared in 1942 [Dodge (1969)]. These sampling procedures later became, with modifications, the Army Service Forces Tables. This led eventually to Military Standard 105A in 1950. Minor modifications to the standard were published as MIL-STD-105B and MIL-STD-105C. Military Standard 105D was the result of a study by a U.S.-British-Canadian working group that sought to develop a common standard for the three countries [Duncan (1986)]. This standard (MIL-STD-105D) was later adopted as a voluntary American National Standard by the American Society for Quality as ANSI/ASQC Z1.4 in 1971. In 1974 this standard, with some further modifications, was adopted as an international standard, ISO 2859, by the International Organization for Standardization. It was also adopted by the International Electrotechnical Committee as IEC 410.

ISO 2859 was revised in 1989 and again in 1999. Subcommittee 5 of ISO Technical Committee 69 is responsible for this standard. Before the 1989 edition, this subcommittee decided to develop four parts to the ISO 2859 standard with the generic title "Sampling Procedures for Inspection by Attributes." A fifth part (Part 4) was added in 1999, and a sixth part is under development as of this writing.

Part 0: Introduction to the ISO 2859 Attributes Sampling System

Part 1: Sampling Plans Indexed by Acceptable Quality Level (AQL) for Lot-by-Lot Inspection

Part 2: Sampling Plans Indexed by Limiting Quality (LQ) for Isolated Lot Inspection

Part 3: Skip-Lot Sampling Procedures

Part 4: Sampling Plans for Assessment of Conformity to Stated Quality Levels

Part 5: Sequential Sampling Plans Indexed by Acceptance Quality Limit (AQL) for Inspection by Attributes

The 1999 revision of Part 1 included a new, more descriptive title, "Sampling Schemes Indexed by Acceptance Quality Limit (AQL) for Lot-by-Lot Inspection." This is in keeping with the discussion in Section 15-1 of the term "AQL" and the definitions above.

MIL-STD-105D was revised again in 1989 as MIL-STD-105E, and ANSI/ASQC Z1.4 was revised in 1981 and in 1993. These revisions included minor revisions to the supplementary tables. In the mid-1990s the U.S. Department of Defense decided to drop MIL-STD-105E in favor of the voluntary standard, ANSI/ASQC Z1.4. The 1999 edition of ISO 2859-1 made a number of significant changes in the basic standard. Because international standards are now considered those to which national standards should conform if possible, it will be used in this chapter. The next revision of ANSI/ASQC Z1.4 is expected to adopt the changes in this edition of ISO 2859-1. The purpose of these changes was (1) to make the standard easier to use; (2) to align it more closely with the variables standard, ISO 3951, to be discussed in Chapter 17; (3) to make further corrections in the supplementary tables; (4) to introduce optional alternative sampling plans called fractional acceptance number plans located between the acceptance number 0 and acceptance number 1 plans; and (5) to revise the double and multiple plans to make a more consistent ASN pattern.

The 1989 edition of ISO 2859-1 and the 1981 edition of ANSI/ASQC Z1.4 were published in an effort to modernize the terminology. The latest editions of these standards also incorporate this modern terminology and are consistent with the terminology standards of ISO TC 69 and TC 176 (ISO 3534-2: 2002 and ISO 9000: 2000).

These versions of the basic sampling plans for attributes are the most commonly used AQL sampling systems. When an Average Outgoing Quality Limit (AOQL) plan is desired, the Dodge-Romig system may be employed. Dodge and Romig's *Sampling Inspection Tables* (1959) are designed to minimize average total inspection for a given AOQL and a specified process average. The tables in the Dodge and Romig book are of two general types, one based on the concept of lot tolerance and the other on AOQL. Tables are provided for both types for single sampling and for double sampling. Each of the individual tables constitutes a collection of solutions to the problem of minimizing the overall amount of inspection when rectification is performed.

The third type of attributes acceptance sampling system covered in this chapter is for limiting quality level (LQL). This type of system is called lot tolerance percent defective (LTPD) in some references, such as Dodge and Romig, but the current nomenclature is LQL or LQ. Although the Dodge-Romig system can be indexed by LQL (LTPD) and used as an LQL system, much interest in recent years has been in LQL acceptance sampling schemes that are compatible with the AQL schemes of ISO 2859-1, ANSI/ASQC Z1.4, and MIL-STD-105E. This demand has been especially strong from the electronics industry, in which there is a need for tight consumer's risk plans for electronic devices such as very large integrated circuits. The AQL and AOQL acceptance sampling systems are often thought of as producer's risk schemes, since they are indexed by the AQL or AOQL values, where a very high percentage of product should be accepted. The LQL schemes are sometimes called consumer's risk schemes because the index (LQL) is a value at which a small fraction of the lots will be accepted.

As was seen in Chapter 15, a single sampling acceptance plan is defined by its sample size and acceptance number, which lead to an operating characteristic curve. Once the operating characteristic curve has been calculated, it is easy to determine the points at which 95%, 90%, 10%, 5%, or any other percent of lots will be accepted.

The purpose of acceptance sampling tables is not to provide answers to what today are not very difficult computations on modern computers, but to supply a set of procedures that have been used in the proving ground of experience. The tables provide acceptance procedures with known properties and verified results. The tables are widely available and are referenced and used around the world. Both producer and consumer can easily understand the risks to both.

▶ 16-1 ISO 2859-1:1999

As was discussed above, ISO 2859-1:1999 will be used as the basic reference for our discussion of AQL acceptance sampling systems because it contains the most recent revisions and is widely available throughout the world. Differences among the three standards will be discussed so that anyone using either of the other two should not have any problems. The emphasis in ISO 2859-1, ANSI/ASQC Z1.4, and MIL-STD-105E is on the scheme aspect of the acceptance sampling procedure.

This emphasis is accomplished by means of a figure describing the operation of the system found in both the ISO and the ANSI standards. In addition scheme performance is described by means of five tables in the ANSI/ASQ Z1.4 standard and a set of normalized OC curves in the ISO 2859-1 standard. The tables in ANSI/ASQC Z1.4 show the average outgoing quality limit factors for scheme performance, the limiting quality for probabilities of acceptance equal to 10% and 5%, the average sample size for scheme performance, and OC curves for scheme performance.

Other changes in the latest editions of ANSI/ASQC Z1.4 and ISO 2859-1 include modern terminology. Perhaps the most obvious terminology difference between these standards and MIL-STD-105E is the use of the terms "nonconformity" and "percent nonconforming" instead of "defect" and "percent defective." The rationale for this change is that in acceptance sampling, they are used for items that are nonconforming to specifications as opposed to defective items, which are items that are unable to perform their intended function. An item that is nonconforming is not always defective.

The rules for switching from one plan to another have been changed in these standards from those in MIL-STD-105E. This change has been made to more closely conform to the switching rules of the corresponding variables plans discussed in Chapter 17.

16-1.1 Description of ISO 2859-1:1999

The International Organization for Standardization (ISO) standard ISO 2859-1, as well as ANSI/ASQC Z1.4 and MIL-STD-105E, is a sampling system indexed by lot size ranges, inspection levels, and AQLs. To use this acceptance sampling system, an agreement is reached by the consumer and producer that a certain level of quality, the AQL, may be accepted most of the time, an inspection level is selected, and the appropriate lot size range is determined. It is assumed that the producer will submit a continuous series of lots for inspection. The use of the acceptance sampling schemes defined in ISO 2859-1 will constrain the producer to provide product of quality at or better than the AQL. If the producer submits a product of quality worse than the AQL the acceptance sampling scheme will switch to tighter inspection. If the quality does not improve during the tightened inspection phase, the sampling scheme calls for discontinuing of inspection and a termination of the contract.

16-1.2 Inspection Levels

The inspection level selected determines the relationship between the lot or batch size and the sample size. In this way the user controls the power of the sampling scheme and the probability of rejecting a lot when the quality is worse than the AQL. Table 16-1 shows

TABLE 16-1   Sample Sizes for Normal Inspection for Different Inspection Levels

Lot or Batch Size	Special Inspection Levels				General Inspection Levels		
	S-1	S-2	S-3	S-4	I	II	III
2–8	2	2	2	2	2	2	3
9–15	2	2	2	2	2	3	5
16–25	2	2	3	3	3	5	8
26–50	2	3	3	5	5	8	13
51–90	3	3	5	5	5	13	20
91–150	3	3	5	8	8	20	32
151–280	3	5	8	13	13	32	50
281–500	3	5	8	13	20	50	80
501–1200	5	5	13	20	32	80	125
1201–3200	5	8	13	32	50	125	200
3201–10,000	5	8	20	32	80	200	315
10,001–35,000	5	8	20	50	125	315	500
35,001–150,000	8	13	32	80	200	500	800
150,001–500,000	8	13	32	80	315	800	1250
500,001 and over	8	13	50	125	500	1250	2000

how the sample sizes for normal inspection vary with production lot sizes for the inspection levels. Three main inspection levels—I, II, and III—are for general use. Level III provides the largest samples and thus the greatest discrimination. Because of the discreteness of the sample size to lot size relationships some cases exist where this is not true. There are four additional special inspection levels: S-1, S-2, S-3, and S-4. These are used when relatively small samples are necessary and large sampling risks can or must be tolerated. In general, it is true that the larger the sample size, the more protection the consumer has, but this may vary slightly because the accept numbers change as the sample sizes change.

The acceptance sampling system, ISO 2859-1:1999, contains three types of sampling schemes: single, double, and multiple. When several types of plans are available for a desired AQL and inspection level, any one may be used. For any fraction nonconforming the average sample size (ASN) for multiple schemes is less than that for double schemes, and the ASN for double schemes is less than that for single schemes. Table 9 in the standard contains ASN curves that illustrate these relationships. Usually, the single sampling procedures are easier to administer than the double or multiple ones.

Operating characteristic curves for the individual plans that are elements of the acceptance sampling schemes are given in all three standards, and the operating characteristic curves for the schemes when the switching rules are used are provided in the ANSI and ISO standards. Operating curves are not included for double or multiple plans; however, they are matched as closely as possible. Some of the work by Schilling and Sheesley (1978a, 1978b) has been incorporated in these standards to show the performance of the sampling schemes under different assumptions. Liebesman (1979) addresses performance of the schemes when the quality level changes during tightened inspection.

The standard also includes average outgoing quality limit (AOQL) values for each of the single sampling plans for normal and tightened inspection. ANSI/ASQC Z1.4 also contains AOQL values for scheme performance under the assumption that the process stays at the same quality level in both normal and tightened inspection phases.

An optional procedure, designated as fractional acceptance number plans, has been added to the 1999 edition of ISO 2859-1. These plans, which will be discussed later, provide single sampling plans between the acceptance number 0 and 1 plans that could not be obtained by using integer acceptance numbers. If used, they replace the arrows found in the single sampling tables. This allows a more consistent operating characteristic pattern to be obtained. In addition, tables giving the percent of lots whose quality level is equal to the AQL expected to be accepted are included in this latest edition of the standard.

16-1.3 Scope and Field of Application

The standards are designed for inspection by attributes and assume a continuous production of lots. They can be applied to a producer, a single nonconformance classification of a product, or a collection of nonconformance classifications. The sampling schemes are applicable to, but not limited to, inspection of the following:

End items

Raw materials and components

Operations

Materials in process

Supplies in storage

Maintenance operations

Data or records

Administrative procedures

16-1.4 Classification of Defects and Nonconformities

The ISO 2859-1 standard uses the term "defect" to mean a nonconformity of sufficient severity to interfere with its intended usage requirements. The term "nonconformity" is used for all other deviations from requirements or specifications. Thus, the acceptance sampling plans given in the standard are in terms of percent of nonconforming items or number of nonconformities per hundred items. Whether they are called defects, nonconformities, or imperfections, the use of the acceptance sampling plans and schemes is the same. A common practice is to classify the defects or nonconformities according to their seriousness. Separate AQLs are set for the different seriousness classifications or the different classifications are combined with some appropriate weighting scheme. A class A nonconformity is the most serious type, with class B next. Nonconforming items are any items having one or more nonconformities. An example of a class A nonconformity could be an improper ground on a toaster that could cause a dangerous shock to a user. An improper solder in the wiring of the toaster that would reduce its useful life could be a class B nonconformity. A scratch in the finish could be classified as a class C nonconformity.

16-1.5 Percent Nonconforming and Nonconformities per Hundred Items

The percent nonconforming of any given quantity of items is just 100 times the number of nonconforming items inspected divided by the number of items inspected. Nonconformities per hundred items are simply the number of nonconformities divided by the number inspected times 100. It is possible for one item to have zero, one, or more nonconformities. All AQLs above 10% are for number of nonconformities per hundred items.

16-1.6 Specifying the AQL

The AQL is used to select a sampling scheme from the standard. Chapter 15 defined the AQL as the maximum percent nonconforming (or the maximum number of nonconformities per hundred items) that, for purposes of sampling inspection, can be considered satisfactory as a process average. The AQL is often designated in the contract between the producer and the consumer. The AQLs given in the tables are called the *preferred AQLs*. The term "preferred" only means that the tables and operating characteristic curves have been constructed for these values. Other values may be used, but the burden of constructing plans and operating characteristic curves is then on the user.

16-1.7 Submission of Product

The plans in this system are sometimes called lot-by-lot acceptance sampling plans because it is assumed that product is grouped in lots or batches of a single type, grade, class, size, and composition manufactured under essentially the same conditions and at essentially the same time. An example of a lot is the product made during one shift of a small group of workers on one assembly line using materials from the same stock. Often the procedure for the formation of a lot is specified in the contract.

16-1.8 Acceptance and Rejection

The sample size is determined by using the tables, the sample is taken, and the nonconformities or nonconforming items are counted. The lot is accepted if the number of nonconformities or nonconforming items is less than or equal to the accept number; otherwise, the lot is rejected. The inspecting organization has the right to reject any item that is found to be nonconforming, whether it was or was not in the sample. Different sampling plans may be used for different types of nonconformities on the same items. For example, every item may be inspected for Class A nonconformities, but a sampling plan could be used for all other classes of nonconformities. When a rejected lot is resubmitted for inspection, every item should have been inspected and replaced if nonconforming, not just those items that are found to be nonconforming in the first sample.

16-1.9 Sampling

Sampling is the drawing of one or more items from a lot. It should be done as randomly as possible unless there is a rationale for representative sampling. In representative sampling, items from each identifiable stratum in the lot should be drawn randomly.

16-1.10 Fractional Acceptance Numbers

An optional procedure has been added to the 1999 edition of the ISO 2859-1 sampling system called *fractional acceptance number plans*. This addition applies only to single sampling plans. The reason for the addition is to make the change in the operating characteristic less abrupt when going from the accept number 1 to the accept number 0 plans. The master tables for single sampling (Figures 16-1 and 16-3) show two arrows between these two plans for normal and tightened plans and three arrows for reduced plans (Figure 16-5). Fractions $1/3$ and $1/2$ are introduced to replace these arrows in the normal and tightened plans, while $1/5$, $1/3$, and $1/2$ are used for the reduced plans. A fractional acceptance number of $1/2$ means that the current lot is to be accepted if there are no nonconforming items in the lot or if there is one nonconforming item and none in the immediately preceding lot. An acceptance number of $1/3$ means the lot is acceptable if there are no nonconforming items in the present lot or if there is one nonconforming item and none in the previous two lots. If there are two or more nonconforming items in the present lot, it is to be rejected. This is a chain sampling procedure, to be discussed in Chapter 18.

16-1.11 Using ISO 2859-1 for Acceptance Sampling

The proper use of an acceptance sampling scheme can best be explained by working through an example. Assume that a consumer wants to purchase a product with an ac-

TABLE 16-2 Sample Size Code Letters

Lot or Batch Size			Special Inspection Levels				General Inspection Levels		
			S-1	S-2	S-3	S-4	I	II	III
2	to	8	A	A	A	A	A	A	B
9	to	15	A	A	A	A	A	B	C
16	to	25	A	A	B	B	B	C	D
26	to	50	A	B	B	C	C	D	E
51	to	90	B	B	C	C	C	E	F
90	to	150	B	B	C	D	D	F	G
151	to	280	B	C	D	E	E	G	H
281	to	500	B	C	D	E	F	H	J
501	to	1200	C	C	E	F	G	J	K
1201	to	3200	C	D	E	G	H	K	L
3201	to	10000	C	D	F	G	J	L	M
10001	to	35000	C	D	F	H	K	M	N
35001	to	150000	D	E	G	J	L	N	P
150001	to	500000	D	E	G	J	M	P	Q
500001	and	over	D	E	H	K	N	Q	R

ceptance quality limit (AQL) of 1% nonconforming. The product is manufactured on one assembly line at a rate of 300 per shift, and the consumer decides that the quality per shift will be fairly homogeneous and decides to use a lot size of 300. The consumer will accept or not accept the lot on the basis of a sample inspection.

The product is not of critical importance but is expensive, and testing is moderately difficult. The consumer decides that general inspection level II seems appropriate. The product will be tested on an automatic test set and deemed conforming only if all tests pass. The product is packaged during manufacture, and the drawing of the sample is rather complicated and time-consuming, but the administrative advantages of single sampling are far more important than reducing the sample size by means of double or multiple sampling.

The first step is to enter Table 1, reproduced here as Table 16-2, with the lot size and general inspection level II to obtain the sample size code letter. Looking under lot size 281 to 500 and general inspection level II, one obtains sample size code letter H. Table 16-2 was reproduced from ANSI/ASQC Z1.4 but the table is identical to Table 1 in ISO 2859-1.

Normal Inspection

The second step is to find the table for single sampling plans for normal inspection which is Table 2-A, found here as Figure 16-1. Entering the table with the sample size code letter H and an AQL of 1.0%, the plan calls for a sample size of 50 and an acceptance number of 1.

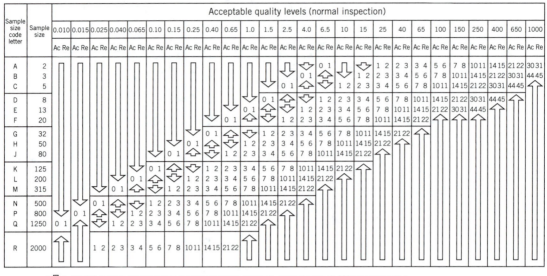

= Use first sampling plan below arrow. If sample size equals, or exceeds, lot or batch size, do 100 percent inspection.
= Use first sampling plan above arrow.
Ac = Acceptance number.
Re = Rejection number.

Figure 16-1 ISO 2859-1, Table 2-A—Single Sampling Plans for Normal Inspection (Master Table)

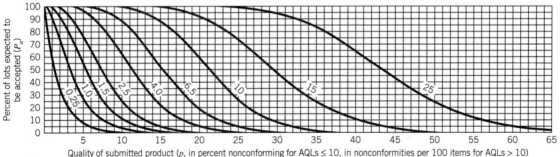

Quality of submitted product (p, in percent nonconforming for AQLs ≤ 10, in nonconformities per 100 items for AQLs > 10)
NOTE: Values on curves are Acceptance Quality Limits (AQLs) for normal inspection.

	Acceptance Quality Limit, normal inspection (in percent nonconforming and nonconformities per 100 items)																
P_a	0.25	1.0	1.5	2.5	4.0	6.5	✕	10	0.25	1.0	1.5	2.5	4.0	6.5	✕	10	✕ 15 ✕ 25
	p (in percent nonconforming)								p (in nonconformities per 100 items)								
99.0	0.0201	0.300	0.886	1.68	3.69	6.07		7.36	10.1	0.0201	0.297	0.872	1.65	3.57	5.81	7.01	9.54 12.2 15.0 20.7 25.1
95.0	0.103	0.715	1.66	2.78	5.36	8.22		9.72	12.9	0.103	0.711	1.64	2.73	5.23	7.96	9.39 12.3 15.4 18.5 24.9 29.8
90.0	0.210	1.07	2.22	3.53	6.43	9.54		11.2	14.5	0.211	1.06	2.20	3.49	6.30	9.31	10.9 14.0 17.3 20.6 27.3 32.5
75.0	0.574	1.92	3.46	5.10	8.51	12.0		13.8	17.5	0.575	1.92	3.45	5.07	8.44	11.9	13.7 17.2 20.8 24.5 31.8 37.4
50.0	1.38	3.33	5.31	7.29	11.3	15.2		17.2	21.2	1.39	3.36	5.35	7.34	11.3	15.3	17.3 21.3 25.3 29.3 37.3 43.3
25.0	2.73	5.29	7.69	10.0	14.5	18.8		21.0	25.2	2.77	5.39	7.84	10.2	14.8	19.4	21.6 26.0 30.4 34.8 43.5 49.9
10.0	4.50	7.56	10.3	12.9	17.8	22.4		24.7	29.1	4.61	7.78	10.6	13.4	18.5	23.5	26.0 30.8 35.6 40.3 49.5 56.4
5.0	5.82	9.14	12.1	14.8	19.9	24.7		27.0	31.6	5.99	9.49	12.6	15.5	21.0	26.3	28.9 33.9 38.9 43.8 53.4 60.5
1.0	8.80	12.6	15.8	18.7	24.2	29.2		31.6	36.3	9.21	13.3	16.8	20.1	26.2	32.0	34.8 40.3 45.6 50.9 61.2 68.7
	0.40	1.5	2.5	4.0	6.5	✕		10	✕	0.40	1.5	2.5	4.0	6.5	✕	10	✕ 15 ✕ 25 ✕
	Acceptance Quality Limit, tightened inspection (in percent nonconforming and nonconformities per 100 items)																

NOTE Binomial distribution used for entries corresponding to inspection for nonconforming items, Poisson for inspection for number of nonconformities.

Figure 16-2 ISO 2859-1, Chart H—Tables for Sample Size Code Letter H and Table 10-H-1 Tabulated Values for Operating Characteristic Curves for Single Sampling Plans

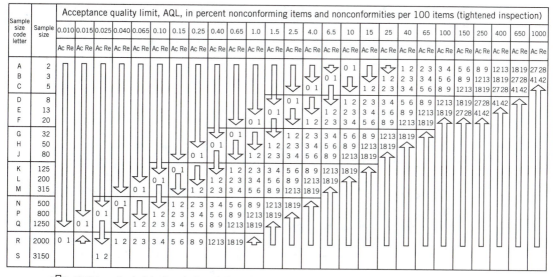

= Use first sampling plan below the arrow. If sample size equals, or exceeds, lot size, carry out 100% inspection.

= Use first sampling plan above the arrow.

Ac = Acceptance number

Re = Rejection number

Figure 16-3 Table 2-B—Single Sampling Plans for Tightened Inspection

The consumer next checks the operating characteristic curve for sample size code letter H in Chart H of Figure 16-2 or the tabulated values for the operating characteristic curve in Table 10-H-1 of Figure 16-2. Here for quality of submitted product equal to 1.07% nonconforming the plan will accept 90% of the submitted lots. For quality of submitted product equal to 0.712% nonconforming the plan will accept 95% of the submitted lots. By using the acceptance sampling scheme as intended, with full use of the switching rules, the consumer feels confident that the product accepted will have a quality no worse than 1% nonconforming.

The consumer now reviews the switching rules with the producer. The normal acceptance sampling plan will be used as long as no two lots in any string of five submitted fail to be accepted. If two or more of five are not accepted, the consumer will switch to tightened inspection.

Tightened Inspection

The consumer checks Table 2-B, reproduced here as Figure 16-3, for single sampling plans for tightened inspection. He or she finds for code letter H and AQL 1% a sample size of 80 and an acceptance number of 1.

As a quick check as to how much tighter this is, the consumer calculates from the binomial distribution the probability of acceptance. Since a sample of 80 from a lot of 300 is a significant proportion, the hypergeometric distribution should be used, but for simplicity here the binomial will be used. For this situation the probability of acceptance is the probability that there are no nonconforming items in the sample of eighty items or that there is only one nonconforming item in the sample. Using the quality of submitted lots equal to 1.07% nonconforming, we calculate

$$P_a = \sum_{x=0}^{1} \binom{n}{x} p^x (1 - p)^{n-x}$$

$$= \binom{80}{0}(0.0107)^0(1 - 0.0107)^{80} + \binom{80}{1}(0.0107)^1(1 - 0.0107)^{79}$$

$$= (0.9893)^{80} + 80(0.0107)(0.9893)^{79} = 0.79$$

For tightened inspection the probability of accepting a lot with 1.07% nonconforming product is 79%, compared to a 90% probability of accepting the lot under normal inspection.

The tables could also be used for a comparison in the following way. Since the acceptance sampling plan for tightened inspection in this case is $n = 80$, $c = 1$, which corresponds to a normal sampling plan for code letter J, use the tabulated or graphical operating characteristic curves for a plan of $n = 80$, $c = 1$ on a different page of the standard (not given here). For a probability of acceptance under tightened inspection of 90%, the quality of submitted lots would have to be 0.666% nonconforming. For a probability of acceptance of 95%, the quality of submitted lots would have to be 0.444% nonconforming. This compares to 1.07% and 0.715% nonconforming for 90% and 95% probabilities of acceptance under normal inspection.

When five consecutive lots are accepted under tightened inspection the acceptance sampling inspection scheme permits returning to normal inspection. If five lots are rejected under tightened inspection, then inspection under this acceptance sampling scheme should be discontinued. This is definitely an indication of a quality problem, and the consumer is no longer assured of receiving product no worse than the AQL. Inspection may be resumed after the problem is corrected to the satisfaction of both parties.

Reduced Inspection
The ANSI/ASQC Z1.4 acceptance sampling system provides for reduced inspection if ten consecutive lots are accepted when on normal inspection, and the total number of nonconforming items in the samples from the ten lots is equal to or less than an applicable number in Table VIII in the standard. This table is not reproduced here, since it is not used in ISO 2859-1. Using Table II-C of the Z1.4 standard (Figure 16-4), the sample size for this example is reduced to 20 with an acceptance number of 0 and a rejection number of 2. This means that if a sample of twenty is taken and one nonconforming item is found, the present lot is accepted but a move back to normal inspection for succeeding lots is necessary. Normal inspection is also used any time a lot is not accepted, production becomes irregular or delayed, or other conditions warrant that normal inspection should be resumed. Examples of these other conditions are when a different material is substituted in the manufacturing process or when a procedure in the manufacturing process changes.

The rule for switching from normal to reduced inspection for ISO 2859-1 is different than that for ANSI/ASQC Z1.4. It introduces a statistic called *switching score*. If this switching score is 30 or more, production is at a steady rate, and the responsible authority permits, the switch to reduced inspection is allowed. The table for reduced inspection in this

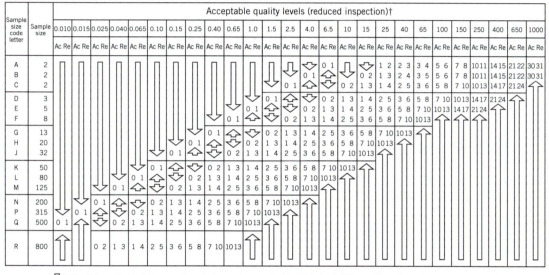

▽ = Use first sampling plan below arrow. If sample size equals, or exceeds, lot or batch size, do 100 percent inspection.
△ = Use first sampling plan above arrow.
Ac = Acceptance number.
Re = Rejection number.
† = If the acceptance number has been exceeded, but the rejection number has not been reached, accept the lot, but reinstate normal inspection (see 10.1.4)

Figure 16-4 ANSI/ASQC Z1.4 Table II-C—Single Sampling Plans for Reduced Inspection (Master Table)

sampling system is also different from that for ANSI/ASQC Z1.4. It is reproduced here as Figure 16-5. It will be noticed that the gap between the acceptance and rejection numbers has been eliminated. As a result, many of the acceptance numbers are different. The sample sizes are the same, however.

The calculation of the switching score begins at the start of a sequence of lots inspected under normal inspection. The switching score is set at zero at the start of the sequence and is updated after each lot is inspected according to the following rules:

Single Sampling Plans

1. When the acceptance number is 2 or more, add 3 to the switching score if the lot would have been accepted if the AQL had been one step tighter; otherwise reset the switching score to zero.

2. When the acceptance number is 0 or 1, add 2 to the switching score if the lot is accepted; otherwise reset the switching score to zero.

Double and Multiple Sampling Plans

1. When a double sampling scheme is in use, add 3 to the switching score if the lot is accepted after the first sample; otherwise reset the switching score to zero.

2. When a multiple sampling scheme is in use, add 3 to the switching score if the lot is accepted by the third sample; otherwise reset the switching score to zero.

This procedure for switching from normal to reduced inspection is statistically equivalent to that for ANSI/ASQC Z1.4, and it is not believed to be any more difficult

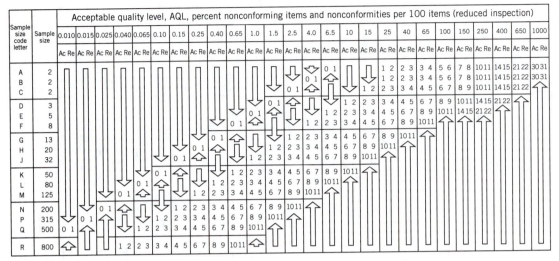

▽ = Use first sampling plan below arrow. If sample size equals, or exceeds, lot or batch size, do 100 percent inspection.

△ = Use first sampling plan above arrow.

Ac = Acceptance number.

Re = Rejection number.

Figure 16-5 ISO 2859-1, Table 2-C—Single Sampling Plans for Reduced Inspection (Master Table)

to manage. The principal advantage is the elimination of the gap between the acceptance and rejection numbers, which many users found to be confusing. The rules for a return to normal inspection are the same as those for ANSI/ASQC Z1.4 discussed above, except for that dealing with the gap between acceptance and rejection numbers.

Using ISO 2859-1, the reduced sampling plan for sample size code letter H and AQL 1% results in a downward arrow. In this case, this means that the user must move to code letter J, where the reduced plan will be $n = 32$ and $Ac = 1$.

Reduced inspection is optional and is often used when the cost of inspection per item is small in comparison to the cost of sampling and inspecting the first item. ISO 2859-1 also allows for the use of the skip-lot plans of ISO 2859-3:1991 in place of the reduced plans. Tightened inspection should always be part of the acceptance sampling inspection scheme. Protection from quality significantly worse than expected cannot be ensured without the use of the tightened inspection provision. B. S. Liebesman (1979) has shown that when normal and tightened inspection are applied according to the rules, with the reasonable assumption that the producer improves the quality of submitted lots during tightened inspection to avoid the discontinue (contract canceled) phase, the average quality received is at least as good as the AQL. Under these assumptions the scheme performs similarly to an AOQL plan.

Scheme Performance

The scheme performance section of ANSI/ASQC Z1.4:1993 is based on the assumption that the percent nonconforming level of a process stays at that level even after switching to tightened inspection [Schilling and Sheesley (1978a, 1978b)]. This assumption is a conservative worst-case description of the performance of the scheme for use as a baseline.

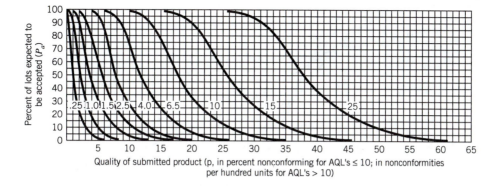

P_a	\multicolumn{7}{c|}{Acceptable Quality Levels (normal inspection)}												
	.25	1.0	1.5	2.5	4.0	6.5	10	.25	1.0	1.5	2.5	4.0	6.5	10	15	25
	\multicolumn{7}{c|}{p (in percent nonconforming)}	\multicolumn{9}{c|}{p (in nonconformities per 100 items)}
99.0	0.416	0.386	1.09	1.87	3.86	6.33	10.4	0.416	0.383	1.08	1.84	3.77	6.14	10.0	15.4	25.6
95.0	0.143	0.733	1.59	2.70	5.03	7.92	12.6	0.143	0.729	1.57	2.66	4.92	7.69	12.1	18.3	29.4
90.0	0.229	0.983	1.93	3.23	5.62	8.76	13.7	0.229	0.979	1.92	3.20	5.53	8.57	13.3	19.9	31.3
75.0	0.445	1.46	2.55	4.15	6.52	10.0	15.4	0.446	1.46	2.55	4.13	6.47	9.90	15.2	22.4	34.2
50.0	0.893	2.17	3.52	5.49	7.74	11.7	17.6	0.898	2.18	3.54	5.52	7.78	11.7	17.7	25.7	37.9
25.0	1.72	3.34	5.30	7.70	10.0	14.5	21.0	1.73	3.37	5.39	7.85	10.2	14.9	21.6	30.4	43.5
10.0	2.84	4.77	7.56	10.3	12.9	17.8	24.7	2.88	4.86	7.78	10.6	13.4	18.5	26.0	35.6	49.5
5.0	3.68	5.79	9.14	12.1	14.8	19.9	27.0	3.74	5.93	9.49	12.6	15.5	21.0	28.9	38.9	53.4
1.0	5.59	8.01	12.5	15.8	18.7	24.1	31.6	5.76	8.30	13.3	16.8	20.1	26.2	34.8	45.7	61.2

Figure 16-6 ANSI/ASQC Z1.4, Chart XV-H—Operating Characteristic Curves for ANSI Z1.4 Scheme Performance and Table XV-H-1—Tabulated Values for Operating Characteristic Curves for ANSI Z1.4 Scheme Performance

Most producers would try very diligently to improve the quality of submitted lots during tightened inspection. To examine the scheme performance, use the tables added to ANSI/ASQC Z1.4. In this case, use Table XV-H-1 or Chart XV-H (Figure 16-6) for tabulated or graphical operating characteristic values. At 1.07% nonconforming, approximately 85% of the lots will be accepted using the scheme with switching rules, compared to 90% of lots submitted accepted by the normal plan alone. It can be seen that for 90% of lots to be accepted under the scheme with switching rules, the quality of submitted lots would have to be 0.983% nonconforming. In general, the operating characteristic curves for scheme performance are approximately similar to those of normal inspection plans for low levels of percent nonconforming. They are approximately equal to those of tightened plans for high levels of percent nonconforming.

ISO 2859-1 also concerns itself with scheme performance. However, it does it with normalized graphs, found in Figure 16-7. Each curve in Figure 16-7 is for a single sampling acceptance number for normal inspection. The abscissa is the submitted percent nonconforming (p) divided by the AQL. For our example ($n = 80$, $Ac = 1$) the percentage of lots expected to be accepted if 1% nonconforming lots are submitted will be about 90. If lots of 3% nonconforming are submitted, approximately 40% will be accepted if the sampling scheme is used properly.

There are also tables in ANSI/ASQC Z1.4 for finding the average outgoing quality limit (AOQL) for each of the single sampling plans for normal and tightened inspection

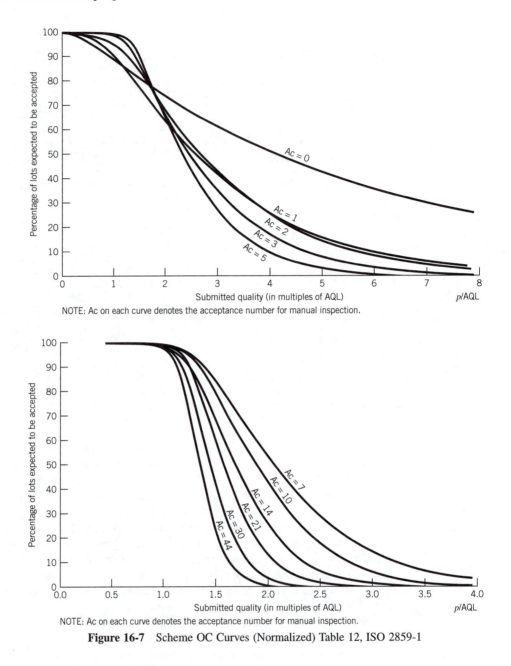

Figure 16-7 Scheme OC Curves (Normalized) Table 12, ISO 2859-1

and for scheme performance. ANSI/ASQC Z1.4:1993 and ISO 2859-1:1999 also contain average sample size curves for double and multiple sampling plans compared to the single sampling plans for each acceptance number. These curves show the average sample sizes that may be expected to occur under the various sampling plans for a given process level. These curves do not apply to scheme performance.

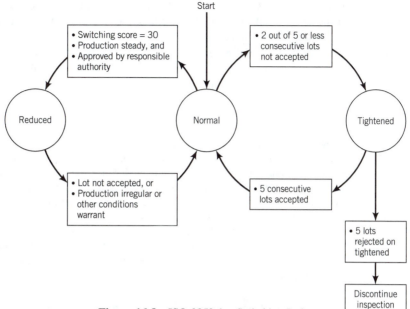

Figure 16-8   ISO 2859-1—Switching Rules

An example will not be presented of how to use ISO 2859-1 for AOQL or LQL plans, since in the rest of this chapter the Dodge-Romig AOQL system and a LQL system developed as ISO 2859-2 will be discussed. ISO 2859-1 and ANSI/ASQC Z1.4 are intended to be used as a scheme for a continuing series of lots to achieve consumer protection while assuring the producer that acceptance will occur most of the time if the quality is better than the AQL. The use of the standard is summarized in Figure 16-8.

▶ 16-2 THE DODGE-ROMIG SYSTEM

In the first part of this chapter the use of the ISO 2859-1:1999 and the ANSI/ASQC Z1.4:1993 acceptance sampling systems was discussed. Each of these systems is made up of AQL schemes, although provisions exist in the standards for constructing AOQL and LQL schemes. The first acceptance sampling system to propose the idea of the average outgoing quality limit (AOQL) as an index was published by Dodge and Romig in the *Bell System Technical Journal* (1924). This system was published subsequently as *Sampling Inspection Tables* (1959) by Dodge and Romig and is still widely used. An abbreviated compilation of the sampling plans along with a guide to their use has been published as ASTM E 259-98, entitled *Standard Practice for the Use of Process Oriented AOQL and LTPD Sampling Plans* (1999).

The AQL acceptance sampling systems are used to provide protection to the buyer or consumer from accepting very bad lots and to encourage the producer to provide good lots consistently. The direct effect on quality of AQL acceptance sampling plans is negligible in most situations. For example, if the quality of each lot is identical (say, $p\%$ nonconforming), any AQL sampling system will accept some fraction of the lots inspected and reject the rest. Except for the minor effect of removing the nonconforming items found in the samples taken from accepted lots, the quality of accepted lots will be the same as the quality of the submitted lots (in this example, $p\%$ nonconforming). The use of AQL acceptance sampling systems has a direct effect on the accepted quality that is proportional to the variance of the quality of the submitted lots. To illustrate this, consider the following simple hypothetical example.

▷ **EXAMPLE 16-1**

A manufacturer has two assembly lots of product. Unknown to the manufacturer, one line is out of calibration and is producing lots that are 100% nonconforming. The other line is working perfectly and producing lots that have no nonconforming items. Any AQL acceptance sampling plan would reject all the lots from the first line and accept all the lots from the second. The quality received by the consumer would be 0% nonconforming, whereas the submitted quality was 50% nonconforming. This example not only shows that the direct effect of an AQL plan on quality received can be substantial if the variance of quality from lot to lot is significant, but also demonstrates the importance of correctly composing and identifying lots. Consider the effect of using the same AQL acceptance sampling plan on lots that were composed of a mixture of items from both assembly lines.

Dodge and Romig addressed the problem of controlling the average quality through sampling inspection more directly. By requiring that all rejected lots be 100% reinspected and the nonconforming items removed and replaced by good items, they found that they could calculate the average outgoing quality limit (AOQL). This limit was the worst average quality that would be passed regardless of the quality of the submitted lots or the distribution of the quality of submitted lots. Obviously, one way perfect quality could be received would be for all lots to be rejected, inspected 100%, nonconforming items replaced with good items, and resubmitted. (The reader has probably noticed that this and preceding discussions make a very strong assumption, that inspection is 100% efficient. That is, every nonconforming item inspected will be detected to be nonconforming. No inspection process is ever 100% efficient. Even automatic inspection with the best computer-driven test set has some positive probability of a nonconforming item being accepted and vice versa.)

What Dodge and Romig have done is to derive acceptance sampling plans that not only give the consumer quality at least as good as the desired AOQL, but do so with a minimum amount of inspection. Minimum amount of inspection refers to the overall inspection: that performed on the initial samples plus that involved with the complete reinspection of rejected lots. These acceptance sampling plans were also designed with the understanding that lots are often "merely quantities whose size was determined by convenience in handling. In contrast with customer lots, which are specific in quantity and which commonly retain their identity, the inspection lots in manufacture were usually convenient subdivisions of a flow of product" [Dodge and Romig (1959)].

The Dodge-Romig plans were designed for use with rectifying inspection. In practice this may not be practical or possible (e.g., with destructive testing). In these cases the Dodge-Romig plans may still be used, but the consumer is no longer guaranteed that the average outgoing quality will be better than the AOQL value. In practice, however, the high rate of rejected lots with quality much worse (two times the AOQL value) and high rate of acceptance for lots with quality better than the AOQL value "will tend to compel the producer in his own interest, to maintain a process quality which at worst will be little, if any, poorer than the AOQL" [Dodge and Romig (1959)].

16-2.1 Choosing a Sampling Plan from the Dodge-Romig Tables

Many factors should be considered when choosing any sampling plan. Dodge and Romig (1959, p. 4) suggest the following sequence of steps:

1. DECIDE what characteristics to include.
2. DECIDE what is to constitute a lot.
3. CHOOSE the type of protection: LQL or AOQL.
4. CHOOSE a suitable value of LQL or AOQL.
5. CHOOSE between single sampling and double sampling.
6. SELECT the appropriate sampling table.
7. OBTAIN an estimate of the process average percent nonconforming.
8. CHOOSE a sampling plan for the given lot size and process average percent nonconforming.
9. FIND the OC curve of the sampling plan. If it is satisfactory, adopt the plan.
10. SELECT sample items from the lot by a random procedure.
11. FOLLOW the prescribed procedure—single sampling or double sampling.
12. KEEP a running check of the process average percent nonconforming. Change the sampling plan as necessary to match shifts in the process average percent nonconforming.

These steps lead the user through several important decisions. The first step, deciding which characteristics to include, is very important. One can have a separate plan for each characteristic to be inspected, but this is often a poor practice. For efficiency characteristics should be grouped collectively when they are expected to have satisfactory quality and treated separately when they are likely to produce a large number of nonconformities. This procedure helps to limit the number of characteristics that must be 100% inspected on rejected lots. Similar characteristics that are inspected or tested at the same time are usually grouped. Modern automated test equipment often makes possible the testing of many functions or characteristics per item. Usually, one separate sampling plan is used for the total results of these tests, with items being classified as good if all tests pass and nonconforming if any test fails.

The determination of a lot (Step 2) also important. Large lots minimize the amount of inspection, but items in a lot should be from as homogeneous a population as possible. Corrective action is much simpler if the source, time and date of manufacture, material used, and manufacturing conditions can be readily identified. The choice between LQL (which Dodge and Romig called LTPD) and AOQL schemes (Step 3) is usually made by considering why a sampling scheme is being used. When the responsible engineer wants great assurance that each individual lot is better than a certain quality level, an LQL scheme is selected. When the engineer wants long-term average quality better than a certain level, an AOQL scheme is chosen. The AOQL schemes are often used by different sections of the same plant or company. They are also useful in final inspection to provide good assurance that a consumer's acceptance sampling scheme will have a high probability of acceptance of the manufacturer's product.

Choosing the AOQL or LQL value should ideally be an economic decision. The goal is to select the value that minimizes both the total cost of purchasing a product manufactured at a certain quality and the cost of using a product of that quality. The calculation of total cost is often difficult, and quality levels are frequently determined on the basis of production capability or competitive decisions.

The choice of single sampling versus double sampling (Step 5) is a choice of economics. When the inspection cost per item is high, double sampling is usually chosen, since this minimizes the average sample size. Single sampling is easier to administer, since the number of items to be inspected does not vary and the inspectors' workload can be better planned. When the acceptance number is necessarily small, there is a strong additional reason for choosing the double sampling schemes. With double sampling, at least one nonconforming item is allowed; however, in single sampling schemes none may be allowed. The shape of the operating characteristic curves for acceptance number equal to zero is far from ideal.

After the above decisions are made, the correct table (Step 6) is selected from Appendices 4, 5, 6, or 7 of *Sampling Inspection Tables* according to whether LQL (LTPD) or AOQL is to be used and whether single or doubling sampling is employed. An estimate of the process average (Step 7) is used to select the most economical sampling plan. When immediately prior data from the process are available, estimates are used based on these data. If no data are available for this product, data from a similar product or process are used for rough estimates. During submission of a series of lots, new estimates of the process average are made. This is the "switching" procedure that makes the system a set of schemes.

The sampling plan is then chosen using the current estimate of process average percent nonconforming (PA) and the given lot size (Step 8). If the PA is unknown or larger than any in the table, use the largest available. Before proceeding, always obtain the OC curve and examine it to be sure that the plan's performance is understood (Step 9). Select the items from the lot for the sample using some procedure that ensures that each item in the lot has an equal chance of being selected (Step 10).

After the sample is selected, all items should be inspected (Step 11). Dodge and Romig emphasize that at least in single sampling or for the first sample of double sampling, all items should be inspected, even if the rejection number is exceeded before all items are inspected. Accurate estimates of the process average percent nonconforming (or number of nonconformities per 100 units) are usually wanted, since the role of process or final inspections is broader than merely accepting or rejecting lots one by one. In addition, a running check on the process average is kept (Step 12) to enable switching to be performed. The continuing estimates of process average also provide information for the shop to make improvements and the inspecting organization to adjust procedures for maximizing efficiency.

16-2.2 Using Dodge-Romig Sampling Inspection Tables

The Dodge-Romig *Sampling Inspection Tables* can be used for selecting sampling plans corresponding to desired limiting quality level (LQL) [or lot tolerance percent defective (LTPD)] or average outgoing quality limit (AOQL). Several things about these plans should be remembered. They are intended to be used in situations in which rejected lots are inspected 100% and nonconforming items are replaced. They are employed most efficiently with estimates of the average process percent nonconforming. The plans selected from these tables will have the minimum sample sizes for the conditions stated. Of course, these minima are only approximate, because of discrete values used for table lookup and ranges used for incoming quality process average and lot size. Exact plans may be calculated by using the methods in Chapter 15.

Using Dodge-Romig Tables for LQL (LTPD)

▶ **EXAMPLE 16-2**

To see how to use the Dodge-Romig tables in a typical practical application, revisit the example in Chapter 15. Assume that lots of size 900 are being submitted for inspection. An LQL of 7% and a consumer's risk of 10% are desired. A sampling plan that minimizes the average total inspection when the incoming lot quality is at a 2% nonconforming level is needed.

In Appendix 4 of Dodge and Romig's tables for single sampling, there are schemes for 7% LTPD (LQL) and 10% LTPD (LQL). The 7% table, reproduced here as Table 16-3, is selected.

For an LQL of 7%, lot size 801–1000, and process average 1.41–2.1% nonconforming a sample size of $n = 110$ and acceptance number of $c = 4$ is indicated. The AOQL associated with this plan is 2.1%. In Chapter 15 a sampling plan with $n = 132$ and $c = 5$ with average total inspection equal to 171 was selected. The sampling plan $n = 114$ and $c = 4$ had a slightly higher average total inspection of 184. From this example it is seen that very satisfactory sampling plans may be selected using the Dodge-Romig tables. The discrete groupings in the tables do lead to jumps and approximate answers, but in practice, these jumps usually matter very little. For example, if the lot size were 1001 rather than 900, with the other conditions being the same, a sampling plan of $n = 130$, $c = 5$ would be selected. This would have resulted in a sample of fourteen more items than if the calculations had been done for LQL = 7%, $N = 1001$, and consumer's risk equal to 10%. Remember that in Chapter 15 the Poisson approximation was used for the calculations. Slight differences with the values in the Dodge-Romig tables may be expected. In fact, the Dodge-Romig tables were also calculated by using Poisson and binomial approximations to the hypergeometric distribution.

▶ **EXAMPLE 16-3**

Consider another example. Assume that business has been continued with the same supplier, and after receiving ten lots, the process average nonconforming is estimated to be 0.5% rather than 2%. In addition, increased production has led to lot sizes of 2000 items. The LQL (LTPD) = 7% table is still used, but now $n = 75$ and $c = 2$. The AOQL for this plan is 1.8%. The sample size is now reduced from 11% of the lot to less than 5% with an improvement in the AOQL. Two generalizations can be made. For a given LQL and consumer's risk, lower values for process average percent nonconforming yield smaller sample sizes. Larger lots yield a smaller fraction of the lot sampled for the same LQL and consumer's risk.

TABLE 16-3 Dodge and Romig Single Sampling Table for Limiting Quality Level $(LQL) = 7.0\%$

Lot Size	Process Average 0 to 0.07%			Process Average 0.08 to 0.70%			Process Average 0.71 to 1.40%			Process Average 1.41 to 2.10%			Process Average 2.11 to 2.80%			Process Average 2.81 to 3.50%		
	n	c	AOQL in %	n	c	AOQL in %	n	c	AOQL in %	n	c	AOQL in %	n	c	AOQL in %	n	c	AOQL in %
1–25	All	0	0	All	0	0	All	0	0	All	0	0	All	0	0	All	0	0
26–50	24	0	0.80	24	0	0.80	24	0	0.80	24	0	0.80	24	0	0.80	24	0	0.80
51–100	28	0	0.95	28	0	0.95	28	0	0.95	28	0	0.95	28	0	0.95	28	0	0.95
101–200	30	0	1.0	30	0	1.0	49	1	1.3	49	1	1.3	49	1	1.3	65	2	1.4
201–300	31	0	1.1	31	0	1.1	50	1	1.4	70	2	1.5	85	3	1.6	85	3	1.6
301–400	32	0	1.1	55	1	1.4	70	2	1.6	90	3	1.7	105	4	1.8	125	5	1.8
401–500	32	0	1.1	55	1	1.4	75	2	1.6	90	3	1.8	110	4	1.9	140	6	2.0
501–600	32	0	1.1	55	1	1.4	75	2	1.7	95	3	1.8	125	5	2.0	145	6	2.1
601–800	32	0	1.1	55	1	1.4	75	2	1.7	110	4	2.0	130	5	2.1	160	7	2.2
801–1000	33	0	1.1	55	1	1.4	95	3	1.9	110	4	2.1	145	6	2.2	180	8	2.4
1001–2000	55	1	1.5	75	2	1.8	95	3	2.0	130	5	2.3	185	8	2.5	230	11	2.8
2001–3000	55	1	1.5	75	2	1.8	115	4	2.1	150	6	2.4	215	10	2.8	300	15	3.0
3001–4000	55	1	1.5	75	2	1.8	115	4	2.2	165	7	2.6	235	11	2.9	330	17	3.2
4001–5000	55	1	1.5	75	2	1.8	130	5	2.4	185	8	2.7	250	12	3.0	350	18	3.3
5001–7000	55	1	1.5	75	2	1.8	130	5	2.4	185	8	2.7	270	13	3.1	385	20	3.4
7001–10,000	55	1	1.5	95	3	2.0	150	6	2.5	200	9	2.9	285	14	3.2	415	22	3.6
10,001–20,000	55	1	1.5	95	3	2.0	150	6	2.5	220	10	2.9	320	16	3.3	470	25	3.7
20,001–50,000	55	1	1.5	115	4	2.2	170	7	2.6	235	11	3.1	355	18	3.5	530	29	3.9
50,001–100,000	55	1	1.5	115	4	2.2	185	8	2.7	270	13	3.1	370	19	3.5	530	29	3.9

Double Sampling Plans

As was explained earlier, double sampling plans trade some increased administrative difficulty for reduced average sample number (ASN). Remember that a double sampling plan has two sample sizes and two sets of accept and reject numbers. By always inspecting all items in the first sample, straightforward estimates of the process average percent nonconforming are obtained. However, items in the second sample are usually not inspected after the number of nonconforming items found exceeds the acceptance number. This practice gives even greater reductions in average sample size than the tables indicate for double sampling. This procedure (curtailing) was discussed in Chapter 15. Double sampling is the standard in many manufacturing plants using Dodge-Romig plans. It is fairly easy to administer and produces substantial savings over single sampling. Multiple sampling plans and sequential sampling plans would reduce even more the total inspected items but are not frequently used because the efficiency gained compared to double is not as great as double compared to single, and the administration becomes more difficult.

▶ **EXAMPLE 16-4**

Use the example from earlier in this chapter to select a double sampling plan with LQL = 7%, consumer's risk = 10%, process average percent nonconforming 2%, and lot size 900. The Dodge-Romig tables contain LQL (LTPD) = 7%. It is seen in Table 16-4 that the first sample is $n_1 = 65$ with an acceptance number of $c = 1$, and the second sample size is $n_2 = 110$ with the combined sample equal to 175 and combined acceptance number of $c = 7$. The rejection number for the first sample is $c_2 + 1$ or 8. A quick calculation using Equation (15-2) gives the probability of 0.63 that the lot will be accepted on the first sample when there are 2% nonconforming items in the lot. The probability of acceptance on the first or second sample (using Equation 15-11) is 0.98.

Using Dodge-Romig Tables for AOQL

The Dodge-Romig tables that are most frequently used are those indexed by the average outgoing quality limit (AOQL). The AOQL may be specified in a contract, negotiated between different sections in a manufacturing plant, or chosen as a way of using final inspection to guarantee good results when the consumer is using the AQL or LQL sampling inspection system.

▶ **EXAMPLE 16-5**

The use of the tables can be illustrated by going back to the corresponding example used in Chapter 15. For the AOQL plan construction, assume a lot size of 900, a process average percent nonconforming of 2%, and a desired sampling plan that gave an AOQL of 4% with minimum ATI. The Dodge-Romig tables contain a single sampling plan for AOQL = 4%. Using Table 16-5, row 801–1000 for lot size and the column for process average percent nonconforming of 1.61 to 2.40%, the plan $n = 46$, $c = 3$ is selected. This agrees exactly with the directly calculated plan in Chapter 15. In those calculations an ATI of 58 was found. It is seen from Table 16-5 that the LQL value for a consumer's risk of 10% is 14.3%. A double sampling plan for these conditions can be found by using Table 16-6. The first sample would be $n_1 = 37$ with acceptance number $c = 1$ and rejection number $c_2 + 1 = 7$. The second sample, if needed, would be $n_2 = 58$ with a total acceptance number of $c_2 = 6$ and rejection number 7.

TABLE 16-4 Dodge and Romig Double Sampling Table for Limiting Quality Level (LQL) = 7.0%

	Process Average 0 to 0.07%						Process Average 0.08 to 0.70%						Process Average 0.71 to 1.40%					
	Trial 1		Trial 2			AOQL in %	Trial 1		Trial 2			AOQL in %	Trial 1		Trial 2			AOQL in %
Lot Size	n_1	c_1	n_2	$n_1 + n_2$	c_2		n_1	c_1	n_2	$n_1 + n_2$	c_2		n_1	c_1	n_2	$n_1 + n_2$	c_2	
1–25	All	0	—	—	—	0	All	0	—	—	—	0	All	0	—	—	—	0
26–50	24	0	—	—	—	0.80	24	0	—	—	—	0.80	24	0	—	—	—	0.80
51–75	31	0	15	46	1	0.90	31	0	15	46	1	0.90	31	0	15	46	1	0.90
76–110	34	0	16	50	1	1.1	34	0	16	50	1	1.1	34	0	16	50	1	1.1
111–200	36	0	19	55	1	1.2	36	0	19	55	1	1.2	36	0	39	75	2	1.4
201–300	37	0	23	60	1	1.3	37	0	23	60	1	1.3	37	0	38	75	2	1.5
301–400	38	0	22	60	1	1.3	38	0	42	80	2	1.5	38	0	57	95	3	1.7
401–500	39	0	21	60	1	1.3	39	0	41	80	2	1.5	39	0	61	100	3	1.7
501–600	39	0	26	65	1	1.3	39	0	46	85	2	1.6	39	0	61	100	3	1.7
601–800	39	0	26	65	1	1.4	39	0	46	85	2	1.6	39	0	81	120	4	1.9
801–1000	39	0	26	65	1	1.4	39	0	46	85	2	1.6	39	0	86	125	4	2.0
1001–2000	40	0	45	85	2	1.7	40	0	65	105	3	1.9	40	0	105	145	5	2.2
2001–3000	40	0	45	85	2	1.7	40	0	65	105	3	1.9	65	1	100	165	6	2.3
3001–4000	40	0	45	85	2	1.7	40	0	65	105	3	1.9	65	1	115	180	7	2.4
4001–5000	40	0	45	85	2	1.7	40	0	85	125	4	2.1	65	1	115	180	7	2.5
5001–7000	40	0	45	85	2	1.7	40	0	85	125	4	2.1	65	1	135	200	8	2.5
7001–10,000	40	0	45	85	2	1.7	40	0	85	125	4	2.1	65	1	135	200	8	2.6
10,001–20,000	40	0	45	85	2	1.7	40	0	85	125	4	2.1	65	1	155	220	9	2.7
20,001–50,000	40	0	45	85	2	1.7	40	0	105	145	5	2.3	65	1	170	235	10	2.8
50,001–100,000	40	0	45	85	2	1.7	40	0	105	145	5	2.3	65	1	170	235	10	2.9

	Process Average 1.41 to 2.10%						Process Average 2.11 to 2.80%						Process Average 2.81 to 3.50%					
	Trial 1		Trial 2			AOQL in %	Trial 1		Trial 2			AOQL in %	Trial 1		Trial 2			AOQL in %
Lot Size	n_1	c_1	n_2	n_1+n_2	c_2		n_1	c_1	n_2	n_1+n_2	c_2		n_1	c_1	n_2	n_1+n_2	c_2	
1–25	All	0	—	—	—	0	All	0	—	—	—	0	All	0	—	—	—	0
26–50	24	0	—	—	—	0.80	24	0	—	—	—	0.80	24	0	—	—	—	0.80
51–75	31	0	15	46	1	0.90	31	0	15	46	1	0.90	31	0	15	46	1	0.90
76–110	34	0	31	65	2	1.2	34	0	31	65	2	1.2	34	0	31	65	2	1.2
111–200	36	0	54	90	3	1.5	36	0	54	90	3	1.5	36	0	69	105	4	1.5
201–300	37	0	58	95	3	1.6	37	0	73	110	4	1.7	60	1	80	140	6	1.9
301–400	38	0	77	115	4	1.8	60	1	85	145	6	1.9	60	1	100	160	7	2.0
401–500	39	0	76	115	4	1.8	60	1	105	165	7	2.1	60	1	135	195	9	2.2
501–600	65	1	90	155	6	2.1	65	1	120	185	8	2.2	85	2	130	215	10	2.3
601–800	65	1	105	170	7	2.2	65	1	140	205	9	2.3	85	2	165	250	12	2.5
801–1000	65	1	110	175	7	2.2	85	2	140	225	10	2.5	105	3	180	285	14	2.7
1001–2000	65	1	150	215	9	2.5	105	3	175	280	13	2.8	145	5	230	375	19	3.1
2001–3000	85	2	165	250	11	2.7	105	3	210	315	15	3.0	165	6	300	465	24	3.3
3001–4000	85	2	185	270	12	2.8	105	3	250	355	17	3.1	180	7	335	515	27	3.4
4001–5000	85	2	185	270	12	2.9	125	4	245	370	18	3.2	180	7	370	550	29	3.6
5001–7000	85	2	205	290	13	3.0	125	4	265	390	19	3.3	200	8	385	585	31	3.8
7001–10,000	85	2	205	290	13	3.1	125	4	300	425	21	3.4	200	8	450	650	35	3.9
10,001–20,000	85	2	220	305	14	3.2	125	4	335	460	23	3.5	220	9	485	705	38	4.0
20,001–50,000	85	2	240	325	15	3.3	145	5	360	505	26	3.5	220	9	565	785	43	4.1
50,001–100,000	105	3	270	375	18	3.4	165	6	390	555	29	3.7	235	10	610	845	47	4.2

Trial 1: n_1 = first sample size; c_1 = acceptance number for first sample.

"All" indicates that each piece in the lot is to be inspected.

Trial 2: n_2 = second sample size; c_2 = acceptance number for first and second samples combined.

AOQL = average outgoing quality limit.

577

TABLE 16-5 Dodge and Romig Single Sampling Table for Average Outgoing Quality Limit (AOQL) = 4.0%

Lot Size	Process Average 0 to 0.08%			Process Average 0.09 to 0.80%			Process Average 0.81 to 1.60%			Process Average 1.61 to 2.40%			Process Average 2.41 to 3.20%			Process Average 3.21 to 4.00%		
	n	c	$p_t\%$	n	c	$p_t\%$	n	c	$p_t\%$	n	c	$p_t\%$	n	c	$p_t\%$	n	c	$p_t\%$
1–10	All	0	—	All	0	—	All	0	—	All	0	—	All	0	—	All	0	—
11–50	8	0	23.0	8	0	23.0	8	0	23.0	8	0	23.0	8	0	23.0	8	0	23.0
51–100	8	0	24.0	8	0	24.0	8	0	24.0	8	0	24.0	17	1	21.5	17	1	21.5
101–200	9	0	22.0	9	0	22.0	19	1	20.0	19	1	20.0	19	1	20.0	19	1	20.0
201–300	9	0	22.5	9	0	22.5	20	1	19.0	20	1	19.0	31	2	16.8	31	2	16.8
301–400	9	0	22.5	20	1	19.1	20	1	19.1	32	2	16.2	32	2	16.2	43	3	15.2
401–500	9	0	22.5	20	1	19.1	20	1	19.1	32	2	16.3	32	2	16.3	44	3	14.9
501–600	9	0	22.5	20	1	19.2	20	1	19.2	32	2	16.3	45	3	14.6	60	4	12.9
601–800	9	0	22.5	20	1	19.2	33	2	15.9	33	2	15.9	46	3	14.3	60	4	13.0
801–1000	9	0	22.5	21	1	18.3	33	2	16.0	46	3	14.3	60	4	13.0	75	5	12.2
1001–2000	9	0	22.5	21	1	18.4	34	2	15.6	47	3	14.1	75	5	12.2	105	7	11.0
2001–3000	9	0	22.5	21	1	18.4	34	2	15.6	60	4	13.2	90	6	11.3	125	8	10.4
3001–4000	21	1	18.4	21	1	18.4	48	3	13.8	65	4	12.2	110	7	10.7	155	10	9.8
4001–5000	21	1	18.5	34	2	15.7	48	3	13.9	80	5	11.6	110	7	10.8	175	11	9.5
5001–7000	21	1	18.5	34	2	15.7	48	3	13.9	80	5	11.6	125	8	10.4	210	13	9.0
7001–10,000	21	1	18.5	34	2	15.7	65	4	12.3	95	6	11.1	145	9	9.8	245	15	8.6
10,001–20,000	21	1	18.5	34	2	15.7	65	4	12.3	110	7	10.8	195	12	9.0	340	20	7.9
20,001–50,000	21	1	18.5	49	3	13.6	80	5	11.6	145	9	9.8	250	15	8.5	460	26	7.4
50,001–100,000	21	1	18.5	49	3	13.6	95	6	11.1	165	10	9.6	310	18	8.0	540	30	7.1

n = sample size; c = acceptance number.

"All" indicates that each piece in the lot is to be inspected.

p_t = limiting quality level with a consumer's risk (P_C) of 0.10.

TABLE 16-6 Dodge and Romig Double Sampling Table for Average Outgoing Quality Limit (AOQL) = 4.0%

Lot Size	Process Average 0 to 0.08%						Process Average 0.09 to 0.80%						Process Average 0.81 to 1.60%					
	Trial 1		Trial 2			p_t %	Trial 1		Trial 2			p_t %	Trial 1		Trial 2			p_t %
	n_1	c_1	n_2	$n_1 + n_2$	c_2		n_1	c_1	n_2	$n_1 + n_2$	c_2		n_1	c_1	n_2	$n_1 + n_2$	c_2	
1–10	All	0	—	—	—	—	All	0	—	—	—	—	All	0	—	—	—	—
11–50	8	0	—	—	—	23.0	8	0	—	—	—	23.0	8	0	—	—	—	23.0
51–100	12	0	7	19	1	22.0	12	0	7	19	1	22.0	12	0	7	19	1	22.0
101–200	13	0	8	21	1	21.0	13	0	8	21	1	21.0	15	0	17	32	2	18.0
201–300	13	0	9	22	1	20.5	16	0	18	34	2	17.4	16	0	18	34	2	17.4
301–400	14	0	8	22	1	20.0	16	0	19	35	2	17.0	18	0	28	46	3	15.5
401–500	14	0	8	22	1	20.0	16	0	19	35	2	17.0	19	0	28	47	3	13.3
501–600	16	0	19	35	2	17.0	16	0	19	35	2	17.0	19	0	29	48	3	15.1
601–800	16	0	20	36	2	16.7	16	0	20	36	2	16.7	19	0	30	49	3	14.9
801–1000	16	0	20	36	2	16.7	16	0	20	36	2	16.7	20	0	45	65	4	13.8
1001–2000	17	0	19	36	2	16.6	19	0	31	50	3	14.8	21	0	44	65	4	13.6
2001–3000	17	0	19	36	2	16.6	19	0	31	50	3	14.8	21	0	44	65	4	13.6
3001–4000	17	0	20	37	2	16.5	19	0	31	50	3	14.8	22	0	58	80	5	13.0
4001–5000	17	0	20	37	2	16.5	19	0	31	50	3	14.8	22	0	58	80	5	13.0
5001–7000	17	0	20	37	2	16.5	19	0	31	50	3	14.8	22	0	58	80	5	13.0
7001–10,000	17	0	20	37	2	16.5	19	0	36	55	3	14.6	23	0	57	80	5	12.7
10,001–20,000	17	0	20	37	2	16.5	21	0	44	65	4	13.6	23	0	72	95	6	12.0
20,001–50,000	17	0	20	37	2	16.5	21	0	44	65	4	13.6	43	1	92	135	8	10.6
50,001–100,000	17	0	20	37	2	16.5	23	0	62	85	5	12.5	44	1	106	150	9	10.3

(continued)

TABLE 16-6 (continued)

	Process Average 1.61 to 2.40%						Process Average 2.41 to 3.20%						Process Average 3.21 to 4.00%					
	Trial 1		Trial 2			p_t	Trial 1		Trial 2			p_t	Trial 1		Trial 2			p_t
Lot Size	n_1	c_1	n_2	$n_1 + n_2$	c_2	%	n_1	c_1	n_2	$n_1 + n_2$	c_2	%	n_1	c_1	n_2	$n_1 + n_2$	c_2	%
1–10	All	0	—	—	—	—	All	0	—	—	—	—	All	0	—	—	—	—
11–50	8	0	—	—	—	23.0	8	0	—	—	—	23.0	8	0	—	—	—	23.0
51–100	13	0	14	27	2	20.5	13	0	14	27	2	20.5	13	0	14	27	2	20.5
101–200	16	0	26	42	3	16.5	16	0	26	42	3	16.5	16	0	26	42	3	16.5
201–300	17	0	28	45	3	16.0	18	0	37	55	4	15.0	33	1	47	80	6	13.2
301–400	19	0	41	60	4	14.3	19	0	41	60	4	14.3	35	1	60	95	7	12.8
401–500	20	0	40	60	4	14.0	34	1	51	85	6	13.0	36	1	74	110	8	12.2
501–600	20	0	45	65	4	13.8	37	1	63	100	7	12.2	50	2	75	125	9	11.6
601–800	22	0	58	80	5	13.0	39	1	81	120	8	11.6	55	2	105	160	11	10.8
801–1000	37	1	58	95	6	12.2	41	1	94	135	9	11.1	55	2	120	175	12	10.5
1001–2000	39	1	71	110	7	11.5	55	2	110	165	11	10.6	80	3	165	245	16	9.5
2001–3000	41	1	89	130	8	11.0	60	2	145	205	13	9.8	95	4	210	305	20	9.2
3001–4000	43	1	102	145	9	10.5	80	3	160	240	15	9.4	115	5	250	365	23	8.8
4001–5000	45	1	120	165	10	10.0	85	3	180	265	16	8.9	160	7	305	465	28	8.1
5001–7000	65	2	120	185	11	9.6	85	3	200	285	17	8.7	210	9	450	660	38	7.4
7001–10,000	65	2	140	205	12	9.3	90	3	230	320	19	8.5	235	10	550	785	44	7.1
10,001–20,000	65	2	160	225	13	9.0	105	4	265	370	22	8.3	270	12	625	895	50	7.0
20,001–50,000	70	2	175	245	14	8.8	125	5	315	440	26	8.1	295	13	725	1020	57	6.9
50,001–100,000	70	2	205	275	16	8.7	150	6	385	535	31	7.7	335	15	845	1180	66	6.8

Trial 1: n_1 = first sample size; c_1 = acceptance number for first sample.

"All" indicates that each piece in the lot is to be inspected.

Trial 2: n_2 = second sample size; c_2 = acceptance number for first and second sample, combined.

p_t = limiting quality level with a consumer's risk (P_C) of 0.10.

▶ 16-3 AN LQL INDEXED SYSTEM

In the preceding section examples were given of how the Dodge-Romig system could be used for limiting quality level (LQL) sampling schemes. The earlier name for these schemes was lot tolerance percent defective (LTPD). How the sampling schemes of ANSI/ASQC Z1.4 (MIL-STD-105E or ISO 2859-1) could be used as LQL schemes or plans was also discussed. There is interest in acceptance sampling plans that are indexed by LQLs (Duncan et al., 1980). Examples of this interest are the Military Specification MIL-S-19500E for Semiconductor Devices, Military Specification MIL-M-38510 for Microcircuits, and MIL-STD-781C on Reliability Design Qualification and Production Tests. An LQL indexed system based on work by the ISO Technical Committee 69 on Statistical Methods was published as ISO 2859-2 (1985). An American version of this standard is designated as ANSI/ASQC Q3-1988.

The basic difference between LQL and AQL systems is that the indexing values for the LQL tables are the quality levels for which a small fraction (approximately 10%) of the lots will be accepted. The AQL systems use quality values for which a large fraction (approximately 95%) of the lots will be accepted. For this reason, LQL plans are sometimes referred to as consumer plans or customer protection plans. The LQL value is a quality level against which the consumer wishes to protect.

The LQL sampling plans are designed to be compatible with ANSI/ASQC Z1.4, MIL-STD-105E, and ISO 2859-1. Compatibility means that the lot sizes and sample sizes are the same as those used in ISO 2859-1. The desire to use the same sample sizes led to the derivation of the tables presented in this section (Figures 16-9 and 16-10). In ISO 2859-1 the sample sizes bear the ratio to each other of $10^{1/5} = 1.585$ and hence have a cycle of size 5. Thus the LQL values in the tables also have the ratio of 1.585 to their nearest neighbors.

It is important to realize that when LQL acceptance sampling plans are used, the producer will want to supply product with quality considerably better than the LQL value. The LQL value is the quality that the consumer does *not* want, and it would not be very economical for a product to have 90% of submitted lots rejected. The LQL sampling plans have thus been carefully constructed to provide information about the quality levels for which the probability of acceptance is 95%.

16-3.1 Using LQL Plans

The following sequence of steps for use of an LQL procedure is very similar to the sequence that was used in selecting the right Dodge-Romig scheme:

1. DECIDE what characteristics to include.
2. DECIDE what is to constitute a lot.
3. CHOOSE the LQL value to be used.
4. SELECT the appropriate inspection level.
5. DETERMINE the sample size for the lot size used.
6. SELECT the appropriate sampling plan.
7. EXAMINE the OC curve to understand the plan's performance.

Table B6. Single sampling plans for limiting quality 5.0%

Lot size for given inspection level					BS 6001 single sampling plan (normal inspection)			Code letter	Submitted quality accepted with given probability* (quality as percent nonconforming)					Acceptance probabilities† (limiting quality)	
S-1 to S-3	S-4	I	II	III	AQL	n	Ac		0.95	0.90	0.50	0.10	0.05	Max.	Min.
									% 0.444	% 0.666	% 2.09	% 4.78	% 5.80		
> 80‡	81‡ to 500,000	81‡ to 10,000	81‡ to 1,200	81‡ to 500	0.65	80	1	J	0.444	0.666	2.09	4.78	5.80	0.086	0.000
	> 500,000	10,001 to 35,000	1,201 to 3,200	501 to 1,200	1.0	125	3	K	1.09	1.40	2.94	5.35	6.20	0.124	0.092
		35,001 to 150,000	3,201 to 10,000	1,201 to 3,200	1.0	200	5	L	1.31	1.58	2.84	4.64	5.26	0.062	0.048
		> 150,000	> 10,000	>3,200	1.5	315	10	M	1.96	2.23	3.39	4.89	5.38	0.061	0.072

AQL is the acceptable quality level;
n   is the sample size:
Ac is the acceptance number.
*Probability calculated by the Poisson approximation.
† The exact acceptance probabilities calculated from the hypergeometric distribution vary with lot size. The maximum and minimum values attained for permitted lot sizes are given for each plan.
‡ For fewer than 126 in the lot, the lot is to be 100% inspected.

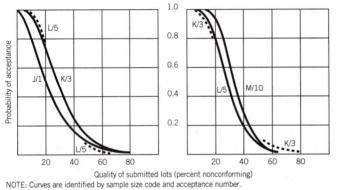

Quality of submitted lots (percent nonconforming)
NOTE: Curves are identified by sample size code and acceptance number.

Figure 16-9   Single Sampling Plans for LQL = 5.0%

8. SELECT the sample items from the lot by a random procedure.

9. FOLLOW the procedure to accept or reject lots based on the acceptance number.

10. KEEP a running estimate of the process average and a count of the lots accepted and rejected. Change plans if necessary.

This sequence of steps will not be discussed in detail because of the similarities to the sequence of steps for the Dodge-Romig plans.

The tables shown here as Figures 16-9 and 16-10 are taken, with permission from ANSI/ASQC Q3. Figure 16-9, which is Table B6 in the standard, contains sampling plans for LQL = 5%. The upper part of the table contains information regarding sample sizes and acceptance numbers for single sampling for inspection levels S1, S2, S3, S4, I, II, and III. The sample size depends on the lot size and inspection level as do the plans in ISO 2859-1.

The right side of the upper portion of the figure contains points on the OC curves, which are shown in the lower portion of the figure. On the far right of the figure are indicated maximum and minimum (based on inspection level) probabilities of acceptance for lots that are 5.0% nonconforming.

When the consumer wants to specify an LQL and use a table of this type, the LQL, lot size, and inspection level are determined. The sample size and acceptance number are

Table 7. Single sampling plans for limiting quality 3.15% (procedure B)

Lot size for given inspection level					BS 6001 single sampling plan (normal inspection)			Code letter	Submitted quality accepted with given probability* (quality as percent nonconforming)					Acceptance probabilities† (limiting quality)	
S-1 to S-3	S-4	I	II	III	AQL	n	Ac		0.95	0.90	0.50	0.10	0.05	Max.	Min.
									%	%	%	%	%		
> 125‡	>125‡	126‡ to 35,000	126‡ to 3,200	126‡ to 1,200	0.40	125	1	K	0.284	0.426	1.34	3.11	3.80	0.093	0.000
		35,001 to 150,000	3,201 to 10,000	1,201 to 3,200	0.65	200	3	L	0.683	0.873	1.84	3.34	3.88	0.122	0.101
		> 150,000	10,001 to 35,000	3,201 to 10,000	0.65	315	5	M	0.829	1.00	1.80	2.94	3.34	0.067	0.058
			> 35,000	>10,000	1.00	500	10	N	1.231	1.40	2.13	3.08	3.39	0.083	0.078

AQL is the acceptable quality level.
n is the sample size.
Ac is the acceptance number.
*Probability calculated by the Poisson approximation for code letters K, L, and M. Binominal distribution for code letter J.
† The exact acceptance probabilities calculated from the hypergeometric distribution vary with lot size. The maximum and minimum values attained for permitted lot sizes are given for each plan.
‡ For fewer than 81 in the lot, the lot is to be 100% inspected.

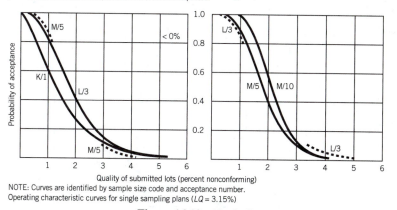

Quality of submitted lots (percent nonconforming)
NOTE: Curves are identified by sample size code and acceptance number.
Operating characteristic curves for single sampling plans (LQ = 3.15%)

Figure 16-10   Single Sampling Plans for LQL = 3.15%

then read from the table. For example, assume that a consumer wishes to purchase capacitors and protect against too high a probability of accepting lots from a process running at 5% nonconforming. If the lot size is 5000 and inspection level II is chosen, it is shown that the plan calls for a sample of 200 capacitors and has an acceptance number of 5. It can also quickly be seen that our consumer protection is better than the nominal 10% probability of acceptance. In this case the probability of accepting a lot from a process running at 5% nonconforming is 0.062. The producer will have to have the process running at 1.3% nonconforming or better to have a probability of acceptance of 0.95. The corresponding plan in ISO 2859-1 has an AQL of 1.0%.

In using these LQL plans, the consumer may want to specify a maximum value for probability of acceptance equal to 0.95 as well as an LQL. The procedure is then similar to specifying a two-point sampling plan. For example, the consumer may want an LQL of 5% and also wish the value at which the probability of acceptance equals 0.95 to be less than 1%. In the above example it is shown that the plan $n = 200$, $c = 3$, which corresponds to an LQL of 3.15% nonconforming, must be used. The tables for LQL = 3.15% are displayed in Figure 16-10.

Lot Size	Nominal Limiting Quality (LQ)									
	0.5	0.8	1.25	2.0	3.15	5.0	8.0	12.5	20.0	32.0
16 to 25						100%/0	17/0 0.9 .26 .30 .29	13/0 .08 .2 .39 .39	9/0 .08 .19 .57 .57	6/0 .07 .15 .85 .85
26 to 50				100%/0	100%/0	28/0 .08 .25 .18 .18	22/0 .09 .17 .23 .23	15/0 .09 .15 .34 .34	10/0 .08 .14 .51 .51	6/0 .08 .15 .85 .85
51 to 90			100%/0	50/0 .19 .37 .10 .09	44/0 .09 .25 .12 .12	34/0 .10 .18 .15 .15	24/0 .10 .15 .21 .21	16/0 .09 .14 .32 .32	10/0 .09 .14 .51 .51	6/0 .09 .15 .85 .85
91 to 150		100%/0	90/0 .16 .32 .06 .06	80/0 .10 .20 .06 .06	55/0 .10 .18 .09 .10	38/0 .10 .15 .13 .13	26/0 .09 .12 .20 .20	18/0 .08 .11 .28 .28	13/0 .05 .07 .39 .39	13/1 .04 .08 2.8 2.7
151 to 280	100%/0	170/0 .10 .26 .03 .03	130/0 .09 .20 .04 .04	95/0 .09 .15 .05 .05	65/0 .09 .13 .08 .07	42/0 .10 .12 .12 .12	28/0 .09 .11 .18 .18	20/0 .06 .08 .26 .26	20/1 .06 .09 1.8 1.8	13/1 .04 .08 2.8 2.7
281 to 500	280/0 .09 .25 .02 .02	220/0 .10 .17 .02 .03	155/0 .09 .14 .03 .03	105/0 .09 .12 .05 .05	80/0 .06 .08 .06 .06	50/0 .07 .08 .10 .10	32/0 .06 .08 .16 .16	32/1 .07 .09 .72 .71	20/1 .07 .09 1.8 1.8	20/3 .07 .12 7.1 6.8
501 to 1,200	380/0 .09 .15 .02 .01	255/0 .08 .13 .02 .02	170/0 .10 .12 .03 .03	125/0 .07 .08 .04 .04	125/0 .08 .10 .29 .30	80/1 .08 .09 .45 .44	50/1 .08 .09 .72 .71	32/1 .07 .09 1.1 1.1	32/3 .09 .12 4.4 4.3	32/5 .03 .06 8.5 8.2
1,201 to 3,200	430/0 .10 .12 .01 .01	280/0 .09 .11 .02 .02	200/0 .07 .08 .02 .02	200/1 .08 .09 .18 .19	125/1 .09 .10 .29 .30	125/3 .12 .13 1.1 1.1	80/3 .11 .12 1.7 1.7	50/3 .11 .13 2.8 2.7	50/5 .05 .07 5.4 5.2	50/10 .04 .08 12.9 12.3
3,201 to 10,000	450/0 .10 .11 .01 .01	315/0 .08 .08 .02 .02	315/1 .09 .10 .11 .12	200/1 .09 .09 .18 .19	200/3 .12 .13 .69 .69	200/5 .06 .07 1.3 1.3	125/5 .06 .07 2.1 2.1	80/5 .05 .07 3.3 3.3	80/10 .06 .08 7.9 7.7	80/18 .04 .07 16.1 15.5
10,001 to 35,000	500/0 .08 .08 .01 .01	500/1 .09 .09 .07 .08	315/1 .09 .10 .11 .12	315/3 .12 .13 .44 .44	315/5 .07 .07 .83 .84	315/10 .08 .09 2.0 2.0	200/10 .07 .08 3.1 3.1	125/10 .08 .09 5.0 4.9	125/18 .07 .09 10.2 10.0	80/18
35,001 to 150,000	800/1 .09 .09 .04 .05	500/1 .09 .09 .07 .08	500/3 .13 .13 .27 .27	500/5 .06 .07 .52 .53	500/10 .08 .09 1.2 1.2	500/18 .09 .09 2.5 2.5	315/18 .08 .09 4.0 3.9	200/18 .08 .09 6.3 6.3	125/18	80/18
150,001 to 500,000	800/1 .09 .09 .04 .05	800/3 .09 .12 .17 .18	800/5 .07 .07 .33 .33	800/10 .08 .08 .77 .78	800/18 .08 .09 1.6 1.6	500/18	315/18	200/18	125/18	80/18
>500,000	1250/3 .13 .13 .11 .11	1250/5 .07 .07 .21 .21	1250/10 .09 .09 .49 .49	1250/18 .09 .08 1.0 1.0	800/18 .08 .09 1.6 1.6	500/18	315/18	200/18	125/18	80/18

Example: For lot size 1,201 to 3,200 and LQ of 2.0% Table A2 gives:

```
200/1
.08 .09
.18 .19
```

which are defined by code below.

Code:

Sample Size/Acceptance Number		
a	b	Use a and c for percent nonconforming
c	d	Use b and d for nonconformities per hundred units

a = hypergeometric P_a at the LQ*
b = Poisson P_a at the LQ
c = process average percent nonconforming for which binomial P_a = 95%
d = process average percent nonconforming for which Poisson P_a = 95%

*These values are calculated on the largest lot size in the group consistent with a whole number of nonconforming units equivalent to the LQ
For the largest lot size, M500,001, a lot size of 1,000,000 was used.

Figure 16-11   Single Sampling Plans Based on the Hypergeometric Distribution (Table A-2 of ANSI/ASQC Q3-1988)

▶ 16-4 OTHER ATTRIBUTE ACCEPTANCE SAMPLING PLANS

Although three attribute sampling systems have been discussed in detail, these are not all of the sampling systems that are in use. They are by far the most common, but many others also exist, and more have been proposed.

Some different plans that appear particularly useful are combination attributes/variables plans, median plans, empirical Bayes and Bayes plans, and reduced limit plans. Of course, many other plans are modifications or close relatives of the sampling systems discussed in this chapter.

One modification should be mentioned because of the number of plans constructed this way. When LQL plans are applied to the inspection of small isolated lots, the probabilities of acceptance as a function of lot quality will be given by the hypergeometric distribution. When the sample size is a significant fraction of the lot size, the results that are calculated can be substantially different from the ones presented in these tables.

The LQL system of ISO 2859-2 (ANSI/ASQC Q3) has a section for hypergeometric plans. The concept is that if the submitted lot is the only one being produced, the hypergeometric plans should be used. These are in Section A of the standards. If the submitted lot is one from a continuing series of lots, even though the customer receives only one lot, the binomial distribution (procedure B) should be used. Procedure B was discussed in Section 16-3.

Figure 16-11 is from Table A2 of ANSI/ASQC Q3. It is essentially the same as the corresponding table in ISO 2859-2. It shows the sample size and acceptance number indexed by LQL, designated LQ, and lot size. In addition the table gives the probability of acceptance, using both the hypergeometric and Poisson distributions, of a lot with percent nonconforming equal to the LQL and the process average percent nonconforming for which the probability of acceptance is 0.95. The purpose of the last figures is to relate the standard to AQL-based plans, specifically ISO 2859-1.

In summary, it should be mentioned that ISO Technical Committee 69 has also published a technical report, ISO TR 8550 (1994) that surveys the entire field of acceptance sampling of discrete items in lots.

▶ 16-5 REFERENCES

American Society for Testing and Materials (1999), ASTM E259-98, *Standard Practice for Use of Process Oriented AOQL and LTPD Sampling Plans,* West Conshohocken, PA.

American Society for Quality (1988), ASQC Q3, *Sampling Procedures and Tables for Inspection of Isolated Lots by Attributes,* ASQ, Milwaukee.

American Society for Quality (1993a), ANSI/ASQC Z1.4-1993, *Sampling Procedures and Tables for Inspection by Attributes,* ASQ, Milwaukee.

American Society for Quality (1993b), ANSI/ASQC Z1.9-1993, *Sampling Procedures and Tables for Inspection by Variables for Percent Nonconforming,* ASQ, Milwaukee.

American Society for Quality (2002), ANSI/ISO/ASQC A3534-2, *Statistics—Vocabulary and Symbols—Applied Statistics,* ASQ, Milwaukee.

Dodge, H. F. (1969), "Notes on the Evolution of Acceptance Sampling Plans, Part II," *Journal of Quality Technology,* Vol. 1, No. 3, pp. 155–62 (July).

Dodge, H. F. and Romig, H. G. (1924), "A Method of Sampling Inspection," *The Bell System Technical Journal,* Vol. 8, No. 10, pp. 613–31.

Dodge, H. F. and Romig, H. G. (1959), *Sampling Inspection Tables,* Second Edition, Wiley, New York. Reprinted as the Wiley Classic Library Edition (1998).

Duncan, A. J. (1986), *Quality Control and Industrial Statistics,* Fifth Edition, Richard D. Irwin, Homewood, IL.

Duncan, A. J., Godfrey, A. B., Mundel, A. B., and Partridge, V. A. (1980), "Single Sampling Plans Indexed by LQLs that are Compatible with the Structure of MIL-STD-105D," *Journal of Quality Technology,* Vol. 12, No. 1, pp. 40–46 (January).

International Organization for Standardization (1985), ISO 2859-2, *Sampling Procedures for Inspection by Attributes—Part 2: Sampling Plans Indexed by Limiting Quality (LQ) for Isolated Lot Inspection*, ISO, Geneva, Switzerland.

International Organization for Standardization (1989), ISO 3951, *Sampling Procedures and Charts for Inspection by Variables for Percent Nonconforming*, ISO, Geneva, Switzerland.

International Organization for Standardization (1991), ISO 2859-3, *Sampling Procedures for Inspection by Attributes—Part 3: Skip-Lot Sampling Procedures*, ISO, Geneva, Switzerland.

International Organization for Standardization (1994), ISO TR 8550, *Guide to the Selection of an Acceptance Sampling System, Scheme or Plan for Inspection of Discrete Items in Lots*, ISO, Geneva, Switzerland.

International Organization for Standardization (1999), ISO 2859-1, *Sampling Procedures for Inspection by Attributes—Part 1: Sampling Schemes Indexed by Acceptance Quality Limit (AQL) for Lot-by-Lot Inspection*, ISO, Geneva, Switzerland.

International Organization for Standardization (2000), ISO 9000: 2000, *Quality Management Systems—Fundamentals and Vocabulary*, ISO, Geneva, Switzerland.

International Organization for Standardization (2002), ISO 3534-2, *Statistics—Vocabulary and Symbols—Part 2: Applied Statistics*, ISO, Geneva, Switzerland.

Liebesman, B. S. (1979), "The Use of MIL-STD-105D to Control Average Outgoing Quality," *Journal of Quality Technology*, Vol. 11, No. 1, Jan.; pp. 36–43.

Schilling, E. G. and Sheesley, J. H. (1978a), "The Performance of MIL-STD-105D under the Switching Rules, Part Evaluation," *Journal of Quality Technology*, Vol. 10, No. 2, April; pp. 76–83.

Schilling, E. G., and Sheesley, J. H. (1978b), "The Performance of MIL-STD-105D under the Switching Rules, Part 2: Tables," *Journal of Quality Technology*, Vol. 10, No. 3, July; pp. 105–24.

U.S. Department of Defense (1957), MIL-STD-414, *Sampling Procedures and Tables for Inspection by Variables for Percent Defective*, Washington, D.C.

U.S. Department of Defense (1989), *Sampling Procedures and Tables for Inspection by Attributes* (MIL-STD-105E), U.S. Government Printing Office, Washington, D.C.

► 16-6 PROBLEMS

1. Assume that a product is produced in lots of 2000 items, the consumer is willing to select the least stringent of the general inspection levels, and an AQL of 4% nonconforming is used. What is the code letter? What sample size is used? What are the acceptance and rejection numbers for normal inspection? What are they for tightened inspection?

2. In the example above, when would the consumer go to reduced inspection? What would be the sample size used? What would be the acceptance and rejection numbers used during reduced inspection? What would happen if the sample had three nonconforming items?

3. In the preceding example, at what percent nonconforming in the lot would 95% of the lots be accepted during normal inspection? At what percent nonconforming in the lot would 95% of the lots be accepted during tightened inspection?

4. Using the same example, what percent of the lots would be accepted using the switching rules correctly and assuming that submitted lots have a quality level of 5.03% nonconforming? At 3.86% nonconforming? At 10% nonconforming?

5. Let 0 designate an accepted lot, and let X designate a lot not accepted. Explain what happens and when with respect to switching rules for the following sequence (assume that no nonconforming items are in accepted lots):

000X00000X000X00X00000000000000X0000

6. Using the procedure discussed in Section 15-3.5, calculate the sampling plan that provides minimum average total inspection for $N = 1000$, $p = 0.02$, LQL = 7%, and a consumer's risk of 10%. Compare this with the sampling plan for these conditions selected in this chapter. How much do they differ? Why?

7. Explain the following statement: "The operating characteristic curves for plans with $c = 0$ have a very undesirable shape."

8. For the same LQL, consumer's risk, and process average percent nonconforming, does the AOQL get better or worse with increasing lot size?

9. Find an example in which the fraction of a lot sampled actually increases when the lot size increases from one value to another.

10. Calculate the average total inspection for the double sampling example LQL = 7%, $N = 1000$, $p = 2\%$, and consumer's risk = 10%.

17

ACCEPTANCE SAMPLING BY VARIABLES

In addition to the acceptance sampling plans based on attributes discussed in the preceding two chapters, there are many acceptance sampling plans based on variables data. These plans have several distinct advantages and disadvantages compared to attribute plans. Their primary advantage is efficiency. Variables carry more information than attributes (a length of 37.5 is more informative, for example, than the fact that it exceeds 30). It is thus often possible to achieve the same power with a sample size in a variables acceptance sampling plan far smaller than the sample size for a comparable attributes acceptance sampling plan. Variables acceptance sampling plans are also often far better suited for the inspection being performed when the specification or requirement is expressed as an average of a measure of variation.

The disadvantages of variables acceptance sampling plans compared to attributes acceptance sampling plans are that they may be more difficult to use, the assumptions on which they are based may not be met or may not be known to be met. They are unwieldy in situations in which several characteristics for each item are being inspected. Usually, the cost of inspecting each item by attributes is less than the cost of inspecting them by variables. This may be because of the method of inspection. A go-no go test may be simpler to perform than measuring a variable. The lower cost may also be the result of the simpler procedure of recording only the number of items failing a test rather than recording a variables measurement on each item. In many modern quality control systems these reasons are no longer valid because measurements are made by automated test equipment. Even the simplest automated test equipment usually has the capability for the simple calculations and data accumulation needed for variables acceptance sampling.

The savings afforded by variables acceptance sampling can be substantial. A recent application in one factory reduced the sample needed for testing a new electronic product to one fourth the previous sample size. Because the testing was done by humans one step at a time, the labor savings were significant. In this case the test procedure was very simple and combined sequential and variables sampling. A small desktop microprocessor wired to a test set was used to make the variables measurements and perform the calculations. The operator performed a test operation and then observed a control panel. If the green light was lit, the operator accepted the item; if yellow, the operator made another test operation; if red, the operator rejected the item. The microprocessor was using the variables data at each step.

In this chapter the basic steps for constructing a variables sampling plan are presented. To understand the fundamental principles, approximate but simple methods will be used to derive a basic variables acceptance sampling plan. Then ANSI/ASQC Z1.9-1993, "Sampling Procedures and Tables for Inspection by Variables for Percent Nonconforming," will be discussed. This is a revised and updated version of MIL-STD 414 (1957). An international version, ISO 3951, of these standards will be presented later, along with proposed changes to the latter standard. The international version uses a graphical procedure covered in Section 17-4. Changes to the standard will include double sampling and sequential sampling procedures.

▶ 17-1 ESTIMATING FRACTION NONCONFORMING WITH THE NORMAL DISTRIBUTION

The basic premise of a variables acceptance sampling plan based on the normal distribution is that a relationship exists between the mean and standard deviation of the distribution and the fraction nonconforming. In most variables acceptance sampling plans, the measured characteristics from the production processes are assumed to be normally distributed. If the mean and standard deviation of this distribution are known, the fraction of the distribution lying above or below any point can be determined.

▶ EXAMPLE 17-1

A copper wire is being produced whose resistance has a known mean of 86.5 ohms per mile and a standard deviation of 2.0 ohms per mile. The specifications for the wire allow no resistance beyond 91 ohms per mile. The fraction nonconforming can be calculated

$$z = \frac{U - \mu}{\sigma} = \frac{91 - 86.5}{2} = \frac{4.5}{2} = 2.25$$

where U is the upper limit, μ is the process mean, and σ is the process standard deviation. Using Table A in the Appendix, calculate that the fraction of the standard normal distribution beyond 2.25 is about 1.2% (see Figure 17-1a). If twelve wires in a thousand beyond the acceptable limit is satisfactory, this production process may be used. If the quality of the wire produced must be better than twelve wires in a thousand beyond 91 ohms per mile, either the mean of the process distribution or the standard deviation of the process must be changed. Alternatively, all wire made could be inspected and those wires exceeding 91 ohms per mile could be discarded. If the inspection were at least 92% effective, this would result in a final product of less than 0.1% beyond 91 ohms per mile. This is seldom the low-cost way to produce high-quality product.

Continuing the example, the equation can be solved in two ways. For quality better than 0.1% nonconforming, from Table A in the Appendix,

$$z = 3.09$$

Then

$$z = \frac{U - \mu}{\sigma}$$

becomes

$$3.09 = \frac{91 - \mu}{2.0}$$

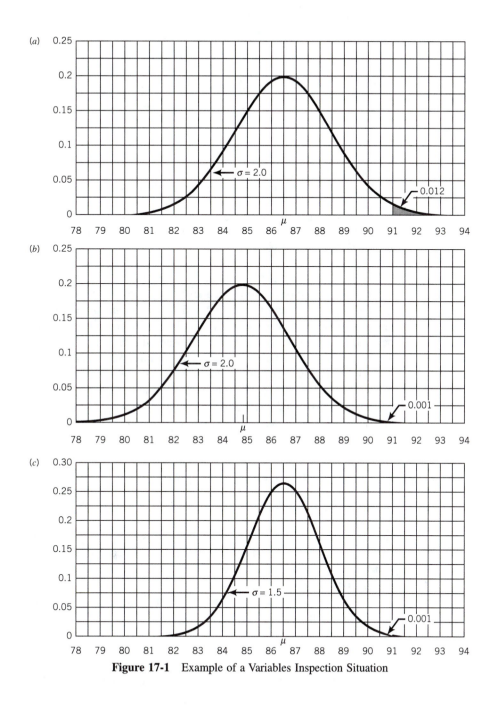

Figure 17-1 Example of a Variables Inspection Situation

which implies

$$\mu = 84.8$$

or

$$3.09 = \frac{91 - 86.5}{\sigma}$$

which implies

$$\sigma = 1.5$$

Either condition satisfies the objective (see Figures 17-1b and 17-1c). Of course, other combinations of μ and σ could give us the same result.

Since the resistance of copper wire is inversely proportional to the square of the diameter of the wire, the additional materials cost to manufacture wire with a diameter that would yield a process average of 84.8 ohms per mile instead of 86.5 ohms per mile may be calculated. It would be more economical to increase the process controls in the manufacturing line than to reduce the process standard deviation to 1.5 ohms per mile.

In the above example the simplest case is studied. The mean and standard deviation are known, and the distribution produced by the process was normal.

This rarely happens. Often, in practice, it is assumed that the distribution is normal on the basis of past experiences with similar production processes, but either the mean or the standard deviation is unknown. The assumption that the distribution is normal should also be checked. This will be discussed in Section 17-5. Variables acceptance sampling is used to estimate the fraction nonconforming based on estimates of either the mean, the standard deviation, or both. The variables acceptance sampling system ANSI/ASQC Z1.9-1993 will be discussed, which provides a general, simple way to do this combined with a test of whether to accept or reject the lot from which the sample was taken.

▶ 17-2 ESTIMATING FRACTION NONCONFORMING WHEN THE STANDARD DEVIATION IS KNOWN

The simplest case in practice is when the standard deviation is known. This assumption is made when experience has shown that the standard deviation of a process is stable because it is governed by fixed process parameters. The only parameter of interest may be the mean, and it is susceptible to shifts and drifts because of variations in raw material quality. Evidence of this condition may be a range or s-chart that stays in control for a long period of time.

In this case the fraction beyond the upper limit, U, may be estimated by calculating the sample mean, $\bar{x}$, and the statistic

$$z = \frac{U - \bar{x}}{\sigma}$$

A better estimate (minimum variance unbiased) is given by Lieberman and Resnikoff (1955):

$$z = \frac{U - \bar{x}}{\sigma} \sqrt{\frac{n}{n - 1}}$$

Although the tables in ANSI/ASQC Z1.9-1993 are based on the best estimates of the various parameters, in this discussion and examples the slightly worse, but simpler, estimates will be used.

A simple variables acceptance sampling plan can now be computed. Select a sample size n, and take the sample. Calculate $\bar{x}$ and estimate the fraction nonconforming, p. If p is greater than some preselected value, M, reject the lot. Otherwise, accept the lot. If the probability of acceptance for this n and M is calculated as a function of possible values of p (which are functions of $\bar{x}$ in this situation), the operating characteristic curve may be obtained for the acceptance sampling plan. In practice, these operating characteristic curves should match the operating characteristic curves for corresponding attributes acceptance sampling plans as closely as possible. This is desirable because they are often compared during deliberations of which plan to use.

17-2.1 Derivation of a Variables Plan

Before learning to use one of the standard variables acceptance sampling systems, it is informative to work through the derivation of a simple plan. This will illustrate both the construction of such a plan and how it is used. For this derivation, assume the quality characteristic can be measured on a continuous scale and is normally distributed with a known standard deviation. For simplicity, also assume that there is a single upper specification limit, U. In the standard sampling systems, two procedures are usually given called Form 1 and Form 2. In Form 1 a value is calculated and compared to a calculated acceptance constant, and a decision is made. In Form 2 the second step of estimating the percent nonconforming is taken, and then this estimate is compared to the maximum allowable percent nonconforming.

In designing the plan, an acceptability constant, k, is determined that gives the desired properties for the plan. Assume that a probability of acceptance of 95% is desired when the product is less than 1% nonconforming and a probability of acceptance of only 10% is needed when the product is 15% nonconforming. In the standard notation this is written as $\alpha = 0.05$, $\beta = 0.10$, $p_1 = 0.01$, and $p_2 = 0.15$. Using Table A in the Appendix it is seen that,

$$P(z_1 > 2.327) = 0.01$$

and

$$P(z_2 > 1.037) = 0.15$$

Values for the mean can then be calculated. Using the criteria from the previous example, $U = 91$ ohms per mile and $\sigma = 2.0$ ohms per mile, μ_1 is calculated from

$$\frac{U - \mu_1}{\sigma} = \frac{91 - \mu_1}{2} = 2.327 = z_1$$

and $\mu_1 = 91 - 4.65 = 86.35$. Consequently, if the true mean of the distribution is 86.35 ohms per mile, fewer than 1% of the wires will have resistance greater than 91 ohms per mile. Similarly, calculate μ_2 from

$$\frac{U - \mu_2}{\sigma} = \frac{91 - \mu_2}{2} = 1.037 = z_2$$

and $\mu_2 = 91 - 2.07 = 88.93$. If the mean is 88.93 ohms per mile, 15% of the wires will have a resistance beyond the 91 ohms per mile upper limit. In the method given by Form 1, accept a lot if

$$\frac{U - \bar{x}}{\sigma} \geq k$$

This can be written as

$$\frac{U - \mu}{\sigma} + \frac{\mu - \bar{x}}{\sigma} \geq k$$

by simply adding and subtracting μ/σ. Multiplying each side by $\sqrt{n}$ and doing some algebra gives

$$\frac{\bar{x} - \mu}{\frac{\sigma}{\sqrt{n}}} \geq \left(k - \frac{U - \mu}{\sigma} \right)\sqrt{n}$$

[see Duncan (1986) for details].

From the earlier discussion it is known that all the stated criteria will be met if k and n are selected such that

$$\text{Probability} \left(\frac{\bar{x} - \mu}{\sigma/\sqrt{n}} \geq (k - z_1)\sqrt{n} \right) = 1 - \alpha = 0.95$$

$$\text{Probability} \left(\frac{\bar{x} - \mu}{\sigma/\sqrt{n}} \geq (k - z_2)\sqrt{n} \right) = \beta = 0.10$$

Since $(\bar{x} - \mu)/(\sigma/\sqrt{n})$ is a normally distributed random variable with mean zero and standard deviation 1, the above equations can be written as

$$\text{Probability} \left[z \geq (k - z_1)\sqrt{n} \right] = 0.95$$

and

$$\text{Probability} \left[z \geq (k - z_2)\sqrt{n} \right] = 0.10$$

where z is distributed $N(0,1)$. From Table A in the Appendix, this leads to

$$(k - z_1)\sqrt{n} = -1.645 \tag{17-1}$$

and

$$(k - z_2)\sqrt{n} = 1.282 \tag{17-2}$$

These equations can be solved as

$$n = \left(\frac{1.282 + 1.645}{z_1 - z_2} \right)^2 \tag{17-3}$$

and

$$k = -\frac{1.645}{\sqrt{n}} + z_1 \tag{17-4}$$

or

$$k = \frac{1.282}{\sqrt{n}} + z_2 \tag{17-5}$$

From the example, $z_1 = 2.327$ and $z_2 = 1.037$. Making the substitutions, from Equation (17-3), $n = 5.148$ or, rounding up, 6. From Equation (17-4), $k = 1.655$ and from Equation (17-5), $k = 1.560$. The value of k depends on whether it is desired to hold α or β. As an alternative, use the average of these two values or $k = 1.608$. The acceptance sampling plan is as follows:

1. Take a random sample of six items.
2. Compute the quantity

$$\frac{U - \bar{x}}{\sigma} = \frac{91 - \bar{x}}{2.0}$$

3. If this quantity is greater than or equal to the acceptability constant $k = 1.608$, the lot is accepted.
4. Otherwise, the lot is rejected.

In the Form 2 method a further step is taken to calculate an estimate of the percent nonconforming. This is done by calculating the quantity

$$\frac{U - \bar{x}}{\sigma} \sqrt{\frac{n}{n - 1}}$$

and treating this quantity as a standard normal variable. Calculate a quantity called the maximum acceptable percent nonconforming:

$$M = \overline{\Phi}\left(k\sqrt{\frac{n}{n - 1}}\right)$$

where $\overline{\Phi}(\bullet)$ denotes 1 minus the normal cumulative distribution function. In this example,

$$M = \overline{\Phi}\left(1.608\sqrt{\frac{6}{5}}\right) = \overline{\Phi}(1.762) = 0.039$$

$$M = 3.9\%$$

Then estimate the percent nonconforming by

$$\hat{p} = \overline{\Phi}\left(\frac{U - \bar{x}}{\sigma}\sqrt{\frac{n}{n - 1}}\right)$$

If $\hat{p}$ is greater than M, reject; if it is less than or equal to M, accept.

In this example, suppose the sampled six values are

$$86.8 \quad 87.3 \quad 86.2 \quad 85.9 \quad 86.1 \quad 86.5$$

Then $\bar{x} = 86.47$, and

$$\frac{U - \bar{x}}{\sigma} = \frac{91.0 - 86.47}{2.0} = 2.27$$

In Form 1, accept immediately, since 2.27 is greater than $k = 1.608$. In Form 2, first estimate the percent nonconforming by

$$\hat{p} = \overline{\Phi}\left(\frac{U - \bar{x}}{\sigma}\sqrt{\frac{n}{n - 1}}\right) = \overline{\Phi}(2.481) = 0.007 \text{ or } 0.7\%$$

Since this is clearly less than the maximum acceptable percent nonconforming, $M = 0.039$, or 3.9%, the lot is accepted. Operating characteristic curves for this plan can be constructed in a straightforward manner [see Duncan (1986)].

▶ 17-3 ACCEPTANCE SAMPLING BY VARIABLES
USING ANSI/ASQC Z1.9-1993 (MIL-STD-414)

The procedure described in the previous section could be used to develop a variables acceptance sampling plan whenever one is needed. A similar derivation could be used for the situation in which the standard deviation is not known. This would be time-consuming and not very efficient, considering the large number of possible situations. Fortunately, published standards contain systems of variables acceptance sampling plans. The most frequently used system is ANSI/ASQC Z1.9-1993 or MIL-STD-414 (1957). It has also been published as an international standard, ISO 3951 (1989). ISO 3951 is being revised as this is written. The revised standard will be broken into parts with ISO 3951-1 corresponding to the version under discussion here. There are slight differences in the ANSI, MIL-STD, and ISO versions. These will be discussed later.

ANSI/ASQC Z1.9-1993 has an introduction and four major sections. Section A gives a general description of the plans. It contains an AQL conversion table, the sample size code letter table, and operating characteristic curves for the sampling plans of section B. Section B is for the case in which the standard deviation is unknown and the sample standard deviation method is used to estimate it. Section C covers the case in which the variability is unknown and the range method is used. Section D is for the situation in which the variability is known. Each section is divided into two major parts: single specification limit and double specification limits. The standard also contains a special procedure for application of mixed variables–attributes sampling plans.

The use of ANSI/ASQC Z1.9-1993 is very similar to the use of ANSI/ASQC Z1.4-1993 (ISO 2859-1:1999). The user first specifies an AQL. There is a conversion table in the standard for converting the specified AQL to one used in the standard. Table 17-1 is a copy of the AQL conversion table. The second step is to determine the sample size code letter. In ANSI/ASQC Z1.9-1993 there are three general inspection levels and two special levels instead of the three general inspection levels and the four special inspection levels

TABLE 17-1   AQL Conversion Table

For Specified AQL Values Falling within These Ranges	Use This AQL Value
— to 0.109	0.10
0.110 to 0.164	0.15
0.165 to 0.279	0.25
0.280 to 0.439	0.40
0.440 to 0.699	0.65
0.700 to 1.09	1.0
1.10 to 1.64	1.5
1.65 to 2.79	2.5
2.80 to 4.39	4.0
4.40 to 6.99	6.5
7.00 to 10.9	10.0

Source: Copyright American Society for Quality Control, Inc. Reprinted by permission.

TABLE 17-2   Sample Size Code Letters

| | | | Inspection Levels | | | |
| | | | Special | | General | | |
Lot Size			S3	S4	I	II	III
2 to	8		B	B	B	B	C
9 to	15		B	B	B	B	D
16 to	25		B	B	B	C	E
26 to	50		B	B	C	D	F
51 to	90		B	B	D	E	G
91 to	150		B	C	E	F	H
151 to	280		B	D	F	G	I
281 to	400		C	E	G	H	J
401 to	500		C	E	G	I	J
501 to	1,200		D	F	H	J	K
1,201 to	3,200		E	G	I	K	L
3,201 to	10,000		F	H	J	L	M
10,001 to	35,000		G	I	K	M	N
35,001 to	150,000		H	J	L	N	P
150,001 to	500,000		H	K	M	P	P
500,001 and over			H	K	N	P	P

Source: Copyright American Society for Quality Control, Inc. Reprinted by permission.

of ANSI/ASQC Z1.4. Unless otherwise specified, general inspection level II is to be used. The sample size code letters and inspection levels are shown in Table 17-2.

17-3.1 Variability Unknown—Standard Deviation Method

In using the procedures of ANSI/ASQC Z1.9-1993, one first selects the AQL value and then determines the sample size code letter. The correct master sampling tables are then consulted to obtain the sample size and the acceptability constant.

Single Specification Limit Plans

The degree of conformance of a quality characteristic with respect to a single specification limit is judged by the quantity

$$\frac{U - \bar{x}}{s} \quad \text{or} \quad \frac{\bar{x} - L}{s}$$

where

U = the upper specification limit

L = the lower specification limit

$\bar{x}$ = the sample average

s = the estimate of lot standard deviation

The quantity $(U - \bar{x})/s$ or $(\bar{x} - L)/s$ is compared with the acceptability constant k. If $(U - \bar{x})/s$ or $(\bar{x} - L)/s$ is equal to or greater than k, the lot meets the acceptability criterion and is accepted. If $(U - \bar{x})/s$ or $(\bar{x} - L)/s$ is less than k or is negative, then the lot does not meet the acceptability criterion and is rejected.

The procedure described above is Form 1. Some users do not like this procedure because no estimate of the percent nonconforming is calculated. In Form 2, an estimate of the percent nonconforming is made and compared with a calculated maximum allowable percent nonconforming. In using Form 2, a quality index

$$Q_U = \frac{U - \bar{x}}{s} \quad \text{or} \quad Q_L = \frac{\bar{x} - L}{s}$$

is computed for an upper limit specification or a lower limit specification, respectively. An estimate of the percent of the lot above the upper specification limit, $\hat{p}_U$, or the percent of the lot below the lower specification limit, $\hat{p}_L$, is made. This estimate is made by entering a table with the value Q_U or Q_L and the sample size. The estimated lot percent nonconforming ($\hat{p}_U$ or $\hat{p}_L$) is compared with the maximum allowable percent nonconforming, M. If $\hat{p}_U$ or $\hat{p}_L$ is greater than M or if Q_U or Q_L is negative, then the lot does not meet the acceptability criterion. The table providing estimates of $\hat{p}_U$ or $\hat{p}_L$ is based on the noncentral t distribution. The theory behind this procedure may be found in Lieberman and Resnikoff (1955).

► **EXAMPLE 17-2** Single Specification Limit—Form 1

A certain transmitter has a maximum allowed voltage output of 30 volts. Lots of twenty items are submitted, and inspection level II, normal inspection, with AQL = 2% is to be used.

Step	Information Needed	Value(s) Obtained	Comments
1	AQL to be used	AQL = 2.5	From Table 17-1
2	Sample size code letter	letter = C	From Table 17-2
3	Sample size n	$n = 4$	From Table 17-3
4	Sample	28,27,25,29	Sample values
5	Sum of measurements: Σx	109.0	
6	Sum of squared measurements: Σx^2	2979.0	
7	Correction factor (CF): $(\Sigma x)^2/n$	2970.25	
8	Corrected sum of squares (SS): $\Sigma x^2 - CF$	8.75	$2979 - 2970.25$
9	Variance (V): SS/$(n - 1)$	2.92	8.75/3
10	Estimate of lot standard deviation s: $\sqrt{V}$	1.71	$\sqrt{2.92}$
11	Sample mean: $\bar{x}$: $\Sigma x/n$	27.25	109/4
12	Specification limit (upper): U	30	
13	$(U - \bar{x})/s$	1.61	
14	Acceptability constant: k	1.17	From Table 17-3
15	Acceptability criterion: $(U - \bar{x})/s > k$	1.61 > 1.17	Accept

► **EXAMPLE 17-3** Single Specification Limit—Form 2

In using Form 2, the same steps 1–12 above would be taken. But from there, the following would be calculated:

TABLE 17-3 Master Table for Normal and Tightened Inspection for Plans Based on Variability Unknown (Single Specification Limit—Form 1)

Sample Size Code Letter	Sample Size	Acceptable Quality Levels (Normal Inspection)											
		T	0.10	0.15	0.25	0.40	0.65	1.00	1.50	2.50	4.00	6.50	10.00
		k	k	k	k	k	k	k	k	k	k	k	k
B	3					⇩	⇩	1.12	0.958	0.765	0.566
C	4					⇩	⇩	1.46	1.34	1.17	1.01	0.815	0.617
D	5		⇩	⇩	⇩	1.77	1.65	1.52	1.40	1.24	1.07	0.874	0.675
E	7	⇩	2.22	2.13	2.00	1.88	1.75	1.62	1.50	1.33	1.15	0.955	0.755
F	10	2.44	2.34	2.24	2.11	1.98	1.84	1.72	1.59	1.41	1.23	1.03	0.828
G	15	2.53	2.42	2.32	2.19	2.06	1.92	1.79	1.65	1.48	1.30	1.09	0.885
H	20	2.58	2.47	2.37	2.23	2.10	1.96	1.83	1.69	1.51	1.33	1.12	0.916
I	25	2.61	2.50	2.40	2.26	2.13	1.98	1.85	1.72	1.53	1.35	1.14	0.935
J	35	2.66	2.55	2.45	2.31	2.18	2.03	1.89	1.76	1.57	1.39	1.18	0.968
K	50	2.71	2.61	2.50	2.36	2.22	2.08	1.94	1.80	1.61	1.42	1.21	1.00
L	75	2.77	2.66	2.55	2.41	2.27	2.12	1.98	1.84	1.65	1.46	1.25	1.03
M	100	2.80	2.69	2.58	2.43	2.29	2.14	2.00	1.86	1.67	1.48	1.26	1.05
N	150	2.84	2.73	2.62	2.47	2.33	2.18	2.03	1.89	1.70	1.51	1.29	1.07
P	200	2.85	2.73	2.62	2.47	2.33	2.18	2.04	1.89	1.70	1.51	1.29	1.08
		0.10	0.15	0.25	0.40	0.65	1.00	1.50	2.50	4.00	6.50	10.00	
		Acceptable Quality Levels (Tightened Inspection)											

All AQL values are in percent nonconforming. T denotes plan used exclusively on tightened inspection and provides symbol for identification of appropriate OC curve.

⇩ Use first sampling plan below arrow; that is, both sample size as well as k value. When sample size equals or exceeds lot size, every item in the lot must be inspected.

Source: Copyright American Society for Quality, Inc. Reprinted by permission.

13	Quality index: $Q_U = (U - \bar{x})/s$	1.61	
14	Estimate of lot percent nonconforming: $\hat{p}_U$	0	From Table 17-4
15	Maximum allowable percent nonconforming: M	10.88	From Table 17-5

Since $\hat{p}_U$ is less than M, accept the lot. The decision is the same as for Form 1, but, in addition, now there is an estimate, $\hat{p}$, of the fraction nonconforming.

Double Specification Limit Plans

A few basic differences exist between double specification limit plans and single specification limit plans. The first is that only one method is used, a method similar to Form 2. It is necessary to calculate the maximum allowable percent nonconforming, and this is complicated because there may be a different AQL value associated with each limit. If separate AQLs are assigned, then the maximum allowable percent nonconforming for the lower limit is designated M_L and for the upper limit by M_U. If one AQL is assigned to both limits combined, the maximum allowable percent nonconforming is designated M, as with the single specification plans.

(text continues on page 606)

TABLE 17-4 Table for Estimating the Lot Percent Nonconforming Using Standard Deviation Method

Q_U or Q_L	Sample Size														
	3	4	5	7	10	15	20	25	30	35	50	75	100	150	200
0	50.00	50.00	50.00	50.00	50.00	50.00	50.00	50.00	50.00	50.00	50.00	50.00	50.00	50.00	50.00
0.1	47.24	46.67	46.44	46.26	46.16	46.10	46.08	46.06	46.05	46.05	46.04	46.03	46.03	46.02	46.02
0.2	44.46	43.33	42.90	42.54	42.35	42.24	42.19	42.16	42.15	42.13	42.11	42.10	42.09	42.09	42.08
0.3	41.63	40.00	39.37	38.87	38.60	38.44	38.37	38.33	38.31	38.29	38.27	38.25	38.24	38.23	38.22
0.31	41.35	39.67	39.02	38.50	38.23	38.06	37.99	37.95	37.93	37.91	37.89	37.87	37.86	37.85	37.84
0.32	41.06	39.33	38.67	38.14	37.86	37.69	37.62	37.58	37.55	37.54	37.51	37.49	37.48	37.47	37.46
0.33	40.77	39.00	38.32	37.78	37.49	37.31	37.24	37.20	37.18	37.16	37.13	37.11	37.10	37.09	37.08
0.34	40.49	38.67	37.97	37.42	37.12	36.94	36.87	36.83	36.80	36.78	36.75	36.73	36.72	36.71	36.71
0.35	40.20	38.33	37.62	37.06	36.75	36.57	36.49	36.45	36.43	36.41	36.38	36.36	36.35	36.34	36.33
0.36	39.91	38.00	37.28	36.69	36.38	36.20	36.12	36.08	36.05	36.04	36.01	35.98	35.97	35.96	35.96
0.37	39.62	37.67	36.95	36.33	36.02	35.83	35.75	35.71	35.68	35.66	35.63	35.61	35.60	35.59	35.58
0.38	39.33	37.33	36.58	35.98	35.65	35.46	35.38	35.34	35.31	35.29	35.26	35.24	35.23	35.22	35.21
0.39	39.03	37.00	36.23	35.62	35.29	35.10	35.02	34.97	34.94	34.93	34.89	34.87	34.86	34.85	34.84
0.40	38.74	36.67	35.88	35.26	34.93	34.73	34.65	34.60	34.58	34.56	34.53	34.50	34.49	34.48	34.47
0.41	38.45	36.33	35.54	34.90	34.57	34.37	34.28	34.24	34.21	34.19	34.16	34.13	34.12	34.11	34.11
0.42	38.15	36.00	35.19	34.55	34.21	34.00	33.92	33.87	33.85	33.83	33.79	33.77	33.76	33.75	33.74
0.43	37.85	35.67	34.85	34.19	33.85	33.64	33.56	33.51	33.48	33.46	33.43	33.40	33.39	33.38	33.38
0.44	37.56	35.33	34.50	33.84	33.49	33.28	33.20	33.15	33.12	33.10	33.07	33.04	33.03	33.02	33.01
0.45	37.26	35.00	34.16	33.49	33.13	32.92	32.84	32.79	32.76	32.74	32.71	32.68	32.67	32.66	32.65
0.46	36.96	34.67	33.81	33.13	32.78	32.57	32.48	32.43	32.40	32.38	32.35	32.32	32.31	32.30	32.29
0.47	36.66	34.33	33.47	32.78	32.42	32.21	32.12	32.07	32.04	32.02	31.99	31.96	31.95	31.94	31.93
0.48	36.35	34.00	33.12	32.43	32.07	31.85	31.77	31.72	31.69	31.67	31.63	31.61	31.60	31.58	31.58
0.49	36.05	33.67	32.78	32.08	31.72	31.50	31.41	31.36	31.33	31.31	31.28	31.25	31.24	31.23	31.22
0.50	35.75	33.33	32.44	31.74	31.37	31.15	31.06	31.01	30.98	30.96	30.93	30.90	30.89	30.88	30.87
0.51	35.44	33.00	32.10	31.39	31.02	30.80	30.71	30.66	30.63	30.61	30.57	30.55	30.54	30.53	30.52
0.52	35.13	32.67	31.76	31.04	30.67	30.45	30.36	30.31	30.28	30.26	30.23	30.20	30.19	30.18	30.17
0.53	34.82	32.33	31.42	30.70	30.32	30.10	30.01	29.96	29.93	29.91	29.88	29.85	29.84	29.83	29.82
0.54	34.51	32.00	31.08	30.36	29.98	29.76	29.67	29.62	29.59	29.57	29.53	29.51	29.49	29.48	29.48
0.55	34.20	31.67	30.74	30.01	29.64	29.41	29.32	29.27	29.24	29.22	29.19	29.16	29.15	29.14	29.13
0.56	33.88	31.33	30.40	29.67	29.29	29.07	28.98	28.93	28.90	28.88	28.85	28.82	28.81	28.80	28.79
0.57	33.57	31.00	30.06	29.33	28.95	28.73	28.64	28.59	28.56	28.54	28.51	28.48	28.47	28.46	28.45
0.58	33.25	30.67	29.73	28.99	28.61	28.39	28.30	28.25	28.22	28.20	28.17	28.14	28.13	28.12	28.11
0.59	32.93	30.33	29.39	28.66	28.28	28.05	27.96	27.92	27.89	27.87	27.83	27.81	27.79	27.78	27.78
0.60	32.61	30.00	29.05	28.32	27.94	27.72	27.63	27.58	27.55	27.53	27.50	27.47	27.46	27.45	27.44
0.61	32.28	29.67	28.72	27.98	27.60	27.39	27.30	27.25	27.22	27.20	27.16	27.14	27.13	27.11	27.11
0.62	31.96	29.33	28.39	27.65	27.27	27.05	26.96	26.92	26.89	26.87	26.83	26.81	26.80	26.78	26.78
0.63	31.63	29.00	28.05	27.32	26.94	26.72	26.63	26.59	26.56	26.54	26.50	26.48	26.47	26.46	26.45
0.64	31.30	28.67	27.72	26.99	26.61	26.39	26.31	26.26	26.25	26.21	26.18	26.15	26.14	26.13	26.12
0.65	30.97	28.33	27.39	26.66	26.28	26.07	25.98	25.93	25.90	25.88	25.85	25.83	25.82	25.81	25.80
0.66	30.63	28.00	27.06	26.33	25.96	25.74	25.66	25.61	25.58	25.56	25.53	25.51	25.49	25.48	25.48
0.67	30.30	27.67	26.73	26.00	25.63	25.42	25.33	25.29	25.26	25.24	25.21	25.19	25.17	25.16	25.16
0.68	29.96	27.33	26.40	25.68	25.31	25.10	25.01	24.97	24.94	24.92	24.89	24.87	24.86	24.85	24.84
0.69	29.61	27.00	26.07	25.35	24.99	24.78	24.70	24.65	24.62	24.60	24.57	24.55	24.54	24.53	24.52

Values tabulated are read in percent.

Q_U or Q_L	Sample Size														
	3	4	5	7	10	15	20	25	30	35	50	75	100	150	200
0.70	29.27	26.67	25.74	25.03	24.67	24.46	24.38	24.33	24.31	24.29	24.26	24.24	24.23	24.22	24.21
0.71	28.92	26.33	25.41	24.71	24.35	24.15	24.06	24.02	23.99	23.98	23.95	23.92	23.91	23.90	23.90
0.72	28.57	26.00	25.09	24.39	24.03	23.83	23.75	23.71	23.68	23.67	23.64	23.61	23.60	23.59	23.59
0.73	28.22	25.67	24.76	24.07	23.72	23.52	23.44	23.40	23.37	23.36	23.33	23.31	23.30	23.29	23.28
0.74	27.86	25.33	24.44	23.75	23.41	23.21	23.13	23.09	23.07	23.05	23.02	23.00	22.99	22.98	22.98
0.75	27.50	25.00	24.11	23.44	23.10	22.90	22.83	22.79	22.76	22.75	22.72	22.70	22.69	22.68	22.68
0.76	27.13	24.67	23.79	23.12	22.79	22.60	22.52	22.48	22.46	22.44	22.42	22.40	22.39	22.38	22.38
0.77	26.76	24.33	23.47	22.81	22.48	22.30	22.22	22.18	22.16	22.14	22.12	22.10	22.09	22.08	22.08
0.78	26.39	24.00	23.15	22.50	22.18	21.99	21.92	21.89	21.86	21.85	21.82	21.80	21.79	21.79	21.78
0.79	26.02	23.67	22.83	22.19	21.87	21.70	21.63	21.59	21.57	21.55	21.53	21.51	21.50	21.49	21.49
0.80	25.64	23.33	22.51	21.88	21.57	21.40	21.33	21.29	21.27	21.26	21.23	21.22	21.21	21.20	21.20
0.81	25.25	23.00	22.19	21.58	21.27	21.10	21.04	21.00	20.98	20.97	20.94	20.93	20.92	20.91	20.91
0.82	24.86	22.67	21.87	21.27	20.98	20.81	20.75	20.71	20.69	20.68	20.65	20.64	20.63	20.62	20.62
0.83	24.47	22.33	21.56	20.97	20.68	20.52	20.46	20.42	20.40	20.39	20.37	20.35	20.35	20.34	20.34
0.84	24.07	22.00	21.24	20.67	20.39	20.23	20.17	20.14	20.12	20.11	20.09	20.07	20.06	20.06	20.05
0.85	23.67	21.67	20.93	20.37	20.10	19.94	19.89	19.86	19.84	19.82	19.80	19.79	19.78	19.78	19.77
0.86	23.26	21.33	20.62	20.07	19.81	19.66	19.60	19.57	19.56	19.54	19.53	19.51	19.51	19.50	19.50
0.87	22.84	21.00	20.31	19.78	19.52	19.38	19.32	19.30	19.28	19.27	19.25	19.24	19.23	19.23	19.22
0.88	22.42	20.67	20.00	19.48	19.23	19.10	19.05	19.02	19.00	18.99	18.98	18.96	18.96	18.95	18.95
0.89	21.99	20.33	19.69	19.19	18.95	18.82	18.77	18.74	18.73	18.72	18.70	18.69	18.69	18.68	18.68
0.90	21.55	20.00	19.38	18.90	18.67	18.54	18.50	18.47	18.46	18.45	18.43	18.42	18.42	18.41	18.41
0.91	21.11	19.67	19.07	18.61	18.39	18.27	18.23	18.20	18.19	18.18	18.17	18.16	18.15	18.15	18.15
0.92	20.66	19.33	18.77	18.33	18.11	18.00	17.96	17.94	17.92	17.92	17.90	17.89	17.89	17.89	17.88
0.93	20.19	19.00	18.46	18.04	17.84	17.73	17.69	17.67	17.66	17.65	17.64	17.63	17.63	17.62	17.62
0.94	19.73	18.67	18.16	17.76	17.56	17.46	17.43	17.41	17.40	17.39	17.38	17.37	17.37	17.37	17.36
0.95	19.25	18.33	17.86	17.48	17.29	17.20	17.17	17.16	17.14	17.13	17.12	17.12	17.11	17.11	17.11
0.96	18.75	18.00	17.55	17.20	17.03	16.94	16.90	16.89	16.88	16.88	16.87	16.86	16.86	16.86	16.86
0.97	18.25	17.67	17.25	16.92	16.76	16.68	16.65	16.63	16.63	16.62	16.61	16.61	16.61	16.61	16.60
0.98	17.74	17.33	16.96	16.65	16.49	16.42	16.39	16.38	16.37	16.37	16.36	16.36	16.36	16.36	16.36
0.99	17.21	17.00	16.66	16.37	16.23	16.16	16.14	16.13	16.12	16.12	16.12	16.11	16.11	16.11	16.11
1.00	16.67	16.67	16.36	16.10	15.97	15.91	15.89	15.88	15.88	15.87	15.87	15.87	15.87	15.87	15.87
1.01	16.11	16.33	16.07	15.83	15.72	15.66	15.64	15.63	15.63	15.63	15.63	15.62	15.62	15.62	15.62
1.02	15.53	16.00	15.78	15.56	15.46	15.41	15.40	15.39	15.39	15.39	15.38	15.38	15.37	15.38	15.39
1.03	14.93	15.67	15.48	15.30	15.21	15.17	15.15	15.15	15.15	15.15	15.15	15.15	15.15	15.15	15.15
1.04	14.31	15.33	15.19	15.03	14.96	14.92	14.91	14.9l	14.91	14.91	14.91	14.91	14.91	14.91	14.91
1.05	13.66	15.00	14.91	14.77	14.71	14.68	14.67	14.67	14.67	14.67	14.68	14.68	14.68	14.68	14.68
1.06	12.98	14.67	14.62	14.51	14.46	14.44	14.44	14.44	14.44	14.44	14.45	14.45	14.45	14.45	14.45
1.07	12.27	14.33	14.33	14.26	14.22	14.20	14.20	14.21	14.21	14.21	14.22	14.22	14.22	14.23	14.23
1.08	11.51	14.00	14.05	14.00	13.97	13.97	13.97	13.98	13.98	13.98	13.99	13.99	14.00	14.00	14.00
1.09	10.71	13.67	13.76	13.75	13.73	13.74	13.74	13.75	13.75	13.76	13.77	13.77	13.77	13.78	13.78
1.10	9.84	13.33	13.48	13.49	13.50	13.51	13.52	13.52	13.53	13.54	13.54	13.55	13.55	13.56	13.56
1.11	8.89	13.00	13.20	13.25	13.26	13.28	13.29	13.30	13.31	13.31	13.32	13.33	13.34	13.34	13.34
1.12	7.82	12.67	12.93	13.00	13.03	13.05	13.07	13.08	13.09	13.10	13.11	13.12	13.13	13.12	13.13
1.13	6.60	12.33	12.65	12.75	12.80	12.83	12.85	12.86	12.87	12.88	12.89	12.90	12.91	12.91	12.92
1.14	5.08	12.00	12.37	12.51	12.57	12.61	12.63	12.65	12.66	12.67	12.68	12.69	12.70	12.70	12.71
1.15	2.87	11.67	12.10	12.27	12.34	12.39	12.42	12.44	12.45	12.46	12.47	12.48	12.49	12.49	12.50
1.16	0.00	11.33	11.83	12.03	12.12	12.18	12.21	12.22	12.24	12.25	12.26	12.28	12.28	12.29	12.29
1.17	0.00	11.00	11.56	11.79	11.90	11.96	12.00	12.02	12.03	12.04	12.06	12.07	12.08	12.07	12.09
1.18	0.00	10.67	11.29	11.56	11.68	11.75	11.79	11.81	11.82	11.84	11.85	11.87	11.88	11.88	11.89
1.19	0.00	10.33	11.02	11.33	11.46	11.54	11.58	11.61	11.62	11.63	11.65	11.67	11.68	11.69	11.69

(continued)

TABLE 17-4 (*continued*)

Q_U or Q_L	Sample Size														
	3	4	5	7	10	15	20	25	30	35	50	75	100	150	200
1.20	0.00	10.00	10.76	11.10	11.24	11.34	11.38	11.41	11.42	11.43	11.46	11.47	11.48	11.49	11.49
1.21	0.00	9.67	10.50	10.87	11.03	11.13	11.18	11.21	11.22	11.24	11.26	11.28	11.29	11.30	11.30
1.22	0.00	9.33	10.23	10.65	10.82	10.93	10.98	11.01	11.03	11.04	11.07	11.09	11.09	11.10	11.11
1.23	0.00	9.00	9.97	10.42	10.61	10.73	10.78	10.81	10.84	10.85	10.88	10.90	10.91	10.92	10.92
1.24	0.00	8.67	9.72	10.20	10.41	10.53	10.59	10.62	10.64	10.66	10.69	10.71	10.72	10.73	10.73
1.25	0.00	8.33	9.46	9.98	10.21	10.34	10.40	10.43	10.46	10.47	10.50	10.52	10.53	10.54	10.55
1.26	0.00	8.00	9.21	9.77	10.00	10.15	10.21	10.25	10.27	10.29	10.32	10.34	10.35	10.36	10.37
1.27	0.00	7.67	8.96	9.55	9.81	9.96	10.02	10.06	10.09	10.10	10.13	10.16	10.17	10.18	10.19
1.28	0.00	7.33	8.71	9.34	9.61	9.77	9.84	9.88	9.90	9.92	9.95	9.98	9.99	10.00	10.01
1.29	0.00	7.00	8.46	9.13	9.42	9.58	9.66	9.70	9.72	9.74	9.78	9.80	9.82	9.83	9.83
1.30	0.00	6.67	8.21	8.93	9.22	9.40	9.48	9.52	9.55	9.57	9.60	9.63	9.64	9.65	9.66
1.31	0.00	6.33	7.97	8.72	9.03	9.22	9.30	9.34	9.37	9.39	9.43	9.46	9.47	9.48	9.49
1.32	0.00	6.00	7.73	8.52	8.85	9.04	9.12	9.17	9.20	9.22	9.26	9.29	9.30	9.31	9.32
1.33	0.00	5.67	7.49	8.32	8.66	8.86	8.95	9.00	9.03	9.05	9.09	9.12	9.13	9.15	9.15
1.34	0.00	5.33	7.25	8.12	8.48	8.69	8.78	8.83	8.86	8.88	8.92	8.95	8.97	8.98	8.99
1.35	0.00	5.00	7.02	7.92	8.30	8.52	8.61	8.66	8.69	8.72	8.76	8.79	8.81	8.82	8.83
1.36	0.00	4.67	6.79	7.73	8.12	8.35	8.44	8.50	8.53	8.55	8.60	8.63	8.65	8.66	8.67
1.37	0.00	4.33	6.56	7.54	7.95	8.18	8.28	8.33	8.37	8.39	8.44	8.47	8.49	8.50	8.51
1.38	0.00	4.00	6.33	7.35	7.77	8.01	8.12	8.17	8.21	8.24	8.28	8.31	8.33	8.35	8.36
1.39	0.00	3.67	6.10	7.17	7.60	7.85	7.96	8.01	8.05	8.08	8.12	8.16	8.18	8.19	8.20
1.40	0.00	3.33	5.88	6.98	7.44	7.69	7.80	7.86	7.90	7.92	7.97	8.01	8.02	8.04	8.05
1.41	0.00	3.00	5.66	6.80	7.27	7.53	7.64	7.70	7.74	7.77	7.82	7.86	7.87	7.89	7.90
1.42	0.00	2.67	5.44	6.62	7.10	7.37	7.49	7.55	7.59	7.62	7.67	7.71	7.73	7.74	7.75
1.43	0.00	2.33	5.23	6.45	6.94	7.22	7.34	7.40	7.44	7.47	7.52	7.56	7.58	7.60	7.61
1.44	0.00	2.00	5.01	6.27	6.78	7.07	7.19	7.26	7.30	7.33	7.38	7.42	7.44	7.46	7.47
1.45	0.00	1.67	4.81	6.10	6.63	6.92	7.04	7.11	7.15	7.18	7.24	7.28	7.30	7.31	7.32
1.46	0.00	1.33	4.60	5.93	6.47	6.77	6.90	6.97	7.01	7.04	7.10	7.14	7.16	7.18	7.19
1.47	0.00	1.00	4.39	5.77	6.32	6.63	6.75	6.83	6.87	6.90	6.96	7.00	7.02	7.04	7.05
1.48	0.00	0.67	4.19	5.60	6.17	6.48	6.61	6.69	6.73	6.77	6.82	6.86	6.88	6.90	6.91
1.49	0.00	0.33	3.99	5.44	6.02	6.34	6.48	6.55	6.60	6.63	6.69	6.73	6.75	6.77	6.78
1.50	0.00	0.00	3.80	5.28	5.87	6.20	6.34	6.41	6.46	6.50	6.55	6.60	6.62	6.64	6.65
1.51	0.00	0.00	3.61	5.13	5.73	6.06	6.20	6.28	6.33	6.36	6.42	6.47	6.49	6.51	6.52
1.52	0.00	0.00	3.42	4.97	5.59	5.93	6.07	6.15	6.20	6.23	6.29	6.34	6.36	6.38	6.39
1.53	0.00	0.00	3.23	4.82	5.45	5.80	5.94	6.02	6.07	6.11	6.17	6.21	6.24	6.26	6.27
1.54	0.00	0.00	3.05	4.67	5.31	5.67	5.81	5.89	5.95	5.98	6.04	6.09	6.11	6.13	6.15
1.55	0.00	0.00	2.87	4.52	5.18	5.54	5.69	5.77	5.82	5.86	5.92	5.97	5.99	6.01	6.02
1.56	0.00	0.00	2.69	4.38	5.05	5.41	5.56	5.65	5.70	5.74	5.80	5.85	5.87	5.89	5.90
1.57	0.00	0.00	2.52	4.24	4.92	5.29	5.44	5.53	5.58	5.62	5.68	5.73	5.75	5.78	5.79
1.58	0.00	0.00	2.35	4.10	4.79	5.16	5.32	5.41	5.46	5.50	5.56	5.61	5.64	5.66	5.67
1.59	0.00	0.00	2.19	3.96	4.66	5.04	5.20	5.29	5.34	5.38	5.45	5.50	5.52	5.55	5.56

Values tabulated are read in percent.

Q_U or Q_L	Sample Size														
	3	4	5	7	10	15	20	25	30	35	50	75	100	150	200
1.60	0.00	0.00	2.03	3.83	4.54	4.92	5.08	5.17	5.23	5.27	5.33	5.38	5.41	5.43	5.44
1.61	0.00	0.00	1.87	3.69	4.41	4.81	4.97	5.06	5.12	5.16	5.22	5.27	5.30	5.32	5.33
1.62	0.00	0.00	1.72	3.57	4.30	4.69	4.86	4.95	5.01	5.04	5.11	5.16	5.19	5.21	5.23
1.63	0.00	0.00	1.57	3.44	4.18	4.58	4.75	4.84	4.90	4.94	5.01	5.06	5.08	5.11	5.12
1.64	0.00	0.00	1.42	3.31	4.06	4.47	4.64	4.73	4.79	4.83	4.90	4.95	4.98	5.00	5.01
1.65	0.00	0.00	1.28	3.19	3.95	4.36	4.53	4.62	4.68	4.72	4.79	4.85	4.87	4.90	4.91
1.66	0.00	0.00	1.15	3.07	3.84	4.25	4.43	4.52	4.58	4.62	4.69	4.74	4.77	4.80	4.81
1.67	0.00	0.00	1.02	2.95	3.73	4.15	4.32	4.42	4.48	4.52	4.59	4.64	4.67	4.70	4.71
1.68	0.00	0.00	0.89	2.84	3.62	4.05	4.22	4.32	4.38	4.42	4.49	4.55	4.57	4.60	4.61
1.69	0.00	0.00	0.77	2.73	3.52	3.94	4.12	4.22	4.28	4.32	4.39	4.45	4.47	4.50	4.51
1.70	0.00	0.00	0.66	2.62	3.41	3.84	4.02	4.12	4.18	4.22	4.30	4.35	4.38	4.41	4.42
1.71	0.00	0.00	0.55	2.51	3.31	3.75	3.93	4.02	4.09	4.13	4.20	4.26	4.29	4.31	4.32
1.72	0.00	0.00	0.45	2.41	3.21	3.65	3.83	3.93	3.99	4.04	4.11	4.17	4.19	4.22	4.23
1.73	0.00	0.00	0.36	2.30	3.11	3.56	3.74	3.84	3.90	3.94	4.02	4.08	4.10	4.13	4.14
1.74	0.00	0.00	0.27	2.20	3.02	3.46	3.65	3.75	3.81	3.85	3.93	3.99	4.01	4.04	4.05
1.75	0.00	0.00	0.19	2.11	2.93	3.37	3.56	3.66	3.72	3.77	3.84	3.90	3.93	3.95	3.97
1.76	0.00	0.00	0.12	2.01	2.83	3.28	3.47	3.57	3.63	3.68	3.76	3.81	3.84	3.87	3.88
1.77	0.00	0.00	0.06	1.92	2.74	3.20	3.38	3.48	3.55	3.59	3.67	3.73	3.76	3.78	3.80
1.78	0.00	0.00	0.02	1.83	2.66	3.11	3.30	3.40	3.47	3.51	3.59	3.64	3.67	3.70	3.71
1.79	0.00	0.00	0.00	1.74	2.57	3.03	3.21	3.32	3.38	3.43	3.51	3.56	3.59	3.62	3.63
1.80	0.00	0.00	0.00	1.65	2.49	2.94	3.13	3.24	3.30	3.35	3.43	3.48	3.51	3.54	3.55
1.81	0.00	0.00	0.00	1.57	2.40	2.86	3.05	3.16	3.22	3.27	3.35	3.40	3.43	3.46	3.47
1.82	0.00	0.00	0.00	1.49	2.32	2.79	2.98	3.08	3.15	3.19	3.27	3.33	3.36	3.38	3.40
1.83	0.00	0.00	0.00	1.41	2.25	2.71	2.90	3.00	3.07	3.11	3.19	3.25	3.28	3.31	3.32
1.84	0.00	0.00	0.00	1.34	2.17	2.63	2.82	2.93	2.99	3.04	3.12	3.18	3.21	3.23	3.25
1.85	0.00	0.00	0.00	1.26	2.09	2.56	2.75	2.85	2.92	2.97	3.05	3.10	3.13	3.16	3.17
1.86	0.00	0.00	0.00	1.19	2.02	2.48	2.68	2.78	2.85	2.89	2.97	3.03	3.06	3.09	3.10
1.87	0.00	0.00	0.00	1.12	1.95	2.41	2.61	2.71	2.78	2.82	2.90	2.96	2.99	3.02	3.03
1.88	0.00	0.00	0.00	1.06	1.88	2.34	2.54	2.64	2.71	2.75	2.83	2.89	2.92	2.95	2.96
1.89	0.00	0.00	0.00	0.99	1.81	2.28	2.47	2.57	2.64	2.69	2.77	2.83	2.85	2.88	2.90
1.90	0.00	0.00	0.00	0.93	1.75	2.21	2.40	2.51	2.57	2.62	2.70	2.76	2.79	2.82	2.83
1.91	0.00	0.00	0.00	0.87	1.68	2.14	2.34	2.44	2.51	2.56	2.63	2.69	2.72	2.75	2.77
1.92	0.00	0.00	0.00	0.81	1.62	2.08	2.27	2.38	2.45	2.49	2.57	2.63	2.66	2.69	2.70
1.93	0.00	0.00	0.00	0.76	1.56	2.02	2.21	2.32	2.38	2.43	2.51	2.57	2.60	2.62	2.64
1.94	0.00	0.00	0.00	0.70	1.50	1.96	2.15	2.25	2.32	2.37	2.45	2.51	2.54	2.56	2.58
1.95	0.00	0.00	0.00	0.65	1.44	1.90	2.09	2.19	2.26	2.31	2.39	2.45	2.48	2.50	2.52
1.96	0.00	0.00	0.00	0.60	1.38	1.84	2.03	2.14	2.20	2.25	2.33	2.39	2.42	2.44	2.46
1.97	0.00	0.00	0.00	0.56	1.33	1.78	1.97	2.08	2.14	2.19	2.27	2.33	2.36	2.39	2.40
1.98	0.00	0.00	0.00	0.51	1.27	1.73	1.92	2.02	2.09	2.13	2.21	2.27	2.30	2.33	2.34
1.99	0.00	0.00	0.00	0.47	1.22	1.67	1.86	1.97	2.03	2.08	2.16	2.22	2.25	2.27	2.29
2.00	0.00	0.00	0.00	0.43	1.17	1.62	1.81	1.91	1.98	2.03	2.10	2.16	2.19	2.22	2.23
2.01	0.00	0.00	0.00	0.39	1.12	1.57	1.76	1.86	1.93	1.97	2.05	2.11	2.14	2.17	2.18
2.02	0.00	0.00	0.00	0.36	1.07	1.52	1.71	1.81	1.87	1.92	2.00	2.06	2.09	2.11	2.13
2.03	0.00	0.00	0.00	0.32	1.03	1.47	1.66	1.76	1.82	1.87	1.95	2.01	2.04	2.06	2.08
2.04	0.00	0.00	0.00	0.29	0.98	1.42	1.61	1.71	1.77	1.82	1.90	1.96	1.99	2.01	2.03
2.05	0.00	0.00	0.00	0.26	0.94	1.37	1.56	1.66	1.73	1.77	1.85	1.91	1.94	1.96	1.98
2.06	0.00	0.00	0.00	0.23	0.90	1.33	1.51	1.61	1.68	1.72	1.80	1.86	1.89	1.92	1.93
2.07	0.00	0.00	0.00	0.21	0.86	1.28	1.47	1.57	1.63	1.68	1.76	1.81	1.84	1.87	1.88
2.08	0.00	0.00	0.00	0.18	0.82	1.24	1.42	1.52	1.59	1.63	1.71	1.77	1.79	1.82	1.84
2.09	0.00	0.00	0.00	0.16	0.78	1.20	1.38	1.48	1.54	1.59	1.66	1.72	1.75	1.78	1.79

(continued)

601

TABLE 17-4 (*continued*)

Q_U or Q_L	Sample Size														
	3	4	5	7	10	15	20	25	30	35	50	75	100	150	200
2.10	0.00	0.00	0.00	0.14	0.74	1.16	1.34	1.44	1.50	1.54	1.62	1.68	1.71	1.73	1.75
2.11	0.00	0.00	0.00	0.12	0.71	1.12	1.30	1.39	1.46	1.50	1.58	1.63	1.66	1.69	1.70
2.12	0.00	0.00	0.00	0.10	0.67	1.08	1.26	1.35	1.42	1.46	1.54	1.59	1.62	1.65	1.66
2.13	0.00	0.00	0.00	0.08	0.64	1.04	1.22	1.31	1.38	1.42	1.50	1.55	1.58	1.61	1.62
2.14	0.00	0.00	0.00	0.07	0.61	1.00	1.18	1.28	1.34	1.38	1.46	1.51	1.54	1.57	1.58
2.15	0.00	0.00	0.00	0.06	0.58	0.97	1.14	1.24	1.30	1.34	1.42	1.47	1.50	1.53	1.54
2.16	0.00	0.00	0.00	0.05	0.55	0.93	1.10	1.20	1.26	1.30	1.38	1.43	1.46	1.49	1.50
2.17	0.00	0.00	0.00	0.04	0.52	0.90	1.07	1.16	1.22	1.27	1.34	1.40	1.42	1.45	1.46
2.18	0.00	0.00	0.00	0.03	0.49	0.87	1.03	1.13	1.19	1.23	1.30	1.36	1.39	1.41	1.42
2.19	0.00	0.00	0.00	0.02	0.46	0.83	1.00	1.09	1.15	1.20	1.27	1.32	1.35	1.38	1.39
2.20	0.000	0.000	0.000	0.015	0.437	0.803	0.968	1.061	1.120	1.161	1.233	1.287	1.314	1.340	1.352
2.21	0.000	0.000	0.000	0.010	0.413	0.772	0.936	1.028	1.087	1.128	1.199	1.253	1.279	1.305	1.318
2.22	0.000	0.000	0.000	0.006	0.389	0.743	0.905	0.996	1.054	1.095	1.166	1.219	1.245	1.271	1.284
2.23	0.000	0.000	0.000	0.003	0.366	0.715	0.874	0.965	1.023	1.063	1.134	1.186	1.212	1.238	1.250
2.24	0.000	0.000	0.000	0.002	0.345	0.687	0.845	0.935	0.992	1.032	1.102	1.154	1.180	1.205	1.218
2.25	0.000	0.000	0.000	0.001	0.324	0.660	0.816	0.905	0.962	1.002	1.071	1.123	1.148	1.173	1.186
2.26	0.000	0.000	0.000	0.000	0.304	0.634	0.789	0.876	0.933	0.972	1.041	1.092	1.117	1.142	1.155
2.27	0.000	0.000	0.000	0.000	0.285	0.609	0.762	0.848	0.904	0.943	1.011	1.062	1.087	1.112	1.124
2.28	0.000	0.000	0.000	0.000	0.267	0.585	0.735	0.821	0.876	0.915	0.982	1.033	1.058	1.082	1.095
2.29	0.000	0.000	0.000	0.000	0.250	0.561	0.710	0.794	0.849	0.887	0.954	1.004	1.029	1.053	1.065
2.30	0.000	0.000	0.000	0.000	0.233	0.538	0.685	0.769	0.823	0.861	0.927	0.977	1.001	1.025	1.037
2.31	0.000	0.000	0.000	0.000	0.218	0.516	0.661	0.743	0.797	0.834	0.900	0.949	0.974	0.998	1.009
2.32	0.000	0.000	0.000	0.000	0.203	0.495	0.637	0.719	0.772	0.809	0.874	0.923	0.947	0.971	0.982
2.33	0.000	0.000	0.000	0.000	0.189	0.474	0.614	0.695	0.748	0.784	0.848	0.897	0.921	0.944	0.956
2.34	0.000	0.000	0.000	0.000	0.175	0.454	0.592	0.672	0.724	0.760	0.824	0.872	0.895	0.919	0.930
2.35	0.000	0.000	0.000	0.000	0.163	0.435	0.571	0.650	0.701	0.736	0.799	0.847	0.870	0.893	0.905
2.36	0.000	0.000	0.000	0.000	0.151	0.416	0.550	0.628	0.678	0.714	0.776	0.823	0.846	0.869	0.880
2.37	0.000	0.000	0.000	0.000	0.139	0.398	0.530	0.606	0.656	0.691	0.753	0.799	0.822	0.845	0.856
2.38	0.000	0.000	0.000	0.000	0.128	0.381	0.510	0.586	0.635	0.670	0.730	0.777	0.799	0.822	0.833
2.39	0.000	0.000	0.000	0.000	0.118	0.364	0.491	0.566	0.614	0.648	0.709	0.754	0.777	0.799	0.810
2.40	0.000	0.000	0.000	0.000	0.109	0.348	0.473	0.546	0.594	0.628	0.687	0.732	0.755	0.777	0.787
2.41	0.000	0.000	0.000	0.000	0.100	0.332	0.455	0.527	0.575	0.608	0.667	0.711	0.733	0.755	0.766
2.42	0.000	0.000	0.000	0.000	0.091	0.317	0.437	0.509	0.555	0.588	0.646	0.691	0.712	0.734	0.744
2.43	0.000	0.000	0.000	0.000	0.083	0.302	0.421	0.491	0.537	0.569	0.627	0.670	0.692	0.713	0.724
2.44	0.000	0.000	0.000	0.000	0.076	0.288	0.404	0.474	0.519	0.551	0.608	0.651	0.672	0.693	0.703
2.45	0.000	0.000	0.000	0.000	0.069	0.275	0.389	0.457	0.501	0.533	0.589	0.632	0.653	0.673	0.684
2.46	0.000	0.000	0.000	0.000	0.063	0.262	0.373	0.440	0.484	0.516	0.571	0.613	0.634	0.654	0.664
2.47	0.000	0.000	0.000	0.000	0.057	0.249	0.359	0.425	0.468	0.499	0.553	0.595	0.615	0.636	0.646
2.48	0.000	0.000	0.000	0.000	0.051	0.237	0.345	0.409	0.452	0.482	0.536	0.577	0.597	0.617	0.627
2.49	0.000	0.000	0.000	0.000	0.046	0.226	0.331	0.394	0.436	0.466	0.519	0.560	0.580	0.600	0.609

Values tabulated are read in percent.

Q_U or Q_L	Sample Size														
	3	4	5	7	10	15	20	25	30	35	50	75	100	150	200
2.50	0.000	0.000	0.000	0.000	0.041	0.214	0.317	0.380	0.421	0.451	0.503	0.543	0.563	0.582	0.592
2.51	0.000	0.000	0.000	0.000	0.037	0.204	0.305	0.366	0.407	0.436	0.487	0.527	0.546	0.565	0.575
2.52	0.000	0.000	0.000	0.000	0.033	0.193	0.292	0.352	0.392	0.421	0.472	0.511	0.530	0.549	0.559
2.53	0.000	0.000	0.000	0.000	0.029	0.184	0.280	0.339	0.379	0.407	0.457	0.495	0.514	0.533	0.542
2.54	0.000	0.000	0.000	0.000	0.026	0.174	0.268	0.326	0.365	0.393	0.442	0.480	0.499	0.517	0.527
2.55	0.000	0.000	0.000	0.000	0.023	0.165	0.257	0.314	0.352	0.379	0.428	0.465	0.484	0.502	0.511
2.56	0.000	0.000	0.000	0.000	0.020	0.156	0.246	0.302	0.340	0.366	0.414	0.451	0.469	0.487	0.496
2.57	0.000	0.000	0.000	0.000	0.017	0.148	0.236	0.291	0.327	0.354	0.401	0.437	0.455	0.473	0.482
2.58	0.000	0.000	0.000	0.000	0.015	0.140	0.226	0.279	0.316	0.341	0.388	0.424	0.441	0.459	0.468
2.59	0.000	0.000	0.000	0.000	0.013	0.133	0.216	0.269	0.304	0.330	0.375	0.410	0.428	0.445	0.454
2.60	0.000	0.000	0.000	0.000	0.011	0.125	0.207	0.258	0.293	0.318	0.363	0.398	0.415	0.432	0.441
2.61	0.000	0.000	0.000	0.000	0.009	0.118	0.198	0.248	0.282	0.307	0.351	0.385	0.402	0.419	0.428
2.62	0.000	0.000	0.000	0.000	0.008	0.112	0.189	0.238	0.272	0.296	0.339	0.373	0.390	0.406	0.415
2.63	0.000	0.000	0.000	0.000	0.007	0.105	0.181	0.229	0.262	0.285	0.328	0.361	0.378	0.394	0.402
2.64	0.000	0.000	0.000	0.000	0.005	0.099	0.172	0.220	0.252	0.275	0.317	0.350	0.366	0.382	0.390
2.65	0.000	0.000	0.000	0.000	0.005	0.094	0.165	0.211	0.242	0.265	0.307	0.339	0.355	0.371	0.379
2.66	0.000	0.000	0.000	0.000	0.004	0.088	0.157	0.202	0.233	0.256	0.296	0.328	0.344	0.359	0.367
2.67	0.000	0.000	0.000	0.000	0.003	0.083	0.150	0.194	0.224	0.246	0.286	0.317	0.333	0.348	0.356
2.68	0.000	0.000	0.000	0.000	0.002	0.078	0.143	0.186	0.216	0.237	0.277	0.307	0.322	0.338	0.345
2.69	0.000	0.000	0.000	0.000	0.002	0.073	0.136	0.179	0.208	0.229	0.267	0.297	0.312	0.327	0.335
2.70	0.000	0.000	0.000	0.001	0.000	0.069	0.130	0.171	0.200	0.220	0.258	0.288	0.302	0.317	0.325
2.71	0.000	0.000	0.000	0.001	0.000	0.064	0.124	0.164	0.192	0.212	0.249	0.278	0.293	0.307	0.315
2.72	0.000	0.000	0.000	0.001	0.000	0.060	0.118	0.157	0.184	0.204	0.241	0.269	0.283	0.298	0.305
2.73	0.000	0.000	0.000	0.001	0.000	0.057	0.112	0.151	0.177	0.197	0.232	0.260	0.274	0.288	0.296
2.74	0.000	0.000	0.000	0.000	0.000	0.053	0.107	0.144	0.170	0.189	0.224	0.252	0.266	0.279	0.286
2.75	0.000	0.000	0.000	0.000	0.000	0.049	0.102	0.138	0.163	0.182	0.216	0.243	0.257	0.271	0.277
2.76	0.000	0.000	0.000	0.000	0.000	0.046	0.097	0.132	0.157	0.175	0.209	0.235	0.249	0.262	0.269
2.77	0.000	0.000	0.000	0.000	0.000	0.043	0.092	0.126	0.151	0.168	0.201	0.227	0.241	0.254	0.260
2.78	0.000	0.000	0.000	0.000	0.000	0.040	0.087	0.121	0.145	0.162	0.194	0.220	0.233	0.246	0.252
2.79	0.000	0.000	0.000	0.000	0.000	0.037	0.083	0.115	0.139	0.156	0.187	0.212	0.225	0.238	0.244
2.80	0.000	0.000	0.000	0.000	0.000	0.035	0.079	0.110	0.133	0.150	0.181	0.205	0.218	0.230	0.237
2.81	0.000	0.000	0.000	0.000	0.000	0.032	0.075	0.105	0.128	0.144	0.174	0.198	0.211	0.223	0.229
2.82	0.000	0.000	0.000	0.000	0.000	0.030	0.071	0.101	0.122	0.138	0.168	0.192	0.204	0.216	0.222
2.83	0.000	0.000	0.000	0.000	0.000	0.028	0.067	0.096	0.117	0.133	0.162	0.185	0.197	0.209	0.215
2.84	0.000	0.000	0.000	0.000	0.000	0.026	0.064	0.092	0.112	0.128	0.156	0.179	0.190	0.202	0.208
2.85	0.000	0.000	0.000	0.000	0.000	0.024	0.060	0.088	0.108	0.122	0.150	0.173	0.184	0.195	0.201
2.86	0.000	0.000	0.000	0.000	0.000	0.022	0.057	0.084	0.103	0.118	0.145	0.167	0.178	0.189	0.195
2.87	0.000	0.000	0.000	0.000	0.000	0.020	0.054	0.080	0.099	0.113	0.139	0.161	0.172	0.183	0.188
2.88	0.000	0.000	0.000	0.000	0.000	0.019	0.051	0.076	0.094	0.108	0.134	0.155	0.166	0.177	0.182
2.89	0.000	0.000	0.000	0.000	0.000	0.017	0.048	0.073	0.090	0.104	0.129	0.150	0.160	0.171	0.176
2.90	0.000	0.000	0.000	0.000	0.000	0.016	0.046	0.069	0.087	0.100	0.125	0.145	0.155	0.165	0.171
2.91	0.000	0.000	0.000	0.000	0.000	0.015	0.043	0.066	0.083	0.096	0.120	0.140	0.150	0.160	0.165
2.92	0.000	0.000	0.000	0.000	0.000	0.013	0.041	0.063	0.079	0.092	0.115	0.135	0.145	0.155	0.160
2.93	0.000	0.000	0.000	0.000	0.000	0.012	0.038	0.060	0.076	0.088	0.111	0.130	0.140	0.149	0.154
2.94	0.000	0.000	0.000	0.000	0.000	0.011	0.036	0.057	0.072	0.084	0.107	0.125	0.135	0.144	0.149
2.95	0.000	0.000	0.000	0.000	0.000	0.010	0.034	0.054	0.069	0.081	0.103	0.121	0.130	0.140	0.144
2.96	0.000	0.000	0.0,00	0.000	0.000	0.009	0.032	0.051	0.066	0.077	0.099	0.117	0.126	0.135	0.140
2.97	0.000	0.000	0.000	0.000	0.000	0.009	0.030	0.049	0.063	0.074	0.095	0.112	0.121	0.130	0.135
2.98	0.000	0.000	0.000	0.000	0.000	0.008	0.028	0.046	0.060	0.071	0.091	0.108	0.117	0.126	0.130
2.99	0.000	0.000	0.000	0.000	0.000	0.007	0.027	0.044	0.057	0.068	0.088	0.104	0.113	0.122	0.126

(*continued*)

TABLE 17-4 (continued)

Q_U or Q_L	Sample Size														
	3	4	5	7	10	15	20	25	30	35	50	75	100	150	200
3.00	0.000	0.000	0.000	0.000	0.000	0.006	0.025	0.042	0.055	0.065	0.084	0.101	0.109	0.118	0.122
3.01	0.000	0.000	0.000	0.000	0.000	0.006	0.024	0.040	0.052	0.062	0.081	0.097	0.105	0.113	0.118
3.02	0.000	0.000	0.000	0.000	0.000	0.005	0.022	0.038	0.050	0.059	0.078	0.093	0.101	0.110	0.114
3.03	0.000	0.000	0.000	0.000	0.000	0.005	0.021	0.036	0.048	0.057	0.075	0.090	0.098	0.106	0.110
3.04	0.000	0.000	0.000	0.000	0.000	0.004	0.019	0.034	0.045	0.054	0.072	0.087	0.094	0.102	0.106
3.05	0.000	0.000	0.000	0.000	0.000	0.004	0.018	0.032	0.043	0.052	0.069	0.083	0.091	0.099	0.103
3.06	0.000	0.000	0.000	0.000	0.000	0.003	0.017	0.030	0.041	0.050	0.066	0.080	0.088	0.095	0.099
3.07	0.000	0.000	0.000	0.000	0.000	0.003	0.016	0.029	0.039	0.047	0.064	0.077	0.085	0.092	0.096
3.08	0.000	0.000	0.000	0.000	0.000	0.003	0.015	0.027	0.037	0.045	0.061	0.074	0.081	0.089	0.092
3.09	0.000	0.000	0.000	0.000	0.000	0.002	0.014	0.026	0.036	0.043	0.059	0.072	0.079	0.086	0.089
3.10	0.000	0.000	0.000	0.000	0.000	0.002	0.013	0.024	0.034	0.041	0.056	0.069	0.076	0.083	0.086
3.11	0.000	0.000	0.000	0.000	0.000	0.002	0.012	0.023	0.032	0.039	0.054	0.066	0.073	0.080	0.083
3.12	0.000	0.000	0.000	0.000	0.000	0.002	0.011	0.022	0.031	0.038	0.052	0.064	0.070	0.077	0.080
3.13	0.000	0.000	0.000	0.000	0.000	0.002	0.011	0.021	0.029	0.036	0.050	0.061	0.068	0.074	0.077
3.14	0.000	0.000	0.000	0.000	0.000	0.001	0.010	0.019	0.028	0.034	0.048	0.059	0.065	0.071	0.075
3.15	0.000	0.000	0.000	0.000	0.000	0.001	0.009	0.018	0.026	0.033	0.046	0.057	0.063	0.069	0.072
3.16	0.000	0.000	0.000	0.000	0.000	0.001	0.009	0.017	0.025	0.031	0.044	0.055	0.060	0.066	0.069
3.17	0.000	0.000	0.000	0.000	0.000	0.001	0.008	0.016	0.024	0.030	0.042	0.053	0.058	0.064	0.067
3.18	0.000	0.000	0.000	0.000	0.000	0.001	0.007	0.015	0.022	0.028	0.040	0.050	0.056	0.062	0.065
3.19	0.000	0.000	0.000	0.000	0.000	0.001	0.007	0.015	0.021	0.027	0.038	0.049	0.054	0.059	0.062
3.20	0.000	0.000	0.000	0.000	0.000	0.001	0.006	0.014	0.020	0.026	0.037	0.047	0.052	0.057	0.060
3.21	0.000	0.000	0.000	0.000	0.000	0.000	0.006	0.013	0.019	0.024	0.035	0.045	0.050	0.055	0.058
3.22	0.000	0.000	0.000	0.000	0.000	0.000	0.005	0.012	0.018	0.023	0.034	0.043	0.048	0.053	0.056
3.23	0.000	0.000	0.000	0.000	0.000	0.000	0.005	0.011	0.017	0.022	0.032	0.041	0.046	0.051	0.054
3.24	0.000	0.000	0.000	0.000	0.000	0.000	0.005	0.011	0.016	0.021	0.031	0.040	0.044	0.049	0.052
3.25	0.000	0.000	0.000	0.000	0.000	0.000	0.004	0.010	0.015	0.020	0.030	0.038	0.043	0.048	0.050
3.26	0.000	0.000	0.000	0.000	0.000	0.000	0.004	0.009	0.015	0.019	0.028	0.037	0.041	0.046	0.048
3.27	0.000	0.000	0.000	0.000	0.000	0.000	0.004	0.009	0.014	0.018	0.027	0.035	0.040	0.044	0.046
3.28	0.000	0.000	0.000	0.000	0.000	0.000	0.003	0.008	0.013	0.017	0.026	0.034	0.038	0.042	0.045
3.29	0.000	0.000	0.000	0.000	0.000	0.000	0.003	0.008	0.012	0.016	0.025	0.032	0.037	0.041	0.043
3.30	0.000	0.000	0.000	0.000	0.000	0.000	0.003	0.007	0.012	0.015	0.024	0.031	0.035	0.039	0.042
3.31	0.000	0.000	0.000	0.000	0.000	0.000	0.003	0.007	0.011	0.015	0.023	0.030	0.034	0.038	0.040
3.32	0.000	0.000	0.000	0.000	0.000	0.000	0.002	0.006	0.010	0.014	0.022	0.029	0.032	0.036	0.038
3.33	0.000	0.000	0.000	0.000	0.000	0.000	0.002	0.006	0.010	0.013	0.021	0.027	0.031	0.035	0.037
3.34	0.000	0.000	0.000	0.000	0.000	0.000	0.002	0.006	0.009	0.013	0.020	0.026	0.030	0.034	0.036
3.35	0.000	0.000	0.000	0.000	0.000	0.000	0.002	0.005	0.009	0.012	0.019	0.025	0.029	0.032	0.034
3.36	0.000	0.000	0.000	0.000	0.000	0.000	0.002	0.005	0.008	0.011	0.018	0.024	0.028	0.031	0.033
3.37	0.000	0.000	0.000	0.000	0.000	0.000	0.002	0.005	0.008	0.011	0.017	0.023	0.026	0.030	0.032
3.38	0.000	0.000	0.000	0.000	0.000	0.000	0.001	0.004	0.007	0.010	0.016	0.022	0.025	0.029	0.031
3.39	0.000	0.000	0.000	0.000	0.000	0.000	0.001	0.004	0.007	0.010	0.016	0.021	0.024	0.028	0.029

Values tabulated are read in percent.

Q_U or Q_L	3	4	5	7	10	15	20	25	30	35	50	75	100	150	200
							Sample Size								
3.40	0.000	0.000	0.000	0.000	0.000	0.000	0.001	0.004	0.007	0.009	0.015	0.020	0.023	0.027	0.028
3.41	0.000	0.000	0.000	0.000	0.000	0.000	0.001	0.003	0.006	0.009	0.014	0.020	0.022	0.026	0.027
3.42	0.000	0.000	0.000	0.000	0.000	0.000	0.001	0.003	0.006	0.008	0.014	0.019	0.022	0.025	0.026
3.43	0.000	0.000	0.000	0.000	0.000	0.000	0.001	0.003	0.005	0.008	0.013	0.018	0.021	0.024	0.025
3.44	0.000	0.000	0.000	0.000	0.000	0.000	0.001	0.003	0.005	0.007	0.012	0.017	0.020	0.023	0.024
3.45	0.000	0.000	0.000	0.000	0.000	0.000	0.001	0.003	0.005	0.007	0.012	0.016	0.019	0.022	0.023
3.46	0.000	0.000	0.000	0.000	0.000	0.000	0.001	0.002	0.005	0.007	0.011	0.016	0.018	0.021	0.022
3.47	0.000	0.000	0.000	0.000	0.000	0.000	0.001	0.002	0.004	0.006	0.011	0.015	0.017	0.020	0.022
3.48	0.000	0.000	0.000	0.000	0.000	0.000	0.001	0.002	0.004	0.006	0.010	0.014	0.017	0.019	0.021
3.49	0.000	0.000	0.000	0.000	0.000	0.000	0.000	0.002	0.004	0.005	0.010	0.014	0.016	0.019	0.020
3.50	0.000	0.000	0.000	0.000	0.000	0.000	0.000	0.002	0.003	0.005	0.009	0.013	0.015	0.018	0.019
3.51	0.000	0.000	0.000	0.000	0.000	0.000	0.000	0.002	0.003	0.005	0.009	0.013	0.015	0.017	0.018
3.52	0.000	0.000	0.000	0.000	0.000	0.000	0.000	0.002	0.003	0.005	0.008	0.012	0.014	0.016	0.018
3.53	0.000	0.000	0.000	0.000	0.000	0.000	0.000	0.001	0.003	0.004	0.008	0.011	0.014	0.016	0.017
3.54	0.000	0.000	0.000	0.000	0.000	0.000	0.000	0.001	0.003	0.004	0.008	0.011	0.013	0.015	0.016
3.55	0.000	0.000	0.000	0.000	0.000	0.000	0.000	0.001	0.003	0.004	0.007	0.011	0.012	0.015	0.016
3.56	0.000	0.000	0.000	0.000	0.000	0.000	0.000	0.001	0.002	0.004	0.007	0.010	0.012	0.014	0.015
3.57	0.000	0.000	0.000	0.000	0.000	0.000	0.000	0.001	0.002	0.003	0.006	0.010	0.011	0.013	0.014
3.58	0.000	0.000	0.000	0.000	0.000	0.000	0.000	0.001	0.002	0.003	0.006	0.009	0.011	0.013	0.014
3.59	0.000	0.000	0.000	0.000	0.000	0.000	0.000	0.001	0.002	0.003	0.006	0.009	0.010	0.012	0.013
3.60	0.000	0.000	0.000	0.000	0.000	0.000	0.000	0.001	0.002	0.003	0.006	0.008	0.010	0.012	0.013
3.61	0.000	0.000	0.000	0.000	0.000	0.000	0.000	0.001	0.002	0.003	0.005	0.008	0.010	0.011	0.012
3.62	0.000	0.000	0.000	0.000	0.000	0.000	0.000	0.001	0.002	0.003	0.005	0.008	0.009	0.011	0.012
3.63	0.000	0.000	0.000	0.000	0.000	0.000	0.000	0.001	0.001	0.002	0.005	0.007	0.009	0.010	0.011
3.64	0.000	0.000	0.000	0.000	0.000	0.000	0.000	0.001	0.001	0.002	0.004	0.007	0.008	0.010	0.011
3.65	0.000	0.000	0.000	0.000	0.000	0.000	0.000	0.001	0.001	0.002	0.004	0.007	0.008	0.010	0.010
3.66	0.000	0.000	0.000	0.000	0.000	0.000	0.000	0.000	0.001	0.002	0.004	0.006	0.008	0.009	0.010
3.67	0.000	0.000	0.000	0.000	0.000	0.000	0.000	0.000	0.001	0.002	0.004	0.006	0.007	0.009	0.010
3.68	0.000	0.000	0.000	0.000	0.000	0.000	0.000	0.000	0.001	0.002	0.004	0.006	0.007	0.008	0.009
3.69	0.000	0.000	0.000	0.000	0.000	0.000	0.000	0.000	0.001	0.002	0.003	0.005	0.007	0.008	0.009
3.70	0.000	0.000	0.000	0.000	0.000	0.000	0.000	0.000	0.001	0.002	0.003	0.005	0.006	0.008	0.008
3.71	0.000	0.000	0.000	0.000	0.000	0.000	0.000	0.000	0.001	0.001	0.003	0.005	0.006	0.007	0.008
3.72	0.000	0.000	0.000	0.000	0.000	0.000	0.000	0.000	0.001	0.001	0.003	0.005	0.006	0.007	0.008
3.73	0.000	0.000	0.000	0.000	0.000	0.000	0.000	0.000	0.001	0.001	0.003	0.005	0.006	0.007	0.007
3.74	0.000	0.000	0.000	0.000	0.000	0.000	0.000	0.000	0.001	0.001	0.003	0.004	0.005	0.007	0.007
3.75	0.000	0.000	0.000	0.000	0.000	0.000	0.000	0.000	0.001	0.001	0.002	0.004	0.005	0.006	0.007
3.76	0.000	0.000	0.000	0.000	0.000	0.000	0.000	0.000	0.001	0.001	0.002	0.004	0.005	0.006	0.007
3.77	0.000	0.000	0.000	0.000	0.000	0.000	0.000	0.000	0.001	0.001	0.002	0.004	0.005	0.006	0.006
3.78	0.000	0.000	0.000	0.000	0.000	0.000	0.000	0.000	0.000	0.001	0.002	0.004	0.004	0.005	0.006
3.79	0.000	0.000	0.000	0.000	0.000	0.000	0.000	0.000	0.000	0.001	0.002	0.003	0.004	0.005	0.006
3.80	0.000	0.000	0.000	0.000	0.000	0.000	0.000	0.000	0.000	0.001	0.002	0.003	0.004	0.005	0.006
3.81	0.000	0.000	0.000	0.000	0.000	0.000	0.000	0.000	0.000	0.001	0.002	0.003	0.004	0.005	0.005
3.82	0.000	0.000	0.000	0.000	0.000	0.000	0.000	0.000	0.000	0.001	0.002	0.003	0.004	0.005	0.005
3.83	0.000	0.000	0.000	0.000	0.000	0.000	0.000	0.000	0.000	0.001	0.002	0.003	0.004	0.004	0.005
3.84	0.000	0.000	0.000	0.000	0.000	0.000	0.000	0.000	0.000	0.001	0.001	0.003	0.003	0.004	0.005
3.85	0.000	0.000	0.000	0.000	0.000	0.000	0.000	0.000	0.000	0.001	0.001	0.002	0.003	0.004	0.004
3.86	0.000	0.000	0.000	0.000	0.000	0.000	0.000	0.000	0.000	0.000	0.001	0.002	0.003	0.004	0.004
3.87	0.000	0.000	0.000	0.000	0.000	0.000	0.000	0.000	0.000	0.000	0.001	0.002	0.003	0.004	0.004
3.88	0.000	0.000	0.000	0.000	0.000	0.000	0.000	0.000	0.000	0.000	0.001	0.002	0.003	0.004	0.004
3.89	0.000	0.000	0.000	0.000	0.000	0.000	0.000	0.000	0.000	0.000	0.001	0.002	0.003	0.003	0.004
3.90	0.000	0.000	0.000	0.000	0.000	0.000	0.000	0.000	0.000	0.000	0.001	0.002	0.003	0.003	0.004

TABLE 17-5   Master Table for Normal and Tightened Inspection for Plans Based on Variability Unknown (Double Specification Limit and Form 2—Single Specification Limit)

Sample Size Code Letter	Sample Size	Acceptance Quality Limit (Normal Inspection)											
		T	0.10	0.15	0.25	0.40	0.65	1.00	1.50	2.50	4.00	6.50	10.00
		M	M	M	M	M	M	M	M	M	M	M	M
B	3	↓	↓	↓	↓	↓	↓	⇩	⇩	7.59	18.86	26.94	33.69
C	4	↓	↓	↓	↓	↓	⇩	1.49	5.46	10.88	16.41	22.84	29.43
D	5	↓	↓	↓	↓	0.041	1.34	3.33	5.82	9.80	14.37	20.19	26.55
E	7	↓	0.005	0.087	0.421	1.05	2.13	3.54	5.34	8.40	12.19	17.34	23.30
F	10	0.077	0.179	0.349	0.714	1.27	2.14	3.27	4.72	7.26	10.53	15.17	20.73
G	15	0.186	0.311	0.491	0.839	1.33	2.09	3.06	4.32	6.55	9.48	13.74	18.97
H	20	0.228	0.356	0.531	0.864	1.33	2.03	2.93	4.10	6.18	8.95	13.01	18.07
I	25	0.250	0.378	0.551	0.874	1.32	2.00	2.86	3.97	5.98	8.65	12.60	17.55
J	35	0.253	0.373	0.534	0.833	1.24	1.87	2.66	3.70	5.58	8.11	11.89	16.67
K	50	0.243	0.355	0.503	0.778	1.16	1.73	2.47	3.44	5.21	7.61	11.23	15.87
L	75	0.225	0.326	0.461	0.711	1.06	1.59	2.27	3.17	4.83	7.10	10.58	15.07
M	100	0.218	0.315	0.444	0.684	1.02	1.52	2.18	3.06	4.67	6.88	10.29	14.71
N	150	0.202	0.292	0.412	0.636	0.946	1.42	2.05	2.88	4.42	6.56	9.86	14.18
P	200	0.204	0.294	0.414	0.637	0.945	1.42	2.04	2.86	4.39	6.52	9.80	14.11
		0.10	0.15	0.25	0.40	0.65	1.00	1.50	2.50	4.00	6.50	10.00	
		Acceptable Quality Levels (Tightened Inspection)											

All AQL values are in percent nonconforming. T denotes plan used exclusively on tightened inspection and provides symbol for identification of appropriate OC curve.

⇩ Use first sampling plan below arrow; that is, both sample size as well as M value. When sample size equals or exceeds lot size, every item in the lot must be inspected.

Source: Copyright American Society for Quality Control, Inc. Reprinted by permission.

The acceptability criterion used is the percent of nonconforming product. The percentage of nonconforming product is estimated by entering Table 17-4 with the quality index and the sample size. Both quality indices $Q_U = (U - \bar{x})/s$ and $Q_L = (\bar{x} - L)/s$ must be computed. Estimates of conformance with the upper limit, $\hat{p}_U$, and of conformance with the lower limit, $\hat{p}_L$, are made. The overall estimate of percent nonconforming, $\hat{p}$, is also calculated by adding $\hat{p}_U$ and $\hat{p}_L$.

When a different AQL value is established for the upper and lower specification limit, all three of the following conditions must be met for acceptance:

1. $\hat{p}_U \leq M_U$.
2. $\hat{p}_L \leq M_L$.
3. $\hat{p} \leq \max{(M_U, M_L)}$.

When a single AQL value is established for the upper and lower specification limits combined, the estimate of the lot percent nonconforming is $\hat{p} = \hat{p}_U + \hat{p}_L$. If $\hat{p}$ is less than or equal to the maximum allowable percent nonconforming, M, the lot meets the acceptability criterion. If $\hat{p}$ is greater than M or if either Q_U, Q_L, or both are negative, then the lot does not meet the acceptability criterion.

▶ **EXAMPLE 17-4** Use of Double Specification Plans—Different
AQL Values for Upper and Lower Specification Limits

The line widths on a memory chip are specified at 1.7 microns. The specifications are a maximum
of 1.75 microns and a minimum of 1.65 microns. The lower limit is more critical and an AQL of
0.25% is selected. For the upper limit an AQL of 1.00% is selected. The chips are made on wafers,
each wafer containing 400 chips. The lot widths have been found to be consistent within a chip.
The decision is made to take one line measurement per chip and to consider each wafer to be a lot
of 400 chips.

Inspection level I is used because the inspections are expensive and the chips have a good quality history. For a lot of 400 chips Table 17-2 indicates code letter G for inspection level I. From
Table 17-5, it is determined that a sample size of 15 is needed. The following measurements are
obtained:

$$
\begin{array}{ccccc}
1.72 & 1.73 & 1.69 & 1.72 & 1.70 \\
1.67 & 1.66 & 1.71 & 1.69 & 1.71 \\
1.69 & 1.69 & 1.73 & 1.68 & 1.70
\end{array}
$$

As before, the straightforward steps outlined in ANSI/ASQC Z1.9-1993 will be used to make the
calculations.

Step	Information Needed	Value(s) Obtained	Explanation
1	Sample size: n	15	
2	Sum of measurements: Σx	25.49	
3	Sum of squared measurements: Σx^2	43.3221	
4	Correction factor (CF): $(\Sigma x)^2/n$	43.3160	$(25.49)^2/15$
5	Corrected sum of squares (SS): $\Sigma x^2 - $ CF	0.0061	$43.3221 - 43.3160$
6	Variance (V): SS/$(n-1)$	0.00044	0.0061/14
7	Estimate of lot standard deviation s: $\sqrt{V}$	0.021	$\sqrt{0.00044}$
8	Sample mean $\bar{x}$: $\Sigma x/n$	1.699	25.49/15
9	Upper specification limit: U	1.75	
10	Lower specification limit: L	1.65	
11	Quality index: $Q_U = (U - \bar{x})/s$	2.429	$(1.75 - 1.699)/0.021$
12	Quality index: $Q_L = (\bar{x} - L)/s$	2.333	$(1.699 - 1.65)/0.021$
13	Estimate of lot nonconforming above U: $\hat{p}_U$	0.302%	See Table 17-4
14	Estimate of lot nonconforming below L: $\hat{p}_L$	0.474%	See Table 17-4
15	Total estimated percent nonconforming in lot: $\hat{p} = \hat{p}_U + \hat{p}_L$	0.776%	0.302 + 0.776
16	Maximum allowable percent nonconforming below L: M_L	0.839%	See Table 17-5
17	Maximum allowable percent nonconforming above U: M_U	3.06%	See Table 17-5
18	Acceptability criteria:		
	(a) Compare $\hat{p}_U$ with M_U	OK	$0.302 \leq 3.06$
	(b) Compare $\hat{p}_L$ with M_L	OK	$0.474 \leq 0.839$
	(c) Compare $\hat{p}$ with M_U	OK	$0.776 \leq 3.06$

In this example the calculated estimates satisfy all three acceptance criteria, so the lot is accepted. The lower specification limit may cause concern, since the estimate (0.474%) is greater than
the AQL (0.25%). It is understood that the sampling plan that has been selected is intended to have

a high probability of acceptance (about 95%) at the AQL value, so it will also have a high probability of acceptance when the true quality is close to the AQL. Also, with a sample size of only 15,
an estimated percent nonconforming of 0.474% would be probable when the true quality is better
than 0.25%.

Maximum Standard Deviation

With double specification limits, there is a maximum value of the standard deviation. If
this value is exceeded, the percent nonconforming of the product will exceed the limit,
M, found in Table 17-5 regardless of where the process is centered. To determine this
value, enter Table B-6 of ANSI/ASQC Z1.9-1993, here reproduced as Table 17-6. From
the table a value of F is obtained corresponding to the sample size and AQL. The maximum standard deviation (MSD) is found by multiplying F by the difference between U
and L. That is,

$$MSD = F(U - L)$$

If the calculated value of the standard deviation exceeds this value, the lot should be
rejected. This step should precede the calculation of the quality indexes and percent nonconforming. For Example 17-4 the MSD would be $0.212(1.75 - 1.65)$, or 0.0212 for the
lower limit and $0.248(1.75 - 1.65) = 0.0248$ for the upper limit. Recall that the calculated value of the standard deviation was 0.021, which just barely meets the lower specification limit.

17-3.2 Variability Known

There are times when it is assumed that the variability of the process with respect to the
quality characteristic is known. There may be a process that has been very stable for a

**TABLE 17-6 Values of F for Maximum Standard Deviation for Variability Unknown Plans,
Double Specification Limits**

Sample Size	T	\multicolumn{12}{c}{Acceptance Quality Limit (AQL)}
		0.10	0.15	0.25	0.40	0.65	1.00	1.50	2.50	4.00	6.50	10.00
3									0.436	0.453	0.475	0.502
4							0.338	0.353	0.374	0.399	0.432	0.472
5					0.281	0.294	0.308	0.323	0.346	0.372	0.408	0.452
7		0.224	0.231	0.242	0.253	0.266	0.280	0.295	0.318	0.345	0.381	0.425
10	0.200	0.206	0.214	0.224	0.235	0.247	0.261	0.275	0.298	0.324	0.359	0.403
15	0.188	0.195	0.202	0.212	0.222	0.235	0.248	0.262	0.284	0.309	0.344	0.386
20	0.183	0.190	0.197	0.206	0.217	0.229	0.242	0.256	0.277	0.302	0.336	0.377
25	0.180	0.187	0.194	0.203	0.213	0.225	0.238	0.252	0.273	0.298	0.331	0.372
30	0.179	0.185	0.192	0.201	0.211	0.223	0.236	0.249	0.271	0.295	0.329	0.369
35	0.176	0.182	0.189	0.198	0.208	0.220	0.232	0.246	0.267	0.291	0.324	0.364
50	0.172	0.178	0.185	0.194	0.204	0.215	0.227	0.241	0.261	0.285	0.317	0.357
75	0.168	0.174	0.181	0.190	0.199	0.211	0.223	0.236	0.256	0.279	0.311	0.349
100	0.167	0.173	0.179	0.188	0.198	0.209	0.220	0.233	0.253	0.276	0.308	0.346
150	0.164	0.170	0.176	0.185	0.195	0.206	0.217	0.230	0.250	0.273	0.304	0.341
200	0.164	0.168	0.176	0.185	0.194	0.205	0.217	0.230	0.249	0.272	0.303	0.340

long time, and many observations over this time period have been obtained. There may also be certain physical characteristics of the process that provide comfort about the certainty of the process variability. In any case the assumption that variability is known makes the use of acceptance sampling by variables easier. The known σ concept is often used until evidence is produced that refutes this concept.

There are several differences from the case in which variability is unknown. In addition to the plans being easier to use, the sample sizes will be smaller. The acceptability criteria for the single specification limit case will be very similar. Calculate the quantities $(U - \bar{x})/\sigma$ or $(\bar{x} - L)/\sigma$, where σ is the assumed known standard deviation and compare this calculation with a constant k. The constant k is obtained from special tables in Section D of ANSI/ASQC Z1.9-1993.

The steps to be used are basically the same as for the previous examples. It is not necessary to compute the standard deviation, which saves several steps. When there is a need to obtain an estimate of the percent nonconforming, a Form 2 procedure may be used as before. Special tables are also provided in ANSI/ASQC Z1.9-1993 for this case. There is one difference here. The quality index is modified by multiplying by a factor v corresponding to the sample size. The factor v is provided in the tables with n and M and is the factor discussed previously [i.e, $\sqrt{n/(n-1)}$]. The quality index is thus

$$Q_U = (U - \bar{x})v/\sigma$$

or

$$Q_L = (\bar{x} - L)v/\sigma$$

The other calculations, estimates of percent nonconforming, and application of the acceptability criteria are as before. In this case the table giving the estimate of percent nonconforming, Table D5 in ANSI/ASQC Z1.9-1993, is a normal area table similar to Table A in the Appendix. The procedures are clearly explained in ANSI/ASQC Z1.9-1993, and excellent examples are also provided.

The use of the acceptance sampling procedures and tables for inspection by variables when variability is known and there are double specification limits is exactly as expected. As in the case in which variability is unknown, only the Form 2 approach may be used with an estimate of the percent nonconforming. The factor v is again used to calculate the quality indices. The same three criteria must be met:

1. $\hat{p}_U \leq M_U$
2. $\hat{p}_L \leq M_L$
3. $\hat{p} \leq \max(M_U, M_L)$

A step-by-step explanation and examples are given in ANSI/ASQC Z1.9-1993 for this procedure also. There is also a table giving values of the maximum process standard deviation.

17-3.3 Switching Rules

One of the biggest differences between MIL-STD-414 and ANSI/ASQC Z1.9-1993 is the switching rules. The switching rules for MIL-STD-414 are described below.

Normal Inspection to Reduced Inspection

"Normal inspection shall be used at the start of inspection unless otherwise designated" (MIL-STD-414, 1957). Reduced inspection is allowed when all of the following conditions are satisfied:

1. The preceding ten lots have been under normal inspection, and none has been rejected.

2. The estimated percent nonconforming for each of these preceding lots is less than the applicable lower limit shown in a special table.

3. Production is at a steady rate.

Normal inspection is to be reinstated from reduced inspection if any one of the following conditions occurs:

1. A lot is rejected.

2. The estimated process average is greater than the AQL.

3. Production becomes irregular or delayed.

4. Other conditions warrant that normal inspection be reinstated.

The revision of the ANSI Z1.9 (1972) standard to ANSI/ASQC Z1.9-1980 and later to ANSI/ASQC Z1.9-1993 was undertaken to allow complete interchangeability with the plans of ISO 3951, which provide a graphical means for implementation of the plans. This revision also roughly matches ANSI/ASQC Z1.9-1993 with ANSI/ASQC Z1.4-1993, which corresponds to MIL-STD-105D. This matching is very noticeable in the switching rules. Switching from normal to reduced inspection under ANSI/ASQC Z1.9-1993 is allowed when all the following conditions are met:

1. The preceding ten lots or batches have been on normal inspection, and none has been rejected.

2. Production is at a steady rate.

3. Reduced inspection is considered desirable by the responsible authority and is permitted by the contract or specification.

Normal inspection is to be reinstituted if any one of the conditions 1, 3, or 4 previously described under MIL-STD-414 occurs. There is no provision for estimating the process average as a part of the switching rules.

Normal Inspection to Tightened Inspection

The biggest difference between ANSI/ASQC Z1.9-1993 and MIL-STD-414 is the rule for switching between normal inspection and tightened. For ANSI/ASQC Z1.9-1993, the new rule is very simple: "When normal inspection is in effect, tightened inspection shall be instituted when two out of five or fewer consecutive lots or batches have been rejected on original inspection" (ANSI/ASQC Z1.9-1993). The rule for returning to normal from tightened inspection is just as simple. When five consecutive lots or batches are considered acceptable on original inspection during tightened inspection, normal inspection may be reinstituted.

The switching rules in MIL-STD-414 are more difficult to use. Switching from normal to tightened is determined by calculating the process average for the preceding ten lots and calculating the number of lots in these ten that have an estimated percent nonconforming exceeding the AQL. If the estimated process average exceeds the AQL and the number of lots with estimated percent nonconforming greater than the AQL exceeds a T value listed in the tables for certain lot sizes, then switch from normal to tightened inspection.

Normal inspection can be reinstituted from tightened under MIL-STD-414 if the estimated process average of lots under tightened inspection is equal to or less than the AQL. No minimum number of lots is given for this criterion.

17-3.4 Other Differences in Acceptance Sampling Plans

The switching rules are probably the most noticeable difference between MIL-STD-414 and ANSI/ASQC Z1.9-1993, but some other differences are worth mentioning. The inspection levels have been relabeled to correspond more closely to MIL-STD-105E and ANSI/ASQC Z1.4-1993. The inspection levels in ANSI/ASQC Z1.9-1993 are S3, S4, I, II, and III instead of I, II, III, IV, and V as used in MIL-STD-414. Recall that in MIL-STD-105E they are S1, S2, S3, S4 and I, II, and III. The lot size ranges in ANSI/ASQC Z1.9-1993 correspond closely to MIL-STD-105E. A new section, "Definitions and Terminology," has been added in place of the old section, "Classification and Defects." And throughout the entire standard the word "defect" has been replaced by "nonconformity," "defective" has been replaced by "nonconforming," and "percent defective" has been replaced by "percent nonconforming."

▶ 17-4 THE GRAPHICAL METHOD—ISO 3951

The international standard ISO 3951(1989), *Sampling Procedures and Charts for Inspection by Variables for Percent Defective,* is a graphical version of ANSI/ASQC Z1.9-1993. It is based on the United Kingdom Defense Standard, *Sampling Procedures and Charts for Inspection by Variables.* The method used in the standard is derived from the one given in ANSI/ASQC Z1.9-1993, but it differs in that a graphical method is applied rather than the Form 2 tabular method in ANSI/ASQC Z1.9-1993.

17-4.1 Variability Unknown

The procedures for the graphical method in ISO 3951 are very similar to the procedures discussed earlier. The graphical methods are most useful for the double specification limit, but they work well also for the single specification limit.

Single Specification Limit
Proceed as before to obtain the sample size and the sample. Then calculate the sample mean and standard deviation. The acceptability constant k is obtained from a table as before. Then the line

$$\bar{x} = U - ks \qquad \text{(for an upper limit)}$$

or

$$\bar{x} = L + ks \qquad \text{(for a lower limit)}$$

is drawn on graph paper or on a computer terminal. Figure 17-2 shows the simple triangular plot that results. The acceptance zone is the area under the line in the case of a single upper limit or above the line for a lower limit. Plot the point $(s, \bar{x})$ on the graph.

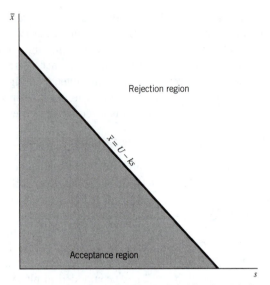

Figure 17-2   Graph for Single Specification Limit

If the point lies in the accept zone, accept the lot or batch. If the point lies outside the accept zone, the lot or batch is rejected.

▶ **EXAMPLE 17-5** Use of Graphical Method for Single Specification Limit

In Example 17-2 a lot of transmitters was to be tested and accepted if voltage levels were satisfactory. A sample of size 4 was taken. The average and the standard deviation of the sample were calculated to be 27.25 and 1.71. The upper specification limit was 30. The acceptability constant, k, was 1.17. The graph is easily drawn and shown here in Figure 17.3. The figure indicates acceptance of the lot. The point $\bar{x} = 27.25$ and $s = 1.71$ lies well within the acceptance region. The graph also shows that the average would need to be above 28 to reject the lot with a standard deviation of 1.71. The standard deviation would have to be greater than 2.5 to reject the lot with an average of 27.25.

Double Specification Limit
The chief advantage of the graphical method is for cases with double specification limits. The ISO 3951 standard contains a series of charts labeled with the sample size code letters. The suggested procedure is for the inspector to copy or trace the appropriate acceptance curve with the AQL specified for the sampling plan. The scale is then adjusted so that the upper limit is plotted instead of 1.0 and the lower limit is plotted instead of 0.0 of the $\bar{x}$ scale. The values of $\bar{x}$ and s can be plotted directly on this graph.

Instead of adjusting the scales, the mean and standard deviation may be standardized by calculating

$$\frac{\bar{x} - L}{U - L} \quad \text{and} \quad \frac{s}{U - L}$$

Proceed again as with ANSI/ASQC Z1.9-1993. First obtain the upper specification limit U and lower specification limit L. The lot size is determined, the inspection level

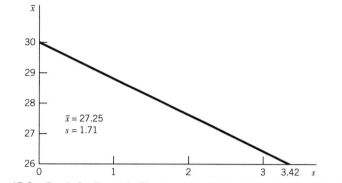

Figure 17-3 Graph for Example Showing Use of Single Specification Limit Plan

is selected, and the AQL is specified. The tables are used to get the code letter and the sample size. After the sample is taken, the sample mean and sample standard deviation are calculated. The appropriate acceptance curve is selected, and the point corresponding to the sample average and standard deviation is plotted. If the point is within the acceptance region, the lot or batch is accepted.

► **EXAMPLE 17-6** Graphical Method with Double Specification Limits

This example is from ISO 3951-1989. Assume that the minimum and maximum temperature of a certain device are specified at 60°C and 70°C, respectively. Production is in lots of size 96. Use general inspection level II, and select an AQL of 1.5%. From Table 17-2 it is seen that sample size code letter F is to be used. From Table 17-5 it is determined that sample size code letter F calls for a sample size of 10. The following measurements in degrees C are obtained:

63.5 62.0 65.2 61.7 69.0

67.1 60.0 66.4 62.8 68.0

Now calculate the average and standard deviation as $\bar{x} = 64.57$ and $s = 3.01$. The appropriate acceptance curve is selected from ISO 3951-1989 and is reproduced here as Figure 17-4. The scales have been adjusted to agree with the limits of 60°C and 70°C. The point (3.01, 64.57) is plotted on the graph. It lies outside of the acceptance region. The lot is rejected.

17-4.2 Variability Known

As with ANSI/ASQC Z1.9-1993, when there is strong evidence that the standard deviation of the process may be considered to be a known constant, the σ method in ISO 3951 may be used. This method will result in smaller sample sizes than with the s method. The procedures to be used are exactly as before, except that σ is used instead of calculating the standard deviation, s, and a different set of tables and charts (the σ series) is used.

17-4.3 Future Revisions of ISO 3951

As this is being written, ISO 3951 is being revised. This next revision of the standard is expected to be published soon after publication of this text. The next revision will consist of five parts. The five parts of ISO 3951 will be:

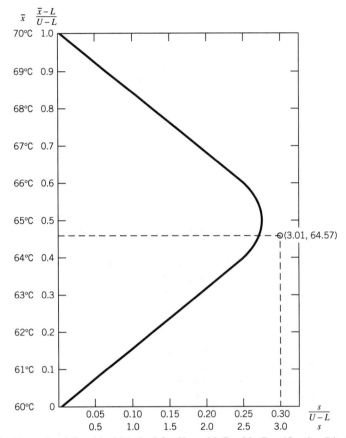

Figure 17-4 Example of Graphical Method for Use with Double Specification Limit Plan [ISO 3951(1989) reproduced with the permission of the International Organization for Standardization, ISO. The complete International Standard can be obtained from the ISO Central Secretariat, Geneva 20 or from any ISO member body]

Part 1. Specification for Single Sampling Plans Indexed by Acceptance Quality Limit (AQL) for Lot-by-Lot Inspection—Single Quality Characteristic and Single AQL

Part 2. General Specification for Single Sampling Plans Indexed by Acceptance Quality Limit (AQL) for Lot-by-Lot Inspection

Part 3. General Specification for Double Sampling Plans Indexed by Acceptance Quality Limit (AQL) for Lot-by-Lot Inspection

Part 4. Procedures for Assessment of Stated Quality Levels for Variables Inspection

Part 5. General Specification for Sequential Sampling Plans Indexed by Acceptance Quality Limit (AQL) for Lot-by-Lot Inspection—Known Process Standard Deviation

ISO 3951-1 will be similar and will replace the 1989 edition of ISO 3951. As of the date of this publication, working drafts of parts 1, 2, and 5 are available. The other parts are still in a very early stage of development.

Changes are being made in the sampling plans to make them agree more closely with the plans of ISO 2859-1. The working group developing the standard has spent a lot of time determining how this agreement should be made. The plans will be organized so either the attributes system (ISO 2859-1) or the variables system (ISO 3951) can be used with the assurance that a sampling scheme from either system that has the same sample size code letter and AQL will have the same operating characteristic.

Because variables plans do not require integer acceptance numbers, the arrows found in the master tables for ISO 2859-1 between the 0 and 1 acceptance numbers are not needed. This is one of the reasons for introducing fractional acceptance numbers into ISO 2859-1. Thus, if fractional acceptance numbers are being used for the attributes scheme, the agreement between the two systems is virtually assured.

▶ 17-5 TESTING NORMALITY

In using the acceptance sampling by variables procedures described in this chapter, several explicit assumptions are made. An assumption is made that the quality characteristic is measurable on a continuous scale and that this characteristic is distributed over the items in a lot according to a normal distribution. If the characteristic is not so distributed, one may be seriously misled by using these acceptance sampling plans. Lots may be accepted that are far worse than expected or needed. Lots may be rejected that meet all specifications.

There should be a routine practice to check the normality assumption when these plans are used. The easiest check is probability plotting. An excellent discussion of probability plotting is given in Shapiro (1980). Shapiro also describes several other useful distribution tests. He cautions that the major drawback to probability plotting is the lack of objectivity. Shapiro describes a regression test for normality (the Shapiro-Wilk W test) that has excellent properties. It is especially effective for detecting differences in the tails compared to other normality tests.

Many other tests for normality exist. These are usually called goodness-of-fit tests. The chi square test is probably the best known. The Kolmogorov-Smirnov test is also widely used. The Anderson-Darling statistic is good for testing for a wide range of alternatives when the parameters are not known [Shapiro (1980)]. Shapiro gives excellent explanations of these tests, along with an annotated bibliography. Shapiro (1998) has also written an excellent discussion of the entire subject of tests for normality as well as other goodness-of-fit tests in a chapter in Wadsworth (1998).

▶ 17-6 SUMMARY

An introduction to acceptance sampling by variables for percent nonconforming is given in this chapter. In addition to the national and international standards, many references are available for further study. Schilling (1982, 1999) gives a thorough treatment of this subject. Stephens (2001) also includes a detailed coverage of sampling, including variables sampling.

Schilling (1979) shows how grand lot acceptance sampling procedures can reduce sample sizes significantly. Bender (1975) and Duncan (1986) review the entire subject of sampling by variables carefully. Kao (1971) describes MIL-STD-414 and gives insight into the reasons behind the methods used for constructing the tables.

The International Organization for Standardization (ISO) has published a standard for acceptance sampling by variables using sequential sampling procedures (see Chapter 15). This standard assumes an underlying normal distribution with known standard deviation. The main part of the standard is for isolated lots, while an appendix contains sequential plans intended to match the known standard deviation plans of ISO 3951. The standard is designated ISO 8423-1991. The appendix will become Part 5 of the revised ISO 3951 series. The main part will be revised as a stand alone document.

▶ 17-7 REFERENCES

American Society for Quality (1993), ANSI/ASQC Z1.9-1993, *Sampling Procedures and Tables for Inspection by Variables for Percent Nonconforming,* ASQ, Milwaukee.

American Society for Quality (1993), ANSI/ASQC Z1.4-1993, *Sampling Procedures for Inspection by Attributes,* ASQ, Milwaukee.

Bender, A. (1975), "Sampling by Variables to Control the Fraction Defective, Part II," *Journal of Quality Technology,* Vol. 7, No. 3, July; pp. 139–45.

Duncan, A. J. (1986), *Quality Control and Industrial Statistics,* Fifth Edition, Richard D. Irwin, Homewood, IL.

International Organization for Standardization (1989), ISO 3951-1989, *Sampling Procedures and Charts for Inspection by Variables,* ISO, Geneva, Switzerland.

International Organization for Standardization (1991), ISO 8423-1991, *Sequential Sampling Plans for Inspection by Variables for Percent Nonconforming (Known Standard Deviation),* ISO, Geneva, Switzerland.

Kao, J. H. K. (1971), "MIL-STD-414 Sampling Procedures and Tables for Inspection by Variables for Percent Defective," *Journal of Quality Technology,* Vol. 3, No. 1, Jan.; pp. 28–37.

Lieberman, G. J. and Resnikoff, G. J. (1955), "Sampling Plans for Inspection by Variables," *Journal of the American Statistical Association,* Vol. 50, June; pp. 457–516.

Schilling, E. G. (1979), "A Simplified Grand Lot Acceptance Sampling Procedure," *Journal of Quality Technology,* Vol. 11, No. 3, July; pp. 116–27.

Schilling, E. G. (1982), *Acceptance Sampling in Quality Control,* Marcel Dekker, New York.

Schilling, E. G. (1999), "Sampling by Variables," in *Juran's Quality Handbook,* Fifth Edition, J. M. Juran and A. B. Godfrey, McGraw-Hill, New York.

Shapiro, S. S. (1980), "How to Test Normality and Other Distributional Assumptions," *The ASQC Basic References in Quality Control: Statistical Techniques,* Vol. 3, American Society for Quality, Milwaukee.

Shapiro, S. S. (1998), "Selection, Fitting, and Testing Statistical Models," in *Handbook of Statistical Methods for Engineers and Scientists,* Second Edition, H. M. Wadsworth, McGraw-Hill, New York.

Stephens, K. S. (2001), *The Handbook of Applied Acceptance Sampling Plans, Procedures, and Principles,* ASQ Quality Press, Milwaukee.

U.S. Department of Defense (1957), MIL-STD 414, *Sampling Procedures and Tables for Inspection by Variables for Percent Defective,* U.S. Government Printing Office, Washington, D.C.

U.S. Department of Defense (1989), MIL-STD 105E, *Sampling Procedures and Tables for Inspection by Attributes,* U.S. Government Printing Office, Washington, D.C.

Wadsworth, H. M., Editor (1998), *Handbook of Statistical Methods for Engineers and Scientists,* Second Edition, McGraw-Hill, New York, NY.

▶ 17-8 PROBLEMS

1. Given the following measurements:

$$104, 93, 107, 95, 100$$

in a 2% AQL variables acceptance sampling plan, lot size 45, inspection level II, variability unknown, upper limit 109, no lower limit.

(a) Should you accept or reject?

(b) What is your estimate of the percent nonconforming in the lot?

(c) Was a sample size of 5 correct for this problem?

2. Assume that in a variables acceptance sampling situation (variability unknown), you wish to use a 0.85% AQL, a lot size of 80, and inspection level II. You have a single lower specification limit of 100 volts, and you obtain the following seven measurements:

$$105, 111, 103, 101, 106, 109, 102$$

(a) Should you accept or reject?

(b) What is your estimate of the percent nonconforming?

(c) Is 7 the correct sample size?

3. Your job is to design a quality system for controlling the fill in cans of coffee. The specification is 16 ounces per can. You set the lower limit at 16.0 ounces and want no more than 0.5% of the cans to be below this limit. You set the upper limit at 16.25 ounces and want no more than 1.0% to exceed this limit. You decide to use general inspection level I. Variability is unknown. The cans are packed 200 to a case, and you decide to use this as a lot.
(a) What sample size do you take?
(b) Assume that you used a sample size of 10 and obtained the following values:

16.14, 16.02, 16.05, 16.07, 16.03, 16.05, l6.03, 16.06, 16.06, 16.01

Should you accept or reject this lot?
(c) What are your estimates of percent nonconforming below lower specification? Above upper specification? Total?

4. In a variability unknown variables acceptance sampling inspection situation, you wish to construct a 1.3% AQL plan with lot size 40, general inspection level II and upper specification limit 164. The sum of the observations in your sample, Σx, is 750, and the sum of squares, Σx^2, is 112,900.
(a) What is the sample size?
(b) What is the estimate of the percent nonconforming?
(c) Should you accept or reject?

5. You are in charge of a process that produces steel bolts. You have been having problems keeping the thickness of the bolts inside the upper specification limit of 10.5 mm. Your inspection results indicate an average of 10.0 mm and a standard deviation of 0.2 mm. You can assume that the thicknesses of the bolts are approximately normally distributed. You wish to have no more than one bolt in a thousand beyond the upper limit.
(a) If you can change the mean, what value would be satisfactory?
(b) If you can change the process variability, what new standard deviation would give acceptable results if the mean remained at 10.0 mm?

6. In Example 17-1 it was determined that the goal of no more than ten wires in a thousand with resistance greater than 91 ohms per mile can be achieved by changing either the mean or the standard deviation. It was also noted that the goal can be achieved by changing both the mean and the standard deviation. Find two other combinations of means and standard deviations that achieve the same result.

7. Assume in Example 17-2 that there is a lower specification limit of 26 volts. Using the graphical method for single specification limit, draw the acceptance region and plot the point $(\bar{x}, s)$. Should you accept or reject?

18

SPECIAL ATTRIBUTE
SAMPLING
PROCEDURES[1]

The acceptance sampling plans of chapters 15–17 may be referred to as general-purpose sampling plans. A large number of sampling procedures have been devised for application to special situations or better quality protection under certain conditions, using variations of statistics. Some of these special attribute sampling procedures are treated in this chapter.

▶ 18-1 CONTINUOUS SAMPLING PLANS—CSP

A common characteristic of the previous sampling plans was their ability to help to make decisions about the acceptability of production lots or similar groupings of items. Some processes do not lend themselves to the formation of discrete lots. Units may flow along a continuous conveyor belt. Inspection may need to be performed at discrete locations along this flow on individual items. For these situations even the simple concept of a sample size is not meaningful. Sampling procedures devised for handling such situations are known as *continuous sampling plans* (CSP). These are employed in production processes in which no separate lots are formed. They are generally used on some type of conveyor but are applicable to any continuous or consecutive-type operation in which it is not convenient to accumulate the items into lots for inspection. Continuous sampling plans were first developed by Dodge (1943, 1947), and subsequent developments represent extensions to and variations on his basic procedure.

18-1.1 Basic Theory, Parameters, Operation, Evaluation, and Application

Continuous sampling plans are sometimes referred to as *random order plans* because they are based on the theory that defects occur in a random series. The theory is similar to that used in lot-by-lot sampling inspection, although the terminology and some of the

---

[1]Portions of this chapter are taken from two companion booklets by one of the authors and are reproduced with some modifications by permission of the American Society for Quality [see Stephens (1995a, 1995b)].

sampling and inspection practices are different. Three common principles for the development of sampling inspection procedures and, in particular, continuous sampling plans, are the following:

1. When samples or individual items are taken from product of a certain quality as measured in percent nonconforming or nonconformities per hundred items, the occurrence of nonconformities forms a certain statistical pattern.

2. When samples of individual items are taken from product of a different quality, the occurrence of nonconformities will form a different statistical pattern.

3. Because of this difference in pattern, it is possible to establish acceptance criteria for sampling inspection that will reject more product when the quality is worse and accept more product when the quality is better.

Basic Theory for CSP

Suppose there is a continuous flow of product that is 4% nonconforming. Inspection of this product is begun by classifying each item in order, as conforming or nonconforming. If 0 represents a conforming item and X a nonconforming one, the record of consecutive inspection results might be similar to the following:

X0000000000000000X 00X 0000000X 00000000X 0000000000000X . . .

The number of items from the occurrence of one nonconforming item to the occurrence of the next is a statistic that follows a predictable pattern and may be referred to as the *nonconforming spacing, s.* In the example above, s is equal to 18, 3, 8, 9, 14, and so on. These values of s can be plotted like any other series of numbers from a process and will form a fluctuating statistical pattern. In fact, s can be seen to follow a geometric distribution (discussed in Chapter 5). If product is worse than 4% nonconforming, the nonconforming items will occur more frequently, and the spacing s will tend to become shorter. If product is less than 4% nonconforming, they will occur less often, and the spacing s tends to become longer. Figures 18-1, 18-2, and 18-3 are actual records of some fifteen observed values of s from a product that was 2%, 4%, and 8% nonconforming, respectively.

Since product of different quality produce different patterns of s, it is possible to set up an acceptance criterion in terms of s. This criterion will reject more product of a bad level of quality and accept more of a good level, where good may be defined as desired.

Parameters for CSP-1

The first plan by Dodge (1943), later designated CSP-1 by Dodge and Torrey (1951), specifies a *clearing interval, i,* which is a fixed parameter for a given continuous sampling plan. This interval denotes the number of consecutive items to be inspected and found clear of nonconforming items before qualifying for sampling. Initially, consecutive items are inspected 100% until the clearing interval, i, qualification is met. Then only a fraction, f, of the items are inspected, with individual items selected one at a time from the flow of product to ensure an unbiased sample of fraction f. The manner of sampling is subsequently considered in greater detail. Hence, f is another parameter of the sampling plan.

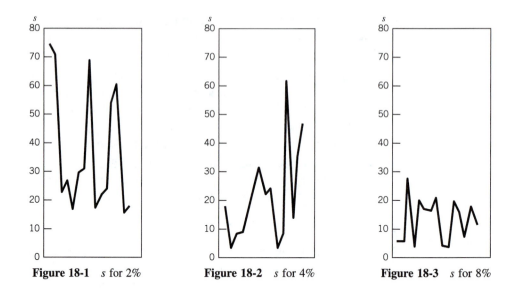

Figure 18-1 *s* for 2%   **Figure 18-2** *s* for 4%   **Figure 18-3** *s* for 8%

When an item is found to be nonconforming during the sampling period, immediate reversion to 100% inspection is required until qualification for sampling by again satisfying the clearing interval, i.

Continuous sampling is generally of the AOQL type involving periods of 100% inspection and periods of sampling. This is to achieve a rectification of an unacceptable or unsatisfactory quality level to one that is more acceptable. The AOQL achieved is determined by the values of i and f chosen, or conversely. Hence, AOQL is another parameter of the sampling plan.

Selection of the parameters for CSP-1 (i.e., AOQL, i, and f) is possible in different ways. Principal among these are the use of nomographs and tables of sampling plans. These are introduced later in this chapter for CSP-1 and its extensions.

Operation of CSP-1

To illustrate the above discussion of the operation of CSP-1, a simple operation schematic for CSP-1 is shown in Figure 18-4. Not explicit in this schematic is the option to correct or replace nonconforming items with good items (replacement) or to simply remove them (nonreplacement).

Evaluation of CSP and CSP-1

It is decided to use a clearing interval of $i = 20$. If the product is 2% nonconforming, about 67% of the nonconforming spacings, as measured by $s - 1$, the length of a series of conforming items would meet this requirement, allowing sampling of f fraction of items quite often. If the product is 4% nonconforming, only about 44% of the spacings would meet it; and if it is 8% nonconforming, only 19% would meet it. Thus, there is an acceptance criteria that can distinguish between product of different quality and does not depend on forming the product into separate lots. There are two other ways in which continuous sampling differs from lot-by-lot sampling.

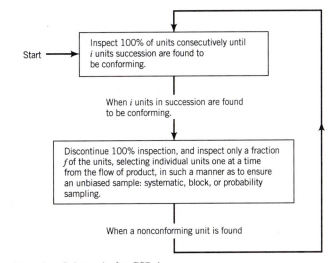

Figure 18-4 Operation Schematic for CSP-1

The Sample.   In continuous sampling, there is no fixed sample size. The sample is expressed as a fraction or percentage of the continuous flow of product. For example, the sample may be expressed as 10% of the product, denoting an f of 0.10 or 1/10. This can mean different things. At least three ways of applying the parameter f to the drawing of sample items have been identified: (1) *systematic sampling,* inspecting every $1/f$th unit produced; (2) *block* or *random sampling*, inspecting a randomly chosen unit from each successive block, "lot," or segment of $1/f$ units produced; and (3) *probability sampling,* inspecting randomly selected units so that f is the overall average frequency of inspected units. Any of these methods of sampling may be used, considering the nature of the process to which it is applied. Systematic sampling is the easiest to use, but block sampling or probability sampling should be used if cycling or some other periodic pattern is present. Block sampling ensures that each $1/f$ item is sampled. For additional discussion on this subject, see Dodge and Torrey (1951) and Derman, Johns, and Lieberman (1959).

The OC Curve.   The operating characteristic (OC) curve for a continuous sampling plan is not the same as for a lot-by-lot sampling plan. In lot-by-lot sampling inspection when using rectification procedures, the probability of acceptance is the probability of accepting a single lot without having to inspect 100%. In continuous sampling, there are no specific lots. Consequently, a different measure of evaluation of the performance of CSP is needed; the most common is the percent of total production accepted on a sampling basis as a function of the incoming percent nonconforming. This will be denoted as P_a.

Other measures of the performance of CSP type plans are (1) average number of items inspected in a 100% screening sequence, (2) average number of items passed under the sampling procedure, (3) average fraction of total produced items inspected in the long run, and (4) average outgoing quality. These and P_a, as defined above, are presented subsequently for CSP-1.

Additional measures of evaluation include spotty quality [Dodge and Torrey (1951)]; stopping rules [Murphy (1958)], Magwire (1956), LeMaster and McKeague (1958)]; minimum average fraction inspected [Resnikoff (1960)]; lack of control [Derman, Johns, and Lieberman (1959), Hillier (1964)]; finite length production runs [Brugger (1972), Blackwell (1977), McShane (1989), McShane and Turnbull (1992)]; robustness [Lasater (1970)]; unrestricted AOQLS [Lieberman (1953), White (1964, 1965), Endres (1967, 1969), Brugger (1967, 1976), Banzhaf and Brugger (1970), Sackrowitz (1975)]; inspection error [Case, Bennett, and Schmidt (1973)]; non-Bernoulli, Markov incoming quality models [Kumar and Rajarshi (1987), McShane (1989), McShane and Turnbull (1991)]; probability limits on AOQL and estimates of incoming quality [McShane and Turnbull (1991)]; economic design [Chiu and Wetherill (1973), Gregory (1956), Satterthwaite (1949), Savage (1959)]; and limiting quality level [Stephens (1981, 1995a)]. Many of these papers address one or more of the additional measures of evaluation. The interested reader should consult the literature for a study of these additional evaluations of CSP to gain understanding of the procedures.

Evaluations for specific plans can be done by direct calculations using formulas developed by Dodge (1943). Modern hand-held calculators are ideally suited to these calculations. A condensed derivation of the formulas for CSP-1 and its immediate extensions is given by Stephens (1995a).

For CSP-1 the five most common measures of performance for evaluation are as follows:

1. The average number of items, denoted u, inspected in a 100% screening sequence following the finding of a nonconforming item:

$$u = (1 - q^i)/pq^i \tag{18-1}$$

where p is the process fraction nonconforming and $q = 1 - p$.

2. The average number of items passed, denoted v, under the sampling procedure before a nonconforming unit is found:

$$v = 1/fp \tag{18-2}$$

3. The average fraction of total produced units inspected in the long run denoted F:

$$F = (u + fv)/(u + v) \tag{18-3}$$

or

$$F = f/[f + (1 - f)q^i] \tag{18-4}$$

4. The average outgoing quality, denoted AOQ:

$$AOQ = p(1 - F) \tag{18-5}$$

or

$$AOQ = p(1 - f)q^i/[f + (1 - f)q^i] \tag{18-6}$$

5. The average fraction of total production accepted on a sampling basis, denoted P_a:

$$P_a = v/(u + v) \tag{18-7}$$

or

$$P_a = AOQ/p(1 - f) \tag{18-8}$$

or

$$P_a = q^i/[f + (1 - f)q^i] \tag{18-9}$$

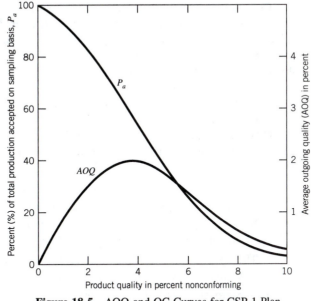

Figure 18-5 AOQ and OC Curves for CSP-1 Plan

These formulas apply when nonconforming items are corrected or replaced with good items, known as the replacement case. Dodge (1943) has noted that the substitution of i by $(i - 1)$ yields the formulas for the nonreplacement assumption. When referring to specific CSP-1 plans with parameters i and f and related AOQ characteristics, Dodge (1955b) further mentions, "It can be shown that i should be increased by one in CSP-1 plans when defective units are removed but not replaced." His Procedure A1 (the replacement case) uses i, and his Procedure A2 (the nonreplacement case) uses $(i + 1)$. Since these developments and related statements by Dodge in the cited papers (1943, 1955b), there have been occasions when these statements were thought to be contradictory and in some cases incorrectly applied. Stephens (1995a) has shown that both statements are correct in that the first substitution pertains to the formulas and the second pertains to the procedures themselves.

To illustrate these evaluations, the AOQ and P_a (OC) curves for the CSP-1 plan with parameters AOQL = 2%, $i = 55$, and $f = 0.10$ are shown in Figure 18-5.

Applications of CSP

CSP procedures are designed for application to situations in which it is neither convenient nor practical to group product articles in collective lots for the purposes of inspection. They are generally applicable to in-line and end-of-line inspections and are most effective when administered to provide an incentive for clearing up the faults in a process promptly. This is commonly achieved by requiring the production organization to perform the 100% screening inspection by a screening crew when the results dictate. An inspector performs the sampling inspection and should continue to sample, even during periods of 100% inspection by the screening crew, as a follow-up on their effectiveness. This procedure has been incorporated in the systems of continuous sampling plans of the U.S. Department of Defense (1988).

Dodge (1943, 1970) developed two procedures referred to as A and B, A being applicable to consecutive articles and B to material offered as a flow of consecutive lots or sublots of articles. Both procedures, under CSP-1, follow the simple diagram of Figure 18-4. Necessary conventions are to substitute the order of production of procedure A with the order of inspection in procedure B, since strict order of production by articles is lost in sublotting. Additionally, in procedure B, when it is necessary to find i inspected items in succession clear of nonconformities, the 100% inspection must extend to the immediately succeeding lots if i items in succession are not found in the current lot.

Other considerations in application of CSP procedures are listed below. They are discussed to illustrate that in the design and implementation of sampling procedures, various factors of logistics must be considered, in addition to statistical aspects.

1. Ample space, equipment, and work force must be provided at or near the site of inspection to permit rapid 100% inspection when required. This may be performed by screening crews who oscillate between production work and inspection work as the sampling inspection results dictate.

2. The inspection should be relatively easy and quick (e.g., attribute inspection by visual observation or automatic inspection).

3. The process should be producing, or be capable of producing, material whose process quality level is stable.

4. The inspection should be nondestructive, since the procedure incorporates 100% inspection.

5. CSP can apply to individual nonconformities, classes of nonconformities, or nonconforming items. When applied to classes of nonconformities, it is possible for one such class to be undergoing a clearing interval for the nonconformity that caused rejection while other classes would still be under sampling.

Application of CSP can be to various entities such as end items, components, raw materials, data or records, or persons. Skip-lot sampling, discussed later in this chapter, is based on the application of continuous sampling procedures to lots as the inspected or skipped entity.

18-1.2 Selection of Plans

Plans having desired properties as determined by Equations (18-1) through (18-9) can be used on a trial-and-error basis. Convenient nomographs as well as tables of plans with specified properties have been developed for use.

CSP-1 Nomograph

An example of a nomograph for CSP-1 is shown in Figure 18-6. It provides a wide range of AOQL values, ranging from 0.1% to 15%, with curves drawn for eighteen specific values. For any of the AOQL curves, a large number of f and i combinations can be selected, resulting in a plan with the given AOQL. An example of this is the plan shown in Figure 18-5. To find values of i for a given f and AOQLs not shown, compute from $i_1/i_2 = AOQL_2/AOQL_1$ approximately.

Aid in the selection of the parameters f and i for a given AOQL is provided by the nomograph in the form of p_t values. For continuous sampling plans, p_t is defined as the

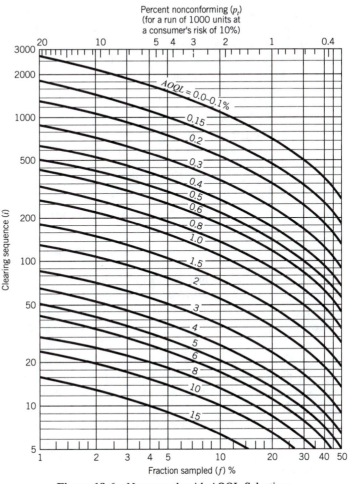

Figure 18-6 Nomograph with AOQL Selections

value of percent nonconforming in a consecutive run of $N = 1000$ product units for which the probability of acceptance, P_{a_s}, *on sampling,* is 0.10 for a sample size of $100f\%$. These values on the upper scale of the nomograph of Figure 18-6 is associated with a level of poor quality for which the probability of acceptance during sampling will be small, of the order of 0.10. This measure was introduced by Dodge and Torrey (1951) as a control on spotty quality such as the clustering of nonconforming items occurring during the sampling phase of continuous sampling. It is not at all similar to the LQL[2] value that

---

[2]LQL, or limiting quality level, was defined and discussed in Chapter 15 for lot-by-lot sampling plans. In earlier papers by Dodge and Romig (1941), including the article by Dodge and Torrey (1951), the LQL concept was called LTPD, for which the shortened symbol, p_t was used. However, p_t, as used by Dodge and Torrey (1951) has the more specific and limited definition given above, applying to the sampling phase of CSP only. LQL, as used here, and in Stephens (1981), applies to the overall performance of CSP-1, combining the sampling and sorting phases of CSP-1.

might be associated with the operating characteristic of CSP as measured by the P_a, average fraction of total production accepted on a sampling basis. This latter measure, P_a for CSP, is dependent on i as well as f. The p_t values, as seen on the nomograph, are functions of f only. The statistic p_t is developed as follows.

Acceptance during sampling occurs in the following two ways for CSP-1:

1. The item is sampled with probability f and is found on inspection to be good with probability $q = 1 - p$, or

2. The item is not sampled with probability $1 - f$ and hence not inspected. Therefore, the probability of acceptance during sampling for CSP-1 is

$$P_{a_s} \text{ (per item)} = fq + (1 - f) = 1 - fp \tag{18-10}$$

and

$$P_{a_s} \text{ (over 1000 items)} = (1 - fp)^{1000} \tag{18-11}$$

and

$$(1 - fp_t)^{1000} = 0.10 \tag{18-12}$$

that is, p_t is that value of p (in fraction nonconforming) for which P_a (over 1000 items) equals 0.10. Hence,

$$p_t = \frac{1}{f}(1 - 0.10^{0.001}) = \frac{1}{f}(2.2999 \times 10^{-3}) \tag{18-13}$$

The p_t scale indicates the necessity to use larger values of f if it is desired to provide for plans with smaller values of p_t. This is similar to the necessity to use larger sample sizes in lot-by-lot sampling plans to allow greater discrimination between good and bad quality.

To enable the selection of f and i values for CSP-1 that prescribe a desired value of LQL (in addition to AOQL) with $P_a = 0.10$ (i.e., the overall probability of acceptance for CSP-1 equal to 0.10), additional curves are provided on the nomograph of Figure 18-7 with the associated LQL values shown on the right-hand scale. Curves associated with LQL (in percent) from 0.5% to 25% are given. Examples, with some approximate values, are given in Table 18-1.

TABLE 18-1   Example CSP-1 Plans with AOQL and LQL

f (%)	i	AOQL (%)	LQL (%)
5	130	1.2	4.0
10	460	0.25	1.0
10	100	1.1	4.5
10	55	2.0	8.0
20	260	0.28	1.5
20	47	1.5	8.0
25	60	1.0	6.0
50	150	0.2	2.0
50	50	0.58	6.0

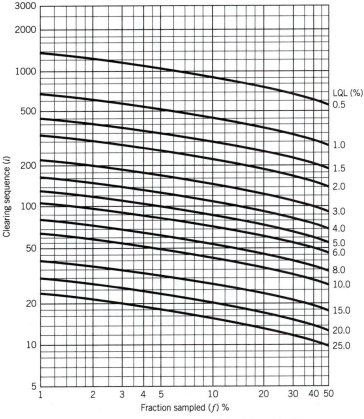

Figure 18-7 CSP-1 Nomograph in f, i, and LQL

CSP-1 Tables

Tables for the selection of the parameters of CSP-1 plans are given in MIL-STD-1235C (1988). The tables first require the selection of a sample frequency code letter from Table 18-2. This is Table 1 from the standard; it associates the number of items in the production interval with sample frequency code letters.

Having selected a code letter, consult Table 18-3 to determine the sample frequency, f. This is Table 2-A from the standard.

Then, for a desired AQL index,[3] the parameter i is obtained from Table 18-3. Two examples may illustrate use of the tables.

---

[3]Continuous sampling plans are AOQL type plans. The AQLs of the referenced military standard serve as indices to identify the plans, as military standard users are accustomed to AQL specifications. AOQLs are directly associated with each AQL index. For a discussion on the use of AQL values for CSP procedures, see Duncan (1986).

TABLE 18-2   Sampling Frequency Code Letters

Number of Units in Production Interval	Permissible Code Letters
2–8	A, B
9–25	A through C
26–90	A through D
91–500	A through E
501–1200	A through F
1201–3200	A through G
3201–10,000	A through H
10,001–35,000	A through I
35,001–150,000	A through J
150,001 up	A through K

▶ **EXAMPLE 18-1**

For Sampling Frequency Code Letter C, associated with the range 501–1200 items in the production interval, we find $f = 1/4$. For $AQL = 0.4\%$, associated with an $AOQL = 0.53\%$, obtain $i = 113$. The CSP-1 plan is $f = 1/4$, $i = 113$, $AOQL = 0.53\%$.

▶ **EXAMPLE 18-2**

For Sampling Frequency Code Letter F, associated with the range 1201–3200 items in the production interval, $f = 1/10$. For $AQL = 1.5\%$, associated with an $AOQL = 1.9\%$, obtain $i = 57$. The CSP-1 plan is $f = 1/10$, $i = 57$, $AOQL = 1.9\%$.

The standard also incorporates a stopping rule for the 100% screening phase in terms of values of S, a critical value on the number of items inspected during 100% screening without finding i consecutive conforming items that, when equaled or exceeded, signals need for corrective action on the process. The table of S values indexed by AQL, f, and sample frequency code letters is shown in Table 18-4. It is Table 2-B from the standard. For the examples above, the appropriate S values are $S = 262$ for Example 18-1 and $S = 221$ for Example 18-2.

Evaluations for CSP-1 plans are contained in Appendix A of the Standard by way of OC, AOQ, and AFI or F curves. The standard should be consulted for additional details, including functional curves for other continuous sampling plans.

18-1.3 Extensions of CSP-1

Continuous sampling procedures and concepts have been presented by way of a certain amount of detail for the basic procedure, CSP-1. This has been done to acquaint the reader with both general and specific information on this subject. It should be understood that CSP-1 is only one of many continuous sampling procedures. A more comprehensive work on CSP by Stephens (1995a) covers other CSP procedures and includes a bibliography of

TABLE 18-3 Values of *i* for CSP-1 Plans

Sample Frequency Code Letter	f	AQL in %*															
		0.010	0.015	0.025	0.040	0.065	0.10	0.15	0.25	0.40	0.65	1.0	1.5	2.5	4.0	6.5	10.0
A	1/2	1540	840	600	375	245	194	140	84	53	36	23	15	10	6	5	3
B	1/3	2550	1390	1000	620	405	321	232	140	87	59	38	25	16	10	7	5
C	1/4	3340	1820	1310	810	530	420	303	182	113	76	49	32	21	13	9	6
D	1/5	3960	2160	1550	965	630	498	360	217	135	91	58	38	25	15	11	7
E	1/7	4950	2700	1940	1205	790	623	450	270	168	113	73	47	31	18	13	8
F	1/10	6050	3300	2370	1470	965	762	550	335	207	138	89	57	38	22	16	10
G	1/15	7390	4030	2890	1800	1180	930	672	410	255	170	108	70	46	27	19	12
H	1/25	9110	4970	3570	2215	1450	1147	828	500	315	210	134	86	57	33	23	14
I	1/50	11730	6400	4590	2855	1870	1477	1067	640	400	270	175	110	72	42	29	18
J	1/100	14320	7810	5600	3485	2305	1820	1302	790	500	330	215	135	89	52	36	22
K	1/200	17420	9500	6810	4235	2760	2178	1583	950	590	400	255	165	106	62	43	26
		0.018	0.033	0.046	0.074	0.113	0.143	0.198	0.33	0.53	0.79	1.22	1.90	2.90	4.94	7.12	11.46
		AOQL in %															

*AQLs are provided as indices to simplify use of this table but have no other meaning relative to the plans.

TABLE 18-4 Values of S for CSP-1 Plans

Sample Frequency Code Letter	f	AQL in %*															
		0.010	0.015	0.025	0.040	0.065	0.10	0.15	0.25	0.40	0.65	1.0	1.5	2.5	4.0	6.5	10.0
A	1/2	1850	925	721	451	295	273	197	119	75	55	36	22	17	11	10	6
B	1/3	4080	1950	1600	993	649	579	442	268	166	120	78	52	36	24	19	16
C	1/4	6010	2915	2360	1460	1010	926	699	421	262	177	115	79	57	36	28	20
D	1/5	8320	3890	3100	1930	1390	1150	975	589	367	258	165	109	76	45	40	27
E	1/7	11400	5670	4660	2895	1980	1750	1355	813	507	376	244	154	109	63	54	34
F	1/10	16900	7590	6640	4120	2800	2595	1985	1245	624	543	352	221	164	90	82	51
G	1/15	24400	11300	9250	5760	4020	3820	2960	1810	922	856	524	327	241	141	138	75
H	1/25	35500	16900	13900	8640	5950	5740	4560	2760	1390	1350	839	524	390	212	189	105
I	1/50	59800	26900	23000	14300	10300	10100	8440	5070	3170	2445	1590	913	733	368	334	212
J	1/100	96000	39800	36400	23300	16900	16500	14300	8710	6020	3980	2600	1640	1360	642	601	352
K	1/200	148100	63700	58000	36000	29000	28500	25400	15200	9470	8030	4365	2835	2150	1080	1025	636
		0.018	0.053	0.046	0.074	0.113	0.143	0.198	0.33	0.53	0.79	1.22	1.90	2.90	4.94	7.12	11.46
		AOQL in %															

*AQLs are provided as indices to simplify use of this table but have no other meaning relative to the plans.

other papers on the subject. See also Stephens (2001) for a more extensive coverage of continuous sampling, including evaluations via Excel spreadsheets.

▶ 18-2 SKIP-LOT SAMPLING PLANS—SkSP

Applying the principles of continuous sampling plan (CSP-1) to a continuing series of lots or batches of material rather than to individual product units led Dodge (1955a) to develop skip-lot sampling plans (SkSP).

18-2.1 Parameters, Operation, Interpretation, and Application

The parameters of SkSP-1 are those of CSP-1: the clearing interval, i, and the sampling fraction, f. The operation is also similar to CSP-1. Two procedures have been proposed for SkSP-1 corresponding to the replacement and nonreplacement options of CSP-1. One applies to reprocessing and correcting nonconforming lots or replacing nonconforming lots with conforming ones. This "replacement" procedure applies when nonconforming lots are readily corrected or replaced. This would be possible if the inspection of the lots is being done between departments within a factory or when the supplier is relatively close and accessible for such corrections or replacements. The second procedure applies to rejecting and removing nonconforming lots without requiring that they be corrected or replaced. It is applicable when rejected lots that are found nonconforming during the inspection are returned to a supplier.

A schematic for these procedures is given in Figure 18-8. This schematic assumes that skip-lot sampling has been chosen for application and that the parameters i and f have been selected to achieve a given AOQL type protection on the average outgoing quality of lots, by quality characteristic.

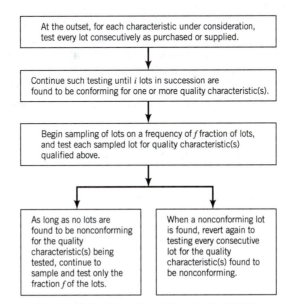

Figure 18-8 Operation Schematic for SkSP-1

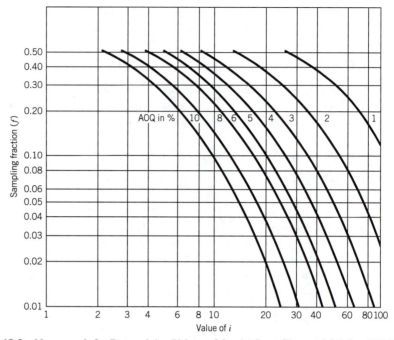

Figure 18-9 Nomograph for Determining Values of f and i for a Given AOQL for CSP-1, Small Values of i

For Procedure 1, all lots found nonconforming are submitted for reprocessing, correction, or replacement and resubmission. For Procedure 2, replace i in the above schematic with $i + 1$, and remove (e.g., return to source of supply) all nonconforming lots.

Specific plans by AOQL, i, and f may be selected from the CSP-1 curves of Figure 18-6. However, it is envisaged that SkSP-1 would not be used with very small AOQLs, large values of i, or small values of f. Hence, a reduced graph of CSP-1 curves is given in Figure 18-9 especially for use in selecting SkSP-1 plans. This nomograph is from Dodge (1955a). Some practical selections from these curves are listed in Table 18-5.

TABLE 18-5   Example SkSP-1 Plans

AOQL (%)	f	i
1.0	1/2	27
2.0	1/2	14
	1/3	23
3.0	1/2	9
	1/3	15
4.0	1/2	7
	1/3	11
	1/4	14

TABLE 18-6   Comparison of Terms for CSP-1 and SkSP-1

CSP-1 (product items)	SkSP-1 (lots of a raw material)
Series of items	Series of lots (or batches)
Inspect an item	Make lab analysis of a sample of material
Nonconforming item (an item that fails to meet the applicable specification requirement)	Nonconforming lot (a lot in which the sample fails to meet the applicable specification requirement)
Items in succession that are found conforming	Lots in succession that are found conforming
Incoming % nonconforming: % of incoming items that do not conform	Incoming % nonconforming: % of incoming lots that are nonconforming
Meaning of 2% AOQL: an average of not more than 2% of accepted items will be nonconforming for the characteristics under consideration	Meaning of 2% AOQL: an average of not more than 2% of accepted lots will be nonconforming for the characteristic under consideration

Dodge (1955a) has summarized the comparison of terms applicable to CSP-1 and SkSP-1. This is reproduced in Table 18-6 and serves to illustrate the interpretations that apply to SkSP-1.

The operating characteristics for SkSP-1 are similar, with some modifications in interpretation, to CSP-1. The differences are outlined in Table 18-6. Equations (18-1) through (18-9) therefore apply equally well to the SkSP-1 plans.

Applications of SkSP are where extensive and costly tests are made on characteristics, such as chemical analyses of composition of raw materials, furnished in successive batches from reliable suppliers. This includes in-plant movement between production departments. More than one quality characteristic may be checked, with each treated separately at the prescribed AOQL or treated collectively against the prescribed AOQL of the plan. Skip-lot sampling often relates to lots for which bulk sampling or composite sampling is used to assess the quality characteristic(s) under study.

Applications have included superimposing skip-lot sampling on ordinary lot-by-lot acceptance sampling systems. These ideas were first formalized in a paper by Dodge and Perry (1971) and three additional papers by Perry (1970, 1973a, 1973b). The ideas expressed in these papers are extensions of SkSP-1 and are referred to as SkSP-2.

A significant application for SkSP-2 is its use as an alternative to the reduced inspection plans in sampling schemes involving switching between various inspection intensities such as those required in ISO 2859-1 and ANSI/ASQC Z1.4. The following quote from Dodge and Perry (1971) describes this use, with additions in brackets by the authors:

> The skip-lot plan SkSP-2 provides a framework that is particularly well-suited as a basis of "reduced inspection" for such structures as the composite scheme of Normal and Reduced Inspection used in MIL-STD-105D [now withdrawn and obsolete, hence substitute ISO 2859-1 or ANSI/ASQC Z1.4 in the following when there is reference to MIL-STD-105D] and like systems of sampling inspection of lots.

For example, MIL-STD-105D uses a complete set of "reduced inspection" sampling plans to be substituted for the set of Normal Inspection sampling plans when certain conditions are met, notably "when the preceding 10 lots or batches have been on Normal Inspection and none has been rejected on original inspection." Basically the plan for reduced inspection calls for a sample of reduced size from each lot about 40% as large as the sample for Normal Inspection together with an appropriate acceptance number, so as to give an OC curve for Reduced Inspection that is suitably looser than the OC curve for Normal Inspection. Instead of using a reduced sample size plan for each lot for Reduced Inspection, there are definite merits in using the Normal Inspection under normal conditions and just skipping the inspection of an appropriate fraction, f, of the lots for reduced inspection. In this way, just the regular sampling plans for Normal Inspection are used—no additional special reduced sample size plans are needed.

Specifically, for MIL-STD-105D, a reduced inspection plan comparable to the one given in 105D would be to use SkSP-2, with the inspection plan given in 105D for Normal Inspection as the "reference plan" together with f = .40 [inspecting only 2 out of each 5 lots] and an i = 10. The reduction in inspection would be about 60% when quality is good [process fraction nonconforming, p, is small], as it is in 105D. Other choices of f and i are of course possible.

With the publication of the ANSI/ASQC Standard S1 (1987) and ISO 2859-3 (1991), a standardized procedure for the use of skip-lot sampling inspection (of the SkSP-2 type) has been established. These two standards are almost identical and were developed by the same people, so they may be used interchangeably. The skip-lot procedure discussed in these standards is intended to be used in conjunction with ISO 2859-1 (1999) or ANSI/ASQC Z1.4 (1993), which are both approximately equivalent to the withdrawn MIL-STD 105E (1989). These standards provide the lot-by-lot phase of the scheme. The Z1.4 standard is referred to in S1, and the 2859-1 standard is referenced in 2859-3. Both ANSI/ASQ Z1.4 and ISO 2859-1 are discussed in Chapter 16.

As discussed in the quote above from Dodge and Perry, the skip-lot standards may be used instead of the reduced inspection plans of ISO 2859-1 and ANSI/ASQC Z1.4, although as a part of their operation they allow reduced inspection during the skip-lot inspection qualification period. This, of course, can be altered by the responsible authority stipulating that reduced inspection is not to be used. Some details of the standards follow.

18-2.2 ANSI/ASQC S1-1987 (2859-3-1991)

Unlike the CSP procedures discussed earlier in this chapter and detailed in Stephens (1955a), except for the S1 and 2859-3 standards, there are no coordinated or extensive tabulations indexed by quality measures for skip-lot sampling inspection. In general, plans must be developed individually with some convenience provided by the brief tabulations of Table 18-5 and the formulas for evaluation. But this table provides no immediate assistance in the selection of a reference sampling plan for SkSP-2 applications.

The reader should note the comments made in the earlier quote from Dodge and Perry (1971). It is used as the basis for the lot-by-lot phase of these skip-lot standards. The single, double, and multiple sampling schemes of ANSI/ASQC Z1.4 and ISO 2859-1 are well documented, including their operating characteristics. These are the potential reference sampling plans for SkSP-2, as are other lot-by-lot acceptance sampling systems for attributes. This is quite different from the use of SkSP-2 as an alternative to reduced inspection plans.

For example for inspection of lots of size 91–150 with a desired *AQL* of 2.5%, the single sampling plan for normal inspection from ANSI/ASQC Z1.4, using sample size code letter F, is $n = 20$, $c = 1$. The OC curves and ASN curves are presented by Perry (1973a) for this scheme for various values of f and i.

The S1 and 2859-3 standards are not collections of f and i values to be used with the skip-lot procedure together with a reference lot-by-lot sampling plan to achieve various AOQL or AQL protection. For all indices of AQL used in these standards, the f and i values are essentially the same. They are part of a standardized procedure, similar to Perry's 2L.3 plan, but with expansion from two to four levels, with i incorporated in the procedure (with values of 20, 10, and 4) and f values fixed at 1/2, 1/3, 1/4, and 1/5.

The attainment of a specified AQL protection is actually achieved by (1) selection of the reference sampling scheme under Z1.4 or 2859-1 and (2) variable criteria incorporated in tabulations of required cumulative sampling results. Hence, the attribute skip-lot sampling programs of ISO 2859-3 and ANSI/ASQC S1 are quite unique and should be distinguished from Dodge's skip-lot plans.

Basic Operation and Evaluation of ANSI/ASQC S1 and ISO 2859-3

The reader is encouraged to obtain a copy of either ANSI/ASQC S1 or ISO 2859-3 and a copy of the reference standard (ANSI/ASQC Z1.4-1993 or ISO 2859-1-1999). Reference should also be to the paper by Liebesman and Saperstein (1983). This paper describes the basic procedure and presents the rationale for structuring the switching rules. Although this is still valid, it should be understood that the procedures finally adopted in these standards differ somewhat from those given by Liebesman and Saperstein. In particular, the initial qualification for skip-lot inspection at fractions of 1/2, 1/3, and 1/4 was modified; the table for individual lot acceptance numbers for skip-lot qualification was changed; and the disqualification from skip-lot interrupt was changed.

An operation schematic for the attribute skip-lot sampling program is shown in Figure 18-10. In the standards, it is expressed as Figure 1 in the form of a flowchart together with criteria for three conditions stipulated in the flowchart. Because both standards are essentially identical, they shall be described using the ANSI/ASQC S1 standard together with its reference standard, ANSI/ASQC Z1.4-1993. For readers using the ISO standards, substitute ISO 2859-3 and 2859-1 in the appropriate places.

In addition to the individual and cumulative lot criteria in the operation schematic of Figure 18-10, the S1 Standard includes other qualifications and approvals for skip-lot inspection.

To enter skip-lot inspection initially and each time after disqualification, it is required to meet supplier and product qualifications. The supplier qualification is stated in the standard as follows:

The Supplier Shall:

    1. Have implemented and maintained a documented system for controlling product quality and design changes. It is assumed that such a system includes inspection by the supplier of every lot produced and recording of inspection results.

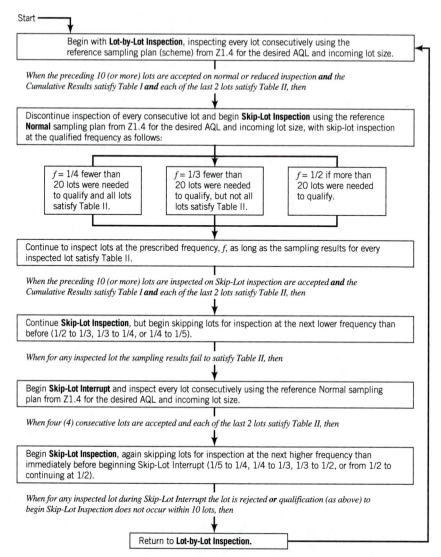

Start ⟶

Begin with **Lot-by-Lot Inspection**, inspecting every lot consecutively using the reference sampling plan (scheme) from Z1.4 for the desired AQL and incoming lot size.

*When the preceding 10 (or more) lots are accepted on normal or reduced inspection **and** the Cumulative Results satisfy Table I **and** each of the last 2 lots satisfy Table II, then*

Discontinue inspection of every consecutive lot and begin **Skip-Lot Inspection** using the reference **Normal** sampling plan from Z1.4 for the desired AQL and incoming lot size, with skip-lot inspection at the qualified frequency as follows:

| $f = 1/4$ fewer than 20 lots were needed to qualify and all lots satisfy Table II. | $f = 1/3$ fewer than 20 lots were needed to qualify, but not all lots satisfy Table II. | $f = 1/2$ if more than 20 lots were needed to qualify. |

Continue to inspect lots at the prescribed frequency, f, as long as the sampling results for every inspected lot satisfy Table II.

*When the preceding 10 (or more) lots are inspected on Skip-Lot inspection are accepted **and** the Cumulative Results satisfy Table I **and** each of the last 2 lots satisfy Table II, then*

Continue **Skip-Lot Inspection**, but begin skipping lots for inspection at the next lower frequency than before (1/2 to 1/3, 1/3 to 1/4, or 1/4 to 1/5).

When for any inspected lot the sampling results fail to satisfy Table II, then

Begin **Skip-Lot Interrupt** and inspect every lot consecutively using the reference Normal sampling plan from Z1.4 for the desired AQL and incoming lot size.

When four (4) consecutive lots are accepted and each of the last 2 lots satisfy Table II, then

Begin **Skip-Lot Inspection**, again skipping lots for inspection at the next higher frequency than immediately before beginning Skip-Lot Interrupt (1/5 to 1/4, 1/4 to 1/3, 1/3 to 1/2, or from 1/2 to continuing at 1/2).

*When for any inspected lot during Skip-Lot Interrupt the lot is rejected **or** qualification (as above) to begin Skip-Lot Inspection does not occur within 10 lots, then*

Return to **Lot-by-Lot Inspection.**

Figure 18-10   Operation Schematic for ANSI/ASQC Standard S1

> 2. *Have instituted a system which is capable of detecting and correcting shifts in quality levels, and monitoring process changes which may adversely affect quality. The supplier's personnel responsible for the application of the system shall exhibit a clear understanding of the applicable standards, systems, and procedures to be followed.*
>
> C *Not have experienced an organization change that might adversely affect quality.*

The product qualification is stated as follows:

The Product shall have met all of the following requirements:

> *1. Be of stable design.*

2. *Have been manufactured on an essentially continuous basis for a period mutually agreed to by the supplier and responsible authority. If no period is specified, the period shall be six months. Whenever production is held pending sample approval, only the time period after approval and resumption of production shall be included. NOTE: Essentially continuous production is considered a stabilizing factor of the manufacturing or assembly process.*

3. *Have been on normal or reduced inspection or a combination of normal and reduced inspection at general inspection levels I, II, or III (see ANSI Z1.4) during the qualification period. A product that has been on tightened inspection during the qualifying period is ineligible for skip-lot inspection.*

4. *Have been maintained at the AQL quality level or better (see ANSI Z1.4) for a period of stability mutually agreed to by both the supplier and responsible authority. If no period is specified, the period shall be six months.*

To begin skip-lot inspection or to continue skip-lot inspection at a lower frequency, application of the S1 standard requires the approval of the responsible authority. While in the skip-lot inspection or the skip-lot interrupt states, the S1 standard also requires return to the lot-by-lot inspection state if there is no production during the agreed period, the supplier violates the requirements of supplier or product qualification, or additional factors apply: if there is a documented complaint, the supplier has knowledge of which lots are to be inspected, the supplier fails to maintain a quality assurance system that includes inspection of each lot produced and records the results, and the responsible authority desires to return to lot-by-lot inspection.

The S1 standard makes provision for the application of skip-lot inspection as a substitute for reduced inspection. In Annex C of the standard are factors for deciding between skip-lot inspection using normal inspection during the skip-lot states and the regular reduced inspection of ANSI/ASQC Z1.4 and ISO 2859-1. [See the earlier quote from Dodge and Perry (1971)].

For all of the above and more, these standards should be consulted. Revised, more accurate tables I and II of the standard are included here as Tables 18-7 and 18-8.

▶ 18-3 CHAIN SAMPLING PLANS—ChSP

Another of the specialized types of sampling procedures developed by Dodge (1955b) is that of chain sampling plans (ChSP). The development was contemporary with that of skip-lot sampling plans. The purpose of ChSP is to achieve a more favorable operating characteristic than that of single sampling, particularly those with an acceptance number of zero. They were originally designed for relatively small samples used in situations of destructive or costly tests, satisfying conditions suitable to the use of cumulative results of samples from several lots in making an acceptance decision on the current lot. Individual lots and samples are considered as links in a chain, hence the name chain sampling.

Many variations have been developed from the basic procedure. However, only the basic procedure will be treated in some detail here, as with CSP and SkSP, with references to the literature for further study.

TABLE 18-7 Mininum Cumulative Sample Size ($n*$), to Initiate Skip-Lot Inspection

Number of nonconforming items or nonconformities	Acceptability quality level, AQL (Percent nonconforming or nonconformities per 100 items)												
	0.10	0.15	0.25	0.40	0.65	1.0	1.5	2.5	4.0	6.5	10	15	25
	Minimum cumulative sample size ($n*$)												
0	2,591	1,727	1,037	648	401	261	173	104	65	41	26	18	11
1	4,249	2,833	1,700	1,063	654	425	284	170	107	66	43	29	17
2	5,733	3,822	2,294	1,434	882	574	383	230	144	89	58	39	23
3	7,135	4,757	2,854	1,784	1,098	714	476	286	179	110	72	48	29
4	8,486	5,658	3,395	2,122	1,306	849	566	340	213	131	85	57	34
5	9,801	6,534	3,921	2,451	1,508	981	654	393	246	151	99	66	40
6	11,090	7,394	4,436	2,773	1,707	1,109	740	444	278	171	111	74	45
7	12,358	8,239	4,944	3,090	1,902	1,236	824	495	309	191	124	83	50
8	13,609	9,073	5,444	3,403	2,094	1,361	908	545	341	210	137	91	55
9	14,847	9,898	5,939	3,712	2,285	1,485	990	594	372	229	149	99	60
10	16,072	10,715	6,429	4,018	2,473	1,608	1,072	643	402	248	161	108	65
11	17,287	11,525	6,915	4,322	2,660	1,729	1,153	692	433	266	173	116	70
12	18,493	12,329	7,397	4,624	2,845	1,850	1,233	740	463	285	185	124	74
13	19,691	13,127	7,877	4,923	3,030	1,970	1,313	788	493	303	197	132	79
14	20,881	13,921	8,353	5,221	3,213	2,089	1,393	836	523	322	209	140	84
15	22,066	14,711	8,827	5,517	3,395	2,207	1,472	883	552	340	221	148	89
16	23,245	15,497	9,298	5,812	3,577	2,325	1,550	930	582	358	233	155	93
17	24,418	16,279	9,768	6,105	3,757	2,442	1,628	977	611	376	245	163	98
18	25,587	17,058	10,235	6,397	3,937	2,559	1,706	1,024	640	394	256	171	103
19	26,751	17,834	10,701	6,688	4,116	2,676	1,784	1,071	669	412	268	179	108
20	27,911	18,608	11,165	6,978	4,294	2,792	1,861	1,117	698	430	280	187	112
21	29,067	19,378	11,627	7,267	4,472	2,907	1,938	1,163	727	448	291	194	117
22	30,220	20,147	12,088	7,555	4,650	3,022	2,015	1,209	756	465	303	202	121
23	31,369	20,913	12,548	7,843	4,826	3,137	2,092	1,255	785	483	314	210	126
24	32,516	21,677	13,007	8,129	5,003	3,252	2,168	1,301	813	501	326	217	131
25	33,659	22,439	13,464	8,415	5,179	3,366	2,244	1,347	842	518	337	225	135
n_d	1,141	761	457	286	176	115	77	46	29	18	12	7.7	4.6

NOTES

1 Percent nonconforming applies only to AQL values of 10 or less.

2 For each additional nonconforming item or nonconformity, add n_d in the bottom row to the minimum cumulative sample size for 25 nonconforming items or nonconformities [$n*(25)$]. For example, at an AQL of 1.0%, 27 nonconforming items are observed. The minimum cumulative sample size for 27 nonconforming items [$n*(27)$] is calculated as follows;

$$n*(27) = 2 \times n_d + n*(25) = 2 \times 115 + 3\,366 = 3\,596$$

If the result has a fraction, round it up to the nearest integer.

TABLE 18-8 Acceptance Numbers to Initiate or Continue Skip-Lot Inspection

Sample size	Acceptable quality level, AQL (Percent nonconforming or nonconformities per 100 items)												
	0.10	0.15	0.25	0.40	0.65	1.0	1.5	2.5	4.0	6.5	10	15	25
	Acceptance numbers (Ac)												
2								→	→	0	→	0	1
3							→	→	0	→	0	1	1
5						→	→	0	→	0	1	1	2
8					→	→	0	→	0	1	1	2	3
13				→	→	0	→	0	1	1	2	3	5
20			→	→	0	→	0	1	1	2	3	5	7
32		→	→	0	→	0	1	1	2	3	5	7	11
50	→	→	0	→	0	1	1	2	3	5	7	11	17
80	→	0	→	0	1	1	2	3	5	7	11	17	
125	0	→	0	1	1	2	3	5	7	11	17		
200	→	0	1	1	2	3	5	7	11	17			
315	0	1	1	2	3	5	7	11	17				
500	1	1	2	3	5	7	11	17					
800	1	2	3	5	7	11	17						
1250	2	3	5	7	11	17							
2000	3	5	7	11	17								

NOTES

1 The acceptance numbers should not be confused with the acceptance numbers in ISO 2859-1, which are used for determination of lot acceptability.

2 Percent nonconforming applies only to AQL values of 10 or less.

3 → = Move to right, where Ac = 0 (only on reduced inspection).

18-3.1 Parameters, Operation, Evaluation, and Application

The first chain sampling plan by Dodge (1955b) designated ChSP-1, employs two parameters, n and i. The first, n, is the sample size or number of items selected at random from each lot (a lot-by-lot procedure) for inspection. The second, i, is the number of preceding samples that, if clear of nonconforming items, allows acceptance of the current lot when one nonconforming item is found in its sample. Otherwise, acceptance of the current lot is permitted when no nonconforming items are found in its sample. The acceptance requirement is fixed at zero or 1 as noted above. An operation schematic, summarizing the above, is shown in Figure 18-11. Evaluation of ChSP-1 is by means of the probability of acceptance, P_a, or operating characteristic, which is readily computed from results derived by Dodge (1955b):

$$P_a = P_{0,n} + P_{1,n}(P_{0,n})^i \tag{18-14}$$

where

$P_{0,n}$ = the probability of finding no nonconforming units in a sample of n units from product of fraction nonconforming, p

$P_{1,n}$ = the probability of finding one nonconforming unit in such a sample

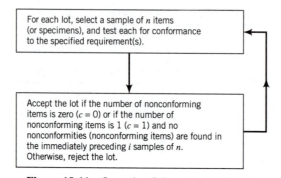

For each lot, select a sample of n items (or specimens), and test each for conformance to the specified requirement(s).

Accept the lot if the number of nonconforming items is zero ($c = 0$) or if the number of nonconforming items is 1 ($c = 1$) and no nonconformities (nonconforming items) are found in the immediately preceding i samples of n. Otherwise, reject the lot.

Figure 18-11   Operation Schematic for ChSP-1

Equation (18-14) may be used to develop the OC curves for values of n and i for a series of p values. An example of such OC curves for several values of i and for $n = 10$ is shown in Figure 18-12. Binomial probabilities are used. The single sampling plan with $n = 10$, $c = 0$ is also illustrated in Figure 18-12 and shows the relationship between chain sampling and single sampling. The OC curves of Figure 18-12 are from Dodge (1955b), reproduced by permission of the American Society for Quality.

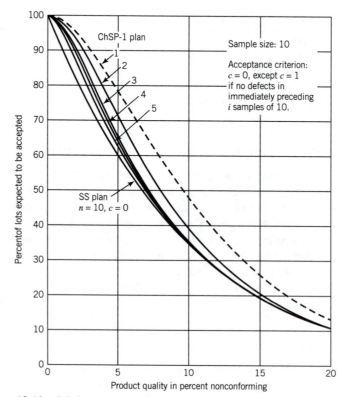

ChSP-1 plan

Sample size: 10

Acceptance criterion:
$c = 0$, except $c = 1$
if no defects in
immediately preceding
i samples of 10.

SS plan
$n = 10, c = 0$

Percent of lots expected to be accepted

Product quality in percent nonconforming

Figure 18-12   OC Curves for ChSP-1 Plans with Values of i from 1 to 5; $n = 10$

These curves have a different meaning from the usual probability of acceptance curves for the ordinary types of lot-by-lot sampling plans because of the cumulative nature of the acceptance requirements. For given n and i, they show the percentage of lots that are expected to be accepted for a given value of product quality p, and the evaluation assumes that p remains fixed over the accumulation period. For ordinary lot-by-lot sampling, decisions are based on information from each lot and are not dependent on previous lots.

The curves of Figure 18-12 also illustrate the ChSP effect that is stated by Dodge (1955b) as follows:

Curves for individual ChSP-1 plans can be compared with the OC curves for basic c = 0 plans of single sampling. It is seen that adding the provision for using cumulative results for i preceding samples has the same effect on the characteristic curve as taking a second sample. It increases the chances of acceptance in the region of principal interest—where the product percent defective is very small. Since in addition it calls for rejection provided only that two defects are fairly close together, it modifies the basically undesirable features of the c = 0 single sampling plans.

Additional OC curves for ChSP-1 plans are presented by Clark (1960). He argues the case for larger sample sizes and presents OC curves for various sample sizes up to $n = 100$. He illustrates an application of ChSP-1 for the sampling inspection of a device for a failure characteristic.

Further evaluations of plans of the ChSP-1 type have been done by Zwickl (1965) and Soundararajan (1978). These relate to determination of AOQL for ChSP-1 and tabulations of ChSP-1 plans for AQL/LTPD and AQL/AOQL requirements. Under conditions suitable to the use of Poisson probabilities (in its own right or as approximations to binomial or hypergeometric probabilities), the following expression can be used to determine the AOQL of ChSP-1 plans:

$$AOQL = k/n - k/N \qquad (18\text{-}15)$$

Values of k for the parameter i for ChSP-1 are given in Table 18-9.

A nomograph for selecting parameters n and i for ChSP-1 and *AOQL*, is given in Figure 18-13, from Zwickl (1965).

TABLE 18-9 k Values for ChSP-1 Plans

i	k
1	0.503
2	0.419
3	0.389
4	0.376
5	0.372
.	.
.	.
.	.
∞*	0.368

*Corresponds to single sampling with $c = 0$.

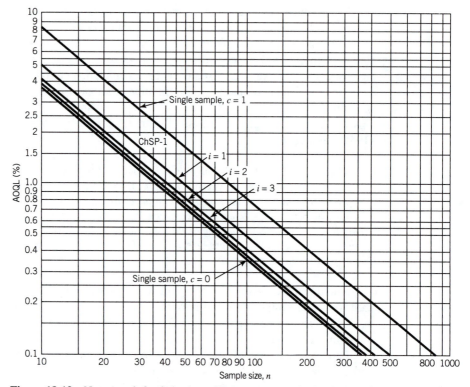

Figure 18-13 Nomograph for Selection of Parameters n and i for ChSP-1 and Desired AOQL

Based on the use of binomial probabilities, the following expressions have been derived for the parameters n and i of ChSP-1 having an OC curve passing approximately through the two points, (p, P_a): $(p_1, 0.95)$ and $(p_2, 0.10)$, with p_1 as AQL and p_2 as LQL:

$$n = \log (0.10)/\log (1 - p_2) \tag{18-16}$$

$$i = \{\log [0.95 - (1 - p_1)^n] - \log (np_1)\}/[n \log (1 - p_1)] - (n - 1)/n \tag{18-17}$$

Chain sampling plans are designed for applications satisfying the following conditions:

1. Lots should be a series of continuous supply, preferably in order of production.

2. Lots are expected to be of essentially the same satisfactory quality.

3. The consumer has confidence in the integrity of the producer.

These plans are particularly suited to situations satisfying the above conditions and involving destructive, complex, or costly tests for which a small sample is desired yielding good quality discrimination. They are also useful for achieving better discrimination (than single and double sampling plans) in situations satisfying the above conditions and requiring larger sample sizes. Zwickl (1965) illustrates an application to transistors requiring an $AOQL = 0.2\%$ for which the ChSP-1 plan is $n = 195$, $i = 2$. This involves less average total inspection (ATI) and less relative total inspection costs than the single sampling plan, $n = 180$, $c = 0$. Frishman (1960) presents an application to the sampling inspection of torpedoes for Naval Ordnance as a check on the control of the production process and test equipment. Hopkins et al. (1972) report an application to acceptance-test firing of missiles.

As with CSP and SkSP, only the single procedure for ChSP-1 is presented here to acquaint the reader with the basic ideas rather than with all varieties of such sampling procedures. The reader may consult a more comprehensive work on ChSP by Stephens (1995b) that includes a reasonably complete bibliography on the subject.

Fractional Acceptance Numbers

An interesting application of the chain sampling principle and procedure is that of *fractional acceptance numbers*. Acceptance numbers for attribute sampling plans apply to the number of nonconforming units allowed in the sample to permit acceptance. Hence, they are discrete numbers. A unique application of the chain sampling principle allows a phenomenon that acts much like fractional acceptance numbers.

It has long been known that the properties of sampling plans with acceptance numbers of zero ($c = 0$) are uniquely different from those with larger acceptance numbers (i.e. for $c \geq 1$). This has presented some difficulties in devising sampling tables, such as ANSI/ASQC Z1.4 and its international equivalent, ISO 2859-1. To achieve a consistent degree of quality protection with various values of index quality, AQLs, and lot size ranges with associated code letters and sample sizes, it is necessary to use arrows in the sampling tables to direct the user to different sample sizes when acceptance numbers of 0 are applicable. The situation has been such that an acceptance number between 0 and 1 would be useful, that is, a fractional acceptance number.

Applying the principle of chain sampling permits the equivalent of these fractional acceptance numbers. The procedure works as follows and has been applied to the latest version of ISO 2859-1, on which the next revision of ANSI/ASQC Z1.4 will be based. Under the normal and tightened sampling plan tables, fractional acceptance numbers, f, of 1/3 and 1/2 are specified for certain combinations of AQL and sample size code letter. Under the reduced sampling plan tables, fractional acceptance numbers, f, of 1/5, 1/3, and 1/2 are specified. These acceptance numbers are applied according to the ChSP-1 operation schematic (of Figure 18-12) with $i = 1/f - 1$. For example, if $f = 1/3$ applies, the current lot is accepted if the number of nonconforming items is zero or if the number of nonconforming units is 1 and no (zero) nonconformities have been found in the immediately preceding 2 $(3 - 1)$ samples from these lots. See also Chapter 16 for a discussion of this procedure in conjunction with attribute acceptance sampling plans.

▶ 18-4 REFERENCES

American Society for Quality Control (1987), ANSI/ASQC S1-1987, *An Attribute Skip-Lot Sampling Program*, ASQC, Milwaukee.

American Society for Quality Control (1993), ANSI/ASQC Z1.4, *Sampling Procedures and Tables for Inspection by Attributes*, ASQC, Milwaukee.

Banzhaf, R. A., and Brugger, R M. (1970), "Review of Standards and Specifications: MIL-STD-1235 (ORD), Single and Multi-Level Continuous Sampling Procedures and Tables for In-spection by Attributes," *Journal of Quality Technology*, Vol. 2, No. 1, Jan.; pp. 41–53.

Blackwell, M. T. R. (1977), "The Effect of Short Production Runs on CSP-1," *Technometrics*, Vol. 19, No. 3, Aug.; pp. 259–63.

Brugger, R. M. (1967), QEM 21-240-9, *The UAOQL of CSP-1, CSP-2, and CSP-R Under the Nonreplacement Assumption*, U.S. Army Ammunition Procurement and Supply Agency, Quality Assurance Directorate, Quality Evaluation Division, Concepts Branch, Joliet, IL, December.

Brugger, R. M. (1972), "Functional Properties of CSP-1 Applied to a Finite Length Production Run," *Proceedings of the 17th Conference on the Design of Experiments in Army Research Development and Testing, Part 2, ARO-D Report 72-2,* pp. 929–53, U.S. Army Research Office, Durham, NC.

Brugger, R. M. (1976), "A Simple Method for Determining the Unrestricted Average Outgoing Quality Limit (UAOQL) of a Continuous Sampling Plan," *Proceedings of the 21st Conference on the Design of Experiments in Army Research Development and Testing, ARO Report 76-2,* pp. 409–16, U.S. Army Research Office, Durham, NC.

Case, K. E., Bennett, E. G., and Schmidt, J. W. (1973), "The Dodge CSP-1 Continuous Sampling Plan under Inspection Error," *AIIE Transactions,* Vol. 5, No. 3, Sept.; pp. 193–202.

Chiu, W. K., and Wetherill, G. B. (1973), "The Economic Design of Continuous Inspection Procedures: A Review Paper," *International Statistical Review,* Vol. 41, No. 3, pp. 357–73.

Clark, C. R. (1960), "OC Curves for ChSP-1 Chain Sampling Plans," *Industrial Quality Control,* Vol. 17, No. 4, Oct.; pp. 10–12.

Derman, C., Johns, M. V., Jr., and Lieberman, G. J. (1959), "Continuous Sampling Procedures Without Control," *The Annals of Mathematical Statistics,* Vol. 30, No. 4, Dec.; pp. 1175–91. (Also published in Technical Report 39, Applied Mathematics and Statistics Laboratory, Stanford University, Stanford, CA, October 10, 1958.)

Dodge, H. F. (1943), "A Sampling Inspection Plan for Continuous Production," *The Annals of Mathematical Statistics,* Vol. 14, No. 3, Sept.; pp. 264–79; and *Transactions of the ASME,* Vol. 66, No. 2, February 1944, pp. 127–33. (Also reprinted in the *Journal of Quality Technology,* Vol. 9, No. 3, pp. 104–19, July 1977.)

Dodge, H. F. (1947), "Sampling Plans for Continuous Production," *Industrial Quality Control,* Vol. 4, No. 3, Nov.; pp. 5–9.

Dodge, H. F. (1955a), "Skip-Lot Sampling Plan," *Industrial Quality Control,* Vol. 11, No. 5, Feb.; pp. 3–5.

Dodge, H. F. (1955b), "Chain Sampling Inspection Plan," *Industrial Quality Control,* Vol. 11, No. 4, Jan.; pp. 10–13.

Dodge, H. F. (1970), "Notes on the Evolution of Acceptance Sampling Plans, Part IV," *Journal of Quality Technology,* Vol. 2, No. 1, Jan.; pp. 1–8.

Dodge, R. F., and Perry, R. L. (1971), "A System of Skip-Lot Plans for Lot by Lot Inspection," *Annual Technical Conference Transactions,* pp. 469–77, American Society for Quality Control, Milwaukee.

Dodge, H. F., and Romig, H. G. (1941), "Single Sampling and Double Sampling Inspection Tables," *Bell System Technical Journal,* Vol. 20, No. 1, Jan.; pp. 1–61.

Dodge, H. F., and Torrey, M. N. (1951), "Additional Continuous Sampling Inspection Plans," *Industrial Quality Control,* Vol. 7, No. 5, March; pp. 7–12.

Duncan, A. J. (1986), *Quality Control and Industrial Statistics,* Fifth Edition, Richard D. Irwin, Homewood, IL.

Endres, A. (1967), QEM 22-240-2, *The Unrestricted AOQL and Its Use in Continuous Sampling Plans,* U.S. Army Ammunition Procurement and Supply Agency, Quality Assurance Directorate, Quality Evaluation Division, Concepts Branch, Joliet, IL.

Endres, A. (1969), "The Computation of the Unrestricted AOQL When Defective Material is Removed but Not Replaced," *Journal of the American Statistical Association,* Vol. 64, No. 326, June; pp. 665–68. (Also published in QEM 21-240-8, U.S. Army Ammunition Procurement and Supply Agency, Quality Assurance Directorate, Quality Evaluation Division, Concepts Branch, Joliet, IL, November 1967.)

Frishman, F. (1960), "An Extended Chain Sampling Inspection Plan," *Industrial Quality Control,* Vol. 17, No. 1, July; pp. 10–12.

Gregory, G. (1956), *An Economic Approach to the Choice of Continuous Sampling Plans,* Technical Report 30, Applied Mathematics and Statistics Laboratory, Stanford University, Stanford, CA.

Hillier, F. S. (1964), "New Criteria for Selecting Continuous Sampling Plans," *Technometrics,* Vol. 6, No. 2, May; pp. 161–78. (Also published in Technical Report 52, Applied Mathematics and Statistics Laboratory, Stanford University, Stanford, CA, May 10, 1961.)

Hopkins, C. L., Nutt, R. L., and Heathcock, R. (1972), *Chain Sampling,* Technical Report QP-TR-72-1, Advanced Techniques Branch, Plans and Programs Analysis Division, Directorate for Product Assurance, U.S. Army Missile Command, Redstone Arsenal, AL.

International Organization for Standardization (1999), ISO 2859-1, *Sampling Procedures for Inspection by Attributes—Part 1: Sampling Schemes Indexed by Acceptance Quality Limit (AQL) for Lot-by-Lot Inspection,* ISO, Geneva, Switzerland.

International Organization for Standardization (1991), ISO 2859-3, *Sampling Procedures for Inspection by Attributes—Part 3: Skip-Lot Sampling Procedures,* ISO, Geneva, Switzerland.

Kumar, V. S. S., and Rajarshi, M. B. (1987), "Continuous Sampling Plans for Markov Dependent Production Processes," *Naval Research Logistics Quarterly,* Vol. 34, pp. 629–44.

Lasater, H. A. (1970), *On the Robustness of a Class of Continuous Sampling Plans Under Certain Types of Process Models,* Unpublished Ph.D. dissertation, Rutgers University, New Brunswick, NJ.

LeMaster, V., and McKeague, R. (1958), *Stopping Rules Used in the Proposed DoD Handbook on Single-Level Continuous Sampling Plans,* ESM 401-0-29, Ordnance Ammunition, Command, National Industrial Operations Division, Engineering Branch, Inspection Engineering and Standards Section, Methods Development Unit, Joliet, IL.

Lieberman, G. J. (1953), "A Note on Dodge's Continuous Inspection Plan," *The Annals of Mathematical Statistics,* Vol. 24, No. 3, Dec.; pp. 480–84. (Also published in Technical Report 12, Applied Mathematics and Statistics Laboratory, Stanford University, Stanford, CA, 1953.)

Liebesman, B. S., and Saperstein, B. (1983), "A Proposed Attribute Skip-Lot Sampling Program," *Journal of Quality Technology,* Vol. 15, No. 3, July; pp. 130–40.

Magwire, C. (1956), *Finite Continuous Sampling Plans Involving a Stopping Rule,* Technical Report 31, Applied Mathematics and Statistics Laboratory, Stanford University, Stanford, CA.

McShane, L. M. (1989), *Statistical Quality Control Procedures for Monitoring Laboratory Analyses,* Unpublished Ph.D. dissertation, Cornell University, Ithaca, NY.

McShane, L. M., and Turnbull, B. W. (1991), "Probability Limits on Outgoing Quality for Continuous Sampling Plans," *Technometrics,* Vol. 33, No. 4, Nov.; pp. 393–404.

McShane, L. M., and Turnbull, B. W. (1992), "New Performance Measures for Continuous Sampling Plans Applied to Finite Production Runs," *Journal of Quality Technology,* Vol. 24, No. 3, July; pp. 153–61.

Murphy, R. B. (1958), "A Criterion to Limit Inspection Effort of Continuous Sampling Plans," *The Bell System Technical Journal,* Vol. 37, No. 1, Jan.; pp. 115–34.

Perry, R. L. (1970), *A System of Skip-Lot Sampling Plans for Lot Inspection,* Unpublished Ph.D. dissertation, Rutgers University Statistics Center, New Brunswick, NJ.

Perry, R. L. (1973a), "Skip-Lot Sampling Plans," *Journal of Quality Technology,* Vol. 5, No. 3, July; pp. 123–30.

Perry, R. L. (1973b), "Two-Level Skip-Lot Sampling Plans—Operating Characteristic Properties," *Journal of Quality Technology,* Vol. 5, No. 4, Oct.; pp. 160–66.

Resnikoff, G. J. (1960), "Minimum Average Fraction Inspected for a Continuous Sampling Plan," *Journal of Industrial Engineering,* Vol. 11, No. 3, May–June; pp. 208–09.

Sackrowitz, H. (1975), "A Note on Unrestricted AOQL's," *Journal of Quality Technology,* Vol. 7, No. 2, April; pp. 77–80.

Satterthwaite, F. E. (1949), *A New Continuous Sampling Inspection Plan Based on an Analysis of Costs,* Report No. 130, Product Service Division, Appliance and Merchandise Department, General Electric Company, Bridgeport, CT.

Savage, I. R. (1959), "A Production Model and Continuous Sampling Plan," *Journal of the American Statistical Association,* Vol. 54, March; pp. 231–47.

Soundararajan, V. (1978), "Procedures and Tables for Construction and Selection of Chain Sampling Plans (ChSP-1), Part 1," *Journal of Quality Technology,* Vol. 10, No. 2, April; pp. 56–60; and Part 2, Vol. 10, July; No. 3, pp. 99–103.

Stephens, K. S. (1981), "CSP-1 for Consumer Protection," *Journal of Quality Technology,* Vol. 13, No. 4, Oct.; pp. 249–53.

Stephens, K. S. (1995a), "How to Perform Continuous Sampling," *The ASQC Basic References in Quality: Statistical Techniques,* Vol. 2, American Society for Quality Control, Milwaukee.

Stephens, K. S. (1995b), "How to Perform Skip-Lot and Chain Sampling," *The ASQC Basic References in Quality Control: Statistical Techniques,* Vol. 4, American Society for Quality, Milwaukee.

Stephens, K. S. (2001), *The Handbook of Applied Acceptance Sampling,* Quality Press, American Society for Quality, Milwaukee.

U.S. Department of Defense (1988), *Single and Multi-Level Continuous Sampling Procedures and Tables for Inspection by Attributes,* MIL-STD-1235C (1988), Washington, D.C.

White, L. S. (1964), *On Finding the AOQL's of a Large Class of Continuous Sampling Plans,* Technical Report 22, Statistical Engineering Group, Columbia University, New York.

White, L. S. (1965), "Markovian Decision Models for the Evaluation of a Large Class of Continuous Sampling Inspection Plans," *The Annals of Mathematical Statistics,* Vol. 36, No. 5, Oct.; pp. 1408–20.

Zwickl, R. D. (1965), *Chain Sampling for Average Quality Protection,* Term paper, Rutgers University Statistics Center, New Brunswick, NJ.

▶ 18-5 PROBLEMS

1. For the CSP-1 plan with parameters, $f = 0.25$, $i = 60$, evaluate the five performance measures given by Equations (18-1) through (18-9) for the series of fraction nonconforming: $p = 0.005, 0.01, 0.02, 0.03, 0.04, 0.05$, and 0.06. Plot the AOQ curve, AOQ versus p, and approximate the AOQL for the plan. Verify this by way of the nomograph of Figure 18-6. Plot the OC curve, P_a versus p, and approximate the LQL (i.e., $p_{0.10}$) for the plan. Verify this by way of the nomograph of Figure 18-7.

2. Repeat Problem 1 for $f = 0.10$, $i = 100$, and $p = 0.005$, 0.010, 0.015, 0.020, 0.025, 0.030, 0.035, 0.040, 0.045, and 0.050.

3. For the CSP-1 plan with parameters $f = 1/7$, $i = 90$, determine the approximate AOQL and LQL.

4. Select from the nomographs of Figure 18-6 and Figure 18-7 some CSP-1 plans (i.e., the approximate parameters, f and i) that meet the following criteria:

(a) $AOQL = 0.5\%$, $LQL = 4\%$
(b) $AOQL = 1.0\%$, $LQL = 4\%$
(c) $AOQL = 1.5\%$, $LQL = 4\%$
(d) $AOQL = 1.0\%$, $LQL = 6\%$
(e) $AOQL = 1.5\%$, $LQL = 6\%$
(f) $AOQL = 2.0\%$, $LQL = 10\%$
(g) Plans for a, b, and c with the same parameter f.
(h) Plans for b and d with the same parameter f.
(i) Plans for c and e with the same parameter f.
(j) Plans for a, b, and c with the same parameter i.
(k) Plans for b and d with the same parameter i.
(l) Plans for c and e with the same parameter i.

5. Select from the tables of Tables 18-2, 18-3, and 18-4 the CSP-1 plans (i.e., f, i, $AOQL$, and S) for the following criteria:

(a) Production interval = 200, $AQL = 0.25\%$
(b) Production interval = 2000, $AQL = 1.5\%$

(c) Production interval = 3000, $AQL = 1.5\%$
(d) Production interval = 12,000, $AQL = 2.5\%$
(e) Production interval = 1,000, $AQL = 0.40\%$

6. Using the cumulative geometric distribution with parameters $p = 0.02, 0.04$, and 0.08, verify the given proportions, $0.67, 0.44$, and 0.19, respectively, of defective spacings $(s - 1)$ meeting the clearing interval criteria, $i = 20$, in the discussion of the evaluation of CSP and CSP-1.

7. From the nomograph of Figure 18-9, select some SkSP plans (i.e., the approximate parameters, i and AOQL) meeting the following sampling criteria:
(a) $f = 1/2$
(b) $f = 1/3$
(c) $f = 1/4$
(d) $f = 1/5$

8. Note that the LQL of CSP-1 has the interpretation of a limiting quality level on the percent of nonconforming lots for SkSP applications. Use the nomographs of Figure 18-6 and Figure 18-7 to select some SkSP-1 plans with the following specifications of f and LQL:
(a) $f = 1/2$, $LQL = 5\%$, 8%, 10%
(b) $f = 1/3$, $LQL = 5\%$, 8%, 10%
(c) $f = 1/4$, $LQL = 5\%$, 8%, 10%
(d) $f = 1/5$, $LQL = 5\%$, 8%, 10%

9. SkSP-2 is the application of SkSP-1 to the inspection of lots with a lot-by-lot acceptance sampling plan, such as a single sampling plan with parameters n and c or the skipping of lots as dictated by the SkSP-1 procedure and outcomes. The p of Equations (18-1) and (18-2) represents the probability that a given entity is nonconforming (rejectable). For SkSP-2 this is the probability of lot rejection, $1 - P$, where P denotes the probability of acceptance (P_a) of a lot according to the chosen acceptance sampling plan. Hence, $q = P$ and $p = 1 - P$ in (18-1) and (18-2) for SkSP-2, and F of (18-3) is determined. Now derive an expression for P_a (f, i), the average fraction of total lots accepted for the SkSP-2 plan. Note that it is not (18-7) with the above substitutions—why?

10. Use the results of Problem 9 to plot the OC curve for the SkSP-2 plan with $f = 1/2$, $i = 14$, $n = 60$, $c = 2$.

11. For the ChSP-1 plan with $n = 50$, $i = 2$, evaluate P_a by Equation (18-14) for the series of fraction nonconforming: $p = 0.002, 0.005, 0.010, 0.015, 0.020$, and 0.025. Plot the OC curve. Determine and plot on the same graph the OC curve for the single sampling plan with $n = 50$, $c = 0$.

12. For the ChSP-1 plan with $n = 5$, $i = 3$, evaluate P_a for the series of fraction nonconforming: $p = 0.01, 0.02, 0.05$,

0.10, 0.20, 0.30, and 0.40. Plot the OC curve. Determine and plot on the same graph the OC curve for the single sampling plan with $n = 5$, $c = 0$.

13. Find the ChSP-1 plan (i.e., the parameters, n and i) by Equations (18-16) and (18-17) meeting the following criteria:
(a) $P_a = 0.95$ for $p_1 = 0.004$ $(p_{0.95} = 0.004)$; $P_a = 0.10$ for $p_2 = 0.05$ $(p_{0.10} = 0.05)$
(b) $p_{0.95} = 0.01$; $p_{0.10} = 0.08$
(c) $p_{0.95} = 0.0025$; $p_{0.10} = 0.03$
(d) $p_{0.95} = 0.01$; $p_{0.10} = 0.10$
(e) $p_{0.95} = 0.01$; $p_{0.10} = 0.13$
(f) $p_{0.95} = 0.04$; $p_{0.10} = 0.20$
(g) $p_{0.95} = 0.01$; $p_{0.10} = 0.15$
(h) Derive the single sampling plans meeting the same criteria and compare with the above.

14. Select from the nomograph of Figure 18-13 some ChSP-1 plans (i.e., the approximate parameters, n and i) meeting the following criteria:
(a) $AOQL = 0.5\%$
(b) $AOQL = 1.0\%$
(c) $AOQL = 2.0\%$
(d) $AOQL = 0.2\%$

15. Sampling is conducted using Z1.4 with the following sampling plan: $AQL = 1.5\%$, $N = 1000$, Code Letter J, $n = 80$, $c = 3$ (see Chapter 16), on normal inspection. Ten lots are inspected, with the following results. Is skip-lot inspection permitted? If so, what are the parameters of the plan?

Lot No.	n	d	Lot No.	n	d
1	80	2	6	80	1
2	80	0	7	80	0
3	80	1	8	80	2
4	80	0	9	80	1
5	80	3	10	80	0

16. The sampling plan of Problem 15 is continued with the following results. Is it permitted to change to skip-lot inspection at any time in this sequence of results? If so, at what lot number and with what parameters of the skip-lot plan?

Lot No.	n	d	Lot No.	n	d
11	80	0	16	80	0
12	80	1	17	80	1
13	80	1	18	80	0
14	80	0	19	80	0
15	80	0	20	80	1

TABLES

TABLE A   Areas Under the Normal Curve, Proportion of Total Area Under the Curve from $-\infty$ to $(x_i - \mu)/\sigma$

$\dfrac{x_i - \mu}{\sigma}$	0.09	0.08	0.07	0.06	0.05	0.04	0.03	0.02	0.01	0.00
-3.5	0.00017	0.00017	0.00018	0.00019	0.00019	0.00020	0.00021	0.00022	0.00022	0.00023
-3.4	0.00024	0.00025	0.00026	0.00027	0.00028	0.00029	0.00030	0.00031	0.00033	0.00034
-3.3	0.00035	0.00036	0.00038	0.00039	0.00040	0.00042	0.00043	0.00045	0.00047	0.00048
-3.2	0.00050	0.00052	0.00054	0.00056	0.00058	0.00060	0.00062	0.00064	0.00066	0.00069
-3.1	0.00071	0.00074	0.00076	0.00079	0.00082	0.00085	0.00087	0.00090	0.00094	0.00097
-3.0	0.00100	0.00104	0.00107	0.00111	0.00114	0.00118	0.00122	0.00126	0.00131	0.00135
-2.9	0.0014	0.0014	0.0015	0.0015	0.0016	0.0016	0.0017	0.0017	0.0018	0.0019
-2.8	0.0019	0.0020	0.0021	0.0021	0.0022	0.0023	0.0023	0.0024	0.0025	0.0026
-2.7	0.0026	0.0027	0.0028	0.0029	0.0030	0.0031	0.0032	0.0033	0.0034	0.0035
-2.6	0.0036	0.0037	0.0038	0.0039	0.0040	0.0041	0.0043	0.0044	0.0045	0.0047
-2.5	0.0048	0.0049	0.0051	0.0052	0.0054	0.0055	0.0057	0.0059	0.0060	0.0062
-2.4	0.0064	0.0066	0.0068	0.0069	0.0071	0.0073	0.0075	0.0078	0.0080	0.0082
-2.3	0.0084	0.0087	0.0089	0.0091	0.0094	0.0096	0.0099	0.0102	0.0104	0.0107
-2.2	0.0110	0.0113	0.0116	0.0119	0.0122	0.0125	0.0129	0.0132	0.0136	0.0139
-2.1	0.0143	0.0146	0.0150	0.0154	0.0158	0.0162	0.0166	0.0170	0.0174	0.0179
-2.0	0.0183	0.0188	0.0192	0.0197	0.0202	0.0207	0.0212	0.0217	0.0222	0.0228
-1.9	0.0233	0.0239	0.0244	0.0250	0.0256	0.0262	0.0268	0.0274	0.0281	0.0287
-1.8	0.0294	0.0301	0.0307	0.0314	0.0322	0.0329	0.0336	0.0344	0.0351	0.0359
-1.7	0.0367	0.0375	0.0384	0.0392	0.0401	0.0409	0.0418	0.0427	0.0436	0.0446
-1.6	0.0455	0.0465	0.0475	0.0485	0.0495	0.0505	0.0516	0.0526	0.0537	0.0548
-1.5	0.0559	0.0571	0.0582	0.0594	0.0606	0.0618	0.0630	0.0643	0.0655	0.0668
-1.4	0.0681	0.0694	0.0708	0.0721	0.0735	0.0749	0.0764	0.0778	0.0793	0.0808
-1.3	0.0823	0.0838	0.0853	0.0869	0.0885	0.0901	0.0918	0.0934	0.0951	0.0968
-1.2	0.0985	0.1003	0.1020	0.1038	0.1057	0.1075	0.1093	0.1112	0.1131	0.1151
-1.1	0.1170	0.1190	0.1210	0.1230	0.1251	0.1271	0.1292	0.1314	0.1335	0.1357
-1.0	0.1379	0.1401	0.1423	0.1446	0.1469	0.1492	0.1515	0.1539	0.1562	0.1587
-0.9	0.1611	0.1635	0.1660	0.1685	0.1711	0.1736	0.1762	0.1788	0.1814	0.1841
-0.8	0.1867	0.1894	0.1922	0.1949	0.1977	0.2005	0.2033	0.2061	0.2090	0.2119
-0.7	0.2148	0.2177	0.2207	0.2236	0.2266	0.2297	0.2327	0.2358	0.2389	0.2420
-0.6	0.2451	0.2483	0.2514	0.2546	0.2578	0.2611	0.2643	0.2676	0.2709	0.2743
-0.5	0.2776	0.2810	0.2843	0.2877	0.2912	0.2946	0.2981	0.3015	0.3050	0.3085
-0.4	0.3121	0.3156	0.3192	0.3228	0.3264	0.3300	0.3336	0.3372	0.3409	0.3446
-0.3	0.3483	0.3520	0.3557	0.3594	0.3632	0.3669	0.3707	0.3745	0.3783	0.3821
-0.2	0.3859	0.3897	0.3936	0.3974	0.4013	0.4052	0.4090	0.4129	0.4168	0.4207
-0.1	0.4247	0.4286	0.4325	0.4364	0.4404	0.4443	0.4483	0.4522	0.4562	0.4602
-0.0	0.4641	0.4681	0.4721	0.4761	0.4801	0.4840	0.4880	0.4920	0.4960	0.5000

Source: Reprinted with permission from Grant, E. L., and R. S. Leavenworth (1980), *Statistical Quality Control,* Fifth Edition, McGraw-Hill, New York.

TABLE A   Areas Under the Normal Curve   (*continued*)

$\dfrac{x_i - \mu}{\sigma}$	0.00	0.01	0.02	0.03	0.04	0.05	0.06	0.07	0.08	0.09
+0.0	0.5000	0.5040	0.5080	0.5120	0.5160	0.5199	0.5239	0.5279	0.5319	0.5359
+0.1	0.5398	0.5438	0.5478	0.5517	0.5557	0.5596	0.5636	0.5675	0.5714	0.5753
+0.2	0.5793	0.5832	0.5871	0.5910	0.5948	0.5987	0.6026	0.6064	0.6103	0.6141
+0.3	0.6179	0.6217	0.6255	0.6293	0.6331	0.6368	0.6406	0.6443	0.6480	0.6517
+0.4	0.6554	0.6591	0.6628	0.6664	0.6700	0.6736	0.6772	0.6808	0.6844	0.6879
+0.5	0.6915	0.6950	0.6985	0.7019	0.7054	0.7088	0.7123	0.7157	0.7190	0.7224
+0.6	0.7257	0.7291	0.7324	0.7357	0.7389	0.7422	0.7454	0.7486	0.7517	0.7549
+0.7	0.7580	0.7611	0.7642	0.7673	0.7704	0.7734	0.7764	0.7794	0.7823	0.7852
+0.8	0.7881	0.7910	0.7939	0.7967	0.7995	0.8023	0.8051	0.8079	0.8106	0.8133
+0.9	0.8159	0.8186	0.8212	0.8238	0.8264	0.8289	0.8315	0.8340	0.8365	0.8389
+1.0	0.8413	0.8438	0.8461	0.8485	0.8508	0.8531	0.8554	0.8577	0.8599	0.8621
+1.1	0.8643	0.8665	0.8686	0.8708	0.8729	0.8749	0.8770	0.8790	0.8810	0.8830
+1.2	0.8849	0.8869	0.8888	0.8907	0.8925	0.8944	0.8962	0.8980	0.8997	0.9015
+1.3	0.9032	0.9049	0.9066	0.9082	0.9099	0.9115	0.9131	0.9147	0.9162	0.9177
+1.4	0.9192	0.9207	0.9222	0.9236	0.9251	0.9265	0.9279	0.9292	0.9306	0.9319
+1.5	0.9332	0.9345	0.9357	0.9370	0.9382	0.9394	0.9406	0.9418	0.9429	0.9441
+1.6	0.9452	0.9463	0.9474	0.9484	0.9495	0.9505	0.9515	0.9525	0.9535	0.9545
+1.7	0.9554	0.9564	0.9573	0.9582	0.9591	0.9599	0.9608	0.9616	0.9625	0.9633
+1.8	0.9641	0.9649	0.9656	0.9664	0.9671	0.9678	0.9686	0.9693	0.9699	0.9706
+1.9	0.9713	0.9719	0.9726	0.9732	0.9738	0.9744	0.9750	0.9756	0.9761	0.9767
+2.0	0.9773	0.9778	0.9783	0.9788	0.9793	0.9798	0.9803	0.9808	0.9812	0.9817
+2.1	0.9821	0.9826	0.9830	0.9834	0.9838	0.9842	0.9846	0.9850	0.9854	0.9857
+2.2	0.9861	0.9864	0.9868	0.9871	0.9875	0.9878	0.9881	0.9884	0.9887	0.9890
+2.3	0.9893	0.9896	0.9898	0.9901	0.9904	0.9906	0.9909	0.9911	0.9913	0.9916
+2.4	0.9918	0.9920	0.9922	0.9925	0.9927	0.9929	0.9931	0.9932	0.9934	0.9936
+2.5	0.9938	0.9940	0.9941	0.9943	0.9945	0.9946	0.9948	0.9949	0.9951	0.9952
+2.6	0.9953	0.9955	0.9956	0.9957	0.9959	0.9960	0.9961	0.9962	0.9963	0.9964
+2.7	0.9965	0.9966	0.9967	0.9968	0.9969	0.9970	0.9971	0.9972	0.9973	0.9974
+2.8	0.9974	0.9975	0.9976	0.9977	0.9977	0.9978	0.9979	0.9979	0.9980	0.9981
+2.9	0.9981	0.9982	0.9983	0.9983	0.9984	0.9984	0.9985	0.9985	0.9986	0.9986
+3.0	0.99865	0.99869	0.99874	0.99878	0.99882	0.99886	0.99889	0.99893	0.99896	0.99900
+3.1	0.99903	0.99906	0.99910	0.99913	0.99915	0.99918	0.99921	0.99924	0.99926	0.99929
+3.2	0.99931	0.99934	0.99936	0.99938	0.99940	0.99942	0.99944	0.99946	0.99948	0.99950
+3.3	0.99952	0.99953	0.99955	0.99957	0.99958	0.99960	0.99961	0.99962	0.99964	0.99965
+3.4	0.99966	0.99967	0.99969	0.99970	0.99971	0.99972	0.99973	0.99974	0.99975	0.99976
+3.5	0.99977	0.99978	0.99978	0.99979	0.99980	0.99981	0.99981	0.99982	0.99983	0.99983

TABLE B **Percentage Points of the Chi Square (χ^2) Distribution**

v^a \ α	.995	.990	.975	.950	.900	.500	.100	.050	.025	.010	.005
1	.00+	.00+	.00+	.00+	.02	.45	2.71	3.84	5.02	6.63	7.88
2	.01	.02	.05	.10	.21	1.39	4.61	5.99	7.38	9.21	10.60
3	.07	.11	.22	.35	.58	2.37	6.25	7.81	9.35	11.34	12.84
4	.21	.30	.48	.71	1.06	3.36	7.78	9.49	11.14	13.28	14.86
5	.41	.55	.83	1.15	1.61	4.35	9.24	11.07	12.83	15.09	16.75
6	.68	.87	1.24	1.64	2.20	5.35	10.65	12.59	14.45	16.81	18.55
7	.99	1.24	1.69	2.17	2.83	6.35	12.02	14.07	16.01	18.48	20.28
8	1.34	1.65	2.18	2.73	3.49	7.34	13.36	15.51	17.53	20.09	21.96
9	1.73	2.09	2.70	3.33	4.17	8.34	14.68	16.92	19.02	21.67	23.59
10	2.16	2.56	3.25	3.94	4.87	9.34	15.99	18.31	20.48	23.21	25.19
11	2.60	3.05	3.82	4.57	5.58	10.34	17.28	19.68	21.92	24.72	26.76
12	3.07	3.57	4.40	5.23	6.30	11.34	18.55	21.03	23.34	26.22	28.30
13	3.57	4.11	5.01	5.89	7.04	12.34	19.81	22.36	24.74	27.69	29.82
14	4.07	4.66	5.63	6.57	7.79	13.34	21.06	23.68	26.12	29.14	31.32
15	4.60	5.23	6.27	7.26	8.55	14.34	22.31	25.00	27.49	30.58	32.80
16	5.14	5.81	6.91	7.96	9.31	15.34	23.54	26.30	28.85	32.00	34.27
17	5.70	6.41	7.56	8.67	10.09	16.34	24.77	27.59	30.19	33.41	35.72
18	6.26	7.01	8.23	9.39	10.87	17.34	25.99	28.87	31.53	34.81	37.16
19	6.84	7.63	8.91	10.12	11.65	18.34	27.20	30.14	32.85	36.19	38.58
20	7.43	8.26	9.59	10.85	12.44	19.34	28.41	31.41	34.17	37.57	40.00
21	8.03	8.90	10.28	11.59	13.24	20.34	29.62	32.67	35.48	38.93	41.40
22	8.64	9.54	10.98	12.34	14.04	21.34	30.81	33.92	36.78	40.29	42.80
23	9.26	10.20	11.69	13.09	14.85	22.34	32.01	35.17	38.08	41.64	44.18
24	9.89	10.86	12.40	13.85	15.66	23.34	33.20	36.42	39.36	42.98	45.56
25	10.52	11.52	13.12	14.61	16.47	24.34	34.28	37.65	40.65	44.31	46.93
26	11.16	12.20	13.84	15.38	17.29	25.34	35.56	38.89	41.92	45.64	48.29
27	11.81	12.88	14.57	16.15	18.11	26.34	36.74	40.11	43.19	46.96	49.65
28	12.46	13.57	15.31	16.93	18.94	27.34	37.92	41.34	44.46	48.28	50.99
29	13.12	14.26	16.05	17.71	19.77	28.34	39.09	42.56	45.72	49.59	52.34
30	13.79	14.95	16.79	18.49	20.60	29.34	40.26	43.77	46.98	50.89	53.67
40	20.71	22.16	24.43	26.51	29.05	39.34	51.81	55.76	59.34	63.69	66.77
50	27.99	29.71	32.36	34.76	37.69	49.33	63.17	67.50	71.42	76.15	79.49
60	35.53	37.48	40.48	43.19	46.46	59.33	74.40	79.08	83.30	88.38	91.95
70	43.28	45.44	48.76	51.74	55.33	69.33	85.53	90.53	95.02	100.42	104.22
80	51.17	53.54	57.15	60.39	64.28	79.33	96.58	101.88	106.63	112.33	116.32
90	59.20	61.75	65.65	69.13	73.29	89.33	107.57	113.14	118.14	124.12	128.30
100	67.33	70.06	74.22	77.93	82.36	99.33	118.50	124.34	129.56	135.81	140.17

Source: Reprinted with permission from Hines, W. W., and D. C. Montgomery (1980), *Probability and Statistics in Engineering and Management Science.* Second Edition, Wiley, New York.

[a] v = degrees of freedom.

TABLE C **Percentage Points of the *t* Distribution**

v \ α	.40	.25	.10	.05	.025	.01	.005	.0025	.001	.0005
1	.325	1.000	3.078	6.314	12.706	31.821	63.657	127.32	318.31	636.62
2	.289	.816	1.886	2.920	4.303	6.965	9.925	14.089	23.326	31.598
3	.277	.765	1.638	2.353	3.182	4.541	5.841	7.453	10.213	12.924
4	.271	.741	1.533	2.132	2.776	3.747	4.604	5.598	7.173	8.610
5	.267	.727	1.476	2.015	2.571	3.365	4.032	4.773	5.893	6.869
6	.265	.718	1.440	1.943	2.447	3.143	3.707	4.317	5.208	5.959
7	.263	.711	1.415	1.895	2.365	2.998	3.499	4.029	4.785	5.408
8	.262	.706	1.397	1.860	2.306	2.896	3.355	3.833	4.501	5.041
9	.261	.703	1.383	1.833	2.262	2.821	3.250	3.690	4.297	4.781
10	.260	.700	1.372	1.812	2.228	2.764	3.169	3.581	4.144	4.587
11	.260	.697	1.363	1.796	2.201	2.718	3.106	3.497	4.025	4.437
12	.259	.695	1.356	1.782	2.179	2.681	3.055	3.428	3.930	4.318
13	.259	.694	1.350	1.771	2.160	2.650	3.012	3.372	3.852	4.221
14	.258	.692	1.345	1.761	2.145	2.624	2.977	3.326	3.787	4.140
15	.258	.691	1.341	1.753	2.131	2.602	2.947	3.286	3.733	4.073
16	.258	.690	1.337	1.746	2.120	2.583	2.921	3.252	3.686	4.015
17	.257	.689	1.333	1.740	2.110	2.567	2.898	3.222	3.646	3.965
18	.257	.688	1.330	1.734	2.101	2.552	2.878	3.197	3.610	3.922
19	.257	.688	1.328	1.729	2.093	2.539	2.861	3.174	3.579	3.883
20	.257	.687	1.325	1.725	2.086	2.528	2.845	3.153	3.552	3.850
21	.257	.686	1.323	1.721	2.080	2.518	2.831	3.135	3.527	3.819
22	.256	.686	1.321	1.717	2.074	2.508	2.819	3.119	3.505	3.792
23	.256	.685	1.319	1.714	2.069	2.500	2.807	3.104	3.485	3.767
24	.256	.685	1.318	1.711	2.064	2.492	2.797	3.091	3.467	3.745
25	.256	.684	1.316	1.708	2.060	2.485	2.787	3.078	3.450	3.725
26	.256	.684	1.315	1.706	2.056	2.479	2.779	3.067	3.435	3.707
27	.256	.684	1.314	1.703	2.052	2.473	2.771	3.057	3.421	3.690
28	.256	.683	1.313	1.701	2.048	2.467	2.763	3.047	3.408	3.674
29	.256	.683	1.311	1.699	2.045	2.462	2.756	3.038	3.396	3.659
30	.256	.683	1.310	1.697	2.042	2.457	2.750	3.030	3.385	3.646
40	.255	.681	1.303	1.684	2.021	2.423	2.704	2.971	3.307	3.551
60	.254	.679	1.296	1.671	2.000	2.390	2.660	2.915	3.232	3.460
120	.254	.677	1.289	1.658	1.980	2.358	2.617	2.860	3.160	3.373
∞	.253	.674	1.282	1.645	1.960	2.326	2.576	2.807	3.090	3.291

Source: This table is adapted from *Biometrika Tables for Statisticians,* Vol. 1, 3rd edition, 1966, by permission of the Biometrika Trustees.

TABLE D Percentage Points of the F Distribution

$$F_{.25, v_1, v_2}$$

Degrees of freedom for the numerator (v_1)

v_2	1	2	3	4	5	6	7	8	9	10	12	15	20	24	30	40	60	120	∞
1	5.83	7.50	8.20	8.58	8.82	8.98	9.10	9.19	9.26	9.32	9.41	9.49	9.58	9.63	9.67	9.71	9.76	9.80	9.85
2	2.57	3.00	3.15	3.23	3.28	3.31	3.34	3.35	3.37	3.38	3.39	3.41	3.43	3.43	3.44	3.45	3.46	3.47	3.48
3	2.02	2.28	2.36	2.39	2.41	2.42	2.43	2.44	2.44	2.44	2.45	2.46	2.46	2.46	2.47	2.47	2.47	2.47	2.47
4	1.81	2.00	2.05	2.06	2.07	2.08	2.08	2.08	2.08	2.08	2.08	2.08	2.08	2.08	2.08	2.08	2.08	2.08	2.08
5	1.69	1.85	1.88	1.89	1.89	1.89	1.89	1.89	1.89	1.89	1.89	1.89	1.88	1.88	1.88	1.88	1.87	1.87	1.87
6	1.62	1.76	1.78	1.79	1.79	1.78	1.78	1.78	1.77	1.77	1.77	1.76	1.76	1.75	1.75	1.75	1.74	1.74	1.74
7	1.57	1.70	1.72	1.72	1.71	1.71	1.70	1.70	1.70	1.69	1.68	1.68	1.67	1.67	1.66	1.66	1.65	1.65	1.65
8	1.54	1.66	1.67	1.66	1.66	1.65	1.64	1.64	1.63	1.63	1.62	1.62	1.61	1.60	1.60	1.59	1.59	1.58	1.58
9	1.51	1.62	1.63	1.63	1.62	1.61	1.60	1.60	1.59	1.59	1.58	1.57	1.56	1.56	1.55	1.54	1.54	1.53	1.53
10	1.49	1.60	1.60	1.59	1.59	1.58	1.57	1.56	1.56	1.55	1.54	1.53	1.52	1.52	1.51	1.51	1.50	1.49	1.48
11	1.47	1.58	1.58	1.57	1.56	1.55	1.54	1.53	1.53	1.52	1.51	1.50	1.49	1.49	1.48	1.47	1.47	1.46	1.45
12	1.46	1.56	1.56	1.55	1.54	1.53	1.52	1.51	1.51	1.50	1.49	1.48	1.47	1.46	1.45	1.45	1.44	1.43	1.42
13	1.45	1.55	1.55	1.53	1.52	1.51	1.50	1.49	1.49	1.48	1.47	1.46	1.45	1.44	1.43	1.42	1.42	1.41	1.40
14	1.44	1.53	1.53	1.52	1.51	1.50	1.49	1.48	1.47	1.46	1.45	1.44	1.43	1.42	1.41	1.41	1.40	1.39	1.38
15	1.43	1.52	1.52	1.51	1.49	1.48	1.47	1.46	1.46	1.45	1.44	1.43	1.41	1.41	1.40	1.39	1.38	1.37	1.36
16	1.42	1.51	1.51	1.50	1.48	1.47	1.46	1.45	1.44	1.44	1.43	1.41	1.40	1.39	1.38	1.37	1.36	1.35	1.34
17	1.42	1.51	1.50	1.49	1.47	1.46	1.45	1.44	1.43	1.43	1.41	1.40	1.39	1.38	1.37	1.36	1.35	1.34	1.33
18	1.41	1.50	1.49	1.48	1.46	1.45	1.44	1.43	1.42	1.42	1.40	1.39	1.38	1.37	1.36	1.35	1.34	1.33	1.32
19	1.41	1.49	1.49	1.47	1.46	1.44	1.43	1.42	1.41	1.41	1.40	1.38	1.37	1.36	1.35	1.34	1.33	1.32	1.30
20	1.40	1.49	1.48	1.47	1.45	1.44	1.43	1.42	1.41	1.40	1.39	1.37	1.36	1.35	1.34	1.33	1.32	1.31	1.29
21	1.40	1.48	1.48	1.46	1.44	1.43	1.42	1.41	1.40	1.39	1.38	1.37	1.35	1.34	1.33	1.32	1.31	1.30	1.28
22	1.40	1.48	1.47	1.45	1.44	1.42	1.41	1.40	1.39	1.39	1.37	1.36	1.34	1.33	1.32	1.31	1.30	1.29	1.28
23	1.39	1.47	1.47	1.45	1.43	1.42	1.41	1.40	1.39	1.38	1.37	1.35	1.34	1.33	1.32	1.31	1.30	1.28	1.27
24	1.39	1.47	1.46	1.44	1.43	1.41	1.40	1.39	1.38	1.38	1.36	1.35	1.33	1.32	1.31	1.30	1.29	1.28	1.26
25	1.39	1.47	1.46	1.44	1.42	1.41	1.40	1.39	1.38	1.37	1.36	1.34	1.33	1.32	1.31	1.29	1.28	1.27	1.25
26	1.38	1.46	1.45	1.44	1.42	1.41	1.39	1.38	1.37	1.37	1.35	1.34	1.32	1.31	1.30	1.29	1.28	1.26	1.25
27	1.38	1.46	1.45	1.43	1.42	1.40	1.39	1.38	1.37	1.36	1.35	1.33	1.32	1.31	1.30	1.28	1.27	1.26	1.24
28	1.38	1.46	1.45	1.43	1.41	1.40	1.39	1.38	1.37	1.36	1.34	1.33	1.31	1.30	1.29	1.28	1.27	1.25	1.24
29	1.38	1.45	1.45	1.43	1.41	1.40	1.38	1.37	1.36	1.35	1.34	1.32	1.31	1.30	1.29	1.27	1.26	1.25	1.23
30	1.38	1.45	1.44	1.42	1.41	1.39	1.38	1.37	1.36	1.35	1.34	1.32	1.30	1.29	1.28	1.27	1.26	1.24	1.23
40	1.36	1.44	1.42	1.40	1.39	1.37	1.36	1.35	1.34	1.33	1.31	1.30	1.28	1.26	1.25	1.24	1.22	1.21	1.19
60	1.35	1.42	1.41	1.38	1.37	1.35	1.33	1.32	1.31	1.30	1.29	1.27	1.25	1.24	1.22	1.21	1.19	1.17	1.15
120	1.34	1.40	1.39	1.37	1.35	1.33	1.31	1.30	1.29	1.28	1.26	1.24	1.22	1.21	1.19	1.18	1.16	1.13	1.10
∞	1.32	1.39	1.37	1.35	1.33	1.31	1.29	1.28	1.27	1.25	1.24	1.22	1.19	1.18	1.16	1.14	1.12	1.08	1.00

Degrees of freedom for the denominator (v_2)

Source: Adapted with permission from Pearson, E. S., and H. O. Hartley, Biometrika Tables for Statisticians, Vol. 1, 3rd edition, Cambridge University Press, Cambridge, 1966.

TABLE D Percentage Points of the F Distribution *(continued)*

$$F_{.10, v_1, v_2}$$

Degrees of freedom for the numerator (v_1)

v_2 \ v_1	1	2	3	4	5	6	7	8	9	10	12	15	20	24	30	40	60	120	∞
1	39.86	49.50	53.59	55.83	57.24	58.20	58.91	59.44	59.86	60.19	60.71	61.22	61.74	62.00	62.26	62.53	62.79	63.06	63.33
2	8.53	9.00	9.16	9.24	9.29	9.33	9.35	9.37	9.38	9.39	9.41	9.42	9.44	9.45	9.46	9.47	9.47	9.48	9.49
3	5.54	5.46	5.39	5.34	5.31	5.28	5.27	5.25	5.24	5.23	5.22	5.20	5.18	5.18	5.17	5.16	5.15	5.14	5.13
4	4.54	4.32	4.19	4.11	4.05	4.01	3.98	3.95	3.94	3.92	3.90	3.87	3.84	3.83	3.82	3.80	3.79	3.78	3.76
5	4.06	3.78	3.62	3.52	3.45	3.40	3.37	3.34	3.32	3.30	3.27	3.24	3.21	3.19	3.17	3.16	3.14	3.12	3.10
6	3.78	3.46	3.29	3.18	3.11	3.05	3.01	2.98	2.96	2.94	2.90	2.87	2.84	2.82	2.80	2.78	2.76	2.74	2.72
7	3.59	3.26	3.07	2.96	2.88	2.83	2.78	2.75	2.72	2.70	2.67	2.63	2.59	2.58	2.56	2.54	2.51	2.49	2.47
8	3.46	3.11	2.92	2.81	2.73	2.67	2.62	2.59	2.56	2.54	2.50	2.46	2.42	2.40	2.38	2.36	2.34	2.32	2.29
9	3.36	3.01	2.81	2.69	2.61	2.55	2.51	2.47	2.44	2.42	2.38	2.34	2.30	2.28	2.25	2.23	2.21	2.18	2.16
10	3.29	2.92	2.73	2.61	2.52	2.46	2.41	2.38	2.35	2.32	2.28	2.24	2.20	2.18	2.16	2.13	2.11	2.08	2.06
11	3.23	2.86	2.66	2.54	2.45	2.39	2.34	2.30	2.27	2.25	2.21	2.17	2.12	2.10	2.08	2.05	2.03	2.00	1.97
12	3.18	2.81	2.61	2.48	2.39	2.33	2.28	2.24	2.21	2.19	2.15	2.10	2.06	2.04	2.01	1.99	1.96	1.93	1.90
13	3.14	2.76	2.56	2.43	2.35	2.28	2.23	2.20	2.16	2.14	2.10	2.05	2.01	1.98	1.96	1.93	1.90	1.88	1.85
14	3.10	2.73	2.52	2.39	2.31	2.24	2.19	2.15	2.12	2.10	2.05	2.01	1.96	1.94	1.91	1.89	1.86	1.83	1.80
15	3.07	2.70	2.49	2.36	2.27	2.21	2.16	2.12	2.09	2.06	2.02	1.97	1.92	1.90	1.87	1.85	1.82	1.79	1.76
16	3.05	2.67	2.46	2.33	2.24	2.18	2.13	2.09	2.06	2.03	1.99	1.94	1.89	1.87	1.84	1.81	1.78	1.75	1.72
17	3.03	2.64	2.44	2.31	2.22	2.15	2.10	2.06	2.03	2.00	1.96	1.91	1.86	1.84	1.81	1.78	1.75	1.72	1.69
18	3.01	2.62	2.42	2.29	2.20	2.13	2.08	2.04	2.00	1.98	1.93	1.89	1.84	1.81	1.78	1.75	1.72	1.69	1.66
19	2.99	2.61	2.40	2.27	2.18	2.11	2.06	2.02	1.98	1.96	1.91	1.86	1.81	1.79	1.76	1.73	1.70	1.67	1.63
20	2.97	2.59	2.38	2.25	2.16	2.09	2.04	2.00	1.96	1.94	1.89	1.84	1.79	1.77	1.74	1.71	1.68	1.64	1.61
21	2.96	2.57	2.36	2.23	2.14	2.08	2.02	1.98	1.95	1.92	1.87	1.83	1.78	1.75	1.72	1.69	1.66	1.62	1.59
22	2.95	2.56	2.35	2.22	2.13	2.06	2.01	1.97	1.93	1.90	1.86	1.81	1.76	1.73	1.70	1.67	1.64	1.60	1.57
23	2.94	2.55	2.34	2.21	2.11	2.05	1.99	1.95	1.92	1.89	1.84	1.80	1.74	1.72	1.69	1.66	1.62	1.59	1.55
24	2.93	2.54	2.33	2.19	2.10	2.04	1.98	1.94	1.91	1.88	1.83	1.78	1.73	1.70	1.67	1.64	1.61	1.57	1.53
25	2.92	2.53	2.32	2.18	2.09	2.02	1.97	1.93	1.89	1.87	1.82	1.77	1.72	1.69	1.66	1.63	1.59	1.56	1.52
26	2.91	2.52	2.31	2.17	2.08	2.01	1.96	1.92	1.88	1.86	1.81	1.76	1.71	1.68	1.65	1.61	1.58	1.54	1.50
27	2.90	2.51	2.30	2.17	2.07	2.00	1.95	1.91	1.87	1.85	1.80	1.75	1.70	1.67	1.64	1.60	1.57	1.53	1.49
28	2.89	2.50	2.29	2.16	2.06	2.00	1.94	1.90	1.87	1.84	1.79	1.74	1.69	1.66	1.63	1.59	1.56	1.52	1.48
29	2.89	2.50	2.28	2.15	2.06	1.99	1.93	1.89	1.86	1.83	1.78	1.73	1.68	1.65	1.62	1.58	1.55	1.51	1.47
30	2.88	2.49	2.28	2.14	2.03	1.98	1.93	1.88	1.85	1.82	1.77	1.72	1.67	1.64	1.61	1.57	1.54	1.50	1.46
40	2.84	2.44	2.23	2.09	2.00	1.93	1.87	1.83	1.79	1.76	1.71	1.66	1.61	1.57	1.54	1.51	1.47	1.42	1.38
60	2.79	2.39	2.18	2.04	1.95	1.87	1.82	1.77	1.74	1.71	1.66	1.60	1.54	1.51	1.48	1.44	1.40	1.35	1.29
120	2.75	2.35	2.13	1.99	1.90	1.82	1.77	1.72	1.68	1.65	1.60	1.55	1.48	1.45	1.41	1.37	1.32	1.26	1.19
∞	2.71	2.30	2.08	1.94	1.85	1.77	1.72	1.67	1.63	1.60	1.55	1.49	1.42	1.38	1.34	1.30	1.24	1.17	1.00

Degrees of freedom for the denominator (v_2)

TABLE D Percentage Points of the F Distribution *(continued)*

$$F_{.05, v_1, v_2}$$

Degrees of freedom for the numerator (v_1)

v_2	1	2	3	4	5	6	7	8	9	10	12	15	20	24	30	40	60	120	∞
1	161.4	199.5	215.7	224.6	230.2	234.0	236.8	238.9	240.5	241.9	243.9	245.9	248.0	249.1	250.1	251.1	252.2	253.3	254.3
2	18.51	19.00	19.16	19.25	19.30	19.33	19.35	19.37	19.38	19.40	19.41	19.43	19.45	19.45	19.46	19.47	19.48	19.49	19.50
3	10.13	9.55	9.28	9.12	9.01	8.94	8.89	8.85	8.81	8.79	8.74	8.70	8.66	8.64	8.62	8.59	8.57	8.55	8.53
4	7.71	6.94	6.59	6.39	6.26	6.16	6.09	6.04	6.00	5.96	5.91	5.86	5.80	5.77	5.75	5.72	5.69	5.66	5.63
5	6.61	5.79	5.41	5.19	5.05	4.95	4.88	4.82	4.77	4.74	4.68	4.62	4.56	4.53	4.50	4.46	4.43	4.40	4.36
6	5.99	5.14	4.76	4.53	4.39	4.28	4.21	4.15	4.10	4.06	4.00	3.94	3.87	3.84	3.81	3.77	3.74	3.70	3.67
7	5.59	4.74	4.35	4.12	3.97	3.87	3.79	3.73	3.68	3.64	3.57	3.51	3.44	3.41	3.38	3.34	3.30	3.27	3.23
8	5.32	4.46	4.07	3.84	3.69	3.58	3.50	3.44	3.39	3.35	3.28	3.22	3.15	3.12	3.08	3.04	3.01	2.97	2.93
9	5.12	4.26	3.86	3.63	3.48	3.37	3.29	3.23	3.18	3.14	3.07	3.01	2.94	2.90	2.86	2.83	2.79	2.75	2.71
10	4.96	4.10	3.71	3.48	3.33	3.22	3.14	3.07	3.02	2.98	2.91	2.85	2.77	2.74	2.70	2.66	2.62	2.58	2.54
11	4.84	3.98	3.59	3.36	3.20	3.09	3.01	2.95	2.90	2.85	2.79	2.72	2.65	2.61	2.57	2.53	2.49	2.45	2.40
12	4.75	3.89	3.49	3.26	3.11	3.00	2.91	2.85	2.80	2.75	2.69	2.62	2.54	2.51	2.47	2.43	2.38	2.34	2.30
13	4.67	3.81	3.41	3.18	3.03	2.92	2.83	2.77	2.71	2.67	2.60	2.53	2.46	2.42	2.38	2.34	2.30	2.25	2.21
14	4.60	3.74	3.34	3.11	2.96	2.85	2.76	2.70	2.65	2.60	2.53	2.46	2.39	2.35	2.31	2.27	2.22	2.18	2.13
15	4.54	3.68	3.29	3.06	2.90	2.79	2.71	2.64	2.59	2.54	2.48	2.40	2.33	2.29	2.25	2.20	2.16	2.11	2.07
16	4.49	3.63	3.24	3.01	2.85	2.74	2.66	2.59	2.54	2.49	2.42	2.35	2.28	2.24	2.19	2.15	2.11	2.06	2.01
17	4.45	3.59	3.20	2.96	2.81	2.70	2.61	2.55	2.49	2.45	2.38	2.31	2.23	2.19	2.15	2.10	2.06	2.01	1.96
18	4.41	3.55	3.16	2.93	2.77	2.66	2.58	2.51	2.46	2.41	2.34	2.27	2.19	2.15	2.11	2.06	2.02	1.97	1.92
19	4.38	3.52	3.13	2.90	2.74	2.63	2.54	2.48	2.42	2.38	2.31	2.23	2.16	2.11	2.07	2.03	1.98	1.93	1.88
20	4.35	3.49	3.10	2.87	2.71	2.60	2.51	2.45	2.39	2.35	2.28	2.20	2.12	2.08	2.04	1.99	1.95	1.90	1.84
21	4.32	3.47	3.07	2.84	2.68	2.57	2.49	2.42	2.37	2.32	2.25	2.18	2.10	2.05	2.01	1.96	1.92	1.87	1.81
22	4.30	3.44	3.05	2.82	2.66	2.55	2.46	2.40	2.34	2.30	2.23	2.15	2.07	2.03	1.98	1.94	1.89	1.84	1.78
23	4.28	3.42	3.03	2.80	2.64	2.53	2.44	2.37	2.32	2.27	2.20	2.13	2.05	2.01	1.96	1.91	1.86	1.81	1.76
24	4.26	3.40	3.01	2.78	2.62	2.51	2.42	2.36	2.30	2.25	2.18	2.11	2.03	1.98	1.94	1.89	1.84	1.79	1.73
25	4.24	3.39	2.99	2.76	2.60	2.49	2.40	2.34	2.28	2.24	2.16	2.09	2.01	1.96	1.92	1.87	1.82	1.77	1.71
26	4.23	3.37	2.98	2.74	2.59	2.47	2.39	2.32	2.27	2.22	2.15	2.07	1.99	1.95	1.90	1.85	1.80	1.75	1.69
27	4.21	3.35	2.96	2.73	2.57	2.46	2.37	2.31	2.25	2.20	2.13	2.06	1.97	1.93	1.88	1.84	1.79	1.73	1.67
28	4.20	3.34	2.95	2.71	2.56	2.45	2.36	2.29	2.24	2.19	2.12	2.04	1.96	1.91	1.87	1.82	1.77	1.71	1.65
29	4.18	3.33	2.93	2.70	2.55	2.43	2.35	2.28	2.22	2.18	2.10	2.03	1.94	1.90	1.85	1.81	1.75	1.70	1.64
30	4.17	3.32	2.92	2.69	2.53	2.42	2.33	2.27	2.21	2.16	2.09	2.01	1.93	1.89	1.84	1.79	1.74	1.68	1.62
40	4.08	3.23	2.84	2.61	2.45	2.34	2.25	2.18	2.12	2.08	2.00	1.92	1.84	1.79	1.74	1.69	1.64	1.58	1.51
60	4.00	3.15	2.76	2.53	2.37	2.25	2.17	2.10	2.04	1.99	1.92	1.84	1.75	1.70	1.65	1.59	1.53	1.47	1.39
120	3.92	3.07	2.68	2.45	2.29	2.17	2.09	2.02	1.96	1.91	1.83	1.75	1.66	1.61	1.55	1.50	1.43	1.35	1.25
∞	3.84	3.00	2.60	2.37	2.21	2.10	2.01	1.94	1.88	1.83	1.75	1.67	1.57	1.52	1.46	1.39	1.32	1.22	1.00

Degrees of freedom for the denominator (v_2)

TABLE D Percentage Points of the F Distribution (continued)

$$F_{.025, v_1, v_2}$$

						Degrees of freedom for the numerator (v_1)												
v_2	1	2	3	4	5	6	7	8	9	10	12	15	20	24	30	40	60	120	∞
1	647.8	799.5	864.2	899.6	921.8	937.1	948.2	956.7	963.3	968.6	976.7	984.9	993.1	997.2	1001	1006	1010	1014	1018
2	38.51	39.00	39.17	39.25	39.30	39.33	39.36	39.37	39.39	39.40	39.41	39.43	39.45	39.46	39.46	39.47	39.48	39.49	39.50
3	17.44	16.04	15.44	15.10	14.88	14.73	14.62	14.54	14.47	14.42	14.34	14.25	14.17	14.12	14.08	14.04	13.99	13.95	13.90
4	12.22	10.65	9.98	9.60	9.36	9.20	9.07	8.98	8.90	8.84	8.75	8.66	8.56	8.51	8.46	8.41	8.36	8.31	8.26
5	10.01	8.43	7.76	7.39	7.15	6.98	6.85	6.76	6.68	6.62	6.52	6.43	6.33	6.28	6.23	6.18	6.12	6.07	6.02
6	8.81	7.26	6.60	6.23	5.99	5.82	5.70	5.60	5.52	5.46	5.37	5.27	5.17	5.12	5.07	5.01	4.96	4.90	4.85
7	8.07	6.54	5.89	5.52	5.29	5.12	4.99	4.90	4.82	4.76	4.67	4.57	4.47	4.42	4.36	4.31	4.25	4.20	4.14
8	7.57	6.06	5.42	5.05	4.82	4.65	4.53	4.43	4.36	4.30	4.20	4.10	4.00	3.95	3.89	3.84	3.78	3.73	3.67
9	7.21	5.71	5.08	4.72	4.48	4.32	4.20	4.10	4.03	3.96	3.87	3.77	3.67	3.61	3.56	3.51	3.45	3.39	3.33
10	6.94	5.46	4.83	4.47	4.24	4.07	3.95	3.85	3.78	3.72	3.62	3.52	3.42	3.37	3.31	3.26	3.20	3.14	3.08
11	6.72	5.26	4.63	4.28	4.04	3.88	3.76	3.66	3.59	3.53	3.43	3.33	3.23	3.17	3.12	3.06	3.00	2.94	2.88
12	6.55	5.10	4.47	4.12	3.89	3.73	3.61	3.51	3.44	3.37	3.28	3.18	3.07	3.02	2.96	2.91	2.85	2.79	2.72
13	6.41	4.97	4.35	4.00	3.77	3.60	3.48	3.39	3.31	3.25	3.15	3.05	2.95	2.89	2.84	2.78	2.72	2.66	2.60
14	6.30	4.86	4.24	3.89	3.66	3.50	3.38	3.29	3.21	3.15	3.05	2.95	2.84	2.79	2.73	2.67	2.61	2.55	2.49
15	6.20	4.77	4.15	3.80	3.58	3.41	3.29	3.20	3.12	3.06	2.96	2.86	2.76	2.70	2.64	2.59	2.52	2.46	2.40
16	6.12	4.69	4.08	3.73	3.50	3.34	3.22	3.12	3.05	2.99	2.89	2.79	2.68	2.63	2.57	2.51	2.45	2.38	2.32
17	6.04	4.62	4.01	3.66	3.44	3.28	3.16	3.06	2.98	2.92	2.82	2.72	2.62	2.56	2.50	2.44	2.38	2.32	2.25
18	5.98	4.56	3.95	3.61	3.38	3.22	3.10	3.01	2.93	2.87	2.77	2.67	2.56	2.50	2.44	2.38	2.32	2.26	2.19
19	5.92	4.51	3.90	3.56	3.33	3.17	3.05	2.96	2.88	2.82	2.72	2.62	2.51	2.45	2.39	2.33	2.27	2.20	2.13
20	5.87	4.46	3.86	3.51	3.29	3.13	3.01	2.91	2.84	2.77	2.68	2.57	2.46	2.41	2.35	2.29	2.22	2.16	2.09
21	5.83	4.42	3.82	3.48	3.25	3.09	2.97	2.87	2.80	2.73	2.64	2.53	2.42	2.37	2.31	2.25	2.18	2.11	2.04
22	5.79	4.38	3.78	3.44	3.22	3.05	2.93	2.84	2.76	2.70	2.60	2.50	2.39	2.33	2.27	2.21	2.14	2.08	2.00
23	5.75	4.35	3.75	3.41	3.18	3.02	2.90	2.81	2.73	2.67	2.57	2.47	2.36	2.30	2.24	2.18	2.11	2.04	1.97
24	5.72	4.32	3.72	3.38	3.15	2.99	2.87	2.78	2.70	2.64	2.54	2.44	2.33	2.27	2.21	2.15	2.08	2.01	1.94
25	5.69	4.29	3.69	3.35	3.13	2.97	2.85	2.75	2.68	2.61	2.51	2.41	2.30	2.24	2.18	2.12	2.05	1.98	1.91
26	5.66	4.27	3.67	3.33	3.10	2.94	2.82	2.73	2.65	2.59	2.49	2.39	2.28	2.22	2.16	2.09	2.03	1.95	1.88
27	5.63	4.24	3.65	3.31	3.08	2.92	2.80	2.71	2.63	2.57	2.47	2.36	2.25	2.19	2.13	2.07	2.00	1.93	1.85
28	5.61	4.22	3.63	3.29	3.06	2.90	2.78	2.69	2.61	2.55	2.45	2.34	2.23	2.17	2.11	2.05	1.98	1.91	1.83
29	5.59	4.20	3.61	3.27	3.04	2.88	2.76	2.67	2.59	2.53	2.43	2.32	2.21	2.15	2.09	2.03	1.96	1.89	1.81
30	5.57	4.18	3.59	3.25	3.03	2.87	2.75	2.65	2.57	2.51	2.41	2.31	2.20	2.14	2.07	2.01	1.94	1.87	1.79
40	5.42	4.05	3.46	3.13	2.90	2.74	2.62	2.53	2.45	2.39	2.29	2.18	2.07	2.01	1.94	1.88	1.80	1.72	1.64
60	5.29	3.93	3.34	3.01	2.79	2.63	2.51	2.41	2.33	2.27	2.17	2.06	1.94	1.88	1.82	1.74	1.67	1.58	1.48
120	5.15	3.80	3.23	2.89	2.67	2.52	2.39	2.30	2.22	2.16	2.05	1.94	1.82	1.76	1.69	1.61	1.53	1.43	1.31
∞	5.02	3.69	3.12	2.79	2.57	2.41	2.29	2.19	2.11	2.05	1.94	1.83	1.71	1.64	1.57	1.48	1.39	1.27	1.00

Degrees of freedom for the denominator (v_2)

TABLE D Percentage Points of the F Distribution (*continued*)

$F_{.01, v_1, v_2}$

v_2 \ v_1	1	2	3	4	5	6	7	8	9	10	12	15	20	24	30	40	60	120	∞
1	4052	4999.5	5403	5625	5764	5859	5928	5982	6022	6056	6106	6157	6209	6235	6261	6287	6313	6339	6366
2	98.50	99.00	99.17	99.25	99.30	99.33	99.36	99.37	99.39	99.40	99.42	99.43	99.45	99.46	99.47	99.47	99.48	99.49	99.50
3	34.12	30.82	29.46	28.71	28.24	27.91	27.67	27.49	27.35	27.23	27.05	26.87	26.69	26.60	26.50	26.41	26.32	26.22	26.13
4	21.20	18.00	16.69	15.98	15.52	15.21	14.98	14.80	14.66	14.55	14.37	14.20	14.02	13.93	13.84	13.75	13.65	13.56	13.46
5	16.26	13.27	12.06	11.39	10.97	10.67	10.46	10.29	10.16	10.05	9.89	9.72	9.55	9.47	9.38	9.29	9.20	9.11	9.02
6	13.75	10.92	9.78	9.15	8.75	8.47	8.26	8.10	7.98	7.87	7.72	7.56	7.40	7.31	7.23	7.14	7.06	6.97	6.88
7	12.25	9.55	8.45	7.85	7.46	7.19	6.99	6.84	6.72	6.62	6.47	6.31	6.16	6.07	5.99	5.91	5.82	5.74	5.65
8	11.26	8.65	7.59	7.01	6.63	6.37	6.18	6.03	5.91	5.81	5.67	5.52	5.36	5.28	5.20	5.12	5.03	4.95	4.86
9	10.56	8.02	6.99	6.42	6.06	5.80	5.61	5.47	5.35	5.26	5.11	4.96	4.81	4.73	4.65	4.57	4.48	4.40	4.31
10	10.04	7.56	6.55	5.99	5.64	5.39	5.20	5.06	4.94	4.85	4.71	4.56	4.41	4.33	4.25	4.17	4.08	4.00	3.91
11	9.65	7.21	6.22	5.67	5.32	5.07	4.89	4.74	4.63	4.54	4.40	4.25	4.10	4.02	3.94	3.86	3.78	3.69	3.60
12	9.33	6.93	5.95	5.41	5.06	4.82	4.64	4.50	4.39	4.30	4.16	4.01	3.86	3.78	3.70	3.62	3.54	3.45	3.36
13	9.07	6.70	5.74	5.21	4.86	4.62	4.44	4.30	4.19	4.10	3.96	3.82	3.66	3.59	3.51	3.43	3.34	3.25	3.17
14	8.86	6.51	5.56	5.04	4.69	4.46	4.28	4.14	4.03	3.94	3.80	3.66	3.51	3.43	3.35	3.27	3.18	3.09	3.00
15	8.68	6.36	5.42	4.89	4.56	4.32	4.14	4.00	3.89	3.80	3.67	3.52	3.37	3.29	3.21	3.13	3.05	2.96	2.87
16	8.53	6.23	5.29	4.77	4.44	4.20	4.03	3.89	3.78	3.69	3.55	3.41	3.26	3.18	3.10	3.02	2.93	2.84	2.75
17	8.40	6.11	5.18	4.67	4.34	4.10	3.93	3.79	3.68	3.59	3.46	3.31	3.16	3.08	3.00	2.92	2.83	2.75	2.65
18	8.29	6.01	5.09	4.58	4.25	4.01	3.84	3.71	3.60	3.51	3.37	3.23	3.08	3.00	2.92	2.84	2.75	2.66	2.57
19	8.18	5.93	5.01	4.50	4.17	3.94	3.77	3.63	3.52	3.43	3.30	3.15	3.00	2.92	2.84	2.76	2.67	2.58	2.49
20	8.10	5.85	4.94	4.43	4.10	3.87	3.70	3.56	3.46	3.37	3.23	3.09	2.94	2.86	2.78	2.69	2.61	2.52	2.42
21	8.02	5.78	4.87	4.37	4.04	3.81	3.64	3.51	3.40	3.31	3.17	3.03	2.88	2.80	2.72	2.64	2.55	2.46	2.36
22	7.95	5.72	4.82	4.31	3.99	3.76	3.59	3.45	3.35	3.26	3.12	2.98	2.83	2.75	2.67	2.58	2.50	2.40	2.31
23	7.88	5.66	4.76	4.26	3.94	3.71	3.54	3.41	3.30	3.21	3.07	2.93	2.78	2.70	2.62	2.54	2.45	2.35	2.26
24	7.82	5.61	4.72	4.22	3.90	3.67	3.50	3.36	3.26	3.17	3.03	2.89	2.74	2.66	2.58	2.49	2.40	2.31	2.21
25	7.77	5.57	4.68	4.18	3.85	3.63	3.46	3.32	3.22	3.13	2.99	2.85	2.70	2.62	2.54	2.45	2.36	2.27	2.17
26	7.72	5.53	4.64	4.14	3.82	3.59	3.42	3.29	3.18	3.09	2.96	2.81	2.66	2.58	2.50	2.42	2.33	2.23	2.13
27	7.68	5.49	4.60	4.11	3.78	3.56	3.39	3.26	3.15	3.06	2.93	2.78	2.63	2.55	2.47	2.38	2.29	2.20	2.10
28	7.64	5.45	4.57	4.07	3.75	3.53	3.36	3.23	3.12	3.03	2.90	2.75	2.60	2.52	2.44	2.35	2.26	2.17	2.06
29	7.60	5.42	4.54	4.04	3.73	3.50	3.33	3.20	3.09	3.00	2.87	2.73	2.57	2.49	2.41	2.33	2.23	2.14	2.03
30	7.56	5.39	4.51	4.02	3.70	3.47	3.30	3.17	3.07	2.98	2.84	2.70	2.55	2.47	2.39	2.30	2.21	2.11	2.01
40	7.31	5.18	4.31	3.83	3.51	3.29	3.12	2.99	2.89	2.80	2.66	2.52	2.37	2.29	2.20	2.11	2.02	1.92	1.80
60	7.08	4.98	4.13	3.65	3.34	3.12	2.95	2.82	2.72	2.63	2.50	2.35	2.20	2.12	2.03	1.94	1.84	1.73	1.60
120	6.85	4.79	3.95	3.48	3.17	2.96	2.79	2.66	2.56	2.47	2.34	2.19	2.03	1.95	1.86	1.76	1.66	1.53	1.38
∞	6.63	4.61	3.78	3.32	3.02	2.80	2.64	2.51	2.41	2.32	2.18	2.04	1.88	1.79	1.70	1.59	1.47	1.32	1.00

Degrees of freedom for the numerator (v_1)

Degrees of freedom for the denominator (v_2)

TABLE E Cumulative Binomial Distribution

					θ				
n	c	0.01	0.02	0.03	0.05	0.07	0.10	0.15	0.20
5	0	.951	.904	.859	.774	.696	.590	.444	.328
	1	.999	.996	.992	.977	.958	.919	.835	.737
	2	1.000	1.000	1.000	.999	.997	.991	.973	.942
	3	1.000	1.000	I.000	1.000	1.000	1.000	.998	.993
	4	1.000	1.000	1.000	1.000	1.000	1.000	1.000	1.000
10	0	.904	.817	.737	.599	.484	.349	.197	.107
	1	.996	.984	.965	.914	.848	.736	.544	.376
	2	1.000	.999	.997	.988	.972	.930	.820	.678
	3	1.000	1.000	1.000	.999	.996	.987	.950	.879
	4	1.000	1.000	1.000	1.000	1.000	.998	.990	.967
	5	1.000	1.000	1.000	1.000	1.000	1.000	.999	.994
	6	1.000	1.000	1.000	1.000	1.000	1.000	1.000	.999
	7	1.000	1.000	1.000	1.000	1.000	1.000	1.000	1.000
15	0	.860	.739	.633	.463	.337	.206	.087	.035
	1	.990	.965	.927	.829	.717	.549	.319	.167
	2	1.000	.997	.991	.964	.917	.816	.604	.398
	3	1.000	1.000	.999	.995	.982	.944	.823	.648
	4	1.000	1.000	1.000	.999	.997	.987	.938	.836
	5	1.000	1.000	1.000	1.000	1.000	.998	.983	.939
	6	1.000	1.000	1.000	1.000	1.000	1.000	.996	.982
	7	1.000	1.000	1.000	1.000	1.000	1.000	.999	.996
	8	1.000	1.000	1.000	1.000	1.000	1.000	1.000	.999
	9	1.000	1.000	1.000	1.000	1.000	1.000	1.000	1.000
20	0	.817	.668	.544	.358	.234	.122	.039	.012
	1	.983	.940	.880	.736	.587	.392	.176	.069
	2	.999	.993	.979	.925	.839	.677	.405	.206
	3	1.000	.999	.997	.984	.953	.867	.648	.411
	4	1.000	1.000	1.000	.997	.989	.957	.830	.630
	5	1.000	1.000	1.000	1.000	.998	.989	.933	.804
	6	1.000	1.000	1.000	1.000	1.000	.998	.978	.913
	7	1.000	1.000	1.000	1.000	1.000	1.000	.994	.968
	8	1.000	1.000	1.000	1.000	1.000	1.000	.999	.990
	9	1.000	1.000	1.000	1.000	1.000	1.000	1.000	.997
	10	1.000	1.000	1.000	1.000	1.000	1.000	1.000	.999
	11	1.000	1.000	1.000	1.000	1.000	1.000	1.000	1.000

n	c	0.01	0.02	0.03	0.05	0.07	0.10	0.15	0.20
25	0	.778	.603	.467	.277	.163	.072	.017	.004
	1	.974	.911	.828	.642	.470	.271	.093	.027
	2	.998	.987	.962	.873	.747	.537	.254	.098
	3	1.000	.999	.994	.966	.906	.764	.471	.234
	4	1.000	1.000	.999	.993	.973	.902	.682	.421
	5	1.000	1.000	1.000	.999	.993	.967	.839	.617
	6	1.000	1.000	1.000	1.000	.999	.991	.931	.780
	7	1.000	1.000	1.000	1.000	1.000	.998	.975	.891
	8	1.000	1.000	1.000	1.000	1.000	1.000	.992	.953
	9	1.000	1.000	1.000	1.000	1.000	1.000	.998	.983
	10	1.000	1.000	1.000	1.000	1.000	1.000	1.000	.994
	11	1.000	1.000	1.000	1.000	1.000	1.000	1.000	.999
	12	1.000	1.000	1.000	1.000	1.000	1.000	1.000	1.000
30	0	.740	.545	.401	.215	.113	.042	.008	.001
	1	.964	.879	.773	.554	.369	.184	.048	.011
	2	.997	.978	.940	.812	.649	.411	.151	.044
	3	1.000	.997	.988	.939	.845	.647	.322	.123
	4	1.000	1.000	.998	.984	.945	.825	.525	.255
	5	1.000	1.000	1.000	.997	.984	.927	.711	.428
	6	1.000	1.000	1.000	.999	.996	.974	.847	.607
	7	1.000	1.000	1.000	1.000	.999	.992	.930	.761
	8	1.000	1.000	1.000	1.000	1.000	.998	.972	.871
	9	1.000	1.000	1.000	1.000	1.000	1.000	.990	.939
	10	1.000	1.000	1.000	1.000	1.000	1.000	.997	.974
	11	1.000	1.000	1.000	1.000	1.000	1.000	.999	.991
	12	1.000	1.000	1.000	1.000	1.000	1.000	1.000	.997
	13	1.000	1.000	1.000	1.000	1.000	1.000	1.000	.999
	14	1.000	1.000	1.000	1.000	1.000	1.000	1.000	1.000
50	0	.605	.364	.218	.077	.027	.005	.000	.000
	1	.911	.736	.555	.279	.126	.034	.003	.000
	2	.986	.922	.811	.541	.311	.112	.014	.001
	3	.998	.982	.937	.760	.533	.250	.046	.006
	4	1.000	.997	.983	.896	.729	.431	.112	.019
	5	1.000	1.000	.996	.962	.865	.616	.219	.048
	6	1.000	1.000	.999	.988	.942	.770	.361	.103
	7	1.000	1.000	1.000	.997	.978	.878	.519	.190
	8	1.000	1.000	1.000	.999	.993	.942	.668	.307
	9	1.000	1.000	1.000	1.000	.998	.975	.791	.444
	10	1.000	1.000	1.000	1.000	.999	.991	.880	.584
	11	1.000	1.000	1.000	1.000	1.000	.997	.937	.711
	12	1.000	1.000	1.000	1.000	1.000	.999	.970	.814
	13	1.000	1.000	1.000	1.000	1.000	1.000	.987	.889
	14	1.000	1.000	1.000	1.000	1.000	1.000	.995	.939
	15	1.000	1.000	1.000	1.000	1.000	1.000	.998	.969
	16	1.000	1.000	1.000	1.000	1.000	1.000	.999	.986
	17	1.000	1.000	1.000	1.000	1.000	1.000	1.000	.994
	18	1.000	1.000	1.000	1.000	1.000	1.000	1.000	.998
	19	1.000	1.000	1.000	1.000	1.000	1.000	1.000	.999
	20	1.000	1.000	1.000	1.000	1.000	1.000	1.000	1.000

TABLE F   Summation of Terms of the Poisson Distribution

1,000 × probability of c or less occurrences of event that has average number of occurrences equal to c or np

λ or np \ c	0	1	2	3	4	5	6	7	8	9
0.02	980	1,000								
0.04	961	999	1,000							
0.06	942	998	1,000							
0.08	923	997	1,000							
0.10	905	995	1,000							
0.15	861	990	999	1,000						
0.20	819	982	999	1,000						
0.25	779	974	998	1,000						
0.30	741	963	996	1,000						
0.35	705	951	994	1,000						
0.40	670	938	992	999	1,000					
0.45	638	925	989	999	1,000					
0.50	607	910	986	998	1,000					
0.55	577	894	982	998	1,000					
0.60	549	878	977	997	1,000					
0.65	522	861	972	996	999	1,000				
0.70	497	844	966	994	999	1,000				
0.75	472	827	959	993	999	1,000				
0.80	449	809	953	991	999	1,000				
0.85	427	791	945	989	998	1,000				
0.90	407	772	937	987	998	1,000				
0.95	387	754	929	984	997	1,000				
1.00	368	736	920	981	996	999	1,000			
1.1	333	699	900	974	995	999	1,000			
1.2	301	663	879	966	992	998	1,000			
1.3	273	627	857	957	989	998	1,000			
1.4	247	592	833	946	986	997	999	1,000		
1.5	223	558	809	934	981	996	999	1,000		
1.6	202	525	783	921	976	994	999	1,000		
1.7	183	493	757	907	970	992	998	1,000		
1.8	165	463	731	891	964	990	997	999	1,000	
1.9	150	434	704	875	956	987	997	999	1,000	
2.0	135	406	677	857	947	983	995	999	1,000	

Source: Reprinted with permission from Grant, E. L., and R. S. Leavenworth (1980), *Statistical Quality Control,* Fifth Edition, McGraw-Hill, New York.

TABLE F   **Summation of Terms of the Poisson Distribution**   (*continued*)

λ or *np* \ *c*	0	1	2	3	4	5	6	7	8	9
2.2	111	355	623	819	928	975	993	998	1,000	
2.4	091	308	570	779	904	964	988	997	999	1,000
2.6	074	267	518	736	877	951	983	995	999	1,000
2.8	061	231	469	692	848	935	976	992	998	999
3.0	050	199	423	647	815	916	966	988	996	999
3.2	041	171	380	603	781	895	955	983	994	998
3.4	033	147	340	558	744	871	942	977	992	997
3.6	027	126	303	515	706	844	927	969	988	996
3.8	022	107	269	473	668	816	909	960	984	994
4.0	018	092	238	433	629	785	889	949	979	992
4.2	015	078	210	395	590	753	867	936	972	989
4.4	012	066	185	359	551	720	844	921	964	985
4.6	010	056	163	326	513	686	818	905	955	980
4.8	008	048	143	294	476	651	791	887	944	975
5.0	007	040	125	265	440	616	762	867	932	968
5.2	006	034	109	238	406	581	732	845	918	960
5.4	005	029	095	213	373	546	702	822	903	951
5.6	004	024	082	191	342	512	670	797	886	941
5.8	003	021	072	170	313	478	638	771	867	929
6.0	002	017	062	151	285	446	606	744	847	916

	10	11	12	13	14	15	16
2.8	1,000						
3.0	1,000						
3.2	1,000						
3.4	999	1,000					
3.6	999	1,000					
3.8	998	999	1,000				
4.0	997	999	1,000				
4.2	996	999	1,000				
4.4	994	998	999	1,000			
4.6	992	997	999	1,000			
4.8	990	996	999	1,000			
5.0	986	995	998	999	1,000		
5.2	982	993	997	999	1,000		
5.4	977	990	996	999	1,000		
5.6	972	988	995	998	999	1,000	
5.8	965	984	993	997	999	1,000	
6.0	957	980	991	996	999	999	1,000

TABLE F   Summation of Terms of the Poisson Distribution   (*continued*)

λ or np \ c	0	1	2	3	4	5	6	7	8	9
6.2	002	015	054	134	259	414	574	716	826	902
6.4	002	012	046	119	235	384	542	687	803	886
6.6	001	010	040	105	213	355	511	658	780	869
6.8	001	009	034	093	192	327	480	628	755	850
7.0	001	007	030	082	173	301	450	599	729	830
7.2	001	006	025	072	156	276	420	569	703	810
7.4	001	005	022	063	140	253	392	539	676	788
7.6	001	004	019	055	125	231	365	510	648	765
7.8	000	004	016	048	112	210	338	481	620	741
8.0	000	003	014	042	100	191	313	453	593	717
8.5	000	002	009	030	074	150	256	386	523	653
9.0	000	001	006	021	055	116	207	324	456	587
9.5	000	001	004	015	040	089	165	269	393	522
10.0	000	000	003	010	029	067	130	220	333	458

	10	11	12	13	14	15	16	17	18	19
6.2	949	975	989	995	998	999	1,000			
6.4	939	969	986	994	997	999	1,000			
6.6	927	963	982	992	997	999	999	1,000		
6.8	915	955	978	990	996	998	999	1,000		
7.0	901	947	973	987	994	998	999	1,000		
7.2	887	937	967	984	993	997	999	999	1,000	
7.4	871	926	961	980	991	996	998	999	1,000	
7.6	854	915	954	976	989	995	998	999	1,000	
7.8	835	902	945	971	986	993	997	999	1,000	
8.0	816	888	936	966	983	992	996	998	999	1,000
8.5	763	849	909	949	973	986	993	997	999	999
9.0	706	803	876	926	959	978	989	995	998	999
9.5	645	752	836	898	940	967	982	991	996	998
10.0	583	697	792	864	917	951	973	986	993	997

	20	21	22
8.5	1,000		
9.0	1,000		
9.5	999	1,000	
10.0	998	999	1,000

TABLE F   Summation of Terms of the Poisson Distribution   (*continued*)

λ or np \ c	0	1	2	3	4	5	6	7	8	9
10.5	000	000	002	007	021	050	102	179	279	397
11.0	000	000	001	005	015	038	079	143	232	341
11.5	000	000	001	003	011	028	060	114	191	289
12.0	000	000	001	002	008	020	046	090	155	242
12.5	000	000	000	002	005	015	035	070	125	201
13.0	000	000	000	001	004	011	026	054	100	166
13.5	000	000	000	001	003	008	019	041	079	135
14.0	000	000	000	000	002	006	014	032	062	109
14.5	000	000	000	000	001	004	010	024	048	088
15.0	000	000	000	000	001	003	008	018	037	070

	10	11	12	13	14	15	16	17	18	19
10.5	521	639	742	825	888	932	960	978	988	994
11.0	460	579	689	781	854	907	944	968	982	991
11.5	402	520	633	733	815	878	924	954	974	986
12.0	347	462	576	682	772	844	899	937	963	979
12.5	297	406	519	628	725	806	869	916	948	969
13.0	252	353	463	573	675	764	835	890	930	957
13.5	211	304	409	518	623	718	798	861	908	942
14.0	176	260	358	464	570	669	756	827	883	923
14.5	145	220	311	413	518	619	711	790	853	901
15.0	118	185	268	363	466	568	664	749	819	875

	20	21	22	23	24	25	26	27	28	29
10.5	997	999	999	1,000						
11.0	995	998	999	1,000						
11.5	992	996	998	999	1,000					
12.0	988	994	997	999	999	1,000				
12.5	983	991	995	998	999	999	1,000			
13.0	975	986	992	996	998	999	1,000			
13.5	965	980	989	994	997	998	999	1,000		
14.0	952	971	983	991	995	997	999	999	1,000	
14.5	936	960	976	986	992	996	998	999	999	1,000
15.0	917	947	967	981	989	994	997	998	999	1,000

TABLE F   Summation of Terms of the Poisson Distribution   (*continued*)

λ or np \ c	4	5	6	7	8	9	10	11	12	13
16	000	001	004	010	022	043	077	127	193	275
17	000	001	002	005	013	026	049	085	135	201
18	000	000	001	003	007	015	030	055	092	143
19	000	000	001	002	004	009	018	035	061	098
20	000	000	000	001	002	005	011	021	039	066
21	000	000	000	000	001	003	006	013	025	043
22	000	000	000	000	001	002	004	008	015	028
23	000	000	000	000	000	001	002	004	009	017
24	000	000	000	000	000	000	001	003	005	011
25	000	000	000	000	000	000	001	001	003	006

	14	15	16	17	18	19	20	21	22	23
16	368	467	566	659	742	812	868	911	942	963
17	281	371	468	564	655	736	805	861	905	937
18	208	287	375	469	562	651	731	799	855	899
19	150	215	292	378	469	561	647	725	793	849
20	105	157	221	297	381	470	559	644	721	787
21	072	111	163	227	302	384	471	558	640	716
22	048	077	117	169	232	306	387	472	556	637
23	031	052	082	123	175	238	310	389	472	555
24	020	034	056	087	128	180	243	314	392	473
25	012	022	038	060	092	134	185	247	318	394

	24	25	26	27	28	29	30	31	32	33
16	978	987	993	996	998	999	999	1,000		
17	959	975	985	991	995	997	999	999	1,000	
18	932	955	972	983	990	994	997	998	999	1,000
19	893	927	951	969	980	988	993	996	998	999
20	843	888	922	948	966	978	987	992	995	997
21	782	838	883	917	944	963	976	985	991	994
22	712	777	832	877	913	940	959	973	983	989
23	635	708	772	827	873	908	936	956	971	981
24	554	632	704	768	823	868	904	932	953	969
25	473	553	629	700	763	818	863	900	929	950

	34	35	36	37	38	39	40	41	42	43
19	999	1,000								
20	999	999	1,000							
21	997	998	999	999	1,000					
22	994	996	998	999	999	1,000				
23	988	993	996	997	999	999	1,000			
24	979	987	992	995	997	998	999	999	1,000	
25	966	978	985	991	994	997	998	999	999	1,000

TABLE G   Control Chart Factors for Central Tendency

n	A	A_1	A_2	A_3	A_4	A_5	A_6	A_7	E_1	E_2	E_3
2	2.121	3.760	1.880	2.659	2.223	2.223	1.880	1.880	5.318	2.660	3.760
3	1.732	2.394	1.023	1.954	1.266	1.137	1.187	1.067	4.146	1.772	3.385
4	1.500	1.880	0.729	1.628	0.828	0.828	0.796	0.796	3.760	1.457	3.256
5	1.342	1.596	0.577	1.427	0.712	0.681	0.691	0.660	3.568	1.290	3.191
6	1.225	1.410	0.483	1.287	0.563	0.595	0.549	0.580	3.454	1.184	3.153
7	1.134	1.277	0.419	1.182	0.521	0.533	0.509	0.521	3.378	1.109	3.127
8	1.061	1.175	0.373	1.099	0.443	0.487	0.434	0.477	3.323	1.054	3.109
9	1.000	1.094	0.337	1.032	0.420	0.453	0.412	0.444	3.283	1.010	3.095
10	0.949	1.028	0.308	0.975	0.371	0.427	0.365	0.419	3.251	0.975	3.084
11	0.905	0.973	0.285	0.927	0.356	0.406	0.350	0.399	3.226	0.946	3.076
12	0.866	0.925	0.266	0.886	0.322	0.388	0.317	0.382	3.205	0.921	3.069
13	0.832	0.884	0.249	0.850	0.311	0.374	0.306	0.368	3.188	0.899	3.063
14	0.802	0.848	0.235	0.817	0.286	0.361	0.282	0.356	3.174	0.881	3.058
15	0.775	0.816	0.223	0.789	0.278	0.351	0.274	0.346	3.161	0.864	3.054
16	0.750	0.788	0.212	0.763	0.260	0.342	0.257	0.337	3.150	0.849	3.050
17	0.728	0.762	0.203	0.739	0.254	0.344	0.250	0.329	3.141	0.836	3.047
18	0.707	0.738	0.194	0.718	0.240	0.327	0.237	0.322	3.133	0.824	3.044
19	0.688	0.717	0.187	0.698	0.234	0.319	0.231	0.315	3.125	0.813	3.042
20	0.671	0.697	0.180	0.680	0.221	0.313	0.218	0.308	3.119	0.803	3.040
21	0.655	0.679	0.173	0.663	0.218	0.307	0.215	0.303	3.113	0.794	3.038
22	0.640	0.662	0.167	0.647	0.207	0.302	0.204	0.298	3.107	0.785	3.036
23	0.626	0.647	0.162	0.633	0.205	0.296	0.202	0.292	3.103	0.778	3.034
24	0.612	0.632	0.157	0.619	0.194	0.292	0.192	0.288	3.098	0.770	3.033
25	0.600	0.619	0.153	0.606	0.193	0.287	0.191	0.284	3.094	0.763	3.032
>25	$3/\sqrt{n}$	$3/(c_2\sqrt{n})$	$3/(d_2\sqrt{n})$	$3/(c_4\sqrt{n})$	$3e_3/d_4$	$3e_4/d_4$	$3e_3/d_2$	$3e_4/d_2$	$3/c_2$	$3/d_2$	$3/c_4$

Values of A, A_1, A_2, A_3, E_2, and E_3 are from the ASTM-STP 15D by permission of the American Society for Testing and Materials.

TABLE H Control Chart Factors for Dispersion—Factors for Range Charts

No. of Observations in Sample n	d_2	d_3	d_4	D_1	D_2	D_3	D_4	D_5	D_6	d_2/c_2	d_2/c_4
2	1.128	0.853	0.954	0	3.686	0	3.269	0	3.68	1.999	1.414
3	1.693	0.888	1.588	0	4.358	0	2.574	0	2.67	2.340	1.910
4	2.059	0.880	1.978	0	4.698	0	2.282	0	2.33	2.581	2.235
5	2.326	0.864	2.257	0	4.918	0	2.114	0	2.14	2.767	2.474
6	2.534	0.848	2.472	0	5.078	0	2.004	0	2.02	2.917	2.663
7	2.704	0.833	2.645	0.205	5.203	0.076	1.924	0.055	1.94	3.044	2.704
8	2.847	0.820	2.791	0.387	5.307	0.136	1.864	0.119	1.88	3.154	2.950
9	2.970	0.808	2.915	0.546	5.394	0.184	1.816	0.168	1.83	3.250	3.064
10	3.078	0.797	3.024	0.687	5.469	0.223	1.777	0.209	1.79	3.336	3.164
11	3.173	0.787	3.120	0.812	5.534	0.256	1.744	0.243	1.75	3.412	3.253
12	3.258	0.778	3.207	0.924	5.592	0.284	1.716	0.272	1.72	3.481	3.333
13	3.336	0.770	3.285	1.026	5.646	0.308	1.692	0.297	1.70	3.545	3.406
14	3.407	0.762	3.356	1.121	5.693	0.329	1.671	0.319	1.68	3.604	3.473
15	3.472	0.755	3.422	1.207	5.737	0.348	1.652	0.338	1.66	3.659	3.535
16	3.532	0.749	3.482	1.285	5.779	0.364	1.636	0.355	1.64	3.709	3.591
17	3.588	0.743	3.538	1.359	5.817	0.379	1.621	0.370	1.63	3.757	3.644
18	3.640	0.738	3.591	1.426	5.854	0.392	1.608	0.383	1.61	3.801	3.694
19	3.689	0.733	3.640	1.490	5.888	0.404	1.596	0.396	1.60	3.843	3.741
20	3.735	0.729	3.686	1.548	5.922	0.414	1.586	0.407	1.59	3.883	3.785
21	3.778	0.724	3.729	1.606	5.950	0.425	1.575	0.418	1.58	3.920	3.825
22	3.819	0.720	3.771	1.659	5.979	0.434	1.566	0.427	1.57	3.955	3.865
23	3.858	0.716	3.810	1.710	6.006	0.443	1.557	0.436	1.56	3.990	3.902
24	3.895	0.712	3.847	1.759	6.031	0.452	1.548	0.445	1.55	4.022	3.938
25	3.931	0.709	3.882	1.804	6.058	0.459	1.541	0.452	1.54	4.054	3.972
>25	$\bar{R}/\sigma$	σ_R/σ	$\tilde{R}/\sigma$	$d_2 - 3d_3$	$d_2 + 3d_3$	$1 - 3d_3/d_2$	$1 + 3d_3/d_2$	$1 - 3d_3/d_4$	$1 + 3d_3/d_4$		

Values of c_4, B_3, B_4, B_5, B_6, d_2, d_3, D_1, D_2, D_3, and D_4 are from ASTM-STP 15D by permission of the American Society for Testing and Materials.

TABLE H Factors for Standard Deviation Charts   (continued)

n	c_2	c_3	c_4	c_5	B_1	B_2	B_3	B_4	B_5	B_6	C	C_1	C_2	C_3	e_3	e_4
2	0.564	0.427	0.798	0.603	0	1.843	0	3.267	0	2.606	0.879	1.558	0.780	1.101	0.707	0.707
3	0.724	0.378	0.886	0.463	0	1.858	0	2.568	0	2.276	1.268	1.752	0.749	1.431	0.602	0.670
4	0.798	0.337	0.921	0.389	0	1.808	0	2.266	0	2.088	1.500	1.880	0.728	1.628	0.546	0.546
5	0.841	0.306	0.940	0.341	0	1.756	0	2.089	0	1.964	1.658	1.972	0.713	1.764	0.512	0.536
6	0.869	0.280	0.952	0.308	0.026	1.711	0.030	1.970	0.029	1.874	1.775	2.044	0.701	1.866	0.490	0.464
7	0.888	0.261	0.959	0.282	0.105	1.672	0.118	1.882	0.113	1.806	1.866	2.101	0.690	1.945	0.470	0.459
8	0.903	0.245	0.965	0.262	0.167	1.638	0.185	1.815	0.179	1.751	1.939	2.148	0.681	2.010	0.453	0.412
9	0.914	0.232	0.969	0.246	0.219	1.609	0.239	1.761	0.232	1.707	2.000	2.189	0.673	2.063	0.440	0.408
10	0.923	0.220	0.973	0.232	0.262	1.584	0.284	1.716	0.276	1.669	2.051	2.223	0.667	2.109	0.430	0.374
11	0.930	0.211	0.975	0.220	0.299	1.561	0.321	1.679	0.313	1.637	2.095	2.253	0.661	2.148	0.422	0.370
12	0.936	0.202	0.978	0.210	0.331	1.541	0.354	1.646	0.346	1.610	2.134	2.280	0.655	2.183	0.415	0.344
13	0.941	0.195	0.979	0.202	0.359	1.523	0.382	1.618	0.374	1.585	2.168	2.304	0.650	2.214	0.409	0.340
14	0.945	0.188	0.981	0.194	0.384	1.507	0.406	1.594	0.399	1.563	2.198	2.326	0.646	2.241	0.404	0.320
15	0.949	0.181	0.982	0.187	0.406	1.492	0.428	1.572	0.421	1.544	2.225	2.345	0.641	2.266	0.400	0.317
16	0.952	0.175	0.984	0.181	0.427	1.478	0.448	1.552	0.440	1.526	2.250	2.362	0.637	2.288	0.397	0.302
17	0.955	0.170	0.985	0.175	0.445	1.465	0.466	1.534	0.458	1.511	2.272	2.379	0.633	2.308	0.394	0.299
18	0.958	0.165	0.985	0.170	0.461	1.454	0.482	1.518	0.475	1.496	2.293	2.395	0.630	2.327	0.391	0.287
19	0.960	0.161	0.986	0.166	0.477	1.443	0.497	1.503	0.490	1.483	2.312	2.408	0.626	2.344	0.387	0.284
20	0.962	0.157	0.987	0.161	0.491	1.433	0.510	1.490	0.504	1.470	2.329	2.422	0.623	2.360	0.384	0.272
21	0.964	0.153	0.988	0.157	0.504	1.424	0.523	1.477	0.516	1.459	2.345	2.434	0.621	2.375	0.382	0.271
22	0.966	0.149	0.988	0.153	0.516	1.415	0.534	1.466	0.528	1.448	2.360	2.445	0.618	2.389	0.379	0.260
23	0.967	0.146	0.989	0.150	0.527	1.407	0.545	1.455	0.539	1.438	2.374	2.456	0.616	2.402	0.376	0.260
24	0.968	0.143	0.989	0.147	0.538	1.399	0.555	1.445	0.549	1.429	2.388	2.466	0.613	2.414	0.374	0.249
25	0.970	0.140	0.990	0.144	0.548	1.392	0.565	1.435	0.559	1.420	2.400	2.475	0.610	2.425	0.372	0.250
>25	$s_{(rms)}/\sigma$	$\sigma_{s(rms)}/\sigma$	$\bar{s}/\sigma$	σ_s/σ	$c_2 - 3c_3$	$c_2 + 3c_3$	$1 - 3c_5/c_4$	$1 + 3c_5/c_4$	$c_4 - 3c_5$	$c_4 + 3c_5$	$3 - A$	$E_1 - A_1$	$E_2 - A_2$	$E_3 - A_3$	σ_M/σ	σ_x/σ

TABLE H   Miscellaneous Factors *(continued)*

No. of Observations in Sample n	c_2/d_2	c_4/d_2	B_1/d_2	B_2/d_2	B_5/d_2	B_6/d_2	D_1/c_2	D_2/c_2	D_1/c_4	D_2/c_4
2	0.500	0.707	0	1.634	0	2.310	0	6.533	0	4.620
3	0.427	0.523	0	1.097	0	1.344	0	6.023	0	4.918
4	0.388	0.447	0	0.878	0	1.014	0	5.888	0	5.099
5	0.361	0.404	0	0.755	0	0.844	0	5.850	0	5.232
6	0.343	0.375	0.010	0.675	0.011	0.740	0	5.486	0	5.337
7	0.328	0.370	0.339	0.618	0.042	0.668	0.231	5.858	0.214	5.423
8	0.317	0.339	0.059	0.575	0.063	0.615	0.429	5.879	0.401	5.499
9	0.308	0.326	0.074	0.542	0.078	0.575	0.597	5.902	0.563	5.565
10	0.300	0.316	0.085	0.515	0.090	0.542	0.745	5.927	0.706	5.622
11	0.293	0.307	0.094	0.492	0.099	0.516	0.873	5.951	0.832	5.674
12	0.287	0.300	0.102	0.473	0.106	0.494	0.987	5.975	0.945	5.720
13	0.282	0.294	0.108	0.457	0.112	0.475	1.090	6.000	1.048	5.765
14	0.277	0.288	0.113	0.442	0.117	0.459	1.186	6.022	1.143	5.803
15	0.273	0.283	0.117	0.430	0.121	0.445	1.272	6.045	1.229	5.840
16	0.270	0.278	0.121	0.418	0.125	0.432	1.349	6.068	1.307	5.876
17	0.266	0.274	0.124	0.408	0.128	0.421	1.423	6.090	1.380	5.909
18	0.263	0.271	0.127	0.399	0.130	0.411	1.489	6.113	1.447	5.941
19	0.260	0.267	0.129	0.391	0.133	0.402	1.552	6.134	1.511	5.970
20	0.258	0.264	0.131	0.384	0.135	0.394	1.609	6.157	1.569	6.001
21	0.255	0.261	0.133	0.377	0.137	0.386	1.666	6.173	1.626	6.025
22	0.253	0.259	0.135	0.371	0.138	0.379	1.718	6.193	1.679	6.050
23	0.251	0.256	0.137	0.365	0.140	0.373	1.768	6.211	1.730	6.075
24	0.249	0.254	0.138	0.359	0.141	0.367	1.816	6.228	1.778	6.097
25	0.247	0.252	0.139	0.354	0.142	0.361	1.861	6.248	1.823	6.122

TABLE I   One-sided Statistical Tolerance Interval, μ, σ Unknown

$$\bar{x} + k_2 s \text{ or } \bar{x} - k_2 s \left[s^2 = \frac{\Sigma(x_i - \bar{x})^2}{n-1} \right]$$

Values of the coefficient $k_2(n, p, 1 - \alpha)$

	$1 - \alpha = 0.95$			$1 - \alpha = 0.99$		
n	$p = 0.90$	$p = 0.95$	$p = 0.99$	$p = 0.90$	$p = 0.95$	$p = 0.99$
5	3.41	4.21	5.75			
6	3.01	3.71	5.07	4.41	5.41	7.33
7	2.76	3.40	4.64	3.86	4.73	6.41
8	2.58	3.19	4.36	3.50	4.29	5.81
9	2.45	3.03	4.14	3.24	3.97	5.39
10	2.36	2.91	3.98	3.05	3.74	5.08
11	2.28	2.82	3.85	2.90	3.56	4.83
12	2.21	2.74	3.75	2.77	3.41	4.63
13	2.16	2.67	3.66	2.68	3.29	4.47
14	2.11	2.61	3.59	2.59	3.19	4.34
15	2.07	2.57	3.52	2.52	3.10	4.22
16	2.03	2.52	3.46	2.46	3.03	4.12
17	2.00	2.49	3.41	2.41	2.96	4.04
18	1.97	2.45	3.37	2.36	2.91	3.96
19	1.95	2.42	3.33	2.32	2.86	3.89
20	1.93	2.40	3.30	2.28	2.81	3.83
22	1.89	2.35	3.23	2.21	2.73	3.73
24	1.85	2.31	3.18	2.15	2.66	3.64
26	1.82	2.27	3.13	2.10	2.60	3.56
28	1.80	2.24	3.09	2.06	2.55	3.50
30	1.78	2.22	3.06	2.03	2.52	3.45
35	1.73	2.17	2.99	1.96	2.43	3.33
40	1.70	2.13	2.94	1.90	2.37	3.25
45	1.67	2.09	2.90	1.86	2.31	3.18
50	1.65	2.07	2.86	1.82	2.27	3.12
60	1.61	2.02	2.81	1.76	2.20	3.04
70	1.58	1.99	2.77	1.72	2.15	2.98
80	1.56	1.97	2.73	1.69	2.11	2.93
90	1.54	1.94	2.71	1.66	2.08	2.89
100	1.53	1.93	2.68	1.64	2.06	2.85
150	1.48	1.87	2.62	1.57	1.97	2.74
200	1.45	1.84	2.57	1.52	1.92	2.68
250	1.43	1.81	2.54	1.50	1.89	2.64
300	1.42	1.80	2.52	1.48	1.87	2.61
400	1.40	1.78	2.49	1.45	1.84	2.57
500	1.39	1.76	2.48	1.43	1.81	2.54
1000	1.35	1.73	2.43	1.38	1.76	2.47
∞	1.28	1.64	2.33	1.28	1.64	2.33

Source: Reprinted with permission from ISO 3207-1975, *Statistical Interpretation of Data—Determination of a Statistical Tolerance Interval*, International Organization for Standardization, Geneva.

TABLE J Two-sided Statistical Tolerance Interval, μ, σ Unknown

$$\bar{x} \pm k'_2 s \left[s^2 = \frac{\Sigma(x_i - \bar{x})^2}{n-1} \right]$$

Values of the coefficient $k'_2(n, p, 1 - \alpha)$

	$1 - \alpha = 0.95$			$1 - \alpha = 0.99$		
n	$p = 0.90$	$p = 0.95$	$p = 0.99$	$p = 0.90$	$p = 0.95$	$p = 0.99$
5	4.28	5.08	6.63	6.61	7.86	10.26
6	3.71	4.41	5.78	5.34	6.35	8.30
7	3.37	4.01	5.25	4.61	5.49	7.19
8	3.14	3.73	4.89	4.15	4.94	6.47
9	2.97	3.53	4.63	3.82	4.55	5.97
10	2.84	3.38	4.43	3.58	4.27	5.59
11	2.74	3.26	4.28	3.40	4.05	5.31
12	2.66	3.16	4.15	3.25	3.87	5.08
13	2.59	3.08	4.04	3.13	3.73	4.89
14	2.53	3.01	3.96	3.03	3.61	4.74
15	2.48	2.95	3.88	2.95	3.51	4.61
16	2.44	2.90	3.81	2.87	3.41	4.49
17	2.40	2.86	3.75	2.81	3.35	4.39
18	2.37	2.82	3.70	2.75	3.28	4.31
19	2.34	2.78	3.66	2.70	3.22	4.23
20	2.31	2.75	3.62	2.66	3.17	4.16
22	2.26	2.70	3.54	2.58	3.08	4.04
24	2.23	2.65	3.48	2.52	3.00	3.95
26	2.19	2.61	3.43	2.47	2.94	3.87
28	2.16	2.58	3.39	2.43	2.89	3.79
30	2.14	2.55	3.35	2.39	2.84	3.73
35	2.09	2.49	3.27	2.31	2.75	3.61
40	2.05	2.45	3.21	2.25	2.68	3.52
45	2.02	2.41	3.17	2.20	2.62	3.44
50	2.00	2.38	3.13	2.16	2.58	3.39
60	1.95	2.33	3.07	2.10	2.51	3.29
70	1.93	2.30	3.02	2.06	2.45	3.23
80	1.91	2.27	2.99	2.03	2.41	3.17
90	1.89	2.25	2.96	2.00	2.38	3.13
100	1.87	2.23	2.93	1.98	2.36	3.10
150	1.83	2.18	2.86	1.91	2.27	2.98
200	1.80	2.14	2.82	1.87	2.22	2.92
250	1.78	2.12	2.79	1.84	2.19	2.88
300	1.77	2.11	2.77	1.82	2.17	2.85
400	1.75	2.08	2.74	1.79	2.14	2.81
500	1.74	2.07	2.72	1.78	2.12	2.78
1000	1.71	2.04	2.68	1.74	2.07	2.72
∞	1.64	1.96	2.58	1.64	1.96	2.58

Source: Reprinted with permission from ISO 3207-1975, *Statistical Interpretation of Data—Determination of a Statistical Tolerance Interval,* International Organization for Standardization, Geneva.

TABLE K   Exact Critical Values for the Analysis of Means

Significance Level = 0.05

df	3	4	5	6	7	8	9	10	11	12	13	14	15	16	17	18	19	20	df
3	4.18																		3
4	3.56	3.89																	4
5	3.25	3.53	3.72																5
6	3.07	3.31	3.49	3.62															6
7	2.94	3.17	3.33	3.45	3.56														7
8	2.86	3.07	3.21	3.33	3.43	3.51													8
9	2.79	2.99	3.13	3.24	3.33	3.41	3.48												9
10	2.74	2.93	3.07	3.17	3.26	3.33	3.40	3.45											10
11	2.70	2.88	3.01	3.12	3.20	3.27	3.33	3.39	3.44										11
12	2.67	2.85	2.97	3.07	3.15	3.22	3.28	3.33	3.38	3.42									12
13	2.64	2.81	2.94	3.03	3.11	3.18	3.24	3.29	3.34	3.38	3.42								13
14	2.62	2.79	2.91	3.00	3.08	3.14	3.20	3.25	3.30	3.34	3.37	3.41							14
15	2.60	2.76	2.88	2.97	3.05	3.11	3.17	3.22	3.26	3.30	3.34	3.37	3.40						15
16	2.58	2.74	2.86	2.95	3.02	3.09	3.14	3.19	3.23	3.27	3.31	3.34	3.37	3.40					16
17	2.57	2.73	2.84	2.93	3.00	3.06	3.12	3.16	3.21	3.25	3.28	3.31	3.34	3.37	3.40				17
18	2.55	2.73	2.82	2.91	2.98	3.04	3.10	3.14	3.18	3.22	3.26	3.29	3.32	3.35	3.37	3.40			18
19	2.54	2.70	2.81	2.89	2.96	3.02	3.08	3.12	3.16	3.20	3.24	3.27	3.30	3.32	3.35	3.37	3.40		19
20	2.53	2.68	2.79	2.88	2.95	3.01	3.06	3.11	3.15	3.18	3.22	3.25	3.28	3.30	3.33	3.35	3.37	3.40	20
24	2.50	2.65	2.75	2.83	2.90	2.96	3.01	3.05	3.09	3.13	3.16	3.19	3.22	3.24	3.27	3.29	3.31	3.33	24
30	2.47	2.61	2.71	2.79	2.85	2.91	2.96	3.00	3.04	3.07	3.10	3.13	3.16	3.18	3.20	3.22	3.25	3.27	30
40	2.43	2.57	2.67	2.75	2.81	2.86	2.91	2.95	2.98	3.01	3.04	3.07	3.10	3.12	3.14	3.16	3.18	3.20	40
60	2.40	2.54	2.63	2.70	2.76	2.81	2.86	2.90	2.93	2.93	2.99	3.02	3.04	3.06	3.08	3.10	3.12	3.14	60
120	2.37	2.50	2.59	2.66	2.72	2.77	2.81	2.84	2.88	2.91	2.93	2.96	2.98	3.00	3.02	3.04	3.06	3.08	120
∞	2.34	2.47	2.56	2.62	2.68	2.72	2.76	2.80	2.83	2.86	2.88	2.90	2.93	2.95	2.97	2.98	3.00	3.02	∞

Number of Means, k

TABLE K Exact Critical Values for the Analysis of Means (*continued*)

Significance Level = 0.01
Number of Means, k

df	3	4	5	6	7	8	9	10	11	12	13	14	15	16	17	18	19	20	df
3	7.51																		3
4	5.74	6.21																	4
5	4.93	5.29	5.55																5
6	4.48	4.77	4.98	5.16															6
7	4.18	4.44	4.63	4.78	4.90														7
8	3.98	4.21	4.38	4.52	4.63	4.72													8
9	3.84	4.05	4.20	4.33	4.43	4.51	4.59												9
10	3.73	3.92	4.07	4.18	4.28	4.36	4.43	4.49											10
11	3.64	3.82	3.96	4.07	4.16	4.23	4.30	4.36	4.41										11
12	3.57	3.74	3.87	3.98	4.06	4.13	4.20	4.25	4.31	4.35									12
13	3.51	3.68	3.80	3.90	3.98	4.05	4.11	4.17	4.22	4.26	4.30								13
14	3.46	3.63	3.74	3.84	3.92	3.98	4.04	4.09	4.14	4.18	4.22	4.26							14
15	3.42	3.58	3.69	3.79	3.86	3.92	3.98	4.03	4.08	4.12	4.16	4.19	4.22						15
16	3.38	3.54	3.65	3.74	3.81	3.87	3.93	3.98	4.02	4.06	4.10	4.14	4.17	4.20					16
17	3.35	3.50	3.61	3.70	3.77	3.83	3.89	3.93	3.98	4.02	4.05	4.09	4.12	4.14	4.17				17
18	3.33	3.47	3.58	3.66	3.73	3.79	3.85	3.89	3.94	3.97	4.01	4.04	4.07	4.10	4.12	4.15			18
19	3.30	3.45	3.55	3.63	3.70	3.76	3.81	3.86	3.90	3.94	3.97	4.00	4.03	4.06	4.08	4.11	4.13		19
20	3.28	3.42	3.53	3.61	3.67	3.73	3.78	3.83	3.87	3.90	3.94	3.97	4.00	4.02	4.05	4.07	4.09	4.12	20
24	3.21	3.35	3.45	3.52	3.58	3.64	3.69	3.73	3.77	3.80	3.83	3.86	3.89	3.91	3.94	3.96	3.98	4.00	24
30	3.15	3.28	3.37	3.44	3.50	3.55	3.59	3.63	3.67	3.70	3.73	3.76	3.78	3.81	3.83	3.85	3.87	3.89	30
40	3.09	3.21	3.29	3.36	3.42	3.46	3.50	3.54	3.58	3.60	3.63	3.66	3.68	3.70	3.72	3.74	3.76	3.78	40
60	3.03	3.14	3.22	3.29	3.34	3.38	3.42	3.46	3.49	3.51	3.54	3.56	3.59	3.61	3.63	3.64	3.66	3.68	60
120	2.97	3.07	3.15	3.21	3.26	3.30	3.34	3.37	3.40	3.42	3.45	3.47	3.49	3.51	3.53	3.55	3.56	3.58	120
∞	2.91	3.01	3.08	3.14	3.18	3.22	3.26	3.29	3.32	3.34	3.36	3.38	3.40	3.42	3.44	3.45	3.47	3.48	∞

Source: Reprinted by permission of Nelson, L. S. (1983), "Exact Critical Values for Use with the Analysis of Means," *Journal of Quality Technology,* Vol. 15, pp. 40–44.

TABLE L   Factors for Acceptance Control Charts

n	$\alpha = \beta = 0.05$			$\alpha = \beta = 0.01$			$\alpha = \beta = 0.001$		
	$C_{0,.05}$	$C_{2,.05}$	$C_{3,.05}$	$C_{0,.01}$	$C_{2,.01}$	$C_{3,.01}$	$C_{0,.001}$	$C_{2,.001}$	$C_{3,.001}$
2	1.837	1.629	2.302	1.356	1.202	1.698	0.815	0.723	1.020
3	2.050	1.211	2.314	1.657	0.979	1.870	1.216	0.718	1.372
4	2.178	1.057	2.363	1.837	0.892	1.994	1.455	0.706	1.579
5	2.264	0.974	2.409	1.960	0.843	2.085	1.618	0.696	1.721
6	2.328	0.919	2.447	2.050	0.810	2.155	1.738	0.686	1.827
7	2.378	0.879	2.479	2.121	0.784	2.211	1.832	0.677	1.909
8	2.418	0.849	2.506	2.177	0.765	2.257	1.907	0.670	1.977
9	2.452	0.825	2.529	2.225	0.749	2.295	1.970	0.663	2.032
10	2.480	0.806	2.549	2.264	0.736	2.328	2.023	0.659	2.079
11	2.504	0.790	2.568	2.298	0.725	2.357	2.068	0.652	2.121
12	2.525	0.775	2.583	2.329	0.715	2.382	2.108	0.647	2.156
13	2.544	0.762	2.597	2.355	0.706	2.404	2.143	0.642	2.187
14	2.560	0.752	2.610	2.378	0.699	2.425	2.174	0.639	2.216
15	2.575	0.742	2.621	2.399	0.691	2.442	2.202	0.634	2.241
16	2.589		2.632	2.419		2.458	2.227		2.264
17	2.601		2.642	2.436		2.474	2.250		2.286
18	2.612		2.650	2.452		2.487	2.272		2.304
19	2.623		2.659	2.467		2.501	2.291		2.323
20	2.632		2.667	2.480		2.513	2.309		2.339
21	2.641		2.674	2.492		2.524	2.325		2.355
22	2.649		2.681	2.504		2.534	2.341		2.369
23	2.657		2.687	2.515		2.543	2.355		2.382
24	2.664		2.694	2.526		2.553	2.369		2.395
25	2.671		2.700	2.535		2.562	2.385		2.408

INDEX